Feminist Social Thought

Feminist Social Thought:

A Reader

Edited by
Diana Tietjens Meyers

Routledge
New York and London

Published in 1997 by
Routledge
29 West 35th Street
New York, NY 10001

Published in Great Britain by
Routledge
11 New Fetter Lane
London EC4P 4EE

Printed in the United States of America on acid-free paper.

Permissions acknowledgments appear on pages 771–772, and on this page by reference.

Library in Congress Cataloging-in-Publication Data

Feminist social thought : a reader / edited by Diana
Tietjens Meyers.
p. cm.
Includes bibliographical references and index.
ISBN 0-415-91536-8 (hb.) — ISBN 0-415-91537-6 (pb)
1. Feminist theory. 2. Feminist ethics. 3. Women—Social
conditions. I. Meyers, Diana T.
HQ1190.F454 1997
305.42′01—dc20 96-41609
CIP

For Eva Feder Kittay

Contents

Acknowledgments

I am particularly grateful to Maureen MacGrogan for offering me the opportunity to prepare this collection and for supporting my work in every way. Among other things, she arranged for many reviewers to read my proposal, and these anonymous reviewers provided much indispensable advice. Although I could not accept all of their recommendations—not because I didn't agree with them, but rather because Routledge insisted on a book of finite length—I did appreciate all of them, and I incorporated many of them. Also, I taught a preliminary version of this collection as a graduate seminar in the spring of 1995. One of the students in that seminar, Jessica Prata Miller, took it upon herself to give me detailed comments on the worthiness and cogency of my selections, and this book has benefited enormously from her many excellent suggestions. Finally, I want to express my thanks to Elise Springer, who did a wonderful job preparing the manuscript.

—D.T.M.

Feminist Social Thought: A Reader

Editor's Introduction

Anything may happen when womanhood has ceased to be a protected occupation, I thought, opening the door.

—Virginia Woolf, *A Room of One's Own*

What is gender? How are gender norms sustained? In what ways do these norms subordinate women? How can women overcome this subordination? These are among the key questions of feminist theory.

The second wave of the women's movement revitalized feminist theory both as a grassroots undertaking in consciousness-raising groups and as a project of academic feminists. In colleges and universities today, feminist theory is an influential intellectual current in many disciplines, including literary studies, sociology, history, anthropology, law, and philosophy. In women's studies programs, which are now well established at most U.S. colleges and universities, feminist theory is central to the curriculum.

With the success of feminist theory in the academy has come specialization. Even within particular areas, such as feminist philosophy (my own field), there is significant specialization. In addition to feminist ethics and social/political theory, feminist history of philosophy, feminist epistemology and philosophy of science, feminist aesthetics, and feminist philosophy of religion have made important contributions. Although some feminist philosophy anthologies try to be comprehensive and include selections from as many subfields as possible, many anthologies accept the reality of specialization and aim for depth of coverage within one or two subfields. This collection, which focuses on feminist ethical, social, and political thought, takes the latter approach.

When feminist philosophers sought to integrate their politics into their scholarship, ethics and social/political theory were among the first areas they worked in. Since feminism aims to transform social relations in order to overcome women's subordination, and since moral, social, and political philosophy seek to account for ethical interpersonal relations and to explicate and defend just social, political, and legal institutions, it seemed natural that many feminist philosophers would choose ethics or social/political theory as a point of departure. Thus, feminist ethics and feminist social/political theory are now well-established fields offering rich literatures. This collection surveys pivotal topics and trends in this vital field.

Some feminist philosophy collections are organized to stress the lines of descent from major philosophical traditions to the feminist philosophy of today. While it is undeniable that feminist philosophy has antecedents in the history of philosophy, it is also undeniable that feminist philosophy has broken with these traditions in striking ways. Feminist philosophy repudiates the sexist assumptions undergirding these traditions, and this commitment to gender equality enables feminists to make distinctive contributions to philosophy. Thus, this collection is organized to highlight salient concerns in contemporary feminist scholarship and the advances feminist philosophers have made. It covers seven main topics:

Part 1: Constructions of Gender
Part 2: Theorizing Diversity—Gender, Race, Class, and Sexual Orientation
Part 3: Figurations of Women/Woman as Figuration
Part 4: Subjectivity, Agency, and Feminist Critique
Part 5: Social Identity, Solidarity, and Political Engagement
Part 6: Care and Its Critics
Part 7: Women, Equality, and Justice

Each part includes articles representing a wide spectrum of feminist thinking.

Parts 1, 2, and 3 survey *gender theory.* What is gender? How are gender norms instilled, enforced, and perpetuated? What are the dangers of essentialism? What are the relationships between gender and other socially demarcated positions, such as race, class, and sexual orientation? How is gender imagery embedded in Western culture? How does this imagery shape people's emotional lives? What opportunities does this imagery open up, and what social liabilities does it impose? Parts 4 and 5 consider theories of *women's subjectivity, social identity, and political agency.* How do prevailing views of choice and action thwart women's agency? What resources for recognizing their subordination and resisting it do women have at their disposal? How is it possible to exercise agency under conditions of oppression? In light of women's diversity, what is the basis for feminist solidarity and political activism? What goals should feminist politics pursue? How should feminists pursue these goals? Parts 6 and 7 turn to feminist work on *care and justice.* Are there ethical insights to be derived from women's experience of giving birth or from the childcare activities customarily assigned to women? How do attention to particular others and empathic feeling contribute to moral judgment? Are care and justice distinct moral orientations? Are most women proponents of the care ethic? Is the care ethic an emancipatory feminist ethic? What political and legal issues does gender raise? How can social and legal equality be reconciled with difference?

This book is divided into parts. But since there are many thematic links between articles in different parts, there are many alternative routes through the text. Individuals who are interested in particular topics may choose to take one of the following routes.

Among the topics to which entire parts are dedicated but that are also threaded throughout the book are the construction of gender (Part 1), gender diversity (Part 2), and figurative representations of women (Part 3). All of these topics are important enough to require parts of their own, but they also play a crucial role in discussions of other topics. Not surprisingly, there is no article in this text that does not in some way touch on the question of the social construction of gender. It may be helpful, however, to mention some places where discussions of the related issues of *gender roles* and *gender psychology* can be found. They include Chapters 10, 11, 12, 14, 16, 20, 23, 24, 25, 27, 30, 31, 32, 33, 34, 36, 37, and 39. The theme of *women's diversity* frequently recurs, as well. For example, Chapters 2, 3, 4, 13, 18, 19, 26, 27, 28, 35, and 39 address issues of gender, race, class, or sexual orientation in conjunction with other topics. Similarly, although Chapters 2, 5, 10, 11, 18, 20, 23, 24 and 34 mainly address other issues, these chapters are also concerned with the *rhetoric of gender* and *cultural representations of women.*

Parts 4 and 5 focus on questions about feminist consciousness and feminist agency, but these topics also come up elsewhere in the volume. For example, the closely related topics of *feminist critique* and *resistance* are discussed in Chapters 3, 4, 5, 6, 7, 8, 11, 12, 13, and 16. Part 6's presentation of the ethic of care is supplemented by discussions of different aspects of *women's caregiving* in Chapters 1, 2, 10, 28, 37, and 38. Materials relevant to Part 7's consideration of *equality and justice* can be found in Chapters 11, 12, 13, 14, 26, 27, 28, 31, and 32. In addition, the liberal and Marxist traditions and their views about justice are discussed in a number of chapters. *Liberalism* is considered in Chapters 4, 12, 20, 23, 26, 28, 31, 32, and 38. *Marxism* (as well as its progeny, socialist feminism) is considered in Chapters 3, 4, 7, 12, 25, and 27.

Two important intellectual movements that have sparked vigorous debate among feminists are *psychoanalysis* and *postmodernism.* Although some scholars hold that psychoanalysis and/or postmodernism is inimical to feminism, I have decided not to focus on these controversies, principally because I am convinced that both of these schools of thought have made valuable contributions to feminist theory. Thus, I have inserted the work of feminist scholars who are sympathetic to psychoanalysis or postmodernism and the work of feminist scholars who are critical of psychoanalysis or postmodernism throughout the text. Aiming to make a couple of frequently cited psychoanalytic texts readily accessible, I have included work by Nancy Chodorow (Chapter 1) and Julia Kristeva (Chapter 16) along with a selection of articles that critically examine the contribution of psychoanalysis to feminist theory or that appropriate psychoanalytic accounts for feminist purposes (Chapters 2, 10, 14, 19, 23, 24, 25, 27). Chapters by feminists who embrace some version of postmodernism include Chapters 5, 6, 7, 15, 27, 28, and 39.

Various additional topics are taken up in the essays in this collection, and I shall conclude by furnishing a brief "roadmap" to assist readers in finding discussions of some topics that have gained prominence in recent feminist thought.

A number of these topics center on the public/private split and the feminist politicization of the private sphere. *Sexuality* is treated in Chapters 3, 4, 13, 18, 23, 24, 27, and 36. *Sexual orientation* is treated in Chapters 4, 6, 11, 19, and 33. *Violence against women* is treated in Chapters 4, 13, 18, 23, 24, and 35. *Motherhood* is treated in Chapters 1, 2, 3, 10, 11, 14, 16, 17, 24, 25, 29, 30, 31, 32, 36, and 37. The *family* is treated in Chapters 1, 3, 10, 11, 12, 24, 27, 30, 31, 32, and 36.

A second group of topics concerns the project of feminist social analysis. *Consciousness raising* is the wellspring of feminist critique, and this activity is discussed in Chapters 4, 19, 20, and 26. Consciousness raising occurs in *feminist communities,* and the role of feminist communities in fostering feminist consciousness is discussed in Chapters 5, 20, 21, 22, 25, and 26. To account for the insights gained through consciousness raising, *feminist moral epistemology* is needed, and Chapters 4, 7, 8, 20, 21, 22, 25, 27, and 34 make contributions to feminist moral epistemology.

A third group of topics concerns women's subordination and feminist emancipatory aims. Views of *male dominance* are offered in Chapters 1, 2, 3, 4, 5, 10, 11, 12, 13, 14, 18, 23, 25, 33, and 37. Anticipatory reflections on the meaning of *emancipation* are offered in Chapters 5, 11, 12, 13, 19, 20, 23, 24, 26, 27, and 28.

Finally, there has been considerable controversy within feminism over the question of *essentialism*. Chapters 1, 2, 7, 9, 15, 27, 28, 35, 37, and 39 address this key issue.

That there are at present many excellent collections of feminist philosophy available testifies to the scope and the vitality of this field. For an anthologist, this scope and vitality are both heartening and frustrating. Heartening because it is abundantly clear that preparing a collection is worthwhile. Frustrating because it is equally clear that no collection can be complete. I have tried to meet the challenge posed by feminist philosophy's flourishing by confining my selections to work in moral, social, and political thought and by including influential and innovative work in these fields. Still, there is a great deal of important work that could not be included, and that I regret. Thus, I submit this volume as one possible snapshot of an endlessly fascinating and rapidly moving subject. Although a whole album of snapshots could be taken using different angles and different lenses, I believe this book is a good portrait—a vivid and revealing likeness of feminist ethics and social/political theory today.

—D.T.M.

Part 1:
Constructions of Gender

Gender, Relation, and Difference in Psychoanalytic Perspective

Chodorow denies that there is an essential difference between women and men. Gender difference is not determined by biology and is not immutable. It must be understood as a "relational construction." For Chodorow, the key to understanding gender difference is the process of "separation-individuation"—the process through which an infant who is cognitively and emotionally fused with its mother comes to understand itself as a distinct individual. Using a psychoanalytic approach to individual development—specifically, an object relations approach—Chodorow argues that one's sense of identity, agency, and authenticity arises as a result of internalizing early nurturing relationships and does not require sharp self-other distinctions. But issues about individual differentiation and identity have become intertwined with issues about gender identity. Masculinity is linked to independence and individualism, whereas femininity is linked to intimacy and emotional ties to other people.

Unfortunately, masculine identity is less secure for boys and men than feminine identity is for girls and women. This asymmetry arises because mothers or other women are primarily responsible for childcare and, as a result, boys must gain their gender identity by negating femininity rather than by positively identifying with a masculine figure. Since men who are raised by women are defensive about their gender identity and have the power to define social norms, identity, agency, and authenticity have come to be equated with isolation from others and with individual control. In contrast, Chodorow advocates a relational account of identity, agency, and authenticity that would enable people to be more tolerant of difference.

—D.T.M.

Chapter 1

Nancy Julia Chodorow

Gender, Relation, and Difference in Psychoanalytic Perspective

> I would go so far as to say that even before slavery or class domination existed, men built an approach to women that would serve one day to introduce differences among us all.
>
> Claude Lévi-Strauss[1]

In both the nineteenth- and twentieth-century women's movements, many feminists have argued that the degendering of society, so that gender and sex no longer determined social existence, would eliminate male dominance. This view assumes that gender differentiating characteristics are acquired. An alternate sexual politics and analysis of sexual inequality has tended toward an essentialist position, posing male-female difference as innate. Not the degendering of society, but its appropriation by woman, with women's virtues, is seen as the solution to male dominance. These virtues are uniquely feminine, and usually thought to emerge from women's biology, which is then seen as intrinsically connected to or entailing a particular psyche, a particular social role (such as mothering), a particular body image (more diffuse, holistic, nonphallocentric), or a particular sexuality (not centered on a particular organ; at times, lesbianism). In this view, women are intrinsically better than men and their virtues are not available to men. Proponents of the degendering model have sometimes also held that "female" virtues or qualities—nurturance, for instance—should be spread throughout society and replace aggression and competitiveness; but these virtues are nevertheless seen as acquired, a product of women's development or social location, and acquirable by men, given appropriate development experience, and social reorganization. (Others who argue for degendering have at times held that women need to acquire certain "male" characteristics and modes of action—autonomy, independence, assertiveness—again, assuming that such characteristics are acquired.)

This essay evaluates the essentialist view of difference and examines the contribution that psychoanalytic theory can make to understanding the question of sex or gender difference. It asks whether gender is best understood by focusing on differences between men and women and on the uniqueness of each and whether gender difference should be a central organizing concept for feminism. The concept of difference to which I refer here, and which is addressed by other writers in this volume, is abstract and irreducible.[2] It assumes the existence of an essence of gender, so that differences between men and women are seen to establish and define each gender as a unique and absolute category.

I will not discuss differences among women. I think we have something else in mind when we speak of differences in this connection. Differences among women—of class, race, sexual preference, nationality, and ethnicity, between mothers and nonmothers—are all significant for feminist theory and practice, but these remain concrete differences, analyzable in terms of specific categories and modes of understanding. We can see how they are socially situated and how they grow from particular social relations and organization; how they may contain physiological elements (race and sexual preference, for example) yet only gain a specific meaning in particular historical contexts and social formations.

I suggest that gender difference is not absolute, abstract, or irreducible; it does not involve an essence of gender. Gender differences, and the experience of difference, like differences among women, are socially and psychologically created and situated. In addition, I want to suggest a relational notion of difference. Difference and gender difference do not exist as things in themselves; they are created relationally, that is, in relationship. We cannot understand difference apart from this relational construction.

The issues I consider here are relevant both to feminist theory and to particular strands of feminist politics. In contrast to the beginning of the contemporary women's movement, there is now a widespread view that gender differences are essential, that women are fundamentally different from men, and that these differences must be recognized, theorized, and maintained. This finds some political counterpart in notions that women's special nature guarantees the emergence of a good society after the feminist revolution and legitimates female dominance, if not an exclusively female society. My conclusions lead me to reject those currents of contemporary feminism that would found a politics on essentialist conceptions of the feminine.

There is also a preoccupation among some women with psychological separateness and autonomy, with individuality as a necessary women's goal. This preoccupation grows out of many women's feelings of not having distinct autonomy as separate selves, in comparison, say, to men. This finds some political counterpart in equal rights arguments, ultimately based on notions of women exclusively as individuals rather than as part of a collectivity or social group. I suggest that we need to situate such a goal in an understanding of psychological development and to indicate the relationship between our culture's individualism and gender differentiation.

Psychoanalysis clarifies for us many of the issues involved in questions of difference, by providing a developmental history of the emergence of separateness, differentiation, and the perception of difference in early childhood. Thus it provides a particularly useful arena in which to see the relational and situated construction of difference, and of gender difference. Moreover, psychoanalysis gives an account of these issues from a general psychological perspective, as well as with specific relation to the question of gender. In this context, I will discuss two aspects of the general subject of separateness, differentiation, and perceptions of difference and their emergence. First, I will consider how separation-individuation occurs relationally in the first "me"–"not-me" division, in the development of the "I," or self. I will suggest that we have to understand this separation-individuation in relation to other aspects of development, that it has particular implications for women, and that differentiation is not synonymous with difference or separateness. Second, I will talk about the ways that difference and gender difference are created distinctly, in different relational contexts, for girls and boys, and, hence, for women and men. The argument here advances a reading of psychoanalysis that stresses the relational ego. It contrasts with certain prevalent (Lacan-influenced) feminist readings of psychoanalysis, in particular with the views advanced by French theorists of difference like Luce Irigaray and with the Freudian orthodoxy of Juliet Mitchell.

DIFFERENTIATION

Psychoanalysis talks of the process of "differentiation" or "separation-individuation."[3] A child of either gender is born originally with what is called a "narcissistic relation to reality": cognitively and libidinally it experiences itself as merged and continuous with the world in general, and with its mother or caretaker in particular. Differentiation, or separation-individuation, means coming to perceive a demarcation between the self and the object world, coming to perceive the subject/self as distinct, or separate from, the object/other. An essential early task of infantile development, it involves the development of ego boundaries (a sense of personal psychological division from the rest of the world) and of a body ego (a sense of the permanence of one's physical separateness and the predictable boundedness of one's own body, of a distinction between inside and outside).

This differentiation requires physiological maturation (for instance, the ability to perceive object constancy), but such maturation is not enough. Differentiation happens *in relation to* the mother, or to the child's primary caretaker. It develops through experiences of the mother's departure and return and through frustration, which emphasizes the child's separateness and the fact that it doesn't control all its own experiences and gratifications. Some of these experiences and gratifications come from within, some from without. If it were not for these frustrations, these disruptions of the experience of primary oneness, total holding, and gratification, the child would not need to begin to perceive the other, the "outer world," as separate, rather than as an extension of itself. Developing separateness thus involves, in particular, perceiving the mother or primary caretaker as separate and "not-me," where once these were an undifferentiated symbiotic unity.

Separateness, then, is not simply given from birth, nor does it emerge from the individual alone. Rather, separateness is defined relationally; differentiation occurs in relationship: "I" am "not-you." Moreover, "you," or the other, is also distinguished. The child learns to see the *particularity* of the mother or primary caretaker in contrast to the rest of the world. Thus, as the self is differentiated from the object world, the object world is itself differentiated into its component parts.

Now, from a psychoanalytic perspective, learning to distinguish "me" and "not-me" is necessary for a person to grow into a functioning human being. It is also inevitable, since experiences of departure, of discontinuity in handling, feeding, where one sleeps, how one is picked up and by whom, of less than total relational and physical gratification, are unavoidable. But for our understanding of "difference" in this connection, the concept of differentiation and the processes that characterize it need elaboration.

First, in most psychoanalytic formulations, and in prevalent understandings of development, the mother, or the outside world, is depicted simply as the other, not-me, one who does or does not fulfill an expectation. This perception arises originally from the infant's cognitive inability to differentiate self and world; the infant does not distinguish between its desires for love and satisfaction and those of its primary love object and object identification. The self here is the infant or growing child, and psychoanalytic accounts take the viewpoint of this child.

However, adequate separation, or differentiation, involves not merely perceiving the separateness, or otherness, of the other. It involves perceiving the person's subjectivity and selfhood as well. Differentiation, separation, and disruption of the narcissistic relation to reality are developed through learning that the mother is a separate being with separate interests and activities that do not always coincide with just what the infant wants at the time. They involve the ability to experience and perceive the object/other (the mother) in aspects apart from its sole relation to the ability to gratify the infant's/subject's needs and wants; they involve seeing the object as separate from the self *and* from the self's needs.[4] The infant must change here from a "relationship to a subjectively conceived object to a relationship to an object objectively perceived."[5]

In infantile development this change requires cognitive sophistication, the growing ability to integrate various images and experiences of the mother that comes with the development of ego capacities. But these capacities are not enough. The ability to perceive the other as a self, finally, requires an emotional shift and a form of emotional growth. The adult self not only experiences the other as distinct and separate. It also does not experience the other solely in terms of its own needs for gratification and its own desires.

This interpretation implies that true differentiation, true separateness, cannot be simply a perception and experience of self-other, of presence-absence. It must precisely involve two selves, two presences, two subjects. Recognizing the other as a subject is possible only to the extent that one is not dominated by felt need and one's own exclusive subjectivity. Such recognition permits appreciation and perception of many aspects of the other person, of her or his existence apart from the child's/the self's. Thus, how we understand differentiation—only from the viewpoint of the infant as a self, or from the viewpoint of two interacting selves—has consequences for what we think of as a mature self. If the mature self grows only out of the infant as a self, the other need never be accorded her or his own selfhood.

The view that adequate separation-individuation, or differentiation, involves not simply perceiving the otherness of the other, but her or his selfhood/subjectivity as well, has important consequences, not only for an understanding of the development of selfhood, but also for perceptions of women. Hence, it seems to me absolutely essential to a feminist appropriation of psychoanalytic conceptions of differentiation. Since women, as mothers, are the primary caretakers of infants, if the child (or the psychoanalytic account) only takes the viewpoint of the infant as a (developing) self, then the *mother* will be perceived (or depicted) only as an object. But, from a feminist perspective, perceiving the particularity of the mother must involve according the mother her own selfhood. This is a necessary part of the developmental process, though it is also often resisted and experienced only conflictually and partially. Throughout life, perceptions of the mother fluctuate between perceiving her particularity and selfhood and perceiving her as a narcissistic extension, a not-separate other whose sole reason for existence is to gratify one's own wants and needs.

Few accounts recognize the import of this particular stance toward the mother. Alice Balint's marvelous proto-feminist account is the best I know of the infantile origins of adult perceptions of mother as object:

> Most men (and women)—even when otherwise quite normal and capable of an "adult," altruistic form of love which acknowledges the interests of the partner—retain towards their own mothers this naive egoistic attitude throughout their lives. For all of us it remains self-evident that the interests of mother and child are identical, and it is the generally acknowledged measure of the goodness or badness of the mother how far she really feels this identity of interests.[6]

Now, these perceptions, as a product of infantile development, are somewhat inevitable as long as women have nearly exclusive maternal responsibilities, and they are one major reason why I advocate equal parenting as a necessary basis of sexual equality. But I think that, even within the ongoing context of women's mothering, as women we can and must liberate ourselves from such perceptions in our personal emotional lives as much as possible, and certainly in our theorizing and politics.[7]

A second elaboration of psychoanalytic accounts of differentiation concerns the affective or emotional distinction between differentiation or separation-individuation, and *difference.* Difference and differentiation are, of course, related to and feed into one another; it is in some sense true that cognitive or linguistic distinction, or division, must imply difference. However, it is possible to be separate, to be differentiated, without caring about or emphasizing difference, without turning the cognitive fact into an emotional, moral, or political one. In fact, assimilating difference to differentiation is defensive and reactive, a reaction to not feeling separate enough. Such assimilation involves arbitrary boundary creation and an assertion of hyperseparateness to reinforce a lack of security in a person's sense of self as a separate person. But one can be separate from and similar to someone at the same time. For example, one can recognize another's subjectivity and humanity as one recognizes one's own, seeing the *commonality* of both as active subjects. Or a woman can recognize her similarity, commonality, even continuity, with her mother, because she has developed enough of an unproblematic sense of separate self. At the same time, the other side of being able to experience separateness and commonality, of recognizing the other's subjectivity, is the ability to recognize differences with a small "d," differences that are produced and situated historically—for instance, the kinds of meaningful differences among women that I mentioned earlier.

The distinction between differentiation/separateness and difference relates to a third consideration, even more significant to our assessment of difference and gender difference. Following Mahler, much psychoanalytic theory has centered its account of early infant development on separation-individuation, on the creation of the separate self, on the "me"–"not-me" distinction. Yet there are other ways of looking at the development of self, other important and fundamental aspects to the self: "me"–"not-me" is not all there is to "me." Separation, the "me"–"not-me" division, looms larger, both in our psychological life and theoretically, to the extent that these other aspects of the self are not developed either in individual lives or in theoretical accounts.

Object-relations theory shows that in the development of self the primary task is not the development of ego boundaries and a body ego.[8] Along with the earliest development of its sense of separateness, the infant constructs an internal set of unconscious, affectively loaded representations of others in relation to its self, and an internal sense of self in relationship emerges. Images of felt good and bad aspects of the mother or primary caretaker, caretaking experiences, and the mothering relationship become part of the self, of a relational ego structure, through unconscious mental processes that appropriate and incorporate these images. With maturation, these early images and fragments of perceived experience become put together into a self. As externality and internality are established, therefore, what comes to be internal includes what originally were aspects of the other and the relation to the other. (Similarly, what is experienced as external may include what was originally part of the developing self's experience.) Externality and internality, then, do not follow easily observable physiological boundaries but are constituted by psychological and emotional processes as well.

These unconscious early internalizations that affect and constitute the internal quality of selfhood may remain more or less fragmented, or they may develop a quality of wholeness. A sense of continuity of experience and the opportunity to integrate a complex of (at least somewhat) complementary and consistent images enables the "I" to emerge as a continuous being with an identity. This more internal sense of self, or of "I," is not dependent on separateness or difference from an other. A "true self," or "central self," emerges through the experience of continuity that the mother or caretaker helps to provide, by protecting the infant from having continually to react to and ward off environmental intrusions and from being continually in need.

The integration of a "true self" that feels alive and whole involves a particular set of internalized feelings about others in relation to the self. These include developing a sense that one is able to affect others and one's environment (a sense that one has not been inhibited by overanticipation of all one's needs), a sense that one has been accorded one's own feelings and a spontaneity about these feelings (a sense that one's feelings or needs have not been projected onto one), and a sense that there is a fit between one's feelings and needs and those of the mother or caretaker. These feelings all give the self a sense of agency and authenticity.

This sense of agency, then, is fostered by caretakers who do not project experiences or feelings onto the child and who do not let the environment impinge indiscriminately. It is evoked by empathic caretakers who understand and validate the infant as a self in its own right, and the infant's experience as real. Thus, the sense of agency, which is one basis of the inner sense of continuity and wholeness, grows out of the nature of the parent-infant relationship.

Another important aspect of internalized feelings about others in relation to the self concerns a certain wholeness that develops through an internal sense of relationship with another.[9] The "thereness" of the primary parenting person grows into an internal sense of the presence of another who is caring and affirming. The self comes into being here first through feeling confidently alone in the presence of its mother, and then through this presence's becoming internalized. Part of its self becomes a good internal mother. This suggests that the central core of self is, internally, a relational ego, a sense of self-in-good-relationship. The presence or absence of others, their sameness or difference, does not then become an issue touching the infant's very existence. A "capacity to be alone," a relational rather than a reactive autonomy, develops because of a sense of the ongoing presence of another.

These several senses of agency, of a true self that does not develop reactively, of a relational self or ego core, and of an internal continuity of being, are fundamental to an unproblematic sense of self and provide the basis of both autonomy and spontaneity. The strength, or wholeness, of the self in this view, does not depend only or even centrally on its degree of separateness, although the extent of confident distinctness certainly affects and is part of the sense of self. The more secure the central self, or ego core, the less one has to define one's self through separateness from others. Separateness becomes, then, a more rigid, defensive, rather fragile, secondary criterion of the strength of the self and of the "success" of individuation.

This view suggests that no one has a separateness consisting only of "me"–"not-me" distinctions. Part of myself is always that which I have taken in; we are all to some degree incorporations and extensions of others. Separateness from the mother, defining oneself as apart from her (and from other women), is not the only or final goal for women's ego strength and autonomy, even if many women must also attain some sense of reliable separateness. In the process of differentiation, leading to a genuine autonomy, people maintain contact with those with whom they had their earliest relationships: indeed this contact is part of who we are. "I am" is not definition through negation, is not "who I am not." Developing a sense of confident separateness must be a part of all children's development. But once this confident separateness is established, one's relational self can become more central to one's life. *Differentiation is not distinctness and separateness, but a particular way of being connected to others.* This connection to others, based on early incorporations, in turn enables us to feel that empathy and confidence that are basic to the recognition of the other as a self.

What does all this have to do with male-female difference and male dominance? Before turning to the question of gender difference, I want to reiterate what we as feminists learn from the general inquiry into "differentiation." First, we learn that we can only think of differentiation and the emergence of the self relationally. Differentiation occurs, and separation emerges, in relationship; they are not givens. Second, we learn that to single out separation as the core of a notion of self and of the process of differentiation may well be inadequate; it is certainly not the only way to discuss the emergence of self or what constitutes a strong self. Differentiation includes the internalization of aspects of the primary caretaker and of the caretaking relationship.

Finally, we learn that essential, important attitudes toward mothers and expectations of mother—attitudes and expectations that enter into experiences of women more generally—emerge in the earliest differentiation of self. These attitudes and expectations arise during the emergence of separateness. Given that differentiation and separation are developmentally problematic, and given that women are primary caretakers, the mother, who is a woman, becomes and remains for children of both genders the other, or object. She is not accorded autonomy or selfness on her side. Such attitudes arise also from the gender-specific character of the early, emotionally charged self and object images that affect the development of self and the sense of autonomy and spontaneity. They are internalizations of feelings about the self in relation to the *mother*, who is then often experienced as either overwhelming or overdenying. These attitudes are often unconscious and always have a basis in unconscious, emotionally charged feelings and conflicts. A precipitate of the early relationship to the mother and of an unconscious sense of self, they may be more fundamental and determining of psychic life than more conscious and explicit attitudes to "sex differences" or "gender differences" themselves.

This inquiry suggests a psychoanalytic grounding for goals of emotional psychic life other than autonomy and separateness. It suggests, instead, an individuality that emphasizes our connectedness with, rather than our separation from, one another. Feelings of inadequate separateness, the fear of merger, are indeed issues for women, because of the ongoing sense of oneness and primary identification with our mothers (and children). A transformed organization of parenting would help women to resolve these issues. However, autonomy, spontaneity, and a sense of agency need not be based on self-other distinctions, on the individual as individual. They can be based on the fundamental interconnectedness, not synonymous with merger, that grows out of our earliest unconscious developmental experience, and that enables the creation of a nonreactive separateness.[10]

GENDER DIFFERENCES IN THE CREATION OF DIFFERENCE

I turn now to the question of gender differences. We are not born with perceptions of gender differences; these emerge developmentally. In the traditional psychoanalytic view, however, when sexual difference is first seen, it has self-evident value. A girl perceives her lack of a penis, knows instantly that she wants one, and subsequently defines herself and her mother as lacking, inadequate, castrated; a boy instantly knows having a penis is better, and fears the loss of his own.[11] This traditional account violates a fundamental rule of psychoanalytic interpretation. When the analyst finds trauma, shock, strong fears, or conflict, it is a signal to look for the roots of such feelings.[12] Because of his inability to focus on the preoedipal years and the relationship of mother to child, Freud could not follow his own rule here.

Clinical and theoretical writings since Freud suggest another interpretation of the emergence of perceptions of gender difference. This view reverses the perception of which gender experiences greater trauma, and retains only the claim that gender identity and the sense of masculinity and femininity develop differently for men and women.[13] These accounts suggest that core gender identity and masculinity are conflictual for men, and are bound up with the masculine sense of self in a way that core gender identity and femininity are not for women. "Core gender identity" here refers to a cognitive sense of gendered self, the sense that one is male or female. It is established in the first two years concomitantly with the development of the sense of self. Later evaluations of the desirability of one's gender and of the activities and modes of behavior associated with it, or of one's own sense of adequacy at fulfilling gender role expectations, are built upon this fundamental gender identity. They do not create or change it.

Most people develop an unambiguous core gender identity, a sense that they are female or male. But because women mother, the sense of maleness in men differs from the sense of femaleness in women. Maleness is more conflictual and more problematic. Underlying, or built into, core male gender identity is an early, nonverbal, unconscious, almost somatic sense of primary oneness with the mother, an underlying sense of femaleness that continually, usually unnoticeably, but sometimes insistently, challenges and undermines the sense of maleness. Thus, because of a primary oneness and identification with his mother, a primary femaleness, a boy's and a man's core gender identity itself—the seemingly unproblematic cognitive sense of being male—is an issue. A boy must learn his gender identity as being not-female, or not-mother. Subsequently, again because of the primacy of the mother in early life and because of the absence of concrete, real, available male figures of identification and love who are as salient for him as female figures, learning what it is to be masculine comes to mean learning to be not-feminine, or not-womanly.

Because of early-developed, conflictual core gender identity problems, and later problems of adequate masculinity, it becomes important to men to have a clear sense of gender difference, of what is masculine and what is feminine, and to maintain rigid boundaries between these. Researchers find, for example, that fathers sex-type children more than mothers. They treat sons and daughters more differently and enforce gender role expectations more vigorously than mothers do.[14] Boys and men come to deny the feminine identification within themselves and those feelings they experience as feminine: feelings of dependence, relational needs, emotions generally. They come to emphasize differences, not commonalities or continuities, between themselves and women, especially in situations that evoke anxiety, because these commonalities and continuities threaten to challenge gender difference or to remind boys and men consciously of their potentially feminine attributes.

These conflicts concerning core gender identity interact with and build upon particular ways that boys experience the processes of differentiation and the formation of the self.[15] Both sexes establish separateness in relation to their mother, and internalizations in the development of self take in aspects of the mother as well. But because the mother is a woman, these experiences differ by gender. Though children of both sexes are originally part of herself, a mother unconsciously and often consciously experiences her son as more of an "other" than her daughter. Reciprocally, a son's male core gender identity develops away from his mother. The male's self, as a result, becomes based on a more fixed "me"–"not-me" distinction. Separateness and difference as a component of differentiation become more salient. By contrast, the female's self is less separate and involves a less fixed "me"–"not-me" distinction, creating the difficulties with a sense of separateness and autonomy that I mentioned above.

At the same time, core gender identity for a girl is not problematic in the sense that it is for boys. It is built upon, and does not contradict, her primary sense of oneness and identification with her mother and is assumed easily along with her developing sense of self. Girls grow up with a sense of continuity and similarity to their mother, a relational connection to the world. For them, difference is not originally problematic or fundamental to their psychological being or identity. They do not define themselves as "not-men," or "not-male," but as "I, who am female." Girls and women may have problems with their sense of continuity and similarity if it is too strong and they have no sense of a separate self. However, these problems are not inevitable products of having a sense of continuity and similarity, since, as I argue here, selfhood does *not* depend only on the strength and impermeability of ego boundaries. Nor are these problems bound up with questions of gender; rather, they are bound up with questions of self.

In the development of gender identification for girls it is not the existence of core gender identity, the unquestioned knowledge that one is female, that is problematic. Rather, it is the later-developed conflicts concerning this identity, and the identifications, learning, and cognitive choices that it implies. The difficulties that girls have in establishing a "feminine" identity do not stem from the inaccessibility and negative definition of this identity, or its assumption by denial (as in the case of boys). They arise from identification with a negatively valued gender category, and an ambivalently experienced maternal figure, whose mothering and femininity, often conflictual for the mother herself, are accessible, but devalued. Conflicts here arise from questions of relative power, and social and cultural value, even as female identification and the assumption of core gender identity are straightforward. I would argue that these conflicts come later in development, and are less pervasively determining of psychological life for women than are masculine conflicts around core gender identity and gender difference.

Men's and women's understanding of difference, and gender difference, must thus be understood in the relational context in which these are created. They stem from the respective relation of boys and girls to their mother, who is their primary caretaker, love object, and object of identification, and who is a woman in a sexually and gender-organized world. This relational context contrasts profoundly for girls and boys in a way that makes difference, and gender difference, central for males—one of the earliest, most basic male development issues—and not central for females. It gives men a psychological investment in difference that women do not have.

According to psychoanalytic accounts since Freud, it is very clear that males are "not-females" in earliest development. Core gender identity and the sense of masculinity are defined more negatively, in terms of that which is not-female or not-mother, than positively. By contrast, females do not develop as "not-males." Female core gender identity and the sense of femininity are defined positively, as that which is female, or like mother. Difference from males is not so salient. An alternative way to put this is to suggest that, developmentally, the maternal identification represents and is experienced as generically human for children of both genders.[16]

But, because men have power and cultural hegemony in our society, a notable thing happens. Men use and have used this hegemony to appropriate and transform these experiences. Both in everyday life and in theoretical and intellectual formulations, men have come to define maleness as that which is basically human, and to define women as not-men. This transformation is first learned in, and helps to constitute, the oedipal transition—the cultural, affective, and sexual learnings of the meaning and valuation of sex differences.[17] Because Freud was not attentive to preoedipal development (and because of his sexism), he took this meaning and valuation as a self-evident given, rather than a developmental and cultural product.

We must remember that this transformed interpretation of difference, an interpretation learned in the oedipal transition, is produced by means of male cultural hegemony and power. Men have the means to institutionalize their unconscious defenses against repressed yet strongly experienced developmental conflicts. This interpretation of difference is imposed on earlier developmental processes; it is not the deepest, unconscious root of either the female or the male sense of gendered self. In fact, the primary sense of gendered self that emerges in earliest development constantly challenges and threatens men, and gives a certain potential psychological security, even liberation, to women. The transformed interpretation of difference is not inevitable, given other parenting arrangements and other arrangements of power between the sexes. It is especially insofar as women's lives and self-definition become oriented to men that difference becomes more salient for us, as does differential evaluation of the sexes. Insofar as women's lives and self-definition become more oriented toward themselves, differences from men become less salient.[18]

EVALUATING DIFFERENCE

What are the implications of this inquiry into psychoanalytic understandings of differentiation and gender difference for our understanding of difference, and for our evaluation of the view that difference is central to feminist theory? My investigation suggests that our own sense of differentiation, of separateness from others, as well as our psychological and cultural experience and interpretation of gender or sexual difference, are created through psychological, social, and cultural processes, and through relational experiences. We can only understand gender difference, and human distinctness and separation, relationally and situationally.[19] They are part of a system of asymmetrical social relationships embedded in inequalities of power, in which we grow up as selves, and as women and men. Our experience and perception of gender are processual; they are produced developmentally and in our daily social and cultural lives.

Difference is psychologically salient for men in a way that it is not for women, because of gender differences in early formative developmental processes and the particular unconscious conflicts and defenses these produce. This salience, in turn, has been transmuted into a conscious cultural preoccupation with gender difference. It has also become intertwined with and has helped to produce more general cultural notions, particularly, that individualism, separateness, and distance from others are desirable and requisite to autonomy and human fulfillment.[20] Throughout these processes, it is women, as mothers, who become the objects apart from which separateness, difference, and autonomy are defined.

It is crucial for us feminists to recognize that the ideologies of difference, which define us as women and as men, as well as inequality itself, are produced, socially, psychologically, and culturally, by people living in and creating their social, psychological, and cultural worlds. Women participate in the creation of these worlds and ideologies, even if our ultimate power and access to cultural hegemony are less than those of men. To speak of difference as a final, irreducible concept and to focus on gender differences as central is to reify them and to deny the reality of those *processes* that create the meaning and significance of gender. To see men and women as qualitatively different kinds of people, rather than seeing gender as processual, reflexive, and constructed, is to reify and deny *relations* of gender, to see gender differences as permanent rather than as created and situated.

We certainly need to understand how difference comes to be important, how it is produced as salient, and how it reproduces sexual inequality. But we should not appropriate differentiation and separation, or difference, for ourselves and take it as a given. Feminist theories and feminist inquiry based on the notion of essential difference, or focused on demonstrating difference, are doing feminism a disservice. They ultimately rely on the defensively constructed masculine models of gender that are presented to us as our cultural heritage, rather than creating feminist understandings of gender and difference that grow from our own politics, theorizing, and experience.

NOTES

I am very grateful to Susan Weisskopf, Michelle Z. Rosaldo, Jessica Benjamin, and Sara Ruddick for criticisms and comments on an earlier version of this essay.

1. From *The Elementary Structures of Kinship*, quoted in Adrienne Rich, *On Lies, Secrets and Silence* (New York: W.W. Norton & Co., 1979), p. 84.
2. See, for example, Alice Jardine, "Prelude: The Future of Difference" and Josette Féral, "The Powers of Difference," both in Eisenstein and Jardine, eds., *The Future of Difference* (Boston: Hall, 1980); "Women's Exile: Interview with Luce Irigaray," *Ideology and Consciousness* 1 (1977): 57–76; and Monique Plaza, " 'Phallomorphic Power' and the 'Psychology of Woman' " *Ideology and Consciousness* 4 (1978): 4–36.
3. The work of Margaret S. Mahler, *On Human Symbiosis and the Vicissitudes of Individuation* (New York: International Universities Press, 1968), is paradigmatic. For a more extended discussion of the earliest development of the self along lines suggested here, see Nancy Chodorow, *The Reproduction of Mothering: Psychoanalysis and the Sociology of Gender* (Berkeley: Univ. of California Press, 1978), chs. 4 and 5.

4. Ernest G. Schachtel, "The Development of Focal Attention and the Emergence of Reality" (1954), in *Metamorphosis* (New York: Basic Books, 1959), provides the best discussion I know of this process.
5. D.W. Winnicott, "The Theory of the Parent-Infant Relationship" (1960), in *The Maturational Processes and the Facilitating Environment* (New York: International Universities Press, 1965).
6. Alice Balint, "Love for the Mother and Mother Love" (1939), in Michael Balint, ed., *Primary Love and Psycho-Analytic Technique* (New York: Liveright Publishing, 1965), p. 97.
7. The new feminist/feminine blame-the-mother literature is one contemporary manifestation of failure in such a task. See esp. Nancy Friday, *My Mother/My Self* (New York: Dell Publishing, 1977). Of course, this is not to ignore or pass over the fact that men have been past masters of such perceptions of women.
8. In what follows, I am drawing particularly on the work of D.W. Winnicott and Michael Balint. See Winnicott, *The Maturational Processes*, and *Playing and Reality* (New York: Basic Books, 1971); and Balint, *Primary Love*, and *The Basic Fault: Therapeutic Aspects of Regression* (London: Tavistock Publications, 1968). See also R.D. Fairbairn, *An Object Relations Theory of the Personality* (New York: Basic Books, 1952); and Hans Loewald, "Internalization, Separation, Mourning and the Superego," *Psychoanalytic Quarterly* 31 (1962): 483–504.
9. See Winnicott, "The Capacity to Be Alone" (1958), in *The Maturational Processes.*
10. My interpretation here of differentiation, the self, and the goals of psychic life contrasts with the traditional Freudian view, which stresses ego and superego autonomy. For an excellent discussion of questions of ego autonomy and psychic structure, see Jessica Benjamin, "The End of Internalization: Adorno's Social Psychology," *Telos* 32 (1977): 42–64.
11. See Sigmund Freud, "The Dissolution of the Oedipus Complex" (1924), in *Standard Edition of the Complete Psychological Works* (SE) (London: The Hogarth Press), vol. 19, pp. 172–79; "Some Psychical Consequences of the Anatomical Distinction between the Sexes" (1925), SE, vol. 19, pp. 243–58; and "Femininity" (1933), in *New Introductory Lectures on Psychoanalysis*, SE, vol. 22, pp. 112–35.
12. See Roy Schafer, "Problems in Freud's Psychology of Women," *Journal of the American Psychoanalytic Association* 22 (1974): 459–85.
13. See Robert Stoller, "Facts and Fancies: An Examination of Freud's Concept of Bisexuality," in Jean Strouse, ed., *Women and Analysis* (New York: Grossman Publishers, 1974), and other Stoller writings.
14. For reviews of the social psychological literature on this point, see Miriam Johnson, "Sex Role Learning in the Nuclear Family," in *Child Development* 34 (1963): 319–34; Johnson, "Fathers, Mothers and Sex-Typing," *Sociological Inquiry* 45 (1975): 15–26; and Eleanor Maccoby and Carol Jacklin, *The Psychology of Sex Differences* (Stanford: Stanford Univ. Press, 1974).
15. For further discussion, see Chodorow, *Reproduction of Mothering*, ch. 5.
16. Johnson, "Fathers, Mothers," makes this suggestion, and suggests further that the father's masculinity introduces gender difference.
17. See Juliet Mitchell, *Psychoanalysis and Feminism* (New York: Pantheon Books, 1974).
18. I have not dealt in this essay with male and female body, and I would like to say a few words about these before concluding, since they clearly have relevance for the question of gender difference. We live an embodied life; we live with those genital and reproductive organs and capacities, those hormones and chromosomes, that locate us physiologically as male or female. But, to turn to psychoanalysis once again, I think it is fair to say that Freud's earliest discovery showed that there is nothing self-evident about this biology. How anyone understands, fantasizes about,

symbolizes, internally represents, or feels about her or his physiology is a product of development and experience in the family and not a direct product of this biology itself. These feelings, moreover, may be shaped by completely nonbiological considerations. Nonbiological considerations also shape perceptions of anatomical "sex differences" and the psychological development of these differences into forms of sexual object choice, mode, or aim; into femininity or masculinity as defined by psychoanalysis; into activity or passivity; into one's choice of the organ of erotic pleasure; and so forth. We cannot know what children would make of their bodies in a nongender or nonsexually organized world, what kind of sexual structuration or gender identities would develop. But it is not obvious that there would be major significance to biological sex differences, to gender difference, or to different sexualities. There might be a multiplicity of sexual organizations, identities, and practices, and perhaps even of genders themselves. Bodies would be bodies (I don't think we want to deny people their bodily experience). But particular bodily attributes would not necessarily be so determining of who we are, what we do, how we are perceived, and who are our sexual partners.

19. See Barrie Thorne, "Gender . . . How Is It Best Conceptualized?" (paper presented at the Annual Meeting of the American Sociological Association, San Francisco, August 1978).
20. For a discussion of these general cultural preoccupations and their psychological origins, see Evelyn Fox Keller, "Gender and Science," *Psychoanalysis and Contemporary Thought* 1 (1978): 409–33.

Is Male Gender Identity the Cause of Male Domination?

Young raises the question of whether gender differentiation can account for male domination, and she argues that it cannot. Examining the work of Nancy Chodorow, Nancy Hartsock, and Sandra Harding, Young claims that all of these theorists hold that masculine personalities lead to social structures that institutionalize women's subordination and also that the hierarchical duality in which masculinity is privileged over femininity establishes a pattern of thought and action that is replicated in race, class, heterosexist, and other forms of social domination and subordination. According to Young, gender differentiation concerns individual psychology, individual experience, and cultural categorization, whereas male domination concerns institutions that determine structural relations between women and men. Psychoanalysis does a good job of accounting for gendered symbolic relations, but it overpsychologizes male dominance and neglects concrete power relations.

There could be a gender-differentiated society that was not male-dominated. To account for male domination, then, feminists need an account of the causes and reproduction of social structures that do not originate in gendered psychology, gendered experience, or gendered cultural categories. Feminists must examine the way in which society's institutions are organized—the lines of power and authority they establish and the ways in which goods and services are produced and distributed. Feminists must develop historically and culturally specific theories that pay attention to concrete material conditions and that acknowledge the complexity of social causation. Attempting to change gender relations through coparenting will not suffice to overcome male dominance.

—D.T.M.

Chapter 2

Iris Marion Young

Is Male Gender Identity the Cause of Male Domination?

In this essay I assess the place of Nancy Chodorow's theory of the development of gender personality with respect to the overall project of a feminist social theory. Without doubt, Chodorow's theory has made a vital contribution to a feminist understanding of the meaning and production of gender identity. Chodorow herself, as well as a number of other writers, however, has suggested that this gender theory can ground a theory of male domination as a whole, as well as other relations of domination. I will argue that such a use of Chodorow's theory is illegitimate.

I examine passages in Chodorow's writing that suggest that she takes her theory as a theory of male domination. I examine as well the accounts of Nancy Hartsock and Sandra Harding, who use Chodorow's theory to account for male domination more explicitly than Chodorow herself does and who also go farther to claim that male personality is a foundation for all domination relations. All three writers tend to claim that the social relations of women's mothering and the gender personalities they produce are a crucial foundation for male domination. I should emphasize that this is only a tendency in their work, and in focusing on this tendency I shall to a certain extent not be doing justice to the subtlety of their arguments. The precise status of the explanatory power they claim for the theory of gender is ambiguous, I argue, because they fail to distinguish adequately the categories of gender differentiation and male domination. Once these categories are distinguished and their references formulated, it becomes clear that a theory of gender personality at best can provide only a small part of the description and explanation of institutions of male domination. By failing to distinguish explicitly these categories and focusing primarily on phenomena relating to gender, these accounts divert the attention of feminist theory from questions of the material and structural bases of power.

I

Nancy Chodorow's theory of the development of gender personalities, along with similar work by Jane Flax and the related but rather different work of Dorothy Dinnerstein,[1] has opened a rich territory of theorizing previously only slightly explored by feminist thinkers. In this feminist psychoanalytic theory we have an approach to conceptualizing typical differences in the behavior and experience of men and women that avoids the disadvantages of the only two alternatives we have had until recently for understanding these differences: a biological account or a role-learning account. Chodorow's theory shows the gender characteristics that are stubbornly typical among men and women in our society to be determined by social factors. Unlike a biological account, then, feminist psychoanalytic theory of gender reveals this structure as changeable. But Chodorow's theory also explains why gender identity is so deep-seated as to be virtually impossible to unlearn, and why so much anxiety surrounds gender issues, even for adults. Socialization theory of gender, which conceptualizes gender characteristics as no different in principle from any other learned role norms, cannot account for the uniquely central place of gender in self-identity.

Briefly, the account that Chodorow gives of the development of gender personality in *The Reproduction of Mothering* is as follows.[2] She starts with the fact that the primary person in the life of both men and women is their mother. The significant stages of psychological development that lead to the formation of a separate sense of identity, personality characteristics, the acquisition of gender identity, and sexual orientation, in her theory, play out for both boys and girls in the context of their relation to their mothers. She explains how this exclusive female parenting produces gender identities and personality characteristics that predispose women to be nurturant and cuts off these dispositions in men.

Because of her own gender identity, the mother identifies with her girl child more than with her boy child. In relating to her daughter she unconsciously replays many of the ambiguities and identifications she experienced with her own mother. The mother thus often tends to relate to her daughter more as an extension of herself than as a separate person. The infant girl also experiences herself as identified with her mother, as does the infant boy. The mutually reinforcing identification of mother and daughter results in the girl's acquiring a sense of separate identity later than boys, and never acquiring a sense of separation from others as strong as the boy's. Feminine personality, Chodorow argues, entails the development of relatively permeable "ego boundaries." The normal woman does develop a sense of identity distinct from other people, an ego. But she tends more than the man to fashion her identity by reference to her relation to other people, and to empathize more easily with other people.

For the boy the story is rather different. Due again to her own gender identity, which usually includes a heterosexual identity, the mother of the boy does not identify with him as much as with a girl. She often tends unconsciously to sexualize her relation to him, thus pushing him into a relation of opposition with her. Unlike the girl, then, the boy is encouraged in his effort to separate his identity from his mother. When the boy himself begins to acquire an understanding of gender, his project of separating from the mother becomes one not merely of defining himself as a different person, but as a different *kind* of person. In separating from the mother and developing a distinct identity, then, the boy sets himself in opposition to the mother and all that is feminine. Chodorow concludes that from this process the masculine personality typically develops rigid ego boundaries. A man's sense of separate identity, that is, entails cutting off a sense of continuity and empathy with others.

Chodorow is ambiguous about the explanatory status of her theory. On one reading, her theory accounts for no more than how persons accommodate to gender-divided and male-dominated social relations in our society. Her theory explains only how the gender division of labor in the modern nuclear family, which gives exclusive responsibilities for early childcare to the mother, produces gender-differentiated persons with desires and capacities that particularly suit them for continuing that gendered division of labor.[3] On this reading, the structures of male domination in our society are presupposed. A separate explanation is required to account for the origin and maintenance of these structures themselves, such as the relations of authority, dependence, and coercion that define this or any other male-dominated society, or the differential access to important resources that underlies gender inequality.

The dominant strain in Chodorow's book, however, suggests that she thinks that at least the basic form of her theory applies to an explanation of male domination in all societies that have existed. Following Gayle Rubin's idea of the "sex/gender system,"[4] Chodorow defines the social organization of gender as the social construction of sexuality, procreation, and kinship that differentiates by gender. She asserts that while logically a society could be gendered without being male-dominated, no such society has ever existed. Thus she seems to conclude that gender differentiation is identical to male domination in at least all hitherto existing societies, and that her theory of the development of gender personalities by women's mothering is a theory of this male-dominated gender system.[5] Hartsock and Harding also tend to collapse the categories of gender differentiation and male domination, at least insofar as they appear to make inferences about male domination directly from claims about gender differentiation.

Alongside passages which suggest that this theory of gender accounts for the motivation of individuals to act in accordance with the institutions of male domination, there are passages such as the following in which Chodorow appears to claim that the theory accounts for male domination itself.

> We can define and articulate certain broad universal sexual asymmetries in the social organization of gender *generated* by women's mothering. Women's mothering *determines* women's primary location in the domestic sphere and creates a *basis* for the structural differentiation of domestic and public spheres. But these spheres operate hierarchically. Kinship rules organize claims of men on domestic units, and men dominate kinship. Culturally and politically, the public sphere dominates the domestic, and *hence* men dominate women.[6]

In my reading of this and similar passages, Chodorow claims that her theory explains the basic causes of male domination in all societies. Following Rosaldo and Lamphere,[7] she assumes that the subordination of women is a function of a universal public-domestic division. This public-domestic division, she says, originates in and is reproduced by the social relations of women's mothering that produce distinctive gender personalities. While a direct argument for this set of claims does not appear in Chodorow's writing, one can be reconstructed from what she does say.

Chodorow argues that in developing a masculine self-identity, boys must not only develop a sense of self distinct from the mother, but also a sense of being a different kind of self. Since the mother provides him with his first model of what it is to be a person, the boy defines masculinity negatively, as what the mother is not. To have a positive sense of masculinity, therefore, boys must denigrate and dissociate themselves from the female. Boys develop a dread of women and a desire to have power over them through this process, because mother poses a threat to their separate masculine identities.[8]

To secure his masculine identity, the boy rejects the mother and joins with other boys and men in a positive, exclusive sphere without the attributes of nurturance and dependence associated with the feminine. This masculine realm takes on a more highly valued character than the domestic, because men must affirm their masculinity by denying and denigrating the female. This would appear to be the argument for Chodorow's above-quoted claim that women's mothering "creates a basis for the structural differentiation of domestic and public spheres" and sets up a hierarchical relation between them.

Women's mothering also creates gender personalities that particularly suit women and men for the domestic and public realms respectively. The relative stability of her identification with the mother gives to the girl's gender identity a personality oriented toward affective relations with others. This suits girls for the particularistic relations of the domestic realm. Women's mothering creates in boys, on the other hand, a more bounded, instrumentally oriented, and abstract personality. This suits them particularly for the formal and instrumental character of the relations in the public realm. This presumably is the argument for Chodorow's above-quoted claim that "women's mothering determines women's primary location in the domestic sphere."

In a paper entitled "The Feminist Standpoint: Developing the Ground of a Specifically Feminist Historical Materialism," Nancy Hartsock uses Chodorow's theory of the development of gender personalities as a central element in her account of the "abstract masculinity" she claims underlies Western culture.[9] Abstract masculinity is a mode of conceptualization that emphasizes mutually exclusive dualities. These dualities—such as same-other, identity-difference, negation-affirmation, life-death, body-mind—have a crucial ground in the structure of the masculine personality, which creates in men an oppositional attitude in human relations, a polarity of self and other.

Hartsock uses the notion of abstract masculinity primarily to account for the logic of much of western metaphysical and political thought. More relevant for the issues of this paper, she also appeals to abstract masculinity to account for the nature of institutions. Abstract masculinity, she claims, accounts for hierarchical dualism in the institutions of society, which underlies relations of class domination and gender domination. She argues that "male rather than female experience and activity replicates itself in both the hierarchical and dualist institutions of class society and the frameworks of thought generated by that experience."[10] A primary determinant of this experience is the self-other dichotomy produced in masculine personality by women's mothering.

It is difficult to tell just what sort of causal relations Hartsock asserts, or how strongly. As I interpret her claims, she asserts that masculine personality causes institutions of domination in the following way. Being mothered by women produces in men a propensity to approach relations with others in an oppositional and competitive way. Thus, men produce institutions defined by opposition, hierarchy, and competition. The masculine personality generated by women's mothering also produces the oppression of women because men tend to denigrate and repress activities associated with the body, and women are most linked to such activities.

Sandra Harding asserts an even stronger and more explicit relationship between women's mothering and institutions of domination. In a paper entitled "What is the Real Material Base of Patriarchy and Capital?" she answers that the social relations of women's mothering are the most fundamental material base of all forms of oppression—not only gender oppression, but also class, race, lesbian, and gay oppression. The theory of the production of gendered personalities, she claims, explains "why it is that *men* control and thus have material interests in maintaining both patriarchy and capital." The social relations of women's mothering "create patterns of dominating social relations which are more general than class oppression and gender oppression."[11]

A later paper by Harding specifies more precisely the nature of her causal claim. The social relations of women's mothering determine the form or structure common to male personalities, institutions of domination, and the ideas associated with them.[12] The social relations of women's mothering constitute the material base of classism, racism, heterosexism and sexism insofar as they are all structured by a dualistic hierarchy of dominance and subordination.

Like Chodorow and Hartsock, Harding does not clearly and explicitly lay out the argument for this claim. As I reconstruct her argument, it appears to be the following: Harding theorizes that women's mothering produces a self-other dichotomy in the masculine personality. Because boys have particular separation problems, their search for a separate identity leads them to form rigid ego boundaries and to tend to regard other persons, especially women, as in antagonistic opposition to themselves. This self-other dichotomy is not merely an opposition, but a hierarchy in which self is of greater value. Men thus have a psychic interest in dominating, in setting themselves up as master in relation to other men, to nature, and of course to women. Since men design and control all of society's institutions, according to Harding, these institutions reflect this psychology of self-other domination. Thus class oppression, racial oppression, gender oppression, and homosexual oppression have a common formal cause in "the stereotypically masculine modes of structuring social relations between self and other which originate *in individuals*, in the psycho/physical labor required to become masculinely gendered social persons."[13]

II

Nancy Chodorow appears to identify gender differentiation with male domination, and thus tends to argue that her theory of the development of gender personalities is a theory of male domination. Hartsock and Harding also tend to collapse the categories of gender differentiation and male domination, at least insofar as they appear to make inferences about male domination directly from claims about gender differentiation. In contrast, I perceive and defend a distinction between these two categories. While gender differentiation is a phenomenon of individual psychology and experience, as well as of cultural categorization, male domination refers to structural relations of genders and institutional forms that determine those structures. Any complete account of a male-dominated society requires an account of gender, but also requires an account of the causes and reproduction of structures not originating from gender psychology. For these reasons a theory of gender cannot, as the three writers here treated think, be used as the basis for a theory of male domination. The failure to distinguish the category of gender differentiation from male domination is not uncommon among feminist theorists, especially those who rely on psychoanalytic theory.[14] Thus the significance of the theoretical remarks in this section extends beyond the three thinkers I focus on to the whole project of feminist social theory.

Gender differentiation refers primarily to phenomena of individual psychology and experience. Chodorow shows how the unconscious inner life of men and women is differently structured because they have different infant relations to their mothers, and Harding follows Chodorow on this. Hartsock defines the phenomena of gender less in terms of personality structure and more in terms of the different experience men and women have of the world because they are mothered by women and because the sexual division of labor allocates to them different sorts of activities.[15] Whether interpreted primarily in terms of personality structure or mode of experiencing the world, gender differentiation also includes propensities of both men and women to behave in certain typical ways. All three of the writers under discussion here appear to think that psychological dispositions associated with gender can themselves explain social structural phenomena, such as a distinction between public and private spheres, or relations of hierarchy in institutions, and I shall argue below that such reasoning is inappropriate.

Gender is not merely a phenomenon of individual psychology and experience. In most cultures it is a basic metaphysical category by which the whole universe is organized. Most languages, for example, are elaborately gendered, with gender-differentiated modes of address, verb and noun forms, and so on. In most cultures, moreover, all the significant elements of the social, natural, and spiritual world are differentiated by gender. This usually means more than merely designating animals, weather phenomena, abstract concepts, and so on, as masculine or feminine; it entails as well that the entities categorized carry a rich set of genderized attributes and relationships. The integrating mythologies of most cultures rely heavily on gender symbols, as do most legitimating ideologies.[16]

As a category, then, gender differentiation is primarily a phenomenon of symbolic life, in both the individual consciousness and the general metaphysical framework and ideologies of a culture. Psychoanalytic theory of gender is the most adequate theory, because more than any other type of theory it can make the connections between individual affectivity, motivation, and desire, on the one hand, and the symbolic and categories of culture, on the other. A psychoanalytic account of gender can explain why gender meanings are so deep-seated in individual identity and cultural categorization, and why discussion of alteration in gender meanings or gender relationships causes most people great anxiety. As a theory of symbolism, and of the unconscious mechanism for symbol substitution and transference, moreover, psychoanalysis can provide a framework for understanding the pervasiveness of gender meanings throughout a culture's categorical and symbolic systems. The feminist theories of gender developed by Chodorow, Flax, Dinnerstein, and others no doubt need more elaboration and refinement, particularly with regard to questions of cross-cultural and historical variation. There is little doubt, however, that they have already contributed significantly to the development of feminist social theory.

To regard male domination as identical with or derivable from gender differentiation, however, is to overpsychologize the social phenomena of male domination.[17] As a category, male domination refers not primarily to psychological and cultural phenomena, but to a different aspect of social reality, institutional structures.[18] This structural aspect of social reality includes at least the following: (a) what the major institutions in a given society are, how differentiated they are from one another, and how they reinforce or conflict with one another; (b) how material resources are produced and distributed within and among these institutions, and how these patterns of production and distribution provide differentiated capacities and satisfactions for different individuals and groups of people; and (c) the rules according to which the institutions are organized and the means of their enforcement, especially as these define relations of authority and subordination.

Male domination refers to the organization of a particular institution or the pattern of institutional organization in a whole society in which men have some degree of unreciprocated authority or control over women, and/or men have greater control than women over the operations of the institutions or set of institutions. Male domination exists within an institution or in a whole society when one or more of the following conditions obtain: (a) men have the power to control aspects of women's lives and actions and the means to enforce their will, and women do not have complementary control over men's lives; (b) men occupy institutionalized positions of social decision-making from which women are excluded, and women do not have their own spheres with comparable privilege or control over men's lives; (c) men benefit from the labor and other activity of women to a greater degree than women benefit from that of men.[19]

It is possible to conceive of a gender-differentiated society, I suggest, in which none of these conditions of male domination exist. It may be true that all hitherto existing societies have been male dominated as well as gender differentiated, although this is a matter of some dispute. Even if it were true that male domination in fact has always existed along with gender differentiation, that would not mean that they are identical, or that the former derives from the latter. Unless we make a clear distinction between these two categories and develop clear criteria for what counts as male domination, we will not be able to discover how culturally and historically widespread male domination is, or how it varies in degree and kind. Only by keeping the distinction clear can we ascertain whether there is any regular relation between phenomena of gender differentiation and phenomena of male domination.

Before continuing the examination of the theories of Chodorow, Harding, and Hartsock, it might be useful to illustrate the categorical distinctions I have been making with an example of phenomena of male domination that cannot be explained by appealing to gender theory.

Evelyn Fox Keller presents a very interesting account of the origins of the style of modern scientific inquiry in the masculine personality women's mothering generates. She argues that the rigid notion of scientific objectivity that excludes all affectivity, value, and human meaning derives from the rigid character of masculine ego-boundaries. She argues that the metaphors of Bacon and other founders of modern science that depict the scientist as conquering and mastering a female nature, moreover, arise from a masculine self-other opposition that identifies the other as female.[20] Her account reveals much about the cognitive styles of modern and contemporary science, and the degree to which we can understand these as bound to the identities of the men who have founded and dominated that science.

It does not itself account for why, since the early modern period, men have dominated scientific activity, however, as Keller suggests it does. Nor does it show how male domination of scientific and technological activity has had crucial implications for the specific forms of women's oppression in the modern world. Explaining why men dominate science, and why that fact enables them to dominate women, entails reference to more structural aspects of social life and their changes.

Important among these structural aspects is specific change in the gendered division of labor that accompanied the rise of science. During the time that Bacon defined science as the domination of nature, men were appropriating from women many of the practical arts whose union with traditional intellectual science Bacon saw as the key to the new method. For example, feminists have most researched the male appropriation of the healing arts, which before that time were dominated by women. An account like Keller's can explain why, once men had dominated medicine and defined it as science, the conceptualization of the body by medicine became more objectified, the use of instruments increased, and so on. The gender theory cannot explain, however, how men were able to take over the formerly female-dominated professions, or even why they wanted to.[21]

III

I have argued that attempts to develop a general theory of women's oppression from gender theory fail to distinguish clearly between gender differentiation and male domination. As a result, as I will show in this section, this use of gender theory tends to divert the attention of feminist social theory from questions of the bases, conditions, and exercise of power.

Chodorow's theory of the development of gender personalities exhibits a curious lack of reference to male power. Unlike earlier feminist attempts to reinterpret psychoanalytic theory, such as those by Firestone, Rubin, and Mitchell,[22] Chodorow does not at all appeal to the power of the father in the family to account for the development of different personalties in boys and girls. On those earlier accounts, which follow Freud more closely than Chodorow does, the boy gives up his attachment to his mother in exchange for the promise that one day he can accede to the power of the father. Thus, when the boy despises the mother and gives up identification with her, he does so not simply because he is uncertain about who he is, but because he despises her powerlessness. For the girl, on the other hand, the discovery that she lacks the phallus as does her mother is a discovery that she belongs to the class of the powerless. Penis envy is her desire to belong to the class of the powerful. The girl drops her desire for her mother and turns her affection to the father as her only avenue to power. Chodorow's theory has an advantage over these accounts in the specific attention she gives to the positive relation the infant has to the mother. This emphasis on the relations of mothering, however, leads her to ignore the power of the father in accounting for gender personality. In her account, the father is primarily an absence, not a power.

This de-emphasis of male power in Chodorow's theory carries over into the use made of it for general feminist social theory. All three of the thinkers summarized above, of course, claim to be concerned with explaining the sources of male power and the oppression of women. The most they explain, however, is a masculine *desire* for power. The social relations of infant care, they argue, produce men with more of a propensity than women to instrumentalize relations with others. Men also emerge from the mothering process with a hierarchical self-other dichotomy that allows them to view all persons as potential subordinates. The three thinkers account for a specific male desire to dominate women, moreover, by appeal to an unconscious dread of women resulting from male insecurity of self as different from the other.

Unless a psychological propensity to wield power itself makes men powerful, however, their accounts do not touch on the question of the sources of male power. Neither Chodorow, Hartsock, nor Harding sees that their theories ignore concrete relations of domination; and as I have already pointed out, they tend to draw conclusions about the latter from arguments about the former. Other elements of gender theory also contribute to a tendency to de-emphasize concrete relations of power. In particular, uses of gender theory to found a theory of male domination tend to (a) ignore historical and cultural specificity, (b) focus on ideational forms, and (c) assume incorrect social ontology.

Omission of Historical and Cultural Specificity

All three of the theorists under discussion abstract from the cultural and historical specificity of concrete social structures. They pose their claims in terms of what is common to all (male-dominated) societies. As a consequence of this universalizing tendency, they make controversial claims about the universality of certain social phenomena. Chodorow and Harding assume, for example, that in all societies women have exclusive responsibility for primary infant care, and that in all societies women have been devalued. Both assumptions, however, would be disputed by many anthropologists.[23] Chodorow appears to assume that all societies have a public-private split, which allocates men to the public and women to the private. Many anthropologists and historians would take issue with this, as well.[24] Finally, many anthropologists and historians would dispute the assumption made by all three writers that in all societies women are oppressed, or at least have a lesser status than men.

From a methodological point of view, this universalizing tendency has several problems. First, claims about the universality of gender structures are usually made without empirical warrant. On most questions about what is common to all societies, the data simply are not in. Second, trans-historical or trans-cultural claims too often carry over assumptions based on the historically specific structures of modern European society to other societies and periods.[25]

The attempt to make universalistic claims about male domination, finally, requires taking a very abstract approach to social reality. For concrete observation shows that there is extraordinary variability in the causes and degrees of male domination in different societies, or even among different subgroups in one society. Since the concrete social relations of gender vary enormously in content and structure, then, gender theory can only make trans-historical or trans-cultural assertions by abstracting from these concrete relations. For Chodorow to regard the public-private distinction as a cultural universal always connected with women's mothering and women's status in the same way, for example, she must conceive it as an abstract and purely formal distinction empty of specific content. Harding says explicitly that gender theory is concerned not with the content of social phenomena, but rather with the formal similarity she claims exists among masculine personality, patriarchal social institutions, and the belief systems that arise within those institutions. These all have in common, she suggests, the formal structure of hierarchical dualism.[26]

Emphasis on Ideational Forms

Relations of power and domination drop out of consideration in the accounts we are examining here precisely because of the level of abstraction at which they operate. The bases, structure, and operation of power and domination are necessarily concrete, and are extraordinarily variable in both form and degree.[27] The inability of this formalism to deal with power becomes apparent in the way that Hartsock and Harding conceptualize domination itself. They do not refer to concrete material conditions to describe the enactment of power and domination, but rather only to the relation among categories. For both, social relations of domination appear to be defined as nothing more than a hierarchical dualism of self and other.

Hartsock, for example, appears to define class society as a social structure in which there is a hierarchical dualism, a ruling group standing in opposition to a ruled group.[28] This merely defines the abstract categorical relations of class society, and excludes reference to the social structures and material relations that also ought to define class society. Class society is indeed hierarchical but, more specifically, it involves relations of power and dependence in which one sector of society enforces the appropriation of the products of the labor of other segments of society.[29]

Despite the fact that the gender theorists claim to be materialist in their account of the bases of male domination, their accounts are idealist in the strict sense. They claim that the nature of institutions is determined by a relation among ideas. To be sure, they attempt to ground the self-other dichotomy they attribute to the masculine personality in the material relations of infant care. They do not argue, however, that material relations determine the institutional structure. They argue, rather, that a certain logical or metaphysical structure determines the structure of social institutions, namely, a conceptualization of experience in terms of a rigid self-other dichotomy.

If I have offered a correct analysis of the categories of gender differentiation and male domination, phenomena related to gender differentiation cannot by themselves explain structures of male domination, because the former category refers to ideas, symbols, and forms of consciousness, and the latter refers to the appropriation of benefit from women by men in a concrete material way. Gender theory can plausibly be used to argue that certain forms of conceptualization that appear in western theories and ideologies have a root in the masculine personality generated by women's mothering.[30] For here the account grounds one set of forms of consciousness in another.

Gender theory surely can contribute a part of the explanation of the nature and relation of social institutions, moreover. But the explanation of any institutional form, especially those relating to power and domination, requires in addition reference to the relation of institutions to one another, and an account of the material means of access, control, enforcement, and autonomy that agents have within those institutions. In not recognizing the categorical difference between gender differentiation and male domination, gender theory ignores these explanatory requirements.

Let me give an example of this sort of confusion. Chodorow's arguments, as well as Harding's, focus on the devaluation of women rather than directly on the question of male domination. In explaining devaluation of women they appear to think they have thereby explained male domination, when in fact no such inference is warranted.

As summarized above, Chodorow explains the source of the devaluation of women by men in a dread of women and anxiety about their masculinity caused by the social relations of mothering. Inasmuch as it argues that one form of consciousness—masculine personality—grounds another—masculine attitude toward women—this is a plausible argument. One cannot pass from such an argument directly to a conclusion about the causes of male domination, however. Even if we find that devaluation of women and male domination always occur together, we cannot conclude that the explanation of one is also the explanation of the other. Description and explanation of male domination still require reference to material relations of dependence and autonomy, access to resources and the material means of coercion, as well as to the structural relations among institutions which reinforce or change these.

Assumption of Incorrect Social Ontology

A final element of the accounts of Hartsock and Harding contributes to their lack of specific attention to the concrete causes and operation of power. They both assume that the institutions of male-dominated society reflect masculine personality, and only masculine personality. Harding most explicitly argues that the nature of institutions of domination is determined by the self-other dichotomy of masculine personality because men design and control all institutions in patriarchal societies and make them in their own image.[31]

This argument falsely assumes that the nature of institutions in patriarchal societies is solely or primarily a product of male action. Even in the most male-dominated societies, many spheres of social life exist in which women's action and temperament have a significant influence. The problem of male domination is not that women are prevented from acting upon and within institutions, but that the benefits of their contribution are systematically transferred to men.

More important, that institutions of domination reflect the structure of masculine personality is an argument that rests on a questionable assumption about the relation of individuals and social structures. It assumes that the nature of institutions is determined by the nature of the individuals whose actions produce and maintain them. There are several problems, however, with this assumption.

While acting persons are indeed the only concrete human entities that exist in the social world, it does not follow that the nature of institutions is isomorphic with the nature of individuals. The assumption mistakes the fundamental unit of institutions, which is not individuals but *interactions* among individuals.[32] Most institutions relevant to a theory of male domination are products of interactions between men and women, and not merely among men. The characteristics of personality, the motives they influence, and the interpretations of events they color are surely important elements in these interactions. But the structure of the institutions cannot be read off from the structure of individual personalities.[33]

Actions and interactions, moreover, are not the only determinants of institutional structures and practices. Individuals always act situated within and oriented toward natural and geographical givens, the possibilities and limits of available technologies and artifacts, and the cultural traditions to which they are heir. Perhaps even more important, the actions and interactions of social life almost always generate unintended consequences. One cannot foresee or control the interpretation others will give to one's actions or how they will respond, nor how others will respond to the response, and so on. Social events are often the result of the cumulative effect of a great many individual actions and interactions, moreover, bringing results neither intended nor predicted by any of the actors. Economic events like depressions, for example, often have this character.

The argument that the nature of institutions of domination is determined by the self-other dichotomy of the masculine personality created by women's mothering, then, erases the complex material and social structural factors involved in the causes, maintenance, and operation of relations of power and domination. These arguments fail to distinguish male domination from gender differentiation insofar as they tend to reduce social structural phenomena to psychological causes. Thus they fail to give adequate focus to those structures of male domination in a particular context which cannot be reduced to individual psychologies.

In sum, gender theory diverts feminist thinking from specific focus on power because it tends to be universalistic, hence to couch its claims in terms of abstract relations of categories, and to reduce social structures to products of individual personality.[34]

IV

Chodorow's theory, as well as Dinnerstein's, has received much discussion and has been absorbed quickly into feminist theorizing, at least partly because it seemed to offer a concrete and workable strategy for transforming gender relations. The theories suggest that exclusive parenting of infants by women is a key cause of male domination and the oppression of women. Thus, if the social relations of infant care were to change such that men participated as much as women, it seems to follow that the whole edifice erected on the base of exclusive female parenting would topple.

Parenting shared by men and women is the key step in eliminating the oppression of women. When that strategy was first put forward, it sounded simple and straightforward. It has not taken feminists long, however, to see that the matter is not so simple. Many wonder whether men with their present masculine personalities, complete with their insecurities and hatred of women, should be anywhere near children. Others have pointed out that in contemporary society, mothering is one of the only activities in which most women have some autonomy and from which they derive a measure of self-respect. If men were encouraged to participate in that sphere as well, under present conditions, it would mean a loss of status for women.

It quickly became apparent, moreover, that to really change the social relations of infant care entails monumental changes in all institutions of society. For shared parenting to be possible, the whole structure of work outside the home would have to change and become more flexible. To encourage men to be childcare workers, outside the home as well as in it, the value of childcare would have to be significantly increased. Without alteration in other elements of male domination, moreover, shared parenting, even if it happened, would not be likely to change greatly the patterns of socialization or the resulting masculine and feminine personalities. If men were to continue to occupy positions of authority, for example, and the idea of authority continued to be associated with masculinity, then children raised by both women and men would be likely to maintain that association. If media images continued to sentimentalize and sexualize women while presenting men as tough and emotionally distant, children and adults of both sexes would be likely to internalize and reproduce those images.

When we ask about feminist strategy, the error of collapsing the categories of male domination and gender differentiation and attributing the key cause of male domination to women's mothering becomes apparent. Gender division in parenting is only one among the many institutional structures that produce and maintain the oppression of women. If the above arguments are sound, moreover, women's mothering may be less fundamental than other institutions of male domination, since it appears that relations of parenting cannot be changed without first changing other structures.

What does it mean, then, for feminist theory to pay attention to issues of power and domination? I have suggested that it entails a structural analysis of relations of authority and dependence, and a description of the transfer and appropriation of benefits of labor. To describe and explain male domination as concrete relations of power, feminist theory must ask questions like the following. Which gender has access to what social resources as a result of performing its gender-differentiated activity, and what do the resources give members of the gender the capacity to do? How much and by what means are members of each gender organized in networks of solidarity?[35] How do the structural relations among various institutions—state and family, for example—affect the concrete relations of dependence and autonomy in which women stand?[36]

If it does not offer us a very full strategy for feminist revolution, what can gender theory offer that will aid in undermining the oppression of women? Gender theory can provide us with an important understanding of the power of symbols and the bases of motivation and desire. It can help sensitize both women and men to the deep sources of some of the ways of experiencing that are particular to each gender. It can also help us understand, as Flax has argued, how in the women's movement itself we may tend to reproduce our relations to our mothers in our relationships with each other. Perhaps most important, gender theory can be an enormous aid in consciousness raising about contemporary masculinist ideologies, by showing some of the sources of their misogyny. All this needs to be supplemented with a concrete analysis of the social structure, however, which cannot be provided by gender theory. To fight against male domination we need to understand how the institutions work in such a way as to promote women's working for men, how the current arrangements are enforced, and who controls the resources that produce and maintain them.

NOTES

I began research for this paper while participating in a National Endowment for the Humanities Summer Seminar Fellowship on "Themes in Cross-Cultural Analysis of Women and Society" directed by Eleanor Leacock, City University of New York, in the summer of 1980. An earlier version of this paper was presented at the Caucus for a New Political Science, American Political Science Association meetings, New York City, September 1981; and at a meeting of the Society for Women in Philosophy, Western Division, Fort Wayne, Indiana, October 1981. I am grateful to women at those meetings for their responses and suggestions. I am also grateful to Nancy Hartsock, Muriel Dimen, Linda Nicholson, Sandra Bartky, Roger Gottlieb, and David Alexander for their helpful suggestions.

1. Jane Flax, "The Conflict Between Nurturance and Autonomy in Mother-Daughter Relationships and within Feminism," *Feminist Studies* 4, no. 2 (1978); Dorothy Dinnerstein, *The Mermaid and the Minotaur: Sexual Arrangements and Human Malaise* (New York: Harper & Row, 1976).
2. Nancy Chodorow, *The Reproduction of Mothering* (Berkeley: University of California Press, 1978).
3. Ibid., pp. 185, 208–9.
4. Gayle Rubin, "The Traffic in Women: Notes Toward a Political Economy of Sex," in *Toward an Anthropology of Women*, edited by Rayna Reiter (New York: Monthly Review Press, 1976).

5. Chodorow, *Reproduction of Mothering*, pp. 8–9.
6. Ibid., pp. 9–10 (italics mine).
7. Michelle Zimbalist Rosaldo and Louise Lamphere, Introduction to *Woman, Culture and Society* (Stanford: Stanford University Press, 1974), pp. 1–16.
8. Chodorow talks most explicitly about dread of women as an element in masculine personality in her paper "Being and Doing: A Cross-Cultural Examination of the Socialization of Males and Females," in *Woman in Sexist Society*, edited by Vivian Gornick and Barbara K. Moran (New York: Basic Books, 1971); see also Chodorow, *Reproduction of Mothering*, pp. 181–83.
9. Included in *Discovering Reality: Feminist Perspectives on Epistemology, Metaphysics, Methodology, and Philosophy of Science*, edited by Sandra Harding and Merrill B. Hintikka (Dordrecht: Reidel Publishing Co., 1983).
10. Hartsock, "The Feminist Standpoint," p. 20.
11. Sandra Harding, "What is the Real Material Base of Patriarchy and Capital?" in *Women and Revolution*, edited by Lydia Sargent (Boston: South End Press, 1981), p. 139.
12. See Sandra Harding, "Gender Politics of Infancy," *Quest* 5, no. 3, p. 63.
13. Ibid., p. 62.
14. For example, Juliet Mitchell, in her book *Psychoanalysis and Feminism* (New York: Vintage Books, 1975), clearly identifies patriarchy with the psychodynamics of gender. See my critique of her failure to make this distinction in "Socialist Feminism and the Limits of Dual Systems Theory," *Socialist Review* 50/51, Summer 1980.
15. Nancy Hartsock, in a personal communication, has pointed out this difference in emphasis between her account and the others. This distinction raises the question, which I do not intend to answer here, of what the relationship is between the concepts of "personality" and "experience."
16. For an incisive definition of gender in these terms, see David Alexander, "Gender Labor and Occupational Segregation by Sex" (unpublished, University of Massachusetts).
17. Susan Bourque and Kay Barbara Warren make this point in *Women of the Andes: Patriarchy and Social Change in Two Peruvian Towns* (Ann Arbor: University of Michigan Press, 1981), pp. 58 and 83. They do not give very thorough reasons for their claim that an understanding of patriarchy requires analysis of the institutional context of sex roles independent of psychology.
18. For an account of the logic of social analysis which distinguishes between psychological and structural aspects without falling into the polarization typical of other sociological frameworks, see Anthony Giddens, *Central Problems in Social Theory* (Berkeley: University of California Press, 1979), Ch. 2–5.
19. Very few feminist theorists have discussed how to define criteria of male domination. Peggy Reeves Sanday has a useful discussion of the way certain anthropologists have defined the concept, and offers an alternative formulation of her own, one somewhat narrower than the one I have articulated. See *Female Power and Male Dominance* (New York: Cambridge University Press, 1981), especially pp. 163–79.

    Naomi Rosenthal has developed a useful notion of the measures of male dominance and female autonomy based on the ability to mobilize resources, including political and ideological resources, which she applies to five Amazonian societies. See her "Women in Amazonia," (unpublished, SUNY at Old Westbury).

    Lisa Leghorn and Katherine Parker, in *Woman's Worth* (New York: Routledge & Kegan Paul, 1981), develop criteria for distinguishing three levels of male-dominated societies: those in which women have no power, those in which women have token power, and those in which women have negotiating power. They measure women's power within three areas: (a) valuation of women's fertility and physical integrity; (b) women's access to and control over crucial resources, including property, paid and collective labor, training and education; and (c) women's networks (p. 22).

20. Evelyn Fox Keller, "Baconian Science: A Hermaphroditic Birth," *Philosophical Forum* II, No. 3 (Spring 1980).
21. To my knowledge, Alice Clark's 1919 book, *The Working Life of Women in the Seventeenth Century* (New York: E.P. Dutton & Co.), is still the best single source on this process of change in women's economic status.
22. Shulamith Firestone, *The Dialectic of Sex* (New York: William Morrow, 1970), chap. 3; Rubin, "The Traffic in Women"; Mitchell, *Psychoanalysis and Feminism.*
23. Sanday, *Female Power and Male Dominance*, Eleanor Leacock, "Women in Egalitarian Society," in *Becoming Visible: Women in European History*, edited by Renate Bridenthal and Claudia Koonz (Boston: Houghton Mifflin, 1977).
24. In an article published shortly before she died, Rosaldo argued against her earlier position that discussion of a universal public-domestic split tends to rely on cultural assumptions based on that particular form of the public-private split that dates from the nineteenth century in western Europe. See Michelle Rosaldo, "The Use and Abuse of Anthropology: Reflections on Feminism and Cross-Cultural Understanding," *Signs* 5, no. 3 (1980): 389–417. Linda Nicholson suggests that feminist theory should conceptualize public-domestic divisions in historically specific ways in *Feminist Theory: The Public and the Private* (SUNY at Albany).
25. Mina Davis Caulfield, "Universal Sex Oppression? A Critique from Marxist Anthropology," *Catalyst* 10/11 (Summer 1977): 60–77.
26. Harding, "Gender Politics of Infancy," p. 63.
27. Rosaldo, "The Use and Abuse of Anthropology," passim.
28. Hartsock, "The Feminist Standpoint," p. 20.
29. It is indicative that in her account of the social relations of class society as grounded in a self-other dichotomy, Hartsock appeals to Hegel's master-slave account. This provides some support for my claim that her conceptualization of the basis of social relations is essentially idealistic.
30. Hartsock and Keller have arguments to this effect in the papers already cited. See also the papers by Jane Flax and Naomi Scheman in Harding and Hintikka, eds., *Discovering Reality.*
31. Harding, "What is the Real Material Base of Patriarchy and Capitalism?" p. 139; here Harding asserts quite strongly that *all* institutions in society are controlled by men. On page 150 Harding gives the argument that institutions reflect male psyches because men design and control them.
32. Cf. Rosaldo, "Use and Abuse."
33. Cf. Giddens, *Central Problems in Social Theory*, pp. 73–95; Sartre conceptualizes the notion of social structure as the result of individual actions that nevertheless do not have attributes that can be assigned to individuals in his concepts of *totalization* and *counter-finality.* See his *Critique of Dialectical Reason* (London: New Left Books, 1976).
34. Harding specifically disclaims that her theory is psychologically reductionist, on the grounds that it says that the psychic structures that cause institutional forms are themselves caused by the social relations of mothering. See "What is the Real Material Base," p. 149. This does not answer my point, however, since I am claiming that she reduces the attributes of institutions to attributes of individuals.
35. Rosenthal, in "Women in Amazonia," takes gender solidarity as a major factor in accounting for male domination or the lack of it. In examining Amazonian societies she concludes that collec-

tive solidarity among men, where such collective solidarity is lacking among women, accounts for the only significant inequality between the genders in those societies.

36. Harding, "Gender Politics of Infancy," p. 68; cf. Chodorow, *Reproduction of Mothering*, pp. 218–19.

On Conceiving Motherhood and Sexuality: A Feminist Materialist Approach

Aiming to provide a "general paradigm of the cross-cultural persistence of male domination," Ferguson begins by pointing out two universal facts: 1) most women are able to conceive and give birth to a baby, and 2) most women were raised by a same-sex parent, that is, by their mothers or other women. These differences between women and men with respect to biological capacity and childhood socialization entail differences with respect to parenting and sexuality. Moreover, since differences with respect to parenting and sexuality are linked to differences in power, they provide a key to understanding male dominance. But since the particulars of these differences vary culturally and historically, Ferguson believes that this conceptual framework does not commit feminists to a false or static universalism.

A socialist feminist, Ferguson denies that there is one fundamental form of social domination and maintains that each form of domination has its own logic. In the case of gender domination, the key to this logic is sex/affective production—that is, the production and reproduction of people in families and kinship networks through sexuality, nurturance, and affection. In the nuclear family, a sex/affective triangle between the father, the mother, and the child leads to contradictory interests for women—conflicts between mother-child ties and mother-father ties. As a result, women develop a double-consciousness that both facilitates their internalization of male dominance and opens up the possibility of their resisting male dominance. Ferguson illustrates her view by applying it to three periods of U.S. history and their respective forms of patriarchy.

—D.T.M.

Chapter 3

Ann Ferguson

On Conceiving Motherhood and Sexuality: A Feminist Materialist Approach

ANALYTIC CATEGORIES

> The cathexis between mother and daughter—essential, distorted, misused—is the great unwritten story. Probably there is nothing in human nature more resonant with charges than the flow of energy between two biologically alike bodies, one of which has lain in amniotic bliss inside the other, one of which has labored to give birth to the other.
>
> The "childless woman" and the "mother" are a false polarity which has served the institutions of both motherhood and heterosexuality. . . . We are, none of us, "either" mothers or daughters; to our amazement, confusion, and greater complexity, we are both.
>
> Adrienne Rich, *Of Woman Born*[1]

Every woman has had at least one mother, and the overwhelming majority of women have had the experience of being mothered. Many women, like me, are also mothers. Having been mothered and being a mother give one some insights into the mothering relationship. But by itself, the experience of mothering can tell us little about the *conception* of motherhood prevalent in a society at a certain time, or differences in the conception of motherhood that are prevalent in different economic classes or different racial and ethnic groups.

To understand conceptions of motherhood and sexuality, their connections and interactions, the changes they undergo in different historical periods in a society, and the differences between conceptions of motherhood and sexuality in different cultures, we require an analytic framework of categories. As a feminist social theorist, I focus on the connections between motherhood and sexuality because I wish to develop a general paradigm of the cross-cultural persistence of male domination based on the two cross-cultural constants common to all or most women: (a) that we are or can become biological mothers and (b) that the vast majority of us were primarily "mothered" rather than "fathered," i.e., socially cared for in infancy and early childhood by mothers/women. These cross-cultural constants ensure that women's experience of parenting and sexuality will be different from men's. Does the sexual division of labor in parenting and the different consequences of sexuality for men and women also suggest a base for the persistence of male dominance cross-culturally?

To answer this question, which is actually a question of power, i.e., the relative power that the relations of parenting and sexuality give to men vs. women, we must introduce an analytic framework of categories that does not attribute a falsely universalist and static quality to male dominance. The relations of motherhood and sexuality, and the relative power of men and women in these relations, vary not only in different societies, but in different societies at different historical periods, and in the same society across class, ethnic, and race lines.

A Multi-Systems Approach to Domination Relations

My approach to understanding motherhood and sexuality is a *multi-systems* feminist materialist (or socialist-feminist) approach. By "multi-system," I mean an approach that is not reductive, that is, one that does not attempt to reduce male domination to a function of capitalist or commodity production economic systems (classic marxism), nor to reduce race and class domination to a function of patriarchy (classic radical feminism). Rather, I assume that much of human history can be understood only by conceiving societies in terms of interacting but semi-autonomous systems of human domination, three important ones having been class, race/ethnic, and sex/gender. These domination systems may not always support each other, particularly in periods of rapid change or social crisis. One way to understand the social movements of a particular historical period, such as the black civil rights movement of the '60s or the Women's Movement of the '70s in the United States, is to conjecture that a dialectical undermining of one domination system by the historical development of another, e.g., race and sex domination undermined by capitalist development, has provoked a social crisis. A multi-systems theory, unlike a reductivist approach, does not posit that social crises are automatically resolved by the development of a new social "equilibrium" that guarantees the same level of class, race, or male domination.

What distinguishes my particular multi-systems socialist-feminist theory of male domination from others is the concept of "sex/affective production." The concept of sex/affective production develops Gayle Rubin's point (Rubin, 1975) that every society has a "sex/gender system" that arranges a sexual division of labor, organizes sexuality and kinship interactions, and teaches sex/gender. It also is connected to Habermas's insight (Habermas, 1979) that what is distinctive about humans as a species is the way human societies construct human nature through different types of family and kinship networks. My theory, unlike one tendency within classic marxist theory, does not privilege the economic realm (the production of *things* to meet human material needs and the manner in which the social surplus gets appropriated) as the material base for all human domination relations. Rather, I conceptualize the production and reproduction of *people* in family and kinship networks as a production process that may take different *forms* or *modes*, depending on the historical relations between parenting, kinship, and sexual structures and economic modes of production. Just as marxism postulates distinctive "logics" (structural rules) that are characteristics of different modes of class production, so I suggest that each mode of sex/affective production will have its own distinctive logic of exchange of the human services of sexuality, nurturance, and affection, and will therefore differently constitute the human nature of its special product: human children. Because I think that infancy and early childhood form a crucial period in the formation of gender identity and attendant masculine and feminine personality structures, I privilege family and kin networks as the material base for sex/affective production. It does not follow, however, that sex/affective production is limited to family and kin networks. On the contrary, I argue that modes of sex/affective production specific to capitalist economic development create problematic and contradictory gender identities in both boys and girls in childhood, identities which then make subsequent experiences in peer interaction in schools and communities, and later in workplaces, very important in determining sexual preference, sexual practices, and the ultimate content of one's gender identity.

The separation between the public and the private, the realm of economic production and the realm of domestic life specific to capitalist society, should not lead us to the error of conceptualizing sex/affective production, or the production of people, as a process occurring in a place or realm different from that where the production of things takes place. The sexual division of wage labor, sexual harassment in the workplace, male decision-making and female obedience roles, and high-status male work versus low-status female work are all specific aspects of the capitalist production process which are its sex/affective production component. In the same way the power of the male wage earner versus the non-paid housewife and class differences in women's ability to pay for childcare and thus obtain leisure time for themselves as mothers are specific example of the capitalist aspect of sex/affective production. The production of things and the production of people thus interpenetrate. The point of conceptualizing them as separate production systems is that they have different logics, logics which must be understood historically and specifically if we are to understand possibilities for change and strategies of resistance to domination relations embedded in both sorts of production.

Before the specific types of sex/affective production are analyzed, the concepts involved and the underlying assumptions about affection, parenting, and sexuality need to be examined.

The Concept of Sex/Affective Production

The conceptual category *sex/affection production* is a way of understanding the social organization of labor and the exchange of services that occur between men and women in the production of children, affection, and sexuality. Every human society has its particular mode or modes of organizing and controlling sexuality, affectionate interactions (e.g., friendships, social bonding, alliances), and parenting relationships. Complex class and race/ethnic-divided societies like our own may have a number of different modes centered in different organizations of family household and kin networks.

Central to all previous modes of organization of this work and service has been a sexual division of labor in the performance of the tasks and the distribution of the services involved. The sexual division of labor in the production and exchange of these sex/affective services (sexuality, affection, parenting) is a central key to the social production of people as "sex/gendered," i.e., as having the consciousness of self as male or female. This consciousness is always relational (i.e., what is male is not-female, and what is female is not-male), thus connecting one to a social sex/gender class which is expected to have certain ideal masculine or feminine characteristics. One of these ideal characteristics is, usually, a sexual attraction for the opposite sex.[2] It is important to note, however, that there is no automatic (merely a strong contingent) connection between sex/gender identity and sexual identity (i.e., sexual preference): one is a deviant male if one is sexually attracted only to men, but one is still a male (and similarly for females who are attracted to females).

In stratified class and caste societies, different economic classes and racial/ethnic groups may hold different sex/gender ideals, although when this happens the lower classes are usually categorized as inferior male and female types "by nature." Often, split categories stereotype the good and bad woman—e.g., the Madonna [Mother]/Whore—exemplifying the hegemony of dominant classes' ideals for men and women, which allows their members (but not those of subordinate classes) to fulfill those preferred ideals.

Many different modes of sex/affective production are male-dominant (or patriarchal).[3] In general, they all have in common an unequal and exploitative production and exchange of sexuality, affection, and parenting between men and women; that is, women have less control over the process of production (e.g., control of human reproductive decisions) and the services exchanged; and men characteristically get more than they give in the exchange of these services. They differ in the specific sexual divisions of labor and the social mechanisms by which men dominate and exploit women, as well as in the female strategies of resistance, escape, and sabotage of male power in parenting, sexuality, and affectional bonding.[4]

In order to understand the "unity" of sex/affective production, we need to explore further its philosophical underpinnings. Why, for example, is it assumed that sexuality, affection, and parenting are intertwined in a way that the production of goods to meet material survival needs are not? What underlying theories of sexuality, affection, and production are assumed? What implications are there for the concepts of human agency, domination, and exploitation that are used in the classification of different modes of sex/affective production? Why link *sexuality* and *affection* in sex/affective production? The underlying assumption is that both sexuality and affection are *bodily* as well as *social* energies, and that they are each specific manifestations of a general type of physical/social energy we can call "sex/affective" energy.[5] We tend to think of affectional bonds as emotional rather than bodily and of sexual bonds as bodily rather than emotional or social. In fact, however, I would claim that this is a distortion that comes about because of western dualistic thought patterns. It may be more helpful to conceive of sex/affective energy as a spectrum ranging from the affectional/spiritual/not-specifically-physical interactions, at one pole, to genital sexual exchanges that are physical but not specifically affectional, at the other. A second way to conceive of sex/affective energy is as presenting two different dimensions or aspects which can admit of degree: a dimension of *physical* involvement, attraction, and interconnection of a human being with (an)other human being(s) or objects symbolizing human beings, and a *social/emotional* dimension of involvement, attraction, and interdefinition of self with (an)other human being(s).

We need now to consider some of the insights and problems of the sex/affective production paradigm.

First, a thesis about human nature: humans do not reproduce themselves (i.e., have children) merely as a means to guarantee that their material needs for physical survival will be met (e.g., that they will have children to care for them in old age). Rather, humans are a social species whose needs to connect to one another in some form of sexual and/or affectional interaction are as basic as their material needs as an animal species to produce a material livelihood. Heterosexual mating leads, intentionally or inadvertently, to human procreation, which leads to parenting. Thus, the sexuality and affection that heterosexual mates give each other requires the social development of parenting systems in which nurturance/affection, socialization, and physical maintenance of the young are organized. Since patriarchal parenting systems also organize adult sexuality (most often by compulsory heterosexuality in marriage arrangements which impose double-standard monogamy), an interaction exists between the type of sexual exchanges engaged in by adults and the nature, amount, and control of parenting work engaged in by each sex/gender.

A second thesis is that the position of sex/affective production systems as a base for male dominance is a feminist *materialist* approach in two specific senses. First, we know that human babies require affection and nurturance in order to survive. Thus, mothering or caretaking that involves more than simply feeding and clothing is a material requirement for the reproduction of the human species. Second, human young, unlike other animal species, have bodily energies (e.g., affectional, sexual, nutritional) that are initially without specific objects. The fact that humans are without instincts with fixed goals requires a period of care and socialization of the young that make some system of parenting, and the organization of sexuality and affection around these tasks, a material necessity for the human species.

We need thus to widen the concept of production as socially necessary labor to satisfy basic human material needs that Marx and Engels introduced in *The German Ideology* to include not merely a transformation of nature to met human needs, but also the production and reproduction of new life, i.e., the production and transformation of *people* via various historical parenting and sexual systems embedded in family and kin networks.[6]

Let me take a moment to contrast the concept of sex/affective production with other feminist revisions of classical marxist categories. Some marxist-feminists attempt to revise the classical marxist emphasis on the primacy of the economic sphere in human social organization (particularly in systems where the production of things involves the creation and distribution of a social surplus). They argue that every economic system involves both production and reproduction, and therefore that modes of reproduction of a system (including the reproduction of labor power and thus modes of procreation) are just as important to the total operation of the system as the production of things. They argue either that we should reject the concept of the social primacy of the economic (the base/superstructure distinction), or that modes of reproduction in family and kin networks are just as much a part of the economic base of a social formation as is the production of things.

The problem with the concepts of modes of reproduction (Brown, 1981) and modes of procreation (McDonough and Harrison, 1978) is that either (a) they ambiguously mean both human biological and human social reproduction, or (b) they emphasize the production of children as the goal and aim of this form of social relations. Neither approach is satisfactory. The former case allows confusion with the marxist categories of production/reproduction (Barrett, 1981), where the mode of social reproduction of an economic system can be said to occur simultaneously at every site of social relations—e.g., in the factory, state, and schools as well as in the family. This concept of social reproduction does not give us any non-functionalist way to conceive of, for example, the relationship between capitalism and patriarchy.

In the second alternative (modes of procreation), human biological production and the regulation of fertility rates would be seen as the goal of these systems. Such an emphasis marginalizes the human incentives to experience the pleasures of sexuality not as reproductive instruments but as intrinsic energizers. We would also miss the ways that affectional and sexual same-sex relations, which develop for their own sake in sexual divisions of labor, are used as mechanisms both to cement (if dominant male) or to resist (if subordinate or deviant male or female) patriarchal sex/affective production processes (Hartmann, 1981).

The sex/affective production paradigm is superior to these other approaches because conceiving of a semi-autonomous system of the organization of sexuality, affection, and the production of children in family and kin networks can allow us to understand how patriarchal relations can persist (since embedded and reproduced in family and kin networks) through changes in modes of production of things (feudalism, capitalism, state socialism). It can conceptualize how changes in family structure due to capitalist development might weaken certain forms of patriarchal sex/affective production while allowing for the possibility that other adaptive forms are developing.

A serious philosophical problem that the concept of sex/affective production raises is how we can distinguish between childcare and sexual or nurturant activities that are work or *labor* and those that are *leisure* activities. Using the concept of production assumes one can empirically distinguish between labor (activity socially necessary to meet human material needs) and activity which may be work (not thought of as leisure by its agent) but not labor per se, and activity which is play. Childcare is an aspect of housework that mothers perform at home while caring for infants and small children, yet we know that the very idea that childcare and housework are separate work activities is a historical development caused by the separation of the homes from economic production with the development of capitalist production. Ehrenreich and English (1975 and 1978) have documented how the combined effect of the domestic science movement, the development of the medical establishment, child development experts, and consumer capitalism in the early twentieth century expanded rather than reduced the tasks thought socially necessary in parenting work.

A parallel historical argument would challenge the view of some feminists that sexual exchanges between men and women in patriarchal societies involve work on the part of women that is not repaid, since the control and sexual satisfaction involved are not equal for both male and female partners. How can we make this argument if we accept recent historical arguments (Foucault, 1980; Weeks, 1979, 1981) that our very conception of sexuality, its exchange and deployment, as at the center of bodily and mental health, is a recent social construction of discourses developed by bourgeois sexologists and therapists? And, if the conception of sexual satisfaction and sexual health itself is historically relative, how can we defend the claim that there is an exchange of socially necessary labor in parenting, sexuality, and affection? Or the claim that patriarchal parenting and sexual systems allow men to control and exploit the productive process of parenting and sexual exchange by contributing less (labor or services) and receiving more (leisure, services, pleasures)?

Even if one admits that there are no historical universal requirements for good parenting, sexuality, or friendship, it does not follow that there is no empirical and historical way to compare male and female inputs, rewards from, and control of these production processes. Marx's concept of socially necessary labor has a "historical and moral element" which in part depends on what has come to be accepted as a decent minimal standard of living, given the available resources and expectations of a society at a particular historical period. Similarly, women's expectations of acceptable sexual satisfaction have changed since the nineteenth century, in part because of the writings of sexologists and in part because of the second wave Women's Movement.

The inequality of patriarchal forms of sexual exchange lies not simply in the fact that men characteristically experience more orgasms and sexual satisfaction than women, although this is certainly relevant and can be empirically measured. It is the aspect of domination, the fact that men usually control the nature of the interaction itself as the sexual initiators, that perpetuates the image of women as the sexual objects of men, and women's bodies as the instruments of men's pleasure. In such a situation it would seem that a woman has less agency in the sexual encounter, even though she may experience more orgasms than the man she relates to.

We will not really be able to measure the relative equality or inequality of sexual exchanges until we have a physical model of sexual satisfaction and sexual agency that allows us to make connections between certain bodily states such as body blocks, orgasms, complete orgiastic release (Reich, 1970), and the experience of sexual agency versus sexual patiency. But that we have no complete theory suggests merely the need for further empirical sexual research rather than a dead end for the sex/affective production paradigm. No matter how we ultimately measure equality in sexual exchange, we do have some intuitive criteria we can use in the meantime: for example, most would agree that any sexual exchange in which one partner but not the other enjoys orgasms regularly and in which the enjoying partner also controls the sexual process is an unequal exchange.

Finally, the question of one's power or control/agency in sexual and parenting exchanges cannot be separated from the economic, political/legal, and cultural constraints that may limit women's freedom of choice more than men's. Such constraints as economic dependence, legal restrictions on reproductive control, lack of strong female bonding networks that support sexual freedom for women or parental responsibilities for men, and physical violence by one's partner are all empirical factors that make women less free in parenting and sexuality than men. This shows the way in which sex/affective production systems are not autonomous from the economic mode of production, the nature of the state, etc.

In determining which parental interactions with children are labor and which are leisure, we can agree that this is historically relative to social (and perhaps class and ethnic) expectations of parents and still find a way to compare the equality or inequality of the exchange between women and men in parenting work. No matter how the line between parenting labor and leisure is culturally drawn, it remains clear that most mothers in patriarchal modes of sex/affective production do more direct and indirect parenting work than men in terms of total labor hours spent (where "indirect parenting work" would include wage-earning as well as unpaid productive work which produces, or exchanges for, goods necessary to the physical maintenance of infants and children). Folbre (1980a) is developing an economic model to compare the waged and nonwaged work (parenting and housework) in the family economy so as to develop a way to measure the relative exploitation of women versus men, and parents versus children. Delphy (1976) argues that the male-dominated family economy continues after divorce, since mothers are saddled with much more direct and indirect parenting work and few fathers provide much in child-support funds. Thus, in this sense male exploitation of women who are mothers increases with divorce, which suggests that the rise of single-mother families should be seen not simply as a decline in husband-patriarchy, but rather as the rise of a new patriarchal sex/affective form, which we might call "single-mother-absent-father patriarchy" and which is connected to the shift from family-centered patriarchal forms to more impersonal forms of state-patriarchy (hooks, 1981; and see below).

A final question concerns the relativity versus universality of the connection between affection, sexuality, and parenting. The analytic categories of sex/affective production would seem to suggest a universal connection (hence a mate-self-child sex/affective triangle) which has historically specific forms. Nevertheless, Ariès (1965) and Shorter (1977) argue that affectionate interaction between children, kin, and spouses is characteristic neither of peasant nor of aristocratic families in the medieval period. Rather, it develops as part of the bourgeois sentimental family, which develops a new conception of childhood and an increased emphasis on affection.

I would agree that we need to conceptualize a different form of patriarchal sex/affective production for aristocratic and peasant families than for bourgeois families. The interpersonal dynamic between parents, children, and mates will obviously be different when affectionate connections are present, or absent, or not exclusive (as when children are cared for by wet nurses, nannies, or extended kin networks). It is obvious that sexual intercourse to produce heirs has a different dynamic than when the resulting children and sexual energy are valued for their own sake.

Despite the relativity of who performs nurturant/affectionate services to children, a caretaker must provide a minimal affection quotient for the child to survive. Thus, the procuring of someone to perform these services is a necessary part of sex/affective production even in aristocratic families. Furthermore, it may be argued that courtly love ideals for extramarital relationships among the medieval aristocracy idealized homosexual love relationships among ancient Greek male aristocracy, and close same-sex bonding among peasants are evidence that affectionate interactions will come to be institutionalized in some form in human societies where they are lacking in parenting and marriage interactions.

Double Consciousness and the Sex/Affective Triangle

In this section I will explore a mechanism for perpetuating male dominance through motherhood in specific modes of patriarchal sex/affective production, particularly nuclear family forms as they develop with the growth of capitalism and the breakdown of feudalism. I call these forms "bourgeois patriarchal family forms," where this is understood to include families in the independent rural production (as in the colonial United States), working-class nuclearized families, and families of the bourgeois classes. These are the dominant family forms of the period of American history that I will consider later.

The family form involves a sex/affective triangle of father-mother-child(ren) that creates a structural contradiction of sex/affective interests for mothers but not fathers, which explains a psychological mechanism through which male dominance is internalized by women: the phenomenon of women's double consciousness. On the other hand, the structural triangle also sets the conditions for mothers' internal resistance to patriarchy and the progressive development of successively less strong patriarchal family forms in American history.

The structural situation is this: the sexual division of labor in childrearing in which women mother, i.e., perform primary infant and childcare, gives the mother a greater, because longer and more intense, affectionate relationship with the offspring. This situation tends to make her identify with the sex/affective interests of the child more than does the father.[7] In addition, the situation of childbirth and breastfeeding, plus the greater physical nurturance the mother gives the young child, arouse maternal erotic and sexual feelings toward the child that are repressed due to the weight of the patriarchal incest taboo. Nonetheless, the persistence of these feelings creates a much stronger mother-child than father-child sex/affective bond (Contratto, 1980; Person, 1980; Rich, 1980).

The greater absorption of mothers than fathers in the sex/affective interests of children may not only be because of the psychological investment of time and energy in the child. Some feminists have argued that the metaphysical and psychological indeterminacy over the boundaries of one's body versus the child's in childbirth and breastfeeding give mothers a special "epistemological standpoint" different from men's (Hartsock, 1981).[8]

The potential contradiction of the sex/affective triangle for the mother is highlighted by her involvement as well in the other leg of the mate-self-child sex/affective triangle, i.e., that as the present and/or former mate of the father, she is also identified with his sex/affective interests. Thus the woman's, but not the man's, own sex/affective interests as a rational agent are bound up with promoting both a woman/mate bond and a woman/child bond. She is forced into the position of negotiator of the sexual and emotional jealousies (conflicts of sex/affective interests) between children and father.

What this imbalance in parenting work creates for mothers is a *double consciousness*: a consciousness of the potential conflict between their own interests as sexual agents/partners in a peer/mate relationship and their interests as mothers in a nonpeer mother/child relationship. Women's sex/affective energy is consequently more bound than men's into adjudicating actual and potential conflicts of interest in the sex/affective family triangle. The relatively greater absorption of energy this involves often occurs at the expense of their other needs. Consider, for example, the routine sacrifices undergone by women for children and mates: given up are leisure time, job-training possibilities, access to greater economic productive resources, political liaisons, and sexual liaisons with other mates.

The structural double consciousness created by the imbalance in parenting work between men and women explains how women internalize the oppression of male domination as long as they are engaged in such a patriarchal parenting process. Double consciousness creates a double or split self-image for women. On the one hand, most mothers have a positive image of themselves and positive gratification from their mothering work with children. On the other hand, most women have a negative self-image when father-and-child jealousy is a factor. Women feel both more responsible than men for adjudicating this conflict and more to blame when they do not succeed in negotiating it.

One implication of this sex/affective triangle in bourgeois patriarchal family forms is the possibility of father/daughter incest as a response by the father to the divided loyalty of the mother (Herman, 1981). Incest is a patriarchal tool of domination by the father which disrupts the strength of the mother-daughter bond by a possessive sexual relationship that forces the daughter's sex/affective involvement away from the mother. Incest occurs when fathers, jealous of the attention that mothers give to daughters and/or angry at the lack of sex/affective attention from mothers, sexualize their relations with their daughters. This turns the daughters into substitute mothers, turns daughters against mothers, and makes mothers feel themselves to be the guilty accomplices of their daughter's sexual abuse. Mothers, on the contrary, are more sensitive than fathers to the power imbalance between adults and children, and are often powerless themselves to escape from the father. Thus, mothers are more likely to refrain from sexual relations with their children, not only for the child's good and from guilt feelings about the father's needs, but also from a powerlessness to escape the oppressive economic, political, and psychological structures of the family household engaged in patriarchal sex/affective production.

We have already alluded to the difficulty of drawing the line between parenting labor and parenting leisure activities with children. For the mother this is due in part, again, to the phenomenon of double consciousness: after all, if cooking and serving a meal to husband and children increases the sex/affective energy available to everyone—mate, self, and children—who can one see it as *work*? Thus many women do not experience unequal sexual division of labor in parenting as exploitative. It is often only when one is forced to change one's social relations of parenting (by divorce, by step-parenting, by a change to lesbian parenting, etc.) that one experiences an alternative arrangement allowing for a higher level of sex/affective energy in both mating and mothering due to a more egalitarian organization of parenting work. In hindsight, one can then see the previous organization of sex/affective production as exploitative.

If the mother's absorption in both legs of the sex/affective triangle immerses her in a self-sacrificing negotiator role vis-à-vis the sex/affective interests of father-mate and child(ren), we could expect to see in history various forms of female resistance to this self-sacrificing role. Women may be oppressed within patriarchal structures, but they are also always partial agents within the structures and, as such, can try to alter the power relations within the structure, often in favorable historical conditions thus altering the structures themselves. Some of the forms of historical resistance we might expect to find to bourgeois patriarchal family forms include the following: (a) women could refuse marriage altogether (in the contemporary period, this includes the possibility of choosing a lesbian relationship); (b) women could marry yet resist childbearing; (c) women could favor one leg of the triangle (eg., relation to child or relation to mate) at the expense of the other; (d) women could emphasize outside kin and friendship networks with peers as a way of withholding energy, either to male mates or to the mother/child bond; or (e) if economically viable, women could engage in serial monogamy and several marriages, which would tend to diminish loyalty to the mate bond and expand loyalty to the mother/child bond (the one that lasts).

I have argued in this section that unequal relations of childrearing create in bourgeois family forms a double consciousness in women due to their structural inequality in the mate-child-self sex/affective parenting triangle. This analysis I find superior to Chodorow's neo-Freudian approach to understanding the way that the reproduction of mothering perpetuates male dominance. In the next section, I will provide a brief historical sketch of changes in patriarchal sex/affective production in American history which will indicate the sex/affective production paradigm's usefulness in explaining historical change in parenting patterns and ideologies.

HISTORICAL APPLICATIONS

I have maintained that a multi-system approach to analyzing male dominance is best; i.e., one that takes account of the economic *class* structure of a given historical period (the mode of economic production), the *racial/ethnic* dominance patterns of the period (what we could call the mode of community relations—Albert and Hahnel, 1978), and the *sex/gender* dominance patterns of the period (the mode of sex/affective production). To understand the relative strengths of each domination system, we will also have to consider other aspects of a society, such as the form of the state and its relation to the economy. The relationship between the three domination systems is dialectical rather than functional: there is no automatic fit between different systems of dominance. Nonetheless, those on top in various domination systems will attempt to maintain their positions. Historical alliance will be created by various representative elements of dominant groups, alliances that during periods of social crisis or protracted change may be undermined or superseded. Ongoing developments in one mode of social organization may undermine social dominance patterns in another, and this will create an intersystemic social crisis. It is at these historical junctures that social change of appreciable dimensions is likely to occur. The structures of sex/affective production as they are reconstituted after a period of major social change will depend in large part on the consciousness and collective power of existing social movements of subordinate groups: women, nonwhites, and subordinate economic classes.

Periods of Sex/Affective Production in American History

Since colonial times, there have been three main periods of patriarchal sex/affective production in American history.[9] Each of these periods involves a different sort of patriarchal relationship between men, women, and children, and each of them has its different basic mechanisms for maintaining (or, in marxist terminology, "reproducing") male dominance. In the colonial period, Father Patriarchy was reproduced by the father's legal/economic control of inheritance through family property vested in sons, not daughters. In the romantic/Victorian period, Husband Patriarchy was reproduced by the institution of the "family wage," which was vested in husbands who were the family breadwinners. And in the present period of the consumer economy, Public Patriarchy has been reproduced through a number of mechanisms; these include laws restricting birth control and abortion, state welfare support of single mothers, the growth of the advertising industry and the manipulation of women's images (Ewen, 1976), and market mechanisms encouraging repressive desublimation (Marcuse, 1964) such as pornography, media violence against women, and sexual advertising, which promote the sexual objectification of women.

Let us consider each period in greater detail.

Period I: Father Patriarchy. White European settlers, primarily English religious Puritans, established a mode of agricultural production based on family households in the New England states that lasted from about 1620 to 1799. The mode of economic production was characterized by farm households producing primarily for use and not for market, and was consolidated by force against existing Native American economies which were hunting/gathering, nomadic societies. Dominance relations between men and women were perpetuated by Father Patriarchy, a combination of economic, political/legal, and childrearing structures in which the father owned property and dispensed it at will to his children, the land to sons and a lesser dowry to daughters. The father was the religious/moral head of the household. Children needed their fathers' permission to marry and were completely dependent on his largesse in inheritance.

The father in a Puritan household was not only the supreme authority in sex/affective production relations with wife and children; he was usually also master to indentured servants and young relatives who were apprenticed from adjacent family households. Thus, class relations were internal family household relations as well. Although a small artisan class grew with the rise of commercial capitalism and urban centers, which afforded an escape for men of the subsumed servant class from the family patriarchal domination in the rural family household, it was not possible for a woman, regardless of economic class, to have any economic independence nor any escape from Father Patriarchy, unless she was a widow and could take over her husband's business, trade, or land.

The conception of motherhood in the Puritan era was derived from Old Testament beliefs that women were weaker in reason and more emotional and therefore in need of practical moral and intellectual control by men. This, in turn, was due to the conception of motherhood as a natural, nearly automatic consequence of women's bodies. Since bodies themselves had evil lusts, women were thought to be more innately subject to sin than men. The ideal standard of parenthood was the same for both sexes, and both men and women were conceived to be innately sexual beings as well as feeling beings. But since feelings uncontrolled by reason were suspect, maternal feeling itself was dangerous and without moral authority and thus had to be subjected to father authority for appropriate correction. Women were often chastised for showing their offspring too much natural affection. Since children were thought to be sinful, depraved creatures in Calvinist ideology, which lacked a developmental theory of the human ego, there was little distinction between appropriate punishment for a child and for an adult. The key feature of the Puritan ideology of childrearing was to break the child's will as soon as possible to create a proper fear of those in authority, i.e., the hierarchy of patriarchs who controlled sinful desire and affections—individually in their homes and collectively as church/state elders (Stewart, 1981).

Some authors have argued (Ryan, 1975) that the Puritan emphasis on women as helpmates to men, the absence of an ideology of romantic love, and a more egalitarian sexual ideology, which posited sexual drives in both men and women were indications that women were more equal as sexual partners in the Puritan period than in the subsequent Romantic era. It certainly is true that there was less of a sexual double standard in the Puritan period than subsequently: men could be punished for raping wives or for fornication outside of marriage. Nonetheless, I think some authors overplay "egalitarian" implications of sexual practices in Puritan society (Mitchell, 1973): sexual double standards still persisted with respect to adultery, and a woman who became pregnant by rape outside of marriage could still be flogged or fined.

Three distinctive features of Puritan sex/affective production indicate that women had *less* power over mothering than in subsequent periods. First, children were regularly sent at young ages (around seven) to live on relatives' farms. This was in part to counter the excessive affection which was thought to permeate natal families (Stewart, 1981). Thus, an intense mother-child bond was not only ideologically suspect but difficult to maintain because of physical distance. This meant that mothers not only had less control over the dispensation of nurturance and discipline than in subsequent periods, but also less ability to "corner the market" on the positive satisfactions of an intense affectionate relationship with children.

Second, the pervasive presence of the father and his ideological hegemony over childrearing undermined an independent authority of mothers over children. Fathers, not mothers, seem to have been the major enforcers of the "breaking of the will" practices that were used on children, particularly during the separation/individuation period around the age of two. (This shows that it is not simply shared childrearing which is necessary to overcome gender-differentiated personality development in childhood.)[10]

Third, Demos (1970) presents a fascinating sketch of Puritan weaning practices which suggests that mother/child identification was rudely severed by the abrupt weaning of the eighteen-month-child at the moment of the birth of the next child. This abrupt separation, in connection with "breaking the will" practices to stifle the child's attempts at separation/autonomy, created an authoritarian (repressed but dependent) individual particularly subject to male-domination structures.

Period II: Husband Patriarchy. American society went through a period of rapid social change after the American Revolution and through the Jacksonian period. The shift from rural production to commercial capitalism, the beginning of industrial capitalism, and the expansion of slavery in the south occurred in the context of the creation of a new political entity, the national state of the United States. These changes also meant changes in the family, mothering, and sexuality.

A new ideology of motherhood and sexuality came into existence at this time in American history: the moral motherhood/cult of domesticity paradigm. In this ideology, which, as we shall see, did not refer to all women, women were no longer conceived as inferior helpmeets to men. Rather, women were "moral mothers." The domestic world was now conceptualized as a separate sphere and motherhood as a chosen vocation, one that required specialized skills (moral perception, intuitive and emotional connection). Men could not achieve these skills, for they were constrained to act within the public sphere of the capitalist marketplace, which required that they develop the skills necessary to survive there: egoism, individualism, cunning, and immorality. Instead of *natural* (sinful) mothers who subjected themselves to the superior moral authority of men, women had become the *chosen* mothers, the moral and spiritual superiors of men in their protected sphere of the home.

My explanation of this shift in the practices and ideology of parenting differs from those theories (Zaretsky, 1976; Benston, 1969; Douglass, 1977) that suggest that moral motherhood ideology was a sentimental response that sought to hide from consciousness the actual devaluation of women's role with the developing split between home and commodity production (i.e., the public/private split). What is wrong with the sentimentalist hypothesis is the assumption that middle-class women were the *victims* of an ideology meant to hide their parasitical dependence on men. Rather, I would argue from the multi-systems approach that the reformation of parenting and sexual practices as reflected by the moral motherhood ideology was the result of a dialectical struggle between middle-class men, women, and ministers/writers; i.e., social groups whose roles were in transition. The evangelical ministers involved in the Great Awakening spiritual revival movement made common cause with middle-class women, who formed the majority of their congregations, to elevate women's spiritual status in the Church. Thus, middle-class women were partial agents in a reformation of bourgeois patriarchal sex/affective production in order to gain greater power as mothers than they had in the Puritan period, while they nonetheless preserved some aspects of men's power in the family as husbands.

Daniel Scott Smith argues for this perspective in an important paper in which he dubs as "domestic feminism" the underground social movement by women in the nineteenth century, in which women increased female control over reproductive sexuality and increased their autonomous control over childrearing (Smith, 1974). He dubs as "matriarchalism" the weaker form of patriarchy that developed during this period, in which men as fathers lost power but women were still controlled by men's economic and legal power as husbands.

Smith's evidence that women essentially gained rather than lost power in nineteenth-century matriarchalist sex/affective production rests primarily on the declining fertility rate. From the sex/affective production paradigm, we can further develop Smith's insight that women, by reducing fertility, increased their control over mothering work. Reduced fertility not only means less risks of maternal mortality, but the possibility of increased attention to each child. Thus, the emphasis on new theories of childhood as a distinctive stage of human life and the conceptualization of childhood through the notion of developmental stages suggest the need for an increased intuitive-affective understanding of each child (possible for women but not for men, since the latter are absent from the home in commodity production). The stage is set for the theory of childrearing that emphasizes the internalization of values through identification and guilt, rather than through the imposition of values by external force (shame). Each of the elements of the romantic view of childhood can be seen as legitimizing the priority of the mother-child bond *over* the father-child bond. In terms of the father-mother-child parenting triangle, sex/affective energy between mother and child is increased at the expense of sex/affective energy between father and mother, thus giving women increased bargaining power in sex/affective power relationships.[11]

The connection of moral motherhood with asexuality is important for understanding nineteenth-century sex/affective ideology. How can conceptualizing good women as asexual (versus men who are naturally lustful) and bad women as sexual (whores) have been used as a tool to increase women's power in the family?

First, the voluntary motherhood and social purity movements of the late 19th century used the notion of the morally pure, asexual woman to insist that sexuality needed to be controlled by women. As Linda Gordon has pointed out (Gordon, 1976, ch. 5), this was not necessarily because advocates of social purity were opposed to sexuality per se. Rather, they argued that sexuality needed to be controlled by women in order to bring men under the same standard of sexual morality as women, thus eliminating the double standard. Not only was this designed to allow women to control the timing and frequency of genital intercourse so as to give more control over reproductive sexuality; it was also used as part of the campaign to eliminate prostitution at its perceived source, i.e., male sexual promiscuity.

The reversal of the emphasis prevalent today in sex/affective relationships seems to have characterized middle-class women's lives in the 19th century. Given that genital sexual relationships were unsatisfactory and men's and women's work worlds so different, it is not surprising that the affectionate relations that women had with other women most often contained higher levels of erotic energy than did relations, whether genital or affectionate, with men (Sahli, 1979; Faderman, 1981). And as we have argued, the primacy of the mother-child bond over the heterosexual couple bond prevalent during this period no doubt involved a similar concentration of sex/affective energy. Thus, we need not assume that Victorian women's lives were devoid of sex/affective gratification in comparison with Puritan women or contemporary women; or that women had "given up" sex in order to get control of mothering. What is needed is a further amplification of the concept of sex/affective energy in order to conceptualize more clearly the conditions under which it is expressed/satisfied versus conditions under which it is frustrated. For example, Victorian women may have gained power in sex/affective production, compared to Puritan women, by emphasizing nonsexual but intensely affectionate relations with children and other women. But in changed historical conditions it also seems true that the twentieth-century sexual revolution, particularly the lesbian-feminist validation of sexual relations between women, contains a revolutionary potential for increased sex/affective energy gratification for contemporary women (Ferguson, 1981b). This is true despite the fact that much of the theory and practice of sexologists and advocates of sexual freedom have been male-dominant (Simons, 1979; Campbell, 1980).

Class and Race Differences in Motherhood and Sexuality. I have argued that the romantic/Victorian ideology of moral motherhood was a tool used by northern, white, middle-class Protestant women to aid in the transformation of sex/affective production in a way that increased their power over the production and distribution of sex/affective energy and also increased the relative quantity of sex/affective energy they received from children and homosocial networks. But by the end of the 19th century, the moral motherhood ideology was almost universally accepted by white working-class families as well. This was ironic, since the emphasis that the Romantic/Victorian ideology placed on women being at home where their standards of sexual purity could be enforced on husbands and taught to children legitimized sexual violence against working-class women who were forced, for economic reasons, to work outside their homes.

For black women the moral motherhood ideology has two dimensions of racist control: the background of slavery, and economic necessity. The historical background of slavery in which black women were raped by white owners in order to produce more slaves created the material base for a racial-sexual stereotype of black women as bestial and sexual. Motherhood for them was not, like that for "full" (white) humans, a chosen career, but a natural involuntary process as it is for all beasts of burden. The image is created of black people mating like dogs. Under this stereotype, black women could not be expected to be moral authorities like white mothers. Rather, they could care for the white mistress's children under her moral supervision. The second part of the slavery stereotype of black women as mothers, then, is as servants caring for (white) children, rather than as mothers in authority caring for their own children. The racial/sexual stereotype thus sets up the dichotomy *white* (good, virginal mother) versus *black* (evil, sexual, bestial, whore).

One explanation for working-class acceptance of the moral motherhood/cult of domesticity is provided by Hartmann (1981). According to her, late nineteenth-century organized trade union movements led by skilled male workers attempted to create a "family wage" in order to protect their challenged interests as family patriarchs. A family wage, i.e., a wage which allowed a wage-earning husband to support a non-wage-earning wife and children, performed two functions for patriarchal control: it cut competition from women wage workers, and it allowed men to keep their wives at home to provide personal services, services that are not so easily forthcoming when women have to deal with the problems of the second shift. The family wage and protective labor legislation for women and children were a "bargain" struck by male capitalists, upper-middle-class women reformers, and workers, which served each group's interests—the capitalists' because their new concern to reproduce a skilled labor force led them to emphasize public schooling and home childcare for children, care most economically provided free by working-class mothers.

It is important to note that contemporary changes in the married women wage labor force have changed the historical dynamic in which women could in fact gain power as mothers by remaining home with children. Working-class white women historically gained power as mothers by the institution of the family wage and protective legislation, but they also lost the power that being economically independent/less dependent on men brings to women who are waged. Black women, however, never gained any power from family wage legislation, for black men were largely excluded from unions. So black male unemployment and/or low wages was one of the reasons so many black married women worked in wage labor.[12]

Period III: Public (Capitalist) Patriarchy. Our contemporary American society is a social totality containing a mode of economic production, welfare state corporate capitalism, and a patriarchal mode of sex/affective production we can call "masculinist" (Ehrenreich and English, 1978). The shift between the first phase of industrial capitalism and our present stage began to occur during the progressive period of the 1890s and has been increasingly consolidated since then by the growth of the welfare state.

In terms of sex/affective production, the content and social relations of women's mothering in the home have changed significantly with the advent of the consumer economy. First, many of the tasks associated with "mothering" maintenance work (e.g., sewing, mending, cooking, gardening, nursing children and old people) are now no longer done primarily at home by mothers. Ready-made clothes, store-bought foods, and fast food restaurants have lessened mothers' domestic work in these areas, although the increasing drain on the male breadwinner's wage that consumerism brings has caused a steady rise in women's wage work in the twentieth century.

The fact that mothers' work as health care workers and isolated mothers in the home has been diminished by the shift to public schools, hospitals, and nursing homes has not brought women a greater equality or control in the societywide sexual division of labor providing these services. Rather, as Ehrenreich and English note, the rise of the male-dominated medical profession in the late nineteenth and early twentieth centuries diminished the control women had in health care, childbearing (by eliminating midwifery), and child nurturing. As male experts came to define what was healthy medicinally (the proliferation of the drug industry), emotionally (child development "experts"), and sexually (Freud and the sexologists), women lost the "moral expert" status *re* children they had gained with the adoption of the moral mother ideology.

Contemporary childbirth and reproductive practices are increasingly a form of "alienated labor" in the market sense, as a male-controlled medical technology is used to limit women's reproductive control (e.g., involuntary sterilizations, and making mothers passive, drugged objects in childbirth (Rich, 1976; Jaggar, 1981).

The increasing dominance of the public school system and the growth of suburban and urban living patterns has meant the isolation of mothers from supportive networks of other women. This has meant an increasing loss of control over their children's emotional and social environment. The nineteenth-century concept of children as private property of their parents is increasingly unbelievable (Ferguson, 1981a). Not only do major socializers of children beside the family (teachers, peers, TV, and the mass media) contribute to personality formation of young people, but the welfare state with its social workers of all kinds has increasing legal power to intervene in family affairs (McIntosh, 1978; Donzelot, 1979).

Contemporary motherhood creates an ambivalent relationship between mother and child that is extreme. Children are no longer apprentices to parents nor may their adult lives be much like those of their parents, so it is hard for mothers to see their children as products reproducing their interests and skills. From the child's point of view, parents become increasingly outmoded authorities whose only value lies in their access to money to pay for children's wants. Children form intense social bonds with their peers that often supplant parents as the objects of sex/affective energy.[13]

Within the nuclear family context itself, the influences of the sexual revolution for women have not so much increased the sexual satisfaction afforded to women as undermined their power as mothers. The late '20s and '30s saw the popularization of Freudian ideas by the development of a new liberal ideal of the "companionate marriage" (Simons, 1979). This involved a new domestic ideal of "mom" as sexy housewife. Mental health within the family required that mothers balance their affectionate involvement with their children by an equally intense, sexually intimate, and affectionately involving relationship with their husbands. Women who attempted to resort to nineteenth-century methods of controlling sexual intercourse by resisting husbands' advances could now be labeled "frigid" and "castrating women." Women who preferred the company of their children to that of their husbands were "narcissistic," had "separation problems," were causing sons to become homosexuals by tying them to their apron strings, and in general were damaging their children's health by excessive "momism" (Ehrenrich and English, 1978). Finally, women who prefer homosocial friendship networks to social time with their husbands, a practice taken for granted in the nineteenth century, can now be stigmatized as "sexually repressed" or, even worse, as *lesbians*, a concept which didn't exist in the nineteenth century (Ferguson, 1981b; Weeks, 1979, 1981).

It is not surprising that motherhood has become devalued in late twentieth-century capitalist countries. Now that the percentage of women in the United States who are wage workers is over 50 percent and the number of married mothers with children under eighteen who do wage work has increased dramatically in the last ten years, the second shift problem has become acute for working mothers. The United States in particular has handled the problem of working mothers in a totally inadequate way: only one out of six children whose mothers seek public childcare are able to find an available slot. Why have the problems of motherhood increased while its consequent social status has decreased?

One explanation is provided by Carol Brown (1981), who argues that since children are no longer economic assets to the family, due to the development of public schooling and child labor laws, men have lost interest in economically supporting children. Thus, what seems to be an advance or even a victory for women—the change from the "father right" characteristic of nineteenth-century divorce law to the "mother right" typical of twentieth-century cases (lesbian mothers of course not included!)—is, in actuality, a breakdown of paternal obligations toward children. Women have won a "right" to child custody that merely guarantees an added unequal burden compared to fathers; not only the total burden of the sex/affective work involved in raising children, but in addition being the "breadwinner" (if only via welfare payments) as well.[14]

Carol Brown's argument has a rather excessive economistic emphasis on the economic costs and benefits of children. From the sex/affective production paradigm we can frame an additional explanation of why fathers have ceased to accept the "family wage" bargain of the nineteenth century and the role of primary breadwinner for wives and children. This is that the "victory" of the nineteenth-century mothers using the moral motherhood ideology in gaining control of the sex/affective energy exchange between parents and children disassociated fathers from direct control and production of this sex/affective good. Thus men don't want to contribute to the support of children to whom they do not experience a close sex/affective connection.

Another reason why the status of motherhood has declined under Public Patriarchy is, ironically, the partial success of the sexual revolution for women. Women's increasing economic independence from men and increased sexual permissiveness (partly as a result of the commoditization of sex through the influence of consumerism) has weakened men's ability to impose sexual double standards on women.

A frustrated male backlash to greater sexual freedom for women has been male recourse to sexual violence (rape, incest, domestic violence) (Easton, 1978) as well as the increased sexual objectification of women (pornography, sexual advertising) (Dworkin, 1981). In sharp contrast to the nineteenth-century split between the moral mother and the whore, many men now experience women simultaneously as both mother and whore, thus devaluing motherhood (hooks, 1981).

The increasing crisis of motherhood in the United States is exacerbated by the phenomenal increase in the divorce rate in the 20th century (up to two-fifths of all marriages) (Bureau of the Census, 1977). Since marriage is no longer for life, women cannot rely on a stable family household and support from a male breadwinner in exchange for mothering and housework. Even though it is easier for divorced women to remarry now that the social stigma of divorce is lessening, many white mothers find divorce creates a crisis in self-identity, in part because single motherhood has been so devalued in white culture. This is an important difference between black and white culture, for American black culture has always valued motherhood, married or not, more than white culture has.[15]

The major increase in alternate families, particularly single motherhood and families formed by remarriage, is creating new social problems. Step-children often resent their new social parent (or mother's new lover), and lack of social precedents for how to facilitate conflicts often keeps the new family from developing equitable decision-making processes. This creates special problems for women, for as mothers and step-mothers (despite the patriarchal image of the "wicked step-mother") women are expected to be the ones to heal the conflicts within the family and to nurture everyone involved.

Racism has kept motherhood a very different experience for American white and black women in the past. Nonetheless, twentieth-century changes in multi-systems domination relations are developing a particular form of white-supremacist capitalist patriarchy. Non-capitalist class white and black women's lives as wage workers, welfare recipients, single mothers, and sexual objects are much more similar with regard to sex/affective production than they use to be. Four key factors are the rise in single motherhood for both black and white women; the general rise in impersonalized violence against all women (rape); the rise in physical mobility of families and individuals, which causes the loosening of extended family networks; and consequently, the increasing isolation of motherhood for all women.

Political strength and emotional survival under these conditions requires for both black and white women a *chosen* as well as a blood kinship networking with other women to handle the fact of motherhood. This is not to deny that racism and classism oppress women differently. Rather, it suggests that, with respect to motherhood, issues of sex/gender class in sex/affective production (e.g., conflicts between men and women over parenting, sexuality, and nurturance) are becoming structurally similar. Black and Third World feminist organizations are thus developing within different racial and ethnic communities as an attempt to resolve intra-community the social crisis of the family and personal intimacy presently occurring across racial/ethnic lines. Influential members and groups within the white women's movement are presently seeking to make coalitions with black feminists, in part by dealing with the racism within the white women's movement.

The Women's Movement has created a rising consciousness of the social inequalities forced on mothers by our current social arrangements of parenting (masculinist sex/affective production). Lesbian-feminism arose in the early '70s as one way to turn the sexual revolution toward egalitarian sexual relationships for women. As a result, many young women who might have married and had children in an earlier era have become lesbians. Many women, lesbian and heterosexual, have coped with the problem of motherhood today by choosing not to become mothers. For them the problem becomes how to challenge the patriarchal ideology that a woman is not successful (indeed has not achieved adult status) until she becomes a mother. Other women are resorting to nontraditional ways of becoming mothers: artificial insemination, the "one-night stand," adoption, etc. In addition to the economic, legal, and social difficulties that single women face in trying to become mothers, there are continuing legal problems of child custody rights faced by lesbian mothers.

It would take another paper to develop in detail the political implications of conceptualizing motherhood as a part of a sex/affective production process. Briefly, however, we can say that, failing a fascist takeover of state capitalism, the New Right will not be able to reconstruct the patriarchal nuclear family of nineteenth-century Husband Patriarchy. Families of choice, viz., social families with alternative egalitarian structures, are here to stay. Rather than accept the terms of the debate posed by the New Right (the family versus lesbian/gay rights, traditional mothers versus career women, etc.), the Women's Movement needs to continue to build an oppositional culture and politics that validates social, egalitarian parenting (parenting characterized by chosen, non-possessive social networks of women and children (social motherhood), or men, women, and children (social parenthood) (Ferguson, 1981a; Allison, 1980). Only in this way can we strengthen ourselves as women and mothers to use the current contradictions between masculinist sex/affective production based in the family and the ongoing development of state capitalist society in a struggle to challenge public patriarchy as a system of male domination.

CONCLUSION

I have argued that male domination can best be understood as perpetuated by the social relations of parenting, affection, and sexuality. These social relations involve different modes of the production and exchange of "sex/affective energy" and the production of gendered producers of this energy (modes of "sex/affective production"). Although different societies have had different modes of sex/affective production at different times, a cross-cultural constant is involved in different modes of bourgeois patriarchal sex/affective production. This is that women as mothers are placed in a structural bind by mother-centered infant and small child care, a bind that ensures that mothers will give more than they get in the sex/affective parenting triangle to which even lesbian and single parents are subjected. The ensuing double consciousness explains the internalization of oppressive structures of parenting in a way that avoids the static, deterministic emphasis of feminist neo-Freudian analyses like those of

Nancy Chodorow. Furthermore, the concept of modes of sex/affective production can be applied to historical changes in parenting in American history to pinpoint changes in the concepts of motherhood and consequent strategies of resistance to male domination.

Historically, there are three main modes of sex/affective production in modern American history: Father Patriarchy (the colonial period), Husband Patriarchy (the Romantic/Victorian period) and Public Patriarchy (the twentieth century). The multi-systems approach shows that each of these periods is characterized by different power relations between men and women in parenting and sexuality, relations which also vary by race and class. Consequently, the *meaning* of motherhood, as a strategy of resistance to male domination or as a capitulation to it, varies in different periods, classes, and races. Further analyses are needed of areas within capitalist patriarchy where different domination systems functionally support each other and where they are in contradiction. Only by such concrete analyses can we develop specific feminist strategies for change in motherhood that make it clear what sorts of families of choice (social families) rather than birth (biological kin networks) we must conceptualize.

NOTES

Thanks to many friends who gave me criticisms of earlier drafts of this essay, including Sam Bowles, Barbara Ehrenreich, Nancy Folbre, Sandra Harding, Annette Kuhn, Elaine MacCrate, Linda Nicolson, Francine Rainone, and Iris Young. Special thanks to Liz, Francine, Kathy, Connie, Sarah, Lisa, and all the mothers and daughters who have provided the nurturance in which this article was born.

1. Adrienne Rich's classic *Of Woman Born* (1976) raises important issues for further thought. I chose these two quotes to begin this article not because I totally agree with them, but because they raise important theoretical questions. The first quote privileges the *biological* bond between mothers and daughters, thus raising the question of whether *social* mothering (adoptive mothers, step- and foster mothers, older sisters, other mother surrogates) involves a secondary or different kind of mother-daughter bond. The second quote is ambiguous on the question of whether the actual *process* of mothering a child, as opposed to having been a child, makes an important difference to one's self-concept and perspective on life. I disagree with one of the implications of this quote, which suggests that actual mothering is irrelevant to one's self-concept. Rather, I maintain that actual mothering, whether biological-social or non-biological social (e.g., adopting, communal living, etc.) does make a difference to one's self-concept, which is not simply one of status in patriarchal societies.
2. The connection between gender identity and sexual preference (sexual identity) is problematic. While some theorists seem to assume an automatic connection (Chodorow, 1978), the gay and lesbian liberation movements of the twentieth century have hypothesized sexual identity as quite separate from gender identity (Ferguson, 1981b). Compare also the view of sexologists and gays of the late nineteenth and early twentieth century that gays constituted a "third sex": "Uranians" (Weeks, 1979).
3. I use the word "patriarchal" in a generic sense to refer to many types of male-dominant sex/affective production processes, and not in the specific sense in which it refers to a *father* patriarchal family where wife and children are economic and legal dependents.
4. In an earlier paper (Ferguson, 1979), I argue that in patriarchal sex/affective production systems, unequal labor time exchanged by men and women in housework, sexuality, nurturance, and

childcare is exploitative in the classic marxist sense; men appropriate the surplus labor time of women in appropriating more of the human goods produced. In a subsequent paper (Ferguson and Folbre, 1981) the argument is advanced that increasing contradictions between patriarchy and capitalism are creating women as a new sex/gender class that cuts across family economic class lines. I owe many of my ideas on the analogies between economic and sex/affective production to Nancy Folbre (Folbre, 1980a, 1980b).

5. I develop the concept of sex/affective energy to improve on the concept of libido introduced by Freud and further developed by Reich (1970, 1974). I have two objections to classic libido theory as developed by Freud and Reich: (1) They posit it as a bodily *drive* or type of *instinct* rather than an *energy.* This suggests a fixed quantity of energy held in check by the psychological mechanisms of repression. Foucault (1980), among others, has creatively criticized that image of sexuality and has suggested, to the contrary, that sexuality is an energy that can be brought into existence, focused, and augmented by social discourses. On this point I tend to agree with Foucault. (2) Freud and Reich's use of the concept of libido seems to assume that *genital sexuality* is the highest expression of this drive: that other forms of sexuality are either stages of arrested development or sublimated forms. I do not wish to assume that any one form of sexuality or affection is a "higher" or more basic expression of the generic form, nor do I wish to imply that affection is simply sublimated genital sexuality. Hence, I hyphenate the concept: sex/affective energy.

6. A much-quoted passage from Engels's *Origin of the Family* is richly suggestive yet ultimately ambiguous on the question of how to conceptualize sexuality, nurturance, and human reproduction:

> According to the materialistic conception, the determining factor in history is, in the final instance, the production and reproduction of immediate life. This again is of a two fold character: on the one side, the production of the means of existence, of food, clothing and shelter and the tools necessary for that production; on the other side, the production of human beings themselves, the propagation of the species. The social organization under which the people of a particular historical epoch and a particular country live is determined by both kinds of production; by the stage of development of labor on the one hand and of the family on the other (Engels, 1972: 71–72).

The quote would seem to suggest that modes of the family are part of the material base of a society. Unfortunately, neither *Origins* nor *The German Ideology* deals seriously with changes in the "production of people" except as a direct function of the production of things (viz., the economy). So, other passages from *The German Ideology* suggest that Marx and Engels thought that the family in capitalist production is no longer part of the material base of society but has become part of the superstructure. This is a position which *reduces* the domination relations involved in the patriarchal production of people to a straight function of the domination relations involved in the production of things. The concept of sex/affective production, on the contrary, is meant to avoid this consequence.

7. Sara Ruddick argues (1980) that the maternal perspective involves a constant adjudication of one's own needs in reference to the child's because of three features of mothering work: concern for the physical survival, social acceptability, and growth (developmental needs) of the child. Her insights here are somewhat flawed by the apparent assumption that these concerns are not seriously altered by (a) the relation to the father, (b) other children or adult parent surrogates, and (c) the responses and options of the child, e.g., whether the child accepts mother's directions in these areas.

8. Marge Piercy's novel (1976) raises all sorts of interesting questions about whether the biological differences between men and women in human reproduction should be totally eliminated in order to permit gender-free childrearing.

9. The history of forms of the Afro-American family differs from these dominant family forms because of the institution of slavery and subsequent attempts by the black family after slavery to cope with the effects of institutionalized racism in the wage labor force. Since the black family has always had a different and more egalitarian internal structure than white family forms, sexism in the Afro-American community needs to be seen as a reflection of dominant white cultural forms (e.g., the sexual division of wage labor, macho images in the media, etc.) rather than as an autonomous structure of the community itself.
10. The theoretical method in use here differs from that followed in Nancy Chodorow's influential work, *The Reproduction of Mothering*, in several respects. First, the claim that mothering in bourgeois nuclear family systems can be seen in terms of a sex/affective triangle between father, mother, and child(ren) places more emphasis on the historically constructed system of parenting and sexual roles than does Chodorow. The nature of the mother-child bond and masculine/feminine gender identities is not simply determined by the fact of primary mother infant care; but by the manner in which the father controls or intervenes, the parents' treatment of sexuality, and the part played by other siblings in the child's interaction with parents. While Chodorow maintains that gender identities are fixed in childhood, she can account neither for the changing conceptions of sexual identities nor for gender identities caused by peer oppositional cultures of the contemporary lesbian/gay and women's movement. In conceptualizing parenting as a historical process that interacts with a historical set of sexual practices, my approach can take into account race, ethnic, and class differences in motherhood. Its emphasis is more dynamic and agent-centered than Chodorow's, for the aim is to show that women have struggled to redefine motherhood (and consequently gender identities) within the parameters of the sex/affective triangle, given the opportunities afforded by changing economic, political, and cultural variables.
11. The gradual transference of parental authority from fathers to mothers and the intensification of the mother-child relationship would seem to have had contradictory effects for middle-class children. On the one hand, children became economic dependents of the family, as the length of time spent in schooling increased while the practice of apprenticing children decreased. As mothers came to feel children to be their exclusive products, children may have felt at once powerless to escape mothers, yet encouraged to develop some autonomy because of the new permissive childrearing practices coming into fashion. We can thus suppose that certain forbidden sexual practices (masturbation, homosexual play) actually increased among children, in part as a psychological distancing and resistance mechanism. This is quite a different explanation for the increased attention to adolescent sexuality evinced by eighteenth- and nineteenth-century writers than that provided by Foucault (1978). According to him, bourgeois sexual discourses (including religious confessional writing, sexual purity writers, and sexologists) created a new bourgeois concern with sexuality not as a response to any changing material conditions, but simply as a spontaneous change of direction in "discourses." My explanation assumes, on the contrary, that a material change in power relations between bourgeois children and parents created new sexual practices, including asexuality among wives and sexuality among children, which then spurred new regulatory discourses.
12. Black women have consistently worked outside the home since the Civil War in proportions that were three to four times higher than for white women. In 1880, for example, about 50 percent of black women were in the labor force, compared to 15 percent of white women. The percentage of married black women working compared to married white women is similarly high. In the 1880s, for example, no more than 10 percent to 15 percent of white native and immigrant wives worked in wage labor (less in certain immigrant groups, e.g., Jews and Italians). Yet in New Or-

leans in the 1880s, 30 percent of black wives worked, and in Cambridge, Mass., Nashville, Tenn., and Atlanta in 1886 the figures were from 44 percent to 65 percent (Degler, 1980, p. 389).

13. Many sources discuss the alienation of contemporary mothers. The classic is Friedan (1963). Others are Wandor (1974) and Bart (1970).
14. Most divorced fathers cop out not only on direct childcare work but also on financial contributions toward child support: 90 percent of divorced women do not receive regular child-support payments from fathers, and those who do do not receive the full payments the legal system entitled them to ("Women and Childcare" in *Women's Agenda*, March/April 1976). Welfare mothers are also subject to a male-headed bureaucracy whose interference in personal life and demeaning regulations attempt to reduce women to menial status.
15. This may be why a recent study of black women found that single black mothers had much higher self-esteem than single white mothers, in part because the latter did not compare themselves with married women, but with other single black others in assessing social status (Myers, 1980).

BIBLIOGRAPHY

Albert, Michael, and Hahnel, Robin. 1978. *UnOrthodox Marxism*. Boston: South End Press.

Allison, Dorothy. 1980. "Weaving the Web of Community." *Quest* 5, no. 1.

Ariès, Philippe. 1965. *Centuries of Childhood: A Social History of Family Life*. Translated by Robert Baldick. New York: Alfred A. Knopf.

Barrett, Michelle. 1981. *Women's Oppression Today*. London: Virago.

Bart, Pauline. 1970. "Mother Portnoy's Complaint." *trans action* 8, nos. 1 and 2.

Benston, Margaret. 1969. "The Political Economy of Women's Liberation." *Monthly Review*. September.

Brown, Carol. 1981. "Mothers, Fathers and Children: From Private to Public Patriarchy." In *Women and Revolution*. Edited by L. Sargent. Boston: South End Press.

Bureau of the Census. 1977. "Marital Status and Living Arrangements: March 1976." *Current Population Reports*. Ser. P-20, no. 306. January.

Campbell, Beatrix. 1980. "A Feminist Sexual Politics," *Feminist Review* 5.

Chodorow, Nancy. 1978. *The Reproduction of Mothering*. Berkeley: University of California.

Contratto, Susan Weisskopf. 1980. "Maternal Sexuality and Asexual Motherhood." *Signs* 6, no. 1.

Degler, Carl. 1980. *At Odds: Women and the Family in America from Revolution to the Present*. Oxford: Oxford University Press.

Delphy, Christine. 1976. "Continuities and Discontinuities in Marriage and Divorce." In *Sexual Divisions and Society: Process and Change*. Edited by D. Leonard-Barker and S. Allen. London: Tavistock.

Demos, John. 1970. *A Little Commonwealth: Family Life in Plymouth Colony*. New York: Oxford University Press.

Donzelot, Jacques. 1979. *The Policing of Families*. New York: Pantheon.

Dworkin, Andrea. 1981. *Pornography: Men Possessing Women*. New York: Perigee/G.P. Putnam Sons.

Easton, Barbara. 1978. "Feminism and the Contemporary Family." *Socialist Review* 39, vol. 8, no. 3.

Ehrenreich, Barbara, and English, Deirdre. 1975. "The Manufacture of Housework." *Socialist Revolution* 26, vol. 5, no. 4.

______. 1978. *For Her Own Good: 150 Years of the Experts' Advice to Women*. Garden City, NJ: Anchor/Doubleday.

Engels, Friedrich. 1972. *Origin of the Family, Private Property and the State*. Edited by E. Leacock. New York: International Publishers.

Ewen, Stewart. 1976. *Captains of Consciousness.* New York: McGraw Hill.

Faderman, Lillian. 1981. *Surpassing the Love of Men.* London: Junction Books.

Ferguson, Ann. 1979. "Women as a New Revolutionary Class in the U.S." In *Between Labor and Capital.* Edited by P. Walker. Boston: South End Press.

______. 1981a. "The Che-Lumumba School: Creating a Revolutionary Family-Community." *Quest* 5, no. 3: 13–26.

______. 1981b. "Patriarchy, Sexual Identity, and the Sexual Revolution." *Signs* 7, no. 1 (Autumn): 158–72.

Ferguson, Ann, and Folbre, Nancy. 1981. "The Unhappy Marriage of Patriarchy and Capitalism." In *Women and Revolution.* Edited by L. Sargent. Boston: South End Press.

Folbre, Nancy. 1980a. "The Reproduction of Labor Power." Unpublished, Economic Growth Center, Yale University.

______. 1980b. "Of Patriarchy Born: The Political Economy of Fertility Decisions." Discussion Paper #350, Economic Growth Center, Yale University.

Foucault, Michel. 1978. *The History of Sexuality*, vol. 1: *An Introduction.* Translated by R. Hurley. New York: Pantheon.

Friedan, Betty. 1963. *The Feminine Mystique.* New York: Dell.

Gordon, Linda. 1976. *Woman's Body, Woman's Right: A Social History of Birth Control.* New York: Grossman.

Habermas, Jurgen. 1979. "Toward a Reconstruction of Historical Materialism." In *Communication and the Evolution of Society.* Translated by Thomas McCarthy. Boston: Beacon Press.

Hartmann, Heidi. 1979. "Capitalism, Patriarchy and Job Segregation by Sex." In *Capitalist Patriarchy and the Case for Socialist Feminism.* Edited by Z. Eisenstein. New York: Monthly Review Press.

______. 1981. "The Unhappy Marriage of Marxism and Feminism." In *Women and Revolution.* Edited by L. Sargent. Boston: South End Press.

Hartsock, Nancy. 1981. "The Feminist Standpoint." In *Discovering Reality.* Edited by S. Harding and M. Hintikka. Dordrecht: Reidel.

Herman, Judith. 1981. *Father-Daughter Incest.* Cambridge: Harvard University Press.

hooks, bell. 1981. *Ain't I a Woman: Black Women and Feminism.* Boston: South End Press.

Jaggar, Alison. 1983. *Feminist Politics and Human Nature.* Totowa, NJ: Rowman & Allanheld.

Marcuse, Herbert. 1964. *One Dimensional Man.* Boston: Beacon Press.

McDonough, Roisin, and Harrison, Rachel. 1978. "Patriarchy and Relations of Production." In *Feminism and Materialism.* Edited by A. Kuhn and A. M. Wolpe. London: Routledge & Kegan Paul.

McIntosh, Mary. 1978. "The State and the Oppression of Women." In *Feminism and Materialism.* Edited by A. Kuhn and A M. Wolpe. London: Routledge & Kegan Paul.

Mitchell, Juliet. 1973. *Woman's Estate.* New York: Vintage/Random House.

Myers, Lena Wright. 1980. *Black Women: Do They Cope Better?* Englewood Cliffs, NJ: Prentice-Hall.

Person, Ethel Spector. 1980. "Sexuality as the Mainstay of Identity." *Psychoanalytic Perspectives* 5, no. 4 (Summer): 605–30.

Piercy, Marge. 1976. *Woman on the Edge of Time.* New York: Fawcett.

Poster, Mark. 1978. *Critical Theory of the Family.* London: Pluto.

Reich, Wilhelm. 1970. *The Discovery of the Orgone: The Function of the Orgasm.* New York: Noonday/Farrar, Straus and Giroux.

______. 1974. *The Sexual Revolution.* New York: Simon & Schuster.

Rich, Adrienne. 1976. *Of Woman Born.* New York: Bantam Books.

______. 1980. "Compulsory Heterosexuality and Lesbian Existence." *Signs* 5, no. 4 (Summer): 342–67.

Rubin, Gayle. 1975. "The Traffic in Women." In *Toward an Anthropology of Women.* Edited by R. Reiter. New York: Monthly Review Press.

Ruddick, Sara. 1980. "Maternal Thinking." *Feminist Studies* 6, no. 2 (Summer): 342–67.

Ryan, Mary. 1975. *Womanhood in America from Colonial Times to the Present.* New York: Franklin-Watts.

Sahli, Nancy. 1979. "Smashing: Women's Relationships Before the Fall." *Chrysalis* 8, pp. 17–28.

Shorter, Edward. 1977. *The Making of the Modern Family.* New York: Basic Books/Harper.

Simons, Christina. 1979. "Companionate Marriage and the Lesbian Threat." *Frontiers* 4, no. 3 (Fall): 54–59.

Smith, Daniel Scott. 1974. "Family Limitation, Sexual Control and Domestic Feminism." In *Clio's Consciousness Raised.* Edited by M. Hartman and L. W. Banner. New York: Harper & Row.

Smith-Rosenberg, Carroll. 1975. "The Female World of Love and Ritual: Relations Between Women in 19th Century America," *Signs* 1, no. 1 (Autumn): 1–29.

Stewart, Katie. 1981. "The Marriage of Capitalist and Patriarchal Ideologies: Meanings of Male Bonding and Male Ranking in U.S. Culture." In *Women and Revolution.* Edited by L. Sargent. Boston: South End Press.

Wandor, Michelene. 1974. "The Conditions of Illusion." In *Conditions of Illusion: Papers for the Women's Movement.* Edited by S. Allan, L. Sanders, and J. Wallis. Leeds: Feminist Books.

Weeks, Jeffrey. 1979. *Coming Out: A History of Homosexuality from 19th Century to the Present.* Boston: Charles River Books.

______. 1981. *Sex, Politics, and Society.* New York: Longman.

Young, Iris. 1980. "Socialist Feminism and the Limits of Dual Systems Theory." *Socialist Review* 10, no. 50/51 (March/June): 169–88.

Zaretsky, Eli. 1976. *Capitalism, the Family and Personal Life.* New York: Harper & Row.

Feminism, Marxism, Method, and the State: An Agenda for Theory

MacKinnon aims to articulate a freestanding account of feminism—"feminism unmodified," as she terms it elsewhere. She begins by examining the alternatives. Liberal feminism is primarily an instrument for the advancement of well-off, talented women. Marxism analyzes feminist concerns in terms of economic class domination and exploitation. Thus, Marxism fails to grasp that, although male dominance assumes different forms in different classes and in different historical periods, it cuts across all class lines. Moreover, Marxism neither grasps nor seeks to rectify forms of exploitation that are specific to women. Likewise, socialist feminism assimilates feminist categories of analysis and feminist issues to Marxist categories and issues. Consequently, socialist feminism neglects the centrality of sexuality to feminism.

MacKinnon holds that sexuality is the foundation of male domination and the central category of feminist analysis. Sexuality is a form of power, and women are those people whose sexuality is expropriated and used by others. Women are "walking embodiments of men's projected needs." Thus, feminine gender identity reduces to attractiveness to men and sexual availability on men's terms. Since sexuality is socially constructed, women have no suppressed, innate sexuality that can be liberated. They are defined by their powerlessness and victimization—their sexual objectification. Through consciousness raising, however, women analyze their experience and gain an understanding of women's collective condition. Gaining feminist consciousness is a form of political practice.

—D.T.M.

Chapter 4

Catharine MacKinnon

Feminism, Marxism, Method, and the State: An Agenda for Theory

Sexuality is to feminism what work is to marxism: that which is most one's own, yet most taken away. Marxist theory argues that society is fundamentally constructed of the relations people form as they do and make things needed to survive humanly. Work is the social process of shaping and transforming material and social worlds, creating people as social beings as they create value. It is that activity by which people become who they are. Class is its structure, production its consequence, capital its congealed form, and control its issue.

Implicit in feminist theory is a parallel argument: the molding, direction, and expression of sexuality organizes society into two sexes—women and men—which division underlies the totality of social relations. Sexuality is that social process which creates, organizes, expresses, and directs desire,[1] creating the social beings we know as women and men, as their relations create society. As work is to marxism, sexuality to feminism is socially constructed yet constructing, universal as activity yet historically specific, jointly comprised of matter and mind. As the organized expropriation of the work of some for the benefit of others defines a class—workers—the organized expropriation of the sexuality of some for the use of others defines the sex, woman. Heterosexuality is its structure, gender and family its congealed forms, sex roles its qualities generalized to social persona, reproduction its consequence, and control its issue.

Marxism and feminism are theories of power and its distribution: inequality. They provide accounts of how social arrangements of patterned disparity can be internally rational yet unjust. But their specificity is not incidental. In marxism to be deprived of one's work, in feminism of one's sexuality, defines each one's conception of lack of power per se. They do not mean to exist side-by-side to insure that two separate spheres of social life are not overlooked, the interests of two groups are not obscured, or the contributions of two sets of variables are not ignored. They exist to argue, respectively, that the relations in which many work and few gain, in which some fuck and others get fucked,[2] are the prime moment of politics.

What if the claims of each theory are taken equally seriously, each on its own terms? Can two social processes be basic at once? Can two groups be subordinated in conflicting ways, or do they merely crosscut? Can two theories, each of which purports to account for the same thing—power as such—be reconciled? Or, is there a connection between the fact that the few have ruled the many and the fact that those few have been men?

Confronted on equal terms, these theories pose fundamental questions for each other. Is male dominance a creation of capitalism or is capitalism one expression of male dominance? What does it mean for class analysis if one can assert that a social group is defined and exploited through means largely independent of the organization of production, if in forms appropriate to it? What does it mean for a sex-based analysis if one can assert that capitalism would not be materially altered if it were sex integrated or even controlled by women? If the structure and interests served by the socialist state and the capitalist state differ in class terms, are they equally predicated upon sex inequality? To the extent their form and behavior resemble one another, could this be their commonality? Is there a relationship between the power of some classes over others and that of all men over all women?

Rather than confront these questions, marxists and feminists have usually either dismissed or, in what amounts to the same thing, subsumed each other. Marxists have criticized feminism as bourgeois in theory and in practice, meaning that it works in the interest of the ruling class. They argue that to analyze society in terms of sex ignores class divisions among women, dividing the proletariat. Feminist demands, it is claimed, could be fully satisfied within capitalism, so their pursuit undercuts and deflects the effort for basic change. Efforts to eliminate barriers to women's personhood—arguments for access to life chances without regard to sex—are seen as liberal and individualistic. Whatever women have in common is considered based in nature, not society; cross-cultural analyses of commonalities in women's social conditions are seen as ahistorical and lacking in cultural specificity. The women's movement's focus upon attitudes and feelings as powerful components of social reality is criticized as idealist; its composition, purportedly of middle-class educated women, is advanced as an explanation for its opportunism.

Feminists charge that marxism is male defined in theory and in practice, meaning that it moves within the world view and in the interest of men. Feminists argue that analyzing society exclusively in class terms ignores the distinctive social experiences of the sexes, obscuring women's unity. Marxist demands, it is claimed, could be (and in part have been) satisfied without altering women's inequality to men. Feminists have often found that working-class movements and the Left undervalue women's work and concerns; neglect the role of feelings and attitudes in a focus on institutional and material change; denigrate women in procedure, practice, and everyday life; and in general fail to distinguish themselves from any other ideology or group dominated by male interests. Marxists and feminists thus accuse each other of seeking (what in each one's terms is) reform—changes that appease and assuage without addressing the grounds of discontent—where (again in each one's terms) a fundamental overthrow is required. The mutual perception, at its most extreme, is not only that the other's analysis is incorrect, but that its success would be a defeat.

Neither set of allegations is groundless. In the feminist view, sex, in analysis and in reality, does divide classes, a fact marxists have been more inclined to deny or ignore than to explain or change. Marxists, similarly, have seen parts of the women's movement function as a special interest group to advance the class-privileged: educated and professional women. To consider this group coextensive with "the women's movement" precludes questioning a definition of coalesced interest and resistance[3] which gives disproportionate visibility to the movement's least broadly based segment. But advocates of women's interests have not always been class conscious; some have exploited class-based arguments for advantage, even when the interests of working-class *women* were thereby obscured.

For example, in 1866, in an act often thought to inaugurate the first wave of feminism, John Stuart Mill petitioned the English parliament for women's suffrage with the following partial justification: "Under whatever conditions, and within whatever limits, men are admitted to suffrage, there is not a shadow of justification for not admitting women under the same. The majority of women of any class are not likely to differ in political opinion from the majority of men in the same class."[4] Perhaps Mill means that, to the extent class determines opinion, sex is irrelevant. In this sense, the argument is (to some persuasively) narrow. It can also justify limiting the extension of the franchise to women who "belong to" men of the same class that already exercises it, to the further detriment of the excluded underclass, "their" women included.[5]

This kind of reasoning is confined neither to the issue of the vote nor to the nineteenth century. Mill's logic is embedded in a theoretical structure that underlies much contemporary feminist theory and justifies much of the marxist critique. That women should be allowed to engage in politics expressed Mill's concern that the state not restrict individuals' self-government, their freedom to develop talents for their own growth, and their ability to contribute to society for the good of humanity. As an empirical rationalist, he resisted attributing to biology what could be explained as social conditioning. As a utilitarian, he found most sex-based inequalities inaccurate or dubious, inefficient, and therefore unjust. The liberty of women as individuals to achieve the limits of self-development without arbitrary interference extended to women his meritocratic goal of the self-made man, condemning (what has since come to be termed) sexism as an interference with personal initiative and laissez-faire.

The hospitality of such an analysis to marxist concerns is problematic. One might extend Mill's argument to cover class as one more arbitrary, socially conditioned factor that produces inefficient development of talent and unjust distribution of resources among individuals. But although this might be in a sense materialist, it would not be a class analysis. Mill does not even allow for income leveling. Unequal distribution of wealth is exactly what laissez-faire and unregulated personal initiative produces. The individual concept of rights that this theory requires on a juridical level (especially but not only in the economic sphere), a concept which produces the tension between liberty for each and equality among all, pervades liberal feminism, substantiating the criticism that feminism is for the privileged few.

The marxist criticism that feminism focuses upon feelings and attitudes is also based on something real: the centrality of consciousness raising. Consciousness raising is the major technique of analysis, structure of organization, method of practice, and theory of social change of the women's movement.[6] In consciousness raising, often in groups, the impact of male dominance is concretely uncovered and analyzed through the collective speaking of women's experience, from the perspective of that experience. Because marxists tend to conceive of powerlessness, first and last, as concrete and externally imposed, they believe that it must be concretely and externally undone to be changed. Women's powerlessness has been found through consciousness raising to be both internalized and externally imposed, so that, for example, femininity is identity to women as well as desirability to men. The feminist concept of consciousness and its place in social order and change emerge from this practical analytic. What marxism conceives as change in consciousness is not a form of social change in itself. For feminism, it can be, but because women's oppression is not just in the head, feminist *consciousness* is not just in the head either. But the pain, isolation, and thingification of women who have been pampered and pacified into nonpersonhood—women "grown ugly and dangerous from being nobody for so long"[7]—is difficult for the materially deprived to see as a form of oppression, particularly for women whom no man has ever put on a pedestal.

Marxism, similarly, has not just been misunderstood. Marxist theory *has* traditionally attempted to comprehend all meaningful social variance in class terms. In this respect, sex parallels race and nation as an undigested but persistently salient challenge to the exclusivity—or even primacy—of class as social explanation. Marxists typically extend class to cover women, a division and submersion that, to feminism, is inadequate to women's divergent and common experience. In 1912 Rosa Luxemburg, for example, addressed a group of women on the issue of suffrage: "Most of these bourgeois women who act like lionesses in the struggle against 'male prerogatives' would trot like docile lambs in the camp of conservative and clerical reaction if they had the suffrage. Indeed, they would certainly be a good deal more reactionary than the male part of their class. Aside from the few who have taken jobs or professions, the bourgeoisie do not take part in social production. They are nothing but co-consumers of the surplus product their men extort from the proletariat. They are parasites of the parasites of the social body."[8] Her sympathies lay with "proletarian women" who derive their right to vote from being "productive for society like the men."[9] With a blind spot analogous to Mill's within her own perspective, Luxemburg defends women's suffrage on class grounds, although in both cases the vote would have benefited women without regard to class.

Women as women, across class distinctions and apart from nature, were simply unthinkable to Luxemburg, as to most marxists. Feminist theory asks marxism: What is class for women? Luxemburg, again like Mill in her own context, subliminally recognizes that women derive their class position, with concomitant privileges and restrictions, from their associations with men. For a feminist, this may explain why they do not unite against male dominance, but it does not explain that dominance, which cuts across class lines even as it takes forms peculiar to classes. What distinguishes the bourgeois woman from her domestic servant is that the latter is paid (if barely), while the former is kept (if contingently). But is this a difference in social productivity or only in its indices, indices which themselves may be products of women's undervalued status?[10] Luxemburg sees that the bourgeois woman of her time is a "parasite of a parasite" but fails to consider her commonality with the proletarian woman who is the slave of a slave. In the case of bourgeois women, to limit the analysis of women's relationship to capitalism to their relations through men is to see only its vicarious aspect. To fail to do this in the case of proletarian women is to miss its vicarious aspect.

Feminist observations of women's situation in socialist countries, although not conclusive on the contribution of marxist theory to understanding women's situation, have supported the theoretical critique.[11] In the feminist view, these countries have solved many social problems, women's subordination not included. The criticism is not that socialism has not automatically liberated women in the process of transforming production (assuming that this transformation is occurring). Nor is it to diminish the significance of such changes for women: "There is a difference between a society in which sexism is expressed in the form of female infanticide and a society in which sexism takes the form of unequal representation on the Central Committee. And the difference is worth dying for."[12] The criticism is rather that these countries do not make a priority of working for women that distinguishes them from nonsocialist societies. Capitalist countries value women in terms of their "merit" by male standards; in socialist countries women are invisible except in their capacity as "workers," a term that seldom includes women's distinctive work: housework, sexual service, childbearing. The concern of revolutionary leadership for ending women's confinement to traditional roles too often seems limited to making their labor available to the regime, leading feminists to wonder whose interests are served by this version of liberation. Women become as free as men to work outside the home while men remain free from work within it. This also occurs under capitalism. When woman's labor or militancy suits the needs of emergency, she is suddenly man's equal, only to regress when the urgency recedes.[13] Feminists do not argue that it means the same to women to be on the bottom in a feudal regime, a capitalist regime, and a socialist regime; the commonality argued is that, despite real changes, bottom is bottom.

Where such attitudes and practices come to be criticized, as in Cuba or China, changes appear gradual and precarious, even where the effort looks major. If seizures of state and productive power overturn work relations, they do not overturn sex relations at the same time or in the same way, as a class analysis of sex would (and in some cases did) predict.[14] Neither technology nor socialism, both of which purport to alter women's role at the point of production, have ever yet equalized women's status relative to men. In the feminist view, nothing has. At minimum, a separate effort appears required—an effort that can be shaped by revolutionary regime and work relations—but a separate effort nonetheless. In light of these experiences, women's struggles, whether under capitalist or socialist regimes, appear to feminists to have more in common with each other than with leftist struggles anywhere.

Attempts to create a synthesis between marxism and feminism, termed socialist-feminism, have not recognized the depth of the antagonism or the separate integrity of each theory. These juxtapositions emerge as unconfronted as they started: either feminist or marxist, usually the latter. Socialist-feminist practice often divides along the same lines, consisting largely in organizational cross-memberships and mutual support on specific issues.[15] Women with feminist sympathies urge attention to women's issues by left or labor groups; marxist women pursue issues of class within feminist groups; explicitly socialist-feminist groups come together and divide, often at the hyphen.[16]

Most attempts at synthesis attempt to integrate or explain the appeal of feminism by incorporating issues feminism identifies as central—the family, housework, sexuality, reproduction, socialization, personal life—within an essentially unchanged marxian analysis.[17] According to the persuasion of the marxist, women become a caste, a stratum, a cultural group, a division in civil society, a secondary contradiction, or a nonantagonistic contradiction; women's liberation becomes a precondition, a measure of society's general emancipation, part of the superstructure, or an important aspect of the class struggle. Most commonly, women are reduced to some other category, such as "women workers," which is then treated as coextensive with all women.[18] Or, in what has become near reflex, women become "the family," as if this single form of women's confinement (then divided on class lines, then on racial lines) can be *presumed* the crucible of women's determination.[19] Or, the marxist meaning of reproduction, the iteration of productive relations, is punned into an analysis of biological reproduction, as if women's bodily differences from men must account for their subordination to men; and as if this social analogue to the biological makes women's definition material, therefore based on a division of *labor* after all, therefore real, therefore (potentially) unequal.[20] Sexuality, if noticed at all, is, like "everyday life,"[21] analyzed in gender-neutral terms, as if its social meaning can be presumed the same, or coequal, or complementary, for women and men.[22] Although a unified theory of social inequality is presaged in these strategies of subordination, staged progression, and assimilation of women's concerns to left concerns, at most an uneven combination is accomplished. However sympathetically, "the woman question" is always reduced to some other question, instead of being seen as *the* question, calling for analysis on its own terms.

Socialist-feminism stands before the task of synthesis as if nothing essential to either theory fundamentally opposes their wedding—indeed as if the union had already occurred and need only be celebrated. The failure to contain both theories on equal terms derives from the failure to confront each on its own ground: at the level of method. Method shapes each theory's vision of social reality. It identifies its central problem, group, and process, and creates as a consequence its distinctive conception of politics as such. Work and sexuality as concepts, then, derive their meaning and primacy from the *way* each theory approaches, grasps, interprets, and inhabits its world. Clearly, there is a relationship between how and what a theory sees: is there a marxist method without class? a feminist method without sex? Method in this sense organizes the apprehension of truth; it determines what counts as evidence and defines what is taken as verification. Instead of engaging the debate over which came (or comes) first, sex, or class, the task for theory is to explore the conflicts and connections between the methods that found it meaningful to analyze social conditions in terms of those categories in the first place.[23]

Feminism has not been perceived as having a method, or even a central argument, with which to contend. It has been perceived not as a systematic analysis but as a loose collection of factors, complaints, and issues which, taken together, describe rather than explain the misfortunes of the female sex. The challenge is to demonstrate that feminism systematically converges upon a central explanation of sex inequality through an approach distinctive to its subject yet applicable to the whole of social life, including class.

Under the rubric of feminism, woman's situation has been explained as a consequence of biology[24] or of reproduction and mothering, social organizations of biology;[25] as caused by the marriage law[26] or, as extensions, by the patriarchal family, becoming society as a "patriarchy";[27] or as caused by artificial gender roles and their attendant attitudes.[28] Informed by these attempts, but conceiving nature, law, the family, and roles as consequences, not foundations, I think that feminism fundamentally identifies sexuality as the primary social sphere of male power. The centrality of sexuality emerges not from Freudian conceptions[29] but from feminist practice on diverse issues, including abortion, birth control, sterilization abuse, domestic battery, rape, incest, lesbianism, sexual harassment, prostitution, female sexual slavery, and pornography. In all these areas, feminist efforts confront and change women's lives concretely and experientially. Taken together, they are producing a feminist political theory centering upon sexuality: its social determination, daily construction, birth to death expression, and ultimately male control.

Feminist inquiry into these specific issues began with a broad unmasking of the attitudes that legitimize and hide women's status, the ideational envelope that contains woman's body: notions that women desire and provoke rape, that girls' experiences of incest are fantasies, that career women plot and advance by sexual parlays, that prostitutes are lustful, that wife beating expresses the intensity of love. Beneath each of these ideas was revealed bare coercion and broad connections to woman's social definition as a sex. Research on sex roles, pursuing Simone de Beauvoir's insight that "one is not born, one rather becomes a woman,"[30] disclosed an elaborate process: how and what one learns to become one. Gender, cross-culturally, was found to be a learned quality, an acquired characteristic, an assigned status, with qualities that vary independent of biology and an ideology that attributes them to nature.[31] The discovery that the female archetype is the feminine stereotype exposed "woman" as a social construction. Contemporary industrial society's version of her is docile, soft, passive, nurturant, vulnerable, weak, narcissistic, childlike, incompetent, masochistic, and domestic, made for child care, home care, and husband care. Conditioning to these values permeates the upbringing of girls and the images for emulation thrust upon women. Women who resist or fail, including those who never did fit—for example, black and lower-class women who cannot survive if they are soft and weak and incompetent,[32] assertively self-respecting women, women with ambitions of male dimensions—are considered less female, lesser women. Women who comply or succeed are elevated as models, tokenized by success on male terms or portrayed as consenting to their natural place and dismissed as having participated if they complain.

If the literature on sex roles and the investigations of particular issues are read in light of each other, each element of the female *gender* stereotype is revealed as, in fact, *sexual.* Vulnerability means the appearance/reality of easy sexual access; passivity means receptivity and disabled resistance, enforced by trained physical weakness; softness means pregnability by something hard. Incompetence seeks help as vulnerability seeks shelter, inviting the embrace that becomes the invasion, trading exclusive access for protection . . . from the same access. Domesticity nurtures the consequent progeny, proof of potency, and ideally waits at home dressed in Saran Wrap.[33] Woman's infantilization evokes pedophilia; fixation on dismembered body parts (the breast man, the leg man) evokes fetishism; idolization of vapidity, necrophilia. Narcissism insures that woman identifies with that image of herself that man holds up: "Hold still, we are going to do your portrait, so that you can begin looking like it right away."[34] Masochism means that pleasure in violation becomes her sensuality. Lesbians so violate the sexuality implicit in female gender stereotypes as not to be considered women at all.

Socially, femaleness means femininity, which means attractiveness to men, which means sexual attractiveness, which means sexual availability on male terms.[35] What defines woman as such is what turns men on. Good girls are "attractive," bad girls "provocative." Gender socialization is the process through which women come to identify themselves as sexual beings, as beings that exist for men. It is that process through which women internalize (make their own) a male image of their sexuality *as* their identity as women.[36] It is not just an illusion. Feminist inquiry into women's own experience of sexuality revises prior comprehensions of sexual issues and transforms the concept of sexuality itself—its determinants and its role in society and politics. According to this revision, one "becomes a woman"—acquires and identifies with the status of the female—not so much through physical maturation or inculcation into appropriate role behavior as through the experience of sexuality: a complex unity of physicality, emotionality, identity, and status affirmation. Sex as gender and sex as sexuality are thus defined in terms of each other, but it is sexuality that determines gender, not the other way around. This, the central but never stated insight of Kate Millett's *Sexual Politics*,[37] resolves the duality in the term "sex" itself: what women learn in order to "have sex," in order to "become women"—woman as gender—comes through the experience of, and is a condition for, "having sex"—woman as sexual object for man, the use of women's sexuality by men. Indeed, to the extent sexuality is social, women's sexuality *is* its use, just as our femaleness *is* its alterity.

Many issues that appear sexual from this standpoint have not been seen as such, nor have they been seen as defining a politics. Incest, for example, is commonly seen as a question of distinguishing the real evil, a crime against the family, from girlish seductiveness or fantasy. Contraception and abortion have been framed as matters of reproduction and fought out as proper or improper social constraints on nature. Or they are seen as private, minimizing state intervention into intimate relations. Sexual harassment was a nonissue, then became a problem of distinguishing personal relationships or affectionate flirtation from abuse of position. Lesbianism, when visible, has been either a perversion or not, to be tolerated or not. Pornography has been considered a question of freedom to speak and depict the erotic, as against the obscene or violent. Prostitution has been understood either as mutual lust and degradation or an equal exchange of sexual need for economic need. The issue in rape has been whether the intercourse was provoked/mutually desired, or whether it was forced: was it sex or violence? Across and beneath these issues, sexuality itself has been divided into parallel provinces: traditionally, religion or biology; in modern transformation, morality or psychology. Almost never politics.

In a feminist perspective, the formulation of each issue, in the terms just described, expresses ideologically the same interest that the problem it formulates expresses concretely: the interest from the male point of view. Women experience the sexual events these issues codify[38] as a cohesive whole within which each resonates. The defining theme of that whole is the male pursuit of control over women's sexuality—men not as individuals nor as biological beings, but as a gender group characterized by maleness as socially constructed, of which this pursuit is definitive. For example, women who need abortions see contraception as a struggle not only for control over the biological products of sexual expression but also over the social rhythms and mores of sexual intercourse. These norms often appear hostile to women's self-protection even when the technology is at hand. As an instance of such norms, women notice that sexual harassment looks a great deal like ordinary heterosexual initiation under conditions of gender inequality. Few women are in a position to refuse unwanted sexual initiatives. That consent, rather than nonmutuality, is the line between rape and intercourse further exposes the inequality in normal social expectations. So does the substantial amount of male force allowed in the focus on the woman's resistance, which tends to be disabled by socialization to passivity. If sex is ordinarily accepted as something men do *to* women, the better question would be whether consent is a meaningful concept. Penetration (often by a penis) is also substantially more central to both the legal definition of rape and the male definition of sexual intercourse than it is to women's sexual violation or sexual pleasure. Rape in marriage expresses the male sense of entitlement to access to women they annex; incest extends it. Although most women are raped by men they know, the closer the relation, the less women are allowed to claim it was rape. Pornography becomes difficult to distinguish from art and ads once it is clear that what is degrading to women is compelling to the consumer. Prostitutes sell the unilaterality that pornography advertises. That most of these issues codify behavior that is neither counter-systematic nor exceptional is supported by women's experience as victims: these behaviors are either not illegal or are effectively permitted on a large scale. As women's experience blurs the lines between deviance and normalcy, it obliterates the distinction between abuses *of* women and the social definition of what a woman *is*.[39]

These investigations reveal rape, incest, sexual harassment, pornography, and prostitution as not primarily abuses of physical force, violence, authority, or economics. They are abuses of sex. They need not and do not rely for their coerciveness upon forms of enforcement other than the sexual; that those forms of enforcement, at least in this context, are themselves sexualized is closer to the truth. They are not the erotization *of* something else; eroticism *itself* exists in their form. Nor are they perversions of art and morality. They *are* art and morality from the male point of view. They are sexual because they express the relations, values, feelings, norms, and behaviors of the culture's sexuality, in which considering things like rape, pornography, incest, or lesbianism deviant, perverse, or blasphemous is part of their excitement potential.

Sexuality, then, is a form of power. Gender, as socially constructed, embodies it, not the reverse. Women and men are divided by gender, made into the sexes as we know them, by the social requirements of heterosexuality, which institutionalizes male sexual dominance and female sexual submission.[40] If this is true, sexuality is the linchpin of gender inequality.

A woman is a being who identifies and is identified as one whose sexuality exists for someone else, who is socially male. Women's sexuality is the capacity to arouse desire in that someone. If what is sexual about a woman is what the male point of view requires for excitement, have male requirements so usurped its terms as to have become them? Considering women's sexuality in this way forces confrontation with whether there is any such thing. Is women's sexuality its absence? If being *for* another is the whole of women's sexual construction, it can be no more escaped by separatism, men's temporary concrete absence, than eliminated or qualified by permissiveness, which, in this context, looks like women emulating male roles. As Susan Sontag said: "The question is: *what* sexuality are women to be liberated to enjoy? Merely to remove the onus placed upon the sexual expressiveness of women is a hollow victory if the sexuality they become freer to enjoy remains the old one that converts women into objects. . . . This already 'freer' sexuality mostly reflects a spurious idea of freedom: the right of each person, briefly, to exploit and dehumanize someone else. Without a change in the very norms of sexuality, the liberation of women is a meaningless goal. Sex as such is not liberating for women. Neither is more sex."[41] Does removing or revising gender constraints upon sexual expression change or even challenge its norms?[42] This question ultimately is one of social determination in the broadest sense: its mechanism, permeability, specificity, and totality. If women are socially defined such that female sexuality cannot be lived or spoken or felt or even somatically sensed apart from its enforced definition, so that it *is* its own lack, then there is no such thing as a woman as such, there are only walking embodiments of men's projected needs. For feminism, asking whether there is, socially, a female sexuality is the same as asking whether women exist.

Methodologically, the feminist concept of the personal as political is an attempt to answer this question. Relinquishing all instinctual, natural, transcendental, and divine authority, this concept grounds women's sexuality on purely relational terrain, anchoring women's power and accounting for women's discontent in the same world they stand against. The personal as political is not a simile, not a metaphor, and not an analogy. It does not mean that what occurs in personal life is similar to, or comparable with, what occurs in the public arena. It is not an application of categories from social life to the private world, as when Engels (followed by Bebel) says that in the family the husband is the bourgeois and the wife represents the proletariat.[43] Nor is it an equation of two spheres which remain analytically distinct, as when Reich interprets state behavior in sexual terms,[44] or a one-way infusion of one sphere into the other, as when Lasswell interprets political behavior as the displacement of personal problems into public objects.[45] It means that women's distinctive experience as women occurs within that sphere that has been socially lived as the personal—private, emotional, interiorized, particular, individuated, intimate—so that what it is to *know* the *politics* of woman's situation is to know women's personal lives.

The substantive principle governing the authentic politics of women's personal lives is pervasive powerlessness to men, expressed and reconstituted daily *as* sexuality. To say that the personal is political means that gender as a division of power is discoverable and verifiable through women's intimate experience of sexual objectification, which is definitive of and synonymous with women's lives as gender female. Thus, to feminism, the personal is epistemologically the political, and its epistemology is its politics.[46] Feminism, on this level, is the theory of women's point of view. It is the theory of Judy Grahn's "common woman"[47] speaking Adrienne Rich's "common language."[48] Consciousness raising is its quintessential expression. Feminism does not appropriate an existing method—such as scientific method—and apply it to a different sphere of society to reveal its preexisting political aspect. Consciousness raising not only comes to know different things as politics; it necessarily comes to know them in a different way. Women's experience of politics, of life as sex object, gives rise to its own method of appropriating that reality: feminist method.[49] As its own kind of social analysis, within yet outside the male paradigm just as women's lives are, it has a distinctive theory of the *relation* between method and truth, the individual and her social surroundings, the presence and place of the natural and spiritual in culture and society, and social being and causality itself.

Having been objectified as sexual beings while stigmatized as ruled by subjective passions, women reject the distinction between knowing subject and known object—the division between subjective and objective postures—as the means to comprehend social life. Disaffected from objectivity, having been its prey, but excluded from its world through relegation to subjective inwardness, women's interest lies in overthrowing the distinction itself. Proceeding connotatively and analytically at the same time, consciousness raising is at once common sense expression and critical articulation of concepts. Taking situated feelings and common detail (common here meaning both ordinary and shared) as the matter of political analysis, it explores the terrain that is most damaged, most contaminated, yet therefore most women's own, most intimately known, most open to reclamation. The process can be described as a collective "sympathetic internal experience of the gradual construction of [the] system according to its inner necessity,"[50] as a strategy for deconstructing it.

Through consciousness raising, women grasp the collective reality of women's condition from within the perspective of that experience, not from outside it. The claim that a sexual politics exists and is socially fundamental is grounded in the claim of feminism *to* women's perspective, not from it. Its claim to women's perspective *is* its claim to truth. In its account of itself, women's point of view contains a duality analogous to that of the marxist proletariat: determined by the reality the theory explodes, it thereby claims special access to that reality.[51] Feminism does not see its view as subjective, partial, or undetermined but as a critique of the purported generality, disinterestedness, and universality of prior accounts. These have not been half right but have invoked the wrong whole. Feminism not only challenges masculine partiality but also questions the universality imperative itself. Aperspectivity is revealed as a strategy of male hegemony.[52]

"Representation of the world," de Beauvoir writes, "like the world itself, is the work of men; they describe it from their own point of view, which they confuse with the absolute truth."[53] The parallel between representation and construction should be sustained: men *create* the world from their own point of view, which then *becomes* the truth to be described. This is a closed system, not anyone's confusion. *Power to create the world from one's point of view is power in its male form.*[54] The male epistemological stance, which corresponds to the world it creates, is objectivity: the ostensibly noninvolved stance, the view from a distance and from no particular perspective, apparently transparent to its reality. It does not comprehend its own perspectivity, does not recognize what it sees as subject like itself, or that the way it apprehends its world is a form of its subjugation and presupposes it. The objectively knowable is object. Woman through male eyes is sex object, that by which man knows himself at once as man and as subject.[55] What is objectively known corresponds to the world and can be verified by pointing to it (as science does) because the world itself is controlled from the same point of view.[56] Combining, like any form of power, legitimation with force, male power extends beneath the representation of reality to its construction: it makes women (as it were) and so verifies (makes true) who women "are" in its view, simultaneously confirming its way of being and its vision of truth. The eroticism that corresponds to this is "the use of things to experience self."[57] As a coerced pornography model put it, "You do it, you do it, and you do it; then you become it."[58] The fetish speaks feminism.

Objectification makes sexuality a material reality of women's lives, not just a psychological, attitudinal, or ideological one.[59] It obliterates the mind/matter distinction that such a division is premised upon. Like the value of a commodity, women's sexual desirability is fetishized; it is made to appear a quality of the object itself, spontaneous and inherent, independent of the social relation which creates it, uncontrolled by the force that requires it. It helps if the object cooperates: hence, the vaginal orgasm;[60] hence, faked orgasms altogether.[61] Women's sexualness, like male prowess, is no less real for being mythic. It is embodied. Commodities do have value, but only because value is a social property arising from the totality of the same social relations which, unconscious of their determination, fetishize it. Women's bodies possess no less real desirability—or, probably, desire. Sartre exemplifies the problem on the epistemological level: "But if I desire a house, or a glass of water or a woman's body, how could this body, this glass, this piece of property reside in my desire and how can my desire be anything but the consciousness of these objects as desirable?"[62] Indeed. Objectivity is the methodological stance of which objectification is the social process. Sexual objectification is the primary process of the subjection of women. It unites act with word, construction with expression, perception with enforcement, myth with reality. Man fucks woman; subject verb object.

The distinction between objectification and alienation is called into question by this analysis. Objectification in marxist materialism is thought to be the foundation of human freedom, the work process whereby a subject becomes embodied in products and relationships.[63] Alienation is the socially contingent distortion of that process, a reification of products and relations which prevents them from being, and being seen as, dependent on human agency.[64] But from the point of view of the object, objectification *is* alienation. For women, there is no distinction between objectification and alienation because women have not authored objectifications, we have been them. Women have been the nature, the matter, the acted upon, to be subdued by the acting subject seeking to embody himself in the social world. Reification is not just an illusion to the reified; it is also their reality. The alienated who can only grasp self as other is no different from the object who can only grasp self as thing. To be man's other *is* to be his thing. Similarly, the problem of how the object can know herself as such is the same as how the alienated can know its own alienation. This, in turn, poses the problem of feminism's account of women's consciousness. How can women, as created, "thingified in the head,"[65] complicit in the body, see our condition as such?

In order to account for women's consciousness (much less propagate it), feminism must grasp that male power produces the world before it distorts it. Women's acceptance of their condition does not contradict its fundamental unacceptability if women have little choice but to *become* persons who freely choose women's roles. For this reason, the reality of women's oppression is, finally, neither demonstrable nor refutable empirically. Until this is confronted on the level of method, criticism of what exists can be undercut by pointing to the reality to be criticized. Women's bondage, degradation, damage, complicity, and inferiority—together with the possibility of resistance, movement, or exceptions—will operate as barriers to consciousness rather than as means of access to what women need to become conscious of in order to change.

Male power is real; it is just not what it claims to be, namely, the only reality. Male power is a myth that makes itself true. To raise consciousness is to confront male power in this duality—as total on one side and a delusion on the other. In consciousness raising, women learn they have *learned* that men are everything, women their negation, but that the sexes are equal. The content of the message is revealed true and false at the same time, in fact, each part reflects the other transvalued. If "men are all, women their negation" is taken as social criticism rather than simple description, it becomes clear for the first time that women *are* men's equals, everywhere in chains. Their chains become visible, their inferiority—their inequality—a product of subjection and a mode of its enforcement. Reciprocally, the moment it is seen that this—life as we know it—is not equality, that the sexes are not socially equal, womanhood can no longer be defined in terms of lack of maleness, as negativity. For the first time, the question of what a woman *is* seeks its ground in and of a world understood as neither of its making nor in its image, and finds, within a critical embrace of woman's fractured and alien image, that world women have made and a vision of its wholeness. Feminism has unmasked maleness as a form of power that is both omnipotent and nonexistent, an unreal thing with very real consequences. Zora Neale Hurston captured its two-sidedness: "The town has a basketful of feelings good and bad about Joe's positions and possessions, but none had the temerity to challenge him. They bowed down to him rather, because he was all of these things, and then again he was all of these things because the town bowed down."[66] If "positions and possessions" and rulership create each other, in relation, the question becomes one of form and inevitability. This challenges feminism to apply its theory of women's standpoint to the regime.[67]

Feminism is the first theory to emerge from those whose interest it affirms. Its method recapitulates as theory the reality it seeks to capture. As marxist method is dialectical materialism, feminist method is consciousness raising: the collective critical reconstitution of the meaning of women's social experience, as women live through it. Marxism and feminism on this level posit a different relation between thought and thing, both in terms of the relationship of the analysis itself to the social life it captures and in terms of the participation of thought in the social life it analyzes. To the extent that materialism is scientific, it posits and refers to a reality outside thought which it considers to have an objective—that is, truly nonsocially perspectival—content. Consciousness raising, by contrast, inquires into an intrinsically social situation, into that mixture of thought and materiality which is women's sexuality in the most generic sense. It approaches its world through a process that shares its determination: women's consciousness, not as individual or subjective ideas, but as collective social being. This method stands inside its own determinations in order to uncover them, just as it criticizes them in order to value them on its own terms—in order to *have* its own terms at all. Feminism turns theory itself—the pursuit of a true analysis of social life—into the pursuit of consciousness and turns an analysis of inequality into a critical embrace of its own determinants. The process is transformative as well as perceptive, since thought and thing are inextricable and reciprocally constituting of women's oppression, just as the state as coercion and the state as legitimizing ideology are indistinguishable, and for the same reasons. The pursuit of consciousness becomes a form of political practice. Consciousness raising has revealed gender relations to be a collective fact, no more simply personal than class relations. This implies that class relations may also be personal, no less so for being at the same time collective. The failure of marxism to realize this may connect the failure of workers in advanced capitalist nations to organize in the socialist sense with the failure of left revolutions to liberate women in the feminist sense.

Feminism stands in relation to marxism as marxism does to classical political economy: its final conclusion and ultimate critique. Compared with marxism, the place of thought and things in method and reality are reversed in a seizure of power that penetrates subject with object and theory with practice. In a dual motion, feminism turns marxism inside out and on its head.

To answer an old question—how is value created and distributed?—Marx needed to create an entirely new account of the social world. To answer an equally old question, or to question an equally old reality—what explains the inequality of women to men? or, how does desire become domination? or, what is male power?—feminism revolutionizes politics.

NOTES

Dedicated to the spirit of Shelly Rosaldo in us all.

The second part of this article, which will appear in a forthcoming issue of *Signs* as "Feminism, Marxism, Method, and the State: Toward Feminist Jurisprudence," applies the critique developed here to theories of the state and to legal materials. Both articles are parts of a longer work in progress. The argument of this essay on the relation between marxism and feminism has not changed since it was first written in 1973, but the argument on feminism itself has. In the intervening years, the manuscript has been widely circulated, in biannual mutations, for criticism. Reflecting on that process, which I hope publication will continue (this *is* "an agenda for theory"), I find the following people, each in their way, contributed most to its present incarnation: Sonia E. Alvarez, Douglas Bennett, Paul Brest, Ruth Colker, Robert A. Dahl, Karen E. Davis, Andrea Dworkin, Alicia Fernandez, Jane Flax, Bert Garskoff, Elbert Gates, Karen Haney, Kent Harvey, Linda Hoaglund, Nan Keohane, Duncan Kennedy, Bob Lamm, Martha Roper, Michelle Z. Rosaldo, Anne E. Simon, Sharon Silverstein, Valier A. Tebbetts, Rona Wilensky, Gaye

Williams, Jack Winkler, and Laura X. The superb work of Martha Freeman and Lu Ann Carter was essential to its production.

I have rendered "marxism" in lower case and "Black" in upper case and have been asked by the publisher to explain these choices. It is conventional to capitalize terms that derive from a proper name. Since I wish to place marxism and feminism in equipoise, the disparate typography would weigh against my analytic structure. Capitalizing both would germanize the text. I also hope feminism, a politics authored by those it works in the name of, is never named after an individual. Black is conventionally (I am told) regarded as a color rather than a racial or national designation, hence is not usually capitalized. I do not regard Black as merely a color of skin pigmentation, but as a heritage, an experience, a cultural and personal identity, the meaning of which becomes specifically stigmatic and/or glorious and/or ordinary under specific social conditions. It is as much socially created as, and at least in the American context no less specifically meaningful or definitive than, any linguistic, tribal, or religious ethnicity, all of which are conventionally recognized by capitalization.

1. "Desire" is selected as a term parallel to "value" in marxist theory to refer to that substance felt to be primordial or aboriginal but posited by the theory as social and contingent. The sense in which I mean it is consonant with its development in contemporary French feminist theories, e.g., in Hélène Cixous, "The Laugh of Medusa: Viewpoint," trans. Keith Cohen and Paula Cohen, *Signs: Journal of Women in Culture and Society* 1, no. 4 (Summer 1976): 875–93; and in works by Gauthier, Irigaray, LeClerc, Duras, and Kristeva in *New French Feminisms: An Anthology*, ed. Elaine Marks and Isabelle de Courtivron (Amherst: University of Massachusetts Press, 1980). My use of the term is to be distinguished from that of Gilles Deleuze and Felix Gauttari, *Anti-Oedipus: Capitalism and Schizophrenia* (New York: Viking Press, 1977); and Guy Hocquenghem, *Homosexual Desire* (London: Allison & Busby, 1978), for example.
2. I know no nondegraded English verb for the activity of sexual expression that would allow a construction parallel to, for example, "I am working," a phrase that could apply to nearly any activity. This fact of language may reflect and contribute to the process of obscuring sexuality's pervasiveness in social life. Nor is there *any* active verb meaning "to act sexually" that specifically envisions a woman's action. If language constructs as well as expresses the social world, these words support heterosexual values.
3. Accepting this definition has tended to exclude from "the women's movement" and make invisible the diverse ways that many women—notably Blacks and working-class women—have *moved* against their determinants.
4. John Stuart Mill, "The Subjection of Women," in *Essays on Sex Equality*, ed. Alice S. Rossi (Chicago: University of Chicago Press, 1970), pp. 184–85.
5. Mill personally supported universal suffrage. As it happened, working-class men got the vote before women of any class.
6. Feminists have observed the importance of consciousness raising without seeing it as method in the way developed here. See Pamela Allen, *Free Space: A Perspective on the Small Group in Women's Liberation* (New York: Times Change Press, 1970); Anuradha Bose, "Consciousness Raising," in *Mother Was Not a Person*, ed. Margaret Anderson (Montreal: Content Publishing, 1972); Nancy McWilliams, "Contemporary Feminism, Consciousness-Raising, and Changing Views of the Political," in *Women in Politics*, ed. Jane Jaquette (New York: John Wiley & Sons, 1974); Joan Cassell, *A Group Called Women: Sisterhood and Symbolism in the Feminist Movement*

(New York: David McKay, 1977); and Nancy Hartsock, "Fundamental Feminism: Process and Perspective," *Quest: A Feminist Quarterly* 2, no. 2 (Fall 1975): 67–80.

7. Toni Cade (now Bambara) thus describes a desperate Black women who has too many children and too little means to care for them or herself in "The Pill: Genocide or Liberation?" in *The Black Woman: An Anthology*, ed. Toni Cade (New York: Mentor, New American Library, 1970), p. 168. By using her phrase in altered context, I do not want to distort her meaning but to extend it. Throughout this essay, I have tried to see if women's condition is shared, even when contexts or magnitudes differ. (Thus, it is very different to be "nobody" as a Black woman than as a white lady, but neither is "somebody" by male standards.) This is the approach to race and ethnicity attempted throughout. I aspire to include all women in the term "women" in some way, without violating the particularity of any woman's experience. Whenever this fails, the statement is simply wrong and will have to be qualified or the aspiration (or the theory) abandoned.
8. Rosa Luxemburg, "Women's Suffrage and Class Struggle," in *Selected Political Writings*, ed. Dick Howard (New York: Monthly Review Press, 1971), pp. 219–20. It may or may not be true that women as a group vote more conservatively than men, on a conventional left-right spectrum. The apparently accurate suspicion that they do may have accounted for left ambivalence on women's suffrage as much as any principled view of the role of reform in a politics of radical change.
9. Ibid., p. 220.
10. This question is most productively explored in the controversy over wages for housework. See Margaret Benston, "The Political Economy of Women's Liberation," *Monthly Review*, vol. 21, no. 4 (September 1969), reprinted in *From Feminism to Liberation*, ed. Edith Hoshino Altbach (Cambridge, Mass.: Schenckman Publishing Co., 1971), pp. 199–210; Peggy Morton, "Women's Work Is Never Done," in *Women Unite* (Toronto: Canadian Women's Educational Press, 1972); Hodee Edwards, "Housework and Exploitation: A Marxist Analysis," *No More Fun and Games: A Journal of Female Liberation*, Issue 4 (July 1971), pp. 92–100; and Mariarosa Dalla Costa and Selma James, *The Power of Women and the Subversion of the Community* (Bristol: Falling Wall Press, 1973). This last work situates housework in a broader theoretical context of wagelessness and potential political power while avoiding support of wages for housework as a program; its authors have since come to support wages for housework, deducing it from the perspective presented here. See also Sylvia Federici, *Wages Against Housework* (Bristol: Falling Wall Press, 1973). Wally Seccombe, "The Housewife and Her Labor under Capitalism," *New Left Review* 83 (January–February 1974): 3–24; Carol Lopate, "Women and Pay for Housework," *Liberation* 18, no. 9 (May–June 1974): 11–19; Nicole Cox and Sylvia Federici, *Counter-Planning from the Kitchen—Wages for Housework: A Perspective on Capital and the Left* (Bristol: Falling Wall Press, 1975); Wendy Edmond and Suzi Fleming, eds., *All Work and No Pay: Women, Housework and the Wages Due* (Bristol: Falling Wall Press, 1975); Jeanette Silveira, *The Housewife and Marxist Class Analysis* (Seattle, Wash.: By the author, 1975) (pamphlet available from the author, P.O. Box 30451, Seattle, Wash. 98103); Jean Gardiner, "Women's Domestic Labor," *New Left Review 89* (January–February 1975) 47–55; Beth Ingber and Cleveland Modern Times Group, "The Social Factory," *Falling Wall Review*, no. 5 (1976), pp. 1–7; Joan Landes, "Wages for Housework: Subsidizing Capitalism?" *Quest: A Feminist Quarterly* 2, no. 2 (Fall 1975): 17–30; Batya Weinbaum and Amy Bridges, "The Other Side of the Paycheck: Monopoly Capital and the Structure of Conscription," *Monthly Review* 28, no. 3 (July–August 1976): 88–103.
11. These observations are complex and varied. Typically they begin with the recognition of the important changes socialism has made for women, qualified by reservations about its potential to

make the remaining necessary ones. Delia Davin, "Women in the Countryside of China," in *Women in Chinese Society*, ed. Margery Wolf and Roxane Witke (Stanford, Calif.: Stanford University press, 1974); Katie Curtin, *Women in China* (New York: Pathfinder Press, 1975); Judith Stacey, "When Patriarchy Kowtows: The Significance of the Chinese Family Evolution for Feminist Theory," *Feminist Studies* 2, no. 2/3 (1975): 64–112; Julia Kristeva, *About Chinese Women* (New York: Urizen Books, 1977); Hilda Scott, *Does Socialism Liberate Women? Experiences from Eastern Europe* (Cambridge, Mass.: Beacon Press, 1974); Margaret Randall, *Cuban Women Now* (Toronto: Women's Press, 1974) (an edited collation of Cuban women's own observations), and *Cuban Women Now: Afterword* (Toronto: Women's Press, 1974); Carollee Bengelsdorf and Alice Hageman, "Emerging from Underdevelopment: Women and Work in Cuba," in *Capitalist Patriarchy and the Case for Socialist Feminism*, ed. Zillah Eisenstein (New York: Monthly Review Press, 1979).

12. Barbara Ehrenreich, "What Is Socialist Feminism?" *Win* (June 3, 1976), reprinted in *Working Papers on Socialism and Feminism* (Chicago: New American Movement, n.d.). Counterpoint is provided by feminsts who have more difficulty separating the two. Susan Brownmiller notes: "It seems to me that a country that wiped out the tsetse fly can by fiat put an equal number of women on the Central Committee" ("Notes of an Ex–China Fan,' *Village Voice*, quoted in Batya Weinbaum, *The Curious Courtship of Women's Liberation and Socialism* [Boston: South End Press, 1978], p. 7).
13. Stacey (n. 11 above); Janet Salaff and Judith Merkle, "Women and Revolution: The Lessons of the Soviet Union and China," *Socialist Revolution* 1, no. 4 (1970): 39–72; Linda Gordon, *The Fourth Mountain* (Cambridge, Mass.: Working Papers, 1973); Richard Stites, *The Women's Liberation Movement in Russia; Feminism, Nihilism, and Bolshevism* (Princeton, N.J.: Princeton University Press, 1978), pp. 392–421.
14. See Fidel Castro, *Women and the Cuban Revolution* (New York: Pathfinder Press, 1970); but compare Fidel's "Speech at Closing Session of the 2d Congress of the Federation of Cuban Women," November 29, 1974, *Cuba Review* 4(December 1974): 17–23. Stephanie Urdang, *A Revolution within a Revolution: Women in Guinea–Bissau* (Boston: New England Free Press, n.d.).This is the general position taken by official documents of the Chinese revolution, as collected by Elisabeth Croll, ed., *The Women's Movement in China: A Selection of Readings*, 1949–1973, Modern China Series, no. 6 (London: Anglo–Chinese Educational Institute, 1974). Mao Tse-Tung recognized a distinctive domination of women by men (see discussion by Stuart Schram, *The Political Thought of Mao Tse-Tung* [New York: Praeger Publishers, 1969], p. 257), but interpretations of his thought throughout the revolution saw issues of sex as bourgeois deviation (see Croll, ed., pp. 19, 22, 32). The Leninist view which the latter documents seem to reflect is expressed in Clara Zetkin's account, "Lenin on the Woman Question," excerpted as appendix in *The Woman Question* (New York: International Publishers, 1951), p. 89. Engels earlier traced the oppression of women to the rise of class society, the patriarchal family, and the state, arguing that woman's status would be changed with the elimination of private property as a form of ownership and her integration into public production (Friedrich Engels, *Origin of the Family, Private Property and the State* [New York: International Publishers, 1942]).
15. Sheila Rowbotham, *Hidden from History: Rediscovering Women in History from the Seventeenth Century to the Present* (New York: Random House, 1973); Mary Jo Buhle, "Women and the Socialist Party, 1901–1914," in Altbach, ed. (n. 10 above); Robert Shaffer, "Women and the Communist Party, USA, 1930–1940," *Socialist Review* 45 (May–June 1979): 73–118. Contemporary attempts to create socialist-feminist groups and strategies are exemplified in position papers:

Chicago Women's Liberation Union, "Socialist Feminism: A Strategy for the Women's Movement," mimeograph (Chicago, 1972) (available from Women's Liberation Union, Hyde Park Chapter, 819 W. George, Chicago, Ill. 60657); Berkeley-Oakland Women's Union, "Principles of Unity," *Socialist Revolution* 4, no. 1 (January–March 1974): 69–82; Lavender and Red Union, *The Political Perspective of the Lavender and Red Union* (Los Angeles: Fanshen Printing Collective, 1975). Rosalind Petchesky, "Dissolving the Hyphen: A Report on Marxist-Feminist Groups 1–5," in Eisenstein, ed., (n. 11 above), and Red Apple Collective, "Socialist-Feminist Women's Unions: Past and Present," *Quest: A Feminist Quarterly* 4, no. 1 (1977): 88–96, reflect on the process.

16. Many attempts at unity began as an effort to justify women's struggles in marxist terms, as if only that could make them legitimate. This anxiety lurks under many synthetic attempts, although feminism has largely redirected its efforts from justifying itself within any other perspective to developing its own.

17. While true from a feminist standpoint, this sweeping characterization does minimize the wide varieties of marxist theories that have produced significantly different analyses of women's situation. Juliet Mitchell, *Women's Estate* (New York: Random House, 1971); Sheila Rowbotham, *Women Resistance and Revolution: A History of Women and Revolution in the Modern World* (New York: Random House, 1972); Zillah Eisenstein, "Some Notes on the Relations of Capitalist Patriarchy," in Eisenstein, ed. (n. 11 above); Eli Zaretsky, "Socialist Politics and the Family," *Socialist Revolution* 19 (January–March 1974): 83–99; Eli Zaretsky, "Capitalism, the Family and Personal Life," *Socialist Revolution* 3, nos. 1 and 2 (January–April 1973): 69–126, and no. 3 (May–June 1973): 19–70; Virginia Held, "Marx, Sex and the Transformation of Society," in *Women and Philosophy: Toward a Theory of Liberation,* ed. Carol C. Gould and Marx W. Wartofsky (New York: G. P. Putnam's Sons, 1976), pp. 168–84; Mihailo Marković, "Women's Liberation and Human Emancipation," ibid., pp. 145–67; Hal Draper, "Marx and Engels on Women's Liberation," in *Female Liberation,* ed. Roberta Salper (New York: Alfred A. Knopf, Inc., 1972), pp. 83–107. No matter how perceptive about the contributions of feminism or sympathetic to women's interests, these attempts cast feminism, ultimately, as a movement *within* marxism: "I want to suggest that the women's movement can provide the basis for building a new and authentic American socialism" (Nancy Hartsock, "Feminist Theory and the Development of Revolutionary Strategy," in Eisenstein, ed. [n. 11 above], p. 57). Attempts at synthesis that push these limits include Gayle Rubin, "The Traffic in Women: Notes on the 'Political Economy' of Sex," in *Toward an Anthropology of Women,* ed. Rayna R. Reiter (New York: Monthly Review Press, 1975), pp. 157–210; Sheila Rowbotham, *Women's Liberation and the New Politics,* Spokesman Pamphlet, no. 17 (Bristol: Falling Wall Press, 1971); Annette Kuhn and AnnMarie Wolpe, "Feminism and Materialism," in *Feminism and Materialism: Women and Modes of Production,* ed. Annette Kuhn and AnnMarie Wolpe (London: Routledge & Kegan Paul, 1978); Ann Foreman, *Femininity as Alienation: Women and the Family in Marxism and Psychoanalysis* (London: Pluto Press, 1977); Meredith Tax and Jonathan Schwartz, "The Wageless Slave and the Proletarian," mimeograph (1972) (available from the author); Heidi I. Hartmann, "Capitalism, Patriarchy, and Job Segregation by Sex," *Signs: Journal of Women in Culture and Society* 1, no. 3, pt. 2 (Spring 1976): 137–69, and "The Unhappy Marriage of Marxism and Feminism: Towards a More Progressive Union," *Capital and Class* 8 (Summer 1979): 1–33; advocates of "wages for housework" mentioned in n. 10 above; and work by Linda Gordon, *Woman's Body, Woman's Right: A Social History of Birth Control in America* (New York: Grossman Publishers, 1976), pp. 403–18.Also see Linda Gordon, "The Struggle for Reproductive Freedom: Three Stages of Fem-

inism," in Eisenstein, ed. (n. 11 above). Charlotte Bunch and Nancy Myron, *Class and Feminism* (Baltimore: Diana Press, 1974) exemplifies, without explicitly articulating, feminist method applied to class.

18. This tendency, again with important variations, is manifest in writings otherwise as diverse as Charnie Guettel, *Marxism and Feminism* (Toronto: Canadian Women's Education Press, 1974); Mary Alice Waters, "Are Feminism and Socialism Related?" in *Feminism and Socialism*, ed. Linda Jenness (New York: Pathfinder Press, 1972), pp. 18–26; Weather Underground, *Prairie Fire* (Underground, U.S.A.: Red Dragon Collective, 1975); Marjorie King, "Cuba's Attack on Women's Second Shift, 1974–1976," *Latin American Perspectives*, 4, nos. 1 and 2 (Winter–Spring 1977): 106–19; Al Syzmanski, "The Socialization of Women's Oppression: A Marxist Theory of the Changing Position of Women in Advanced Capitalist Society," *Insurgent Sociologist* 6, no. 11 (Winter 1976): 31–58; "The Political Economy of Women," *Review of Radical Political Economics* 4, no. 3 (July 1972). See also Selma James, *Women, the Unions and Work, or What Is Not to Be Done* (Bristol: Falling Wall Press, 1976). This is true for "wages for housework" theory in the sense that it sees women as exploited because they do work—housework.
19. Engels (n. 14 above); Leon Trotsky, *Women and the Family*, trans. Max Eastman et al. (New York: Pathfinder Press, 1970); Evelyn Reed, *Women's Evolution: From Matriarchal Clan to Patriarchal Family* (New York: Pathfinder Press, 1975); Lise Vogel, "The Earthly Family," *Radical America* 7, nos. 4–5 (July–October 1973): 9–50; Kollontai Collective, "The Politics of the Family: A Marxist View" (paper prepared for Socialist Feminist Conference at Yellow Springs, Ohio, July 4–6, 1975); Linda Limpus, *Liberation of Women: Sexual Repression and the Family* (Boston: New England Free Press, n.d.); Marlene Dixon, "On the Super-Exploitation of Women," *Synthesis* I, no. 4 (Spring 1977): 1–11; David P. Levine and Lynn S. Levine, "Problems in the Marxist Theory of the Family," photocopied (Department of Economics, Yale University, July 1978). A common approach to treating women's situation as coterminous with the family is to make women's circumstances the incident or focus for a reconciliation of Marx with Freud. This approach, in turn, often becomes more Freudian than marxist, without yet becoming feminist in the sense developed here. Juliet Mitchell, *Psychoanalysis and Feminism: Freud, Reich, Laing and Women* (New York: Pantheon Books, 1974); Eli Zaretsky, "Male Supremacy and the Unconscious," *Socialist Revolution* 21, no. 22 (January 1975): 7–56; Nancy Chodorow, *The Reproduction of Mothering: Psychoanalysis and the Sociology of Gender* (Berkeley: University of California Press, 1978). See also Herbert Marcuse, "Socialist Feminism: The Hard Core of the Dream," *Edcentric: A Journal of Educational Change*, no. 31–32 (November 1974), pp. 7–44.
20. Sometimes "reproduction" refers to biological reproduction, sometimes to the "reproduction" of daily life, as housework, sometimes both. Political Economy of Women Group, "Women, the State and Reproduction since the 1930s," *On the Political Economy of Women*, CSE Pamphlet no. 2, Stage 1 (London: Conference of Socialist Economists, 1977). Family theories (n. 19 above) often analyze biological reproduction as a part of the family, while theories of women as workers often see it as work (n. 18 above). For an analysis of reproduction as an aspect of *sexuality*, in the context of an attempted synthesis, see Gordon, "The Struggle for Reproductive Freedom: Three Stages of Feminism" (n. 17 above).
21. Henri Lefebvre, *Everyday Life in the Modern World* (London: Penguin Books, 1971); Bruce Brown, *Marx, Freud and the Critique of Everyday Life: Toward a Permanent Cultural Revolution* (New York: Monthly Review Press, 1973).
22. Herbert Marcuse, *Eros and Civilization: A Philosophical Inquiry into Freud* (New York: Random House, 1955); Wilhelm Reich, *Sex-Pol: Essays, 1929–1934* (New York: Random House, 1972);

Reimut Reiche, *Sexuality and Class Struggle* (London: New Left Books, 1970); Bertell Ollman, *Social and Sexual Revolution: Essays on Marx and Reich* (Boston: South End Press, 1979); Red Collective, *The Politics of Sexuality in Capitalism* (London: Red Collective, 1973). This is also true of Michel Foucault, *The History of Sexuality*, vol. 1, *An Introduction* (New York: Random House, 1980). Although Foucault understands that sexuality must be discussed at the same time as method, power, class, and the law, he does not systematically comprehend the specificity of gender—women's and men's relation to these factors—as a primary category for comprehending them. As one result, he cannot distinguish between the silence about sexuality that Victorianism has made into a noisy discourse and the silence that has *been* women's sexuality under conditions of subordination by and to men. Lacan notwithstanding, none of these theorists grasps sexuality (*including desire itself*) as social, nor the content of its determination as a sexist social order that eroticizes potency (as male) and victimization (as female).

23. Marxist method is not monolithic. Beginning with Marx, it has divided between an epistemology that embraces its own historicity and one that claims to portray a reality outside itself. In the first tendency, all thought, including social analysis, is ideological in the sense of being shaped by social being, the conditions of which are external to no theory. The project of theory is to create what Lukàcs described as "a theory of theory and a consciousness of consciousness" (Georg Lukàcs, "Class Consciousness," in *History and Class Consciousness: Studies in Marxist Dialectics* [Cambridge, Mass.: MIT Press, 1968], p. 47). Theory is a social activity engaged in the life situation of consciousness. See Jane Flax, "Epistemology and Politics: An Inquiry into Their Relation" (Ph.D. diss., Yale University, 1974). In the second tendency, theory is acontextual to the extent that it is correct. Real processes and thought processes are distinct; being has primacy over knowledge. The real can only be unified with knowledge of the real, as in dialectical materialism, because they have previously been separated. Nicos Poulantzas, *Political Power and Social Classes* (London: Verso, 1978), p. 14. Theory as a form of thought is methodologically set apart both from the illusions endemic to social reality—ideology—and from reality itself, a world defined as thinglike, independent of both ideology and theory. Ideology here means thought that is socially determined without being conscious of its determinations. Situated thought is as likely to produce "false consciousness" as access to truth. Theory, by definition, is, on the contrary, nonideological. Since ideology is interested, theory must be disinterested in order to penetrate myths that justify and legitimate the status quo. As Louis Althusser warned, "We know that a 'pure' science only exists on condition that it continually frees itself from ideology which occupies it, haunts it, or lies in wait for it" (*For Marx* [London: Verso, 1979], p. 170). When this attempt is successful, society is seen "from the point of view of class exploitation" (Louis Althusser, *Lenin and Philosophy* [New York: Monthly Review Press, 1971], p. 8). A theory that embraced its own historicity might see the scientific imperative itself as historically contingent. (On the objective standpoint, see text, pp. 70–76.) The problem with using scientific method to understand women's situation is that it is precisely unclear and crucial what is thought and what is thing, so that the separation itself becomes problematic. The second tendency grounds the marxist claim to be scientific; the first, its claim to capture as thought the flux of history. The first is more hospitable to feminism; the second has become the dominant tradition.

24. Simone de Beauvoir, *The Second Sex* (New York: Alfred A. Knopf, Inc., 1970). Her existential theory merges, in order to criticize, social meaning with biological determination in "anatomical destiny": "Here we have the key to the whole mystery. On the biological level a species is maintained only by creating itself anew; but this creation results only in repeating the same Life in more individuals. But man assures the repetition of Life while transcending life through Exis-

tence; by this transcendence he creates values that deprive pure repetition of all value. . . . Her misfortune is to have been biologically destined for the repetition of Life when even in her own view Life does not carry within itself its reasons for being, reasons that are more important than life itself" (p. 59). She does not ask, for example, whether the social value placed upon "repetition of life," the fact that it is seen as iterative rather than generative, or the fact that women are more identified with it than are men, are themselves social artifacts of women's subordination, rather than existential derivations of biological fiat. Shulamith Firestone substitutes the contradiction of sex for class in a dialectical analysis, but nevertheless takes sex itself as presocial: "Unlike economic class, sex class sprang directly from a biological reality; men and women were created different, and not equally privileged. . . . The biological family is an inherently unequal power distribution" (*The Dialectic of Sex: The Case For Feminist Revolution* [New York: William Morrow & Co., 1972], p. 3). Her solutions are consistent: "The freeing of women from the tyranny of their reproductive biology by every means available, and the diffusion of childbearing and the childrearing role to the society as a whole, men as well as women" (p. 206). Susan Brownmiller (in *Against Our Will: Men, Women and Rape* [New York: Simon & Schuster, 1976]) expresses a biological theory of rape within a social critique of the centrality of rape to women's subordination: "Men's structural capacity to rape and woman's corresponding structural vulnerability are as basic to the physiology of both our sexes as the primal act of sex itself. Had it not been for this accident of biology, an accommodation requiring the locking together of two separate parts, penis and vagina, there would be neither copulation nor rape as we know it. . . . By anatomical fiat—the inescapable construction of their genital organs—the human male was a natural predator and the human female served as his natural prey" (pp. 4, 6). She does not seem to think it necessary to explain why women do not engulf men, an equal biological possibility. Criticizing the law for confusing intercourse with rape, she finds them biologically indistinguishable, leaving one wondering whether she, too, must alter or acquiesce in the biological.

25. Adrienne Rich, *Of Woman Born: Motherhood as Experience and Institution* (New York: W. W. Norton & Co., 1976); Chodorow (n. 19 above); Dorothy Dinnerstein, *The Mermaid and the Minotaur: Sexual Arrangements and Human Malaise* (New York: Harper & Row, 1977); Suzanne Arms, *Immaculate Deception: A New Look at Women and Childbirth in America* (Boston: Houghton Mifflin Co., 1975).
26. I take Mill's "The Subjection of Women" (n. 4 above) to be the original articulation of the theory, generalized in much contemporary feminism, that women are oppressed by "patriarchy," meaning a system originating in the household wherein the father dominates, the structure then reproduced throughout the society in gender relations.
27. In her "notes toward a theory of patriarchy" Kate Millett comprehends "sex as a status category with political implications," in which politics refers to "power-structured relationships, arrangements whereby one group of persons is controlled by another. . . . Patriarchy's chief institution is the family" (*Sexual Politics* [New York: Ballentine Books, 1969], pp. 32, 31, 45.
28. Sandra L. Bem and Daryl J. Bem, "Case Study of Nonconscious Ideology: Training the Woman to Know Her Place," in *Beliefs, Attitudes and Human Affairs*, ed. D. J. Bem (Belmont, Calif.: Brooks/Cole, 1970); Eleanor Emmons Maccoby and Carol Nagy Jacklin, *The Psychology of Sex Differences* (Stanford, Calif.: Stanford University Press, 1974); and Shirley Weitz, *Sex Roles: Biological, Psychological and Social Foundations* (New York: Oxford University Press, 1977).
29. Nor does it grow directly from Lacanian roots, although French feminists have contributed much to the developing theory from within that tradition.
30. De Beauvoir (n. 24 above), p. 249.

31. J. H. Block, "Conceptions of Sex Role: Some Cross-cultural and Longitudinal Perspectives," *American Psychologist* 28, no. 3 (June 1973): 512–26; Nancy Chodorow, "Being and Doing" A Cross-cultural Examination of the Socialization of Males and Females," in *Women in Sexist Society*, ed. V. Gornick and B. K. Moran (New York: Basic Books, 1971); R. R. Sears, "Development of Gender Role," in *Sex and Behavior*, ed. F. A. Beach (New York: John Wiley & Sons, 1965).
32. National Black Feminist Organization, "Statement of Purpose," *Ms* (May 1974): "The black woman has had to be strong, yet we are persecuted for having survived" (p. 99). Jonnie Tillmon, "Welfare Is a Women's Issue," *Liberation News Service* (February 26, 1972), in *America's Working Women: A Documentary History, 1600 to the Present*, ed. Rosalyn Baxandall, Linda Gordon, and Susan Reverby (New York: Vintage Books, 1976): "On TV a woman learns that human worth means beauty and that beauty means being thin, white, young and rich. . . . In other words, an A.F.D.C. mother learns that being a 'real woman' means being all the things she isn't and having all the things she can't have" (pp. 357–58).
33. Marabel Morgan, *The Total Woman* (Old Tappan, N.J.: Fleming H. Revell Co., 1973). "Total Woman" makes blasphemous sexuality into a home art, redomesticating what prostitutes have marketed as forbidden.
34. Cixous (n. 1 above), p. 892.
35. Indications are that this is true not only in Western industrial society; further cross-cultural research is definitely needed.
36. Love justifies this on the emotional level. Firestone (n. 24 above), chap. 6.
37. Millett's analysis is pervasively animated by the sense that women's status is sexually determined. It shapes her choice of authors, scenes, and themes and underlies her most pointed criticisms of women's depiction. Her explicit discussion, however, vacillates between clear glimpses of that argument and statements nearly to the contrary.
38. Each of these issues is discussed at length in the second part of this article "Toward Feminist Jurisprudence"), forthcoming.
39. On abortion and contraception, see Kristin Luker, *Taking Chances: Abortion and the Decision Not to Contracept* (Berkeley: University of California Press, 1975). On rape, see Diana E. H. Russell, *Rape: The Victim's Perspective* New York: Stein & Day, 1977); Andrea Medea and Kathleen Thompson, *Against Rape* (New york: Farrar, Straus & Giroux, 1974); Lorenne N. G. Clark and Debra Lewis, *Rape: The Price of Coercive Sexuality* (Toronto: Women's Press, 1977); Susan Griffin, *Rape: The Power of Consciousness* (San Francisco: Harper & Row, 1979); Kalamu ya Salaam, "Rape: A Radical Analysis from the African-American Perspective," in his *Our Women Keep Our Skies from Falling* (New Orleans: Nkombo, 1980), pp. 25–40. On incest, see Judith Herman and Lisa Hirschman, "Father-Daughter Incest," *Signs: Journal of Women in Culture and Society* 2, no. 1 (Summer 1977): 735–56. On sexual harassment, see my *Sexual Harassment of Working Women* (New Haven, Conn.: Yale University Press, 1979). On pornography, see Andrea Dworkin, *Pornography: Men Possessing Women* (New York: G. P. Putnam's Sons, 1981).
40. Ellen Morgan, *The Erotization of Male Dominance/Female Submission* (Pittsburgh: Know, Inc., 1975); Adrienne Rich, "Compulsory Heterosexuality and Lesbian Existence," *Signs: Journal of Women in Culture and Society* 5, no. 4 (Summer 1980): 631–60.
41. Susan Sontag, "The Third World of Women," *Partisan Review* 40, no. 2 (1973): 180–206, esp. 188.
42. The same question could be asked of lesbian sadomasochism: when women engage in ritualized sexual dominance and submission, does it express the male structure or subvert it? The answer depends upon whether one has a social or biological definition of gender and of sexuality and

then upon the content of these definitions. Lesbian sex, simply as sex between women, does not by definition transcend the erotization of dominance and submission and their social equation with masculinity and femininity. Butch/femme as *sexual* (not just gender) role playing, together with parallels in lesbian sadomasochism's "top" and "bottom," suggest to me that sexual conformity extends far beyond gender object mores. For a contrary view see Pat Califia, *Sapphistry: The Book of Lesbian Sexuality* (Tallahassee, Fla.: Naiad Press, 1980); Gayle Rubin, "Sexual Politics, the New Right and the Sexual Fringe," in *What Color Is Your Handkerchief: A Lesbian S/M Sexuality Reader* (Berkeley, Calif.: Samois, 1979), pp. 28–35.

43. Engels (n. 14 above); August Bebel, *Women under Socialism*, trans. Daniel DeLeon (New York: New York Labor News Press, 1904).
44. Reich (n. 22 above). He examines fascism, for example, as a question of how the masses can be made to desire their own repression. This might be seen as a precursor to the feminist question of how female desire *itself* can become the lust for self–annihilation.
45. Harold Lasswell, *Psychoanalysis and Politics* (Chicago: University of Chicago Press, 1930).
46. The aphorism "Feminism is the theory; lesbianism is the practice" has been attributed to TiGrace Atkinson by Anne Koedt, "Lesbianism and Feminism," in *Radical Feminism*, ed. Anne Koedt, Ellen Levine, and Anita Rapone (New York: New York Times Book Co., 1973); p. 246. See also Radicalesbians, "The Woman Identified Woman," ibid., pp. 24–45; TiGrace Atkinson, "Lesbianism & Feminism," *Amazon Odyssey: The First Collection of Writings by the Political Pioneer of the Women's Movement* (New York: Links Books, 1974), pp. 83–88; Jill Johnston, *Lesbian Nation: The Feminist Solution* (New York: Simon & Schuster, 1973), pp. 167, 185, 278. This aphorism accepts a simplistic view of the relationship between theory and practice. Feminism reconceptualizes the connection between being and thinking such that it may be more accurate to say that feminism is the epistemology of which lesbianism is an ontology. But see n. 56 below on this latter distinction as well.
47. Judy Grahn, *The Work of a Common Woman* (New York: St. Martin's Press, 1978). "The Common Woman" poems are on pp. 61–73.
48. Adrienne Rich, "Origins and History of Consciousness," in *The Dream of a Common Language: Poems, 1974–1977* (New York: W. W. Norton & Co., 1978), p. 7. This means that a women's movement exists wherever women identify collectively to resist/reclaim their determinants as such. This feminist redefinition of consciousness requires a corresponding redefinition of the process of mobilizing it: feminist *organizing*. The transformation from subordinate group to movement parallels Marx's distinction between a class "in itself" and a class "for itself." See Karl Marx, *The Poverty of Philosophy* (New York: International Publishers, 1963), p. 195.
49. In addition to the references in n. 1, see Sandra Lee Bartky, "Toward a Phenomenology of Feminist Consciousness," in *Feminism and Philosophy*, ed. Mary Vetterling-Braggin et al. (Totowa, N.J.: Littlefield, Adams & Co., 1977). Susan Griffin reflects/creates the process: "We do not rush to speech. We allow ourselves to be moved. We do not attempt objectivity. . . . We said we had experienced this ourselves. I felt so much for her then, she said, with her head cradled in my lap, she said, I knew what to do. We said we were moved to see her go through what we had gone through. We said this gave us some knowledge" (*Woman and Nature: The Roaring Inside Her* [New York: Harper & Row, 1978], p. 197). Assertions such as "our politics begin with our feelings" have emerged from the practice of consciousness raising. Somewhere between mirror-reflexive determination and transcendence of determinants, "feelings" are seen as both access to truth—at times a bit phenomenologically transparent—and an artifact of politics. There is both suspicion of feelings and affirmation of their health. They become simultaneously an inner

expression of outer lies and a less contaminated resource for verification. See San Francisco Redstockings, "Our Politics Begin with Our Feelings," in *Masculine/Feminine: Readings in Sexual Mythology and the Liberation of Women*, ed. Betty Roszak and Theodore Roszak (New York: Harper & Row, 1969).

50. Fredric Jameson, *Marxism and Form* (Princeton, N.J.: Princeton University Press, 1971), p. xi. Jameson is describing dialectical method: "I have felt that the dialectical method can be acquired only by a concrete working through of detail, by a sympathetic internal experience of the gradual construction of a system according to its inner necessity."

51. This distinguishes both feminism and at least a strain in marxism from Freud: "My self-analysis is still interrupted and I have realized the reason. I can only analyze my self with the help of knowledge obtained objectively (like an outsider). Genuine self-analysis is impossible, otherwise there would be no [neurotic] illness." (Sigmund Freud, Letter to Wilhelm Fleiss, #71, October 15, 1887, quoted in Mitchell, *Psychoanalysis and Feminism: Freud, Reich, Laing and Women* [n. 19 above], pp. 61–62, see also p. 271). Given that introspection is not analytically dispositive to Freud, the collective self-knowledge of feminism might be collective neurosis. Although it is interpersonal, it is still an insider to its world.

52. Feminist scholars are beginning to criticize objectivity from different disciplinary standpoints, although not as frontally as here, nor in its connection with objectification. Julia Sherman and Evelyn Torton Beck, eds., *The Prism of Sex: Essays in the Sociology of Knowledge* (Madison: University of Wisconsin Press, 1979): Margrit Eichler, *The Double Standard: A Feminist Critique of Feminist Social Science* (New York: St. Martin's Press, 1980); Evelyn Fox Keller, "Gender and Science," *Psychoanalysis and Contemporary Thought* 1, no. 3 (1978): 409–33. Adrienne Rich, "Toward a Woman-centered University," in *Woman and the Power to Change*, ed. Florence Howe (New York: McGraw-Hill Book Co., 1975).

53. De Beauvoir (n. 24 above). De Beauvoir had not pursued the analysis to the point I suggest here by 1979, either. See her "Introduction," in Marks and de Courtivron, eds. (n. 1 above), pp. 41–56.

54. This does not mean all men *have* male power equally. American Black men, for instance have substantially less of it. But to the extent that they cannot create the world from their point of view, they find themselves unmanned, castrated, literally or figuratively. This supports rather than qualifies the sex specificity of the argument without resolving the relationship between racism and sexism, or the relation of either to class. Although historically receiving more attention, race and nation are otherwise analogous to sex in the place they occupy for, and the challenge they pose to, marxist theory. If the real basis of history and activity is class and class conflict, what, other than "false consciousness," is one to make of the historical force of sexism, racism, and nationalism? Similarly, positing a supra-class unit with true meaning, such as "Black people," is analytically parallel to positing a supra-class (and supra-racial) unit "women." Treating race, nation, and sex as lesser included problems has been the major response of marxist theory to such challenges. Any relationship *between* sex and race tends to be left entirely out of account, since they are considered parallel "strata." Attempts to confront the latter issue include Adrienne Rich, "Disloyal to Civilization: Feminism, Racism and Gynephobia," in *On Lies, Secrets and Silence: Selected Essays, 1966–1978* (New York: W. W. Norton & Co., 1979); Selma James, *Sex, Race and Class* (Bristol: Falling Wall Press, 1967); R. Coles and J. H. Coles, *Women of Crisis* (New York: Dell Publishing Co, Delacorte Press, 1978); Socialist Women's Caucus of Louisville, "The Racist Use of Rape and the Rape Charge" (Louisville, Ky., ca. 1977); Angela Davis, "The Role of Black Women in the Community of Slaves," *Black Scholar* 3, no. 4 (De-

cember 1971): 2–16; The Combahee River Collective, "A Black Feminist Statement," in Eisenstein, ed., (n. 11 above); Karen Getman, "Relations of Gender and Sexuality during the Period of Institutional Slavery in the Southern Colonies" (working paper, Yale University, 1980); E. V. Spelman, "Feminism, Sexism and Racism" (University of Massachusetts, 1981); Cherrié Moraga and Gloria Anzaldúa, eds., *This Bridge Called My Back: Writings of Radical Women of Color* (Watertown, Mass.: Persephone Press, 1981).

55. This suggests a way in which marxism and feminism may be reciprocally illuminating, without, for the moment, confronting the deep divisions between them. Marxism comprehends the *object* world's *social* existence: how objects are constituted, embedded in social life, infused with meaning, created in systematic and structural relation. Feminism comprehends the *social* world's *object* existence: how women are created in the image of, and as, things. The object world's social existence varies with the structure of production. Suppose that wherever the sexes are unequal, women are objects, but what it means to be an object varies with the productive relations that create objects as social. Thus, under primitive exchange systems, women are exchange objects. Under capitalism, women appear as commodities. That is, women's sexuality as object for men is valued as objects are under capitalism, namely as commodities. Under true communism, women would be collective sex objects. If women have universally been sex objects, it is also true that matter as the acted-upon in social life has a history. If women have always been things, it is also true that things have not always had the same meaning. Of course, this does not explain sex inequality. It merely observes, once that inequality exists, the way its dynamics may interact with the social organization of production. Sexual objectification may also have a separate history, with its own periods, forms, structures, technology, and, potentially, revolutions.

56. In a sense, this realization collapses the epistemology/ontology distinction altogether. What is purely an ontological category, a category of "being" free of social perception? Surely not the self/other distinction. Ultimately, the feminist approach turns social inquiry into political hermeneutics: inquiry into situated meaning, one in which the inquiry itself participates. A feminist political hermeneutics would be a theory of the answer to the question, What does it mean? that would comprehend that the first question to address is, To whom? within a context that comprehends gender as a social division of power. Useful general treatments of hermeneutical issues (which nevertheless proceed as if feminism, or a specific problematic of women, did not exist) include Josef Bleicher, *Contemporary Hermeneutics: Hermeneutics as Method, Philosophy and Critique* (London: Routledge & Kegan Paul, 1980); Hans-Georg Gadamer, *Philosophical Hermeneutics*, trans. David E. Linge (Berkeley: University of California Press, 1976); Rosalind Coward and John Ellis, *Language and Materialism: Developments in Semiology and the Theory of the Subject* (London: Routledge & Kegan Paul, 1977). Mary Daly approaches the ontological issue when she says that ontological theory without an understanding of sex roles cannot be "really ontological" (*Beyond God the Father: Toward a Philosophy of Women's Liberation* [Boston: Beacon Press, 1973], p. 124). But both in this work, and more pervasively in *Gyn/Ecology: The Metaethics of Radical Feminism* (Boston: Beacon Press, 1978), the extent of the *creation* of women's *reality* by male epistemology, therefore the extent and nature of women's damage, is slighted in favor of a critique of its lies and distortions. Consider her investigation of suttee, a practice in which Indian widows are supposed to throw themselves upon their dead husband's funeral pyres in grief (and to keep pure), in which Daly focuses upon demystifying its alleged voluntary aspects. Women are revealed drugged, pushed, browbeaten, or otherwise coerced by the dismal and frightening prospect of widowhood in Indian society (Daly, *Gyn/Ecology*, pp. 113–33). Neglected—both as to the women involved and as to the implications for the entire di-

agnosis of sexism as illusion—are suttee's deepest victims: women who want to die when their husband dies, who volunteer for self-immolation because they believe their life is over when his is. See also Duncan Kennedy, "The Structure of Blackstone's Commentaries," *Buffalo Law Review* 28, no. 2 (1979): 211–12.

57. Dworkin (n. 39 above), p. 124. Explicitness is the aesthetic, the allowed sensibility, of objectified eroticism. Under this norm, written and pictured evocations of sexuality are compulsively literal. What it is to arouse sexuality through art is to recount events "objectively," i.e., verbally and visually to re-present who did what to whom. On the "dynamic of total explicitness" as stylization, explored in the context of the "foremost insight of the modern novel: the interweaving, the symbolic and structural interchange between economic and sexual relations," see George Steiner, "Eros and Idiom: 1975," in *On Difficulty and Other Essays* (New York: Oxford University Press, 1978), p. 100: "Chasteness of discourse [in George Eliot's work] acts not as a limitation but as a liberating privacy within which the character can achieve the paradox of autonomous life" (p. 107). This connects the lack of such liberating privacy for women—in life, law, or letters—with women's lack of autonomy and authentic erotic vocabulary.

58. Linda Lovelace, *Ordeal* (Secaucus, N.J.: Citadel Press, 1980). The same may be true for class. See Richard Sennett and Jonathan Cobb, *The Hidden Injuries of Class* (New York: Alfred A. Knopf, Inc., 1972). Marxism teaches that exploitation/degradation somehow necessarily produces resistance/revolution. Women's experience with sexual exploitation/degradation teaches that it also produces grateful complicity in exchange for survival and self-loathing to the point of the extinction of the self, respect for what makes resistance conceivable. The problem here is not to explain why women acquiesce in their condition but why they ever do anything but.

59. The critique of sexual objectification first became visibly explicit in the American women's movement with the disruption of the Miss America Pageant in September 1968. Robin Morgan, "Women Disrupt the Miss America Pageant," *Rat* (September 1978), reprinted in *Going Too Far: The Personal Chronicle of a Feminist* (New York: Random House, 1977), pp. 62–67. The most compelling account of sexual objectification I know is contained in the following description of women's depiction in art and the media: "According to usage and conventions which are at last being questioned but have by no means been overcome, the social presence of a woman is different in kind from that of a man. . . . A man's presence suggests what he is capable of doing to you or for you. By contrast, a woman's presence expresses her own attitude to herself, and *defines what can and cannot be done to her*. . . . To be born a woman has been to be born, within an allotted and confined space, into the keeping of men. The social presence of women has developed as a result of their ingenuity in living under such tutelage within such a limited space. But this has been at the cost of a woman's self being split into two. A woman must continually watch herself. She is almost continually accompanied by her own image of herself. . . . she comes to consider the surveyor and the surveyed within her as the two constituent yet always distinct elements of her identity as a woman. She has to survey everything she is and everything she does because how she appears to others, and ultimately how she appears to men, *is of crucial importance for what is normally thought of as the success of her life*. Her own sense of being in herself is supplanted by a sense of being appreciated as herself by another. One might simplify this by saying: men act; women appear. *Men look at women. Women watch themselves being looked at.* This determines not only most relations between men and women but also the relation of women to themselves. The surveyor of woman in herself is male: the surveyed, female. Thus she turns herself into an object—and most particularly an object of vision: a sight" (John Berger, *Ways of Seeing* [New York: Viking Press, 1972], pp. 46, 47 [my emphasis]). All that is missing here is an explicit recognition

that this process embodies what the sexuality of women is about and that it expresses an inequality in social power. In a feminist context, aesthetics, including beauty and imagery, becomes the most political of subjects. See Purple September Staff, "The Normative Status of Heterosexuality," in *Lesbianism and the Women's Movement*, ed. Charlotte Bunch and Nancy Myron (Baltimore: Diana Press, 1975), pp. 79–83, esp. pp. 80–81.

Marxist attempts to deal with sexual objectification have not connected the issue with the politics of aesthetics or with subordination: "She becomes a sexual object only in a relationship, when she allows man to treat her in a certain depersonalizing, degrading way; and vice versa, a woman does not become a sexual subject simply by neglecting her appearance. There is no reason why a women's liberation activist should not try to look pretty and attractive. One of the universal aspirations of all times was to raise reality to the level of art. . . . Beauty is a value in itself" (Marković [n. 17 above], pp. 165–66). Other attempts come closer, still without achieving the critique, e.g., Power of Women Collective, "What Is a Sex Object?" *Socialist Woman: A Journal of the International Marxist Group* 1, no. 1 (March/April 1974): 7; Dana Densmore, "On the Temptation to Be a Beautiful Object," in *Toward a Sociology of Women*, ed. C. Safilios-Rothschild (Lexington, Mass.: Xerox Publication, 1972); Rita Arditti, "Women as Objects: Science and Sexual Politics," *Science for the People*, vol. 6, no. 5 (September 1974); Charley Shively, "Cosmetics as an Act of Revolution," *Fag Rag* (Boston), reprinted in *Pink Triangles: Radical Perspectives on Gay Liberation*, ed. Pam Mitchell (Boston: Alyson Publication, 1980). Resentment of white beauty standards is prominent in Black feminism. Beauty standards incapable of achievement by any woman seem to fulfill a dual function. They keep women buying products (to the profit of capitalism) and competing for men (to be affirmed by the standard that matters). That is, they make women feel ugly and inadequate so we need men and money to defend against rejection/self-revulsion. Black women are further from being able concretely to achieve the standard that no woman can ever achieve, or it would lose its point.

60. Anne Koedt, "The Myth of the Vaginal Orgasm," in Koedt et al., eds. (n. 46 above), pp. 198–207; TiGrace Atkinson, "Vaginal Orgasm as a Mass Hysterical Survival Response," in *Amazon Odyssey* (n. 46 above), pp. 5–8.
61. Shere Hite, *The Hite Report: A Nationwide Study of Female Sexuality* (New York: Dell Publishing Co., 1976), "Do you ever fake orgasms?" pp. 257–66.
62. Jean-Paul Sartre, *Existential Psychoanalysis*, trans. Hazel E. Barnes (Chicago: Henry Regnery Co., 1973), p. 20. A similar treatment of "desire" occurs in Deleuze and Guattari's description of man as "desiring-machine," of man in relation to the object world: "Not man as the king of creation, but rather as the being who is in intimate contact with the profound life of all forms or all types of beings, who is responsible for even the stars and animal life, and how ceaselessly plugs an organ-machine into an energy-machine, a tree into his body, a breast into his mouth, the sun into his asshole: the eternal custodian of the machines of the universe" (Deleuze and Guattari [n. 1 above], p. 4). Realizing that women, socially, inhabit the object realm transforms this discourse into a quite accurate description of the feminist analysis of women's desirability to man—the breast in his mouth, the energy machine into which he ceaselessly plugs an organ machine. Extending their inquiry into the extent to which this kind of objectification of woman is specific to capitalism (either as a process or in its particular form) does little to redeem the sex blindness (blind to the sex of its standpoint) of this supposedly general theory. Women are not desiring-machines.
63. Peter Berger and Stanley Pullberg, "Reification and the Sociological Critique of Consciousness," *New Left Review*, vol. 35 (January–February 1966); Herbert Marcuse, "The Foundation of His-

torical Materialism," in *Studies in Critical Philosophy*, trans. Joris De Bres (Boston: Beacon Press, 1972); Karl Klare, "Law-Making as Praxis," *Telos* 12, no. 2 (Summer 1979): 123–35, esp. 131.

64. Istvan Meszaros, *Marx's Theory of Alienation* (London: Merlin Press, 1972); Bertrell Ollman, *Alienation: Marx's Conception of Man in Capitalist Society* (London: Cambridge University Press, 1971); Marcuse, *Eros and Civilization* (n. 22 above), pp. 93–94, 101–02.
65. Rowbotham, *Women's Liberation and the New Politics* (n. 17 above), p. 17.
66. Zora Neale Hurston, *Their Eyes Were Watching God* (Urbana: University of Illinois Press, 1978), pp. 79–80.
67. In the second part of this article, "Feminism, Marxism, Method, and the State: Toward Feminist Jurisprudence" (forthcoming in *Signs*), I argue that the state is male in that objectivity is its norm.

Foucault, Femininity, and the Modernization of Patriarchal Power

Bartky appropriates Michel Foucault's account of the deployment of power in disciplinary practices in order to understand the contemporary Western feminine body. She begins by cataloging various ways in which women are induced to systematically discipline their bodies through, for example, diet, exercise, restricted movement, smiling, make-up, and skin-care. The feminine body, though elaborately cared for, is nonetheless a mark of inferiority. Women feel deficient and ashamed as a result of trying and failing to measure up to unattainable ideals of feminine beauty. The prescribed feminine look makes women appear vulnerable and childlike. Feminine comportment requires ingratiating behavior and constricted posture. Despite their compliance with these demanding regimes, women are held in contempt for their vanity and preoccupation with such trivial matters.

Feminine bodily discipline is deeply insidious. It renders women "docile and compliant companions of men." Because women have internalized this discipline and embraced its conception of femininity, their adherence to it seems voluntary and natural. Thus, it creates a barrier to feminist consciousness, for refusing to practice this discipline entails disavowing knowledge and skills that are central to women's identity. Still, Bartky maintains that the costs and contradictions internal to this discipline lay the ground for resistance to it. She concludes that compliance with the regime of the feminine body is incompatible with achieving women's emancipation. On the contrary, feminism calls for a "radical and as yet unimagined transformation of the female body."

—D.T.M.

Chapter 5

Sandra Lee Bartky

Foucault, Femininity, and the Modernization of Patriarchal Power

I

In a striking critique of modern society, Michel Foucault has argued that the rise of parliamentary institutions and of new conceptions of political liberty was accompanied by a darker counter-movement, by the emergence of a new and unprecedented discipline directed against the body. More is required of the body now than mere political allegiance or the appropriation of the products of its labor: the new discipline invades the body and seeks to regulate its very forces and operations, the economy and efficiency of its movements.

The disciplinary practices Foucault describes are tied to peculiarly modern forms of the army, the school, the hospital, the prison, and the manufactory; the aim of these disciplines is to increase the utility of the body, to augment its forces:

> What was then being formed was a policy of coercions that act upon the body, a calculated manipulation of its elements, its gestures, its behaviour. The human body was entering a machinery of power that explores it, breaks it down and rearranges it. A "political anatomy", which was also a "mechanics of power", was being born; it defined how one may have a hold over others' bodies, not only so that they may do what one wishes, but so that they may operate as one wishes, with the techniques, the speed and the efficiency that one determines. Thus, discipline produces subjected and practiced bodies, "docile" bodies.[1]

The production of "docile bodies" requires that an uninterrupted coercion be directed to the very processes of bodily activity, not just their result; this "micro-physics of power" fragments and partitions the body's time, its space, and its movements.[2]

The student, then, is enclosed within a classroom and assigned to a desk he cannot leave; his ranking in the class can be read off the position of his desk in the serially ordered and segmented space of the classroom itself. Foucault tells us that "Jean-Baptiste de la Salle dreamt of a classroom in which the spatial distribution might provide a whole series of distinctions at once, according to the pupil's progress, worth, character, application, cleanliness, and parents' fortune."[3] The student must sit upright, feet upon the floor, head erect; he may not slouch or fidget; his animate body is brought into a fixed correlation with the inanimate desk.

The minute breakdown of gestures and movements required of soldiers at drill is far more relentless:

> Bring the weapon forward. In three stages. Raise the rifle with the right hand, bringing it close to the body so as to hold it perpendicular with the right knee, the end of the barrel at eye level, grasping it by striking it with the right hand, the arm held close to the body at waist height. At the second stage, bring the rifle in front of you with the left hand, the barrel in the middle between the two eyes, vertical, the right hand grasping it at the small of the butt, the arm outstretched, the triggerguard resting on the first finger, the left hand at the height of the notch, the thumb lying along the barrel against the moulding. At the third stage. . . .[4]

These "body-object articulations" of the soldier and his weapon, the student and his desk, effect a "coercive link with the apparatus of production." We are far indeed from older forms of control that "demanded of the body only signs or products, forms of expression or the result of labour."[5]

The body's time, in these regimes of power, is as rigidly controlled as its space: the factory whistle and the school bell mark a division of time into discrete and segmented units that regulate the various activities of the day. The following timetable, similar in spirit to the ordering of my grammar school classroom, was suggested for French "écoles mutuelles" of the early nineteenth century:

> 8:45 entrance of the monitor, 8:52 the monitor's summons, 8:56 entrance of the children and prayer, 9:00 the children go to their benches, 9:04 first slate, 9:08 end of dictation, 9:12 second slate, etc.[6]

Control this rigid and precise cannot be maintained without a minute and relentless surveillance.

Jeremy Bentham's design for the Panopticon, a model prison, captures for Foucault the essence of the disciplinary society. At the periphery of the Panopticon, a circular structure; at the center, a tower with wide windows that opens onto the inner side of the ring. The structure on the periphery is divided into cells, each with two windows, one facing the windows of the tower, the other facing the outside, allowing an effect of backlighting to make any figure visible within the cell "All that is needed, then, is to place a supervisor in a central tower and to shut up in each cell a madman, a patient, a condemned man, a worker or a schoolboy."[7] Each inmate is alone, shut off from effective communication with his fellows but constantly visible from the tower. The effect of this is "to induce in the inmate a state of conscious and permanent visibility that assures the automatic functioning of power"; each becomes to himself his own jailer.[8] This "state of conscious and permanent visibility" is a sign that the tight, disciplinary control of the body has gotten a hold on the mind as well. In the perpetual self-surveillance of the inmate lies the genesis of the celebrated "individualism" and heightened self-consciousness which are hallmarks of modern times. For Foucault, the structure and effects of the Panopticon resonate throughout society: Is it surprising that "prisons resemble factories, schools, barracks, hospitals, which all resemble prisons?"[9]

Foucault's account in *Discipline and Punish* of the disciplinary practices that produce the "docile bodies" of modernity is a genuine *tour de force*, incorporating a rich theoretical account of the ways in which instrumental reason takes hold of the body with a mass of historical detail. But Foucault treats the body throughout as if it were one, as if the bodily experiences of men and women did not differ and as if men and women bore the same relationship to the characteristic institutions of modern life. Where is the account of the disciplinary practices that engender the "docile bodies" of women, bodies more docile than the bodies of men? Women, like men, are subject to many of the same disciplinary practices Foucault describes. But he is blind to those disciplines that produce a modality of embodiment that is peculiarly feminine. To overlook the forms of subjection that engender the feminine body is to perpetuate the silence and powerlessness of those upon whom these disciplines have been imposed. Hence, even though a liberatory note is sounded in Foucault's critique of power, his analysis as a whole reproduces that sexism which is endemic throughout Western political theory.

We are born male or female, but not masculine or feminine. Femininity is an artifice, an achievement, "a mode of enacting and reenacting received gender norms which surface as so many styles of the flesh."[10] In what follows, I shall examine those disciplinary practices that produce a body which in gesture and appearance is recognizably feminine. I consider three categories of such practices: those that aim to produce a body of a certain size and general configuration; those that bring forth from this body a specific repertoire of gestures, postures, and movements; and those directed toward the display of this body as an ornamented surface. I shall examine the nature of these disciplines, how they are imposed, and by whom. I shall probe the effects of the imposition of such discipline on female identity and subjectivity. In the final section I shall argue that these disciplinary practices must be understood in the light of the modernization of patriarchal domination, a modernization that unfolds historically according to the general pattern described by Foucault.

II

Styles of the female figure vary over time and across cultures: they reflect cultural obsessions and preoccupations in ways that are still poorly understood. Today, massiveness, power, or abundance in a woman's body is met with distaste. The current body of fashion is taut, small-breasted, narrow-hipped, and of a slimness bordering on emaciation; it is a silhouette that seems more appropriate to an adolescent boy or newly pubescent girl than to an adult woman. Since ordinary women have normally quite different dimensions, they must of course diet.

Mass-circulation women's magazines run articles on dieting in virtually every issue. The *Ladies' Home Journal* of February 1986 carries a "Fat-Burning Exercise Guide," while *Mademoiselle* offers to "Help Stamp Out Cellulite" with "Six Sleek-Down Strategies." After the diet-busting Christmas holidays and later, before summer bikini season, the titles of these features become shriller and more arresting. The reader is now addressed in the imperative mode: Jump into shape for summer! Shed ugly winter fat with the all-new Grapefruit Diet! More women than men visit diet doctors, while women greatly outnumber men in self-help groups such as Weight Watchers and Overeaters Anonymous—in the case of the latter, by well over 90 percent.[11]

Dieting disciplines the body's hungers: Appetite must be monitored at all times and governed by an iron will. Since the innocent need of the organism for food will not be denied, the body becomes one's enemy, an alien being bent on thwarting the disciplinary project. Anorexia nervosa, which has now assumed epidemic proportions, is to women of the late twentieth century what hysteria was to women of an earlier day: the crystallization in a pathological mode of a widespread cultural obsession.[12] A survey taken recently at UCLA is astounding: Of 260 students interviewed, 27.3 percent of the women but only 5.8 percent of men said they were "terrified" of getting fat; 28.7 percent of women and only 7.5 percent of men said they were obsessed or "totally preoccupied" with food. The body images of women and men are strikingly different as well: 35 percent of women but only 12.5 percent of men said they felt fat though other people told them they were thin. Women in the survey wanted to weigh ten pounds less than their average weight; men felt they were within a pound of their ideal weight. A total of 5.9 percent of women and no men met the psychiatric criteria for anorexia or bulimia.[13]

Dieting is one discipline imposed upon a body subject to the "tyranny of slenderness"; exercise is another.[14] Since men as well as women exercise, it is not always easy in the case of women to distinguish what is done for the sake of physical fitness from what is done in obedience to the requirements of femininity. Men as well as women lift weights, do yoga, calisthenics, and aerobics, though "jazzercise" is a largely female pursuit. Men and women alike engage themselves with a variety of machines, each designed to call forth from the body a different exertion: there are Nautilus machines, rowing machines, ordinary and motorized exercycles, portable hip and leg cycles, belt massagers, trampolines, treadmills, arm and leg pulleys. However, given the widespread female obsession with weight, one suspects that many women are working out with these apparatuses in the health club or at the gym with a different aim in mind and in quite a different spirit than the men.

But there are classes of exercises meant for women alone, these designed not to firm or to reduce the body's size overall, but to resculpture its various parts on the current model. M. J. Saffron, "international beauty expert," assures us that his twelve basic facial exercises can erase frown lines, smooth the forehead, raise hollow cheeks, banish crow's feet, and tighten the muscles under the chin.[15] There are exercises to build the breasts and exercises to banish "cellulite," said by "figure consultants" to be a special type of female fat. There is "spot-reducing," an umbrella term that covers dozens of punishing exercises designed to reduce "problem areas" like thick ankles or "saddlebag" thighs. The very idea of "spot-reducing" is both scientifically unsound and cruel, for it raises expectations in women that can never be realized: The pattern in which fat is deposited or removed is known to be genetically determined.

It is not only her natural appetite or unreconstructed contours that pose a danger to women: the very expressions of her face can subvert the disciplinary project of bodily perfection. An expressive face lines and creases more readily than an inexpressive one. Hence, if women are unable to suppress strong emotions, they can at least learn to inhibit the tendency of the face to register them. Sophia Loren recommends a unique solution to this problem: a piece of tape applied to the forehead or between the brows will tug at the skin when one frowns and act as a reminder to relax the face.[16] The tape is to be worn whenever a woman is home alone.

III

There are significant gender differences in gesture, posture, movement, and general bodily comportment: women are more restricted than men in their manner of movement and in their lived spatiality. In her classic paper on the subject, Iris Young observes that a space seems to surround women in imagination which they are hesitant to move beyond. This manifests itself both in a reluctance to reach, stretch, and extend the body to meet resistances of matter in motion—as in sport or in the performance of physical tasks—and in a typically constricted posture and general style of movement. Woman's space is not a field in which her bodily intentionality can be freely realized but an enclosure in which she feels herself positioned and by which she is confined.[17] The "loose woman" violates these norms: Her looseness is manifest not only in her morals, but in her manner of speech, and quite literally in the free and easy way she moves.

In an extraordinary series of over two thousand photographs, many candid shots taken in the street, the German photographer Marianne Wex has documented differences in typical masculine and feminine body posture. Women sit waiting for trains with arms close to the body, hands folded together in their laps, toes pointing straight ahead or turned inward, and legs pressed together.[18] The women in these photographs make themselves small, narrow and harmless; they seem tense; they take up little space. Men, on the other hand, expand into the available space; they sit with legs far apart and arms flung out at some distance from the body. Most common in these sitting male figures is what Wex calls the "proffering position": the men sit with legs thrown wide apart, crotch visible, feet pointing outward, often with an arm and casually dangling hand resting comfortably on an open, spread thigh.

In proportion to total body size, a man's stride is longer than a woman's. The man has more spring and rhythm to his step; he walks with toes pointed outward, holds his arms at a greater distance from his body, and swings them farther; he tends to point the whole hand in the direction he is moving. The woman holds her arms closer to her body, palms against her sides; her walk is circumspect. If she has subjected herself to the additional constraint of high-heeled shoes, her body is thrown forward and off-balance; the struggle to walk under these conditions shortens her stride still more.[19]

But women's movement is subjected to a still finer discipline. Feminine faces, as well as bodies, are trained to the expression of deference. Under male scrutiny, women will avert their eyes or cast them downward; the female gaze is trained to abandon its claim to the sovereign status of seer. The "nice" girl learns to avoid the bold and unfettered staring of the "loose" woman, who looks at whatever and whomever she pleases. Women are trained to smile more than men, too. In the economy of smiles, as elsewhere, there is evidence that women are exploited, for they give more than they receive in return; in a smile-elicitation study, one researcher found that the rate of smile return by women was 93 percent, by men only 67 percent.[20] In many typical women's jobs, graciousness, deference, and the readiness to serve are part of the work; this requires the worker to fix a smile on her face for a good part of the working day, whatever her inner state.[21] The economy of touching is out of balance, too: men touch women more often and on more parts of the body than women touch men: female secretaries, factory workers, and waitresses report that such liberties are taken routinely with their bodies.[22]

Feminine movement, gesture, and posture must exhibit not only constriction, but grace as well, and a certain eroticism restrained by modesty: all three. Here is field for the operation for a whole new training: A woman must stand with stomach pulled in, shoulders thrown slightly back, and chest out, this to display her bosom to maximum advantage. While she must walk in the confined fashion appropriate to women, her movements must, at the same time, be combined with a subtle but provocative hip-roll. But too much display is taboo; women in short, low-cut dresses are told to avoid bending over at all, but if they must, great care must be taken to avoid an unseemly display of breast or rump. From time to time, fashion magazines offer quite precise instructions on the proper way of getting in and out of cars. These instructions combine all three imperatives of women's movement: a woman must not allow her arms and legs to flail about in all directions; she must try to manage her movements with the appearance of grace—no small accomplishment when one is climbing out of the back seat of a Fiat—and she is well-advised to use the opportunity for a certain display of leg.

All the movements we have described so far are self-movements; they arise from within the woman's own body. But in a way that normally goes unnoticed, males in couples may literally steer a woman everywhere she goes: down the street, around corners, into elevators, through doorways, into her chair at the dinner table, around the dance floor. The man's movement "is not necessarily heavy or pushy or physical in an ugly way; it is light and gentle but firm in the way of the most confident equestrians with the best trained horses."[23]

IV

We have examined some of the disciplinary practices a woman must master in pursuit of a body of the right size and shape that also displays the proper styles of feminine motility. But woman's body is an ornamented surface too, and there is much discipline involved in this production as well. Here, especially in the application of make-up and the selection of clothes, art and discipline converge, though, as I shall argue, there is less art involved than one might suppose.

A woman's skin must be soft, supple, hairless, and smooth; ideally, it should betray no sign of wear, experience, age, or deep thought. Hair must be removed not only from the face but from large surfaces of the body as well, from legs and thighs, an operation accomplished by shaving, buffing with fine sandpaper, or foul-smelling depilatories. With the new high-leg bathing suits and leotards, a substantial amount of pubic hair must be removed too.[24] The removal of facial hair can be more specialized. Eyebrows are plucked out by the roots with a tweezer. Hot wax is sometimes poured onto the mustache and cheeks and then ripped away when it cools. The woman who wants a more permanent result may try electrolysis;

this involves the killing of a hair root by the passage of an electric current down a needle which has been inserted into its base. The procedure is painful and expensive.

The development of what one "beauty expert" calls "good skin-care habits" requires not only attention to health, the avoidance of strong facial expressions, and the performance of facial exercises, but the regular use of skin-care preparations, many to be applied more often than once a day: cleansing lotions (ordinary soap and water "upsets the skin's acid and alkaline balance"), wash-off cleansers (milder than cleansing lotions), astringents, toners, make-up removers, night creams, nourishing creams, eye creams, moisturizers, skin balancers, body lotions, hand creams, lip pomades, suntan lotions, sunscreens, facial masks. Provision of the proper facial mask is complex: there are sulfur masks for pimples; hot or oil masks for dry areas; also cold masks for dry areas; tightening masks; conditioning masks; peeling masks; cleansing masks made of herbs, cornmeal, or almonds; mud packs. Black women may wish to use "fade creams" to "even skin tone." Skin-care preparations are never just sloshed onto the skin, but applied according to precise rules: eye cream is dabbed on gently in movements toward, never away from, the nose; cleansing cream is applied in outward directions only, straight across the forehead, the upper lip, and the chin, never up but straight down the nose and up and out on the cheeks.[25]

The normalizing discourse of modern medicine is enlisted by the cosmetics industry to gain credibility for its claims. Dr. Christiaan Barnard lends his enormous prestige to the Glycel line of "cellular treatment activators"; these contain "glycosphingolipids" that can "make older skin behave and look like younger skin." The Clinique computer at any Clinique counter will select a combination of preparations just right for you. Ultima II contains "procollagen" in its anti-aging eye cream that "provides hydration" to "demoralizing lines." "Biotherm" eye cream dramatically improves the "biomechanical properties of the skin."[26] The Park Avenue clinic of Dr. Zizmor, "chief of dermatology at one of New York's leading hospitals," offers not only medical treatments such as dermabrasion and chemical peeling but "total deep skin cleaning" as well.[27]

Really good skin-care habits require the use of a variety of aids and devices: facial steamers; faucet filters to collect impurities in the water; borax to soften it; a humidifier for the bedroom; electric massagers; backbrushes; complexion brushes, loofahs; pumice stones; blackhead removers. I will not detail the implements or techniques involved in the manicure or pedicure.

The ordinary circumstances of life as well as a wide variety of activities cause a crisis in skin-care and require a stepping up of the regimen as well as an additional laying on of preparations. Skin-care discipline requires a specialized knowledge: a woman must know what to do if she has been skiing, taking medication, doing vigorous exercise, boating, or swimming in chlorinated pools; if she has been exposed to pollution, heated rooms, cold, sun, harsh weather, the pressurized cabins on airplanes, saunas or steam rooms, fatigue, or stress. Like the schoolchild or prisoner, the woman mastering good skin-care habits is put on a timetable: Georgette Klinger requires that a shorter or longer period of attention be paid to the complexion at least four times a day.[28] Hair care, like skin care, requires a similar investment of time, the use of a wide variety of preparations, the mastery of a set of techniques, and, again, the acquisition of a specialized knowledge.

The crown and pinnacle of good hair care and skin care is, of course, the arrangement of the hair and the application of cosmetics. Here the regimen of hair care, skin care, manicure, and pedicure is recapitulated in another mode. A woman must learn the proper manipulation of a large number of devices—the blow dryer, styling brush, curling iron, hot curlers, wire curlers, eyeliner, lipliner, lipstick brush, eyelash curler, mascara brush—and the correct manner of application of a wide variety of products—foundation, toner, covering stick, mascara, eye shadow, eye gloss, blusher, lipstick, rouge, lip gloss, hair dye, hair rinse, hair lightener, hair "relaxer," etc.

In the language of fashion magazines and cosmetic ads, making up is typically portrayed as an aesthetic activity in which a woman can express her individuality. In reality, while cosmetic styles change every decade or so and while some variation in make-up is permitted depending on the occasion, making up the face is, in fact, a highly stylized activity that gives little rein to self-expression. Painting the face is not like painting a picture; at best, it might be described as painting the same picture over and over again with minor variations. Little latitude is permitted in what is considered appropriate make-up for the office and for most social occasions; indeed, the woman who uses cosmetics in a genuinely novel and imaginative way is liable to be seen not as an artist but as an eccentric. Furthermore, since a properly made-up face is, if not a card of entrée, at least a badge of acceptability in most social and professional contexts, the woman who chooses not to wear cosmetics at all faces sanctions of a sort which will never be applied to someone who chooses not to paint a watercolor.

V

Are we dealing in all this merely with sexual *difference*? Scarcely. The disciplinary practices I have described are part of the process by which the ideal body of femininity—and hence the feminine body-subject—is constructed; in doing this, they produce a "practiced and subjected" body, i.e., a body on which an inferior status has been inscribed. A woman's face must be made up, that is to say, made over, and so must her body: she is ten pounds overweight; her lips must be made more kissable; her complexion dewier; her eyes more mysterious. The "art" of make-up is the art of disguise, but this presupposes that a woman's face, unpainted, is defective. Soap and water, a shave, and routine attention to hygiene may be enough for *him*; for *her* they are not. The strategy of much beauty-related advertising is to suggest to women that their bodies are deficient, but even without much more or less explicit teaching, the media images of perfect female beauty which bombard us daily leave no doubt in the minds of most women that they fail to measure up. The technologies of femininity are taken up and practiced by women against the background of a pervasive sense of bodily deficiency: this accounts for what is often their compulsive or even ritualistic character.

The disciplinary project of femininity is a "set-up": it requires such radical and extensive measures of bodily transformation that virtually every woman who gives herself to it is destined in some degree to fail. Thus, a measure of shame is added to a woman's sense that the body she inhabits is deficient: she ought to take better care of herself; she might after all have jogged that last mile. Many women are without the time or resources to provide themselves with even the minimum of what such a regimen requires, e.g., a decent diet. Here is an additional source of shame for poor women who must bear what our society regards as the more general shame of poverty. The burdens poor women bear in this regard are not merely psychological, since conformity to the prevailing standards of bodily acceptability is a known factor in economic mobility.

The larger disciplines that construct a "feminine" body out of a female one are by no means race- or class-specific. There is little evidence that women of color or working-class women are in general less committed to the incarnation of an ideal femininity than their more privileged sisters. This is not to deny the many ways in which factors of race, class, locality, ethnicity, or personal taste can be expressed within the kinds of practices I have described. The rising young corporate executive may buy her cosmetics at Bergdorf-Goodman while the counter-server at McDonald's gets hers at K-Mart; the one may join an expensive "upscale" health club, while the other may have to make do with the $9.49 GFX Body-Flex II Home-Gym advertised in the *National Enquirer*: Both are aiming at the same general result.[29]

In the regime of institutionalized heterosexuality woman must make herself "object and prey" for the man: it is for him that these eyes are limpid pools, this cheek baby-smooth.[30] In contemporary patriarchal culture, a panoptical male connoisseur resides within the consciousness of most women: they stand perpetually before his gaze and under his judgment. Woman lives her body as seen by another, by an anonymous patriarchal Other. We are often told that "women dress for other women." There is some truth in this: Who but someone engaged in a project similar to my own can appreciate the panache with which I bring it off? But women know for whom this game is played: They know that a pretty young woman is likelier to become a flight attendant than a plain one and that a well-preserved older woman has a better chance of holding on to her husband than one who has "let herself go."

Here it might be objected that performance for another in no way signals the inferiority of the performer to the one for whom the performance is intended. The actor, for example, depends on his audience but is in no way inferior to it; he is not demeaned by his dependency. While femininity is surely something enacted, the analogy to theater breaks down in a number of ways. First, as I argued earlier, the self-determination we think of as requisite to an artistic career is lacking here: femininity as spectacle is something in which virtually every woman is required to participate. Second, the precise nature of the criteria by which women are judged, not only the inescapability of judgment itself, reflects gross imbalances in the social power of the sexes that do not mark the relationship of artists and their audiences. An aesthetic of femininity, for example, that mandates fragility and a lack of muscular strength produces female bodies that can offer little resistance to physical abuse, and the physical abuse of women by men, as we know, is widespread. It is true that the current fitness movement has permitted women to develop more muscular strength and endurance than was heretofore allowed; indeed, images of women have begun to appear in the mass media that seem to eroticize this new muscularity. But a woman may by no means develop more muscular strength than her partner; the bride who would tenderly carry her groom across the threshold is a figure of comedy, not romance.[31]

Under the current "tyranny of slenderness" women are forbidden to become large or massive; they must take up as little space as possible. The very contours a woman's body takes on as she matures—the fuller breasts and rounded hips—have become distasteful. The body by which a woman feels herself judged and which by rigorous discipline she must try to assume is the body of early adolescence, slight and unformed, a body lacking flesh or substance, a body in whose very contours the image of immaturity has been inscribed. The requirement that a woman maintain a smooth and hairless skin carries further the theme of inexperience, for an infantilized face must accompany her infantilized body, a face that never ages or furrows its brow in thought. The face of the ideally feminine woman must never display the marks of character, wisdom, and experience that we so admire in men.

To succeed in the provision of a beautiful or sexy body gains a woman attention and some admiration but little real respect and rarely any social power. A woman's effort to master feminine body discipline will lack importance just because she does it; her activity partakes of the general depreciation of everything female. In spite of unrelenting pressure to "make the most of what they have," women are ridiculed and dismissed for the triviality of their interest in such "trivial" things as clothes and make-up. Further, the narrow identification of woman with sexuality and the body in a society that has for centuries displayed profound suspicion toward both does little to raise her status. Even the most adored female bodies complain routinely of their situation in ways that reveal an implicit understanding that there is something demeaning in the kind of attention they receive. Marilyn Monroe, Elizabeth Taylor, and Farrah Fawcett have all wanted passionately to become actresses-artists and not just "sex objects."

But it is perhaps in their more restricted motility and comportment that the inferiorization of women's bodies is most evident: women's typical body language, a language of relative tension and constriction, is understood to be a language of subordination when it is enacted by men in male status hierarchies. In groups of men, those with higher status typically assume looser and more relaxed postures; the boss lounges comfortably behind the desk while the applicant sits tense and rigid on the edge of his seat. Higher-status individuals may touch their subordinates more than they themselves get touched; they initiate more eye contact and are smiled at by their inferiors more than they are observed to smile in return.[32] What is announced in the comportment of superiors is confidence and ease, especially ease of access to the Other. Female constraint in posture and movement is no doubt overdetermined: the fact that women tend to sit and stand with legs, feet, and knees close or touching may well be a coded declaration of sexual circumspection in a society that still maintains a double standard or an effort, albeit unconscious, to guard the genital area. In the latter case, a woman's tight and constricted posture must be seen as the expression of her need to ward off real or symbolic sexual attack. Whatever proportions must be assigned in the final display to fear or deference, one thing is clear: Woman's body language speaks eloquently, though silently, of her subordinate status in a hierarchy of gender.

VI

If what we have described is a genuine discipline—a "system of micro-power that is essentially non-egalitarian and asymmetrical"—who then are the disciplinarians?[33] Who is the top sergeant in the disciplinary regime of femininity? Historically, the law has had some responsibility for enforcement; in times gone by, for example, individuals who appeared in public in the clothes of the other sex could be arrested. While cross-dressers are still liable to some harassment, the kind of discipline we are considering is not the business of the police or the courts. Parents and teachers, of course, have extensive influence, admonishing girls to be demure and ladylike, to "smile pretty," to sit with their legs together. The influence of the media is pervasive, too, constructing as it does an image of the female body as spectacle, nor can we ignore the role played by "beauty experts" or by emblematic public personages such as Jane Fonda and Lynn Redgrave.

But none of these individuals—the skin-care consultant, the parent, the policeman—does in fact wield the kind of authority that is typically invested in those who manage more straightforward disciplinary institutions. The disciplinary power that inscribes femininity in the female body is everywhere and it is nowhere; the disciplinarian is everyone and yet no one in particular. Women regarded as overweight, for example, report that they are regularly admonished to diet, sometimes by people they scarcely know. These intrusions are often softened by reference to the natural prettiness just waiting to emerge: "People have always said that I had a beautiful face and 'if you'd only lose weight you'd be really beautiful.' "[34] Here, "people"—friends and casual acquaintances alike—act to enforce prevailing standards of body size.

Foucault tends to identify the imposition of discipline upon the body with the operation of specific institutions, e.g., the school, the factory, the prison. To do this, however, is to overlook the extent to which discipline can be institutionally *unbound* as well as institutionally bound.[35] The anonymity of disciplinary power and its wide dispersion have consequences which are crucial to a proper understanding of the subordination of women. The absence of a formal institutional structure and of authorities invested with the power to carry out institutional directives creates the impression that the production of femininity is either entirely voluntary or natural. The several senses of "discipline" are instructive here. On the one hand, discipline is something imposed on subjects of an "essentially inegalitarian and asymmetrical" system of authority. Schoolchildren, convicts, and draftees are subject to discipline in this sense. But discipline can be sought voluntarily as well, as, for example, when an individual seeks initiation into the spiritual discipline of Zen Buddhism. Discipline can, of course, be both at once: the volunteer may seek the physical and occupational training offered by the army without the army's ceasing in any way to be the instrument by which he and other members of his class are kept in disciplined subjection. Feminine bodily discipline has this dual character: on the one hand, no one is marched off for electrolysis at the end of a rifle, nor can we fail to appreciate the initiative and ingenuity displayed by countless women in an attempt to master the rituals of beauty. Nevertheless, insofar as the disciplinary practices of femininity produce a "subjected and practiced," an inferiorized body, they must be understood as aspects of a far larger discipline, an oppressive and inegalitarian system of sexual subordination. This system aims at turning women into the docile and compliant companions of men just as surely as the army aims to turn its raw recruits into soldiers.

Now the transformation of oneself into a properly feminine body may be any or all of the following: a rite of passage into adulthood; the adoption and celebration of a particular aesthetic; a way of announcing one's economic level and social status; a way to triumph over other women in the competition for men or jobs; or an opportunity for massive narcissistic indulgence.[36] The social construction of the feminine body is all these things, but it is at base discipline, too, and discipline of the inegalitarian sort. The absence of formally identifiable disciplinarians and of a public schedule of sanctions serves only to disguise the extent to which the imperative to be "feminine" serves the interest of domination. This is a lie in which all concur: making up is merely artful play; one's first pair of high-heeled shoes is an innocent part of growing up and not the modern equivalent of foot-binding.

Why aren't all women feminists? In modern industrial societies, women are not kept in line by fear of retaliatory male violence; their victimization is not that of the South African black. Nor will it suffice to say that a false consciousness engendered in women by patriarchal ideology is at the basis of female subordination. This is not to deny the fact that women are often subject to gross male violence or that women and men alike are ideologically mystified by the dominant gender arrangements. What I wish to suggest instead is that an adequate understanding of women's oppression will require an appreciation of the extent to which not only women's lives but also their very subjectivities are structured within an ensemble of systematically duplicitous practices. The feminine discipline of the body is a case in point: The practices which construct this body have an overt aim and character far removed, indeed radically distinct, from their covert function. In this regard, the system of gender subordination, like the wage-bargain under capitalism, illustrates in its own way the ancient tension between what is and what appears: The phenomenal forms in which it is manifested are often quite different from the real relations which form its deeper structure.

VII

The lack of formal public sanctions does not mean that a woman who is unable or unwilling to submit herself to the appropriate body discipline will face no sanctions at all. On the contrary, she faces a very severe sanction indeed in a world dominated by men: the refusal of male patronage. For the heterosexual woman, this may mean the loss of a badly needed intimacy; for both heterosexual women and lesbians, it may well mean the refusal of a decent livelihood.

As noted earlier, women punish themselves too for the failure to conform. The growing literature on women's body size is filled with wrenching confessions of shame from the overweight:

> I felt clumsy and huge. I felt that I would knock over furniture, bump into things, tip over chairs, not fit into VW's, especially when people were trying to crowd into the back seat. I felt like I was taking over the whole room. . . . I felt disgusting and like a slob. In the summer I felt hot and sweaty and I knew people saw my sweat as evidence that I was too fat.
>
> I felt so terrible about the way I look that I cut off connection with my body. I operate from the neck up. I do not look in mirrors. I do not want to spend time buying clothes. I do not want to spend time with make-up because it's painful for me to look at myself.[37]
>
> I can no longer bear to look at myself. Whenever I have to stand in front of a mirror to comb my hair I tie a large towel around my neck. Even at night I slip my nightgown on before I take off my blouse and pants. But all this has only made it worse and worse. It's been so long since I've really looked at my body.[38]

The depth of these women's shame is a measure of the extent to which all women have internalized patriarchal standards of bodily acceptability. A fuller examination of what is meant here by "internalization" may shed light on a question posed earlier: Why isn't every woman a feminist?

Something is "internalized" when it gets incorporated into the structure of the self. By "structure of the self" I refer to those modes of perception and of self-perception that allow a self to distinguish itself both from other selves and from things which are not selves. I have described elsewhere how a generalized male witness comes to structure woman's consciousness of herself as a bodily being.[39] This, then, is one meaning of "internalization." The sense of oneself as a distinct and valuable individual is tied not only to the sense of how one is perceived but also to what one knows, especially to what one knows how to do; this is a second sense of "internalization." Whatever its ultimate effect, discipline can provide the individual upon whom it is imposed with a sense of mastery as well as a secure sense of identity. There is a certain contradiction here: While its imposition may promote a larger disempowerment, discipline may bring with it a certain development of a person's powers. Women, then, like other skilled individuals, have a stake in the perpetuation of their skills, whatever it may have cost to acquire them and quite apart from the question whether, as a gender, they would have been better off had they never had to acquire them in the first place. Hence, feminism, especially a genuinely radical feminism that questions the patriarchal construction of the female body, threatens women with a certain de-skilling, something people normally resist. Beyond this, it calls into question that aspect of personal identity that is tied to the development of a sense of competence.

Resistance from this source may be joined by a reluctance to part with the rewards of compliance; further, many women will resist the abandonment of an aesthetic that defines what they take to be beautiful. But there is still another source of resistance, one more subtle perhaps, but tied once again to questions of identity and internalization. To have a body felt to be "feminine"—a body socially constructed through the appropriate practices—is in most cases crucial to a woman's sense of herself as female and, since persons currently can *be* only as male or female, to her sense of herself as an existing individual. To possess such a body may also be essential to her sense of herself as a sexually desiring and desirable subject. Hence, any political project that aims to dismantle the machinery that turns a female body into a feminine one may well be apprehended by a woman as something that threatens her with desexualization, if not outright annihilation.

The categories of masculinity and femininity do more than assist in the construction of personal identities: they are critical elements in our informal social ontology. This may account to some degree for the otherwise puzzling phenomenon of homophobia and for the revulsion felt by many at the sight of female bodybuilders; neither the homosexual nor the muscular woman can be assimilated easily into the categories that structure everyday life. The radical feminist critique of femininity, then, may pose a threat not only to a woman's sense of her own identity and desirability but also to the very structure of her social universe.

Of course, many women *are* feminists, favoring a program of political and economic reform in the struggle to gain equality with men.[40] But many "reform" or liberal feminists, indeed, many orthodox Marxists, are committed to the idea that the preservation of a woman's femininity is quite compatible with her struggle for liberation.[41] These thinkers have rejected a normative femininity based upon the notion of "separate spheres" and the traditional sexual division of labor while accepting at the same time conventional standards of feminine body display. If my analysis is correct, such a feminism is incoherent. Foucault has argued that modern bourgeois democracy is deeply flawed in that it seeks political rights for individuals constituted as unfree by a variety of disciplinary micropowers that lie beyond the realm of what is ordinarily defined as the "political." "The man described for us whom we are invited to free," he says, "is already in himself the effect of a subjection much more profound than himself."[42] If, as I have argued, female subjectivity is constituted in any significant measure in and through the disciplinary practices that construct the feminine body, what Foucault says here of "man" is perhaps even truer of "woman." Marxists have maintained from the first the inadequacy of a purely liberal feminism: We have reached the same conclusion through a different route, casting doubt at the same time on the adequacy of traditional Marxist prescriptions for women's liberation as well. Liberals call for equal rights for women, traditional Marxists for the entry of women into production on an equal footing with men, the socialization of housework, and proletarian revolution; neither calls for the deconstruction of the categories of masculinity and femininity.[43] Femininity as a certain "style of the flesh" will have to be surpassed in the direction of something quite different, not masculinity, which is in many ways only its mirror opposite, but a radical and as yet unimagined transformation of the female body.

VIII

Foucault has argued that the transition from traditional to modern societies has been characterized by a profound transformation in the exercise of power, by what he calls "a reversal of the political axis of individuation."[44] In older authoritarian systems, power was embodied in the person of the monarch and exercised upon a largely anonymous body of subjects; violation of the law was seen as an insult to the royal individual. While the methods employed to enforce compliance in the past were often quite brutal, involving gross assaults against the body, power in such a system operated in a haphazard and discontinuous fashion; much in the social totality lay beyond its reach.

By contrast, modern society has seen the emergence of increasingly invasive apparatuses of power; these exercise a far more restrictive social and psychological control than was heretofore possible. In modern societies, effects of power "circulate through progressively finer channels, gaining access to individuals themselves, to their bodies, their gestures and all their daily actions."[45] Power now seeks to transform the minds of those individuals who might be tempted to resist it, not merely to punish or imprison their bodies. This requires two things: a finer control of the body's time and its movements—a control that cannot be achieved without ceaseless surveillance and a better understanding of the specific person, of the genesis and nature of his "case." The power these new apparatuses seek to exercise require a new knowledge of the individual; modern psychology and sociology are born. Whether the new modes of control have charge of correction, production, education, or the provision of welfare, they resemble one another; they exercise power in a bureaucratic mode—faceless, centralized, and pervasive. A reversal has occurred: power has now become anonymous, while the project of control has brought into being a new individuality. In fact, Foucault believes that the operation of power constitutes the very subjectivity of the subject. Here, the image of the Panopticon returns: knowing that he may be observed from the tower at any time, the inmate takes over the job of policing himself. The gaze which is inscribed in the very structure of the disciplinary institution is internalized by the inmate; modern technologies of behavior are thus oriented toward the production of isolated and self-policing subjects.[46]

Women have their own experience of the modernization of power, one which begins later but follows in many respects the course outlined by Foucault. In important ways, a woman's behavior is less regulated now than it was in the past. She has more mobility and is less confined to domestic space. She enjoys what to previous generations would have been an unimaginable sexual liberty. Divorce, access to paid work outside the home, and the increasing secularization of modern life have loosened the hold over her of the traditional family and, in spite of the current fundamentalist revival, of the church. Power in these institutions was wielded by individuals known to her. Husbands and fathers enforced patriarchal authority in the family. As in the *ancien régime*, a woman's body was subject to sanctions if she disobeyed. Not Foucault's royal individual but the Divine Individual decreed that her desire be always "unto her husband," while the person of the priest made known to her God's more specific intentions concerning her place and duties. In the days when civil and ecclesiastical authority were still conjoined, individuals formally invested with power were charged with the correction of recalcitrant women whom the family had somehow failed to constrain.

By contrast, the disciplinary power that is increasingly charged with the production of a properly embodied femininity is dispersed and anonymous; there are no individuals formally empowered to wield it; it is, as we have seen, invested in everyone and in no one in particular. This disciplinary power is peculiarly modern; it does not rely upon violent or public sanctions, nor does it seek to restrain the freedom of the female body to move from place to place. For all that, its invasion of the body is well-nigh total: the female body enters "a machinery of power that explores it, breaks it down and rearranges it."[47] The disciplinary techniques through which the "docile bodies" of women are constructed aim at a regulation which is perpetual and exhaustive—a regulation of the body's size and contours, its appetite, posture, gestures, and general comportment in space and the appearance of each of its visible parts.

As modern industrial societies change and as women themselves offer resistance to patriarchy, older forms of domination are eroded. But new forms arise, spread, and become consolidated. Women are no longer required to be chaste or modest, to restrict their sphere of activity to the home, or even to realize their properly feminine destiny in maternity. Normative femininity is coming more and more to be centered on woman's body—not its duties and obligations or even its capacity to bear children, but its sexuality, more precisely, its presumed heterosexuality and its appearance. There is, of course, nothing new in women's preoccupation with youth and beauty. What is new is the growing power of the image in a society increasingly oriented toward the visual media. Images of normative femininity, it might be ventured, have replaced the religiously oriented tracts of the past. New too is the spread of this discipline to all classes of women and its deployment throughout the life cycle. What was formerly the specialty of the aristocrat or courtesan is now the routine obligation of every woman, be she a grandmother or a barely pubescent girl.

To subject oneself to the new disciplinary power is to be up-to-date, to be "with-it"; as I have argued, it is presented to us in ways that are regularly disguised. It is fully compatible with the current need for women's wage labor, the cult of youth and fitness, and the need of advanced capitalism to maintain high levels of consumption. Further, it represents a saving in the economy of enforcement: since it is women themselves who practice this discipline on and against their own bodies, men get off scot-free.

The woman who checks her make-up half a dozen times a day to see if her foundation has caked or her mascara run, who worries that the wind or rain may spoil her hairdo, who looks frequently to see if her stockings have bagged at the ankle, or who, feeling fat, monitors everything she eats, has become, just as surely as the inmate of Panopticon, a self-policing subject, a self committed to a relentless self-surveillance. This self-surveillance is a form of obedience to patriarchy. It is also the reflection in woman's consciousness of the fact that *she* is under surveillance in ways that *he* is not, that whatever else she may become, she is importantly a body designed to please or to excite. There has been induced in many women, then, in Foucault's words, "a state of conscious and permanent visibility that assures the automatic functioning of power."[48] Since the standards of female bodily acceptability are impossible fully to realize, requiring as they do a virtual transcendence of nature, a woman may live much of her life with a pervasive feeling of bodily deficiency. Hence, a tighter control of the body has gained a new kind of hold over the mind.

Foucault often writes as if power constitutes the very individuals upon whom it operates:

> The individual is not to be conceived as a sort of elementary nucleus, a primitive atom, a multiple and inert material on which power comes to fasten or against which it happens to strike. . . . In fact, it is already one of the prime effects of power that certain bodies, certain gestures, certain discourses, certain desires, come to be identified and constituted as individuals.[49]

Nevertheless, if individuals were wholly constituted by the power/knowledge regime Foucault descries, it would make no sense to speak of resistance to discipline at all. Foucault seems sometimes on the verge of depriving us of a vocabulary in which to conceptualize the nature and meaning of those periodic refusals of control which, just as much as the imposition of control, mark the course of human history.

Peter Dews accuses Foucault of lacking a theory of the "libidinal body," i.e., the body upon which discipline is imposed and whose bedrock impulse toward spontaneity and pleasure might perhaps become the locus of resistance.[50] Do women's "libidinal" bodies, then, not rebel against the pain, constriction, tedium, semistarvation, and constant self-surveillance to which they are currently condemned? Certainly they do, but the rebellion is put down every time a woman picks up her eyebrow tweezers or embarks upon a new diet. The harshness of a regimen alone does not guarantee its rejection, for hardships can be endured if they are thought to be necessary or inevitable.

While "nature," in the form of a "libidinal" body, may not be the origin of a revolt against "culture," domination and the discipline it requires are never imposed without some cost. Historically, the forms and occasions of resistance are manifold. Sometimes, instances of resistance appear to spring from the introduction of new and conflicting factors into the lives of the dominated. The juxtaposition of old and new and the resulting incoherence or "contradiction" may make submission to the old ways seem increasingly unnecessary. In the present instance, what may be a major factor in the relentless and escalating objectification of women's bodies—namely, women's growing independence—produces in many women a sense of incoherence that calls into question the meaning and necessity of the current discipline. As women (albeit a small minority of women) begin to realize an unprecedented political, economic, and sexual self-determination, they fall ever more completely under the dominating gaze of patriarchy. It is this paradox, not the "libidinal body," that produces, here and there, pockets of resistance.

In the current political climate, there is no reason to anticipate either widespread resistance to currently fashionable modes of feminine embodiment or joyous experimentation with new "styles of the flesh"; moreover, such novelties would face profound opposition from material and psychological sources identified earlier in this essay (see Section VII). In spite of this, a number of oppositional discourses and practices have appeared in recent years. An increasing number of women are "pumping iron," a few with little concern for the limits of body development imposed by current canons of femininity. Women in radical lesbian communities have also rejected hegemonic images of femininity and are struggling to develop a new female aesthetic. A striking feature of such communities is the extent to which they have overcome the oppressive identification of female beauty and desirability with youth. Here, the physical features of aging—"character" lines and greying hair—not only do not diminish a woman's attractiveness, they may even enhance it. A popular literature of resistance is growing, some of it analytical and reflective, like Kim Chernin's *The Obsession*, some oriented toward practical self-help, like Marcia Hutchinson's recent *Transforming Body Image: Learning to Love the Body You Have.*[51] This literature reflects a mood akin in some ways to that other and earlier mood of quiet desperation to which Betty Friedan gave voice in *The Feminine Mystique.* Nor should we forget that a mass-based women's movement is in place in this country which has begun a critical questioning of the meaning of femininity—if not yet in this, then in other domains of life. We women cannot begin the re-vision of our own bodies until we learn to read the cultural messages we inscribe upon them daily and until we come to see that even when the mastery of the disciplines of femininity produce a triumphant result, we are still only women.

NOTES

1. Michel Foucault, *Discipline and Punish* (New York: Vintage Books, 1979), p. 138.
2. Ibid., p. 28.
3. Ibid., p. 147.
4. Ibid., p. 153. Foucault is citing an eighteenth-century military manual, "Ordonance du Ier Janvier 1766 . . . , titre XI, article 2."
5. Ibid., p. 153.
6. Ibid., p. 150.
7. Ibid., p. 200.
8. Ibid., p. 201.
9. Ibid., p. 228.
10. Judith Butler, "Embodied Identity in De Beauvoir's *The Second Sex*," unpublished manuscript, p. 11, presented to American Philosophical Association, Pacific Division, March 22, 1985. See also Butler's recent monograph *Gender Trouble: Feminism and the Subversion of Identity* (New York: Routledge, 1990).
11. Marcia Millman, *Such a Pretty Face—Being Fat in America* (New York: Norton, 1980) p. 46.
12. Susan Bordo, "Anorexia Nervosa: Psychopathology as the Crystallization of Culture," *Philosophical Forum*, Vol. XVII, No. 2, Winter 1985–86, pp. 73–104. See also Bordo's *Food, Fashion and Power: The Body and The Reproduction of Gender* (forthcoming, v. of California Press).
13. *USA Today*, May 30, 1985.
14. Phrase taken from the title of Kim Chernin's *The Obsession: Reflections on the Tyranny of Slenderness* (New York: Harper and Row, 1981), an examination from a feminist perspective of women's eating disorders and of the current female preoccupation with body size.
15. M. J. Saffon, *The 15-Minute-A-Day Natural Face Lift* (New York: Warner Books, 1981).
16. Sophia Loren, *Women and Beauty* (New York: William Morrow, 1984), p. 57.

17. Iris Young, "Throwing Like a Girl: A Phenomenology of Feminine Body Comportment, Motility and Spatiality," *Human Studies*, Vol. 3, (1980), pp. 137–156.
18. Marianne Wex, *Let's Take Back Our Space: "Female" and "Male" Body Language as a Result of Patriarchal Structures* (Berlin: Frauenliteraturvelag Hermine Fees, 1979). Wex claims that Japanese women are still taught to position their feet so that the toes point inward, a traditional sign of submissiveness (p. 23).
19. In heels, the "female foot and leg are turned into ornamental objects and the impractical shoe, which offers little protection against dust, rain and snow, induces helplessness and dependence. . . . The extra wiggle in the hips, exaggerating a slight natural tendency, is seen as sexually flirtatious while the smaller steps and tentative, insecure tread suggest daintiness, modesty and refinement. Finally, the overall hobbling effect with its sadomaschistic tinge is suggestive of the restraining leg irons and ankle chains endured by captive animals, prisoners and slaves who were also festooned with decorative symbols of their bondage." Susan Brownmiller, *Femininity* (New York: Simon and Schuster, 1984), p. 184.
20. Nancy Henley, *Body Politics* (Englewood Cliffs, N.J.: Prentice-Hall, 1977), p. 176.
21. For an account of the sometimes devastating effects on workers, like flight attendants, whose conditions of employment require the display of a perpetual friendliness, see Arlie Hochschild, *The Managed Heart: The Commercialization of Human Feeling* (Berkeley, Calif.: University of California Press, 1983).
22. Henley, *Body Politics*, p. 108.
23. Ibid., p. 149.
24. Clairol has just introduced a small electric shaver, the "Bikini," apparently intended for just such use.
25. Georgette Klinger and Barbara Rowes, *Georgette Klinger's Skincare* (New York: William Morrow, 1978, pp. 102, 105, 151, 188, and passim.
26. *Chicago Magazine*, March 1986, pp. 43, 10, 18, and 62.
27. *Essence*, April 1986, p. 25. I am indebted to Laurie Shrage for calling this to my attention and for providing most of these examples.
28. Klinger, *Skincare*, pp. 137–140.
29. In light of this, one is surprised to see a two-ounce jar of "Skin Regeneration Formula," a "Proteolytic Enzyme Cream with Bromelain and Papain," selling for $23.95 in the tabloid *Globe* (April 8, 1986, p. 29) and an unidentified amount of Tova Borgnine's "amazing new formula from Beverly Hills" (otherwise unnamed) going for $41.75 in the *National Enquirer* (April 8, 1986, p. 15).
30. "It is required of woman that in order to realize her femininity she must make herself object and prey, which is to say that she must renounce her claims as sovereign subject." *Simone De Beauvoir, The Second Sex* (New York: Bantam Books, 1968), p. 642.
31. The film *Pumping Iron II* portrays very clearly the tension for female bodybuilders (a tension that enters into formal judging in the sport) between muscular development and a properly feminine appearance.
32. Henley, *Body Politics*, p. 101, 153, and passim.
33. Foucault, *Discipline and Punish*, p. 222.
34. Millman, *Such a Pretty Face*, p. 80. These sorts of remarks are made so commonly to heavy women that sociologist Millman takes the most clichéd as title of her study of the lives of the overweight.
35. I am indebted to Nancy Fraser for the formulation of this point.

36. See Chapter 3.
37. Millman, *Such a Pretty Face*, pp. 80 and 195.
38. Chernin, *The Obsession*, p. 53.
39. See Chapter 3.
40. For a claim that the project of liberal or "mainstream" feminism is covertly racist, see Bell Hooks, *Ain't I Woman: Black Women and Feminism* (Boston: South End Press, 1981), Chap. 4. For an authoritative general critique of liberal feminism, see Alison Jaggar, *Feminist Politics and Human Nature* (Totowa, N.J.: Rowman and Allanheld, 1983), Chaps. 3 and 7.
41. See, for example, Mihailo Markovic, "Women's Liberation and Human Emancipation," in *Women and Philosophy*, ed. Carol C. Gould and Marx W. Wartofsky (New York: G. P. Putnam's Sons, 1976, pp. 165–166.
42. Foucault, *Discipline and Punish*, p. 30.
43. Some radical feminists have called for just such a deconstruction. See especially Monique Wittig, *The Lesbian Body* (New York: Avon Books, 1976), and Butler, *Gender Trouble.*
44. Foucault, *Discipline and Punish*, p. 44.
45. Foucault, Colin Gordon, ed., *Power/Knowledge* (Brighton, 1980), p. 151. Quoted in Peter Dews, "Power and Subjectivity in Foucault," *New Left Review*, No. 144, March–April 1984, p. 17.
46. Dews, op. cit., p. 77.
47. Foucault, *Discipline and Punish*, p. 138.
48. Ibid., p. 201.
49. Foucault, *Power/Knowledge*, p. 98. In fact, Foucault is not entirely consistent on this point. For an excellent discussion of contending Foucault interpretations and for the difficulty of deriving a consistent set of claims from Foucault's work generally, see Nancy Fraser, "Michel Foucault: A 'Young Conservative'?" *Ethics*, Vol. 9(?) October 1985, pp. 165–184.
50. Dews, op. cit., p. 92.
51. See Marcia Hutchinson, *Transforming Body Image—Learning to Love the Body You Have* (Trumansburg, N.Y.: Crossing Press, 1985). See also Bordo, "Anorexia Nervosa: Psychopathology as the Crystallization of Culture."

Excerpt from *Gender Trouble*

Butler questions several categories that serve as markers of personal identity and as organizing principles for politics—biological sex, polarized gender, and determinate sexuality. According to Butler, materiality is itself a concept that has a cultural history, and bodies are not fundamental, brute realities. Rather, bodies are delimited though the inscription of cultural discourses. On this view, gender identity is a discipline that constructs a gendered body and that enforces compulsory heterosexuality. Through personal experience of received meanings and participation in a set of imitative practices, individuals come to think of themselves as having innate and deep-seated gender identities. Yet gender is a discursive effect; it is neither a biological nor a psychological necessity. Gendered behavior—that is, enactments of prescribed corporeal styles—is "performative," for it creates the illusion of primary, interior gender identity. This illusion conceals the political underpinnings of gender identity, namely, male dominance and heterosexism.

Butler's account of gender puts feminist politics on a new footing. Parodic gender performances, such as drag, are politically significant, for they reveal the imitative structure of gender and subvert its claim to be natural or necessary. Such performances suggest an alternative understanding of political agency—a discourse-based conception, as opposed to an identity-based conception.

—D.T.M.

Chapter 6

Judith Butler

Excerpt from *Gender Trouble*

> "Garbo 'got in drag' whenever she took some heavy glamour part, whenever she melted in or out of a man's arms, whenever she simply let that heavenly-flexed neck . . . bear the weight of her thrown-back head. . . . How resplendent seems the art of acting! It is all *impersonation,* whether the sex underneath is true or not."
>
> Parker Tyler, "The Garbo Image,"
> quoted in Esther Newton, *Mother Camp*

Categories of true sex, discrete gender, and specific sexuality have constituted the stable point of reference for a great deal of feminist theory and politics. These constructs of identity serve as the points of epistemic departure from which theory emerges and politics itself is shaped. In the case of feminism, politics is ostensibly shaped to express the interests, the perspectives, of "women." But is there a political shape to "women," as it were, that precedes and prefigures the political elaboration of their interests and epistemic point of view? How is that identity shaped, and is it a political shaping that takes the very morphology and boundary of the sexed body as the ground, surface, or site of cultural inscription? What circumscribes that site as "the female body"? Is "the body" or "the sexed body" the firm foundation on which gender and systems of compulsory sexuality operate? Or is "the body" itself shaped by political fores with strategic interests in keeping that body bounded and constituted by the markers of sex?

The sex/gender distinction and the category of sex itself appear to presuppose a generalization of "the body" that preexists the acquisition of its sexed significance. This "body" often appears to be a passive medium that is signified by an inscription from a cultural source figured as "external" to that body. Any theory of the culturally constructed body, however, ought to question "the body" as a construct of suspect generality when it is figured as passive and prior to discourse. There are Christian and Cartesian precedents to such views which, prior to the emergence of vitalistic biologies in the nineteenth century, understand "the body" as so much inert matter, signifying nothing or, more specifically, signifying a profane void, the fallen state: deception, sin, the premonitional metaphorics of hell, and the eternal feminine. There are many occasions in both Sartre's and Beauvoir's work where "the body" is figured as a mute facticity, anticipating some meaning that can be attributed only by a transcendent consciousness, understood in Cartesian terms as radically immaterial. But what establishes this dualism for us? What separates off "the body" as indifferent to signification, and signification itself as the act of a radically disembodied consciousness or, rather, the act that radically disembodies that consciousness? To what extent is that Cartesian dualism presupposed in phenomenology adapted to the structuralist frame in which mind/body is redescribed as culture/nature? With respect to gender discourse, to what extent do these problematic dualisms still operate within the very descriptions that are supposed to lead us out of that binarism and its implicit hierarchy? How are the contours of the body clearly marked as the taken-for-granted ground or surface upon which gender significations are inscribed, a mere facticity devoid of value, prior to significance?

Wittig suggests that a culturally specific epistemic *a priori* establishes the naturalness of "sex." But by what enigmatic means has "the body" been accepted as a *prima facie* given that admits of no genealogy? Even within Foucault's essay on the very theme of genealogy, the body is figured as a surface and the scene of a cultural inscription: "the body is the inscribed surface of events."[1] The task of genealogy, he claims, is "to expose a body totally imprinted by history." His sentence continues, however, by referring to the goal of "history"—here clearly understood on the model of Freud's "civilization"—as the "destruction of the body" (148). Forces and impulses with multiple directionalities are precisely that which history both destroys and preserves through the *entstehung* (historical event) of inscription. As "a volume in perpetual disintegration" (148), the body is always under siege, suffering destruction by the very terms of history. And history is the creation of values and meanings by a signifying practice that requires the subjection of the body. This corporeal destruction is necessary to produce the speaking subject and its significations. This is a body, described through the language of surface and force, weakened through a "single drama" of domination, inscription, and creation (150). This is not the *modus vivendi* of one kind of history rather than another, but is, for Foucault, "history" (148) in its essential and repressive gesture.

Although Foucault writes, "Nothing in man [*sic*]—not even his body—is sufficiently stable to serve as the basis for self-recognition or for understanding other men [*sic*]" (153), he nevertheless points to the constancy of cultural inscription as a "single drama" that acts on the body. If the creation of values, that historical mode of signification, requires the destruction of the body, much as the instrument of torture in Kafka's *In the Penal Colony* destroys the body on which it writes, then there must be a body prior to that inscription, stable and self-identical, subject to that sacrificial destruction. In a sense, for Foucault, as for Nietzsche, cultural values emerge as the result of an inscription on the body, understood as a medium, indeed, a blank page; in order for this inscription to signify, however, that medium must itself be destroyed—that is, fully transvaluated into a sublimated domain of values. Within the metaphorics of this notion of cultural values is the figure of history as a relentless writing instrument, and the body as the medium which must be destroyed and transfigured in order for "culture" to emerge.

By maintaining a body prior to its cultural inscription, Foucault appears to assume a materiality prior to signification and form. Because this distinction operates as essential to the task of genealogy as he defines it, the distinction itself is precluded as an object of genealogical investigation. Occasionally in his analysis of Herculine, Foucault subscribes to a prediscursive multiplicity of bodily forces that break through the surface of the body to disrupt the regulating practices of cultural coherence imposed upon that body by a power regime, understood as a vicissitude of "history." If the presumption of some kind of precategorical source of disruption is refused, is it still possible to give a genealogical account of the demarcation of the body as such as a signifying practice? This demarcation is not initiated by a reified history or by a subject. This marking is the result of a diffuse and active structuring of the social field. This signifying practice effects a social space for and of the body within certain regulatory grids of intelligibility.

Mary Douglas's *Purity and Danger* suggests that the very contours of "the body" are established through markings that seek to establish specific codes of cultural coherence. Any discourse that establishes the boundaries of the body serves the purpose of instating and naturalizing certain taboos regarding the appropriate limits, postures, and modes of exchange that define what it is that constitutes bodies:

> Ideas about separating, purifying, demarcating and punishing transgressions have as their main function to impose system on an inherently untidy experience. It is only by exaggerating the difference between within and without, above and below, male and female, with and against, that a semblance of order is created.[2]

Although Douglas clearly subscribes to a structuralist distinction between an inherently unruly nature and an order imposed by cultural means, the "untidiness" to which she refers can be redescribed as a region of *cultural* unruliness and disorder. Assuming the inevitably binary structure of the nature/culture distinction, Douglas cannot point toward an alternative configuration of culture in which such distinctions become malleable or proliferate beyond the binary frame. Her analysis, however, provides a possible point of departure for understanding the relationship by which social taboos institute and maintain the boundaries of the body as such. Her analysis suggests that what constitutes the limit of the body is never merely material, but that the surface, the skin, is systemically signified by taboos and anticipated transgressions; indeed, the boundaries of the body become, within her analysis, the limits of the social *per se.* A poststructuralist appropriation of her view might well understand the boundaries of the body as the limits of the socially *hegemonic.* In a variety of cultures, she maintains, there are

> pollution powers which inhere in the structure of ideas itself and which punish a symbolic breaking of that which should be joined or joining of that which should be separate. It follows from this that pollution is a type of danger which is not likely to occur except where the lines of structure, cosmic or social, are clearly defined.
>
> A polluting person is always in the wrong. He [*sic*] has developed some wrong condition or simply crossed over some line which should not have been crossed and this displacement unleashes danger for someone.[3]

In a sense, Simon Watney has identified the contemporary construction of "the polluting person" as the person with AIDS in his *Policing Desire: AIDS, Pornography, and the Media.*[4] Not only is the illness figured as the "gay disease," but throughout the media's hysterical and homophobic response to the illness there is a tactical construction of a continuity between the polluted status of the homosexual by virtue of the boundary-trespass that *is* homosexuality and the disease as a specific modality of homosexual pollution. That the disease is transmitted through the exchange of bodily fluids suggests within the sensationalist graphics of homophobic signifying systems the dangers that permeable bodily boundaries present to the social order as such. Douglas remarks that "the body is a model that can stand for any bounded system. Its boundaries can represent any boundaries which are threatened or precarious."[5] And she asks a question which one might have expected to read in Foucault: "Why should bodily margins be thought to be specifically invested with power and danger?"[6]

Douglas suggests that all social systems are vulnerable at their margins, and that all margins are accordingly considered dangerous. If the body is synecdochal for the social system *per se* or a site in which open systems converge, then any kind of unregulated permeability constitutes a site of pollution and endangerment. Since anal and oral sex among men clearly establishes certain kinds of bodily permeabilities unsanctioned by the hegemonic order, male homosexuality would, within such a hegemonic point of view, constitute a site of danger and pollution prior to and regardless of the cultural presence of AIDS. Similarly, the "polluted" status of lesbians, regardless of their low-risk status with respect to AIDS, brings into relief the dangers of their bodily exchanges. Significantly, being "outside" the hegemonic order does not signify being "in" a state of filthy and untidy nature. Paradoxically, homosexuality is almost always conceived within the homophobic signifying economy as *both* uncivilized and unnatural.

The construction of stable bodily contours relies upon fixed sites of corporeal permeability and impermeability. Those sexual practices in both homosexual and heterosexual contexts that open surfaces and orifices to erotic signification or close down others effectively reinscribe the boundaries of the body along new cultural lines. Anal sex among men is an example, as is the radical re-membering of the body in Wittig's *The Lesbian Body*. Douglas alludes to "a kind of sex pollution which expresses a desire to keep the body (physical and social) intact,"[7] suggesting that the naturalized notion of "the" body is itself a consequence of taboos that render that body discrete by virtue of its stable boundaries. Further, the rites of passage that govern various bodily orifices presuppose a heterosexual construction of gendered exchange, positions, and erotic possibilities. The deregulation of such exchanges accordingly disrupts the very boundaries that determine what it is to be a body at all. Indeed, the critical inquiry that traces the regulatory practices within which bodily contours are constructed constitutes precisely the genealogy of "the body" in its discreteness that might further radicalize Foucault's theory.[8]

Significantly, Kristeva's discussion of abjection in *The Powers of Horror* begins to suggest the uses of this structuralist notion of a boundary-constituting taboo for the purposes of constructing a discrete subject through exclusion.[9] The "abject" designates that which has been expelled from the body, discharged as excrement, literally rendered "Other." This appears as an expulsion of alien elements, but the alien is effectively established through this expulsion. The construction of the "not-me" as the abject establishes the boundaries of the body which are also the first contours of the subject. Kristeva writes:

> *nausea* makes me balk at that milk cream, separates me from the mother and father who proffer it. "I" want none of that element, sign of their desire; "I" do not want to listen, "I" do not assimilate it, "I" expel it. But since the food is not an "other" for "me," who am only in their desire, I expel *myself*, I spit *myself* out, I abject *myself* within the same motion through which "I" claim to establish myself.[10]

The boundary of the body as well as the distinction between internal and external is established through the ejection and transvaluation of something originally part of identity into a defiling otherness. As Iris Young has suggested in her use of Kristeva to understand sexism, homophobia, and racism, the repudiation of bodies for their sex, sexuality, and/or color is an "expulsion" followed by a "repulsion" that founds and consolidates culturally hegemonic identities along sex/race/sexuality axes of differentiation.[11] Young's appropriation of Kristeva shows how the operation of repulsion can consolidate "identities" founded on the instituting of the "Other" or a set of Others through exclusion and domination. What constitutes through division the "inner" and "outer" worlds of the subject is a border and boundary tenuously maintained for the purposes of social regulation and control. The boundary between the inner and the outer is confounded by those excremental passages in which the inner effectively becomes outer, and this excreting function becomes, as it were, the model by which other forms of identity-differentiation are accomplished. In effect, this is the mode by which Others become shit. For inner and outer worlds to remain utterly distinct, the entire surface of the body would have to achieve an impossible impermeability. This sealing of its surfaces would constitute the seamless boundary of the subject; but this enclosure would invariably be exploded by precisely that excremental filth that it fears.

Regardless of the compelling metaphors of the spatial distinctions of inner and outer, they remain linguistic terms that facilitate and articulate a set of fantasies, feared and desired. "Inner" and "outer" make sense only with reference to a mediating boundary that strives for stability. And this stability, this coherence, is determined in large part by cultural orders that sanction the subject and compel its differentiation from the abject. Hence, "inner" and "outer" constitute a binary distinction that stabilizes and consolidates the coherent subject. When that subject is challenged, the meaning and necessity of the terms are subject to displacement. If the "inner world" no longer designates a topos, then the internal fixity of the self and, indeed, the internal locale of gender identity, become similarly suspect. The critical question is not *how* did that identity become *internalized*? as if internalization were a process or a mechanism that might be descriptively reconstructed. Rather, the question is: From what strategic position in public discourse and for what reasons has the trope of interiority and the disjunctive binary of inner/outer taken hold? In what language is "inner space" figured? What kind of figuration is it, and through what figure of the body is it signified? How does a body figure on its surface the very invisibility of its hidden depth?

From Interiority to Gender Performatives

In *Discipline and Punish* Foucault challenges the language of internalization as it operates in the service of the disciplinary regime of the subjection and subjectivation of criminals.[12] Although Foucault objected to what he understood to be the psychoanalytic belief in the "inner" truth of sex in *The History of Sexuality*, he turns to a criticism of the doctrine of internalization for separate purposes in the context of his history of criminology. In a sense, *Discipline and Punish* can be read as Foucault's effort to rewrite Nietzsche's doctrine of internalization in *On the Genealogy of Morals* on the model of *inscription.* In the context of prisoners, Foucault writes, the strategy has been not to enforce a repression of their desires, but to compel their bodies to signify the prohibitive law as their very essence, style, and necessity. That law is not literally internalized, but incorporated, with the consequence that bodies are produced which signify that law on and through the body; there the law is manifest as the essence of their selves, the meaning of their soul, their conscience, the law of their desire. In effect, the law is at once fully manifest and fully latent, for it never appears as external to the bodies it subjects and subjectivates. Foucault writes:

> It would be wrong to say that the soul is an illusion, or an ideological effect. On the contrary, it exists, it has a reality, it is produced permanently *around, on, within,* the body by the functioning of a power that is exercised on those that are punished.[13] (my emphasis)

The figure of the interior soul understood as "within" the body is signified through its inscription *on* the body, even though its primary mode of signification is through its very absence, its potent invisibility. The effect of a structuring inner space is produced through the signification of a body as a vital and sacred enclosure. The soul is precisely what the body lacks; hence, the body presents itself as a signifying lack. That lack which *is* the body signifies the soul as that which cannot show. In this sense, then, the soul is a surface signification that contests and displaces the inner/outer distinction itself, a figure of interior psychic space inscribed *on* the body as a social signification that perpetually renounces itself as such. In Foucault's terms, the soul is not imprisoned by or within the body, as some Christian imagery would suggest, but "the soul is the prison of the body."[14]

The redescription of intrapsychic processes in terms of the surface politics of the body implies a corollary redescription of gender as the disciplinary production of the figures of fantasy through the play of presence and absence on the body's surface, the construction of the gendered body through a series of exclusions and denials, signifying absences. But what determines the manifest and latent text of the body politic? What is the prohibitive law that generates the corporeal stylization of gender, the fantasied and fantastic figuration of the body? We have already considered the incest taboo and the prior taboo against homosexuality as the generative moments of gender identity, the prohibitions that produce identity along the culturally intelligible grids of an idealized and compulsory heterosexuality. That disciplinary production of gender effects a false stabilization of gender in the interests of the heterosexual construction and regulation of sexuality within the reproductive domain. The construction of coherence conceals the gender discontinuities that run rampant within heterosexual, bisexual, and gay and lesbian contexts in which gender does not necessarily follow from sex, and desire, or sexuality generally, does not seem to follow from gender—indeed, where none of these dimensions of significant corporeality express or reflect one another. When the disorganization and disaggregation of the field of bodies disrupt the regulatory fiction of heterosexual coherence, it seems that the expressive model loses its descriptive force. That regulatory ideal is then exposed as a norm and a fiction that disguises itself as a developmental law regulating the sexual field that it purports to describe.

According to the understanding of identification as an enacted fantasy or incorporation, however, it is clear that coherence is desired, wished for, idealized, and that this idealization is an effect of a corporeal signification. In other words, acts, gestures, and desire produce the effect of an internal core or substance, but produce this *on the surface* of the body, through the play of signifying absences that suggest, but never reveal, the organizing principle of identity as a cause. Such acts, gestures, enactments, generally construed, are *performative* in the sense that the essence or identity that they otherwise purport to express are *fabrications* manufactured and sustained through corporeal signs and other discursive means. That the gendered body is performative suggests that it has no ontological status apart from the various acts which constitute its reality. This also suggests that if that reality is fabricated as an interior essence, that very interiority is an effect and function of a decidedly public and social discourse, the public regulation of fantasy through the surface politics of the body, the gender border control that differentiates inner from outer, and so institutes the "integrity" of the subject. In other words, acts and gestures, articulated and enacted desires, create the illusion of an interior and organizing gender core, an illusion discursively maintained for the purposes of the regulation of sexuality within the obligatory frame of reproductive heterosexuality. If the "cause" of desire, gesture, and act can be localized within the "self" of the actor, then the political regulations and disciplinary practices which produce that ostensibly coherent gender are effectively displaced from view. The displacement of a political and discursive origin of gender identity onto a psychological "core" precludes an analysis of the political constitution of the gendered subject and its fabricated notions about the ineffable interiority of its sex or of its true identity.

If the inner truth of gender is a fabrication and if a true gender is a fantasy instituted and inscribed on the surface of bodies, then it seems that genders can be neither true nor false, but are only produced as the truth effects of a discourse of primary and stable identity. In *Mother Camp: Female Impersonators in America*, anthropologist Esther Newton suggests that the structure of impersonation reveals one of the key fabricating mechanisms through which the social construction of gender takes place.[15] I would suggest as well that drag fully subverts the distinction between inner and outer psychic space and effectively mocks both the expressive model of gender and the notion of a true gender identity. Newton writes:

> At its most complex, [drag] is a double inversion that says, "appearance is an illusion." Drag says [Newton's curious personification] "my 'outside' appearance is feminine, but my essence 'inside' [the body] is masculine." At the same time it symbolizes the opposite inversion; "my appearance 'outside' [my body, my gender] is masculine but my essence 'inside' [myself] is feminine."[16]

Both claims to truth contradict one another and so displace the entire enactment of gender significations from the discourse of truth and falsity.

The notion of an original or primary gender identity is often parodied within the cultural practices of drag, cross-dressing, and the sexual stylization of butch/femme identities. Within feminist theory, such parodic identities have been understood to be either degrading to women, in the case of drag and cross-dressing, or an uncritical appropriation of sex-role stereotyping from within the practice of heterosexuality, especially in the case of butch/femme lesbian identifies. But the relation between the "imitation" and the "original" is, I think, more complicated than that critique generally allows. Moreover, it gives us a clue to the way in which the relationship between primary identification—that is, the original meanings accorded to gender—and subsequent gender experience might be reframed. The performance of drag plays upon the distinction between the anatomy of the performer and the gender that is being performed. But we are actually in the presence of three contingent dimensions of significant corporeality: anatomical sex, gender identity, and gender performance. If the anatomy of the performer is already distinct from the gender of the performer, and both of those are distinct from the gender of the performance, then the performance suggests a dissonance between not only sex and performance, but also sex and gender, and gender and performance. As much as drag creates a unified picture of "woman" (what its critics often oppose), it also reveals the distinctness of those aspects of gendered experience which are falsely naturalized as a unity through the regulatory fiction of heterosexual coherence. *In imitating gender, drag implicitly reveals the imitative structure of gender itself—as well as its contingency.* Indeed, part of the pleasure, the giddiness of the performance is in the recognition of a radical contingency in the relation between sex and gender in the face of cultural configurations of causal unities that are regularly assumed to be natural and necessary. In the place of the law of heterosexual coherence, we see sex and gender denaturalized by means of a performance which avows their distinctness and dramatizes the cultural mechanism of their fabricated unity.

The notion of gender parody defended here does not assume that there is an original which such parodic identities imitate. Indeed, the parody is *of* the very notion of an original; just as the psychoanalytic notion of gender identification is constituted by a fantasy of a fantasy, the transfiguration of an Other who is always already a "figure" in that double sense, so gender parody reveals that the original identity after which gender fashions itself is an imitation without an origin. To be more precise, it is a production which, in effect—that is, in its effect—postures as an imitation. This perpetual displacement constitutes a fluidity of identities that suggests an openness to resignification and recontextualization; parodic proliferation deprives hegemonic culture and its critics of the claim to naturalized or essentialist gender identities. Although the gender meanings taken up in these parodic styles are clearly part of hegemonic, misogynist culture, they are nevertheless denaturalized and mobilized through their parodic recontextualization. As imitations which effectively displace the meaning of the original, they imitate the myth of originality itself. In the place of an original identification which serves as a determining cause, gender identity might be reconceived as a personal/cultural history of received meanings subject to a set of imitative practices which refer laterally to other imitations and which, jointly, construct the illusion of a primary and interior gendered self or parody the mechanism of that construction.

According to Fredric Jameson's "Postmodernism and Consumer Society," the imitation that mocks the notion of an original is characteristic of pastiche rather than parody:

> Pastiche is, like parody, the imitation of a peculiar or unique style, the wearing of a stylistic mask, speech in a dead language: but it is a neutral practice of mimicry, without parody's ulterior motive, without the satirical impulse, without laughter, without that still latent feeling that there exists something *normal* compared to which what is being imitated is rather comic. Pastiche is blank parody, parody that has lost its humor.[17]

The loss of the sense of "the normal," however, can be its own occasion for laughter, especially when "the normal," "the original" is revealed to be a copy, and an inevitably failed one, an ideal that no one *can* embody. In this sense, laughter emerges in the realization that all along the original was derived.

Parody by itself is not subversive, and there must be a way to understand what makes certain kinds of parodic repetitions effectively disruptive, truly troubling, and which repetitions become domesticated and recirculated as instruments of cultural hegemony. A typology of actions would clearly not suffice, for parodic displacement, indeed, parodic laughter, depends on a context and reception in which subversive confusions can be fostered. What performance where will invert the inner/outer distinction and compel a radical rethinking of the psychological presuppositions of gender identity and sexuality? What performance where will compel a reconsideration of the *place* and stability of the masculine and the feminine? And what kind of gender performance will enact and reveal the performativity of gender itself in a way that destabilizes the naturalized categories of identity and desire.

If the body is not a "being," but a variable boundary, a surface whose permeability is politically regulated, a signifying practice within a cultural field of gender hierarchy and compulsory heterosexuality, then what language is left for understanding this corporeal enactment, gender, that constitutes its "interior" signification on its surface? Sartre would perhaps have called this act "a style of being," Foucault, "a stylistics of existence." And in my earlier reading of Beauvoir, I suggest that gendered bodies are so many "styles of the flesh." These styles are never fully self-styled, for styles have a history, and those histories condition and limit the possibilities. Consider gender, for instance, as *a corporeal style*, an "act," as it were, which is both intentional and performative, where *"performative"* suggests a dramatic and contingent construction of meaning.

Wittig understands gender as the workings of "sex," where "sex" is an obligatory injunction for the body to become a cultural sign, to materialize itself in obedience to a historically delimited possibility, and to do this, not once or twice, but as a sustained and repeated corporeal project. The notion of a "project," however, suggests the originating force of a radical will, and because gender is a project that has cultural survival as its end, the term *strategy* better suggests the situation of duress under which gender performance always and variously occurs. Hence, as a strategy of survival within compulsory systems, gender is a performance with clearly punitive consequences. Discrete genders are part of what "humanizes" individuals within contemporary culture; indeed, we regularly punish those who fail to do their gender right. Because there is neither an "essence" that gender expresses or externalizes nor an objective ideal to which gender aspires, and because gender is not a fact, the various acts of gender create the idea of gender, and without those acts, there would be no gender at all. Gender is, thus, a construction that regularly conceals its genesis; the tacit collective agreement to perform, produce, and sustain discrete and polar genders as cultural fictions is obscured by the credibility of those productions—and the punishments that attend not agreeing to believe in them; the construction "compels" our belief in its necessity and naturalness. The historical possibilities materialized through various corporeal styles are nothing other than those punitively regulated cultural fictions alternately embodied and deflected under duress.

Consider that a sedimentation of gender norms produces the peculiar phenomenon of a "natural sex" or a "real woman" or any number of prevalent and compelling social fictions, and that this is a sedimentation that over time has produced a set of corporeal styles which, in reified form, appear as the natural configuration of bodies into sexes existing in a binary relation to one another. If these styles are enacted, and if they produce the coherent gendered subjects who pose as their originators, what kind of performance might reveal this ostensible "cause" to be an "effect"?

In what sense, then, is gender an act? As in other ritual social dramas, the action of gender requires a performance that is *repeated.* This repetition is at once a reenactment and reexperiencing of a set of meanings already socially established; and it is the mundane and ritualized form of their legitimation.[18] Although there are individual bodies that enact these significations by becoming stylized into gendered modes, this "action" is a public action. There are temporal and collective dimensions to these actions, and their public character is not inconsequential; indeed, the performance is effected with the strategic aim of maintaining gender within its binary frame—an aim that cannot be attributed to a subject, but, rather, must be understood to found and consolidate the subject.

Gender ought not to be construed as a stable identity or locus of agency from which various acts follow; rather, gender is an identity tenuously constituted in time, instituted in an exterior space through a *stylized repetition of acts.* The effect of gender is produced through the stylization of the body and, hence, must be understood as the mundane way in which bodily gestures, movements, and styles of various kinds constitute the illusion of an abiding gendered self. This formulation moves the conception of gender off the ground of a substantial model of identity to one that requires a conception of gender as a constituted *social temporality.* Significantly, if gender is instituted through acts which are internally discontinuous, then the *appearance of substance* is precisely that, a constructed identity, a performative accomplishment which the mundane social audience, including the actors themselves, come to believe and to perform in the mode of belief. Gender is also a norm that can never be fully internalized; "the internal" is a surface signification, and gender norms are finally phantasmatic, impossible to embody. If the ground of gender identity is the stylized repetition of acts through time and not a seemingly seamless identity, then the spatial metaphor of a "ground" will be displaced and revealed as a stylized configuration, indeed, a gendered corporealization of time. The abiding gendered self will then be shown to be structured by repeated acts that seek to approximate the idea of a substantial ground of identity, but which, in their occasional *dis*continuity, reveal the temporal and contingent groundlessness of this "ground." The possibilities of gender transformation are to be found precisely in the arbitrary relation between such acts, in the possibility of a failure to repeat, a de-formity, or a parodic repetition that exposes the phantasmatic effect of abiding identity as a politically tenuous construction.

If gender attributes, however, are not expressive but performative, then these attributes effectively constitute the identity they are said to express or reveal. The distinction between expression and performativeness is crucial. If gender attributes and acts, the various ways in which a body shows or produces its cultural signification, are performative, then there is no preexisting identity by which an act or attribute might be measured; there would be no true or false, real or distorted acts of gender, and the postulation of a true gender identity would be revealed as a regulatory fiction. That gender reality is created through sustained social performances means that the very notions of an essential sex and a true or abiding masculinity or femininity are also constituted as part of the strategy that conceals gender's performative character and the performative possibilities for proliferating gender configurations outside the restricting frames of masculinist domination and compulsory heterosexuality.

Genders can be neither true nor false, neither real nor apparent, neither original nor derived. As credible bearers of those attributes, however, genders can also be rendered thoroughly and radically *incredible.*

CONCLUSION: FROM PARODY TO POLITICS

I began with the speculative question of whether feminist politics could do without a "subject" in the category of women. At stake is not whether it still makes sense, strategically or transitionally, to refer to women in order to make representational claims in their behalf. The feminist "we" is always and only a phantasmatic construction, one that has its purposes, but which denies the internal complexity and indeterminacy of the term and constitutes itself only through the exclusion of some part of the constituency that it simultaneously seeks to represent. The tenuous or phantasmatic status of the "we," however, is not cause for despair or, at least, it is not *only* cause for despair. The radical instability of the category sets into question the *foundational* restrictions on feminist political theorizing and opens up other configurations, not only of genders and bodies, but of politics itself.

The foundationalist reasoning of identity politics tends to assume that an identity must first be in place in order for political interests to be elaborated and, subsequently, political action to be taken. My argument is that there need not be a "doer behind the deed," but that the "doer" is variably constructed in and through the deed. This is not a return to an existential theory of the self as constituted through its acts, for the existential theory maintains a prediscursive structure for both the self and its acts. It is precisely the discursively variable construction of each in and through the other that has interested me here.

The question of locating "agency" is usually associated with the viability of the "subject," where the "subject" is understood to have some stable existence prior to the cultural field that it negotiates. Or, if the subject is culturally constructed, it is nevertheless vested with an agency, usually figured as the capacity for reflexive mediation, that remains intact regardless of its cultural embeddedness. On such a model, "culture" and "discourse" *mire* the subject, but do not constitute that subject. This move to qualify and enmire the preexisting subject has appeared necessary to establish a point of agency that is not fully *determined* by that culture and discourse. And yet, this kind of reasoning falsely presumes (a) agency can only be established through recourse to a prediscursive "I," even if that "I" is found in the midst of a discursive convergence, and (b) that to be *constituted* by discourse is to be *determined* by discourse, where determination forecloses the possibility of agency.

Even within the theories that maintain a highly qualified or situated subject, the subject still encounters its discursively constituted environment in an oppositional epistemological frame. The culturally enmired subject negotiates its constructions, even when those constructions are the very predicates of its own identity. In Beauvoir, for example, there is an "I" that does its gender, that becomes its gender, but that "I," invariably associated with its gender, is nevertheless a point of agency never fully identifiable with its gender. That *cogito* is never fully *of* the cultural world that it negotiates, no matter the narrowness of the ontological distance that separates that subject from its cultural predicates. The theories of feminist identity that elaborate predicates of color, sexuality, ethnicity, class, and able-bodiedness invariably close with an embarrassed "etc." at the end of the list. Through this horizontal trajectory of adjectives, these positions strive to encompass a situated subject, but invariably fail to be complete. This failure, however, is instructive: what political impetus is to be derived from the exasperated "etc." that so often occurs at the end of such lines? This is a sign of exhaustion as well as of the illimitable process of signification itself. It is the *supplément*, the excess that necessarily accompanies any effort to posit identity once and for all. This illimitable *et cetera*, however, offers itself as a new departure for feminist political theorizing.

If identity is asserted through a process of signification, if identity is always already signified, and yet continues to signify as it circulates within various interlocking discourses, then the question of agency is not to be answered through recourse to an "I" that preexists signification. In other words, the enabling conditions for an assertion of "I" are provided by the structure of signification, the rules that regulate the legitimate and illegitimate invocation of that pronoun, the practices that establish the terms of intelligibility by which that pronoun can circulate. Language is not an *exterior medium or instrument* into which I pour a self and from which I glean a reflection of that self. The Hegelian model of self-recognition that has been appropriated by Marx, Lukàcs, and a variety of contemporary liberatory discourses presupposes a potential adequation between the "I" that confronts its world, including its language, as an object, and the "I" that finds itself as an object in that world. But the subject/object dichotomy, which here belongs to the tradition of Western epistemology, conditions the very problematic of identity that it seeks to solve.

What discursive tradition establishes the "I" and its "Other" in an epistemological confrontation that subsequently decides where and how questions of knowability and agency are to be determined? What kinds of agency are foreclosed through the positing of an epistemological subject precisely because the rules and practices that govern the invocation of that subject and regulate its agency in advance are ruled out as sites of analysis and critical intervention? That the epistemological point of departure is in no sense inevitable is naively and pervasively confirmed by the mundane operations of ordinary language—widely documented within anthropology—that regard the subject/object dichotomy as a strange and contingent, if not violent, philosophical imposition. The language of appropriation, instrumentality, and distanciation germane to the epistemological mode also belong to a strategy of domination that pits the "I" against an "Other" and, once that separation is effected, creates an artificial set of questions about the knowability and recoverability of that Other.

As part of the epistemological inheritance of contemporary political discourses of identity, this binary opposition is a strategic move within a given set of signifying practices, one that establishes the "I" in and through this opposition and which reifies that opposition as a necessity, concealing the discursive apparatus by which the binary itself is constituted. The shift from an *epistemological* account of identity to one which locates the problematic within practices of *signification* permits an analysis that takes the epistemological mode itself as one possible and contingent signifying practice. Further, the question of *agency* is reformulated as a question of how signification and resignification work. In other words, what is signified as an identity is not signified at a given point in time after which it is simply there as an inert piece of entitative language. Clearly, identities *can* appear as so many inert substantives; indeed, epistemological models tend to take this appearance as their point of theoretical departure. However, the substantive "I" only appears as such through a signifying practice that seeks to conceal its own workings and to naturalize its effects. Further, to qualify as a substantive identity is an arduous task, for such appearances are rule-generated identities, ones which rely on the consistent and repeated invocation of rules that condition and restrict culturally intelligible practices of identity. Indeed, to understand identity as a *practice*, and as a signifying practice, is to understand culturally intelligible subjects as the resulting effect of a rule-bound discourse that inserts itself in the pervasive and mundane signifying acts of linguistic life. Abstractly considered, language refers to an open system of signs by which intelligibility is insistently created and contested. As historically specific organizations of language, discourses present themselves in the plural, coexisting within temporal frames, and instituting unpredictable and inadvertent convergences from which specific modalities of discursive possibilities are engendered.

As a process, signification harbors within itself what the epistemological discourse refers to as "agency." The rules that govern intelligible identity, i.e., that enable and restrict the intelligible assertion of an "I," rules that are partially structured along matrices of gender hierarchy and compulsory heterosexuality, operate through *repetition.* Indeed, when the subject is said to be constituted, that means simply that the subject is a consequence of certain rule-governed discourses that govern the intelligible invocation of identity. The subject is not *determined* by the rules through which it is generated because signification is *not a founding act, but rather a regulated process of repetition* that both conceals itself and enforces its rules precisely through the production of substantializing effects. In a sense, all signification takes place within the orbit of the compulsion to repeat; "agency," then, is to be located within the possibility of a variation on that repetition. If the rules governing signification not only restrict but also enable the assertion of alternative domains of cultural intelligibility, i.e., new possibilities for gender that contest the rigid codes of hierarchical binarisms, then it is only *within* the practices of repetitive signifying that a subversion of identity becomes possible. The injunction *to be* a given gender produces necessary failures, a variety of incoherent configurations that in their multiplicity exceed and defy the injunction by which they are generated. Further, the very injunction to be a given gender takes place through discursive routes: to be a good mother, to be a heterosexually desirable object, to be a fit worker, in sum, to signify a multiplicity of guarantees in response to a variety of different demands all at once. The coexistence or convergence of such discursive injunctions produces the possibility of a complex reconfiguration and redeployment; it is not a transcendental subject who enables action in the midst of such a convergence. There is no self that is prior to the convergence or who maintains "integrity" prior to its entrance into this conflicted cultural field. There is only a taking up of the tools where they lie, where the very "taking up" is enabled by the tool lying there.

What constitutes a subversive repetition within signifying practices of gender? I have argued ("I" deploy the grammar that governs the genre of the philosophical conclusion, but note that it is the grammar itself that deploys and enables this "I," even as the "I" that insists itself here repeats, redeploys, and—as the critics will determine—contests the philosophical grammar by which it is both enabled and restricted) that, for instance, within the sex/gender distinction, sex poses as "the real" and the "factic," the material or corporeal ground upon which gender operates as an act of cultural *inscription.* And yet gender is not written on the body as the torturing instrument of writing in Kafka's *In the Penal Colony* inscribes itself unintelligibly on the flesh of the accused. The question is not: what meaning does that inscription carry within it, but what cultural apparatus arranges this meeting between instrument and body, what interventions into this ritualistic repetition are possible? The "real" and the "sexually factic" are phantasmatic constructions —illusions of substance—that bodies are compelled to approximate, but never can. What, then, enables the exposure of the rift between the phantasmatic and the real whereby the real admits itself as phantasmatic? Does this offer the possibility for a repetition that is not fully constrained by the injunction to reconsolidate naturalized identities? Just as bodily surfaces are enacted *as* the natural, so these surfaces can become the site of a dissonant and denaturalized performance that reveals the performative status of the natural itself.

Practices of parody can serve to reengage and reconsolidate the very distinction between a privileged and naturalized gender configuration and one that appears as derived, phantasmatic, and mimetic—a failed copy, as it were. And surely parody has been used to further a politics of despair, one which affirms a seemingly inevitable exclusion of marginal genders from the territory of the natural and the real. And yet this failure to become "real" and to embody "the natural" is, I would argue, a constitutive failure of all gender enactments for the very reason that these ontological locales are fundamentally uninhabitable. Hence, there is a subversive laughter in the pastiche-effect of parodic practices in which the original, the authentic, and the real are themselves constituted as effects. The loss of gender norms would have the effect of proliferating gender configurations, destabilizing substantive identity, and depriving the naturalizing narratives of compulsory heterosexuality of their central protagonists: "man" and "woman." The parodic repetition of gender exposes as well the illusion of gender identity as an intractable depth and inner substance. As the effects of a subtle and politically enforced performativity, gender is an "act," as it were, that is open to splittings, self-parody, self-criticism, and those hyperbolic exhibitions of "the natural" that, in their very exaggeration, reveal its fundamentally phantasmatic status.

I have tried to suggest that the identity categories often presumed to be foundational to feminist politics, that is, deemed necessary in order to mobilize feminism as an identity politics, simultaneously work to limit and constrain in advance the very cultural possibilities that feminism is supposed to open up. The tacit constraints that produce culturally intelligible "sex" ought to be understood as generative political structures rather than naturalized foundations. Paradoxically, the reconceptualization of identity as an *effect*, that is, as *produced* or *generated*, opens up possibilities of "agency" that are insidiously foreclosed by positions that take identity categories as foundational and fixed. For an identity to be an effect means that it is neither fatally determined nor fully artificial and arbitrary. That the *constituted* status of identity is misconstrued along these two conflicting lines suggests the ways in which the feminist discourse on cultural construction remains trapped within the unnecessary binarism of free will and determinism. Construction is not opposed to agency; it is the necessary scene of agency, the very terms in which agency is articulated and becomes culturally intelligible. The critical task for feminism is not to establish a point of view outside of constructed identities; that conceit is the construction of an epistemological model that would disavow its own cultural location and, hence, promote itself as a global subject, a position that deploys precisely the imperialist strategies that feminism ought to criticize. The critical task is, rather, to locate strategies of subversive repetition enabled by those constructions, to affirm the local possibilities of intervention through participating in precisely those practices of repetition that constitute identity and, therefore, present the immanent possibility of contesting them.

This theoretical inquiry has attempted to locate the political in the very signifying practices that establish, regulate, and deregulate identity. This effort, however, can only be accomplished through the introduction of a set of questions that extend the very notion of the political. How to disrupt the foundations that cover over alternative cultural configurations of gender? How to destabilize and render in their phantasmatic dimension the "premises" of identity politics?

This task has required a critical genealogy of the naturalization of sex and of bodies in general. It has also demanded a reconsideration of the figure of the body as mute, prior to culture, awaiting signification, a figure that cross-checks with the figure of the feminine, awaiting the inscription-as-incision of the masculine signifier for entrance into language and culture. From a political analysis of compulsory heterosexuality, it has been necessary to question the construction of sex as binary, as a hierarchical binary. From the point of view of gender as enacted, questions have merged over the fixity of gender identity as an interior depth that is said to be externalized in various forms of "expression." The implicit construction of the primary heterosexual construction of desire is shown to persist even as it appears in the mode of primary bisexuality. Strategies of exclusion and hierarchy are also shown to persist in the formulation of the sex/gender distinction and its recourse to "sex" as the prediscursive as well as the priority of sexuality to culture and, in particular, the cultural construction of sexuality as the prediscursive. Finally, the epistemological paradigm that presumes the priority of the doer to the deed establishes a global and globalizing subject who disavows its own locality as well as the conditions for local intervention.

If taken as the grounds of feminist theory or politics, these "effects" of gender hierarchy and compulsory heterosexuality are not only misdescribed as foundations, but the signifying practices that enable this metaleptic misdescription remain outside the purview of a feminist critique of gender relations. To enter into the repetitive practices of this terrain of signification is not a choice, for the "I" that might enter is always already inside: there is no possibility of agency or reality outside of the discursive practices that give those terms the intelligibility that they have. The task is not whether to repeat, but how to repeat or, indeed, to repeat and, through a radical proliferation of gender, *to displace* the very gender norms that enable the repetition itself. There is no ontology of gender on which we might construct a politics, for gender ontologies always operate within established political contexts as normative injunctions, determining what qualifies as intelligible sex, invoking and consolidating the reproductive constraints on sexuality, setting the prescriptive requirements whereby sexed or gendered bodies come into cultural intelligibility. Ontology is, thus, not a foundation, but a normative injunction that operates insidiously by installing itself into political discourse as its necessary ground.

The deconstruction of identity is not the deconstruction of politics; rather, it establishes as political the very terms through which identity is articulated. This kind of critique brings into question the foundationalist frame in which feminism as an identity politics has been articulated. The internal paradox of this foundationalism is that it presumes, fixes, and constrains the very "subjects" that it hopes to represent and liberate. The task here is not to celebrate each and every new possibility *qua* possibility, but to redescribe those possibilities that *already* exist, but which exist within cultural domains designated as culturally unintelligible and impossible. If identities were no longer fixed as the premises of a political syllogism, and politics no longer understood as a set of practices derived from the alleged interests that belong to a set of ready-made subjects, a new configuration of politics would surely emerge from the ruins of the old. Cultural configurations of sex and gender might then proliferate or, rather, their present proliferation might then become articulable within the discourses that establish intelligible cultural life, confounding the very binarism of sex and exposing its fundamental unnaturalness. What other local strategies for engaging the "unnatural" might lead to the denaturalization of gender as such?

NOTES

1. Michel Foucault, "Nietzsche, Genealogy, History," in *Language, Counter-Memory, Practice: Selected Essays and Interviews by Michel Foucault,* trans. Donald F. Bouchard and Sherry Simon, ed. Donald F. Bouchard (Ithaca: Cornell University Press, 1977), p. 148. References in the text are to this essay.
2. Mary Douglas, *Purity and Danger* (London, Boston, and Henley: Routledge and Kegan Paul, 1969), p. 4.
3. Ibid., p. 113.
4. Simon Watney, *Policing Desire: AIDS, Pornography, and the Media* (Minneapolis: University of Minnesota Press, 1988).
5. Douglas, *Purity and Danger,* p. 115.
6. Ibid., p. 121.
7. Ibid., p. 140.
8. Foucault's essay "A Preface to Transgression" (in *Language, Counter-Memory, Practice*) does provide an interesting juxtaposition with Douglas' notion of body boundaries constituted by incest taboos. Originally written in honor of Georges Bataille, this essay explores in part the metaphorical "dirt" of transgressive pleasures and the association of the forbidden orifice with the dirt-covered tomb. See pp. 46–48.
9. Kristeva discusses Mary Douglas work in a short section of *The Powers of Horror: An Essay on Abjection,* trans. Leon Roudiez (New York: Columbia University Press, 1982), originally published as *Pouvoirs de l'horreur* (Paris: Éditions de Seuil, 1980). Assimilating Douglas' insights to her own reformulation of Lacan, Kristeva writes, "Defilement is what is jettisoned from the *symbolic system.* It is what escapes that social rationality, that logical order on which a social aggregate is based, which then becomes differentiated from a temporary agglomeration of individuals and, in short, constitutes a *classification system* or *a structure*" (p. 65).
10. Ibid., p. 3.
11. Iris Marion Young, "Abjection and Oppression: Unconscious Dynamics of Racism, Sexism, and Homophobia," paper presented at the Society of Phenomenology and Existential Philosophy Meetings, Northwestern University, 1988. The paper will be published in the proceedings of the 1988 meetings by the State University of New York Press. It is also included as part of a larger chapter in her *Justice and the Politics of Difference* (Princeton: Princeton University Press, 1990).
12. Parts of the following discussion were published in two different contexts, in my "Gender Trouble, Feminist Theory, and Psychoanalytic Discourse," in *Feminism/Postmodernism,* ed. Linda J. Nicholson (New York: Routledge, 1989) and "Performative Acts and Gender Constitution: An Essay in Phenomenology and Feminist Theory," *Theatre Journal,* Vol. 20, No. 3, Winter 1988.
13. Michel Foucault, *Discipline and Punish: the Birth of the Prison,* trans. Alan Sheridan (New York: Vintage, 1979), p. 29.
14. Ibid., p. 30.
15. See the chapter "Role Models" in Esther Newton, *Mother Camp: Female Impersonators in America* (Chicago: University of Chicago Press, 1972).
16. Ibid., p. 103.
17. Fredric Jameson, "Postmodernism and Consumer Society," in *The Anti-Aesthetic: Essays on Postmodern Culture,* ed. Hal Foster (Port Townsend, WA.: Bay Press, 1983), p. 114.
18. See Victor Turner, *Dramas, Fields and Metaphors* (Ithaca: Cornell University Press, 1974). See also Clifford Geertz, "Blurred Genres: The Refiguration of Thought," in *Local Knowledge, Further Essays in Interpretive Anthropology* (New York: Basic Books, 1983).

Part 2:
Theorizing Diversity—
Gender, Race, Class, and Sexual Orientation

Social Criticism without Philosophy: An Encounter between Feminism and Postmodernism

Fraser and Nicholson see feminism and postmodernism as contemporary intellectual currents with complementary strengths and weaknesses. After examining influential postmodern and feminist theories, they sketch a postmodern-feminist approach to social critique.

Fraser and Nicholson endorse postmodernism's critique of philosophical foundationalism and essentialism. Feminists should not rely on "grand narratives of legitimation," such as Marxism, and they should embrace a dynamic, nonreifying account of individual identity and social relations. However, Fraser and Nicholson are troubled by the constraints that Jean-François Lyotard's postmodernism places upon social theorizing. His view confines social critique to identifying and contesting oppressive local norms and practices, and it rules out large-scale normative theorizing. Thus, his postmodernism disallows critique of unjust macrostructures and repudiates broad categories like race, class, and gender. In contrast, Fraser and Nicholson maintain that feminists cannot assume that there are no systemic wrongs undergirding local injustices. Indeed, they hold that large-scale theorizing is necessary for feminism, but they are critical of much of the large-scale theorizing that feminists have done. In their view, Shulamith Firestone's biologist feminism, Nancy Chodorow's account of the reproduction of mothering, Ann Ferguson's theory of sex-affective production, Catharine MacKinnon's view of sexuality, and Carol Gilligan's theory of gender identity all incorporate essentialist elements. As a result, these "quasi-metanarratives" block solidarity among women from diverse social groups and block alliances with other progressive movements. Still, Fraser and Nicholson hold that postmodern feminism needs the scope of large historical narratives and the power of analyses of macrostructures. What is crucial is that these theories be genealogized, historically and culturally specific, comparativist, pragmatic, and fallibilistic.

—D.T.M.

Chapter 7

Nancy Fraser and Linda J. Nicholson

Social Criticism without Philosophy: An Encounter between Feminism and Postmodernism

Feminism and postmodernism have emerged as two of the most important political-cultural currents of the last decade. So far, however, they have kept an uneasy distance from one another. Indeed, so great has been their mutual wariness that there have been remarkably few extended discussions of the relations between them.[1]

Initial reticences aside, there are good reasons for exploring the relations between feminism and postmodernism. Both have offered deep and far-reaching criticisms of the institution of philosophy. Both have elaborated critical perspectives on the relation of philosophy to the larger culture. And, most central to the concerns of this essay, both have sought to develop new paradigms of social criticism which do not rely on traditional philosophical underpinnings. Other differences notwithstanding, one could say that during the last decade feminists and postmodernists have worked independently on a common nexus of problems: They have tried to rethink the relation between philosophy and social criticism so as to develop paradigms of criticism without philosophy.

On the other hand, the two tendencies have proceeded from opposite directions. Postmodernists have focused primarily on the philosophy outside of the problem. They have begun by elaborating antifoundational metaphilosophical perspectives and from there have drawn conclusions about the shape and character of social criticism. For feminists, on the other hand, the question of philosophy has always been subordinate to an interest in social criticism. Consequently, they have begun by developing critical political perspectives and from there have drawn conclusions about the status of philosophy. As a result of this difference in emphasis and direction, the two tendencies have ended up with complementary strengths and weaknesses. Postmodernists offer sophisticated and persuasive criticisms of foundationalism and essentialism, but their conceptions of social criticism tend to be anemic. Feminists offer robust conceptions of social criticism, but they tend at times to lapse into foundationalism and essentialism.

Thus, each of the two perspectives suggests some important criticisms of the other. A postmodernist reflection on feminist theory reveals disabling vestiges of essentialism, while a feminist reflection on postmodernism reveals androcentrism and political naivete.

It follows that an encounter between feminism and postmodernism will initially be a trading of criticisms. But there is no reason to suppose that this is where matters must end. In fact, each of these tendencies has much to learn from the other; each is in possession of valuable resources which can help remedy the deficiencies of the other. Thus, the ultimate stake of an encounter between feminism and postmodernism is the prospect of a perspective which integrates their respective strengths while eliminating their respective weaknesses. It is the prospect of a postmodernist feminism.

In what follows, we aim to contribute to the development of such a perspective by staging the initial, critical phase of the encounter. In the first section, we examine the ways in which one exemplary postmodernist, Jean-François Lyotard, has sought to derive new paradigms of social criticism from a critique of the institution of philosophy. We argue that the conception of social criticism so derived is too restricted to permit an adequate critical grasp of gender dominance and subordination. We identify some internal tensions in Lyotard's arguments, and we suggest some alternative formulations which could allow for more robust forms of criticism without sacrificing the commitment to antifoundationalism. In the second section, we examine some representative genres of feminist social criticism. We argue that in many cases feminist critics continue tacitly to rely on the sorts of philosophical underpinnings which their own commitments, like those of the postmodernists, ought in principle to rule out. We identify some points at which such underpinnings could be abandoned without any sacrifice of social-critical force. Finally, in a brief conclusion, we consider the prospects for a postmodernist feminism. We discuss some requirements which constrain the development of such a perspective, and we identify some pertinent conceptual resources and critical strategies.

POSTMODERNISM

Postmodernists seek, *inter alia*, to develop conceptions of social criticism which do not rely on traditional philosophical underpinnings. The typical starting point for their efforts is a reflection on the condition of philosophy today. Writers like Richard Rorty and Jean-François Lyotard begin by arguing that Philosophy with a capital *P* is no longer a viable or credible enterprise. They go on to claim that philosophy and, by extension, theory in general, can no longer function to *ground* politics and social criticism. With the demise of foundationalism comes the demise of the view that casts philosophy in the role of *founding* discourse vis-à-vis social criticism. That "modern" conception must give way to a new "postmodern" one in which criticism floats free of any universalist theoretical ground. No longer anchored philosophically, the very shape or character of social criticism changes; it becomes more pragmatic, *ad hoc*, contextual, and local. With this change comes a corresponding change in the social role and political function of intellectuals.

Thus, in the postmodern reflection on the relationship between philosophy and social criticism, the term "philosophy" undergoes an explicit devaluation; it is cut down to size, if not eliminated altogether. Yet, even as this devaluation is argued explicitly, the term "philosophy" retains an implicit structural privilege. It is the changed condition of philosophy which determines the changed character of social criticism and of engaged intellectual practice. In the new postmodern equation, then, philosophy is the independent variable while social criticisms and political practice are dependent variables. The view of theory which emerges is not determined by considering the needs of contemporary criticism and engagement. It is determined, rather, by considering the contemporary status of philosophy. This way of proceeding has important consequences, not all of which are positive. Among the results is a certain underestimation and premature foreclosing of possibilities for social criticism and engaged intellectual practice. This limitation of postmodern thought will be apparent when we consider its results in the light of the needs of contemporary feminist theory and practice.

Let us consider as an example the postmodernism of Jean-François Lyotard, since it is genuinely exemplary of the larger tendency. Lyotard is one of the few social thinkers widely considered postmodern who actually uses the term; indeed, it was he himself who introduced it into current discussions of philosophy, politics, society, and social theory. His book *The Postmodern Condition* has become the *locus classicus* for contemporary debates, and it reflects in an especially acute form the characteristic concerns and tensions of the movement.[2]

For Lyotard, postmodernism designates a general condition of contemporary Western civilization. The postmodern condition is one in which "grand narratives of legitimation" are no longer credible. By grand narratives he means overarching philosophies of history like the Enlightenment story of the gradual but steady progress of reason and freedom, Hegel's dialectic of Spirit coming to know itself, and, most importantly, Marx's drama of the forward march of human productive capacities via class conflict culminating in proletarian revolution. For Lyotard, these metanarratives instantiate a specifically modern approach to the problem of legitimation. Each situates first-order discursive practices of inquiry and politics within a broader totalizing metadiscourse which legitimates them. The metadiscourse narrates a story about the whole of human history, which purports to guarantee that the pragmatics of the modern science and of modern political processes—the norms and rules which govern these practices, determining what counts as a warranted move within them—are themselves legitimate. The story guarantees that some sciences and some politics have the *right* pragmatics and, so, are the *right* practices.

We should not be misled by Lyotard's focus on narrative philosophies of history. In his conception of legitimating metanarrative, the stress properly belongs on the *meta* and not on the *narrative.* For what most interests him about the Enlightenment, Hegelian, and Marxist stories is what they share with other nonnarrative forms of philosophy. Like ahistorical epistemologies and moral theories, they aim to show that specific first-order discursive practices are well formed and capable of yielding true and just results. *True* and *just* here mean something more than results reached by adhering scrupulously to the constitutive rules of some given scientific and political games. They mean, rather, results which correspond to Truth and Justice as they really are in themselves independent of contingent, historical social practices. Thus, in Lyotard's view, a metanarrative is *meta* in a very strong sense. It purports to be a privileged discourse capable of situating, characterizing, and evaluating all other discourses but not itself to be infected by the historicity and contingency which render first-order discourses potentially distorted and in need of legitimation.

In *The Postmodern Condition*, Lyotard argues that metanarratives, whether philosophies of history or nonnarrative foundational philosophies, are merely modern and dépassé. We can no longer believe, he claims, in the availability of a privileged metadiscourse capable of capturing once and for all the truth of every first-order discourse. The claim to *meta* status does not stand up. A so-called metadiscourse is in fact simply one more discourse among others. It follows for Lyotard that legitimation, both epistemic and political, can no longer reside in philosophical metanarratives. Where, then, he asks, does legitimation reside in the postmodern era?

Much of *The Postmodern Condition* is devoted to sketching an answer to that question. The answer, in brief, is that in the postmodern era legitimation becomes plural, local, an immanent. In this era, there will necessarily be many discourses of legitimation dispersed among the plurality of first-order discursive practices. For example, scientists no longer look to prescriptive philosophies of science to warrant their procedures of inquiry. Rather, they themselves problematize, modify, and warrant the constitutive norms of their own practice even as they engage in it. Instead of hovering above, legitimation descends to the level of practice and becomes immanent in it. There are no special tribunals set apart from the sites where inquiry is practiced. Rather, practitioners assume responsibility for legitimizing their own practice.

Lyotard intimates that something similar is or should be happening with respect to political legitimation. We cannot have and do not need a single, overarching theory of justice. What is required, rather, is a "justice of multiplicities."[3] What Lyotard means by this is not wholly clear. On one level, he can be read as offering a normative vision in which the good society consists in a decentralized plurality of democratic, self-managing groups and institutions whose members problematize the norms of their practice and take responsibility for modifying them as situations require. But paradoxically, on another level, he can be read as ruling out the sort of larger-scale, normative political theorizing which, from a modern perspective at least, would be required to legitimate such a vision. In any case, his justice of multiplicities conception precludes one familiar, and arguably essential, genre of political theory: identification and critique of macrostructures of inequality and injustice which cut across the boundaries separating relatively discrete practices and institutions. There is no place in Lyotard's universe for critique of pervasive axes of stratification, for critique of broad-based relations of dominance and subordination along lines like gender, race, and class.

Lyotard's suspicion of the large extends to historical narrative and social theory as well. Here, his chief target is Marxism, the one metanarrative in France with enough lingering credibility to be worth arguing against. The problem with Marxism, in his view, is twofold. On the one hand, the Marxian story is too big, since it spans virtually the whole of human history. On the other hand, the Marxian story is too theoretical, since it relies on a *theory* of social practice and social relations which claims to *explain* historical change. At one level, Lyotard simply rejects the specifics of this theory. He claims that the Marxian conception of practice as production occludes the diversity and plurality of human practices; and that the Marxian conception of capitalist society as a totality traversed by one major division and contradiction occludes the diversity and plurality of contemporary societal differences and oppositions. But Lyotard does not conclude that such deficiencies can and should be remedied by a better social theory. Rather, he rejects the project of social theory *tout court*.

Once again, Lyotard's position is ambiguous, since his rejection of social theory depends on a theoretical perspective of sorts of its own. He offers a postmodern conception of sociality and social identity, a conception of what he calls "the social bond." What holds a society together, he claims, is not a common consciousness or institutional substructure. Rather, the social bond is a weave of crisscrossing threads of discursive practices, no single one of which runs continuously throughout the whole. Individuals are the nodes or posts where such practices intersect, and so they participate in many practices simultaneously. It follows that social identities are complex and heterogeneous. They cannot be mapped onto one another nor onto the social totality. Indeed, strictly speaking, there is no social totality and *a fortiori* no possibility of a totalizing social theory.

Thus, Lyotard insists that the field of the social is heterogeneous and nontotalizable. As a result, he rules out the sort of critical social theory which employs general categories like gender, race, and class. From his perspective, such categories are too reductive of the complexity of social identities to be useful. There is apparently nothing to be gained, in his view, by situating an account of the fluidity and diversity of discursive practices in the context of a critical analysis of large-scale institutions and social structures.

Thus, Lyotard's postmodern conception of criticism without philosophy rules out several recognizable genres of social criticism. From the premise that criticism cannot be grounded by a foundationalist philosophical metanarrative, he infers the illegitimacy of large historical stories, normative theories of justice, and social-theoretical accounts of macrostructures which institutionalize inequality. What, then, *does* postmodern social criticism look like?

Lyotard tries to fashion some new genres of social criticism from the discursive resources that remain. Chief among these is smallish, localized narrative. He seeks to vindicate such narrative against both modern totalizing metanarrative and the scientism that is hostile to all narrative. One genre of postmodern social criticism, then, consists in relatively discrete, local stories about the emergence, transformation, and disappearance of various discursive practices treated in isolation from one another. Such stories might resemble those told by Michel Foucault, although without the attempts to discern larger synchronic patterns and connections that Foucault sometimes made.[4] Like Michael Walzer, Lyotard evidently assumes that practitioners would narrate such stories when seeking to persuade one another to modify the pragmatics or constitutive norms of their practice.[5]

This genre of social criticism is not the whole postmodern story, however. For it casts critique as strictly local, *ad hoc*, and ameliorative, thus supposing a political diagnosis according to which there are no large-scale, systemic problems which resist local, *ad hoc*, ameliorative initiatives. Yet, Lyotard recognizes that postmodern society does contain at least one unfavorable structural tendency which requires a more coordinated response. This is the tendency to universalize instrumental reason, to subject *all* discursive practices indiscriminately to the single criterion of efficiency, or "performativity." In Lyotard's view, this threatens the autonomy and integrity of science and politics, since these practices are not properly subordinated to performative standards. It would pervert and distort them, thereby destroying the diversity of discursive forms.

Thus, even as he argues explicitly against it, Lyotard posits the need for a genre of social criticism which transcends local mininarrative. Despite his strictures against large, totalizing stories, he narrates a fairly tall tale about a large-scale social trend. Moreover, the logic of this story, and of the genre of criticism to which it belongs, calls for judgments which are not strictly practice-immanent. Lyotard's story presupposes the legitimacy and integrity of the scientific and political practices allegedly threatened by performativity. It supposes that one can distinguish changes or developments which are *internal* to these practices from externally induced distortions. But this drives Lyotard to make normative judgments about the value and character of the threatened practices. These judgments are not strictly immanent in the practices judged. Rather, they are metapractical.

Thus, Lyotard's view of postmodern social criticism is neither entirely self-consistent nor entirely persuasive. He goes too quickly from the premise that Philosophy cannot ground social criticism to the conclusion that criticism itself must be local, *ad hoc*, and nontheoretical. As a result, he throws out the baby of large historical narrative with the bathwater of philosophical metanarrative and the baby of social-theoretical analysis of large-scale inequalities with the bathwater of reductive Marxian class theory. Moreover, these allegedly illegitimate babies do not in fact remain excluded. They return like the repressed within the very genres of postmodern social criticism with which Lyotard intends to replace them.

We began this discussion by noting that postmodernists orient their reflections on the character of postmodern social criticism by the falling star of foundationalist philosophy. They posit that, with Philosophy no longer able credibly to ground social criticism, criticism itself must be local, *ad hoc*, and untheoretical. Thus, from the critique of foundationalism, they infer the illegitimacy of several genres of social criticism. For Lyotard, the illegitimate genres include large-scale historical narrative and social-theoretical analyses of pervasive relations of dominance and subordination.[6]

Suppose, however, one were to choose another starting point for reflecting on postfoundational social criticism. Suppose one began, not with the condition of Philosophy, but with the nature of the social object one wished to criticize. Suppose, further, that one defined that object as the subordination of women to and by men. Then, we submit, it would be apparent that many of the genres rejected by postmodernists are necessary for social criticism. For a phenomenon as pervasive and multifaceted as male dominance simply cannot be adequately grasped with the meager critical resources to which they would limit us. On the contrary, effective criticism of this phenomenon requires an array of different methods and genres. It requires at minimum large narratives about changes in social organization and ideology, empirical and social-theoretical analyses of macrostructures and institutions, interactionist analyses of the micropolitics of everyday life, critical-hermeneutical and institutional analyses of cultural production, historically and culturally specific sociologies of gender, and so on. The list could go on.

Clearly, not all of these approaches are local and untheoretical. But all are nonetheless essential to feminist social criticism. Moreover, all can in principle be conceived in ways that do not take us back to foundationalism, even though, as we argue in the next section, many feminists have not wholly succeeded in avoiding that trap.

FEMINISM

Feminists, like postmodernists, have sought to develop new paradigms of social criticism which do not rely on traditional philosophical underpinnings. They have criticized modern foundationalist epistemologies and moral and political theories, exposing the contingent, partial, and historically situated character of what has passed in the mainstream for necessary, universal, and ahistorical truths. They have called into question the dominant philosophical project of seeking objectivity in the guides of a "God's eye view" which transcends any situation or perspective.[7]

However, if postmodernists have been drawn to such views by a concern with the status of philosophy, feminists have been led to them by the demands of political practice. This practical interest has saved feminist theory from many of the mistakes of postmodernism: Women whose theorizing was to serve the struggle against sexism were not about to abandon powerful political tools merely as a result of intramural debates in professional philosophy.

Yet, even as the imperatives of political practice have saved feminist theory from one set of difficulties, they have tended at times to incline it toward another. Practical imperatives have led some feminists to adopt modes of theorizing which resemble the sorts of philosophical metanarrative rightly criticized by postmodernists. To be sure, the feminist theories we have in mind here are not pure metanarratives; they are not ahistorical normative theories about the transcultural nature of rationality or justice. Rather, they are very large social theories—theories of history, society, culture, and psychology—which claim, for example, to identify causes and constitutive features of sexism that operate cross-culturally. Thus, these social theories purport to be empirical rather than philosophical. But, as we open to show, they are actually quasi-metanarratives. They tacitly presuppose some commonly held but unwarranted and essentialist assumptions about the nature of human beings and the conditions for social life. In addition, they assume methods and concepts which are uninflected by temporality or historicity and which therefore function *de facto* as permanent, neutral matrices for inquiry. Such theories then, share some of the essentialist and ahistorical features of metanarratives: They are insufficiently attentive to historical and cultural diversity, and they falsely universalize features of the theorist's own era, society, culture, class, sexual orientation, and ethnic or racial group.

On the other hand, the practical exigencies inclining feminists to produce quasi-metanarratives have by no means held undisputed sway. Rather, they have had to coexist, often uneasily, with counterexigencies which have worked to opposite effect, for example, political pressures to acknowledge differences among women. In general, then, the recent history of feminist social theory reflects a tug of war between forces which have encouraged and forces which have discouraged metanarrative-like modes of theorizing. We can illustrate this dynamic by looking at a few important turning points in this history.

When in the 1960s, women in the New Left began to extend prior talk about women's rights into the more encompassing discussion of women's liberation, they encountered the fear and hostility of their male comrades and the use of Marxist political theory as a support for these reactions. Many men of the New Left argued that gender issues were secondary because they were subsumable under more basic modes of oppression, namely, class and race.

In response to this practical-political problem, radical feminists such as Shulamith Firestone resorted to an ingenious tactical maneuver: Firestone invoked biological differences between women and men to explain sexism. This enabled her to turn the tables on her Marxist comrades by claiming that gender conflict was the most basic form of human conflict and the source of all other forms, including class conflict.[8] Firestone drew on the pervasive tendency within modern culture to locate the roots of gender differences in biology. Her coup was to use biologism to establish the primacy of the struggle against male domination rather than to justify acquiescence to it.

The trick, of course, is problematic from a postmodernist perspective in that appeals to biology to explain social phenomena are essentialist and monocausal. They are essentialist insofar as they project onto all women and men qualities which develop under historically specific social conditions. They are monocausal insofar as they look to one set of characteristics, such as women's physiology or men's hormones, to explain women's oppression in all cultures. These problems are only compounded when appeals to biology are used in conjunction with the dubious claim that women's oppression is the cause of all other forms of oppression.

Moreover, as Marxists and feminist anthropologists began insisting in the early 1970s, appeals to biology do not allow us to understand the enormous diversity of forms which both gender and sexism assume in different cultures. In fact, it was not long before most feminist social theorists came to appreciate that accounting of the diversity of the forms of sexism was as important as accounting for its depth and autonomy. Gayle Rubin aptly described this dual requirement as the need to formulate theory that could account for the oppression of women in its "endless variety and monotonous similarity."[9] How were feminists to develop a social theory adequate to both demands?

One approach that seemed promising was suggested by Michelle Zimbalist Rosaldo and other contributors in the influential 1974 anthropology collection, *Women, Culture, and Society*. They argued that common to all known societies was some type of separation between a domestic sphere and a public sphere, the former associated with women and the latter with men. Because in most societies to date, women have spent a good part of their lives bearing and raising children, their lives have been more bound to the domestic sphere. Men, on the other hand, have had both the time and mobility to engage in those out of the home activities which generate political structures. Thus, as Rosaldo argued, while in many societies women possess some or even a great deal of power, women's power is always viewed as illegitimate, disruptive, and without authority.[10]

This approach seemed to allow for both diversity and ubiquity in the manifestations of sexism. A very general identification of women with the domestic and of men with the extradomestic could accommodate a great deal of cultural variation both in social structures and in gender roles. At the same time, it could make comprehensible the apparent ubiquity of the assumption of women's inferiority above and beyond such variation. This hypothesis was also compatible with the idea that the extent of women's oppression differed in different societies. It could explain such differences by correlating the extent of gender inequality in a society with the extent and rigidity of the separation between its domestic and public spheres. In short, the domestic/public theorists seemed to have generated an explanation capable of satisfying a variety of conflicting demands.

However, this explanation turned out to be problematic in ways reminiscent of Firestone's account. Although the theory focused on differences between men's and women's spheres of activity rather than on differences between men's and women's biology, it was essentialist and monocausal nonetheless. It posited the existence of a domestic sphere in all societies and thereby assumed that women's activities were basically similar in content and significance across cultures. (An analogous assumption about men's activities lay behind the postulation of a universal public sphere.) In effect, the theory falsely generalized to all societies an historically specific conjunction of properties: women's responsibility for early child rearing, women's tendency to spend more time in the geographical space of the home, women's lesser participation in the affairs of the community, a cultural ascription of triviality to domestic work, and a cultural ascription of inferiority to women. The theory thus failed to appreciate that, while each individual property may be true of many societies, the conjunction is not true of most.[11]

One source of difficulty in these early feminist social theories was the presumption of an overly grandiose and totalizing conception of theory. Theory was understood as the search for the one key factor which would explain sexism cross-culturally and illuminate all of social life. In this sense, to theorize was by definition to produce a quasi-metanarrative.

Since the late 1970s, feminist social theorists have largely ceased speaking of biological determinants or a cross-cultural domestic/public separation. Many, moreover, have given up the assumption of monocausality. Nevertheless, some feminist social theorists have continued implicitly to suppose a quasi-metanarrative conception of theory. They have continued to theorize in terms of a putatively unitary, primary, culturally universal type of activity associated with women, generally an activity conceived as domestic and located in the family.

One influential example is the analysis of mothering developed by Nancy Chodorow. Setting herself to explain the internal, psychological dynamics which have led many women willingly to reproduce social divisions associated with female inferiority, Chodorow posited a cross-cultural activity, mothering, as the relevant object of investigation. Her question thus became: How is mothering as a female-associated activity reproduced over time? How does mothering produce a new generation of men not so inclined? The answer she offered was in terms of gender identity: Female mothering produces women whose deep sense of self is relational and men whose deep sense of self is not.[12]

Chodorow's theory has struck many feminists as a persuasive account of some apparently observable psychic differences between men and women. Yet, the theory has clear metanarrative overtones. It posits the existence of a single activity, mothering, which, while differing in specifics in different societies, nevertheless constitutes enough of a natural kind to warrant one label. It stipulates that this basically unitary activity gives rise to two distinct sorts of deep selves, one relatively common across cultures to women, the other relatively common across cultures to men. It claims that the difference thus generated between feminine and masculine gender identity causes a variety of supposedly cross-cultural social phenomena, including the continuation of female mothering, male contempt for women, and problems in heterosexual relationships.

From a postmodern perspective, all of these assumptions are problematic because they are essentialist. But the second one, concerning gender identity, warrants special scrutiny, given its political implications. Consider that Chodorow's use of the notion of gender identity presupposes three major premises. One is the psychoanalytic premise that everyone has a deep sense of self which is constituted in early childhood through one's interactions with one's primary parent and which remains relatively constant thereafter. Another is the premise that this deep self differs significantly for men and for women but is roughly similar among women, on the one hand, and among men, on the other hand, both across cultures and within cultures across lines of class, race, and ethnicity. The third premise is that this deep self colors everything one does; there are no actions, however trivial, which do not bear traces of one's masculine or feminine gender identity.

One can appreciate the political exigencies which made this conjunction of premises attractive. It gave scholarly substance to the idea of the pervasiveness of sexism. If masculinity and femininity constitute our basic and ever present sense of self, then it is not surprising that the manifestations of sexism are systemic. Moreover, many feminists had already sensed that the concept of sex-role socialization, an ideal Chodorow explicitly criticized, ignored the depth and intractability of male dominance. By implying that measures such as changing images in school textbooks or allowing boys to play with dolls would be sufficient to bring about equality between the sexes, this concept seemed to trivialize and co-opt the message of feminism. Finally, Chodorow's depth-psychological approach gave a scholarly sanction to the idea of sisterhood. It seemed to legitimate the claim that the ties that bind women are deep and substantively based.

Needless to say, we have no wish to quarrel with the claim of the depth and pervasiveness of sexism nor with the idea of sisterhood. But we do wish to challenge Chodorow's way of legitimating them. The idea of a cross-cultural, deep sense of self, specified differently for women and men, becomes problematic when given any specific content. Chodorow states that women everywhere differ from men in their greater concern with "relational interaction." But what does she mean by this term? Certainly not any and every kind of human interaction, since men have often been more concerned than women with some kinds of interactions—for example, those which have to do with the aggrandizement of power and wealth. Of course, it is true that may women in modern Western societies have been expected to exhibit strong concern with those types of interactions associated with intimacy, friendship, and love, interactions which dominate one meaning of the late twentieth-century concept of relationship. But surely this meaning presupposes a notion of private life specific to modern Western societies of the last two centuries. Is it possible that Chodorow's theory rests on an equivocation on the term *relationship*?[13]

Equally troubling are the aporias this theory generates for political practice. While gender identity gives substance to the idea of sisterhood, it does so at the cost of repressing differences among sisters. Although the theory allows for some differences among women of different classes, races, sexual orientations, and ethnic groups, it construes these as subsidiary to more basic similarities. But it is precisely as a consequence of the request to understand such differences as secondary that many women have denied an allegiance to feminism.

We have dwelt at length on Chodorow because of the great influence her work has enjoyed. But she is not the only recent feminist social theorist who has constructed a quasi-metanarrative around a putatively cross-cultural female-associated activity. On the contrary, theorists like Ann Ferguson and Nancy Folbre, Nancy Hartsock, and Catharine MacKinnon have built similar theories around notions of sex-affective production, reproduction, and sexuality, respectively.[14] Each claims to have identified a basic kind of human practice found in all societies which has cross-cultural explanatory power. In each case, the practice in question is associated with a biological or quasi-biological need and is construed as functionally necessary to the reproduction of society. It is not the sort of thing, then, whose historical origins need be investigated.

The difficulty here is that categories like sexuality, mothering, reproduction, and sex-affective production group together phenomena which are not necessarily conjoined in all societies while separating off from one another phenomena which are not necessarily separated. As a matter of fact, it is doubtful whether these categories have any determinate cross-cultural content. Thus, for a theorist to use such categories to construct a universalistic social theory is to risk projecting the socially dominant conjunctions and dispersions of her own society onto others, thereby distorting important features of both. Social theorists would do better first to construct genealogies of the *categories* of sexuality, reproduction, and mothering before assuming their universal significance.

Since around 1980, many feminist scholars have come to abandon the project of grand social theory. They have stopped looking for *the* causes of sexism and have turned to more concrete inquiry with more limited aims. One reason for this shift is the growing legitimacy of feminist scholarship. The institutionalization of women's studies in the United States has meant a dramatic increase in the size of the community of feminist inquirers, a much greater division of scholarly labor, and a large and growing fund of concrete information. As a result, feminist scholars have come to regard their enterprise more collectively, more like a puzzle whose various pieces are being filled in by many different people than like a construction to be completed by a single grand theoretical stroke. In short, feminist scholarship has attained its maturity.

Even in this phase, however, traces of youthful quasi-metanarratives remain. Some theorists who have ceased looking for *the* causes of sexism still rely on essentialist categories such as gender identity. This is especially true of those scholars who have sought to develop gynocentric alternatives to mainstream androcentric perspectives but who have not fully abandoned the universalist pretensions of the latter.

Consider, as an example, the work of Carol Gilligan. Unlike most of the theorists we have considered so far, Gilligan has not sought to explain the origins or nature of cross-cultural sexism. Rather, she set herself the more limited task of exposing and redressing androcentric bias in the model of moral development of psychologist Lawrence Kohlberg. Thus, she argued that it is illegitimate to evaluate the moral development of women and girls by reference to a standard drawn exclusively from the experience of men and boys. She proposed to examine women's moral discourse on its own terms in order to uncover its immanent standards of adequacy.[15]

Gilligan's work has been rightly regarded as important and innovative. It challenged mainstream psychology's persistent occlusion of women's lives and experiences and its insistent but false claims to universality. Yet, insofar as Gilligan's challenge involved the construction of an alternative feminine model of moral development, her position was ambiguous. On the one hand, by providing a counterexample to Kohlberg's model, she cast doubt on the possibility of any single, universalist development schema. On the other hand, by constructing a female countermodel, she invited the same charge of false generalization she had herself raised against Kohlberg, although now from other perspectives such as class, sexual orientation, race, and ethnicity. Gilligan's disclaimers notwithstanding,[16] to the extent that she described women's moral development in terms of *a* different voice; to the extent that she did not specify which women, under which specific historical circumstances have spoken with the voice in question; and to the extent that she grounded her analysis in the explicitly cross-cultural framework of Nancy Chodorow, her model remained essentialist. It perpetuated in a newer, more localized fashion traces of previous more grandiose quasi-metanarratives.

Thus, vestiges of essentialism have continued to plague feminist scholarship, even despite the decline of grand theorizing. In many cases, including Gilligan's, this represents the continuing subterranean influence of those very mainstream modes of thought and inquiry with which feminists have wished to break.

On the other hand, the practice of feminist politics in the 1980s has generated a new set of pressures which have worked against metanarratives. In recent years, poor and working-class women, women of color, and lesbians have finally won a wider hearing for their objections to feminist theories which fail to illuminate their lives and address their problems. They have exposed the earlier quasi-metanarratives, with their assumptions of universal female dependence and confinement to the domestic sphere, as false extrapolations from the experience of the white, middle-class, heterosexual women who dominated the beginnings of the second wave. For example, writers like bell hooks, Gloria Joseph, Audre Lord, María Lugones, and Elizabeth Spelman have unmasked the implicit reference to white Anglo women in many classic feminist texts. Likewise, Adrienne Rich and Marilyn Frye have exposed the heterosexist bias of much mainstream feminist theory.[17] Thus, as the class, sexual, racial, and ethnic awareness of the movement has altered, so has the preferred conception of theory. It has become clear that quasi-metanarratives hamper rather than promote sisterhood, since they elide differences among women and among the forms of sexism to which different women are differentially subject. Likewise, it is increasingly apparent that such theories hinder alliances with other professive movements, since they tend to occlude axes of domination other than gender. In sum, there is growing interest among feminists in modes of theorizing which are attentive to differences and to cultural and historical specificity.

In general, then, feminist scholarship of the 1980s evinces some conflicting tendencies. On the one hand, there is decreasing interest in grand social theories as scholarship has become more localized, issue-oriented, and explicitly fallibilistic. On the other, essentialist vestiges persist in the continued use of ahistorical categories like gender identity without reflection as to how, when, and why such categories originated and were modified over time. This tension is symptomatically expressed in the current fascination, on the part of U.S. feminists, with French psychoanalytic feminisms: the latter propositionally decry essentialism even as they performatively enact it.[18] More generally, feminist scholarship has remained insufficiently attentive to the *theoretical* prerequisites of dealing with diversity, despite widespread commitment to accepting it politically.

By criticizing lingering essentialisms in contemporary feminist theory, we hope to encourage such theory to become more consistently postmodern. This is not, however, to recommend merely any form of postmodernism. On the contrary, as we have shown, the version developed by Jean-François Lyotard offers a weak and inadequate conception of social criticism without philosophy. It rules out genres of criticism, such as large historical narrative and historically situated social theory, which feminists rightly regard as indispensable. But it does not follow from Lyotard's shortcomings that criticism without philosophy is in principle incompatible with criticism with social force. Rather, as we argue next, a robust postmodern-feminist paradigm of social criticism without philosophy is possible.

TOWARD A POSTMODERN FEMINISM

How can we combine a postmodernist incredulity toward metanarratives with the social-critical power of feminism? How can we conceive a version of criticism without philosophy which is robust enough to handle the tough job of analyzing sexism in all its endless variety and monotonous similarity?

A first step is to recognize, *contra* Lyotard, that postmodern critique need forswear neither large historical narratives nor analyses of societal macrostructures. This point is important for feminists, since sexism has a long history and is deeply and pervasively embedded in contemporary societies. Thus, postmodern feminists need not abandon the large theoretical tools needed to address large political problems. There is nothing self-contradictory in the idea of a postmodern theory.

However, if postmodern-feminist critique must remain theoretical, not just any kind of theory will do. Rather, theory here would be explicitly historical, attuned to the cultural specificity of different societies and periods and to that of different groups within societies and periods. Thus, the categories of postmodern-feminist theory would be inflected by temporality, with historically specific institutional categories like the modern, restricted, male-headed, nuclear family taking precedence over ahistorical, functionalist categories like reproduction and mothering. Where categories of the latter sort were not eschewed altogether, they would be genealogized, that is, framed by a historical narrative and rendered temporally and culturally specific.

Moreover, postmodern-feminist theory would be nonuniversalist. When its focus became cross-cultural or transepochal, its mode of attention would be comparativist rather than universalizing, attuned to changes and contrasts instead of to covering laws. Finally, postmodern-feminist theory would dispense with the idea of a subject of history. It would replace unitary notions of woman and feminine gender identity with plural and complexly constructed conceptions of social identity, treating gender as one relevant strand among others, attending also to class, race, ethnicity, age, and sexual orientation.

In general, postmodern-feminist theory would be pragmatic and fallibilistic. It would tailor its methods and categories to the specific task at hand, using multiple categories when appropriate and forswearing the metaphysical comfort of a single feminist method or feminist epistemology. In short, this theory would look more like a tapestry composed of threads of many different hues than one woven in a single color.

The most important advantage of this sort of theory would be its usefulness for contemporary feminist political practice. Such practice is increasingly a matter of alliances rather than one of unity around a universally shared interest or identity. It recognizes that the diversity of women's needs and experiences means that no single solution, on issues like child care, social security, and housing, can be adequate for all. Thus, the underlying premise of this practice is that, while some women share some common interests and face some common enemies, such commonalities are by no means universal; rather, they are interlaced with differences, even with conflicts. This, then, is a practice made up of a patchwork of overlapping alliances, not one circumscribable by an essential definition. One might best speak of it in the plural as the practice of feminisms. In a sense, this practice is in advance of much contemporary feminist theory. It is already implicitly postmodern. It would find its most appropriate and useful theoretical expression in a postmodern-feminist form of critical inquiry. Such inquiry would be the theoretical counterpart of a broader, richer, more complex, and multilayered feminist solidarity, the sort of solidarity which is essential for overcoming the oppression of women in its "endless variety and monotonous similarity."

NOTES

We are grateful for the helpful suggestions of many people, especially Jonathan Arac, Ann Ferguson, Marilyn Frye, Nancy Hartsock, Alison Jaggar, Berel Lang, Thomas McCarthy, Karsten Struhl, Iris Young, Thomas Wartenburg, and the members of SOFPHIA. We are also grateful for word-processing help from Marina Rosiene.

1. Exceptions are Jane Flax, "Gender as a Social Problem: In and For Feminist Theory," *American Studies/Amerika Studien*, June 1986 (an earlier version of the paper in this book); Sandra Harding, *The Science Question in Feminism* (Ithaca, NY: Cornell University Press, 1986) and "The Instability of the Analytical Categories of Feminist Theory," *Signs: Journal of Women in Culture and*

Society, Vol. 11, No. 4, 1986, pp. 645–64; Donna Haraway, "A Manifesto for Cyborgs; Science, Technology, and Socialist Feminism in the 1980s," *Socialist Review*, No. 80, 1983, pp. 65–107; Alice A. Jardine, *Gynesis: Configurations of Women and Modernity* (Ithaca, NY: Cornell University Press, 1985); Jean-François Lyotard, "Some of the Things at Stake in Women's Struggles," trans. Deborah J. Clarke, Winifred Woodhull, and John Mowitt, *Sub-Stance*, No. 20, 1978; Craig Owens, "The Discourse of Others: Feminists and Postmodernism," *The Anti-Aesthetic: Essays on Postmodern Culture*, ed. Hal Foster (Port Townsend, WA: Bay Press, 1983).

2. Jean-François Lyotard, *The Postmodern Condition: A Report on Knowledge*, trans. G. Bennington and B. Massumi (Minneapolis: University of Minnesota Press, 1984).
3. Ibid. Cf. Jean-François Lyotard and Jean-Loup Thebaud, *Just Gaming* (Minneapolis: University of Minnesota Press, 1987); also Jean-François Lyotard, "The Differend," *Diacritics*, Fall 1984, trans. George Van Den Abbeele, pp. 4–14.
4. See, for example, Michel Foucault, *Discipline and Punish: The Birth of the Prison*, trans. Alan Sheridan (New York: Vintage Books, 1979).
5. Michael Walzer, *Spheres of Justice: A Defense of Pluralism and Equality* (New York: Basic Books, 1983).
6. It should be noted that, for Lyotard, the choice of philosophy as a starting point is itself determined by a metapolitical commitment, namely, to antitotalitarianism. He assumes erroneously, in our view, that totalizing social and political theory necessarily eventuates in totalitarian societies. Thus, the "practical intent" that subtends Lyotard's privileging of philosophy (and which is in turn attenuated by the latter) is anti-Marxism. Whether it should also be characterized as neoliberalism is a question too complicated to be explored here.
7. See, for example, the essays in *Discovering Reality: Feminist Perspectives on Epistemology, Metaphysics, Methodology, and Philosophy of Science*, ed. Sandra Harding and Merrill B. Hintikka (Dordrecht, Holland: D. Reidel, 1983).
8. Shulamith Firestone, *The Dialectic of Sex* (New York: Bantam, 1970).
9. Gayle Rubin, "The Traffic in Women," in *Toward an Anthropology of Women*, ed. Rayna R. Reiter, (New York: Monthly Review Press, 1975), p. 160.
10. Michelle Zimbalist Rosaldo, "Woman, Culture, and Society: A Theoretical Overview," *Woman, Culture, and Society*, ed. Michelle Zimbalist Rosaldo and Louise Lamphere (Stanford: Stanford University Press, 1974), pp. 17–42.
11. These and related problems were soon apparent to many of the domestic/public theorists themselves. See Rosaldo's self-criticism, "The Use and Abuse of Anthropology: Reflections on Feminism and Cross-cultural Understanding," *Signs: Journal of Women in Culture and Society*, Vol. 5, No. 3, 1980, pp. 389–417. A more recent discussion, which points out the circularity of the theory, appears in Sylvia J. Yanagisako and Jane F. Collier, "Toward a Unified Analysis of Gender and Kinship," in *Gender and Kinship: Essays Toward a Unified Analysis*, ed. Jane Fishburne Collier and Sylvia Junko Yanagisako (Stanford: Stanford University Press, 1987).
12. Nancy Chodorow, *The Reproduction of Mothering: Psychoanalysis and the Sociology of Gender* (Berkeley: University of California Press, 1978).
13. A similar ambiguity attends Chodorow's discussion of the family. In response to critics who object that her psychoanalytic emphasis ignores social structures, Chodorow has rightly insisted that the family is itself a social structure, one frequently slighted in social explanations. Yet, she generally does not discuss families as historically specific social institutions whose specific relations with other institutions can be analyzed. Rather, she tends to invoke the family in a very abstract and general sense defined only as the locus of female mothering.

14. Ann Ferguson and Nancy Folbre, "The Unhappy Marriage of Patriarchy and Capitalism," in *Women and Revolution*, ed. Lydia Sargent (Boston: South End Press, 1981), pp. 313–38; Nancy Hartsock, *Money, Sex, and Power: Toward a Feminist Historical Materialism* (New York: Longman, 1983); Catharine A. MacKinnon, "Feminism, Marxism, Method, and the State: An Agenda for Theory," reprinted here, Ch. 4.
15. Carol Gilligan, *In a Different Voice: Psychological Theory and Women's Development* (Cambridge, MA: Harvard University Press, 1983).
16. Cf. Ibid., p. 2.
17. Marilyn Frye, *The Politics of Reality: Essays in Feminist Theory* (Trumansburg, NY: The Crossing Press, 1983); bell hooks, *Feminist Theory: From Margin to Center* (Boston: South End Press, 1984); Gloria Joseph, "The Incompatible Menage à Trois: Marxism, Feminism and Racism," in *Women and Revolution*, ed. Lydia Sargent (Boston: South End Press, 1981), pp. 91–107; Audre Lord, "An Open Letter to Mary Daly," in *This Bridge Called My Back: Writings by Radical Women of Color*, ed. Cherríe Moraga and Gloria Anzaldúa (Watertown, MA: Persephone Press, 1981), pp. 94–97; María C. Lugones and Elizabeth V. Spelman, "Have We Got a Theory for You! Feminist Theory, Cultural Imperialism and the Demand for the Woman's Voice," *Hypatia, Women's Studies International Forum*, Vol. 6, No. 6, 1983, pp. 578–81; Adrienne Rich, "Compulsory Heterosexuality and Lesbian existence," *Signs: Journal of Women in Culture and Society*, Vol. 5, No. 4, Summer 1980, pp. 631–60; Elizabeth Spelman, "Theories of Race and Gender: The Erasure of Black Women," *Quest*, Vol. 5, No. 4, 1980/81, pp. 36–62.
18. See, for example, Hélène Cixous, "The Laugh of the Medusa," trans. Keith Cohen and Paula Cohen, in *New French Feminisms*, ed. Elaine Marks and Esabelle de Courtivron (New York: Schocken Books, 1981), pp. 245–61; Hélène Cixous and Catherine Clément, *The Newly Born Woman*, trans. Betsy Wing (Minneapolis: University of Minnesota Press, 1986); Luce Irigaray, *Speculum of the Other Woman* (Ithaca, NY: Cornell University Press, 1985) and *This Sex Which Is Not One* (Ithaca, NY: Cornell University Press, 1985); Julia Kristeva, *Desire in Language: A Semiotic Approach to Literature and Art*, ed. Lon S. Roudiez (New York: Columbia University Press, 1980), and "Women's Time," trans. Alice Jardine and Harry Blake, *Signs: Journal of Women in Culture and Society*, Vol. 7, No. 1, Autumn 1981, pp. 13–35. See also the critical discussions by Ann Rosalind Jones, "Writing the Body: Toward an Understanding of l'Écriture Féminine," in *The New Feminist Criticism: Essays on Women, Literature and Theory*, ed. Elaine Showalter (New York: Pantheon Books, 1985), and Toril Moi, *Sexual/Textual Politics: Feminist Literary Theory* (London: Methuen, 1985).

Playfulness, "World"-Travelling, and Loving Perception

Lugones raises the question of how divisions between women who are members of different social groups can be overcome. To explore these issues Lugones develops the concept of a "world" and the concept of "world"-travelling. A "world" is a social universe that has a language and norms, within which many people approve of those norms, where many of the inhabitants have affectionate ties to one another, and which endows inhabitants with a common history and common knowledge. Each "world" constructs the individuals who are in it, including "outsiders," in distinctive ways. Thus, "world"-travelling involves entering into different worlds and, as a result, undergoing changes in one's identity.

Lugones tells how her failure to travel to her mother's world alienated her from her mother. Likewise, she points out that women of color in the United States are commonly obliged to travel to the worlds of White/Anglo women, but White/Anglo women seldom reciprocate and travel to the worlds of women of color. According to Lugones, loving and playful "world"-travelling is the key to breaking down barriers between women from different social groups. A loving approach requires giving oneself over to the other's world—seeing the other as she is constructed in her world and seeing oneself as one is constructed in the other's world. A playful approach requires abandoning rules, being creative, welcoming surprise, and being receptive to self-construction. "World"-travelling in this spirit enables one to see that members of other social groups have complex subjective and agentic lives that are denied in the "world" where one is at home.

—D.T.M.

Chapter 8

María Lugones

Playfulness, "World"-Travelling, and Loving Perception

This paper weaves two aspects of life together. My coming to consciousness as a daughter and my coming to consciousness as a woman of color have made this weaving possible. This weaving reveals the possibility and complexity of a pluralistic feminism, a feminism that affirms the plurality in each of us and among us as richness and as central to feminist ontology and epistemology.

The paper describes the experience of "outsiders" to the mainstream of, for example, White/Anglo organization of life in the U.S. and stresses a particular feature of the outsider's existence: the outsider has necessarily acquired flexibility in shifting from the mainstream construction of life where she is constructed as an outsider to other constructions of life where she is more or less "at home." This flexibility is necessary for the outsider but it can also be willfully exercised by the outsider or by those who are at ease in the mainstream. I recommend this willful exercise which I call "world"-travelling and I also recommend that the willful exercise be animated by an attitude that I describe as playful.

As outsiders to the mainstream, women of color in the U.S. practice "world"-travelling, mostly out of necessity. I affirm this practice as a skillful, creative, rich, enriching, and, given certain circumstances, as a loving way of being and living. I recognize that much of our travelling is done unwillfully to hostile White/Anglo "worlds." The hostility of these "worlds" and the compulsory nature of the "travelling" have obscured for us the enormous value of this aspect of our living and its connection to loving. Racism has a vested interest in obscuring and devaluing the complex skills involved in it. I recommend that we affirm this travelling across "worlds" as partly constitutive of cross-cultural and cross-racial loving. Thus I recommend to women of color in the U.S. that we learn to love each other by learning to travel to each other's "worlds."

On the other hand, the paper makes a connection between what Marilyn Frye has named "arrogant perception" and the failure to identify with persons that one views arrogantly or has come to see as the products of arrogant perception. A further connection is made between this failure of identification and a failure of love, and thus between loving and identifying with another person. The sense of love is not the one Frye has identified as both consistent with arrogant perception and as promoting unconditional servitude. "We can be taken in by this equation of servitude with love," Frye (1983, 73) says, "because we make two mistakes at once: we think, of both servitude and love that they are selfless or unselfish." Rather, the identification of which I speak is constituted by what I come to characterize as playful "world"-travelling. To the extent that we learn to perceive others arrogantly or come to see them only as products of arrogant perception and continue to perceive them that way, we fail to identify with them—fail to love them—in this particularly deep way.

IDENTIFICATION AND LOVE

As a child, I was taught to perceive arrogantly. I have also been the object of arrogant perception. Though I am not a White/Anglo woman, it is clear to me that I can understand both my childhood training as an arrogant perceiver and my having been the object of arrogant perception without any reference to White/Anglo men, which is some indication that the concept of arrogant perception can be used cross-culturally and that White/Anglo men are not the only arrogant perceivers. I was brought up in Argentina watching men and women of moderate and of considerable means graft the substance[1] of their servants to themselves. I also learned to graft my mother's substance to my own. It was clear to me that both men and women were the victims of arrogant perception and that arrogant perception was systematically organized to break the spirit of all women and of most men. I valued my rural "gaucho" ancestry because its ethos has always been one of independence in poverty through enormous loneliness, courage, and self-reliance. I found inspiration in this ethos and committed myself never to be broken by arrogant perception. I can say all of this in this way only because I have learned from Frye's "In and Out of Harm's Way: Arrogance and Love." She has given me a way of understanding and articulating something important in my own life.

Frye is not particularly concerned with women as arrogant perceivers but as the objects of arrogant perception. Her concern is, in part, to enhance our understanding of women "untouched by phallocratic machinations" (Frye 1983, 53), by understanding the harm done to women through such machinations. In this case she proposes that we could understand women untouched by arrogant perception through an understanding of what arrogant perception does to women. She also proposes an understanding of what it is to love women that is inspired by a vision of women unharmed by arrogant perception. To love women is, at least in part, to perceive them with loving eyes. "The loving eye is a contrary of the arrogant eye" (Frye 1983, 75).

I am concerned with women as arrogant perceivers because I want to explore further what it is to love women. I want to explore two failures of love: my failure to love my mother and White/Anglo women's failure to love women across racial and cultural boundaries in the U.S. As a consequence of exploring these failures I will offer a loving solution to them. My solution modifies Frye's account of loving perception by adding what I call playful "world"-travel.

It is clear to me that at least in the U.S. and Argentina women are taught to perceive many other women arrogantly. Being taught to perceive arrogantly is part of being taught to be a woman of a certain class in both the U.S. and Argentina; it is part of being taught to be a White/Anglo woman in the U.S., and it is part of being taught to be a woman in both places: to be both the agent and the object of arrogant perception. My love for my mother seemed to me thoroughly imperfect as I was growing up because I was unwilling to become what I had been taught to see my mother as being. I thought that to love her was consistent with my abusing her (using, taking for granted, and demanding her services in a far reaching way that, since four other people engaged in the same grafting of her substance onto themselves, left her little of herself to herself) and was to be in part constituted by my identifying with her, my seeing myself in her: to love her was supposed to be of a piece with both my abusing her and with my being open to being abused. It is clear to me that I was not supposed to love servants: I could abuse them without identifying with them, without seeing myself in them. When I came to the U.S. I learned that part of racism is the internalization of the propriety of abuse without identification: I learned that I could be seen as a being to be used by White/Anglo men and women without the possibility of identification, i.e. without their act of attempting to graft my substance onto others, rubbing off on them at all. They could remain untouched, without any sense of loss.

So, women who are perceived arrogantly can perceive other women arrogantly in their turn. To what extent those women are responsible for their arrogant perceptions of other women is certainly open to question, but I do not have any doubt that any women have been taught to abuse women in this particular way. I am not interested in assigning responsibility. I am interested in understanding the phenomenon so as to understand a loving way out of it.

There is something obviously wrong with the love that I was taught and something right with my failure to love my mother in this way. But I do not think what is wrong is my profound desire to identify with her, to see myself in her; what is wrong is that I was taught to identify with a victim of enslavement. What is wrong is that I was taught to practice enslavement of my mother and to learn to become a slave through this practice. There is something obviously wrong with my having been taught that love is consistent with abuse, consistent with arrogant perception. Notice that the love I was taught is the love that Frye (1983, 73) speaks of when she says, "We can be taken in by this equation of servitude with love." Even though I could both abuse and love my mother, I was not supposed to love servants. This is because in the case of servants one is and is supposed to be clear about their servitude and the "equation of servitude with love" is never to be thought clearly in those terms. So, I was not supposed to love and could not love servants. But I could love my mother because deception (in particular, self-deception) is part of this "loving." Servitude is called abnegation, and abnegation is not analyzed any further. Abnegation is not instilled in us through an analysis of its nature but rather through a heralding of it as beautiful and noble. We are coaxed, seduced into abnegation not through analysis but through emotive persuasion. Frye makes the connection between deception and this sense of "loving" clear. When I say that there is something obviously wrong with the loving that I was taught, I do not mean to say that the connection between this loving and abuse is obvious. Rather I mean that once the connection between this loving and abuse has been unveiled, there is something obviously wrong with the loving given that it is obvious that it is wrong to abuse others.

I am glad that I did not learn my lessons well, but it is clear that part of the mechanism that permitted my not learning well involved a separation from my mother: I saw us as beings of quite a different sort. It involved an abandoning of my mother while I longed not to abandon her. I wanted to love my mother, though given what I was taught, "love" could not be the right word for what I longed for.

I was disturbed by my not wanting to be what she was. I had a sense of not being quite integrated, my self was missing because I could not identify with her, I could not see myself in her, I could not welcome her world. I saw myself as separate from her, a different sort of being, not quite of the same species. This separation, this lack of love, I saw, and I think that I saw correctly as a lack in myself (not a fault, but a lack). I also see that if this was a lack of love, love cannot be what I was taught. Love has to be rethought, made anew.

There is something in common between the relation between myself and my mother as someone I did not use to be able to love and the relation between myself or other women of color in the U.S. and White/Anglo women: there is a failure of love. I want to suggest here that Frye has helped me understand one of the aspects of this failure, the directly abusive aspect. But I also think that there is a complex failure of love in the failure to identify with another woman, the failure to see oneself in other women who are quite different from oneself. I want to begin to analyze this complex failure.

Notice that Frye's emphasis on independence in her analysis of loving perceptions is not particularly helpful in explaining this failure. She says that in loving perception, "The object of the seeing is another being whose existence and character are logically independent of the seer and who may be practically or empirically independent in any particular respect at any particular time" (Frye 1983, 77). But this is not helpful in allowing me to understand how my failure of love toward my mother (when I ceased to be her parasite) left me not quite whole. It is not helpful since I saw her as logically independent from me. It also does not help me to understand why the racist or ethnocentric failure of love of White/Anglo women—in particular of those White/Anglo women who are not pained by their failure—should leave me not quite substantive among them. Here I am not particularly interested in cases of White women's parasitism onto women of color but more pointedly in cases where the failure of identification is the manifestation of the "relation." I am particularly interested here in those many cases in which White/Anglo women do one or more of the following to women of color: they ignore us, ostracize us, render us invisible, stereotype us, leave us completely alone, interpret us as crazy. All of this *while we are in their midst.* The more independent I am, the more independent I am left to be. Their world and their integrity do not require me at all. There is no sense of self-loss in them for my own lack of solidity. But they rob me of my solidity through indifference, an indifference they can afford and which seems sometimes studied. (All of this points, of course, toward separatism in communities where our substance is seen and celebrated, where we become substantive through this celebration. But many of us have to work among White/Anglo folk and our best shot at recognition has seemed to be among White/Anglo women because many of them have expressed a *general* sense of being pained at their failure of love.)

Many times White/Anglo women want us out of their field of vision. Their lack of concern is a harmful failure of love that leaves me independent from them in a way similar to the way in which, once I ceased to be my mother's parasite, she became, though not independent from all others, certainly independent from me. But of course, because my mother and I wanted to love each other well, we were not whole in this independence.

White/Anglo women are independent from me, I am independent from them, I am independent from my mother, she is independent from me, and none of us loves each other in this independence.

I am incomplete and unreal without other women. I am profoundly dependent on others without having to be their subordinate, their slave, their servant.

Frye (1983, 75) also says that the loving eye is "the eye of one who knows that to know the seen one must consult something other than one's own will and interests and fears and imagination." This is much more helpful to me so long as I do not understand Frye to mean that I should not consult my own interests nor that I should exclude the possibility that my self and the self of the one I love may be importantly tied to each other in many complicated ways. Since I am emphasizing here that the failure of love lies in part in the failure to identify and since I agree with Frye that one "must consult something other than one's own will and interests and fears and imagination," I will proceed to try to explain what I think needs to be consulted. To love my mother was not possible for me while I retained a sense that it was fine for me and others to see her arrogantly. Loving my mother also required that I see with her eyes, that I go into my mother's world, that I see both of us as we are constructed in her world, that I witness her own sense of herself from within her world. Only through this travelling to her "world" could I identify with her because only then could I cease to ignore her and to be excluded and separate from her. Only then could I see her as a subject even if one subjected and only then could I see at all how meaning could arise fully between us. We are fully dependent on each other for the possibility of being understood, and without this understanding we are not intelligible, we do not make sense, we are not solid, visible, integrated; we are lacking. So travelling to each other's "worlds" would enable us to *be* through *loving* each other.

Hopefully the sense of identification I have in mind is becoming clear. But if it is to become clearer, I need to explain what I mean by a "world" and by "travelling" to another "world."

In explaining what I mean by a "world" I will not appeal to traveling to other women's worlds. Rather I will lead you to see what I mean by a "world" the way I came to propose the concept to myself: through the kind of ontological confusion about myself that we, women of color, refer to half-jokingly as "schizophrenia" (we feel schizophrenic in our goings back and forth between different "communities") and through my effort to make some sense of this ontological confusion.

"WORLDS" AND "WORLD"-TRAVELLING

Some time ago I came to be in a state of profound confusion as I experienced myself as both having and not having a particular attribute. I was sure I had the attribute in question and, on the other hand, I was sure that I did not have it. I remain convinced that I both have and do not have this attribute. The attribute is playfulness. I am sure that I am a playful person. On the other hand, I can say, painfully, that I am not a playful person. I am not a playful person in certain worlds. One of the things I did as I became confused was to call my friends, far away people who knew me well, to see whether or not I was playful. Maybe they could help me out of my confusion. They said to me, "Of course you are playful" and they said it with the same conviction that I had about it. Of course I am playful. Those people who were around me said to me, "No, you are not playful. You are a serious woman. You just take everything seriously." They were just as sure about what they said to me and could offer me every bit of evidence that one could need to conclude that they were right. So I said to myself: "Okay, maybe what's happening here is that there is an attribute that I do have but there are certain worlds in which I am not at ease and it is because I'm not at ease in those worlds that I don't have that attribute in those worlds. But what does that mean?" I was worried both about what I meant by "worlds" when I said "in some worlds I do not have the attribute" and what I meant by saying that lack of ease was what led me not to be playful in those worlds. Because, you see, if it was just a matter of lack of ease, I could work on it.

I can explain some of what I mean by a "world." I do not want the fixity of a definition at this point, because I think the term is suggestive and I do not want to close the suggestiveness of it too soon. I can offer some characteristics that serve to distinguish between a "world," a utopia, a possible world in the philosophical sense, and a world view. By a "world" I do not mean a utopia at all. A utopia does not count as a world in my sense. The "worlds" that I am talking about are possible. But a possible world is not what I mean by a "world" and I do not mean a world-view, though something like world-view is involved here.

For something to be a "world" in my sense it has to be inhabited at present by some flesh and blood people. That is why it cannot be a utopia. It may also be inhabited by some imaginary people. It may be inhabited by people who are dead or people that the inhabitants of this "world" met in some other "world" and now have in this "world" in imagination.

A "world" in my sense may be an actual society given its dominant culture's description and construction of life, including a construction of the relationships of production, of gender, race, etc. But a "world" can also be such a society given a nondominant construction, or it can be such a society or *a* society, given an idiosyncratic construction. As we will see, it is problematic to say that these are all constructions of the same society. But they are different "worlds."

A "world" need not be a construction of a whole society. It may be a construction of a tiny portion of a particular society. It may be inhabited by just a few people. Some "worlds" are bigger than others.

A "world" may be incomplete in that things in it may not be altogether constructed or some things may be constructed negatively (they are not what "they" are in some other "world.") Or the "world" may be incomplete because it may have references to things that do not quite exist in it, references to things like Brazil, where Brazil is not quite part of that "world." Given lesbian feminism, the construction of "lesbian" is purposefully and healthily still up in the air, in the process of becoming. What is it to be a Hispanic in this country is, in a dominant Anglo construction purposefully incomplete. Thus one cannot really answer questions of the sort "What is a Hispanic?" "Who counts as a Hispanic?" "Are Latinos, Chicanos, Hispanos, black Dominicans, white Cubans, Korean-Colombians, Italian-Argentineans Hispanic?" What it is to be a "Hispanic" in the varied so-called Hispanic communities in the U.S. is also yet up in the air. We have not yet decided whether there is something like a "Hispanic" in our varied "worlds." So, a "world" may be an incomplete visionary non-utopian construction of life or it may be a traditional construction of life. A traditional Hispano construction of Northern New Mexican life is a "world." Such a traditional construction, in the face of a racist, ethnocentrist, money-centered Anglo construction of Northern New Mexico life is highly unstable because Anglos have the means for imperialist destruction of traditional Hispano "worlds."

In a "world," some of the inhabitants may not understand or hold the particular construction of them that constructs them in that "world." So, there may be "worlds" that construct me in ways I do not even understand. Or it may be that I understand the construction but do not hold it of myself. I may not accept it as an account of myself, a construction of myself. And yet, I may be *animating* such a construction.

One can "travel" between these "worlds" and one can inhabit more than one of these "worlds" at the very same time. I think that most of us who are outside the mainstream of, for example, the U.S. dominant construction or organization of life are "world"-travellers as a matter of necessity and of survival. It seems to me that inhabiting more than one "world" at the same time and "travelling" between "worlds" is part and parcel of our experience and our situation. One can be at the same time in a "world" that constructs one as stereotypically latin, for example, and in a "world" that constructs one as latin. Being stereotypically latin and being simply latin are different simultaneous constructions of persons that are part of different "worlds." One animates one or the other or both at the same time without necessarily confusing them, though simultaneous enactment can be confusing if one is not on one's guard.

In describing my sense of a "world," I mean to be offering a description of experience, something that is true to experience even if it is ontologically problematic. Though I would think that any account of identity that could not be true to this experience of outsiders to the mainstream would be faulty even if ontologically unproblematic. Its ease would constrain, erase, or deem aberrant experience that has within it significant insights into non-imperialistic understanding between people.

Those of us who are "world"-travellers have the distinct experience of being in different "worlds" and of having the capacity to remember other "worlds" and ourselves in them. We can say, "That is me there, and I am happy in that 'world.' " So, the experience is of being a different person in different "worlds" and yet of having memory of oneself as different without quite having the sense of there being an underlying "I." So I can say "That is me there and I am so playful in that 'world.' " I say "That is *me* in that 'world' " not because I recognize myself in that person, rather the first person statement is non-inferential. I may well recognize that that person has abilities that I do not have and yet the having or not having of the abilities is always an "I have . . ." and "I do not have . . .", i.e. it is always experienced in the first person.

The shift from being one person to being a different person is what I call "travel." This shift may not be willful or even conscious, and one may be completely unaware of being different from how one is in a different "world," and may not recognize that one is in a different "world." Even though the shift can be done willfully, it is not a matter of acting. One does not pose as someone else, one does not pretend to be, for example, someone of a different personality or character or someone who uses space or language differently from the other person. Rather one is someone who has that personality or character or uses space and language in that particular way. The "one" here does not refer to some underlying "I." One does not *experience* any underlying "I."

BEING AT EASE IN A "WORLD"

In investigating what I mean by "being at ease in a 'world'," I will describe different ways of being at ease. One may be at ease in one or in all of these ways. There is a maximal way of being at ease, viz. being at ease in all of these ways. I take this maximal way of being at ease to be somewhat dangerous because it tends to produce people who have no inclination to travel across "worlds" or have no experience of "world"-travelling.

The first way of being at ease in a particular "world" is by being a fluent speaker in that "world." I know all the norms that there are to be followed. I know all the words that there are to be spoken. I know all the moves. I am confident.

Another way of being at ease is by being normatively happy. I agree with all the norms, I could not love any norms better. I am asked to do just what I want to do or what I think I should do. At ease.

Another way of being at ease in a "world" is by being humanly bonded. I am with those I love and they love me too. It should be noticed that I may be with those I love and be at ease because of them in a "world" that is otherwise as hostile to me as "worlds" get.

Finally one may be at ease because one has a history with others that is shared, especially daily history, the kind of shared history that one sees exemplified by the response to "Do you remember poodle skirts?" question. There you are, with people you do not know at all. The question is posed and then they all begin talking about their poodle skirt stories. I have been in such situations without knowing what poodle skirts, for example, were and I felt so ill at ease because it was not *my* history. The other people did not particularly know each other. It is not that they were humanly bonded. Probably they did not have much politically in common either. But poodle skirts were in their shared history.

One may be at ease in one of these ways or in all of them. Notice that when one says meaningfully "This is *my* world," one may not be at ease in it. Or one may be at ease in it only in some of these respects and not in others. To say of some "world" that it is "*my* world" is to make an evaluation. One may privilege one or more "worlds" in this way for a variety of reasons: for example because one experiences oneself as an agent in a fuller sense than one experiences "oneself" in other "worlds." One may disown a "world" because one has first-person memories of a person who is so thoroughly dominated that she has no sense of exercising her own will or has a sense of having serious difficulties in performing actions that are willed by herself and no difficulty in performing actions willed by others. One may say of a "world" that it is "my world" because one is at ease in it, i.e., being at ease in a "world" may be the basis for the evaluation.

Given the clarification of what I meant by a "world," "world"-travel, and being at ease in a "world," we are in a position to return to my problematic attribute, playfulness. It may be that in this "world" in which I am so unplayful, I am a different person than in the "world" in which I am playful. Or it may be that the "world" in which I am unplayful is constructed in such a way that I could be playful in it. I could practice, even though that "world" is constructed in such a way that my being playful in it is kind of hard. In describing what I take a "world" to be, I emphasize the first possibility as both the one that is truest to the experience of "outsider" to the mainstream and as ontologically problematic because the "I" is identified in some sense as one and in some sense as a plurality. I identify myself as myself through memory and I train myself as different in memory. When I travel from one "world" to another, I have this image, this memory of myself as playful in this other "world." I can then be in a particular "world" and have a double image of myself as, for example, playful and as not playful. But this is a very familiar and recognizable phenomenon to the outsider to the mainstream in some central cases: when in one "world" I animate, for example, that "world's" caricatures of the person I am in the other "world." I can have both images of myself, and to the extent that I can materialize or animate both images at the same time I become an ambiguous being. This is very much a part of trickery and foolery. It is worth remembering that the trickster and the fool are significant characters in many nondominant or outsider culture. One then sees any particular "world" with these double edges and sees absurdity in them and so inhabits oneself differently. Given that latins are constructed in Anglo "worlds" as stereotypically intense—intensity being a central characteristic of at least one of the Anglo stereotypes of latins—and given that many latins, myself included, are genuinely intense, I can say to myself "I am intense" and take a hold of the double meaning. And furthermore, I can be stereotypically intense or be the real thing and, if you are Anglo, you do not know when I am which *because* I am Latin-American. As Latin-American I am an ambiguous being, a two-imaged self: I can see that gringos see me as stereotypically intense because I am, as a Latin-American, constructed that way but I may or may not *intentionally* animate the stereotype or the real thing knowing that you may not see it in anything other than in the stereotypical construction. This ambiguity is funny and it is not just funny, it is survival-rich. We can also make the picture of those who dominate us funny precisely because we can see the double edge, we can see them doubly constructed, we can see the plurality in them. So we know truths that only the fool can speak and only the trickster can play out without harm. We inhabit "worlds" and travel across them and keep all the memories.

Sometimes the "world"-traveler has a double image of herself and each self includes as important ingredients of itself one or more attributes that are *incompatible* with one or more of the attributes of the other self: for example being playful and being unplayful. To the extent that the attribute is an important ingredient of the self she is in that "world," i.e., to the extent that there is a particularly good fit between that "world" and her having that attribute in it and to the extent that the attribute is personality or character central, that "world" would have to be changed if she is to be playful in it. It is not the case that if she could come to be at ease in it, she would be her own playful self. Because the attribute is personality or character central and there is such a good fit between that "world" and her being constructed with that attribute as central, *she* cannot become playful, she is unplayful. To become unplayful would be for her to become a contradictory being. So I am suggesting that the lack of ease solution cannot be a solution to my problematic case. My problem is not one of lack of ease. I am suggesting that I can understand my confusion about whether I am or am not playful by saying that I am both and that I am different persons in different "worlds" and can remember myself in both as I am in the other. I am a plurality of selves. This is to understand my confusion because *it is to come to see it as a piece* with much of the rest of my experience as an outsider in some of the "worlds" that I inhabit and of a piece with significant aspects of the experience of nondominant people in the "worlds" of their dominators.

So, though I may not be at ease in the "worlds" in which I am not constructed playful, it is not that I am not playful *because* I am not at ease. The two are compatible. But lack of playfulness is not caused by lack of ease. Lack of playfulness is not symptomatic of lack of ease but of lack of health. I am not a healthy being in the "worlds" that construct me as unplayful.

PLAYFULNESS

I had a very personal stake in investigating this topic. Playfulness is not only the attribute that was the source of my confusion and the attitude that I recommend as the loving attitude in travelling across "worlds." I am also scared of ending up a serious human being, someone with no multidimensionality, with no fun in life, someone who is just someone who has had the fun constructed out of her. I am seriously scared of getting stuck in a "world" that constructs me that way. A world that I have no escape from and in which I cannot be playful.

I thought about what it is to be playful and what it is to play and I did this thinking in a "world" in which I only remember myself as playful and in which all of those who know me as playful are imaginary beings. A "world" in which I am scared of losing my memories of myself as playful or have them erased from me. Because I live in such a "world," after I formulated my own sense of what it is to be playful and to play I decided that I needed to "go to the literature." I read two classics on the subject: Johan Huizinga's *Homo Ludens* and Hans-Georg Gadamer's chapter on the concept of play in his *Truth and Method.* I discovered, to my amazement, that what I thought about play and playfulness, if they were right, was absolutely wrong. Though I will not provide the arguments for this interpretation of Gadamer and Huizinga here, I understood that both of them have an agonistic sense of "play." Play and playfulness have, ultimately, to do with contest, with winning, losing, battling. The sense of playfulness that I have in mind has nothing to do with those things. So, I tried to elucidate both senses of play and playfulness by contrasting them to each other. The contrast helped me see the attitude that I have in mind as the loving attitude in traveling across "worlds" more clearly.

An agonistic sense of playfulness is one in which *competence* is supreme. You better know the rules of the game. In agonistic play there is risk, there is *uncertainty,* but the uncertainty is about who is going to win and who is going to lose. There are rules that inspire hostility. The attitude of *playfulness is conceived as secondary to or derivative from play.* Since play is agon, then the only conceivable playful attitude is an agonistic one (the attitude does not turn an activity into play, but rather presupposes an activity that is play). One of the paradigmatic ways of playing for both Gadamer and Huizinga is role-playing. In role-playing, the person who is a participant in the game has a *fixed conception for him or herself.* I also think that the players are imbued with *self-importance* in agonistic play since they are so keen on winning given their own merits, their very own competence.

When considering the value of "world"-travelling and whether playfulness is the loving attitude to have while travelling, I recognized the agonistic attitude as inimical to travelling across "worlds." The agonistic traveller is a conqueror, an imperialist. Huizinga, in his classic book on play, interprets Western civilization as play. That is an interesting thing for Third World people to think about. Western civilization has been interpreted by a white Western man as play in the agonistic sense of play. Huizinga reviews Western law, art, and many other aspects of Western culture and sees agon in all of them. Agonistic playfulness leads those who attempt to travel to another "world" with this attitude to failure. Agonistic travellers fail consistently in their attempt to travel because what they do is to try to conquer the other "world." The attempt is not an attempt to try to erase the other "world." That is what assimilation is all about. Assimilation is the destruction of other people's "worlds." So, the agonistic attitude, the playful attitude given Western man's construction of playfulness, is not a healthy, loving attitude to have in travelling across "worlds." Notice that given the agonistic attitude one *cannot* travel across "worlds," though one can kill other "worlds" with it. So for people who are interested in crossing racial and ethnic boundaries, an arrogant Western man's construction of playfulness is deadly. One cannot cross the boundaries with it. One needs to give up such an attitude if one wants to travel.

So then, what is the loving playfulness that I have in mind? Let me begin with one example: We are by the river bank. The river is very, very low. Almost dry. Bits of water here and there. Little pools with a few trout hiding under the rocks. But mostly it is wet stones, grey on the outside. We walk on the stones for awhile. You pick up a stone and crash it onto the others. As it breaks, it is quite wet inside and it is very colorful, very pretty. I pick up a stone and break it and run toward the pieces to see the colors. They are beautiful. I laugh and bring the pieces back to you and you are doing the same with your pieces. We keep on crashing stones for hours, anxious to see the beautiful new colors. We are playing. The playfulness of our activity does not presuppose that there is something like "crashing stones" that is a particular form of play with its own rules. Rather *the attitude that carries us through the activity, a playful attitude, turns the activity into play.* Our activity has no rules, though it is certainly intentional activity and we both understand what we are doing. The playfulness that gives meaning to our activity includes uncertainty, but in this case the uncertainty is an *openness to surprise.* This is a particular metaphysical attitude that does not expect the world to be neatly packaged, ruly. Rules may fail to explain what we are doing. We are not self-important, we are not fixed in particular constructions of ourselves, which is part of saying that we are *open to self-construction.* We may not have rules, and when we do have rules, *there are no rules that are to us sacred.* We are not worried about competence. We are not wedded to a particular way of doing things. While playful we have not abandoned ourselves to, nor are we stuck in, any particular "world." We *are there creatively.* We are not passive.

Playfulness is, in part, an openness to being a fool, which is a combination of not worrying about competence, not being self-important, not taking norms as sacred and finding ambiguity and double edges a source of wisdom and delight.

So, positively, the playful attitude involves openness to surprise, openness to being a fool, openness to self-construction or reconstruction and to construction or reconstruction of the "worlds" we inhabit playfully. Negatively, playfulness is characterized by uncertainty, lack of self-importance, absence of rules or a not taking rules as sacred, a not worrying about competence and a lack of abandonment to a particular construction of oneself, others and one's relation to them. In attempting to take a hold of oneself and of one's relation to others in a particular "world," one may study, examine and come to understand oneself. One may then see what the possibilities for play are for the being one is in that "world." One may even decide to inhabit that self fully in order to understand it better and find its creative possibilities. All of this is just self-reflection and it is quite different from resigning or abandoning oneself to the particular construction of oneself that one is attempting to take a hold of.

CONCLUSION

There are "worlds" we enter at our own risk, "worlds" that have agon, conquest, and arrogance as the main ingredients in their ethos. These are "worlds" that we enter out of necessity and which would be foolish to enter playfully in either the agonistic sense or in my sense. In such "worlds" *we* are not playful.

But there are "worlds" that we can travel to lovingly, and travelling to them is part of loving at least some of their inhabitants. The reason why I think that travelling to someone's "world" is a way of identifying with them is because by travelling to their "world" we can understand *what it is to be them and what it is to be ourselves in their eyes.* Only when we have travelled to each other's "worlds" are we fully subjects to each other (I agree with Hegel that self-recognition requires other subjects, but I disagree with his claim that it requires tension or hostility).

Knowing other women's "worlds" is part of knowing them and knowing them is part of loving them. Notice that the knowing can be done in greater or lesser depth, as can the loving. Also notice that traveling to another's "world" is not the same as becoming intimate with them. Intimacy is constituted in part by a very deep knowledge of the other self and "world"-travelling is only part of having this knowledge. Also notice that some people, in particular those who are outsiders to the mainstream, can be known only to the extent that they are known in several "worlds" and as "world"-travellers.

Without knowing the other's "world," one does not know the other, and without knowing the other one is really alone in the other's presence because the other is only dimly present to one.

Through travelling to other people's "worlds" we discover that there are "worlds" in which those who are the victims of arrogant perception are really subjects, lively beings, resistors, constructors of visions even though in the mainstream construction they are animated only by the arrogant perceiver and are pliable, foldable, file-awayable, classifiable. I always imagine the Aristotelian slave as pliable and foldable at night or after he or she cannot work anymore (when he or she dies as a tool). Aristotle tells us nothing about the slave *apart from the master.* We know the slave only through the master. The slave is a tool of the master. After working hours he or she is folded and placed in a drawer till the next morning. My mother was apparent to me mostly as a victim of arrogant perception. I was loyal to the arrogant perceiver's construction of her and thus disloyal to her in assuming that she was exhausted by that construction. I was unwilling to be like her and thought that identifying with her, seeing myself in her necessitated that I become like her. I was wrong both in assuming that she was exhausted by the arrogant perceiver's construction of her and in my understanding of identification, though I was not wrong in thinking that identification was part of loving and that it involved in part my seeing myself in her. I came to realize through travelling to her "world" that she is not foldable and pliable, that she is not exhausted by the mainstream Argentinean patriarchal construction of her. I came to realize that there are "worlds" in which she shines as a creative being. Seeing myself in her through travelling to her "world" has meant seeing how different from her I am in her "world."

So, in recommending "world"-travelling and identification through "world"-travelling as part of loving other women, I am suggesting disloyalty to arrogant perceivers, including the arrogant perceiver in ourselves, and to their constructions of women. In revealing agonistic playfulness as incompatible with "world"-travelling, I am revealing both its affinity with imperialism and arrogant perception and its incompatibility with loving and loving perception.

NOTE

1. Grafting the substance of another to oneself is partly constitutive of arrogant perception. See M. Frye (1983, 66).

REFERENCES

Frye, Marilyn. 1983. *The Politics of Reality: Essays in Feminist Theory.* Trumansburg, N.Y.: Crossing Press.

Gadamer, Hans-Georg. 1975. *Truth and Method.* New York: Seabury Press.

Huizinga, Johan. 1968. *Homo Ludens.* Buenos Aires, Argentina: Emecé Editores.

Woman: The One and the Many

Many people have no difficulty answering questions about their gender and their race, but it is not clear what, if anything, follows from the ability to do this. Does it follow that there are isolable parts of one's identity that determine one's gender and one's race? Spelman's answer is NO. She maintains that gender and racial identity must be understood in terms of the imposition of classification systems, not in terms of psychological or biological states inhering in individuals.

Spelman challenges the thesis that gender is separate from race by inviting her readers to imagine James Baldwin, Angela Davis, Spelman herself, and Spelman's brother lined up on a stage. What, she asks, do she and Angela Davis have in common, apart from the fact that they are both gendered as women, that distinguishes the two of them from both of the men? The answer is far from obvious since experiencing gender as a Black woman differs in many salient respects from experiencing gender as a white woman. Now, it may seem that we need more facts about Black women and white women in order to settle this question. But Spelman denies that empirical studies can establish what these two groups of women have in common. Empirical research rests on normatively conditioned beliefs about what similarities and differences are worth studying, criteria of sameness and difference, and the significance of the similarities and differences that are found. Objective investigation that transcends social power relations and cultural values is not possible. Thus, Spelman turns to an examination of the way in which different classification systems locate individuals in a social order. Spelman models social classification schemes as a customs hall where people are required to pass through doors labeled according to gender or race. This model shows that differences among women are obscured when gender is considered primary, and that the self-understandings of white women then tend to be privileged. Also, the customs-hall model exposes the artificiality and alterability of classification schemes and opens up the possibility of politically resisting and reshaping them.

—D.T.M.

Chapter 9

Elizabeth V. Spelman

Woman: The One and the Many

> Women don't lead their lives like, "Well, this part is race, and this is class, and this part has to do with women's identities," so it's confusing.
>
> Beverly Smith

Most everyone has no trouble at all answering questions such as "What gender are you?" "What race are you?" and so on. This is not to say that there are not, for example, debates about the "racial" categories on United States census forms. Nor is it to forget that in countries like the United States the pretense of there being no class differences makes it very hard for many people to answer questions about what class they belong to. But I may seem to have forgotten that at least some of these questions about one's identity are easy to answer. I agree: I don't have any trouble answering that I am a woman and that I am white. These appear to be two separate questions, which I can answer separately; my brother answers one of them as I do, the other not. So it seems that I can easily pick out the "woman part" of me and the "white part" of me and, moreover, tell the difference between them.

But does this mean that there is a "woman part" of me, and that it is distinct, for example, from something that is the "white part" of me? If there is a "woman part" of me, it doesn't seem to be the kind of thing I could point to—not because etiquette demands that nice people don't point to their private or covered parts, but because even if I broke a social rule and did so, nothing I might point to would meet the requirements of being a "part" of me that was a "woman part" that was not also a "white part." Any part of my body is part of a body that is, by prevailing criteria, female and white. And now that I have moved surreptitiously from talking about a "woman part" to talking about a "female part," you will remember another reason why pointing to the "woman part" of myself would be no mean feat: being a "woman" is not the same thing as, nor is it reducible to, being a "female." "Women" are what females of the human species become, or are supposed to become, through learning how to think, act, and live in certain ways. What females in one society learn about how they are to think, act, and live can differ enormously from what females in another society learn; in fact, as we have been reminded often, there can be very significant differences within a given society. Moreover, those females who don't learn their lessons very well, or who resist being and doing what they're taught, or who, as we saw in Aristotle's view, are born into the "wrong" group, may have their credentials as "real women" questioned even while their status as females remains intact. Indeed, unless their female status is assumed, there can be no grounds for wondering whether they are really "women." Being a woman—or a man, for that matter—is a complicated business, and apparently a precarious one, given the number of societal institutions instructing us about how to be women or men and punishing us for failing to act appropriately.

Maybe I could tell you better about that aspect of myself in virtue of which I am called a "woman" and show you how it is different from that aspect of myself in virtue of which I am called "white" by talking about how as a woman I am distinguished from men, while as a white person I am distinguished from, for example, Black people. I can metaphorically point to my womanness by reminding you of how I am different from men, to my whiteness by reminding you of how I am different from Black people. For example, I can attend to the different expectations my parents and teachers had for me and my two sisters, on the one hand, and our two brothers, on the other, or *à la* Nancy Chodorow, I can try to describe the difference between how we three girls related to our mother and how our brothers related to her, and how that affected our senses of ourselves. And this might appear to have nothing to do with whether I am white or Black, Anglo or Hispana, Christian or Jewish. But it is only because whiteness is taken as a given that there is even the appearance of being able to distinguish simply between a person's being a woman and a person's being a man, and thus of being able somehow to point to the "woman part" of me in isolation from the "white part" of me. Even if the idea is that I am to be distinguished simply from men, it may turn out that I am distinguished from white men in ways different from the ways in which I am distinguished from Black men. We have discussed this before, but it's worth trying one more approach to it.

Let's suppose I have the chance to stand up on a stage next to James Baldwin. He is a man and I am a woman, but there are other differences between us, including of course the fact that he is Black and I am white. How, then, will contrasting myself to him enable you to see what my "woman part" is and how it is isolatable from my "white part"? Is my difference from him as a woman separable from my difference from him as a white person? To find out whether my gender difference is isolatable from my racial difference from him, it would help to add some more people on the stage. So now Angela Davis joins us. Is there some respect in which I am different from James Baldwin in just the same way Angela Davis is different from him—is there something she and I share such that we are different from him in just the same ways? And now let's add a white man up here—say my brother Jon. Are Angela Davis and I different from Jon in just the same way, since we both are women and he is a man?

Now in what respect could Angela and I be said to be different from Jon in just the same way? Well, we're both called "women" and he is not. But does our being called "women" mean the same thing to us and for us? Are there any situations in which my being white and her being Black does not affect what it means to us and for us to be women? To whom is it not going to make a difference that my "womanness" is the womanness of a white woman, that hers is the womanness of a Black woman? To our mothers? our fathers? our sisters? our brothers? our children? our teachers? our students? our employers? our lovers? ourselves?

If it were possible to isolate a woman's "womanness" from her racial identity, then we should have no trouble imagining that had I been Black I could have had just the same understanding of myself as a woman as I in fact do, and that no matter how differently people would have treated me had I been Black, nevertheless what it would have meant to them that I was a woman would have been just the same. To rehearse this imaginary situation is to expose its utter bizarreness.

The identities of persons are much more complicated than what might be suggested by the simple and straightforward use of terms like "Black," "white," "woman," "man." Conceptual tidiness would suggest that if Angela's a woman and I am too, while James is a man and so is Jon, then unless our language misleads us there must be something Angela and I share that distinguishes us from James and Jon and distinguishes us from them indistinguishably. Similarly, if Angela is Black and so is James, while Jon is white and so am I, then unless our language misleads us there must be something Angela and James share that distinguishes them from Jon and me and distinguishes them from us indistinguishably.

However, as some philosophers have been trying to tell us now for decades, we can't blame language for our failure to examine its use in context. And if we examine the use of "woman" in particular contexts, then we might be encouraged to ask when descriptions of what-it-is-to-be-a-woman really are descriptions of what-it-is-to-be-a-woman-in-culture-X or subculture-Y. Being a woman, as we surely know by now from cross-cultural studies, is something that is constructed by societies and differs from one society to another. Hence unless I know something more about two women than the fact that they are women, I can't say anything about what they might have in common. What is the "womanness" that Angela Davis and I are said to share? Prior to any actual investigation, all we can say for sure is that being a woman is constructed in contrast to (even if the contrast is minimal) being a man (or to some other gender as well—not all cultures are as stingy as those that countenance only "men" and "women").[1] While all women are gendered, and are gendered as women in contrast to men, nothing follows from that alone about what it means to be so gendered. For it is simply a tautology to say that all women are gendered, since women are by definition gendered females. (We are referring to gender and not to sex; not all human females end up gendered as women.)

It is thus evident that thinking about a person's identity as made up of neatly distinguishable "parts" may be very misleading, despite the impetus from philosophers such as Plato and Descartes to so describe ourselves. Just as in their cases we may get the impression that the whole person is a composite of soul (or mind) and body, so in the case of much feminist thought we may get the impression that a woman's identity consists of a sum of parts neatly divisible from one another, parts defined in terms of her race, gender, class, and so on. We may infer that the oppressions she is subject to are (depending on who she is) neatly divisible into racism, sexism, classism, or homophobia, and that in her various political activities she works clearly now out of one part of herself, now out of another. This is a version of personal identity we might call Tootsie Roll metaphysics: each part of my identity is separable from every other part, and the significance of each part is unaffected by the other parts. On this view of personal identity (which might also be called pop-bead metaphysics), my being a woman means the same whether I am white or Black, rich or poor, French or Jamaican, Jewish or Muslim.[2] As a woman, I'm like other women; my difference from other women is only along the other dimensions of my identity. Hence it is possible on this view to imagine my being the same woman even if my race were different—the pop-bead or Tootsie Roll section labeled "woman" is just inserted into a different strand or roll. According to a powerful tradition within Western philosophy (thought not limited to it), if my soul is separable from my body, it might become attached to or lodge in another body; and if my soul is who I really am, then this new combination of soul and body is still me. Similarly, if my "womanness" is separable from other aspects of my identity, then I as woman would still be the same woman I am even if I happen to have been born into a body of a different color, or even a body of the same color at a different moment in history.[3]

I

There is much new and recently recovered work by and about women, in history, anthropology, psychology, economics, and sociology, not to mention literature. It is the result of painstaking and often undervalued labor. Surely in such investigations we can expect to find people refusing to let either logical or political assumptions of the kind we discussed in earlier chapters take the place of good empirical research: rather than assuming that women must have something in common as women, these researchers should help us look to see whether they do, to investigate not only the respects in which women of different races, classes, nationalities, historical periods, religions, sexual orientations, and so forth, are similar but the respects in which they are different. On the basis of such studies we may find a way to isolate what is true of women as women.

This way of trying to get at what is true about women is quite different from the two ways we have already explored: (1) to look within a single racial or ethnic or religious or cultural group for the effects of gender, eliminating other differences in an individual's development or treatment; (2) to examine the effects of gender on women not otherwise subject to oppression. Both of these methods are based on the unwarranted assumption that what is constant doesn't affect what is variable, that race or class disappear because they are held constant or because they are not a factor in a woman's oppression. Neither method requires us to investigate differences among women or to go beyond a single group of women.

This ought to tell us that rather than first finding out what is true of some women as women and then inferring that this is true of all women and thus is common to all women, we have to investigate different women's lives and see what they have in common *other* than being female and being called "women." Only then (if at all) can we talk about what is true of any and all of them as women.

Plato, as we saw, thought that only especially gifted thinkers could discern what differences between men and women, or differences among men and among women, mattered; only they could know how and why the differences made a difference; and only by virtue of such knowledge were they philosopher-rulers. If we take nothing else away from a reading of the *Republic*, surely we ought to question how the kind of authority about sameness and difference vested in philosopher-rulers ever becomes the bailiwick of any particular person or group (for example, of the justices of the Supreme Court of the United States, who are taken to have not merely the right but the obligation to decide what the relevant similarities and differences are between men and women, whites and Blacks, Christians and Jews, "normal" and mentally retarded people, etc., and what those similarities and differences mean).[4] The philosopher-rulers do not merely notice some interesting features about the world around them when they describe two people as being the same or different in particular ways—for example, when they claim that male and female philosopher-rulers are more alike than male philosophers and male cobblers. Whatever else they are doing, philosopher-rulers are implicitly insisting that this is the way the world really is. Moreover, they think that their actions and those of everyone else ought to be based on a picture of the way things really are and not on some less accurate account.

Reading Plato ought to encourage us to look at the degree of metaphysical and political authority presupposed by those who claim the right to point out commonality, who assert or exercise the privilege of determining just what it means in terms of others' identities, social locations, and political priorities. It is useful to remember, for example, that Plato didn't consult with women around him to find out if they thought they were like men in the significant ways he thought they were; he claimed to know how and to what extent men and women of a given class were similar and what that meant about how their lives ought to be organized. This as much as any other consideration should make us wonder about the extent to which Plato ought to be called a feminist. One can have a theory about the equality between men and women that itself violates the conditions under which real equality can exist: for simply telling a group of heretofore subjugated people "You are like us in the following respects and hence ought to be treated in the following way" is an assertion of the very power and authority that the claims about equality are supposed to make illicit. As James Baldwin said: "There is no reason for you to try to become like white people and there is no basis whatever for their impertinent assumption that *they* must accept *you*."[5]

It is no wonder, then, that women of color have been distrustful of white women who point to similarities between them when it seems politically expedient to do so and to dissimilarities when it does not.[6] They have wanted to know just why and when white women become interested in similarities and differences among women. At issue is not so much whether there are or are not similarities or differences, but about how white, middle-class feminists try to use claims about similarity and differences among women in different directions, depending on what they believe such similarity or dissimilarity implies. For example, as we have seen, sometimes feminists have insisted on the similarity between the treatment of "women" and that of "slaves"; other times they have insisted that the situation of free women and slave women is different enough that the situation of slave women cannot be useful guide to that of free women.[7] The issue is thus not so much a metaphysical one as a political one. Given the highly charged political atmosphere in which claims about sameness and difference are made, challenged, and negotiated, and the consequences of such claims for access to resources, status, and power, we cannot assume that they are simple descriptive reports on the basis of which we can come to see what women of different races, cultures, and so on, have in common, what is true of them as women. Investigations into ways in which women are similar and ways we are different must always be looked at in the light of the following questions: Who is doing the investigating? Whose views are heard and accepted? Why? What criteria are used for similarity and difference? Finally, and most important, what is said to follow from the supposed existence of similarity or difference?[8] Have those under investigation been asked what they think?

Someone might tell me that we have something in common, but even if I agree, I may find that utterly insignificant in terms of my identity and my plans for action. This reminds us that the claim of commonality can be very arrogant indeed: the caller may be attempting to appropriate the other's identity. We are aware of this whenever we find it annoying for a stranger or even an acquaintance to claim something in common with us. In such cases we resent the implication that because we have something in common there is some special connection between us, some reason for spending time together, making plans together.

Nevertheless, not all claims about commonality are arrogant. Let us take for example the following case:

> You have described yourself as having certain properties or characteristics by virtue of which you justify the claim to a certain position or status or certain entitlements.
>
> I claim that I am like you in that respect and that I therefore also ought to be enjoying that status or those entitlements.
>
> You have the power and authority to recognize our similarity and your doing so will make a significant difference as to whether my claim is attended to.

This history of the civil rights movement and women's rights movements provide familiar examples of this claim. A subordinated people insist that they have characteristics in common with their dominators (e.g., humanity, reason, vulnerability to suffering) and therefore that they are owed a higher regard than presently afforded them by the dominators.

In stark contrast we have the following case:

> You have described yourself as having certain properties or characteristics.
>
> You claim that I am like you in having the same characteristics, but you have not consulted me as to whether I think I am like you in this way or whether I attach the same significance you do to having such characteristics.
>
> You have more power and authority than I to make your claims heard and attended to.

White feminists have fallen into this trap whenever they have assumed that women of color are like themselves and hence ought to have the same priorities. Although it is not arrogant, for example, for a Black woman in the United States to claim that she is like me in having characteristics I say entitle me to citizenship, it is arrogant for me to simply declare to the same woman that she is like me and tell her what that means about the two of us. What makes my claim untenable is my presumption that I have the power and the authority to legislate her identity. She makes no such presumptions in her assertion of her rights; she merely refers to my own description of my identity and rights as a basis for asserting her own. Of course none of this means that I can't help but be arrogant in all ways or that she couldn't possibly be in any way. The two cases we've described do not exhaust the possibilities; variations along a spectrum of claims about commonality will be the more interesting cases for feminist examination.

We have begun to realize that I don't necessarily correct my picture of what is true of women "as women" by doing "empirical research" rather than simply generalizing from my own case.[9] For I can't simply "look and see" to find out what we have or don't have in common. First of all, I have to have decided what kind of similarity or difference I am interested in. It makes no sense to ask simply whether women are similar or different—I have to specify in what way they might be similar or different. Moreover, I have to employ criteria of sameness and difference—I have to use some measure by which I decide whether they are the same or different in the specified way. And finally, I have to determine the significance of the similarities and differences I find.

Let us suppose that I am interested in finding out how much economic and political power various groups of women have. Let us also suppose that the criterion for similarity or difference I use is whether women have as much economic and political power as the most powerful men. Using this criterion, I say I find—perhaps I may be challenged by some anthropologists—that there are no significant differences among women with respect to their having that degree of economic and political power. Finally, I judge that being the same in this way is a very significant fact about women, more significant than any other similarity or difference among us. The most important fact about us is what we have in common: namely, that none of us has the power the most powerful men do.

On the other hand, I might employ another criterion. I might ask not simply whether any women have as much power as the most powerful men, but rather investigate the degree to which and ways in which different groups of women have access to such power, even on borrowed terms. Using this criterion I am much more likely to see differences among women; and while I may not be sure just what significance to attach to those differences, I am at least prepared to give them some weight. For example, using the first criterion I cannot attach any significance to the fact that because the wives of white slaveowners in the United States were of a different race and class, they had many more privileges than the Black women who were their slaves (including the privilege of whipping their female slaves at will and with impunity). If my working criterion is the kind of power women lack rather than the degree of power they have, then I have to say that the wives did not have the economic and political power their husbands did, and hence that there is no significant difference between them and the Black slave women. But by the second criterion, I do not discount the power women have (however derivative it might be) in trying to see what women do or do not have in common. I note that while neither the white wife nor the Black female slave had the power the white male slaveowner did, this did not mean they were subject to the same abuses of his power, nor did it mean that the women were equally powerless in relation to each other.

Let us explore a related example. Suppose my criterion for deciding how similar women are with respect to economic and political power is whether they have as much power as men of their own racial, class, or ethnic group. Let us suppose—contrary to some anthropological findings and to the facts of slavery before us—that according to this criterion, all women are the same: none of us has as much or more power than the men of our group. But if we use this criterion for deciding how similar or different we are, then we completely leave aside the differences in power between men of different groups, between women of different groups, and between men of one group and women of another. If we suppose, for example, that upper-class white women in the United States are as subject to the whims of their husbands' desire to abuse them as poor white women are, we leave out of the picture the power upper-class white women and their husbands have over poor white men and poor white women.

An example from Kenneth Stampp brings to mind yet another decision that has to be made when I try to "look and see" what different groups of people have in common: how shall I describe what they share? Stampp describes a working assumption of his investigations in this way:

> I have assumed that the slaves were merely ordinary human beings, that innately Negroes *are*, after all, only white men with black skins, nothing more, nothing less.[10]

What Blacks and whites have in common, according to Stampp, is an essential "whiteness." Stampp is willing to countenance similarity to members of a different racial group, historically despised by his own, as long as it is on his terms (he gets to decide who is like whom and what that means) and as long as it is favorable to him (it preserves his identity and erases that of the formerly despised group). He is hardly being "color-blind" here, but rather is insisting that Black people aren't the color some of us might have thought; they actually are white.

In short, I may have a great deal at stake when I explore similarities and differences among groups of people. Just what I have at stake may show up at the many points in my investigation at which I must make some crucial decisions: decisions about the kind of similarity or difference I am interested in, decisions about the criteria I will employ to see what similarities and differences there are, decisions about what I take them to mean, decisions about how I describe those similarities or differences. We feminists are no less subject to the biases such decisions can introduce than anyone else is. A description of the common world we share "as women" may be simply a description of my world with you now as an honorary member.

II

Let us return for a moment to the knowledge about our identities that most of us find easy to express. Most of us (in perhaps most societies) are asked at regular intervals to indicate whether we are men or women, what racial or ethnic category describes us, and so on (what we are asked will depend on the society we live in). Indeed, our knowledge of such facts about our identities is called upon all the time—for example, in filing out new patient forms at the dentist's, in choosing which bathroom to enter, in providing information for demographic studies (to say nothing about the information we constantly give out to others about aspects of our identities, through our speech patterns, gestures, accents, inflections, gait, and clothing). No doubt we can lie about these identities—by checking the wrong box, for example. No doubt we can refuse to act the way we might be expected to on the basis of this self-knowledge—my knowing I'm a woman doesn't mean I won't use a bathroom marked "men." But lying and "misbehaving" presuppose the kind of knowledge in question, that is, knowledge of one's gender, one's race, one's ethnicity, one's nationality. What is it I know if I know that I am a woman or a man, Black or Hispana or white, Jewish or Christian, straight or gay or lesbian? Could I be wrong? If others disagree with me, is there a way of deciding which of us is right?

Descartes argued that given good grounds for doubt about anything else he might have come to believe, there was only one thing he could know for certain: that he existed.

> This proposition, "I am," "I exist," whenever I utter it or conceive it in my mind, is necessarily true.[11]

Indeed, the fact of his doubting was the very condition of his certain knowledge—for doubting (itself a kind of thinking) couldn't take place unless there was someone to do the doubting. To paraphrase Walt Kelley's Pogo: I have met the doubter and he is I. I think, therefore I am. This knowledge of his own existence was something Descartes took himself to have apart from the mediation of his senses (those, he had satisfied himself, were deceptive until proven otherwise) and apart from the mediation of his culture (there was no good reason to believe anything he had been taught).[12] And he was in many ways quite attuned to the reach of his senses and his culture: for having found the nugget of certainty in the fact that he existed, he was very cautions about describing who or what the "I" that exists *is*:

> But I do not yet sufficiently understand what is this "I" that necessarily exists. I must take care, then, that I do not rashly take something else for the "I," and thus go wrong even in the knowledge that I am maintaining to be the most certain and evident of all. . . . What, then, did I formerly think I was?[13]

He trots out, only to dismiss on the skeptical grounds he already has laid, several possible candidates for what he is—reasonable animal, man, body, soul. I can't say for certain that I have a face, hands, arms, Descartes reasoned, even though I can say for certain that I exist, because I have said that I have reason to doubt that such things exist.

I bring up Descartes here, not because I think a program of skeptical calisthenics along the lines he proposed is the right antidote for the habits of thought that lie at the root of tendencies toward ethnocentrism in dominant Western feminist thought. But I do find instructive his caution about *what* or *who* he is, as well as his general point about the deceptive ease with which we use words, the facile certainty with which we describe what we might think we know best—ourselves. Descartes—certain as he is about some facts about himself—is concerned about how much our understanding of ourselves is due, not to unmediated introspection, but to concepts and categories we inherit from other people, concepts and categories that presuppose the existence of the very things Descartes thinks we have reason to doubt.[14] I might well be a man, Descartes is saying, but I have to convince myself that I know some other things before I'll agree to this description of myself.

I say that I know I am a woman, I know that I am white, and so on. But if I know that, surely I know what I mean by saying these things. What properties am I ascribing to myself? Are there circumstances under which I might have doubts about what or who I am? Is being a woman something I could cease being? Is being white something I could cease being?

What have I learned, when I learn that I am a woman? When I learn that I am white? What have I agreed to, in agreeing to say that I am a woman? In agreeing to say that I am white? What am I refusing, if I were to insist that neither of these terms applies to me?

Imagine a huge customs hall with numerous doors, marked "women," "men," "Afro-American," "Asian-American," "Euro-American," "Hispanic-American," "working class," "middle class," "upper class," "lesbian," "gay," "heterosexual," and so forth. (You may add to or subtract from the number of doors to your heart's content; we'll return in a minute to the question of who decides how many doors there are, what the doors say, and other questions about the legislation and orchestration of identity.) The doors are arranged in banks, so that each person faces first a bank of doors that sort according to gender, then a bank that sort according to race, or alternatively sort first according to race, then according to class, then according to gender, and so on. We'll all give notice of who we are by going through the requisite doors.

Assume that the doors at the first bank are marked

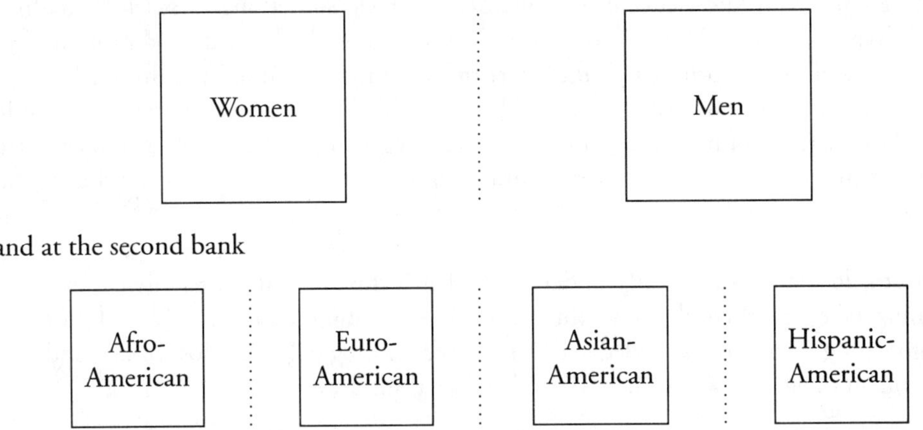

and at the second bank

If the sorting done at the first bank is still in effect at the second, then there will have to be two sets of doors at the second, like so:

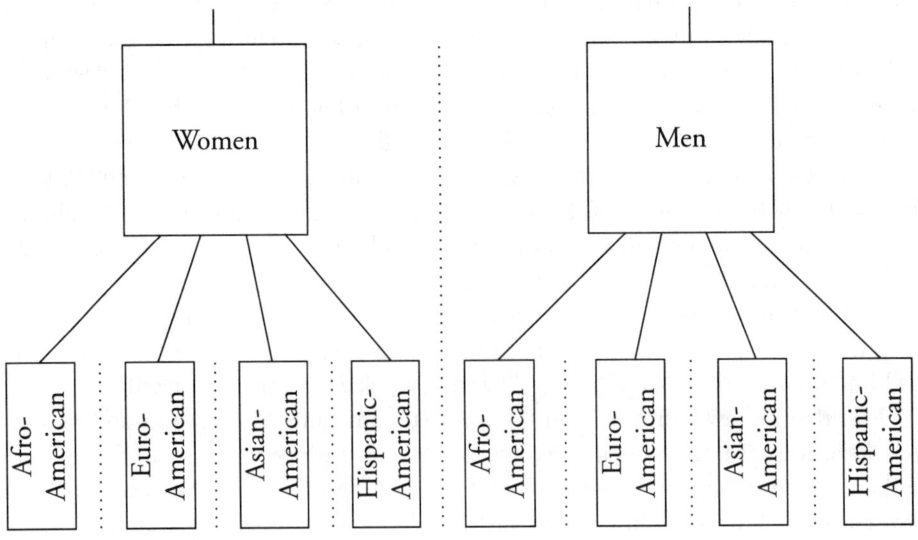

That is, if the original division is maintained between women and men, then Afro-American women and men will not go through the same doors—for there will be two doors marked "Afro-American," one at the other side of the door marked "women," the other at the other side of the door marked "men."[15] Notice that in this case whatever the Afro-Americans have in common, they will not end up on the other side of the same door; they won't be in the same place. For their Afro-Americanness, whatever that is, will be seen to exist in the context of their being women or men, and more particularly as in some sense subordinate to their being women or men. In accordance with this way of sorting people, there is only one category of "woman," but two categories of each racial or cultural identity.

Let us see what happens if we change the order of the doors or if we do not insist that one sorting have effect on the next: for example, the Afro-American men and women would have ended up on the other side of the same door marked "Afro-American" if after the division into women and men all the people involved in the sorting had come back together again in a big group and started afresh. Though they once would have been divided for another purpose, that fact about them does not show up in the next division. Or let us suppose that the first division was not between men and women but between Afro-American, Euro-American, and so forth. In this situation, Afro-American women and the other women would not end up in the same location after the first sorting.

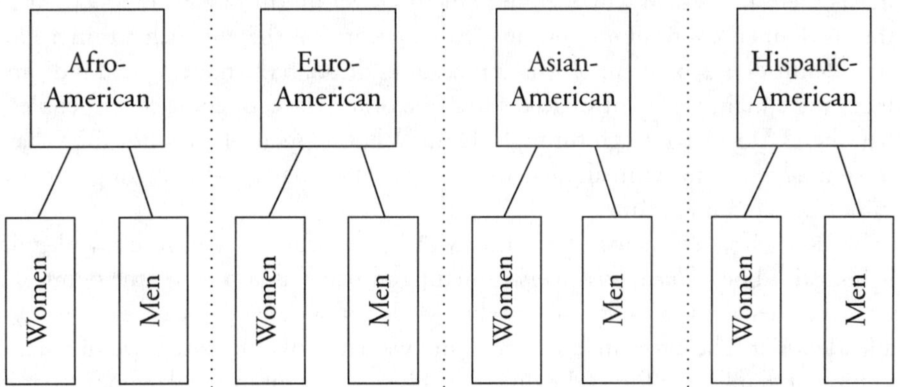

Notice that according to this schema, there are four categories of women, while according to the first sorting there was but one; and there is only one category for each racial or cultural group, while according to the first division there were several. Whether and how people are divided up further depends on what the next set of doors is.

As you already can see, we get different pictures of people's identities and of the extent to which one person shares some aspect of identity with another, depending on what the doors are, how they are ordered, and how people are supposed to proceed through them. For example, according to the first schema, a woman who is "Asian-American" has more in common with all other women than she does with Asian-American men while according to the second, Asian-American men and women have more in common than Asian-American women and other women. According to the first schema, I can in some sense think about myself as a woman in isolation from other facts about myself; if I couldn't, I wouldn't know how to go through the doors. Yet according to the second schema, my thinking about myself as a woman is in the context of being Asian-American or Afro-American, or some other racial group.

We will need to know more about these doors: Who makes them, and who guards them? That is, who decides what will be on them, how many there will be, in what order they occur? Who decides which one you are supposed to take if there is any doubt? Is one free to ignore a door or to go around a given set of doors? We surely also need to know what facts about you and your experiences and history make it seem likely—to you and others—that you will go through one door rather than another, or that you will find the order of the doors appropriate to your identity.

Questions will also arise about what the designations on the doors mean. For example, there is a certain ambiguity about the doors marked "men" and "women." That isn't the same as having them marked "male" and "female."[16] Many questions will come up about the accuracy of the designations: What if someone refused to go through a door marked simply "Woman" or simply "Asian-American," on the grounds that she found those categories too crude and as suspicious of the point of being catalogued in these ways? Suppose someone didn't know what the point of door-dividing is and was not sure of what the designations mean? Moreover, if I think that things are better behind one door than another, I might try very hard to convince the guards and the people scheduled to be sorted that I ought to go behind that one even though I know it is not the one they expect me to go through. Do some people know better than I what doors I really belong behind? Is there any reason why I should not try to get on the far side of any door I want to? Are the doors there to pinpoint one's "true identity," if there is such a thing? Do people have identities independent of what proceeding through the doors would indicate? Are the doors there mainly to control access to some other place, or some other people? Why are they there? Do I have to go through them? What happens if I try not to? What happens if someone tries to claim an identity as an act of solidarity—by wearing a yellow star or a pink triangle, for example?

The doors imagery helps us to deal with some issues that have been plaguing us throughout this book [*Inessential Woman*—ed.] and helps us also to see the point of questions raised earlier about what it is to have knowledge of one's gender, race, class or any other possible identifier. The alternative schemas (and we have only presented two of indefinitely many) present graphically for us the different things it can mean to talk about what is true of women "as women" and about what women have in common. According to the first schema, what is true of me "as a woman" seems to be what I have in common with all other women in contrast to all other men. According to the second schema, what is true of me "as a woman" would seem to be what I have in common with other women of my ethnic and racial background in contrast to men of the same background. The second schema suggests that one's womanness is to be understood in the context of one's ethnic and racial background, while the first makes it look as if one's womanness can be specified quite independently of such background. According to the second schema, even if a case could be made for there being a "woman part" of each woman that was isolatable from her other "parts," that wouldn't necessarily show that all women have something substantial in common "as women," that the "woman part" would be the same in all cases. In order to know whether all the people who end up behind the doors marked "women" share anything substantial in common, we'd have to know the criteria used for dividing women from men in each case and see if they were similar in all cases (and this, as noted earlier, will require us to decide in what respect and by what criteria we want to see whether they are similar). Of course we could assure that all women have something substantial in common by insisting that anyone who does not have some particular characteristic is not a "woman"; then "all women have something in common" would be as secure, and as trivial, as any other tautology.

The schemas enable us to see how the situation of white, middle-class women can be conflated with the situation of "women," thus securing the privileged position of one group of women over others. If we use the first schema, differences among women are recognized but treated as secondary to whatever it is that distinguishes all women from all men. The first schema doesn't tell us what this common distinguishing feature is. But if our description of what distinguishes "women" from "men" in fact ends up being what distinguishes one group of women from the men like them, then what is true of that one group of women will be taken to characterize all women. This is in effect what we saw happening in de Beauvoir's account. If we keep the second schema in mind, we might be less likely to take the case of one group of women for the case of all, since the second schema implies that gender distinctions exist in the context of ethnic and racial distinctions. Indeed, it suggests that the distinctions between any two ethnic or racial groups are more significant (according to those who devise the system) than the distinctions between men and women within any such group. It makes it harder for us to take any particular group of women's experience as representative of all, but surely it does not prohibit us from asking what different groups of women have or might come to have in common.

Since people can be classified and catalogued in any number of ways, overlapping ways, how we catalog them, in particular how we sort out the overlapping distinctions, will depend on our purposes and our sense of what the similarities and differences among them are and how they ought to be weighed. (Think of the different classifactory schemas implicitly proposed by those who insist "I am a woman who is a writer," or "I am a writer who is a woman.") Purposes may clash, indeed may clash somewhat predictably along the lines of certain differences among us; and not all of us have the same degree of power and authority about which schema or schemas are the most appropriate or revealing means of presenting the significance of similarities and differences among people.

By thinking of cataloguing schemes as being like doors in an imaginary customs house, or like doors in some version of the immigration bureau that existed at Ellis Island, or like bathroom doors in segregated areas of the United States, we may be more likely to keep in mind the constant human effort it takes to create and maintain classifactory schemas, the continual human battles over which schemes are to prevail, and the purposes of such schemes.

Perhaps we need to add a door that says "officials only" to remind us of another very important difference—that between people who create and maintain the schemes and those simply subject to them. On the other hand, it may well be that those with the most power of all don't have doors—especially not doors labeled "makers and keepers of the doors"—for that would only reveal that the scheme is not a "natural" one and also enable those upset with the scheme to know where to begin to look for its creators and enforcers.[17] This points to another useful feature of the doors analogy: it reminds us how certain human artifacts can come to be regarded as things found or forged in nature, facts to be discovered or unearthed by human investigators. It has been crucial for those who make much of certain differences among humans to portray those differences as givens that humanity disregards at its peril.[18]

Classificatory names on doors have an important kind of official status: while they reflect the particular purposes of powerful members of human communities (purposes that may be shared by less powerful members, a point to which we shall return below), they at the same time obscure those purposes through the suggestion that the categories are uncreated, that they exist in themselves. In this view, each of us is either man or woman, either white or Black or brown, either Jewish or Christian, heterosexual or gay or lesbian, and that like it or not, one or some of those elements of our identities are more fundamentally descriptive of us than others. No doubt it is true that once those categories have been created, and once social and political and economic institutions have been built around them, there will be criteria in accordance with which we can say with assurance into what categories any particular person fits. And even if we had no part in the creation of such categories, if we have learned the ways of our society, we have learned which doors we will be expected to pass through. Indeed, we may joyfully embrace the identities they draw attention to.

Our learning of the categories and where we fit into them is unlikely to include learning about their historical character. That is, it is unlikely that we learn about the point at which a category came into being. (For example, the creation of "homosexual" as a category of person as opposed to a category of action dates apparently from the late nineteenth century).[19] It is also unlikely that we learn about the battles over what the categories mean (for example, battles over definitions among white men about what constitutes "Negro blood," or over definitions among contemporary Blacks in the United States over what constitutes being "Black").[20]

If we think of such distinctions in terms of the doors, then we might begin to ask a number of questions that would challenge the assumption that the distinctions we make among people are simple and straightforward responses to the distinctions found in them in nature. (It also helps to challenge a somewhat more complicated assumption: that the categories are indeed created for human purposes, but not for those of any particular group—as if all humans have the same authority over the creation and maintenance of the categories.) First of all, the door imagery implies some ambiguity about whether the process of going (or being made to go) through the doors represents a recognition of differences among people or a creation of them. Insofar as there are criteria for the appropriateness of particular people passing through particular doors, and insofar as those who pass through and those who monitor their passage seem to have no questions about the passage, it looks as if the doors simply represent a moment at which people are processed in accordance with characteristics that inhere in them. Moreover, the monitors or guards seem to be there, not to keep making up categories, but to make sure that the people whom the guards know (and whom the guards assume know they know) to belong to one category rather than another go through the right door. A further but only occasionally called-upon role of the monitors is to decide about borderline cases.

On the other hand, the process by which people are channeled into one category rather than another can be seen as creating distinctions. We need to ask why people are being processed through these doors, whether social and political positions and privileges are at stake in this processing. We need also to inquire whether (and how) those subject to such processing ever challenge the categories or their significance. It is important to know whether they are punished for questioning the appropriateness of the categories or challenging the authority of those who seem to have most power over the maintenance of them. Whether categories come into and go out of existence, and if so, why. We must ask whether there are battles over what the categories ought to be, or over what they mean, or over who gets to decide these issues.

We may also want to know more about just how people are processed through the doors: by this we mean to ask not simply whether people resist going through or help others who resist going through; but also whether if they do resist they are forced through anyway. It is not enough to know whether people do something without resistance to decide whether they are made to do it. For we can come to do without apparent coercion what we were encouraged to do and punished for not doing from an early age. We have to ask what happens when we do not do what we are expected to. I should be wary of describing my actions as "willing" if I would have been punished for not acting in that way. The existence of known punishments for failure to do something strongly suggests that one is being made to do that thing—that in the absence of such punishments one probably wouldn't do it.

In light of such considerations we might go back to some questions raised earlier in this chapter about what one knows when one answers such questions as "Are you a man or a woman?" "Are you white or Black or . . .?" To answer the first by saying "I am a woman" is to agree to what one understands to be the criteria for being a woman and to say that one meets those criteria. But one could be challenge either on the grounds that one isn't using the right criteria or on the grounds that one doesn't meet them. And insofar as the doors analogy helps us to see the extent to which gender identity is, not only as de Beauvoir argued the ongoing creation of a society (women are made, not born), but something over which some members of society have more authority than others, my claim about being a woman may well be challenged by those who have that authority. Sojourner Truth had to argue for the proposition that she was a "woman." Someone who refused to indicate whether one is a "woman" or a "man," or someone who refuses to specify their "race" or "ethnicity" on a census form, may be punished by those who distribute such forms. Some women may be told by white feminists that they aren't properly distinguishing their voices as "women" from their voices as "Afro-Americans" or "Jews" or members of the "working class."[21] Jan Morris decided that rather than contest the meaning of "woman" or "man" she would change her bodily appearance and her gestures and "lifestyle" so that she would be counted as a "woman."[22] (I don't know what it says on her passport about her sexual identity, or who exactly is in the position to decide what she is entitled to put there, but I feel certain she uses bathrooms marked "women" and presents herself in social life as a woman—indeed, as an upper-middle-class, white Englishwoman.)

Given the possibility of questions about and challenges to the categories, it may be more important to ask, not what I know when I answer such questions about my identity, but what I acquiesce in, what I do not resist, when I agree to answer them. I am agreeing to some schema of identity, forged in accordance with some individual's or some group's or some society's classificatory purposes. Unless I register some kind of protest or qualification, I accept (willingly or not) the appropriateness of the classification and the significance attached to it. So, for example, I might gladly use the word "woman" to refer to myself but try in concert with others to resist what I take to be the prevailing meaning of the term or the prevailing significance attached to it. Or I might think it important to resist a term altogether—for example, "handicapped." I might think it important to embrace joyfully such a term as "lesbian" or "Black" and to try with others to invest it with new meaning.

Insofar as we don't regard the kinds of exercises in which we are asked to indicate our gender, race, and so on, as problematic, we may have forgotten to ask how we came to use those categories to refer to ourselves or to others. It may seem to us as if who we are, who others are, and what we do and don't have in common are matters of simple observation. Perhaps because we learn the categories so early and are continually asked to reflect our knowledge of them, they seem unproblematic. Ease of application of the categories can be confused with justified certainty about how "natural" they are.

Furthermore, if we think about identities and points of similarity and difference as things that are always being negotiated and challenged, we may think more about ways in which these categories depend upon the particular purposes of those who create and maintain them. This is not to say that it is easy to identify those who create and maintain them. It often seems as if none of us created these categories but all of us help to maintain them. But insofar as we feel moved to do battle over them, we exhibit both a sense of being subject to them against our will and a sense of being able to do something about the power they have over the articulation of our identities and thus over our social and political positions to the extent that they depend on those identities.

In some ways it ought to be quite surprising that describing who we are and how we are like and unlike others is not always the straightforward process it appears to be. For first of all, the ability to compare and contrast things by seeing what categories they do or don't fit into is crucial to thinking and to using language. Second, in societies in which great significance is attached to sexual, racial, and class categories, we learn early and well which of those categories we and everyone around us belong to. Indeed, most of the time we probably are showing ourselves and others which of these categories we belong to, even when we are not explicitly saying so. Unless categorization is made problematic for us, we are not likely to raise questions about the categories we use; and it seems likely that the more a society has invested in its members' getting the categories right, the more occasions there will be for reinforcing them, and the fewer occasions there will be for raising questions about them.[23] . . .

IV

This chapter tries to respond to quite reasonable questions about our capacity to distinguish our gender from other aspects of our identities. Indeed, this capacity is part of a more general ability to distinguish anyone's gender from her or his race, class, or any other identities. To know what "woman" means is to know that it applies to me and to Angela Davis and doesn't apply to my brother Jon or to James Baldwin. (Similarly, I couldn't be said to know what "white" means if I only applied it to myself and didn't know how it also applies to Jon but not to Angela Davis or James Baldwin.) The question for us is not whether we have such capacities but what, if anything, follows from them.

It certainly doesn't follow that there is an essential "womanness" that Angela and I share and that Jon and James lack. That is, what makes it true that Angela and I are women is not some "woman" substance that is the same in each of us and interchangeable between us. Selves are not made up of separable units of identity strung together to constitute a whole person. It is not as if there is a goddess somewhere who made lots of little identical "woman" units and then, in order to spruce up the world a bit for herself, decided to put some of those units in black bodies, some in white bodies, some in the bodies of kitchen maids in seventeenth-century France, some in the bodies of English, Israeli, and Indian prime ministers.

Indeed, positing an essential "womanness" has the effect of making women inessential in a variety of ways. First of all, if there is an essential womanness that all women have and have always had, then we needn't know anything about any woman in particular. For the details of her situation and her experience are irrelevant to her being a woman. Thus if we want to understand what "being a woman" means, we needn't investigate her individual life or any other woman's individual life. All those particulars become inessential to her being and our understanding of her being a woman. And so she also becomes inessential in the sense that she is not needed in order to produce the "story of woman." If all women have the same story "as women," we don't need a chorus of voices to tell the story.

Moreover, to think of "womanness" in this way obscures three related facts about the meaning of being a woman: first of all, that whatever similarities there are between Angela Davis and me, they exist in the context of differences between us; second, that there is ongoing debate about what effect such differences have on those similarities (different arrangements of the doors express different positions on this matter); third, not all participants in that debate get equal air time or are invested with equal authority.

The problem with the "story of man" was that women couldn't recognize themselves in it. So those who produce the "story of woman" want to make sure they appear in it. The best way to ensure that is to be the storyteller and hence to be in a position to decide which of all the many facts about women's lives ought to go into the story, which ought to be left out. Essentialism works well in behalf of these aims, aims that subvert the very process by which women might come to see where and how they wish to make common cause. For essentialism invites me to take what I understand to be true of me "as a woman" for some golden nugget of womanness all women have as women; and it makes the participation of other women inessential to the production of the story. How lovely: the many turn out to be one, and the one that they are is me.

NOTES

1. See, for example, Robert B. Edgerton, "Pokot Intersexuality: An East African Example of the Resolution of Sexual Incongruity," *American Anthropologist* 66, no. 1 (1964): 1288–99.
2. Many thanks to Barbara Cottle Johnson for the pop-bead imagery.
3. A white woman might think her gender is thoroughly distinct from her race because she appears to experience sexism in isolation from racism: she is subjected to sexism but not to racism. (I say "appears" because we cannot understand the sexism she experiences without understanding its connection to the racism she does not.) It does not follow from that apparent isolation that her gender is distinct from her race; but neither does it follow, from the fact that a woman experiences sexism *and* racism, that her gender is distinct from her race. We discussed reasons for this earlier in chapter 2 [of *Inessential Woman* (Boston: Beacon Press, 1988)] and they are explored further below.

   It is important to note that this composite, collection-of-parts view of personhood, as well as its accompanying view of political activity, is held implicity by a wide range of feminist political and social theorists—not only those who treat gender as distinct from and isolatable from racial, ethnic, or other identity, but those who treat racial, class, and ethnic identity as isolatable from gender identity.
4. For extremely illuminating accounts of the role of the judiciary in making such decisions, see Martha Minow, "When Difference Has Its Home: Group Homes for the Mentally Retarded, Equal Protection, and Legal Treatment of Difference," *Harvard Civil Rights Civil Liberties Review* 22, no. 1 (1987), 111–89; and her "Foreword: Justice Engendered," in "The Supreme Court 1986 Term," *Harvard Law Review* 101, no. 1 (1987): 10–95.
5. *The Fire Next Time* (New York: Dell, 1962), 19. James Baldwin died while I was writing this book.

6. See Lorraine Bethel, "What Chou Mean *WE*, White Girl?" in *Conditions* 5 (1979): 86–92.
7. See the discussion of Richards and Cantarella in chapter 2 of *Inessential Woman.*
8. See Minow references in note 4 above.
9. I hardly begin to dip into the issues raised by reflection on what actual or desirable social science methodology is.
10. Stampp, *The Peculiar Institution* (New York: Knopf, 1954), vii–viii.
11. René Descartes, *Meditations on First Philosophy*, in *Descartes: Philosophical Writings*, translated and edited by Elizabeth Anscombe and Peter Geach (London: Nelson, 1969). Meditation 2: 67. Further citations are from this edition.
12. See Descartes, *Discourse on Method.*
13. Meditation 2: 67.
14. That is, he would agree with the later Wittgenstein (see, for example, *The Philosophical Investigations* [New York: Macmillan, 1953]) to some extent that the language we use to talk about ourselves is itself an intersubjective product and project and that therefore if we want to locate a kind of knowledge that does not depend on such products and projects we can't use language that imports them. Descartes does not realize how this undermines the method of the *Meditations.*
15. This pattern of sorting was not used by those who constructed segregated bathrooms in the United States.
16. This reminds us to ask whether the kinds of questions we referred to earlier that we are so adept at answering are questions about our sexual identity or our gender identity. It is worth thinking about why many bathroom doors are marked "men" and "women" rather than "male" and "female," since applications and census forms typically use the latter and seem to have to do simply with sexual identity. (Forms that ask one to pick from among "Mr.," "Mrs.," "Miss," and now "Ms." have more to do with gender identity and social role than sexual identity, since there are only two sexes referred to.) Perhaps it is because bathrooms have a lot to do with the maintenance of gender identity, insofar as they are places where females are expected to engage in the titivating activities necessary for maintaining one's womanly appearance—brushing one's hair, putting on makeup, adjusting one's skirt, attending to small children, spraying on perfume, and so forth.

    In regard to accuracy of designation, one knows why doors are marked "men" and "women," and one knows what is in store behind those doors—even if one thinks bathrooms oght to be co-ed. I also note that it is perfectly within the rules about bathroom doors that humans below a certain age can go into either—or rather, that little boys can go into rooms marked "women" even though little girls don't usually go into rooms marked "men."
17. It is not without reason that trustees of colleges and universities typically don't have campus offices.
18. Sociobiology is perhaps the most recent field to define human differences in this way. For another illustration of the creation of difference in the guise of discovering it, see the legal and medical documents collected by Michel Foucault together with the memoirs of a nineteenty-century French hermaphrodite in *Herculine Barbin* (New York: Random, 1980).
19. For a recent discussion of this, see Ian Hacking, "Making Up People," in *Reconstructing Individualism*, ed. Thomas C. Heller, Morton Sosna, and David E. Wellerby (Stanford: Stanford University Press, 1986), 222–36. See also "On 'Compulsory Hexterosexuality and Lesbian Existence': Defining the Issues," a collection of comments by Ann Ferguson, Jacquelyn N. Zita, and Kathryn Pyne Adelson, *Signs 7* (1981): 158–99.
20. See, for example, "Woman Seeks Change in Racial Designation," *The New York Times*, Friday, 28 November 1984, A28. Also see Michael Omi and Howard Winant, "By the Rivers of Babylon: Race in the United States," parts 1 and 2, *Socialist Review* 71 and 72 (1983).

21. See Lugones and Spelman, "Have We Got a Theory for You!" *Women's Studies International Forum* 6, no. 6 (1983), 573–81.
22. Jan Morris, *Conundrum* (New York: Signet, 1974).
23. There will be tension between these two things, since being too obvious about reinforcing categories may make people suspicious.

Race, Class, and Psychoanalysis? Opening Questions

Many feminists have criticized psychoanalysis for its failure to address race and class specificity and thus for its privileging of a conception of gender based on the white, middle-class, nuclear family. Abel acknowledges the merits of this critique. Nevertheless, she maintains that psychoanalysis is capable of accommodating race and class difference, and she discusses two texts in which psychoanalysis is used effectively to situate gender in the context of race and class.

In "Mama's Baby, Papa's Maybe: An American Grammar Book," Hortense Spillers uses Lacanian theory to analyze slavery and to draw out its implications with respect to gender. She documents a number of ways in which gender was deconstructed under slavery. These include the slave mother's centrality to kinship relations as a result of the suppression of the African-American father's name, the stark contrast between the culture's figuring of the slave woman as a breeder and the white woman as a revered mother, and the slave mother's dynamic role in the formation of her son's subjectivity. In *Landscape for a Good Woman: A Story of Two Lives,* Carolyn Kay Steedman explores some relations between class and gender. Two stories about her childhood—one about an encounter between her father and a forest-keeper and the other about an encounter between her mother and a health official—displace the sexualized Oedipal account of gender formation and replace it with an account of class, authority, power, and gender. Steedman's text also interrogates the empathic, nurturant conception of mothering that is associated with middle-class values and with object relations psychoanalytic theory by contrasting this image with a conception of purely material mothering that originates in the working class. Steedman's ambivalence about these alternatives is poignantly and subversively expressed through a pair of fairy tales. Abel concludes that, although feminists must be wary of race and class bias in psychoanalytic theory, psychoanalytic discourse has great potential as a medium in which feminists can articulate and negotiate race, class, and gender boundaries.

—D.T.M.

Chapter 10

Elizabeth Abel

Race, Class, and Psychoanalysis? Opening Questions

> Although psychoanalytic theory has done a great deal to improve our understanding of sexual difference, it has done little or nothing to change the concrete social conditions of sex-relations and of gender-stratification. The latter is precisely the target of feminist practice.
>
> Rosi Braidotti, "The Politics of Ontological Difference"

> It would seem fairly obvious by now that feminism's struggle to infuse into psychoanalytical theory the breath of an efficacious politics has not been a major success. Feminist approaches in recent years to Lacanian psychoanalysis, for example . . . have been thwarted by the obstinacy of psychoanalytic *universalist* theories of subjective construction.
>
> Paul Smith, "Julia Kristeva Et Al.; or, Take Three or More"[1]

Repudiating psychoanalysis has become a familiar gesture of contemporary feminist discourse—and with some good reasons.[2] Seduced by psychoanalytic accounts of subjectivity, much feminist theory of the 1970s has come to seem, from the vantage point of the late 1980s, to have lost its material groundings and with them the possibility of interpreting (and thereby promoting) social change. The traditional indifference of psychoanalysis to racial, class, and cultural differences, and the tendency of psychoanalysis to insulate subjectivity from social practices and discourses all run contrary to a feminism increasingly attuned to the power of social exigencies and differences in the constitution of subjectivity. It is clear that a psychoanalysis useful for contemporary feminism needs some infusion of the social—whether the "social" is construed as the technologies that regulate desire or (in this essay's terms) as the roles of race and class in a diversified construction of subjectivity.[3] It is less clear whether the resistance of psychoanalysis to the social is adventitious or intrinsic. If we agree (as I do) with Paul Smith that psychoanalysis has no innate political desire, we nevertheless can ask how labile psychoanalysis is, how far its boundaries can expand to incorporate issues of social difference into a discourse useful, if not for changing the social order, at least for theorizing this order's intervention in the production of diversely gendered subjects.

Psychanalysis, of course, is not a monolithic discourse and has no uniform relation to the social domain. Freud's resistance to a culturally inflected psychoanalysis is overt and infamous.[4] The recent revisions of Freud that have been more influential for feminism, however, have opened possibilities for new negotiations between the psychoanalytic and the social domains. Introducing the category of the social into Lacanian discourse requires a deliberate intervention, since this discourse collapses the social into a symbolic register that is always everywhere the same. While de-essentializing gender by relocating it in a cultural arena that is severed from biology, orthodox Lacanians essentialize a dehistoricized paternal law, derived from the symbolic Father, "the dead father of the law who . . . is there however weak or absent his real representative may be."[5] According to Jacqueline Rose, "the force of psychoanalysis is . . . precisely that it gives an account of patriarchal culture as a trans-historical and cross-cultural force. It therefore conforms to a feminist demand for a theory which can explain women's subordination across specific cultures and different historical moments."[6] By insisting that the father's law is necessary and tantamount to culture, however, the official Lacanian account prohibits alternative conceptualizations of culture and renders variations within patriarchal social forms (and thus in the degree and kind of women's subordination) either inconsequential or invisible. Yet the very erasures accomplished by this discourse have pointed its most revisionist practitioners toward a reading of the ways that gender is diversely (de)constructed by the gaps between the social and symbolic domains.[7]

A less deliberate intervention is required within feminist object relations theory, which explicitly locates the production of gendered subjectivity in historically specific and socially variable caretaking arrangements. To foreground these diverse social arrangements would entail not a revision of this theory but, rather, a fulfillment of its claims to explain how the "inexorably social" self that is "constructed in a relational matrix" varies, along with that matrix, "by individual, culture, period, gender."[8] In principle, this matrix is not restricted to an invariant or insulated nuclear family; instead, it functions as a permeable membrane through which a wide range of changing social relations inform the evolution of the gendered subject. Jane Flax, for example, insists: "The caretaker brings to the relationship . . . the whole range of social experience—work, friends, interaction with political and economic institutions, and so on. The seemingly abstract and suprapersonal relations of class, race, and male dominance enter into the construction of 'individual' human development."[9] In practice, however, object relations discourse has confined itself to the Western middle-class nuclear family and has bracketed all variables other than gender; while avoiding the homogeneity of the Lacanian symbolic, this discourse has tended to homogenize gender by implying that children learn within the family a single uniform masculinity or femininity. Elizabeth Spelman has mounted a powerful critique of this homogenizing tendency by arguing that "children learn what it means to be men or women by learning what it is to be men or women of their race, class, ethnicity" since "women mother in a social and political context in which they not only are distinguished from men, but are, along with men of their same cultural background, distinguished from men and women of their cultural backgrounds."[10] But the inadequately textured accounts produced by object relations are not limitations intrinsic to the theory. In her response to a methodological debate on *The Reproduction of Mothering*, Nancy Chodorow invites further research into "class and ethnic differences, differences in family and household structure, differences in sexual orientation of parents, and historical and cross-cultural variations in these relationships" and claims that if she were to write a new *Reproduction of Mothering* she would "examine the link between what seems exclusively gender-related and the construction of other aspects of society, politics, and culture."[11] This is not the direction her own work has pursued; but there is no intrinsic incompatibility between the governing principles of object relations theory and socially inflected qualifications of that theory.[12]

Posing the question of the social enables us to redraw the map of psychoanalytic feminism, so sharply and hierarchally split over the last decade between Lacan and object relations. Both psychoanalytic discourse now seem guilty, either in theory or in practice, of privileging a decontextualized gender as the constitutive factor in subjectivity; and both discourses are (diversely) subject to revision. When difference is interpreted within a social as well as a linguistic framework, moreover, the Lacanian critique of the unitary subject loses some of its special edge, and the heterogeneity of the Lacanian subject seems insufficiently textured and less radically different from the intersubjectively constituted self of object relations.[13] Most importantly, the urgency of theorizing subjectivity within a range of social contexts has made it less productive to reiterate the old oppositions within psychoanalytic feminism, or between psychoanalysis and contemporary feminism, than to imagine more fluid intersections.

Toward this end, I want to ground this essay in a reading of two dense and brilliant texts that address the intersections of gender with race or class from perspectives both indebted to and critical of psychoanalysis. Both published in this country in 1987, Hortense J. Spillers's "Mama's Baby, Papa's Maybe: An American Grammar Book," a psychoanalytically informed meditation on the devastations wrought by slavery on African-American kinship and gender structures, and Carolyn Kay Steedman's *Landscape for a Good Woman: A Story of Two Lives*, a reading of class analysis against and with psychoanalysis, are teasingly and deliberately polyphonic texts. Although Spillers works primarily with Lacan, and Steedman primarily with object relations, each asserts and subverts a range of psychoanalytic and social discourses and propels them into provocative and complicated play.

II

> Is the Freudian landscape an applicable text (say nothing of appropriate) to social and historical situations that do not replicate moments of its own cultural origins and involvements?
>
> Hortense J. Spillers,
> " 'The Permanent Obliquity of an In[pha]llibly Straight':
> In the Time of the Daughters and the Fathers"[14]

"Mama's Baby, Papa's Maybe: An American Grammar Book" offers a qualified "yes" to the question of the applicability of psychoanalysis to the African-American social landscape, although, as the shift from the epigraph's spatial metaphor to the figure of the "grammar book" suggests, Lacanian rather than Freudian discourse is at issue here. The essay's title also offers an intertextual clue to one function of Lacanian theory in Spillers's own discourse. In "Interstices: A Small Drama of Words," an earlier essay, Spillers introduces the folksy "Mama's baby, papa's maybe" to signal the importance of the "hidden and impermissible" paternal origins of feminist analysis in the dominant culture's master discourses, whose boundaries feminism can explode while exploiting an extended heritage of discursive strategies.[15] In "Mama's Baby, Papa's Maybe: An American Grammar Book," a discourse on the "grammar" of the European-American eradication of African kinship structures serves to destabilize Anglo-American universalizations of gender difference, to ally black feminist analyses of degendering under slavery with the larger theoretical project of poststructuralism, and to recast the Lacanian symbolic in the terms of cultural domination. Overtly, a Lacanian discourse politicized through the African-American context authorizes a critique of an Anglo-American feminism identified with object relations and dismissed as "the reproduction of mothering"—as an account, that is, of female gender transmission entirely irrelevant to the brutally disrupted kinship bonds of persons in captivity. Nevertheless, as the essay's title indicates, there is a contradictory (although largely disavowed) alliance with the mother—both with the biological mother whose determinative role in the social definition of the slave child complicates Spillers's allegiance to the paternal discourse and the Name of the Father it privileges, and, consequently, with the discursive mother (an Anglo-American feminism allied with object relations) that, despite its different social context, also underscores the mother's centrality. This discursive genealogy is both irreducibly heterogeneous and necessary to Spillers's project of specifying the complex (de)constructions of gender under slavery.

Spillers invokes the Lacanian divorce between biology and culture in order to subvert the assumption she ascribes to Anglo-American feminism that shared biology entails a common gender, that all biological females participate in a single womanhood reproduced across the generations. In quite an orthodox Lancanian claim, she asserts that " 'gendering' takes place within the confines of the domestic, an essential metaphor that then spreads its tentacles for male and female subjects over a wider ground of human and social purposes. Domesticity appears to gain its power by way of a common origin of cultural fictions that are grounded in the specificity of proper names, more exactly, a patronymic."[16] Violently dislocated from their own kinship (and consequently gender) structures and situated outside the domestic realm in the New World, captive persons in Spillers's account are deprived of gender. This pulverization is also played out on the body. It is not only that gender is severed from biology but also that "biology" shifts in this account from the arena of sexual difference to the Lacanian zone of the fragmented body imperfectly effaced by our illusions of coherence.[17] During both slavery and the Middle Passage (for Spillers, at once a horrific historical reality and a metaphor of the slave's perpetually suspended social definition), violent assaults deprived the captive person's body of any integrity and, consequently, of gender. Distinguishing the socially conceptualized "body" from the undifferentiated, ungendered "flesh" subtending it, Spillers argues that the European capture of African bodies constituted "High crimes against the *flesh*. . . . If we think of the 'flesh' as a primary narrative, then we mean its seared, divided, ripped-apartness, riveted to the ship's hole, fallen, or 'escaped' overboard," or with "eyes beaten out, arms, backs, skulls branded, a left jaw, a right ankle, punctured; teeth missing, as the calculated work of iron, whips, chains, knives, the canine patrol, the bullet" (67). Torture deliberately undoes, and thus exposes the factitiousness of, the integrated body.

Spillers reads the degendering of captive persons through Lacan, but she also politicizes Lacan by focusing on the sites of cultural domination at which kinship, gender, and bodies are deconstructed. Rather than detailing a universal law of culture to which all speaking beings are "subjected," she examines relations of power among cultures, the encounters between different symbolic orders instead of the passage from infancy to culture. By delineating the practices of cultural domination, she renders their violence palpable: the slave's abused flesh bears "the marks of a cultural text whose inside has been turned outside" (67). These inscriptions are in turn perpetuated across generations by the symbolic substitutions of language, as violent (in this account) as the slaveowner's branding iron: "Sticks and bricks *might* break our bones, but words will most certainly *kill* us" (68). It is not, as for Lacan, that "language" speaks "us" but that a dominant symbolic order marks the bodies of its captives. For the African-American female, seizing the power to name within this system is both an imperative of survival and the condition of possibility for a new social subject undetermined by either the dichotomy phallus/castration that has vexed the efforts of Lacan's feminist heirs to theorize the place of "the feminine" in "language" or by the conventions of domesticity that have produced the Anglo-American "gendered female."

Spillers also politicizes Lacan by highlighting the fissures between the social and symbolic realms within the culture of slavery, in which the Name of the Father establishes not gender but property. Since slavery prohibits the African-American male from participating in "the prevailing social fiction of the Father's name, the Father's law," slave children (and their heirs) in Spillers's argument have a distinctive relation to the patriarchal symbolic register, a relation in which masculinity, constituted through a "dual fatherhood . . . comprised of the African father's *banished* name and body and the captor father's mocking presence," is inevitably divided (80). Within this fractured configuration, moreover, the position of the enslaved mother acquires special prominence. Probing the gaps between the social and symbolic fields opens a space for the mother and the mode of feminism that orthodox Lacanian rhetoric critiques.

Overtly, the enslaved mother is the locus of Spillers's sharpest distinction between biology and gender, between ungendered black "female bodies in the raw" and the white "gendered female" defined preeminently in terms of a revered maternity (75). Reproduction under slavery is breeding, not maternity; denied all maternal claims to her children, the enslaved mother simply increases her owner's stock; " 'motherhood' as female blood-rite/right" is destroyed (75). Nevertheless, Spillers accords the slave mother a critical, albeit transient, role in the formation of her children's subjectivity. Working from Frederick Douglass's account of the impact of his enforced early separation from his mother, which he claims eventually dissolved his sense of kinship with his siblings, Spillers locates the experience of kinship in the presence of the mother: "If the child's humanity is mirrored initially in the eyes of its mother, or the maternal function, then we might be able to guess that the social subject grasps the whole dynamic of resemblance and kinship by way of the same source" (76). Using a language of mirroring reminiscent of D. W. Winnicott, Spillers relocates the origin of the social subject in the maternal rather than the paternal function.[18] To underscore the eradication of kinship under slavery, Spillers envisages a maternal function that slavery (imperfectly) destroys.

By the end of the essay, where the subversive matricentric discourse culminates, it is clear that some maternal imprint survives the master culture's attacks. Unmediated by a father empowered by the Father's name, the enslaved child's relation to the mother gains an almost tangible proximity. Spillers carefully differentiates this relationship from the pathological structure that the Moynihan Report ascribes to the black family, since the mother's absolute disempowerment precludes any presumption of matriarchy; but at the same time that "motherhood as female blood-rite is outraged, is denied . . . it becomes the founding term of a human and social enactment" (80). According to the American slave code, the "condition" of the mother determines that of " 'all her remotest posterity' " (79). But, Spillers asks, "What is the 'condition' of the mother? Is it the 'condition' of enslavement the writer means, or does he mean the 'mark' and the 'knowledge' of the *mother* upon the child that here translates into the culturally forbidden and impure?" (79). This culturally forbidden maternal mark is a redemptive antidote to the marks the patriarchal symbolic order inscribes on the bodies of its slaves. Spillers examines the consequences of this marking for the African-American male, who "has been touched, therefore, by the *mother, handed* by her in ways that he cannot escape, and in ways that the white American male is allowed to temporize by a fatherly reprieve. . . . It is the heritage of the *mother* that the African-American must regain as an aspect of his own personhood—the power of 'yes' to the 'female' within" (80).

This invocation of androgynous Afro-American masculinity—seemingly a regendering rather than a degendering—introduces at the end of Spillers's text an anomalous Afro-American discourse of "personhood" and gender that raises some important unanswered questions. Does the Afro-American mother mark her son and her daughter identically? If the mother's mark on her son enables some access to the " 'female' within," what does it enable for the daughter? Why is the daughter so conspicuously absent from this text? Shrouded in silence, she enters only as a double of the delegitimized Afro-American father, the mirroring pair with which the essay begins, and in apposition to the mother, as if mother and daughter were indistinguishable: "the Afro-American woman, the mother, the daughter" (80).[19] Allowed, like the son, no "fatherly reprieve," does the daughter merge with the mother—as she does in Chodorow's account of female identity formation in mother-centered (i.e., normative Western) families? Does the context of slavery, with its enforced alienation of the father, undo the fluidity of mother-daughter boundaries that Chodorow represents as the "reproduction of mothering," or, as Toni Morrison's *Beloved* suggests, does it exaggerate this loss of boundaries? Must the daughter be banned from Spillers's text to ward off the threat that possible gender differences between son and daughter pose to a discourse on degendering?

Addressing these questions directly might have complicated in productive ways Spillers's already dazzlingly complex analysis. Perhaps the contradictions involved in representing both an undoing and a redoing of gender in a language informed by the Lacanian critique of the subject and by the Anglo-American valorization of the female—a language (dis)loyal to both the identity-subverting Name of the Father and to the boundary-transgressing body of the mother—should be asserted and analyzed more fully as the necessary heteroglossia of a discourse bridging race, gender, psychoanalysis, and history.

III

> Class and gender, and their articulations, are the bits and pieces from which psychological selfhood is made.
>
> Carolyn Kay Steedman, *Landscape for a Good Woman*[20]

More self-consciously polyphonic, *Landscape for a Good Woman: A Story of Two Lives* takes a different contradiction for its subject. Written from the perspective of the daughter, this extraordinary hybrid text splices a double biography (the narrator's and her working-class mother's) with a feminist psychoanalytic critique of cultural criticism and a class critique of feminist psychoanalysis. The text gains its power from dizzying reversals that undo its own neatly mapped social and discursive landscape, bifurcated by a gate dividing an affluent terrain of "bourgeois household[s] where doors shut along the corridor"—the landscape that generates, and thus is rendered normative by, our dominant narratives of childhood subjectivity (psychoanalysis and fairy tales, affiliated forms in Steedman's account)—from the working-class terrain of the narrator's own childhood, the council houses of South London's long streets, "the world outside the gate" that has been represented only in the discourses of class (77). Despite the construction of these clear oppositions, the boundaries of class and discourse frequently dissolve. There is no stable narrative perspective: the adult narrator's ambiguously classed voice both merges with and ironically echoes the working-class child's, which itself frequently mimics her mother's. No individual discourse can adequately represent the complexity of feeling and class positioning. Overtly repudiated for its class specificity, psychoanalysis re-enters through a carefully crafted subtext of fairy tales that disclose the unruly features of the narrator's subjectivity, and through the narrative structure of the text, which, like a case history (Steedman's own analogy for it), "presents the ebb and flow of memory, the structure of dreams, the stories that people tell to explain themselves to others" (21). More provocative than the text's articulated claims are its unstated but clearly signaled contradictions and self-critiques, which open a different narrative scene.

Direct feminist psychoanalytic challenges to class analysis are the least successful aspects of this text. Steedman's most emphatic project is to grant her mother the subjectivity denied by the conventions of a (masculine) cultural criticism that construct the working-class mother as " 'Mum, the formidable and eternal Mum, virago, domestic law giver, comforter and martyr' "(92).[21] Stereotyped and misdescribed (Steedman insists on her mother's nondomestic roles as worker and economic provider), the figure of "our mam" epitomizes the absence of individuality in (even sympathetic) representations of the working class. "When the sons of the working class, who have made their earlier escape from this landscape of psychological simplicity, put so much effort into accepting and celebrating it . . . then something important, and odd, and possibly promising of startling revelation, is actually going on. This refusal of a complicated psychology to those living in conditions of material distress is a central theme of this book" (12). Writing as a daughter of the working class, Steedman strives to articulate and to validate her mother's desires, to fill in the psychological content absent from the accounts of such cultural critics as Jeremy Seabrook and Richard Hoggart, to revise a canonical class perspective through the lenses of gender and psychoanalysis. But her portrait has its own monolithic features. By insisting on the overriding centrality and legitimacy of her mother's craving for "the things of the earth," on her unresigned response to material deprivation, Steedman circumscribes the subjectivity whose complexity she asserts but does not demonstrate. The metonymic series that characterizes her mother's desire tends to unfold within a single register. "From a Lancashire mill town and a working-class twenties childhood she came away wanting: fine clothes, glamour, money; to be what she wasn't" (6).[22] Sexuality, love, loneliness, and loss barely inflect this story of thwarted desire and legitimate envy. Psychological complexity reduces in this context to a more nuanced narrative of class consciousness.

Privileging the politics of envy constricts the psychoanalytic complication of working-class maternal subjectivity; class, however, powerfully and variously revises psychoanalysis, most succinctly in two "primal" scenes that crystallize the narrator's childhood relation to her parents. In both these scenes, as in Freud's primal scene, the narrator is an observer rather than a participant: watching from the sidelines is *the* working-class child's position in this text. What she sees, in contrast to the scenario witnesses by the Freudian child, however, is a class rather than a sexual encounter, for her developmental task entails negotiating subjectivity between class as well as gender positions. The first (chronologically) of these scenes revises Lacan's revision of Freud in a way that suggests a daughterly counterpart to Spillers's analysis of Afro-American fathers and sons. The narrator's father takes his three-year-old daughter for a walk in the bluebell wood. After gathering the flowers, they are suddenly accosted by an angry forest-keeper who reprimands the father for picking the flowers and, snatching them from his hands, scatters them on the ground, "their white roots glimmering, unprotected" (50). Recalling "the roots and their whiteness, and the way in which they had been pulled away, to wither exposed on the bank," the narrator remembers her father as "the loser, feminized, undone" by "the very solid and powerful" forest-keeper (50–51).

Recasting oedipal conflict in terms of class, the scene dramatizes the narrator's perception of her father's "castration" and her consequent disbelief in the equation of power with masculinity: "the iron of patriarchy didn't enter into my soul" (19). Like Spillers, and *contra* Lacan, Steedman argues that the disenfranchised father's difference from the Name of the Father critically shapes his child's gender and sexuality. (And like Spillers, Steedman depicts a situation of illegitimacy, in which the father can't legally transmit his family name.) If the Afro-American son, in Spillers's account, has access, through the gap between the Afro-American father and the Name of the (symbolic) Father, to an intimacy with the " 'female' within," the working-class daughter, in Steedman's account, undergoes a different form of gender blurring by identifying with, rather than desiring, a socially castrated father. The narrator is called by one of her father's names for her, Kay, which Steedman signs here (and in no other text) as her middle name. As a young girl, she identifies with her father's body rather than her mother's: "A little girl's body, its neat containment, seems much more like that of a man than it does of a woman. . . . His body was in some way mine" (94). Without power as a gender differential, without the phallus giving meaning to the penis, genital differences lose their significance. Defined through neither opposition nor attraction to masculinity, the narrator's working-class femininity positions her outside the dominant psychoanalytic narratives, and their affiliated fairy tales, of heterosexuality. "In the fairy-stories the daughters love their fathers because they are mighty princes, great rulers, and because such power seduces. The modern psychoanalytic myths posit the same plot, old tales are made manifest: secret longings, doors closing along the corridors of the bourgeois household. But daddy, you never knew me like this . . . the iron didn't enter into the soul" (61). In her own household the mother, not the father, is the potent presence behind closed doors;

marginalized both outside the family and (partially as a consequence) within, the father is an object of the daughter's pity rather than desire.[23]

Through the other primal scene, given far more weight than the one with the father and preceding it in the narrative (although, chronologically, it occurs a few months later), the narrator's relation to her mother calls into question the construction of femininity within different psychoanalytic discourses. As in the scene in the bluebell wood, the child is a spectator rather than a participant; once again, she observes a class encounter between two same-sex adults, here, her mother (who has just given birth to the narrator's sister) and a health visitor who censors the mother's provision of physical—and, by implication, psychological—nurture: 'This house isn't fit for a baby' " (2).[24] In both scenes, a disciplinary figure bearing class authority intervenes in the narrator's relation to a parent and introduces a difference within gender. Watching from the curtainless window as the health visitor recedes, the child makes a silent pact of class solidarity with her mother, articulated by the adult narrator's vow: "I will do everything and anything until the end of my days to stop anyone ever talking to me like that woman talked to my mother. . . . I read a [middle-class] woman's book, meet such a woman at a party (a woman now, like me) and think quite deliberately as we talk: we are divided. . . . I know this and you don't" (2). The interaction simultaneously revises and conflates oedipal and preoedipal scenarios, for it is the middle-class woman (rather than the father) who both interrupts and consolidates the mother-daughter bond. The daughter's identification with her mother is not produced in a dyadic sphere created by the mother's mirroring gaze but through a common position at the window and a shared perception of a third term. Identification with the mother is disidentification with the health visitor; it is triadic rather than dyadic and triangulated by class instead of patriarchy.

To defend her mother from the middle-class critique personified by the health visitor, the narrator must avoid participating in psychoanalytic discourses that might signal her complicity with this critique. As a child, she approvingly echoes her mother's class-appropriate definition of good mothering —"we'd never gone hungry; she went out to work for us; we had warm beds to lie in at night"—and insists on the sufficiency of a purely material mothering (1). As an adult, she both reiterates this definition, with some ironic distance, and displaces it with Winnicott's notion of good enough mothering (in her one eager unequivocal appropriation of psychoanalysis) to argue that her own childhood desire to have children demonstrates, as Winnicott suggests, her mother's adequacy; but her case is unconvincing, and perhaps intentionally so, since her childhood desire for two children, one resembling herself and the other her mother, just as plausibly attests to a longing to repair insufficient mothering by remothering both her mother and herself. What the class configuration consistently inhibits is the direct articulation of anger and the endorsement of psychoanalytic accounts of childhood ambivalence that might seem, through their contaminating association with the health visitor's judgment, to blame the (maternal) victim. The middle-class intervention thus shapes the mother-daughter bond both by disallowing ambivalence and by seemingly resoling it through providing an alternative focus for the daughter's anger, deflecting it away from the mother. This female triangle enables a version of the splitting that Melanie Klein attributes to the infant, who divides the inevitably frustrating mother into a "good" breast and "bad" breast: the "bad" breast, by drawing anger to itself, preserves the idealization of the mother.[25] But rather than overtly asserting her ambivalence (which she occasionally enacts indirectly through sudden, unexplained outbursts of tears), Steedman's narrator represents ambivalence as the psychic property of the working-class mother who loves her children but simultaneously resents the hardships they impose. Steedman renders maternal ambivalence as a temporal structure produced by economic exigencies (although the imagery seems, as I shall argue later, to return ambivalence to the child): "What came free could be given freely, like her milk: loving a baby costs very little. But feeding us during our later childhood was a tense struggle between giving and denial. We never went hungry, we were well nourished, but fed in the cheapest possible way. I knew this, I think, when I conjured her under the kitchen table, the thin wounds across her breasts pouring forth blood, not milk" (93). In contrast to her apostrophe to her father, the narrator never blames or even retrospectively addresses her mother. The only overt sign of trouble is a brief unexplained allusion to a nine-year period when the adult narrator refused to see her mother.

Declining to theorize the daughter's ambivalence both invokes and revokes the discourse of Klein; insisting on the mother's ambivalence differentiates Steedman's account from that of Klein's most influential feminist descendant, Nancy Chodorow, whom Steedman faults for the middle-class assumption that mothers identify and merge with daughters, who themselves become mothers in order to reproduce the original merger with their own mothers. There is a primary identification with the mother in this text—"she, myself, walks my dreams"—but no normative reproduction of mothering, most obviously because the narrator deliberately does not become a mother (61). (Her sister, however, does become a mother, in an untold story that haunts the fringes of this text.) More importantly, this daughter internalizes from her mother not relationality and fluid ego boundaries but stoicism in the face of inequality. What she learns from her mother's response to the health visitor—"she [the mother] had cried. . . . And then she stopped crying, my mother, got by, the phrase that picks up after all difficulty"—she learns again through the story of her great-grandmother, sent from home at age eleven to work as a maid in a distant town: "She cried, because tears are cheap; and then she stopped, and got by, because no one gives you anything in this world" (1–2, 31). The femininity (re)produced through this working-class female genealogy has more to do with self-sufficiency than with relationality. Replacing the tears that figure fluid boundaries is a maternal voice commanding self-restraint; under her mother's tutelage, the narrator learns to dry her "sentimental" tears over nineteenth-century accounts of child labor, as well as any tears she might shed for herself. The withholding, not the offer, of empathic merger here structures female subjectivity. In her description of her final visit to her mother, two weeks before her mother's death, the narrator represents this withholding as an inevitable function of a class position that makes its members feel endangered and illegitimate, threatened by emotions that are perilous for victims and denied the self-esteem that enables mirroring: "I was really a ghost who came to call. That feeling, the sense of being absent in my mother's presence, was nothing to do with illness, was what it had always been like. We were truly illegitimate, outside any law of recognition: the mirror broken, a lump of ice for a heart" (142).

Steedman's metaphors, however, signal a different discourse, with a less forgiving account of broken mirroring. The disavowed story of daughterly ambivalence returns through the middle-class discourse of fairy tales, ingeniously manipulated to encode a subversive psychoanalytic subtext to the daughter's faithful narrative of class. Never represented as coherent narrative, but nonetheless evoked through recurrent allusions, two interwoven fairy tales, "The Snow Queen" and "The Little Mermaid," create a violent imaginary of glass, mirrors, ice, tears, milk, and blood. By depicting scenarios in which the mother, absent from the family, assumes a terrifying mythic guise (as the Snow Queen and the sea witch), these tales call into question the narrator's legitimization of working-class mothering.

"The Snow Queen" offers the least threatening and most explicit counternarrative, in which the narrator openly identifies with the (male) protagonist who shares her name, Kay. In the opening section of the fairy tale, the devil makes a distorting mirror that transforms beauty into ugliness; it falls and breaks into hundreds of millions of billions of pieces which pierce people's eyes, distorting their vision, and penetrate their hearts, turning them to ice. During a snowstorm, Kay (who lives with his grandmother) is visited by the Snow Queen, whose power he has defied by boasting he would melt her on the stove. "She was delicately lovely, but all ice, glittering, dazzling ice. . . . her eyes shone like two bright stars, but there was no rest or peace in them."[26] After this visit, two splinters from the devil's mirror suddenly enter Kay's eyes and heart; his vision transformed and his heart frozen, he becomes the Snow Queen's icy subject. Only the empathic tears of his devoted playmate, Gerda, who travels to the Snow Queen's arctic palace in search of him, melt Kay's frozen heart, and his tears of gratitude wash the splinters from his eye. Steedman's recurrent allusions to this story—"the mirror breaks . . . and a lump of ice is lodged in the heart" (97)—indict the mother she overtly justifies. The stoical voice, from this perspective, is a frozen voice; the repudiation of tears, a form of death rather than of strength. The fairy tale intimates the unstated cost of "getting by" without empathic mothering. What the broken mirror (re)produces is a frozen heart.

Through its story of chosen mutilation, "The Little Mermaid" introduces a more violent psychoanalytic discourse, which replaces the Winnicottian language of mirroring with a Kleinian language of passion and blood.[27] Although the story itself focuses on the heterosexual romance between the mermaid and the prince, Steedman's choice of images highlights the relationship of the mermaid and the sea witch, whom the mermaid begs to transform her fishtail into legs in order to win the prince's love. The witch warns her: "It hurts; it is as if a sharp sword were running through you. . . . Every step you take will be as if you were treading upon sharp knives, so sharp as to draw blood" (132). As payment for this service, to be rendered through a potion made with her own blood, the witch demands the mermaid's beautiful voice: "She [the witch] punctured her breast and let the black blood drop into the caldron . . . thereupon she cuts off the tongue of the little mermaid, who was dumb now and could neither sing nor speak" (133–34). Although these sacrifices prove futile in the fairy tale, they constitute the central symbolic episode of Steedman's text, which circulates the images of knives and sacrifice without specifying who is cutting whom. Whereas the mermaid elects her sacrifice to gain the love of the prince, the violent sacrificial relationships in Steedman's text bind mothers and daughters, not women and men: "Somehow the iron of patriarchy didn't enter into my soul. . . . [I]n the dreams it is a woman who holds the knife, and only a woman can kill" (19). (Steedman's final description of her dying mother as looking "like a witch" [140]—thin, dark, gaunt—secures the connection to the fairy tale.) During her first reading of the two fairy tales, at age seven, the narrator imagines her parents naked under the kitchen table, holding sharp-edged knives with which they "cut each other, making thin surface wounds like lines drawn with a sharp red pencil, from which the blood poured. . . . Downstairs I thought, the thin blood falls in sheets from my mother's breasts; she was the most cut, but I knew it was she who did the cutting. I couldn't always see the knife in my father's hand" (54). By the time she is twelve, her father has dropped out of the picture and sexual warfare has become self-dramatizing maternal self-mutilation, as the narrator reimagines "the knife in my mother's hand, and the thin red lines of blood drawn across her breasts:

displaying to my imagination the mutilation involved in keeping and feeding us" (82). Lacing milk with blood, the imagery reveals at once the narrator's guilty conviction that she has, however inadvertently, bloodied her mother's breasts, and her anger at her mother's self-display. Through the parallel scene from "The Little Mermaid," it is clear that the sacrifice is mutual: the witch/mother mutilates herself to enable the mermaid/daughter's upward mobility (to the land/to the middle class), and in exchange the daughter relinquishes her voice, parroting instead her mother's working-class discourse on good mothering. Instead of being mirrored by her mother, the daughter faithfully echoes her voice.

Through the fairy-tale subtext, then, Steedman launches a subversive psychoanalytic critique of her own class-based critique of psychoanalysis. Both discourses are necessary to represent the subjectivity produced by a position straddling the class divide, for the narrator (in contrast to the mother with whom she so strongly identifies) is not confined to the working-class world of her childhood: she gains continued access, through education, to the middle-class culture she began at age seven to consume through fairy tales. Steedman doesn't speculate whether a contemporary child rooted entirely in the working class feels anger at her mother; instead, she demonstrates the prohibitions on that child's recognition of her anger and subtly devises strategies for representing her own complex position on the boundary.

She figures this position most deftly through the contrast between two narratives; the story of the little watercress girl recounted by Henry Mayhew in *London Labour and the London Poor* and the story of "Dora" recounted by Freud, the story "we" know intimately because it is "*the* story . . . of the bourgeois household and the romances of the family and the fairy-tales that lie behind its closed doors" (137–39). These narratives mark the range of her contradictory identifications: between working-class femininity (defined by labor) and middle-class femininity (defined by sexuality), between harmonious and disharmonious mother-daughter relationships, between history and psychoanalysis, and between coherent and hysterical (contradictory, disrupted) narrative modes. Steedman valorizes the story of the little watercress girl for resisting our dominant cultural narratives and insists that she finds a mirror image in this "good and helpful child, who eased her mother's life" (141); but her own troubled story far more closely resembles Dora's inconclusive tale. (The narrator's childhood failure to come home from rehearsing a school play in time to buy the watercress her mother wants for tea underlines her distance from the dutiful watercress girl.) For all its incoherence, Dora's narrative is legible to the narrator, while the watercress girl's remains opaque. Insisting that lives "outside the gate" be allowed to preserve their inscrutability, Steedman refuses to recuperate the watercress girl's story to familiar (psychoanalytic) narratives. But her own heterogeneous narrative, as full as Dora's of gaps, contradictions, repetitions, and revisions that interrupt and interlard the exposition, unfolds within a psychoanalytic register that seemingly operates for the person on the boundary as well as the one inside the gate.

IV

> However unfeasible and inefficient it may sound, I see no way to avoid insisting that there has to be a simultaneous other focus: not merely who am I? but who is the other woman? How am I naming her? How does she name me?
>
> Gayatri Chakravorty Spivak,
> "French Feminism in an International Frame"[28]

Steedman's focus on the boundary affiliates her with a current trend in readings of class and psychoanalysis. The boundary is the critical position in these readings, for it both destabilizes and extends the psychoanalytic enclosure, as Jane Gallop and Mary Poovey suggest in their investigations of the threshold figure of the governess, who exists at once outside and inside the middle-class family.[29] As a duplicate mother who is "castrated" by passing through the circuit of money, the governess disrupts the imaginary wholeness of the middle-class family and of psychoanalytic theory. Yet psychoanalysis is well suited to describe this disruption, which Gallop represents as an intervention of the symbolic in the imaginary. Poovey depicts psychoanalysis as the most appropriate discourse for articulating the splits, identifications, and displacements that characterize both the person on the boundary and the current historical situation of feminist criticism itself, positioned "between the powerful guardians of culture, among whom we do and do not belong, and a vast, heterogeneous majority who feel excluded from what we say, and between an outdated ideology of individualism and an ideology of decentered subjects whose hour is not yet here."[30]

Poovey's account of feminism's double loyalties returns us to Spillers's representation of feminism's discursive genealogy. Like Steedman, Gallop, and Poovey, moreover, Spillers locates psychoanalysis (as well as feminism) at the boundaries, rather than exclusively on either side. When she explicitly invokes psychoanalysis (as opposed to the analogies she implies between the effects of the Lacanian symbolic and of cultural domination), it is in relation to negotiations across racial and gender boundaries. Spillers examines a specific discursive moment in the representation of slavery, Harriet Jacobs's *Incidents in the Life of a Slave Girl.* Written by an escaped female slave and dictated to a woman abolitionist, Jacobs's text succinctly embodies these negotiations through the representation of a triangulated scene between Linda Brent, the autobiographical protagonist, and Mr. and Ms. Flint, the white couple that owns her. By acting out her husband's desire for the captive woman, Mrs. Flint dissolves the boundaries of gender on both sides of the racial divide, "degendering" both herself and Linda Brent by subjecting Brent to female as well as male sexual desire (and thereby contrasting her to the "gendered female," who is defined by a relation of vulnerability solely to the male). There is an identification, however, not only between the Anglo-American woman and man but also between the Anglo-American and Afro-American women, "twin actants on a common psychic landscape" created by the sovereignty of the Anglo-American male: "Neither could claim her body and its various productions—for quite different reasons, albeit—as her own . . . we cannot unravel one female's narrative from the other's, cannot decipher one without tripping over the other" (77). These multiple interwoven identifications make this scene resemble "casebook narratives from psychoanalysis" (76). It is less the experience of captive persons themselves than the " 'threads cable-strong' of an incestuous interracial genealogy [that] uncover slavery in the United States as one of the richest displays of the psychoanalytic dimensions of culture before the science of European psychoanalysis takes hold" (77).

Spillers and Steedman share (along with Gallop and Poovey) a preference for delineating situations and figures at the boundary and a reticence about representing the subjectivity of persons entirely dominated by oppression. Steedman explores her own liminal position and refuses to interpret the watercress girl's story; Spillers details the positioning, but not the subjectivity, of persons in captivity and suggests that the twentieth-century "black woman," rather than the captive person, constitutes the "profoundest revelation of the "split subject that psychanalytic theory posits" (65). Their caution raises a critical question about the limits of psychoanalysis. How do we know when social and cultural boundaries should be crossed, when "naming" the "other woman," as Spivak and others have exhorted us to do, simply appropriates "her" to "us"?[31] Rather than groping after some definitive answer, I want to end by gesturing toward a countertext that crosses, instead of lingering at, a boundary, a text that has been a kind of subtext to my own. *Beloved* deliberately represents captive persons as subjects rather than as objects of oppression, and does so primarily in a discourse on the hunger, passion, and violence generated in the "too thick" mother-daughter bond produced by the conditions of slavery.[32] This extraordinary project has its attendant risks, of course, discernible perhaps in the novel's enormous popularity with women readers across racial lines. But the text circumvents any easy delimitation of the boundaries of psychoanalysis.

It is too early for feminism to foreclose on psychoanalysis. Vast cultural terrains unfold beyond the boundaries of this essay, and beyond those of psychoanalysis as well, undoubtedly. But rather than fixing those boundaries, my goal has been to forestall the sense that we know exactly where they lie and what they necessarily exclude. Psychoanalysis has been resistant to the social, but it need not always, uniformly, be. It is better for feminism to challenge that resistance than to renounce psychoanalysis entirely or succumb to its seductions.

NOTES

1. Rosi Braidotti, "The Politics of Ontological Difference," in *Between Feminism and Psychoanalysis*, ed. Teresa Brennan (London: Routledge, 1989), pp. 97–98. Paul Smith, "Julia Kristeva Et Al.; or, Take Three or More," in *Feminism and Psychoanalysis*, ed. Richard Feldstein and Judith Roof (Ithaca: Cornell University Press, 1989), pp. 84–85.

   I am grateful to Marianne Hirsch and Evelyn Fox Keller for their boundless patience and support during the composition of this essay. I am also grateful for Mary M. Childers's helpful criticism, which I have been able only in part to incorporate into this version of the essay.
2. There are diverse reasons for the pervasive current disrepute of psychoanalysis, ranging from the politics of academic discourse, in which the hegemony of psychoanalysis within "theory" has been displaced by more historical and socially nuanced discourses, to the politics of public discourse on the family, in which psychoanalysis has been tainted by its alleged complicity in the cover-up of child abuse. The exemplary case of the latter charge is Jeffrey Moussaieff Masson, *The Assault on Truth: Freud's Suppression of the Seduction Theory* (New York: Farrar, Straus, and Giroux, 1984). See also Judith Lewis Herman, with Lisa Hirschman, *Father-Daughter Incest* (Cambridge, Mass.: Harvard University Press, 1981); and Louise DeSalvo, *Virginia Woolf: The Impact of Childhood Sexual Abuse on Her Life and Work* (Boston: Beacon Press, 1989). These diverse discursive arenas share a perception of the social irresponsibility of psychoanalysis. For a response to this charge, see Jacqueline Rose, "Where Does the Misery Come From? Psychoanalysis, Feminism, and the Event," in *Feminism and Psychoanalysis*, pp. 25–39. For a similar attempt to rescue psychoanalysis for feminism, see Rachel Bowlby on the gendered implications of "repudiation," in "Still Crazy After All These Years," in *Between Feminism and Psychoanalysis*, pp. 40–60.
3. For an integration of psychoanalysis and the social realm under the aegis of Foucault, see Julian Henriques, Wendy Hollway, Cathy Urwin, Couze Venn, Valerie Walkerdine, *Changing the Subject: Psychology, Social Regulation and Subjectivity* (London and New York: Methuen, 1984).
4. *Totem and Taboo* is devoted to demonstrating that all culture originates in patricide, which is universally preserved in the psyche as the oedipus complex. In "Mother-Right and the Sexual Igno-

rance of Savages" Freud's British representative Ernest Jones defends the universality of the oedipus complex against the cultural relativism of Bronislaw Malinowski by arguing that only "primordial Oedipus tendencies" could generate the denial of paternity enabling the matrilinear Melanesian societies Malinowski studied. See Sigmund Freud, *Totem and Taboo* [1913–14], *The Standard Edition of the Complete Psychological Works of Sigmund Freud*, trans. and ed. James Strachey (London: Hogarth Press, 1953–66), vol. 13; Ernest Jones, "Mother-Right and the Sexual Ignorance of Savages" [1924], in *Essays in Applied Psycho-Analysis*, 2 vols. (London: Hogarth Press and the Institute of Psycho-Analysis, 1951, 2:170); and Bronislaw Malinowski, *Sex and Repression in Savage Society* (1927) Chicago: University of Chicago Press, 1985).

5. Juliet Mitchell, *Psychoanalysis and Feminism: Freud, Reich, Laing, and Women* (New York: Random House, 1974), p. 395.
6. Jacqueline Rose, *Sexuality in the Field of Vision* (London: Verso, 1986), p. 90. Here, and in her essay "Where Does the Misery Come From?" (see n. 2 above), Rose mounts the most eloquent defenses of the utility of Lacanian psychoanalysis for feminism.
7. This revision has emerged only from theorists with primary commitments to questions of race and class. In the Lacanian anthology *Between Feminism and Psychoanalysis*, for example, the editor, Teresa Brennan, comments in her Introduction that "real changes in either parenting patterns or the social position of women and men must have consequences for the symbolic" (p. 3), but neither the Introduction nor the rest of the anthology examines these changes or their consequences. Despite Brennan's claim that the anthology unsettles the "relation of psychical structures to the political realities of women's social conditions" (p. 12), all of the essays (except for Rosi Braidotti's overt critique of psychoanalysis) either define the "social," the "political," and the "historical" within the terms of psychoanalysis (so that the "social" is coterminous with the death drive, for example) or circumscribe them radically (the only social context analyzed, for example, is the academy). The anthology bears witness to Paul Smith's charge that psychoanalysis cannot generate political desire and has tended to deplete that of feminism—unless, I would argue, feminism demands that psychoanalysis address specific social configurations.
8. Nancy J. Chodorow, *Feminism and Psychoanalytic Theory* (Cambridge: Polity Press, 1989), pp. 157, 159. Object relations theory has consistently emphasized the social context of development, in opposition to the intrapsychic terrain of drive theory; some slippage between the "social" as the narrowly interpersonal and as a more inclusive historical field has bolstered the discourse's political claims. For a recent critique, from an entirely different perspective, of the place of the social in object relations, see Daniel N. Stern, *The Interpersonal World of the Infant: A View from Psychoanalysis and Developmental Psychology* (New York: Basic Books, 1985).
9. Jane Flax, *Thinking Fragments: Psychoanalysis, Feminism, and Postmodernism in the Contemporary West* (Berkeley and Los Angeles: University of California Press, 1989), p. 122. This position is also presented in various ways throughout Nancy Chodorow's *Feminism and Psychoanalytic Theory.*
10. Elizabeth V. Spelman, *Inessential Woman: Problems of Exclusion in Feminist Thought* (Boston: Beacon Press, 1988), pp. 95, 157. For a recent critique of Chodorow's "cultural essentialism" from a Lacanian perspective that faults the assumptions that gender is constant with the subject and that psychological differences between the sexes are universal, see Toril Moi, "Patriarchal Thought and the Drive for Knowledge," in *Between Feminism and Psychoanalysis*, pp. 189–205. For a related critique of Chodorow from a Foucauldian perspective, see Cathy Urwin's contribution to *Changing the Subject*, which insists on the ways that the mother's response to her child, and hence the child's perception and internalization of the mother's gender, is always mediated by the mother's own "positioning within particular discourses which enter into the constitution of her role" (p. 320).

11. Chodorow, "On *The Reproduction of Mothering:* A Methodological Debate," *Signs* 6, no. 3 (Spring 1981): 514. At the end of her early essay "Family Structure and Feminine Personality" (in *Woman, Culture, and Society*, ed. Michelle Zimbalist Rosaldo and Louise Lamphere [Stanford: Stanford University press, 1974]), Chodorow launches this cross-cultural work by drawing from ethnographies of Java and East London to contrast the pathological dimension of the mother-daughter bond in Western middle-class families with the higher self-esteem transmitted from mother to daughter in cultures in which mothers have authority and important connections with other women both outside and within the home. The complaint that Chodorow privileges (rather than simply represents) of Western middle-class femininity seems to me based on a misperception.
12. Hence the recurrent claim that object relations theory is intrinsically inapplicable to diverse social configurations seems misguided to me. Recent explorations of multiple mothering in extended African-American families, for example, seem perfectly congruent with Chodorow's emphasis on the psychological consequences of female caretakers. See, for example, Patricia Hill Collins, "The Meaning of Motherhood in Black Culture and Black Mother/Daughter Relationships," in *Sage: A Scholarly Journal on Black Women* 4, no. 2 (Fall 1987): 3–10.
13. On the insufficiency of the Lacanian subject for a feminist politics, see Teresa de Lauretis, "Feminist Studies/Critical Studies: Issues, Terms, and Contexts," in *Feminist Studies/Critical Studies*, ed. Teresa de Lauretis (Bloomington: Indiana University Press, 1986), pp. 1–19. In her Introduction to *Between Feminism and Psychoanalysis*, Teresa Brennan eloquently argues for undoing the hierarchialized polarization of object relations and Lacan. For a reading of object relations theory as incorporating, rather than opposing, some basic principles of deconstruction, see Leslie Wahl Rabine, "A Feminist Politics of Non-Identity," *Feminist Studies* 14, no. 1 (Spring 1988): 11–31. For a partially comparable project, in another arena, of undoing the opposition between Anglo-American and French feminisms, see Betsy Draine, "Refusing the Wisdom of Solomon: Some Recent Feminist Literary Theory," *Signs* 15, no. 1 (Autumn 1989): 144–70. Reworking the opposition sometimes generates reversals. In *Thinking Fragments*, Jane Flax argues surprisingly that "Object relations theory is more compatible with postmodernism than Freudian or Lacanian analysis because it does not require a fixed or essentialist view of 'human nature' . . . . As social relations and family structures change, so would human nature" (p. 110). This assertion is based on privileging history as the *only* form of difference and on overlooking the radically disruptive, de-essentializing function of the unconscious in Lacan; it is important to remember that the intersubjectivity constituted and historically variable self of object relations remains more integrated than the split subject of Lacan. Nevertheless, Flax's assertion usefully calls into question the oversimplified opposition between the allegedly unitary self of object relations and the heterogeneous Lacanian subject.
14. Hortense J. Spillers, " 'The Permanent Obliquity of an In[pha]llibly Straight': In the Time of the Daughters and the Fathers," in *Daughters and Fathers*, ed. Lydna E. Boose and Betty S. Flowers (Baltimore: Johns Hopkins University Press, 1989), p. 158.
15. Hortense J. Spillers, "Interstices: A Small Drama of Words," in *Pleasure and Danger*, ed. Carol Vance (Boston: Routledge and Kegan Paul, 1984), p. 88.
16. Hortense J. Spillers, "Mama's Baby, Papa's Maybe: An American Grammar Book," *diacritics* 17, no. 2 (Summer 1987): 72; subsequent citations of this work will be placed in parentheses in the text. For a non-Lacanian account of the ways that slavery undoes the meaning of domesticity, see Hortense J. Spillers, "Changing the Letter: The Yokes, the Jokes of Discourse, or, Mrs. Stowe, Mr. Reed," in *Slavery and the Literary Imagination*, ed. Deborah E. McDowell and Arnold Rampersad (Baltimore: Johns Hopkins University Press, 1989), pp. 25–61.

17. See Jacques Lacan, "The Mirror Stage as Formative of the Function of the I," *Ecrits: A Selection*, trans. Alan Sheridan (New York: W. W. Norton, 1977), pp. 1–7.
18. See D. W. Winnicott, "Mirror-role of Mother and Family in Child Development," *Playing and Reality* (Harmondworth, Middlesex: Penguin Books, 1971). I cite Winnicott rather than Lacan (whose essay on the mirror stage influenced Winnicott) because Spillers's emphasis on the child's humanity and the social implications of the mother's responsive gaze are much closer to the discourse of object relations than to Lacan's insistence on the alienating structure of the ego produced by the mirror stage. For Lacan, the social subject is produced by the symbolic.
19. In " 'The Permanent Obliquity of an In[pha]llibly Straight': In the Time of the Daughters and the Fathers," Spillers offers a detailed analysis of the African-American father-daughter relationship, which has captured her attention more fully than the mother-daughter relationship.
20. Carolyn Kay Steedman, *Landscape for a Good Woman: A Story of Two Lives* (London: Virago, 1986; New Brunswick, N.J.: Rutgers University Press, 1987), p. 7; subsequent citations of this work will be to the American edition and will be placed in parentheses in the text. I am grateful to Tricia Moran for calling this text to my attention.
21. From Jeremy Seabrook, *What Went Wrong?* (London: Victor Gollancz, 1978), cited by Steedman.
22. Or note another characteristic example: "Born into 'the old working class,' she wanted: A New Look skirt, a timbered country cottage, to marry a prince" (p. 9). Rather than introducing a new direction, the last term in these series encompasses the others.
23. As Julie Abraham points out in her review of *Landscape for a Good Woman* in the *Women's Review of Books* 5, no. 9 (June 1988), Steedman is reticent about her own sexuality. Her story, however, puts her at a distance from the dominant narratives of heterosexuality. Although as a daughter she desires to be marked by the father, or by the law he (inadequately) represents, she expresses no desire for the person that he is.
24. Steedman represents the boundaries of the working-class home as more permeable than the locked doors of the middle-class houses behind the gate. Curtainless windows and unlocked doors characterize the narrator's family home, whose domestic boundaries are also subverted by the frequent presence of boarders. That the marginalized father, who sleeps in the attic, is sometimes mistaken for another boarder underlines the blurring of the inside/outside dichotomy. On the psychoanalytic fiction of the insular middle-class family, see Jane Gallop, *The Daughter's Seduction: Feminism and Psychoanalysis* (Ithaca: Cornell University Press, 1982), p. 144.
25. See Melanie Klein, *"Love, Guilt, and Reparation" and Other Works, 1921–45* (New York: Dell, 1975). Conspicuously absent (repressed?) from Steedman's text, Klein is mentioned only in relation to the pathologization of envy, never in relation to the mother-daughter bond.
26. Dulac's *"The Snow Queen" and Other Stories from Hans Andersen* (Garden City: Doubleday, 1976), p. 16; subsequent citations of "The Snow Queen" will be placed in parentheses in the text. Citations of "The Little Mermaid" will also be to this edition and will be placed in parentheses in the text.
27. On the evolution of object relations from the Kleinian emphasis on hunger and aggression to Winnicott's more benign accounts of mother-infant mirroring, see Jay R. Greenberg and Stephen A. Mitchell, *Object Relations in Psychoanalytic Theory* (Cambridge, Mass.: Harvard University Press, 1983); Judith M. Hughes, *Reshaping the Psychoanalytic Domain: The Work of Melanie Klein, W.R.D. Firbairn, and D.W. Winnicott* (Berkeley and Los Angeles: University of California Press, 1989); and D.W. Winnicott, "A Personal View of the Kleinian Contribution," in *The Maturational Processes and the Facilitating Environment* (London: Hogarth Press, 1965), pp. 171–78.

28. Gayatri Chakravorty Spivak, "French Feminism in an International Frame," *Yale French Studies* 62 (1981): 179.
29. Jane Gallop, *The Daughter's Seduction: Feminism and Psychoanalysis* (Ithaca: Cornell University Press, 1982), pp. 141–48; Mary Poovey, "The Anathematized Race: The Governance and *Jane Eyre*," in *Feminism and Psychoanalysis*, pp. 230–54.
30. Poovey, "The Anathematized Race," p. 254.
31. Spivak's line has been cited in numerous places. See especially Jane Gallop, "The Monster in the Mirror: The Feminist Critic's Psychoanalysis," in *Feminism and Psychoanalysis*, pp. 13–24; Jane Gallop, "Annie Leclerc Writing a Letter, with Vermeer," in *The Poetics of Gender*, ed. Nancy K. Miller (New York: Columbia University Press, 1986), pp. 137–56; and Helena Michie's extremely interesting comparison and critique of these two essays in "Not One of the Family: The Repression of the Other Woman in Feminist Theory," in *Discontented Discourses: Feminism/Textual Intervention/Psychoanalysis*, ed. Marleen S. Barr and Richard Feldstein (Urbana: University of Illinois Press, 1989), pp. 15–28.
32. Toni Morrison, *Beloved* (New York: Knopf, 1987), p. 164. "Too thick" is the charge made by Paul D. and does not, of course, represent Morrison's perspective. The whole question of *Beloved* and psychoanalysis is, obviously, the subject of another essay.

Separating Lesbian Theory from Feminist Theory

A number of lesbian theorists have treated lesbian theory as a species of feminist theory. Calhoun rejects collapsing lesbian theory into feminist theory. On her view, heterosexism and patriarchy are analytically distinct social systems. Thus, the interests of heterosexual feminists and lesbians diverge in some respects, and emancipatory lesbian political programs may not always coincide with feminist politics.

Calhoun is skeptical of attempts to assimilate lesbian politics to gay rights, for this movement fails to address the overlap between women's oppression and lesbian oppression, and it ignores patriarchal attitudes among gay men. Still, lesbian politics does not merge well with feminist politics, either, for lesbians are oppressed in ways that heterosexual women are not. Whereas heterosexual feminists mainly want to reconstruct the category of "woman" in ways that sever it from male dominance, lesbians are positioned as "not-women" and thus are denied the option of reconstructing the category to make it fit them better. Calhoun characterizes lesbian experience as being oppressed by being a not-woman in a society that requires everyone to be a woman or a man and by a norm of womanliness that denies the lesbian's love for and sexual attraction to a particular woman. Moreover, she characterizes heterosexuality as a political system that is related to, yet distinct from patriarchy. Heterosexuality identifies male-female couples as fundamental to the social structure and as the only legitimate site of sexuality, childbearing, childrearing, and kinship. Only heterosexual couples have socio-politico-legal standing. Since lesbians are denied these heterosexual privileges, it is important for them, though not for heterosexual feminists, to demand the right of access to sexual-romantic-marital-familial relationships. Calhoun concludes that prohibiting discrimination based on sexual orientation and legalizing domestic partnerships will not give lesbians and gays genuine socio-politico-legal standing, for anti-discrimination laws do not touch on domestic relations, and domestic partnerships are inferiorized marriages.

—D.T.M.

Chapter 11

Cheshire Calhoun

Separating Lesbian Theory from Feminist Theory

Heidi Hartmann once said of the marriage of Marxism and feminism that it "has been like the marriage of husband and wife depicted in English common law: marxism and feminism are one, and that one is marxism."[1] Lesbian theory and feminism, I want to suggest, are at risk of falling into a similar unhappy marriage in which "the one" is feminism.

Although lesbian feminist theorizing has significantly contributed to feminist thought, it has also generally treated lesbianism as a kind of applied issue. Feminist theories developed outside of the context of lesbianism are brought to bear on lesbianism in order to illuminate the nature of lesbian oppression and women's relation to women within lesbianism. So, for example, early radical lesbians played off the feminist claim that all male-female relationships are dominance relationships. They argued either that the lesbian is *the* paradigm case of patriarchal resister because she refuses to be heterosexual or that she fits on a continuum of types of patriarchal resisters.[2] In taking this line, lesbian theorists made a space for lesbianism by focusing on what they took to be the inherently feminist and antipatriarchal nature of lesbian existence. Contemporary lesbian theorists are less inclined to read lesbianism as a feminist resistance to male dominance.[3] Instead, following the trend that feminist theory has itself taken, the focus has largely shifted to women's relation to women: the presence of ageism, racism, and anti-Semitism among lesbians; the problem of avoiding a totalizing discourse that speaks for all lesbians without being sensitive to differences; the difficulty of creating community in the face of political differences (e.g., on the issue of sadomasochism [s/m]); and the need to construct new conceptions of female agency and female friendship.[4] All of these are issues that have their birthplace in feminist theory. They become lesbian issues only because the general concern with women's relation to women is narrowed to lesbians' relation to fellow lesbians. Once again, lesbian thought becomes applied feminist thought.

Now, there is nothing wrong with using feminist tools to analyze lesbianism. Indeed, something would be wrong with feminist theory if it could not be usefully applied to lesbianism in a way that both illuminates lesbianism and extends feminist theory itself. And there would surely be something lacking in lesbian thought if it did not make use of feminist insights. My worry is that if this is all that lesbian feminism amounts to then there is no lesbian *theory*. Lesbian theory and feminist theory are one, and that one is feminist theory. What more could one want?

When Hartmann complained that Marxism had swallowed feminism, her point was that because traditional Marxism lacks a notion of sex-class, and thus of patriarchy as a political system distinct from capitalism, it must treat women's oppression as a special case of class oppression. Marxism is of necessity blind to the irreducibly gendered nature of women's lives. A parallel complaint might be raised about feminist theory. To the extent that feminist theory lacks a concept of heterosexuals and nonheterosexuals as members of different sexuality classes and thus of heterosexuality as a political structure separable from patriarchy, feminist theory must treat lesbian oppression as a special case of patriarchal oppression and remain blind to the irreducibly lesbian nature of lesbian lives.

Lesbian feminism is for several reasons at high risk of doing just that. First, the most extensive analyses of heterosexuality available to feminists are those developed in the late 1970s and early 1980s by Charlotte Bunch, Gayle Rubin, Adrienne Rich, Monique Wittig, and Kate Millett.[5] Heterosexuality, on this account, is both product and essential support of patriarchy. Women's heterosexual orientation perpetuates their social, economic, emotional and sexual dependence on and accessibility by men. Heterosexuality is thus a system of male ownership of women, participation in which is compulsory for men and especially for women. The lesbian's and heterosexual woman's relation to heterosexuality on this account is fundamentally the same. Both experience it as the demand that women be dependent on and accessible by men. Both are vulnerable to penalties if they resist that demand. Thus heterosexuality is equally compulsory for heterosexual women and lesbians; and compulsory heterosexuality means the same thing for both. There is no specifically lesbian relation to heterosexuality.

Second, lesbian feminists have had to assert their differences from gay men and thus their distance from both the political aims and the self-understanding of the gay movement. The gay rights movement has suffered from at least two defects. On the one hand, in focusing on lesbians' and gays' shared status as sexual deviants, the gay rights movement was unable to address the connection between lesbian oppression and women's oppression. On the other hand, it tended to equate gay with gay male and failed to address the patriarchal attitudes embedded in the gay movement itself.[6] Making clear the difference between lesbians and gay men meant that lesbian feminists' focus had to be on the experience of lesbians in a patriarchal culture, not on their experience as deviants in a heterosexist culture.

Third, the fact that to be lesbian is to live out of intimate relation with men and in intimate relation with women encourages the reduction of "lesbian" to "feminist."[7] Early radical feminists were quite explicit about this, claiming that lesbians are the truly woman-identified women. Contemporary lesbian feminists, recognizing that lesbians may share patriarchal attitudes toward women, resist such grand claims. But even if lesbian feminism is no longer at risk of equating being lesbian with being a "true" feminist, the danger remains that it may equate "lesbian issue" with "feminist issue." If what count as lesbian issues are only those visible through a feminist lens, then lesbian issues will simply be a special class of feminist ones.

Finally, the historical circumstances that gave birth to lesbian feminism had a decided impact on the direction that lesbian feminism took. The first major lesbian feminist statement, "The Woman-Identified Woman," was a direct response to Betty Friedan's charge that lesbians posed a "lavender menace" to the women's movement.[8] In Friedan's and many National Organization for Women (NOW) members' view, the association of feminism with lesbianism, and thus with deviancy, undermined the credibility of women's rights claims. Threatened with ostracism from the women's movement, the Radicalesbians argued in "The Woman-Identified Woman" that lesbians, because they love women and refuse to live with or devote their energies to the oppressor, are the paradigm feminists.[9] The political climate of the 1970s women's movement thus required lesbian feminists to assert their allegiance to feminist aims and values rather than calling attention to lesbians' differences from their heterosexual sisters. It was neither the time nor the place for lesbians to entertain the possibility that heterosexuality might itself be a political system and that heterosexual women and men, as a consolidated and powerful class, might have strong interests in maintaining a system of heterosexual privileges. In affirming their commitment to opposing patriarchy, lesbian feminists instead committed themselves to a specifically feminist account of the interests motivating the maintenance of a heterosexual system: men have patriarchal interests in securing sexual/emotional access to women, and heterosexual women have complicitous interests in securing access to a system of male privileges. This move effectively barred lesbian feminists from asking whether heterosexual women and men have, as heterosexuals, a class interest in constructing heterosexual sex as the only real, nonimitative sex; in eliminating historical, literary, and media representations of lesbian and gay men; in reserving jobs, public accommodations, and private housing for heterosexuals only; in barring lesbians and gay men from access to children in the education system, children's service organizations, and adoption and artificial insemination agencies; in reducing lesbianism and homosexuality to biologically or psychodevelopmentally rooted urges while propagating the myth of a magical heterosexual romantic love; and in securing for the married heterosexual couple exclusive pride of place in the social world. Nor could or did lesbian feminists ask whether these privileges taken as a set could provide a sufficient motivating interest for maintaining a heterosexual system even in the absence of patriarchy.

For all four reasons, treating sexual orientation on a par with gender, race, and economic class—that is, as a distinct and irreducible dimension of one's political identity—may not come naturally to lesbian feminist thinking. But separating sexuality politics from gender politics is exactly what must happen if there is to be a specifically *lesbian* feminist theory rather than simply feminist theory applied to lesbians. A lesbian feminist theory would need, among other things, to focus on what is distinctive about the lesbian's relation to heterosexuality, to the category "woman," and to other women. That is, it would need to put into clear view the difference between being a *lesbian* who loves women, resists heterosexuality, and resists being a woman, and being a (possibly heterosexual) *feminist* who loves women, resists heterosexuality, and resists being a woman.

In what follows, I will be arguing that, like patriarchy and capitalism, or white imperialism, patriarchy and heterosexual dominance are two in principle, separable systems. Even where they work together, it is possible conceptually to pull the patriarchal aspect of male-female relationships apart from their heterosexual dimensions. In arguing for the conceptual separability of the political structure of heterosexuality from patriarchy, I hope to establish two main points. First, lesbianism ought not to be read solely as resistance to patriarchal male-female relationships. One misses a good deal of what it means to live life as a lesbian as well as much of the political significance of lesbian practices by doing so. Second, even if empirically and historically heterosexual dominance and patriarchy are completely intertwined, it does not follow from this fact that the collapse of patriarchy will bring about the collapse of heterosexual dominance.[10] Heterosexual society may simply adapt to new social conditions. Thus it is a mistake for feminists to assume that work to end gender subordination will have as much payoff for lesbians as it would for heterosexual women. Only a political strategy that keeps clearly in mind the duality of the heterosexual-patriarchal structure, as well as the potential for conflict between feminist and lesbian strategies, could have such a payoff.

In making this argument, I will take the category "woman" and the institution of heterosexuality in turn. My aim in both cases is to illustrate the difference between being a lesbian and being a feminist, between lesbian politics and feminist politics, and to sketch the directions that I think lesbian theory would need to go in order to make a space for fully lesbian theorizing within feminist thought. I begin with the category "woman."

THE LESBIAN NOT-WOMAN

Monique Wittig ends "The Straight Mind" with this sentence: "Lesbians are not women."[11] Wittig denies that "man" and "woman" are natural categories, arguing instead that the two sex-classes—men, women—are the product of heterosexual social relations in which "men appropriate for themselves the reproduction and production of women and also their physical persons by means of a contract called the marriage contract."[12] Thus, "it is oppression that creates sex and not the contrary."[13] Lesbians, however, refuse to participate in heterosexual social relations. Like runaway slaves who refuse to have their labor appropriated by white masters, lesbians are runaways who refuse to allow men to control their productive and reproductive labor within a nuclear family. Thus Wittig observes, "Lesbianism is the only concept I know of which is beyond the categories of sex (woman and man), because the designated subject (lesbian) is not a woman, either economically, or politically, or ideologically. For what makes a woman is a specific social relation to a man, a relation that we have previously called servitude, a relation which implies personal and physical obligation as well as economic obligation ('forced residence', domestic corvée, conjugal duties, unlimited production of children, etc.), a relation which lesbians escape by refusing to become or to stay heterosexual."[14] What I want to highlight in Wittig's explanation of what bars lesbians from the category "woman" is that it claims both too much and too little for lesbians as well as reads lesbianism from a peculiarly heterosexual viewpoint. To say that only lesbians exist beyond sex categories (in Wittig's particular sense of what this means) claims too much for lesbians. If to be a woman just means living in a relation of servitude to men, there will be other ways short of lesbianism of evading the category "woman". The heterosexual celibate, virgin, single-parent head of household, marriage resister, or the married woman who insists on an egalitarian marriage contract all apparently qualify as escapees from the category "woman."[15]

Although Wittig does remark that runaway wives are also escaping their sex class, she clearly thought that lesbians are in some special sense *not-women.* But her own analysis does not capture lesbians' special deviancy from the category "woman." There is indeed no conceptual space in Wittig's framework for pursuing the question of how a heterosexual woman's refusal to be a woman differs from a lesbian's refusal to be a woman. It is in that failure that she claims too little for lesbians. Because lesbians and heterosexual resisters must have, on her account, the same relation to the category "woman", there can be no interesting differences between the two. This, I think, is a mistake, and I will argue in a moment that lesbians are in a quite special sense not-women.

Finally, to equate lesbians' escape from heterosexuality and the category "woman" with escape from male control is to adopt a peculiarly heterosexual viewpoint on lesbianism. The fact that heterosexuality enables men to control women's domestic labor is something that would be salient only to a *heterosexual* woman. Only heterosexual women do housework for men, raise children for men, have their domiciles determined by men, and so on. Thus, from a heterosexual standpoint lesbianism may indeed appear to offer a liberating escape from male control. But from the standpoint of a woman unaccustomed to living with men, that is, from a lesbian standpoint, lesbianism is not about a refusal to labor for men. Nor is heterosexuality experienced primarily as a form of male dominance over women, but instead as heterosexual dominance over lesbians and gay men. Nor is the daily experience of lesbianism one of liberation but, instead, one of acute oppression.

Because Wittig looks at lesbianism from a (heterosexual) feminist perspective, asking how lesbians escape the kinds of male control to which paradigmatically heterosexual women are subject, she misses the penalties attached to lesbians' exit from heterosexuality. Indeed, contrary to Wittig's claim, the lesbian may as a rule have *less* control over her productive and reproductive labor than her married heterosexual sister. Although the lesbian escapes whatever control *individual* men may exercise over tier wives within marriage, she does not thereby escape control of her productive and reproductive labor either in her personal life with another woman or in her public life. To refuse to be heterosexual is simply to leap out of the frying pan of individual patriarchal control into the fire of institutionalized heterosexual control. Wittig's claim that "lesbianism provides for the moment the only social form in which we can live freely" vastly underestimates the coercive forces brought to bear on the lesbian for her lesbianism.[16] She may be unable to adopt children or be denied custody of and visiting privileges to her children. In order to retain her job, she will most likely have to hide her lesbianism and pretend to be heterosexual. She will likely be punished for public displays of affection. She may be denied the housing of her choice or be forced to move from her home as a result of harassment by neighbors. If she is "out," she will find herself alternately abused and subjected to lascivious interest by heterosexual men. Even if she is no longer at risk of being burned at the stake or subjected to clitoridectomy or electroshock, she may still be subjected to "therapies" that insist that she cannot be both lesbian and a healthy, mature adult. She will be labeled a dyke and scrutinized for symptoms of mannishness in her anatomy, dress, behavior, and interests. She will not see her lesbian sexuality or romantic love for another woman reflected in the public media. And both because there are no publicly accessible models of lesbian relationships and because such coercive pressure is brought to bear against lesbian relationships, sustaining a stable personal life will be very difficult. The lesbian may be free from an individual man in her personal life, but she is not free.

What these criticisms suggest is, first, that the political structure that oppresses heterosexual women is patriarchy; but the political structure that most acutely oppresses lesbians is more plausibly taken to be heterosexuality. Second, these criticisms suggest that heterosexual women's (especially heterosexual feminists') and lesbians' relation to the category "woman" are not the same.

From a feminist point of view, the problem with the category "woman" is not so much that there is one. The problem lies in its specific construction within patriarchal society. "Woman" has been constructed as the Other and the deficient in relation to "man." To "woman" have been assigned all those traits that would both rationalize and perpetuates women's lack of power in relation to men. Women are weak, passive, dependent, emotional, irrational, nurturant, closer to nature, maternal, and so on. This is to say that, from a feminist point of view, the problem with the category "woman" is that "woman" has been equated with subordination to men. The feminist task, then, is to rupture that equation. With the exception of early liberal feminists' recommendation of androgyny and possibly contemporary French feminists' deconstruction of "woman," the feminist project has not been the elimination of the category "woman." Instead, the project has been one of reconstructing that category. That reconstructive project has had two phases within feminism. The first phase tried to reconstruct the category "woman" so that it could no longer be used to rationalize male dominance. So, for example, some feminine traits were rejected, others, such as nurturance, were revalued and/or redefined, and some masculine traits (e.g., strength) were appropriated with or without redefinition.[17] The more recent phase has been devoted to reconstructing the category "woman" employed within feminism itself so that it cannot be used to rationalize white, middle-class, college-educated, heterosexual, Christian women's dominance within feminism.[18] This latter reconstruction has required the postulate of multiple categories of "woman" to capture the intersection of gender with other political identities.[19]

The feminist experience of her relation to the category "woman", thus, has been the experience of *being* a woman in a male dominant, as well as racist and classist, society, which imposes on her a conception of what it means to be a woman that she rejects. Her refusal to be a woman has extended only to refusal to be the kind of woman that a patriarchal, racist, and classist society demands that she be. And that refusal has gone hand in hand with claiming the category "woman" (or categories of 'women') for herself and insisting on a woman-identified construction of that category.

This is not the lesbian relation to the category "woman". Although partly mistaken, I think, in her reasons, Wittig was correct to say that to be lesbian is to exit the category "woman" altogether. It is to be ungendered, unsexed, neither woman nor man. This is because (here following Wittig) sex/gender is the result of institutionalized heterosexuality.[20] Heterosexual systems are ones that organize reproduction via hetero*sexual* practice. That practice requires the production of two sex/genders so that sexual desire can be heterosexualized. It also requires that sex/gender map onto reproductive differences. Thus, within heterosexual systems, " 'intelligible' genders are those which in some sense institute and maintain relations of coherence and continuity among sex, gender, sexual practice, and desire."[21] Individuals who violate the unity of reproductive anatomy, heterosexual desire, and gender behavior fall out of the domain of intelligible gender identity. At best, lesbians are not-women. That is, for them the closet available category of sex/gender identity is one that does not fit. Neither anatomy nor desire nor gender can link her securely to the category "woman." Within heterosexist ideology her anatomy itself is suspect. Much was made, for example, in the sexologists' literature of physical masculinity in the lesbian, including reports of an enlarged clitoris. The postulate of a biological basis of homosexuality and lesbianism continues to guide research today. And many lesbians' insistence on having been born lesbian reinforces such suspicions about anatomical differences from heterosexual women. In addition, her anatomy cannot link her to "woman" because what lesbianism reveals is the fundamental lie that differences in male and female anatomy destine a difference in males' and females' sexual and social relations to females, that is, destine one to be functionally a man or a woman. The lesbian's female body in no way bars her from functioning as a man in relation to women. She shares with members of the category "man" a sexual desire for and love of women. Also, the very traits that Wittig took to be definitive of "man"—the enactment of masculine dominance over women, physically, psychologically, socially, and economically—are an option for her in a way that they are not an option for heterosexual women. The lesbian thus exits the category of "woman", though without thereby entering the category "man."

Gender-deviant heterosexual women (i.e., women who resist patriarchal understandings of what it means to be a woman) do not similarly exit the category "woman". Gender deviance would result in not-woman status only if the content of the category "woman" were fully exhausted by a description, such as Wittig's, of what it means to be a woman. I have been suggesting, on the contrary, that heterosexuality is a critical component of the category "woman." Heterosexuality secures one's status as a "natural" woman, which is to say, as having a body whose sex as female is above suspicion. Heterosexuality also guarantees a significant nonidentity between one's own and men's relation to women. The heterosexual woman will not have a sexual, romantic, marital, coparenting relation to other women; she will have instead a *woman's* relation to women. Thus even in her gender deviance, the heterosexual resister of patriarchally defined gender remains unambiguously a woman.

Because the lesbian stands outside the category "woman", her experience of womanliness and its oppressive nature is not identical to that of the heterosexual feminist, who stands within the category of "woman," even if resistantly. Womanliness is not something the lesbian has the option of refusing or reconstructing for a better fit. It is a fundamental impossibility for her. To be a not-woman is to be incapable of *being* a woman within heterosexual society. The lesbian can thus be womanly only in the modes of being in drag and of passing. And if she experiences womanliness—the demand that she look like a woman, act like a woman—as oppressive, it is not because womanliness requires subordination to men (although this may also be her experience). It is instead because the demand that she be womanly is the demand that she pretend that the sex/gender "woman" is a natural possibility for her and that she pass as a woman. It is thus also a demand that she not reveal the nonexhaustiveness and, potentially, the nonnaturalness of the binary categories "woman" and "man."

The lesbian experience of her relation to the category "woman", thus, is the experience of being a not-woman in a heterosexual society that compels everyone to be either a woman or a man and requires that she be a woman.[22] It is also the experience of being oppressed by a womanliness that denies her desire for women, and of being deviantly outside of sex/gender categories. That deviancy is harshly punished. In an attempt to compel her back into the category "woman", her lesbian desire and unwomanly relation to women are punished or treated. At the same time, she is denied the heterosexual privileges to which "real" women have access.

From a lesbian perspective, the category "woman" is oppressive because, within heterosexual societies, that category is compulsory for all anatomically female individuals. Feminist reconstructions of "woman" do not typically challenge compulsory sex/gender. They implicitly assume that "woman" and "man" exhaust the field of possible sorts of persons to be (even if it takes multiple categories of each to exhaust the taxonomy). Furthermore, insofar as lesbians are automatically and uncritically subsumed under the feminist category "woman," feminist theorizing presumes that membership in that category is determined by anatomy and ignores the extent to which the femaleness of the lesbian body is suspect. The lesbian objection to being a woman is not met by admissions that the category "woman" as well as what it means to be anatomically female are open to social construction and reconstruction. Nor is it met by the suggestion that there is no single category "woman" but instead multiple categories of women. From a lesbian perspective, what has to be challenged is heterosexual society's demand that females be women. For that demand denies the lesbian option. The lesbian option is to be a not-woman, where being a not-woman is played out by insisting on being neither identifiably woman nor man, nor by enacting femininity as drag, nor by insisting on switching gender categories and thus being a man, which within patriarchy means being dominant in relation to women and potentially also misogynistic.

Failure to see the difference between feminist and lesbian relations to the category "woman" may well result in mislocating lesbian politics and failing to see the potential friction between feminist and lesbian politics. I take the feminist critique of butch and femme lesbianism as a case in point. On that critique, both the lesbian appropriation of femininity by femmes (and more recently by lipstick lesbians) and the lesbian appropriation of masculinity through butch sexual-social dominance repeat between women the power politics and misogyny that typifies male-female relations in a patriarchal society. Julia Penelope, for instance, argues that "those aspects of behavior and appearance labeled 'femininity' in HP [heteropatriarchy] are dangerous for us. We still live *in* a heteropatriarchy and Lesbians who incorporate male ideas of appropriate female behaviors into their lives signal their acceptance of the HP version of reality."[23] In particular, the feminine lesbian confirms heteropatriarchy's acceptance of the feminine woman and rejection of any trace of mannishness in women.

From a feminist point of view there is no way of rendering politically harmless the appropriation of a role that requires sexual-social passivity and subordination, even if the appropriation is by a not-woman and even if she is not passive or subordinate primarily in relation to men. Here the argument against femininity in lesbians directly parallels the argument against the masochist role in lesbian s/m. The femme's and masochist's appeal to the voluntariness of their choices, the privacy of their practices, and the pleasure they derive from femininity and masochism, respectively, do not go all the way toward making what they do purely personal. Both femininity and female masochism acquire their meaning from what Penelope calls "heteropatriarchal semantics" as well as from the historical and material conditions of women's oppression. Those meanings cannot be dissolved at will.[24] To adopt either femininity or female masochism for oneself is to make use of a set of meanings produced through and sustained by men's oppression of women. It is thus to reveal one's personal failure to come to critical grips with the politics of women's position within patriarchy. Even if the femme's or masochist's personal choices are not political in the sense that they also publicly endorse femininity or masochism in women, they are still political in the sense that they also make use of public meanings which are tied to gender politics.

Nor, the feminist critic might add, can the appropriation of masculine dominance, aggression, and misogyny be rendered politically harmless. What the butch (as well as the sadist in lesbian s/m) confirms is the patriarchal equation of power with sexual dominance and superiority with masculinity. Janice Raymond's caustic remarks about lesbian s/m might equally express the feminist critique of butch-femme roles: "It is difficult to see what is so advanced or progressive about a position that locates 'desire', and that imprisons female sexual dynamism, vitality, and vigor, in old forms of sexual objectification, subordination, and violence, this time initiated by women and done with women's consent. The libertarians offer a supposed sexuality stripped naked of feminine taboo, but only able to dress itself in masculine garb. It is a male-constructed sexuality in drag."[25]

I have no intention of disagreeing with the claim that butch-femme role-playing runs contrary to feminist politics. What I do intend to take issue with is the assumption that feminist politics are necessarily lesbian politics. Judith Butler gives a quite different reading of the multiple appropriations of femininity and masculinity within the lesbian/gay community by butches, femmes, queens, dykes, and gay male girls. It is a reading that I take to be closer to a lesbian perspective, even if farther from a feminist one.

What the feminist critique omits is the fact that "within lesbian contexts, the 'identification' with masculinity that appears as butch identity is not a simple assimilation of lesbianism back to the terms of heterosexuality. As one lesbian femme explained, she likes her boys to be girls. . . . As a result, that masculinity, if that it can be called, is always brought into relief against a culturally intelligible 'female body.' It is precisely this dissonant juxtaposition and the sexual tension that its transgression generates that constitute the object of desire."[26] It is also precisely this dissonant juxtaposition of masculinity and female body that enables the butch to enact a comedic parody of masculinity that denaturalizes the category "man". Heterosexual society assumes that masculinity is naturally united to the male body and desire for women. Similarly, it assumes that femininity is naturally united to the female body and desire for men. Butler argues, however, that gender identity is not natural but the result of continuous gender performances. One can be a man, for example, only by continuously performing masculinity and desire for women through a male body. Heterosexual society sustains the illusion of natural gender identities—"heterosexual man," "heterosexual woman"—by outlawing alternative performances. The butch lesbian gives an outlawed performance. She performs masculinity and desire for women through a female body. The butch gay man similarly gives and outlaws performance by performing masculinity in tandem with desire for men through a male body. Such multiple locations of masculinity—on the heterosexual male body, the lesbian body, the gay man's body—help create a condition in which "after a while, everyone starts to look like a drag queen."[27] The categories "woman" and "man" cease to appear natural. Without such clearly natural or original gender identities, lesbians' subordinate status cannot be rationalized on the grounds that lesbians are unnatural, imitative beings. And, one might add, the exclusively heterosexual organization of sexuality, romantic love, marriage, and the family begin to appear arbitrary.

Because challenging heterosexual dominance and compulsory compliance with heterosexual sex/gender categories depends on deviating performances that reconfigure the elements of "man" and "woman," Butler rejects feminist attempts to "outlaw" butch and femme lesbian identities.

> Lesbianism that defines itself in radical exclusion from heterosexuality deprives itself of the capacity to resignify the very heterosexual constructs by which it is partially and inevitably constituted. As a result, that lesbian strategy would consolidate compulsory heterosexuality in its oppressive forms.
>
> The more insidious and effective strategy it seems is a thoroughgoing appropriation and redeployment of the categories of identity themselves.[28]

Terralee Bensinger gives a similar reading of butch-femme representations within lesbian pornography. Like Butler, she stresses the political significance of displacing "traditional heterosexual postures" of masculinity and femininity from their supposedly natural home on the heterosexual couple's bodies to the lesbian couple's bodies.[29] "The important thing here is that the reworking of these codes, within a lesbian context, de-naturalizes the illusion of a 'natural' heterosexuality (where such codes are 'appropriately' attached to female and male bodies in a sex/gender suture)."[30] In her view, however, the effectiveness of butch-femme representations depends not only upon the displacement of masculinity and femininity onto nonheterosexual bodies but also upon their shifting and ambivalent inscription on lesbian bodies. When elements of masculinity and femininity appear on the same body or shift back and forth between the bodies of the lesbian couple, gender is most fully destabilized and denaturalized.

But have Butler and Bensinger really responded to the *feminist* critique of butch-femme role-playing? I think not. A feminist might well raise the following objection: butch and femme lesbianism may indeed undermine heterosexual society. It does not follow, however, that butch-femme lesbianism undermines patriarchy. The original objection still stands: butch lesbianism leaves in place the patriarchal equation of masculinity with power and dominance, while femme lesbianism leaves in place the patriarchal equation of femininity with weakness and subordination. Butler's, and perhaps also Bensinger's, political program would at best simply replace heterosexuality-based patriarchy (male power) with masculinity-based patriarchy (masculine power). Under masculinity-based patriarchy, anatomical females and males would have an equal opportunity to appropriate masculine power over feminine individuals, who themselves could be either anatomically male or female.

What the disagreement between Butler and many feminists reveals is the fact that challenging heterosexual society and challenging patriarchy are not the same thing. The feminist political opposition to patriarchal power relations disables lesbians from effectively challenging heterosexual society. The lesbian political opposition to compulsory heterosexual gender performances disables feminists from effectively challenging patriarchal society. But neither Butler nor feminists who critique butch and femme lesbians see this. Both assume the *identity* of feminist politics and lesbian politics. This is simply a mistake. Heterosexuality and patriarchy are analytically distinct social systems, just as capitalism and patriarchy are distinct. Patriarchy can survive just as easily in a nonheterosexual society as it can in a noncapitalist society. Butch-femme culture is a case in point. On the flip side, heterosexuality can survive in a nonpatriarchal society. Heterosexual societies simply require that masculinity be united with a male body and desire for women and that femininity be united with a female body and desire for men. Heterosexual systems do *not* depend on femininity and masculinity being defined and valued the way they are in patriarchal societies. Matriarchies are heterosexual systems.[31]

Given this, one should expect that feminist politics and lesbian politics, though typically overlapping, may sometimes part company. Moreover, when those politics do conflict, there is no reason to expect that feminist lesbians will or should give priority to feminist politics. Being a woman (or better, being mistaken for a woman) and being oppressed as a woman are often not the most important facts in a lesbian's life. Being a lesbian and being oppressed as a lesbian often matter more.

WHICH HETEROSEXUALITY?

I said at the beginning that one main reason why "lesbian issue" tends to collapse into "feminist issue" is that the most well-developed model of heterosexuality available to lesbian feminist theorizing is one that takes heterosexuality to be both product and essential support of patriarchy. The Radicalesbians, Monique Wittig, Charlotte Bunch, Adrienne Rich, and more recently Marilyn Frye all take this view.[32] On this feminist reading of heterosexuality, what defines heterosexuality is the requirement that women be in a dependent and subordinate relation to men. I have already argued that looking at heterosexuality this way results in claiming too much for lesbians. Lesbianism is mistakenly read as the quintessential form of feminist revolt. I intend to begin this section by expanding on the argument against reducing the institution of heterosexuality to (a part of) the institution of male dominance. I will then turn to Janice Raymond's and Sarah Hoagland's feminist attempts to avoid claiming too much for lesbians. Their strategy involves locating the political problem in a particular *style* of heterosexualist interaction rather than in heterosexuality itself. This strategy, I will argue, results in claiming too little for lesbians by denying that there is anything intrinsically political in lesbians' revolt against the rule of heterosexuality. I will conclude with a quite different reading of heterosexuality, one that I take to be closer to a lesbian view, if farther from a feminist one.

Heterosexuality as Male Dominance

Heterosexuality, in Wittig's view, is a political and economic system of male dominance. The heterosexual social contract (to which only men have consented) stipulates that women belong to men. In particular, women's reproductive labor, including both childrearing and domestic chores, belongs to men by "natural" right much as a slave's labor belongs to its master by natural right. It is thus heterosexuality that enables men to appropriate women's labor and that supports a system of male dominance. In Wittig's view, lesbian refusal to be heterosexual challenges this system of male dominance because being lesbian fundamentally means refusing to accept the "economic, ideological and political power of men."[33] Wittig's equation of lesbian resistance with feminist resistance is both obvious and explicit. She claims that to be a feminist is to fight for the disappearance of the sex-class "woman" by refusing to participate in the heterosexual relations that created the sex-class "woman" in the first place.[34] To be a feminist just *is* to be a lesbian.

In "Lesbians in Revolt," Charlotte Bunch similarly equates heterosexuality with male control over women's labor; and like Wittig, she regards lesbianism as a political revolt against a system in which neither a woman nor her labor belong to herself. "The lesbian . . . refuses to be a man's property, to submit to the unpaid labor system of housework and childcare. She rejects the nuclear family as the basic unit of production and consumption in capitalist society."[35] In Bunch's view, commitment to heterosexuality is necessarily a commitment to supporting a male world, and thus a barrier to struggle against women's oppression. "Being a lesbian means ending identification with, allegiance to, dependence on, and support of heterosexuality. It means ending your personal stake in the male world so that you join women individually and collectively in the struggle to end oppression."[36]

At least two different objections might be raised to Wittig's and Bunch's implicit claim that one must be a lesbian to be a feminist. First, lesbianism only challenges male control of women in the family. But women's labor power is also extensively controlled in the public sphere through male bosses, absence of maternity leave, sexual harassment, the job requirement of an "appropriately" feminine appearance, insufficient availability of day care, sex segregation of women into lower paid jobs and so on. As Ann Ferguson observes, enforced heterosexuality "may be one of the mechanisms [of male dominance], but it surely is not the single or sufficient one. Others, such as the control of female biological reproduction, male control of state and political power, and economic systems involving discrimination based on class and race, seem analytically distinct from coercive heterosexuality, yet are causes which support and perpetuate male dominance."[37] Moreover, given both the decline of male power within the nuclear family and of the nuclear family itself, one might well claim that the public control of women's productive and reproductive labor is far more critical to the maintenance of patriarchy than the private control of women's labor within the nuclear family.

While the first objection focuses on the way that lesbianism may not be the only or even most fundamental means of resisting patriarchy, a second objection focuses on the fact that the kind of resistance being claimed for lesbians in fact belongs generally to feminists. As an empirical generalization about heterosexual relations, it is true that men continue to exercise control over women's private and public work lives. As Wittig might put it, it "goes without saying" in the heterosexual social contract that women will assume primary responsibility for child rearing and domestic labor, that they will adjust their public work lives to the exigencies of their male partner's, and that they will be at least partially economically dependent on their male partner's income. But there are any number of ways of evading the terms of this contract without ceasing to be heterosexual. Thus the claim that heterosexual relations are male dominant ones is insufficient to support the claim that only lesbians are genuine resisters. Indeed, the heterosexual feminist who insists on a more equal partnership may resist patriarchy more effectively than many lesbians. As both Janice Raymond and Sarah Hoagland have argued, the importation of hetero-relations into lesbian relationships enables patriarchal ways of thinking to be sustained within lesbian relationships themselves.[38]

Heterosexualism versus Heterosexuality

Both Raymond and Hoagland avoid equating "lesbian" with "feminist" by distinguishing heterosexuality from "hetero-relations" (Raymond) and "heterosexualism" (Hoagland). Within their writing, "heterosexuality" retains its customary referent to sexual object choice. "Hetero-relations" and "heterosexualism" refer to the patriarchal nature of male-female relations in both the private and public spheres. According to Raymond, in a hetero-relational society, "most of women's personal, social, political, professional, and economic relations are defined by the ideology that woman is for man."[39] Hoagland similarly claims that heterosexualism "is a particular economic, political, and emotional relationship between men and women: men must dominate women and women must subordinate themselves to men in any number of ways. As a result, men presume access to women while women remain riveted on men and are unable to sustain a community of women."[40] It is, in their view, hetero-relationalism, not heterosexuality, per se, that subordinates women to men.

By distinguishing hetero-relations and heterosexualism from heterosexuality Raymond and Hoagland avoid exaggerating the feminist element in lesbianism. Both recognize the potential failure of lesbians to disengage from heterosexualism. Lesbians themselves may be misogynistic and may engage in the same dominance-subordinance relations that typify heterosexualism. Thus lesbian resistance to heterosexuality is not automatically a resistance to patriarchy. Because Raymond and Hoagland are sensitive to this fact, they are able to subject lesbian relations to feminist critique in a productive way. In addition, by recognizing that heterosexual women can redefine their relations to men in such a way that they both leave space for gyn-affectionate relations with women and refuse to participate in hetero-relations with men, Raymond avoids pitting lesbians against heterosexual women within the feminist community in a battle over who counts as a "true" feminist.

Their attempt, however, to avoid claiming too much for lesbianism comes at the cost of ultimately claiming too little for it. By putting the concept of hetero-relations or heterosexualism at the center of their lesbian feminism, both effectively eliminate space for a *lesbian* theory. Within their work, lesbian resistance to heterosexuality does not, in itself, have either political or conceptual significance. Whatever political significance lesbian personal lives may have is due entirely to the presence of or resistance to hetero-relations within those lives. The reduction of lesbian politics to feminist politics is quite obvious in Raymond's "Putting the Politics Back into Lesbianism."[41] There, Raymond sharply criticizes lesbian lifestyles and sexual libertarians for failure to see that in advocating an anything-goes sexuality (including lesbian pornography and s/m) as the path to liberation, they are simply repeating the patriarchal image of woman as essentially sexual being. Moreover, as I mentioned earlier, insofar as lesbian lifestyles advocate aggressive and violent forms of sexuality, they are simply putting a "male-constructed sexuality in drag."[42] What I want to underscore in Raymond's critique is that putting politics into lesbianism means putting *feminist* politics into lesbianism. She does not demand that lesbians put resistance to heterosexuality and to lesbian oppression at the center of their lives. Thus she does not ask whether or not lesbian s/m promotes *lesbian* politics.

One important consequence of equating lesbian with feminist politics in this way is that lesbians who have suffered the worst oppression; for example, the 1950s butches and femmes who risked repeated arrest and police harassment, often turn out to be the least politically interesting from a feminist point of view. Shane Phelan's criticism of Adrienne Rich for marginalizing "real" lesbians who resisted heterosexuality and for giving nonlesbians who resisted dependency on men pride of place on her lesbian continuum applies generally to those who equate lesbian politics with feminist politics: "It becomes clear that the existence of these women [lesbians], those who have been targets of abuse for decades, is less interesting to lesbian feminists than the existence of women who never called themselves lesbians, never thought of themselves as such, and never faced the consequences of that. The sort of lesbian who laid the groundwork, built the urban subcultures, that allowed lesbians to find one another before feminism, is remembered primarily in the works of male historians. The relevant community is lesbian feminist, with the emphasis, curiously, on the feminist rather than the lesbian."[43]

From a feminist point of view whose political yardstick measures only distance from patriarchal practices and institutions, butches and femmes, lesbian sex radicals who promote pornography and s/m, lesbian mothers, and married lesbians all fail to measure up. All are vulnerable to the charge of appropriating for women and between women the very practices and institutions that have served so well to oppress women. Yet it is precisely these women who insist on the reality and value of romance, sexuality, parenting, and marriage between women, who resist most strongly heterosexual society's reservation of the private sphere for male-female couples only. From a lesbian point of view whose political yardstick measures resistance to heterosexuality and heterosexual privilege, they are neither politically uninteresting nor assimilationist.

Not only does this focus on heterosexualism rather than heterosexuality leave no space for understanding the inherently political nature of lesbianism, it also leaves no space for understanding the significance of specifically lesbian love. For instance, like Rich's notion of a lesbian continuum that includes both lesbians and heterosexual women, Raymond's "use of the term *Gyn/affection* expresses a *continuum* of female friendship" that includes some (but not all) lesbian love as well as friendship between heterosexual women.[44] In her view, it is in gyn/affection that women seize power from men and engage in a woman-identified act. Thus it is gyn/affection that is politically significant. Specifically lesbian sexual and romantic attraction to women is left without any politically or conceptually interesting place to be. Raymond is by no means the first or only lesbian feminist to marginalize lesbian love in favor of a form of love between women that is more directly tied to feminist solidarity. Bunch, for example, claims that "the lesbian, woman-identified-woman commits herself to women not only as an alternative to oppressive male-female relationships but primarily because she *loves* women."[45] That this is not a particularized conception of love but rather feminist "love" of women as a class becomes clear in the way she connects lesbian love with class solidarity: "When women do give primary energies to other women, then it is possible to concentrate fully on building a movement for our liberation."[46] In a more recent piece, Nett Hart similarly equates lesbian love with love of women as a class: "We love women as a class and we love specific women. We embrace the concept that women can be loved, that women are inherently worthy of love."[47] In both Bunch and Hart, there is a conceptual slide from "love" in the sense of a sexual-romantic love of a particular woman to "love" in the sense of valuing and respecting members of the category "woman." Although Raymond differs in being much more careful to keep the two sorts of love conceptually separated, all three prioritize love of women as a class. From a feminist point of view it is indeed the capacity to value members of the category "woman" and to form strong primary bonds of friendship with many women that matters politically. But this is not lesbian love. Lesbians fall in love with, want to make love to, decide to set up a household with a particular other woman, not a class of women. It is for this particularized, sexualized love that lesbians are penalized in heterosexual society. Because of this, lesbian theory needs to move specifically lesbian love to the center of its political stage.

These remarks are not intended either to undercut the value for feminists of work being done by lesbians or the need to subject lesbian practice to feminist critique. They are meant to suggest that a full-blown lesbian feminism cannot afford to reduce the political institution of heterosexuality to an institution of male dominance.

Heterosexuality as a Political System

I have been arguing so far that reading heterosexuality and lesbianism solely in relation to patriarchal gender politics fails to yield an adequate picture of lesbians' political position. I turn now to an exploration of the thesis that heterosexuality is itself a political system that shapes our social structure as systematically as do patriarchal, racial imperialist, and class systems.

I do not mean to deny that in patriarchal societies heterosexuality enables what Gayle Rubin called the "traffic in women." I *do* mean to deny that heterosexual systems' only function is to support a system of male privilege. I suggest instead that heterosexual systems, whether patriarchal or not, function to insure reproduction by making the male-female unit fundamental to social structure, particularly, though not exclusively, to the structure of what might broadly be called the private sphere. That is, heterosexual systems assign the heterosexual couple-based family a privileged social status as the only legitimate site of sexuality, childbearing, childrearing, the care of individuals' physical and emotional needs, the maintenance of a household, and the creation of kinship bonds. It is because the purpose of heterosexual systems is to sustain reproduction that threats to that system—for example the education of women, or homosexuality—inevitably evoke in Anglo-American history some version of the race suicide argument.

Heterosexuality then is not just a matter of the orientation of individual sexual desire. It is a method of socially organizing a broad spectrum of reproductive activities. Accordingly, the taboo on homosexuality does not simply outlaw same-sex desire. More basically it outlaws the female-female or male-male couple as the site of any reproductive activities.[48] Thus, if one wants a complete set of the regulations that constitute the taboo on lesbianism and homosexuality, one needs to look at all of the practices that directly or indirectly insure that the family will be built around a male-female pair. The social and legal prohibition of same-sex sex is only the tip of the iceberg of the systematic heterosexualization of social life.

This socially foundational status of the male-female couple gets ideologically expressed and reinforced through the language of naturalness: the individuals who make up society are taken to be naturally gendered as men or women, naturally heterosexual, and naturally inclined to establish a family based around the male-female reproductive unit. The alleged natural inevitability of gender differences, heterosexual desire, and heterosexually reproductive families enables heterosexual societies to take it for granted that "of course" the social, economic, and legal structure of any society will, and ought to, reflect these basic facts.

Social practices, norms, and institutions are designed to meet heterosexual systems' need to produce sex/gender dimorphism—masculine males and feminine females—so that desire can then be heterosexualized. Gendered behavioral norms, gendered rites of passage, a sexual division of labor, and the like produce differently gendered persons out of differently sexed persons. Prohibitions against gender crossing (e.g., against cross-dressing, effeminacy in men, mannishness in women) also help sustain the dimorphism necessary to heterosexualize desire.

Children and especially adolescents are carefully prepared for heterosexual interaction. They are given heterosexual sex education, advice for attracting the opposite sex, norms for heterosexual behavior, and appropriate social occasions (such as dances or dating rituals) for enacting desire. Adult heterosexuality is further sustained through erotica and pornography, heterosexualized humor, heterosexualized dress, romance novels, and so on.

Heterosexual societies take it for granted that men and women will bond in an intimate relationship, ultimately founding a family. As a result, social conventions, economic arrangements, and the legal structure treat the heterosexual couple as a single, and singularly important, social unit. The couple is represented linguistically (boyfriend-girlfriend, husband-wife) and is treated socially as a single unit (e.g., in joint invitations or in receiving joint gifts). It is legally licensed and legally supported through such entitlements as communal property, joint custody or adoption of children, and the power to give proxy consent within the couple. The couple is also recognized in the occupational structure via such provisions as spousal healthcare benefits and restrictions on nepotism. Multiple practices and institutions help heterosexual individuals to couple and create families and support the continuation of those couples and couple-based families. These include dating services, matchmakers, introductions to eligible partners, premarital counseling, marriage counseling, marriage and divorce law, adoption services, reproductive technologies, family rates, family healthcare benefits, tax deductions for married couples, and so on.

The sum total of all the social, economic, and legal arrangements that support the sexual and relational coupling of men with women constitutes heterosexual privilege. And it is privilege of a peculiar sort. Heterosexuals do not simply claim *greater* socio-politico-legal standing than nonheterosexuals. They claim as natural and normal an arrangement where *only* heterosexuals have socio-political-legal standing. Lesbians and gay men are not recognized as social beings because they cannot enter into the most basic social unit, the male-female couple. Within heterosexual systems, the only social arrangements that apply to nonheterosexuals are eliminative in nature. The coercive force of the criminal law, institutionalized discrimination, "therapeutic" treatment, and individual prejudice and violence is marshaled against the existence of lesbians and gay men. At best, lesbians and gay men have negative social reality. Lesbians are not-women engaged in nonsex with nonrelationships that may constitute a nonfamily.

It would be a mistake to think that legal prohibitions of discrimination on the basis of sexual orientation or legal recognition of domestic partnerships would give lesbians and gay men any genuine socio-politico-legal standing. The legal reduction of lesbianism to mere sexuality which is implicitly in "sexual orientation" legislation only reconfirms the heterosexual assumption that lesbianism cannot itself provide the site for the broad spectrum of reproductive activities. Only heterosexuality, which "everyone knows" is more than mere sexual desire, can provide this site in the form of the heterosexual couple. Because lesbianism is supposedly mere sex and not a mode of sociality, no fundamental alteration needs to be made in the social practices and institutions that constitute the private sphere. Domestic partnership laws fall in the same boat. They set up what amount to separate but allegedly equal spheres for heterosexuals and nonheterosexuals. Heterosexuals retain coverage by marriage laws. All other possible private arrangements are covered under domestic partnerships. The point of excluding lesbian and gay marriages from marriage law itself is, of course, to reaffirm heterosexual society's most basic belief that only the male-female couple constitutes a natural, basic social unit.

In short, unlike the heterosexual woman, including the heterosexual feminist, the lesbian experience of the institution of heterosexuality is of a system that makes her sexual, affectional, domestic, and reproductive life unreal. With heterosexual society, the experience between women of sexual fulfillment, of falling in love, of marrying, of creating a home, of starting a family have no social reality. Unlike the heterosexual feminist, the lesbian has no socially supported private sphere, not even an oppressive one.

Failure to see the difference between the heterosexual feminist's and the lesbian's relation to the institution of heterosexuality may well result in mislocating lesbian politics. From a feminist point of view, sexual interaction, romantic love, marriage, and the family are all danger zones because all have been distorted to serve male interests. It thus does not behoove feminist politics to begin by championing the importance of sexual interaction, romantic love, marriage, and the (couple-based) family. But it does behoove lesbian politics to start in precisely these places. Her recognition as a social being, and thus as an individual with socio-political-legal standing, depends upon the female-female couple being recognized as a primary social unit. That in turn cannot be done without directly challenging the reservation of the primary structures of the private sphere for heterosexuals. Just as the heart of male privilege lies in the "right" of access to women, so the heart of heterosexual privilege lies in the "right" of access to sexual-romantic-marital-familial relationships.

NOTES

1. Heidi Hartmann, "The Unhappy Marriage of Marxism and Feminism," in *Feminist Frameworks*, ed. Alison M. Jaggar and Paula S. Rothenberg, 2d ed. (New York: McGraw-Hill, 1984), p. 172.
2. On the former, see, e.g., Charlotte Bunch, "Lesbians in Revolt," in her *Passionate Politics, Essays 1968–1986* (New York: St. Martin's, 1987); and Monique Wittig, *The Straight Mind and Other Essays* (Boston: Beacon, 1992). Regarding the latter, see Adrienne Rich, "Compulsory Heterosexuality and the Lesbian Continuum," in *The Signs Reader: Women, Gender, and Scholarship*, ed. Elizabeth Abel and Emily K. Abel (Chicago: University of Chicago Press, 1983).
3. For instance, Jeffner Allen states in her introduction to the anthology *Lesbian Philosophies and Cultures*, ed. Jeffner Allen (Albany, N.Y.: SUNY Press, 1990), "The primary emphasis of this book is *lesbian* philosophies and cultures, rather than lesbianism considered in relation to or in contrast to, patriarchy, or heterosexuality" (p. 1).
4. See, e.g., the recent anthology, Allen, ed., *Lesbian Philosophies and Cultures*; as well as Sarah Lucia Hoagland's *Lesbian Ethics: Toward New Value* (Palo Alto, Calif.: Institute of Lesbian Studies, 1990); and Janice G. Raymond's *A Passion for Friends* (Boston: Beacon, 1986).
5. Charlotte Bunch, "Lesbians in Revolt," "Learning from Lesbian Separatism," and "Lesbian-Feminist Theory," all in her *Passionate Politics*; Gayle Rubin, "The Traffic in Women," in *Toward an Anthropology of Women*, ed. Rayna Reiter (New York: Monthly Review, 1975); Kate Millett, *Sexual Politics* (New York: Doubleday, 1969); Rich; Wittig, *The Straight Mind.*
6. See, e.g., Marilyn Frye's critical assessment of the gay rights movement in "Lesbian Feminism and the Gay Rights Movement: Another View of Male Supremacy, Another Separatism," in her *The Politics of Reality* (Freedom, Calif.: Crossing, 1983); as well as John Stoltenberg's "Sadomasochism: Eroticized Violence, Eroticized Powerlessness," in *Against Sadomasochism*, ed. Robin Ruth Linden et al. (San Francisco: Frog in the Well, 1982).
7. Charlotte Bunch, e.g., observes that "lesbianism and feminism are both about women loving and supporting women and women revolting against the so-called supremacy of men and the patriarchal institutions that control us" ("Lesbian-Feminist Theory," p. 196).
8. For brief historical discussions of this event, see Shane Phelan's "The Woman-identified Woman," in her *Identity Politics: Lesbian Feminism and the Limits of Community* (Philadelphia: Temple University Press, 1989); and Terralee Bensinger's "Lesbian Pornography: The Re/Making of (a) Community," *Discourse* 15 (1992):69–93.
9. Radicalesbians, "The Woman Identified Woman," in *Radical Feminism*, ed. Anne Koedt et al. (New York: Quadrangle, 1973).
10. I thank Ann Ferguson for pointing out that capitalism and patriarchy are empirically and historically intertwined, even if conceptually separate, and for suggesting that the same might be true of the heterosexual and patriarchal aspects of male/female relationships.
11. Monique Wittig, "The Straight Mind," in *The Straight Mind and Other Essays*, p. 32.
12. Monique Wittig, "The Category of Sex," in *The Straight Mind and Other Essays*, p. 6.
13. Ibid., p. 2.

14. Monique Wittig, "One Is Not Born a Woman," in *The Straight Mind and Other Essays*, p. 20.
15. This point has been made by a number of authors, including Marilyn Frye ("Some Refections on Separatism and Power," in *The Politics of Reality)* and Kathryn Pyne Addelson ("Words and Lives," *Signs* 7 [1981]: 187–99).
16. Wittig, "One Is Not Born a Woman," p. 20.
17. Joyce Trebilcott neatly summarizes these reconstructive strategies in "Conceiving Women: Notes on the Logic of Feminism," *Sinister Wisdom*, vol. 11 (1979), reprinted in *Women and Values: Readings in Recent Feminist Philosophy*, ed. Marilyn Pearsall (Belmont, Calif.: Wadsworth, 1986).
18. See, e.g., Marilyn Frye's "A Response to *Lesbian Ethics*: Why Ethics?" in *Feminist Ethics*, ed. Claudia Card (Lawrence: University Press of Kansas, 1991); and Elizabeth V. Spelman's *Inessential Woman: Problems of Exclusion in Feminist Thought* (Boston: Beacon, 1988).
19. Spelman argues elegantly for the necessity of multiple categories in *Inessential Woman.*
20. I use "sex/gender" rather than "gender" throughout the argument that lesbians are not-women in order to avoid implying that what makes lesbians not-women is simply their gender deviance (e.g., their butchness or refusal to be subordinate to men). I want to stress instead that lesbians are not clearly female. It is sex deviance combined with gender deviance that I think results in lesbians' exit from the category "woman".
21. Judith Butler, *Gender Trouble: Feminism and the Subversion of Identity* (New York: Routledge, 1990), p. 17.
22. Frye quite vividly describes the phenomenon of compulsory sex/gender in "Sexism," in *The Politics of Reality.*
23. Julia Penelope, "Heteropatriarchal Semantics and Lesbian Identity: The Ways a Lesbian Can Be," in her *Call Me Lesbian: Lesbian Lives, Lesbian Theory* (Freedom, Calif.: Crossing, 1992).
24. For critical discussions of the meanings employed within s/m, see esp. Susan Leigh Star, "Swastikas: The Street and the University," in Linden et al., eds.; and Stoltenberg.
25. Janice G. Raymond, "Putting the Politics Back into Lesbianism," *Women's Studies International Forum* 12 (1989): 149–56.
26. Butler, *Gender Trouble*, p. 123. For additional discussion of the creation of an apparently natural gender identity through repetitive gender performances, see Judith Butler, "Imitation and Gender Insubordination," in *Inside/Out: Lesbian Theories, Gay Theories*, ed. Diana Fuss (New York: Routledge, 1991).
27. Quote of the week from Allan Berubé in *City on a Hill* 26, no. 30 (1992): 10. In "Sexism," Frye similarly comments that "heterosexual critics of queers' 'role-playing' ought to look at themselves in the mirror on their way out for a night on the town to see who's in drag. The answer is, everybody is" (p. 29).
28. Butler, *Gender Trouble*, p. 128.
29. Bensinger, p. 84.
30. Ibid.
31. Wittig makes this point in "One Is Not Born a Woman," p. 10.
32. Marilyn Frye, "Willful Virgin or Do You Have to Be a Lesbian to Be a Feminist?" in *Willful Virgin: Essays in Feminism* (Freedom, Calif.: Crossing, 1992).
33. Wittig, "One Is Not Born a Woman," p. 13.
34. Ibid., p. 14.
35. Bunch, "Lesbians in Revolt," p. 165.
36. Ibid., p. 166.

37. Ann Ferguson, "Patriarchy, Sexual Identity, and the Sexual Revolution," in Ann Ferguson, Jacqueline N. Zita, and Kathryn Pyne Addelson, "Viewpoint: On 'Compulsory Heterosexuality and Lesbian Existence': Defining the Issues," *Signs* 7 (1981): 147–88, p. 159.
38. Hoagland.
39. Raymond, *A Passion for Friends*, p. 11.
40. Hoagland, p. 29.
41. Raymond, "Putting the Politics Back into Lesbianism." See also her criticisms of lesbian s/m in the chapter "Obstacles to Female Friendship," in *A Passion for Friends.*
42. Raymond, "Putting the Politics Back into Lesbianism," p. 150.
43. Phelan, p. 69.
44. Raymond, *A Passion for Friends*, p. 15.
45. Bunch, "Lesbians in Revolt," p. 162.
46. Ibid.
47. Nett Hart, "Lesbian Desire as Social Action," in Allen, ed., p. 297.
48. This helps explain why it is relatively easy to garner toleration of lesbianism and homosexuality as private bedroom practices, while attempts to sanction lesbian and gay parenting and marriages meet with intense resistance. I thank Mary Going for bringing me to see the critical importance of challenging the heterosexual couple–based family.

Multiple Jeopardy, Multiple Consciousness: The Context of a Black Feminist Ideology

King examines the ways in which race, sex, and class inequality compound one another and the issues this complex oppression raises for black women. Sex oppression is often likened to race oppression, but this analogy obscures the oppression of black women either by equating it with the oppression of black men or by equating it with the oppression of white women. It is necessary to recognize that black women confront multiple jeopardy—discrimination based on sex, race, class, and sexual orientation. These forms of discrimination are not additive. They are interdependent, and they interact. In some respects, black women are disadvantaged relative to white women. In other respects, black women are relatively advantaged.

The complexity of black women's social position creates difficulties in regard to their political alliances. In groups dedicated to the goal of racial justice, issues of special concern to black women, such as high rates of violence against them and high poverty rates among them, are often sidelined. In feminist groups, black women are alienated by white women's critique of the family as an inherently patriarchal institution, by their advocacy of separatism, by their individualistic preoccupation with professional advancement, and by their failure to mount a sustained challenge to systemic class oppression. Historically, trade unionism has been hostile to the interests of both women and minorities. Moreover, the union focus on the work conditions, wages, and benefits of the individual worker does not address issues of class stratification. However, anticapitalist leftist groups do not provide a satisfactory alternative. They generally ignore racism and sexism, and they fail to appreciate that women and minorities want a "piece of the American Dream, not its destruction." In view of the narrow, monistic analysis of each of these movements, black women must "define and sustain a multiple consciousness" that is committed to feminism, though not exclusively so.

—D.T.M.

Chapter 12

Deborah K. King

Multiple Jeopardy, Multiple Consciousness: The Context of a Black Feminist Ideology

Black women have long recognized the special circumstances of our lives in the United States: the commonalities that we share with all women, as well as the bonds that connect us to the men of our race. We have also realized that the interactive oppressions that circumscribe our lives provide a distinctive context for black womanhood. For us, the notion of double jeopardy is not a new one. Near the end of the nineteenth century, Anna Julia Cooper, who was born a slave and later became an educator and earned a Ph.D., often spoke and wrote of the double enslavement of black women and of our being "confronted by both a woman question and a race problem."[1] In 1904, Mary Church Terrell, the first president of the National Association of Colored Women, wrote, "Not only are colored women . . . handicapped on account of their sex, but they are almost everywhere baffled and mocked because of their race. Not only because they are women, but because they are colored women."[2]

The dual and systematic discriminations of racism and sexism remain pervasive, and, for many, class inequality compounds those oppressions. Yet, for as long as black women have known our numerous discriminations, we have also resisted those oppressions. Our day-to-day survival as well as our organized political actions have demonstrated the tenacity of our struggle against subordination. In the mid-nineteenth century, Sojourner Truth, an antislavery activist and women's rights advocate, repeatedly pronounced the strength and perseverance of black women.[3] More than one hundred years later, another black woman elaborated on Truth's theme. In addressing the National Association for the advancement of Colored People (NAACP) Legal Defense Fund in 1971, Fannie Lou Hamer, the daughter of sharecroppers and a civil rights activist in Mississippi, commented on the special plight and role of black women over 350 years: "You know I work for the liberation of all people because when I liberate myself, I'm liberating other people. . . . Her [the white woman's] freedom is shackled in chains to mine, and she realizes for the first time that she is not free until I am free."[4] The necessity of addressing all oppressions is one of the hallmarks of black feminist thought.

THE THEORETICAL INVISIBILITY OF BLACK WOMEN

Among the first and perhaps most widely used approaches for understanding women's status in the United States has been the race-sex analogy. In essence, the model draws parallels between the systems and experiences of domination for blacks and those for women, and, as a result, it assumes that political mobilizations against racism and sexism are comparable. In 1860, Elizabeth Cady Stanton observed, "Prejudice against color, of which we hear so much, is no stronger than that against sex."[5] Scholars in various disciplines have drawn similar analogies between racism and sexism. Sociologist Helen Hacker and historian William Chafe have both noted that, unlike many ethnic groups, women and blacks possess ineradicable physical attributes that function "systematically and clearly to define from birth the possibilities to which members of a group might aspire."[6] In the first formal topology of the race-sex analogy, Helen Hacker identifies four additional dimensions on which the castelike status of blacks and women are similar: (1) ascribed attributes of emotionality, immaturity, and slyness; (2) rationalizations of status as conveyed in the notions of appropriate "place" and the contented subordinate; (3) accommodating and guileful behaviors; and (4) economic, legal, educational, and social discriminations.[7] Feminist theorists, including Simone de Beauvoir, Kate Millett, Mary Daly, and Shulamith Firestone have all drawn extensively on this analogy in their critiques of the patriarchy.[8]

This analogy has served as a powerful means of conveying an image of women's subordinate status and of mobilizing women and men for political action. The social movements for racial equality in the United States, whether the abolitionist movement in the nineteenth century or the civil rights movement in the mid-twentieth century, were predecessors, catalysts, and prototypes for women's collective action. A significant segment of feminist activists came to recognize and understand their own oppression, as well as to develop important organizing skills through their participation in efforts for racial justice.[9] In sum, the race-sex correspondence has been used successfully because the race model was a well-established and effective pedagogical tool for both the theoretical conceptualization of and the political resistance to sexual inequality.

We learn very little about black women from this analogy.[10] The experience of black women is apparently assumed, though never explicitly stated, to be synonymous with that of either black males or white females; and since the experiences of both are equivalent, a discussion of black women in particular is superfluous. It is mistakenly granted that either there is no difference in being black and female from being generically black (i.e., male) or generically female (i.e., white). The analogy obfuscates or denies what Chafe refers to as "the profound substantive differences" between blacks and women. The scope, both institutionally and culturally, and the intensity of the physical and psychological impact of racism is qualitatively different from that of sexism. The group experience of slavery and lynching for blacks, genocide for Native Americans, and military conquest for Mexican-Americans and Puerto

Ricans is not substantively comparable to the physical abuse, social discrimination, and cultural denigration suffered by women. This is not to argue that those forms of racial oppressions are greater or more unjust but that the substantive differences need to be identified and to inform conceptualizations. Althea Smith and Abigail Stewart point out that "the assumption of parallelism led to research that masked the differences in these processes [i.e., racism, sexism, and their effects on self-image] for different groups."[11] A similar point has been forcefully made by bell hooks: "No other group in America has so had their identity socialized out of existence as have black women. We are rarely recognized as a group separate and distinct from black men, or a present part of the larger group "women" in this culture. . . . When black people are talked about the focus tends to be on black men; and when women are talked about the focus tends to be on white women."[12] It is precisely those differences between blacks and women, between black men and black women, between black women and white women, that are crucial to understanding the nature of black womanhood.

THE PROMISE AND LIMITATIONS OF DOUBLE JEOPARDY

In 1972, Frances Beale, a founding member of the Women's Liberation Committee of the Student Nonviolent Coordinating Committee (SNCC) and, later, a member of the Third World Women's Alliance, introduced the term "double jeopardy" to describe the dual discriminations of racism and sexism that subjugate black women. Concerning black women, she wrote, "As blacks they suffer all the burdens of prejudice and mistreatment that fall on anyone with dark skin. As women they bear the additional burden of having to cope with white and black men.[13] Beale also astutely observed that the reality of dual discriminations often entailed economic disadvantage; unfortunately she did not incorporate that understanding into the conceptualization. Perhaps she viewed class status as a particular consequence of racism rather than as an autonomous source of persecution; but such a preponderant majority of black women have endured the very lowest of wages and very poorest conditions of rural and urban poverty that some scholars have argued that economic class oppression must necessarily constitute a third jeopardy.[14] Still others have suggested that heterosexism or homophobia represents another significant oppression and should be included as a third or perhaps fourth jeopardy.[15] The triple jeopardy of racism, sexism, and classism is now widely accepted and used as the conceptualization of black women's status. However, while advancing our understanding beyond the erasure of black women with the confines of the race-sex analogy, it does not yet fully convey the dynamics of multiple forms of discrimination.

Unfortunately, most applications of the concepts of double and triple jeopardy have been overly simplistic in assuming that the relationships among the various discriminations are merely additive. These relationships are interpreted as equivalent to the mathematical equation, racism plus sexism plus classism equals triple jeopardy. In this instance, each discrimination has a single, direct, and independent effect on status, wherein the relative contribution of each is readily apparent. This simple incremental process does not represent the nature of black women's oppression but rather, I would contend, leads to nonproductive assertions that one factor can and should supplant the other. For example, class oppression is the largest component of black women's subordinate status, therefore the exclusive focus should be on economics. Such assertions ignore the fact that racism, sexism, and classism constitute three, interdependent control systems. An interactive model, which I have termed multiple jeopardy, better captures those processes.[16]

The modifier "multiple" refers not only to several simultaneous oppressions but also to the multiplicative relationships among them. In other words, the equivalent formulation is racism multiplied by sexism multiplied by classism. The sexual exploitation of black women in slavery is a historical example. While black women workers suffered the same demanding physical labor and brutal punishments as black men, as females, we were also subject to forms of subjugation only applicable to women. Angela Davis, in *Women, Race and Class*, notes, "If the most violent punishments of men consisted in floggings and mutilations, women were flogged and mutilated, as well as raped."[17] At the same time, our reproductive and child-rearing activities served to enhance the quantity and quality of the "capital" of a slave economy. Our institutionalized exploitation as the concubines, mistresses, and sexual slaves of white males distinguished our experience from that of white females' sexual oppression because it could only have existed in relation to racist and classist forms of domination.

The importance of any one factor in explaining black women's circumstances thus arises depending on the particular aspect of our lives under consideration and the reference groups to whom we are compared. In some cases, race may be the more significant predictor of black women's status; in others, gender or class may be more influential. Table 1 presents the varied and conditional influence of race and gender and, presumably, of racism and sexism on socioeconomic and educational status. White males earn the highest median incomes, followed in decreasing order by black males, white females, and black females. The educational rankings are different. White males are again on top; but whites, males and females, have more years of schooling than black males and females. While gender is more critical in understanding black women's income ranking, race is more important in explaining their level of educational attainment. But in both examples, black females have the lowest status.

Table 2 shows a more complex relationship between race, gender, and class (here represented by educational attainment), and the influence of these variables on income. Overall, education is an important determinant of income, and despite race or gender, those with more education earn more money than those with less. Men earn more than women at the same level of education, and whites earn more than blacks at the same level of education. But among women, the relationship of education to income is confounded by race. Given our subordinate statuses as female and black, we might expect black women to receive the lowest incomes regardless of their educational attainment. However, the returns of postsecondary education, a college degree or higher, are greater for black females than for white

Table 1 Race and Gender Interactive Effects on Socioeconomic Status

	Economic Status ($)	*Educational Status (yrs.)*
White males	16,467	12.7
Black males	9,448	12.2
White females	6,949	12.6
Black females	6,164	12.2

Note: Income figures are 1984 median incomes for those fifteen years or older. Educational attainment is for 1984, median years of school completed.

Source: U.S. Department of Commerce, Bureau of the Census, *Statistical Abstract of the United States, 1987* (Washington, D.C.: Government Printing Office, 1987).

Table 2 Multiplicative Effects of Race, Gender, and Class on Income

	Income ($)			
	White males	*Black males*	*White females*	*Black females*
Less than a high school diploma	9,525	6,823	3,961	3,618
4 years of high school	13,733	9,260	6,103	5,954
1–3 years of college	14,258	10,532	6,451	6,929
Bachelor's degree	19,783	14,131	9,134	10,692
5 or more years of post-baccalaureate education	23,143	18,970	12,980	14,537

Note: Income is 1979 median income. Educational attainment is used as a measure of economic class.
Source: *Detailed Population Characteristics,* U.S. Summary, Sec. A. 1980 (Washington, D.C.: Government Printing Office, 1980).

females, while among those with less than a college degree, black females earn less than white females. A similar pattern is not found among males. In this three-way analysis, black women are not consistently in the lowest status, evidence that the importance of the multiple discriminations of race, gender, and class is varied and complex.

In the interactive model, the relative significance of race, sex, or class in determining the conditions of black women's lives is neither fixed nor absolute but, rather, is dependent on the sociohistorical context and the social phenomenon under consideration. These interactions also produce what to some appears a seemingly confounding set of social roles and political attitudes among black women. Sociologist Bonnie Thornton Dill has discussed the importance of scholars' recognizing, incorporating, and interpreting the complex variety of social roles that black women have performed in reaction to multiple jeopardies. She argues that the constellation of "attitudes, behaviors, and interpersonal relationships . . . were adaptations to a variety of factors, including the harsh realities of their environment, Afro-American cultural images of black womanhood, and the sometimes conflicting values and norms of the wider society."[18]

A black woman's survival depends on her ability to use all the economic, social, and cultural resources available to her from both the larger society and within her community. For example, black women historically have had to assume economically productive roles as well as retain domestic ones, and until recently our labor force participation rate well exceeded that of white women.[19] Labor, whether unpaid and coerced (as under slavery) or paid and necessary employment, has been a distinctive characteristic of black women's social roles. It has earned us a small but significant degree of self-reliance and independence that has promoted egalitarian relations with black women and active influence within the black family and community.[20] But it also has had costs. For instance, black women have most often had to work in low-status and low-paying jobs since race and sex discrimination have historically limited our employment options. The legacy of the political economy of slavery under capitalism is the fact that employers, and not black women, still profit the most from black women's labor. And when black women become the primary or sole earners for households, researchers and public analysts interpret this self-sufficiency as pathology, as deviance, as a threat to black family life.[21] Yet, it is black women's well-documented facility to encompass seemingly contradictory role expectations of worker, homemaker, and mother that has contributed to the confusion in understanding black womanhood.[22] These competing demands (each requiring its own set of resistances to multiple forms of oppression) are a primary influence on the black woman's definition of her womanhood and her relationships to the people around her. To reduce this complex of negotiations to an addition problem (racism + sexism = black women's experience) is to define the issues, and indeed black womanhood itself, within the structural terms developed by Europeans and especially white males to privilege their race and their sex unilaterally. Sojourner's declaration, "Ain't I a woman?" directly refutes this sort of conceptualization of womanhood as one-dimensional rather than dialectical.

MULTIPLE JEOPARDY WITHIN THE POLITICS OF LIBERATION

In order to understand the concept of multiple jeopardy, it is necessary to look beyond the social structure and process of the dominant society that insidiously pervade even the movements for race, gender, and class liberation. Thus, the confrontations among blacks about sexism and classism, among women about racism and classism, and among the various economic classes about racism and sexism compose a second feature of the context of black feminist ideology. A formidable impediment in these battles is the "monist" approach of most liberation ideologies. In *Liberating Theory*, monism is described as a political claim "that one particular domination precipitates all really important oppressions. Whether Marxist, anarchist, nationalist, or feminist, these 'ideal types' argue that important social relations can all be reduced to the economy, state, culture, or gender."[23] For example, during the suffrage debates, it was routinely asserted that only one group might gain voting privileges—either blacks or women, that is black men or white women. For black women, the granting of suffrage to either group would still mean our disenfranchisement because of either our sex or our race. Faced with this dilemma, many black women and most black men believed that the extension of suffrage to black males was imperative in order to protect race interests in the historical period of postbellum America. But because political empowerment for black women would require that both blacks and women gained the right to vote, some of these same black women also lobbied strenuously for women's suffrage.[24]

The contemporary efforts of black women to achieve greater equal opportunity and status present similar dilemmas, whether in the areas of reproductive rights, electoral politics, or poverty. Our history of resistance to multiple jeopardies is replete with the fierce tensions, untenable ultimatums, and bitter compromises between nationalism, feminism, and class politics. In a curious twist of fate, we find ourselves marginal to both the movements for women's liberation and black liberation irrespective of our victimization under the dual discriminations of racism and sexism. A similar exclusion or secondary status typifies our role within class movements. Ironically, black women are often in conflict with the very same subordinate groups with which we share some interests. The groups in which we find logical allies on certain issue are the groups in which we may find opponents on others. To the extent that we have found ourselves confronting the exclusivity of monistic politics, we have had to manage ideologies and activities that did not address the dialectics of our lives. We are asked to decide with whom to ally, which interests to advance. Should black women's primary ideological and activist commitment be to race, sex, or class-based social movement? Can we afford to be monist? Can we afford not to be?

In the following consideration of the dialectics within each of three liberation movements, I hope to describe the tensions and priorities that influence the construction of a black feminist ideology. To the extent that any politic is monistic, the actual victims of racism, sexism, or classism may be absent from, invisible within, or seen as antagonistic to that politic. Thus, prejudicial attitudes and discriminatory actions may be overt, subtle, or covert; and they may have various manifestations through ideological statements, policies and strategies, and interpersonal relations. That is, black and/or poor women may be marginal to monistic feminism, women's concerns may be excluded from nationalistic activism, and indifference to race and gender may pervade class politics. This invisibility may be due to actual exclusion or benign neglect, while marginality is represented in tokenism, minimization, and devalued participation. Antagonism involves two subordinate groups whose actions and beliefs are placed in opposition as mutually detrimental. From this conceptual framework, the following discussion highlights the major aspects of multiple jeopardy within liberation politics.

Intraracial Politics

Racial solidarity and race liberation have been and remain fundamental concerns for black Americans. Historically and currently, slavery, segregation, and institutional as well as individual discrimination have been formative experiences in most blacks' socialization and political outlook. The inerasable physical characteristics of race have long determined the status and opportunities of black women in the United States. Since race serves as a significant filter of what blacks perceive and how blacks are perceived, many black women have claimed that their racial identity is more salient than either their gender or class identity.[25] Diane Lewis, an anthropologist, has remarked that when racism is seen as the principal cause of their subordinate status, "their interests as blacks have taken precedence over their interests as women."[26] This political importance of race is evident for other reasons as well. Certainly, the chronological order of the social movements for racial, gender, and class justice in part explains the priority given to racial interests. In both the nineteenth and twentieth centuries, the abolition and civil rights movements predate women's suffrage and the women's movement. Similarly, collective efforts that addressed economic deprivation and exploitation, such as trade unionism beginning in the late 1800s, communists organizing in the 1920s and 1930s, and the anti-imperialist activism of the 1960s were preceded by or simultaneous with race-oriented movements. Considering the order of events, it is reasonable to expect that most black women would have made commitments to and investments in the race movements such that they would not or could not easily abandon those for later movements.

Furthermore, through the necessity of confronting and surviving racial oppression, black women have assumed responsibilities atypical of those assigned to white women under Western patriarchy. Black women often held central and powerful leadership roles within the black community and within its liberation politics. We founded schools, operated social welfare services, sustained churches, organized collective work groups and unions, and even established banks and commercial enterprises. That is, we were the backbone of racial uplift, and we also played critical roles in the struggle for racial justice.[27] Harriet Tubman led slaves to freedom on the underground railroad; Ida Wells Barnett led the crusade against lynching; Fannie Lou Hamer and Ella Baker were guiding political spirits of the southern black efforts that gave birth to SNCC and the Mississippi Freedom Democratic Party; the "simple" act of

Rosa Parks catapulted Martin Luther King to national prominence. Black women, therefore, did not experience sexism with the race movement in quite the ways that brought many white women to feminist consciousness within either civil rights or New Left politics.[28]

All together this history constitutes a powerful impetus toward a monistic race approach as the means of liberation for black women. Michelle Wallace concludes that black women simply lack a feminist consciousness as a matter of choice, out of ignorance, misguided beliefs, or an inability to recognize sexual domination both within and without the black community.[29] Since the 1800s, however, the writings of such prominent black women as Sojourner Truth, Maria Stewart, Anna Julia Cooper, Josephine St. Pierre Ruffin, Frances Watkins Harper, Pauli Murray, Frances Beale, Audre Lorde, and Angela Davis have described a broader view of black consciousness.[30] Even among those black women who expressed grave reservations about participating in the women's movement, most recognized sexism as a factor of their subordination in the larger society and acknowledged sexual politics among blacks. They could identify the sexual inequalities that resulted in the images of black women as emasculating matriarchs; in the rates of sexual abuse and physical violence; and in black men assuming the visible leadership positions in many black social institutions, such as the church, the intelligentsia, and political organizations.[31] During the civil rights and black nationalist movements of the 1960s and 1970s, men quite effectively used the matriarchy issue to manipulate and coerce black women into maintaining exclusive commitments to racial interests and redefining and narrowing black women's roles and images in ways to fit a more traditional Western view of women. Black feminists Pauli Murray and Pauline Terrelonge Stone both agree that the debates over this issue became an ideological ploy to heighten guilt in black women over their supposed collusion with whites in the oppression of black men.[32] Consequently, these intraracial tensions worked against the public articulations of a feminist consciousness by most black women. Nevertheless, a point of concern and contention within the black community was how sexual inequalities might best be addressed, not whether they existed. A few black women responded by choosing monistic feminism, others sought a distinct black feminist activism. While many organized feminist efforts within race-oriented movements, some also adopted a strict nationalist view. Over time, there were also transformations of perspectives. For example, the black women of SNCC created within it a women's liberation group which later became an independent feminists-of-color organization, the Third World Women's Alliance, which is today the only surviving entity of SNCC.

The politics of race liberation have rarely been exclusively race-based. Because so many blacks historically have been economically oppressed, race liberation has out of necessity become more pluralistic through its incorporation of economic interests. Whether civil rights or a nationalist activism, the approach to class injustice generally promotes greater economic opportunities and rewards within the existing capitalist order. At the turn of the century, for instance, the collective action known as racial uplift involved the efforts of educated, middle-class blacks to elevate the moral, physical, social, and economic conditions of lower income blacks. The National Association of Wage Earners was established in the 1920s by women like Nannie Burroughs, Maggie Wallace, and Mary McCleod Bethune to assist black female domestic and factory workers.[33]

The civil rights movement initially seemed to avoid the value-laden implications of this pattern of middle-class beneficence toward those with fewer economic resources. Both Aldon Morris, a sociologist, and Clayborne Carson, a historian, have written of the genuine grass roots orientation of the black southern strategy in the 1950s and early 1960s.[34] The majority of the participants were rural, poorly educated, and economically disadvantaged, but more important, these same individuals set the priorities and the strategies of the movement. The legacy was an affirmation of the strength of seemingly powerless people, and particularly of the black women who were among the principal organizers and supporters.[35]

Despite these auspicious beginnings, Cornel West, a black theologian, described the 1960s as a time when the interests of poor blacks were often betrayed.[36] Middle-class blacks were better able to take advantage of the relatively greater opportunities made possible through the race-oriented, legal liberalism of equal opportunity and affirmative action policies and electoral politics. Only such groups as the Nation of Islam and the League of Revolutionary Black Workers, like Marcus Garvey's United Negro Improvement Association earlier in this century, continued to represent the interests of working class and impoverished blacks. The contemporary controversy over class polarization in the black community is a consequence of the movement not effectively addressing the economic status of all blacks. Given the particularly precarious economic status of black women, this neglect and marginalization of class is especially problematic for them. The National Welfare Rights Organization, founded in 1967, was one of the few successful, though short-lived, efforts to address the class divisions. Only recently have race-focal groups, including the Urban League and the National Association for the Advancement of Colored People, addressed the plight of impoverished black women.

Racial solidarity has been a fundamental element of black women's resistance to domination. However, the intraracial politics of gender and class have made a strictly nationalistic approach overly restrictive and incalculably detrimental to our prospects for full liberation. Given a social condition that is also compounded by other oppressions, black women have necessarily been concerned with effecting, at the very least, an amelioration of economic and gender discriminations. Consequently, some black women have sought an association with feminism as one alternative to the limitations of monistic race politics.

Politics Among Women

At one level, black women, other women of color, and white women, share many common contemporary concerns about their legal status and rights, encounters with discrimination, and sexual victimization. It is on these shared concerns that feminists have sought to forge a sense of sisterhood and to foster solidarity. This effort is manifest in a variety of ways, but the slogan "sisterhood is powerful" best exemplifies the importance and the hoped-for efficacy of such solidarity in the achievement of women's equality and liberation. For example, all-female restrictions for consciousness-raising sessions, intellectual and artistic programs and publications, organizations, businesses, and communities reflect this singular orientation; and lesbian feminist separatism represents the absolute ideological expression of the monistic tendencies in feminism.

Presumably, black women are included in the sisterhood, but, nonetheless, invisibility and marginality characterize much of our relationship to the women's movement. The assertion of commonality, indeed of the universality and primacy of female oppression, denies the other structured inequalities of race, class, religion, and nationality, as well as the diverse cultural heritages that affect the lives of many women. While contending that feminist consciousness and theory emerged from the personal, everyday reality of being female, the reality of millions of women was ignored. The phrase, "the personal is the political," not only reflects a phenomenological approach to women's liberation—that is, of women defining and constructing their own reality—but also has come to describe the politics of imposing and privileging a few women's personal lives over all women's lives by assuming that these few could be prototypical. For black women, the personal is bound up in the problems peculiar to multiple jeopardies of race and class, not the singular one of sexual inequality. This has not necessarily meant that black women rejected feminism, but merely that they were not singlehandedly committed to the organizations and some of the agenda that have come to be called the women's movement, that is, the movement of white, often Protestant, middle-class women.

Feminism has excluded and devalued black women, our experiences, and our interpretations of our own realities at the conceptual and ideological level. Black feminists and black women scholars have identified and critically examined other serious flaws in feminist theorizing. The assumption that the family is by definition patriarchal, the privileging of an individualistic worldview, and the advocacy of female separatism are often antithetical positions to many of the values and goals of black women and thus are hindrances to our association with feminism.[37] These theoretical blinders obscure the ability of certain feminists first to recognize the multifaceted nature of women's oppressions and then to envision theories that encompass those realities. As a consequence, monistic feminism's ability to foresee remedies that would neither abandon women to the other discriminations, including race and class, nor exacerbate those burdens, is extremely limited. Without theories and concepts that represent the experiences of black women, the women's movement has and will be ineffectual in making ideological appeals that might mobilize such women. Often, in fact, this conceptual invisibility has led to the actual strategic neglect and physical exclusion or nonparticipation of black women. Most black women who have participated in any organizations or activities of the women's movement are keenly aware of the racial politics that anger, frustrate, and alienate us.

The case of the struggle for suffrage in the nineteenth century again is an instructive example of the complexity of multiple jeopardy and its politics. Initially, there was an alliance of blacks and women for universal suffrage. However, as the campaign ensued, opponents of universal suffrage, and of any extension of voting privileges, were successful in transforming the debate into one of whom should receive the vote—women or black males. Many prominent white suffragists, including Elizabeth Cady Stanton, Susan B. Anthony, and Carrie Chapman Catt abandoned the alliance and demanded a "women only" enfranchisement. The question of black women's suffrage should have been especially problematical for them. In fact, it was never seriously considered. More damning, however, were their politics of expediency. They cooperated with avowed racists in order to gain the southern vote and liberally used racial slurs and epithets arguing that white women's superior character and intellect made them more deserving of the right to vote than blacks, Native Americans, and Eastern European and Asian immigrants.

As Angela Davis observes in her examination of race and class in the early women's rights campaign, even the Seneca Falls Declaration "all but ignored the predicament of white working-class women, as it ignored the condition of black women in the South and North alike."[38] Barbara Andolsen, in one of the most comprehensive studies of racism in the woman suffrage movement observed: "[it] had a bold vision and noble principles . . . but this is a story of a vision betrayed. For the white women who led this movement came to trade upon their privilege as the daughters (sisters, wives, and mothers) of powerful white men in order to gain for themselves some share of the political power those men possessed. They did not adequately identify ways in which that political power would not be accessible to poor women, immigrant, women, and black women."[39] Yet despite the blatant racism and class bias of the women's suffrage movement, black women, discouraged and betrayed, continued to work for their right to vote, both as blacks and as women, through their own suffrage organizations.

This history of racism in the early women's movement has been sustained by contemporary white feminists. Within organizations, most twentieth-century black women encounter myriad experiences that deny their reality. In some instances, it is the absence of materials, information, speeches, readings, or persons representing black women. When present at all, women of color are underrepresented and have marginal and subordinate roles. Recently, Paula Giddings has reported that the National Organization of Women (NOW) remains insensitive to such problematic issues as rape, abortion, sterilization, poverty, and unions. Women of color are rarely elected as officers or appointed to major positions, and NOW has actually encouraged minority women's chapters rather than the incorporation of their concerns into the "regular" chapters.[40] Lawyer and educator Mary Frances Berry, in her analysis of the politics of amending the constitution, has argued that one reason for the defeat of the Equal Rights Amendment was the failure of its proponents to campaign, educate, and mobilize the black community, and especially black women.[41]

Many white feminist activists have often assumed that their anti-sexism stance abolished all racial prejudice or discriminatory behaviors. At best, this presumption is naive and reflects a serious ignorance of the pervasiveness of racism in this society. Many blacks, women and men alike, see such postures as arrogant, racist, and dangerous to their own interests. Diane Lewis concluded that the status of black women and our interests within the women's movement and its organizations essentially replicates our structurally subordinate position to white women in the larger society.[42] Different opportunity structures and life options make interracial alliances and feminist solidarity problematic. Conceptually invisible, interpersonally misunderstood and insulted, and strategically marginal, black women have found that much in the movement has denied important aspects of our history and experience. Yet, despite the critical obstacles and limitations, the imperatives of multiple jeopardy necessitate recognizing and resisting sexism.

Beyond the race politics in feminism, many black women share concerns of impoverished and working-class women about class politics. What has become mainstream feminism rests on traditional, liberal economic aspirations of equal employment opportunities for women. In practice, however, the emphasis is often on the professional careers of those women who are already economically privileged and college educated. It could be argued, for instance, that equal access to all types of vocational training and jobs may not be desirable as a necessary or primary goal. While it is true that men on average earn more than women, all men do not have equally attractive jobs in terms of working conditions, compensation and benefits, prestige, and mobility. Those male jobs may represent, at best, only a minimal improvement over the jobs of many working women. White feminist economic concerns have concentrated on primary sector employment, but these are not the positions that are most critical and accessible to lower- or no-income women. Referring to the equal opportunity approach, Karen Kollias points out that "the majority of nonwhite, lower- and working-class women don't have the power to utilize these benefits because their primary, objective economic conditions haven't changed."[43]

Class stratification becomes an insignificant issue if economic disadvantage is seen as relevant only for feminism to the extent that women are unequal vis-à-vis men. The difference between male and female incomes is dramatically less among blacks than among whites (see table 1), suggesting that sex alone is not the sole determinant of economic status. From a monist feminist perspective, class exploitation is not understood as an independent system of oppression. Consequently, broad class dynamics are not addressed in liberal and some radical feminisms. Marxist and socialist feminists have sought to correct this biased view of class.[44] While the Marxists attempted to incorporate a concern for gender within traditional Marxist analysis, socialist feminists tried to develop a nonmonist perspective of feminism that saw sexism and classism as co-equal oppressions. Ellen Willis concludes that within various feminisms there was limited politics beyond an assertion that class hierarchy was oppressive. A radical feminist, she observes that the consciousness-raising, personal politics approach did not effectively challenge the structural, political economy of class oppression. She concludes that as a consequence, "women were implicated in the class system and had real class interests, that women could oppress men on the basis of class, and that class differences among women could not be resolved within a feminist context alone."[45]

First, the memberships of these class-oriented groups remained mostly middle class. Economically disadvantaged women have not directly contributed to a feminist theoretical understanding of class dynamics or the development of programs and strategies. bell hooks, black feminist and literary critic, notes that "had poor women set the agenda for feminist movement, they might have decided that class struggle would be a central feminist issue."[46] She further contends that class oppression has not become central among women liberationists because their "values, behaviors, and lifestyles continue to be shaped by privilege."[47] In a similar fashion, feminist and race politics have not informed or reestablished ties between poor and working-class black and white women. Phyllis M. Palmer reasons that from the perspective of a poor black woman, white women individually may suffer wage discrimination because of their sex, but their relations to white males, the top income earners, as daughters and wives grants them a relatively better quality of material well-being. "Most white women do not *in reality* live on what they earn; they have access to the resources of white male income earners."[48] Rejecting what she views as the hollow efforts of "slumming" or nonhierarchical organizing, she observes that no serious strategies have been developed for convincing bourgeois women that class liberation is critical for women's liberation or for organizing with poor and working-class women.

This lack of attention to economic issues has significant implications for the participation of black women. Many of the differences in priorities between black and white women are related to class. Issues of welfare, hunger, poor housing, limited health care, and transportation are seldom seen as feminist interests and are rarely the subject of feminist social policies. As Brenda Eichelberger maintains, "The black woman's energy output is more often directed toward such basic survival issues, while the white woman's is more often aimed at fulfillment."[49] The economic concerns of women from lower-income backgrounds are relatively ignored and distorted in the contemporary women's movement. The feminist interpretation of the "feminization" of poverty is a case in point. While noting that some women, again middle class, have indeed experienced a recent drastic decline in life circumstances as a consequence of divorce, the feminization analysis has misrepresented many of the causes of female poverty. For example, most impoverished women have been poor throughout their lives as a consequence of their class position or of racial oppression. Linda Burnham writes that race and class are more significant causative factors in black women's impoverishment than is gender. In the thesis of the feminization of poverty, she contends, "The vulnerability of white women to impoverishment is overstated; the impoverishment of Black men is ignored or underestimated; and the fundamental basis in working-class exploitation for the continual regeneration of poverty is abandoned for a focus on gender."[50]

In summary, feminism's neglect, misunderstanding, or deemphasis of the politics of race and class have direct implications for the actions of black women in relationship to the movement. Often, our response has been to avoid participation in white female, middle-class–dominated organizations and to withhold our support from policies that are not in our race and class interests. Nevertheless, just as the importance of race led many black women to commitments to racially based politics, and gender interests compelled our feminist efforts, economic injustices have brought many to consider class politics as a major avenue of liberation.

Class Politics

Economic exploitation is the third societal jeopardy constraining the lives of black women. Historically, the three major movements to address the deprivations of class in the United States have been trade unionism and the anticapitalist politics of the 1930s and 1960s, which are colloquially referred to as the Old and the New Left, respectively. Having their origins in responses to the degradations that accompanied urbanization and industrialization, labor unionists and leftists organized to address the problems of wage labor and economic stratification in a capitalistic society, including the excessive working hours in poor, unsafe conditions, low pay and limited job security, fluctuations in the labor demand, the decline in work satisfaction, the loss of worker autonomy, and poverty. Each movement, although monistic, possessed different objectives. Unionism was reformist in orientation, seeking to ameliorate the worst of the above conditions. In contrast, the socialist and communist ideologies of the Left were revolutionary in that they aspired to eradicate capitalism and ostensibly to establish a classless society.

Into the first quarter of this century, organized labor's approach to economic disadvantage held little promise for blacks or women, and thus no promise for black women. Samuel Gompers, the leading force of trade unionism and president of the American Federation of Labor (AFL, founded in 1886), believed that the best means of improving wages for Anglo males was to restrict the labor supply. His strategy was to advocate the return of women to the home and the banning of blacks and Asians from the unions. Although the AFL never formally adopted these restrictions at the national level, many local chapters did so through both formal rules and informal practices.[51] Trade unionists cultivated a cultural image of the worker as a married male who required a family wage to support a wife and children. Labor actively supported protective labor legislation, which effectively excluded women from the jobs that would provide them with sufficient incomes to support themselves and their families. These efforts against women were coupled with the exclusion of blacks, other racial minorities, and initially southern and eastern European immigrant males from the most economically rewarding labor in the unionized crafts and the closed shops. Blacks, in particular, were specifically denied union membership or else relegated to the unskilled, low-paying jobs. Consequently, the denial of a family wage to black males exacerbated the circumstances of already economically distressed black families and individuals. In occupations where blacks were well represented, unionization often meant their forcible expulsion. Many of the race riots in the early 1900s were related to the tensions between black laborers and white laborers in competition for employment. So, an effective two-prong strategy for improving white men's incomes required the demand for a family wage and the restriction of labor competition from women and racial minorities.

In response to union discrimination, white women and black women and men organized. The Working Women's Association, formed in 1868, was one of the earliest attempts at synthesizing feminist and white female workers concerns; the Women's Trade Union League, established in 1903, allied white working- and middle-class women, while the International Ladies' Garment Workers' Union publicized the conditions of white working women, demanded equal pay, demanded female representation in the national labor unions, formed female unions, and organized strikes.[52] Ironically, most of the women's trade union organizations as well as many socialist feminsts supported protective legislation but with the mistaken belief that involving the state would ensure safer work environments and reasonable labor requirements for both women and men. However, an unintended consequence of this strategy was that many women's economic situations declined because protective legislation could be used to reinforce occupational segregation and thus limit women's wage earning opportunities.

As the wives and daughters of men who did not earn a family wage, black women's participation in the labor market was crucial to the survival of themselves and their families. Yet, black women benefited little from the unionization efforts among white women. First, they were disproportionately situated in those occupations least likely to be unionized, such as domestic and nonhousehold service and agricultural labor. In large industrial workplaces, they were segregated from white female workers, where the organizing took place, and were often pawns in the labor-management contests.[53] Second, white trade unionists failed to recruit black females actively, and they often were denied membership because of their race. The protective legislation further hampered their opportunities by closing off numerous employment opportunities simply on the basis of sex. Black women wanted better paying jobs, but they often had to settle for the jobs that were considered too hazardous, dirty, or immoral for white women, and for which they were not fairly compensated. During the Depression, race-gender discrimination was so pervasive that employment in federal work-relief projects often was closed to them. Thus, significant numbers of black women were unemployed and/or underemployed and, therefore, untouched by union activism.

Despite their exclusion from the major unions, black women and men organized caucuses within predominantly white unions and formed their own unions, such as the Urban League's Negro Workers Councils, African Blood Brotherhood, Negro American Labor Council, National Negro Labor Council, and Dodge Revolutionary Union Movement (DRUM). A. Phillip Randolph, founder of the Brotherhood of Sleeping Car Porters, called for a march on Washington in the 1940s to demand the end of wage and job discrimination, the desegregation of schools and public accommodations, protection of immigrant workers, cessation of lynching, and the unionization of black women. During the Depression, trade unions and unemployed councils held demonstrations demanding immediate cash relief and unemployment compensation, as well as advocating race solidarity. For blacks in the first half of this century, class and race interests were often inseparable. Black women benefited indirectly from black men's labor activism, and they often supported those efforts by participating on picket lines, providing food and clothing for strikers and their families, and, most importantly, making financial contributions to the households from their own paid labor. Black women also engaged in labor organizing directly, both through existing, predominantly white, unions and through their own activism. Black domestics, tobacco workers, garment workers, and others organized strikes and fought for union representation.[54]

Not all unions and economic organizations excluded white women and black women and men. The Knights of Labor, established in 1886, the Industrial Workers of the World, created in 1905, and the Congress of Industrial Organizations, formed in 1938, are noted for encouraging the unionization of millions of black men and black and white women workers. But overall, the record of organized labor on issues of import to black women and men and white women has not been outstanding. Until 1971, the major unions opposed the Equal Rights Amendment; today, many challenge affirmative action and comparable worth policies. The continued need for black and women's labor organizations suggest that the historic barriers remain to their full participation and rewards in unions. But it is also important to recognize that the trade unionist approach has many limitations, and first among these is its focus on the individual worker. As a result, the broad issues of poverty and economic inequality are perceived as beyond the purview of most labor activism. While seeking to ameliorate the worst of industrial society, unionists seldom challenge the economic order of capitalism.

This challenge was left to the socialist and communist activists, but this radical critique of the political economy has never been a part of the political mainstream of the United States as it has in other nations. Nevertheless, a small but significant group of activists and intellectuals have advanced radicalism throughout this century.[55] The political left, in general, supported black women and men and white working women during the Progressive Era. In fact, leading intellectuals, including Emma Goldman, Margaret Sanger, Charlotte Perkins Gilman, Elizabeth Gurley Flynn, Langston Hughes, Paul Robeson, W.E.B. DuBois, and C.L.R. James saw socialism as the route for liberation. Two black women, Lucy Parsons and Claudia Jones, were among the early labor activists and socialists of the Old Left. And even Angela Davis, who describes the important role of individual women within the Socialist and Communist Parties during the first half of the twentieth century, does not offer us much insight into the general status of black women, besides noting the Socialist Party's indifference to blacks, both males and females.[56]

But even within these efforts, there still were gaps in recognizing the needs of black women. In 1900, the Socialist Party was founded and immediately began campaigning for women's suffrage and labor rights through its Woman's National Committee. Because it focused on the industrial proletariat, it paid no particular attention to blacks since they were mostly agricultural laborers. Consequently, the party also paid minimal attention to the black women who were not industrially employed. In contrast, members of the Communist Party were actively involved in organizing industrial workers, sharecroppers, and the unemployed during the Depression and in championing racial as well as economic justice for blacks.[57] However, the Communist Party remained relatively silent on various feminist concerns. Its vigorous defense of the Scottsboro boys and other victims of racial bigotry linked with its call for black self-determination initially attracted numerous blacks to the party in the 1930s and 1940s. Nevertheless, it became increasingly clear that the international Communist Party was concerned with the liberation of blacks only as long as those efforts advanced its overall objective of aiding the revolutionary leadership of a European working class. Eventually, the collusion of the American Communist Party with racism and sexism dissuaded many blacks and women from the advantages of Soviet-oriented communist activism.

The second surge of anticapitalism was an integral part of the so-called New Left of the 1960s. Sociologist Stanley Aronowitz has described the sixties' radicalism as the movements of a generation, which were not oriented around any particular class or race issue.[58] While this might characterize certain aspects of the radical critique of the liberal society, his interpretation does not account for the ideological and activist history that informed both the black and women's liberation efforts of that decade. In an analysis of the contradictions and dilemmas of the New Left, Peter Clecak described the era as one that lacked a vision of a new society beyond the negation of the present ills of poverty, racism, imperialism, and hegemony. Its apocalyptic perspectives on American society and utopian images of community were founded on a fundamental acceptance of capitalist notions of individualism, personal gain, and personal liberty.[59] By implication, much of the New Left lacked a basic, critical understanding of the dynamics of oppression as group and systemic processes.

The disillusionment that characterized the New Left movement was compounded by the frustration of its failure to organize the urban poor and racial minorities. The free speech and antiwar activists, Students for a Democratic Society and the Weather Underground (i.e., the Weathermen), mistakenly attempted to organize northern urban communities using SNCC's southern mobilization model. At another level, New Leftists did not understand that most members of oppressed groups desired a piece of the American Dream, not its destruction. The efforts to create coalitions with civil rights and black nationalist groups were strained and defeated because of the conflicting objectives and tactics. The aims of civil rights groups were integrationist through nonviolent means; and while black militants advocated armed defense or even revolution and adopted a Maoist, anticapitalist program, their separatist orientation made black-white alliances almost impossible. Moreover, while the Left condemned the role of U.S. imperialism in Southeast Asia, it ignored the advance of Western, capitalist interests into the continent of Africa, especially South Africa.

At the same time, women active in the New Left became increasingly frustrated with the theoretical and strategic indifference to the woman question. The sexual politics within the movement subjected women to traditional gender role assignments, sexual manipulation, male leadership and domination, plus a concentration on an essentially male issue, the draft.[60] Once again, invisibility typifies the role of black women in New Left radical politics. Black women responded by incorporating class interests into their race and gender politics. In the founding documents of various black feminist organizations, scathing critiques of the political economy are a cornerstone of the analysis of domination. For example, the *Combahee River Collective Statement* pointedly declared that "the liberation of all oppressed peoples necessitates the destruction of the political-economic systems of capitalism and imperialism, as well as patriarchy. . . . We are not convinced, however, that a socialist revolution that is not also a feminist and anti-racism revolution will guarantee our liberation."[61] This excerpt clearly articulates an understanding of multiple jeopardy and its function in the dominant society and within liberation politics. Out of necessity, black women have addressed both narrow labor and broad economic concerns.

Political theorist Manning Marable has argued that progressive forces must uproot racism and patriarchy in their quest for a socialist democracy through a dedication to equality.[62] Yet a major limitation of both unionism and radical class politics is their monist formulations, wherein economics are exaggerated at the expense of understanding and confronting other oppressions such as racism and sexism. Despite the historical examples of black women and men and white women as union activists and socialists, and the examples of the sporadic concern of organized labor and leftists with race and gender politics, class politics have not provided the solution to black women's domination because they continue to privilege class issues within a white male framework. Given the inability of any single agenda to address the intricate complex of racism, sexism, and classism in black women's lives, black women must develop a political ideology capable of interpreting and resisting that multiple jeopardy.

MULTIPLE CONSCIOUSNESS IN BLACK FEMINIST IDEOLOGY

Gloria Joseph and Jill Lewis have suggested that black women face a dilemma analogous to that of Siamese twins, whose interests are distinct and incompatible.[63] Black women cannot, they argue, be wholeheartedly committed and fully active in both the black liberation struggle and the women's liberation movement, because of sexual and racial politics within each respectively. The authors recognize the demands of multiple jeopardy politics and the detrimental effect of neglecting these dual commitments. But what they fail to consider are the multiple and creative ways in which black women address their interdependent concerns of racism, sexism, and classism.

Black women have been feminists since the early 1800s, but our exclusion from the white women's movement and its organizations has led many to assume incorrectly that we were not present in the (white) women's movement because we were not interested in resisting sexism both within and without the black community. What appears recently to be a change in black women's position, from studied indifference to disdain and curiosity to cautious affirmation of the women's movement, may be due to structural changes in relationships between blacks and whites that have made black women "more sensitive to the obstacles of sexism and to the relevance of the women's movement."[64] Black women's apparent greater sensitivity to sexism may be merely the bolder, public articulation of black feminist concerns that have existed for well over a century. In other words, black women did not just become feminists in the 1970s. We did, however, grant more salience to those concerns and become more willing to organize primarily on that basis, creating the Combahee River Collective, the National Black Feminist Organization, and Sapphire Sapphos. Some black women chose to participate in predominantly white women's movement activities and organizations, while others elected to develop the scholarship and curriculum that became the foundation of black women's studies, while still others founded black feminist journals, presses, and political organizations.[65]

Several studies have considered the relevance of black women's diverse characteristics in understanding our political attitudes; these reports seem fairly inconsistent, if not contradictory.[66] The various findings do suggest that the conditions that bring black women to feminist consciousness are specific to our social and historical experiences. For black women, the circumstances of lower socioeconomic life may encourage political, and particularly feminist, consciousness.[67] This is in contrast to feminist as well as traditional political socialization literature, which suggests that more liberal, that is, feminist, attitudes are associated with higher education attainment and class standing. Many of the conditions that middle-class, white feminists have found oppressive are perceived as privileges by black women, especially those with low incomes. For instance, the option not to work outside of the home is a luxury that historically has been denied most black women. The desire to struggle for this option can, in such a context, represent a feminist position, precisely because it constitutes an instance of greater liberty for certain women. It is also important to note, however, that the class differences among black women regarding our feminist consciousness are minimal. Black women's particular history thus is as essential ingredient in shaping our feminist concerns.

Certainly the multifaceted nature of black womanhood would meld diverse ideologies, from race liberation, class liberation, and women's liberation. The basis of our feminist ideology is rooted in our reality. To the extent that the adherents of any one ideology insist on separatist organizational forms, assert the fundamental nature of any one oppression, and demand total cognitive, affective, and behavioral commitment, that ideology and its practitioners exclude black women and the realities of our lives.

A black feminist ideology, first and foremost, thus declares the visibility of black women. It acknowledges the fact that two innate and inerasable traits, being both black and female, constitute our special status in American society. Second, black feminism asserts self-determination as essential. Black women are empowered with the right to interpret our reality and define our objectives. While drawing on a rich tradition of struggle as blacks and as women, we continually establish and reestablish our own priorities. As black women, we decide for ourselves that relative salience of any and all identities and oppressions, and how and the extent to which those features inform our politics. Third, a black feminist ideology fundamentally challenges the interstructure of the oppressions of racism, sexism, and classism both in the dominant society and within movements for liberation. It is in confrontation with multiple jeopardy that black women define and sustain a multiple consciousness essential for our liberation, of which feminist consciousness is an integral part.

Finally, a black feminist ideology presumes an image of black women as powerful, independent subjects. By concentrating on our multiple oppressions, scholarly descriptions have confounded our ability to discover and appreciate the ways in which black women are not victims. Ideological and political choices cannot be assumed to be determined solely by the historical dynamics of racism, sexism, and classism in this society. Although the complexities and ambiguities that merge a consciousness of race, class, and gender oppressions make the emergence and praxis of a multivalent ideology problematical, they also make such a task more necessary if we are to work toward our liberation as blacks, as the economically exploited, and as women.

NOTES

I am greatly indebted to Elsa B. Brown, Elaine Upton, Patricia Palmieri, Patricia Hill Collins, Dianne Pinderhughes, Rose Brewer, and *Signs*' referees for their thoughtful and critical comments on this paper.

1. Gerda Lerner, ed., *Black Women in White America: A Documentary History* (New York: Vintage, 1973), 573.
2. Mary Church Terrell, "The Progress of Colored Women," *Voice of the Negro* 1, no. 7 (July 1904): 292
3. See Lerner, ed., esp. 566–72; and Bert James Loewenberg and Ruth Bogin, eds., *Black Women in Nineteenth-Century American Life* (University Park: Pennsylvania State University Press, 1976), 234–42.

4. See Lerner, ed., 609, 610, 611.
5. Elizabeth Cady Stanton as quoted by William Chafe, *Women and Equality: Changing Patterns in American Culture* (New York: Oxford University Press, 1977), 44. Some eighty years after Stanton's observation, Swedish social psychologist Gunnar Myrdal, in an appendix to his *An American Dilemma: The Negro Problem and Modern Democracy* (New York: Harper & Row, 1962), also saw the woman problem as parallel to the Negro problem.
6. Chafe, 77.
7. Helen Hacker, "Women as a Minority Group," *Social Forces* 30 (1951): 60–69.
8. For examples of feminist writings using the race-sex analogy or the master-slave model, see Simone de Beauvoir, *The Second Sex*, trans. and ed. H. M. Parshley (New York: Random House, 1974); Kate Millett, *Sexual Politics* (New York: Avon, 1969); Shulamith Firestone, *The Dialectic of Sex* (New York: Morrow, 1970); and Mary Daly, *Beyond God the Father: Toward a Philosophy of Women's Liberation* (Boston: Beacon, 1973).
9. See Sara Evans, *Personal Politics: The Roots of Women's Liberation in the Civil Rights Movement and the New Left* (New York: Vintage, 1980); Catharine Stimpson, "Thy Neighbor's Wife, Thy Neighbor's Servants: Women's Liberation and Black Civil Rights," in *Woman in Sexist Society: Studies in Power and Powerlessness*, ed. Vivian Gornick and Barbara Moran (New York: Basic, 1971), 452–79; and Angela Davis, *Women, Race and Class* (New York: Random House, 1981). Recently there has been some debate concerning precisely what lessons, if any, women learned from their participation in the abolitionist and civil rights movements. For an argument against the importance of race-oriented movements for feminist politics, see E. C. DuBois, *Feminism and Suffrage* (Ithaca, N.Y.: Cornell University Press, 1978).
10. Other limitations have been noted by Linda LaRue, who contents that the analogy is an abstraction that falsely asserts a common oppression of blacks and women for rhetorical and propagandistic purposes ("The Black Movement and Women's Liberation," in *Female Psychology: The Emerging Self*, ed. Sue Cox [Chicago: Science Research Assoc., 1976]). In *Ain't I a Woman* (Boston: South End Press, 1981), bell hooks questions whether certain women, particularly those self-identified feminists who are white and middle class, are truly oppressed as opposed to being discriminated against. Stimpson bluntly declares that the race-sex analogy is exploitative and racist. See also Margaret A. Simons, "Racism and Feminism: A Schism in the Sisterhood," *Feminist Studies* 5 (1979): 384–401, for a critical review of this conceptual approach in feminist theorizing.
11. Chafe, 76; Althea Smith and Abigail J. Stewart, "Approaches to Studying Racism and Sexism in Black Women's Lives," *Journal of Social Issues* 39 (1983): 1–15.
12. hooks, *Ain't I a Woman*, 7.
13. Frances Beale, "Double Jeopardy: To Be Black and Female," in *The Black Woman: An Anthology*, ed. Toni Cade (New York: New American Library, 1979), 90–100.
14. See, e.g., Beverly Lindsay, "Minority Women in America: Black American, Native American, Chicana, and Asian American Women," in *The Study of Woman: Enlarging Perspectives of Social Reality*, ed. Eloise C. Snyder (New York: Harper & Row, 1979), 318–63. She presents a paradigm wherein whiteness, maleness, and money are advantageous; a poor, black woman is triply disadvantaged. Lindsay argues that triple jeopardy, the interaction of sexism, racism and economic oppression, is "the most realistic perspective for analyzing the position of black American women; and this perspective will serve as common linkage among the discussions of other minority women" (328).
15. See Barbara Smith, ed., *Home Girls: A Black Feminist Anthology* (New York: Kitchen Table Press, 1983), esp. sec. 3; and Audre Lorde, "Scratching the Surface: Some Notes on Barriers to Women

and Loving," *Black Scholar* 13 (Summer 1982): 20–24, and *Sister Outsider: Essays and Speeches* (Trumansburg, N.Y.: Crossing Press, 1984).

16. For other attempts at nonadditive models, see Smith and Stewart; Elizabeth M. Almquist, "Untangling the Effects of Race and Sex: The Disadvantaged Status of Black Women," *Social Quarterly* 56 (1975): 129–42; Margaret L. Andersen, *Thinking about Women: Sociological and Feminist Perspectives* (New York: Macmillan, 1983). The term "ethnogender" is introduced in Vincent Jeffries and H. Edward Ransford, *Social Stratification: A Multiple Hierarchy Approach* (Boston: Allyn & Bacon, 1980); and Edward Ransford and Jon Miller, "Race, Sex, and Feminist Outlook," *American Sociological Review* 48 (1983): 46–59.
17. Davis, *Women, Race and Class*, 7.
18. Bonnie Thornton Dill, "The Dialectics of Black Womanhood," *Signs: Journal of Women in Culture and Society* 4 (1979): 543–55, esp. 547. Smith and Stewart make a similar point.
19. In slavery, there was 100 percent labor force participation by black women. In 1910, 34 percent were in the official labor force. In 1960, the figure was 40 percent, and by 1980, it was over 50 percent. Comparable figures for white women are 18 percent in 1890, 22 percent in 1910, 37 percent in 1960, and 51 percent in 1980. For a more detailed discussion, see Phyllis A. Wallace, *Black Women in the Labor Force* (Cambridge, Mass.: MIT Press, 1980).
20. Angela Davis, "Reflections of the Black Woman's Role in the Community of Slaves," *Black Scholar* 3 (December 1971): 2–16, offers an enlightening discussion of the irony of independence out of subordination. See also Deborah Gray White, *Ar'n't I a Woman? Female Slaves in the Plantation South* (New York: Norton, 1985), for a more detailed analysis of the contradictions of the black female role in slavery. For a discussion of the role of black women in the family, see Robert Staples, *The Black Woman in America* (Chicago: Nelson Hall, 1973); Robert Hill, *The Strengths of Black Families* (New York: Emerson Hall, 1972); Herbert Guttman, *The Black Family in Slavery and Freedom, 1750 to 1925* (New York: Random House, 1976); Carol Stack, *All Our Kin: Strategies for Survival in a Black Community* (New York: Harper & Row, 1974); and Charles Willie, *A New Look at Black Families* (New York: General Hall, 1976). For a discussion of black women's community roles, see Bettina Aptheker, *Woman's Legacy: Essays on Race, Sex, and Class in American History* (Amherst: University of Massachusetts Press, 1982); Paula Giddings, *When and Where I Enter: The Impact of Black Women on Race and Sex in America* (New York: William Morrow, 1983); Lerner, ed. (n. 1 above); Sharon Harley and Rosalyn Terborg-Penn, eds., *The Afro-American Woman: Struggles and Images* (Port Washington, N.Y.: Kennikat Press, 1978); Linda Perkins, "The Impact of the 'Cult of True Womanhood' on the Education of Black Women," *Journal of Social Issues* 39 (1983): 17–28; and the special issue, "The Impact of Black Women in Education," *Journal of Negro Education*, 51, no. 3 (Summer 1982).
21. See Robert Staples, "The Myth of the Black Matriarchy," in his *The Black Family: Essays and Studies* (Belmont, Calif.: Wadsworth, 1971), and *The Black Woman in America*. Also see hooks, *Ain't I a Woman* (n. 10 above); and Cheryl T. Gilkes, "Black Women's Work as Deviance: Social Sources of Racial Antagonism within Contemporary Feminism," Working Paper no. 66 (Wellesley, Mass.: Wellesley College, Center for Research on Women, 1979). However, more recently Robert Staples has argued that black women who are too independent will be unable to find black mates and that black men are justified in their preference for a more traditionally feminine partner ("The Myth of Black Macho: A Response to Angry Black Feminists," *Black Scholar* 10 [March–April 1979]: 24–32).
22. See White; and Jacqueline Jones, *Labor of Love, Labor of Sorrow: Black Women, Work and the Family, From Slavery to the Present* (New York: Basic Books, 1985).

23. Michael Albert et al., *Liberating Theory* (Boston: South End Press, 1986), 6.
24. For further discussion of suffrage and racism, see Davis, *Women, Race and Class* (n. 9 above); Giddings; Harley and Terborg-Penn; and Barbara H. Andolsen, "*Daughters of Jefferson, Daughters of Bootblacks": Racism and American Feminism* (Macon, Ga.: Mercer University Press, 1986).
25. See Gloria Joseph and Jill Lewis, *Common Differences: Conflicts in Black and White Feminist Perspectives* (New York: Avon, 1981); Diane K. Lewis, "A Response to Inequality: Black Women, Racism, and Sexism," *Signs* 3 (1977): 339–61; and bell hooks, *Feminist Theory: From Margin to Center* (Boston: South End Press, 1984), for extended discussions of the dynamics of structural subordination to and social conflict with varying dominant racial and sexual groups.
26. Lewis, 343.
27. Giddings; Harley and Terborg-Penn; and Davis, "Reflections on the Black Woman's Role in the Community of Slaves."
28. See Evans (n. 9 above); and Clayborne Carson, *In Struggle: SNCC and the Black Awakening of the 1960s* (Cambridge, Mass.: Harvard University Press, 1981).
29. Michelle Wallace, *Black Macho and the Myth of the Superwoman* (New York: Dial, 1979). See also Linda C. Powell, "Black Macho and Black Feminism," in Smith, ed. (n. 15 above), 283–92, for a critique of Wallace's thesis.
30. For statements by Truth, Stewart, Cooper, Ruffin, and Harper, see Loewenberg and Bogin, eds. (n. 3 above); and Lerner, ed. (n. 1 above); for Lorde, see Lorde (n. 15 above); for Davis, see Dais, *Women, Race and Class;* for Beale, see Frances Beale, "Double Jeopardy" (n. 13 above), and "Slave of a Slave No More: Black Women in the Struggle," *Black Scholar* 12, no. 6 (November/December 1981): 16–24; and for Murray, see Pauli Murray, "The Liberation of Black Women," in *Women: A Feminist Perspective*, ed. Jo Freeman (Palo Alto, Calif.: Mayfield, 1975), 351–63.
31. Regarding the church, see Pauline Terrelonge Stone, "Feminist Consciousness and Black Women," in Freeman, ed., 575–88; Joseph and Lewis; Jacqueline Grant, "Black Women and the Church," in *But Some of Us Are Brave: Black Women's Studies*, ed. Gloria T. Hull et al. (Old Westbury, N.Y.: Feminist Press, 1982), 141–52; and Cheryl Townsend Gilkes, " 'Together and in Harness': Women's Traditions in the Sanctified Church," *Signs* 10, no. 4 (Summer 1985): 678–99. Concerning politics, see LaRue (n. 10 above); Mae C. King, "The Politics of Sexual Stereotypes," *Black Scholar* 4 (March/April 1973): 12–22; and Manning Marable, *How Capitalism Underdeveloped Black America* (Boston: South End Press, 1983), esp. chap. 3. For a discussion of sexual victimization, see Barbara Smith, "Notes for Yet Another Paper on Black Feminism, or Will the Real Enemy Please Stand Up," *Conditions* 5 (1979): 123–27, as well as Joseph and Lewis. For a critique of the notion of the matriarch, see Stone; and Staples, "The Myth of the Black Matriarchy" (n. 21 above).
32. See Murray; and Stone.
33. Evelyn Brooks Bennett, "Nannie Burroughs and the Education of Black Woman," in Harley and Terborg-Penn (n. 20 above), 97–108.
34. Aldon Morris, *The Origins of the Civil Rights Movement: Black Communities Organizing for Change* (New York: Free Press, 1984); and Carson.
35. See the recent publication by Jo Ann Gibson Robinson, *The Montgomery Bus Boycott and the Women Who Started It* (Knoxville: University of Tennessee Press, 1987).
36. Cornel West, "The Paradox of the Afro-American Rebellion," in *The Sixties without Apology*, ed. Sohnya Sayres, Anders Stephanson, Stanley Aronowitz, Fredric Jameson (Minneapolis: University of Minnesota Press, 1984).

37. Lorde, *Sister Outsider*, esp. 66–71; hooks, *Feminist Theory* (n. 25 above); Linda Burnham, "Has Poverty Been Feminized in Black America?" *Black Scholar* 16, no. 2 (March/April 1985): 14–24; María C. Lugones and Elizabeth V. Spelman, "Have We Got A Theory for you! Feminist Theory, Cultural Imperialism and the Demand for 'The Woman's Voice,' " *Women's Studies International Forum* 6, no. 6 (1983): 573–81.
38. Davis, *Women, Race and Class* (n. 9 above), 53–54.
39. Andolsen (n. 24 above), 78.
40. Giddings (n. 20 above), 348.
41. Mary Frances Berry, *Why ERA Failed: Politics, Women's Rights, and the Amending Process of the Constitution* (Bloomington: Indiana University Press, 1986).
42. Lewis (n. 25 above).
43. Karen Kollias, "Class Realities: Create a New Power Base," in *Building Feminist Theory: Essays from Quest*, ed. *Quest* staff (New York: Longman, 1981), 125–38, esp. 134.
44. See Josephine Donovan, *Feminist Theory: The Intellectual Traditions of American Feminism* (New York: Ungar, 1985); Lydia Sargent, ed., *Woman and Revolution: A Discussion of the Unhappy Marriage of Marxism and Feminism* (Boston: South End Press, 1981); and Zillah R. Eisenstein, ed., *Capitalist Patriarchy and the Case for Socialist Feminsm* (New York: Monthly Review Press, 1979), for fuller discussions.
45. Ellen Willis, "Radical Feminism and Feminist Radicalism," in Sayres et al., eds. (n. 36 above), 91–118, esp. 110–11.
46. hooks, *Feminist Theory* (n. 25 above), 60–61.
47. Ibid., 61
48. Phyllis Marynick Palmer, "White Women/Black Women: The Dualism of Female Identity and Experiences in the United States," *Feminist Studies* 91 (Spring 1983): 162.
49. Brenda Eichelberger, "Voices on Black Feminism," *Quest: A Feminist Quarterly* 4 (1977): 16–28, esp. 16.
50. Burnham (n. 37, above), 15.
51. For discussion of women, employment, and the labor movement, see Diane Balser, *Sisterhood and Solidarity: Feminism and Labor in Modern Times* (Boston: South End Press, 1987); Carol Groneman and Mary Beth Norton, eds., "*To Toil the Livelong Day*": *America's Women at Work, 1780–1980* (Ithaca, N.Y.: Cornell University Press, 1987); Philip S. Foner, *Women and the American Labor Movement: From World War I to the Present* (New York: Free Press, 1980); Bettina Berch, *The Endless Day: The Political Economy of Women and Work* (New York: Harcourt Brace Jovanovich, 1982); and Mary Frank Fox and Sharlene Hesse-Biber, *Women at Work* (Palo Alto, Calif.: Mayfield, 1984). For blacks, see Marable (n. 31 above); Richard Polenberg, *One Nation Divisible: Class, Race, and Ethnicity in the United States since 1938* (New York: Penguin, 1980); Philip S. Foner, *Organized Labor and the Black Worker, 1619–1973* (New York: International Publishers, 1976); and Dorothy K. Newman et al., *Protest, Politics, and Prosperity; Black Americans and White Institutions, 1940–75* (New York: Pantheon, 1978).
52. See Balser for a detailed consideration of the contemporary union activities of women, especially their efforts to organize clerical and other pink-collar workers.
53. See Jones (n. 22 above); Giddings (n. 20 above); and Davis, *Women, Race and Class* (n. 9 above), for an examination of black women's work roles and labor activism.
54. See Dolores Janiewski, "Seeking 'a New Day and a New Way': Black Women and Unions in the Southern Tobacco Industry"; and Elizabeth Clark-Lewis, " 'This Work Had a End': African-American Domestic Workers in Washington, D.C., 1910–1940," both in Groneman and Norton, eds.

55. See Peter Clecak, *Radical Paradoxes: Dilemmas of the American Left: 1945–1970* (New York: Harper & Row, 1973), for an illuminating analysis of the Old and New Left.
56. Davis, *Women, Race and Class.*
57. See Vincent Harding, *The Other American Revolution* (Los Angeles and Atlanta: University of California, Los Angeles, Center for Afro-American Studies, and Institute of the Black World, 1980), for discussion of blacks and communist organizing.
58. Stanley Aronowitz, "When the New Left Was New," in Sayres et al., eds. (n. 36 above), 11–43.
59. Clecak.
60. Heidi Hartmann and Zillah Eisenstein provide theoretical critiques of monist Marxism as an adequate avenue for women's liberation. Both Lydia Sargent and Sara Evans detail the sexual politics on the Left (see Heidi Hartmann, "The Unhappy Marriage of Marxism and Feminism," in Sargent, ed. [n. 44 above]; Eisenstein, "Reform and/or Revolution: Toward a Unified Women's Movement," in Sargent, ed. [n. 44 above], 339–62; Sargent, "New Left Women and Men: The Honeymoon Is Over," in Sargent, ed. [n. 44 above], xi–xxxii; and Evans [n. 9 above]).
61. See Combahee River Collective, *Combahee River Collective Statement: Black Feminist Organizing in the Seventies and Eighties* (New York: Kitchen Table Press, 1986), 12–13.
62. Marable (n. 31 above).
63. Joseph and Lewis (n. 25 above), 38.
64. Lewis (n. 25 above), 341.
65. For more information on the development of black feminist scholarship and academic programs, see Patricia Bell Scott, "Selective Bibliography on Black Feminism" in Hull et al., eds. (n. 31 above); Black Studies/Women's Studies Faculty Development Project, "Black Studies/Women's Studies: An Overdue Partnership" (Women's Studies, University of Massachusetts—Amherst, mimeograph, 1983); Nancy Conklin et al., "The Culture of Southern Black Women: Approaches and Materials" (Tuscaloosa: University of Alabama Archives of American Minority Cultures and Women's Studies Program, Project on the Culture of Southern Black Women, 1983); the premier issue of *Sage: A Scholarly Journal on Black Women* 1, no. 1 (Spring 1984); and the establishment of Kitchen Table: A Women of Color Press, New York. The Center for Research on Women at Memphis State University, the Women's Research and Resource Center at Spelman College, and the Minority Women's Program at Wellesley College are among the academic centers.
66. See Andrew Cherlin and Pamela Waters, "Trends in United States Men's and Women's Sex-Role Attitudes: 1972–1978," *American Sociological Review* 46 (1981): 453–60. See also, Janice Gump, "Comparative Analysis of Black Women's and White Women's Sex-role Attitudes," *Journal of Consulting and Clinical Psychology* 43 (1975): 858–63; and Marjorie Hershey, "Racial Difference in Sex-Role Identities and Sex Stereotyping: Evidence Against a Common Assumption," *Social Science Quarterly* 58 (1978): 583–96. For various opinion polls, see "The 1972 Virginia Slims American Women's Opinion Poll" and "The 1974 Virginia Slims American Women's Opinion Poll," conducted by the Roper Organization (Williamstown, Mass.: Roper Public Opinion Research Center, 1974). See Barbara Everitt Bryant, "American Women: Today and Tomorrow," National Commission on the Observance of International Women's Year (Washington, D.C.: Government Printing Office, March 1977); Gloria Steinem, "Exclusive Louis Harris Survey: How Women Live, Vote and Think," *Ms. Magazine* 13 (July 1984): 51–54.
67. For analyses of the influence of socioeconomic class and race on feminist attitudes, see Willa Mae Hemmons, "The Women's Liberation Movement: Understanding Black Women's Attitudes," in *The Black Woman*, ed. LaFrances Rodgers-Rose (Beverly Hills, Calif.: Sage Publications, 1980), 285–99; and Ransford and Miller (n. 16 above).

Part 3: Figurations of Women/Woman as Figuration

Beyond Racism and Misogyny: Black Feminism and 2 Live Crew

Many feminists have maintained that there is a tie between the way in which women are portrayed in the arts and in popular entertainment and the way in which women are treated. Crenshaw examines this claim from the standpoint of black women and violence against black women. She maintains that stereotypical media representations of black women incite violence against them, discredit victims' accounts of the harm inflicted on them, and trivialize their suffering.

Crenshaw's discussion of this problem is premised on an intersectional analysis of the relation between gender, race, and class. Cultural imagery depicts women of color in singularly abhorrent ways—as crass, promiscuous, predatory monsters or as pathetic, witless victims. In addition to movies, African-American rap music has been a major source of misogynistic imagery, and there has been a great deal of controversy recently over violent rap lyrics. For example, 2 Live Crew was prosecuted for obscenity in Florida in 1990. Crenshaw expresses sympathy with both positions in the debate that ensued. As an African American, she feels loyalty to these black men, who she argues were targeted for prosecution for racist reasons. Yet, as a woman, she is troubled by the social impact of lyrics that gloat over the degradation of African-American women and by the readiness of some black male intellectuals to celebrate this mode of expression. Ultimately, Crenshaw takes a position that reflects her intersectional analysis. She critiques the unjust prosecution of 2 Live Crew, and she also critiques their lyrics. In this way, she affirms the need of black women for positive cultural representations that challenge their subordination, and she avoids becoming complicit in racist policies.

—D.T.M.

Chapter 13

Kimberlè Williams Crenshaw

Beyond Racism and Misogyny: Black Feminism and 2 Live Crew

Violence against women is a central issue in the feminist movement. As part of an overall strategy to change patterns of individual and institutional behavior to better women's lives, academics and activists have challenged the ways violence against women—primarily battering and rape—is perpetuated and condoned within our culture.

Much of this challenge has occurred within legal discourse because it is within the law that cultural attitudes are legitimized through organized state power. Feminists have struggled with some success to end the representation of battering and rape as a "private family matter" or as "errant sexuality" and make clear these are specific sites of gender subordination. These battles have taken place over issues such as mandatory arrest for batterers, the admissibility of a victim's sexual history in sexual assault cases, and the admissibility of psychological evidence, such as the battered women's syndrome in cases involving women who kill their batterers and rape trauma syndrome in sexual assault cases.

If recent events are indicative, the process may continue to bear some political fruit. The governors of Ohio and Maryland have commuted sentences of women convicted of murdering abusive husbands, and other states are considering similar actions. Moreover, legislation is pending before Congress that would make violence "motivated by gender" a civil rights violation.[1]

The emphasis on gender, however, tends to downplay the interaction of gender subordination with race and class. The attitude is largely consistent with doctrinal and political practices that construct racism and sexism as mutually exclusive. Given the assumption that all women stand to benefit from efforts to politicize violence against women, concerns about race may initially seem unnecessarily divisive. Indeed, it seems that what women have in common—the fact that they are primary targets of rape and battering—not only outweighs the differences among them but may render bizarre the argument that race should play a significant role in the analysis if these issues.

Although racial issues are not explicitly part of the politicization of gender, public controversies show that racial politics are often linked to gender violence in the way that the violence is experienced, how the interventions are shaped, or the manner in which the consequences are politicized and represented. The controversies over the Central Park jogger case, the 2 Live Crew case, the St. John's rape trial, and the perhaps lesser known issue of Shahrazad Ali's *The Blackman's Guide to the Blackwoman*,[2] all present issues of gender violence in which racial politics are deeply implicated but in ways that seem impossible to capture fully within existing frameworks that separate racial politics from gender politics. These separations are linked to the overall problem of the way racism and sexism are understood and how these understandings inform organizing around antiracism and feminism.

Reformist efforts to politicize these issues exclusively around gender are thus problematic both for women of color and for those engaged in feminist and antiracist politics generally. Discursive and political practices that separate race from gender and gender from race create complex problems of exclusion and distortion for women of color. Because monocausal frameworks are unlikely to provide a ready means for addressing the interplay of gender and race in cultural and political discourse on violence, it is necessary to recenter inquiries relating to violence against women from the vantage point of women of color. On the simplest level, an intersectional framework uncovers how the dual positioning of women of color as women and as members of a subordinated racial group bears upon violence committed against us. This dual positioning, or as some scholars have labeled it, double jeopardy, renders women of color vulnerable to the structural, political and representational dynamics of both race and gender subordination. A framework attuned to the various ways that these dynamics intersect is a necessary prerequisite to exploring how this double vulnerability influences the way that violence against women of color is experienced and best addressed.

Second, an intersectional framework suggests ways in which political and representational practices connected to race and gender interrelate. This is relevant because the separate rhetorical strategies that characterize antiracist and feminist politics frequently intersect in ways that create new dilemmas for women of color. For example, political imperatives are frequently constructed from the perspectives of those who are dominant within either the race or gender categories in which women of color are situated, namely white women or men of color. These priorities are grounded in efforts to address only racism or sexism—as those issues are understood by the dominant voices within these communities. Political strategies that challenge only certain subordinating practices while maintaining existing hierarchies not only marginalize those who are subject to multiple systems of subordination but also often result in oppositionalizing race and gender discourses. As intersectional critique is thus important in uncovering the ways in which the reformist politics of one discourse enforce subordinating aspects of another.

The observations that follow are meant to explore the ways in which intersections of race and gender bear upon depictions of violence against women, particularly women of color. My observations are also meant to explore the bearing of these intersections on the broader efforts to politicize violence against all women. I explicitly adopt a Black feminist stance in my attempt to survey violence against women of color. I do this with cognizance of several tensions that this perspective entails. The significant one relates to the way in which feminism has been subject to the dual criticism of speaking *for* women of color through its invocation of the term "woman" even as it fails to examine differences and the problem of *excluding* women of color through grounding feminism in the experiences and interests of white women. I think it is important to name the perspective from which my own analysis is constructed, and that is as a Black feminist. I also think it is important to acknowledge that the materials upon which my analysis is based relate primarily to Black women. At the same time, I see my own work as part of a broader effort among feminist women of color to broaden feminism to include, among other factors, an analysis of race. Thus, I attempt to reach across racial differences to share my thinking and tentatively suggest ways in which the theory may apply to other women of color.

This chapter focuses on the problem of representational intersectionality. After a brief introduction to the theory of intersectionality, I will consider the ways in which media representations of women of color reinforce race and gender stereotypes. These stereotyped representations encourage and incite violence against us. But they do much more than that: They create a dominant narrative that forces actual women of color to the margins of the discourse and renders our own accounts of such victimization less credible. These media images define the spaces that women of color may occupy in dominant consciousness and problematize our efforts to construct a political practice and cultural critique that address the physical and material violence we experience.

This project is not oppositional to the overall effort to recode violence against women; rather, it is an attempt to broaden and strengthen the strategies available by exploring sites where race and gender converge to create the cultural and political grounding for gender violence. It is important also to ensure that these reform efforts do not reinforce racist sensibilities within the larger culture or ignore the need to challenge patriarchy within subcultures.

AN EXAMINATION OF INTERSECTIONALITY

Intersectionality is a core concept both provisional and illustrative. Although the primary intersections that I explore here are between race and gender, the concept can and should be expanded by factoring in issues such as class, sexual orientation, age, and color. I conceive of intersectionality as a provisional concept that links contemporary politics with postmodern theory. In examining the intersections of race and gender, I engage the dominant assumptions that these are essentially separate; by tracing the categories to their intersections, I hope to suggest a methodology that will ultimately disrupt the tendencies to see race and gender as exclusive or separable categories. Intersectionality is thus in my view a transitional concept that links current concepts with their political consequences, and real world politics with postmodern insights. It can be replaced, and our understanding of each category becomes more multidimensional. The basic function of intersectionality is to frame the following inquiry: How does the fact that women of color are simultaneously situated within at least two groups that are subjected to broad societal subordination bear upon problems traditionally viewed as monocausal—that is, gender discrimination or race discrimination? I believe three aspects of subordination are important: the structural dimensions of domination (structural intersectionality), the politics engendered by a political system of domination (political intersectionality), and the representations of the dominated (representational intersectionality). These intersectionalities serve as metaphors for different ways in which women of color are situated between categories of race and gender when the two are regarded as mutually exclusive. I hope that a framework of intersection will facilitate a merging of race and gender discourses to uncover what lies hidden between them and to construct a better means of conceptualizing and politicizing violence against women of color. It is important to note that although I use these concepts in fairly specific ways, as metaphors their boundaries are neither finite nor rigid. Indeed, representational intersectionality is not only implicated in the political interactions of race and gender discourses, it also can be inclusive of these intersections. Moreover, political and representational intersectionality can also be included as aspects of structural intersectionality.

Structural Intersectionality

I use the term structural intersectionality to refer to the way in which women of color are situated within overlapping structures of subordination. Any particular disadvantage or disability is sometimes compounded by yet another disadvantage emanating from or reflecting the dynamics of a separate system of subordination. An analysis sensitive to structural intersectionality explores the lives of those at the bottom of multiple hierarchies to determine how the dynamics of each hierarchy exacerbates and compounds the consequences of another. The material consequences of the interaction of these multiple hierarchies in the lives of women of color is what I call structural intersectionality. Illustrations of structural intersectionality suggest that violence toward women usually occurs within a specific context that may vary considerably depending on the woman's race, class, and other social characteristics. These constraints can be better understood and addressed through a framework that links them to broader structures of subordination that intersect in fairly predictable ways.

One illustration of structural intersectionality is the way in which the burdens of illiteracy, responsibility of child care, poverty, lack of job skills, and passive discrimination weigh down many battered women of color who are trying to escape the cycle of abuse. That is, gender subordination—manifested in this case by battering—intersects with race and class disadvantage to shape and limit the opportunities for effective intervention.

Another illustration of structural intersectionality is the way in which battered immigrant women's vulnerabilities were particularly exploited by the Immigration Marriage Fraud Amendments of 1986,[3] which imposed a two-year wait for permanent-resident status on women who moved to this country to marry U.S. citizens or permanent residents, and which required that both spouses file the application for the wife's permanent-resident status. When faced with what they saw as a choice between securing protection from their batterers and securing protection from deportation, many women, not surprisingly, chose the latter. Even now that these provisions have been amended—primarily at the urging of immigration activists, not feminists, which is perhaps another testament to immigrant women's isolation under intersecting structures of subordination—immigrant women are still at risk. The amendment waives the two-year wait only for battered women who produce evidence of battering from authorities (such as police officers, psychologists, and school officials) to which immigrant women may have little access, and immigrant women may still lack the English-language skills, the privacy on the telephone, and the courage to transgress cultural barriers to ask for help. Further, women married to undocumented workers may suffer in silence for fear that the security of their entire family will be jeopardized should they seek help.

A final illustration of structural intersectionality is the way in which rape crisis centers in poor minority or immigrant communities must address rape survivors' homelessness, unemployment, poverty, hunger, distrust of law-enforcement officers, and perhaps their lack of English-language skills as well, often hindered by funding agency policies premised on the needs of middle-class white rape survivors.

Political Intersectionality

I use the term political intersectionality to refer to the different ways in which political and discursive practices relating to race and gender interrelate, often erasing women of color. On some issues, the frameworks highlighting *race* and those highlighting *gender* are oppositional and potentially contradictory. These discourses are sometimes presented as either/or propositions with the validity of each necessarily precluding the validity of the other. Manifestations of this oppositionality are found in antiracist and feminist rhetorical postures that implicitly or explicitly legitimize the dynamics of either racial or gender subordination. An extreme example is Shahrazad Ali's controversial book, *The Blackman's Guide to the Blackwoman* (1989), which blames the deteriorating conditions within the Black community on the failure of the Black men to control their women. Ali recommends, among other practices, that Black men "discipline" disrespectful Black women by slapping them in the mouth—the mouth "because it is from that hole, in the lower part of her face. that all her rebellion culminates into words. Her unbridled tongue is a main reason she cannot get along with the Blackman."[4] More commonly, the need to protect the political or cultural integrity of the community is interpreted as precluding any public discussion of domestic violence. But suppressing information about domestic violence in the name of antiracism leaves unrevealed, and thus unaddressed in public discourse within our communities, the real terror in which many women of color live.

In other instances, women of color are erased when race and gender politics proceed on grounds that exclude or overlook the existence of women of color. Such an erasure took place in the rhetorical appeals made by sponsors of the Violence Against Women Act (1991).[5] White male senators eloquently urged passage of the bill because violence against women occurs everywhere, not just in the inner cities. That is, the senators attempted to persuade other whites that domestic violence is a problem because "these are *our* women being victimized." White women thus came into focus, and any authentic, sensitive attention to our images and our experience, which would have probably jeopardized the bill, faded into darkness.

But an erasure need not take place for us to be silenced. Tokenistic, objectifying, voyeuristic inclusion is at least as damaging as exclusion. We are as silenced when we appear in the margins as we are when we fail to appear at all.

Political intersectionality as it relates to violence against women of color reveals the ways in which politics centered around exclusive notions of race and gender leave women of color without a political framework that will adequately conceptualize the violence that occurs in our lives.

Representational Intersectionality

A final variant on the intersectional theme is representational intersectionality, referring to the way that race and gender images, readily available in our culture, converge to create unique and specific narratives deemed appropriate for women of color. Not surprisingly, the clearest convergences are those involving sexuality. Perhaps because it is through sexuality that images of minorities and women are most sharply focused. Representational intersectionality is significant in exploring violence against women of color because it provides cues to the ways in which our experiences are weighed against counternarratives that cast doubt upon the validity and harm of such violence. I will analyze examples of representational intersectionality in images of violence against women—images that wound—in the next section.

REPRESENTATIONAL INTERSECTIONALITY AND IMAGES THAT WOUND

Representational intersectionality is manifest in the familiar images of women of color within popular culture. Here I examine the cultural images widely disseminated in the mainstream movies *Angel Heart, Colors, Year of the Dragon,* and *Tales From the Darkside: The Movie.* Next, I will discuss a video game called *General Custer's Revenge.* Finally, I will consider in more detail the debate surrounding the obscenity prosecution of 2 Live Crew's album *As Nasty as They Wanna Be.*

Media images provide cues to understanding the ways in which women of color are imagined in our society. The images of Latina, African-American, Asian-American, and Native American women are constructed through combinations of readily available race and gender stereotypes. Because the stereotypes depicted in these presentations are quite familiar, collectively they form images of women of color that are specific and categorically unique.

Consider first the film *Colors. Colors* was a controversial film, but unfortunately, none of the criticism addressed its portrayal of women. Yet the film was rife with familiar stereotypes. The obligatory sexual relationship in that movie occurred between a hot-headed white cop played by Sean Penn and a young Latina played by Maria Conchito Alonso, whom he encountered working at a fast-food stand. Their relationship and her characterization progressed as follows: In Scene 1, he flirts, she blushes. In Scene 2, she accompanies him to a family outing at his partner's home. In Scene 3, the crucial scene, he drops her off at her home. She almost maintains the "good girl" image that had been carefully constructed from the onset, but when she reaches her door, she reconsiders and turns back to invite him in for a night of sex. In subsequent scenes this nice, hardworking ethnic girl increasingly turns into a promiscuous schizophrenic Latina. In her final appearance, the transformation is complete. The scene begins with the young cop arriving to investigate a noisy house party. She is seen putting on her clothes in a bedroom from which a black man has departed. She wears a low-cut, loud dress and six-inch heels. She is very loud and brash now, laughingly tormenting the distraught and disappointed Sean Penn who, upon seeing her, attempts to escape. She follows him and with her hands on her hips, demanding now in a very heavy and exaggerated accent: "Look at me. This is part of me too!"

The image of the good ethnic fiery Latina is contrasted with an image of Black sexuality also constructed in *Colors.* In another scene, the police converge on a house to serve a warrant on a suspect named Rock-it. As they approach the house, the viewer hears a rhythmic squeaking and loud screams. The camera takes several seconds to track through the ramshackle house. There is little in the house except a stereo apparently playing the loud, pulsating music accenting the sound track. The camera turns a corner and finds a Black man and a Black woman on a bed, atop a single white sheet, so earnestly and frantically copulating that they are wholly oblivious to the several police officers surrounding them with guns drawn. When they finally become aware of the officers' presence, the man makes a sudden move and is shot several times in the back. As his lover screams hysterically, he gasps that he was simply reaching for his clothes.

In *Angel Heart*, the descent of an African-American woman into her own uncontrolled sexuality ends in tragic horror. Epiphany Proudfoot, played by Cosby-kid Lisa Bonet, is introduced washing her hair at a well. She appears at first the model of youth, reticent and exotic. Yet she is slightly fallen: she has a child whose father is unknown. Later we see her as a voodoo priestess dancing a blood-curdling ritual and collapsing in an uncontrolled sexual frenzy. The movie culminates in a vicious pornographic scene between Epiphany and Harry Angel (played by Mickey Rourke) that gives new meaning to the phrase "sex and violence." Sex—initiated by Epiphany—soon becomes gruesome as dripping water turns to blood, intercut with rivers of blood, deep thrusting, and screams of agony and horror. The visual narrative splits after this scene: Epiphany appears normal, singing a lovely lullaby and wistfully twisting her hair as she bathes, but later we discover that Epiphany is in fact dead. Her body sprawls across the bed, her legs spread open. A deep pool of blood surrounds her pelvic area. The movie's final scene plays out across her dead body. We discover the cause of her death when the southern sheriff questioning Angel drawls, "Is that your gun up her snatch?" The horror is not yet complete, for we have still to discover that not only has Harry Angel killed his lover, but that his lover is actually his daughter. So this Cosby-kid hits big time, being multiply victimized by incest, rape and murder.

Perhaps it is happenstance that Lisa Bonet played Epiphany and that the imagery in this big-budget Hollywood film is so violent. Yet I wonder whether a Michelle Pfeiffer, a Kim Bassinger, or even a Madonna would be asked to play such a role? I don't think so. The film, by relying on race-sex exoticism, works differently from the way it would with a white female. In fact, the presence of a woman of color often "makes" the story, as is still more clearly shown in an episode from *Tales from the Dark Side: The Movie*. The life of a young white artist is spared by a sixteen-foot talking gargoyle upon the artist's promise that he will never tell anyone that he has ever seen this gargoyle. Later that night he meets a Black woman, played here by Rae Dawn Chong, whom he later marries and with whom he has two lovely children. With the support of his wife he becomes enormously successful, and they live a happy, fulfilled life. On their tenth anniversary, he decides to tell his wife this secret as part of his expression of affection to her. Presenting her with a full-sized sculpture of the monster, he tells her how his life was spared upon making a vow never to reveal that the monster exists. After he tells her the story, she becomes hysterical and, as "fate" would have it, begins to turn into the sixteen-foot gargoyle. Their two children emerge from the adjoining room as baby gargoyles. The wife disregards the artist's frantic efforts to profess his love for her, stating that she "loved him too but when the vow was broken their fate was sealed." She monstrously tears out his throat, gathers up the "children," and swoops through the ceiling. Here the drop-of-blood rule really works: The children, although half-human, are little monsters too. Can anyone doubt the message?—white male miscegenators, beware! Exotica and danger go hand in hand.

Mickey Rourke, apparently bidding to be everybody's favorite racist/sadomasochist/rapist/murderer, turns up again in *Year of the Dragon*. There he plays Captain Stanley White, a New York cop, who pursues a brash and independent Asian-American TV newscaster. He encounters her on the street, addresses her as a prostitute, taunts her with racist epithets (apparently learned from his days in Vietnam). After she invites him up to her apartment, he continues to assault her verbally, before physically doing so. He tells her that he hates everything about her, and then taking down his pants, he queries, "So why do I want to fuck you so badly?" The worst is yet to come: As our heroine rallies enough outrage to ask him to leave, he calls her a slant-eyed cunt. She slaps him once, pauses, and slaps again. He then grabs her, throws her down, rips off her clothes, and has forcible sex with her.

The next image comes not from a movie but from a video game, *General Custer's Revenge.* A Native American woman is tied to a pole. The player, General Custer, must traverse an obstacle course to get to the woman before getting shot. His saberlike penis leads him forward. The player wins when General Custer reaches the Native American woman and pounces on her. She "Kicks up her legs in dubious delight" as he commits "what opponents call a rape and the manufacturer claims is a willing sex act." (A spokesman for the manufacturer commented, "There is a facsimile of intercourse. The woman is smiling.") Every stroke is a point. The motto: "When you score, you score."[6]

These four representations confirm both the feminist claim that women are legitimate targets for violence and the more specific observation that these targets are often represented with distinct racialized images. The Latina is two sided: she is both a sweet, hardworking ethnic and a loud, unscrupulous, racialized "other." The Black woman is wild and animal-like. In *Tales from the Darkside: The Movie,* she is an animal, or, worse yet, a monster. The Asian-American woman is passive. She is verbally abused and physically assaulted, yet she still stands ready to please. The Native American woman is a savage. She has no honor and no integrity. She doesn't fight rape; in fact, being tied up and ravished makes her smile. She enjoys it.

In each of these cases the specific image is created within the intersection of race and gender. Although some claim that these images reflect certain attitudes that make women of color targets of sexual violence, the actual effect of images on behavior is still hotly contested. Whatever the relationship between imagery and actions is, it seems clear that these images do function to create counternarratives to the experiences of women of color that discredit our claims and render the violence that we experience unimportant. These images not only represent the devaluation of women of color, they may also reproduce it by providing viewers with both conscious and unconscious cues for interpreting the experiences of "others." Because both the actual experience of violence and the representations of those experiences constitute the "problem" of gender violence, feminists of color must address how race and gender intersect in popular discourse as well as in feminist and antiracist politics.

ADDRESSING THE INTERSECTIONALITIES IN THE 2 LIVE CREW CONTROVERSY

The different intersectionalities discussed above converge in my thinking on the controversy surrounding the obscenity prosecution of 2 Live Crew. The entire problem spurred by the prosecution of 2 Live Crew—the question of how to construct a Black feminist approach to the virulent misogyny in some rap music—has vexed me for some time, and as I suggested at the outset, prompted my attempt to construct a Black feminist understanding of gender violence.

The prosecution of 2 Live Crew began several months after the release of their *As Nasty As They Wanna Be* album. In the midst of the Mapplethorpe controversy and Tipper Gore's campaign to label offensive rock music, the Broward County sheriff, Nick Navarro, began investigating 2 Live Crew's *Nasty* recording at the behest of Jack Thompson, a fundamentalist attorney in Miami, Florida. The sheriff obtained an ex parte order declaring the recording obscene and presented copies of the order to local store owners, threatening them with arrest if they continued to sell the recording. 2 Live Crew filed a civil rights suit, and Sheriff Navarro sought a judicial determination labeling 2 Live Crew's *Nasty* recording obscene.[7] A federal court ruled that *Nasty* was obscene but granted 2 Live Crew permanent injunctive relief because the sheriff's action had subjected the recording to unconstitutional prior restraint. Two days after the judge declared the recording obscene, 2 Live Crew members were charged with giving an obscene performance at a club in Hollywood, Florida. Additionally, deputy sheriffs arrested a merchant who was selling copies of the *Nasty* recording. These events received national attention and the controversy quickly polarized into two camps. Writing in *Newsweek*, political columnist George Will staked a case for the prosecution. He argued that *Nasty* was misogynistic filth. Will characterized the performance as a profoundly repugnant "combination of extreme infantilism and menace" that objectified Black women and represented them as suitable targets for sexual violence.[8]

The most prominent defense of 2 Live Crew was advanced by Professor Henry Louis Gates, Jr., an expert on African-American literature. In a *New York Times* op-ed piece and in testimony at the criminal trial, Gates contended that 2 Live Crew were literary geniuses operating within and inadvertently elaborating distinctively African-American forms of cultural expression.[9] Furthermore, the characteristic exaggeration featured in their lyrics served a political end: to explode popular racist stereotypes in a comically extreme form. Where Will saw a misogynistic assault on Black women by social degenerates, Gates found a form of "sexual carnivalesque" with the promise to free us from the pathologies of racism.

As a Black feminist, I felt the pull of each of these poles but not the compelling attractions of either. My immediate response to the criminal charges against 2 Live Crew was a feeling of being torn between standing with the brothers against a racist attack and standing against a frightening explosion of violent imagery directed to women like me. This reaction, I have come to believe, is a consequence of the location of Black women at the intersection of racial and sexual subordination. My experience of sharp internal division—if dissatisfaction with the idea that the "real issue" is race or gender is inertly juxtaposed—is characteristic of that location. Black feminism offers an intellectual and political response to that experience. Bringing together the different aspects of an otherwise divided sensibility, Black feminism argues that racial and sexual subordination are mutually reinforcing, that Black women are marginalized by a politics of race and gender, and that a political response to each form of subordination must at the same time be a political response to both. When the controversy over 2 Live Crew is approached in light of such Black feminist sensibilities, an alternative to the dominant poles of the public debate emerges.

At the legal bottom line I agree with the supporters of 2 Live Crew that the obscenity prosecution was wrongheaded. But the reasons for my conclusion are not the same as the reasons generally offered in support of 2 Live Crew. I will come to those reasons shortly, but first I must emphasize that after listening to 2 Live Crew's lyrics along with those of other rap artists, my defense of 2 Live Crew, however careful, did not come easily.

On first hearing 2 Live Crew I was shocked; unlike Gates I did not "bust out laughing." One trivializes the issue by describing the images of women in *As Nasty As They Wanna Be* as simply "sexually explicit." We hear about cunts being fucked until backbones are cracked, asses being busted, dicks rammed down throats, and semen splattered across faces.

Black women are cunts, bitches, and all-purpose "hos." Images of women in some of the other rap acts are even more horrifying: battering, rape, and rape-murder are often graphically detailed. Occasionally, we do hear Black women's voices, and these voices are sometimes oppositional. But the response to opposition typically returns to the central refrain: "Shut up, bitch. Suck my dick."

This is no mere braggadocio. Those of us who are concerned about the high rates of gender violence in our communities must be troubled by the possible connections between such images and violence against women. Children and teenagers are listening to this music, and I am concerned that the range of acceptable behavior is broadened by the constant propagation of antiwomen imagery. I'm concerned, too, about young Black women who together with men are learning that their value lies between their legs. Unlike that of men, however, women's sexual value is portrayed as a depletable commodity: By expending it, boys become men and girls become whores.

Nasty is misogynist, and a Black feminist response to the case against 2 Live Crew should not depart from a full acknowledgment of that misogyny. But such a response must also consider whether an exclusive focus on issues of gender risks overlooking aspects of the prosecution of 2 Live Crew that raise serious questions of racism. And here is where the roots of my opposition to the obscenity prosecution lie.

An initial problem concerning the prosecution was its apparent selectivity. Even the most superficial comparison between 2 Live Crew and other mass-marketed sexual representations suggest the likelihood that race played some role in distinguishing 2 Live Crew as the first group ever to be prosecuted for obscenity in connection with a musical recording, and one of only a handful of recording groups or artists to be prosecuted for a live performance. Recent controversies about sexism, racism, and violence in popular culture point to a vast range of expression that might have provided targets for censorship, but that were left untouched. Madonna has acted out masturbation, portrayed the seduction of a priest, and simulated group sex on stage. But she has never been prosecuted for obscenity. Whereas 2 Live Crew was performing in an adults-only club in Hollywood, Florida, Andrew Dice Clay was performing nationwide on HBO. Well known for his racist "humor," Clay is also comparable to 2 Live Crew in sexual explicitness and misogyny. In his show, for example, Clay offers: "Eeny, meeny, miney, mo, suck my [expletive] and swallow slow," or "Lose the bra bitch." Moreover, graphic sexual images—many of them violent—were widely available in Broward County where 2 Live Crew's performance and trial took place. According to the trial testimony of a vice detective named McCloud, "Nude dance shows and adult bookstores are scattered throughout the county where 2 Live Crew performed."[10] But again, no obscenity charges were leveled against the performers or producers of these representations.

In response to this charge of selectivity, it might be argued that the successful prosecution of 2 Live Crew demonstrates that its lyrics were uniquely obscene. In a sense, this argument runs, the proof is in the prosecution—if they were not uniquely obscene, they would have been acquitted. However the elements of 2 Live Crew's performance that contributed initially to their selective arrest continued to play out as the court applied the obscenity standard to the recording. To clarify this argument, we need to consider the technical use of "obscenity" as a legal term of art. For the purposes of legal argument, the Supreme Court in the 1973 case of *Miller v. California* held that a work is obscene if and only if it meets each of three conditions: (1) "the average person, applying community standards, would find that the work, taken as a whole, appeals to the prurient interest"; (2) "the work depicts or describes, in a patently offensive way, sexual conduct specifically defined by the applicable state law"; and (3) "the work, taken as a whole, lacks serious literary, artistic, political, or scientific value."[11] The Court held that it is consistent with first amendment guarantees of freedom of expression for states to subject work that meets each of the three prongs of the *Miller* test to very restrictive regulations.

Focusing first on the prurient interest prong of the *Miller* test, we might wonder how 2 Live Crew could have been seen as uniquely obscene by the lights of the "community standards" of Broward County. After all, as Detective McCloud put it, "Patrons [of clubs in Broward] can see women dancing with at least their breasts exposed" and bookstore patrons can "view and purchase films and magazines that depict vaginal, oral and anal sex, homosexual sex and group sex."[12] In arriving at this finding of obscenity, the court placed little weight on the available range of films, magazines, and live shows as evidence of the community's sensibilities. Instead the court apparently accepted the sheriff's testimony that the decision to single out *Nasty* was based on the number of complaints against 2 Live Crew "communicated by telephone calls, anonymous messages, or letters to the police."[13]

Evidence of this popular outcry was never substantiated. But even if it were, the case for selectivity would remain. The history of social repression of Black male sexuality is long, often violent, and all too familiar. Negative reactions against the sexual conduct of Black males have traditionally had racist overtones, especially where the conduct threatens to "cross over" into the mainstream community. So even if the decision to prosecute did reflect a widespread community perception of the purely prurient character of 2 Live Crew's music, that perception itself might reflect an established pattern of vigilante attitudes directed toward the sexual expression of Black males. In short, the appeal to community standards does not undercut a concern about racism; rather, it underscores that concern.

A second troubling dimension of the case against 2 Live Crew was the court's apparent disregard for the culturally rooted aspects of 2 Live Crew's music. Such disregard was essential to a finding of obscenity given the third prong of the *Miller* test, requiring that obscene material lack literary, artistic, or political value. 2 Live Crew argued that this test was not met because the recording exemplified such African-American cultural modes as "playing the dozens," "call and response," and "signifying." As a storehouse of such cultural modes, it could not be said that *Nasty* could be described as completely devoid of literary or artistic value. In each case the court denied the group's claim of cultural specificity by recharacterizing these modes claimed to be African-American in more generic terms. For example, the court reasoned that playing the dozens is "commonly seen in adolescents, especially boys, of all ages." "Boasting," the court observed, appears to be "part of the universal human condition." And the court noted that the cultural origins of one song featuring call and response—a song about fellatio in which competing groups chanted "less filling" and "tastes great"—were to be found in a Miller beer commercial, not in African-American cultural tradition. The possibility that the Miller beer commercial may have itself evolved from an African-American cultural tradition was lost on the court.

In disregarding this testimony the court denied the artistic value in the form and style of *Nasty* and, by implication, rap music more generally. This disturbing dismissal of the cultural attributes of rap and the effort to universalize African-American modes of expression flattens cultural differences. The court's analysis here manifests in the law a frequently encountered strategy of cultural appropriation. African-American contributions accepted by the mainstream culture are considered simply "American" or found to be the "universal."

Other modes associated with African-American culture that resist absorption and remain distinctive are neglected or dismissed as "deviant."

An additional concern has as much to do with the obscenity doctrine itself as with the court's application of it in this case. The case illustrates the ways in which obscenity doctrine asks the wrong questions with respect to sexual violence and facilitates wrong conclusions with respect to racially selective enforcement. As I mentioned earlier, obscenity requires a determination that the material be intended to appeal to prurient interest. In making this determination, the court rejected the relevance of 2 Live Crew's admitted motives—both their larger motive of making money and their secondary motive of doing so through the marketing of outrageous sexual humor. Although the prurient interest requirement eludes precise definition—recall Potter Stewart's infamous declaration that "I know it when I see it"—it seems clear that it must appeal in some immediate way to sexual desire. It would be difficult to say definitively what does or does not constitute an appeal to this prurient interest, but one can surmise that the twenty-five cent peep shows that are standard fare in Broward County rank considerably higher on his scale than the sexual tall tales told by 2 Live Crew.

2 Live Crew is thus one of the lesser candidates in the prurient interest sweepstakes mandated by the obscenity standard, and it is also a lesser contender by another measure that lies explicitly outside the obscenity doctrine: violence. Compared to groups such as N.W.A., Too Short, Ice Cube, and the Geto Boys, 2 Live Crew's misogynistic hyperbole sounds minor league. Sometimes called gangsta' rap, the lyrics offered by these other groups celebrate violent assault, rape, rape-murder, and mutilation. Had these other groups been targeted rather than the comparatively less offensive 2 Live Crew, they may have been more successful in defeating the prosecution. The graphic violence in their representations militates against a finding of obscenity by suggesting an intent to appeal not to prurient interests but instead to the fantasy of the social outlaw. Indeed, these appeals might even be read as political. Against the historical backdrop against which the image of the Black male as the social outlaw is a prominent theme, gangsta' rap might be read as a rejection of a conciliatory stance aimed at undermining fear through reassurance in favor of a more subversive form of opposition that attempts to challenge the rules precisely by becoming the very social outlaw that society has proscribed. Thus, so long as obscenity remains preoccupied with finding prurient interests and violent imagery is seen as distinct from sexuality, obscenity doctrine is ineffectual against more violent rappers.

Yet even this somewhat formal dichotomy between sex, which obscenity is concerned about, and violence, which lies beyond its purview, may provide little solace to the entire spectrum of rappers ranging from the Geto Boys to 2 Live Crew. Given the historical linkages between Black male sexuality and violence, the two are likely to be directly linked in the prurient interest inquiry, even if subconsciously. In fact, it may have been the background images of Black male sexual violence that rendered 2 Live Crew an acceptable target for obscenity in a lineup that included many stronger contenders.

My point here is not to suggest that the distinction between sex and violence should be maintained in obscenity, nor more specifically, that the more violent rappers ought to be protected. To the contrary, these groups trouble me much more than 2 Live Crew. My point instead is to suggest that obscenity doctrine does nothing to protect the interests of those who are most directly implicated in such rap—Black women. On a formal level, obscenity separates out sexuality and violence, thus shielding the more violently misogynistic groups from prosecution. Yet the historical linkages between images of Black male sexuality and violence simultaneously single out lightweight rappers for prosecution among all other purveyors of explicit sexual imagery. Neither course furthers Black women's simultaneous interests in opposing racism and misogyny.

Although Black women's interests were quite obviously irrelevant in this obscenity judgment, their bodies figured prominently in the public case supporting the prosecution. George Will's *Newsweek* essay provides a striking example of how Black women's bodies were appropriated and deployed in the broader attack against 2 Live Crew. In "America's Slide into the Sewers," Will told us, "America today is capable of terrific intolerance about smoking, or toxic waste that threatens trout. But only a deeply confused society is more concerned about protecting lungs than minds, trout than black women. We legislate against smoking in restaurants; singing 'Me So Horny' is a constitutional right. Secondary smoke is carcinogenic; celebration of torn vaginas is 'mere words.' "[14]

Notwithstanding these expressions of concern about Black women, Will's real worry is suggested by his repeated references to the Central Park jogger. He writes, "Her face was so disfigured a friend took 15 minutes to identify her. 'I recognized her ring.' Do you recognize the relevance of 2 Live Crew?" Although the connection between the threat of 2 Live Crew and the image of the Black male rapist was suggested subtly in the public debate, it is manifest throughout Will's discussion and in fact bids to be its central theme. "Fact: Some members of a particular age and societal cohort—the one making 2 Live Crew rich—stomped and raped the jogger to the razor edge of death, for the fun of it." Will directly indicts 2 Live Crew in the Central Park jogger rape through a fictional dialogue between himself and the defendants. Responding to one defendant's alleged confession that the rape was fun, Will asks: "Where can you get the idea that sexual violence against women is fun? From a music store, through Walkman earphones, from boom boxes blaring forth the rap lyrics of 2 Live Crew"; because the rapists were young Black males and *Nasty* presents Black men celebrating sexual violence, surely 2 Live Crew was responsible. Apparently, the vast American industry that markets misogynistic representation in every conceivable way is irrelevant to understanding this particular incident of sexual violence.

Will invokes Black women—twice—as victims of this music. But if he were really concerned with the threat to Black women, why does the Central Park jogger figure so prominently in his argument? Why not the Black woman from Brooklyn who, within weeks of the Central Park assault, was gang-raped and then thrown down an air shaft? What about the twenty-eight other women—mostly women of color—who were raped in New York City the same week the Central Park jogger was raped? Rather than being centered in Will's display of concern, Black women appear to function as stand-ins for white women. The focus on sexual violence played out on Black women's bodies seems to reflect concerns about the threat to Black male violence against the strategy of the prosecutor in Richard Wright's novel *Native Son.*[15] Bigger Thomas, the Black male protagonist, is on trial for killing Mary Dalton, a white woman. Because Bigger burned her body, however, it cannot be established whether Mary was raped. So the prosecution brings in the body of Bessie, a Black woman raped by Bigger and left to die, to establish that Bigger has raped Mary.

Further evidence that Will's concern about sexual imagery and rape is grounded in familiar narratives of Black sexual violence and white victimhood is suggested by his nearly apoplectic reaction to similar attempts to regulate racist speech. In his assault on 2 Live Crew, Will decries liberal tolerance for lyrics that "desensitize" our society and that will certainly have "behavioral consequences." Proponents of campus speech regulations have made arguments that racist speech facilitates racist violence in much the same way that Will links rap to sexual violence. Yet Will has excoriated such proponents.

Despite his anguish that sexual lyrics "coarsen" our society and facilitate a "slide into the sewer," in Will's view,[16] racist speech is situated on a much higher plane. Apparently, the "social cohort" that is most likely to engage in racial violence—young white men—has sense enough to distinguish ideas from action whereas the "social cohort" that identifies with 2 Live Crew is made up of mindless brutes who will take rap as literal encouragement to rape. Will's position on racist speech not only indicates how readily manipulable the link between expression and action is, but suggests further reasons why his invocation of Black women seems so disingenuous. One can't help but wonder why Will is so outraged about attacks on Black women's vaginal walls and not concerned about attacks on our skin.

These concerns about selectivity in prosecution, about the denial of cultural specificity, and about the manipulation of Black women's bodies convince me that race played a significant if not determining role in the shaping of the case against 2 Live Crew. While using antisexist rhetoric to suggest a concern for omen, the attack simultaneously endorsed traditional readings of Black male sexuality. The fact that most sexual violence involves intraracial assault fades to the background as the Black male is represented as the agent of sexual violence and the white community is represented as his victim. The subtext of the 2 Live Crew prosecution thus becomes a rereading of the sexualized racial politics of the past.

Although concerns about racism fuel my opposition to the obscenity prosecution, I am also troubled by the uncritical support for and indeed celebration of 2 Live Crew by other opponents of that prosecution. If the rhetoric of antisexism provided an occasion for racism, so too, the rhetoric of antiracism provided an occasion for defending the misogyny of Black male rappers.

The defense of 2 Live Crew took two forms, one political and one cultural, both of which were advanced most prominently by Henry Louis Gates, Jr. The political argument was that 2 Live Crew represents an attack against Black sexual stereotypes. The strategy of the attack is, in Gates's words, to "exaggerate [the] stereotypes" and thereby "to show how ridiculous the portrayals are."[17] For the strategy to succeed, it must of course highlight the sexism, misogyny, and violence stereotypically associated with Black male sexuality. But far from embracing that popular methodology, the idea is to fight the racism of those who accept it. Thus, the argument goes, 2 Live Crew and other rap groups are simply pushing white society's buttons to ridicule its dominant sexual images.

I agree with Gates that the reactions by Will and others to 2 Live Crew confirm that the stereotypes still exist and still evoke basic fears. But even if I were to agree that 2 Live Crew intended to explode these mythic fears, I still would argue that this strategy is wholly misguided. These fears are too active and African Americans are too closely associated with them not to be burned when the myths are exploded. More fundamentally, however, I am deeply skeptical about the claim that the Crew was engaged—either in intent or effects—in a postmodern guerrilla war against racist stereotypes.

Gates argues that when one listens to 2 Live Crew, the ridiculous stories and the hyperbole make the listener "bust out laughing." Apparently, the fact that Gates and many other people react with laughter confirms and satisfies Crew's objective of ridiculing the stereotypes. The fact that the Crew is often successful in achieving laughter neither substantiates Gates's reading nor forecloses serious critique of its subordinating dimensions.

In disagreeing with Gates, I do not mean to suggest that 2 Live Crew's lyrics are to be taken literally. But rather than exploding stereotypes as Gates suggests, I believe that the group simply uses readily available sexual images in trying to be funny. Trading in racial stereotypes and sexual hyperbole are well-rehearsed strategies for achieving laughter; the most extreme representations often do more to reinforce and entrench the image than to explode it. 2 Live Crew departs from this tradition only in its attempt to up the ante through more outrageous boasts and more explicit manifestations of misogyny.

The acknowledgment, however, that the Crew was simply trying to be funny should not be interpreted as constituting a defense against its misogyny. Neither the intent to be funny nor Gates's loftier explanations negate the subordinating qualities of such humor. An examination of the parallel arguments in the context of racist humor suggests why neither claim functions as a persuasive defense for 2 Live Crew.

Gates's use of laughter as a defensive maneuver in the attack on 2 Live Crew recalls similar strategies in defense of racist humor. Racist humor has sometimes been defended as antiracist—an effort to poke fun at or to show the ridiculousness of racism. More simply, racist humor has often been excused as just joking; even racially motivated assaults are often defended as simple pranks. Thus, the racism and sexism of Andrew Dice Clay could be defended either as an attempt to explode the stereotypes of white racists or more simply as simple humor not meant to be taken seriously. Implicit in these defenses is the assumption that racist representations are injurious only if they are devoid of any other objective or are meant to be taken literally. Although these arguments are familiar within the Black community, I think it is highly unlikely that they would be viewed as a persuasive defense of Andrew Dice Clay. Indeed, the historical and ongoing criticism of such humor suggests widespread rejection of such disclaimers. Operating instead under a premise that humor can be nonliteral, perhaps even well intended, but racist nonetheless, African Americans have protested such humor. This practice of opposition suggests a general recognition within the Black community that "mere humor" is not inconsistent with subordination. The question of what people find humorous is of course a complicated one that includes considerations of aggression, reinforcement of group boundaries, projection and other issues. The claim of intending only a joke may be true, but representations function as humor within a specific social context and frequently reinforce patterns of social power. Even though racial humor may sometimes be intended to ridicule racism, the close relationship between the stereotypes and the prevailing images of marginalized people as well as a presumed connection between the humorist and the dominant audience complicates this strategy. Clearly, racial humor does not always undermine the racism of the character speaking nor indict the wider society in which the jokes have meaning. The endearment of Archie Bunker seems to suggest at least this much.

Thus, in the context of racist humor, neither the fact that people actually laughed at racist humor nor the usual disclaimer of intent have functioned to preclude incisive and quite often angry criticism of such humor within the African-American community. Although a similar set of arguments could be offered in the context of sexist humor, images marketed by 2 Live Crew were not condemned but, as Gates illustrates, defended, often with great commitment and skill. Clearly, the fact that the Crew is Black, as are the women it objectifies, shaped this response. There is of course an ongoing issue of how one's positioning vis-à-vis a targeted group colors the way the group interprets a potentially derisive stereotype or gesture. Had 2 Live Crew been whites in blackface, for example, all of the readings would have been different. Although the question of whether one can defend the broader license given to Black comedians to market stereotypical images is an interesting one, it is not the issue here. 2 Live Crew cannot claim an in-group privilege to perpetuate misogynistic humor against Black women. Its members are not Black women, and more important, they enjoy a power relationship over them.

Sexual humor in which women are objectified as packages of bodily parts to serve whatever male-bonding/male-competition the speakers please subordinates women in much the same way that racist humor subordinates African Americans. That these are "just jokes" and are not taken as literal claims does little to blunt their demeaning quality—nor, for that matter, does it help that the jokes are told within a tradition of intragroup humor.

Gates offered a second, cultural defense of 2 Live Crew: the idea that *Nasty* is in line with distinctively African-American traditions of culture. It is true that the "dozens" and other forms of verbal boasting have been practiced within the Black community for some time. It is true as well that raunchy jokes, insinuations, and boasts of sexual prowess were not meant to be taken literally. Nor, however, were they meant to disrupt conventional myths about Black sexuality. They were meant simply to be laughed at and perhaps to gain respect for the speaker's word wizardry.

Ultimately, however, little turns on whether the "wordplay" performed by 2 Live Crew is a postmodern challenge to racist sexual mythology or simply an internal group practice that has crossed over to mainstream U.S. society. Both versions of the defense are problematic because both call on Black women to accept misogyny and its attendant disrespect in the service of some broader group objective. Whereas one version argues that accepting misogyny is necessary to antiracist politics, the other argues that it is necessary to maintain the cultural integrity of the community. Neither presents sufficient justification for requiring Black women to tolerate such misogyny. The message that these arguments embrace—that patriarchy can be made to serve antiracist ends—is a familiar one, with proponents ranging from Eldridge Cleaver in the 1960s to Shahrazad Ali in the 1990s. In Gates's variant, the position of Black women is determined by the need to wield gargantuan penises in efforts to ridicule racist images of Black male sexuality. Even though Black women may not be the intended targets, they are necessarily called to serve these gargantuan penises and are thus in the position of absorbing the impact. The common message of all such strategies is that Black women are expected to be vehicles for notions of "liberation" that function to preserve Black female subordination.

To be sure, Gates's claim about the cultural aspects of 2 Live Crew's lyrics do address the legal issue about the applicability of the obscenity standard. As I indicated earlier, the group's music does have artistic and potentially political value; I believe the court decided this issue incorrectly and Will was all too glib in his critique. But these criticisms do not settle the issue within the community. Dozens and other wordplays have long been within the Black oral tradition, but acknowledging this fact does not eliminate the need to interrogate either the sexism within that tradition or the objectives to which that tradition has been pressed. To say that playing the dozens, for example, is rooted in a Black cultural tradition or that themes represented by mythic folk heroes such as Stagolee are Black does not settle the question of whether such practices are oppressive to women and others within the community. The same point can be made about the relentless homophobia in the work of Eddie Murphy and many other comedians and rappers. Whether or not the Black community has a pronounced tradition of homophobic humor is beside the point; the question instead is how these subordinating aspects of tradition play out in the lives of people in the community, people who are otherwise called upon to share the benefits and the burdens of a common history, culture, and political agenda. Although it may be true that the Black community is more familiar with the cultural forms that have evolved into rap, that familiarity should not end the discussion of whether the misogyny within rap is acceptable.

Moreover, we need to consider the possible relationships between sexism in our cultural practices and violence against women. Violence against women of color is not centered as a critical issue in either the antiracist or antiviolence discourses. The "different culture" defense may contribute to a disregard for women of color victimized by rape and violence that reinforces the tendency within the broader community not to take intraracial violence seriously. Numerous studies have suggested that Black victims of crime can count on less protection from the criminal justice system than whites receive. This is true for Black rape victims as well—their rapists are less likely to be convicted and on average serve less time when they are convicted. Could it be that perpetuating the belief that Blacks are different with respect to sexuality and violence contributes to the disregard of Black female rape victims like Bessie in *Native Son* or the woman thrown down an air shaft in Brooklyn?

Although there are times when Black feminists should fight for the integrity of Black culture, this does not mean that criticism must end when a practice or form of expression is traced to an aspect of culture. We must also determine whether the practices and forms of expression are consistent with other tests that we must define. The legal question of obscenity may be settled by finding roots in the culture. But traditional obscenity is not our central issue. Performances and representations that do not appeal principally to "prurient interests" or that may reflect expressive patterns that are culturally specific may still encourage self-hatred, disrespect, subordination, and various other forms of manifestations of intragroup pathology. These problems require an internal group dialogue. Although we have no plenary authority to grapple with these issues, we do need to find ways of using group formation mechanisms and other social spaces to reflect upon and reformulate our cultural and political practices.

I said earlier that the political goals of Black feminism are to construct and empower a political sensibility that opposes misogyny and racism simultaneously. Merging this double vision in an analysis of the 2 Live Crew controversy makes clear that, despite the superficial defense of the prosecution as being in the interests of women, nothing about the anti–2 Live Crew movement is about Black women's lives. The political process involved in the legal prosecution of 2 Live Crew's representational subordination of Black women does not seek to empower Black women; indeed, the racism of that process is injurious to us.

The implication of this conclusion is not that Black feminists should stand in solidarity with the supporters of 2 Live Crew. The spirited defense of 2 Live Crew was no more about defending the Black community than the prosecution was about defending women. After all, Black women—whose assault is the very subject of the representation—are part of that community. Black women can hardly regard the right to be represented as rape-deserving bitches and whores as essential to their interests. Instead the defense primarily functions to protect the cultural and political prerogative of male rappers to be as misogynistic as they want to be.

The debate over 2 Live Crew illustrates how the discursive structures of race and gender politics continue to marginalize Black women, rendering us virtually voiceless. Fitted with a Black feminist sensibility, one uncovers other issues in which the unique situation of Black women renders a different formulation of the problem than the version that dominates in current debate. Ready examples include rape, domestic violence, and welfare dependency. A Black feminist sensibility might also provide a more direct link between the women's movement and traditional civil rights movements, helping them both to shed conceptual blinders that limit the efficacy of their efforts. In the recent controversy over the nomination of Clarence Thomas to the U.S. Supreme Court, for example, organized groups in both camps—in particular women's groups—initially struggled to produce evidence showing Thomas's negative disposition toward their respective constituencies. Thomas's repeated derogatory references to his sister as the quintessential example of welfare dependency might have been profitably viewed from a Black framework as the embodiment of his views on race, gender, and class, permitting an earlier formulation of a more effective coalition.

The development of a Black feminist sensibility is no guarantee that Black women's interests will be taken seriously. For that sensibility to develop into empowerment, Black women will have to make it clear that patriarchy is a critical issue that negatively impacts the lives of not only African-American women but men as well. Within the African-American political community, this recognition might reshape traditional practices so that evidence of racism would not constitute sufficient justification for uncritical rallying around misogynistic politics and patriarchal values. Although collective opposition to racist practice has been and continues to be crucially important in protecting Black interests, an empowered Black feminist sensibility would require that the terms of unity no longer reflect priorities premised upon the continued marginalization of Black women.

NOTES

1. 137 Cong. Rec. S597, S610 (1991) (S. 15, H.R. 1502).
2. S. Ali, *The Blackman's Guide to the Blackwoman* (1989).
3. Pub. L. 99–639 (Nov. 10, 1986), Pub. L. 100–525, § 7(a)–(c) (Oct. 24, 1988).
4. S. Ali, *supra* note 2, at 169.
5. H.R. 1502, S. 15 (102d Cong.).
6. Coraham, *Custer May Be Shot Down Again in Battle of Sexes over X-Rated Video Game*, People Magazine, Nov. 15, 1982.
7. Santoro, *How 2B Nasty: Rap Musicians 2 Live Crew Arrested*, The Nation, July 2, 1990, at 4.
8. Will, *America's Slide into the Sewer*, Newsweek, July 30, 1990, at 64.
9. Gates, *2 Live Crew Decoded*, N.Y. Times, June 19, 1990, at A23.
10. *2 Live Crew*, UPI (Oct. 19, 1990).
11. 413 U.S. 15, 24 (1973).
12. *2 Live Crew*, UPI (Oct. 19, 1990).
13. 739 F. Supp. 578, 589 (S.D. Fla. 1990).
14. Will, *supra* note 8.
15. R. Wright, Native Son (1966).
16. Will, *supra* note 8.
17. *An Album Is Judged Obscene; Rap: Slick, Violent, Nasty, and Maybe Helpful*, N.Y. Times, June 17, 1990, at 1.

Chapter 14

Eva Feder Kittay

Woman as Metaphor[1]

Women's activities and women's relation to man persistently are used as metaphors for men's activities and projects. In these metaphors, man mediates his engagement with the world through a representation of it as Woman and metaphorically transposes this relation to Woman on to his relation to the world. Many of these metaphors are transcultural and transhistorical. Man speaks of conquering the mountain as he would woman, of raping the land, of his plow penetrating a female earth in order that he may sow his seed therein. He symbolically mimics a woman's birthgiving in initiation rites when man gives birth to man, concretizing metaphors into ritualistic enactments.[2] And he uses exclusively female activities as metaphors to help him structure his own relations to his exclusively male enterprises.

Plato uses the midwife and the female domain of procreation as metaphor for intellectual activity which, within the setting of fifth-century Athens, is virtually an exclusively male domain.[3] Rilke speaks of "the thought of being creator, of procreating, of making," as "nothing without the thousandfold concordance of things and animals—and enjoyment of it is so indescribably beautiful and rich only because it is full of inherited memories of the conceiving and the bearing of millions" (Rilke 1934). Nietzsche, situates—however problematically—in the male domain of philosophy, opens *Beyond Good and Evil* with the invitation to suppose that truth is woman. Contrariwise (or perhaps given Nietzsche's ironical stance, contrapuntally) the arts of deception are spoken of as Woman. Locke, eloquently deriding eloquence, writes: "Eloquence, like the fair sex, has too prevailing beauties in it to suffer itself ever to be spoken against. And it is vain to find fault with those arts of deceiving wherein men find pleasure to be deceived." (Locke 1689)

Images of sexual conquest, particularly since the seventeenth century, are regularly used to describe the relation of the male scientist who investigates a female Nature, Mother Nature, penetrating her and forcing her to yield up her secrets. Or man speaks gently of the earth as his mother and Nature as his nurse:

> Earth fills her lap with pleasures of her own;
> Yearnings she has in her own natural kind,
> And, even with something of a Mother's mind,
> And no unworthy aim,
> The homely nurse doth all she can
> To make her Foster-child, her Inmate Man,
> Forget the glories he hath known,
> And that imperial palace whence he came.
>
> Wordsworth (From *"Ode, Intimations of Immortality from Recollections of Early Childhood."*)

Man identifies that which he wants and desires, or has acquired or fears acquiring, as Woman. The earth, the sea, the hurricane, Truth, Freedom, Liberty, Sexuality are all called Woman, as is Death itself. These examples direct us to consider the importance of woman's metaphorization in the conceptual organization of man's experience.

The use of the vehicle of Woman to form man's conceptualization of the world and his relation to it is pervasive and goes unquestioned because Woman, both as Other and as Mother, occupies a position in men's lives that both reflects the structure of metaphorical thought and mirrors the role of metaphor in language and thought. To the extent that the structuring of our conceptualizations depends on the use of metaphor (see Lakoff and Johnson 1980; Kittay 1987), to that extent we can expect that the articulation of men's experiences, in large measure, will be modeled on their relationship to women.

Let me suggest how there is a congruence between man's relation to women and the structure of metaphorical language. Simone de Beauvoir argues convincingly that woman is Other for man: man regards himself as the norm against which woman is postulated as Other. Alterity is itself a crucial requirement for metaphor. A minimal, but essential requirement for metaphor is that its topic and its vehicle come from two distinct conceptual domains, that is, the vehicle must be Other with regard to the topic. Consider, for example, the difficulty of using "knife" metaphorically for "fork" when both are used as they come from the one domain of eating utensils; or consider using "apple" for "pear" where both come from the domain of common fruit.

Women and metaphors alike are at once mediational and relational. As Other, woman serves to mediate between man and man, man and Nature, man and spirit. In metaphor the domain of the vehicle mediates between that which is not well known, or that about which we want to learn more, and what is familiar or ready to hand. That is, metaphors mediate between an assimilated (or rather relatively assimilated) conceptual domain and a distinct and separate domain which needs to be newly assimilated or reconceptualized. My claim, then, is that as women are the Other, mediating for men between one stage of life and the next, between the familiar and the new, so Woman serves symbolically, through metaphor, to mediate man's conceptualizations between himself and those alterities he must encounter.

Woman has served not only as other and as Mediator. Woman has been the fulcrum of relations, of those associations into which men enter—the life of a woman has traditionally been dominated by relations born to others. It is this role as the locus of human relations that makes possible woman's capacity as mediator. While women are the loci of sets of human relations, metaphors acquire meaning by exploiting semantic relations.

Metaphors accomplish their mediational cognitive function, the mediation between distinctive domains, through a *transference of semantic relations* (Kittay and Lehrer 1981; Kittay 1987). Metaphors are best understood if we regard the metaphorical transfer of meaning to be a transfer of the relations of contrast and affinity which pertain to the vehicle term on to the domain of the topic. For example, if I say of a tennis player that she is "hot" this game, "hot" is the vehicle, and its semantic field is the field of temperature terms; the domain of the topic is athletics. "Hot" and "cold" are graded antonyms in the temperature field; when transferred to athletics, a "hot" player is one who plays well and scores while a "cold" player does not. The antonymy of the pair is preserved. Moreover, if a player scores only moderately well mid-game, we can say "she was lukewarm in the third quarter." Since "hot" and "cold" are not absolute but graded antonyms, we can capture all sorts of performances in between, and even on the outer extremes, e.g., "Her performance on the court today is sizzling." In this way metaphor can, through a relational transposition, structure an as yet unstructured conceptual domain, thereby altering, sometimes transiently, sometimes permanently, our ways of regarding our world.

To the extent that man uses Woman as metaphor he has a conceptual domain available that is already schematized by proximate and familiar relations that can be transferred to make intelligible more distant and obscure conceptual and experiential domains. Woman provides man with a set of richly articulated domains by which he can conceptualize even his earliest mediations between himself and his self, his fellows and his world.

The congruence of the structural features of metaphor and the structural features of man's relations to woman makes the metaphorical use of Woman a central feature in man's conceptualization of his cosmos—some central, that were men's relations to women to change, men will need to abandon conceptualizations even of parts of their experience which appear to have little to do with their relations with women. The study of the persistent use of woman's domain as the vehicle, where the domain of man is the topic, is then a philosophical investigation, spurred by feminist theorizing, into the nature and source of some of our most significant conceptions.

I. THE "OTHER" AND GENDER THEORY

Woman As "Other"

If the structure of metaphor is such that the vehicle and the topic must come from two distinct domains, the Simone de Beauvoir's understanding of women's secondary status already provides motivation for the metaphoric use of women. For Beauvoir contended that women's inferior status was rooted in man's conception of woman as Other.[4] If woman is Other, then she is always available as the vehicle for the self-conception and activities of man, the subject, the topic.

Following a Hegelian metaphysics, Beauvoir claimed that "Other" was a basic category of human thought. As the subject sets itself up as the essential one, it does so in opposition to an other: "The subject can be posed, only in being opposed" (Beauvoir 1952, xvii). But if otherness is a fundamental category of human thought, necessary to the very formation of self-consciousness, women too should set themselves up as the essential Subject in opposition to another self which they posit as Other. Women's positing men as Other would then generate metaphors in which men were the vehicles for the self-conceptions and activities of women. Indeed, within the Hegelian dialectic the claim of the other consciousness cannot long be ignored, and one must acknowledge the reciprocal claim on the part of the other. When that consciousness which has been posed as the Other sets itself up as the One, it then poses the first consciousness as the Other.[5] And yet man's relation to woman differs from his relations to the other self-conscious beings, i.e., men, in that this otherness is not reciprocal. Women have not similarly asserted their own essentiality and posited the otherness of man. And the dearth of metaphors where man serves as the vehicle for the topic, woman, attests to this lack of reciprocity.

Beauvoir was herself unable to explain the lack of reciprocity. As she noted, other groups, notably minorities or colonized peoples, have lacked the full reciprocity of Otherness for extended periods, but have in time asserted their subjectivity and posited their oppressors as other. Only in the case of women has the lack of reciprocity seemed so material and so inexorable. Neither the apparent lack of historical contingency nor the apparent "primordial *Mitsein*" of the sexes explains this lack of reciprocity. "In truth," she writes, "the nature of things is no more immutable given, once for all, than historical reality. If woman seems to be the inessential which never becomes the essential, it is because she herself fails to bring about this change" (Beauvoir 1952, xviii). This suggests that in the end we are forced to attribute woman's continued otherness to her own complicity with her oppressors. It is a complicity which Beauvoir analyzes as arising from woman's exclusion from production and her historic enslavement to reproduction—a condition over which she has had little control—as well as men's resistance to her assumption of the status of subject.[6] But it is also a complicity that comes from a "temptation to forego liberty and become a thing," a temptation which coexists in the person along with the "ethical urge" towards transcendence.

But if this is so, how did women come to assume the position of dependency, of otherness in the first place? Why should women have been permitted themselves to be excluded from production? And why should women's role in reproduction have doomed her to otherness and subordination rather than ascendancy and power? Why, in the final analysis, should women and not men have yielded to "the temptation to forego liberty?" Without retreating to that essentialism, be it biological or metaphysical, that Beauvoir so significantly repudiated when she declared that woman was not born but made, we are left without a fully satisfactory answer to the question Beauvoir poses: Why is otherness not reciprocally posited by woman?

I suggest that with the arrival of current gender theory we have an explanation that can help resolve our perplexity. Gender theory has provided a justification for claiming that the category of Otherness is not as essential to the self of a woman as it is for a man. Once we understand the source of the asymmetry of otherness, we will also understand why woman serves as metaphor for men, and why man does not perform a similar service for women. Furthermore, this justification explains why woman, in particular, has functioned as a mediation and predicts the sort of relations we can expect when we examine metaphors in which woman is the vehicle. We shall see exactly how Nancy Chodorow's (1978) psychological tale of the formation of the self illumines Beauvoir's question and consequently frames the investigation of Woman as Metaphor.

Chodorow and Gender Theory

Perhaps we first need to consider whether an empirically based study such as Chodorow's can have a bearing on the philosophical concept of the Other. I adopt the position that the most metaphysical concepts, apparent spinnings of ethereal webs *ex nihilo*, are, if *only* through metaphoric transpositions, grounded in experiential reality. Such experience in turn presents itself, in its particularity, through the articulation of concepts. In fact, the very thrust of this paper is to show, more or less specifically, how an entire series of such conceptualizations is grounded in men's experience of women as nurturers, an experience which itself reflects culturally defined conditions shaping the lives of both men and women.

Primary among the important psychological consequences of asymmetrical gender-differentiated relations between mother and child, consequences that result from the production of gender, is the fact that men establish their identity, their sense of self, in opposition to the mother, while daughters establish their sense of self through a continuing identity with the mother. If this thesis is correct, it explains why otherness is essential to the self-formation of men but not of women. For men the category of Other is crucial because men establish their relation both to themselves and to their world through an opposition to one whose otherness is marked not only by the limits of one's skin, but by the saliency of sexual and gender differences. Woman, in contradistinction, does not establish herself in *opposition* to one who is so fundamentally differentiated from herself. [7]

Chodorow argues that the young boy must repress his primary identification with his mother in order to develop his proper sexual identity, that is, more precisely, his gender. Foremost among the salient sexual differences which the young boy comes to perceive are the procreative ones. Therefore the boy comes to understand that because he is male, and his mother is female, he cannot reproduce in his experience the birthgiving which brought him into existence and which justifies the remarkable power that the mother holds over him (Kittay 1983).

Certainly, the young girl learns, as does the young boy, to distinguish herself from the mother, that the limits of her skin are not coincident with that of the woman who cares for her and has power over her. But as Chodorow's use of "object-relations" psychoanalytic theory allows her to demonstrate, the differentiation, the separation is never complete in the girl. And to Chodorow's analysis we can add that the young girl can maintain the identification in the knowledge that she can one day bear the same relationship to her children that the mother bears to her: her dependency on her mother and the power she thus grants her mother is the very power that she can look forward to having when she herself becomes a mother. For women, the category of Otherness never has the fundamental status and pervasive character it has for men, because women's own understanding of themselves and their affiliations is mediated through one who, insofar as she has the same gender identity, is not fundamentally Other.

In recasting Chodorow's object-relations psychoanalytic theory into the philosophical concept of alterity, we can say that for the boy and girl alike, the mother, as the first important Other, serves as the first mediation between the child and the child's sense of who s/he is—one's consciousness of oneself as a separate conscious being in a world with other separate conscious beings. She is simultaneously the mediator between the child and the world. But for the boy, his relations to himself, his relations to other persons, and his relations to the world about him are all first mediated by the Mother, as fundamentally and absolutely

Other, in her sexual (and perhaps particularly procreative) differentiation from the boy. The significance of the biological sexual difference attains its particular saliency by virtue of the cultural significance of gender (itself a cultural, not a biological concept) to identity itself. In order to establish his appropriate gender identity, he must establish himself both as separate and as distinct from her.

Before moving on, then, to apply these feminist analyses to metaphor, we see how Chodorow, in effect, explains why women have never reciprocally constituted man as Other. For women, Otherness need not have the oppositional and absolute character it has for men. For better and for worse, the self that women develop may well be more accommodating to Otherness. If gender theory is correct, then the key to women's liberation may not lie in the reciprocity of Otherness. Instead women will be liberated by creating new social conditions that will be alternatives to men's current conception of the relation between self and other. It may now be the historical moment for philosophers to rewrite Hegel's master-slave dialectic from the standpoint of the maternal consciousness which has been formed to accommodate the otherness of the child and which in turn develops that same accommodating otherness in the female child. This is a dialectic in which the self and other are such that the self comprehends itself not through an opposition, but through a connectedness, an emphatic bond with an other. This still-to-be-developed dialectic, together with other feminist efforts, may throw light both on the familiar limitation of women's dependency and lack of autonomy that emerge from the relative lack of separation and differentiation from the mother; but it will also illuminate the excessive valuation of autonomy and the undervaluation of mutuality that feminists have begun to identify.

These remarks are meant as a contribution to the efforts of feminists to see how far gender theory can tackle us in understanding the gender-based nature of out theoretical constructs. The utilization of this perspective to the question of Woman as metaphor is part of the exploration of the new terrain opened up by examining the consequences of woman's mothering.[8]

II. MOTHER/OTHER—WOMAN/METAPHOR

It is the initial positing of Mother as Other that makes Woman a particularly suitable vehicle to mediate later (re)definitions of oneself and one's connections to the world. Because man's first and most significant attempt to define himself and to establish his relationships arises out of his experience with a woman, women serve metaphorically to represent those activities and domains in which man will redefine himself and establish new associations in a world which expands for him as he matures and gains knowledge. This conceptual move is facilitated by the structure of metaphor itself. Because it is in the very structure of metaphor to exploit such relationships, woman's situation as Other is solidified through the metaphorization of these early experiences and their metaphorical transposition on to man's later life. Woman performing her role as Mother/Mediator is propitiously situated in man's life to become the metaphor which mediates between assimilated and as-yet-unassimilated experience in later life.

Furthermore, the very relations the Woman as Mother bears to her young son obtain the potential—through their saliency in the boy's mental representations of himself and his position in the world—to serve as the model for the various possible relations he will later need to establish between himself and his world. On many accounts of metaphor, models are elaborated and extended metaphors which have the possibility of greater conceptual stability than most metaphors. As such, the models of the relations of the man to his early mother figure become the source of many possible metaphors in which those relations are transferred to the domains occupied by man and his various projects. They will be relations which reflect the metaphoric transpositions of the ways in which the child views his relation to his mother given the gender differential, combined, we must add, with devaluation of the female gender.

They will be relations which reverse the power the mother has over the child, yielding metaphors of conquest and forced submission. Others will reflect the fact of man having been born of woman. These are the metaphors of man giving birth to himself, to his products, to other men (in initiation rites). They are metaphors of man giving life (Pygmalion), saving life, or—though a metaphorical reversal of death for life where woman is death or the victim to receive death—taking life. Still others will reflect man's dependency, with all the ambivalence such dependency evokes. These give us the ambivalence of metaphors of the good and nurturing Mother Earth and the "Earth Mother [who] engulfs the bones of her children" (Beauvoir 1952, 166), the glorification of women's sensual body and the devaluation of the bodily (Flesh as Woman), the life-giving yet fearsome powers of a female Sea, the welcoming and enveloping or suffocating and confining arms of the city as Woman.

And they will reflect the mediation of the Mother with the greater and more powerful forces of the Father (the Virgin Mary), the female incarnation of Justice, Liberty, Truth, Death; her mediation between the young boy and his future self, the female Muses who mediate between the poet and his art (men's brainchildren, born of the male creator mating with the female Muse); and her mediation with the social world, woman as keeper of the hearth, the feminine as the compassionate, empathetic, moralizing element, and woman herself as a metaphoric transaction binding together groups of men in the rites of marriage. (see Lévi-Strauss 1949). These latter mediations also have a negative side, as when the woman thought to bridge man not with the higher, but with the lower powers, aligning man with the forces of Evil: the witch copulating with the Devil is the symbolic incarnation of this metaphoric mediation. Images of woman "on top," of woman taking over, have metaphorically represented anarchy, the overturning of properly constituted power, as in Bruegel's painting of Mad Megg.[9]

The metaphorical image of woman has been used to represent man's emotional and irrational elements, his (sic) "darker side." Here woman mediates negatively between man and himself so that he can displace onto woman those components of his nature from which he wants to disassociate himself—just as he utilized the psychological mechanism of "splitting" his mother into a "good mother" and a "bad mother" (see Klein 1957), so he splits himself into a good self and an evil self and uses the "bad mother" as the one onto whom he can project his evil self, producing the metaphor of Woman as Evil, Irrational Witch.

The dark side of woman as mediator between man and other men, between man and his social world, has its representation in metaphors of Woman as Artifice, Woman as Deception, and the mythic representation of Helen, whose "mediation" between men was that of war and destruction, although ambivalent figure that she is, she was also the source of unity among Greeks: woman as she who binds men together is the positive mediation, while woman as she who causes discord among men is its negative side. The metaphoric use of women who belong to social groups thought to be Other is pertinent here. The Other Other has perhaps a unique role in mediating between man and women of his own social group—

especially in the context of sexual relations. The iconography of the black female servant in paintings with strong erotic content, e.g., Manet's *Olympia* or Daniel Rossetti's painting *The Beloved*, can be analyzed as an intensification of the erotic—itself paradigmatically Other—achieved by the sexualization of the woman who is doubly other.[10]

In regard to both its relational and mediational aspects, metaphor is the instrument, *par excellence*, for such relational transfers across distinct domains, where the metaphor mediates between such distinct domains. Man's metaphorization of his relations to women is thereby used to order man's subsequent relations to others and that which is Other.

The work of Evelyn Fox Keller (1984), Sandra Harding (1986), Carolyn Merchant (1980), and others strongly suggests that scientific developments are associated in some systematic way (the directionality of a causal link, if any, remains unclear) with changing metaphors regarding "gender politics," and the many forms and shifts in this politics of gender. Harding (1986, 115), speaking of the Renaissance and Elizabethan periods, writes:

> Thinkers of the period consistently perceived unruly, wild nature as rising up against man's attempt to control his fate. Machiavelli appealed to sexual metaphors in his proposition that the potential violence of fate could be mastered: "Fortune is a Woman and it is necessary if you wish to master her to conquer her by force; and it can be seen that she lets herself be overcome by the bold rather than by those who proceed coldly, and therefore like a woman, he is always a friend to the young because they are less cautious, fierce and master her with greater audacity."

The violent images recur in Bacon ([1623] 1870, 296):

> You have but to follow and as it were hound nature in her wanderings, and you will be able, when you like, to lead and drive her afterward to the same place again. . . . Neither ought a man to make scruple of entering and penetrating into those holes and corners, when the inquisition of truth is his whole object.

Harding (1986) maintains that the canons of science retain the *structure*, if not the content, of the metaphors because the contentful metaphors have proven so fruitful in empirical research.[11]

Mediations/Metaphors

A child emerging into personhood engages in many mediations that utilize Mother/Other. These become the source of future metaphoric mediations. Such a flow of mediation/metaphor has at least three distinctive tributaries. And in looking at the vast assortment of metaphors, it may be helpful to have a typology to guide us.

The developing child must mediate between its present self and its evolving self, between itself and its world (as object), and between itself and other subjects (its social world). In a world where the subject is thought of as male, these three mediations are reflected in three metaphor-types: (male)self/(male)self, (male)self/object world, (male)self/social world. The typology provides, at once, three ways in which women or women's activities are used to form metaphorical identifications based on women's role in a man's early life and which are the sources of potent metaphorical conceptualizations.

(Male)Self/(Male) Self. We have said that the mother first mediates between the young child and his sense of self. Attaining that sense of self comes through an increase in his activities and his growth. According to early child theorists, the child's early attainment of his sense of self proceeds through activities in which he identifies with his mother. In the self/self metaphors, we have man's later replication of precisely this relationship to his mother—again he mediates between a current self and a developing self by identifying with the active woman and through a mimetic relation, an imitation not of the actual activity but of the structure of that activity, man incorporates these activities into a newly articulated self-definition.

Here Woman is vehicle in the sense that some exclusively male activity is modeled on her activities, as in, for example, the midwife metaphor.[12] In this type of metaphor, man vis-à-vis his domain locates himself in a position homologous to that of the woman vis-à-vis her domain.[13] This results in a metaphoric identification of the man with a woman: Socrates in the domain of philosophy is a midwife. Notice that in the *Theaetetus* metaphor, Socrates points to one disanalogy which he takes to be critical, namely, that his job as a philosopher-teacher is far more important than the midwife's since he, unlike the midwife, must be able to discern true from false births.

Where man metaphorically identifies himself with a woman, we can almost always find an accompanying statement in which the man, at once, disassociates himself from the devaluation of the literal female activity by supervaluating his metaphorically identified male activity. When men of New Guinea structure their male initiation rites on the model of women's birthgiving, they make clear to all that their birthgiving is far superior to the birthgiving of women. And Rilke (1903) writes in the "Book of Hours:"

> Bestow on us man's real motherhood (not of the kind of woman's labor), install the he-man in his right as he who giveth birth; birth to Death—Messiah: fulfill his longings, for they are greater than the dream of the virgin giving birth to God.[14]

It is woman's agency within her own domain that is modeled by man when he seeks a representation for his own activity. But man's metaphoric identification with woman is combined with a supervaluation of man's activities and a metaphoric *appropriation* of the relevant relations which pertain in the female domain via a transposition of these relations onto an exclusively male domain.

(Male)Self/Object World. This metaphor type does not require the topic of the metaphor to be a domain of man's activities per se. It only requires the topic to be a domain which is Other for man. Here the relation of man to some alterity is mediated through a chosen relation (or set of relations) to Woman: not man but the alterity (which is the topic) is metaphorically identified with woman, and it is man who is the utterer of the metaphor. The alterity is just that otherness which man wants in some way to engage. Or else, it is the alterity he wants to mediate between himself as utterer and a force greater than himself. When an alterity is metaphorically identified as woman, and man relates to it as he would to a woman, the ensuing relation is generally modeled on the mother guiding her child in the child's interaction with the external world. The confidence, security, anger, and fear—all the ambivalences evoked by the move away from the dependency on the mother—is reflected in the metaphors in which another alterity is metaphorically named Woman. His attitudes and behavior toward the Other mimic his relations (or rather some chosen subset of

possible relations) to women. In a telling passage from the Prelude, Wordsworth, deriding "that false secondary power / By which we multiply distinctions," praises that association of the babe to its mother which instills in us a yearning to regain the wholeness of Being, the unity of ourselves and the world of Nature. The effort to reestablish unity is the creative urge of the poet. The babe, in his experience of oneness with his mother, is "the first / Poetic spirit of our human life" (Prelude, bk 2, lines 216–17, 260–61).

The ambivalence of the closeness and dependency that the young child experiences in regard to its mother becomes reflected in the contrary and contradictory nature of the images of those alterities identified as woman. Biblical images of the cities of Jerusalem and Babylon, for instance, exemplify both sides of the ambivalence. St. Paul in the Epistle to the Galatians speaks of that "Jerusalem which now is, and is in bondage with her children," and of that "Jerusalem which is above which is free, which is the mother of us all" (Gal. 4: 25). The city of Babylon is simply "the great whore."

(Male)Self/(Male)Social World. In this metaphor-type, the woman herself, not a mere representation, linguistic or otherwise, becomes the metaphoric vehicle. The metaphoric identification is between woman and that value which *woman signifies* but which *man possesses.* Possession of such value places him in an interactive relation with other men. This metaphor is based on the mediative role of the mother to the child as she integrates the child to the social order, which under patriarchy is the world of the Father. To a large extent, the value the mother takes on is both value that the child attaches to her and which other, grown men (the father) attach to her. It is the shift in her value from protector, nurturer, omnipotent figure to her value as erotic object.

Once she loses her omnipotence (becomes viewed as a castrate in Freudian idiom) and is seen to be valued by others for her erotic qualities, she can be exchanged for another erotic object. It is an exchange which binds men together. The Oedipal complex can itself be viewed as such a metaphoric exchange. The boy gives up the Mother as a love object—gives her over to the Father—in exchange for the father's social identity in and through the superego. This is also how to understand Lévi-Strauss's explanation of the primordial and universal character of the incest taboo: that "in human society a man must obtain a woman from another man who gives him a daughter or a sister" (Lévi-Strauss 1967, 44). Through the exchange of women, men establish social circles of interaction with men not from the same maternal line. In this exchange, actual women function as *signifiers* whose value comes from their mediating role in the interaction between men.

Within social structures where kinship plays a less critical role in establishing social relations, woman is still the metaphoric vehicle for the value controlled by a man, value through which he establishes his position in the social order. Thus the "possession" of a Beautiful Woman takes on the metaphoric role of signifying the greater virility (or money or power) of the man "possessing" her. Similar signification is given to a woman's clothing, jewels, leisure, or today, perhaps, to her professional achievement. We have already cited the destructive (although ambivalent) character of such mediation in the figure of Helen. To this we need to add the rape of women in wartime, which is as much a symbolic act as an actual assault. Woman as the metaphor, the mediation of one social group of men and another, is precisely the vehicle for expression of the domination of one group over the other. If the sexual exchange of women marks the bond between men, the victor's sexual "expropriation" solidifies a conquest.[15]

Within patriarchy, those men who possess value do not signify value. Men who do not possess value but who are productive, e.g. slaves and laborers, do signify value; however, the signification is literal, not metaphorical. In social and metaphorical orders where women are actively engaged in "productive" labor, they too signify literal rather than symbolic or metaphorical value—that is, they exemplify the value they produce for others. But it is that which neither possesses value of itself, nor is engaged in "productive" labor (labor productive of value), which is best suited as the metaphorical vehicle for value. It is reasonable to conjecture that the less she is engaged in utility and needed productive labor, the more geared to leisure and luxury, the more she is capable of being metaphorically identified with the value which belongs to man.

Yet women who are productive will still take on a metaphoric import, but it is not the positive value accorded to the women of leisure; it is rather negative value which is accorded to the Witch, the Whore, the Temptress. It is not only productive women who acquire a negative valence, but also, especially in hierarchical and racist societies, those women who are the Other Other. The Other Other is a woman who, like the mother, is female but, unlike the mother, comes from some group already marked by salient differences—differences conceptualized as threatening or desirable, as imbuing its bearers with power or rendering them vulnerable prey. Sexual transgressions along the lines of class and race invite danger, excitement, even disaster, but also allow men who are regarded as Other to deny their alterity (e.g., the sailor in *Swept Away* [see n. 15]; also see Cleaver 1967), and allow men who are the One to affirm their mastery or assert their sexuality—especially where upper class males are conceptualized as effete or as lacking a robust sexuality (e.g., the Cary Grant figure in *I'm No Angel* [see n. 16]). The Other Other, the dark woman, the Jewess, the working-class woman, is sexualized—she is conceptualized as unusually voluptuous or yielding, or as perversely or exaggeratedly sexual.

The Other Other may be regarded as mediating between man and other men of his own class and race, but also between himself and his sexual relations with women of his own group or between himself and his ambivalence toward his own sexuality. The ambivalence toward sexuality in Western cultures is mirrored in the contradictory images of the diseased or perverse or bestial sexuality of the Negress, the Hottentot, the Jewess, or the prostitute; and the sexually stimulating, the desirable, the irresistible Negress, Jewess, prostitute; or the sexually accommodating, pliant, self-effacing Asian woman (see Gilman 1985).[16]

Gilman (1985, 122–3) writes, "All the world is the womb, according to Lawrence, Miller and Durrell, but the black womb is quite different" and cites a remarkable passage from Durrell in *The Black Book* (1973, 123), which features a black English student, Miss Smith:

> The creeds and mores of a continent, clothed in an iridescent tunic of oil. I turn always to those rivers running between the black thighs for ever and for ever. A cathartic Zambesi which never freezes over, fighting its way through, but flowing as chastely as if it were clothed in an iridescent tunic of oil. I turn always to those exquisite horrors, the mutilations and deformations, which cobble the history of the dark continent in little ulcers of madness. Strange streaks here and there you will find: hair trigger insanities barely showing, like flaws in ice, but running in a steady, heavy river, the endless tributary of sex . . . All this lives in the wool of Miss Smith, plainly visible, but dying.

As a mediator between a man and his own social class, the Other Other is generally destructive of the social order. In the same novel, Durrell speaks of the black woman: "The strange stream of sex which beats in the heavy arteries, faster and faster, until the world is shaken to pieces about one's ears, and you are left with an indeterminate vision of the warm African fissure, opened . . . to swallow all the white races and their enervate creeds, their arks, their olive branches."

The Witch, generally a peasant woman, is thought to derive her powers by her intercourse with the Devil. In this she mediates between men and the Devil—the father who would destroy the order among men given by God, the Father. The Whore, the working-class woman who sells herself rather than her labor, is the communal repository of men's lust, that is, of those men who can pay for her. Within the hypocritical morality of those societies which support prostitution while condemning it, the Whore is at once destructive of the social order of marriage and supportive of an order in which the upper-class women, desexualized, are kept "pure" of all utility, including the rendering of sexual services.[17]

The Temptress, again generally a woman of the "lower classes" (the Siren, the Golddigger, the Actress), both distracts men from obligations within the social order and tempts them to take a woman from outside his appropriate class. Given that marriage is a social and economic bond between men who exchange their daughters and sisters, the temptress succeeds in marrying the man and thus displacing a woman from the appropriate group; she disrupts the prevailing exchange of value among men and diverts wealth away from the class of men with whom "her catch" has a bond, and amongst whose heirs the wealth is supposed to be distributed. In the film *I'm No Angel*, Mae West, the irresistible seductive showgirl, triumphs over the blue blooded family of heir, Cary Grant, who inadvertently has fallen under her spell. As she winningly counters their assaults on her chastity and morality, love and Mae West win the day; thus playing out the scenario in accordance with Hollywood's version of romance, virtue and democratic opportunity.

In a counterpart to this Hollywood fantasy, the negative value of the Temptress is converted to positive currency when the man of wealth turns the temptress into his mistress (or turns a former prostitute into a kept woman, e.g., Camille). In supporting her in addition to his legitimate wife, he obtains still another sign of his worth.

Otherness for the Woman as Subject

The category of Otherness is not without significance for woman as well. She too must establish her sense of separateness from her mother and from the world in which she exists. But women do not posit men as Other in establishing their own sense of identity. For women, the first Other is not a sexual opposite in a world where, as we have said, sexual difference is fundamental to identity. Of the three kinds of metaphor, we see that the self/self metaphor has limited applicability to the female subject. She *can* posit the mother's domain of activity for activities which are literally nonmotherly. After all, she too develops a sense of self in relation, if not in fundamental opposition to the mother. She can speak of "giving birth to herself," for example. But what we do not seem to find is a similar genre of metaphors in which domains of exclusively male activities are utilized as vehicles for exclusively female activities.

Women can also posit some alterity as Woman (the self/object world metaphor)—the Earth is Mother to women as much as it is to men. However, the opposition, the alterity is not so fundamental. It involves at once an identification between the speaker and the metaphoric vehicle, resulting in a metaphor with a very different configuration than the same metaphor uttered by man. For again, in the case of the young girl, as in the case of the young boy, it is the mother who mediates between the girl and the world she encounters. The father, to some small extent, may play a mediating role in relation to the exterior world in such a way that his relation can be metaphorically exploited. We have the use of the male vehicle of the Shepherd as Protector, the Spiritual Guide, etc. for men and women alike.[18] But such male vehicles for activities and alterities which women engage in (usually along with, rather than instead of, men) do not predominate.

It is difficult to ascertain the extent to which women use actual women (the self/social world metaphor) to mediate metaphorically between themselves and their social sphere. If Chodorow and object relations theorists are right, women never fully renounce the mother as a love object. Instead, the father is simply added as another love object. In their erotic attachments to men, there is often an affective relation to another woman. Does this "other woman" perform a metaphoric function comparable to the metaphoric function women perform for men? Or does the man have a metaphoric value in the association of the two women? However we describe the psychological reality, there appear to be few resonances comparable to the mediation women provide for men in either actual or symbolic social structures. An anthropologist, for example, would be hard pressed to reinterpret incest taboos and kinship structures so that marriages could be viewed as an exchange among women of men: in our own culture, it is the father who gives the bride away, not the mother who gives away the groom.

Women who mother mediate literally for infant males and females alike. But while women become metaphoric mediators for adult men, men rarely play this metaphoric role for women. Instead, for the adult woman, her place in the world, even her identity is *literally* mediated by her relationship to a man. Women will speak metaphorically of their "battle scars" using the male domain of war for the actual scars left from childbirth or the psychological (and metaphorical) scars left by life's hardships. When puerperal fever took the lives of so many women, one might have said that the lying-in chambers of the hospital were women's "gory battlefields." But while we speak of men giving birth to new ideas, to works of art, etc., childrearing is not spoken of as "inseminating" the child with the values of society. Metaphors in which women's activities are the topic and men's activities the vehicle, or in which the man is the Other, or in which actual men metaphorically are identified with the power or value which inheres in the woman and through which woman relates to the social world of women, are all less frequent and less likely—and certainly constitute an insignificant number of standard metaphors within our language.

The metaphor of Woman is, nonetheless, both accessible and understandable to women—and yet problematic. For in order to comprehend the metaphor a woman must see herself at once as the Other—in the vehicle—and as the One, occupying man's position in the topic of the metaphor. Woman, insofar as she shares man's relation to the Mother/Other, is capable of comprehending the metaphor from the position of the topic (man's world) but insofar as she identifies with Mother/Woman she finds herself as the Other and the vehicle rather than the subject who can utter the metaphor.

Insofar as metaphor, on my account, requires that the domain represented by the vehicle be distinct from the one represented by the topic, the use of Woman as metaphor for the activities that are generally regarded as limited to man solidifies as well as reflects the alterity of woman. And the shifts in relationships man establishes to various alterities echo back to those he experiences with women. This leads to the following hypothesis: where woman and her domains are employed as a metaphor for some other human enterprise, the latter is viewed as belonging exclusively to man. Where she is thought to be an equal citizen in the latter domain, she would cease to serve as a metaphor.[19]

To pursue this admittedly speculative line, consider the Socratic midwife metaphor once more. The metaphor plays on the relation between creation and procreation and the field to which these notions belong. The conceptual fields generated result in the identification of female creation as corporeal and male creation as mental or spiritual—an identification which makes of woman the vehicle for intellectual creativity, and at once excludes her as a participant in that cerebral creativity. The transference in this metaphor is one from the field of the physical, palpable reality of corporeal birth—as accomplished by women—to the field of mental activity, and by a simultaneous transference of the antonymous relation of male and female to the *male sphere* of intellectual activity. Since one thing is always a metaphor for something other than itself, a woman's pro-creativity could only be a metaphor for a man's creativity. Unfortunately, woman has served in our intellectual *his*/story, as a symbol of or as a metaphor for, but not as an actor in the life of the mental and spiritual. Once she becomes a full participant, will she still serve as a metaphor?

As woman becomes a participant, and if the progress toward that end proceeds without significant regressions, she will slowly cease to serve as metaphor. Once her entire participation is secure, though, the metaphor of woman's procreativity for intellectual creativity may reenter the language, but with a different resonance. For woman's intellectual creativity, which she would now share with men, would be recognized as distinct from her unique role in birthgiving. When these two capacities are no longer in danger of being conflated and her role as the creator of ideas, poems, paintings, etc., is not in danger of being abrogated, then the one function can again be metaphor for the other.

This speculation is based on the observation that in a period of transition, when old roles and assumptions are questioned and new ones are still unformulated, but in which the direction of the new order is set forth, metaphor is often too threatening to the establishment of the new order. Either it incorporates regressive assumptions (as in the case of woman as metaphor *only*) or because it is too radical in already using assumptions of the new order as a basis for building new incongruities. Metaphors, curiously, while crucially important conceptual tools for bringing about conceptual change, need a stable order for their meaningful formulation as metaphor.

A final observation with regard to the birth metaphor. As women are more fully engaged in intellectual life while still fulfilling their procreative function, we may find more metaphors in which former exclusively male activities are the vehicles for childbirth. A woman who is a musician may speak of the "symphonic climax of the head emerging," or the female philosopher may ponder the metaphysical perplexities of embodying two separate beings while having only a single consciousness, employing figures from philosophy to help her illumine the situation of pregnancy.

CONCLUSION

If the claims put forward here are valid and the speculative hypotheses prove true, there would be profound consequences for man's conceptual organization were women to cease functioning as man's "double and mediator" (Beauvoir 1952, 687). This condition, if the claims of gender theorists are correct, will come about only if women no longer serve as the sole nurturers of young children. Add to this the claims of Lakoff and Johnson (1980) and others that our conceptual system is substantially metaphoric, structuring (and being structured by) our language, our experience, and our actions. Then we see how an investigation of Woman as metaphor and its dependence on the early mother-child relation (in which the mother is Other for the boy) will reveal that much of the conceptual and experiential organization of men's lives depends on retaining the Otherness of Woman—i.e., her potential as metaphor.

Little has been done to analyze how a general image such as Woman contributes to and operates in the conceptualizations articulated by a culture.[20] Indeed, generally metaphor is far too context-bound to yield interesting results on such a scale. Lakoff and Johnson deal broadly with a number of metaphors which they take to be key metaphors within the conceptual system of contemporary Western man, e.g. "time is money," "up is good," etc., but they do not consider the metaphors utilizing women such as "nature (or earth or body or the irrational) is a woman," "intellectual creativity (or artistic activity) is giving birth," "becoming a man (or gaining knowledge—coming into the light) is emerging from the womb (or being born anew)," etc. Certainly, literary studies and some anthropological work have dealt more specifically with the use of woman as some particular vehicle in particular metaphors. We need more general studies of the underlying metaphors employing woman as vehicle. And we need studies directed at cultural differences in the symbolic use of Woman, as well as differences in the metaphors generated by the use of women from various social classes or racial groups. Here I have been less concerned with the specific content of the metaphors of Woman than in claiming that the structure of metaphor and the structure of relations between men and Mother/Woman as Other contribute to the conceptual importance of the metaphorization of Woman.

NOTES

This paper was read at the City University of New York Women in Philosophy Colloquium at the Graduate School of the City of New York and at the World Congress of Philosophy, Montreal, August 1983. I want to thank the members of both audiences for their useful comments. I also want to thank the graduate students of Society for Women in Philosophy, Stony Brook, State University of New York, especially Janice McLane, for their remarks and suggestions. The paper has further profited from the comments of Diana Meyers, Edward Casey, Elfie Raymond, Margaret Simons, and the two anonymous reviewers for *Hypatia*.

1. There is an ambiguity in the title due to a feature of metaphor first brought to light by I. A. Richards (1936). There are metaphors in which women are metaphorically described and there are metaphors in which women are used to metaphorically describe something else. Richards introduced the view that the meaning of metaphor emerges from an interaction of the *subject*, or *topic* of the metaphor, that which is represented by the metaphor, and the *vehicle*, the representation used to speak of the subject. When a woman's beauty is represented as a flower, fruit or some other delight of nature, we say Woman is the *topic* and Nature the metaphor's *vehicle*. While the vehicle offers a perspective through which we view and understand the topic, the choice of the vehicle itself can reveal much about the way in which the topic is conceived.

Simone de Beauvoir's superb chapters from *The Second Sex*, "Dreams, Fears and Idols" and "Myth and Reality," display the numerous and contrary vehicles that metaphorically speak of woman. Beauvoir concludes that woman is a cipher, an Other onto which man can project all his "dreams, fears and idols." Woman is thus metaphorically represented by whatever alterity man seeks to engage, and so becomes myth rather than subject. On the other side of the ambiguity we find that she can also be used to represent the alterity. Beauvoir's focus is on metaphoric and mythic representations of women, although she points to many examples where woman serves as a metaphor for some other alterity. It is in this latter sense that I want to look at woman as metaphor.

2. See Mead (1949); Bettelheim (1954); Kittay (1983).
3. Plato, at the same time, was among the few men within philosophy to challenge that exclusivity, though interestingly enough, not in the same dialogues in which he utilizes the vehicle of woman. In these dialogues, especially in the *Theaetetus* and the *Symposium*, the presumption is that the intellectual and creative sphere are the province of males—and this despite the fact that the wisdom concerning love is learned from a woman, Diotima. The ascent to the absolute form of Beauty is described for men only.
4. My reading of Beauvoir does not depend on an understanding of woman's Otherness as being the primary, that is the primordial, source of woman's oppression. Otherness is fundamentally a representational, not a causal notion and can well co-exist with a more materially grounded notion of the ultimate sources of women's oppression. Nonetheless the representation of a class or caste as Other serves to encapsulate for the oppressed, and in turn justify for the oppressor, the behaviors that constitute the oppression. As such the concept has not only representational but also causal force.
5. Ironically, within the Hegelian dialectic, self-consciousness is ultimately the achievement of the slave, one made possible by the slave's relation to his labor.
6. I thank Margaret Simons for reminding me of this aspect of Beauvoir's analysis.
7. Some feminists, e.g., Young (1983) challenge the universality of Chodorow's thesis, suggesting that because it relies on an analysis of gender formation within the nuclear family, the thesis cannot be generalized to situations where familial structures are different. And some feminists resist all attempts to fashion universalistic theories about women.

   I hold on to the view that the varieties of women's situation, of her oppressions, and her symbolization are not disjoint but can be encompassed in a theory that has within it the possibility of accounting for differences; a theory that sees, for example, different forms of oppression as transformations of one another that take their specific form in virtue of constraining and shaping conditions unique to each culture, race, and class. I take the theory that Chodorow gives us, especially when we consider *The Reproduction of Mothering* together with Chodorow's articles, e.g., "Mothering, Male Domination and Capitalism" (1979) to be such a theory.

   The universality of Chodorow's thesis lies not in its specific account of gender formation in the nuclear family, but in two theses: the universality of women's nurturance of very young children and the universality of women's subordination to men. Only if one seriously questions these must one question the possibility of an appropriate variation of a Chodorow-like account to accommodate differences in family structure.

   While few have contested the universality of women's mothering, some have posed serious challenges to the thesis of universal male domination, e.g., Allen (1986). It is still not clear how we should receive accounts of genuine gynocentric societies. On the one hand, they evince data, apparently ignored by male, white anthropologists, of institutions granting women considerable power, even an egalitarian status. On the other hand, the claim is made that these egalitarian features were destroyed in large measure by colonialism and imperialism. The societies studied by anthropologists, significantly adulterated and infected with the patriarchalism of the colonial powers, lack the strong and alive egalitarianism of former times. Those who speak of their native cultures as thus contaminated by white man's patriarchy, speak of the power of the native women still present in an attenuated form. But harkening back to a time and place when women were powerful in an unattenuated form, to a genuinely sexually egalitarian society, when the existence of such structures was based on artifacts, myths, folktales and various oral traditions, is not nearly as satisfactory as the direct evidence of a healthy vigorous, and *extant* sexually egalitarian society. For instance, in reading an account such as that of Paula Gunn Allen, one is genuinely impressed by her evidence and arguments that the women of the Laguna Pueblo exercised considerable power. But given that matters of war and peace and the external affairs of the society were in the hands of men, one wants to ask if the external and internal affairs were equally valued, or did the men hand over the internal affairs to women so that they would be left free to occupy themselves with what they may have taken as the more important external affairs? That is to say, before concluding that this was genuinely an egalitarian society, one wants to know much more.

Evidence may be mounting for a reversal of the thesis of universal male domination. To the extent that there is evidence for genuine, though historical instances of gynocentric societies, to that extent feminist theories will have to reconsider theories based on universal male domination and will have reason to glean visions of what a gynocentric society of the future might look like and what the preconditions for patriarchy are. Perhaps for now, both the thesis of universal male domination and its negation are conjectures; still, we have surer reasons for adopting the thesis. At the very least, we can say that the thesis, if not universal, is a true generalization. And a theory such as Chodorow's is generalizable to the extent that the generalization is true.

8. As Carol Gilligan's provocative book, *In a Different Voice* (1981) suggests, a self which regards itself as a self-in-relation rather than as autonomous develops distinctive ways of dealing with moral problems. According to Freud, a boy's oedipal complex is resolved by the castration complex, which, in turn, is completed by incorporating the father's authoritative morality into the boy's own self. As this feat is not possible for women—their castration complex precedes their oedipal stage—Freud claimed that women are incapable of forming a fully authoritative superego. With Chodorow and Gilligan, Freud's claim is turned on its head. We have here not a failing of women, but an excess on the part of men to compensate themselves for the repression of a former identification with their mothers. These views, though new and in need of further research and argument, are, for many, tantalizing and intuitively convincing (see Kittay and Meyers 1987). If this line of research is as productive as it now seems, we will have at hand a set of tools by which to begin a profound reexamination of our representation and study of human nature and enterprises.
9. I owe this observation to Linda Nochlin in a personal communication.
10. I recommend the discussion in Gilman (1985), especially part I, in which he not only draws our attention to the sexual iconography of the black female servant in European painting, but also discusses the sexualization of women who belong to nonwhite, non-Christian, or lower socioeconomic groups.
11. See Harding (1986), especially chapters 5 and 9 for a fuller discussion.
12. It is interesting to note that Socrates' mother was herself a midwife.
13. Today not only is it the case that the profession of philosopher is occasionally occupied by women, but the role of midwife has been largely usurped by male physicians. When we under-

stand the metaphor, we bracket those contemporary facts which we know to be at odds with the sexual differentiation of the two domains presupposed by the metaphor. Our comprehension is facilitated by the scarcity of women philosophers and the embedded feminine word in "midwife."

14. Note that one cannot understand "man" in the generic sense, since it becomes the anaphoric reference of "*he*-man."
15. I use the term "expropriation" rather than "theft" because wartime rape, rather than rape which occurs under the normalized circumstances of peace, often has an almost semi-official status. Men are rarely brought to trial for wartime rape, much less actually convicted and punished for such activities. It is often assumed to be the normal booty one is entitled to as victor.

    But as the sailor in Lina Wertmuller's movie *Swept Away* discovers to his dismay, the rape and conquest of a woman of the social class that constitutes his oppressors does not in and of itself a revolution make. When the sailor and the wife of his employer are swept off to a desert island, he lords over her as she had once lorded over him—and goes far beyond that in his sexual mastery of the woman who becomes his willing sexual slave. For the sailor the possession of his master's wife signifies that he is at least as much of a man, if not more, than his former employer and all the men of his ilk—men of the upper bourgeoisie. But this signification gets lost as soon as the couple leave their island and return to their former surrounding. The husband reclaims his wife, she her privileged existences as an upper bourgeois woman, and the sailor is again just another hired hand.
16. This sexualizing of the Other Other has a corollary in the sexualized and feminized images of the black man and the Jew in racist and anti-Semitic societies. The African man, pictured with a pendulous abdomen, was likened to the pregnant European woman. As such, his physiology was believed to be of a lower order than that of the European man. The Jewish male was characterized as having effeminate features and possessing feminine personality traits and, once again, placed lower on the scale of human development than the European male (Gilman 1985). One can understand the feminization of the male other as yet other use of woman (here the feminized traits) as an effort of the males belonging to the dominant groups to mediate their own relation to men who are distinctly Other. By imbuing them with feminine traits and identifying them with a feminized Other, the privileged men legitimize excluding other men from sexual access to women from the dominant social group.
17. We see here again how the Other Other mediates not only between a man and other men, but also between a man and the women of his class. This is perhaps paradigmatic of the way in which working-class women and women of color and, in the context of anti-Semitism, Jewish women have been used by the men of the dominant group to exclude the women of their own class from productive labor, from sexual fulfillment, and from forming genuine connections to all women. And it is also paradigmatic of the way in which women of the dominant class have been pitted against other women—so the former see the latter as more sexually available, desirable, useful, and so forth, while the latter see themselves as excluded from a womanhood exemplified by the former. The woman who is the Other Other bears the social cost that makes possible the rarified femininity of women of the upper classes. The metaphorization of the Other Other is one more obstacle to an inclusive feminist movement.
18. Rozemund Rosenberg called these to my attention.
19. This hypothesis is formulate for societies that are patriarchies and may be moving toward a more sexually egalitarian society. If there are, or have been genuine gynocentric societies that have never moved through an androcentric period, this hypothesis would not necessarily hold. For in

a truly gynocentric society the relation to the mother, for both male and female, must be importantly different, since the mother would not be a devalued Other. Patriarchies depend on the expropriation of the power of women—of her sexual and procreative powers (see Kittay 1983), a condition which, by definition, would not hold for a gynocracy. Gender identity formation for both men and women take place in the context of this expropriation and concomitant devaluation of women. The discussion which follows and which has predominated in this paper presumes, with Chodorow, that gender identity formation and women's subordination are intimately entwined, and that woman's mothering is the linchpin in the complex.

As Iris Young (1984) has pointed out, it is perfectly possible that gender identity formation is not necessarily tied to woman's subordination and that a society in which mothering is the work of women can also be a society in which women are not subordinated. Allen (1986) who argues that Laguna Pueblos have, or rather have had such a gynocracy (see n. 7), claims that American Indian culture generally is gynocentric. It is therefore worth examining the images of American Indian cultures and seeing whether we find the same metaphoric use of woman. A detailed study is beyond the confines of this paper. But two points are noteworthy.

First, the image of woman and Mother seems to be an especially salient one even in such a presumably egalitarian society. Allen writes:

> There is a spirit that pervades, that is capable of powerful song and radiant movement, and that moves in and out of the mind . . . Old Spider Woman is one name for this quintessential spirit, and Serpent Woman is another, Corn Woman is one aspect of her, and Earth Woman is another, what they together have made is called Creation, Earth, creatures, plants, and light.

She cites a portion of the Thought Woman story:

> In the beginning Tse che nako, Thought Woman finished everything, thought, and the names of all things. She finished everything, thoughts, and the names of all things. She finished also all the languages. And then our mothers, Uretsete and Naotsete said they would make names and they would make thoughts. Thus they said. Thus they did.

Furthermore, the Mother/Woman image is importantly mediational. For example, in speaking of the Corn Mother, Allen says that without her presence, "no ceremony can produce the power it is designed to create or release. The story of Abanaki, the First Woman, is even more clearly mediational. During a great famine she has her husband kill her so that her corpse should be transformed into a fertile field which would provide food for her children and their descendants" (Allen 1986, 13, 13, 17, 23).

But the second point to note is that nature of the symbolism in the context of Native American culture is importantly different from Western societies. Allen emphasizes that the symbols are statements of a perceived reality, not metaphors which stand for something else. Therefore it is not that the Earth, for example, is metaphorically conceptualized as woman, but it *is* a woman, from a certain point of view, just as Allen says "The color red, as used by the Lakota, doesn't stand for sacred or earth, but it is the quality of being, the color of it, when perceived 'in a sacred manner' or from the point of view of the earth itself" (1986). If this is how we are to understand the images of Woman in Native American cultures, then, perhaps Woman is neither Other, nor metaphor, in spite of her evident importance in the symbolic fabric of Native American life. In that case, the thesis of this paper—that it is by virtue of her Otherness that woman is a central metaphor in our conceptualization—is not challenged by the role of Woman in the symbolic structure of gynocentric societies. And the importance of woman's mediational role, which I have claimed derives from her position as mother, is evident in both modes of symbolization.

20. There is of course the notable exception of Beauvoir's two chapters cited above from *The Second Sex*. Also see Griffin (1978), Merchant (1980), Harding (1986), and Keller (1985) for useful analyses of scientific metaphors, and Gilman's (1985) analysis of the images of women from groups thought to be Other.

REFERENCES

Allen, Paula Gunn. 1987. *The Sacred Hoop*. Boston: Beacon Press.

Bacon, Francis. [1623]. *De Dignatate et Augmentis Scientiarum*. Vol. 4. Longman's Green. London: 1870. Cited by Merchant 1980, 168; and Harding 1986, 116.

Beauvoir, Simone de. 1952. *The Second Sex*. Trans. H.M. Parshley. New York: Alfred Knopf.

Bettleheim, Bruno. 1954. *Symbolic Wounds*. New York: Macmillan Press.

Chodorow, Nancy. 1978. *The Reproduction of Mothering*. Berkeley: University of California Press.

______. 1979. "Mothering, Male Dominance and Capitalism." In Zillah Eisenstein, ed. *Capitalist Patriarchy and the Case for Socialist Feminism*. New York: Monthly Review Press, 83–106.

Cleaver, Eldridge, 1967. *Soul on Ice*. New York: McGraw-Hill.

Dinnerstein, Dorothy. 1976. *The Mermaid and the Minotaur: Sexual Arrangements and the Human Malaise*. New York: Harper and Row.

Durrell, Lawrence. 1973. *The Black Book*. London: Farber and Farber. Cited in Gilman 1985, 123.

Gilligan, Carol. 1981. *In a Different Voice*. Cambridge: Harvard University Press.

Gilman, Sander. 1985. *Difference and Pathology: Stereotypes of Sexuality, Race and Madness*. Ithaca: Cornell University Press.

Griffin, Susan. 1978. *Woman and Nature: The Roaring inside Her*. New York: Harper and Row.

Harding, Sandra. 1986. *The Science Question in Feminism*. Ithaca: Cornell University Press.

Hegel, G.W. [1807]. *The Phenomenology of Mind*. Trans. by J.B. Baillie. New York: Harper and Row. 1967.

Keller, Evelyn Fox. 1985. *Reflections on Gender and Science*. New Haven: Yale University Press.

Kittay, Eva Feder. 1983. "Womb Envy as an Explanatory Concept." In Joyce Trebilcot, ed. *Mothering: Essays in Feminist Theory*. New Jersey: Littlefield and Adams, 94–129.

______. 1987. *Metaphor: Its Cognitive Force and Linguistic Structure*. Oxford: Oxford University Press.

Kittay, E.F., and A. Lehrer. 1981. "Semantic Fields and the Structure of Metaphor." *Studies in Language* 5, 31–64.

Kittay, E.F., and Diana T. Meyers. 1987. *Women and Moral Theory*. Totowa, New Jersey: Rowman and Littlefield.

Klein, Melanie. [1957]. "Envy and Gratitude." *Envy and Gratitude and Other Works: 1946–1963*. New York: Delacorte. 1975.

Lakoff, G., and Johnson, M. 1980. *Metaphors We Live By*. Chicago: University of Chicago Press.

______. [1963]. *Structural Anthropology*. New York: Anchor Books, 1967.

Lévi-Strauss, Claude. 1949. *Les Structures Elémentaires de la Parenté*, Paris.

______. 1967. *Structural Anthropology*. Garden City, NY: Anchor Books.

Locke, John. 1689. *An Essay on the Human Understanding*, bk. 3, ch. 10.

Machiavelli, Niccolo. [1531]. *The Prince and the Discourses*. Ch. 13, p. 64; ch. 25, pp. 91, 94. Modern Library. 1950. Cited by Merchant 1980, 130.

Mead, Margaret. 1949. *Male and Female*. New York: William Morrow and Company.

Merchant, Carolyn. 1980. *The Domination of Nature*. San Francisco: Harper and Row.

Plato. 1968. *The Theaetetus*. In *The Dialogues of Plato*. Trans. Jowett. London: Oxford University Press.

Richards, I.A. 1936. *The Philosophy of Rhetoric.* London: Oxford University Press.

Rilke, Rainer Maria. 1903. *The Book of Hours.* Cited and translated by Simenauer 1954, 242.

______. 1934. Letter of the 16th of July, 1903. *In Letters to a Young Poet.* Trans. M.D. Herder, 36–38. New York: Norton. Cited by Simenauer 1954, 239.

Simenauer, Erich, 1954. "Pregnancy Envy." In Rainer Maria Rilke, *The American Imago* 11. 235–48.

Young, Iris Marion. 1983. "Is Male Gender Identity the Cause of Male Domination?" in *Mothering,* ed. Joyce Trebilcot. Totowa, NJ: Rowman & Allanheld.

Maleness, Metaphor, and the "Crisis" of Reason

Many feminists have critiqued the "maleness" of reason, but it is not clear what the implications of this criticism are. Should feminists abandon reason and seek alternative modes of thought? Does it follow that women are less rational than men? Lloyd examines the way in which figuring reason as male operates in culture by taking up two issues: 1) the contrast between biological sex and gender and 2) the contrast between the literal and the figurative.

Lloyd questions the distinction between biological sex and the real mental processes of women and men, on the one hand, and gender and the social construction of feminine and masculine identities (individual gender) and masculine and feminine social positions (structural gender), on the other hand. This dichotomy is problematic, for it obscures symbolic gender—the operations of Man and Woman as symbols. Moreover, she takes issue with theorists who confuse the metaphorical exclusion of women from reason with a literal claim that women are not rational and should identify with an alternative, ostensibly feminine discursive position. Likewise, she questions Derrida's using Woman to symbolize multiplicity and *différance*, for these tropes reiterate and reinforce orthodox gender polarities. We can grasp the significance of symbolizing reason as male without endorsing the claim that a discursive excess or residue is female. Gender neutrality is not a tenable option either. Representing reason as gender-neutral depends on the opposition between masculinity and femininity, for Woman is used to symbolize gender opposition. Here, the maleness metaphor is invoked but concealed, and it retains its full power. Lloyd concludes by examining figurations of the mental in Descartes' texts. She argues that, although some of these figurations are extraneous theoretical ornamentation, others are constitutive of the philosophical content.

—D.T.M.

Chapter 15

Genevieve Lloyd

Maleness, Metaphor, and the "Crisis" of Reason

Umberto Eco, in a bemused discussion of the "crisis" of reason in his *Travels in Hyper-Reality,*[1] suggests that it is perhaps not so much reason as the notion of its "crisis" that is currently in critical condition. What exactly, he asks, is this crisis? If we feel all right, whose crisis is it? And can we clear it up? Should we be looking for a new instrument to replace reason—"feeling, delirium, poetry, mystical silence, a sardine can opener?" There is, of course, an obviously appropriate response to Eco's feigned perplexity. His facetious search for a new instrument mislocates the alleged crisis. The crisis concerns nor the reliability of instrumental reason but the privileged position it has assumed.

The current "rage against reason," as Richard Bernstein has called it, is directed not at its reliability as an instrument, but rather at the extent to which instrumental reason has come to dominate the traditionally rich and varied senses of the concept.[2] In Max Horkheimer's metaphor, in *The Eclipse of Reason,*[3] instrumental reason has eclipsed the richer dimensions of "objective" reason that traditionally expressed the ideal of a meaningful human life in a rational world. If the "fully enlightened" world is seen as radiating "disaster triumphant,"[4] it is because of what rationality has come to be in the modern world—because of the predominance of one form of reason. Such critics of reason are seeking not a new instrument but the recovery—less in forms appropriate to the modern world—of older ways of thinking of reason. Horkheimer's "objective" reason, grounding meaningful human lives, and Jurgen Habermas's "communicative" reason, articulated in the ideal of free, undistorted speech, are attempts to remedy the impoverishment of modern reason by shifting away from its preoccupations with instrumentality.

Eco's whimsical incredulity about the crisis does nonetheless carry a salutary message for feminists and for other contemporary ragers against reason. Some feminist dismissals of reason as male do seem to come perilously close to Eco's picture of a poignant search for a sardine can opener. The feminist critique of reason is centered on its alleged maleness, but it shares in the strengths and confusions of broader criticism of reason. And "maleness" can function in this context as a general term of disapprobation, encompassing all the negative features of post-Enlightenment reason. It should be no surprise that attempts by feminist philosophers to articulate the alleged maleness of reason evoke the same bemused responses as other articulations of the "crisis." What exactly, we may ask, is the maleness of reason, and what is supposed to follow from it? For whom is it a problem? What does it have to do with real men and women? Is the claim about reason itself or about ways in which past philosophers have talked of it? Is this maleness real or metaphorical? And, having discerned its presence in reason, what are women supposed to do? Stop reasoning? Look for another instrument?

For some feminists, accepting the maleness of reason involves trying to find or develop new female or feminine thought styles. Others have responded to these developments with dismay, seeing in them an insidious reinforcement of the old stereotypes of female irrationality. Eco's plea of clarity about what or who is in crisis is worth taking seriously, even if we think his interpretation of the issue is misguided. But, whereas Eco deplores "metaphoric irresponsibility" as exacerbating rather than illuminating the "crisis" of reason, I want to explore the issues of reason's alleged maleness not by rejecting metaphor but by trying to get a deeper understanding of how metaphor operates.

"MALE" AND "FEMALE" AS METAPHORS

The reflections on metaphor in this chapter have been stimulated by two kinds of critical response to my book *The Man of Reason: "Male" and "Female" in Western Philosophy* (London: Methuen, 1984). On the one hand, some feminist critics have suggested that the book's treatment of the maleness of reason slides between "sex" and "gender"—between claims about the mental processes of real men and women and the social construction of masculinity and femininity in Western culture. Another kind of criticism, mostly from nonfeminists, has suggested that the book slides between the metaphorical and the literal—that it mistakes for real features of reason what are in fact mere superficial accretions of metaphor in its philosophical articulation.

Both criticisms have their point. The book directly addressed neither the sex-gender distinction nor the distinction between the metaphoric and the literal. And it does contain slides within those distinctions. But I am not at all sure that they result from a failure to observe distinctions that are in themselves unproblematic. Both sets of distinction are unstable. And the claims of the book resist encapsulation as either sex or gender, literal or metaphorical. I doubt that all the offending slides in the book result from lack of care with well-established distinctions. They come, rather, from trying to articulate—perhaps with only limited success—perceptions that those distinctions themselves help to obscure.

The distinction between "biological" sex and "socially constructed" gender has undoubtedly been useful for understanding some aspects of sex difference, providing a way of conceptualizing the rejection of biological determinism and allowing the formulation of ideals of sexual equality. But what feminists have tried to articulate as the maleness of reason cannot be readily expressed as either sex or gender. Although it does have effects for real men and women, it certainly does not pertain to them as biologically sexed beings. Can it then be treated as a feature or product of social construction? In some trivial ways, yes. Forced to choose, we would locate it with gender. Women can, of course, participate in male reason. And part of what that means can be captured in the cumbersome platitude that persons who are biologically female can exhibit traits that are socially regarded as masculine. But there are aspects of the maleness of reason that are not captured in the idea of socially constructed masculinity. We are here dealing with the content of symbols. That, of course, belongs—if anything does—in the realm of the social. But this maleness, though it does have consequences for the social construction of gender, cannot be equated with socially produced masculinity.

Sandra Harding, in her discussion of gender in *The Science Question in Feminism*, has drawn some useful distinctions between "symbolic gender" on the one hand and "structural gender" on the other: the ways in which human activity and labor are divided by gender; and "individual gender" (that is, what counts as masculine or feminine identity and behavior).[5] My concern in this chapter is with what Harding calls "symbolic gender"—with the operations of male and female as symbols. These symbolic operations interact, of course, with gender division and with the social formation of gender identity. Masculine socialization influences which symbols male authors choose and how they operate with them. And those uses of symbols influence in turn the social formation of gender identity. But if we are to understand those interactions, there are aspects of the symbols that we must first separate from gender.

Despite their differences from biological sex, the concepts Harding calls "structural gender" and "individual gender" both apply directly to real men and women. The connections between symbolic gender and real men and women are more complex. The content of symbolic gender can be appropriated by men and women. But even though people can identify with symbolic maleness or femaleness, their proper subjects are not men and women but concepts. The maleness of reason belongs in this category of the symbolic. Equating it with gender can obscure just how different it is from the gender that has as its proper subjects real men and women, making it harder to grasp how it does interact with their biological or socially produced properties.

The distinction between sex and gender, important though it is in other contexts, can distract us from how "male" and "female" act as symbols, which is where our attention should be focused if we are to understand this aspect of reason. *The Man of Reason* was certainly concerned with male and female as symbolic content (metaphors); it was concerned with the literary dimensions of philosophical texts. This male and female symbolism is also the concern of much of contemporary French philosophy and feminist theory now being appropriated by English-speaking feminists. I suspect that the real import of this material—especially that inspired by Jacques Derrida—has been obscured by older and different concerns with sexual difference that have found expression through the sex-gender distinction.

Let me now turn to the idea of metaphor and the distinction between the literal and the metaphorical. The maleness of reason, which is sometimes, perhaps, taken all too literally by feminists, has also often been dismissed as "mere" metaphor, of no consequence for reason itself. What I want to resist in this is not the claim that the maleness of reason is metaphorical but the dismissiveness implicit in the qualification of "mereness." We can recognize this maleness as metaphorical without relegating it to the margins of truth. Like many other metaphors in the history of philosophy, this maleness is not a superficial accretion to the real being of reason. Those who talk of mere metaphor here imply that we can keep our received ideals of reason while cleaning up the offensive metaphors through which they have been articulated. But the problem goes deeper than this—not just because metaphors have their nonmetaphorical effects on our self-understanding, but also for reasons that pertain to the relations between reason and the metaphors that express it. Metaphors have their philosophical import as well as their cultural effects.

Evelyn Fox Keller has offered some illuminating accounts of the complex interactions between the metaphors of a culture and the social formation of gender, especially in relation to the collective consciousness of science.[6] My own concern is not with the processes by which social gender and symbolic gender interact but rather with getting a better understanding of symbolic maleness and symbolic femaleness independently of that interaction. This is something that can be masked by concern with the social formation of gender. It is illuminating to focus directly on it, although adequate understanding of sexual difference in relation to reason may involve bringing all the elements together again.

Contemporary French feminist theory, especially the work of Luce Irigaray, has helped bring these metaphorical dimensions of the male-female distinction into focus.[7] I want now to look at a discussion of Irigaray in a recent paper by Margaret Whitford: "Luce Irigaray's Critique of Rationality."[8] This interesting and enlightening treatment of Irigaray serves to highlight some aspects of the current use of her work that I think need close examination.

Whitford's reading focuses on Irigaray's strategy of appropriating the feminine position that has traditionally been created through a conceptualization of reason as male. Irigaray is presented as offering an alternative to what Whitford calls "exclusion" models of rationality (p. 111), although this alternative, Whitford says, is not to be understood as an "essentialist description of what women are really like," but rather as a "description of the female as she appears in, and is symbolized by, the Western cultural imaginary" (p. 114). In this respect, Whitford notes, Irigaray's work draws on that of Derrida. She uses deconstructive strategies to undermine the constraining power of male reason over its female opposites. So for Irigaray the problem is not so much that women are treated as incapable of reason as that the female has been assigned a particular function in symbolic processes. Whitford sums this process up as "to subtend them, to be that which is outside discourse" (p. 118). The female, Whitford says, is taken as representing "that original state of non-differentiation" from which distinctions and determinate identities emerge. This state outside discourse is traditionally conceptualized as female. Here, within Irigaray's "female imaginary," the laws of identity and noncontradiction do not apply. Whitford points out that all this may well sound dangerously irrationalist, but she stresses that Irigaray's point is not that *women* are irrational but that there is always a "residue" that exceeds determinate categories and that this excess has been conceptualized as female.

This description of how the female functions in Western symbolism brings out the contingency of symbolic processes and thus opens up space for questions about the relations between real women and symbolic Woman. The problem for real women, as Whitford sums it up, is that although they may be symbolized as the outside, they are not in fact outside society and its symbolic structures. We have here, she suggests, a "social imaginary"—a symbolic construction—that is taken to be real, with damaging consequences for women. Women, unlike men, find themselves homeless in the symbolic order (p. 121). What emerges from Whitford's reading of Irigaray is that sexual difference does not yet exist in the "social imaginary" of the West. Rather than being located within the operations of symbolism, sexual difference is aligned with the distinction between the symbolic and what lies outside its operation. Sexual difference symbolizes the distinction between the symbolic and what lies beyond it. Where, then, are women supposed to go from here? Symbolic meanings, Whitford stresses, cannot be altered by fiat. The symbolism cannot be simply reversed. Nor is it enough to insist that women are in fact rational, because that is not the point. The point is, rather, the relation of women to the symbolic structures that exclude them (p. 123).

There is much about Whitford's elaboration of the upshot of Irigaray's work that illuminates the operations of Woman as symbol. But I think clarification is needed of her presentation of the relations between women and symbolic Woman. Should the claim really be that women are excluded from the symbolic structures? Does this follow from the fact that Woman symbolically represents exclusion? Or has something gone awry with this application of deconstructive strategies to the understanding of women's relations to symbols? What does it mean to say that women are outside the symbolic structures? In one sense it is, of course, clearly true. It is not women but men who have created the symbolic structures we have inherited in the philosophical tradition. Men have conceptualized reason through Woman, symbolizing what is opposite to maleness and, to that extent, what is opposite to themselves as men. The symbolization of reason as male derives historically from the contingent fact that it was largely men—to the literal exclusion of women—who devised the symbolic structures. This is a symbolism appropriate to men as exclusive symbol users. If this were all that is involved in the claimed exclusion of women from the symbolic structures, it would be an uncontroversial point—and also a relatively uninteresting one. The more substantive claim concerns the ramifications of this past exclusion for women's current relations to the symbolic structures. And here the upshot of Irigary's use of deconstructive strategies is by no means straightforward.

Irigaray herself describes her strategy in terms of mimicry or "mimesis"—a conscious appropriation of the position outside symbolism in order from this vantage point to offer readings or interpretations of texts in the Western tradition. This is supposed to yield, in her own metaphor, a jamming of the theoretical machinery. The strategy, of course, cannot but be an ironic one—it is itself an operation with symbols. And the outsideness of the speaking position also has to be metaphorical. Women as symbol users are no more outside the operations of symbols than men, whatever may be the content of Woman as symbol. Irigaray, ironically, appropriates a position outside the symbolic structures in order, by speaking from it, to make visible the role played by the projected excluded other. It is the strategy for laying bare the operations of a text; it is often a very effective one. What concerns me is a nonironic version of this deconstructive strategy that seems evident in some English-speaking versions of that strategy—as if it were literally the unspoken but real feminine that is captured through deconstruction. To be assured that this feminine is not "essential" but rather a contingent product of the symbolic structures themselves does not remove my skepticism about this vein in contemporary feminist theory.

For Whitford, what Irigaray shows is that the conceptualization of rationality in Western thought involves the domination, repression, or transcending of the symbolic female. It is, she suggests, an "exclusion" model of rationality that reflects the way the "male imaginary" deals with sexual difference. And she sees Irigaray's strategies as pointing to a more adequate conceptualization of rationality, in which the male does not repress or split off from the "unconscious" female but acknowledges or integrates it (p. 125). This issue of the connections between the use of Woman as symbol and the understanding of sexual difference needs more discussion than it has received. It is undoubtedly true that the symbolic representation of Woman has influenced the formation of gender identity in Western culture. Sexual difference provided the symbolism. And the operations of the symbolism in turn affect the constitution of sexual difference. But if we are to understand those processes of interaction and influence between symbolism and the formation of gender identity, it is important, as I stressed earlier, to first understand the symbolic operations themselves. The connections between the content of Woman as symbol and the conceptualization of sexual difference—the understanding of what it is to be a man or a woman—are, I suggest, less immediate than Whitford's application of deconstructive strategies would have us think.

What exactly is being suggested in the claim that (real) women are "homeless" in the symbolic order of Western thought? Are they homeless *in* it or *beyond* it, where the content of Woman as symbol is projected? If the point is not that (real) women are excluded from (real) rationality, why should it be any more acceptable to claim that they are excluded from the symbolic order? What does the excluded feminine have to do with real women? The ironic exercise in miming, as a real woman, the speaking position to which Woman is relegated in the symbolic order can be a powerful reading strategy. But what is supposed to emerge for the understanding of (real) sexual difference?

Whitford rightly insists that Irigaray is not prescribing what the female should be; rather, she is describing how the female functions within the symbolic operations (p. 120); that the female imaginary is not the essential feminine common to all women but is, rather, a "place in the symbolic structures" (p. 124); and that Irigary's *mimesis* is a strategy rather than a solution (p. 123). These are all important acknowledgments. Clearly, symbolic Woman is not to be identified with an essential feminine. What concerns me, however, is a general lack of clarity about the status of this nonessential feminine. In claiming it as a new conceptualization of both reason and the feminine, are feminists perpetuating the link between sexual difference and the symbolization of reason that is the heart of the problem? Does this Irigarayan mode of criticizing the maleness of reason perpetuate a symbolic use of sexual difference that we would do better to part company with altogether?

DERRIDA AND DECONSTRUCTIVE STRATEGIES

It may help extricate us from these perplexities to focus more directly on some aspects of Derrida's deconstructive strategies that, as Whitford points out, underlie Irigaray's treatment of the symbolic dimensions of the male-female distinction and that have also had a more direct influence on contemporary feminist discussions of the maleness of reason. Susan Hekman, for example, in her discussion of Derrida in *Gender and Knowledge*,[9] presents his strategies for the displacement of traditional epistemological assumptions as providing a way of reconceptualizing the feminine in nondualistic terms. Here again my doubts about the exercise concern the swiftness of the move from understanding the operations of male and female as metaphors to the conceptualizing of sexual difference or the feminine.

Hekman makes the same important acknowledgment as Whitford: Deconstruction is not supposed to reveal an essential feminine. In Derrida's discussion, in *Spurs/Eperons*, of Nietzsche's commentary on woman, Hekman points out, Derrida makes it clear that in turning away from the "metaphysics of presence," he is explicitly embracing what the feminine has represented: qualities of multiplicity and ambiguity. But Derrida does not see this as endorsing a feminine essence. His concern is not with the elevation of a unitary feminine but with the replacement of the unitary with the multiple. What is supposed to emerge is not a feminist epistemology but a "structure that has been feminized in a metaphorical sense through a replacement of oppositions with multiplicity" (Hekman, p. 166). The content of the traditional symbolism of woman—multiplicity as against oneness, indeterminacy as against determination—is to be exploited to break open binary oppositions. Woman as metaphor is supposed to offer a revolutionary force, a disruptive potential by which the binary logic of Western thought can be replaced. Derrida, we are told, offers a constructive way forward from the sterile debates about difference and sameness—a new option, not abandoning difference, but conceptualizing it in a new way, in terms of multiplicities and pluralities rather than polarities (Hekman, p. 174). Masculine and feminine become not opposites but representations of multiple differences. The traditional metaphorical content of Woman is used to overthrow the polarities of the metaphysics of presence. But for Hekman, Derrida's positive appropriation of the metaphor is also supposed to open a "new discourse on women and sexuality," a discourse on multiplicity that "can and should be central to feminists' attempts to reconceptalize sexual difference." This is to be a discourse that "has no center, neither masculine nor feminine," but that still does not "erase" either the masculine or the feminine (Hekman, p. 175).

It may well seem that the multiplicity of the content of Woman as metaphor in this new "decentered" but nor "erased" understanding of the feminine has here reached the point of a literal, as distinct from metaphorical, contradiction. What exactly is the point supposed to be? If to affirm the content of Woman is to reject polarity in favor of multiplicity, is not that to say that the metaphor destroys itself? Why should we want to continue to affirm multiplicity—through the polarizing metaphor par excellence—as feminine? It is all very well to be told that this transformed metaphor of the feminine affirms multiplicity rather than opposition. But if multiplicity was always the content of the polarized Woman, what exactly is the content of this new, nonpolarized feminine?

The content of Woman as metaphor is, of course, closely associated with Derrida's general repudiation of what he calls the "metaphysics of presence"—the illusion of total presence of thought to object, of meaning to origin in thinking subject. Woman traditionally represents what cannot be contained or accommodated within determinate limits. It is not surprising, then, that for Derrida the metaphorical feminine should be associated with *différance*—the concept that is not a concept —through which he tries to unsettle the metaphysics of presence. *Différance* is supposed to belong neither to voice nor to writing—at any rate, not in the usual sense, which would see writing as transcription of the real bearer of meaning: self-present speech. Like Woman, *différance* connotes fluidity, endless deferral, which links it with the theme of strategy without finality. Here, Derrida says in "Differance,"[10] everything is strategic and adventurous. To talk of *différance* is to talk of what is not, of what is never present, of what is always deferred.

These connotations of endless strategy, constant deferral of meaning—blind tactics, wandering, play—can give Derrida's *différance* and the deconstructive strategies associated with it the appearance of a license to complete lack of restraint in textual interpretation, a self-indulgent free play of meanings. But it is for him part of a serious intellectual project, bringing out what lies behind the meaning of central texts in the philosophical tradition—understanding and intervening in what he sees as most irreducible about our era. It is not surprising, then, that Derrida's strategies should have been taken up by feminist philosophers. But the connections between deconstructive reading strategies and the positive evaluation of the content of Woman as metaphor are by no means clear. We are told that sexual difference should be nonexclusionary; that feminine fluidity and indeterminateness are not irrational excesses but rather values to be defended. But what justifies the move from use of the metaphor of Woman as a reading strategy to the affirmation of its content in the understanding of sexual difference? And can it be used in this way without perpetuating stereotypes of femininity? Should it be as "feminine" that fluidity or indeterminacy are extolled? And is the identification of such values as feminine perhaps itself an implicit departure from Derrida's insistence that *différance*, if it is seen as a strategy, is one without finality? Does this idea of the feminine admit of a fixed content that would allow it to be applied to the understanding of sexual difference any more than could be done with the associated notion of *différance?*

Such misgivings are no doubt supposed to be allayed by the constant insistence that this is a "nonessentialist" feminine. But the identification of it as feminine at all may put at risk what is most valuable for feminism in these Derridean insights. The repudiation of essentialism here can give a false security, masking perhaps a more elusive perpetuation of damaging sexual stereotypes. The linking of the symbolism of the male-female distinction with the understanding of rationality is a contingent feature of Western thought , the elusive but real effects of which are still with us. Does the feminist appropriation of the symbolic content of Woman risk perpetuating that contingent alignment? Might not deconstructive strategies be better employed exposing that contingent link—trying to understand its operations in order to break its grip?

Seeing the maleness of reason is part of coming to understand how the symbolic structures work, realizing that there are speaking positions that, though supposedly gender-neutral, in fact depend on the male-female opposition. There can be real discomfort for women in attempting to speak from those supposedly neutral positions that have been constituted by and for male thinking subjects for whom the oppositions came naturally. But what can appropriately be said in the diagnosis of the maleness of reason does not necessarily carry over into an appropriate response to the problem. We can gain the crucial insights into the maleness of reason without appropriating the residue or "excess" as female.

The metaphor of the feminine is supposed to direct us to fluidity—to the impossibility of fixing stable contents to meaning. It is supposed to make visible a variety of "subject positions." Feminists using this Derridean approach insist that the content of the feminine here is not an essence. But should it be seen as a fixed semantic content at all? Derrida's feminine lacks determinate content in the same way that *différance* lacks determinate content. It plays a role in getting us to see what underlies all determinate content and thus alerts us to the contingency of meaning. It is misleading, then, to apply it to the understanding of what it is to be feminine, even contingently. It is not clear that this indeterminacy can be appropriated, as if it were itself a determinate meaning. It does not bring a feminine indeterminacy in from the cold to operate within the bounds of meaning.

Ironic enactments of the "unbounded feminine" can be powerful and illuminating. My concern is that nonironic enactments of feminine fluidity—as if determinacy were itself a determinate (though nonessentialist) meaning—perpetuate what has been objectionable in the symbolic use of Woman. Intelligent applications of the insights of deconstruction to reveal the operations of Woman as metaphor have passed over into dubious affirmations of indeterminacy in the name of the feminine. Having acknowledged that properties such as indeterminacy, vagueness, and fluidity should not be seen as the essential feminine, feminist thinkers should question whether they should be appropriated as feminine at all. There are some indications the Derrida was aware of the problem. In his own remarks about the significance of the metaphorical feminine in *Spurs/Eperons*, he warns against mistaking the perception that what will not be pinned down by truth is feminine for a claim about woman's femininity or about female sexuality.[11] But the dismissal of essentialism can too readily be taken as leaving space for a nonessential feminine. And the lure of the new Woman is strong.

The problem, however, is that in resisting the feminizing of the results of deconstruction, we risk falling back into an old posture—the affirmation of a sexless ideal of knowledge. The alleged sexlessness of reason is already part of the symbolic structure—a sexlessness that, as many feminist critics have pointed out, is often a covert form of privileging maleness. The idea of the sexless soul coexists with the maleness of reason, despite the appearance of tension. Sexlessness is here enmeshed in inherited operations of metaphor, although it may pose as a repudiation of metaphor.

These unstable and contradictory alignments of reason with the male-female distinction reach back into the conceptualization of reason in the Western philosophical tradition. Derrida has pointed out that it is not always Woman or femininity that is secondary in these oppositions. Sometimes it is the division between male and female that is secondary in relation to an ideal of mind as transcending all sexual difference. Woman has been used not only to symbolize what is opposed to male reason but also to symbolize sexual difference itself, in opposition to lack of sexual differentiation. The philosophical tradition has constructed reason as male in opposition to female emotion, sense, imagination, and so on. But it has also constructed the soul, of which it is the attribute, as sexless, as transcending bodily difference. And the two themes although they may appear to be in tension are interconnected.

Derrida, in a rather cryptic remark in an interview, referred to this inner tension in the symbolization of reason as one of the paradoxes of phallocentrism.[12] When sexual difference is determined by a Hegelian opposition, he said, the resulting war between the sexes is predetermined to a male victory, but in such a way that difference is erased. The dialectal opposition neutralizes or supersedes the difference. According to a surreptitious operation, however, phallocentric mastery is assured under the cover of neutralization every time.

Contemporary feminists have grasped this tension independently of the insights of deconstruction. Catharine MacKinnon, in her analysis of the subtle privileging of masculinity that underpins our ideas of sameness and difference, makes a similar point: Sameness means the same as men, difference means different from men.[13] Deconstructive techniques can offer some insight into the complexities of this maneuver with symbols. What emerges is not a contradiction between different ways of thinking about reason; instead, it is a complex symbolic operation in which the metaphor of maleness is both used and erased. The apparently sexless soul can be seen as itself an erased metaphor of maleness.

Deconstructive play with the representation of Woman can give us a better understanding of this spurious neutrality. The metaphors of male and female come into the conceptualization of reason in two ways. On the one hand, male reason is opposed to female, nonrational traits; on the other, sexless reason is opposed to all that pertains to body, including sexual difference. Here sexual difference is itself equated with the female. The supposed sexual neutrality of reason demands a male viewpoint—it coincides with the male position, which can take the female as its opposite. Woman therefore becomes the symbol of sexual difference.[14] In the spurious sexlessness of reason, then, we can see a shadowy maleness that is neither the full masculinity of gender nor the metaphoric maleness explicit in other constructions. This is a maleness that comes from the shedding of "feminine" sexual difference. Because sexlessness is here defined oppositionally to sexual difference, it takes on an implicit but powerful symbolic maleness. It is here that the maleness of reason is most embedded and elusive.

The interplay between the conceptualizations of reason as sexless and as male may appear to involve a contrast between literal and metaphorical treatments of reason. But it can also be seen as a complex interaction between different constructions of metaphor. There are similar interplays in other aspects of the conceptualization of reason that have been illuminated through Derrida's deconstructive reading strategies. One of his most important insights, developed especially in "White Mythology,"[15] has been into the elusiveness of the supposed separability of the metaphorical from the literal in the understanding of philosophical texts and their relations to the "writing" that is diffused through a culture. Before concluding my discussion of the metaphor of maleness, I want to try to bring out what is relevant in Derrida's treatment of metaphor by applying it to the complex play of metaphors involved in René Descartes' treatment of mental activity.

DESCARTES' METAPHORS OF THE MIND IN MOTION

The metaphor of the mind in motion is so familiar to us—so inextricable from our thought about thinking—that it is difficult to see how we could shed it. It is a basic metaphor, like those drawn from the bodily senses, which Derrida discusses in "White Mythology"—so much part of our thought that it can be difficult to see that they are metaphorical at all. In Descartes' discussion of reason, metaphors of movement interact with metaphors drawn from sight.[16] The ideal of intellect is an attentive gaze, which leaves behind the unstable, erratic motion of inferior forms of knowledge drawn from sense and infected by the intrusions of body. The ideal is a form of stasis, with intellectual contemplation construed on the model of vision. The only real or proper activity of the mind that Descartes allows is that of the will—the mind's self-movement in response to intellectual clear and distinct perception. The other kinds of mental motion presented in the text are marks of instability—legacies of the intermingling of mind and body. But their description—as is often the case with philosophical metaphors—communicates a richness and vitality that is lacking in the preferred term in the opposition.

Temporality is here seen as a threat to selfhood, as a source of fragmentation. The benevolent and veracious God must secure the continued existence of the self through time. His sustaining causal force provides an essential continuity to mental life. The literary dimensions of the *Meditations* reinforce this theme of the temporal continuity of mental life. It is the story of a mind in motion; it is a narrative of an intellectual journey. The *Meditations* enacts an intellectual process that transcends the idiosyncrasies of any single mind. But it is nonetheless the narration of something past—the very thoughts that enabled Descartes to arrive at a certain and evident knowledge of the truth are set out to allow others to test what has convinced him, thereby convincing all.

Metaphors of sight and motion interact in this narrative. Images of darkness and light interweave with images of restlessness and turmoil. This is an arduous undertaking, Descartes says at the end of the Second Meditation; a kind of laziness brings him back to normal life.

He is like a prisoner enjoying imaginary freedom while he sleeps; he dreads waking up and ending the pleasant illusion. He slides back into old opinions, fearing that peaceful sleep will be followed by hard labor, toiling not in the light but in the inextricable darkness of the problems he has raised. He feels as if he has fallen into a deep whirlpool that tumbles him around, so that he can neither stand on the bottom nor swim to the top. Even the uncertainty that comes from awareness of his own thinking is threatened by the movement of time. "I am, I exist—that is certain. But for how long? For as long as I am thinking. For it could be that were I totally to cease from thinking I should totally cease to exist" (Cottingham et al., vol. 2, p. 18). The way out of the instability is the cultivation of a form of mental gaze—an intellectual contemplation that will extricate him from the turmoil of change.

This refrain of emergence from instability into the stasis of intellectual contemplation recurs throughout the *Meditations.* Fixing in his mind what he has already attained is an important part of the process for Descartes. At the end of the Second Meditation, he stops to reflect on the new knowledge gained in order to fix it more deeply in his memory. And by the end of the Third Meditation, the analogies with religious contemplation are explicit and have become, indeed, rather more than mere analogy. Descartes now pauses to spend time in the contemplation of God—to reflect on his attributes and to "gaze with wonder and adoration on the beauty of this immense light, so far as the eye of my darkened intellect can bear it" (Cottingham et al., vol. 2, p. 36). This is, he thinks the same contemplation, although less perfect, that we shall have in the contemplation of the divine majesty in the next life.

Descartes' need to "fix" the mind in contemplation is frustrated by the unavoidability of time. Although our nature is such that so long as we perceive something clearly and distinctly we cannot but believe it to be true, our nature is also such that we cannot fix our mental vision continually on the same thing so as to keep perceiving it clearly. If shifting and changeable opinions are to give way to true and certain knowledge, the mind must learn to transform instability into mental vision. And this involves learning to control its motion. The mind must learn to distinguish two kinds of motion: its restless impulses to assent to what it does not understand; and the movement of assent that springs from its own true nature. Then, in a famous metaphorical passage in the Second Mediation, Descartes compares the restless mind to a wandering horse whose movements must at first be unrestrained so that one can better control it. It is surely surprising, Descartes comments, that he should have a more distinct grasp of things that he realizes are doubtful, unknown, and foreign to him than of what is true and known—that is, his own self. "But I see what it is: my mind enjoys wandering off and will not yet submit to being restrained within the bounds of truth. Very well then; just this once let us give it completely free rein, so that after a while, when it is time to tighten the reins, it may more readily submit to being curbed" (Cottingham et al., vol. 2, p. 20).

The process of turning instability into the stasis of intellectual contemplation echoes Descartes' treatment in the *Rules for the Direction of the Mind* of the transformation of deduction into intuition. There, too, the distinction is drawn in terms of motion. In deduction we are aware of a movement or "a sort of sequence," he says in Rule Three (Cottingham et al., vol. 1, p. 15). And because deduction, unlike intuition, does not require immediate self-evidence, it gets its certainty, in a sense, from memory. But the movement of deduction can in the practiced mind come to approximate the superior state of intuition. We can redress the sluggishness of our intelligence and enlarge its capacity by practicing an uninterrupted movement of the imagination, Descartes says in Rule Seven, "simultaneously intuiting one relation and passing on to the next until we learn to pass from the first to the last so swiftly that memory is left with practically no role to play, and we seem to intuit the whole thing at once" (Cottingham et al., vol. 1, p. 25). When we think of deduction as a process of inference that does not take place all at once, it seems to be a kind of movement of our minds. We are then justified in distinguishing it from intuition. But if we look on it as a completed process, it no longer signifies movement but rather the completion of a movement (Cottingham et al., vol. 1, p. 37).

Also in the *Rules*, metaphors of motion interact with metaphors of light. We can best learn how mental intuition is to be employed, Descartes says in Rule Nine, by comparing it with ordinary vision.

> If one tries to look at many objects at one glance, one sees none of them distinctly. Likewise, if one is inclined to attend to many things at the same time in a single act of thought, one does so with a confused mind. Yet craftsmen who engage in delicate operations, and are used to fixing their eyes on a single point, acquire through practice the ability to make perfect distinctions between things, however minute and delicate. The same is true of those who never let their thinking be distracted by many different objects at the same time, but always devote their whole attention to the simplest and easiest of matters: they become perspicacious (Cottingham et al., vol. 1, p. 33).

And in Rule Two, Descartes relates the point, as he does in the *Meditations*, to memory: "Conclusions which embrace more than we can grasp in a single intuition depend for their certainty on memory, and since memory is weak and unstable, it must be refreshed and strengthened through the continuous and repeated movement of thought" (Cottingham et al., vol. 1, p. 38).

I have looked in some detail at these metaphors of mental motion in order to bring out certain aspects of philosophical metaphor that are also involved in the operation of maleness as a metaphor. There is no clear answer to the question whether the movement of the mind is literal or metaphorical. Descartes' treatment seems to "move," often imperceptibly, between the two. In some passages, as in the extended metaphor of the wandering horse, the language is straightforwardly metaphorical. But what of the passage that urges us to practice the process of deduction until we attain the state approximating intuition? Does the mind really "move" here? If not, what exactly is it that we are supposed to transform into the intellectual contemplation? Yet, surely, at some level, all talk of mind in motion must be a metaphorical extension from the movement of bodies. Is the horse passage just a more colorful metaphor than the others? Clearly it is easier to find a nonmetaphorical rendering of what is being said into apparently more literal ways of talking of the mind's motion. But do these translations just terminate in deeper metaphors of which we cannot rid ourselves? What of the talk of the mind's activity? Is that also metaphorical? Could there be a nonmetaphorical rendering of Descartes' distinction between mental activity and passivity? Can such concepts really straddle the gap between mind and body? And if not, what are we to make of Descartes' talk of the passions of the soul as caused by the movements of bodily animal spirits? The consideration of these metaphors clearly has implications for philosophical content. They are not mere embellishment.

Our difficulty in thinking of thought without the idea of activity can make it appear that activity is the essence of thought, as if we had something that does not rest on the contingency of metaphor. But perhaps such impossibilities are always retrospective. Derrida has shown in "White Mythology" that the metaphors through which we describe thought itself are particularly difficult to think away. But his approach also stresses the contingency of metaphors, even those we cannot shed. The insight into contingency that comes with awareness of the operations of metaphor give us valuable understanding of our ways of thinking, even where we cannot begin to articulate what it would be like to think otherwise.

What would it be to think of thought—or to think at all —without thinking of the mind as active? But the activity/passivity distinction is itself, of course, not a straightforward description of the mind's operations. It is also, like the male/female distinction with which it often interacts in philosophical texts, a vehicle of evaluation. It serves to privilege, through oppositional contrasts, some aspects of mind over others. And the privileging operates, as usual, in an unstable way. On the one hand, Descartes downgrades the "motion" of the mind. It represents an instability that must be transcended. On the other hand, the privileged state of mind is also presented as a form of activity. But this superior form of mental activity belongs to the proper nature of the soul—the movement of the will. The mental motion figured in the horse metaphor turns out to be really a form of passivity. The mind is pushed by the body into a motion not its own. The will must exert a counterforce "reining it in."

The model is fundamentally the same as that which will be elaborated in *The Passions of the Soul* through other metaphors, often military ones. The mind is rendered passive by the movements of the animal spirits. The will must fight back, exerting a counterforce through the pineal gland, redirecting the movements of the spirits. It is a struggle in which the soul is strengthened through its own "proper arms"—the determinate judgments of good and evil. The metaphors play out the privileging of one side in an oppositional contrast. And tensions in their operations reflect more than mere accidental features of the mixing of metaphors—these tensions alert us to unresolved problems in Descartes' theory of the mind and its relation with the body. Spinoza later exploits the tensions to collapse the Cartesian substantial difference between mind and body and the distinction between intellect and will to yield a different version of the contrasts between mental activity and mental passivity.

THE MALENESS OF REASON

Let me conclude by bringing all this back to bear on the maleness of reason. Some of the symbolic operations of maleness and femaleness in relation to reason can be compared to Descartes' metaphors of the mind as a horse. Francis Bacon's metaphors of nature as a chaste bride to be wooed by male science, for example, can be shed without leaving us with nothing to say. This sexual symbolism is not merely retrospectively contingent; it is also clearly not constitutive of the thought. Other symbolic operations of male and female are more deeply embedded in the conceptualization of reason—more akin to Descartes' elusive metaphors of the mind in motion, with their slides into literal talk of mental activity. Sexual symbolism operates in this embedded way in, for example, the conceptualization of reason as an attainment, as a transcending of the feminine. Embeddedness is also a feature of the metaphors of containment that link reason and its opposites with the public/private distinction. The conceptual containment of the feminine nonrational subtly reinforces—and is reinforced by—the literal containment of women in the domestic domain. And the sexual symbolism is, of course, particularly difficult to separate from more literal claims about reason in conceptualizations of the soul as sexless, where what looks like a repudiation of metaphor can be a subtle privileging of maleness coinciding with sexlessness in opposition to "female" sexual difference.

What is interesting and important from a Derridean perspective about these slides between the literal and the metaphorical is not the discovery of the metaphorical intrusions into philosophical thought—as if they should or could be shed; or as if it means the end of philosophy if they cannot. What is interesting is the tensions between different layers of metaphor and the insight these tensions give us into philosophical content. To grasp the contingency of philosophical metaphor is often to gain insight into philosophical content, even where this does not bring with it any clear idea of how we might think differently.

Feminist rage against narrowly instrumental conceptions of rationality—and against the more blatant use of sexual symbolism in formulations of ideals of reason—can distract attention from the more subtle operations of sexual symbolism in relation to reason. And the expectation that women can now come up with an alternative to male reason can reflect a lingering commitment to the primacy of instrumental reason. The maleness of reason is not a unitary representation; rather, it is a network of symbolic operations—some relatively superficial, others deeply embedded in our conceptualizations of what it is to think at all. To some of these symbolic operations, the appropriate response may well be a reevaluation and affirmation of neglected aspects of being human that have traditionally been associated with women. But I remain skeptical about the generalized affirmation of the feminine that has characterized some contemporary feminist critiques of reason. Here debate about reason joins the familiar paradoxes of other feminist debates about sameness and difference. But, as Joan Scott has argued convincingly in her excellent discussion of the relevance of deconstructive strategies, "Deconstructing Equality-Versus-Difference",[17] all this really rests on a false choice. In some contexts, it is appropriate to demand sameness; in others, difference. And this, I think, is also the real upshot of deconstructive strategies in feminist readings of the history of philosophy. There are times and contexts in which the struggle to affirm the feminine is crucial. And there are other times and contexts in which the attempt to find feminine truth, or the truth of the feminine, is as forlorn and misconceived as Eco's feigned search for a new sardine can opener. There is, of course, room for constructive disagreement about which stance is appropriate in particular contexts.

NOTES

1. Umberto Eco, "On the Crisis of the Crisis of Reason," in *Travels in Hyper-Reality*, tr. W. Weaver (London: Picador, 1987), pp. 125–32.
2. Richard Bernstein, "The Rage against Reason," *Philosophy and Literature* 10 (1986): 186–210.
3. Max Horkheimer, *The Eclipse of Reason* (New York: Continuum, 1985).
4. T. Adorno and M. Horkheimer, *The Dialectic of Enlightenment*, tr. J. Cumming (London: Verso, 1979).
5. Sandra Harding, *The Science Question in Feminism* (Ithaca, N.Y.: Cornell University Press, 1986), p. 52.
6. See especially Evelyn Fox Keller, *Reflections on Gender and Science* (New Haven, Conn./London: Yale University Press, 1985), pt. 2, ch. 4.

7. See especially Luce Irigary, *Speculum of the Other Woman*, tr. Gillian C. Gill (Ithaca, N.Y.: Cornell University Press, 1985), and *This Sex Which is Not One*, tr. C. Porter with C. Burke (Ithaca, N.Y.: Cornell University Press, 1985).
8. In M. Griffiths and Margaret Whitford, *Feminist Perspectives in Philosophy* (London: Macmillan, 1988), p. 109–130.
9. Susan J. Hekman, *Gender and Knowledge: Elements of a Postmodern Feminism* (London: Polity Press, 1990), pp. 163–175.
10. Jacques Derrida, "Différance," in *Margins of Philosophy*, tr. Alan Bass (Brighton, Sussex: Harvester, 1982), pp. 1–28.
11. Jacques Derrida, *Spurs/Eperons* (Chicago: University of Chicago Press, 1978).
12. Jacques Derrida and Christie V. McDonald, "Choreographies," *Diacritics* 12 (1982): esp. pp. 68–72.
13. Catharine MacKinnon, "Difference and Dominance," in MacKinnon, *Feminism Unmodified* (Cambridge, Mass.: Harvard University Press, 1987), pp. 32–45.
14. Derrida describes this conceptual maneuver in his remarks in the "Choreographies" interview (p. 73) on Levinas's treatment of the symbolism of the Genesis story: A masculine sexual marking is given to what is presented either as a neutral origin or, at least, before and superior to all sexual markings. Differentiated humanity is placed beneath an undifferentiated humanity. Masculinity is left "in command and at the beginning, on a par with the Spirit." This gesture, the most "self-interested of contradiction," Derrida observes, has repeated itself since Adam and Eve and persists in analogous form into modernity.
15. Jacques Derrida, "White Mythology: Metaphor in the Text of Philosophy," in *Margins of Philosophy*, pp. 207–272.
16. Quotations are from *The Philosophical Writings of Descartes*, 2 vols, tr. John Cottingham and Dugald Murdoch (Cambridge: Cambridge University Press, 1985).
17. Joan W. Scott, "Deconstructing Equality-Versus-Difference, Or the Uses of Poststructuralist Theory for Feminism," reprinted here, chap. 39.

Stabat Mater

Kristeva's topic is motherhood—the way in which Western culture symbolizes motherhood and also the way in which women experience motherhood. Much of Kristeva's text is divided into two columns. For the most part, the left-hand column is a poetic evocation of her own experience of pregnancy and maternity, whereas the right-hand column is a theoretical analysis of the figure of the Virgin Mary. It is worth noting, however, that Kristeva does not rigidly segregate theory and poetry. The right-hand column sometimes expands to fill the page, and the text of the left-hand column sometimes turns theoretical.

According to Kristeva, figurations of maternity do not describe mothers. Rather, they express a fantasy of the infant's primordial bond with its mother. Since this fantasy of fusion represents both a comforting state of security and a threat to the individual's distinct identity, effective maternal figurations must accent the reassuring side of this fantasy and defuse the threatening side. Kristeva maintains that for centuries the Virgin Mary succeeded in striking this balance by symbolizing the mother as both ethereally spiritual and humble before her child. Moreover, she urges that women have found the image appealing, for it represents motherhood as an incomparable accomplishment of which women can be proud. Still, this figuration places women in a double-bind. Either they can be "hyper-abstract," or they can be "merely different." The image denies that women can be individuals in their own right, and it fails to address such important issues as the mother's role in transmitting culture and relations between mothers and daughters. Thus, Kristeva calls for women to refigure maternity, and her alternately lyrical and jarring prose poem in the left-hand column is a contribution to that project of emancipatory refiguration. In the closing lines of her essay, Kristeva christens this project "heretical ethics."

—D.T.M.

Chapter 16

Julia Kristeva

Stabat Mater

THE PARADOX: MOTHER OR PRIMARY NARCISSISM

If it is not possible to say of a *woman* what she *is* (without running the risk of abolishing her difference), would it perhaps be different concerning the *mother*, since that is the only function of the "other sex" to which we can definitely attribute existence? And yet, there too, we are caught in a paradox. First, we live in a civilization where the *consecrated* (religious or secular) representation of femininity is absorbed by motherhood. If, however, one looks at it more closely, this motherhood is the *fantasy* that is nurtured by the adult, man or woman, of a lost territory; what is more, it involves less an idealized archaic mother than the idealization of the *relationship* that binds us to her, one that cannot be localized—an idealization of primary narcissism. Now, when feminism demands a new representation of femininity, it seems to identify motherhood with that idealized misconception and, because it rejects the image and its misuse, feminism circumvents the real experience that fantasy overshadows. The result?—a negation or rejection of motherhood by some avant-garde feminist groups. Or else an acceptance—conscious or not—of its traditional representations by the great mass of people, women and men.

FLASH—instant of time or of dream without time; inordinately swollen atoms of a bond, a vision, a shiver, a yet formless, unnamable embryo. Epiphanies. Photos of what is not yet visible and that language

Christianity is doubtless the most refined symbolic construct in which femininity, to the extent that it transpires through it—and it does so incessantly—is focused on *Maternality*.[1] Let us call "maternal" the

necessarily skims over from afar, allusively. Words that are always too distant, too abstract for this underground swarming of seconds, folding in unimaginable spaces. Writing them down is an ordeal of discourse, like love. What is loving, for a woman, the same thing as writing. Laugh. Impossible. Flash on the unnameable, weavings of abstractions to be torn. Let a body venture at last out of its shelter, take a chance with meaning under a veil of words. WORD FLESH. From one to the other, eternally, broken up visions, metaphors of the invisible.

ambivalent principle that is bound to the species, on the one hand, and on the other stems from an identity catastrophe that causes the Name to topple over into the unnamable that one imagines as femininity, nonlanguage, or body. Thus Christ, the Son of man, when all is said and done, is "human" only through his mother—as if Christly or Christian humanism could only be a maternalism (this is, besides, what some secularizing trends within its orbit do not cease claiming in their esotericism). And yet, the humanity of the Virgin mother is not always obvious, and we shall see how, in her being cleared of sin, for instance, Mary distinguishes herself from mankind. But at the same time the most intense revelation of God, which occurs in mysticism, is given only to a person who assumes himself as "maternal." Augustine, Bernard of Clairvaux, Meister Eckhart, to mention but a few, played the part of the Father's virgin spouses, or even, like Bernard, received drops of virginal milk directly on their lips. Freedom with respect to the maternal territory then becomes the pedestal upon which love of God is erected. As a consequence, mystics, those "happy Schrebers" (Sollers) through a bizarre light on the psychotic sore of modernity: it appears as the incapability of contemporary codes to tame the maternal, that is, primary narcissism. Uncommon and "literary," their present-day counterparts are always somewhat oriental, if not tragical—Henry Miller, who says he is pregnant; Artaud, who sees himself as "his daughters" or "his mother"... It is the orthodox constituent of Christianity, through John Chrysostom's golden mouth, among others, that sanctioned the transitional function of the Maternal by calling the Virgin a "bond," a "medium," or an "interval," thus opening the door to more or less heretical identifications with the Holy Ghost.

This resorption of femininity within the Maternal is specific to many civilizations, but Christianity, in its own fashion, brings it to its peak. Could it be that such a reduction represents no more than a masculine appropriation of the Maternal, which, in line with our hypothesis, is only a fantasy masking primary narcissism? Or else, might one detect in it, in other respects, the workings of enigmatic sublimation? These are perhaps the workings of masculine sublimation, a sublimation just the same, if it be true that for Freud picturing da Vinci, and even for da Vinci himself, the taming of that economy (of the Maternal or of primary narcissism) is a requirement for artistic, literary, or painterly accomplishment?

Within that perspective, however, there are two questions, among others, that remain unanswered. What is there, in the portrayal of the Maternal in general and particularly in its Christian, virginal, one, that reduces social anguish and gratifies a male being; what is there that also satisfies a woman so that a commonality of the sexes is set up, beyond and in spite of their glaring incompatibility and permanent warfare? Moreover, is there something in that Maternal notion that ignores what a woman might say or want—as a result, when women speak out today it is in matters of conception and motherhood that their annoyance is basically centered. Beyond social and political demands, this takes the well-known "discontents" of our civilization to a level where Freud would not follow—the discontents of the species.

A TRIUMPH OF THE UNCONSCIOUS IN MONOTHEISM

It would seem that the "virgin" attribute for Mary is a translation error, the translator having substituted for the Semitic term that indicates the sociolegal status of a young unmarried woman the Greek word *parthenos*, which on the other hand specifies a physiological and psychological condition: virginity. One might read into this the Indo-European fascination (which Dumezil analyzed)[2] with the virgin daughter as guardian of paternal power; one might also detect an ambivalent conspiracy, through excessive spiritualization, of the mother-goddess and the underlying matriarchy with which Greek culture and Jewish monotheism kept struggling. The fact remains that western Christianity has organized that "translation error," projected its own fantasies into it, and produced one of the most powerful imaginary constructs known in the history of civilizations.

The story of the virginal cult in Christianity amounts in fact to the imposition of pagan-rooted beliefs in, and often against, dogmas of the official Church. It is true that the Gospels already posit Mary's existence. But they suggest only very discreetly the immaculate conception of Christ's mother, they say nothing concerning Mary's own background and speak of her only seldom at the side of her son or during crucifixion. Thus Matthew 1:20 (". . . the angel of the Lord appeared to him in a dream and said, 'Joseph, son of David, do not be afraid to take Mary home as your wife, because she has conceived what is in her by the Holy Spirit' "), and Luke 1:34 ("Mary said to the angel, 'But how can this come about since I do not know man?' ") open a door, a narrow opening for all that, but one that would soon widen thanks to apocryphal additions on impregnation without sexuality; according to this notion a woman, preserved from masculine intervention, conceives alone with a "third party," a nonperson, the Spirit. In the rare instances when the Mother of Jesus appears in the Gospels, she is informed that filial relationship rests not with the flesh but with the name or, in other words, that any possible matrilinearism is to be repudiated and the symbolic link alone is to last. We thus have Luke 2:48–49 ("his mother said to him, 'My child, why have you done this to us? See how worried your father and I have been, looking for you.' 'Why were you looking for me?' he replied. 'Did you not know that I must be busy with my father's affairs?' "), and also John 2:3–5 ("the mother of Jesus said to him, 'They have no wine.' Jesus said, 'Woman, why turn to me?[3] My hour has not come yet.' ") and 19:26–27 ("Seeing his mother and the disciple he loved standing near her, Jesus said to his mother, 'Woman, this is your son.' Then to the disciple he said, 'This is your mother.' And from that moment the disciple made a place for her in his home.")

Starting from this programmatic material, rather skimpy nevertheless, a compelling imaginary construct proliferated in essentially three directions. In the first place, there was the matter of drawing a parallel between Mother and Son by expanding the theme of the immaculate conception, inventing a biography of Mary similar to that of Jesus, and, by depriving her of sin, depriving her of death. Mary leaves by way of Dormition or Assumption. Next, she needed letters patent of nobility, a power that, even though exercised in the beyond, is nonetheless political, since Mary was to be proclaimed queen, given the attributes and paraphernalia of royalty and, in parallel fashion, declared Mother of the divine institution on earth, the Church. Finally, the relationship with Mary and from Mary was to be revealed as the prototype of a love relationship and followed two fundamental aspects of western love: courtly love and child love, thus fitting the entire range that goes from sublimation to asceticism and masochism.

NEITHER SEX NOR DEATH

Mary's life, devised on the model of the life of Jesus, seems to be the fruit of apocryphal literature. The story of her own miraculous conception, called "immaculate conception," by Ann and Joachim, after a long, barren marriage, together with her biography as a pious maiden, show up in apocryphal sources as early as the end of the first century. Their entirety may be found in the *Secret Book of James* and also in one of the pseudoepigrapha, the Gospel according to the Hebrews (which inspired Giotto's frescoes, for instance). Those "facts" were quoted by Clement of Alexandria and Origen but not officially accepted; even though the Eastern Church tolerated them readily, they were translated into Latin only in the sixteenth century. Yet the West was not long before glorifying the life of Mary on its own but always under orthodox guidance. The first Latin poem, "Maria," on the birth of Mary was written by the nun Hrotswith von Gandersheim (who died before 1002), a playwright and poet.

Fourth-century asceticism, developed by the Fathers of the Church, was grafted on that apocryphal shoot in order to bring out and rationalize the immaculate conception postulate. The demonstration was based on a simple logical relation: the intertwining of sexuality and death. Since they are mutually implicated with each other, one cannot avoid the one without fleeing the other. This asceticism, applicable to both sexes, was vigorously expressed by John Chrysostom (*On Virginity:* "For where there is death there is also sexual copulation, and where there is no death there is no sexual copulation either"); even though he was attacked by Augustine and Aquinas, he nonetheless fueled Christian doctrine. Thus, Augustine condemned "concupiscence" (*epithumia*) and posited that Mary's virginity is in fact only a logical precondition of Christ's chastity. The Orthodox Church, heir no doubt to a matriarchy that was more intense in Eastern European societies, emphasized Mary's virginity more boldly. Mary was contrasted with Eve, life with death (Jerome, *Letter 22*, "Death came through Eve but life came through Mary"; Irenaeus, "Through Mary the snake becomes a dove and we are freed from the chains of death"). People even got involved in tortuous arguments in order to demonstrate that Mary remained a virgin after childbirth (thus the second Constantinople council, in 381, under Arisanistic influence, emphasized the Virgin's role in comparison to official dogma and asserted Mary's perpetual virginity; the 451 council called her *Aeiparthenos*—ever virgin). Once this was established, Mary, instead of being referred to as Mother of man or Mother of Christ, would be proclaimed Mother of God: *Theotokos*. Nestorius, patriarch of Constantinople, refused to go along; Nestorianism, however, for all practical purposes died with the patriarch's own death in 451, and the path that would lead to Mary's deification was then clear.

Head reclining, nape finally relaxed, skin, blood, nerves warmed up, luminous flow: stream of hair made of ebony, of nectar, smooth darkness through her fingers, gleaming honey under the wings of bees,

Very soon, within the complex relationship between Christ and Mother where relations of God to mankind, man to woman, son to mother, etc., are hatched, the problematics of *time* similar to that of cause

sparkling strands burning bright . . . silk, mercury, ductile copper: frozen light warmed under fingers. Mane of beast—squirrel, horse, and the happiness of a faceless head, Narcissuslike touching without eyes, sight dissolving in muscles, hair, deep, smooth, peaceful colors. Mamma: anamnesis.

Taut eardrum, tearing sound out of muted silence. Wind among grasses, a seagull's faraway call, echoes of waves, auto horns, voices, or nothing? Or his own tears, my newborn, spasm of syncopated void. I no longer hear anything, but the eardrum keeps transmitting this resonant vertigo to my skull, the hair. My body is no longer mine, it doubles up, suffers, bleeds, catches cold, puts its teeth in, slobbers, coughs, is covered with pimples, and it laughs. And yet, when its own joy, my child's, returns, its smile washes only my eyes. But the pain, its pain—it comes from inside, never remains apart, other, it inflames me at once, without a second's respite. As if that was what I had given birth to and, not willing to part from me, insisted on coming back, dwelled in me permanently. One does not give birth in pain, one gives birth to pain: the child represents it and henceforth it settles in, it is continuous. Obviously you may close your eyes, cover up your ears, teach courses, run errands, tidy up the house, think about objects, subjects. But a mother is always branded by pain, she yields to it. "And a sword will pierce your own soul too . . ."

Dream without glow, without sound, dream of brawn. Dark twisting, pain in the back, the arms, the thighs—pincers turned into fibers, infernos bursting veins, stones breaking bones: grinders of volumes, expanses, spaces, lines, points. All those words, now, ever visible things to register the roar of a silence that hurts all

loomed up. If Mary preceded Christ and he originated in her if only from the standpoint of his humanity, should not the conception of Mary herself have been immaculate? For, if that were not the case, how could a being conceived in sin and harboring it in herself produce a God? Some apocryphal writers had not hesitated, without too much caution, to suggest such an absence of sin in Mary's conception, but the Fathers of the Church were more careful. Bernard of Clairvaux is reluctant to extol the conception of Mary by Anne, and thus he tries to check the homologation of Mary with Christ. But it fell upon Duns Scotus to change the hesitation over the promotion of a mother goddess within Christianity into a logical problem, thus saving them both, the Great Mother as well as logic. He viewed Mary's birth as a *praeredemptio*, as a matter of congruency: if it be true that Christ alone saves us through his redemption on the cross, the Virgin who bore him can but be preserved from sin in "recursive" fashion, from the time of her own conception up to that redemption.

For or against, with dogma or logical shrewdness, the battle around the Virgin intensified between Jesuits and Dominicans, but the Counter-Reformation, as is well known, finally ended the resistance: henceforth, Catholics venerated Mary in herself. The Society of Jesus succeeded in completing a process of popular pressure distilled by patristic asceticism, and in reducing, with neither explicit hostility nor brutal rejection, the share of the Maternal (in the sense given above) useful to a certain balance between the two sexes. Curiously and necessarily, when that balance began to be seriously threatened in the nineteenth century, the Catholic Church—more dialectical and subtle here than the Protestants, who were already spawning the first suffragettes—raised the Immaculate Conception to dogma status in 1854. It is often

over. As if a geometry ghost could suffer when collapsing in a noiseless tumult . . . Yet the eye picked up nothing, the ear remained deaf. But everything swarmed, and crumbled, and twisted, and broke—the grinding continued . . . Then, slowly, a shadowy shape gathered, became detached, darkened, stood out: seen from what must be the true place of my head, it was the right side of my pelvis. Just bony, sleek, yellow, misshapen, a piece of my body jutting out unnaturally, asymmetrically, but slit: severed scaly surface, revealing under this disproportionate pointed limb the fibers of a marrow . . . Frozen placenta, live limb of a skeleton, monstrous graft of life on myself, a living dead. Life . . . death . . . undecidable. During delivery it went to the left with the afterbirth . . . my removed marrow, which nevertheless acts as a graft, which wounds but increases me. Paradox: deprivation and benefit of childbirth. But calm finally hovers over pain, over the terror of this dried branch that comes back to life, cut off, wounded, deprived of its sparkling bark. The calm of another life, the life of that other who wends his way while I remain henceforth like a framework. Still life. There is him, however, his own flesh, which was mine yesterday. Death, then, how could I yield to it?

suggested that the blossoming of feminism in Protestant countries is due, among other things, to the greater initiative allowed women on the social and ritual plane. One might wonder if, in addition, such a flowering is not the result of a *lack* in the Protestant religious structure with respect to the Maternal, which, on the contrary, was elaborated within Catholicism with a refinement to which the Jesuits gave the final touch, and which still makes Catholicism very difficult to analyze.

The fulfillment, under the name of Mary, of a totality made of woman and God is finally accomplished through the avoidance of death. The Virgin Mary experiences a fate more radiant than her son's: she undergoes no calvary, she has no tomb, she doesn't die and hence has no need to rise from the dead. Mary doesn't die but—as if to echo oriental beliefs, Taoists' among others, according to which human bodies pass from one place to another in an eternal flow that constitutes a carbon copy of the maternal receptacle—she is transported.

Her transition is more passive in the Eastern Church: it is a Dormition (*Koimesis*) during which, according to a number of iconographic representations, Mary can be seen changed into a little girl in the arms of her son who henceforth becomes her father; she thus reverses her role as Mother into a Daughter's role for the greater pleasure of those who enjoy Freud's "Theme of the Three Caskets."

Indeed, *mother* of her son and his *daughter* as well, Mary is also, and besides, his *wife*: she therefore actualizes the threefold metamorphosis of a woman in the tightest parenthood structure. From 1135 on, transposing the Song of Songs, Bernard of Clairvaux glorifies Mary in her role of beloved and wife. But Catherine of Alexandria (said to have been martyred in 307) already pictured herself as receiving the wedding ring from Christ, with the Virgin's help, while Catherine of Siena (1347–80) goes through a mystical wedding with him. Is it the impact of Mary's function as Christ's beloved and wife that is responsible for the blossoming out of the Marian cult in the West after Bernard and thanks to the Cistercians? "*Vergine Madre, figlia del tuo Figlio,*" Dante exclaims, thus probably best condensing the gathering of the three feminine functions (daughter-wife-mother) within a totality where they vanish as specific corporealities while retaining their psychological functions. Their bond makes up the basis of unchanging and timeless spirituality; "the set time limit of an eternal design" (*Termine fisso d'eterno consiglio*), as Dante masterfully points out in his *Divine Comedy.*

The transition is more active in the West, with Mary rising body and soul toward the other world in an *Assumption.* That feast, honored in Byzantium as early as the fourth century, reaches Gaul in the seventh under the influence of the Eastern Church; but the earliest Western visions of the Virgin's assumption, women's visions (particularly that of Elizabeth von Schönau, who died in 1164) date only from the twelfth century. For the Vatican, the Assumption became dogma only in 1950. What death anguish was it intended to soothe after the conclusion of the deadliest of wars?

IMAGE OF POWER

On the side of "power," *Maria Regina* appears in imagery as early as the sixth century in the church of Santa Maria Antiqua in Rome. Interestingly enough, it is she, woman and mother, who is called upon to represent supreme earthly power. Christ is king but neither He nor His Father are pictured wearing crowns, diadems, costly paraphernalia, and other external signs of abundant material goods. That opulent infringement to Christian idealism is centered on the Virgin Mother. Later, when she assumed the title of *Our Lady,* this would also be an analogy to the earthly power of the noble feudal lady of medieval courts. Mary's function as guardian of power, later checked when the Church became wary of it, nevertheless persisted in popular and pictorial representation, witness Piero della Francesca's impressive painting, *Madonna della Misericordia,* which was disavowed by Catholic authorities at the time. And yet, not only did the papacy revere more and more the Christly mother as the Vatican's power over cities and municipalities was strengthened, it also openly identified its own institution with the Virgin: Mary was officially proclaimed Queen by Pius XII in 1954 and *Mater Ecclesiae* in 1964.

EIA MATER, FONS AMORIS!

Fundamental aspects of Western love finally converged on Mary. In a first step, it indeed appears that the Marian cult homologizing Mary with Jesus and carrying asceticism to the extreme was opposed to courtly love for the noble lady, which, while representing social transgression, was not at all a physical or moral sin. And yet, at the very dawn of a "courtliness" that was still very carnal, Mary and the Lady shared one common trait: they are the focal point of men's desires and aspirations. Moreover, because they were unique and thus excluded all other women, both the Lady and the Virgin embodied an absolute authority [the more attractive as it appeared removed] from paternal sternness. This feminine power must have been experienced as denied power, more pleasant to seize because it was both archaic and secondary, a kind of substitute for effective power in the family and the city but no less authoritarian, the underhand double of explicit phallic power. As early as the thirteenth century, thanks to the implantation of ascetic Christianity and especially, as early as 1328, to the promulgation of Salic laws, which excluded daughters from the inheritance and thus made the loved one very vulnerable and colored one's love for her with all the hues of the impossible, the Marian and courtly streams came together. Around the time of Blanche of Castile (who died in 1252), the Virgin explicitly became the focus of courtly love, thus gathering the attributes of the desired woman and of the holy mother in a totality as accomplished as it was inaccessible. Enough to make any woman suffer, any man dream. One finds indeed in a *Miracle de Notre Dame* the story of a young man who abandons his fiancée for the Virgin: the latter came to him in a dream and reproached him for having left her for an "earthy woman."

Nevertheless, besides that ideal totality that no individual woman could possibly embody, the Virgin also became the fulcrum of the humanization of the West in general and of love in particular. It is again about the thirteenth century, with Francis of Assisi, that this tendency takes shape with the representation of Mary as poor, modest, and humble—madonna of humility at the same time as a devoted, fond mother. The famous nativity of Piero della Francesca in London, in which Simone de Beauvoir too hastily saw a feminine defeat because the mother kneeled before her barely born son, in fact consolidates the new cult of humanistic sensitivity. It replaces the high spirituality that assimilated the Virgin to Christ with an earthly conception of a wholly human mother. As a source for the most popularized pious images, such maternal humility comes closer to "lived" feminine experience than the earlier representations did. Beyond this, however, it is true that it integrates a certain feminine masochism but also displays its counterpart in gratification and jouissance. The truth of it is that the lowered head of the mother before her son is accompanied by the immeasurable pride of the one who knows she is also his wife and daughter. She knows she is destined to that eternity (of the spirit or of the species) of which every mother is unconsciously aware, and with regard to which maternal devotion or even sacrifice is but an insignificant price to pay. A price that is borne all the more easily since, contrasted with the love that binds a mother to her son, all other "human relationships" burst like blatant shams. The Franciscan representation of the Mother conveys many essential aspects of maternal psychology, thus leading up to an influx of common people to the churches and also a tremendous increase in the Marian cult—witness the building of many churches dedicated to her

Scent of milk, dewed greenery, acid and clear, recall of wind, air, seaweed (as if a body lived without waste): it slides under the skin, does not remain in the mouth or nose but fondles the veins, detaches skin from bones, inflates me like an ozone balloon, and I hover with feet firmly planted on the ground in order to carry him, sure, stable, ineradicable, while he dances in my neck, flutters with my hair, seeks a smooth shoulder on the right, on the left, slips on the breast, swingles, silver vivid blossom of my belly, and finally flies away on my navel in his dream carried by my hands. My son.

Nights of wakefulness, scattered sleep, sweetness of the child, warm mercury in my arms, cajolery, affection, defenseless body, his or mine, sheltered, protected. A wave swells again, when he goes to sleep, under my skin—tummy, thighs, legs: sleep of the muscles, not of the brain, sleep of the flesh. The wakeful tongue quietly remembers another withdrawal, mine: a blossoming heaviness in the middle of the bed, of a hollow, of the sea . . . Recovered childhood, dreamed peace restored, in sparks, flash of cells, instants of laughter, smiles in the blackness of dreams, at night, opaque joy that roots me in her bed, my mother's, and projects him, a son, a butterfly soaking up dew from her hand, there, nearby, in the night. Alone: she, I, and he.

He returns from the depths of the nose, the vocal chords, the lungs, the ears, pierces their smothering stopping sickness swab, and awakens in his eyes. Gentleness of the sleeping face, contours of pinkish jade—forehead, eyebrows, nostrils, cheeks,

parted features of the mouth, delicate, hard, pointed chin. Without fold or shadow, neither being nor unborn, neither present nor absent, but real, real inaccessible innocence, engaging weight and seraphic lightness. A child?—An angel, a glow on an Italian painting, impassive, peaceful dream—dragnet of Mediterranean fishermen. And then, the mother-of-pearl bead awakens: quicksilver. Shiver of the eyelashes, imperceptible twitch of the eyebrows, quivering skin, anxious reflections, seeking, knowing, casting their knowledge aside in the face of my nonknowledge: fleeting irony of childhood gentleness that awakens to meaning, surpasses it, goes past it, causes me to soar in music, in dance. Impossible refinement, subtle rape of inherited genes: before what has been learned comes to pelt him, harden him, ripen him. Hard, mischievous gentleness of the first ailment overcome, innocent wisdom of the first ordeal undergone, yet hopeful blame on account of the suffering I put you through, by calling for you, desiring, creating . . . Gentleness, wisdom, blame: your face is already human, sickness has caused you to join our species, you speak without words but your throat no longer gurgles—it harkens with me to the silence of your born meaning that draws my tears toward a smile.

The lover gone, forgetfulness comes, but the pleasure of the sexes remains, and there is nothing lacking. No representation, sensation, or recall. Inferno of vice. Later, forgetfulness returns but this time as fall—leaden—grey, dull, opaque. Forgetfulness: blinding, smothering foam, but on the quiet. Like the fog that devours the park, wolfs down the branches, erases the green, rusty ground, and mists up my eyes.

Absence, inferno, forgetfulness. Rhythm of our lives.

A hunger remains, in place of the heart. A spasm that spreads, runs through

("Notre Dame"). Such a humanization of Christianity through the cult of the mother also led to an interest in the humanity of the father-man: the celebration of "family life" showed Joseph to advantage as early as the fifteenth century.

WHAT BODY?

We are entitled only to the ear of the virginal body, the tears, and the breast. With the female sexual organ changed into an innocent shell, holder of sound, there arises a possible tendency to eroticize hearing, voice, or even understanding. By the same token, however, sexuality is brought down to the level of innuendo. Feminine sexual experience is thus rooted in the universality of sound, since wit is distributed *equally* among all men, all women. A woman will only have the choice to live her life either *hyperabstractly* ("immediately universal," Hegel said) in order thus to earn divine grace and homologation with symbolic order; or merely *different*, other, fallen ("immediately particular," Hegel said). But she will not be able to accede to the complexity of being divided, of heterogeneity, of the catastrophic-fold-of-"being" ("never singular," Hegel said).

Under a full, blue gown, the maternal, virginal body allowed only the breast to show, while the face, with the stiffness of Byzantine icons gradually softened, was covered with tears. Milk and tears became the privileged signs of the *Mater Dolorosa* who invaded the West beginning with the eleventh century, reaching the peak of its influx in the fourteenth. But it never ceased to fill the Marian visions of those, men or women (often children), who were racked by the anguish of a maternal frustration. Even though orality—threshold of infantile regression—is displayed in the area of the breast, while the spasm at the slipping away of eroticism is translated into tears, this

the blood vessels to the tips of the breasts, to the tips of the fingers. It throbs, pierces the void, erases it, and gradually settles in. My heart: a tremendous pounding wound. A thirst.

Anguished, guilty. Freud's Vaterkomplex on the Acropolis? The impossibility of being without repeated legitimation (without books, man, family). Impossibility—depressing possibility—of "transgression."

Either repression in which *I* hand the Other what I want from others.

Or this squalling of the void, open wound in my heart, which allows me to be only in purgatory.

I yearn for the Law. And since it is not made for me alone, I venture to desire outside the law. Then, narcissism thus awakened—the narcissism that wants to be sex—roams, astonished. In sensual rapture I am distraught. Nothing reassures, for only the law sets anything down. Who calls such a suffering jouissance? It is the pleasure of the damned.

should not conceal what milk and tears have in common: they are the metaphors of nonspeech, of a "semiotics" that linguistic communication does not account for. The Mother and her attributes, evoking sorrowful humanity, thus become representatives of a "return of the repressed" in monotheism. They reestablish what is nonverbal and show up as the receptacle of a signifying disposition that is closer to so-called primary processes. Without them the complexity of the Holy Ghost would have been mutilated. On the other hand, as they return by way of the Virgin Mother, they find their outlet in the arts—painting and music—of which the Virgin necessarily becomes both patron saint and privileged object.

The function of this "Virginal Maternal" may thus be seen taking shape in the Western symbolic economy. Starting with the high Christly sublimation for which it yearns and occasionally exceeds, and extending to the extralinguistic regions of the unnamable, the Virgin Mother occupied the tremendous territory on this and that side of the parenthesis of language. She adds to the Christian Trinity and to the Word that delineates their coherence the heterogeneity they salvage.

The ordering of the maternal libido reached its apotheosis when centered in the theme of death. The *Mater Dolorosa* knows no masculine body save that of her dead son, and her only pathos (which contrasts with the somewhat vacant, gentle serenity of the nursing Madonnas) is her shedding tears over a corpse. Since resurrection there is, and, as Mother of God, she must know this, nothing justifies Mary's outburst of pain at the foot of the cross, unless it be the desire to experience within her own body the death of a human being, which her feminine fate of being the source of life spares her. Could it be that the love, as puzzling as it is ancient, of mourners for corpses relates to the same longing of a woman whom nothing fulfills—the longing to experience the wholly masculine pain of a man who expires at every moment on account of jouissance due to obsession with his own death? And yet, Marian pain is in no way connected with tragic outburst: joy and even a kind of triumph follow upon tears, as if the conviction that death does not exist were an irrational but unshakable maternal certainty, on which the principle of resurrection had to rest. The brilliant illustration of the wrenching between desire for the masculine corpse and negation of death, a wrenching whose paranoid logic cannot be overlooked, is masterfully presented by the famous *Stabat Mater*. It is likely that all beliefs in resurrections are rooted in mythologies marked by the strong dominance of a mother goddess. Christianity, it is true, finds its calling in the displacement of that bio-maternal

Belief in the mother is rooted in fear, fascinated with a weakness—the weakness of language. If language is powerless to lo-

cate myself for and state myself to the other, I assume—I want to believe—that there is someone who makes up for that weakness. Someone, of either sex, *before* the id speaks, before language, who might make me be by means of borders, separations, vertigos. In asserting that "in the beginning was the Word," Christians must have found such a postulate sufficiently hard to believe and, for whatever it was worth, they added its compensation, its permanent lining: the maternal receptacle, purified as it might be by the virginal fantasy. Archaic maternal love would be an incorporation of my suffering that is unfailing, unlike what often happens with the lacunary network of signs. In that sense, any belief, anguished by definition, is upheld by the fascinated fear of language's impotence. Every God, even including the God of the Word, relies on a mother Goddess. Christianity is perhaps also the last of the religions to have displayed in broad daylight the bipolar structure of belief: on the one hand, the difficult experience of the Word—a passion; on the other, the reassuring wrapping in the proverbial mirage of the mother—a love. For that reason, it seems to me that there is only one way to go through the religion of the Word, or its counterpart, the more or less discreet cult of the Mother, it is the "artists' " way, those who make up for the vertigo of language weakness with the oversaturation of sign systems. By this token, all art is a kind of counter-Reformation, an accepted baroqueness. For is it not true that if the Jesuits finally did persuade the official Church to accept the cult of the Virgin, following the puritanical wave of the Reformation, that dogma was in fact no more than a pretext, and its efficacy lay elsewhere? It did not become the opposite of the cult of the mother but its inversion through expenditure in the wealth of signs that constitutes the baroque. The latter determinism through the postulate that immortality is mainly that of the name of the Father. But it does not succeed in imposing *its* symbolic revolution without relying on the feminine representation of an immortal biology. Mary defying death is the theme that has been conveyed to us by the numerous variations of the *Stabat Mater*, which, in the text attributed to Jacopone da Todi, enthralls us today through the music of Palestrina, Pergolesi, Haydn, and Rossini.

Let us listen to the baroque style of the young Pergolesi (1710–36), who was dying of tuberculosis when he wrote his immortal *Stabat Mater*. His musical inventiveness, which, through Haydn, later reverberated in the work of Mozart, probably constitutes his one and only claim to immortality. But when this cry burst forth, referring to Mary facing her son's death—"*Eia Mater, fons amoris!*" ("Hail mother, source of love!")—was it merely a remnant of the period? Man overcomes the unthinkable of death by postulating maternal love in its place—in the place and stead of death and thought. This love, of which divine love is merely a not always convincing derivation, psychologically is perhaps a recall, on the near side of early identifications, of the primal shelter that insured the survival of the newborn. Such a love is in fact, logically speaking, a surge of anguish at the very moment when the identity of thought and living body collapses. The possibilities of communication having been swept away, only the subtle gamut of sound, touch, and visual traces, older than language and newly worked out, are preserved as an ultimate shield against death. It is only "normal" for a maternal representation to set itself up at the place of this subdued anguish called love. No one escapes it. Except perhaps the saint, the mystic, or the writer who, through the power of language, nevertheless succeeds in doing no better than to take apart the fiction of the mother as mainstay of love, and to identify with

renders belief in the Mother useless by overwhelming the symbolic weakness where she takes refuge, withdrawn from history, with an overabundance of discourse.

The immeasurable, unconfinable maternal body.

First there is the separation, previous to pregnancy, but which pregnancy brings to light and imposes without remedy.

On the one hand—the pelvis: center of gravity, unchanging ground, solid pedestal, heaviness and weight to which the thighs adhere, with no promise of agility on that score. On the other—the torso, arms, neck, head, face, calves, feet: unbounded liveliness, rhythm, and mask, which furiously attempt to compensate for the immutability of the central tree. We live on that border, crossroads beings, crucified beings. A woman is neither nomadic nor a male body that considers itself earthly only in erotic passion. A mother is a continuous separation, a division of the very flesh. And consequently a division of language—and it has always been so.

Then there is this other abyss that opens up between the body and what had been its inside: there is the abyss between the mother and the child. What connection is there between myself, or even more unassumingly between my body and this internal graft and fold, which, once the umbilical cord has been severed, is an inaccessible other? My body and . . . him. No connection. Nothing to do with it. And this, as early as the first gestures, cries, steps, long before its personality has become my opponent. The child, whether *he* or *she*, is irremediably an other. To say that there are no sexual relationships constitutes a skimpy assertion when confronting the flash that bedazzles me when I confront the abyss between what was mine and is henceforth but irreparably alien. Trying to think through that abyss: love itself and what he is in fact—*a fire of tongues*, an exit from representation. Might not modern art then be, for the few who are attached to it, the implementation of that maternal love—a veil over death, in death's very site and with full knowledge of the facts? A sublimated celebration of incest . . .

ALONE OF HER SEX

Freud collected, among other objects of art and archeology, countless statuettes representing mother goddesses. And yet his interest in them comes to light only in discreet fashion in his work. It shows up when Freud examines artistic creation and homosexuality in connection with Leonardo da Vinci and deciphers there the ascendancy of an archaic mother, seen therefore from the standpoint of her effects on man and particularly on this strange function of his sometimes to change languages. Moreover, when Freud analyzes the advent and transformations of monotheism, he emphasizes that Christianity comes closer to pagan myths by integrating, through and against Judaic rigor, a preconscious acknowledgment of a maternal feminine. And yet, among the patients analyzed by Freud, one seeks in vain for mothers and their problems. One might be led to think that motherhood was a solution to neurosis and, by its very nature, ruled out psychoanalysis as a possible other solution. Or might psychoanalysis, at this point, make way for religion? In simplified fashion, the only thing Freud tells us concerning motherhood is that the desire for a child is a transformation of either penis envy or anal drive, and this allows her to discover the neurotic equation child-penis-feces. We are thus enlightened concerning an essential aspect of male phantasmatics with respect to childbirth, and female phantasmatics as well, to the extent that it embraces, in large part and in its hysterical labyrinths, the male one.

staggering vertigo. No identity holds up. A mother's identity is maintained only through the well-known closure of consciousness within the indolence of habit, when a woman protects herself from the borderline that severs her body and expatriates it from her child. Lucidity, on the contrary, would restore her as cut in half, alien to its other—and a ground favorable to delirium. But also and for that very reason, motherhood destines us to a demented jouissance that is answered, by chance, by the nursling's laughter in the sunny waters of the ocean. What connection is there between it and myself? No connection, except for that overflowing laughter where one senses the collapse of some ringing, subtle, fluid identity or other, softly buoyed by the waves.

Concerning that stage of my childhood, scented, warm, and soft to the touch, I have only a spatial memory. No time at all. Fragrance of honey, roundness of forms, silk and velvet under my fingers, on my cheeks. Mummy. Almost no sight—a shadow that darkens, soaks me up, or vanishes amid flashes. Almost no voice in her placid presence. Except, perhaps, and more belatedly, the echo of quarrels: her exasperation, her being fed up, her hatred. Never straightforward, always held back, as if, although the unmanageable child deserved it, the daughter could not accept the mother's hatred—it was not meant for her. A hatred without recipient or rather whose recipient was no "I" and which, perturbed by such a lack of recipience, was toned down into irony or collapsed into remorse before reaching its destination. With others, this maternal aversion may be worked up to a spasm that is held like a delayed orgasm. Women doubtless reproduce among themselves the strange gamut of forgotten body relationships with their mothers. Complicity in the unspoken,

The fact remains, as far as the complexities and pitfalls of maternal experience are involved, that Freud offers only a massive *nothing*, which, for those who might care to analyze it, is punctuated with this or that remark on the part of Freud's mother, proving to him in the kitchen that his own body is anything but immortal and will rumble away like dough; or the sour photograph of Marthe Freud, the wife, a whole mute story . . . There thus remained for his followers an entire continent to explore, a black one indeed, where Jung was the first to rush in, getting all his esoteric fingers burnt, but not without calling attention to some sore points of the imagination with regard to motherhood, points that are still resisting analytical rationality.[4]

There might doubtless be a way to approach the dark area that motherhood constitutes for a woman; one needs to listen, more carefully than ever, to what mothers are saying today, through their economic difficulties and, beyond the guilt that a too existentialist feminism handed down, through their discomforts, insomnias, joys, angers, desires, pains, and pleasures . . . One might, in similar fashion, try better to understand the incredible construct of the Maternal that the West elaborated by means of the Virgin, and of which I have just mentioned a few episodes in a never-ending history.

What is it then in this maternal representation that, alone of her sex, goes against both of the two sexes,[5] and was able to attract women's wishes for identification as well as the very precise interposition of those who assumed to keep watch over the symbolic and social order?

Let me suggest, by way of hypothesis, that the virginal maternal is a way (not among the less effective ones) of dealing with feminine paranoia.

—The Virgin assumes her feminine denial of the other sex (of man) but overcomes him by setting up a third person: *I* connivance of the inexpressible, of a wink, a tone of voice, a gesture, a tinge, a scent. We are in it, set free of our identification papers and names, on an ocean of preciseness, a computerization of the unnamable. No communication between individuals but connections between atoms, molecules, wisps of words, droplets of sentences. The community of women is a community of dolphins. Conversely, when the other woman posits herself as such, that is, as singular and inevitably in opposition, "I" am startled, so much that "I" no longer know what is going on. There are then two paths left open to the rejection that speaks the recognition of the other woman as such. Either, not wanting to experience her, I ignore her and, "alone of my sex," I turn my back on her in friendly fashion. It is a hatred that, lacking a recipient worthy enough of its power, changes to unconcerned complacency. Or else outraged by her own stubbornness, by that other's belief that she is singular, I unrelentingly let go at her claim to address me and find respite only in the eternal return of power strokes, bursts of hatred—blind and dull but obstinate. I do not see her as herself, but beyond her I aim at the claim to singularity, the unacceptable ambition to be something other than a child or a fold in the plasma that constitutes us, an echo of the cosmos that unifies us. What an inconceivable ambition it is to aspire to singularity, it is not natural, hence it is inhuman; the mania smitten with Oneness ("There is only One woman") can only be impugn it by condemning it as "masculine" . . . Within this strange feminine seesaw that makes "me" swing from the unnameable community of women over to the war of individual singularities, it is unsettling to say "I." The languages of the great formerly matriarchal civilizations must avoid, do avoid, personal pronouns: they leave to the context the burden of distinguishing ... do not conceive with *you* but with *Him*. The result is an immaculate conception (therefore with neither man nor sex), conception of a God with whose existence a woman has indeed something to do, on condition that she acknowledge being subjected to it.

—The Virgin assumes the paranoid lust for power by changing a woman into a Queen in heaven and a Mother of the earthly institutions (of the Church). But she succeeds in stifling that megalomania by putting it on its knees before the child-god.

—The Virgin obstructs the desire for murder or devouring by means of a strong oral cathexis (the breast), valorization of pain (the sob), and incitement to replace the sexed body with the ear of understanding.

—The Virgin assumes the paranoid fantasy of being excluded from time and death through the very flattering representations of Dormition or Assumption.

—The Virgin especially agrees with the repudiation of the other woman (which doubtless amounts basically to a repudiation of the woman's mother) by suggesting the image of a woman as Unique: alone among women, alone among mothers, alone among humans since she is without sin. But the acknowledgement of a longing for uniqueness is immediately checked by the postulate according to which uniqueness is attained only through an exacerbated masochism: a concrete woman, worthy of the feminine ideal embodied by the Virgin as an inaccessible goal, could only be a nun, a martyr, or, if she is married, one who leads a life that would remove her from that "earthly" condition and dedicate her to the highest sublimation alien to her body. A bonus, however; the promised jouissance.

A skillful balance of concessions and constraints involving feminine paranoia, the representation of virgin motherhood appears to crown the efforts of a society to reconcile the social remnants of matrilin-

tinguishing protagonists and take refuge in tones to recover an underwater, transverbal communication between bodies. It is a music from which so-called oriental civility tears away suddenly through violence, murder, blood baths. A woman's discourse, would that be it? Did not Christianity attempt, among other things, to freeze that see-saw? To stop it, tear women away from its rhythm, settle them permanently in the spirit? Too permanently . . .

earism and the unconscious needs of primary narcissism on the one hand, and on the other the requirements of a new society based on exchange and before long on increased production, which require the contribution of the superego and rely on the symbolic paternal agency.

While that clever balanced architecture today appears to be crumbling, one is led to ask the following: What are the aspects of the feminine psyche for which that representation of motherhood does not provide a solution or else provides one that is felt as too coercive by twentieth-century women?

The unspoken doubtless weighs first on the maternal body: as no signifier can uplift it without leaving a remainder, for the signifier is always meaning, communication, or structure, whereas a woman as mother would be, instead, a strange fold that changes culture into nature, the speaking into biology. Although it concerns every woman's body, the heterogeneity that cannot be subsumed in the signifier nevertheless explodes violently with pregnancy (the threshold of culture and nature) and gives the child's arrival (which extracts woman out of her oneness and gives her the possibility—but not the certainty—of reaching out to the other, the ethical). Those particularities of the maternal body compose woman into a being of folds, a catastrophe of being that the dialectics of the Trinity and its supplements would be unable to subsume.

Silence weighs heavily nonetheless on the corporeal and psychological suffering of childbirth and especially the self-sacrifice involved in becoming anonymous in order to pass on the social norm, which one might repudiate for one's own sake but within which *one must* include the child in order to educate it along the chain of generations. A suffering lined with jubilation—ambivalence of masochism—on account of which a woman, rather refractory to perversion, in fact allows herself a coded, fundamental, perverse behavior, ultimate guarantee of society, without which society will not reproduce and will not maintain a constancy of standardized household. Feminine perversion does not reside in the parceling or the Don Juan–like multiplying of objects of desire; it is at once legalized, if not rendered paranoid, through the agency of masochism: all sexual "dissoluteness" will be accepted and hence become insignificant, provided a child seals up such outpourings. Feminine perversion [*père-version*] is coiled up in the desire for law as desire for reproduction and continuity; it promotes feminine masochism to the rank of structure stabilizer (against its deviations); by assuring the mother that she may thus enter into an order that is above that of humans, it gives her her reward of pleasure. Such coded perversion, such close combat between maternal masochism and the law, have been utilized by totalitarian powers of all times to bring women to their side, and, of course, they succeed easily. And yet, it is not enough to "declaim against" the reactionary role of mothers in the service of "male dominating power." One would need to examine to what extent that role corresponds to the biosymbolic latencies of motherhood and, on that basis, to try and understand, since the myth of the Virgin does not subsume them, or no longer does, how their surge lays women open to the most fearsome manipulations, not to mention blinding, or pure and simple rejection by progressive activists who refuse to take a close look.

Among things left out of the virginal myth there is the war between mother and daughter, a war masterfully but too quickly settled by promoting Mary as universal and particular, but never singular—as "alone of her sex." The relation to the other woman has presented our culture, in massive fashion during the past century, with the necessity to reformulate its representations of love and hatred—inherited from Plato's *Symposium*, the troubadours, or Our Lady. On that level, too, motherhood opens out a vista: a woman seldom (although not necessarily) experiences her passion (love and hatred) for another woman without having taken her own mother's place—without having herself become a mother, and especially without slowly learning to differentiate between same beings—as being face to face with her daughter forces her to do.

Finally, repudiation of the other sex (the masculine) no longer seems possible under the aegis of the third person, hypostatized in the child as go-between: "neither me, nor you, but him, the child, the third person, the nonperson, God, which I still am in the final analysis . . ." Since there is repudiation, and if the feminine being that struggles within it is to remain there, it henceforth calls for, not the deification of the third party, but countercathexes in strong values, in strong *equivalents of power*. Feminine psychosis today is sustained and absorbed through passion for politics, science, art . . . The variant that accompanies motherhood might be analyzed perhaps more readily than the others from the standpoint of the rejection of the other sex that it comprises. To allow what? Surely not some understanding or other on the part of "sexual partners" within the pre-established harmony of primal androgyny. Rather, to lead to an acknowledgement of what is irreducible, of the irreconcilable interest of both sexes in asserting their differences, in the quest of each one—and of women, after all—for an appropriate fulfillment.

These, then, are a few questions among others concerning a motherhood that today remains, after the Virgin, without a discourse. They suggest, all in all, the need of an ethics for this "second" sex, which, as one asserts it, is reawakening.

Nothing, however, suggests that a feminine ethics is possible, and Spinoza excluded women from his (along with children and the insane). Now, if a contemporary ethics is no longer seen as being the same as morality; if ethics amounts to not avoiding the embarrassing and inevitable problematics of the law but giving it flesh, language, and jouissance—in that case its reformulation demands the contribution of women. Of women who harbor the desire to reproduce (to have stability). Of women

The love of God and for God resides in a gap: the broken space made explicit by sin on the one side, the beyond on the other. Discontinuity, lack, and arbitrariness: topography of the sign, of the symbolic relation that posits my otherness as impossible. Love, here, is only for the impossible.

For a mother, on the other hand, strangely so, the other as arbitrary (the child) is taken for granted. As far as she is concerned—impossible, that is just the way it is: it is reduced to the implacable. The other is inevitable, she seems to say, turn it into a God if you wish, it is nevertheless natural, for such an other has come out of myself, which is yet not myself but a flow of unending germinations, an eternal cosmos. The other goes much without saying and without my saying that, at the limit, it does not exist for itself. The "just the same" of motherly peace of mind, more persistent than philosophical doubt, gnaws, on account of its basic disbelief, at the symbolic's almightiness. It bypasses perverse negation ("I know, but just the same") and constitutes the basis of the social bond in its generality, in the sense of "resembling others and eventually the species." Such an atti-

tude is frightening when one imagines that it can crush everything the other (the child) has that is specifically irreducible: rooted in that disposition of motherly love, besides, we find the leaden strap it can become, smothering any different individuality. But it is there, too, that the speaking being finds a refuge when his/her symbolic shell cracks and a crest emerges where speech causes biology to show through: I am thinking of the time of illness, of sexual-intellectual-physical passion, of death . . .

who are available so that our speaking species, which knows it is mortal, might understand death. Of mothers. For an heretical ethics separated from morality, an *herethics*, is perhaps no more than that which in life makes bonds, thoughts, and therefore the thought of death, bearable: herethics is undeath [*a-mort*], love . . . *Eia mater, fons amoris* . . . So let us again listen to the *Stabat Mater*, and the music, all the music . . . it swallows up the goddesses and removes their necessity.

NOTES

1. Between the lines of this section one should be able to detect the presence of Marina Warner, *Alone of All Her Sex: The Myth and Cult of the Virgin Mary* (New York: Knopf, 1976) and Ilse Barande, *Le Maternel singulier* (Paris: Aubier-Montaigne, 1977), which underlay my reflections.
2. Georges Dumezil, *La Religion romaine archaïque* (Paris: Payot, 1974).
3. [The French version quoted by Kristeva ("Woman, what is there in common between you and me?") is even stronger than the King James translation, "Woman, what have I to do with thee?"—Trans.]
4. Jung thus noted the "hierogamous" relationship between Mary and Christ as well as the overprotection given the Virgin with respect to original sin, which places her on the margin of mankind; finally, he insisted very much on the Vatican's adoption of the Assumption as dogma, seeing it as one of the considerable merits of Catholicism as opposed to Protestantism. C. G. Jung, *Answer to Job* (Princeton: Princeton University Press, 1969).
5. As Caelius Sedulius wrote, "She . . . had no peer/Either in our first mother or in all women/Who were to come. But alone of all her sex/She pleased the Lord." ("Paschalis Carminis," Book II, lines 68ff. of *Opera Omnia* [Vienna, 1885]). Epigraph to Marina Warner, *Alone of All Her Sex.*

And the One Doesn't Stir Without the Other

The relationship between mothers and their daughters is among the most vexing problems for feminist theory. Irigaray's meditation on the obstacles to women's identity and individuality is cast in the form of an extended apostrophe, in which she confronts her mother with her frustrations, with the ways in which their relationship stifles her. A torrent of tropes—milk as ice, mothers and daughters as living mirrors, women as prisoners—this essay rages against the conflation of daughters with their mothers, against mothers' vicarious identification with their daughters' lives, and against women's confinement to the single role of motherhood. Also, it pleads for a conception of womanhood that would allow both the mother and the daughter to be distinct individuals and to achieve this without abandoning their ties to one another and without necessitating a liberating bond to a man.

—D.T.M.

Chapter 17

Luce Irigaray

And the One Doesn't Stir Without the Other

Translated by Hélène Vivienne Wenzel

With your milk, Mother, I swallowed ice. And here I am now, my insides frozen. And I walk with even more difficulty than you do, and I move even less. You flowed into me, and that hot liquid became poison, paralyzing me. My blood no longer circulates to my feet or my hands, or as far as my head. It is immobilized, thickened by the cold. Obstructed by icy chunks which resist its flow. My blood coagulates, remains in and near my heart.

And I can no longer race toward what I love. And the more I love, the more I become captive, held back by a weightiness that immobilizes me. And I grow angry, I struggle, I scream—I want out of this prison.

But what prison? Where am I cloistered? I see nothing confining me. The prison is within myself, and it is I who am its captive.

How to get out? And why am I thus detained?

You take care of me, you keep watch over me. You want me always in your sight in order to protect me. You fear that something will happen to me. Do you fear that something will happen? But what could happen that would be worse than the fact of my lying supine day and night? Already full-grown and still in the cradle. Still dependent upon someone who carries me, who nurses me. Who *carries* me? Who *nurses* me?

A little light enters me. Something inside me begins to stir. Barely. Something new has moved me. As though I'd taken a first step inside myself. As if a breath of air had penetrated a completely petrified being, unsticking its mass. Waking me from a long sleep. From an ancient dream. A dream which must not have been my own, but in which I was captive. Was I a participant, or was I the dream itself—another's dream, a dream about another?

I start to breathe, or rather I start to breathe again. It's strange. I stay very still, and I feel this something moving inside me. It enters me, leaves me, comes back, leaves again. I make this movement all by myself. No one assists. I have a home inside me, another outside, and I take myself from the one to the other, from the one into the other. And I no longer need your belly, your arms, your eyes, or your words to return or to leave. I am still so close to you, and already so far way. It's morning, my first morning. Hello. You're there. I'm here. Between us so much air, light, space to share with each other. I no longer kick impatiently, for I've got time now.

The day dawns. I'm hungry. I wish I had the energy to walk. To run all by myself, near or far from you. To go toward what I love.

You've prepared something to eat. You bring it to me. You feed me/yourself.[1] But you feed me/yourself too much, as if you wanted to fill me up completely with your offering. You put yourself in my mouth, and I suffocate. Put yourself less in me, and let me look at you. I'd like to see you while you nurse me; not lose my/your eyes when I open my mouth for you; have you stay near me while I drink you. I'd like you to remain outside, too. Keep yourself/me outside, too. Don't engulf yourself or me in what flows from you into me. I would like both of us to be present. So that the one doesn't disappear in the other, or the other in the one. So that we can taste each other, feel each other, listen to each other, see each other—together.

I look like you, you look like me. I look at myself in you, you look at yourself in me. You're already big, I'm still little. But I came out of you, and here, in front of your very eyes, I am another living you.

But, always distracted, you turn away. Furtively, you verify your own continued existence in the mirror, and you return to your cooking. You change yourself according to the clock. You adorn yourself depending upon the time. What time? Time for what? Time for whom? I would like you to break this watch and let me watch you. And look at me. I would like us to play together at being the same and different. You/I exchanging selves endlessly and each staying herself. Living mirrors.

We would play catch, you and I. But who would see that what bounces between us are images? That you give them to me, and I to you without end. And that we don't need an object to throw back and forth at each other for this game to take place. I throw an image of you to you, you throw it back, catch it again.

But then you seem to catch yourself, and once more you throw back to me: "Do you want some honey? It's time to eat. You must eat to become big."

You've gone again. Once more you're assimilated into nourishment. We've again disappeared into this act of eating each other. Hardly do I glimpse you and walk toward you, when you metamorphose into a baby nurse. Again you want to fill my mouth, my belly, to make yourself into a plenitude for mouth and belly. To let nothing pass between us but blood, milk, honey, and meat (but no, no meat; I don't want you dead inside me).

Will there never be love between us other than this filling up of holes? To close up and seal off everything that could happen between us, indefinitely, is that your only desire? To reduce us to consuming and being consumed, is that your only need?

I want no more of this stuffed, sealed-up, immobilized body. No, I want air. And if you lead me back again and again to this blind assimilation of you—but who are you?—if you turn your face from me, giving yourself to me only in an already inanimate form, abandoning me to competent men to undo my/your paralysis, I'll turn to my father. I'll leave you for someone who seems more alive than you. For someone who doesn't prepare anything for me to eat. For someone who leaves me empty of him, mouth gaping on his truth. I'll follow him with my eyes, I'll listen to what he says, I'll try to walk behind him.

He leaves the house, I follow in his steps. Farewell, Mother, I shall never become your likeness.

I do gymnastics. I practice the body exercises suited to my disorder. I'll become a schooled robot. I move my body, completely unmoved. I advance and move about to the rhythm prescribed for my cure. Will, not love, regulates my gestures, my leaps, my dancing about. Each hour of the day finds me applying myself: trying to obey the doctors' orders. I concur totally with their diagnosis of my condition. I give them my complete attention, all my energy. I'll be the living demonstration of the correctness of their principles. Animated, reanimated by their understanding.

See from afar how I move with measured steps, me, once frozen in anger? Aren't I good now? A nearly perfect girl? I lack only a few garments, a little jewelry, some makeup, a disguise, some ways of being or doing to appear perfect. I'm beginning to look like what's expected of me. One more effort, a little more anger against you who want me to remain little, you who want me to eat what you bring me rather than to see me dress like you, and I'll step out of the dream. Out of my disorder. Out of you in me, me in you. I'll leave us. I'll go into another home. I'll live my own life, my story.

Look at how healthy I am now. I don't even have to run after a man, he comes toward me. He approaches me. I await him, immobile, rooted. He's very near. I'm paralyzed with emotion. My blood no longer circulates very well. I hardly breathe. I leave.

I can't tell you where I am going. Forget me, Mother. Forget you in me, me in you. Let's just forget us. Life continues . . .

* * *

You look at yourself in the mirror.[2] And already you see your own mother there. And soon your daughter, a mother. Between the two, what are you? What space is yours alone? In what frame must you contain yourself? And how to let your face show through, beyond all the masks?

It's evening. As you're alone, as you've no more image to maintain or impose, you strip off your disguises. You take off your face of a mother's daughter, of a daughter's mother. You lose your mirror reflection. You thaw. You melt. You flow out of your self.

But no one is there to gather you up, and nothing stops this overflow. Before day's end you'll no longer exist if this hemorrhaging continues. Not even a photographic remembrance as a mark of your passage between your mother and your daughter. And, maybe, nothing at all. Your function remains faceless. Nourishing takes place before there are any images.[3] There's just a pause: the time for the one to become the other. Consuming comes before any vision of her who gives herself. You've disappeared, unperceived—imperceptible if not for this flow that fills up to the edge. That enters the other in the container of her skin. That penetrates and occupies the container until it takes away all possible space from both the one and the other, removes every interval between the one and the other. Until there is only this liquid that flows from the one into the other, and that is nameless.

No one to take you into herself tonight, Mother. No one to thirst for you, to receive you into herself. No one to open her lips and to let you flow into her, thus to keep you alive. No one to mark the time of your existence, to evoke in you the rise of a passage out of yourself, to tell you: Come here, stay here. No one to tell you: Don't remain caught up between the mirror and this endless loss of yourself. A self separated from another self. A self missing some other self. Two dead selves distanced from each other, with no ties binding them. The self that you see in the mirror severed from the self that nurtures. And, as I've gone, you've lost the place where proof of your subsistence once appeared to you.

Or so you thought. But by pouring your ice into me, didn't you quench my thirst with your paralysis? And never having known your own face, didn't you nourish me with lifelessness? In your blood, in your milk there flowed sandy mirages. Mixed in with these was the still-liquid substance which would soon freeze in all our exchanges, creating the impossible between us. Of necessity I became the uninhabitable region of your reflections. You wanted me to grow up, to walk, to run in order to vanquish your own infirmity.

So that your body would move to the rhythm of your desire to see yourself alive, you imprisoned me in your blindness to yourself. In the absence of love that provoked or accompanied the mobility of your features, your gestures. You desired me, such is this love of yours.[4] Imprisoned by your desire for a reflection, I became a statue, an image of your mobility.[5]

In the place where you wanted yourself seen you received only transparency or inertness. An atmosphere indefinitely void of any reflection of you, a body uninhabited by self-knowledge. You could traverse every landscape or horizon, over and over again, without ever encountering yourself. Or bump against this thing that you are, and that you have made me, hindering your/my progress. Opacity eclipsing any movement toward the light.

Who are you? Who am I? Who answers for our presence in this translucency, before this blind obstacle?

And if I leave, you no longer find yourself. Was I not the bail to keep you from disappearing? The stand-in for your absence? The guardian of your nonexistence? She who reassured you that you could always find yourself again, hold yourself, at any hour, in your arms? Keep yourself alive? Nurture yourself indefinitely in your attempt to subsist? Feed yourself blood and milk and honey over and over again (I never wanted your meat), to try to restore yourself to the world?[6]

But so it is when one waits;[7] this evening no one comes. You move toward a future that is lacking. There is no one in whom to remember the dream of yourself. The house, the garden, everywhere is empty of you. You search for yourself everywhere in vain. Nothing before your eyes, in your hands, against your skin to remind you of yourself. To allow you to see yourself in another self. And this makes you empty yourself even more into my body—to maintain the memory of yourself, to nourish the appearance of yourself. No, Mother, I've gone away.

But have I ever known you otherwise than gone? And the home of your disappearance was not in me. When you poured yourself into me, you'd already left. Already become captive elsewhere. Already entered into someone else's gaze. You were already moving into a world to which I had no access. I received from you only your obliviousness of self, while my presence allowed you to forget this oblivion. So that with my tangible appearance I redoubled the lack of your presence.

But forgetfulness remembers itself when its memorial disappears. And here you are, this very evening, facing a mourning with no remembrance. Invested with an emptiness that evokes no memories. That screams at its own rebounding echo. A materiality occupying a void that escapes its grasp. A block sealing the wall of your prison. A buttress to a possible future, which, taken away, lets everything crumble indefinitely.

Where are you? Where am I? Where to find the traces of our passage? From the one to the other? From the one into the other?

You go down, you go down again, alone, under the ground. Under the ground where we seemed to be walking. The one, the other. The one or the other. You abandon your firmness, your uprightness. Your steps, your features hardened by the determination that accompanies solitude. You return to this cave whose entrance you couldn't find. To this cellar whose doorway you've forgotten. To this hole in your memory where the silence of my birth from you was buried—the silence of my separation, inseparable from you. To the obscurity of your conception of me.

What happened in the nighttime of your belly to make you no longer know I existed? Of the two of us, who was the one, who the other? What shadow or what light grew inside you while you carried me? And did you not grow radiant with light while I lived, a thing held in the horizon of your body? And did you not grow dim when I took root in your soil? A flower left to its own growth. To contemplate itself without necessarily seeking to see itself. A blossoming not subject to any mold. An effluorescence obeying no already known contours. A design that changed itself endlessly according to the hour of the day. Open to the flux of its own becoming. Turning, turning away, turning around as it was drawn or pushed toward the burst of growth, or held back near the hiding place of its first watering; unfolding in an atmosphere as yet free of images. Becoming ecstatic with its own rhythm and measure, not yet under the constraint of eyes in quest of its mystery. Full-blossomed, bound by the ring of a lost vision. Encircled in the blind periphery of a question without answer.

Was I not your predestined guarantor? The profile of yourself that another would have stolen from you? The skin that another would have taken away? Wandering without identity, discharging upon me this endless, and at each step excruciating, wandering of yours. In me, shaping your destiny of an unknown. The yet-undeveloped negative images of your coming to yourself/me.

Here is she who I shall be, or was, or would like to be—was that not your response to my birth? What place remained for me into which to be born? Where to start my birth outside of you? For even when I was yet inside you, you kept me outside yourself.

With your milk, Mother, you fed me ice. And if I leave, you lose the reflection of life, of your life. And if I remain, am I not the guarantor of your death? Each of us lacks her own image; her own face, the animation of her own body is missing. And the one mourns the other. My paralysis signifying your abduction in the mirror.

And when I leave, is it not the perpetuation of your exile? And when it's my turn, of my own disappearance? I, too, a captive when a man holds me in his gaze; I, too, am abducted from myself. Immobilized in the reflection he expects of me. Reduced to the face he fashions for me in which to look at himself. Traveling at the whim of his dreams and mirages. Trapped in a single function—mothering.

* * *

Haven't you let yourself be touched by me? Haven't I held your face between my hands? Haven't I learned your body? Living its fullness. Feeling the place of its passage—and of the passage between you and me. Making from your gaze an airy substance to inhabit me and shelter me from our resemblance. From your/my mouth, an unending horizon. In you/me and out of you/me, clothed or not, because of our sex. In proportion to our skin. Neither too large nor too small. Neither wide open nor sutured. Not rent, but slightly parted.

And why would any other hurt be inflicted upon me? Didn't I already have my/your lips? And this body open on what we would never have stopped giving each other, saying to each other? This breach of silence where we constantly re-envelope ourselves in order to be reborn. Where we come to relearn ourselves and each other, in order to become women, and mothers, again and again.

But we have never, never spoken to each other. And such an abyss now separates us that I never leave you whole, for I am always held back in your womb. Shrouded in shadow. Captives of our confinement.

And the one doesn't stir without the other. But we do not move together.[8] When the one of us comes into the world, the other goes underground. When the one carries life, the other dies. And what I wanted from you, Mother, was this: that in giving me life, you still remain alive.

NOTES

1. The French here—*Tu me/te donnes à manger*—carries several nuanced meanings: "You give me [something] to eat"; "You give yourself [something] to eat"; and "You give me yourself to eat." (Note—All footnotes are translator's comments.)

2. The word in French, *la glace,* has the second meaning of "ice" that carries more strongly than the English "mirror" a sense of movement frozen and rigidified.
3. The French is more elegant than the English can be: *Nourir a lieu avant toute figure.* Implied also in the word *figure* is the concept of "face" and of "identity."
4. The phrase *tel cet amour de toi* carries the meaning "such is this love of yours," but also suggested is "such is this love *of yourself,*" underlining the confusion/fusion of identities between mother and daughter.
5. Irigaray's own words—*j'étais pétrifiée dans la représentation de ta mouvance*—brings together ideas of fear and immobility as the English cannot. In these passages Irigaray creates a locus of coexisting opposites that contrast actual paralysis and potential movement: *paralysie, inanimée, gel, infirmité, enfermée, figée, petrifiée;* and *coulait, fluide, marche, coure, meuve, mobilité, mouvance.*
6. The phrase used by Irigaray—*se remettre au monde*—carries the implication of physical birth (*mettre au monde*) as well as of giving birth to the self or of self-restoration.
7. The phrase *telle l'attente de toi* carries the meaning "such is your wait," but also suggested is "so it is when one waits *for you,*" in recognition of the daughter's waiting for the mother.
8. The sentence in French—*Mais ce n'est ensemble que nous nous mouvons*—creates a sense of ambiguity since it suggests as well that "it is only together that we (can) move."

Part 4:
Subjectivity, Agency, and Feminist Critique

Mirrors and Windows: An Essay on Empty Signs, Pregnant Meanings, and Women's Power

Williams examines the Tawana Brawley case and draws out the implications of this case with respect to race, gender, and agency. In the fall of 1987 in upstate New York, a black teenager, Tawana Brawley, was found in a dazed and abused condition lying in a vacant lot. When questioned by authorities, she indicated that six white men had kidnapped and raped her. Sensationalized by the press, the case galvanized and polarized public opinion. After a lengthy investigation punctuated by charges of a racially motivated cover-up, prosecutors concluded that Brawley had inflicted the injuries on herself and fabricated her accusations. No one was indicted in the case.

Williams begins by introducing the themes of laughter and mirroring. She recalls how her law school colleagues told her to laugh off her students' racist behavior when she solicited their help in addressing this problem. Also, she describes mocking media coverage of a sting operation in which one hundred black male parole violators were lured to a party where they expected to receive tickets to a professional football game, but found themselves under arrest instead. For Williams, socially marginalized people who can be harmed and laughed at with impunity and who are expected to join in the merriment act as mirrors that reveal hidden structures of domination. When Williams turns to Tawana Brawley, she documents unexplained shifts in press accounts of Brawley's condition when she was found, the deflection of media attention away from what happened to Brawley and toward her family and advisors, and the stereotyping of African-American sexuality in the popular imagination. Moreover, Williams stresses that Brawley was both exposed and silenced by white male legal authorities and by black male leaders. A pawn in a politics in which she had no voice, Brawley is seen at a comedy show at the Apollo Theater laughing at a joke about her own disempowerment, in which she has no choice but to collaborate.

—D.T.M.

Chapter 18

Patricia J. Williams

Mirrors and Windows: An Essay on Empty Signs, Pregnant Meanings, and Women's Power

At a faculty meeting once, I raised several issues: racism among my students, my difficulty in dealing with it by myself, and my need for the support of colleagues. I was told by a white professor that "we" should be able to "break the anxiety by just laughing about it." Another nodded in agreement and added that "the key is not to take this sort of thing too seriously."

Sometime after that, the *New York Times* ran a story about the arrest of one hundred parole violators who had been lured to a brunch with promises of free tickets to a Washington Redskins–Cincinnati Bengals football game: "The suspects reported to the Washington Convention Center after receiving a letter saying they had won the tickets from a cable television company, which had been set up as part of the police operation."[1] That evening, the televised news accounts of this story were infinitely more graphic. They showed one hundred black men entering a hall dressed for a party, some in tuxedos, some with fresh shiny perms, some with flowers in their lapels, some clearly hungry and there for the promised food, some dressed in the outfits of anticipatory football spectators, in raccoon coats and duckbill hats that said "Redskins." One hundred black men rolling up the escalators to the convention hall were greeted by smiling white (undercover) masters of ceremony, popping flashbulbs, lots of cameras, and pretty white women in skimpy costumes. Everyone smiled and laughed, like children at a birthday party. Everyone looked as though they were about the business of having a good time together. We saw the one hundred black men being rounded up by a swarm of white men, white women (also undercover agents) dressed as cheerleaders bouncing up and down on the side, a policeman dressed as a chicken with an automatic hidden in the lining, a SWAT team dressed in guerrilla-warfare green bursting in with weapons drawn.

My faculty colleagues have urged me not to give the voices of racism "so much power." Laughter is the way to disempower the forces of evil, I am told. But is it the racism I am disempowering if I laugh? Wouldn't this betray the deadly seriousness of it all? Laughing purposefully at what is hurtful seems somehow related to a first lesson in the skill of staged humiliation. Racism will thus be reduced to fantasy, a slapstick vaunting of good over evil—except that it is real. The cultural image of favored step-siblings laughing and pointing at such stupidity, at the sheer disingenuousness of bad children falling for the promise that they will get gifts, of even daring to imagine that they will get wonderful gifts too . . . if I laugh, don't I risk becoming that or, worse, a caricature of that image, that glossy marketing of despair?

Those who compose the fringe of society have always been the acceptable scapegoats, the butts of jokes, and the favored whipping boys. It resembles the pattern within psychotic families, where one child is set up as "sick" and absorbs the whole family's destructiveness. The child may indeed be sick in unsociably visible and dramatically destructive ways, but the family is unhealthy in its conspiracy not to see in themselves the emanation of such sickness. The child becomes the public mirror of quietly enacted personality slaughter. Resistance to seeing the full reality is played out in the heaving of blame and, most cowardly of all, in disempowering others and ourselves by making fun of serious issues. The alternative (and infinitely more difficult) course is to face the interconnectedness, the enmeshed pattern of public dismissiveness and private humiliation, of private crimes and publicly righteous wrongs, of individual disappointments and national tragedies.

In sum, I see the problem at hand not as one of *my* giving racism too much power, but of how we may all give more power to the voices that racism suppresses.

I am attending a conference called The Sounds of Silence. The topic of the day is the social construction of race and gender and oppression. People hurl heavy names at one another: Hegel, Foucault, Adorno. The discussion is interesting, but the undercurrent is dialectical war; there are lots of authority-bullets whizzing through the air.

I think: my raciality is socially constructed, and I experience it as such. I feel my black-self as an eddy of conflicted meanings—and meaninglessness—in which my self can get lost, in which agency and consent are tumbled in constant motion. This sense of motion, this constant windy sound of manipulation whistling in my ears, is a reminder of society's constant construction of my blackness.

Somewhere at the center, my heart gets lost. I transfigure the undesirability of my racial ambiguity into the necessity of deference, the accommodation of condescension. It is very painful when I permit myself to see all this. I shield myself from it wherever possible. Indeed, at the conference it feels too dangerous to say any of this aloud, so I continue to muse to myself, pretending to doze. I am awakened suddenly to a still and deadly serious room: someone has asked me to comment on the rape of black women and the death of our children.

Caught with my guard down, I finesse the question with statistics and forgotten words. What actually comes to my mind, however, is a tragically powerful embodiment of my ambiguous, tenuous social positioning: the case of Tawana Brawley, a fifteen-year-old black girl from Wappinger Falls, New York. In late November 1987, after a four-day disappearance, she was found in a vacant lot, clothed only in a shirt and a plastic garbage bag into which she had apparently crawled; she was in a dazed state, not responding to noise, cold, or ammonia;

there was urine-soaked cotton stuffed in her nose and ears; her hair had been chopped off; there were cigarette burns over a third of her body; "KKK" and "Nigger" had been inscribed on her torso; her body was smeared with dog feces.[2] This much is certain, "certain" because there were objective third persons to testify as to her condition in that foundling state (and independent "objective" testimony is apparently what is required before experience gets to be labeled truth), although even this much certainty was persistently recast as nothing-at-all in the subsequent months. By September the *New York Times* was reporting that "her ears and nose were *protected* by cotton wads;" that it was not her *own* hair that was cut, but hair extensions "woven into her own short hair" that had either been torn or cut out; that only her clothes and not her body had been burned; that, from the moment she was found, "*seemingly* dazed and degraded, [she] assumed the mantle of victim;" and that her dazed condition was "ephemeral" because, in the emergency room, after resisting efforts to pull open her eyes, "Dr. Pena concluded that Tawana was not unconscious and was aware of what was going on around her. . . . In a moment of quiet drama, Dr. Pena confronted Miss Brawley: 'I know you can hear me so open your eyes,' she commanded. Tawana opened her eyes and was able to move them in all directions by following Pena's finger."[3]

This much is certainly worth the conviction that Tawana Brawley has been the victim of some unspeakable crime. No matter how she got there. No matter who did it to her—and even if she did it to herself. Her condition was clearly the expression of some crime against her, some tremendous violence, some great violation that challenges comprehension. And it is this much that I grieve about. The rest of the story is lost, or irrelevant in the worst of all possible ways.

But there is a second version of the story. On July 14, 1988, New York State Attorney General Robert Abrams stated that "there may not have been any crime committed here."[4] A local television call-in poll showed that the vast majority of New Yorkers—the vast majority of any potential jury pool, in other words—agreed with him. Most people felt either that if she were raped it was "consensual" (as cruel an oxymoron that ever was) or that she "did it to herself" (as if self-mutilation and attempted suicide are free-enterprise, private matters of no social consequence with reference to which the concern of others is an invasion of privacy). It was a surprise to no one, therefore, when a New York grand jury concluded that Tawana Brawley had made the whole thing up.[5]

When Tawana Brawley was finally able to tell her story—she remained curled in fetal position for several days after she was found—she indicated that she had been kidnapped and raped by six white men:

> Nodding or shaking her head to questions . . . Miss Brawley gave contradictory answers. She indicated that she had been subjected to acts of oral sex, and after first indicating she had not been raped, she suggested she had been assaulted by three white men. . . . Asked who assaulted her, she grabbed the silver badge on his uniform but did not respond when he asked if the badge she saw was like this. He then gave her his notebook and she wrote "white cop." Asked where, she wrote "woods." He then asked her if she had been raped, and she wrote: "a lot" and drew an arrow to "white cop." . . . This response was the closest Miss Brawley ever came to asserting to authorities that she had been raped; her family and advisers, however, asserted many times that she was raped, sodomized and subjected to other abuse.[6]

The white men she implicated included the district attorney of Wappinger Falls, a highway patrolman, and a local police officer. This accusation was not only the first but also the last public statement Tawana Brawley ever made. (One may well question why she, a minor and a rape victim, was ever put in the position of making public statements at all. One might also inquire why the Child Protective Services Agency, which is supposed to intervene in such cases, did not.[7])

What replaced Tawana's story was a thunderous amount of media brouhaha, public offerings of a thousand and one other stories, fables, legends, and myths. A sampling of these enticing distractions includes:

> —Tawana's mother, Glenda Brawley, who fled to the sanctuary of a church to avoid arrest for failing to testify before a grand jury and to protest the failure of the same grand jury to subpoena the men named by her daughter.
>
> —Tawana's stepfather, from whom she had allegedly run away on prior occasions; by whom she had allegedly been beaten many times before—once even in a police station, in the presence of officers before they had a chance to intervene; and who served seven years for manslaughter in the death of his first wife, whom he stabbed fourteen times and, while awaiting trial for that much, then shot and killed.
>
> —Tawana's boyfriend, who was serving time on drug charges in an upstate facility and whom she had gone to visit shortly before her disappearance.
>
> —Tawana's lawyers, civil-rights activists Alton Maddox and C. Vernon Mason, who advised their client not to cooperate with investigating authorities until an independent prosecutor was appointed to handle the case.
>
> —Tawana's spiritual counselor, the Reverend Al Sharpton, described variously as a "minister without a congregation" ("Mr. Sharpton, who is still a member of the Washington Temple Church of God in Christ, does not serve as the pastor of any church. 'My total time is civil rights,' he said. 'It's kind of hard to do both' "[8]) and as an informer for the FBI ("The Rev. Al Sharpton, a Brooklyn minister who has organized civil disobedience demonstrations and has frequently criticized the city's predominantly white political leadership, assisted law-enforcement officials in at least one recent criminal investigation of black community groups, Government sources said. He also allowed investigators to wiretap a telephone in his home, the sources said"[9]). Al Sharpton, a man who had a long and well-publicized history of involvement in the wiretapping of civil rights leaders, yet—*miribile dictu*—a sudden but "trusted adviser" to the Brawley family. Al Sharpton, tumbling off the stage in a bout of fisticuffs with Roy Innis on the Morton Downey television show, brought to you Live! From the Apollo Theater.[10] Al Sharpton, railing against the court order holding Glenda Brawley in contempt, saying to the television cameras, "Their arms are too short to box with God."

It was Al Sharpton who proceeded to weave the story where Tawana left off. It was he who proceeded, on the Phil Donahue show, to implicate the Irish Republican Army, a man with a missing finger, and the Mafia. And it was he who spirited Tawana Brawley off into hiding, shortly after the police officer she had implicated in her rape committed suicide.

More hiding. As if it were a reenactment of her kidnap, a re-reenactment of her disappearing into the middle of her own case. It was like watching the Pied Piper of Harlem, this slowly replayed television spectacle of her being led off by the hand, put in a car, and driven to "a secret location"; a dance into thin air that could be accounted for by nothing less than sheer enchantment. I had a terrible premonition, as I watched, that Tawana Brawley would never be heard from again.

She has not been heard from again. From time to time there are missives from her advisers to the world: Tawana is adjusting well to her new school; Tawana wants to be a model; Tawana approves of the actions of her advisers; and, most poignantly, Tawana is "depressed," so her advisers are throwing her a party.

But the stories in the newspapers are no longer about Tawana anyway. They are all about black manhood and white justice; a contest of wills between her attorneys, the black community, and the New York state prosecutor's office. Since Tawana's statement implicated a prosecutor, one issue was the propriety of her case's being handled through the usual channels, rather than setting up a special unit to handle this and other allegations of racial violence. But even this issue was not able to hold center stage with all the thunder and smoke of raucous male outcry, curdling warrior accusations, the flash of political swords and shields—typified by Governor Cuomo's gratuitous offer to talk to Tawana personally; by Al Sharpton's particularly gratuitous statement that Tawana might show up at her mother's contempt hearing because "most children want to be in court to say good-bye to their mothers before they go to jail;"[11] by Phil Donahue's interview with Glenda Brawley, which he began with "No one wants to jump on your bones and suggest that you are not an honorable person but . . . ;" by the enlistment or the support of Louis Farrakhan and a good deal of anti-Semitic insinuation; by the mishandling and loss of key evidence by investigating authorities; by the commissioning of a so-called Black Army to encircle Glenda Brawley on the courthouse steps; by the refusal of the New York attorney general's office to take seriously the request for an independent prosecutor; and by the testimony of an associate of Sharpton's, a former police officer named Perry McKinnon, that Mason, Maddox, and Sharpton did not believe Tawana's story. (On television I hear this story reported in at least three different forms: McKinnon says Tawana lied; McKinnon says Sharpton lied about believing Tawana's story; McKinnon says that Mason and Maddox made up the whole thing in order to advance their own political careers. Like a contest, or a lottery with some drunken, solomonic game-show host at the helm, the truth gets sorted out by a call-in poll. Channel 7, the local ABC affiliate, puts the issue to its viewers: Do you believe Sharpton? Or do you believe McKinnon? I forgot to listen to the eleven o'clock news, when the winner and the weather were to have been announced.)

To me, the most ironic thing about this whole bad business—as well as the thread of wisdom that runs at the heart of the decision not to have Tawana Brawley testify—is that were she to have come out of hiding and pursued trial in the conventional manner, she would no doubt have undergone exactly what she did undergo, in the courts and in the media. Without her, the script unfolded at a particularly abstract and fanatical level, but the story would be the same: wild black girl who loves to lie, who is no innocent (New York television newscasters inadvertently, but repeatedly, referred to her as the "defendant") and whose wiles are the downfall of innocent, jaded, desperate white men; this whore-lette, the symbolic consort of rapacious, saber-rattling, buffoonish black men asserting their manhood, whether her jailbird boyfriend, her smooth-headed FBI drugbuster informant of a spiritual adviser, or her grandstanding, unethically boisterous so-called lawyers who have yet to establish "a *single* cognizable legal claim."[12]

Tawana's terrible story has every black woman's worst fears and experiences wrapped into it. Few will believe a black woman who has been raped by a white man. In one of the more appallingly straightforward statements to this effect, Pete Hamill, while excoriating the "racist hustlers" Sharpton, Mason, and Maddox for talking "about 'whites' as if they were a monolith," asked: "After Tawana Brawley, who will believe the next black woman who says she was raped by white men? Or the one after her?"[13] A slightly more highbrow version of the same sentiment was put forth in a *New York Times* editorial: "How can anyone know the depths of cynicism and distrust engendered by an escapade like this? Ask the next black person who is truly victimized—and meets skepticism and disbelief. Ask the next skeptic, white or black."[14]

If anyone believes that some white man even wanted her, no one will believe that she is not a whore. (White women are prostitutes; black women are whores. White women sell themselves, in implied Dickensian fashion, because they are jaded and desperate; black women *whore* as a way of being, as an innateness of sootiness and contamination, as a sticky-sweet inherency of black womanhood persistently imaged as overripe fruit—so they whore, according to this fantasy script, as easily as they will cut your throat or slit open said deep sweet fruit, spitting out afterwards a predictable stream of blood and seeds and casual curses.) Black women whore because it is sensual and lazy and vengeful. How can such a one be raped? Or so the story goes.

It is no easier when a black woman is raped by a black man (many of the newspapers have spun eager nets of suspicion around Tawana's stepfather[15] or a boyfriend). Black-on-black rape is not merely the violation of one woman by one man; it is a sociological event, a circus of stereotypification.[16] It is a contest between the universalized black man and the lusty black female. The intimacy of rape becomes a public display, full of passion, pain and gutsy blues.

Tawana Brawley herself remains absent from all this. She is a shape, a hollow, an emptiness at the center. Joy Kogawa's "white sound":

> There is a silence that cannot speak.
> There is a silence that will not speak.
> Beneath the grass the speaking dreams and beneath the dreams is a sensate sea. The speech that frees comes forth from that amniotic deep. To attend its voice, I can hear it say, is to embrace its absence. But I fail the task. The word is stone.[17]

There is no respect or wonder for her silence. The world that created her oppression now literally countenances it, filling the void of her suffering with sacrilegious noise, clashing color, serial tableaux of lurid possibility. Truth, like a fad, takes on a life of its own, independent of action and limited only by the imagination of self-proclaimed visionaries; untruth becomes truth through belief, and disbelief untruths the truth. The world turns upside-down; the quiet, terrible, nearly invisible story of her suffering may never emerge from the clamor that overtook the quest for "what happened" and polarized it into the bizarre and undecidable litigation of "something happened" versus "nothing happened."

In the face of all this, there is some part of me that wanted this child to stay in hiding, some part of me that understands the instinct to bury her rather than expound. Exposure is the equivalent of metarape, as hiding with Al Sharpton is the equivalent of metakidnap. It feels as if there are no other options than hiding or exposing. There is danger everywhere for her, no shelter, no protection. There is no medicine circle for her, no healing society, no stable place to testify and be heard, in the unburdening of one heart.

There are three enduring pictures I have of Tawana Brawley. The first is drawn from the images that both signaled and sensationalized the public controversy: the "television cameras invading the Brawley home to zoom in for a close-up of Tawana lying on a couch, looking brutalized, disoriented, almost comatose." And the pictures that were either leaked or "escaped" from the attorney general's office, the "police-evidence photographs showing Tawana Brawley as she looked when she was first brought by ambulance to a hospital following her rape; unconscious, dirty, half-naked, a 'censorship band' on the pictures covering only the nipples on her otherwise exposed breasts."[18] Her body so open and public; her eyes closed, her face shuttered, her head turned always away from the cameras.

The second image I carry of her is the widely circulated picture of her standing just behind Al Sharpton as he spoke for her. It is an image retained from innumerable photographs, taken from every angle and published over and over again, for months, everywhere: Al Sharpton with his mouth open, the perpetually open mouth. Tawana standing in his shadow clothed in silence, obedient and attentive, patient, wide-eyed, and unremittingly passive.

The third image is one described by a student of mine. At the height of the controversy, Tawana attended a comedy show at the Apollo Theater in Harlem. One of the comedians called attention to her presence in the audience and, in a parody of the federal antisex and antidrug campaigns, advised her to "just say no next time." As the audience roared with merriment and the spotlight played on her, Tawana threw back her head and laughed along with the crowd. She opened her mouth and laughed, in false witness of this cruel joke. It is the only image I have of Tawana with her mouth open—caught in a position of compromise, of satisfying the pleasure and expectations of others, trapped in the pornography of living out other people's fantasy.

I also take away three images of the men in whose shadow Tawana always stood. The first, and just plain weirdest, is that of Al Sharpton boxing with Roy Innis on the ultraconservative and ultrapsychotic *Morton Downey Show:*

> Conservative black leader Roy Innis toppled Tawana Brawley adviser Al Sharpton while taping a TV program on black leadership, and the two civil rights gadflies vowed yesterday to settle their dispute in a boxing ring. . . . "He tried to 'Bogart' me in the middle of my statement," said Innis. . . . "I said no dice. . . . We stood up and the body language was not good. So I acted to protect myself. I pushed him and he went down." . . . As the rotund preacher tumbled backward, Downey and several bodyguards jumped between the pair. Neither man was hurt. . . . Sharpton said he hoped boxing promoter Don King would help organize a Sharpton-Innis charity boxing match. . . . but said he would promote it himself if necessary. . . . "The best part is that we will be giving a very positive lesson to young black people in this city about conflicting resolution—but not on the street with guns and knives," Innis said. "It will be an honest, clean and honorable contest."[19]

The second image I have is of heavyweight champion Mike Tyson, whose own tumultuous home life was momentarily overshadowed when, with a great deal of public ceremony, he presented Tawana with a gold Rolex watch and ringside tickets for his next match. Yet there was an odd intersection in the Brawley and Tyson stories: in the contemporaneous coverage of the marital spats between Tyson and his wife, actress Robin Givens—and in the face of uncontested allegations that Tyson used his lethal million-dollar fists to beat her up—it was somehow Givens and her mother, like Tawana and hers, who became everyone's favorite despised object in supermarket-checkout conversation.[20] Tyson's image as a big harmless puppy whose uncontrolled paws were only a feature of his exuberant lovability found ultimate and ironic expression, as cultured in the media, with his visit and gifts to the Brawley family.

The last image is one I saw in the newspaper shortly after the grand-jury report had been published, of Louis Farrakhan, unkindly captured with his mouth wide open. The story says that Tawana Brawley has surfaced from her long silence and

> expressed a desire to become a Muslim and will receive a new Muslim name. . . . Mr. Farrakhan [leader of the Nation of Islam] . . . told an audience of 10,000 on Sunday that he . . . rejected the grand jury's findings, and he vowed vengeance on those who, he said, had attacked the girl. "You raped my daughter and I will kill you and dismember your body and feed it to the fowl of the air."[21]

The photo also showed Tawana, standing just behind Farrakhan. She is wrapped and turbaned in white, the image of chastity, of rigid propriety, of womanhood's submission to rule and ritual in a world where obedience is an unendingly complicated affair. There is a prayerful expression on her face. Her eyes are unreadable, and her mouth is closed.

NOTES

1. "Police, Marshals and Chicken Lure Fugitives into Custody," *New York Times*, December 16, 1985, p. B17.
2. E. Diamond, "The Brawley Fiasco," *New York Magazine*, July 18, 1988, p. 22.
3. "Evidence Points to Deceit by Brawley," *New York Times*, September 27, 1988, p. A1, italics added.
4. M. Cottman, "Abrams' Brawley Update: There Might Be No Crime," *New York Newsday*, July 15, 1988, p. 5.
5. Robert McFadden "Brawley Made Up Story of Assault, Grand Jury Finds," *New York Times*, October 7, 1988, p. 1.
6. *New York Times*, September 27, 1988, p. A1.
7. "What first signalled to me that a Black girl was about to bcome a public victim was hearing the *name* of an alleged rape victim—Tawana Brawley—given on a local radio news show. Since when does the press give the name of any rape victim, much less one who is underage? Obviously when the victim is Black, and thus not worthy of the same respect and protection that would be given a white child." Audrey Edwards, "The Rape of Tawana Brawley," *Essence*, November 1988, p. 80.

   As NAACP attorney Conrad Lynn observed, "State law provides that if a child appears to have been sexually molested, then the Child Protective Services Agency is supposed to take jurisdiction and custody of that child. Now, Tawana Brawley was 15 at the time of the incident. If that had been done, as I proposed early on, the agency would have given her psychiatric attention and preserved evidence, if ther wer evidence . . . But there was a state decision that the agency shouldn't be involved." Editorial, "What Happened to Tawana Brawley's Case—and to Attitudes about Race and Justice," *New York Times*, October 9, 1988, p. E8.

8. E. R. Shipp, "A Flamboyant Leader of Protests," *New York Times*, January 21, 1988, p. B6.
9. M. A. Farber, "Protest Figure Reported To Be a U. S. Informant," *New York Times*, January 21, 1988, p. B1. "Mr. Sharpton said that he—not investigators—had put a recording device on his phone, but only to serve as a 'hot line' for people turning in crack dealers" (p. B6).
10. "Roy Innis Pushes Al Sharpton: Fracas at 'Downey Show' Taping; Boxing Match Planned," *Washington Post*, August 11, 1988, p. D4.
11. A. Bollinger, "Tawana's Mom to Get 'Black Army' Escort," *New York Post*, June 3, 1988, p. 7.
12. Howard Kurtz, "New York Moves Against Brawley Lawyers," *Washington Post*, October 7, 1988, p. A1.
13. Pete Hamill, "Black Media Should Tell the Truth," *New York Post*, September 29, 1988, p. 5.
14. "The Victims of the Brawley Case," *New York Times*, September 28, 1988, p. A22.
15. "One witness said Mr. King 'would watch her exercise' and talked to the girl 'in a real sexual way,' sometimes describing her as a 'fine fox,' " *New York Times*, September 27, 1988, p. A16.
16. "Then it was off to the airport cafeteria for a strategy session and some cheeseburgers with adversers Alton Maddox, C. Vernon Mason and the Rev. Al Sharpton. 'The fat one, he ate the most,' said Carmen, the cashier. 'He and the skinny one [an aide] bought about $50 or $60 of cheeseburgers, orange juice, chocolate cake, pasta salad and pie,' she added." J. Nolan, "Traveling Circus Has 'Em Rollin' in Aisles," *New York Post*, September 29, 1988, p. 4.
17. Joy Kogawa, *Obasan* (Boston: David Godine, 1981), p. 1.
18. Edwards, "The Rape of Tawana Brawley," p. 80.
19. *Washington Post*, August 11, 1988, p. D4.
20. Under the caption "Robin Givens: Waiter, a Tonic with Slime for the Lady," even *Ms* magazine wrote: "We sympathized with the fights. We understood the divorce. But this crazy libel suit we don't get. Was it his personality and his pecs, or did you just want the bucks all along?" E. Combs and M. Suh, "Women Who Made Us Cringe," *Ms*, January–February 1989, p. 96.
21. "Brawley To Get Muslim Name," *New York Times*, October 11, 1988, p. B3.

Though This Be Method, Yet There Is Madness in It: Paranoia and Liberal Epistemology

Enlightenment philosophers acknowledge the rationality of all persons and affirm that every rational individual is capable of grasping the truth. Since no person need defer to a higher authority for knowledge, Enlightenment epistemologies are egalitarian. Yet, Scheman urges that the social import of these epistemologies depends on the historical context in which they are adopted. Despite the democratic intentions of the philosophers who developed Enlightenment epistemologies, and despite the emancipatory purposes that these epistemologies served in their time, they serve retrograde ends today.

Scheman makes her case by drawing parallels between the logic of paranoia and the logic of Cartesian epistemology. Paranoia develops as a result of cruel, fiercely disciplinary childrearing practices designed to repress taboo desires. Hating the repressed desires that threaten unified identity and disrupt control, the paranoid projects them onto others. Thus, paranoiacs believe that others are hostile and that this hostility justifies hating them. They defend their own egos at the cost of estranging themselves from everyone else. Similarly, Scheman urges, Descartes's skeptical method requires that knowers discipline themselves—that they cut themselves off from their bodies, police their passions and perceptions, and rely exclusively on reason for knowledge. Alienated from and suspicious of sensual, embodied experience, they project this dimension of human existence onto subordinated social groups. Identified with the non-rational, women, workers, gays, lesbians, and the disabled are denied the status of knowers, and an epistemological elite is formed. How can epistemology be democratized? Scheman recommends conceiving the epistemic subject as internally multiplicitous, and she advocates an "emancipatory practice of subjectivity" through which diverse parts of the self can be brought into dialogue with one another and through which the need to project "bad" parts of the self onto others can be eliminated.

—D.T.M.

Chapter 19

Naomi Scheman

Though This Be Method, Yet There Is Madness in It: Paranoia and Liberal Epistemology

> When you do not see plurality in the very structure of a theory, what do you see?
>
> —María Lugones, "On the Logic of Pluralist Feminism"

> Somewhere every culture has an imaginary zone for what it excludes, and it is that zone we must try to remember today.
>
> —Catherine Clément, *The Newly Born Woman*

In an article entitled "The Politics of Epistemology," Morton White argues that it is not in general possible to ascribe a unique political character to a theory of knowledge.[1] In particular, he explores what he takes to be the irony that the epistemologies developed by John Locke and John Stuart Mill for explicitly progressive and democratic ends have loopholes that allow for undemocratic interpretation and application. The loopholes White identifies concern in each case the methods by which authority is granted or recognized.

Neither Locke nor Mill acknowledges any higher epistemic authority than human reason, which they take (however differently they define it) as generic to the human species and not the possession of some favored few. But for both of them, as for most other democratically minded philosophers (White discusses also John Dewey and Charles Sanders Peirce), there needs to be some way of distinguishing between the exercise of reason and the workings of something else, variously characterized as degeneracy, madness, immaturity, backwardness, ignorance, passion, prejudice, or some other state of mind that permanently or temporarily impairs the development or proper use of reason. That is, democracy is seen as needing to be defended against "the excesses of unbridled relativism and subjectivism" (White, "Politics," p. 90).

The success of such a defense depends on the assumption that if we eliminate the voices of those lacking in the proper use of reason, we will be eliminating (or at least substantially "bridling") relativism. This, I take it, can only mean that those whose voices are listened to will (substantially) agree, at least about those things that are thought to be matters of knowledge, whether they be scientific or commonsense statements of fact, fundamental moral and political principles, or specific judgments of right or wrong. To some extent this assumption is tautological: it is frequently by "disagreeing" about things the rest of us take for granted that one is counted as mad, ignorant, or otherwise not possessed of reason. But precisely that tautologousness is at the root of what White identifies as the loophole through which the antidemocratic can pass. Moral, political, and epistemological elitism is most attractive (to the elite) and most objectionable (to others) when the nonelite would say something different from what gets said on their behalf, allegedly in the name of their own more enlightened selves.

White argues that the democratic nature of an epistemology cannot be read off its face but is in part a matter of its historically specific application: "Whether such a philosophy will be democratic in its effect depends on the ease with which the ordinary man may attain the privileged status described in the epistemology of the democratically oriented thinker. Where, because of social conditions, large numbers of persons in the community are not thought by such a philosopher to be able to see what their moral duties and rights are because they lack the attributes of a fully equipped moral judge, then the democratic intentions stand a good chance of being subverted" (White, "Politics," pp. 91–92). It's unclear to me why White thinks that the anti-democratic subversion of an intentionally democratic epistemology depends specifically on the philosophers' beliefs about who can exemplify their theories. Surely, such subversion depends at least as much on the ways in which that theory is understood and applied by others and on the beliefs of those others about who does and does not satisfy the philosophers' criteria of enfranchisement. Such beliefs may even, as I will argue is the case with René Descartes, contradict the philosopher's own explicit statements. Authorial intent is not determinative of how democratic an epistemology is: having constructed a loophole, theorists do not retain the authority to determine what can pass through it.

White's own unselfconscious use of "man" in what I assume he intends to be a generic sense is, ironically, a case in point. As has been argued by many feminist theorists,[2] masculine nouns and pronouns do not, in fact, have genuinely generic senses. Rather, in designating the masculine *as* generic, they designate the feminine as different, thereby requiring an act of self-estrangement on the part of female readers who would take themselves to be included in their scope. And all too often (frequently despite the stated beliefs of philosophers themselves), women have *not* been included among the rational, the mature, the unprejudiced. Historically, more often than not, in the real worlds in which philosophers' theories have been interpreted, the vast majority of women—along with many men—have been barred from or thought incapable of attaining "the privileged status described in the epistemology (or the moral philosophy) of the democratically oriented thinker[s]."

A striking feature of the advance of liberal political and epistemological theory and practice over the past three hundred years has been the increase in the ranks of the politically and epistemically enfranchised. It would seem that the loopholes have been successively narrowed, that fewer and fewer are being relegated to the hinterlands of incompetence or unreliability. In one sense, of course, this is true: race, sex, and property ownership are no longer explicit requirements for voting, office holding, or access to education in most countries. But just as exclusionary gestures can operate to separate off groups of people, so similar gestures can operate intrapsychically to separate those aspects of people that, if acknowledged, would disqualify them from full enfranchisement. We can understand the advance of liberalism as the progressive internalization—through regimes of socialization and pedagogy—of norms of self-constitution that (oxymoronically) "democratize privilege."

Thus various civil rights agendas in the United States have proceeded by promulgating the idea that underneath the superficial differences of skin color, genitalia, or behavior in the bedroom, blacks, women, and gays and lesbians are really just like straight white men. Not, of course, the other way around: difference and similarity are only apparently symmetrical terms. In the logic of political identity, to be among the privileged is to be among the same, and for the different to join those ranks has demanded the willingness to separate the difference-bearing aspects of their identity, to demonstrate what increasingly liberal regimes were increasingly willing to acknowledge: that one didn't need, for example, to be a man to embrace the deep structure of misogyny. It is one of my aims to argue that the norms that have structured modern epistemic authority have required the internalization of such exclusionary gestures, the splitting off and denial of (or control over) aspects of the self that have been associated with the lives of the disenfranchised, and that those gestures exhibit the logic of paranoia.

This process of "democratizing privilege" is inherently unstable. Materially, it runs up against the requirement of capitalism for significant numbers of people who are outside the reasonably affluent, paid labor force: the vast majority of people in the Third World, as well as those in affluent countries who are unemployed or marginally employed or who work only in the home—that is, those whose bodies literally are the foundation on which privileged subjectivity rests. As more and more of those others lay claim to stand on the ground their bodies have constituted, that ground gets predictably unstable.[3] Ideologically, expanding the ranks of the same runs up against the rise of the wide varieties of nationalisms and identity politics that have followed on the recognition by large numbers of people that they have all been attempting to impersonate a small minority of the world's population, and that it might instead be both desirable and possible to claim enfranchisement as the particular peoples they happen to be. Recent work in epistemology and philosophy of science, much of it explicitly influenced by Ludwig Wittgenstein or W. V. Quine (neither of whom would embrace either the explanations or the political agenda at issue here), can be seen as responsive to the need, given these challenges, for an epistemology that breaks with the structures of modernity by eschewing the homogenization of foundationalism and allowing for the democratic enfranchisement of explicitly and irreducibly diverse subjects. Knowledge rests not on universally recognizable and unassailable premises but on the social labor of historically embodied communities of knowers.

Part of my aim is to provide an account of what I think underlies this shift in mainstream Anglo-American epistemology and philosophy of science, to place that shift in social and historical context. But I am also concerned with the extent to which much current work is still captive to older pictures, notably in the continuing dominance of individualism in the philosophy of psychology. A fully social conception of knowledge that embraces diversity among knowers requires a corresponding conception of persons as irreducibly diverse and essentially interconnected. The individualism of modern personhood entails a denial both of connection and of individuality: modern subjects are distinct but not distinctive. Philosophers have taken this subject as theirs: it is his (*sic*) problems that have defined the field, the problems of anyone who takes on the tasks of internalizing the norms of privilege. As these norms change, so must the corresponding conceptions of personhood.

It is in this light that I want to examine the influence of Descartes's writings, works of intentionally democratic epistemology that explicitly include women in the scope of those they enfranchise. I have argued elsewhere, as have many others,[4] for the undemocratic nature of the influence of Cartesian epistemology, an influence that extends even to those epistemologies standardly treated as most antithetical to it (notably, empiricism). In particular, I want to argue that the structures of characteristically modern epistemic authority (with science as the central paradigm) normalized strategies of self-constitution drawn from Cartesian method. The discipline that is meant to ensure that proper use of the method will not lead to "unbridled relativism and subjectivism," although intended by Descartes to be both liberatory and democratic, has come to mirror the repressions that mark the achievement of privilege. Those strategies find, I believe, a peculiarly revelatory echo in the autobiographical writings of Daniel Paul Schreber and in their use in Freud's theory of paranoia.[5] Ironically, by the very moves that were meant to ensure universal enfranchisement, the epistemology that has grounded modern science and liberal politics not only has provided the means for excluding, for most of its history, most of the human race but has constructed, for those it authorizes, a normative paranoia.

I. SCHREBER

> The pedagogical conviction that one must bring a child into line . . . has its origin in the need to split off the disquieting parts of the inner self and project them onto an available object. . . . The enemy within can at last be hunted down on the outside.[6]

> [Anti-Semites] are people who are afraid. Not of the Jews, to be sure, but of themselves, of their own consciousness, of their instincts, of their responsibilities, of solitariness, of change, of society, and of the world—of everything except the Jews. . . . Anti-Semitism, in short, is fear of the human condition. The Anti-Semite is a person who wishes to be a pitiless stone, a furious torrent, a devastating thunderbolt—anything except a human being.[7]

Daniel Paul Schreber, a German judge, was thrice hospitalized for mental illness. After a brief confinement in a Leipzig clinic in 1884–1885, he recovered sufficiently to serve as *Senatspräsident* (head of a panel of judges) in Dresden. He was rehospitalized from 1893 until 1903, when he left the asylum after succeeding in a legal suit for his release from "tutelage" (that is, involuntary state guardianship). He returned to the asylum in 1907 and remained there until his death in 1911, the same year Freud published the case history based on the *Memoirs of My Nervous Illness*, which Schreber published in 1903 to draw attention to what he took to be happening to him.

Subsequent discussions of Schreber's case and of the *Memoirs* have taken issue with Freud's account. Sam Weber, in his introduction to recent re-publications (in German and

English) of the *Memoirs*, gives a Lacanian reading of the text, and Morton Schatzman, in *Soul Murder: Persecution in the Family*,[8] takes Schreber's account as a transformed but intelligible description of what was done to him as a child by his father, Daniel Gottlieb Moritz Schreber. The elder Schreber was a renowned doctor whose theories of child rearing were exceedingly influential in the development of some of the more extreme forms of what Alice Miller describes as "poisonous pedagogy,"[9] by which she means the accepted, even normative, use of coercion and violence against children supposedly "for their own good." I find helpful correctives to Freud both in Weber's Lacanian remarks and, especially, in Schatzman's antipsychoanalytic analysis[10] (to which I will return); but I want to start with Freud's account, in part because its logical structure mirrors that of the *Meditations* and the *Discourse on Method*.

Freud suggests that central to symptom formation in paranoia is the process of projection, but that this process can't be definitive of paranoia, in part because it appears elsewhere—for example, "when we refer the causes of certain sensations to the external world, instead of looking for them (as we do in the case of others) inside ourselves" (Freud, *SE*, 12, p. 66). He expresses the intention of returning to a general theory of (nonpathological as well as pathological) projection, but he never does. I want to suggest that the account he does give—of projection as a mechanism of paranoia—is closer to such a general theory than he thought it to be, because the relationship to the external world that was epistemically normative in his time and in ours is, by that account, paranoid.

Paranoia, for Freud, starts with the repression of a homosexual wishful fantasy—that is, for a man, sexual desire for another man.[11] In paranoia, as in all cases of repression more generally, there is a detachment of libido: what is previously cathected becomes "indifferent and irrelevant" (Freud, *SE*, 12, p. 70). In paranoia this decathexis spreads from its original object to the external world as a whole, and the detached libido attaches itself to the ego, resulting in megalomania.[12] It is the subsequently megalomaniacally re-created world that is permanently hostile to the paranoid: "The human subject has recaptured a relation, and often a very intense one, to the people and things in the world, even though the relation is a hostile one now, where formerly it was hopefully affectionate" (Freud, *SE*, 12, p. 71).

The hostility of the re-created world is a function of the mechanism of projection. The repression of the fantasy of loving a man takes the form of its contradiction: "I *hate* him," which is transformed by projection into "*he* hates—and persecutes—*me*, which justifies my hating him." Freud says only that the "mechanism of symptom-formation in paranoia requires that internal perceptions—feelings—shall be replaced by external perceptions" (Freud, *SE*, 12, p. 63). Presumably an account of just why such replacement should be required was to await the never-delivered general account of projection, but the mechanism isn't very mysterious. Placing all the initiating feeling out there, on what had been its object, is a far more effective way of shielding the ego from the acknowledgement of its own forbidden desires than would be a simple transformation of love into (inexplicable) hate.

The hostile forces in Schreber's world—God and his "rays"—are unequivocally male, and he believes that part of their plan is to transform him into a woman. The meaning of the transformation is twofold. Men, according to Schreber, have "nerves of voluptuousness" only in and immediately around their penises, whereas women's entire bodies are suffused with such nerves (Schreber, *Memoirs*, p. 204). God is directing toward Schreber, who has captured all of God's attention, rays that stimulate these nerves, requiring Schreber to "strive to give divine rays the impression of a woman in the height of sexual delight," by imagining himself "as man and woman in one person having intercourse with myself," an activity that Schreber insists, obviously protesting too much, "has nothing whatever to do with any idea of masturbation or anything like it" (Schreber, *Memoirs*, p. 208). The rays also impose demands, in the form of compulsive thinking, on Schreber's "nerves of intellect," and he is forced to strike a balance between intellectual thought and sensual ecstasy. But, most important, he must attempt always to be engaged in one or the other:

> As soon as I allow a pause in my thinking without devoting myself to the cultivation of voluptuousness—which is unavoidable as nobody can either think all the time or always cultivate voluptuousness—the following unpleasant consequences . . . occur: attacks of bellowing and bodily pain; vulgar noises from the madmen around me, and cries of "help" from God. Mere common sense therefore commands that as far as humanly possible I fill every pause in my thinking—in other words the periods of rest from intellectual activity—with the cultivation of voluptuousness. (Schreber, *Memoirs*, pp. 210–11)

In addition to being provided with soul-voluptuousness, God's other aim in "unmanning" him was eventual "fertilization with divine rays for the purpose of creating new human beings." Schreber was cognizant of the humiliating aspects of his position. The rays themselves taunted him, saying such things as, "Fancy a person who was a *Senatspräsident* allowing himself to be f . . . d [*sic*]." He initially entered into complicity with his transformation into a woman at a time when he believed that he was the only real person existing: "All the human shapes I saw were only 'fleeting and improvised,' so that there could be no question of any ignominy being attached to unmanning" (Schreber, *Memoirs*, p. 148). He subsequently defends the essential honor of his position as an accommodation with necessity and with God's will: "Since then I have wholeheartedly inscribed the cultivation of femininity on my banner. . . . I would like to meet the man who, faced with the choice of either becoming a demented human being in male habitus or a spirited woman, would not prefer the latter" (Schreber, *Memoirs*, p. 149).

The logic of Schreber's madness seems to me not that of homosexuality, repressed or otherwise. His delusions mirror his treatment as a boy at the hands of his father, and his madness indicts the treatment even while preserving the idealization of the powerful father who administered it. What that combination of terror and enthralled submission in the face of remembered or imagined male power does reflect is the logic of male homophobia. "Homophobia" is often used as though it meant the same thing for women as for men, but, given the very different social constructions of female and male sexuality, there is no reason to think this should be so. In particular, male homophobia attaches with greatest force not to the general idea of sexual desire for another man, but to the specific idea of being in the receptive position sexually. Given a culturally normative definition of sexuality in terms of male domination and female subordination, there is an understandable anxiety attached to a man's imagining another man's doing to him what men are expected to do to women: real men, *Senatspräsidenten* or not, are not supposed to allow themselves to be fucked. (Thus in men's prisons, the stigma attaches not to rapists, but to their victims.)

Male homophobia combines this anxiety with its corresponding desire, that of being, as we might say, ravished,[13] or swept away. It's notoriously difficult to speak—or think—

clearly about such desires or pleasures, a difficulty made apparent by the intertwinings of rape and rapture (which themselves share a common Latin root) in the *Oxford English Dictionary*'s definition of "ravish." The story seems to be the bad old one of the woman falling in love with the man who rapes her, a staple of pornography and Gothic romance, and barely veiled in Freudian accounts of normative femininity and in fairy tales. (Did Sleeping Beauty consent to the Prince's kiss?) Part of what is so insidious about these stories is that they link violence and domination to the pleasures of release—for example, the pleasure that sneezing can be, the sudden unwilled flood of sensation. Not, that is, *against* our will, inflicted upon us and a threat to our integrity, but *un*willed, a respite from will, a momentary reprieve from the exigencies of bodily discipline, an affront not to our humanity but to our solemnity, not to our self-respect but to our self-conceit. (The unblinking of such pleasure from the sadomasochistic structure of normative sexuality—the uncoupling of rape from rapture—is a fairy tale worth believing in, even if we can't quite tell it clearly.)

Schreber enacts both the anxiety and the desire. His body and mind are wracked by the struggle to resist what he ultimately succumbs to—being "unmanned" in the name of perpetual feminine "voluptuousness." His compensation for being subjected to such humiliating pleasure is the knowledge both that God has singled him out to receive it and that from his feminized loins will issue a new race of humans to re-create the world. Homophobia thus gets joined to another venerable fantasy structure: the usurpation by men of women's reproductive power. At least as far back as Socrates, men have taken the imagery of childbirth to describe their allegedly nobler, sublimated creative activities. Schreber's fantasies expose the homophobic anxieties that underlie the use of this imagery: you can't give birth without being fucked.

II. DESCARTES

> They are, in essence, captives of a peculiar arrogance, the arrogance of not knowing that they do not know what it is they do not know, yet they speak as if they know what all of us need to know.[14]

Cartesian philosophy is a paradigmatic example of White's thesis about the subversion of the democratic intent of an epistemology, although not because of Descartes's own views about whom it authorized. Descartes's explicit intent was the epistemic authorization of individuals as such—not as occupiers of particular social locations, including the social location of gender.[15] Most important, Descartes wanted to secure epistemic authority for individual knowers who would depend on their own resources and not on the imprimatur of those in high places, and, he argues, those resources could only be those of mathematized reason, not those of the senses. Only such a use of reason could ensure the sort of stability that distinguishes knowledge from mere opinion. Descartes's method was designed to allow anyone who used it to place him- or herself beyond the influence of anything that could induce error. Human beings, he argued, were not created as naturally and inevitably subject to error: God wouldn't have done that. What we are is finite, hence neither omniscient nor infallible. But if we recognize our limits and shield ourselves from the influence of what we cannot control, we can be assured that what we take ourselves to know is, in fact, true.

The method is a form of discipline requiring acts of will to patrol a perimeter around our minds, allowing in only what can be determined to be trustworthy, and controlling the influence of the vicissitudes of our bodies and of other people. Purged of bad influences, we will be struck by the "clarity and distinctness" of truths like the cogito.[16] We will have no real choice but to acknowledge their truth, but we ought not to find in such lack of choice any diminution of our freedom. Because the perception of truth comes from within us, not "determined by any external force," we are free in assenting to it, just as we are free when we choose what we fully and unambivalently want, even though it makes no sense to imagine that, given our desire, we might just as well have chosen otherwise.[17]

Freedom from determination by any external force requires, for Descartes, freedom from determination by the body, which is, with respect to the mind, an external force. Thus when Descartes invokes the malicious demon at the end of the First Meditation to help steel him against lazily slipping back into credulity,[18] his efforts are of a piece with his presentation at the end of *The Passions of the Soul* of "a general remedy against the passions."[19] Passions are no more to be dispensed with entirely than are perceptions (or, strictly speaking, *other* perceptions, given that passions are for Descartes a species of perception). But no more than other perceptions are passions to be taken at face value: they can be deceptive and misleading. Still less are they to be taken uncritically as motives to act, whether the action in question be running in fear from the dagger I perceive before me, or assenting to its real existence. In both cases, I (my mind) need to exercise control over my perceptions or, at least, over what I choose to do in the face of them. Seeing ought *not* to be believing in the case of literal, embodied vision, but when ideas are seen by the light of reason in the mind's eye, assent does and should follow freely.[20]

The individualism of Cartesian epistemology is yoked to its universalism. Though we are each to pursue knowledge on our own, freed from the influence of any other people, what we come up with is not supposed to be our own view of the world—it is supposed to be the truth, unique and invariable. When Descartes extols, in the *Discourse*,[21] the greater perfection of buildings or whole towns that are the work of a single planner over those that sprang up in an uncoordinated way, he may seem to be extolling the virtues of individuality. But what he finds pleasing are not the signs of individual style; it is the determining influence of reason as opposed to chance. Individualism is the route not to the idiosyncrasies of individuality but to the universality of reason.

This consequence is hardly accidental. Skepticism, which was a tool for Descartes, was for some of his contemporaries the ultimate, inevitable consequence of ceding epistemic authority to individual reason. If epistemic democratization was not to lead to the nihilism of the Pyrrhonists or the modesty of Montaigne, Descartes needed to demonstrate that what his method produced was knowledge, not a cacophony of opinion.[22] It could not turn out to be the case that the world appeared quite different when viewed by people differently placed in it. More precisely, everyone had to be persuaded that if it *did* appear different from where they stood, the remedy was to move to the Archimedean point defined by the discipline of Cartesian method. Those who could not so move were, in the manner of White's discussion, relegated to the ranks of the epistemically disenfranchised.

Descartes himself does not, so far as I know, consider the possibility that not everyone of sufficient maturity could actually use his method. The only disqualifying attribute I know that he explicitly discusses is youth.[23] He does, of course, briefly consider in the First Meditation the possibility that he is mad, or asleep and dreaming, but his aim there is to argue that it makes no difference: the cogito would still be true and knowable. Later, when he needs to go beyond those confines to areas in which sanity and a certain degree of consciousness can be presumed to make a difference, he needs, for the sake of his argument, to rely on first-person accessible signs that his mind is in working order: there's no way in which the judgment of others could be allowed to undercut the agent's own sense of being epistemically trustworthy.

It is central to Descartes's project, as it is to the social and political significance of that project, that no one and nothing other than agents themselves can confer or confirm epistemic authority (despite God's being its ultimate guarantor, His guarantee consists precisely in our each individually possessing such authority). Epistemic authority resides in the exercise of will that disciplines one's acts of assent—principally to refrain from assenting to whatever is not perceived clearly and distinctly.[24] And the will, for Descartes, is not only equally distributed among all people, but is also, in each of us, literally infinite. What is required is not the acquisition of some capacity, the exercise of which might be thought to be unequally available to all; rather it is the curbing of a too-ready willingness to believe.

Of course, such restraint will lead only to the avoidance of error; in order actually to acquire knowledge, one has also clearly and distinctly to perceive ideas to which one will, freely and inevitably, assent. But even such acquisition is, for Descartes, not reserved for the few, and even it is more a matter of disciplining the interference of distracting and misleading influences from the body, and from the external world through the body, than it is a positive matter of access to recondite truths. We need to train ourselves to quiet the ceaseless chatter of inner and outer perception, to curb, for example, the wonder we feel at the appearance of what seems to us unusual and extraordinary. A certain degree of wonder is useful for retaining in memory what we might otherwise fail to register sufficiently, but wonder, if unchecked, draws our attention hither and yon, when we should be intentionally directing it along the lines of thoughtful investigation. In his discussion of wonder Descartes does distinguish among people who are "dull and stupid," or "ignorant" because "not naturally inclined to wonder," or inclined to excessive, distracting wonder because "though equipped with excellent common sense, [they] have no high opinion of their abilities."[25] But none of these differences are differences in *intellect*: in our active capacities as knowers we are all, for Descartes, absolutely equal, and by disciplining our overactive wills, we can all bring our problematic (and unequal) bodies into line.

But, as I argued above, there is no reason why philosophers' own views about who can and cannot fully exemplify their requirements of epistemic enfranchisement should carry any special weight when the question concerns the democratic or antidemocratic effect of their theories, especially as those theories have been influential far beyond those philosophers' lifetimes. Descartes is a paradigmatic case in point.

The Cartesian subject was revolutionary. The individual bearer of modern epistemic authority became, through variations on the originating theme of self-constitution, the bourgeois bearer of rights, the self-made capitalist, the citizen of the nation state, and the Protestant bound by conscience and a personal relationship to God. In Descartes's writings we find the lineaments of the construction of that new subject, and we see the centrality of discipline to its constitution. Such discipline is supposed in theory to be available to all, not only to those whose birth gave them a privileged place in the world. If one was placed where one could not see the truth, or obtain riches, or exercise political or religious freedom, the solution was to move to some more privileged and privileging place. The "New World" was precisely constituted by the self-defining gestures of those who moved there from Europe and who subsequently got to determine who among those who followed would be allowed to take a stand on the common ground. (That constitution of the "New World" is one reason why the people who already lived there merited so little consideration in the eyes of those who invaded their home. The relationship the Indians took—and take—themselves to have to the land, a relationship grounded in their unchosen, unquestionable ties to it, was precisely the wrong relationship from the perspective of those who came to that land in order to define themselves anew by willfully claiming it, unfettered by history.)

With the success of the revolutions prefigured in the Cartesian texts, it became clear that the theoretical universalism that was their underpinning existed in problematic tension with actual oppression. Those who succeeded in embodying the ideals of subjecthood oppressed those whose places in the world (from which, for various reasons, they could not move)[26] were (often) to perform the labor on which the existence and well-being of the enfranchised depended and (always) to represent the aspects of embodied humanness that the more privileged denied in themselves.

The "often" and "always" in the preceding sentence reflect differences in the form taken by the oppression of various groups and the concomitant applicability of various methods for explaining that oppression. With respect to certain groups, most clearly the working class but also many women and people of color, oppression has been in large measure a matter of exploitation. Members of privileged groups benefit directly from the labor done by the exploited, whose oppression is a function both of the theft of their labor and of the ideological representation of that labor as disenfranchising. Such labor is disenfranchising either positively, in that its nature (for example, the bearing and rearing of children) is taken to be incompatible with intellection, or negatively, in that it doesn't allow for the leisure to cultivate the "higher" capacities that authorize the enfranchised.

For other oppressed groups, notably gay men, lesbians, and the disabled, the element of exploitation is either missing or at least far less evident, and an economic analysis of why they are oppressed is less evidently promising. It is striking, however, that such groups share with the others the representation of their supposed natures as incompatible with full social, political, and epistemic authority. For various reasons they are portrayed in hegemonic discourses as incapable of full participation in public life: they are put into one or more of the categories of disenfranchisement that White discusses. All the oppressed—the obviously exploited and the others—share in the minds of the privileged a defining connection to the body, whether it is seen primarily as the laboring body, the sexual body, the body insufficiently under the control of the rational will, or some combination of these. The privileged are precisely those who are defined not by the meanings and uses of their bodies for others but by their ability either to control their bodies for their own ends or to seem to exist virtually bodilessly. They are those who have conquered the sexual, dependent, mortal, and messy parts of themselves—in part by projecting all those qualities onto others, whom they thereby earn the right to dominate and, if the occasion arises, to exploit.

Exploitation and oppression are, of course, enormous and enormously complicated phenomena, and there is no reason to believe that one theory will account for all their aspects and ramifications, all their causes and effects.[27] There are also reasons for being generally suspicious of the felt need for, what are called by their critics, grand or totalizing theories or master narratives.[28] It is certainly not my intent either to give or to invoke any such theory. Rather, as Sandra Harding argues,[29] we (those who would seek to understand these phenomena with the aim of ending them) need to embrace not only methodological pluralism but even the "instabilities and incoherencies" (Harding, *Science Question*, p. 244) that come with theorizing during times of large-scale intellectual, social, and political change. In that spirit, I see this essay as part of what we might call the social psychology of privilege, an examination not of the apparently economically rational grounds for exploitation-based oppression, but of the deep springs that feed such oppression as well as the oppressions that seem on their face less rational.

Privilege, as it has historically belonged to propertied, heterosexual, able-bodied, white men, and as it has been claimed in liberal terms by those who are variously different, has rested on the successful disciplining of one's mind and its relation to one's body and to the bodies and minds of others. The discourses of gender, race, class, and physical and cognitive ability have set up dichotomies that, in each case, have normalized one side as the essentially human and stigmatized the other, usually in terms that stress the need for control and the inability of the stigmatized to control themselves. Acts of violence directed against oppressed groups typically are presented by their oppressors as preemptive strikes, justified by the dangers pose by the supposedly less-civilized, less-disciplined natures of those being suppressed. Workplace surveillance through lie detectors and drug testing (procedures in which subjects' bodies are made to testify to the inadequacies of their minds and wills), programs of social control to police the sexual behavior of homosexuals, the paternalistic disempowerment of the disabled, increasing levels of verbal and physical attacks on students of color by other students, and the pervasive terrorism of random violence against women all bespeak the need on the part of the privileged to control the bodies and behavior of those who are "different," a need that both in its targets and in its gratuitous fierceness goes beyond securing the advantages of exploitation.

Cartesian strategies of epistemic authorization, viewed through the lens of Schreber's paranoia, are illuminating here. As the authorized subject constitutes himself by contrast with the disenfranchised others, so he constitutes himself by contrast with the world that is the object of his knowledge. He also, by the same gestures, reciprocally constitutes that world. Freud, in his discussion of Schreber, quotes Goethe's *Faust*:

> Woe! Woe!
> Thou hast it destroyed,
> The beautiful world,
> With powerful fist!
> In ruins 'tis hurled,
> By the blow of a demigod shattered!
>
> Mightier
> For the children of men,
> More splendid
> Build it again,
> In thine own bosom build it anew![30]

The gesture is not only Schreber's; it is, of course, Descartes's. Like Schreber, Descartes imaginatively destroys the world through the withdrawal of his attachment to it (he becomes agnostic about its very existence), and like Schreber, his ego is thereby aggrandized and goes about the task of reconstituting the world, or a semblance of it, under the problematic aegis of an all-powerful father. This reconstituted world is perceived as hostile—made up as it is of everything the ego has split off—and as permanently in need of vigilant control. It is also perceived, and needs to be perceived, as independent of the self as the self needs to be perceived as independent of it. There can be no acknowledgement of the self's complicity in the constitution of the world as an object of knowledge. "Indeed," as Paul Smith puts it, "it is the desired fate of both paranoia and classical realism to be construed as interpretations of an already existing world, even though the world they both create is their own."[31]

Smith notes the need of the paranoiac (or of the humanist intellectual—he has in mind, in particular, hermeneutically inclined anthropologists such as Clifford Geertz) "to objectify or *realize* a reality and yet to proclaim the 'subject's' innocence of its formation" (Smith, *Discerning the Subject*, p. 87; emphasis in the original). Not only as hostile—or exotic—but as *real*, the world has to be regarded as wholly independent of the self. And the very activity of securing that independence has to be repressed; the subject and the world have to be innocent of each other, unimplicated in each other's identity.[32]

Despite Descartes's genuinely democratic intentions, as his epistemology was taken up by those who followed him, it authorized those—and only those—whose subject positions were constituted equally by their relationship into a purportedly objective world and by their relationship to the disenfranchised others, defined by their inescapable, undisciplined bodies.

III. PARANOIA, DISCIPLINE, AND MODERNITY

> Whatever we seek in philosophy, or whatever leads us to ask philosophical questions at all, must be something pretty deep in human nature, and what leads us to ask just the questions we do in the particular ways we now ask them must be something pretty deep in our tradition.[33]

The most influential theorist of surveillance, discipline, and control is Michel Foucault. *Discipline and Punish: The Birth of the Prison* traces the development and deployment of characteristically modern systems of power as pervasively applied to the bodies of the subjugated; *The History of Sexuality*, volume 1, looks at those systems largely as they shape subjectivity, desire, and knowledge.[34] In both cases power is not the simple possession of certain individuals or groups; rather, it is omnipresent, constitutive as much as constraining, expressed through the tissue of our personal and institutional lives.[35] But whereas the forms of administrative power discussed in *Discipline and Punish* construct individuals as objects, the discursive constructions of sex construct us rather *as subjects* in what we take to be our freedom, the expression of our desire. As we struggle against what we have learned to call repression, we speak our desire in terms that construct it—and us—according to a distinctively modern regime, even as we take ourselves to be striving toward the liberation of timelessly human wants and needs.[36]

I want to use Foucault to bring together Descartes and Schreber. With the success of the economic, social, cultural, and political revolutions that empowered the Cartesian subject,[37] the discipline Descartes called for moved from being the self-conscious work of self-constituting radicals to finding expression in the pedagogy of the privileged.[38] The soul-shaping regimes of the elder Schreber are a particularly stark version of that pedagogy, which finds coded expression in the *Memoirs* of Freud's Schreber and a chilling critique in the works of Alice Miller.

Morton Schatzman's *Soul Murder* is a detailed argument for the thesis that Schreber's *Memoirs* recount in coded form what his father did to him when he was a child. Daniel Gottlieb Moritz Schreber wrote prolifically about child-rearing regimes aimed at suppressing a child's will and replacing it with automatic obedience to the will of the parent while simultaneously inculcating in the child enormous powers of self-control, which the child was to exercise over his or her own body and desires. That is, the goal was not an attitude of subservient obedience, such that children would have no idea of what they were to do until commanded by their parents. Rather, the child's will was to be replaced by the will of the parent in such a way that the child would not notice (or, at least, would not remember)[39] that this was done and would henceforth act "autonomously," as though the now-internalized commands came from her or his own true self. And that commanding self needs precisely not to be weak and unassertive, charged as it is with keeping under control the child's unruly body, emotions, and desires.

Not surprisingly, prominent among the desires and unruly impulses that need to be kept under control are those connected with masturbation and sexual curiosity. Foucault's characterization of modern Europe as hardly silent about sexuality is borne out by Miller's examples of instructional techniques for extracting from children confessions of masturbation (Miller, *For Your Own Good*, pp. 18–21) and of arguments that sexual curiosity needs to be (albeit perhaps fraudulently) satisfied, lest it grow obsessive. One recommended means is to have children view naked corpses, because "the sight of a corpse evokes solemnity and reflection, and this is the most appropriate mood for a child under such circumstances" (Miller, *For Your Own Good*, p. 46). J. Oest, whose advise this was in 1787, also advised

> that children be cleansed from head to foot every two to four weeks by an old, dirty, and ugly woman, without anyone else being present; still, parents should make sure that even this old woman doesn't linger unnecessarily over any part of the body. This task should be depicted to the children as disgusting, and they should be told that the old woman must be paid to undertake a task that, although necessary for purposes of health and cleanliness, is yet so disgusting that no other person can bring himself to do it (Miller, *For Your Own Good*, pp. 46–47).

Miller quotes extensively from the elder Schreber as well as from these and other, similar eighteenth- and nineteenth-century pedagogues who counseled parents on how, for example, "exercises can aid in the complete suppression of affect" (Miller, *For Your Own Good*, p. 25; the counsel comes from J. Sulzer, whose *Essay on the Education and Instruction of Children* was published in German in 1748). The same theorist made it clear that such suppression of autonomy was not intended only or even primarily for those whose place in society was subordinate:

> Obedience is so important that all education is actually nothing other than learning how to obey. It is a generally recognized principle that persons of high estate who are destined to rule whole nations must learn the art of governance by way of first learning obedience. . . . [T]he reason for this is that obedience teaches a per-

son to be zealous in observing the law, which is the first quality of the ruler (Miller, *For Your Own Good*, pp. 12–13).

The choreography of will breaking and will strengthening has one additional turn: the shaping fiction of the enterprise is that the unruliness of children, however omnipresent, is nonetheless unnatural. In Schreber's words, "the noble seeds of human nature sprout upwards in their purity almost of their own accord if the ignoble ones, the weeds, are sought out and destroyed in time."[40] Thus the parental will that replaces the child's is in fact more truly expressive of the child's true nature than was the "bad" will the child took to be her or his own; it is not only that children should come to think so.

All this is, of course, much more reminiscent of Kant than of Descartes. It is Kant who argued that our passions are not expressive of our true, autonomous selves and, hence, that acting on them is neither morally right nor autonomous, and that those categories—the law-bound and the free—are actually identical. It is Kant who most clearly taught us to control our passions[41] and to identify with a self that we experience not as idiosyncratic but as speaking in the voice of impartial reason. Descartes, on the other hand, seems far more human, more playful, more respectful of the body and the emotions, more intrigued by the diversity in the world around him, more—and this is the crucial difference—anti-authoritarian than Kant.

As, of course, he was. He was in the midst of making the revolution that the pedagogues and Kant inherited, and it was a revolution precisely against entrenched authority, a revolution waged in the name of the individual. There is an exhilaration that even today's undergraduates can find in reading Descartes; he can speak, for example, to the woman student who is in the midst of discovering for herself that she has been systematically lied to about the world and her place in it, that authorities she had trusted disagree with each other and that none of them seems to have it right, and that even her own body can be untrustworthy. She may, for example, find food repulsive because even as she becomes emaciated she sees herself as hideously fat, or she may have learned from a sexual abuser to desire her own humiliation.

But, I want to argue, the Descartes we have inherited (and, more broadly, the liberal politics his epistemology partially grounds)[42] is a problematic ally for this young woman, as he is for the other women and men who have been the excluded others. Though he is not Kant, let alone Schreber (either the paranoid son or the "paranoidogenic" father),[43] the discipline of the method that lies at the heart of Descartes's constitution of himself as epistemically authoritative bears the seeds of paranoia, seeds that germinated as the revolution he helped to inaugurate moved from marginality to hegemony.

As Freud argues, the central mechanism of paranoia is projection, that process by which something that had been recognized as a part of the self is detached from it (a process called "splitting") and reattached on to something or someone other than the self. An underlying motivation for such splitting is narcissism: what is split off is incompatible with the developing ego. But it is significant to note that one obvious effect is the diminution of the self—it no longer contains something it once did. One consequence of that recognition is that it provides a motivation for thinking of that which is split off as wholly bad, perhaps even worse than it was thought to be when it was split off. It has to be clear that the self really is better off without it.

This is one way of thinking about the fate of the body in Cartesian and post-Cartesian epistemology. The self of the cogito establishes its claim to authority precisely by its separation from the body, a separation that is simultaneously liberating and totally isolating.

Although Descartes goes on, under the protection of God, to reclaim his body and to place himself in intimate and friendly relation to it, the loss to the self remains. René Descartes, along with all those who would follow his method, really is a *res cogitans*, not a sensual, bodily person. One can glimpse the magnitude of the loss in Descartes's attempts to theorize his relationship to the body he calls his own, an attempt he finally abandons,[44] but the full force of it is found elsewhere, when the demand that one separate from and control one's body is joined both to Christian associations of the body with sin and to the pedagogical practices that replaced Descartes's self-conscious self-constitution.

It became impossible to empower the mind without disempowering and stigmatizing the body, or, in Foucauldian terms, anatomizing, administering, scrutinizing, and disciplining it. The body Descartes regains and bequeaths to his heirs is mechanical, not the lived body but the object of scientific practices, a body best known by being, after its death, dissected. It became the paradigmatic object in an epistemology founded on a firm and unbridgeable subject-object distinction.[45] And it became bad—because it had once been part of the self and it had had to be pushed away, split off, and repudiated. So, too, with everything else from which the authorized self needed to be distinguished and distanced. The rational mind stood over and against the mechanical world of orderly explanation, while the rest—the disorderly, the passionate, the uncontrollable—was relegated to the categories of the "primitive or exotic . . . two new interests in bourgeois society, to compensate for the estranged experience of the bourgeois self."[46]

The Cartesian God—the poisonously pedagogical parent, seen by the successfully reared child as wholly benevolent—conscripts the infinite will of the privileged son and sets it the task of "autonomously" disciplining the body, the perceptions, and the passions, with the promised reward being the revelation of guaranteed truths and the power that goes with knowledge. Evelyn Fox Keller is discussing Bacon, but she could as well be discussing Descartes—or the paranoid Schreber:

> What is sought here is the proper stance for mind necessary to insure the reception of truth, and the conception of science. To receive God's truth, the mind must be pure and clean, submissive and open—it must be undefiled and female. Only then can it give birth to a masculine and virile science. That is, if the mind is pure, receptive and submissive—female—in its relation to God, it can be transformed by God into a forceful, potent and virile agent—male—in its relation to nature. Cleansed of contamination, the mind can be impregnated by God, and, in that act, virilized—made potent and capable of generating virile offspring in its union with nature.[47]

Such a self, privileged by its estrangement from its own body, from the "external" world, and from other people, will, in a culture that defines such estrangements as normal, express the paranoia of such a stance not only through oppression but, more benignly, through the problems that are taken as the most fundamental, even if not the most practically pressing: the problems of philosophy. Those problems—notably, the mind-body problem, problems of reference and truth, the problem of other minds, and skepticism about knowledge of the external world—all concern the subject's ability or inability to connect with the split-off parts of itself—its physicality, its sociability. Such problems are literally and unsurprisingly unsolvable so long as the subject's very identity is constituted by those estrangements. A subject whose authority is defined by his location on one side of a gulf cannot authoritatively theorize that gulf away. Philosophers' problems are the neuroses of privilege; discipline makes the difference between such problems and the psychosis of full-blown paranoia.

IV. BEYOND MADNESS AND METHOD

> The new *mestiza* copes by developing a tolerance for ambiguity. . . . She has a plural personality, she operates in a pluralistic mode—nothing is thrust out, the good, the bad and the ugly, nothing rejected, nothing abandoned.[48]

> The alternative to relativism is partial, locatable, critical knowledges sustaining the possibility of webs of connections called solidarity in politics and shared conversations in epistemology.[49]

The authorized subject thus achieves and maintains his authority by his ability to keep his body and the rest of the world radically separated from his ego, marked off from it by policed boundaries.[50] Within those boundaries, the self is supposed to be unitary and seamless, characterized by the doxastic virtue of noncontradiction and the moral virtue of integrity. The social mechanisms of privilege aid in the achievement of those virtues by facilitating splitting and projection: the unity of the privileged self is maintained by dumping out of the self—onto the object world or onto the different, the stigmatized others—everything that would disturb its pristine wholeness.

Various contemporary theorists are articulating alternative conceptions of subjectivity, conceptions that start from plurality and diversity, not just among but, crucially, within subjects.[51] From that starting point flow radically transformed relationships among subjects and between subjects and the world they would know.

One way to approach these discussions is to return to Freud. Mental health for Freud consisted in part in the acknowledgement by the ego of the impulses of the id: "Where id was, there ego shall be."[52] The German is more striking than the English: the German words for "ego" and "id" are "ich" and "es";[53] the sense is "Where *it* was, there *I* shall be." One can take this in two ways. Under the sorts of disciplinary regimes that constitute epistemic privilege, the exhortation has a colonizing ring to it. The not-I needs to be brought under the civilizing control of the ego; the aim is not to split it off but to tame it. Splitting represents the failure of colonization, the loss of will for the task of domestication. The healthy ego is unified not because it has cast out parts of itself, but because it has effectively administered even the formerly unruly outposts of its dominion. Or so goes the story one is supposed to tell. (Any splitting goes unacknowledged.)

There is another way to take Freud's exhortation. The aim might be not to colonize the "it" but to break down the distinction between "it" and "I," between object and subject. "Where it was, there I shall be," not because I am colonizing it, but because where I am is always shifting. As Nancy Chodorow puts it, in giving an object-relational alternative to the classical Freudian account, "where fragmented internal objects were, there shall harmoniously related objects be."[54] Moving becomes not the installment of oneself astride the Archimedean point, the self-made man taming the frontier of the "New World," but the sort of "world"-travel María Lugones discusses as the ground of what she calls, following Marilyn Frye, "loving perception."[55] By putting ourselves in settings where we are perceived as—and hence are able (or unable not) to be—different people from who we are at home, we learn about ourselves, each other, and the world. And part of what we learn is that the unity of the self is an illusion of privilege, as when, to use Lugones's example (from a talk she gave at the University of Minnesota), we think there is a natural, unmediated connection between intention, will, and action, because if we are privileged, the world collaborates with us, making it all work, apparently seamlessly, and giving us the credit. As Frye puts it, we are trained not to notice the stagehands, all those whose labor enables the play to proceed smoothly.[56]

What is problematic about Descartes's Faustian gesture is not the idea that the world is in some sense our creation. Rather, it is on the one hand the individualism of the construction (or, what comes to the same thing, the unitary construction by all and only those who count as the same, the not-different) and on the other the need to deny any construction, to maintain the mutual independence of the self and the world. Realism ought not to require such independence on the side of the world, any more than rationality ought to require it on the side of the knowing subject, if by realism we mean the recognition that the world may not be the way anyone (or any group, however powerful) thinks it is, and if by rationality we mean ways of learning and teaching that are reliably useful in collective endeavors.

Philosophical realism has typically stressed the independence of the world from those who would know it, a formulation that, at least since Kant, has been linked with the intractability of skepticism. But it's hard to see exactly why independence should be what is required. A world that exists in complex interdependence with those who know it (who are, of course, also part of it) is nonetheless real. Lots of real things are not independent of what we think about them, without being simply what anyone or any group takes them to be—the economy, to take just one obvious example. The interdependencies are real, as are the entities and structures shaped by them. One way we know they are real is precisely that they look different to those differently placed in relation to them. (There aren't a variety of diverse takes on my hallucinations.) The only way to take diversity of perspectives seriously is to be robustly realist, both about the world viewed and about the material locations of those doing the viewing. Archimedean, difference-denying epistemology ought to be seen as incompatible with such a robust realism. How could there possibly be one account of a world shaped in interaction with subjects so diversely constituted and with such diverse interests in constructing and knowing it?

A specifically Cartesian feature of the conception of the world as independent is the world as inanimate, and consequently not reciprocally engaged in the activities through which it comes to be known. Thus, for example, the social sciences, which take as their objects bearers of subjectivity and the entities and structures they create, have been seen as scientifically deficient precisely because of the insufficiently independent status of what they study. (The remedy for such deficiency has typically been the dehumanizing objectification of the "subjects" of the social sciences, an objectification especially damaging when those subjects have been otherwise oppressed.) But it's far from obvious that being inert should make something more knowable. Why not take "subject" and "object" to name not ontological categories, but reciprocal, shifting positions? Why not think of knowledge emerging paradigmatically in mutual interaction, so that what puzzles us is how to account not for the objectivity of the social sciences but for the intersubjectivity of the natural sciences?[57]

In a discussion of the problems, from an African-American perspective, with the critical legal theorists' rejection of rights, Patricia Williams suggests that rather than discarding rights, "society must *give* them away. Unlock them from reification by giving them to slaves. Give them to trees. Give them to cows. Give them to history. Give them to rivers and rocks. Give to all of society's objects and untouchables the rights of privacy, integrity, and self-assertion; give them distance and respect. Flood them with the animating spirit that rights mythology fires in this country's most oppressed psyches, and wash away the shrouds of inanimate-object status."[58] One might respond similarly to the suggestion from postmodernist quarters that we discard subjectivity and agency. Rather, we should profligately give them away, invest the things of the world with subjectivity, with the ability and interest to return our gaze.[59] Realism can mean that we take ourselves as inhabiting a world in which the likes of us (whoever we may be) are not the only sources of meaning, that we see ourselves as implicated in, reciprocated by, the world.

The world as real is the world as precisely not dead or mechanistic; the world as trickster, as protean, is always slipping out from under our best attempts to pin it down.[60] The real world is not the world of our best physics but the world that defeats any physics that would be final, that would desire to be the last world, "the end of the story, the horizon of interpretation, the end of 'the puzzlement'," a desire Paul Smith calls "claustrophilic."[61] Donna Haraway imaginatively sketches an epistemology for the explicitly partial, fragmentary, un-unified knowers we are and need to be if we are to move within and learn from the complexities of the world and the complexities of how we are constructed in it. As she puts it, "Splitting, not being, is the privileged image for feminist epistemologies of scientific knowledge" (Haraway, "Situated Knowledges," p. 586).

A trickster reality is thus matched by a trickster subjectivity, a subjectivity that finds expression in African and African-American oral and written traditions. In *The Signifying Monkey*, Henry Louis Gates, Jr., builds "a theory of African-American literary criticism" (the book's subtitle) on the ground of African-American vernacular traditions.[62] Literature, the written word, was the privileged site for the attainment and display of Enlightenment rationality, the place for former slaves and the descendants of slaves to stake a claim to full membership in the human community. The signifying monkey and other traditional African trickster figures from oral traditions are for Gates a way of exploring the simultaneous appropriations and subversions of the site of writing, the attempts of African-American writers not to mimic the texts of the masters but to write themselves and their communities into history and culture by transforming the nature of writing itself, by giving voice to the written word. Gates's central trope of "Signifyin(g)" complexly spins a story about the multivocality of African-American texts, the weaving of vernacular voices into literature, and the subversions, parodies, and appropriations of earlier texts. Even when the singular voice is seen as a desirable ideal, its achievement is never a simple matter, never seen as a birthright; there are always other voices playing around the edges of the text.

The unity of privileged subjectivity is mirrored in the demand that language be transparent, a demand most explicit in the now-discredited ideal languages of the logical positivists but lingering in the demands of present-day analytic philosophers for (a certain picture of) clarity, as though the point of language was to be seen through. When June Jordan writes of Black English that one of its hallmarks is "clarity: If the sentence is not clear it's not Black English," she might seem to be endorsing such a demand, but the clarity she extols is contextual and "person-centered": "If your idea, your sentence, assumes the presence of at least two living and active people, you will make it understandable because the motivation behind every sentence is the wish to say something real to somebody real."[63] The clarity of analytic philosophy, by contrast, is best exhibited in argumentative contexts, detached from the specificities of anyone's voice, in avoidance of ad hominem and other genetic fallacies. The clarity of Black English, Jordan explains, is grounded in the rhythms and intonations of speech, in the immediacy of the present indicative, and in an abhorrence of abstraction and the eschewal of the passive (non)voice: it is the clarity of illumination, not of the transparent medium. In contrast to the language of philosophy, which assumes its adequacy as a vessel for fully translatable meaning, Black English does not take its authority for granted. It is a language "constructed by people constantly needing to insist that we exist, that we are present."[64] It aims not at transparent representation but at subversive transformation; it is an act of intervention, used by communities of resistance and used within those communities for collective self-constitution.

There are many other theorists of trickster subjectivity. Gloria Anzaldúa, for example, in *Borderlands/La Frontera* writes in a combination of English and Spanish, refusing the demand to choose one or another "pure" language, as she moves along and across the borders that are supposed to define and separate, finding/creating herself by refusing the definitions and separations.

Teresa de Lauretis finds in some women's films a challenge to the unity of the subject. For example, Lizzie Borden's *Born in Flames* discomfits some privileged women viewers precisely in not addressing them alone, in not (re)presenting the women of color in the film *to* them, but rather addressing an audience of women as diverse as the women on the screen. There is no unitary viewer for the film, a move that de Lauretis takes to express the feminist understanding "that the female subject is en-gendered, constructed and defined in gender across multiple representations of class, race, language, and social relations; and that, therefore, differences among women are differences *within* women."[65]

In *The American Evasion of Philosophy*, Cornel West finds in pragmatism a challenge to the Enlightenment that can make room for a historical subject constituted otherwise than by the norms of European epistemology.[66] He sees what he calls "prophetic pragmatism" as an intellectual stance for liberationist struggles, in part because of its inheritance from earlier pragmatists, notably Dewey, of a rejection of foundationalism and individualism and an openness to the "fluidity, plurality, and diversity of experience" (West, *American Evasion*, p. 91). Knowledge and the knowing subject emerge together from continuous engagement with the world; such engagement (with our actual lives at stake) and not the abstractions of epistemology ought to be the stuff of our reflection.[67]

There is, however, an obvious problem with taking splitting and internal multiplicity as the hallmarks of liberatory subjectivity. The most striking and clear-cut cases of internal multiplicity are cases of multiple personality, a pathological condition typically caused by severe childhood abuse, that is, by the most poisonous of pedagogies.[68] Recent clinical work with people with multiple personalities suggests such multiplicity is a means of coping with the terror and pain of the child's situation.[69] Part of that coping consists of a protective amnesia of what the child can neither stop nor understand nor tell anyone about. Consequently the lines of communication between the different selves become blocked, and some of the relations between them become antagonistic as some of the selves adopt coping strategies that are at odds with those of others. Multiple personality, on such a view, is a comprehensible, perhaps even rational, response to an intolerable situation, a way of maintaining some degree of agency in the face of profoundly soul-destroying attacks on one's ability to construct a sense of self. Such construction, throughout life, but especially when one is a child, proceeds interactively. We all are, to use Annette Baier's term, "second persons,"[70] and when those we most trust to mirror us abuse that trust, the conditions for wholeness are shattered.

In reflecting on the experiences of "multiples," Claudia Card (to whom I owe much of this discussion) suggests that we can see the main difference between them and the rest of us as lying not in their internal multiplicity but in the amnesia that both guards it and keeps it at odds. Therapy can succeed not by integrating all the personalities into one, nor by making all but one go away, but by creating the possibility for respectful conversation among them, facilitating their mutual recognition and acceptance. Analogously with oppressed communities, Card argues, multiples are internally in strife, unable to confront those who have damaged them, needing not seamless unity but effective alliance building.[71] They need from trusted others a mirror of themselves not as unitary but as united, which requires, in part, that those others be committed to the joint survival of all the selves they are and to at least some of the projects in which those selves might engage, either jointly or individually, with mutual respect.

Such an account parallels María Lugones's account of her experiences as a "multiplicitous being," a U.S. Latina lesbian who could not be unitary without killing off a crucial part of who she is, without betraying both herself and others with whom she identifies and for whom she cares.[72] Without identification with and engagement in struggle within *la cultura hispana Nuevamejicana,* the imperiled community in which she "has found her grounding," she risks becoming "culturally obsolete," but as a lesbian within that culture, she is not a lover of women—she is an "abomination." Needing to be both of the very different people she is in the *Nuevamejicana* and lesbian cultures, she works not for unity but for connection, for the not-to-be-taken-for-granted understanding of each of her selves by the other, understanding that is cultivated by work in the "borderlands," "the understanding of liminals." Victoria Davion contends that it is such connection that can ground a conception of integrity that does justice—as she argues any usable feminist notion of integrity must—to the experiences of multiplicitous beings,[73] and it is just that connection that it would seem multiple personalities need to acquire within/among themselves.

Thus we can see the splitting characteristic of multiple personality as a response to oppression that needs resolution by the achievement not of unity but of mutual respect, an achievement that requires the loving collaboration of others. On such a view, such splitting is the most striking example of a far more common phenomenon, seen also in experiences such as those María Lugones theorizes. I want to suggest that, without blurring the specificities of such experiences, we can recognize that the experiences even of those who identify with dominant cultures can lead in different ways to multiplicitous identities. Gloria Anzaldúa, for example, stresses the importance for *mestizas* of the acceptance of all of who they are, "the white parts, the male parts, the queer parts, the vulnerable parts."[74] But she equally calls for such self-acceptance on the part of the privileged, as the only alternative to the splitting and projection that underwrite domination: "Admit that Mexico is your double, that we are irrevocably tied to her. Gringo, accept the doppelganger in your psyche. By taking back your collective shadow the intracultural split will heal" (Anzaldúa, *Borderlands/La Frontera,* p. 86).

Erica Sherover-Marcuse suggests that all children are subject to what she calls "adultism," a form of mistreatment that targets all young people who are born into an oppressive society.[75] Such mistreatment, she argues, is "the 'training ground' for other forms of oppression," a crucial part of the socialization of some as oppressor, some as oppressed, and most of us into complex combinations of both. Central to such socialization is its normalization, the denial of its traumatic nature, the forgetting of the pain; and central to emancipation is "a labor of *affective remembrance.*"[76] Alice Miller argues similarly in *For Your Own Good* that only those who have been abused become abusers, and her account focuses on the mechanisms of splitting and projection: "Children who have grown up being assailed for qualities the parents hate in themselves can hardly wait to assign those qualities to someone else so they can once gain regard themselves as good, 'moral,' noble, and altruistic" (Miller, *For Your Own Good*, p. 91).

The abuse of which Alice Miller writes, which ranges from normative to the horrific, shares the requirement of amnesia, which means that the split-off parts of the self, whether they be the survival-ensuring "alters" of the multiple or the stigmatized others of the privileged, are emphatically inaccessible. What Sherover-Marcuse calls "an emancipatory practice of subjectivity" (Sherover-Marcuse, *Emancipation and Consciousness*, p. 140) requires memory, connection, and the learning of respect for the others outside of us. Schreber, as privileged jurist and as incarcerated madman, emblematizes the victimized child who grows up to become the dominating adult, the possessor of power—which, while real enough (as is the privilege it secures), rests on a history of abuse. As long as we hold on to the ideal of the self as a seamless unity, we will not only be marginalizing the experiences of those like María Lugones and Gloria Anzaldúa, for whom such unity could only be bought at the price of self-betrayal, but we will be fundamentally misrepresenting the experiences of even the most privileged among us, whose apparent unity was bought at the price of the projection onto stigmatized others of the split-off parts of themselves they were taught to despise.

As Quine has persuasively argued,[77] epistemology cannot come from thin air: to naturalize epistemology is to acknowledge that we need to study how actual people actually know. But one thing we ought to know about actual people is that they inhabit a world of systematic inequality, in which authority—centrally including epistemic authority—is systematically given to some and withheld from others. If our interest is in changing that world, we need to look critically at the terms of epistemic authority. Certainly there is no reason why those who have historically been dominated by the epistemology of modernity—the objects to its subjects—should accept the terms of that epistemology as the only route to empowerment.

That epistemology presents itself as universal, a universal defined by precisely that which is not different in the ways that some are defined as different: women (not men), people of color (not white people), the disabled (not the able-bodied), gays and lesbians (not heterosexuals). To echo Foucault again, none of these categories is natural or ahistorical, and they all came into existence as strategies of regimentation and containment. They all represent aspects of the multiple, shifting, unstable ways that people can be, aspects that have been split off from the psyches of the privileged, projected onto the bodies of others, and concertized as identities. The privileged, in turn, having shucked off what would threaten their sense of control, theorize their own subjectivity (which they name generically human) as unitary and transparent to consciousness, characterized by integrity and consistency. Not only is such subjectivity a myth; its logic is that of paranoia.[78]

NOTES

1. Morton White, "The Politics of Epistemology," *Ethics 100* (October 1989): 77–92.
2. For one of the earliest and most thorough of such arguments, see Janice Moulton, "The Myth of the Neutral 'Man'," in *Feminism and Philosophy*, ed. Mary Vetterling-Braggin, Frederick Elliston, and Jane English (Totowa, N.J.: Littlefield, Adams & Co., 1977).

3. I have argued for this dependence in "Your Ground Is My Body: Strategien des Anti-Fundamentalismus."
4. See Genevieve Lloyd, *The Man of Reason* (Minneapolis: University of Minnesota Press, 1984); Susan Bordo, *The Flight to Objectivity: Essays on Cartesianism and Culture* (Albany: SUNY Press, 1987); my "Othello's Doubt/Desdemona's Death: The Engendering of Scepticism" in *Engenderings* (NY: Routledge, 1993); and Jacquelyn Zita, "Transsexualized Origins: Reflections on Descartes's *Meditations,*" *Genders* 5 (Summer 1989): 86–105.
5. Daniel Paul Schreber, *Memoirs of My Nervous Illness*, tr. and ed. Ida Macalpine and Richard A. Hunter (Cambridge: Harvard University Press, 1988); Sigmund Freud, "Psycho-Analytic Notes upon an Autobiographical Account of a Case of Paranoia (Dementia Paranoides),: *Standard Edition* (hereafter *SE*) 12 (London: Hogarth Press, 1958): 9–82.
6. Alice Miller, *For Your Own Good: Hidden Cruelty in Child-Rearing and the Roots of Violence*, tr. Hildegarde Hannum and Hunter Hannum (New York: Farrar, Straus and Giroux, 1984), p. 91.
7. Jean-Paul Sarte, *Anti-Semite and Jew*, quoted in Erica Sherover-Marcuse, *Emancipation and Consciousness: Dogmatic and Dialectical Perspectives in the Early Marx* (Oxford: Basil Blackwell, 1986), p. 158.
8. Morton Schatzman, *Soul Murder: Persecution in the Family* (New York: Random House, 1973).
9. Miller, *For Your Own Good.*
10. It is antipsychoanalytic in the manner of Jeffrey Moussaieff Masson's later but better-known work, *The Assault on Truth: Freud's Suppression of the Seduction Theory* (New York: Farrar, Straus and Giroux, 1984), i.e., in reading patients' reports and symptoms as expressions not of fantasies but of what was actually done to them as children.
11. Freud's account is almost entirely in masculine terms, but here, as elsewhere, he took his analysis to apply also to women, *mutatis mutandis.* As I will go on to argue, the phenomena he describes are, in fact, wholly gender inflected and are grounded in distinctively masculine experiences.
12. Freud gives two reasons for the attachment of the libido to the ego: that, detached from the entire external world, it has nowhere else to go (*SE*, 12, p. 65), and that narcissism is the stage at which paranoids are characteristically fixated, hence the stage to which they regress (SE, 12, p. 72). This latter view is connected to Freud's notorious association of homosexuality with narcissism, a stage intermediate between auto-eroticism and object-love (*SE*, 12, pp. 60–61).
13. The term "ravished" comes from a conversation with Gary Thomas about music and sexuality: "ravishing" seems the best word for the effect on us of certain, especially Romantic, music.
14. Molefi Kete Asante, *The Afrocentric Idea* (Philadelphia: Temple University Press, 1987), p. 4.
15. Cartesian philosophy was, in fact, influential on and in some ways empowering for contemporary feminists. See Ruth Perry, "Radical Doubt and the Liberation of Women," *Eighteenth Century Studies* 18 (1985): 472–93.
16. It is a frequently remarked problem that the original argumentative role of the cogito depends on the absolute uniqueness of its claim to our credulity, yet it is then supposed to stand as a paradigm for other successful claimants.
17. Descartes, Meditation 4, in *The Philosophical Writings of Descartes*, 2 vols., tr. John Cottingham, Robert Stoothoff, and Dugald Murdoch (Cambridge: Cambridge University Press, 1985) (hereafter CS&M), p. 40.
18. Descartes, Meditation 1, CS&M, p. 15.
19. Descartes, *The Passions of the Soul*, part 3, sec. 211, CS&M, 1, p. 123. I owe the suggestion to look again at *The Passions of the Soul* to Adam Morton, who may, however, have had something else entirely in mind.

20. Evelyn Fox Keller and Christine R. Grontkowski provide an excellent account of the role and fate of vision in Cartesian dualism in "The Mind's Eye," in *Discovering Reality: Feminist Perspectives on Epistemology, Metaphysis, Methodology, and Philosophy of Science*, ed. Sandra Harding and Merrill B. Hintikka (Dordrecht: Reidel, 1983).
21. Descartes, *Discourse on the Method*, part 2, CS&M, 1, pp. 116–17.
22. On Pyrrhonist and Montaignean scepticism, see Richard Popkin, *The History of Scepticism from Erasmus to Descartes* (New York: Humanities Press, 1960).
23. See, for example, part 2 of the *Discourse on the Method*, CS&M, 1, p. 123.
24. See Margaret Dauler Wilson, *Descartes* (London: Routledge & Kegan Paul, 1978), pp. 17–31.
25. Descartes, *The Passions of the Soul*, part 2, secs. 75–79, CS&M, 1, pp. 354–56.
26. The most heinous case of such oppression is in slavery, and the U.S. slave trade, of course, required the movement of slaves from their homes. But such movement was the denial, rather than the expression, of those people's will, and it served to confirm what, in the nonliteral sense, was their place in the world, as defined by Europeans and Euro-Americans, part of which was that they had no say over where, literally, their place in the world was to be.
27. For a helpful discussion of the intertwinings of oppression and exploitation, see Marilyn Frye, "In and Out of Harm's Way: Arrogance and Love," in *Politics of Reality: Essays in Feminist Theory* (Freedom, Calif.: The Crossing Press, 1983).
28. The literature on these disputes is vast and growing. For an introduction and overview, see Sandra Harding, *The Science Question in Feminism* (Ithaca, N.Y.: Cornell University Press, 1986), pp. 163–96; and Linda Nicholson, ed., *Feminism/Postmodernism* (New York: Routledge, 1989). For some of us, myself included, the later Wittgenstein is an independent source of a deep skepticism toward theories, though not necessarily toward the activity of theorizing. For a discussion of that distinction, see Barbara Christian, "The Race for Theory," *Cultural Critique* 6 (Spring 1987): 51–63.
29. Harding, *The Science Question in Feminism*, and "The Method Question," *Hypatia* 2, no. 3 (Fall 1987): 19–35.
30. Freud, "Notes on a Case of Paranoia," *SE*, 12, p. 70. The quotation is from Part I, scene 4 of *Faust*.
31. Paul Smith, *Discerning the Subject* (Minneapolis: University of Minnesota Press, 1988), p. 98. Smith's parallels between paranoia and what he calls "humanist epistemology," which I came across in the very final stages of writing this paper, are very similar to mine, as is his aim to articulate a conception of human subjectivity and agency that is politically and socially usable.
32. See my "From Hamlet to Maggie Verver: The History and Politics of the Knowing Subject"; and "Missing Mothers/Desiring Daughters: Framing the Sight of Women."
33. Barry Stroud, *The Significance of Philosophical Scepticism* (New York: Oxford University Press, 1984), p. x.
34. I owe this juxtaposition of the two books to a suggestion by Michael Root. See Hubert L. Dreyfus and Paul Rabinow, *Michel Foucault: Beyond Structuralism and Hermeneutics*, 2d ed. (Chicago: University of Chicago Press, 1983), pp. 143–83.
35. Feminists and others have expressed concerns that despite the attractiveness of Foucauldian theory we need to be wary that by following him we risk losing politically indispensable notions like oppression and power (as something some people have unjustly more of). It is similarly unclear how in Foucauldian terms to formulate effectively coordinated strategies of resistance. See, for example, *Feminism and Foucault: Reflections on Resistance*, eds., Irene Diamond and Lee Quinby (Boston: Northeastern University Press, 1988); and Cornel West, *The American Evasion of Phi-*

losophy: A Genealogy of Pragmatism (Madison: University of Wisconsin Press, 1989), pp. 223–26. I share these concerns but find some of Foucault's analyses helpfully illuminating. I want to "go a piece of the way with him," a notion I owe to an unpublished paper by Angelita Reyes, "Derrida . . . Don't Leave Home without Him, or, Going a Piece of the Way with Them."

36. The unspecified 'we' in these sentences is a reflection of one thing many feminists and other liberationist theorists find problematic in Foucault—the homogenization of subject positions. It is striking to me how difficult it is not to do this, to be always conscious of the diversity of different people's experiences. Philosophy as a discipline makes such consciousness especially difficult, because the philosophical subject is defined precisely by its (alleged) universality.
37. See, for example, Francis Barker, *The Tremulous Private Body: Essays on Subjection* (London: Methuen, 1984), for an account of the emergence of the distinctively modern subject.
38. The echo of Paulo Freire's *Pedagogy of the Oppressed* is intentional. Freire's aim is to develop an explicit pedagogy that will be empowering to those who are currently oppressed; I want to examine the implicit pedagogy that actually empowers the currently privileged.
39. Alice Miller stresses the importance for the success of "poisonous pedagogy" that its victims not have any memory of what was done to them, that they never see their parents as anything other than good and loving. My discussion draws heavily on her *For Your Own Good*.
40. Quoted in Miller, *For Your Own Good*, p. 90; from Schatzman, Soul Murder, p. 19, quoting Schreber.
41. But we should not obliterate them. Kant suggests, for example, that we should visit places that house the poor and the ill to reinvigorate in ourselves sympathetic feelings that can be enlisted on the side of motivating us to do what duty commands. Immanuel Kant, *The Doctrine of Virtue: Part II of the Metaphysics of Morals*, tr. Mary J. Gregor (Philadelphia: University of Pennsylvania Press, 1964), sec. 35, p. 126.
42. This is as good a place as any to note that what I find problematic in Cartesian epistemology is not peculiar to him or even to rationalism. The gender associations are, in fact, far clearer in Bacon. (See Evelyn Fox Keller, "Baconian Science: A Hermaphroditic Birth," *The Philosophical Forum* XL, 3 [Spring 1980]: 299–308; reprinted in Keller, *Reflections on Gender and Science* [New Haven: Yale University Press, 1985].) For a fuller statement of what I take to be in common in views that the usual accounts of the history of philosophy put in opposition, see my "Othello's Doubt/Desdemona's Death."
43. The term is Schatzman's in *Soul Murder*, p. 137.
44. For the attempt, see Descartes, Meditation 6, CS&M, 1, pp. 56–57; the Fourth Set of Replies (to Arnauld), CS&M, 2, p. 60; Sixth Set of Replies (to Mersenne), CS&M, 2, pp. 297–99. For further attempts and, in the face of her persistent questioning, his abandonment of the possibility of getting a rationally grounded theoretical account of the union of mind and body, see Descartes's Letters IX (a and b) and X (a and b) to Princess Elizabeth, in *Descartes: Philosophical Writings*, eds., Elizabeth Anscombe and Peter Thomas Geach (Indianapolis: Bobbs-Merrill, 1954).
45. Barker, *The Tremulous Private Body*. See also my "From Hamlet to Maggie Verver."
46. Donald M. Lowe, *History of Bourgeois Perception* (Chicago: The University of Chicago Press, 1982), p. 22.
47. Keller, "Baconian Science," p. 304.
48. Gloria Anzaldúa, *Borderlands/La Frontera: The New Mestiza* (San Francisco: Spinsters/Aunt Lute, 1987), p. 79.
49. Donna Haraway, "Situated Knowledges: The Science Question in Feminism and the Privilege of Partial Perspective," *Feminist Studies* 14, no. 3 (Fall 1988): 584.

50. Firm ego-boundaries are typically taken as a measure of mental health: one is supposed to be clear about where one's self leaves off and the rest of the world begins. An alternative view—that part of mental health, or of an adequate epistemology, consists in the acceptance of a sizable intermediate domain—has been developed by the object-relations theorist D. W. Winnicott. For a discussion of the relevance of his work to feminist theory, see Keller, *Reflections on Gender and Science*, pp. 83, 99–102; and Jane Flax, *Thinking Fragments: Psychoanalysis, Feminism, and Postmodernism in the Contemporary West* (Berkeley and Los Angeles: University of California Press, 1990), pp. 116–32.
51. Sandra Harding and Donna Haraway are two such theorists, who also give excellent overviews of work in this area. See, especially, Haraway, "Situated Knowledges," pp. 575–99; and Harding, "Reinventing Ourselves as Other: More New Agents of History and Knowledge," in Harding, *Whose Science? Whose Knowledge? Thinking from Women's Lives* (Ithaca, N.Y.: Cornell University Press, 1991), pp. 286–95. See also three papers in which María Lugones develops a pluralistic theory of identity: "Playfulness, 'World'-Traveling, and Loving Perception," *Hypatia* 2, no. 2 (Summer 1987): 3–19; "Hispaneando y Lesbiando: On Sarah Hoagland's *Lesbian Ethics*," *Hypatia* 5, no. 3 (Fall 1990); 138–46; and "On the Logic of Pluralistic Feminism," in *Feminist Ethics*, ed. Claudia Card (Wichita: Kansas University Press, 1991).
52. Sigmund Freud, "New Introductory Lectures on Psychoanalysis," *SE*, 22, p. 80.
53. See Bruno Bettelheim, *Freud and Man's Soul* (New York: A. A. Knopf, 1983). "The New Introductory Lectures" were written originally in English, but the point still holds: Freud used the English of his translators.
54. Nancy Chodorow, "Toward a Relational Individualism: The Mediation of Self through Psychoanalysis," in *Reconstructing Individualism: Autonomy, Individuality, and the Self in Western Thought*, ed. Thomas C. Heller, Morton Sosna, and David E. Wellbery (Stanford: Stanford University Press, 1986), pp. 197–207.
55. Lugones, "Playfulness, 'World'-Travel, and Loving Perception"; Frye, "In and Out of Harm's Way."
56. Frye, "To Be and Be Seen," *The Politics of Reality*, pp. 167–73.
57. For a start on such an account, as well as an argument for why we should seek one, see Lorraine Code, *What Can She Know? Feminist Theory and the Construction of Knowledge* (Ithaca, N.Y.: Cornell University Press, 1991), esp. chaps. 3 and 4; and Sandra Harding, *Whose Science? Whose Knowledge?* esp. chap. 4.
58. Patricia J. Williams, *The Alchemy of Race and Rights: Diary of a Law Professor* (Cambridge, Mass.: Harvard University Press, 1991), p. 165.
59. See Rainer Maria Rilke's "Archaic Torso of Apollo": "There is no place / that does not see you. You must change your life." *Translations from the Poetry of Rainer Maria Rilke*, tr. M. D. Herter Norton (New York: W. W. Norton & Co., 1938).
60. Haraway, "Situated Knowledges," p. 596.
61. Smith, *Discerning the Subject*, p. 98.
62. Henry Louis Gates, Jr., *The Signifying Monkey: A Theory of African-American Literary Criticism* (New York and Oxford: Oxford University Press, 1988).
63. June Jordan, "Nobody Mean More to Me than You / And the Future Life of Willie Jordan," in *On Call: Political Essays* (Boston: South End Press, 1985), pp. 129ff. Such accounts make evident the Eurocentrism of deconstructive sorties against such notions as presence, voice, and authorship. See, for example, Jacques Derrida, "Plato's Pharmacy," in *Dissemination*, tr. Barbara Johnson (Chicago: University of Chicago Press, 1981).
64. Ibid.

65. Theresa de Lauretis, "Rethinking Women's Cinema: Aesthetics and Feminist Theory," in *Technologies of Gender: Essays on Theory, Film, and Fiction* (Bloomington: Indiana University Press, 1987), p. 139.
66. West, *The American Evasion of Philosophy.*
67. George Herbert Mead has also inspired theorists of subjectivity concerned with sociality and internal diversity. See, in particular, Karen Hanson, *The Self Imagined: Philosophical Reflections on the Social Character of Psyche* (New York: Routledge and Kegan Paul, 1986); and Catherine Keller, *From a Broken Web: Separation, Sexism, and Self* (Boston: Beacon Press, 1986).
68. Thanks to Louise Antony for stressing the importance of dealing with these issues.
69. "Dissociative Disorder," *Diagnostic and Statistical Manual of Mental Disorders,* 3rd ed., rev. (Washington, D.C.: American Psychiatric Association, 1987), pp. 269–79.
70. Annette Baier, "Cartesian Persons," in *Postures of the Mind: Essays on Mind and Morals* (Minneapolis: University of Minnesota Press, 1985), pp. 79–92. See also the chapter on "Second Persons," in Code, *What Can She Know?* pp. 71–109.
71. Claudia Card, "Responsibility and Moral Luck: Resisting Oppression and Abuse," manuscript, 1989.
72. María Lugones, "Hispaneando y Lesbiando."
73. Victoria M. Davion, "Integrity and Radical Change," in *Feminist Ethics,* ed. Card.
74. Anzaldúa, *Borderlands/La Frontera,* p. 88.
75. Sherover-Marcuse, *Emancipation and Consciousness,* p. 139.
76. Ibid., p. 140. Emphasis in the original.
77. W. V. Quine, "Epistemology Naturalized," *Ontological Relativity and Other Essays* (New York: Columbia University Press, 1969).
78. Louise Antony's detailed and erudite response to an earlier draft was a model of friendly, feminist criticism. It is a rare thing to have one's writing so thoroughly disagreed with and at the same time taken so seriously and with so much care. Ruth Wood was, as usual, of enormous help in clarifying the convolutions.

Feminism and Objective Interests: The Role of Transformation Experiences in Rational Deliberation

Babbitt appreciates certain virtues of the liberal account of autonomous choice. Its definition of autonomous choice as choice with full information, good reasoning skills, and vivid awareness of the likely consequences respects the individual without entailing that whatever an individual chooses is good. However, Babbitt doubts that the liberal view is adequate to address the problem of ideological oppression or false consciousness. Ideological oppression forms one's preferences in ways that deny or diminish the interest in one's own human flourishing. According to Babbitt, the idealized cognitive conditions that liberals rely on will not counteract such distortions if they stem from an individual's "not possessing a sense of self that would support a full sense of flourishing."

A deferential wife need not lack self-concern or imagination, and she may be actively constructing a life around service to her husband. Thus, she may be expressing her actual self and may resist liberal autonomy until her self is changed. To change her self, argues Babbitt, she would have to undergo a transformative experience. Yet, there are reasons to be skeptical about conversion experiences—the results can be bad for the individual, and advocating them may clear the way for objectionable paternalism. Still, Babbitt contends that a different interpretive background is needed to dislodge false consciousness and that gaining the requisite interpretive background may require transformation. By participating in a political movement, for example, a person's emotional situation might be transformed. Moreover, this emotional transformation might give rise to nonpropositional knowledge in the form of intuitions, attitudes, or ways of behaving, which in turn might prompt a radical social critique. Still, it remains to be asked which transformation experiences are good. Babbitt urges that good transformation experiences promote self-respect, dignity, and liberation and that these values constitute objective epistemic standards.

—D.T.M.

Chapter 20

Susan E. Babbitt

Feminism and Objective Interests: The Role of Transformation Experiences in Rational Deliberation

The importance of the particular and the personal in feminist accounts of ethics and epistemology has suggested to some that feminist epistemologies are irrationalist or at best relativistic. Feminist theorists have emphasized the importance of interpersonal relations and particular connections in making ethical and epistemic judgments. They have thus sometimes been accused of ignoring the importance of general principles.[1] Although it has sometimes been true in feminist debates that emphasizing the particular *is* set in opposition to the development of general theories, it is often the case that such emphasis is advanced as part of a broader reconception of personal relations and knowledge. What is especially insightful in some recent feminist treatments of epistemological issues is the recognition that adequate understanding, both personal and political, often depends upon the actual bringing about of alternative social relations and political structures. Although such discussions are not often advanced as theories about knowledge, in some recent feminist discussions of personal and political relations there exist resources for rethinking and answering some general epistemological and metaphysical issues.[2]

In this article I will argue that some feminist treatments of the role of personal experience in political theorizing ought to be understood as part of a reconception of the notion of objective rational interests. In particular, I suggest that some feminist discussions have offered important criticisms of a standard (liberal) notion of what it means for someone to act in her real interests, as opposed to doing what is right for her according to accepted social norms and values. They have done so by advancing implicit reconceptions of self-knowledge and hence of autonomy. I will argue that the emphasis on personal experience in recent feminist theorizing ought to be understood as an emphasis on the occasional role of personal development and experience in the acquiring of nonpropositional understanding, the understanding people possess in the form of intuitions, attitudes, and so on. When feminist insights about personal development are understood in a more straightforwardly epistemological fashion, it will turn out that rather than undermining the possibility of objective knowledge and general rational principles, as feminist theorists have sometimes been accused of doing, the treatment of personal experience found in some feminist accounts in fact advances the possibility of objective justification for claims about social and political realities.

There is a tradition in political philosophy of distinguishing between actions and interests that people engage in and possess, and actions and interests that are rational for them. We may wonder, for instance, whether the decisions a person makes on the basis of her preferences at a particular time really represent her long-term interests. It may be that the individual's decisions rest on very little information or are the result of dubious influences. Or, even when someone's projects and interests are carefully chosen and reflected upon in light of available facts, we may think she is choosing irrationally because she fails to value the right kinds of things for herself. In some cases in which we think someone falls short of choosing rationally, we may want to say not just that she chooses irrationally because she fails to choose correctly given her ends, but also that she is mistaken about her ends.

The most interesting and controversial formulations of issues about rational interests arise in relation to cases of false consciousness. In situations involving ideological oppression, an individual may fail to possess preferences and desire that adequately reflect an interest in her own human flourishing because she has been beaten down by the circumstances of her situation. She may have been deprived of information about her personal prospects and, more importantly, denied the possibility to develop the self-assurance and integrity that would allow her to pursue her options if they were made available to her. Moreover, individuals who are discriminated against in a society are sometimes not aware of that discrimination, and even when people do become aware of discrimination, they may not be aware of the full extent to which discriminatory practices affect them. The effects of oppression may be such that people are psychologically damaged, possessing interests and desires that reflect their subservient social status. They fail to recognize that social and institutional structures discriminate against them in deep ways and that as a result many of their own perceptions and reactions are not fully representative of their own real needs and aspirations. In such cases we may want to say that an individual possesses an objective interest in goods that go beyond what she would desire for herself even if she were not mistaken about her options or the consequences of pursuing them. We may think, for instance, that an individual has an objective interest in full self-respect and integrity even though it may be true that this is for her both inconceivable and unavailable given current structures.

Questions about the relation between rational choice and objective interests have been approached in several ways. The liberal approach to the question has been to define rational choice in terms of what someone would choose under various types of idealized cognitive conditions.[3] The idea is that an act is rational for a person if it is accessible to that person through a process of rational deliberation in which the conditions for rational deliberation are idealized in a suitably specified way. John Rawls argues, for instance, that a person's rational choice is what she would choose if she possessed adequate instrumental reasoning abilities, full and complete information, and the capacity to vividly imagine the consequences of her actions.[4] In his discussion of paternalism, Rawls argues that in any judgment about what is good for someone, we had better be able to argue that the individual herself would have so decided if she had been able to choose under the right conditions.[5] Otherwise, it would be possible to rationalize "totalitarian" actions. Rawls's view permits identifying desires and aims as a person's rational desires and aims even if they are not the person's current desires and aims but precludes the justification of actions aimed at making the person into someone she previously wasn't—that is, conversion experiences. As long as a person would so choose if she *were* fully rational and adequately informed, we can say that the choices in question are in her real interests.

The liberal view has the virtue, first, that it preserves the centrality of the individual perspective. It defines rational choice in terms of what the individual herself would choose under idealized conditions, so that what might be called a person's objective rational choice is determined by the person's idiosyncratic initial perspective. Thus, the liberal can say that the idealization defines an *individual's* good as opposed to what is good for all people (or all relevant sorts of people, according to general social or moral theories). Especially in cases in which paternalism is justified on the liberal view by the individual's incompetence or incapacity, the argument is that the individual herself would have so chosen under the right conditions. For instance, we might feel justified in preventing someone from harming himself even though he has reflected carefully on his decision and strongly desires the result. If intervention were justified in such a case, the argument would be that the person would not have reasoned as he had been able to consider his options in the absence of certain psychological constraints or distorting circumstantial pressures. The concern here is that if individuals' goods were not defined in terms of current interests and desires, it could turn out that detrimental processes of brainwashing and other wrong licensing of intervention could be held to be rational for an individual.

The second virtue of the liberal account is that it avoids saying that something is in someone's interest if, as a result of just any chances that come about, she ends up desiring it; that is, the liberal view acknowledges the centrality of the individual's perspective but does not claim that anything a person comes to desire is rational for her. If a person is adequately indoctrinated, subjected to psychological pressure, she will indeed desire the situation that results from the process, even if it is quite wrong for her. The liberal view suggests that a future desire is rational for a person at a time if it is desirable to her when reflected upon at that time in light of full and complete information and vivid awareness of the consequences of desiring it. That is, it defines a person's good in terms of what the current person, given her basic desires and interests, would choose for her future self if only she could choose under idealized conditions (i.e., conditions of full information and capacity to reason well instrumentally). It does not consider relevant to defining someone's good what that individual would choose for herself if she were to become some other person—if, for instance, she were to undergo a conversion experience and come to assess her options in terms of a fundamentally different personal perspective.

But there are some cases in which this conception of what is in someone's real interests gives the wrong result. The central insight of this standard account is that what makes a choice rational for someone is that she herself would choose such an option if she were able to choose under the right conditions; it precludes consideration of what the person would choose if she were psychologically pressured or were to undergo a conversion experience. Yet there are some cases in which the effects of social conditioning on a person are such that if rationality is defined ultimately in terms of a person's current desires and interests, even under conditions of more adequate beliefs, continued subordination and degradation turn out to be in the person's best interests. In cases in which someone is the victim of ideological oppression, the failure to act in what we would think to be her real interests may not be just a matter of her mistaken beliefs and inadequate reasoning capacities; it may also be a matter of her not possessing a sense of her self—or even a self at all—that would support a full sense of flourishing. Equipped with ideal cognitive capacities and resources, it is not clear that a person who is degraded and diminished by social conditioning would have reason to choose goods typically thought to represent flourishing.

Consider, for instance, the case of Thomas Hill's Deferential Wife, the wife who is utterly devoted to and derives happiness from deferring to her husband.[6] The person in the example does not just subordinate herself to her husband as a means of acquiring happiness; for instance, she does not defer to him in some spheres in return for his deference to her in other spheres. The Deferential Wife defines herself in terms of her subordination. She is proud to subordinate herself to her husband and derives much of her happiness from the fact that she serves him well. As Hill describes the temperament and outlook of the Deferential Wife, aspiring toward and being in control of her life would cause her more suffering than would be balanced out by the resulting benefits. His proposal is that we can account for our intuitions that she is acting irrationally in subordinating herself by suggesting that she would choose to pursue a sense of self-respect if she were fully informed as to her rights as a moral being and were able to accord the right kind of importance to such rights. Hill uses the example to show that although there are some cases in which it is apparently not instrumentally rational for a person to pursue her rational interest, we might still want to say that that person *has* a rational interest in becoming a fully self-respecting and autonomous human being.

Suppose, however, that in fact the Deferential Wife *is* in control of her life and that deferring to her husband *is* the realization of her actual sense of self—not a result of mistaken beliefs about her self. Suppose she controls the life that she has, appreciates her rights, and has full respect for what she is; suppose, in other words, that her problem is that the life she has and the person she really is are diminished and defective due to deep and longstanding forms of social oppression. If this is so, an alternative interpretation of Hill's example is that rather than failing to have the right beliefs about her situation, the Deferential Wife fails to have an appropriate situation—in particular, she fails to possess an adequate self and sense of integrity. She may not be lacking in imagination or self-concern at all; on the contrary, she may have carved out carefully defined limits as regards deference to her husband and be actively engaged in fulfilling herself in accordance with them.

Of course, in some formulations of this view Rawls adds the restriction that under idealized conditions the person whose good is in question should be concerned about autonomy.[7] He does this in order to guarantee that it be in everyone's good to become an autonomous, valuing agent. But if autonomy is defined so as to rule out the kind of servility that characterizes the Deferential Wife's relationship to her husband, it may not in fact turn out that, with full and complete information, she would desire autonomy. For given her actual sense of her self, which is the position from which she approaches idealized information on liberal views, she may have no reason to desire *that* kind of autonomy. If her social and historical situation is such that it is part of her identity to be inferior to men—in particular to her husband—deferring to him in all decisions *is* a valuing of her autonomy. She already is autonomous and self-respecting to the extent available to her.[8]

In other words, one might think that Rawls's view can account for people in situations like that of the Deferential Wife by simply building into the model the notion that under idealized cognitive conditions people would desire the right kind of autonomy. However, it is important to note that to the extent that some people are in fact deprived of dignity and self-respect in their actual lives, desiring the kind of self-determination that we usually think characteristic of a good life would depend upon their undergoing a change to their actual selves. Insofar as the model would turn out to accommodate the situations of people who are actually degraded, it would risk giving up the very feature supposedly making it a model that preserves individuals' autonomy.

Thus, in situations in which a person's self is degraded, the result of the person's choosing under Rawls-type idealized conditions may be a sense of autonomy that is somewhat thin. It is central to the liberal definition of interests that the self that chooses under idealized conditions be untransformed; that is, it is important that the individual's choices be defined in terms of her own perspective. However, in the case of the Deferential Wife, if she is to choose what is best for *her*—even if she has access to full and complete information about what would be good for her under different conditions—she has no reason to choose a full sense of autonomy. She has not the kind of self to which such a sense of autonomy could be applied. And if Rawls were to stipulate that under idealized conditions the Deferential Wife desires a thick sense of autonomy, he would have to include in his idealization transformations to her self. In order for it to be rational for her to desire autonomy in the sense that rules out her habitual servility, her actual sense of self would have to be transformed so that habitual servility is not what defines it. But defining a person's objective interest in terms of a perspective the person might have but in fact does not is just what the liberal view rules out.[9]

The reasons for denying a role for conversion experiences in defining someone's rational interest are clear. For one thing, it would be hard, otherwise, to see how the *individual's* good is at issue. If, under idealized conditions, a person chooses from among her various options from a perspective that is not that of her actual self, it is hard to see how such a choice should carry any weight for the actual person whose choices are at issue. Second, if potential psychological transformations are relevant to defining rational choice, it may become possible to rationalize dubious life choices. Not all transformation experiences are beneficial for individuals, and some are quite detrimental. For instance, it might turn out to be possible to say that something is in someone's best interest because if she were to spend weeks being indoctrinated by a religious (or other) cult, she would then desire the thing in question. A third consideration is the rationalization of undesirable forms of paternalism. Given that people may in fact come to desire certain choices after having been coerced into them, we might be forced to say that such coercive interventions are for their own good.

But in some cases, like that of the Deferential Wife, a person's rational interests—or at least what we might intuitively think to be in her individual rational interests—depend precisely upon other kinds of personal and political transformations experiences the liberal accounts want to rule out. In fact, it sometimes looks as though the disruption of a person's secure sense of self is just what is required to make a full state of flourishing individually rational for a person. Consider the member of a marginalized group who has the talent to be a medical researcher but who aspires toward a job in the local pharmacy. The liberal view would attempt to account for our intuitions that the person's aspirations are irrational by suggesting that if the person had access to full and complete information, then he would know that his low expectations for himself are socially induced and that he would desire more for himself than a career in the local drugstore. But if the person has access to full and complete information, then he will not only find out that his aspirations are a result of adverse social conditioning but also that if he pursues a career as a medical researcher, he will then suffer harassment, job discrimination, alienation, and so on. Moreover he will find out that although he has the ability to do such a job well, that fact is irrelevant. For he will not be taken seriously in his work and will spend more of his time fighting civil rights cases than doing what he had desired. At least at the drugstore he has the possibility of doing reasonably satisfying work and gaining a steady income. If he inserts himself into the medical establishment, he may then achieve other goals and acquire other goods, but he may not be acting rationally given his current desires and interests.

Now, of course it may *not* be in his rational interests to pursue a career in medical research. It is certainly sometimes true of individuals that they could not cope with the consequences of pursuing what we would intuitively think to be in their long-term interests as human beings. But there *are* cases in which a person actually acquires greater self-respect, strength, and a quite different sense of priorities as a result of the effects upon her of undertaking just such an apparently irrational pursuit. As a result of social and political engagement, she does not just acquire different aims and desires; she also becomes personally changed so as to possess a different interpretive background on the basis of which to weight her desires and interests. Hill's Deferential Wife may in fact be right in thinking she is not being personally deprived by acting out her deferential relationship. Given the dependence of her identity on her social situation, she may really have as part of her self-concept the feature of being inferior to her husband. However, it is likely that if the Deferential Wife were to act in certain ways or even were compelled to act in certain ways by circumstances or forceful persuasion, she would *acquire* desires and interests that would change her position and provide her with a different interpretive background. If she were to acquire, say, greater power or self-respect, she would in fact become such that the actual denial of power and control to her *is* a personal deprivation. Now if Rawls were to include under the effects of vivid imagining the insight people acquire as a result of having their condition and situation transformed in this sort of way, he would in fact be including the role of conversion experiences in his account of a person's good. But he would then have to answer the question, which he does not address, of why some conversion experiences and not others can be beneficial for someone.

The second closely related feature of note about the liberal view is that the full and complete information assumed in the idealizations is mostly propositional; that is, the kind of information in light of which an individual considers her choices is of the type that could be expressed in words and concepts. The individual reflects upon her options in light of a full and complete body of truths that could be put into the form of sentences in her idiolect. The idealizations do not include complete access to a different kind of knowledge—knowledge that people possess in the form of intuitions, attitudes, ways of behaving, orientation, and so on. It is true that for Rawls, a kind of nonpropositional understanding is involved in the idealizations insofar as people are able to vividly imagine being in certain circumstances. But his account does not include the kind of understanding that a person acquires in virtue of being transformed—precisely the kind that is often needed for understanding ideological oppression. This is because this sort of transformation constitutes a different interpretive position; the vivid imaginings provided in a Rawlsian idealization are dependent for their interpretation upon the person's *initial* interpretive position.

It seems clear that people usually know things about their situation that cannot be expressed now. There is always something about an experience of a situation that cannot be expressed, even in principle. But in certain cases what a person knows as a result of being in a situation constitutes understanding of a larger situation. That is, being in a particular personal state and relationship to society sometimes constitutes a kind of understanding of that society that could not be obtained through an examination of the expressible truths about that society. Literary critic Barbara Christian describes something like this knowledge in her discussion of Alice Walker's *The Color Purple.*[10] She cites a passage in which Mister taunts Celie: "Look at you. You black, you pore, you ugly, you a woman. Goddam . . . you nothing at all." Celie retorts: "I'm pore, I'm black, I may be ugly and can't cook . . . but I'm here." Celie is nothing according to the categories that Mister possesses for interpreting the world. Her existence as a person is an anomaly in his terms because according to the conceptual framework he applies, the concept "people" does not include black women. Christian writes that "Celie's affirmation of her existence does not deny [Mister's] categories of powerlessness; rather she insists that nonetheless she exists, that she knows something as a result of being at that intersection of categories that attempt to 'camouflage her existence.' "[11]

But we might think that Celie does indeed challenge Mister's categories, and it is in fact *because* she challenges his categories that she knows something that could not otherwise be known. Celie's experience of existing as a person puts her outside of the categories in terms of which Mister, and the rest of society, make sense of their experience. Not only is there something about Celie's experience that cannot be expressed—that is, something that it feels like to be in her situation—but there is also something about her experience that, if it could be expressed, would contradict presuppositions of the dominant conceptual framework. Celie's assertion of her existence challenges Mister's categories, but it is because her knowledge is in fact a way of existing and acting that her assertion constitutes a threat. If her challenge to Mister's categories were merely verbal or intellectual, it could be answered within the terms of the framework that Mister employs, just as anomalies can usually be explained away in terms of a dominant conceptual framework. However, to the extent that Celie's understanding of what it is like to be in her situation consists in her *acting* against the grain of that conceptual framework, her nonpropositional understanding of her position constitutes a critical interpretive position. As Christian writes, "The contrariness [between prevailing traditional and alternative modes of representing reality] is a measure of health, of the insistence that counter to the societal perception of black women as being 'nothing at all,' their existence is knowledge that relates to us all."[12]

Celie's existing in a certain relation to society constitutes a kind of understanding of that society that cannot entirely be expressed in propositions. In one sense the inexpressibility of Celie's experience is explained simply by the difficulty of expressing any experience of what it is like to be somewhere or in some state. But there is more to be said about inexpressibility in this particular case. In Celie's situation, the inexpressibility of her experience is of particular epistemic significance. For it is not just another dimension of her expressible experience. What she understands but is incapable of expressing provides, or potentially provides, the interpretive standards that could make a more adequate *expressed* experience possible. That is, the conceptual framework that she currently operates with is not adequate for Celie's deliberations about her life and actions because according to that conceptual framework, she doesn't exist as a person. A better conceptual framework, however, cannot be got simply by revising language and concepts because the only available theoretical instruments for carrying out such revision disallow the full humanity of people like Celie. Instead, Celie's proper deliberations depend upon the bringing about of a critical perspective as result of acting on the basis of that part of her experience that is inexpressible—her nonpropositional understanding of her situation. In this kind of case, then, nonpropositional understanding provides not just another level of understanding but perhaps the only possible access to the kinds of epistemic standards that would permit effective radical criticism.

In another Walker story, a young African-American woman's understanding of her personal situation depends importantly upon the bringing about of social relations in terms of which she can properly interpret her personal perceptions. In *Meridian*, the protagonist comes to understand her political goals primarily as a result of her experiencing what it is like to be part of the "togetherness, communal spirit [and] righteous convergence" of the civil rights movement.[13] Perhaps due in part to her youth, Meridian is at first unable to define her own political commitment. When asked whether she would kill for the revolution, she is unable to make a judgment because she lacks a clear understanding of what such a commitment would entail. At the point in the story when Meridian *does* decide that she can kill for the revolution, the difference is not that she has acquired more theoretical understanding; she had quite a bit of that at the point where she had been confused. Instead, what is different is her situation, particularly her emotional situation. Sitting in the church, feeling the political impetus of the music and the tradition, she recognizes that "the years in America had created them One Life."[14] Certainly, this latter is propositional understanding, but the understanding of this proposition depends heavily on Meridian's changed personal state. The intellectual element of her experience in the church is made possible, it seems, by her emotionally experiencing what it is like to be part of a developing set of social and political interrelations. Her actual situatedness within a network of political and emotional relationships itself provides her with epistemic standards making interpretations possible that were not so previously. What Meridian acquires during her experience in the church is not knowledge of when and where she would or could kill for the revolution; rather, what appears to be the case is that she has acquired relations, attitudes, and ways of behaving that constitute a more adequate interpretive framework.

It looks as though one sort of nonpropositional understanding consists largely in a person, or a group of persons, existing or acting in ways that constitute an interpretive framework. A person's existing in a certain state or a group of persons bringing about certain sets of social or political relations can sometimes constitute understanding of a situation that cannot be entirely expressed theoretically. This kind of understanding is different from the experience of vivid imagination that liberals typically include in their idealizations. In the case of someone like the Deferential Wife, it would be the acquiring of new aims and interests altogether—in fact, her becoming a different person—that would explain her possession of an individual rational interest in human flourishing. Vividly imagining oneself in some position does not usually involve transformations. This is why vivid imaginings are usually different from something like a mind-altering drug experience or a hallucination. When we vividly imagine ourselves in some situation, we are usually in control of the interpretation of that event. In a drug experience or a hallucination, the control is not there, so that often a person experiences herself in a state of emotion, desire, commitment, or relationship that she does not choose. Not only does that person experience herself in that situation, but she also acts and engages according to what she is in this other state, experiencing the consequences and so on. The kind of transformation that would make it possible for the Deferential Wife to properly understand her real possibilities as a person would be one that would provide her with different grounds, and such a transformation would most likely have to be one which transformed *herself.*

Now, it is not just in the case of oppressed people that transformation experiences are relevant to the acquisition of a more adequate understanding of one's life and situation. bell hooks has made the point that it is often difficult for white liberals to acknowledge that there are perspectives that they cannot have access to.[15] By this, I take it that she does not mean that whites can have no understanding of racist oppression at all but rather that there are some things that cannot be understood by whites in advance of somewhat radical change to the social structures and power relations that define the way people see themselves. In particular, I suspect that she means that adequate understanding of racism, on the part of white people, requires personal change, a giving up of power, and an actual change of behavior and commitment. There are plenty of examples of people possessing large amounts of theoretical information about sexism and racism and failing to understand what it means; they fail in particular to grasp the implications of such information for their own behavior and relations. hooks's point appears to be that it is not possible for the relatively nonoppressed to acquire adequate understanding of racism simply by reading or listening to what people of color have to say, unless that reading or listening is of an emotionally and politically engaged sort. Instead, understanding often requires undergoing some kind of transformation experience, particularly of the sort that results in the unsettling of the person's self and position.

The two features of the liberal view noted above are related in a way that helps explain the inadequacy of the liberal idealization. I have suggested that it is a mistake to think that a person acts autonomously when she chooses in light of correct information in a way that preserves her basic sense of self. For it is often a person's *self* that is diminished and deprived by ideological oppression, and correcting a person's *beliefs* is not an adequate response. But there is definitely a strong grain of truth in the intuition reflected in the liberal view that it is wrong to interfere in a person's carefully thought-out choices. It is certainly true that we are often rightly reluctant to try to persuade someone that we care about that she is living her life wrongly, that she is mistaken in her view of what is good for her. It is also true, however, that in some cases in which we might be reluctant to say such a thing to someone, we would take action to change that person's situation. We might supply her with increased economic resources, introduce her to different sets of relations, and so on. The grain of truth in our intuitions that it is wrong to tell people how to live their lives may not be that people act autonomously when they act on the basis of their own basic preferences and value and that their choices therefore ought to be respected; rather, it may be that it is often painfully futile and startlingly insensitive to try to help someone out of a difficult situation by simply giving her more information. Telling someone that she is living her life wrongly is not usually helpful and often quite damaging. However, by changing someone's situation we are sometimes in fact supplying that person with relevant information. The notion that we ought not to interfere with someone's choices does not correctly reflect a concern for autonomy if that person is deprived of the resources to act autonomously. It may, however, correctly reflect the insight that in any case supplying people with information that would be useful to them in individual deliberations is not a matter of providing increased access to propositional truths; instead, it is a matter of the bringing about of different, more appropriate, social and political situations. The idea that a person acts or chooses in her interests when she proceeds as she would under liberal idealized conditions is mistaken both epistemologically and metaphysically; it mistakenly excludes the role of important kinds of nonpropositional understanding in rational deliberation, and it ignores the occasional importance to proper individual development of the bringing about of conditions that transform a person's aims and values.

Gayatri Spivak is one feminist theorist who sometimes appears to be talking about the role of nonpropositional understanding. Many feminists have talked about the importance of bodily understanding, but such discussions do not often hook up discussion about the body to questions about the development of radical critique. In her intriguing discussion of "The Breastgiver," Spivak suggests that the body is the *place* of knowledge and not merely the instrument.[16] This claim by itself is not striking, but Spivak goes on to suggest that bodily experience can often be the bringing about of different sets of relations, relations that can make things understandable that could not have been understandable previously. Women's full sexual identity, for instance, cannot be properly understood within a conceptual framework that denies women any identity at all. But the *experience* of orgasmic pleasure—*jouissance*—is "the place where an unexchangeable excess can be imagined and figured forth."[17] The bodily experience, the bringing about of relations, is necessary in order that experiences that would have no meaning within a dominant conceptual framework are able to be understood. Spivak appears, at least here, to be suggesting that in order for some situations to be understood, it is not just new concepts that need to be introduced but new relations, and new relations sometimes constitute epistemic standards according to which concepts can be more properly evaluated and supplied.

Sometimes an alternative conceptual background can be acquired imaginatively through fiction. Spivak points out that emotional involvement in fiction can sometimes "perform the ideological mobilization" that an adequate propositional understanding of the situation cannot.[18] People always understand information from a particular (biased) perspective. If what needs to be understood is the nature and wrongness of the structures and assumptions in terms of which people are interpreting information and themselves, "scholarly demonstrations" are not going to do the job. What is needed is a different perspective, one that can often only be acquired through transformative emotional involvement. Certainly, not just any reading of fiction can help to bring about the "counter-hegemonic ideological production" that Spivak has in mind, for one can read fiction without being unsettled and transformed. The point is that one often *has* to become unsettled in order to understand properly, and fiction is sometimes a vehicle for this.

Audre Lorde is another theorist who sometimes treats personal involvement and commitment epistemically and who also appears to have in mind the important political role of understanding acquired through personal engagement and activity.[19] In her "Uses of the Erotic," she appears to be attributing to experiences of passionate involvement the kind of epistemic significance that can explain radical understanding. The passionate involvement she appears to have in mind is sometimes sexual but also includes activities such as building a bookcase; specifically, she seems to have in mind the occasional spiritual experiences people undergo when they become intensely, creatively involved—with people, art, things, nature, or whatever. In suggesting that the erotic is a source of power and information in our lives, Lorde does not appear to be suggesting that there is propositional information that can be gained through passionate involvement in activities and relationships; she speaks of the erotic as a "lens through which we scrutinize . . . [and] evaluate" aspects of our existence.[20] She speaks of the capacity to experience and to engage as a "measure" of the possibilities for a more full human experience, suggesting that the entering into and the bringing about of states, not primarily a theoretical body of truths, provides a more adequate basis for individual deliberation.

There is an important scientific source for this notion of nonpropositional knowledge. In Kuhn's discussion of scientific paradigms, he treats the acquiring of scientific skills as an acquiring of knowledge.[21] He insists that scientific practices and procedures amount to more than the explicit theories that they depend upon and inform, and that precisely for this reason part of the training of professional scientists must be experimental. Whether or not they accept Kuhn's constructivist conclusions about the status of scientific knowledge, philosophers of science are generally agreed that good scientific practice depends upon the acquiring of experimental know how, including good scientific "hunches" and intuitions. Moreover, one explanation for this is that the practices and procedures of science often constitute a kind of nonpropositional, or tacit, knowledge.[22] One reason the role of nonpropositional understanding of this type would be important in explaining scientific progress is that what needs to be explained in regard to the possibility of objective scientific knowledge in how it is that scientists acquire rational standards that guide them to knowledge of an independent world.[23] To the extent that it is uncontroversial that all aspects of scientific practice are deeply theory-dependent, the possibility that scientists develop practices and skills as a result of interaction with the physical world would help explain how it is that scientific standards are appropriate for the investigation of an independent world and not simply the consequence of the development of a particular tradition. The role of nonpropositional knowledge in explaining reliable scientific practice is thus not *just* the acquisition of skills necessary for carrying out previously defined projects. Rather, it appears importantly to involve the development of standards for defining and evaluating new directions in theory development.

Knowledge people acquire of oppression appears to be of this sort. If it is true, as it seems to be, that all thinking is dependent upon a person's social and historical situation, there is a question about how people can ever know that their current situation is in fact wrong for them. To the extent that people interpret their lives in terms of a conceptual background that represents the status quo, how do they come to learn that that background is in fact mistaken? One answer to this is that in order to continue to act and to make sense of his situation, a person who is a member of an oppressed group will learn certain behaviors and attitudes. For instance, he learns to become aware of racist biases and to make allowance for them. Now it could be that someone learns how to behave appropriately for a situation and continues to understand things in the same way. But often an individual's learning of coping skills in such a situation constitutes a way of interpreting things differently. As a result of learning certain procedures, he comes to see his situation differently and to apply different considerations in deliberating about it.

It seems reasonable that some feminist discussions of personal development could plausibly be understood as a working out of the political implications of the importance of acquiring nonpropositional understanding in choosing and acting rationally. Sarah Hoagland, for instance, makes the important point that engaging in projects and commitments is necessary for discovering one's proper sense of self, and that such "self-interest" in fact provides the ground for effective moral action.[24] She emphasizes that her point is *not* that people sometimes need to engage with others to discover the submerged self, but rather that engaging with others in personally and politically appropriate ways is necessary to bring about the conditions that make being an integrated self possible in the first place. Her point appears to be that *self*-interest ought not always to be considered egotistical, because serving one's real self-interest often depends upon engaging oneself socially and politically in appropriate ways. The development of the right kinds of community relations provides the social network—especially the transformed power relations—that makes options conceivable that otherwise would not be for a given individual. This makes it look as though the role of community building in Hoagland's account is partly epistemic; it consists, at least in part, in providing a more appropriate background for individual rational deliberation. The striking consequence of the potential epistemic role of personal engagement and community building is that it looks as though rather than requiring information in order to make the right choices, individuals sometimes have to make certain choices and take actions *first* in order to bring about the conditions under which information, if it is available, can be properly approached.

The importance of Hoagland's treatment of rational interests, I suggest, is her emphasis on the ontological significance of social and political engagement. While philosophers commonly note that it is old hat to recognize the social dimensions of personal identity,[25] there are important questions to be raised about the implications of recognizing the fully social nature of identity that are not often addressed. Hoagland's account contributes to this development in demonstrating a more thoroughgoing denial of the centrality of a person's given psychological state in defining an individual's individuality or proper sense of integrity. In particular, her account is important in pointing out the political aspects of defining and acquiring an adequate sense of personal integrity. The suggestion is not that a person's self has to be *discovered* through interaction and engagements—as if it were *always* there to begin with—but rather that in some cases a person's self has to be brought about and discovered through her experience of the effects of actual social and political change and moreover by changes to the external circumstances.

But Hoagland does not herself emphasize the epistemic dimensions of her account. In fact, one finds no answer to the question of why not just any way we choose to create ourselves is rational as long as it emerges from the right kind of community. It is clear that she does not intend that just any kind of interrelational patterns emerging from lesbian community provide conditions for more adequate personal development, for she criticizes the racism and violence of some lesbian communities. She even suggests that people (within lesbian communities) sometimes need to be jolted out of their stupidity and bigotry.[26] Insofar as her emphasis is strictly on community and interaction and not on the occasional epistemological role of transformative personal and political experiences, it is not at all clear how she explains the possibility of justifiably criticizing some community practices and promoting others.

The epistemic component of personal development provides part of an answer to the question of how some transformations can be considered beneficial for someone and others not. The capacity of personal transformations to sometimes provide the insight and capacity to act in ways that promote self-respect, dignity, greater liberation, and so on provides part of a basis for measuring the rational adequacy of such experiences. Now one might think that the appeal to general human goods, such as self-respect, dignity, and liberation, or even to a notion of adequacy amounts to the importation of abstract, removed ideals, of the sort that the liberal accounts of an individual's good are rightly concerned to avoid. But the constraints on individual development provided by a concern to achieve greater human flourishing, both for individuals and for society, need not be abstract and removed any more than the principles that guide the acquiring of objective scientific knowledge are of this sort.

It is especially significant here that if knowledge is acquired through processes of action and engagement and if in fact some such knowledge is tacit, it is a mistake to think that a theory of knowledge must provide criteria, justifiable a priori, for distinguishing knowledge from nonknowledge.[27] The worry expressed by some feminists about developing theories of knowledge is sometimes that the development of such theories imposes, a priori, legislative conditions for knowledge. But, in fact, it is one of the virtues of developing an alternative general account of the nature of knowledge and objectivity that it becomes possible to see why such epistemological demands are misguided. If political knowledge depends upon the acquisition of nonpropositional understanding as a result of engagement, then the status of epistemic principles raises a contingent question about the role of such principles in a general process of social, political, and moral development; it is not a question that can be answered, or should be answered, in advance of engagement in and application to that process.

Feminist accounts of the role of personal relations and commitments in self- and social understanding provide reasons for thinking that the standard (liberal) formulations of the issue of an individual's rational interests gets the question backwards. If it is true that the acquiring of adequate personal integrity often depends upon the bringing about of more appropriate personal and political conditions, the question of what is good for someone cannot be a question about what an initial individual does *with* information; instead, to the extent that the acquiring of information *is* the bringing about of a more adequate personal situation, the proper formulation of the issue is as a question about what the right kind of information does *to* the individual. The deep problem with liberal views—and with any view that identifies what is good for someone with what the person would herself choose if only she possessed the right amount of propositional information—is that such a model for rational choices misconstrues the metaphysics of individuality. In particular it misconstrues how the acquiring of adequate personal integrity depends upon actual changes to a person's self and situation. Not only do some feminist accounts contribute to our understanding of how we can really know about our social and political situations; in doing so they also indicate the mistake in thinking that issues about genuinely autonomous action are fundamentally issues about an individual's psychological state.

NOTES

I am greatly indebted to Richard Boyd for frequent and fruitful discussion on the issues of this paper. I am also grateful to him for extensive and insightful written comments on countless drafts of the dissertation from which this paper emerges. Others who have offered helpful discussion and comments are Linda Alcoff, Richmond Campbell, Jackie Davies, Libby Potter, Phyllis Rooney, Nicholas Sturgeon, and an audience at the Canadian Philosophical Association Meetings in Kingston, Ontario, May 1991.

1. See, for example, Kai Nielson, "Afterword" in Kai Nielson and Marsha Hanen, eds., *Science, Morality and Feminist Theory* (Calgary, Alta.: University of Calgary Press, 1987).
2. I should say here that I do not agree with characterization of feminist work according to which feminist epistemology is opposed to the development of theories of knowledge, or even, as is often said, to "mainstream" epistemology. Feminists, it seems to me, are clearly developing gen-

eral theories of knowledge, and in many ways feminist work is continuous with some strains of postpositivist, naturalistic epistemology. While I cannot here make the arguments for this, I suggest that the radical, subversive potential of feminist work is undermined when it is thought of as being somehow *opposed* to the development of general epistemology and metaphysics.

3. I have called this a "liberal" view, not just because it is advanced by liberals but also because it is characterized primarily by its ultimate preservation of the initial individual's perspective and a certain conception of knowledge. I have argued elsewhere ("Rationality and Integrity: The Role of Transformation Experiences in Defining Individual Rational Standards," chapter 2, Ph.D. dissertation, Cornell University, 1991) that Peter Railton, a Marxist, offers an account that shares the same liberal features. While Railton does indeed introduce nonliberal insights that could provide the resources for accommodating the kinds of case I discuss below, I argue that he fails to exploit them properly.
4. John Rawls, *A Theory of Justice* (Cambridge: Harvard University Press, 1971), 417 ff. Similar views have been advanced by Henry Sidgwick, *The Methods of Ethics* (London: Macmillan & Co., Ltd., 1907); Richard Brandt, *A Theory of the Right and the Good* (Oxford: Clarendon Press, 1979); and R. M. Hare, *Moral Thinking* (Oxford: Clarendon Press, 1981).
5. Rawls, *A Theory of Justice*, 248 ff.
6. Thomas Hill, "Servility and Self Respect," in *The Monist* 57 (1973): 87.
7. John Rawls, *A Theory of Justice*, 417; "Kantian Constructivism in Moral Theory," in *Journal of Philosophy* 87 (1980): 525–26.
8. There are plenty of examples available to show that people can fail to understand or be motivated by information that they possess and believe and in which the failure can be attributed to the possession of a particular self-concept. When I lived for years in Italy, I failed to learn to make fresh pasta even though I was shown in detail many times and possessed a great desire to learn. I knew all the steps but did not understand the procedure. One main reason for this, I presume, is that I possessed a concept of people who make pasta from scratch as being unusually competent in culinary affairs and of myself as not being such a person. Had I become integrated enough to be able to see making pasta as part of what one does to get along, I would have understood better. A self-concept, including understanding of social positioning, is not something that people are often fully aware of but which is assumed in the interpretation and application of much information. That the possession of a certain self-concept prevents or makes possible understanding of one's situation is indicated by the fact that people often acquire an understanding of their actual situations when they discover the ways in which their self-concepts, unbeknownst to them, are racist, sexist, or whatever.
9. See especially Rawls, *A Theory of Justice:* 248. In fact, liberal accounts allow significant criticism of a person's particular desires—even strongly held ones—but they stop at criticism of the standards and perspective according to which the current person assesses her desires and options.
10. Barbara Christian, "What Celie Knows That You Should Know," in David T. Goldberg, ed. *The Anatomy of Racism* (Minneapolis: University of Minnesota Press, 1990), 135.
11. Ibid., 135.
12. Ibid., 141–42.
13. Alice Walker, *Meridian* (New York: Pocket Books, 1976), 199–200.
14. Ibid.
15. bell hooks, "Talking Race, Resisting Racism," presented at Feminism and Cultural Imperialism conference, Cornell University, April 23, 1989.
16. Gayatri Spivak, "A Literary Representation of the Subaltern," in *In Other Worlds* (New York: Methuen Press, 1987), 241–68, esp. 258–61.

17. Ibid., 259.
18. Ibid., 256.
19. Audre Lorde, "Uses of the Erotic: The Erotic as Power," in *Sister Outsider* (Freedom, CA: The Crossing Press, 1984), 53–59.
20. Ibid., 53, 57.
21. See Thomas Kuhn, *The Structure of Scientific Revoutions* (Chicago: University of Chicago Press, 1970).
22. For discussion of scientific intuitions and their explanation, see Richard Boyd, "Naturalistic Epistemology and Scientific Realism," *Philosophy of Science Association* 2 (1980); and "How to be a Moral Realist," in G. Sayre-MacCord, ed., *Essays on Moral Realism* (Ithaca: Cornell University Press, 1989).
23. In particular, Boyd op. cit.; and "On the Current Status of Scientific Realism," *Erkenntnis* 19 (1983): 45–90.
24. Sarah Hoagland, *Lesbian Ethics* (Palo Alto, CA: Institute for Lesbian Studies, 1988), esp. chap. 2.
25. Peter Railton, for instance, in "Alienation, Consequentialism and the Demands of Morality," in *Philosophy and Public Affairs* 13 (1984): 167.
26. This point was made in a presentation, "Lesbian Ethics," at Cornell University, March 9, 1990.
27. This point has been made by naturalistic epistemologies. For an overview see Philip Kitcher "The Naturalist's Return" in *The Philosophical Review* 101, January (1992): 33–114.

Love and Knowledge: Emotion in Feminist Epistemology

Many classic epistemological theories regard emotions as disruptive, nonrational forces that need to be channeled or suppressed if knowledge is to be gained. Jaggar argues that these views are misguided. Not only is emotion implicated in all knowledge claims, but also emotion can help feminists and other emancipatory movements develop critical social theory.

After examining the positivist and the cognitivist accounts of emotion, Jaggar presents some features of emotions that bear on epistemology. Emotions are socially constructed, and understandings of emotion vary from culture to culture and in different historical epochs. Values and norms reflect emotional experience, but emotions presuppose values and norms and express valuations. Emotional attitudes shape perception, and facts embed cultural understandings about appropriate emotional responses. It follows, argues Jaggar, that dispassionate, objective inquiry is unattainable. Yet, this epistemological standard has significant political consequences, for it discredits the epistemic authority of subordinated social groups and legitimates the political power of dominant groups. Seeking to overcome this inequity, Jaggar proposes an alternative epistemology that integrates emotion and theorizing. Jaggar points out that subordinated individuals sometimes experience emotions that are conventionally deemed inappropriate, and she urges that these "outlaw emotions" may provide clues to unjust practices and oppressive conditions. When these emotions are shared or validated by other group members, they can become the basis for oppositional perceptions, norms, and values—in other words, for critical social theory. Moreover, critical social theory can help to reconfigure emotions in ways that promote feminist aims. Thus, Jaggar concludes that emotion is indispensable to knowledge and that the reconstruction of knowledge is necessary to the reconstruction of our emotional lives.

—D.T.M.

Chapter 21

Alison M. Jaggar

Love and Knowledge: Emotion in Feminist Epistemology

INTRODUCTION: EMOTION IN WESTERN EPISTEMOLOGY

Within the western philosophical tradition, emotions usually have been considered as potentially or actually subversive of knowledge.[1] From Plato until the present, with a few notable exceptions, reason rather than emotion has been regarded as the indispensable faculty for acquiring knowledge.[2]

Typically, although again not invariably, the rational has been contrasted with the emotional, and this contrasted pair then often has been linked with other dichotomies. Not only has reason been contrasted with emotion, but it has also been associated with the mental, the cultural, the universal, the public and the male, whereas emotion has been associated with the irrational, the physical, the natural, the particular, the private, and, of course, the female.

Although western epistemology has tended to give pride of place to reason rather than emotion, it has not always excluded emotion completely from the realm of reason. In the *Phaedrus*, Plato portrayed emotions, such as anger or curiosity, as irrational urges (horses) that must always be controlled by reason (the charioteer). On this model, the emotions did not need to be totally suppressed, but rather needed to be directed by reason: for example, in a genuinely threatening situation, it was thought not irrational but foolhardy not to be afraid.[3] The split between reason and emotion was not absolute, therefore, for the Greeks. Instead, the emotions were thought to provide indispensable motive power that needed to be channeled appropriately. Without horses, after all, the skill of the charioteer would be worthless.

The contrast between reason and emotion was sharpened in the seventeenth century by redefining reason as a purely instrumental faculty. For both the Greeks and the medieval philosophers, reason had been linked with value insofar as reason provided access to the objective structure or order of reality, seen as simultaneously natural and morally justified. With the rise of modern science, however, the realms of nature and value were separated: nature was stripped of value and reconceptualized as an inanimate mechanism of no intrinsic worth. Values were relocated in human beings, rooted in human preferences and emotional responses. The separation of supposedly natural fact from human value meant that reason, if it were to provide trustworthy insight into reality, had to be uncontaminated by or abstracted from value. Increasingly, therefore, though never universally,[4] reason was reconceptualized as the ability to make valid inferences from premises established elsewhere, the ability to calculate means but not to determine ends. The validity of logical inferences was thought independent of human attitudes and preferences; this was now the sense in which reason was taken to be objective and universal.[5]

The modern redefinition of rationality required a corresponding reconceptualization of emotion. This was achieved by portraying emotions as nonrational and often irrational urges that regularly swept the body, rather as a storm sweeps over the land. The common way of referring to the emotions as the "passions" emphasized that emotions happened to or were imposed upon an individual, something she suffered rather than something she did.

The epistemology associated with this new ontology rehabilitated sensory perception that, like emotion, typically had been suspected or even discounted by the western tradition as a reliable source of knowledge. British empiricism, succeeded in the nineteenth century by positivism, took its epistemological task to be the formulation of rules of inference that would guarantee the derivation of certain knowledge from the "raw data" supposedly given directly to the senses. Empirical testability became accepted as the hallmark of natural science; this, in turn, was viewed as the paradigm of genuine knowledge. Epistemology often was equated with the philosophy of science, and the dominant methodology of positivism prescribed that truly scientific knowledge must be capable of intersubjective verification. Because values and emotions had been defined as variable and idiosyncratic, positivism stipulated that trustworthy knowledge could be established only by methods that neutralized the values and emotions of individual scientists.

Recent approaches to epistemology have challenged some fundamental assumptions of the positivist epistemological model. Contemporary theorists of knowledge have undermined once-rigid distinctions between analytic and synthetic statements, between theories and observations and even between facts and values. Thus, far, however, few have challenged the purported gap between emotion and knowledge. In this paper, I wish to begin bridging this gap through the suggestion that emotions may be helpful and even necessary rather than inimical to the construction of knowledge. My account is exploratory in nature and leaves many questions unanswered. It is not supported by irrefutable arguments or conclusive proofs; instead, it should be viewed as a preliminary sketch for an epistemological model that will require much further development before its workability can be established.

EMOTION

What are Emotions?

The philosophical question "What are emotions?" requires both explicating the ways in which people ordinarily speak about emotion and evaluating the adequacy of those ways for expressing and illuminating experience and activity. Several problems confront someone trying to answer this deceptively simple question. One set of difficulties results from the variety, complexity, and even inconsistency of the ways in which emotions are viewed, both in daily life and in scientific contexts. It is in part this variety that makes emotions into a "question" and at the same time precludes answering that question by a simple appeal to ordinary usage. A second difficulty is the wide range of phenomena covered by the term "emotion": these extend from apparently instantaneous "knee-jerk" responses of fright to lifelong dedication to an individual or a cause; from highly civilized aesthetic responses to undifferentiated feelings of hunger and thirst;[6] from background moods such as contentment or depression to intense and focused involvement in an immediate situation. It may well be impossible to construct a manageable account of emotion to cover such apparently diverse phenomena.

A further problem concerns the criteria for preferring one account of emotion to another. The more one learns about the ways in which other cultures conceptualize human faculties, the less plausible it becomes that emotions constitute what philosophers call a "natural kind." Not only do some cultures identify emotions unrecognized in the West, but there is reason to believe that the concept of emotion itself is a historical invention, like the concept of intelligence (Lewontin 1982) or even the concept of mind (Rorty 1979). For instance, anthropologist Catherine Lutz argues that the "dichotomous categories of 'cognition' and 'affect' are themselves Euroamerican cultural constructions, master symbols that participate in the fundamental organization of our ways of looking at ourselves and others, both in and outside of social science" (Lutz 1987: 308, citing Lutz 1985, 1986). If this is true, then we have even more reason to wonder about the adequacy of ordinary western ways of talking about emotion. Yet we have no access either to our own emotions or to those of others independent of or unmediated by the discourse of our culture.

In the face of these difficulties, I shall sketch an account of emotion with the following limitations. First, it will operate within the context of western discussions of emotion: I shall not question, for instance, whether it would be possible or desirable to dispense entirely with anything resembling our concept of emotion. Second, although this account attempts to be consistent with as much as possible of western understandings of emotion, it is intended to cover only a limited domain, not every phenomenon that may be called an emotion. On the contrary, it excludes as genuine emotions both automatic physical responses and nonintentional sensations, such as hunger pangs. Third, I do not pretend to offer a complete theory of emotion; instead, I focus on a few specific aspects of emotion that I take to have been neglected or misrepresented, especially in positivist and neopositivist accounts. Finally, I would defend my approach not only on the ground that it illuminates aspects of our experience and activity that are obscured by positivist and neopositivist construals but also on the ground that it is less open than these to ideological abuse. In particular, I believe that recognizing certain neglected aspects of emotion makes possible a better and less ideologically biased account of how knowledge is, and so ought to be, constructed.

Emotions as Intentional

Early positivist approaches to understanding emotion assumed that an adequate account required analytically separating emotion from other human faculties. Just as positivist accounts of sense perception attempted to distinguish the supposedly raw data of sensation from their cognitive interpretations, so positivist accounts of emotion tried to separate emotion conceptually from both reason and sense perception. As one way of sharpening these distinctions, positivist construals of emotion tended to identify emotions with the physical feelings or involuntary bodily movements that typically accompany them, such as pangs or qualms, flushes or tremors; emotions were also assimilated to the subduing of physiological function or movement, as in the case of sadness, depression, or boredom. The continuing influence of such supposedly scientific conceptions of emotion can be seen in the fact that "feeling" is often used colloquially as a synonym for emotion, even though the more central meaning of "feeling" is physiological sensation. On such accounts, emotions were not seen as being *about* anything; instead, they were contrasted with and seen as potential disruptions of other phenomena that *are* about some thing, phenomena such as rational judgments, thoughts, and observations. The positivist approach to understanding emotion has been called the Dumb View (Spelman 1982).

The Dumb View of emotion is quite untenable. For one thing, the same feeling or physiological response is likely to be interpreted as various emotions, depending on the context of experience. This point often is illustrated by reference to the famous Schachter and Singer experiment; excited feelings were induced in research subjects by the injection of adrenalin, and the subjects then attributed to themselves appropriate emotions depending on their context (Schachter and Singer 1969). Another problem with the Dumb View is that identifying emotions with feelings would make it impossible to postulate that a person might not be aware of her emotional state, because feelings by definition are a matter of conscious awareness. Finally, emotions differ from feelings, sensations, or physiological responses in that they are dispositional rather than episodic. For instance, we may assert truthfully that we are outraged by, proud of, or saddened by certain events, even if at that moment we are neither agitated nor tearful.

In recent years, contemporary philosophers have tended to reject the Dumb View of emotion and have substituted more intentional or cognitivist understandings. These newer conceptions emphasize that intentional judgments as well as physiological disturbances are integral elements in emotion.[7] They define or identify emotions not by the quality or character of the physiological sensation that may be associated with them but rather by their intentional aspect, the associated judgment. Thus, it is the content of my associated thought or judgment that determines whether my physical agitation and restlessness are defined as "anxiety about my daughter's lateness" rather than as "anticipation of tonight's performance."

Cognitivist accounts of emotion have been criticized as overly rationalist and inapplicable to allegedly spontaneous, automatic, or global emotions, such as general feelings of nervousness, contentedness, angst, ecstasy, or terror. Certainly, these accounts entail that infants and animals experience emotions, if at all, in only a primitive, rudimentary form. Far from being unacceptable, however, this entailment is desirable because it suggests that humans develop and mature in emotions as well as in other dimensions, increasing the range, variety and subtlety of their emotional responses in accordance with their life experiences and their reflections on these.

Cognitivist accounts of emotion are not without their own problems. A serious difficulty with many is that they end up replicating within the structure of emotion the very problem they are trying to solve—namely, that of an artificial spilt between emotion and thought—because most cognitivist accounts explain emotion as having two "components": an affective or feeling component, and a cognition that supposedly interprets or identifies the feelings. Such accounts, therefore, unwittingly perpetuate the positivist distinction between the shared, public, objective world of verifiable calculations, observations, and facts, and the individual, private, subjective world of idiosyncratic feelings and sensations. This sharp distinction breaks any conceptual links between our feelings and the "external" world: if feelings still are conceived as blind or raw or undifferentiated, then we can give no sense to the notion of feelings fitting or failing to fit our perceptual judgments, that is, being appropriate or inappropriate. When intentionality is viewed as intellectual cognition and moved to the center of our picture of emotion, the affective elements are pushed to the periphery and become shadowy conceptual danglers whose relevance to emotion is obscure or even negligible. An adequate cognitive account of emotion must overcome this problem.

Most cognitivist accounts of emotion thus remain problematic insofar as they fail to explain the relation between the cognitive and the affective aspects of emotion. Moreover, insofar as they prioritize the intellectual aspect over feelings, they reinforce the traditional western preference for mind over body.[8] Nevertheless, they do identify a vital feature of emotion overlooked by the Dumb View—namely, its intentionality.

Emotions as Social Constructs

We tend to experience our emotions as involuntary individual responses to situations, responses that are often (though, significantly, not always) private in the sense that they are not perceived as directly and immediately by other people as they are by the subject of the experience. The apparently individual and involuntary character of our emotional experience often is taken as evidence that emotions are presocial, instinctive responses, determined by our biological constitution. This inference, however, is quite mistaken. Although it is probably true that the physiological disturbances characterizing emotions (facial grimaces, changes in the metabolic rate, sweating, trembling, tears, and so on) are continuous with the instinctive responses of our prehuman ancestors, and also that the ontogeny of emotions to some extent recapitulates their phylogeny, mature human emotions are neither instinctive nor biologically determined. Instead, they are socially constructed on several levels.

The most obvious way in which emotions are socially constructed is that children are taught deliberately what their culture defines as appropriate responses to certain situations: to fear strangers, to enjoy spicy food, or to like swimming in cold water. On a less conscious level, children also learn what their culture defines as the appropriate ways to express the emotions that it recognizes. Although there may be cross-cultural similarities in the expression of some apparently universal emotions, there are also wide divergences in what are recognized as expressions of grief, respect, contempt, or anger. On an even deeper level, cultures construct divergent understandings of what emotions are. For instance, English metaphors and metonymies are said to reveal a "folk" theory of anger as a hot fluid contained in a private space within an individual and liable to dangerous public explosion (Lakoff and Kovecses 1987). By contrast, the Ilongot, a people of the Philippines, apparently do not understand the self in terms of a public/private distinction and consequently do not experience anger as an explosive internal force: for them, rather, it is an interpersonal phenomenon for which an individual may, for instance, be paid (Rosaldo 1984).

Further aspects of the social construction of emotion are revealed through reflection on emotion's intentional structure. If emotions necessarily involve judgments, then obviously they require concepts, which may be seen as socially constructed ways of organizing and making sense of the world. For this reason, emotions simultaneously are made possible and limited by the conceptual and linguistic resources of a society. This philosophical claim is borne out by empirical observation of the cultural variability of emotion. Although there is considerable overlap in the emotions identified by many cultures (Wierzbicka 1986), at least some emotions are historically or culturally specific, including perhaps *ennui, angst,* the Japanese *amai* (in which one clings to another, affiliative love), and the response of "being a wild pig," which occurs among the Gururumba, a horticultural people living in the New Guinea Highlands (Averell 1980: 158). Even apparently universal emotions, such as anger or love, may vary cross-culturally. We have just seen that the Ilongot experience of anger apparently is quite different from the contemporary western experience. Romantic love was invented in the Middle Ages in Europe and since that time has been modified considerably; for instance, it is no longer confined to the nobility, and it no longer needs to be extramarital or unconsummated. In some cultures, romantic love does not exist at all.[9]

Thus there are complex linguistic and other social preconditions for the experience, that is, for the existence of human emotions. The emotions that we experience reflect prevailing forms of social life. For instance, one could not feel or even be betrayed in the absence of social norms about fidelity: it is inconceivable that betrayal or indeed any distinctively human emotion could be experienced by a solitary individual in some hypothetical presocial state of nature. There is a sense in which any individual's guilt or anger, joy or triumph, presupposes the existence of a social group capable of feeling guilt, anger, joy, or triumph. This is not to say that group emotions historically precede or are logically prior to the emotions of individuals; it is to say that individual experience is simultaneously social experience.[10] In later sections, I shall explore the epistemological and political implications of this social rather than individual understanding of emotion.

Emotions as Active Engagements

We often interpret our emotions as experiences that overwhelm us rather than as responses we consciously choose: that emotions are to some extent involuntary is part of the ordinary meaning of the term "emotion." Even in daily life, however, we recognize that emotions are not entirely involuntary and we try to gain control over them in various ways, ranging from mechanistic behavior modification techniques designed to sensitize or desensitize our feeling responses to various situations to cognitive techniques designed to help us think differently about situations. For instance, we might try to change our response to an upsetting situation by thinking about it in a way that will either divert our attention from its more painful aspects or present it as necessary for some larger good.

Some psychological theories interpret emotions as chosen on an even deeper level, interpreting them as actions for which the agent disclaims responsibility. For instance, the psychologist Averell likens the experience of emotion to playing a culturally recognized role: we ordinarily perform so smoothly and automatically that we do not realize we are giving a performance. He provides many examples demonstrating that even extreme and apparently totally involving displays of emotion in fact are functional for the individual and/or the society.[11] For example, when students were asked to record their experiences of anger or annoyance over a two-week period, they came to realize that their anger was not as uncontrollable and irrational as they had assumed previously, and they noted the usefulness and effectiveness of anger in achieving various social goods. Averell notes, however, that emotions often are useful in attaining their goals only if they are interpreted as passions rather than as actions. He cites the case of one subject led to reflect on her anger, who later wrote that it was less useful as a defense mechanism when she became conscious of its function.

The action/passion dichotomy is too simple for understanding emotion, as it is for other aspects of our lives. Perhaps it is more helpful to think of emotions as habitual responses that we may have more or less difficulty in breaking. We claim or disclaim responsibility for these responses depending on our purposes in a particular context. We could never experience our emotions entirely as deliberate actions, for then they would appear nongenuine and unauthentic, but neither should emotions be seen as nonintentional, primal, or physical forces with which our rational selves are forever at war. As they have been socially constructed, so may they be reconstructed, although describing how this might happen would require a long and complicated story.

Emotions, then, are wrongly seen as necessarily passive or involuntary responses to the world. Rather, they are ways in which we engage actively and even construct the world. They have both "mental" and "physical" aspects, each of which conditions the other; in some respects, they are chosen, but in others they are involuntary; they presuppose language and a social order. Thus, they can be attributed only to what are sometimes called "whole persons," engaged in the ongoing activity of social life.

Emotion, Evaluation and Observation

Emotions and values are closely related. The relation is so close, indeed, that some philosophical accounts of what it is to hold or express certain values reduce these phenomena to nothing more than holding or expressing certain emotional attitudes. When the relevant conception of emotion is the Dumb View, then simple emotivism certainly is too crude an account of what it is to hold a value; on this account, the intentionality of value judgments vanishes and value judgments become nothing more than sophisticated grunts and groans. Nevertheless, the grain of important truth in emotivism is its recognition that values presuppose emotions to the extent that emotions provide the experiential basis for values. If we had no emotional responses to the world, it is inconceivable that we should ever come to value one state of affairs more highly than another.

Just as values presuppose emotions, so emotions presuppose values. The object of an emotion—that is, the object of fear, grief, pride, and so on—is a complex state of affairs that is appraised or evaluated by the individual. For instance, my pride in a friend's achievement necessarily incorporates the value judgment that my friend has done something worthy of admiration.

Emotions and evaluations, then, are logically or conceptually connected. Indeed, many evaluative terms derive directly from words for emotions: "desirable," "admirable," "contemptible," "despicable," "respectable," and so on. Certainly it is true (*pace* J. S. Mill) that the evaluation of a situation as desirable or dangerous does not entail it is universally desired or feared but it does entail that desire (or fear) is viewed generally as an appropriate response to the situation. If someone is unafraid in a situation generally perceived as dangerous, her lack of fear requires further explanation; conversely, if someone is afraid without evident danger, then her fear is denounced as irrational or pathological. Thus, every emotion presupposes an evaluation of some aspect of the environment while, conversely, every evaluation or appraisal of the situation implies that those who share that evaluation will share, *ceteris paribus*, a predictable emotional response to the situation.

The rejection of the Dumb View and the recognition of intentional elements in emotion already incorporate a realization that observation influences and indeed partially constitutes emotion. We have seen already that distinctively human emotions are not simple instinctive responses to situations or events; instead, they depend essentially on the ways that we perceive those situations and events, as well on the ways that we have learned or decided to respond to them. Without characteristically human perceptions of and engagements in the world, there would be no characteristically human emotions.

Just as observation directs, shapes, and partially defines emotion, so too emotion directs, shapes, and even partially defines observation. Observation is not simply a passive process of absorbing impressions or recording stimuli; instead, it is an activity of selection and interpretation. What is selected and how it is interpreted are influenced by emotional attitudes. On the level of individual observation, this influence always has been apparent to common sense, which notes that we remark very different features of the world when we are happy, depressed, fearful, or confident. Social scientists are now exploring this influence of emotion on perception. One example is the so-called Honi phenomenon, named after the subject Honi who, under identical experimental conditions, perceived strangers' heads as changing in size but saw her husband's head as remaining the same.[12]

The most obvious significance of this sort of example is to illustrate how the individual experience of emotion focuses our attention selectively, directly, shaping and even partially defining our observations, just as our observations direct, shape, and partially define our emotions. In addition, the example argues for the social construction of what are taken in any situation to be undisputed facts. It shows how these facts rest on intersubjective agreements that consist partly in shared assumptions about "normal" or appropriate emotional responses to situations (McLaughlin 1985). Thus these examples suggest that certain emotional attitudes are involved on a deep level in all observation, in the intersubjectively verified and so supposedly dispassionate observations of science as well as in the common perceptions of daily life. In the next section, I shall elaborate this claim.

EPISTEMOLOGY

The Myth of Dispassionate Investigation

As we have seen already, western epistemology has tended to view emotion with suspicion and even hostility.[13] This derogatory western attitude toward emotion, like the earlier western contempt for sensory observation, fails to recognize that emotion, like sensory perception, is necessary to human survival. Emotions prompt us to act appropriately, to approach some people and situations and to avoid others, to caress or cuddle, fight or flee. Without emotion, human life would be unthinkable. Moreover, emotions have an intrinsic as well as an instrumental value. Although not all emotions are enjoyable or even justifiable, as we shall see, life without any emotion would be life without any meaning.

Within the context of western culture, however, people often have been encouraged to control or even suppress their emotions. Consequently, it is not unusual for people to be unaware of their emotional state or to deny it to themselves and others. This lack of awareness, especially combined with a neopositivist understanding of emotion that construes it just as a feeling of which one is aware, lends plausibility to the myth of dispassionate investigation. But lack of awareness of emotions certainly does not mean that emotions are not present subconsciously or unconsciously, or that subterranean emotions do not exert a continuing influence on people's articulated values and observations, thoughts and actions.[14]

Within the positivist tradition, the influence of emotion usually is seen only as distorting or impeding observation or knowledge. Certainly it is true that contempt, disgust, shame, revulsion, or fear may inhibit investigation of certain situations or phenomena. Furiously angry or extremely sad people often seem quite unaware of their surroundings or even their own conditions; they may fail to hear or may systematically misinterpret what other people say. People in love are notoriously oblivious to many aspects of the situation around them.

In spite of these examples, however, positivist epistemology recognizes that the role of emotion in the construction of knowledge is not invariably deleterious and that emotions may make a valuable contribution to knowledge. But the positivist tradition will allow emotions to play only the role of suggesting hypotheses for investigation. Emotions are allowed this because this so-called logic of discovery sets no limits on the idiosyncratic methods that investigators may use for generating hypotheses.

When hypotheses are to be tested, however, positivist epistemology imposes the much stricter logic of justification. The core of this logic is replicability, a criterion believed capable of eliminating or canceling out what are conceptualized as emotional as well as evaluative biases on the part of individual investigators. The conclusions of western science thus are presumed "objective," precisely in the sense that they are uncontaminated by the supposedly "subjective" values and emotions that might bias individual investigators (Nagel 1968: 33–34).

But if, as has been argued, the positivist distinction between discovery and justification is not viable, then such a distinction is incapable of filtering out values in science. For example, although such a split, when built into the western scientific method, generally is successful in neutralizing the idiosyncratic or unconventional values of individual investigators, it has been argued that it does not, indeed cannot, eliminate generally accepted social values. These values are implicit in the identification of the problems that are considered worthy of investigation, in the selection of the hypotheses that are considered worthy of testing, and in the solutions to the problems that are considered worthy of acceptance. The science of past centuries provides ample evidence of the influence of prevailing social values, whether seventeenth-century atomistic physics (Merchant 1980) or nineteenth-century competitive interpretations of natural selection (Young 1985).

Of course, only hindsight allows us to identify clearly the values that shaped the science of the past and thus to reveal the formative influence on science of pervasive emotional attitudes, attitudes that typically went unremarked at the time because they were shared so generally. For instance, it is now glaringly evident that contempt for (and perhaps fear of) people of color is implicit in nineteenth-century anthropology's interpretations and even constructions of anthropological facts. Because we are closer to them, however, it is harder for us to see how certain emotions, such as sexual possessiveness or the need to dominate others, currently are accepted as guiding principles in twentieth-century sociobiology or even defined as part of reason within political theory and economics (Quinby 1986).

Values and emotions enter into the science of the past and the present not only on the level of scientific practice but also on the metascientific level, as answers to various questions: What is science? How should it be practiced? And what is the status of scientific investigation versus nonscientific modes of enquiry? For instance, it is claimed with increasing frequency that the modern western conception of science, which identifies knowledge with power and views it as a weapon for dominating nature, reflects the imperialism, racism, and misogyny of the societies that created it. Several feminist theorists have argued that modern epistemology itself may be viewed as an expression of certain emotions alleged to be especially characteristic of males in certain periods, such as separation anxiety and paranoia (Flax 1983; Bordo 1987) or an obsession with control and fear of contamination (Scheman 1985; Schott 1988).

Positivism views values and emotions as alien invaders that must be repelled by a stricter application of the scientific method. If the forgoing claims are correct, however, the scientific method and even its positivist construals themselves incorporate values and emotions. Moreover, such an incorporation seems a necessary feature of all knowledge and conceptions of knowledge. Therefore, rather than repressing emotion in epistemology it is necessary to rethink the relation between knowledge and emotion and construct a conceptual model that demonstrates the mutually constitutive rather than oppositional relation between reason and emotion. Far from precluding the possibility of reliable knowledge, emotion as well as value must be shown as necessary to such knowledge. Despite its classical antecedents and like the ideal of disinterested enquiry, the ideal of dispassionate inquiry is an impossible dream, but a dream nonetheless, or perhaps a myth that has exerted enormous influence on western epistemology. Like all myths, it is a form of ideology that fulfills certain social and political functions.

The Ideological Function of the Myth

So far, I have spoken very generally of people and their emotions, as though everyone experienced similar emotions and dealt with them in similar ways. It is an axiom of feminist theory, however, that all generalizations about "people" are suspect. The divisions in our society are so deep, particularly the divisions of race, class, and gender, that many feminist theorists would claim that talk about people in general is ideologically dangerous because such talk obscures the fact that no one is simply a person but instead is constituted fundamentally by race, class, and gender. Race, class, and gender shape every aspect of our lives, and our emotional constitution is not excluded. Recognizing this helps us to see more clearly the political functions of the myth of the dispassionate investigator.

Feminist theorists have pointed out that the western tradition has not seen everyone as equally emotional. Instead, reason has been associated with members of dominant political, social, and cultural groups and emotion with members of subordinate groups. Prominent among those subordinate groups in our society are women of color, except for supposedly "inscrutable orientals," and women.[15]

Although the emotionality of women is a familiar cultural stereotype, its grounding is quite shaky. Women appear to be more emotional than men because they, along with some groups of people of color, are permitted and even required to express emotion more openly. In contemporary western culture, emotionally inexpressive women are suspect as not being real women,[16] whereas men who express their emotions freely are suspected of being homosexual or in some other way deviant from the masculine ideal. Modern western men, in contrast with Shakespeare's heroes, for instance, are required to present a facade of coolness, lack of excitement, even boredom, to express emotion only rarely and then for relatively trivial events, such as sporting occasions, where the emotions expressed are acknowledged to be dramatized and so are not taken entirely seriously. Thus, women in our society form the main group allowed or even expected to feel emotion. A woman may cry in the face of disaster, and a man of color may gesticulate, but a white man merely sets his jaw.[17]

White men's control of their emotional expression may go to the extremes of repressing their emotions, failing to develop emotionally, or even losing the capacity to experience many emotions. Not uncommonly, these men are unable to identify what they are feeling, and even they may be surprised, on occasion, by their own apparent lack of emotional response to a situation, such as a death, where emotional reaction is perceived appropriate. In some married couples, the wife implicitly is assigned the job of feeling emotion for both of them. White, college-educated men increasingly enter therapy in order to learn how to "get in touch with" their emotions, a project other men may ridicule as weakness. In therapeutic situations, men may learn that they are just as emotional as women but less adept at identifying their own or others' emotions. In consequence, their emotional development may be relatively rudimentary; this may lead to moral rigidity or insensitivity. Paradoxically, men's lacking awareness of their own emotional responses frequently results in their being more influenced by emotion rather than less.

Although there is no reason to suppose that the thoughts and actions of women are any more influenced by emotion than the thoughts and actions of men, the stereotypes of cool men and emotional women continue to flourish because they are confirmed by an uncritical daily experience. In these circumstances, where there is a differential assignment of reason and emotion, it is easy to see the ideological function of the myth of the dispassionate investigator. It functions, obviously, to bolster the epistemic authority of the currently dominant groups, composed largely of white men, and to discredit the observations and claims of the currently subordinate groups including, of course, the observations and claims of many people of color and women. The more forcefully and vehemently the latter groups express their observations and claims, the more emotional they appear, and so the more easily they are discredited. The alleged epistemic authority of the dominant groups then justifies their political authority.

The previous section of this paper argued that dispassionate inquiry was a myth. This section has shown that the myth promotes a conception of epistemological justification vindicating the silencing of those, especially women, who are defined culturally as the bearers of emotion and so are perceived as more "subjective," biased, and irrational. In our present social context, therefore, the ideal of the dispassionate investigator is a classist, racist, and especially masculinist myth.[18]

Emotional Hegemony and Emotional Subversion

As we have seen already, mature human emotions are neither instinctive nor biologically determined, although they may have developed out of presocial, instinctive responses. Like everything else that is human, emotions in part are socially constructed; like all social constructs, they are historical products, bearing the marks of the society that constructed them. Within the very language of emotion, in our basic definitions and explanations of what it is to feel pride or embarrassment, resentment or contempt, cultural norms and expectations are embedded. Simply describing ourselves as angry, for instance, presupposes that we view ourselves as having been wronged, victimized by the violation of some social norm. Thus, we absorb the standards and values of our society in the very process of learning the language of emotion, and those standards and values are built into the foundation of our emotional constitution.

Within a hierarchical society, the norms and values that predominate tend to serve the interest of the dominant groups. Within a capitalist, white-supremacist, and male-dominant society, the predominant values will tend to be those that serve the interests of rich white men. Consequently, we are all likely to develop an emotional constitution that is quite inappropriate for feminism. Whatever our color, we are likely to feel what Irving Thalberg has called "visceral racism"; whatever our sexual orientation, we are likely to be homophobic; whatever our class, we are likely to be at least somewhat ambitious and competitive; whatever our sex, we are likely to feel contempt for women. The emotional responses may be rooted in us so deeply that they are relatively impervious to intellectual argument and may recur even when we pay lip service to changed intellectual convictions.[19]

By forming our emotional constitution in particular ways, our society helps to ensure its own perpetuation. The dominant values are implicit in responses taken to be precultural or acultural, our so-called gut responses. Not only do these conservative responses hamper and disrupt our attempts to live in or prefigure alternative social forms but also, and insofar as we take them to be natural responses, they limit our vision theoretically. For instance, they limit our capacity for outrage; they either prevent us from despising or encourage us to despise; they lend a plausibility to the belief that greed and domination are inevitable human motivations; in sum, they blind us to the possibility of alternative ways of living.

This picture may seem at first to support the positivist claim that the intrusion of emotion only disrupts the process of seeking knowledge and distorts the results of that process. The picture, however, is not complete; it ignores the fact that people do not always experience the conventionally acceptable emotions. They may feel satisfaction rather than embarrassment when their leaders make fools of themselves. They may feel resentment rather than gratitude for welfare payments and hand-me-downs. They may be attracted to forbidden modes of sexual expression. They may feel revulsion for socially sanctioned ways of treating children or animals. In other words, the hegemony that our society exercises over people's emotional constitution is not total.

People who experience conventionally unacceptable, or what I call "outlaw," emotions often are subordinated individuals who pay a disproportionately high price for maintaining the status quo. The social situation of such people makes them unable to experience the conventionally prescribed emotions: for instance, people of color are more likely to experience anger than amusement when a racist joke is recounted, and women subjected to male sexual banter are less likely to be flattered than uncomfortable or even afraid.

When unconventional emotional responses are experienced by isolated individuals, those concerned may be confused, unable to name their experience; they may even doubt their own sanity. Women may come to believe that they are "emotionally disturbed" and that the embarrassment or fear aroused in them by male sexual innuendo is prudery or paranoia. When certain emotions are shared or validated by others, however, the basis exists for forming a subculture defined by perceptions, norms, and values that systematically oppose the prevailing perceptions, norms, and values. By constituting the basis for such a subculture, outlaw emotions may be politically (because epistemologically) subversive.

Outlaw emotions are distinguished by their incompatibility with the dominant perceptions and values, and some, though certainly not all, of these outlaw emotions are potentially or actually feminist emotions. Emotions become feminist when they incorporate feminist perceptions and values, just as emotions are sexist or racist when they incorporate sexist or racist perceptions and values. For example, anger becomes feminist anger when it involves the perception that the persistent importuning endured by one woman is a single instance of a widespread pattern of sexual harassment, and pride becomes feminist pride when it is evoked by realizing that a certain person's achievement was possible only because that individual overcame specifically gendered obstacles to success.[20]

Outlaw emotions stand in a dialectical relation to critical social theory: at least some are necessary to developing a critical perspective on the world, but they also presuppose at least the beginnings of such a perspective. Feminists need to be aware of how we can draw on some of our outlaw emotions in constructing feminist theory and also of how the in creasing sophistication of feminist theory can contribute to the reeducation, refinement, and eventual reconstruction of our emotional constitution.

Outlaw Emotions and Feminist Theory

The most obvious way in which feminist and other outlaw emotions can help in developing alternatives to prevailing conceptions of reality is by motivating new investigations. This is possible because, as we saw earlier, emotions may be long-term as well as momentary; it makes sense to say that someone continues to be shocked or saddened by a situation, even if she is at the moment laughing heartily. As we have seen already, theoretical investigation is always purposeful, and observation is always selective. Feminist emotions provide a political motivation for investigation and so help to determine the selection of problems as well as the method by which they are investigated. Susan Griffin makes the same point when she characterizes feminist theory as following "a direction determined by pain, and trauma, and compassion and outrage" (Griffin 1979: 31).

As well as motivating critical research, outlaw emotions may also enable us to perceive the world differently than we would from its portrayal in conventional descriptions. They may provide the first indications that something is wrong with the way alleged facts have been constructed, with accepted understandings of how things are. Conventionally unexpected or inappropriate emotions may precede our conscious recognition that accepted descriptions and justifications often conceal as much as reveal the prevailing state of affairs. Only when we reflect on our initially puzzling irritability, revulsion, anger, or fear may we bring to consciousness our "gut-level" awareness that we are in a situation of coercion, cruelty, injustice, or danger. Thus, conventionally inexplicable emotions, particularly—though not exclusively—those experienced by women, may lead us to make subversive observations that challenge dominant conceptions of the status quo. They may help us to realize that what are taken generally to be facts have been constructed in a way that obscures the reality of subordinated people, especially women's reality.

But why should we trust the emotional responses of women and other subordinated groups? How can we determine which outlaw emotions we should endorse or encourage and which reject? In what sense can we say that some emotional responses are more appropriate than others? What reason is there for supposing that certain alternative perceptions of the world, perceptions informed by outlaw emotions, are to be preferred to perceptions informed by conventional emotions? Here I can indicate only the general direction of an answer, whose full elaboration must await another occasion.[21]

I suggest that emotions are appropriate if they are characteristic of a society in which all humans (and perhaps some nonhuman life too) thrive, or if they are conducive to establishing such a society. For instance, it is appropriate to feel joy when we are developing or exercising our creative powers, and it is appropriate to feel anger and perhaps disgust in those situations where humans are denied their full creativity or freedom. Similarly, it is appropriate to feel fear if those capacities are threatened in us.

This suggestion obviously is extremely vague and may even verge on the tautological. How can we apply it in situations where there is disagreement over what is or is not disgusting or exhilarating or unjust? Here I appeal to a claim for which I have argued elsewhere: the perspective on reality that is available from the standpoint of the oppressed, which in part at least is the standpoint of women, is a perspective that offers a less partial and distorted and therefore more reliable view (Jaggar 1983: chap. 11). Oppressed people have a kind of epistemological privilege insofar as they have easier access to this standpoint and therefore a better chance of ascertaining the possible beginnings of a society in which all could thrive. For this reason, I would claim that the emotional responses of oppressed people in general, and often of women in particular, are more likely to be appropriate than the emotional responses of the dominant class. That is, they are more likely to incorporate reliable appraisals of situations.

Even in contemporary science, where the ideology of dispassionate inquiry is almost overwhelming, it is possible to discover a few examples that seem to support the claim that certain emotions are more appropriate than others in both a moral and epistemological sense. For instance, Hilary Rose claims that women's practice of caring, even though warped by its containment in the alienated context of a coercive sexual division of labor, nevertheless has generated more accurate and less oppressive understandings of women's bodily functions, such as menstruation (Rose 1983). Certain emotions may be both morally appropriate and epistemologically advantageous in approaching the nonhuman and even the inanimate world. Jane Goodall's scientific contribution to our understanding of chimpanzee behavior seems to have been made possible only by her amazing empathy with or even love for these animals (Goodall 1987). In her study of Barbara McClintock, Evelyn Fox Keller describes McClintock's relation to the objects of her research—grains of maize and their genetic properties—as a relation of affection, empathy and "the highest form of love: love that allows for intimacy without the annihilation of difference." She notes that McClintock's "vocabulary is consistently a vocabulary of affection, of kinship, of empathy" (Keller 1984: 164). Examples like these prompt Hilary Rose to assert that a feminist science of nature needs to draw on heart as well as hand and brain.

Some Implications of Recognizing the Epistemic Potential of Emotion

Accepting that appropriate emotions are indispensable to reliable knowledge does not mean, of course, that uncritical feeling may be substituted for supposedly dispassionate investigation. Nor does it mean that the emotional responses of women and other members of the underclass are to be trusted without question. Although our emotions are epistemologically indispensable, they are not epistemologically indisputable. Like all our faculties, they may be misleading, and their data, like all data, are always subject to reinterpretation and revision. Since emotions are not presocial, physiological responses to unequivocal situations, they are open to challenge on various grounds. They may be dishonest or self-deceptive, they may incorporate inaccurate or partial perceptions, or they may be constituted by oppressive values. Accepting the indispensability of appropriate emotions to knowledge means no more (and no less) than that discordant emotions should be attended to seriously and respectfully rather than condemned, ignored, discounted, or suppressed.

Just as appropriate emotions may contribute to the development of knowledge, so the growth of knowledge may contribute to the development of appropriate emotions. For instance, the powerful insights of feminist theory often stimulate new emotional responses to past and present situations. Inevitably, our emotions are affected by the knowledge that the women on our faculty are paid systematically less than the men, that one girl in four is subjected to sexual abuse from heterosexual men in her own family, and that few women reach orgasm in heterosexual intercourse. We are likely to feel different emotions toward older women or people of color as we reevaluate our standards of sexual attractiveness or acknowledge that Black is beautiful. The new emotions evoked by feminist insights are likely in turn to stimulate further feminist observations and insights, and these may generate new directions in both theory and political practice. There is a continuous feedback loop between our emotional constitution and our theorizing such that each continually modifies the other and is in principle inseparable from it.

The ease and speed with which we can reeducate our emotions unfortunately is not great. Emotions are only partially within our control as individuals. Although affected by new information, they are habitual responses not quickly unlearned. Even when we come to believe consciously that our fear or shame or revulsion is unwarranted, we may still continue to experience emotions inconsistent with our conscious politics. We may still continue to be anxious for male approval, competitive with our comrades and sisters, and possessive with our lovers. These unwelcome, because apparently inappropriate, emotions should not be suppressed or denied; instead, they should be acknowledged and subjected to critical scrutiny. The persistence of such recalcitrant emotions probably demonstrates how fundamentally we have been constituted by the dominant world view, but it may also indicate superficiality or other inadequacy in our emerging theory and politics.[22] We can only start from where we are—beings who have been created in a cruelly racist, capitalist, and male-dominated society that has shaped our bodies and our minds, our perceptions, our values and our emotions, our language and our systems of knowledge.

The alternative epistemological model that I suggest displays the continuous interaction between how we understand the world and who we are as people. It shows how our emotional responses to the world change as we conceptualize it differently and how our changing emotional response then stimulates us to new insights. The model demonstrates the need for theory to be self-reflexive, to focus not only on the outer world but also on ourselves and our relation to that world, to examine critically our social location, our actions, our values, our perceptions, and our emotions. The model also shows how feminist and other critical social theories are indispensable psychotherapeutic tools because they provide some insights necessary to a full understanding of our emotional constitution. Thus, the model explains how the reconstruction of knowledge is inseparable from the reconstruction of ourselves.

A corollary of the reflexivity of feminist and other critical theory is that it requires a much broader construal than positivism accepts of the process of theoretical investigation. In particular, it requires acknowledging that a necessary part of the theoretical process is critical self-examination. Time spent in analyzing emotions and uncovering their sources should be viewed, therefore, neither as irrelevant to theoretical investigation nor even as a prerequisite for it; it is not a kind of clearing of the emotional decks, "dealing with" our emotions so that they will not influence our thinking. Instead, we must recognize that our efforts to reinterpret and refine our emotions are necessary to our theoretical investigation, just as our efforts to reeducate our emotions are necessary to our political activity. Critical reflection on emotion is not a self-indulgent substitute for political analysis and political action. It is itself a kind of political theory and political practice, indispensable for an adequate social theory and social transformation.

Finally, the recognition that emotions play a vital part in developing knowledge enlarges our understanding of women's claimed epistemic advantage. We can now see that women's subversive insights owe much to women's outlaw emotions, themselves appropriate responses to the situations of women's subordination. In addition to their propensity to experience outlaw emotions, at least on some level, women are relatively adept at identifying such emotions, in themselves and others, in part because of their social responsibility for caretaking, including emotional nurturance. It is true that women (like all subordinated peoples, especially those who must live in close proximity with their masters) often engage in emotional deception and even self-deception as the price of their survival. Even so, women may be less likely than other subordinated groups to engage in denial or suppression of outlaw emotions. Women's work of emotional nurturance has required them to develop a special acuity in recognizing hidden emotions and in understanding the genesis of those emotions. This emotional acumen can now be recognized as a skill in political analysis and validated as giving women a special advantage both in understanding the mechanisms of domination and in envisioning freer ways to live.

CONCLUSION

The claim that emotion is vital to systematic knowledge is only the most obvious contrast between the conception of theoretical investigation that I have sketched here and the conception provided by positivism. For instance, the alternative approach emphasizes that what we identify as emotion is a conceptual abstraction from a complex process of human activity that also involves acting, sensing, and evaluating. This proposed account of theoretical construction demonstrates the simultaneous necessity for and interdependence of faculties that our culture has abstracted and separated from each other: emotion and reason, evaluation and perception, observation and action. The model of knowing suggested here is nonhierarchical and antifoundationalist; instead, it is appropriately symbolized by the radical feminist metaphor of the upward spiral. Emotions are neither more basic than observation, reason, or action in building theory, nor secondary to them. Each of these human faculties reflects an aspect of human knowing inseparable from the other aspects. Thus, to borrow a famous phrase from a Marxian context, the development of each of these faculties is a necessary condition for the development of all.

In conclusion, it is interesting to note that acknowledging the importance of emotion for knowledge is not an entirely novel suggestion within the western epistemological tradition. The arch-rationalist, Plato himself, came to accept in the end that knowledge required a (very purified) form of love. It may be no accident that in the *Symposium* Socrates learns this lesson from Diotima, the wise woman!

NOTES

This paper was written originally as a contribution to the Women's Studies Chair Seminar at Douglass College, Rutgers University. I wish to thank the following individuals who commented helpfully on earlier drafts of this paper or made me aware of further resources: Lynne Arnault, Susan Bordo, Martha Bolton, Cheshire Calhoun, Randy Cornelius, Shelagh Crooks, Ronald De Sousa, Tim Diamond, Dick Foley, Ann Garry, Judy Gerson, Mary Gibson, Sherry Gorelick, Marcia Lind, Helen Longino, Catherine Lutz, Andy McLaughlin, Uma Narayan, Linda Nicholson, Bob Richardson, Sally Ruddick, Laurie Shrage, Alan Soble, Vicky Spelman, Karsten Struhl, Joan Tronto, Daisy Quarm, Naomi Quinn and Alison Wylie. I am also grateful to my colleagues in the fall of 1985 Women's Studies Chair Seminar at Douglass College, Rutgers University, and to audiences at Duke University, Georgia University Centre, Hobart and William Smith Colleges, Northeastern University, the University of North Carolina at Chapel Hill and Princeton University, for their responses to earlier versions of this paper. In addition, I received many helpful comments from members of the Canadian Society for Women in Philosophy and from students in Lisa Heldke's classes in feminist epistemology at Carleton College and Northwestern University. Thanks, too, to Delia Cushway, who provided a comfortable environment in which I wrote the first draft.

1. Philosophers who do not conform to this generalization and constitute part of what Susan Bordo calls a "recessive" tradition in western philosophy include Hume and Nietzsche, Dewey and James (Bordo 1987: 114–18).
2. The western tradition as a whole has been profoundly rationalist, and much of its history may be viewed as a continuous redrawing of the boundaries of the rational. For a survey of this history from a feminist perspective, see Lloyd 1984.
3. Thus, fear and other emotions were seen as rational in some circumstances. To illustrate this point, E. V. Spelman quotes Aristotle as saying (in the *Nicomachean Ethics*, Bk. IV, ch. 5): "[Anyone] who does not get angry when there is reason to be angry, or who does not get angry in the right way at the right time and with the right people, is a dolt" (Spelman 1982: 1).
4. Descartes, Leibnitz, and Kant are among the prominent philosophers who did not endorse a wholly stripped-down, instrumentalist conception of reason.
5. The relocation of values in human attitudes and preferences in itself was not grounds for denying their universality, because they could have conceived as grounded in a common or universal human nature. In fact, however, the variability, rather than the commonality, of human preferences and responses was emphasized; values gradually came to be viewed as individual, particular, and even idiosyncratic rather than as universal and objective. The only exception to the variability of human desires was the supposedly universal urge to egoism and the motive to maximize one's own utility, whatever that consisted of. The value of autonomy and liberty, consequently, was seen as perhaps the only value capable of being justified objectively because it was a precondition for satisfying other desires.
6. For instance, Julius Moravcsik has characterized as emotions what I would call "plain" hunger and thirst, appetites that are not desired for any particular food or drink (Moravcsik 1982: 207–224). I myself think that such states, which Moravcsik also calls instincts or appetites, are understood better as sensations than emotions. In other words, I would view so-called instinctive, nonintentional feelings as the biological raw material from which full-fledged human emotions develop.

7. Even adherents of the Dumb View recognize, of course, that emotions are not entirely random or unrelated to an individual's judgments and beliefs; in other words, they note that people are angry or excited *about* something, afraid or proud *of* something. On the Dumb View, however, the judgments or beliefs associated with an emotion are seen as its causes and thus as related to it only externally.
8. Cheshire Calhoun pointed this out to me in private correspondence.
9. Recognition of the many levels on which emotions are socially constructed raises the question of whether it makes sense even to speak of the possibility of universal emotions. Although a full answer to this question is methodologically problematic, one might speculate that many of what we westerners identify as emotions have functional analogues in other cultures. In other words, it may be that people in every culture behave in ways that fulfill at least some social functions of our angry or fearful behavior.
10. The relationship between the emotional experience of an individual and the emotional experience of the group to which the individual belongs may perhaps be clarified by analogy to the relation between a word and the language of which it is a part. That a word has meaning presupposes that it is part of a linguistic system without which it has no meaning; yet the language itself has no meaning over and above the meaning of the words of which it is composed, together with their grammatical ordering. Words and language presuppose and mutually constitute each other. Similarly, both individual and group emotion presuppose and mutually constitute each other.
11. Averell cites dissociative reactions by military personnel at Wright Paterson Air Force Base and shows how these were effective in mustering help to deal with difficult situations while simultaneously relieving the individual of responsibility or blame (Averell 1980: 157).
12. These and similar experiments are described in Kilpatrick 1961: ch. 10, cited by McLaughlin 1985: 296.
13. The positivist attitude toward emotion, which requires that ideal investigators be both disinterested and dispassionate, may be a modern variant of older traditions in western philosophy that recommended that people seek to minimize their emotional responses to the world and develop instead their powers of rationality and pure contemplation.
14. It is now widely accepted that the suppression and repression of emotion has damaging if not explosive consequences. There is general acknowledgement that no one can avoid at some time experiencing emotions she or he finds unpleasant, and there is also increasing recognition that the denial of such emotions is likely to result in hysterical disorders of thought and behavior, in projecting one's own emotions onto others, in displacing them to inappropriate situations, or in psychosomatic ailments. Psychotherapy, which purports to help individuals recognize and "deal with" their emotions, has become an enormous industry, especially in the U.S. In much conventional psychotherapy, however, emotions still are conceived as feelings or passions, "subjective" disturbances that afflict individuals or interfere with their capacity for rational thought and action. Different therapies, therefore, have developed a wide variety of techniques for encouraging people to "discharge" or "vent" their emotions, just as they would drain an abscess. Once emotions have been discharged or vented, they are supposed to be experienced less intensely, or even to vanish entirely, and consequently to exert less influence on individuals' thoughts and actions. This approach to psychotherapy clearly demonstrates its kinship with the "folk" theory of anger mentioned earlier, and it equally clearly retains the traditional western assumption that emotion is inimical to rational thought and action. Thus, such approaches fail to challenge and indeed provide covert support for the view that "objective" knowers are not only disinterested but also dispassionate.

15. E. V. Spelman (1982) illustrates this point with a quotation from the well known contemporary philosopher, R. S. Peters, who wrote "we speak of emotional outbursts, reactions, upheavals and women" (*Proceedings of the Aristotelian Society*, New Series, vol. 62).
16. It seems likely that the conspicuous absence of emotion shown by Mrs. Thatcher is a deliberate strategy she finds necessary to counter the public perception of women as too emotional for political leadership. The strategy results in her being perceived as a formidable leader, but as an Iron Lady rather than a real woman. Ironically, Neil Kinnock, leader of the British Labor Party and Thatcher's main opponent in the 1987 General Election, was able to muster consider public support through television commercials portraying him in the stereotypically feminine role of caring about the unfortunate victims of Thatcher economics. Ultimately, however, this support was not sufficient to destroy public confidence in Mrs. Thatcher's "masculine" competence and to gain Kinnock the election.
17. On the rare occasions when a white man cries, he is embarrassed and feels constrained to apologize. The one exception to the rule that men should be emotionless is that they are allowed and often even expected to experience anger. Spelman (1982) points out that men's cultural permission to be angry bolsters their claim to authority.
18. Someone might argue that the viciousness of this myth was not a logical necessity. In the egalitarian society, where the concepts of reason and emotion were not gender-bound in the way they still are today, it might be argued that the ideal of the dispassionate investigator could be epistemologically beneficial. Is it possible that, in such socially and conceptually egalitarian circumstances, the myth of the dispassionate investigator could serve as an heuristic device, an ideal never to be realized in practice but nevertheless helping to minimize "subjectivity" and bias? My own view is that counterfactual myths rarely bring the benefits advertised, and that this one is no exception. This myth fosters an equally mythical conception of pure truth and objectivity, quite independent of human interests or desires, and in this way it functions to disguise the inseparability of theory and practice, science and politics. Thus, it is part of an antidemocratic world view that mystifies the political dimension of knowledge and unwarrantedly circumscribes the arena of political debate.
19. Of course, the similarities in our emotional constitutions should not blind us to systematic differences. For instance, girls rather than boys are taught fear and disgust for spiders and snakes, affection for fluffy animals, and shame for their naked bodies. It is primarily, though not exclusively, men rather than women whose sexual responses are shaped by exposure to visual and sometimes violent pornography. Girls and women are taught to cultivate sympathy for others; boys and men are taught to separate themselves emotionally from others. As I have noted already, more emotional expression is permitted for lower-class and some nonwhite men than for ruling-class men, perhaps because the expression of emotion is thought to expose vulnerability. Men of the upper classes learn to cultivate an attitude of condescension, boredom, or detached amusement. As we shall see shortly, differences in the emotional constitution of various groups may be epistemologically significant in so far as they both presuppose and facilitate different ways of perceiving the world.
20. A necessary condition for experiencing feminist emotions is that one already be a feminist in some sense, even if one does not consciously wear that label. But many women and some men, even those who would deny that they are feminist, still experience emotions compatible with feminist values. For instance, they may be angered by the perception that someone is being mistreated just because she is a woman, or they may take special pride in the achievement of a woman. If those who experience such emotions are unwilling to recognize them as feminist, their emotions are probably better described as potentially feminist or prefeminist emotions.

21. I owe this suggestion to Marcia Lind.
22. Within a feminist context, Berenice Fisher suggests that we focus particular attention on our emotions of guilt and shame as part of a critical reevaluation of our political ideas and our political practice (Fisher 1984).

REFERENCES

Averell, James R. 1980. "The Emotions." In *Personality: Basic Aspects and Current Research*, ed. Ervin Staub. Englewood Cliffs, N.J.: Prentice-Hall.

Bordo, Susan R. 1987. *The Flight to Objectivity: Essays on Cartesianism and Culture.* Albany, N.Y.: SUNY Press.

Fisher, Berenice. 1984. "Guilt and Shame in the Women's Movement: The Radical Ideal of Action and its Meaning for Feminist Intellectuals." *Feminist Studies* 10: 185–212.

Flax, Jane. 1983. "Political Philosophy and the Patriarchal Unconscious: A Psychoanalytic Perspective on Epistemology and Metaphysics." In *Discovering Reality: Feminist Perspectives on Epistemology, Metaphysics, Methodology and Philosophy of Science*, ed. Sandra Harding and Merrill Hintikka. Dordrecht, Holland: D. Reidel Publishing.

Goodall, Jane. 1986. *The Chimpanzees of Bombe: Patterns of Behavior.* Cambridge, Mass.: Harvard University Press.

Griffin, Susan. 1979. *Rape: The Power of Consciousness.* San Francisco: Harper & Row.

Hinman, Lawrence. 1986. "Emotion, Morality and Understanding." Paper presented at Annual Meeting for the Central Division of the American Philosophical Association, St. Louis, Missouri, May 1986.

Jaggar, Alison M. 1983. *Feminist Politics and Human Nature.* Totowa, N.J.: Rowman and Allanheld; Brighton, UK: Harvester Press.

Keller, Evelyn Fox. 1984. *Gender and Science.* New Haven, Conn.: Yale University Press.

Kilpatrick, Franklin P., ed. 1961. *Explorations in Transactional Psychology.* New York: New York University Press.

Lakoff, George, and Zoltan Kovecses. 1987. "The Cognitive Model of Anger Inherent in American English." In *Cultural Models in Language and Thought*, ed. N. Quinn and D. Holland. New York: Cambridge University Press.

Lewontin, R. C. 1982. "Letter to the Editor." *New York Review of Books*, 4 (February): 40–41. This letter was drawn to my attention by Alan Soble.

Lloyd, Genevieve. 1984. *The Man of Reason: "Male" and "Female" in Western Philosophy.* Minneapolis: University of Minnesota Press.

Lutz, Catherine. 1985. "Depression and the Translation of Emotional Worlds." In *Culture and Depression: Studies in the Anthropology and Cross-cultural Psychiatry of Affect and Disorder*, ed. A. Kleinman and B. Good. Berkeley, Calif: University of California Press, 63–100.

______. 1986. "Emotion, Thought, and Estrangement: Emotion as a Cultural Category." *Cultural Anthropology* 1: 287–309.

______. 1987. "Goals, Events and Understanding in Ifaluck and Emotion Theory." In *Cultural Models in Language and Thought*, ed. N. Quinn and D. Holland. New York: Cambridge University Press.

McLaughlin, Andrew. 1985. "Images and Ethics of Nature." *Environmental Ethics* 7: 293–319.

Merchant, Carolyn M. 1980. *The Death of Nature: Women, Ecology and the Scientific Revolution.* New York: Harper & Row.

Moravcsik, J.M.E. 1982. "Understanding and the Emotions." *Dialectica* 36, 2–3: 207–24.

Nagel, Earnest. 1968. "The Subjective Nature of Social Subject Matter." In *Readings in the Philosophy of the Social Sciences*, ed. May Brodbeck. New York: Macmillan.

Quinby, Lee. 1986. Discussion following talk at Hobart and William Smith Colleges, April 1986.

Rorty, Richard.1979. *Philosophy and the Mirror of Nature.* Princeton: Princeton University Press.

Rosaldo, Michelle Z. 1984. "Toward an Anthropology of Self and Feeling." In *Culture Theory*, ed. Richard A. Shweder and Robert A. LeVine. New York: Cambridge University Press.

Rose, Hilary. 1983. "Hand, Brain, and Heart: A Feminist Epistemology for the Natural Sciences." *Signs: Journal of Women in Culture and Society* 9, 1: 73–90.

Schachter, Stanley and Jerome B. Singer. 1969. "Cognitive, Social and Psychological Determinants of Emotional State." *Psychological Review* 69: 379–99.

Scheman, Naomi. "Women in the Philosophy Curriculum." Paper presented at the Annual Meeting of the Central Division of the American Philosophical Association, Chicago, April, 1985.

Schott, Robin M. 1988. *Cognition and Eros: A Critique of the Kantian Paradigm.* Boston, Mass: Beacon Press.

Spelman, Elizabeth V. 1982. "Anger and Insubordination." Manuscript; early version read to Mid-Western chapter of the Society for Women in Philosophy, Spring 1982. (Later version appears in Garry and Pearsall, ed., *Women, Knowledge, and Reality* (Boston: Unwin and Hyman, 1989).

Wierzbicka, Anna. 1986. "Human Emotions: Universal or Culture-Specific?" *American Anthropologist* 88: 584–94.

Young, Robert M. 1985. *Darwin's Metaphor: Nature's Place in Victorian Culture.* Cambridge: Cambridge University Press.

Some Reflections on Separatism and Power

Frye maintains that feminism invariably includes a separatist dimension—for example, in the legally sanctioned form of divorce, in the form of alternative institutions like battered women's shelters, or in the radical form of independent lesbian communities. Yet, feminists and nonfeminists alike commonly find the idea of separatism threatening. Frye speculates about why this is so and defends the need for feminist separatism.

According to Frye, contrary to the popular belief that women are dependent on men, it is actually the case that men are profoundly dependent on women. Thus, separatist initiatives jeopardize men's interests in emotional sustenance and various material services. To secure these interests, men must have access to women, and, since separatism denies them access, they resist separatism. Women, too, are uneasy about separatism. They fear being punished for such blatant insubordination, and, since women are socialized to regard confrontation as unfeminine, separatism conflicts with their sense of their gender identity. Still, Frye urges that feminists cannot shrink from the separatist imperative. To have asymmetrical access to another person is to have power over that person. To equalize the balance of power between women and men, therefore, women must deny men access to them. Furthermore, it is only by denying men access that women can escape from patriarchal definitions of womanhood and create social contexts in which women can begin to define themselves. Finally, when women exclude men, this practice itself changes the meaning of "man" along with the meaning of "woman."

—D.T.M.

Chapter 22

Marilyn Frye

Some Reflections on Separatism and Power

I have been trying to write something about separatism almost since my first dawning of feminist consciousness, but it has always been for me somehow a mercurial topic that, when I tried to grasp it, would softly shatter into many other topics like sexuality, man-hating, so-called reverse discrimination, apocalyptic utopianism, and so on. What I have to share with you today is my latest attempt to get to the heart of the matter.

In my life, and within feminism as I understand it, separatism is not a theory or a doctrine, nor a demand for certain specific behaviors on the part of feminists, though it is undeniably connected with lesbianism. Feminism seems to me to be kaleidoscopic—something whose shapes, structures, and patterns alter with every turn of feminist creativity; and one element that is present through all the changes is an element of separation. This element has different roles and relations in different turns of the glass—it assumes different meanings, is variously conspicuous, variously determined or determining, depending on how the pieces fall and who is the beholder. The theme of separation, in its multitude variations, is there in everything from divorce to exclusive lesbian separatist communities, from shelters for battered women to witch covens, from women's studies programs to women's bars, from expansion of day care to abortion on demand. The presence of this theme is vigorously obscured, trivialized, mystified, and outright denied by many feminist apologists, who seem to find it embarrassing, while it is embraced, explored, expanded, and ramified by most of the more inspiring theorists and activists. The theme of separation is noticeably absent or heavily qualified in most of the things I take to be personal solutions and band-aid projects, like legalization of prostitution, liberal marriage contracts, improvement of the treatment of rape victims, and affirmative action. It is clear to me, in my own case at least, that the contrariety of assimilation and separation is one of the main things that guides or determines assessments of various theories, actions, and practices as reformist or radical, as going to the root of the thing or being relatively superficial. So my topical question comes to this: What is it about separation, in any or all of its many forms and degrees, that makes it so basic and so sinister, so exciting and so repellent?

Feminist separation is, of course, separation of various sorts or modes from men and from institutions, relationships, roles and activities that are male-defined, male-dominated, and operating for the benefit of males and the maintenance of male privilege—this separation being initiated or maintained, at will, *by women.* (Masculist separatism is the partial segregation of women from men and male domains *at the will of men.* This difference is crucial.) The feminist separation can take many forms. Breaking up or avoiding close relationships or working relationships; forbidding someone to enter your house; excluding someone from your company or from your meeting; withdrawal from participation in some activity or institution, or avoidance of participation; avoidance of communications and influence from certain quarters (not listening to music with sexist lyrics, not watching TV); withholding commitment or support; rejection or rudeness toward obnoxious individuals.[1] Some separations are subtle realignments of identification, priorities, and commitments, or working with agendas which only incidentally coincide with the agendas of the institution one works in. Ceasing to be loyal to something or someone is a separation; and ceasing to love. The feminist's separations are rarely if ever sought or maintained directly as ultimate personal or political ends. The closest we come to that, I think, is the separation that is the instinctive and self-preserving recoil from the systematic misogyny that surrounds us.[2] Generally, the separations are brought about and maintained for the sake of something else like independence, liberty, growth, invention, sisterhood, safety, health, or the practice of novel or heretical customs.[3] Often the separations in question evolve, unpremeditated, as one goes one's way and finds various persons, institutions, or relationships useless, obstructive, or noisome and leaves them aside or behind. Sometimes the separations are consciously planned and cultivated as necessary prerequisites or conditions for getting on with one's business. Sometimes the separations are accomplished or maintained easily, or with a sense of relief or even joy; sometimes they are accomplished or maintained with difficulty, by dint of constant vigilance, or with anxiety, pain, or grief.

Most feminists, probably all, practice some separation from males and male-dominated institutions. A separatist practices separation consciously, systematically, and probably more generally then the others, and advocates thorough and "broad-spectrum" separation as part of the conscious strategy of liberation. And, contrary to the image of the separatist as a cowardly escapist, hers is the life and program that inspires the greatest hostility, disparagement, insult, and confrontation, and generally she is the one against whom economic sanctions operate most conclusively. The penalty for refusing to work with or for men is usually starvation (or, at the very least, doing without medical insurance); and if one's policy of noncooperation is more subtle, one's livelihood is still constantly on the line, since one is not a loyal partisan, a proper member of the team, or what have you. The penalties for being a lesbian are ostracism, harassment, and job insecurity or joblessness. The penalty for rejecting men's sexual advances is often rape and, perhaps even more often, forfeit of such things as professional or job opportunities. And the separatist lives with the added burden of being assumed by many to be a morally depraved man-hating bigot. But there is a clue here: if you are doing something that is so strictly forbidden by the patriarchs, you must be doing something right.

There is an idea floating around in both feminist and antifeminist literature to the effect that females and males generally live in a relation of parasitism,[4] a parasitism of the male on the female . . . that is, generally speaking, the strength, energy, inspiration, and nurturance of women that keeps men going, and not the strength, aggression, spirituality, and hunting of men that keeps women going.

It is sometimes said that the parasitism goes the other way around, that the female is the parasite. But one can conjure the appearance of the female as parasite only if one takes a very narrow view of human living—historically parochial, narrow with respect to class and race, and limited in conception of what are the necessary goods. Generally, the female's contribution to her material support is and always has been substantial; in many times and places it has been independently sufficient. One can and should distinguish between a partial and contingent material dependence created by a certain sort of money economy and class structure, and the nearly ubiquitous spiritual, emotional and material dependence of males on females. Males presently provide, off and on, a portion of the material support of women, within circumstances apparently designed to make it difficult for women to provide them for themselves. But females provide and generally have provided for males the energy and spirit for living; the males are nurtured by the females. And this the males apparently cannot do for themselves, even partially.

The parasitism of males on females is, as I see it, demonstrated by the panic, rage, and hysteria generated in so many of them by the thought of being abandoned by women. But it is demonstrated in a way that is perhaps more generally persuasive by both literary and sociological evidence. Evidence cited in Jesse Bernard's work in *The Future of Marriage* and in George Gilder's *Sexual Suicide* and *Men Alone* convincingly shows that males tend in shockingly significant numbers and in alarming degree to fall into mental illness, petty crime, alcoholism, physical infirmity, chronic unemployment, drug addiction, and neurosis when deprived of the care and companionship of a female mate, or keeper. (While on the other hand, women without male mates are significantly healthier and happier than women with male mates.) And masculinist literature is abundant with indications of male cannibalism, of males deriving essential sustenance from females. Cannibalistic imagery, visual and verbal, is common in pornography: images likening women to food, and sex to eating. And, as documented in Millett's *Sexual Politics* and many other feminist analyses of masculinist literature, the theme of men getting high off beating, raping or killing women (or merely bullying them) is common. These interactions with women, or rather, these actions upon women, make men feel good, walk tall, feel refreshed, in*vigor*ated. Men are drained and depleted by their living by themselves and with and among other men, and are revived and refreshed, re-created, by going home and being served dinner, changing to clean clothes, having sex with the wife; or by dropping by the apartment of a woman friend to be served coffee or a drink and stroked in one way or another; or by picking up a prostitute for a quicky or for a dip in favorite sexual escape fantasies; or by raping refugees from their wars (foreign and domestic). The ministrations of women, be they willing or unwilling, free or paid for, are what restore in men the strength, will, and confidence to go on with what they call living.

If it is true that a fundamental aspect of the relations between the sexes is male parasitism, it might help to explain why certain issues are particularly exciting to patriarchal loyalists. For instance, in view of the obvious advantages of easy abortion to population control, to control of welfare rolls, and to ensuring sexual availability of women to men, it is a little surprising that the loyalists are so adamant and riled up in their objection to it. But look . . .

The fetus lives parasitically. It is a distinct animal surviving off the life (the blood) of another animal creature. It is incapable of surviving on its own resources, of independent nutrition; incapable even of symbiosis. If it is true that males live parasitically upon females, it seems reasonable to suppose that many of them and those loyal to them are in some way sensitive to the parallelism between their situation and that of the fetus. They could easily identify with the fetus. The woman who is free to see the fetus as a parasite[5] might be free to see the man as a parasite. The woman's willingness to cut off the lifeline to one parasite suggests a willingness to cut off the lifeline to another parasite. The woman who is capable (legally, psychologically, physically) of decisively, self-interestedly, independently rejecting the one parasite is capable of rejecting, with the same decisiveness and independence, the like burden of the other parasite. In the eyes of the other parasite, the image of the wholly self-determined abortion, involving not even a ritual submission to male veto power, is the mirror image of death.

Another clue here is that one line of argument against free and easy abortion is the slippery slope argument that if fetuses are to be freely dispensed with, old people will be next. Old people? Why are old people next? And why the great concern for them? Most old people are women, indeed, and patriarchal loyalists are not generally so solicitous of the welfare of any women. Why old people? Because, I think, in the modern patriarchal divisions of labor, old people too are parasites on women. The antiabortionist folks seem not to worry about wife beating and wife murder—there is no broad or emotional popular support for stopping these violences. They do not worry about murder and involuntary sterilization in prisons, nor murder in war, nor murder by pollution and industrial accidents. Either these are not real to them or they cannot identify with the victims; but anyway, killing in general is not what they oppose. They worry about the rejection *by women, at women's discretion,* of something that lives parasitically on women. I suspect that they fret not because old people are next, but because men are next.

There are other reasons, of course, why patriarchal loyalists should be disturbed about abortion on demand; a major one being that it would be a significant form of female control of reproduction, and at least from certain angles it looks like the progress of patriarchy *is* the progress toward male control of reproduction, starting with possession of wives and continuing through the invention of obstetrics and the technology of extrauterine gestation. Giving up that control would be giving up patriarchy. But such an objection to abortion is too abstract, and requires too historical a vision, to generate the hysteria there is now in the reaction against abortion. The hysteria is, I think, to be accounted for more in terms of a much more immediate and personal presentiment of ejection by the woman-womb.

I discuss abortion here because it seems to me to be the most publicly emotional and most physically dramatic ground on which the theme of separation and male parasitism is presently being played out. But there are other locales for this play. For instance, women with newly raised consciousness tend to leave marriages and families, either completely, through divorce, or partially, through unavailability of their cooking, housekeeping, and sexual services. And women academics tend to become alienated from their colleagues and male mentors and no longer serve as sounding board, ego booster, editor, mistress, or proofreader. Many awakening women become celibate or lesbian, and the others become a very great deal more choosy about when, where and in what relationships they will have sex with men.

And the men affected by these separations generally react with defensive hostility, anxiety, and guilt-tripping, not to mention descents into illogical argument that match and exceed their own most fanciful images of female irrationality. My claim is that they are very afraid because they depend very heavily upon the goods they receive from women, and these separations cut them off from those goods.

Male parasitism means that males *must have access* to women; it is the Patriarchal Imperative. But feminist no-saying is more than a substantial removal (redirection, reallocation) of goods and services, because Access is one of the faces of Power. Female denial of male access to females substantially cuts off a flow of benefits, but it has also the form and full portent of assumption of power.

Differences of power are always manifested in asymmetrical access. The president of the United States has access to almost everybody for almost anything he might want of them, and almost nobody has access to him. The super-rich have access to almost everybody; almost nobody has access to them. The resources of the employee are available to the boss as the resources of the boss are not to the employee. The parent has unconditional access to the child's room; the child does not have similar access to the parent's room. Students adjust to professors' office hours; professors do not adjust to students' conference hours. The child is required not to lie; the parent is free to close out the child with lies at her discretion. The slave is unconditionally accessible to the master. Total power is unconditional access; total powerlessness is being unconditionally accessible. The creation and manipulation of power is constituted of the manipulation and control of access.

All-woman groups, meetings, projects seem to be great things for causing controversy and confrontation. Many women are offended by them; many are afraid to be the one to announce the exclusion of men; it is seen as a device whose use needs much elaborate justification. I think this is because conscious and deliberate exclusion of men by women, from anything, is blatant insubordination and generates in women fear of punishment and reprisal (fear which is often well-justified). Our own timidity and desire to avoid confrontations generally keep us from doing very much in the way of all-woman groups and meetings. But when we do, we invariably run into the male champion who challenges our right to do it. Only a small minority of men go crazy when an event is advertised to be for women only—just one man tried to crash our women-only Rape Speak-Out, and only a few hid under the auditorium seats to try to spy on a women-only meeting at a NOW convention in Philadelphia. But these few are onto something their less rabid compatriots are missing. The woman-only meeting is a fundamental challenge to the structure of power. It is always the privilege of the master to enter the slave's hut. The slave who decides to exclude the master from her hut is declaring herself not a slave. The exclusion of men from the meeting not only deprives them of certain benefits (which they might survive without); it is also a controlling of access, hence an assumption of power. It is not only mean, it is arrogant.

It becomes clearer now why there is always an off-putting aura of negativity about separatism—one that offends the feminine pollyanna in us and smacks of the purely defensive to the political theorist in us. It is this: First: When those who control access have made you totally accessible, your first act of taking control must be denying access, or must have denial of access as one of its aspects. This is not because you are charged up with (unfeminine or politically incorrect) negativity; it is because of the logic of the situation. When we start from a position of total accessibility, there *must* be an aspect of no-saying (which is the beginning of control) in *every effective* act and strategy, the effective ones being precisely those that *shift power*, i.e., ones that involve manipulation and control of access. Second: Whether or not one says "no," or withholds or closes out or rejects, on this occasion or that, the capacity and ability to say "no" (with effect) is logically necessary to control. When we are in control of access to ourselves there will be some no-saying, and when we are more accustomed to it, when it is more common, an ordinary part of living, it will not seem so prominent, obvious, or strained . . . we will not strike ourselves or others as being particularly negative. In this aspect of ourselves and our lives, we will strike ourselves pleasingly as active beings with momentum of our own, with sufficient shape and structure—with sufficient integrity—to generate friction. Our experience of our no-saying will be an aspect of our experience of our definition.

When our feminist acts or practices have an aspect of separation, we are assuming power by controlling access and simultaneously by undertaking definition. The slave who excludes the master from her hut thereby declares herself *not a slave.* And *definition* is another face of power.

The powerful normally determine what is said and sayable. When the powerful label something or dub it or baptize it, the thing becomes what they call it. When the Secretary of Defense calls something a peace negotiation, for instance, then whatever it is that he called a peace negotiation is an instance of negotiating peace. If the activity in question is the working out of terms of a trade-off of nuclear reactors and territorial redistributions, complete with arrangements for the resulting refugees, that is peacemaking. People laud it, and the negotiators get Nobel Piece Prizes for it. On the other hand, when I call a certain speech act a rape, my "calling" it does not make it so. At best, I have to explain and justify and make clear exactly what it is about this speech act which is assaultive in just what way, and then the others acquiesce in saying the act was *like* rape or could figuratively be called a rape. My counterassault will not be counted a simple case of self-defense. And what I call rejection of parasitism, they call the loss of the womanly virtues of compassion and "caring." And generally, when renegade women call something one thing and patriarchal loyalists call it another, the loyalists get their way.*

---

* This paragraph and the succeeding one comprise the passage which has provoked the most substantial questions from women who read this paper. One thing that causes trouble here is that I am talking from a stance or position that is ambiguous—it is located in two different and noncommunicating systems of thought-action. *Re* the patriarchy and the English language, there is general usage over which I/we do not have the control that elite males have (with the cooperation of all the ordinary patriarchal loyalists). *Re* the new being and meaning which are being created now by lesbian-feminists, we *do* have semantic authority, and, collectively, can and do define with effect. I think it is only by maintaining our boundaries through controlling concrete access to us that we can enforce on those who are not-us our definitions for ourselves, hence force on them *the fact of our existence* and thence open up the *possibility* of our having semantic authority with them. (I wrote some stuff that's relevant to this in the last section of my paper "Male Chauvinism—a Conceptual Analysis.")[6] Our unintelligibility to patriarchal loyalists is a source of pride and delight, in some contexts; but if we don't have an effect on their usage while we continue, willy nilly, to be subject to theirs, being totally unintelligible to them could be fatal. (A friend of mine had a dream where the women were meeting in a cabin at the edge of town, and they had a sort of inspiration through the vision of one of them that they should put a sign on the door which would connect with the patriarchs' meaning-system, for otherwise the men would be too curious/frightened about them and would break the door down to get in. They put a picture of a fish on the door.) Of course, you might say that *being* intelligible to them might be fatal. Well, perhaps it's best to be in a position to make tactical decisions about when and how to be intelligible and unintelligible.

Women generally are not the people who do the defining, and we cannot from our isolation and powerlessness simply commence saying different things than others say and make it stick. There is a humpty-dumpty problem in that. But we are able to arrogate definition to ourselves when we repattern access. Assuming control of access, we draw new boundaries and create new roles and relationships. This, though it causes some strain, puzzlement, and hostility, is to a fair extent within the scope of individuals and small gangs, as outright verbal redefinition is not, at least in the first instance.

One may see access as coming in two sorts, "natural" and humanly arranged. A grizzly bear has what you might call natural access to the picnic basket of the unarmed human. The access of the boss to the personal services of the secretary is humanly arranged access; the boss exercises institutional power. It looks to me, looking from a certain angle, like institutions are humanly designed patterns of access—access to persons and their services. But institutions are artifacts of definition. In the case of intentionally and formally designed institutions, this is very clear, for the relevant definitions are explicitly set forth in by-laws and constitutions, regulations and rules. When one defines the term "president," one defines presidents in terms of what they can do and what is owed them by other offices, and "what they can do" is a matter of their access to the services of others. Similarly, definitions of *dean, student, judge,* and *cop* set forth patterns of access, and definitions of *writer, child, owner,* and, of course, *husband, wife,* and *man* and *girl.* When one changes the pattern of access, one forces new uses of words on those affected. The term "man" has to shift in meaning when rape is no longer possible. When we take control of sexual access to us, of access to our nurturance and to our reproductive function, access to mothering and sistering, we redefine the word "woman." The shift of usage is pressed on others by a change in social reality; it does not await their recognition of our definitional authority.

When women separate (withdraw, break out, regroup, transcend, shove aside, step outside, migrate, say *no*), we are simultaneously controlling access and defining. We are doubly insubordinate, since neither of these is permitted. And access and definition are fundamental ingredients in the alchemy of power, so we are doubly, and radically, insubordinate.

If these, then, are some of the ways in which separation is at the heart of our struggle, it helps to explain why separation is such a hot topic. If there is one thing women are queasy about it is *actually taking power.* As long as one stops just short of that, the patriarchs will for the most part take an indulgent attitude. We are afraid of what will happen to us when we really frighten them. This is not an irrational fear. It is our experience in the movement generally that the defensiveness, nastiness, violence, hostility, and irrationality of the reaction to feminism tends to correlate with the blatancy of the element of separation in the strategy or project that triggers the reaction. The separations involved in women leaving homes, marriages and boyfriends, separations from fetuses, and the separation of lesbianism are all pretty dramatic. That is, they are dramatic and blatant when perceived from within the framework provided by the patriarchal world view and male parasitism. Matters pertaining to marriage and divorce, lesbianism, and abortion touch individual men (and their sympathizers) because they can feel the relevance of these to themselves—they can feel the threat that they might be the next. Hence, heterosexuality, marriage, and motherhood, which are the institutions which most obviously and individually maintain female accessibility to males, form the core triad of antifeminist ideology; and all-woman spaces, all-woman organizations, all-woman meetings, all-woman classes, are outlaws, suppressed, harassed, ridiculed, and punished—in the name of that other fine and enduring patriarchal institution, Sex Equality.

To some of us these issues can seem almost foreign . . . strange ones to be occupying center stage. We are busily engaged in what seem to *us* our blatant insubordinations: living our own lives, taking care of ourselves and one another, doing our work, and, in particular, telling it as we see it. Still, the original sin is the separation that these presuppose, and it is that, not our art or philosophy, not our speechmaking nor our "sexual acts" (or abstinences), for which we will be persecuted, when worse comes to worst.

NOTES

Some notes from *The Politics of Reality* are deleted.

1. Adrienne Rich: "Makes me question the whole idea of 'courtesy' or 'rudeness'—surely *their* constructs, since women become 'rude' when we ignore or reject male obnoxiousness, while male 'rudeness' is usually punctuated with the 'Haven't you a sense of humor' tactic." Yes; me too. I embrace rudeness; our compulsive/compulsory politeness so often is what coerces us into their "fellowship."
2. Ti-Grace Atkinson: "Should give more attention here to our vulnerability to assault and degradation, and to separation as *protection.*" Okay, but then we have to re-emphasize that it has to be separation at *our* behest—we've had enough of their imposed separation for our "protection." (There's no denying that in my real-life life, protection and maintenance of places for healing are major motives for separation.)
3. See "Separatism and Sexual Relationships," in *A Philosophical Approach to Women's Liberation*, ed. S. Hill and M. Weinzweig (Belmont, Calif.: Wadsworth, 1978).
4. I first noticed this when reading *Beyond God the Father*, by Mary Daly (Boston: Beacon Press, 1973). See also *Women's Evolution*, by Evelyn Reed (New York: Pathfinder Press, 1975) for rich hints about male cannibalism and male dependence.
5. Caroline Whitbeck: "Cross-cultural evidence suggests it's not the fetus that gets rejected in cultures where abortion is common, it is the role of motherhood, the burden, in particular, of 'illegitimacy'; where the institution of illegitimacy does not exist, abortion rates are pretty low." This suggests to me that the woman's rejection of the fetus is even more directly a rejection of the male and his world than I had thought.
6. In (improbably enough) *Philosophy and Sex*, edited by Robert Baker and Frederick Elliston (Buffalo: N.Y.: Prometheus Books, 1976).

Glancing at Pornography: Recognizing Men

The male gaze sexually objectifies women, and pornography eroticizes male domination. Yet, feminists are sharply divided over the question of pornography. Is it a violation of women's civil rights that should be suppressed? Or is it a permissible, possibly liberating form of expression? Mann situates this debate in the context of the issue of women's agency, and she argues that the prevalence of pornography does not foreclose feminist critique and action.

For Mann, understanding the relation between pornography and women's subordination requires understanding the asymmetries between male and female sexual agency, the social significance that men and women ascribe to these asymmetries, and the resulting asymmetries of recognition between women and men. Since women fear rape and pregnancy resulting from rape, they are vulnerable to inegalitarian family structures in which they provide services and accept subservience to men in exchange for protection from extrafamilial violence. Yet, women have recently gained control over their reproductive capacities through contraception and also a measure of economic power, and these changes threaten male dominance. According to Mann, men's enjoyment of pornographic representations of female availability and male sexual potency is a form of patriarchal resistance to these emancipatory developments. Moreover, Freud's theory of castration anxiety explains the psychological appeal of pornography—these depictions allow men to experience sexual desire without worrying about their sexual performance. Mann contends that women now have an opportunity to reposition themselves in the dynamic of social recognition. Still, the sexual subordination of women remains a problem, for some educators and employers continue to treat women as erotic playthings. Mann rejects the antipornography solution, however. Appealing to the psychoanalytic theory of Jacques Lacan, she discerns a female agentic potentiality. Since women are socially constructed as critics of patriarchal discourses, they can appropriate feminine modalities selectively and instrumentally, and they can tentatively and revocably seek out egalitarian relationships with men.

—D.T.M.

Chapter 23

Patricia S. Mann

Glancing at Pornography: Recognizing Men

Pornography, like housework, may appear at first sight to warrant a quite straightforward feminist analysis. What woman has not suddenly felt herself the object of a humiliating, leering male gaze? When a radical-feminist antipornography movement developed in the late 1970s, anger in the face of this everyday modern female experience galvanized scores of women who had never before identified with feminist causes to join an emotion-charged crusade against the pornography industry's sexual exploitation and degradation of women. At the height of the movement in 1983, two feminist theorists, Catharine MacKinnon and Andrea Dworkin, drafted a human rights ordinance that declared pornography to be a practice of sex discrimination and a violation of women's civil rights. Under this ordinance, it became a civil offense to "traffic" in pornography or to coerce participation in its making or use. First proposed and debated in Minneapolis, the ordinance was adopted in Indianapolis on May 1, 1984.[1] Within a year, however, a federal appeals court had struck down the ordinance as unconstitutional, and in 1986 the Supreme Court affirmed this decision.[2] The antipornography ordinance had run afoul of First Amendment concerns with protecting the freedom of expression, and with its immediate hopes of political victory dashed, the antipornography movement faded.

As a political issue pornography turned out to be more complicated than anyone might have imagined; it proved highly divisive even within feminism. While opinion polls taken during the height of the controversy showed a majority of Americans believing that pornography is degrading and harmful to women and supporting legal restrictions on its production and distribution, large numbers of feminists were vehemently opposed to legal sanctions against pornography.[3] I will begin this chapter by briefly analyzing the different feminist perspectives occasioned by the pornography controversy. In hindsight, this bitter debate forecast a disconcerting broadening of feminist concerns and heralded the politically transgressive quality of the multiple voices of women.

Sexuality is such a ubiquitous and yet intangible medium of gendered communication and exchange that the apparent concreteness of "pornography" renders it as seductive for social analysis as for politics. In the remaining sections of this chapter, I will attempt to articulate the issues of sexual agency and identity that began to emerge in the course of the pornography debates. . . . My primary concern lies in probing and evaluating current processes of gendered conflict and change as they develop in diverse social locations. The pornography debates provide a good framework for investigating a gendered dimension of agency involving both active and passive forms of sexual and social recognition. Typically overlooked as a dimension of agency even now, patriarchal regimes of sexual recognition are finally, a decade after the pornography controversy, being challenged on a variety of legal and political fronts. But the processes of social renegotiation in sexual harassment and date rape cases, to name two contemporary examples, will succeed only if we appreciate the dynamic underlying structure of recognition relations, which I investigate in this chapter.

I. THE FEMINIST DEBATE OVER PORNOGRAPHY

Antipornography feminists emphasize the relationship between pornography and the institutionalization of male supremacy in our society. Insofar as pornography objectifies women's bodies, sexualizes their human presence, and eroticizes the male subordination of women, the very existence of pornography does violence to the desires of women for equality and relations of mutual respect with men, according to antipornography theorists Andrea Dworkin and Catharine MacKinnon.[4] They argue that male violence against women is endemic to all aspects of pornography: (1) in the production of pornography, where women and children are sometimes coerced into participating;[5] (2) in the images of pornography whether in "snuff films"—in which women are murdered—or in representations of female sexual degradation by means of boots, whips, or just physical force;[6] (3) in the social reception of pornography by men as well as by women. The political psychology here is that the identities of men and women in our society are heavily influenced by the eroticization of male domination of women within pornography—to such an extent that, in MacKinnon's opinion, "women will never have the dignity, security, compensation that is the promise of equality so long as pornography exists as it does now."[7]

Of course, the portrayal of women as sexual playthings and servants is hardly confined to pornography. One need only turn on the television or scan one of innumerable mass-market magazines while in line at the supermarket to gain a quite definitive sense of gendered social hierarchies, and whether it is one's masculine lot in life to actively express sexual desire or instead to accept one's feminine responsibility for satisfying the desires of a man. No law regulating pornography could possibly begin to eradicate all the graphic sexual representations of patriarchy that bombard us in our daily lives. While this might seem a conclusory argument against legal sanctions, MacKinnon justifies her antipornography ordinance in terms that sidestep this criticism. For her, the goal of a civil rights ordinance against pornography does not lie in eradicating it, but in revealing the pervasive eroticization of male power in the visual media, and enabling women to speak out against it in such a way that they can be heard. Representations of women as sexual objects undermine women's social authority so effectively that they make it difficult for women to protest its effects. "To the extent pornography succeeds in constructing social reality," MacKinnon argues, "it becomes invisible as harm. . . . So the issue is . . . how the harm of pornography is to become visible." By enacting into law the antipornography ordinance, MacKinnon believes that women "would have this recognition and institutional support for our equality [and] . . . there could come a day when she would speak in her own voice and you would hear her."[8] Pornography silences women. The antipornography ordinance intends to restore to women their voice.

The antipornography movement's goals, at least as articulated by its most sophisticated theorists, were those of a symbolic politics. There was no question of eliminating all images demeaning to women, and not even the hope of putting an end to the production and distribution of pornography per se. The aim was rather to make people aware of the ideological power of such images, and to empower women to give voice to their anger at being so portrayed. Indeed, the antipornography movement served as an important focal point for the outrage of a great many women who were just beginning to be conscious of how men "looked at" them in a variety of situations. Women were beginning to become wary of possible links between a boss's casual reading of *Hustler* on his lunch break, his embarrassing sexual innuendos in the hallways, and his refusal to pay them the same salary as male coworkers. The antipornography movement was fueled by a growing fury on the part of women newly confronting the fact that the male world looks most readily at women with a sexual gaze, disdaining to recognize women's accomplishments, even disregarding their presence in nonsexual context.[9]

Those feminists opposed to the regulation of pornography do not so much dispute the anger of the antipornography feminists as question its efficacy. They offer two related critiques of the antipornography movement. In the first place, they insist that no matter how reprehensible the images and ideas it communicates, pornography is merely a form of speech or expression; they contrast the repellent images of pornography with actual physical forms of abuse suffered by women at the hands of men. Never denying the psychological forms of male tyranny and domination experienced by women within sexual relationships, these feminists question the significance of pornographic representations in creating the conditions for such forms of domination. Second-wave feminists coming out of a Marxist tradition of material social analysis are skeptical of claims that pornography is any more than a cultural reflection of more basic forms of patriarchal power. As Varda Burstyn confidently asserts, "Sexist pornography is a product of the economic and social conditions of our society—not vice versa. . . . It follows that these are the conditions we must change if we want sexist pornography to disappear."[10]

In the second place, "pro-sex" feminists, as they often identify themselves, celebrate the goal of sexual freedom and the new possibilities for liberatory and egalitarian sexual relationships created by the social enfranchisement of women. Rejecting the tendency of the antipornography movement to focus on the sexual victimization of women by pornography, they emphasize that pornography is a transgressive form of sexual expression in a culture with a long tradition of sexual repression. Insofar as women today are casting off oppressive patriarchal notions of sexuality, they need to see themselves (and are surely seen by others) as engaging in sexually transgressive forms of speech and behavior.[11] For feminists to align themselves with the religious fundamentalists and social conservatives, who most typically call for laws regulating pornography on the grounds of its sinfulness, is both foolish and dangerous, argue these theorists. Such allies are quite likely to turn around and demand the suppression of what they perceive to be radical feminist depictions of deviant and immoral sexuality. Ironically, feminist-inspired antipornography laws will provide "a useful tool in antifeminist moral crusades," and small feminist journals challenging the boundaries of conventional sexuality will be more vulnerable to censorship than financially successful mass-market publishers of pornography.[12]

There were persuasive feminist arguments on their side of the pornography controversy. At the time, it seemed as if discussion of the issue was short-circuited by the legal framework of American liberalism. Any proposal for regulating individual behavior in our legal system must qualify according to the standards of the Harms Principle, first articulated by J. S. Mill in the mid-nineteenth century. Alarmed by the regulatory enthusiasm of Utilitarian social reformers Jeremy Bentham and James Mill, his father, J. S. Mill famously argued in *On Liberty* that governmental restraints upon individual behavior must be justified by the goal of preventing a harm from occurring. And in addition, he maintained, governmental action is warranted to prevent a harm only if the goal can be achieved without creating greater harms as a result of the regulatory procedures themselves.[13] In the United States, a hallowed tradition of First Amendment law has created a strong presumption that there are very great harms in regulating forms of speech or expression, and it has generally been accepted that restrictions should be placed upon speech only if there is shown to be a compelling state interest requiring such restrictions.

In ruling that the Indianapolis antipornography ordinance was unconstitutional, Judge Frank Easterbrook said, "We accept the premises of this legislation. Depictions of subordination tend to perpetuate subordination. The subordinate status of women in turn leads to affront and lower pay at work, insult and injury at home, battery and rape on the streets." That is, he did not deny claims that pornography is a harm to women. On the other hand, he did not find the state's interest in sex-based equality, according to the Fourteenth Amendment, sufficiently compelling to justify what he deemed the even greater harm of infringing upon First Amendment guarantees of free expression.[14] Constitutional norms seemed to weigh in heavily on behalf of the anticensorship, pro-sex feminist position.

In recent years, however, a surprising variety of theoretically compelling arguments have been made that suggest the legal issue might deserve to be reopened. According to Rae Langton, pornography places the state's interest in promoting the equality of women under the equal protection clause of the Fourteenth Amendment in direct conflict with its commitment to an individual freedom of speech. She suggests that if we apply currently accepted forms of legal reasoning to the pornography issue, the equality interest will be seen as "trumping" the state's concern for free expression.[15] Taking another legal tack, Yale law professor Owen Fiss argues for a broader reading of the state's obligation to protect the freedom of speech. He maintains that the state's interest in the freedom of speech should be interpreted not simply as a commitment to protecting individual speech acts, but as a responsibility for promoting a democratic process of discussion. Insofar as pornography serves to silence women to any significant degree, restrictions upon pornography may well enhance a democratic process of free and uninhibited discussion.[16] David Dyzenhaus contends that J. S. Mill himself might have supported restrictions upon pornography, out of his strong concern for opposing male tyranny over women and encouraging the autonomy of women.[17]

Despite the availability of plausible legal arguments for reopening the pornography issue, there seems little political impetus for doing so. The reason, I think, is that many of the issues first raised in the context of pornography are now being joined more effectively in a number of other legal venues. In later chapters [of *Micro-Politics*], I trace the legal and political legacy of the pornography debates in struggles over abortion rights, sexual harassment, and date rape. In the rest of the present chapter, however, I will attempt to unravel the confusing strands of fraying sexual agency and identity that continue to make the theme of pornography a rich fabric for social analysis.

II. AN INTERACTIVE MODEL OF SEXUAL AGENCY

Pornography has a deceptive simplicity about it, representing quite viscerally the reality of female objectification and passivity under the eye of a patriarchal sexual gaze. Lying unselfconsciously and nakedly on a table before us, the pornographic object also seems quite vulnerable to either feminist wrath or defanging. On the one hand, we can imagine reaching out with both fists to crumple it and toss it with little further ado into a wastebasket. Perhaps if enough women rumpled enough pieces of paper we could finally be free of the demeaning images of women in our society. On the other hand, we can imagine this pornographic magazine or video undergoing a sex change. In the place of female bodies it would be filled with male bodies passively displayed for female sexual approval. Artfully posed to emphasize unusually large or perfectly formed sexual parts in states of erotic tumescence, the complete sexual objectification of these men would prove the existence of a female sexual gaze to rival that of the male sexual gaze. The sexual gaze would no longer be associated with patriarchal oppression insofar as it had either been destroyed or become symmetrical.

But pornography is not immediately vulnerable to either the wrathful destruction or the liberatory mimicry of feminist responses. For pornography is not so much a literal record of obnoxious male psychological patterns as it is a sign system constructed atop a set of late patriarchal social asymmetries that cannot be destroyed or reversed so readily.[18] We need to investigate the asymmetries in patriarchal relationships, and particularly the asymmetries within patriarchal systems of recognition, in order to understand the social context for current responses to pornography.

Without succumbing to biological essentialisms of sexual difference we may begin by emphasizing the quite radical asymmetry in biologically based male and female forms of sexual agency.[19] Historically, the male ability to rape and impregnate a woman provided an important ground for patriarchal sexual and social power relationships. Consider the immediate asymmetries indicated by male spermatic agency. A man, qua man, was physically capable of getting a woman, any woman, with child, and leaving her with child. Because of his relative size and strength he was generally able to do this with or without her consent. He was thus able to leave an indelible mark of his momentary pleasure or release upon a woman, imposing upon her a nine-month labor of physical reproduction as well as a future life of motherhood. Any man could thus act upon any woman in a way she could neither refuse, nor reciprocate, nor forget (given pregnancy as a consequence). While such a man might not disavow his physiological paternity, the social anonymity of his sperm after conception made it possible for him to do so. The rather amazing temporal asymmetry of immediate male spermatic potency and long-term female connection and obligation thus provided a material and social basis for more general forms of male domination over women.[20] . . .

Male sexual domination of women is not based upon notions of male sexual rationality or upon the exclusion of women from the site of male sexual activities. Men celebrate the irrationality of their sexual passions, and ardently solicit the participation of women in their sexual scenarios. Male sexual superiority seems to have been a contingent historical function of a man's physical ability to unilaterally act upon a woman in a socially significant way. This ability to act unilaterally upon women anchors the social discourses that represent men as active and women as passive, men as having desire and the sexual gaze and women as lacking sexual desire and being the object of the sexual gaze.

When we seek to make the social mechanisms of male sexual domination explicit, its interactive quality becomes evident. We need to understand complementary forms of male and female sexual agency involving the shared recognition of the social significance of the male ability to act upon a woman. We may say that patriarchal forms of sexual agency are defined dialectically in terms of such recognition relations. A man's ability to rape or impregnate a woman only gains its social significance insofar as this ability is recognized by women as having particular social implications; a woman's recognition of male abilities to rape and/or impregnate her will correspond with particular female strategies to control the conditions under which this may occur. Thus forms of social recognition become both actively and passively a component of gendered agency and identity within patriarchy.

We may even consider this sociosexual interaction in terms of a ritualized male-female dialogue of asymmetrical forms of recognition. Given the shared social knowledge that a man had the capacity at any moment to act sexually upon a woman, a mere look of sexual interest was enough to convey this possibility to a woman, and to constitute an act of sexual intimidation. A woman was required to recognize herself as the object of this male's sexual desire, as the potential repository of his seed, along with the extensive physical and social obligations this seed carried with it. Thus threatened, a woman was forced to accept her generic sexual vulnerability, and was rendered subject to male demands for lesser acts of service or obedience. In other words, through a word or a mere glance communicating his sexual interest, a man could assert his sexual power to act in some future moment upon a particular woman. And he could use this sexual communication as grounds for exerting social control and subordination over a woman, exacting various acts of service from any woman wishing to forestall his sexual threats.[21]

Seen in this light, patriarchal marriage, as an institutionalized structure of kinship placing social boundaries on the physical vulnerability of women, offered obvious advantages for a woman. By accepting the sexual and social demands of one man, by agreeing to provide him with heirs and to serve him, a woman could secure his protection from the sexual threats of other men. Such protection would operate most effectively, of course, insofar as a woman was willing to remain in private familial spaces except when accompanied by her male protector. To be present in the public spaces of social recognition and acclaim meant for a lone woman to be vulnerable to multiple glances of male sexual recognition, reduction, and intimidation. We may well associate women's recognition of the asymmetries of gendered asexual agency with women's "willingness" to accept the confines of a familial sphere, thereby articulating the drastic male exclusion of women from public spaces of social interaction with a strategic female withdrawal. Insofar as the asymmetry of sexual agency imposed kinship boundaries upon women's social participation, we may directly link male spermatic potency to exclusionary male social agency.

Within the normal orderings of social metaphysics we are accustomed to thinking that events occur, or people perform actions, and then recognition follows eventually in response. Recognition is a secondary, cognitive phenomenon, and is even a bit capricious, sometimes failing to occur altogether, at other times exaggerated or distorted in its relationship to the prior performance or occurrence. But whatever its degree of reliability, social recognition exists within the order of social perception or knowledge, and follows or presumes to follow consequentially upon some prior social phenomenon. I am proposing, however, that the asymmetries of sexual agency were such as to reverse the ordering of social metaphysics and epistemology, and most dramatically so in the lives of women.

The social logic ordering women's existence began with their recognition of what men could potentially do to them, and their own sense of agency could only be predicated upon their strategies for dealing with this possibility. Women's position within patriarchy must be understood in the context of asymmetrical relations of sexual recognition, and specifically in terms of women's *anticipatory recognition* of male sexual and social potency. In women's anticipatory recognition of what men could do to them sexually lay the grounds for seeking out marriage so as to avoid becoming prey to random, unexpected acts of male sexual assertion, and for accepting the obligations of a subsumed nurturer within patriarchal kinship relationships.

In women's anticipatory recognition of what men could do to them sexually, we can also discover the seed of a further form of characteristically female anticipatory recognition. The male gaze of sexual interest gained its power as a phallic promissory note, and the responding female gaze not only acknowledged male sexual potential but also elaborated on it. Having accepted her exclusion from direct participation in the public sphere, it made sense for a woman to invest her male partner with all the powers of social activity she could now only imagine and plan. Renouncing the possibility of accomplishing worldly projects herself, female self-realization could vicariously root itself in the nurturance and support of male social potential. Insofar as she could identify with the prospective agency of a particular man, a woman could experience herself as participating in worldly events.[22]

Female fear and acquiescence in anticipatory recognition of male sexual power was transformed by patriarchal institutions of kinship into a generous, supportive, potentially manipulative faith of wives (and mothers) in the capacity of their husbands (and sons) to accomplish worldly goals that women might initiate or help to formulate in the protected space of the home. This anticipatory female recognition and encouragement of prospective male deeds served an important role in empowering the individual economic and political activities of men within liberalism. Romantic modes of mutual recognition whereby men and women sought completion in marital union can be understood as resting upon such a dynamic of gendered anticipation. We can only appreciate the scope of women's social agency by acknowledging the importance of these anticipatory forms of recognition.

Notice that anticipatory forms of social recognition not only preceded performance but were quite capable of existing independently of it. It was not the male act of rape or impregnation so much as the communication of his capacity to do so that socially signified. It was the chain of recognitions ensuing upon a male sexual gaze and the female reception of this gaze; it was the mutual accord as to the meaning of the male gaze that made sense of gendered subjectivities under patriarchy. *Patriarchal power was a power that existed at its very source in the subjective form, in the communication of possibility.* Unlike the whip of the slave master, the violent, coercive meaning of which could not be denied, male sexual potency was long ago accepted, domesticated, and submerged within elaborate rituals of patriarchal love and kinship, providing a foundation for male forms of social agency and identity extending far beyond the private sphere.[23]

The interactive and subjunctive qualities of gendered recognition relations provide insight into some peculiar, and from the perspective of feminism quite disappointing, features of the present social moment. Technologies of contraception have given women the power to contravene male sexual potency, and to become "determinate in the last instance" with respect to reproduction.[24] And social enfranchisement has given women rights and responsibilities to participate directly in political and economic forms of agency. Women's lives can no longer be understood in terms of strategies dictated by the anticipatory recognition of male agency and power. Mary O'Brien has gone so far as to herald a Contraceptive Revolution, proclaiming that the social transformations resulting from women's new procreative control within relations of human reproduction will be as dramatic as the changes Marx predicted from a Communist revolution.[25]

Yet the subjunctive quality of the dialogue of sexual recognition has provided men with a certain cushion against acknowledging their loss of an important material component of patriarchal sexual agency. Male sexual performance could always be deferred in the past, a veiled phallic power source that men and women anticipated and finally took for granted. It seems today that the patriarchal sexual gaze and the ritualized forms of recognition between men and women that it mandated have attained a degree of social autonomy. Many women's current sense of being victimized by pornography, despite having achieved positions of social power and authority countervailing pornography's message of subordination and silencing in their own lives, bears witness to a disheartening autonomy of the patriarchal sexual gaze. It would not be logically impossible for the "memory" of patriarchal sexual and social forms of power to persist indefinitely in this perverse, two-dimensional form.

Yet recognition relations comprise a practical dimension of social agency; we cannot afford to dismiss patriarchal modes of recognition as merely the stuff of bad memories. Neither pornography nor the persistently low wages of women, to mention another currency of social recognition, are merely cognitive artifacts of a senile patriarchal culture. If men still fail to "get it" with respect to women's capacities for worldly achievements, then it must be that they do not want to "get it." Insofar as we are dealing with male resistance to changing relationships between men and women, a failure of recognition can often be interpreted as a refusal of recognition.

In fact, such refusals of recognition are on a continuum with more overtly negative reactions to women's changing status. We may link the impassive denial/recognition of women's changing sexual and social status in the gaze of pornography, for example, with more active forms of denial/recognition within personal relationships. Recent reports indicate that domestic forms of abuse against women increase as women assert greater social independence, and women incur the greatest levels of violence, even death, at the hands of sexual partners they have decided to leave.[26] Confident patriarchal power could once assert itself with a mere glance—no longer. Women may still cower psychologically and feel victimized by the patriarchal gaze of pornography. But increasingly women stand up for themselves within patriarchal institutions of power, saying "No" in the face of coercive sexual and nonsexual demands. Male violence in response to women who leave them and male responsiveness to pornographic images of women who cannot say "No" are surely both acts of patriarchal resistance. In a sense, they constitute an anticipatory male recognition of the radical implications of women's changing status.

We saw that recognition relations were a constitutive part of gendered forms of agency and power in the past. It should hardly surprise us that they continue to play a primary, practical role in the struggle to transform, and to resist the transformation, of gendered relationships. We need to develop better strategies for critically engaging with defensive patriarchal recognition relations, however—which brings us back to the politics of pornography and the sexual gaze.

III. FREUDIAN STORIES, WORLDLY MOTHERS, GENDERED DISENGAGEMENT, AND PORNOGRAPHY

My reconstruction of patriarchal sexual interactions highlights the importance of both active and passive forms of recognition within gendered social relationships. There remains, however, quite a distance between an understanding of how recognition operates within actual social interactions and an understanding of the disembodied form of sexual "recognition" found in pornography. Pornography, and more generally the ubiquity of objectified images of women surrounding us today, are a feature of modern life that cannot be explained directly by means of the asymmetries of interactive patriarchal sexual agency and power described above. They represent (literally) a culturally dominant, impersonal male sexual gaze that has developed quite recently. In order to comprehend such contemporary forms of sexual recognition, we need to investigate what I will designate as "late patriarchal" elaborations upon the earlier sociosexual asymmetries. Our investigation properly begins with Sigmund Freud's psychoanalytic theory of sexual agency and identity.

In the liberal democratic political milieu of late-nineteenth-century Europe, not only radical women but even a few thinkers with the stature of J. S. Mill had begun to challenge the natural as well as the social foundations of patriarchy. Women's demands for economic and political rights seriously threatened to undermine male social authority so long as it seemed to rest upon physiological differences between men and women. Egalitarian doctrines of human potential called into question the moral and political relevance of merely physiological differences.

A universal recognition of male superiority and authority could no longer be taken for granted, despite the fact that patriarchal structures of power remained firmly entrenched. What was needed was a revised explanation of patriarchy's legitimacy, and Freud managed to provide just that. His great achievement was to install psychological metaphysics of "male sexual desire" as a new basis for male sexual and social dominance. It became much harder to criticize the social domination of men insofar as Freud appeared to have demonstrated its psychic necessity, duly linking his "discoveries" of basic psychic differences with evident physiological differences of men and women, and explaining both in terms of enduring myth-laden social and symbolic structures of patriarchy.

The originality and narrative power of Freudian theory has made its theoretical status highly confusing; controversies over whether it is a science or an ideology obscure its historical role as both a response to and a denial of the changing place of women in society. Judith Kegan Gardiner contrasts radical feminists who condemn Freudian theory "as part of the ideological apparatus that oppresses women" and psychoanalytic feminists who "agree that Freud was a sexist product of his time and deplore his belief in anatomical female inferiority but defend the importance of psychoanalytic thinking."[27] My point is that neither group of feminists understands patriarchy in sufficiently dynamic terms: Freud creatively extended and adapted patriarchal ideology in an effort (whether conscious or unconscious) to provide psychological legitimacy for gendered power relationships whose social base was eroding. The success of Freud's effort was very much bound up with his ability to make patriarchy fashionable again by clothing it in new psychic garb. The frequent feminist habit of identifying psychoanalytic theory as "the unconscious of patriarchal society" is misleading, as this implies it is a report of historically enduring features of patriarchal domination. Freud *invented* this (patriarchal) unconscious, and although it may offer us insights into earlier thinking, it serves first and foremost as a report on the historically specific concerns of his late nineteenth-century Western society.[28] If we focus on revealing the historical specificity of Freud's late patriarchal narrative, we may declare certain portions of Freudian theory already anachronistic and psychically implausible, without rejecting the continuing relevance of other aspects of his psychic worldview.

Having said this, I think that what most distinguishes Freudian theory from earlier patriarchal belief systems is its singular emphasis upon the castrated woman, as well as its related obsession with various dynamics of separation from women. Earlier thinkers, from Aristotle to John Locke, generally explained women's inferiority in terms of their incompleteness, or their lesser strength relative to men. Although the image of a woman as a castrated man was hardly new with Freud, only in his system does it become the primary characterization of women. The violence and the instability of this image of women's inferiority is, after all, quite extraordinary. In order to be castrated, a woman must have once possessed the phallus. This means that her inferiority has been violently imposed upon her through taking from her something originally hers. In contrast to Plato's, Aristotle's, or Locke's complacent conceptions of women's natural inferiority, Freud proffers what is in his own terms a guilt-ridden image suggesting a mysteriously unnatural source of women's inferiority. The castrated woman would seem a cruelly defensive emblem of late patriarchal uncertainty about the legitimacy of male domination.

The separation dynamic that the castrated woman initiates, and that structures the Freudian narrative of sexual desire, is also symptomatic of late patriarchy. In Freud's Oedipal account of boyhood, the child begins by desiring his mother. Having recognized his mother's castration, not only must the boy child break away from his mother to avoid being similarly castrated by his father, but also all further contacts with women, and even images of women, are presumed to evoke castration anxiety in boys and in the men they become. It is not the phenomenon of male anxiety when confronted by women's bodies that is new to Freud; rather, it is the dominant place of his desire-based anxiety in his theory of male behavior. Relationships with mothers and wives were taken for granted by earlier thinkers; women were not perceived as occupying the sort of social place that could make them threatening to a man's psychic well-being. Freud, on the other hand, makes the successful repression of the boy's early desire for his mother the foundation for all further relationships, even deriving a man's mature public goals and accomplishments from his successful sublimation of childhood desires for his mother. One of the seductive aspects of psychoanalytic theory for feminists is surely the fact that Freud is the only major thinker ever to take the traditional role of women so seriously, if in a perverse way.

Notice that the Freudian narrative of sexual desire involves a radical turn away from traditional interactive relationships of sexual recognition. Freudian psychoanalysis suggests that each person must seek to discover the psychic origins of their adult sexual desires in childhood relationships. Adult desires, despite their appearance of social immediacy, are always a replay of original Oedipal desires, and in analysis the individual narrates his life story in terms of the significance of the permutations he works upon these original sexual desires. This means that psychoanalysis provides a powerful rhetorical framework for distancing oneself from the psychic give-and-take within adult sexual relationships. As mere replays of the initial relationship of desire and separation from the mother, mature sexual relationships are ultimately about sexual self-recognition.

The sexual objectification of women in the mass media today is a phenomenon highly compatible with this turn away from interactive forms of sexual recognition in adult relationship. Put simply, male erotic pleasure becomes generally problematic insofar as the mere image of a woman is presumed to evoke castration anxiety. One typical solution, according to Laura Mulvey, is "fetishistic scopophilia": the extreme visual beauty of the female portrayed on the movie screen enables men to escape, momentarily, their castration anxiety.[29] Extending Mulvey's analysis to visual representations of women generally, the Freudian narrative explains all too clearly why we are surrounded by idealized sexual images of women in our society, and why women as well as men often find them appealing. With his Oedipal narrative of childhood separation from castrated mothers, Freud emphasized the intrinsically fearful quality of the sexual desire for women, providing a sympathetic perspective on modern alienated forms of erotic desire. Fetishistic representations of women provide men with the occasion for experiencing sexual desire with the least possible anxiety about (castrating) female responses.

Today, however, the social enfranchisement of women, and the advent of what I will refer to as "worldly mothers," throw a bit of a wrench into the Freudian characterization of women and into his story of sexual desire. The image of a castrated mother relied upon the patriarchal opposition between a father whose penis identified him with society's language and laws and a mother whose lack of a penis signified her presocial, bodily existence within the home. Such a binary opposition is increasingly called into question by the new demographics of daily family existence. Mothers today are worldly working mothers, for the most part. Accordingly, it makes increasingly less sense to explain childhood development in terms of an initial bond with a presocial maternal nurturer, and a traumatic break from this primary nurturer in order to enter a social world identified with the father. When a child's mother and father both work outside the home, the presence or absence of a penis will not signify a necessary difference in either parenting roles or in worldly status. When a child lives with a single mother or several women who work outside the home, society's law and language will be personally associated with the lack of a penis. It no longer makes obvious psychic sense to assume that an infant will identify penises with sexual desire or with personhood, and the lack of a penis with castration.[30]

The patriarchal mythology of women's castration represents women as violated and degraded in their female bodily existence. Women cannot afford to accept Freudian versions of a gendered separation dynamic as grounded in a meaningful childhood fear of women as castrated. Having recently acquired the means to control procreation, however, along with expectations of participation in the public sphere, women may have their own interest in narratives of separation from men and children. As women cease to think of themselves as subsumed nurturers and begin to act publicly under their own names, a mythical narrative of female separation from the patriarchal family seems highly appropriate. Despite its troubling implications, a gendered separation dynamic has become historically meaningful to women as well as to men in this late patriarchal moment.

Given the oppositional quality of gender relations during this transitional period, women might be expected to generate a mythology that places the blame for the dynamic of gendered disengagement upon men and their continuing efforts to dominate women. I think it is even possible to interpret the pornography controversy in symbolic sexual terms, as a struggle to define a female mythology of separation from the individual men who have sexually intimidated women. This feminist separation dynamic originates in a male threat of rape rather than a female threat of castration. It will involve the girl child's attraction to, and finally recognition and fear of, "the father who could rape her."

In this context, pornography becomes interesting not for its representations of women, which are hardly unique to pornography, but for its attendant phenomenon of "men looking at pornography." It so happens that this "man looking at pornography" provides a nicely delineated image of male sexual desire for the separating, postmodern woman to focus upon. In critically observing this "man looking at pornography," women are able to objectify and delimit the desiring—and thus obviously lacking and incomplete—male sexual being. In thus focusing on the sexual neediness of men, women can experience their own sexual agency of wanting to position themselves as the object of this male desire, while also finally seeing the dangers inherent in the situation. Male fears of castration are supposedly initially grounded in threats of the father, gradually coming to be associated with the very existence of the desirable woman. In a similar way, female fears of rape can be initially grounded in the exemplary fates of oppressed mothers or grandmothers, gradually coming to be embodied in the very existence of the man who desires the two-dimensional women of pornography.

Both sides of the feminist pornography debate can be understood in terms of a female Ur-separation mythology generated in this context. When Laura Mulvey analyzed the male anxiety evoked by images of women in films, she suggested two distinct modes of cinematic compensation for male anxieties. She designates one male response to women in films as "voyeurism," involving a male preoccupation with the trauma of the guilty castrating female. In certain films, "pleasure lies in ascertaining guilt, asserting control, and subjecting the guilty woman to punishment and/or forgiveness."[31] In our feminist inversion of this male separation schema, antipornography feminists respond to the rape anxiety produced by the father in a similarly "voyeuristic" manner. They exorcise a preoccupation with the female trauma of rape at the hands of the father by projecting their fears onto the "man who looks at pornography," gaining pleasure and release by asserting his guilt and attempting to punish him.

The second cinematic strategy for allaying the male anxiety of the castrating woman involves the aforementioned "fetishistic scopophilia," whereby the physical beauty of the female body is emphasized.[32] This fetishization of the female body is accomplished within films by focusing attention on the erotic alluring quality of a woman, outside of any particular narrative context, and thus denying the traumatic original story of castration. Pro-sex feminists may be understood as engaging in a similar displacement of female rape anxiety through focusing on the erotic quality of the "man looking at pornography." When Ann Snitow insists, for example, that "men looking at pornography" ought to be seen as engaging in a form of sexual fantasy similar to women's enjoyment of Harlequin novels, she may be seen as choosing a fetishistic response to the anxiety evoked by the original story of male rape.[33] By focusing on the passivity of the man viewing pornography, such feminists abstract male desire from its frequent social context of intimidation and hostility. Thus can women fantasize control over the erotic scenario of heterosexual desire, gaining pleasure from this gentler, almost effete representation of male sexuality.

There is incontrovertible evidence today of a broad social phenomenon of *gendered disengagement.* Demographic statistics are compelling, recording trends (in some cases extending back a hundred years) toward later ages of first marriage, greater divorce rates, increasing patterns of unmarried adults and single-motherhood. The figures indicate a separation dynamic of major social proportions. By analyzing Freud's theory of the castrated woman as a late patriarchal separation mythology, and by proposing a corresponding feminist separation mythology founded upon a fear of men as rapists, I have attempted to highlight the historical specificity of this process. The process of gendered disengagement, which began a century ago as a defensive male strategy *within* patriarchy, has now become a feature of women's struggle for social enfranchisement *beyond* patriarchy.

IV. JACQUES LACAN AND WOMEN'S DESIRE FOR RECOGNITION

The social position of women has changed radically in the last quarter of a century. Not only have women achieved unprecedented rights to social participation, but the obligations and burdens that correspond with possessing individual economic and political rights within liberalism have also been redistributed with amazing rapidity from men to women. Gendered disengagement, in the form of declining marriage rates, increasing divorce rates, and increasing rates of motherhood outside of marriage, has contributed to this redistribution of social responsibility. *Yet the gendered redistribution of social recognition lags far behind the redistribution of social responsibilities.* Not only are women still looked at as sexual objects in inappropriate situations, but women also fail to be positively recognized and rewarded in their new social roles. For example, women who are heads of households are not paid the sorts of wages long apportioned exclusively to men as heads of households. Women who perform as effectively as men in various social capacities are not paid equivalent wages and salaries, nor do they receive equivalent opportunities for promotion. Women, as well as members of various culturally devalued groups, need active strategies for gaining appropriate forms of social recognition.

When patriarchal authority began to be questioned a century ago, Freud could propose a psychic regimen of self-recognition for men as a reprieve from the turmoil and anxieties of changing gender relationships. The superior power of men within a patriarchal society meant that they could defensively maintain their power by ignoring those who would not recognize it. But women begin from a position of social inferiority. Unless women are going to create their own autonomous society, no strategy of self-recognition will do; the social empowerment of women within a patriarchal society requires that men alter their previous beliefs and recognize the new status of women. The antipornography movement was an expression of women's frustration at being denied forms of social recognition appropriate to their new social roles and responsibilities. It was hardly a constructive strategy, however, for attaining the kinds of social recognition women currently yearn for and deserve.[34]

Jacques Lacan, perhaps the most significant theorist of psychoanalysis after Freud, makes the individual's desire for recognition by others the central feature of psychic life. While Lacan had rather conventional assumptions about the social positions women and men were destined to take up, his innovative rearticulation of a still-patriarchal Desire in terms of each person's impossible quest to be socially recognized has interesting feminist implications. In fact, Lacan provides a useful theoretical approach to a global situation in which not only gendered but also racial and ethnic conflict and disengagement have heightened everyone's concerns about social recognition. Moreover, in making language the primary site for our efforts to attain recognition, he posits a complexly interactive social framework for addressing issues of recognition.

Lacan himself never contemplates the critical, interactive strategies of social recognition for which I believe his theory helps to lay the groundwork. He remains firmly committed to the psychoanalytic project articulated by Freud, never questioning the notion that an individual's psychic needs are best addressed through helping him to explore his unconscious desires. Lacan's seminal theoretical contribution lies in his emphasis upon the socially mediated forms, specifically the linguistic forms, which provide the fabric of this psychic drive for self-recognition. The feminist challenge lies in showing how Lacan's vision of desiring subjects constructed within language provides a unique basis for understanding gender oppression, while at the same time suggesting that women and others who are not privileged within a particular symbolic system are likely to develop a critical relationship to it and to those subjects it does privilege.

Freud's theory of sexual desire and self-recognition remained grounded in the male possession of a penis and the female lack of a penis. Lacan's theory of desire and recognition is not linked to the physical possession of a penis or to any gender-specific biological features. Desire, for Lacan, is grounded in the human baby's physical helplessness and lack of coordination at the time of birth, which he refers to as "the specific prematurity of birth in man." Lacan posits that from the time of birth onward, the infant "magically" experiences "images of castration, mutilation, dismemberment, dislocation, evisceration, devouring, bursting open of the body, in short . . . *imagos of the fragmented body.*" This early sense of anatomical incompleteness structures all further psychic development, and from this experience of an inherent "lack" in being comes the lifelong desire to be recognized as a unified self. For Lacan, it is this "narcissistic passion" for recognition that underlies all other forms of desire and most basically fuels human behavior.[35]

His theory of early childhood development also does not differentiate between boy and girl children; it explicates what Lacan considers a basic human fixation upon gaining a unified sense of selfhood through various modes of social recognition.[36] He believed that at about six months of age the child entered what he called a "mirror stage," during which the child first perceived itself as a complete object in the reflection of a mirror, as well as in the gaze of its mother or primary caretaker. The infant's mirror-stage image of wholeness, like all later ones, is only illusory, insofar as the first and most basic body image remains one of fragmentation. At about eighteen months of age, the infant's fascination with its mirror gestalt diminishes, and what has begun as a specular identity gradually becomes a social identity, constituted in terms of language.[37]

Lacan associates the mirror stage with a "natural" consciousness and a primary identification with the mother, and he considers the end of the mirror stage to involve the child's passage into social forms of consciousness, achieved through submitting to alienating patriarchal symbolic structures of law and language. He uses the notion of castration to designate the traumatic end of the infant's primary identification with the mother, and he posits that the actual father functions as a Phallus, or as a symbolic agent of separation making this transition possible.[38] Having made the transition into the realm of the patriarchal symbolic, each individual must forever after seek a sense of his or her unity/identity within language and other social systems of signification, which can, however, only "misrecognize" the self.

Notice that Lacan's perspective on gender relations becomes a bit confusing at the point when the child begins to use language because Lacan adopts Freud's naturalistic sexual categories to explain the process of becoming a social subject. Lacan consciously articulates his theory in terms of patriarchal symbolic structures, accepting "paternal metaphors" inherited from Freud, while at the same time denying the existence of any natural foundations of patriarchy. For example, Lacan emphasizes that all his talk of phalluses is purely metaphorical, having no reference to the male penis or the female lack of a penis.[39] It is for this reason that Ellie Ragland-Sullivan can deny an "a priori Lacanian support for phallocentrism" and even argue that his theory is helpful to feminists in offering "a picture of the place of man and woman within a history of symbolization and meaning."[40] Psychoanalysis was formulated as a social practice, however, a means whereby contemporary women and men attempt to better understand themselves and their desires. In the context of its application, Lacan's psychoanalytic discourse encourages a continuing assumption of patriarchal relationships and hierarchies.

I maintain, however, that Lacan's theory of the constitution of desiring subjects within a patriarchal symbolic system only makes complete sense for those male subjects who have a privileged relationship to the signifying structures of the system. For those subjects who are un-named or otherwise devalued within the dominant signifying systems, we will need to comprehend the logic of their desiring behavior in more complicated ways. Insofar as women have become socially enfranchised today as women within a patriarchal signifying system, we may presume their desires to have been constituted in fundamentally conflicted ways, and expect their relationships with various signifying systems to be contentious. Women's psychic need for recognition will lead them to interact critically with the patriarchal signifying systems that Lacan assumes as foundational structures of psychic desire.

Let us look closely at Lacan's theory of how individuals come to understand themselves. Remember that according to Lacan we begin life with a fragmented sense of self that leads to a lifelong effort to substantiate a vision of personal wholeness through social forms of recognition. After the mirror stage has come to an end, we gain our sense of identity within language, becoming a subject of language and in some sense subject to this symbolic order. But language is, for psychological purposes, merely the medium through which we experience the desires and recognition of other human beings. Lacan expresses this social function of language by positing that we gain our sense of identity as a man or as a woman, as well as in other respects, by seeing ourselves in terms of the hypothetical gaze of an Other within signifying systems. Of course, no one signifier, or even many signifiers, can adequately represent who we are. As Lacan says, "It functions as a signifier only to reduce the subject in question to being no more than a signifier, to petrify the subject in the same movement in which it calls the subject to function, to speak, as subject."[41] "Mis-recognition" is thus the paradigmatic dynamic of selfhood for Lacan, the ongoing signifying process within which individuals are necessarily and imperfectly constituted in language and in the gaze of the Other.

As an account of the inevitable inadequacy of language confronted with human particularity, this notion of misrecognition makes sense. It elides the difference between the practical and the cognitive dimensions of recognition rather too quickly, however. It also implies that all forms of misrecognition are equal. Of course they are not, and this becomes evident once we consider that people interact within hierarchically organized social structures in accordance with differential modes of (mis)recognizing one another. As Lacan himself pointed out in a late essay, there are particularly deep-seated problems with being misrecognized as a woman. "By her being in the sexual relation radically Other, in relation to what can be said of the unconscious, the woman is that which relates to this Other. . . . How can we conceive that the Other might, somewhere, be that to which one half—since that is roughly the biological proportion—one half of speaking beings relates? And yet that is what is written up on the blackboard. . . . Nothing can be said of the woman."[42] Lacan is truly puzzled by the effort to think about how the gaze of the Other can misrecognize something it only recognizes as the Other in the first place. Concluding that there can be "no Other of the Other," Lacan accepts the situation as an interesting paradox created by a patriarchal symbolic system.

For individual women who are recognized in an infinite variety of social roles today, but always *in spite* of being women, it is a rather more serious issue. Until recently, women were indeed subject to an all-too-consistent sense of inferior female identity, insofar as the available social roles for women corresponded with the forms of recognition mandated by patriarchal signifying systems. Today, however, with their social enfranchisement, women experience themselves within radically disjunctive social gazes. They are expected to position themselves and to participate within various liberal social structures alongside men. And yet, patriarchal signifying systems continue to recognize them in terms of the old modalities of female inferiority. This patriarchal gaze is newly experienced as a denial of female selfhood, however, insofar as women experience *themselves* as full social selves within various roles. Operating within a confusing tangle of symbolic systems that make recognition of women as contemporary social agents both inevitable and impossible, women must contend with repeated instances of what I will call the "anticipatory nonrecognition" of patriarchal signifying systems.

Lacan focused on the desires of male subjects for recognition within a patriarchal symbolic system, which led him to assume that misrecognition was primarily a form of positive recognition. He theorized the desiring behavior of individuals in the context of the symbolic privileges enjoyed by such subjects, not realizing that the desires of women or other subjects not privileged within a particular signifying system would be constituted differently in response to experiences of *nonrecognition.* In fact, with his discussion of the peculiar quality of misrecognition accorded to women in a patriarchal symbolic system, Lacan inadvertently demonstrates that anticipatory nonrecognition is a quite obvious limit form of language-based misrecognition.

Moreover, the phenomenon of misrecognition as nonrecognition is not peculiar to relationships between men and women; it commonly occurs in situations of cultural dissonance as well. At one point, Lacan writes of an episode in which he himself experienced nonrecognition, still managing to avoid noticing its implications for his theory of misrecognition and the constitution of desiring subjects. He reminisces that many years before, he had visited the coast of Brittany for a week's vacation, and each day he had enthusiastically put out to sea in the boat of a local sardine fisherman. As a young intellectual visiting from Paris, Lacan had imagined himself to be sharing a practical, physical experience of work and danger with this fisherman. At some point, however, the fisherman pointed to a small sardine can floating in the water, exclaiming, "You can see that? Do you see it? Well, it doesn't see you!" The fisherman found this "highly amusing," while Lacan did not.[43] Seeking an explanation, Lacan decides that the fisherman's laughter stems from the fact that he, like the sardine can, could reflect light or apparent awareness in Lacan's presence, without really seeing Lacan at all. Lacan uses this incident to demonstrate that cognition is not merely a matter of physical perception but also a matter of subjective desires. We may think and desire to see ourselves as in a particular place, and then find that, according to someone next to us who surely ought to be able to perceive our presence, we are not there at all. The fisherman's worldly vision, as reflected in his relationship to the floating sardine can, simply did not include Lacan, even as they were sitting side by side in the boat.

This situation of nonrecognition is for Lacan an exceptional one brought on by his own desires to escape his everyday life. He has very little stake in being properly (mis)recognized by the Brittany fisherman, and despite a moment of personal discomfort at the sardine fisherman's dismissive response to his presence, Lacan can put this instance of nonrecognition behind him as merely a bizarre experience. His solution to the problem of not being recognized by the Brittany fisherman is obvious; he will simply return to Paris, to the company of people whose desires are compatible with his own. What is significant is that Lacan does not consider the possibility of attempting to engage with the fisherman in such a way as to bring about a greater degree of mutual understanding and thus the cognitive grounds for mutual recognition.

Lacan's example resonates all too intimately with the experiences of women and cultural minorities, typically more close to home. A woman might recollect a hundred instances when she felt like the young Lacan earnestly out to sea off Brittany, brought up short by the fisherman and the sardine can that glinted at him knowingly in the sun, while explicitly failing to recognize his presence. But a woman invites the alienating experience of anticipatory nonrecognition merely by entering a public space dominated by patriarchal symbolic codes of desire and recognition. It is often within a chosen professional or social group that the startling incident of nonrecognition occurs. Sometimes a woman, or a relevant part of a woman, fails to be acknowledged in any fashion. For example, a woman is not called on when she raises her hand at a meeting, as if female hands themselves became invisible within patriarchal social spaces. At other times a woman will speak in the midst of a discussion, and someone else will immediately take up her point, and somehow it will become his point. Her voice can be heard within a patriarchal discourse, but only if appropriated by a male body.

Everyone is misrecognized within society, according to Lacan. Psychic agency in response to this phenomenon of misrecognition is indefatigable and personally dynamic; we seek out the Other's gaze in a multiplicity of locations, always disappointed, and always hopeful. Yet socially our relationship to the Other and to language is quite static, according to Lacan; we accept each instance of misrecognition as inevitable. We can always move on to another. We do not find it necessary to engage critically with a particular instance of misrecognition—for we do not presume to question the desire of the Other, or the linguistic form it takes.

I have tried to show, however, that women are paradigmatically on a boat off Brittany within their daily existence, not merely misrecognized in the typical sense but frequently unrecognized by male colleagues or lovers for important contributions they make to a shared enterprise. Women cannot simply leave the boat or the boardroom or the relationship and return "home" to be amid people whose subjective desires allow them to include women in their vision. Where would they find such a home? The anticipatory nonrecognition of women is built into the very symbolic codes women grow up articulating their own identities and agency within. For this reason, women can also ill afford to respond to instances of nonrecognition in the passive psychic mode assumed by psychoanalysis. To simply swallow instances of nonrecognition alongside other forms of (mis)recognition is for women to continue to recognize themselves according to a traditional code of female inferiority that their activities and social positions now belie.

Women, in fact, tend to remain on the boat, in the meeting, in the relationship, attempting to negotiate for more viable relationships of (mis)recognition with men. Women are driven by the same narcissistic passions by which Lacan explains the uncritical relationship of men to patriarchal symbolic systems. Their psychic struggle for recognition can hardly leave these patriarchal symbolic systems behind. But for a woman to remain tolerant of the capricious gaze of a signifying system that recognizes her in one instant for her achievements and in the next moment denies her female subjectivity is quite unthinkable if we take Lacan's notion of the narcissistic passion for recognition seriously. A woman will be impelled to engage critically in social discourses where insulting instances of nonrecognition occur. She will find herself proceeding in opposition to such a signifying system, necessarily seeking to rewrite its codes of recognition. In the context of the larger social formation in which women's rights and responsibilities are now being transformed, this will not be an idle project; women are potentially capable of transforming retrograde patriarchal signifying structures that no longer correspond sufficiently with social practices.

The personal psychic struggles of women for recognition can thus only be comprehended by acknowledging this immediately political dimension of their desire for recognition. Narcissistic passion will lead women to break out of the self-contained circuits of desiring (mis)recognition when disparities between the patriarchal gaze and more affirmative social gazes become apparent. The normal desire for recognition will lead women to become activated or critical in relation to both the signifying systems as well as in relation to Others utilizing these systems. Lacanian theory can help us comprehend the social trajectory of women's desires if we attend to the current implications of the social enfranchisement of women as signifying agents within patriarchal systems of recognition.

V. VITAL FEMINIST GLANCES: PAINTING OURSELVES INTO THE PICTURE

In pornography the patriarchal gaze of nonrecognition stares with naked hostility out at women today. I have argued that women are psychically constituted as critical in relation to this gaze. The question is: How may women best act to transform it? Antipornography feminists are quite appropriately angry about the demeaning way in which women are represented in pornography. Their solution is appealing, and appalling, insofar as it operates on the same visceral level as does the pornographic image. In effect, the antipornography ordinances would allow women to scratch out the eyes of the pornographer, as traditional Moslem law allows victims the solace of cutting off the guilty hands of criminals. Opposition to the antipornography ordinances presumably springs, in part, from a deep-seated sense of outrage at the presumptuousness of this feminist desire to molest the male gaze in such a fashion. The most important failing of the antipornography ordinances, however, lies in their narrowing of the feminist project. In a yet-patriarchal world order, the demeaning gaze is everywhere, although typically much more repressed than in pornography. An effectively critical stance of women in relation to pornography must be based upon an understanding of the connections between the pornographic gaze and all the other social discourses that perpetuate an oppressive patriarchal gaze in our society.

It is imperative, in the first place, that women be capable of looking at a pornographic image without seeing themselves in it. Lacan interprets the Gospel, "They have eyes that they might not see," as suggesting the capacity of individuals to choose to look at other people in order not to submit to their gaze. Yet he points out that we typically respond to paintings and other visual representations by "laying down our gaze," even sometimes feeling ourselves "caught in the trap" of the artist's vision.[44] From his psychoanalytic perspective, Lacan is not interested in the social power relationships that determine who actively looks and who passively experiences the gaze of the Other. In fact, a dominant patriarchal gaze is typically embedded in paintings and other representations, as well as in written texts. We are lured into laying down our own gaze and participating in that which is presented to us. It is this seductive quality that is so unnerving about pornography and other sexist texts today. But socially enfranchised women can resist seduction by an overtly patriarchal gaze insofar as it does not accord with the rest of their experiences of themselves in various positions of social engagement and authority today.

Twenty years ago, when the second wave of feminism was just beginning, many women dramatically refused to wear makeup, bras, and other codified symbols of femininity. It was important to publicly express the fact that we refused to identify with sexist images of women. Now that many women, and even feminists, have returned to wearing makeup and bras, there is a tendency to interpret this as a defeat for feminist principles. In fact, a contrary reading is more appropriate. Feminists can don makeup and other signifiers of femininity again insofar as the point has long since been made that women need not identify with or submit to sexist images of women. June Cleaver (the mother of Beaver) is no longer the norm for women, and Marilyn Monroe is not the feminine ideal. Both have become identifiable as cultural stereotypes of womanhood. As Norman Bryson explains, "The stereotype exists and is known at just those points where it does not tally with the evidence, where it comes away from the surface of practice: it establishes two zones, of enchanted representation and disenchanted experience."[45] Women who wear makeup today participate in both zones of cultural experience.

Feminists can clothe themselves in traditional signifiers of femininity instrumentally rather than ecstatically. Stereotypical modes of presentation evoke positive responses socially, but it is dangerous for a female self to identify strongly with these responses or to succumb to the gaze that appreciates her self-consciously codified femininity. Women have the capacity to be self-conscious social actors now rather than traditional passive objects of the patriarchal gaze. Narcissistic passion propels women into signifying engagements and interactions, playing to the expectations of the patriarchal gaze while hoping to rewrite the patriarchal codes that deny women, ahead of time, the quality of recognition they aspire to. Participation in such risky signifying enterprises is increasingly a part of everyday life for women.

Women have no choice but to attempt to rewrite the patriarchal codes of recognition. Yet in setting themselves in opposition to the patriarchal gaze, feminist theorists find themselves in a particularly difficult position. The patriarchal gaze is eroding in various spots, but it is still associated with all the dominant social discourses. The theoretical status of any feminist critique is thus necessarily precarious. In attempting to characterize the status of a feminist theoretical critique in relation to an entrenched patriarchal gaze, it may be helpful to extend our use of visual metaphors and contrast the distant ubiquity of the patriarchal gaze with the ephemeral intensity of feminist glances. Norman Bryson has pointed out that by visually emphasizing the brushstrokes that constitute a particular painting, Chinese art represents the temporal process of producing the picture. It thus offers us an immediate, shifting, fragile *glance* at the world rather than the timeless, disembodied *gaze* idealized within the modern European painting.[46] The glance is thus the viewpoint of the actual painter as she paints or of the writer as she writes; it is the creative envisioning of new subjects of discursive recognition. The feminist theoretical or artistic glance is actively signifying meanings that may or may not endure as part of a disembodied social gaze.

Women are engaging critically and creatively with the dominant theoretical and practical discourses in a diverse array of situations, and there are signs that their interventions are having an effect. But feminist critiques are glancing blows to a still-patriarchal firmament. We set off momentarily blinding fireworks which cast an eerie glow upon an everyday life that tends to go on as before. Various commentators have remarked, for example, that the continuing notoriety of Andrea Dworkin's and Catharine MacKinnon's views is evidence that pornography does not successfully silence women. Dworkin and MacKinnon would surely reply that their personal fame/notoriety has little effect on the degradation of women's daily lives in and through pornography. Ultimately, of course, we may hope that the many glancing blows of feminist critiques will lead dominant social discourses to attempt to exorcise their patriarchal features, but it will be a messy process. The hoary old patriarchal gaze tends to be at once so ambient and so distant that the intense local discourses of feminism have difficulty connecting with it, despite the fact that they are structurally constituted in opposition to it.

The pornographic gaze does not seem distant at all, flagrantly exposing its desires for all to see. Yet it is a desiring gaze that refuses even to flirt with existing feminist glances, sacrificing carnal immediacy in order to gird itself against transgressive female sexual agency. From a feminist perspective, it is far easier to disengage from the stark, unyielding pornographics of the patriarchal gaze than it is to reengage with it critically. We may choose to disengage in the passionate mode of the pornography separation mythologies I suggested above in section III, recognizing men behind the gaze as "fathers who would rape daughters." Or we may disengage in the calmer practical mode of the contemporary woman who recognizes the preferences of men for passive, "two-dimensional" women in both professional and personal relationships. In either case, it is difficult to imagine how to recognize constructively the men behind pornography in modes that would require them to recognize contemporary "multidimensional" women.[47]

Pornography finally confronts us with a potentially tragic dimension of the current feminist struggle for recognition. Women can industriously work within and upon the various discourses of social power, attempting to rearticulate them so that women and women's achievements are more likely to be recognized. Feminist thinkers can brilliantly rewrite social theories to put men and women in their rightful places theoretically. But women cannot finally force men to recognize them. Women cannot act directly to dissolve the patriarchal gaze.[48] Some such dimension of existential uncertainty is present in any radical social project, of course. Women need to be both wary and hopeful in recognizing the men behind the patriarchal gaze.

NOTES

1. See Deborah Rhode, *Justice and Gender* (Cambridge, Mass.: Harvard University Press, 1989), p. 266.
2. See *American Booksellers Association v. Hudnut*, 771 F. 2d 323 (7th Cir. 1985), aff'd sub nom. *Hudnut v. American Booksellers Association*, 106 S. Ct. 1172, rehearing denied 106 S. Ct. 1664 (1986).
3. Rhode, *Justice*, p. 271. Rhode reports that "according to public-opinion surveys in the mid-1980s, some two-thirds of Americans favored prohibition on sexual violence in magazines and movies." See Varda Burstyn, ed., *Women Against Censorship* (Vancouver: Douglas and McIntyre, 1985).
4. See Andrea Dworkin, *Pornography: Men Possessing Women* (New York: Perigee, 1979); Catharine MacKinnon, *Feminist Unmodified* (Cambridge, Mass.: Harvard University Press, 1987).
5. Linda Lovelace's account of her experiences while filming *Deep Throat* is cited as one of the primary examples of such coercion. See Linda Lovelace and Michael McGrady, *Ordeal* (1981).
6. See MacKinnon, *Feminism*, p. 171, where she states that "pornography sexualizes rape, battery, sexual harassment, prostitution, and child sexual abuse; it thereby celebrates, promotes, authorizes, and legitimizes them."
7. Ibid., p. 195.
8. Ibid., pp. 155, 196.
9. There is an interesting comparison to be made between nineteenth-century "social purity" movements in which women focused their ire upon common male practices concerning alcohol and prostitution, and the twentieth-century antipornography movement, which directed its anger at male sexual objectification of women. The social purity movements displaced their underlying criticism of customary male behavior with their focus on an abuse of alcohol or consorting with "bad women." Individual men thus had grounds for exempting themselves from the criticism and proclaiming their own personal virtue. The twentieth-century antipornography movement homed in on a more elmental level of conflict between men and women, potentially indicting all men for their sexualized visions of women. The frequent decision of religious fundamentalists and right-wing conservatives to make alliances with the antipornography struggles of radical feminists betrays a failure to recognize the much more radical social ramifications of the twentieth-century antipornography movement.

   See Judith Walkowitz, "Male Vice and Female Virtue: Feminism and the Politics of Prostitution in Nineteenth-Century Britain," in *Powers of Desire*, ed. Ann Snitow, Christine Stansell, and Sharon Thompson (New York: Monthly Review Press, 1983), on the dangers of a radical feminist analysis slipping back into a nineteenth-century politics of sexual repression.
10. Varda Burstyn, "Political Precedents and Moral Crusades: Women, Sex, and the State," in *Women Against Censorship*, ed. Varda Burstyn, p. 24.
11. See Kate Ellis, "I'm Black and Blue from the Rolling Stones and I'm Not Sure How I Feel about It: Pornography and the Feminist Imagination," *Socialist Review*, nos. 75, 76 (vol. 14, nos. 3, 4), May–August 1984, for a flamboyant statement of this position. Several male members of the (then) New York Collective of *Socialist Review* were highly offended by Kate's blithe discussion of the potential value of fantasies of violence, and opposed publication of her piece on these grounds—thus exemplifying just how close to home the forces of censorship may reside.
12. See Lisa Duggan, Nan Hunter, and Carole S. Vance, "False Promises: Feminist Antipornography Legislation in the U.S.," in Burstyn, ed., *Women Against Censorship*, p. 151. See *Coming To*

Power: Writings and Graphics on Lesbian S/M, ed. SAMOIS (Boston: Alyson Publications, 1982), for a good example of the sort of feminist text likely to become an object of conservative censorship efforts.

13. John Stuart Mill, *On Liberty* (New York: Penguin, 1984), pp. 61, 68, 141.
14. See *American Booksellers Inc. v. Hudnut*, 598 F. Supp. 1326 (S.D. Ind. 1984). See also Rae Langton, "Whose Right? Ronald Dworkin, Women, and Pornographers," *Philosophy and Public Affairs* 19, 4 (Fall 1990), p. 336.
15. Rae Langton maintains that Ronald Dworkin's much esteemed account of a liberal democratic government's responsibility to "treat those whom it governs with equal concern and respect" has straightforward implications for the pornography issue. She challenges Dworkin's analysis of pornography in "Do We Have a Right to Pornography?" in *A Matter of Principle* (Cambridge, Mass.: Harvard Univeristy Press, 1985), confronting Dworkin's pornography analysis with the theory of rights he articulated earlier in *Taking Rights Seriously* (Cambridge, Mass.: Harvard University Press, 1977). See Langton's "Whose Right? Ronald Dworkin, Women, and Pornographers," *Philosophy and Public Affairs* 19, 4 (Fall 1990).
16. Owen Fiss, "Freedom and Feminisim," a talk presented to the New York University Colloquium in Law, Philosophy, and Politicial Theory, November 14, 1991.
17. David Dyzenhaus, "John Stuart Mill and the Harm of Pornography," *Ethics* 102 (April, 1992).
18. See Norman Bryson, *Vision and Painting: The Logic of the Gaze* (New Haven: Yale University Press, 1983), p. xii, for an explanation of this distinction in relation to the interpretation of paintings.
19. See Donna Haraway, " 'Gender' for a Marxist Dictionary: The Sexual Politics of a Word," in *Simians, Cyborgs, and Women* (New York: Routledge, 1991), for a clear critique of both tendencies.
20. I am quite aware of the historical and anthropological limitations of any such account of "traditional" forms of sexual or social agency. Compare my analysis, which begins with the gendered aspects of social agency, with Claude Lévi-Strauss's account in *The Elementary Structures of Kinship* (Boston: Beacon Press, 1969). Lévi-Strauss posits that a universal principle of exchange(!) is the basis for all systems of kinship.
21. It is interesting that such sexualized power relationships exist between men today in prisons. See Wilbert Rideau and Ron Wikberg, *Life Sentences: Rage and Survival Behind Bars* (New York: Random House, 1992). Rideau and Wikberg are award-winning journalists who are also prisoners, and they write that "while homosexual rape in prison is initially a macho/power thing, slaves are created because a need exists for slaves—to serve as women-substitutes, for the expression and reinforcement of one's masculinity, for a sexual outlet, for income and/or service." They quote one fellow prisoner, Dunn, as explaining that "During my first week here, I saw 14 guys rape one youngster 'cause he refused to submit. . . . Man, I didn't want none of that kind of action, and my only protection was in sticking with my old man, the guy who raped me."
22. Notice how common this vicarious sense of participation in worldly events has become in contemporary society. We all derive much of our sense of political participation through identifying with the actions of those we view on the various screens of the electronic media. See my "Representing the Viewer," *Social Text* 27 (Spring, 1991).
23. See Orlando Patterson, *Slavery and Social Death* (Cambridge, Mass.: Harvard University Press, 1982), p. 4.
24. I borrow this felicitous phrase from Louis Althusser. See Louis Althusser and Etienne Balibar, *Reading Capital* (London: New Left Books, 1970).
25. Mary O'Brien, *The Politics of Reproduction* (Boston: Routledge and Kegan Paul, 1981).

26. See Alison Bass, "Domestic Violence: The Roots Go Deep," *Boston Globe*, June 5, 1992. According to the New York State Office for the Prevention of Domestic Violence, domestic violence was responsible for the deaths of three out of four women killed in the United States in 1991. See Diana Jean Schemo, "Amid the Gentility of the East End, A Town Confronts Domestic Abuse," *New York Times*, August 13, 1992.
27. Judith Kegan Gardiner, "Psychoanalysis and Feminism: An American Humanist's View," *Signs* (Winter 1992), pp. 438–39.
28. See Juliet Mitchell's *Psychoanalysis and Feminism* (New York: Vintage, 1975).
29. Laura Mulvey, "Visual Pleasure and Narrative Cinema," *Screen* 16, 3 (Autumn 1975).
30. See Ellie Ragland-Sullivan, *Jacques Lacan and the Philosophy of Psychoanalysis* (Urbana: University of Illinois Press, 1986). As Ragland-Sullivan says, "The sexual identity of both boys and girls is established in relation to the mother's attitudes toward the Phallus" (p. 294). It would thus seem that even if the worldly mother remains the primary early nurturer of the child, her new status in relationship to men and to society will impact directly upon her child's understanding of sexual identity.
31. Laura Mulvey, "Visual Pleasure and Narrative Cinema," *Screen* 16, 3 (Autumn 1975), p. 13.
32. Ibid., p. 14.
33. See Ann Barr Snitow, "Mass Market Romance: Pornography for Women Is Different," in *Powers of Desire.*
34. See the Milan Women's Bookstore Collective's *Sexual Difference: A Theory of Social-Symbolic Practice* (Bloomington: Indiana University Press, 1991), for a compelling argument for developing relations of recognition between women. Disillusioned after two decades of conventional feminist political struggle, these theorists argue for an anti-institutional political project that puts an "entrustment" relationship of symbolic exchange between women, and an articulation of female difference at its center.
35. Jacques Lacan, *Écrits*, trans. Alan Sheridan (New York: Norton, 1977), pp. 4, 11, 21. See also Ellie Ragland-Sullivan, *Jacques Lacan and the Philosophy of Psychoanalysis* (Urbana: University of Illinois Press, 1986), pp. 19–34, 40–41.
36. See Ellie Ragland-Sullivan, *Jacques Lacan*, p. 282. "Although there is no intrinsic gender meaning to this structural drama, it first becomes confused at a secondary, substantive level with gender, and later with sexual organs." See Lacan, *Seminaire XX*, p. 69. See also p. 292, where she cites Lacan as maintaining that sexual desire becomes part of the larger drama of Desire (*Seminaire XX*, p. 14).
37. See Jacques Lacan, "The Mirror Stage," in *Écrits*, trans. Alan Sheridan (New York: Norton, 1977), pp. 1–7.
38. See Ragland-Sullivan, *Jacques Lacan*, p. 55.
39. Lacan, *Écrits*, p. 198.
40. Ragland-Sullivan, *Jacques Lacan*, pp. 282, 298. See Lacan, *Seminaire XX*, p. 69.
41. Jacques Lacan, "The Subject and the Other: Alienation," in *Four Fundamental Concepts of Psycho-Analysis*, trans. Alan Sheridan (New York: Norton, 1981), p. 207.
42. Jacques Lacan, "A Love Letter," in *Feminine Sexuality*, ed. Juliet Mitchell and Jacqueline Rose (New York: Norton, 1985), pp. 151–52.
43. Jacques Lacan, "The Line and Light," in *The Four Fundamental Concepts*, pp. 95–96.
44. Lacan, *The Four Fundamental Concepts*, pp. 92, 99–101, 109.
45. Norman Bryson, *Vision and Painting: The Logic of the Gaze* (New Haven: Yale University Press, 1983), p. 156.

46. Bryson, *Vision and Painting*, p. 89.
47. We might be tempted by a notion of a feminist anticipatory gaze modeled on the anticipatory gazes of women within traditional sexual recognition relationships. Yet the wifely gaze creatively anticipating the social accomplishments of husbands operated under the sanction of the patriarchal sexual gaze. Having accepted patriarchal social orderings, women participated through recognizing husbands and sons in ways that empowered them to act on behalf of women as well as men. This anticipatory gaze of women was socially effective precisely insofar as it was subsumed under the patriarchal gaze. A feminist anticipatory gaze is a utopian idea so long as patriarchal social institutions prevail.
48. One possible response to this potentially tragic dimension of the feminist project is to accept the inability of patriarchal signifying systems to capture the experiences of women. There is a recent tradition of French feminists ("*écriture feminine*") who have insisted that instead of seeking to participate in masculine traditions of law and language, women must affirm feminine sexual difference, and attempt to write a new language of the feminine body. See Luce Irigaray, *This Sex Which Is Not One*, trans. Catherine Porter (Ithaca: Cornell University Press, 1985). See also Drucilla Cornell, *Beyond Accommodation* (New York: Routledge, 1991), for an attempt to meld a feminism of sexual difference with Jacques Derrida.

    The sexual metaphysics of such theorists are unpersuasive to me. The language I write in is a patriarchal language insofar as it assumes and perpetuates gendered oppositions and hierarchies—as does the society I live in. But it is nonetheless my language and my society, for all that. My relationship to language and society is different from that of men whom it privileges, yet it is not necessarily less serious than theirs. In fact, my engagement with language and society may be more intense than that of the men it privileges, insofar as I am compelled to attempt to alter it.

    The Milan Women's Bookstore Collective offers a more socially grounded and thereby more poignant version of the French feminist advocacy of a woman's language. Weary after several decades of activism, and persuaded that women today continue to enter society as "a losing sex," they propose "relationships of entrustment" between women, in which women articulate their respect and gratitude for other women. See their *Sexual Difference* (Bloomington: Indiana University Press, 1991).

    Surely such relationships are an important basis of psychic support for women in a patriarchal society. But they hardly take the place of what I deem to be the necessarily critical and constructive engagements of women today within the late-patriarchal discourses of theory and daily life.

The Family Romance: A Fin-de-Siècle Tragedy

In recovered memory, an adult woman who for many years has had no recollection of being sexually abused during her childhood recalls incidents of such abuse. Recent years have seen a marked rise in cases of recovered memory, and this phenomenon raises difficult questions about the reliability of memory after lengthy periods of amnesia. Meyers shifts the focus of debate away from questions about whether memories can be repressed and how to decide whether recovered memories are accurate. She examines the imagery of femininity and heterosexuality that psychoanalysis helped to bring into cultural currency, considers how this imagery shapes memory, and argues that feminists should regard this imagery as pernicious.

The Oedipus complex that Freud describes is commonly referred to as the family romance, for Freud believed that children fantasize incestuous relations with their parents, and that these fantasies are instrumental in the development of gender and heterosexuality. Meyers points out that the version of the family romance that is currently in circulation has taken a sadistic turn. Moreover, she urges that the family romance should be seen not as a childhood fantasy, but rather as a culturally furnished scenario that figures gender and heterosexuality and that may be literalized to yield autobiographical narratives of incestuous abuse. Although many memories of childhood sexual abuse are no more disputable than other types of childhood memory, some recovered memories are questionable, and there is no reliable way to determine whether the memories are veridical. In cases in which the past is epistemically opaque, Meyers urges that it is best to regard the family romance as a figuration of one's present psychic condition and to adopt an agnostic view of its depiction of one's past. She then turns to an assessment of the desirability of the cultural entrenchment of this figuration. Meyers contends that both from the standpoint of women who have doubts about their recovered memories and from the standpoint of women who have been sexually abused the cultural ubiquity of this imagery is harmful. Finally, she considers the impact of the incest scenario on feminist efforts to reclaim a multiplicitous self, and she concludes that feminists must refigure multiplicity in order to conceive a multiplicitous self that is tenable from a feminist point of view.

—D.T.M.

Chapter 24

Diana Tietjens Meyers

The Family Romance: A Fin-de-Siècle Tragedy

A century ago in the midst of the political, artistic, and intellectual foment of fin-de-siècle Vienna, Freud published "The Aetiology of Hysteria" (1896). This paper contains the shocking revelation that patients suffering from hysteria were sexually abused during childhood and the provocative explanatory hypothesis that the symptoms of hysteria are consequences of this abuse. Some scholars maintain that Freud never denied the high incidence of sexual abuse of children and was troubled by it throughout his life; others maintain that Freud's handling of this matter calls into question his personal and scientific integrity.[1] What is incontrovertible is that Freud soon repudiated the explanatory hypothesis put forward in "The Aetiology of Hysteria." In subsequent accounts of the genesis of neurosis, veridical recollections of early sexual abuse are replaced by recollections of incestuous childhood desires and fantasies of their consummation. Embellishing his initial account by interiorizing the substance of his patients' poignant testimony, Freud invented the elegant baroque conceit that became known as psychoanalysis.

On centennial, not to say millennial, cue, the issue of father-daughter incest has recently resurfaced with all the ferocity and vitriol that psychoanalysts associate with the return of the repressed. The revival of this dormant controversy has unsettled contemporary family life and injected a note of urgency into the by-and-large sluggish political, artistic, and intellectual climate of fin-de-siècle postindustrial society. Especially in the United States, large numbers of women are accusing their fathers[2] of sexually abusing them when they were young, and their supporters are engaged in pitched scholarly, media, and courtroom battles defending recovered memory against skeptics.

My aim in this paper is to propose a way of interpreting the phenomenon of recovered memory that moves beyond the prevailing "Did it happen, or didn't it?" construal of the debate. In Section 1, I critically examine four prominent views of recovered memory, and I argue that none strikes the right balance between the epistemic opacity of the past and the obligation to respect women who claim to remember childhood sexual abuse after a long period of amnesia. In Section 2, I turn to the role of culturally furnished figurations in autobiographical memory, and I consider how different versions of Freud's family romance are used to figure disparate adult outcomes for women—marriage and motherhood, on the one hand, and hysteria or multiple personality disorder, on the other. Focusing on the rhetoric of autobiographical memory in conjunction with the contribution of autobiographical memory to self-definition reorients the discussion of recovered memory. Instead of stubbornly trying to answer the often unanswerable question "Which of these two people is telling the truth?" we can ask which psychological conditions the trope of sadistic incest aptly figures and whether this figuration is necessary or fruitful. Section 3 argues that feminist therapists and scholars have reason to develop alternatives to the family romance. In Section 4, I explore some implications of my analysis with respect to a basic issue in feminist theory, namely, how to conceive the self. Some feminists have sought to reclaim women's experience of multiplicity and to defend the multiplicitous self. I urge, however, that using the trope of sadistic incest to figure multiplicity impedes this reclamation project. Both for purposes of psychotherapy and for purposes of feminist theory, it is time to displace the family romance and to replace it with tropes that support feminist emancipatory aims.

1. THE CONTROVERSY OVER RECOVERED MEMORY

That autobiographical reality is as much a matter of literary form as documentable content seems to be a truism among psychologists who study memory. Still, it does not follow that autobiographical reality is merely subjective. On the contrary, it is intersubjective in many and sundry ways. What does follow is that the personal past is not straightforwardly retrievable and also that the personal past is highly malleable. Of course, neither of these facts stops anyone from confidently representing her past—the minor details as well as the momentous crises and formative watersheds—to herself and others. This is by no means surprising, for however contestable, manipulable, and revisable memory may be, it anchors personal identity. The continuity of one's memory sequence sustains one's sense of ongoing individual existence, and one interprets one's experience and choices and ascribes meaning to one's life in part by invoking memories.

In this context, it is obvious why recovered memories of childhood sexual abuse are both explosive and problematic. Likewise, it is predictable that accounts of the standing of these reports would proliferate. There are three principal accounts currently in contention. Jeffrey Masson, Judith Herman, and Lenore Terr are prominent among those who credit the memories.[3] They believe that child victims commonly repress experience of trauma, especially repeated trauma, and although Herman cautions against injudiciously using hypnosis or drugs to extract memories of abuse, she joins Masson and Terr in holding that there should be a presumption that patients' memories are veridical reports of actual incidents. Taking sharp issue with this view, Frederick Crews debunks recovered memories as suggestions implanted in vulnerable and pliant women by irresponsible, perhaps nefarious, psychotherapists and authors of self-help books.[4]

Ian Hacking proposes a more complex view of recovered memory. He does not deny that some patients are accurately reporting specific abuses, nor that therapists and self-help books can induce susceptible individuals to believe they were abused. However, he observes that these alternatives do not account for all of the cases. According to Hacking, intentional action is indeterminate, for there are many correct ways to describe a single act.[5] Moreover, as new descriptions become available, people can redescribe and reexperience past events.[6] Consider, for example, a "less flagrant" form of abuse that gave a child a "shady feeling of sexual discomfort" at the time.[7] She may not forget her feelings of peril and intimidation even though she is not familiar with the concept of child abuse. If at a later time, she becomes acquainted with the concept of child abuse and the narrative possibilities this concept authorizes, she may fill in scenes that blame her distress on the other person's conduct.[8] Now she remembers being sexually abused as a child. Even conduct that was considered innocuous at the time can be interpreted in light of new concepts. Retroactively revising the past, such recasting accounts for additional cases of recovered memory.[9]

Plainly, it is a virtue of Hacking's view that it respects the testimony of women who are remembering childhood trauma. Yet, some will surely find his view promiscuously inclusive. His account of "semantic contagion" entails that there is almost no woman alive today who could not reasonably profess to having been sexually abused in childhood. That girls are victims of incest becomes a historically conditioned tautology. Yet, Hacking draws back from this conclusion. Insisting on preserving the distinction between true and false beliefs about one's past, he defends the value of lucid self-knowledge.[10]

The territory of memory is notoriously treacherous. Once we relinquish the untenable idea that remembering is like playing a tape one has recorded on an interior video camera (this is Hacking's simile), we are obliged to acknowledge that memory is full of holes. Moreover, it is often impossible to determine which features of an incident one registered at the time and which features one picked up in later conversations with other participants or from other reports. The miscellaneous materials of memory are cobbled into narratives that include selected materials while omitting others, and that could be framed and organized in indefinitely many ways.[11] Rehearsal helps to preserve memories. Yet, people relate their experiences in stories fashioned for particular audiences, and these retellings may erode memory.[12] It is amazingly easy to induce people to believe that they are remembering major events that never happened to them.[13] It is extremely difficult to persuade people that they are misremembering events if their recollections are vivid and detailed, form a coherent sequence, and maintain characterological consistency.[14] Dissolving the distinction between recalling an experience, on the one hand, and believing an experience took place or imagining that it did, on the other hand, is an ever-present danger. Although Hacking resists subjectivizing memory by appealing to shared, though contestable and modifiable, conventions of language use, it is not clear that he altogether avoids conflating these phenomena.

The obligation to show respect for rememberers and their recollections, coupled with the overwhelming evidence of the incompleteness, the variability, indeed, the downright unreliability of memory is confounding. This baffling conjunction of a compelling moral imperative with insuperable epistemic opacity may make Freud's psychoanalytic solution seem attractive. In his view, recovered memories are reports of repressed childhood fantasies of seduction, and these fantasies are constituents of psychic reality. Psychic reality is the unconscious inner world where wishing is indistinguishable from doing a certain act or being subjected to a certain treatment, and where the effects of wishing on personal well-being may be as profound as the effects of acting or undergoing. A girl's repressed fantasies of incest may lead to neurosis later in her life. Women who report childhood sexual abuse but whose parents and siblings adamantly and convincingly deny it are neither lying, nor are they altogether deluding themselves. They are reporting actual past experience of a riveting fantasy.

By positing psychic reality, Freud supplies real events for psychoanalytic interpretations to correspond to and a way out of the either-it-happened-or-it-didn't dilemma. Although psychoanalytic theory holds that the deliverances of memory require quite a bit of professional decoding, since they may conflate fantasies with interpersonal incidents, it upholds the veracity of psychoanalytic patients and the basic reliability of memory. Thus, Freud's fantasy-packed psychic reality secures the truthfulness of women suffering from hysteria or multiple personality disorder and vindicates a qualified affirmation of the veridicality of their memories. Concomitantly, it avoids besmirching the reputations of their fathers.

Recovered memory generates a triadic antinomy of memory and morals. By consigning recovered memories to psychic reality, Freud obtains a neat correspondence between his patients' recollections of sexual molestation and their childhood experience at the price of suppressing or, at least, sidelining the possibility that their father really raped or otherwise molested them. Moreover, he opens his clinical practices to the charge of suggestion, for psychic reality may be nothing more than a fabrication that the therapist persuades the impressionable patient to embrace. Masson, Herman, and Crews revert to a more commonsensical distinction between true and false memories, but at the cost of indiscriminately countenancing or dismissing recovered memories. Masson and Herman merely pay lip service to what they seem to regard as the remote possibility that a father accused of incest is innocent. However, unqualified support for recovered memory claims neglects a substantial body of empirical data demonstrating the mercurial workings of memory, and it scorns out of hand the testimony of anyone who denies the truth of these accusations. In contrast, Crews's impatience with women who report recovered memories of childhood sexual abuse and his contempt for therapists who ally themselves with these women are undisguised. Crews's apostate antipathy for psychoanalysis blinds him to the real possibility that the long-run psychological impact of incest may assume a number of different forms. Hacking proffers a subtle account of memory that is faithful to related social practices. Although Hacking distances himself from many women who allege that they were sexually abused, his account does not preclude solidarity with them. However, his account blurs the line between beliefs representing facts about the past and beliefs projecting present anxieties onto the past. Evidently, no account of memory and recovered memory is free of serious liabilities.

2. FIGURATIONS OF SEXUALITY AND THE FAMILY—THE CULTURAL CACHE

A second truism among psychologists who study autobiographical memory is that people generally rely on a cultural stock of figurations to recount their past. Literary and artistic originality are rare, and most people appropriate culturally furnished figurations. It would be a mistake, though, to think of recollection as a two-stage process in which one starts with a bit of raw memory material and then articulates it via selected figurations. Rather, the figurations guide and shape recollection from the start.[15] To some extent, people are captives of their culture's repertory of figurations. It takes a conscious effort to become aware of and to criticize ubiquitous figurations, especially those that are integral to a cultural worldview, and it takes a great deal of assiduous self-monitoring to begin to extricate one's thinking from these figurations. To understand recovered memory, then, we must consider what culturally entrenched figurations are fueling this phenomenon.

Figurations of gender, sexuality, and family relations are multifarious, pervasive, and captivating.[16] Among the most potent of these figurations is Freud's family romance. According to Freud, the Oedipus complex and its resolution explain the emergence of normal gender, that is, heterosexuality with the aim of procreation. For a girl, the Oedipus complex commences when she discovers that she lacks a penis, a deprivation which she takes for castration.[17] Angry with her mother for not endowing her with this supremely valuable organ, and repelled by her mother who is castrated too, the girl falls in love with her father. Not only does her father have a penis, but also he can give her a penis substitute in the form of a baby. Eventually, the girl will detach her affection from her father and transfer it to a male peer, whom she will marry and have children with. Having made this transition, she achieves "femininity," and the curtain rings down.

But, of course, the family romance is a drama that is never out of production. The culmination of psychic development, the Oedipus complex is reenacted in every generation of every family with mother, father, and daughter or son as conscripted dramatis personae. Its plot embodies the meaning of the family as a site of procreative heterosexuality and as a transmitter of procreative heterosexuality. Its continuous run ceaselessly reaffirms that meaning.[18] Incest is, then, the reigning metaphor of the heterosexual mother (or father).

Although Freud regards the family romance as a childhood fantasy that becomes a prime component of psychic reality, I have classified it as a figuration. Here, I follow Elizabeth Abel, who likens psychoanalysis to fairy tales.[19] Both genres situate prototypical characters in memorable stories that interpret experience and guide conduct, and both are widely disseminated. In this view, we can understand the power of the family romance without becoming embroiled in sterile controversy over infantile sexuality and the fantasies it may or may not kindle. As long as this image of family relations is a cultural staple that is imparted to each new generation, it will be constitutive of the cognitive and emotional substrate of perception and memory, including self-perception and autobiographical memory.

In a discussion of Freud's theory of original fantasies, Jean Laplanche and J.B. Pontalis characterize these fantasies in a way that also illuminates the view I am proposing. Laplanche and Pontalis claim that original fantasies take the form of skeletal, impersonal, present-tense scenarios, and they urge that this form facilitates psychological assimilation of these fantasies.[20] The daughter's version of the family romance might be schematized as follows: A daughter falls in love with a father, and she becomes a wife and a mother. This deceptively simple scenario resonates with the solemn grandeur of ancient Greek mythic tragedy, with the fatuous yet needling taunt of Freud's more recent portrayal of women's anatomical deficit and characterological shortcomings, and with the unnerving cacophony of current news exposés of epidemic child abuse. Consolidating all of these cultural currents in a single emblematic narrative, the family romance is so culturally and psychically entrenched that it seems impervious to critique and virtually impossible to dislodge. The trope of father-daughter incest structures our conception of womanhood and hence our beliefs, expectations, and feelings about women.

Still, the family romance is not our sole source of imagery for gender and sexuality. Indeed, the family romance derives some of its power from its parasitic tie-in to other figurations in a vast cultural cache. Here I shall only adumbrate the dimensions of this cache by mentioning a few well-known images that are plainly relevant to recovered memory. Male heterosexuality is commonly personified as a predatory and voracious hunter or beast.[21] Correlatively, women are commonly figured as sexual targets or prey, although they may also be figured as lascivious whores bent on leading upright men astray.[22] Eroticized images of prepubescent girls often depict these minors as seductive gamines or waifs.[23] The oscillation between figurations representing women and girls as innocent and ones representing them as depraved, and between figurations representing men as violent and ones representing them as honorable, sets the stage for what we might think of as unauthorized productions of the family romance.

I have considered the scenario for happy wives and fulfilled mothers. But what about other women? Freud supplied a number of plots with different denouements—including the lesbian, the female professional, and the hysteric. How is the hysteric, the precursor of the multiple, portrayed? Here is a synopsis of Freud's nineteenth-century staging of the family romance with that plot twist interpolated: A father seduces a daughter, and she represses this shameful experience and develops hysteria. And the twentieth-century update of this tragic scenario: A father forces sex upon a daughter, and she dissociates and develops multiple personality disorder. A rather whimsical tenor offsets the sordidness of the fin-de-siècle Viennese figuration of hysteria—a father romancing a daughter.[24] In the United States today, however, the figuration of multiple personality disorder, which presages recovered memory, is obscene and stark—a father savagely violating and wantonly exploiting a daughter. Unambiguous sadism supplants ambiguous romance.

3. FIGURING ONE'S LIFE

In many cases, memories of childhood sexual abuse raise no more doubt than any other memory. Either the individual has always remembered these assaults (I mean, the memories have never been less retrievable than other memories), or credible corroboration of a recovered memory is forthcoming.[25] However, there are also many bewildering cases in which a recovered memory is met with resolute denial. The woman making the allegations is sincere and deeply wounded, while the man denying the charges is honest and loving. If there is no reason to believe that the woman has fallen into the clutches of an overzealous therapist, and if there is no feasible way to obtain relevant evidence about the past, it is impossible to decide between the irreconcilably opposed positions. These impasses that pit the obligation to respect persons in the present against the epistemic opacity of the past are best approached by placing autobiographical rhetoric in the context of the functions of autobiographical memory.

Memory can resemble a radio announcer's blow-by-blow description of a sporting event: I said, ". . . ;" you said, ". . . ;" I said, ". . . ;" and so on. Sometimes this sort of bare word-for-word recall is precisely what is needed—say, to settle a dispute about the terms of an agreement. But obviously this kind of account leaves out important facts about how one perceived the interaction at the time. Thus, memory often introduces elements of manner and subjectivity: I said, ". . . ;" you acidly joked, ". . . ;" I blanched and retorted, ". . . ;" and so on. This sort of recollection might be germane, for example, to a determination of provocation. Such memory is informationally packed and motivationally intelligible. But except in the immediate aftermath of an incident (and not always then), people are seldom able to recall such minute detail. They are left with summaries: We fought bitterly over such-and-such, or, maybe just, we quarreled. Thin though these memories may seem by comparison, they suffice for many purposes, such as explaining the awkwardness of an encounter or seeing the need to initiate a rapprochement. Not only is the content of memories of particular actions, responses, or exchanges restricted by the limits of human retentive and retrieval capacities, but it is also edited and re-edited depending on how the memory is being used to conduct social relationships or to make sense of one's life.

The case of life stories is parallel. People remember their lives by telling stories that excerpt key episodes and string these episodes together according to themes, such as traits of character, values, aims, norms, exigencies, and so forth. These stories are varied to suit different audiences and different purposes. A politician would hardly tell the same life story to her lesbian partner, to the voters, and to her five-year-old grandchild. Moreover, these narratives can be distilled and condensed. One's story of one's scientific quest might be captured in an image of oneself as an astronaut, or one's story of one's erotic escapades might be captured in an image of oneself as a Don Juan. When autobiographical narratives are encoded in self-figurations, memory's contribution to self-definition becomes salient.

Self-definition pursues the intrinsic value of self-knowledge along with the instrumental value of figuring out how to lead as rewarding a life as one can. Sometimes, one takes a retrospective view and searches one's past in order to better understand oneself and anticipate one's future prospects.[26] In the process of self-definition, the distinction between memory and self-description can dissolve, for self-figuration easily elides the present and the past. In summing up one's life in a trope, one simultaneously represents one's past experience and one's present condition. This may seem unexceptionable, since most people believe that they are largely, if not wholly, products of their past experience. However, the trope of summing up misleadingly suggests that memory works by digesting a superfluity of detail and extracting a figuration. Remembered experience constrains autobiographical figuration, but the relation between remembered experience and figuration is not unidirectional. As we have seen, people seldom derive narrative forms and figurations from their experience. They typically adopt ready-made plot templates and tropes of life trajectories or personality types, and they remember their experience as these culturally furnished literary devices ordain. Thus, a self-definitional trope one embraces in the present is constitutive of one's recollected past—it provides thematic threads for life stories; it highlights certain incidents and obscures others; it prompts one to impute certain attitudes and intentions to oneself and others and to dismiss other interpretations as implausible.[27] The past inherits the present.

Still, figurative self-definition can seem paradoxical, for a figuration can aptly symbolize one's present and can provide an advantageous springboard into the future without accurately representing one's past. A timid scientist whose research has been rather pedestrian might accent an emerging self-confidence and perhaps improve her chances of doing more innovative work in the future by figuring herself as an adventurous explorer. But because people generally believe that the past determines the present, and because they see memory as a guarantor of personal identity, they are disposed to see continuity between their past and their present. This disposition poses a danger that self-figuration will lead people to falsify the past. The danger becomes acute when an apt figuration of oneself in the present has not been derived from one's past and has instead been appropriated from a cultural cache. The trope of the adventurous explorer may color the scientist's memory in rosy hues. Downplaying the disappointing results of her research program while underscoring the boldness of the (indefensible) hypothesis she proposed, she may remember her professional persona as less mousy and more forceful. Slightly exaggerating the extent to which her present self-confidence is latent in the past may be harmless. But if her self-figuration persuades her to remember the lackluster work she has done as a trove of momentous discoveries and to convert decisive refutations of her work into plaudits, her memories of her professional accomplishments run squarely afoul of the facts. She is falsifying the past and deceiving herself.

Trouble arises when people misapprehend and misuse the rhetoric of self-definition. They may mistake figurations for literal truths, and they may proceed to literalize these images by filling in mundane details that personalize them and expand them into autobiographical narratives.[28] Whereas self-figuration is a way of answering the question, "What does it mean to be this way—to have these needs, to lack these skills, to experience these feelings, etc.?" literalization transmutes a self-figuration into an answer to the question, "What caused me to be this way?" Since memory plays a pivotal role in self-definition, and since self-figuration structures memory, keeping these questions disentangled is no mean task.

The temptation to literalize self-figurative discourse is almost irresistible when the figurations are images of childhood scenes. Indeed, it seems that Freud surrendered to this siren call. His theory of psychic reality is a sophisticated compromise between the therapeutic value of figurative discourse and the allure of literal discourse. According to Freud, a girl's infantile desire latches onto an iconic tableau—a father seducing a daughter. By individualizing the features of the daughter and the father to match her own and those of her father, and by locating the action in a familiar setting, the girl spins a personalized fantasy of incest that will prove devilishly difficult to distinguish from a childhood incestuous assault. In contrast, Julia Kristeva trenchantly characterizes psychoanalysis as "a scene of metaphor production."[29] Psychoanalytic interpretations are animated mainly by imagination, and their primary medium is figurative language.[30] For Kristeva, memory is incidental to the talking cure, and nothing is gained by recasting self-figurations as life stories.

Plainly, feminists cannot endorse a conception of self-definition or a psychotherapeutic method that altogether excludes memory. Such an approach would distract women from identifying the social causes of their suffering and induce them to personalize the political. Whether a woman's problems stem from discrimination at work or from childhood sexual abuse, curtailing unfair or persecutorial practices presupposes recognizing them, and recognizing them presupposes remembering being harmed by them. If victims of wrongful practices turn inward and figure their selves in an upbeat way that enables them to feel better instead of tracing their suffering to its source, they will never challenge oppressive institutions or call malign individuals to account. Feminist analysis and activism cannot dispense with memory.

Still, it is not always possible to trace one's problems to their cause(s). The aetiologies of many of one's traits, desires, feelings, and the like are sketchy and speculative at best. In many cases of recovered memory, there is no way to reach a well-supported judgment about the accuracy of one's memories. In such cases, I believe, the best course is to regard the sadistic incest scenario as a figurative window onto one's present and to remain agnostic about its relation to one's past. Where the past is epistemically opaque, self-definition must be insulated from memory.

Psychic states that a sadistic incest scenario could aptly figure readily come to mind. They include feeling damaged where one is most vulnerable and least mendable; suffering from persistent, unsoothable anxiety; living in fear of spontaneity that might reveal one's terrible deficiencies; and feeling aggrieved by a vague, unrectifiable wrong. All of these complaints are amenable to this figuration, and, to judge by my experience, all of them are appallingly widespread among contemporary women. If it is true that people tend to adopt culturally furnished figurations and elaborate these figurations into autobiographical narratives, it is understandable that some fathers are perplexed and injured by their daughters' allegations of sexual abuse. Likewise, it is understandable that many of the women making these charges are unshakable in their conviction that they were sexually assaulted. After all, the sadistic incest scenario does aptly figure their present psychic condition, and the narrative analogue of figurative aptness is factual accuracy. Moreover, since shifting from the self-definitional figurative mode to the autobiographical narrative mode produces closure and relieves the terrible anguish attendant upon agnosticism about childhood trauma, the benefits of believing in a literalized sadistic incest scenario may overpower an individual's qualms about its credibility. Nevertheless, I would submit that gaining a subtle and complex understanding of the meaning of one's psychic make-up is both emotionally satisfying and helpful in bringing about felicific change.[31] When identifying the causal antecedents of one's suffering is not possible, figuring one's life is the key to figuring out one's life.

4. THE FAMILY ROMANCE AND FEMINIST POLITICS—CULTURAL CRITIQUE AND SOCIAL CHANGE

Apart from the light the sadistic incest scenario may or may not shed on a particular individual's past, there are several perspectives from which feminists must evaluate this trope. One is the prospective aim of self-definition. It is necessary to ask not only whether a self-figuration aptly symbolizes one's present condition but also whether it is conducive to a more rewarding life. Does the sadistic incest scenario now in currency help women to overcome constraints and to lead satisfying lives, or, like its predecessor, the trope of castration and penis envy, does it stifle women's potential and divert them into a cramped, subordinate social niche? Since the clinical evidence that is now available is spotty and contradictory, it would be premature to hazard an answer to these questions.

From another angle, however, assessing the merits of the sadistic incest scenario need not await well-wrought, longitudinal studies. I have furnished no protocol for distinguishing literalized self-figurations from ordinary autobiographical narratives in controversial cases, nor, as my recommendation for agnosticism implies, do I expect one to materialize. Certainly, an apparently honest and loving father's vigorous protestations of innocence do not suffice to identify literalized self-figurations. Those who are principally concerned with issues of legal and moral responsibility for child abuse might consider this lacuna fatal to my account. However, I would argue that on the contrary my account has the virtue of pinpointing the menace of the family romance while at the same time showing why this menace need not be tolerated. What is most deplorable about the sadistic incest scenario is the grave disservice it does to women who are not entirely certain about their memories of abuse and to incest victims, both those who are certain about their abuse and those who are not.

For women who have recovered memories of incest but who also have reason to question whether these memories are accurate, the cultural circulation of this trope together with its widespread use to figure various sorts of dissatisfaction, frustration, and dislocation virtually guarantees that their doubts will never be satisfactorily resolved. Since nothing internal to these memories distinguishes them from literalizations of self-figurations, many of these individuals are doomed to a tormenting state of autobiographical limbo. However, if this trope were taken out of circulation, there would be no more reason to doubt memories of childhood sexual abuse than there is to doubt memories of affectionate paternal nurturance. Thus, the pruning of the figurative repertory that I am proposing would redound to the benefit of women in psychotherapy and their therapists. They would have less difficulty determining whether the problem needing treatment was childhood incest, and better diagnosis would presumably speed recovery. For the sake of women who are confused and distraught by recovered memories, then, I would urge feminists to repudiate the family romance.

In addition and even more sobering, the ubiquity of the sadistic incest scenario impeaches the testimony of individuals whose fathers have sexually assaulted them. The fact that it is always possible that a woman has seized upon this figuration and literalized it provides a ready and credible defense for the most scurrilous fathers. To countenance the cultural prevalence of this figuration is to perpetuate a major obstacle to prosecuting real villains. Since other figurations could be devised to represent the miseries and sorrows that the sadistic incest scenario is presently being used to represent, feminists have every reason to oppose it and to champion alternative figurations. For the sake of the untold numbers of real incest victims, then, I would urge feminist therapists and theorists to marshall their critical powers to dispose of the family romance once and for all and to dedicate their imaginative powers to crafting counterfigurations that better serve the interests of women.[32]

Nothing I have said blunts feminist critiques of gender and the family that take aim at child abuse in the home, nor does my view of recovered memory stymie feminist initiatives that seek to reform the criminal law in ways that make it more likely that child abusers will be convicted and punished. It is indisputable that incestuous child abuse is sufficiently prevalent to justify concerted feminist opposition. Moreover, since displacing the family romance would create a cultural climate in which victims' claims would be less suspect, my view complements these other feminist approaches. Once the family romance and its pathological variants have been retired from repertory, there will cease to be any respectable excuse for distrusting women who accuse their fathers of sexually abusing them.

5. THE FAMILY ROMANCE AND FEMINIST RECLAMATION—OBSTACLES AND PROSPECTS

I would like to conclude by reflecting on the implications of the foregoing view of recovered memory for the larger project of feminist theory. Reclaiming women's experience has been an important dimension of this project. So far, it seems to me that feminists have had their greatest success in reclaiming women's experience of motherhood. Lately, however, feminist reclamation efforts have moved in an intriguing new direction, namely, women's experience of multiplicity. I would like to offer some observations regarding the impact of the figurations I have been discussing on this undertaking. Before I do, however, let me stress that my conjectures should not be blown out of proportion. I am not claiming that culturally entrenched figurations of multiplicity exhaust the obstacles impeding feminist reclamation, but I do think these figurations are obstacles that should not be underestimated.

To put the view I want to advance in context, it is worth briefly reviewing the history of the feminist bid to reclaim motherhood. Central to the overall critique developed at the beginning of second-wave feminism was a critique of motherhood. The economic disadvantages were documented; the missed opportunities for personal fulfillment were chronicled; the undercurrent of social contempt for motherhood was exposed. This critique alienated many women who already were mothers or who wanted to become mothers. Yet, it is indisputable that it fastened on real and serious problems. Subsequently, feminists sought to address the needs of mothers and to increase their options by demanding concrete changes like family leave, affordable, high-quality daycare, flex-time work schedules, and so forth. A change in feminist rhetoric accompanied these policy demands—a change that was not limited to toning down the critique. More significantly, motherhood was reconceived and revalued partly through feminist counterfigurations.

Freud's family romance looks like it has a happy ending—girls grow up to be mothers. But if maternity means pursuing a penis equivalent to compensate for an irremediable anatomical lack, maternity can hardly be cause for feminist rejoicing. For motherhood to be reclaimed, it must be refigured in ways that express auspicious meanings, like gladly bestowing life on and/or caring for a precious child. To the extent that Freud's family romance clings to the activity of mothering, motherhood eludes feminist reclamation. That, I would venture, explains why so many psychoanalytic feminists have devoted so much attention to creating counterfigurations of motherhood.[33] They are seeking to displace established figurations of maternity that distort its meaning and belittle the contributions of mothers. They are seeking to figure maternity in a way that is conducive to women's emancipatory aims.

Turning now to the project of reclaiming multiplicity, I think it is possible to discern a similar pattern. No feminist account of the self would be complete without an account of oppositional agency and, specifically, an account of how feminist critique can emerge and how feminist initiatives can be mounted. Many feminist theorists have pointed out that a complex, nontransparent self is needed to undergird an account of feminist agency. A number of feminists who are sympathetic to postmodernism have proposed to understand the complex, nontransparent self as a multiplicitous or plural self.

María Lugones's influential work illustrates the turn to multiplicity. Lugones maintains that she is constructed differently in different social worlds—in the Anglo world, she is serious; in the Latino world, she is playful.[34] For Lugones, this is not a case of being a playful person who is inhibited in some social milieux but not in others.[35] Rather, she insists that she is a different person in each social context (albeit a person who remembers what it is like to be the other person), and she concludes that she is a multiplicitous self.[36]

What is at stake in this line of thought becomes clear in an important paper by Naomi Scheman. After explicating the evils consequent upon fetishizing a unified self, Scheman embraces the multiplicitous self.[37] But plainly a multiplicitous self is in danger of succumbing to terrifying and paralyzing fragmentation. Scheman concedes this liability: "The most striking and clear-cut cases of internal multiplicity are cases of multiple personality, a pathological condition typically caused by severe childhood abuse."[38] Multiple personality is a defense against devastating child abuse, often including incestuous sexual assault. By creating a "bad" alter who deserves the brutality heaped upon her, a child can rationalize her suffering and avoid condemning an adult whom she needs to trust and whose love she needs.[39] Her need to protect herself from knowledge of the vicious harm she has endured may eventually bring about a proliferation of alters, that is, multiple personality disorder.

For women, the multiplicitous self is associatively linked to multiple personality disorder and incestuous childhood sexual assault. In other words, a dysfunctional condition brought on by unforgivable parental behavior figures multiplicity. It is no wonder, then, that the road to reclaiming multiplicity has proven nearly impassable—it is booby-trapped. No one wants to embrace pathology and victimization, and there is an alternative course that is by no means unattractive. Arguably, working to eradicate child abuse—to reform family relations and create a family environment in which dissociation would not be psychologically necessary—makes more sense than identifying with multiplicity. More tellingly, feminists cannot maintain that culturally entrenched figurations of gender generally have a profound effect on thought and yet theorize as if they were exempt from this pernicious influence. Accordingly, there is reason for feminists to proceed cautiously in conceptualizing multiplicity, since the trope of incest-driven alter formation is presumably shaping this theorizing.

Incest is a shattering experience that often leads to a shattered condition. As Scheman points out, therapists seek to repair this damage by persuading different alters to communicate with one another and to agree to some cooperative arrangements.[40] Unfortunately, the alters of multiple personality disorder are a fractious throng, and they mightily resist collaboration.

Now, this description of multiple personality disorder is strikingly reminiscent of some well-known philosophical accounts of the state of nature, and it brings to mind feminist critiques of social contract theory. Feminists have argued that the contractarian conception of the individual as an independent, self-interested atom denies interdependency and the need for care, and also that modeling justice on a bargain reached by wary rivals yields an impoverished vision of social relations.[41] Feminists must reject conceptions of the self that repeat the mistakes they have diagnosed in social contract theory. Conceiving the self as an internal population of self-interested, mutually competitive, unitary individuals would be counterproductive as a foundation for an account of feminist agency. Feminist values and demands cannot be construed as those that no internal self would veto. Since living in a society structured by male dominance ensures that most women have internalized traditional feminine norms, most women have an internal self that will refuse to endorse emancipatory values and demands. Women may have other internal selves that support feminist aims, but these selves need not prevail in the negotiation process.

I am not arguing for jettisoning the multiplicitous self.[42] Nor am I accusing Scheman of lapsing into theorizing the self as an internal population of possessive individualists. Indeed, her text guards against this very trap by tendering a diverse array of figurations of multiplicity.[43] This leads me to believe that Scheman would agree that feminists need to vigilantly resist some of the implications of figuratively linking multiplicity to multiple personality disorder.[44]

My point is that reclamation requires reconception, as well as revaluation. Reconceiving the multiplicitous self requires figuring it in a more felicitous way, for multiplicity will remain in the grip of the picture of an internal mob of warring alters and the connotations of pathology and victimization that this picture conjures up unless it is refigured. It would be naive to suppose that the figurative connection between multiplicity and incest in Anglo-European culture can be severed by counterfigurative fiat,[45] and it would also be a betrayal of women who have been subjected to unspeakable abuse to try to suppress this figurative history. Nevertheless, it would be self-defeating to let multiplicity be absorbed by the trope of incest.

Happily, the counterfiguration project I am advocating is already underway. As I mentioned a moment ago, Scheman cites African, African-American, Latino, and lesbian figurations of multiplicity. I would also like to commend Ruth Leys's psychoanalytic counterfiguration to readers' attention. Ironically dubbing multiplicity "the scandal of dedifferentiation," Leys refigures multiplicity as primordial mimetic identification with the mother.[46] Since I do not have space to explore these counterfigurations here, I must confine myself to urging feminists to build on this groundbreaking counterfigurative work. Thus, I close by opening another inquiry—an inquiry that I believe holds promise for preventing this fin-de-siècle from turning into a dead end for feminism.[47]

NOTES

1. For defense of Freud, see Jean Laplanche and J.-B. Pontalis, "Fantasy and the Origins of Sexuality," *The International Journal of Psychoanalysis* 49 (1968): 1–18 at 6; and Teresa Brennan, *The Interpretation of the Flesh* (New York: Routledge, 1992), p. 29. For criticism of Freud, see Jeffrey Moussaieff Masson, *The Assault on Truth: Freud's Suppression of the Seduction Theory* (New York: Harper Collins, 1992), p. xxxiii and throughout; Judith Lewis Herman, *Trauma and Recovery* (New York: Basic Books, 1992), pp. 13–14.
2. These allegations are not exclusively against biological fathers. Stepfathers, cohabiting male partners, visiting boyfriends, and male relatives are often charged with sexual abuse of girls, as well. However, for the sake of parsimony, I shall use "father" to refer to all of these possible culprits.
3. Masson, *Assault on Truth*; Herman, *Trauma and Recovery*; Lenore Terr, *Unchained Memories: True Stores of Traumatic Memories, Lost and Found* (New York: Basic Books, 1994).
4. Frederick Crews, "The Revenge of the Repressed," *New York Review of Books* 41, no. 19 (1994): 54–60 and 41, no. 20 (1994): 49–58.
5. Ian Hacking, *Rewriting the Soul: Multiple Personality and the Sciences of Memory* (Princeton: Princeton University Press, 1995), p. 235.
6. Ibid., p. 241.
7. Ibid., p. 247.
8. Ibid., p. 256.
9. Ibid., p. 249.
10. Ibid., pp. 258–67.
11. Jerome Bruner, "The 'Remembered' Self," in *The Remembering Self: Construction and Accuracy in the Self-narrative*, ed. Ulric Neisser and Robyn Fivush (New York: Cambridge University Press, 1994), p. 53.
12. Elizabeth F. Loftus and Leah Kaufman, "Why Do Traumatic Experiences Sometimes Produce Good Memory (Flashbulbs) and Sometimes No Memory (Repression)?" in *Affect and Accuracy in Recall*, ed. Eugene E. Winograd and Ulric Neisser (New York: Cambridge University Press, 1992), pp. 215–16, 219.
13. Elizabeth F. Loftus, "The Reality of Repressed Memories," *American Psychologist* 48, no. 5 (1993): 518–37 at 532–33.
14. Michael Ross and Roger Buehler, "Creative Remembering," in *The Remembering Self: Construction and Accuracy in the Self-narrative,* ed Ulric Neisser and Robyn Fivush (New York: Cambridge University Press, 1994), pp. 227–229.
15. For discussion of the role of figurations in structuring thought and feeling, see Helen Haste, *The Sexual Metaphor* (Cambridge: Harvard University Press, 1994), pp. 36–47.
16. See Haste, *The Sexual Metaphor*; Sander L. Gilman, *Difference and Pathology: Stereotypes of Sexuality, Race, and Madness* (Ithaca: Cornell University Press, 1985); Eva Feder Kittay, "Woman as Metaphor," reprinted here, chap. 14; Phyllis Rooney, "Gendered Reason: Sex, Metaphor, and

Conceptions of Reason." *Hypatia* 6, no. 2 (1991): 77–103; Genevieve Lloyd, "Maleness, Metaphor, and the 'Crisis' of Reason," reprinted here, chap. 15; Diana Tietjens Meyers, *Subjection and Subjectivity: Psychoanalytic Feminism and Moral Philosophy* (New York: Routledge, 1994).

17. Since it is not relevant to recovered memory, I shall leave aside the boy's Oedipus complex.
18. For discussion of the inextricability of the Oedipus complex from the meaning of the institution of the family, see Kaja Silverman, *Male Subjectivity at the Margins* (New York: Routledge, 1992), pp. 35–51.
19. Elizabeth Abel, "Race, Class, and Psychoanalysis? Opening Questions," reprinted here, ch. 10
20. Laplanche and Pontalis, "Fantasy and the Origins of Sexuality," pp. 13–14.
21. Wendy W. Williams, "The Equality Crisis: Some Reflections on Culture, Courts, and Feminism," in *Feminist Legal Theory*, ed. Katharine T. Bartlett and Rosanne Kennedy (Boulder, Col.: Westview Press, 1991), p. 20; Patricia S. Mann, *Micro-Politics: Agency in a Postfeminist Era* (Minneapolis, Minn.: University of Minnesota Press, 1994), pp. 29–30.
22. Haste, *The Sexual Metaphor*, pp. 172–73; Catharine MacKinnon, "Feminism, Marxism, Method and the State: An Agenda for Theory," reprinted here, ch. 4; Sandra Lee Bartky, *Femininity and Domination* (New York: Routledge, 1990), pp. 73–74.
23. In addition to child pornography, see the photographs of Charles Dodgson and the paintings of Balthus. For a discussion of nineteenth-century literary treatments of this theme, see Sander L. Gilman, *Difference and Pathology: Stereotypes of Sexuality, Race, and Madness.* (Ithaca: Cornell University Press, 1985), pp. 39–58.
24. I find it an interesting sidelight that Freud also figures the mother as a child molester—in the course of routine bathing and dressing, the mother stimulates her baby's genitals and sexually arouses it. However, the image of the mother/seductress has never caught on. Perhaps, these two roles are too much at odds to fuse. As long as a sexualized childhood is seen as unhealthy and perverse, at least one parent's chaste relations to children must be preserved if anyone is to remain indisputably competent and reliable as a caregiver for children. If women's credentials as benign caregivers were figuratively compromised, who could be trusted to do this work? This suggests a second source of resistance to this image, namely, that it is highly threatening to the sexual division of labor. If women were figured as untrustworthy with small children, how could their continued subordination as designated unpaid caregivers be rationalized? There is too much at stake socially and politically for womanhood to be figured as a sexually aggressive mother.
25. The hyperprivacy in which sexuality is shrouded in many cultures complicates matters. Not only are there usually no nonparticipating witnesses to sex acts, but also we don't usually talk about our sexual experience. To the extent that memory depends on rehearsal then, sex memory is weak. In this connection, it is interesting that the typical abuser's efforts to create a conspiracy of silence around the incestuous acts may counteract the frailty of sex memory. In order to secure the child's silence, the abuser reminds the child not to tell. Thus, abusers may speak of incest more than people usually speak of sex, and, if so, memories of incest may be strengthened.
26. Near the end of her recounting of a Parisian concierge's autobiographical history of modern France, Bonnie G. Smith comments, "It now became clear that during the past few weeks Mme Lucie had reached the end of memory. In the depths of old age, present and future prospects had disappeared from her perspective on life, so she lost sight of the past" (*Confessions of a Concierge* [New Haven: Yale University Press, 1985], p. 150).
27. Notice, by the way, that if cultures are thought to be implanting suggestions by purveying figurations, hardly any perception or memory will be uncontaminated by suggestion. On this sweep-

ing view of the scope of suggestion, the charge of suggestion that is pivotal to Crews's critique of recovered memory would lose all force.

28. I want to distinguish this claim from Hacking's account of memories constituted through semantic contagion (*Rewriting the Soul*, pp. 238, 257). As Hacking points out, once people have categorized their experience (say, as child abuse), they may proceed to fill in their memory of this experience with category-appropriate events (say, incidents of sexual molestation). If I understand Hacking correctly, his view is that semantic contagion is part of the phenomenon of veridical memory formation. Whether a memory derived from semantic contagion is veridical or not depends on the memory practices that are in force in a particular culture at a particular time, and these practices are shaped by memoro-politics.

    I agree that literalizing a self-figuration could yield a veridical memory. Memory is cued in many different, sometimes mysterious ways, and there is no reason to deny that self-figuration can prompt veridical memories. But contrary to Hacking's view, I am suggesting that literalizing figurations often confuses backward-looking memory with forward-looking self-direction and also that, although memoro-politics may determine what people count as a veridical memory, it does not determine what is a veridical memory. Suppose that a scenario of being subjected to clitoridectomy in childhood gained currency as a trope expressing certain psychic scars. It seems unlikely that there would be any temptation to literalize this figuration, but if there were, it is obvious that no memory practice could by itself transform a literalization of this trope into a veridical memory. Only a woman's discovery that her clitoris had been surgically removed (without her knowing it at the time or despite her having forgotten it in the meantime) could certify the accuracy of the memory. Why, then, suppose that whether a memory that liberalizes a figuration of an event for which there is no lasting physical evidence is veridical or not depends entirely on memory practices shaped by memoro-politics? When Hacking affirms that he regards truth and factuality as basic and unproblematic (*Rewriting the Soul*, p. 250), he seems sympathetic to this line of thought, for in these passages he seems to be denying that memory reduces to a circumlocutious discourse of prospective self-definition. Yet, his predominant concern with the malleability of memory practices and the power of these practices to authenticate people's recollections seems to belie his sympathy.

    It is clear, however, that Elizabeth Loftus and Katherine Ketcham share my concern with distinguishing between discourses of autobiographical memory and discourses of self-definition (*The Myth of Repressed Memory* [New York: St. Martin's Press, 1994], pp. 265–67). I strongly object to the tone of relentless skepticism about recovered memory that pervades their book, and I do not endorse their suggestion that psychotherapy abandon its concern with autobiographical memory—if a patient has suffered childhood trauma, remembering it may be crucial to her recovery. Nevertheless, I think it is important to recognize that the incest scenario can be appropriated as a self-figuration and that the aptness of this figuration does not depend on the individual's having been sexually assaulted in childhood.

29. Julia Kristeva, *Tales of Love*, trans. Leon S. Roudiez (New York: Columbia University Press, 1987), p. 276.

30. Jerome Bruner remarks, "If the Self is a remembered self, the remembering reaches far back beyond our own birth, back to the cultural and language forms that specify the defining properties of a Self" ("The 'Remembered' Self," p. 53). This observation is instructive with respect to the drift I have noted from self-figuration to autobiographical narrative. If a key feature of the self is its temporal continuity, self-definition cannot rest with self-figuration, for self-figuration is atemporal and leaves out the sequences of episodes that endow the self with continuity through time.

Thus, the self-definitional discourse of "metaphorization" that Kristeva advocates will be liable to deteriorate into the discourse of autobiographical narrative unless adjustments are made in our conception of the self. Kristeva is right, then, to couple her enthusiasm for self-definition through self-figuration with a call for a nonunitary, destabilized conception of the self.

31. For discussion of psychoanalysis' harnessing of the transformative power of metaphor, see Kristeva, *Tales of Love*, pp. 13–16; also see, Marcia Cavell, *The Psychoanalytic Mind: From Freud to Philosophy* (Cambridge: Harvard University Press, 1993), pp. 96–97.
32. My critique of the family romance raises interesting questions about the history of this trope in Western culture. It is possible that Freud and his followers did women an unintended service by bringing this trope into cultural currency, for its presence in the figurative repertory may have been instrumental in enabling many women to remember and testify to childhood incest. Thus, this trope may have helped to gain attention for this heretofore well-concealed harm. Whether or not this is so, I am convinced that this stock figuration has now become counterproductive from the standpoint of women's interests.
33. See, for example, Nancy Chodorow, *The Reproduction of Mothering* (Berkeley: University of California Press, 1978); and Julia Kristeva, "Stabat Mater," reprinted here, ch. 16. For discussion of feminist psychoanalysis as counterfiguration, see my *Subjection and Subjectivity*, pp. 62–91.

    It is worth noting here that a parallel line of argument could be developed with respect to women's heterosexual desire. If female heterosexuality means repudiating the castrated mother and pining for the forbidden father, as Freud's family romance would have it, feminists cannot reclaim heterosexuality unless it is refigured to express the possibility of affectional attachment to and erotic satisfaction with a beloved male individual. Though there is a rich critical literature on conventional psychoanalytic figurations of heterosexuality, feminists have done relatively little to figuratively redeem heterosexuality.
34. María C. Lugones, "Playfulness, 'World'-Travelling, and Loving Perception." *Hypatia* 2, no. 2 (1987): 3–19, at 9.
35. Ibid., p. 14.
36. Ibid., p. 14.
37. Naomi Scheman, *Engenderings: Constructions of Knowledge, Authority, and Privilege* (New York: Routledge, 1993), pp. 96–105.
38. Scheman, *Engenderings*, p. 102.
39. Herman, *Trauma and Recovery*, pp. 103–107.
40. Scheman, *Engenderings*, p. 103.
41. Annette C. Baier, "The Need for More than Justice," in *Science, Morality, and Feminist Theory*, ed. Marsha Hanen and Kai Nielsen (Calgary: The University of Calgary Press, 1987); Virginia Held, "Feminism and Moral Theory," reprinted here, chap. 32.
42. Elsewhere I have defended a version of the multiplicitous self; see Meyers, *Subjection and Subjectivity*, pp. 146–47. For a promising proposal to model the dynamics of the multiplicitous self on strategies for forging "responsible agency" among the members of an oppressed community, see Claudia Card, *Character and Moral Luck* (Philadelphia: Temple University Press, 1996), ch. 2.
43. Scheman, *Engenderings*, pp. 100–103. It is worth noting that none of Scheman's alternatives to figuring multiplicity as multiple personality disorder stem from the dominant Anglo-European culture that gave us the family romance. Scheman's alternative figurations originate in African, African-American, Latino, and lesbian cultures.
44. In conversation, she has assured me that she does.

45. This point should be underscored. As I remarked earlier, although Freud articulated the family romance in a particularly compelling way and popularizations of psychoanalysis subsequently broadcast this figuration far and wide, in various versions this figuration has been in circulation virtually throughout recorded Western history. The family romance is, then, deeply embedded in Western culture, and it is durable. While I fully recognize how difficult it will be to supplant it (for related discussion, see Meyers, *Subjection and Subjectivity*, pp. 52–56, 113–15), I would nevertheless maintain that it is a task that feminists must undertake.
46. Ruth Leys, "The Real Miss Beauchamp: Gender and the Subject of Imitation," in *Feminists Theorize the Political*, ed. Judith Butler and Joan W. Scott (New York: Routledge, 1992), pp. 189, 201–203. I hope that Leys will not object to my characterizing her view as a counterfiguration of multiplicity. She positions her view as an explanation of why memories of childhood sexual abuse are not recoverable, but I think my reading is faithful to the spirit of her work. For my reasons for reading psychoanalytic developmental theory as an extended trope, see Meyers, *Subjection and Subjectivity*, pp. 12–14.
47. I am grateful to Susan Brison, Hilde Nelson, and Jennifer Radden for helpful comments on an earlier draft of this paper.

Part 5:
Social Identity, Solidarity, and Political Engagement

The Feminist Standpoint: Developing the Ground for a Specifically Feminist Historical Materialism

Hartsock adapts Marxist epistemology to feminist purposes and defends a specifically feminist standpoint. A standpoint is a socioeconomic position from which social reality can be understood and from which emancipatory action can be undertaken. The material position of those who are most exploited by an economic system gives them experience of oppression that the dominant ideology denies and that more advantaged members of society do not see. Still, the wrongs inflicted by an economic system are not obvious to anyone. To perceive them, the victims must organize politically and engage with social reality both intellectually and through political practice. A standpoint is an achievement, not a gift.

What is distinctive about the feminist standpoint is its grounding in the sexual division of labor. Hartsock sets aside differences among women in order to identify commonalities in women's lives. Women, she maintains, are "institutionally responsible for producing both goods and human beings, and all women are forced to become the kinds of people who can do both." Whether or not women work outside the home, they produce "use-value"—cooking, mending, etc.—at home. They do more work than men, and more of women's work is devoted to producing goods that are immediately consumed rather than sold for a profit. By virtue of their reproductive biology, women are less separate from the physical world than men are. By virtue of their socialization, women are less separate from other people than men are. According to Hartsock, women's experience is antithetical to "abstract masculinity." Moreover, the feminist standpoint anchored in women's experience grounds a critique of social relations based on competition and free market exchange, and it argues for creating a society of propertyless producers both of use-values and of human beings.

—D.T.M.

Chapter 25

Nancy C.M. Hartsock

The Feminist Standpoint: Developing the Ground for a Specifically Feminist Historical Materialism

The power of the Marxian critique of class domination stands as an implicit suggestion that feminists should consider the advantages of adopting a historical materialist approach to understanding phallocratic domination. A specifically feminist historical materialism might enable us to lay bare the laws of tendency that constitute the structure of patriarchy over time and to follow its development in and through the Western class societies on which Marx's interest centered. A feminist materialism might in addition enable us to expand the Marxian account to include all human activity rather than focusing on activity more characteristic of males in capitalism. The development of such a historical and materialist account is a very large task, one which requires the political and theoretical contributions of many feminists. Here I will address only the question of the epistemological underpinnings such a materialism would require. Most specifically, I will attempt to develop, on the methodological base provided by Marxian theory, an important epistemological tool for understanding and opposing all forms of domination—a feminist standpoint.

Despite the difficulties feminists have correctly pointed to in Marxian theory, there are several reasons to take over much of Marx's approach. First, I have argued elsewhere that Marx's method and the method developed by the contemporary women's movement recapitulate each other in important ways.[1] This makes it possible for feminists to take over a number of aspects of Marx's method. Here, I will adopt his distinction between appearance and essence, circulation and production, abstract and concrete, and use these distinctions between dual levels of reality to work out the theoretical forms appropriate to each level when viewed not from the standpoint of the proletariat but from a specifically feminist standpoint. In this process I will explore and expand the Marxian argument that socially mediated interaction with nature in the process of production shapes both human beings and theories of knowledge. The Marxian category of labor, including as it does both interaction with other humans and with the natural world, can help to cut through the dichotomy of nature and culture and, for feminists, can help to avoid the false choice of characterizing the situation of women as either "purely natural" or "purely social." As embodied humans we are of course inextricably both natural and social, though feminist theory to date has, for important strategic reasons, concentrated attention on the social aspect.

I set off from Marx's proposal that a correct vision of class society is available from only one of the two major class positions in capitalist society. On the basis of this metatheoretical claim, he was able to develop a powerful critique of class domination. The power of Marx's critique depended on the epistemology and ontology supporting this metatheoretical claim. Feminist Marxists and materialist feminists more generally have argued that the position of women is structurally different from that of men, and that the lived realities of women's lives are profoundly different from those of men.[2] They have not yet, however, given sustained attention to the epistemological consequences of such a claim. Faced with the depth of Marx's critique of capitalism, feminist analysis, as Iris Young has correctly pointed out, often

> accepts the traditional Marxian theory of production relations, historical change, and analysis of the structure of capitalism in basically unchanged form. It rightly criticizes that theory for being essentially gender-blind, and hence seeks to supplement Marxist theory of capitalism with feminist theory of a system of male domination. Taking this route, however, tacitly endorses the traditional Marxian position that "the woman question" is auxiliary to the central questions of a Marxian theory of society.[3]

By setting off from the Marxian metatheory, I am implicitly suggesting that this, rather than his critique of capitalism, can be most helpful to feminists. I will explore some of the epistemological consequences of claiming that women's lives differ structurally from those of men. In particular, I will suggest that, like the lives of proletarians according to Marxian theory, women's lives make available a particular and privileged vantage point on male supremacy, a vantage point that can ground a powerful critique of the phallocratic institutions and ideology that constitute the capitalist form of patriarchy. After a summary of the nature of a standpoint as an epistemological device, I will address the question of whether one can discover a feminist standpoint on which to ground a specifically feminist historical materialism. I will suggest that the sexual division of labor forms the basis for such a standpoint and will argue that, on the basis of the structures that define women's activity as contributors to subsistence and as mothers, one could begin, though not complete, the construction of such an epistemological tool. I hope to show how just as Marx's understanding of the world from the standpoint of the proletariat enabled him to go beneath bourgeois ideology, so a feminist standpoint can allow us to understand patriarchal institutions and ideologies as perverse inversions of more humane social relations.

THE NATURE OF A STANDPOINT

A standpoint is not simply an interested position (interpreted as bias) but is interested in the sense of being engaged. It is true that a desire to conceal real social relations can contribute to an obscurantist account, and it is also true that the ruling gender and class have material interests in deception. A standpoint, however, carries with it the contention that there are some perspectives on society from which, however well-intentioned one may be, the real relations of humans with each other and with the natural world are not visible. This contention should be sorted into a number of distinct epistemological and political claims: (1) Material life (class position in Marxist theory) not only structures but sets limits on the understanding of social relations. (2) If material life is structured in fundamentally opposing ways for two different groups, one can expect that the vision of each will represent an inversion of the other, and in systems of domination the vision available to the rulers will be both partial and perverse. (3) The vision of the ruling class (or gender) structures the material relations in which all parties are forced to participate, and therefore cannot be dismissed as simply false. (4) In consequence, the vision available to the oppressed group must be struggled for and represents an achievement that requires both science to see beneath the surface of the social relations in which all are forced to participate, and the education which can only grow from struggle to change those relations. (5) As an engaged vision, the understanding of the oppressed, the adoption of a standpoint exposes the real relations among human beings as inhuman, points beyond the present, and carries a historically liberatory role.

The concept of a standpoint structures epistemology in a particular way. Rather than a simple dualism, it posits a duality of levels of reality, of which the deeper level or essence both includes and explains the "surface" or appearance, and indicates the logic by means of which the appearance inverts and distorts the deeper reality. In addition, the concept of a standpoint depends on the assumption that epistemology grows in a complex and contradictory way from material life. Any effort to develop a standpoint must take seriously Marx's injunction that "all mysteries which lead theory to mysticism find their rational solution in human practice and in the comprehension of this practice."[4] Marx held that the source both for the proletarian standpoint and the critique of capitalism it makes possible is to be found in practical activity itself. The epistemological (and even ontological) significance of human activity is made clear in Marx's argument not only that persons are active but that reality itself consists of "sensuous human activity, practice."[5] Thus Marx can speak of products as crystallized or congealed human activity or work, of products as conscious human activity in another form. He can state that even plants, animals, light, etc. constitute theoretically a part of human consciousness, and a part of human life and activity.[6] As Marx and Engels summarize their position,

> As individuals express their life, so they are. What they are, therefore, coincides with their production, both with *what* they produce and with *how* they produce. The nature of individuals thus depends on the material conditions determining their production.[7]

This starting point has definite consequences for Marx's theory of knowledge. If humans are not what they eat but what they do, especially what they do in the course of production of subsistence, each means of producing subsistence should be expected to carry with it *both* social relations *and* relations to the world of nature which express the social understanding contained in that mode of production. And in any society with systematically divergent practical activities, one should expect the growth of logically divergent world views. That is, each division of labor, whether by gender or class, can be expected to have consequences for knowledge. Class society, according to Marx, does produce this dual vision in the form of the ruling class vision and the understanding available to the ruled.

On the basis of Marx's description of the activity of commodity exchange in capitalism, the ways in which the dominant categories of thought simply express the mystery of the commodity form have been pointed out. These include a dependence on quantity, duality and opposition of nature to culture, a rigid separation of mind and body, intention and behavior.[8] From the perspective of exchange, where commodities differ from each other only quantitatively, it seems absurd to suggest that labor power differs from all other commodities. The sale and purchase of labor power from the perspective of capital is simply a contract between free agents, in which "the agreement [the parties] come to is but the form in which they give legal expression of their common will." It is a relation of equality,

> because each enters into relations with the other, as with a simple owner of commodities, and they exchange equivalent for equivalent. . . . The only force that brings them together and puts them in relation with each other, is the selfishness, the gain and the private interests of each. Each looks to himself only, and no one troubles himself about the rest, and just because they do so, do they all, in accordance with the pre-established harmony of things, or under the auspices of an all shrewd providence, work together to their mutual advantage, for the common weal and in the interest of all.

This is the only description available within the sphere of circulation or exchange of commodities, or as Marx might put it, at the level of appearance. But at the level of production, the world looks far different. As Marx puts it,

> On leaving this sphere of simple circulation or of exchange of commodities . . . we can perceive a change in the physiognomy of our *dramatis personae*. He who before was the money-owner, now strides in front as capitalist; the possessor of labor-power follows as his laborer. The one with an air of importance, smirking, intent on business; the other timid and holding back, like one who is bringing his own hide to market and has nothing to expect but—a hiding.[9]

This is a vastly different account of the social relations of the buyer and seller of labor power. Only by following the two into the realm of production and adopting the point of view available to the worker could Marx uncover what is really involved in the purchase and sale of labor power, i.e., uncover the process by which surplus value is produced and appropriated by the capitalist, and the means by which the worker is systematically disadvantaged.[10]

If one examines Marx's account of the production and extraction of surplus value, one can see in it the elaboration of each of the claims contained in the concept of a standpoint. First, the contention that material life structures understanding points to the importance of the epistemological consequences of the opposed models of exchange and production. It is apparent that the former results in a dualism based on both the separation of exchange from use, and on the positing of exchange as the only important side of the dichotomy. The epistemological result if one follows through the implications of exchange is a series of opposed and hierarchical dualities—mind/body, ideal/material, social/nature, self/other—even a kind of solipsism—replicating the devaluation of use relative to exchange. The proletarian and Marxian valuation of use over exchange on the basis of involvement in production, in labor, results in a dialectical rather than dualist epistemology: the dialectical and interactive unity (distinction within a unity) of human and natural worlds, mind and body, ideal and material, and the cooperation of self and other (community).

As to the second claim of a standpoint, a Marxian account of exchange versus production indicates that the epistemology growing from exchange not only inverts that present in the process of production but in addition is both partial and fundamentally perverse. The real point of the production of goods and services is, after all, the continuation of the species, a possibility dependent on their use. The epistemology embodied in exchange then, along with the social relations it expresses, not only occupies just one side of the dualities it constructs, but also reverses the proper ordering of any hierarchy in the dualisms: use is primary, not exchange.

The third claim for a standpoint indicates a recognition of the power realities operative in a community, and points to the ways the ruling group's vision may be *both* perverse *and* made real by means of that group's power to define the terms for the community as a whole. In the Marxian analysis, this power is exercised in both control of ideological production, and in the real participation of the worker in exchange. The dichotomous epistemology which grows from exchange cannot be dismissed either as simply false or as an epistemology relevant to only a few: the worker as well as the capitalist engages in the purchase and sale of commodities, and if material life structures consciousness, this cannot fail to have an effect. This leads into the fourth claim for a standpoint—that it is achieved rather than obvious, a mediated rather than immediate understanding. Because the ruling group controls the means of mental as well as physical production, the production of ideals as well as goods, the standpoint of the oppressed represents an achievement both of science (analysis) and of political struggle on the basis of which this analysis can be conducted.

Finally, because it provides the basis for revealing the perversion of both life and thought, the inhumanity of human relations, a standpoint can be the basis for moving beyond these relations. In the historical context of Marx's theory, the engaged vision available to the producers, by drawing out the potentiality available in the actuality—that is, by following up the possibility of abundance capitalism creates—leads toward transcendence. Thus, the proletariat is the only class which has the possibility of creating a classless society. It can do this simply (!) by generalizing its own condition, that is, by making society itself a propertyless producer.[11]

These are the general characteristics of the standpoint of the proletariat. What guidance can feminists take from this discussion? I hold that the powerful vision of both the perverseness and reality of class domination made possible by Marx's adoption of the standpoint of the proletariat suggests that a specifically feminist standpoint could allow for a much more profound critique of phallocratic ideologies and institutions than has yet been achieved. The effectiveness of Marx's critique grew from its uncompromising focus on material life activity, and I propose here to set out from the Marxian contention that not only are persons active, but that reality itself consists of "sensuous human activity, practice." But rather than beginning with men's labor, I will focus on women's life activity and on the institutions which structure that activity in order to raise the question of whether this activity can form the ground for a distinctive standpoint, that is, to determine whether it meets the requirements for a feminist standpoint. (I use the term "feminist" rather than "female" here to indicate both the achieved character of a standpoint and that a standpoint by definition carries a liberatory potential.)

Women's work in every society differs systematically from men's. I intend to pursue the suggestion that this division of labor is the first and in some societies the only division of labor, and moreover, that it is central to the organization of social labor more generally. On the basis of an account of the sexual division of labor, one should be able to begin to explore the oppositions and differences between women's and men's activity and their consequences for epistemology. While I cannot attempt a complete account, I will put forward a schematic and simplified account of the sexual division of labor and its consequences for epistemology. I will sketch out a kind of ideal type of the social relations and world view characteristic of male and female activity in order to explore the epistemology contained in the institutionalized sexual division of labor. In so doing, I do not mean to attribute this vision to individual women or men any more than Marx (or Lukacs) meant their theory of class consciousness to apply to any particular worker or group of workers. My focus is instead on institutionalized social practices and on the specific epistemology and ontology manifested by the institutionalized sexual division of labor. Individuals, as individuals, may change their activity in ways that move them outside the outlook embodied in these institutions, but such a move can be significant only when it occurs at the level of society as a whole.

I will discuss the "sexual division of labor" rather than the "gender division of labor" to stress, first, my belief that the division of labor between women and men cannot be reduced to purely social dimensions. One must distinguish between what Sara Ruddick has termed "invariant and *nearly* unchangeable" features of human life, and those which despite being "*nearly* universal" are "certainly changeable."[12] Thus, the fact that women and not men *bear* children is not (yet) a social choice, but that women and not men rear children in a society structured by compulsory heterosexuality and male dominance is clearly a societal choice. A second reason to use the term "sexual division of labor" is to keep hold of the bodily aspect of existence—perhaps to grasp it overfirmly in an effort to keep it from evaporating altogether. There is some biological, bodily component to human existence. But its size and substantive content will remain unknown until at least the certainly changeable aspects of the sexual division of labor are altered.

On a strict reading of Marx, of course, my enterprise here is illegitimate. While on the one hand Marx remarked that the very first division of labor occurred in sexual intercourse, he argues that the division of labor only becomes "truly such" when the division of mental and manual labor appears. Thus, he dismisses the sexual division of labor as of no analytic importance. At the same time, a reading of other remarks—such as his claim that the mental/manual division of labor is based on the "natural" division of labor in the family—would seem to support the legitimacy of my attention to the sexual division of labor and even add weight to the radical feminist argument that capitalism is an outgrowth of male dominance, rather than vice versa.

On the basis of a schematic account of the sexual division of labor, I will begin to fill in the specific content of the feminist standpoint and begin to specify how women's lives structure an understanding of social relations, that is, begin to follow out the epistimological consequences of the sexual division of labor. In addressing the institutionalized sexual division of labor, I propose to lay aside the important differences among women across race and class boundaries and instead search for central commonalities. I take some justification from the fruitfulness of Marx's similar strategy in constructing a simplified, two-class, two-man model in which everything was exchanged at its value. Marx's schematic account in Volume 1 of *Capital* left out of account such factors as imperialism; the differential wages, work, and working conditions of the Irish; the differences between women, men, and children; and so on. While all of these factors are important to the analysis of contemporary capitalism, none changes either Marx's theories of surplus value or alienation, two of the most fundamental features of the Marxian analysis of capitalism. My effort here takes a similar form in an attempt to move toward a theory of the extraction and appropriation of women's activity and women themselves. Still, I adopt this strategy with some reluctance, since it contains the danger of making invisible the experience of lesbians or women of color.[13] At the same time, I recognize that the effort to uncover a feminist standpoint assumes that there are some things common to all women's lives in Western class societies.

The feminist standpoint that emerges through an examination of women's activities is related to the proletarian standpoint, but deeper going. Women and workers inhabit a world in which the emphasis is on change rather than stasis, a world characterized by interaction with natural substances rather than separation from nature, a world in which quality is more important than quantity, a world in which the unification of mind and body is inherent in the activities performed. Yet, there are some important differences, differences marked by the fact that the proletarian (if male) is immersed in this world only during the time his labor power is being used by the capitalist. If, to paraphrase Marx, we follow the worker home from the factory, we can once again perceive a change in the *dramatis personae.* He who before followed behind as the worker, timid and holding back, with nothing to expect but a hiding, now strides in front while a third person, not specifically present in Marx's account of the transaction between capitalist and worker (both of whom are male), follows timidly behind, carrying groceries, baby and diapers.

THE SEXUAL DIVISION OF LABOR

Women's activity as institutionalized has a double aspect—their contribution to subsistence, and their contribution to childrearing. Whether or not all of us do both, women as a sex are institutionally responsible for producing both goods and human beings, and all women are forced to become the kinds of people who can do both. Although the nature of women's contribution to subsistence varies immensely over time and space, my primary focus here is on capitalism, with a secondary focus on the Western class societies that preceded it.[14] In capitalism, women contribute both production for wages and production of goods in the home, that is, they like men sell their labor power and produce both commodities and surplus value, and produce use-values in the home. Unlike men, however, women's lives are institutionally defined by their production of use-values in the home.[15] And there we begin to encounter the narrowness of the Marxian concept of production. Women's production of use-values in the home has not been well understood by socialists. It is no surprise to feminists that Engels, for example, simply asks how women can continue to do the work in the home and also work in production outside the home. Marx too takes for granted women's responsibility for household labor. He repeats, as if it were his own, the question of a Belgian factory inspector: If a mother works for wages, "how will [the household's] internal economy be cared for; who will look after the young children; who will get ready the meals, do the washing and mending?"[16]

Let us trace both the outlines and the consequences of woman's dual contribution to subsistence in capitalism. Women's labor, like that of the male worker, is contact with material necessity. Their contribution to subsistence, like that of the male worker, involves them in a world in which the relation to nature and to concrete human requirements is central, both in the form of interaction with natural substances whose quality, rather than quantity, is important to the production of meals, clothing, etc., and in the form of close attention to the natural changes in these substances. Women's labor both for wages and even more in household production involves a unification of mind and body for the purpose of transforming natural substances into socially defined goods. This too is true of the labor of the male worker.

There are, however, important differences. First, women as a group work more than men. We are all familiar with the phenomenon of the "double day," and with indications that women work many more hours per week than men.[17] Second, a larger proportion of women's labor time is devoted to the production of use-values than men's. Only some of the goods women produce are commodities (however much they live in a society structured by commodity production and exchange). Third, women's production is structured by repetition in a different way than men's. While repetition for both the woman and the male worker may take the form of production of the same object, over and over—whether apple pies or brake linings—women's work in housekeeping involves a repetitious cleaning.[18]

Thus, the male worker in the process of production is involved in contact with necessity and interchange with nature as well as with other human beings, but the process of production or work does not consume his whole life. The activity of a woman in the home as well as the work she does for wages keeps her continually in contact with a world of qualities and change. Her immersion in the world of use—in concrete, many-qualified, changing material processes—is more complete than his. And if life itself consists of sensuous activity, the vantage point available to women on the basis of their contribution to subsistence represents an intensification and deepening of the materialist world view and consciousness available to the producers of commodities in capitalism, an intensification of class consciousness. The availability of this outlook to even non-working-class women has been strikingly formulated by Marilyn French in *The Women's Room.*

> Washing the toilet used by three males, and the floor and walls around it, is, Mira thought, coming face to face with necessity. And that is why women were saner than men, did not come up with the mad, absurd schemes men developed; they were in touch with necessity, they had to wash the toilet bowl and floor.[19]

The focus on women's subsistence activity rather than men's leads to a model in which the capitalist (male) lives a life structured completely by commodity exchange and not at all by production, and at the furthest distance from contact with concrete material life. The male worker marks a way station on the path to the other extreme of the constant contact with material necessity in women's contribution to subsistence. There are of course important differences along the lines of race and class. For example, working-class men seem to do more domestic labor than men higher up in the class structure—car repairs, carpentry, etc. And until very recently, the wage work done by most women of color replicated the housework required by their own households. Still, there are commonalities present in the institutionalized sexual division of labor that make women responsible for both housework and wage work.

The female contribution to subsistence, however, represents only a part of women's labor. Women also produce/reproduce men (and other women) on both a daily and a long-term basis. This aspect of women's "production" exposes the deep inadequacies of the concept of production as a description of women's activity. One does not (cannot) produce another human being in anything like the way one produces an object such as a chair. Much more is involved, activity that cannot easily be dichotomized into play or work. Helping another to develop, the gradual relinquishing of control, the experience of the human limits of one's action—all these are important features of women's activity as mothers. Women as mothers, even more than as workers, are institutionally involved in processes of change and growth and, more than workers, must understand the importance of avoiding excessive control in order to help others grow.[20] The activity involved is far more complex than the instrumental working with others to transform objects. (Interestingly, much of women's wage work—nursing, social work, and some secretarial jobs in particular—requires and depends on the relational and interpersonal skills women learned by being mothered by someone of the same sex.)

This aspect of women's activity too is not without consequences. Indeed, it is in the production of men by women and the appropriation of this labor and women themselves by men that the opposition between feminist and masculinist experience and outlook is rooted, and it is here that features of the proletarian vision are enhanced and modified for the woman and diluted for the man. The female experience in reproduction represents a unity with nature that goes beyond the proletarian experience of interchange with nature. As another theorist has put it, "reproductive labor might be said to combine the functions of the architect and the bee: like the architect, parturitive woman knows what she is doing; like the bee, she cannot help what she is doing." And just as the worker's acting on the external world changes both the world and the worker's nature, so too "a new life changes the world and the consciousness of the woman."[21] In addition, in the process of producing human beings, relations with others may take a variety of forms with deeper significance than simple cooperation with others for common goals—forms which range from a deep unity with another through the many-leveled and changing connections mothers experience with growing children. Finally, the female experience in bearing and rearing children involves a unity of mind and body more profound than is possible in the worker's instrumental activity.

Motherhood in the large sense, i.e., motherhood as an institution rather than experience, including pregnancy and the preparation for motherhood almost all female children receive as socialization, results in the construction of female existence as centered on a complex relational nexus.[22] One aspect of this relational existence is centered on the experience of living in a female rather than male body. There is a series of boundary challenges inherent in the female physiology—challenges that make it impossible to maintain rigid separation from the object world. Menstruation, coitus, pregnancy, childbirth, lactation—all represent challenges to bodily boundaries.[23] Adrienne Rich has described the experience of pregnancy as one in which the embryo was both inside and

> daily more separate, on its way to becoming separate from me and of itself. In early pregnancy the stirring of the fetus felt like ghostly tremors of my own body,

> later like the movements of a being imprisoned in me; but both sensations were *my* sensations, contributing to my own sense of physical and psychic space.[24]

In turn, the fact that women but not men are primarily responsible for young children means that the infant first experiences itself as not fully differentiated from the mother, and then as an I in relation to an It that it later comes to know as female.[25]

Jane Flax and Nancy Chodorow have argued that the object relations school of psychoanalytic theory puts forward a materialist psychology, one which I propose to treat as a kind of empirical hypothesis. If the account of human development provided by object relations is correct, one ought to expect to find consequences—both psychic and social. According to object relations theory, the process of differentiation from a woman by both male and female children reinforces boundary confusion in female egos and boundary strengthening in males. Individuation is far more conflictual for male than for female children, in part because both mother and son experience the other as a definite "other." The experience of oneness on the part of both mother and infant seems to last longer with girls.[26]

The complex relational world inhabited by women has its start in the experience and resolution of the oedipal crisis, cleanly resolved for the boy, whereas the girl is much more likely to retain both parents as love objects. The nature of the crisis itself differs by sex: the boy's love for the mother is an extension of mother-infant unity and thus essentially threatening to his ego and independence. Male ego-formation necessarily requires repressing this first relation and negating the mother.[27] In contrast, the girl's love for the father is less threatening both because it occurs outside this unity and because it occurs at a later stage of development. For boys, the central issue to be resolved concerns gender identification; for girls the issue is psychosexual development.[28] Chodorow concludes that girls' gradual emergence from the oedipal period takes place in such a way that empathy is built into their primary definition of self, and they have a variety of capacities for experiencing another's needs or feelings as their own. Put another way, girls, because of female parenting, are less differentiated from others than boys, more continuous with and related to the external object world. They are differently oriented to their inner object world as well.[29]

The more complex female relational world is reinforced by the process of socialization. Girls learn roles from watching their mothers; boys must learn roles from rules that structure the life of an absent male figure. Girls can identify with a concrete example present in daily life; boys must identify with an abstract set of maxims only occasionally concretely present in the form of the father. Thus, not only do girls learn roles with more interpersonal and relational skills, but also the process of role learning itself is embodied in the concrete relation with the mother. The male, in contrast, must identify with an abstract, cultural stereotype and learn abstract behaviors not attached to a well-known person. Masculinity is idealized by boys whereas femininity is concrete for girls.[30]

Women and men, then, grow up with personalities affected by different boundary experiences, differently constructed and experienced inner and outer worlds, and preoccupations with different relational issues. This early experience forms an important ground for the female sense of self as connected to the world and the male sense of self as separate, distinct, and even disconnected. By retaining the preoedipal attachment to the mother, girls come to define and experience themselves as continuous with others. In sum, girls enter adulthood with a more complex layering of affective ties and a rich, ongoing inner set of object relations.

Boys, with a simpler oedipal situation and a clear and early resolution, have repressed ties to another. As a result, women define and experience themselves relationally and men do not.[31]

ABSTRACT MASCULINITY AND THE FEMINIST STANDPOINT

This excursion into psychoanalytic theory has served to point to the differences in the male and female experiences of self due to the sexual division of labor in childrearing. These different (psychic) experiences both structure and are reinforced by the differing patterns of male and female activity required by the sexual division of labor, and are thereby replicated as epistemology and ontology. The differential male and female life activity in class society leads on the one hand toward a feminist standpoint and on the other toward an abstract masculinity.

Because the problem for the boy is to distinguish himself from the mother and to protect himself against the real threat she poses for his identity, his conflictual and oppositional efforts lead to the formation of rigid ego boundaries. The way Freud takes for granted the rigid distinction between the "me and not-me" makes the point well: "Normally, there is nothing of which we are more certain than the feeling of ourself, of our own ego. This ego appears to us as something autonomous and unitary, marked off distinctly from everything else." At least toward the outside, "the ego seems to maintain clear and sharp lines of demarcation."[32] Thus, the boy's construction of self in opposition to unity with the mother, his construction of identity as differentiation from the other, sets a hostile and combative dualism at the heart of both the community men construct and the masculinized world view by means of which they understand their lives.

I do not mean to suggest that the totality of human relations can be explained by psychoanalysis. Rather I want to point to the ways male rather than female experience and activity replicates itself in both the hierarchical and dualist institutions of class society and in the frameworks of thought generated by this experience. It is interesting to read Hegel's account of the relation of self and other as a statement of male experience: the relation of the two consciousnesses takes the form of a trial by death. As Hegel describes it, "each seeks the death of the other."

> Thus, the relation of the two self-conscious individuals is such that they provide for themselves and each other through a life-and-death struggle. They must engage in this struggle, for they must raise their certainty *for themselves* to truth, both in the case of the other and in their own case.[33]

The construction of the self in opposition to another who threatens one's very being reverberates throughout the construction of both class society and the masculinized world view and results in a deep-going and hierarchical dualism. First, the male experience is characterized by the duality of concrete versus abstract. Material reality as experienced by the boy in the family provides no model, and is unimportant in the attainment of masculinity. Nothing of value to the boy occurs with the family, and masculinity becomes an abstract ideal to be achieved over the opposition of daily life.[34] Masculinity must be attained by means of opposition to the concrete world of daily life, by escaping from contact with the female world of the household into the masculine world of public life. This experience of two worlds, one valuable, if abstract and deeply unattainable, the other useless and demeaning, if concrete and necessary, lies at the heart of a series of dualisms—abstract/concrete, mind/body, culture/nature, ideal/real, stasis/change. And these dualisms are overlaid by gender: only the first of each pair is associated with the male.

Dualism, along with the dominance of one side of the dichotomy over the other, marks phallocentric society and social theory. These dualisms appear in a variety of forms—in philosophy, technology, political theory, and the organization of class society itself. One can, for example, see them very clearly worked out in Plato, although they appear in many other forms.[35] There, the concrete/abstract duality takes the form of an opposition of material to ideal, and a denial of the relevance of the material world to the attainment of what is of fundamental importance: love of knowledge, or philosophy (masculinity). The duality between nature and culture takes the form of a devaluation of work or necessity, and the primacy instead of purely social interaction for the attainment of undying fame. Philosophy itself is separate from nature, and indeed, exists only on the basis of the domination of (at least some) of the philosopher's own nature.[36] Abstract masculinity, then, can be seen to have structured Western social relations and the modes of thoughts to which these relations give rise at least since the founding of the *polis.*

The oedipal roots of these hierarchical dualisms are memorialized in the overlay of female and male connotations: it is not accidental that women are associated with quasi-human and nonhuman nature, that the female is associated with the body and material life, that the lives of women are systematically used as examples to characterize the lives of those ruled by their bodies rather than their minds.[37]

Both the fragility and fundamental falseness of the masculinized ideology and the deeply problematic nature of the social relations from which it grows are apparent in its reliance on a series of counterfactual assumptions and contentions. Consider how the following contentions are contrary to lived experience: the body is both irrelevant and in opposition to the (real) self, an impediment to be overcome by the mind; the female mind either does not exist (do women have souls?) or works in such incomprehensible ways as to be unintelligible (the "enigma of woman"); what is real and primary is imperceptible to the senses and impervious to nature and natural change. What is remarkable is not only that these contentions have absorbed a great deal of philosophical energy, but, along with a series of outer counterfactuals, have structured social relations for centuries.

Interestingly enough, the epistemology and society constructed by men suffering from the effects of abstract masculinity have a great deal in common with that imposed by commodity exchange. The separation and opposition of social and natural worlds, of abstract and concrete, of permanence and change, the effort to define only the former of each pair as important, the reliance on a series of counterfactual assumptions—all this is shared with the exchange abstraction. Abstract masculinity shares still another of its aspects with the exchange abstraction: it forms the basis for an even more problematic social synthesis. Hegel's analysis makes clear the problematic social relations available to the self that maintains itself by opposition: each of the two subjects struggling for recognition risks its own death in the struggle to kill the other, but if the other is killed the subject is once again alone.[38] In sum, then, the male experience when replicated as epistemology leads to a world conceived as, and (in fact) inhabited by, a number of fundamentally hostile others whom one comes to know by means of opposition (even death struggle) and yet with whom one must construct a social relation in order to survive.

The female construction of self in relation to others leads in an opposite direction—toward opposition to dualisms of any sort, valuation of concrete, everyday life, a sense of a variety of connectednesses and continuities both with other persons and with the natural world. If material life structures consciousness, women's relationally defined existence, bodily experience of boundary challenges, and activity of transforming both physical objects and human beings must be expected to result in a world view to which dichotomies are foreign. Women experience others and themselves along a continuum whose dimensions are evidenced in Adrienne Rich's argument that the child carried for nine months can be defined "*neither* as me or as not-me," and she argues that inner and outer are not polar opposites but a continuum.[39] What the sexual division of labor defines as women's work turns on issues of change rather than stasis, the changes involved in producing both use-values and commodities, but more profoundly in the activity of rearing human beings who change in both more subtle and more autonomous ways than any inanimate object. Not only the qualities of things but also the qualities of people are important in women's work: quantity becomes peripheral. In addition, far more than the instrumental cooperation of the workplace is required; the mother-child relation and the maintenance of the family, while it has instrumental aspects, is not defined by them. Finally, the unity of mental and manual labor, and the directly sensuous nature of much of women's work leads to a more profound unity of mental and manual labor, social and natural worlds, than is experienced by the male worker in capitalism. The unity grows from the fact that women's bodies, unlike men's, can be themselves instruments of production: in pregnancy, giving birth, or lactation, arguments about a division of mental from manual labor are fundamentally foreign.

That this is indeed women's experience is documented in both the theory and practice of the contemporary women's movement and needs no further development here.[40] The more important question here is whether female experience and the world view constructed by female activity can meet the criteria for a standpoint. If we return to the five claims carried by the concept of a standpoint, it seems clear that women's material life activity has important epistemological and ontological consequences for both the understanding and construction of social relations. Women's activity, then, does satisfy the first requirement of a standpoint.

I can now take up the second claim made by a standpoint: that the female experience not only inverts that of the male, but forms a basis on which to expose abstract masculinity as both partial and fundamentally perverse, as not only occupying only one side of the dualities it has constructed, but reversing the proper valuation of human activity. The partiality of the masculinized vision and of the societies that support this understanding is evidenced by its confinement of activity proper to the male, to only one side of the dualisms. Its perverseness, however, lies elsewhere. Perhaps the most dramatic (though not the only) reversal of the proper order of things characteristic of the male experience is the substitution of death for life.

The substitution of death for life results at least in part from the sexual division of labor in childrearing. The self surrounded by rigid ego-boundaries, certain of what is inner and what is outer, the self experienced as walled city, is discontinuous with others. Georges Bataille has made brilliantly clear the ways in which death emerges as the only possible solution to this discontinuity and has followed the logic through to argue that reproduction itself must be understood not as the creation of life, but as death. The core experience to be understood is that of discontinuity and its consequences. As a consequence of this experience of discontinuity and aloneness, penetration of ego-boundaries, or fusion with another is experienced as violent. Thus, the desire for fusion with another can take the form of domination of the other. In this form, it leads to the only possible fusion with a threatening other: when the other ceases to exist as a separate, and for that reason, threatening being. Insisting that another submit to one's will is simply a milder form of the destruction of discontinuity in the death of the other, since in this case one is no longer confronting a discontinuous and opposed will, despite its discontinuous embodiment. This is perhaps one source of the links between sexual activity, domination, and death.

Bataille suggests that killing and sexual activity share both prohibitions and religious significance. Their unit is demonstrated by religious sacrifice, since the latter

> is intentional like the act of the man who lays bare, desires and wants to penetrate his victim. The lover strips the beloved of her identity no less than the blood-stained priest his human or animal victim. The woman in the hands of her assailant is despoiled of her being . . . loses the firm barrier that once separated her from others . . . is brusquely laid open to the violence of the sexual urges set loose in the organs of reproduction; she is laid open to the impersonal violence that overwhelms her from without.[41]

Note the use of the term "lover" and "assailant" as synonyms and the presence of the female as victim.

The importance of Bataille's analysis lies in the fact that it can help to make clear the links among violence, death, and sexual fusion, links that are not simply theoretical but actualized in rape and pornography. Images of women in chains, being beaten, or threatened with attack carry clear social messages, among them that "the normal male is sexually aggressive in a brutal and demeaning way."[42] Bataille's analysis can help to understand why "men advertise, even brag, that their movie is the 'bloodiest thing that ever happened in front of a camera.' "[43] The analysis is supported by the psychoanalyst who suggested that although one of the important dynamics of pornography is hostility, "one can raise the possibly controversial question whether in humans (especially males) powerful sexual excitement can ever exist without brutality also being present."[44]

Bataille's analysis can help to explain what is erotic about "snuff" films, which not only depict the torture and dismemberment of a woman, but also claim that the actress is *in fact* killed. His analysis suggests that perhaps she is a sacrificial victim whose discontinuous existence has been succeeded in her death by "the organic continuity of life drawn into the common life of the beholders."[45] Thus, the pair "lover-assailant" is not accidental. Nor is the connection of reproduction and death.

"Reproduction," Bataille argues, "implies the existence of *discontinuous* beings." This is so because "beings which reproduce themselves are distinct from one another and those reproduced are likewise distinct from each other, just as they are distinct from their parents. Each being is distinct from all others. His birth, his death, the events of his life may have an interest for others, but he alone is directly concerned in them. He is born alone. He dies alone. Between one being and another, there is a *gulf*, a discontinuity."[46] (Clearly it is not just a gulf, but is better understood as a chasm.) In reproduction, sperm and ovum unite to form a new entity, but they do so from the death and disappearance of two separate beings. Thus, the new entity bears within itself "the transition to continuity, the fusion, fatal to both, of two separate beings."[47] Thus, death and reproduction are intimately linked, yet Bataille stresses that "it is only death which is to be identified with continuity." Thus, despite the unity of birth and death in this analysis, Bataille gives greater weight to a "tormenting fact: the urge towards love, pushed to its limit, is an urge toward death."[48] Bataille holds to this position despite his recognition that reproduction is a form of growth. The growth, however, he dismisses as not being "ours," as being only "impersonal."[49] This is not the female experience, in which reproduction is hardly impersonal nor experienced as death. It is, of course, in a literal sense, the sperm which is cut off from its source and lost. No wonder, then, at the masculinized occupation with death, and the feeling that growth is "impersonal," not of fundamental concern to oneself. But this complete dismissal of the experience of another bespeaks a profound lack of empathy and refusal to recognize the very being of another. It is a manifestation of the chasm that separates each man from every other being and from the natural world, the chasm that both marks and defines the problem of community.

The preoccupation with death instead of life appears as well in the argument that it is the ability to kill (and for centuries, the practice) which sets humans above animals. Even Simone de Beauvoir has accepted that "it is not in giving life but in risking life that man is raised above the animal: that is why superiority has been accorded in humanity not to the sex that brings forth but to that which kills."[50] That superiority has been accorded to the sex that kills is beyond doubt. But what kind of experience and vision can take reproduction, the creation of new life, and the force of life in sexuality, and turn it into death—not just in theory but in the practice of rape, pornography, and sexual murder? And why give pride of place to killing? This is not only an inversion of the proper order of things, but also a refusal to recognize the real activities in which men as well as women are engaged. The producing of goods and the reproducing of human beings are certainly life-sustaining activities. And even the deaths of the ancient heroes in search of undying fame were pursuits of life and represented the attempt to void death by attaining immortality. The search for life, then, represents the deeper reality which lies beneath the glorification of death and destruction.

Yet one cannot dismiss the substitution of death for life as simply false. Men's power to structure social relations in their own image means that women too must participate in social relations that manifest and express abstract masculinity. The most important life activities have consistently been held by the powers that be to be unworthy of those who are fully human most centrally because of their close connections with necessity and life: motherwork (the rearing of children), housework, and, until the rise of capitalism in the West, any work necessary to subsistence. In addition, these activities in contemporary capitalism are all constructed in ways that systematically degrade and destroy the minds and bodies of those who perform them.[51] The organization of motherhood as an institution in which a woman is alone with her children, the isolation of women from each other in domestic labor, the female pathology of loss of self in service to others—all mark the transformation of life into death, the distortion of what could have been creative and communal activity into oppressive toil, and the destruction of the possibility of community present in women's relational self-definition. The ruling gender's and class's interest in maintaining social relations such as these is evidenced by the fact that women set up other structures in which the mother is not alone with her children, isolated from others—as is frequently the case in working-class communities or communities of people of color—these arrangements are categorized as pathological deviations.

The real destructiveness of the social relations characteristic of abstract masculinity, however, is now concealed beneath layers of ideology. Marxian theory needed to go beneath the surface to discover the different levels of determination which defined the relation of capitalist and (male) worker. These levels of determination and laws of motion or tendency of phallocratic society must be worked out on the basis of female experience. This brings me to the fourth claim for a standpoint—its character as an achievement of both analysis and political struggle occurring in a particular historical space. The fact that class divisions should have proven so resistent to analysis and required such a prolonged political struggle before Marx was able to formulate the theory of surplus value indicates the difficulty of this accomplishment. And the rational control of production has certainly not been achieved.

Feminists have only begun the process of revaluing female experience, searching for common threads that connect the diverse experiences of women, and searching for the structural determinants of the experiences. The difficulty of the problem faced by feminist theory can be illustrated by the fact that it required a struggle even to define household labor, if not done for wages, as work, to argue that what are held to be acts of love instead must be recognized as work whether or not wages are paid.[52] Both the valuation of women's experience, and the use of this experience as a ground for critique are required. A feminist standpoint may be present on the basis of the common threads of female experience, but it is neither self-evident nor obvious.

Finally, because it provides a way to reveal the perverseness and inhumanity of human relations, a standpoint forms the basis for moving beyond these relations. Just as the proletarian standpoint emerges out of the contradiction between appearance and essence in capitalism, understood as essentially historical and constituted by the relation of capitalist and worker, the feminist standpoint emerges both out of the contradiction between the systematically differing structure of male and female life activity in Western cultures. It expresses female experience at a particular time and place, located within a particular set of social relations. Capitalism, Marx noted, could not develop fully until the notion of human equality achieved the status of universal truth.[53] Despite women's exploitation both as unpaid reproducers of the labor force and as a sex-segregated labor force available for low wages, then, capitalism poses problems for the continued oppression of women. Just as capitalism enables the proletariat to raise the possibility of a society free from class domination, so too it provides space to raise the possibility of a society free from all forms of domination. The articulation of a feminist standpoint based on women's relational self-definition and activity exposes the world men have constructed and the self-understanding which manifests these relations as partial and perverse. More importantly, by drawing out the potentiality available in the actuality and thereby exposing the inhumanity of human relations, it embodies a distress that requires a solution. The experience of continuity and relation—with others, with the natural world, of mind with body—provides an ontological base for developing a nonproblematic social synthesis, a social synthesis which need not operate through the denial of the body, the attack on nature, or the death struggle between the self and other, a social synthesis which does not depend on any of the forms taken by abstract masculinity.

What is necessary is the generalization of the potentiality made available by the activity of women—the defining of society as a whole as propertyless producer both of use-values and of human beings. To understand what such a transformation would require, we should consider what is involved in the partial transformation represented by making the whole of society into propertyless producers of use-values—i.e., socialist revolution. The abolition of the division between mental and manual labor cannot take place simply by means of adopting worker self-management techniques, but instead requires the abolition of private property, the seizure of state power, and lengthy postrevolutionary class struggle. Thus, I am not suggesting that shared parenting arrangements can abolish the sexual division of labor. Doing away with this division of labor would of course require institutionalizing the participation of both women and men in childrearing; but just as the rational and conscious control of the production of goods and services requires a vast and far-reaching social transformation, so the rational and conscious organization of reproduction would entail the transformation both of *every* human relation, and of human relations to the natural world. The magnitude of the task is apparent if one asks what a society without institutionalized gender differences might look like.

CONCLUSION

An analysis which begins from the sexual division of labor—understood not as taboo, but as the real, material activity of concrete human beings—could form the basis for an analysis of the real structures of women's oppression, an analysis that would not require that one sever biology from society, nature from culture, an analysis that would expose the ways women both participate in and oppose their own subordination. The elaboration of such an analysis cannot but be difficult. Women's lives, like men's, are structured by social relations that manifest the experience of the dominant gender and class. The ability to go beneath the surface of appearances to reveal the real but concealed social relations requires both theoretical and political activity. Feminist theorists must demand that feminist theorizing be grounded in women's material activity and must as well be a part of the political struggle necessary to develop areas of social life modeled on this activity. The outcome could be the development of a political economy which included women's activity as well as men's, and could as well be a step toward the redefining and restructuring of society as a whole on the basis of women's activity.

Generalizing the activity of women to the social system as a whole would raise, for the first time in human history, the possibility of a fully human community, a community structured by connection rather than separation and opposition. One can conclude then that women's life activity does form the basis of a specifically feminist materialism, a materialism that can provide a point from which both to critique and to work against phallocratic ideology and institutions.

My argument here opens a number of avenues for future work. Clearly, a systematic critique of Marx on the basis of a more fully developed understanding of the sexual division of labor is in order. And this is indeed being undertaken by a number of feminists. A second avenue for further investigation is the relation between exchange and abstract masculinity. An exploration of Mauss's *The Gift* would play an important part in this project, since he presents the solipsism of exchange as an overlay on and substitution for a deeper-going hostility, the exchange of gifts as an alternative to war. We have seen that the necessity for recognizing and receiving recognition from another to take the form of a death struggle memorializes the male rather than female experience of emerging as a person in opposition to a woman in the context of a deeply phallocratic world. If the community of exchangers (capitalists) rests on the more overtly and directly hostile death struggle of self and other, one might be able to argue that what underlies the exchange abstraction is abstract masculinity. One might then turn to the question of whether capitalism rests on and is a consequence of patriarchy. Perhaps then feminists can produce the analysis which could amend Marx to read: "Though class society appears to be the source, the cause of the oppression of women, it is rather its consequence."[54] Thus, it is "only at the last culmination of the development of class society [that] this, its secret, appear[s] again, namely, that on the one hand it is the *product* of the oppression of women, and that on the other it is the *means* by which women participate in and create their own oppression."[55]

NOTES

I take my title from Iris Young's call for the development of a specifically feminist historical materialism. See "Socialist Feminism and the Limits of Dual Systems Theory," in *Socialist Review* 10, 2/3 (March–June, 1980). My work on this paper is deeply indebted to a number of women whose ideas are incorporated here, although not always used in the ways they might wish. My discussions with Donna Haraway and Sandra Harding have been intense and ongoing over a period of years. I have also had a number of important and useful conversations with Jane Flax, and my project here has benefited both from these contacts and from the opportunity to read her paper, "Political Philosophy and the Patriarchal Unconscious: A Psychoanalytic Perspective on Epistemology and Metaphysics." In addition I have been helped immensely by collective discussions with Annette Bickel, Sarah Begus, and Alexa Freeman. All of these people (along with Iris Young and Irene Diamond) have read and commented on drafts of this paper. I would also like to thank Alison Jaggar for continuing to question me about the basis on which one could claim the superiority of a feminist standpoint and for giving me the opportunity to deliver the paper at the University of Cincinnati Philosophy Department Colloquium; and Stephen Rose for taking the time to read and comment on a rough draft of the paper at a critical point in its development.

1. See my "Feminist Theory and the Development of Revolutionary Strategy," in Zillah Eisenstein, ed., *Capitalist Patriarchy and the Case for Socialist Feminism* (New York: Monthly Review, 1978).
2. The recent literature on mothering is perhaps the most detailed on this point. See Dorothy Dinnerstein, *The Mermaid and the Minotaur* (New York: Harper and Row, 1976); Nancy Chodorow, *The Reproduction of Mothering* (Berkeley: University of California Press, 1978).
3. Iris Young, "Socialist Feminism and the Limits of Dual Systems Theory," in *Socialist Review* 10 2/3 (March–June, 1980), p. 180.
4. Eighth Thesis on Feuerbach, by Karl Marx, "Theses on Feuerbach," in *The German Ideology*, ed. C.J. Arthur (New York: International Publishers, 1970), p. 121.
5. Ibid. Conscious human practice, then, is at once both an epistemology category and the basis for Marx's conception of the nature of humanity itself. To put the case even more strongly, Marx argues that human activity has both an ontological and epistemological status, that human feelings are not "merely anthropological phenomena," but are "truly ontological affirmations of being." See Karl Marx, *Economic and Philosophic Manuscripts of 1844*, ed. Dirk Struik (New York: International Publishers, 1964), pp. 113, 165, 188.
6. Marx, *1844*, p. 112. Nature itself, for Marx, appears as a form of human work, since he argues that humans duplicate themselves actively and come to contemplate themselves in a world of their own making (ibid., p. 114). On the more general issue of the relation of natural to human worlds, see the very interesting account by Alfred Schmidt, *The Concept of Nature in Marx*, tr. Ben Foukes (London: New Left Books, 1971).
7. Marx and Engels, *The German Ideology*, p. 42.

8. See Alfred Sohn-Rethel, *Intellectual and Manual Labor: A Critique of Epistemology* (London: Macmillan, 1978). I should note that my analysis both depends on and is in tension with Sohn-Rethel's. Sohn-Rethel argues that commodity exchange is a characteristic of all class societies—one which comes to a head in capitalism or takes its most advanced form in capitalism. His project, which is not mine, is to argue that (a) commodity exchange, a characteristic of all class societies, is an original source of abstraction, (b) that this abstraction contains the formal element essential for the cognitive faculty of conceptual thinking, and (c) that the abstraction operating in exchange, an abstraction in practice, is the source of the ideal abstraction basic to Greek philosophy and to modern science (see ibid., p. 28). In addition to a different purpose, I should indicate several major differences with Sohn-Rethel. First, he treats the productive forces as separate from the productive relations of society and ascribes far too much autonomy to them. (See, for example, his discussions on pp. 84–85, 95.) I take the position that the distinction between the two is simply a device used for purposes of analysis rather than a feature of the real world. Second, Sohn-Rethel characterizes the period preceding generalized commodity production as primitive communism (see p. 98). This is, however, an inadequate characterization of tribal societies.
9. Karl Marx, *Capital*, I (New York: International Publishers, 1967), p. 176.
10. I have done this elsewhere in a systematic way. For the analysis, see my discussion of the exchange abstraction in *Money, Sex, and Power: An Essay on Domination and Community* (New York: Longman, Inc., 1983).
11. This is Iris Young's point. I am indebted to her persuasive arguments for taking what she terms the "gender differentiation of labor" as a central category of analysis (Young, "Dual Systems Theory," p. 185). My use of this category, however, differs to some extent from hers. Young's analysis of women in capitalism does not seem to include marriage as a part of the division of labor. She is more concerned with the division of labor in the productive sector.
12. See Sara Ruddick, "Maternal Thinking," *Feminist Studies* 6, 2 (Summer 1980), p. 364.
13. See, for discussions of this danger, Adrienne Rich, "Disloyal to Civilization: Feminism, Racism, Gynephobia," in *On Lies, Secrets, and Silence* (New York: W.W. Norton & Co., 1979), pp. 275–310; Elly Bulkin, "Racism and Writing: Some Implications for White Lesbian Critics," in *Sinister Wisdom*, No. 6 (Spring 1980).
14. Some cross-cultural evidence indicates that the status of women varies with the work they do. To the extent that women and men contribute equally to subsistence, women's status is higher than it would be if their subsistence work differed profoundly from that of men; that is, if they do none or almost all of the work of subsistence, their status remains low. See Peggy Sanday, "Female Status in the Public Domain," in Michelle Rosaldo and Louise Lamphere, eds., *Women, Culture, and Society* (Stanford: Stanford University Press, 1974), p. 199. See also Iris Young's account of the sexual division of labor in capitalism, mentioned above.
15. It is irrelevant to my argument here that women's wage labor takes place under different circumstances than men's—that is, their lower wages, their confinement to only a few occupational categories, etc. I am concentrating instead of the formal, structural features of women's work. There has been much effort to argue that women's domestic labor is a source of surplus value, that is, to include it within the scope of Marx's value theory as productive labor, or to argue that since it does not produce surplus value it belongs to an entirely different mode of production, variously characterized as domestic or patriarchal. My strategy here is quite different from this. See, for the British debate, Mariarosa Dalla Costa and Selma James, *The Power of Women and the Subversion of the Community* (Bristol: Falling Wall Press, 1975); Wally Secombe, "The Housewife and Her Labor Under Capitalism," *New Left Review* 83 (January–February 1974); Jean Gardiner,

"Women's Domestic Labour," *New Left Review* 89 (March 1975); and Paul Smith, "Domestic Labour and Marx's Theory of Value," in Annette Kuhn and Ann Marie Wolpe, eds., *Feminism and Materialism* (Boston: Routledge and Kegan Paul, 1978). A portion of the American debate can be found in Ira Gerstein, "Domestic Work and Capitalism," and Lisa Vogel, "The Earthly Family," *Radical America* 7, 4/5 (July–October 1973); Ann Ferguson, "Women as a New Revolutionary Class," in Pat Walker, ed., *Between Labor and Capital* (Boston: South End Press, 1979).

16. Frederick Engels, *Origins of the Family, Private Property and the State* (New York: International Publishers, 1942); Karl Marx, *Capital,* Vol. I, p. 671. Marx and Engels have also described the sexual division of labor as natural or spontaneous. See Mary O'Brien, "Reproducing Marxist Man," in Lorenne Clark and Lynda Lange, eds., *The Sexism of Social and Political Theory: Women and Reproduction from Plato to Nietzsche* (Toronto: University of Toronto Press, 1979).
17. For a discussion of women's work, see Elise Boulding, "Familial Constraints on Women's Work Roles," in Martha Blaxall and B. Reagan, Eds., *Women and the Workplace* (Chicago: University of Chicago Press, 1976), esp. the charts on pp. 111, 113.

    An interesting historical note is provided by the fact that even Nausicaa, the daughter of a Homeric king, did the household laundry (see M. I. Finley, *The World of Odysseus* [Middlesex, England: Penguin, 1979], p. 73). While aristocratic women were less involved in actual labor, the difference was one of degree. And as Aristotle remarked in *The Politics,* supervising slaves is not a particularly uplifting activity. The life of leisure and philosophy, so much the goal for aristocratic Athenian men, then, was almost unthinkable for any woman.
18. Simone de Beauvoir holds that repetition has a deeper significance and that women's biological destiny itself is repetition (see *The Second Sex,* tr. H. M. Parshley [New York: Knopf, 1953], p. 59). But see also her discussion of housework in ibid., pp. 434ff. There her treatment of housework is strikingly negative. For de Beauvoir, transcendence is provided in the historical struggle of self with others and with the natural world. The oppositions she sees are not really stasis vs. change, but rather transcendence, escape from the muddy concreteness of daily life, from the static, biological, concrete repetition of "placid femininity."
19. Marilyn French, *The Women's Room* (New York: Jove, 1978), p. 214.
20. Sara Ruddick, "Maternal Thinking," presents an interesting discussion of these and other aspects of the thought which emerges from the activity of mothering. Although I find it difficult to speak the language of interests and demands she uses, she brings out several valuable points. Her distinction between maternal and scientific thought is very intriguing and potentially useful (see esp. pp. 350–53).
21. O'Brien, "Reproducing Marxist Man," p. 115, n. 11.
22. It should be understood that I am concentrating here on the experience of women in Western culture. There are a number of cross-cultural differences which can be expected to have some effect. See, for example, the differences which emerge from a comparison of childrearing in Ancient Greek society with that of the contemporary Mbuti in central Africa. See Phillip Slater, *The Glory of Hera* (Boston: Beacon, 1968); and Colin Turnbull, "The Politics of Non-Aggression," in Ashley Montague, ed., *Learning Non-Aggression* (New York: Oxford University Press, 1978).
23. See Nancy Chodorow, "Family Structure and Feminine Personality," in Michelle Rosaldo and Louise Lamphere, eds., *Women, Culture, and Society* (Stanford: Stanford University Press, 1974), p. 59.
24. Adrienne Rich, *Of Woman Born* (New York: Norton, 1976), p. 63.
25. See Chodorow, *The Reproduction of Mothering;* and Flax, "The Conflict Between Nurturance and Autonomy in Mother-Daughter Relations and in Feminism," *Feminist Studies,* 4 2 (June,

1978). I rely on the analyses of Dinnerstein and Chodorow but there are difficulties in that they are attempting to explain why humans, both male and female, fear and hate the female. My purpose here is to invert their arguments and to attempt to put forward a positive account of the epistemological consequences of this situation. What follows is a summary of Chodorow, *The Reproduction of Mothering.*

26. Chodorow, *Reproduction,* pp. 105–109.
27. This is Jane Flax's point.
28. Chodorow, *Reproduction,* pp. 127–31, 163.
29. Ibid., p. 166.
30. Ibid., p. 174–78. Chodorow suggests a correlation between father absence and fear of women (p. 213), and one should, treating this as an empirical hypothesis, expect a series of cultural differences based on the degree of father absence. Here the ancient Greeks and the Mbuti provide a fascinating contrast. (See above, note 22.)
31. Ibid., p. 198. The flexible and diffuse female ego boundaries can of course result in the pathology of loss of self in responsibility for and dependence on others (the obverse of the male pathology of experiencing the self as walled city).
32. Sigmund Freud, *Civilization and Its Discontents* (New York: Norton, 1961), pp. 12–13.
33. Hegel, *Phenomenology of Spirit* (New York: Oxford University Press, 1979), tr. A.V. Miller, p. 114. See also Jessica Benjamin's very interesting use of this discussion in "The Bonds of Love: Rational Violence and Erotic Domination," *Feminist Studies* 6, 1 (June 1980).
34. Alvin Gouldner has made a similar argument in his contention that the Platonic stress on hierarchy and order resulted from a similarly learned opposition to daily life, which was rooted in the young aristocrat's experience of being taught proper behavior by slaves who could not themselves engage in this behavior. See *Enter Plato* (New York: Basic Books, 1965), pp. 351–55.
35. One can argue, as Chodorow's analysis suggests, that their extreme form in his philosophy represents an extreme father-absent (father-deprived?) situation. A more general critique of phallocentric dualism occurs in Susan Griffin, *Women and Nature* (New York: Harper & Row, 1978).
36. More recently, of course, the opposition to the natural world has taken the form of destructive technology. See Evelyn Fox Keller, "Gender and Science," *Psychoanalysis and Contemporary Thought* 1, 3 (1978), reprinted in this volume.
37. See Elizabeth Spelman, "Metaphysics and Misogyny: The Soul and Body in Plato's Dialogues," mimeo. One analyst has argued that its basis lies in the fact that "the early mother, monolithic representative of nature, is a source, like nature, of ultimate distress as well as ultimate joy. Like nature, she is both nourishing and disappointing, both alluring and threatening . . . The infant loves her . . . and it hates her because, like nature, she does not perfectly protect and provide for it. . . . The mother, then—like nature, which sends blizzards and locusts as well as sunshine and strawberries—is perceived as capricious, sometimes actively malevolent." Dinnerstein, *Mermaid,* p. 95.
38. See Benjamin, p. 152. The rest of her analysis goes in a different direction than mine, though her account of *The Story of O* can be read as making clear the problems for any social synthesis based on the Hegelian model.
39. Rich, *Of Woman Born,* p. 64, p. 167. For a similar descriptive account, but a dissimilar analysis, see David Bakan, *The Duality of Human Existence* (Boston: Beacon, 1966).
40. My arguments are supported with remarkable force by both the theory and practice of the contemporary women's movement. In theory, this appears in different forms in the work of Dorothy Riddle, "New Visions of Spiritual Power," *Quest: A Feminist Quarterly* 1, 3 (Spring, 1975); Susan Griffin, *Women and Nature,* esp. Book IV: "The Separate Rejoined"; Rich, *Of Woman Born,* esp.

pp. 62–68; Linda Thurston, "On Male and Female Principle," *The Second Wave* 1, 2 (Summer 1971). In feminist political organizing, this vision has been expressed as an opposition of leadership and hierarchy, as an effort to prevent the development of organizations divided into leaders and followers. It has also taken the form of an insistence on the unity of the personal and the political, a stress on the concrete rather than on abstract principles (an opposition to theory), and a stress on the politics of everyday life. For a fascinating and early example, see Pat Mainardi, "The Politics of Housework," in Leslie Tanner, ed. *Voices of Women's Liberation* (New York: New American Library, 1970).

41. Georges Bataille, *Death and Sensuality* (New York: Anro Press, 1977), p. 90.
42. *Women Against Violence Against Women Newsletter*, June, 1976, p. 1.
43. *Aegis: A Magazine on Ending Violence Against Women*, November/December, 1978, p. 3.
44. Robert Stoller, *Perversion: The Erotic Form of Hatred* (New York: Pantheon, 1975), p. 88.
45. Bataille, p. 91. See pp. 91ff. for a more complete account of the commonalities of sexual activity and ritual sacrifice.
46. *Death and Sensuality*, p. 12 (italics mine). See also de Beauvoir's discussion in *The Second Sex*, pp. 135, 151.
47. Bataille, p. 14.
48. Ibid., p. 42. While Adrienne Rich acknowledges the violent feelings between mothers and children, she quite clearly does not put these at the heart of the relation (*Of Woman Born*).
49. Bataille, pp. 95–96.
50. de Beauvoir, *The Second Sex*, p. 58. It should be noted that killing and risking life are ways of indicating one's contempt for one's body, and as such are of a piece with the Platonic search for disembodiment.
51. Consider, for example, Rich's discussion of pregnancy and childbirth, chs. 6 and 7, *Of Woman Born*. And see also Charlotte Perkins Gilman's discussion of domestic labor in *The Home* (Urbana, Ill.: The University of Illinois Press, 1972).
52. The Marxist-feminist efforts to determine whether housework produces surplus value and the feminist political strategy of demanding wages for housework represent two (mistaken) efforts to recognize women's nonwage activity as work. Perhaps domestic labor's nonstatus as work is one of the reasons why its wages—disproportionately paid to women of color—are so low, and working conditions so poor.
53. Marx, *Capital*, Vol. I, p. 60.
54. The phrase is O'Brien's, p. 113.
55. See Marx, *1844*, p. 117.

Sisterhood: Political Solidarity between Women

hooks distinguishes two forms of sisterhood. The first is an empty, if not repressive and hypocritical, claim on the part of middle-class white women that all women are sisters in virtue of their common oppression. Women's diversity in terms of race, class, ethnicity, and sexual orientation belies this claim. But there is a second form of sisterhood that is based on solidarity among diverse women. Solidarity is built through hard, ongoing political work—work confronting conflicts, work finding common interests and goals, and work opposing sexist oppression in all its forms. hooks advocates this second form of sisterhood.

She considers the obstacles to and the potential for feminist unity based on solidarity. Internalized sexism and internalized racism must be overcome, for both divide women from each other. But, according to hooks, it is not enough for feminists to extirpate their personal prejudices. Feminists need to realize that sexist oppression cannot be effectively resisted unless racist oppression, class oppression, and heterosexist oppression are resisted, as well. Thus, hooks favors a multipronged approach to feminist politics. Women from different social groups may choose to focus their political activities on issues that are especially compelling to them, but their thinking and their initiatives must be informed by an awareness of other women's needs and concerns. In this way, feminist solidarity can be achieved without eradicating women's difference.

—D.T.M.

Chapter 26

bell hooks

Sisterhood: Political Solidarity between Women

Women are the group most victimized by sexist oppression. As with other forms of group oppression, sexism is perpetuated by institutional and social structures; by the individuals who dominate, exploit, or oppress; and by the victims themselves who are socialized to behave in ways that make them act in complicity with the status quo. Male supremacist ideology encourages women to believe we are valueless and obtain value only by relating to or bonding with men. We are taught that our relationships with one another diminish rather than enrich our experience. We are taught that women are "natural" enemies, that solidarity will never exist between us because we cannot, should not, and do not bond with one another. We have learned these lessons well. We must unlearn them if we are to build a sustained feminist movement. We must learn to live and work in solidarity. We must learn the true meaning and value of Sisterhood.

Although the contemporary feminist movement should have provided a training ground for women to learn about political solidarity, Sisterhood was not viewed as a revolutionary accomplishment women would work and struggle to obtain. The vision of Sisterhood evoked by women's liberationists was based on the idea of common oppression. Needless to say, it was primarily bourgeois white women, both liberal and radical in perspective, who professed belief in the notion of common oppression. The idea of "common oppression" was a false and corrupt platform disguising and mystifying the true nature of women's varied and complex social reality. Women are divided by sexist attitudes, racism, class privilege, and a host of other prejudices. Sustained woman bonding can occur only when these divisions are confronted and the necessary steps are taken to eliminate them.

Divisions will not be eliminated by wishful thinking or romantic reverie about common oppression despite the value of highlighting experiences all women share.

In recent years Sisterhood as slogan, motto, rallying cry no longer evokes the spirit of power in unity. Some feminists now seem to feel that unity between women is impossible given our differences. Abandoning the idea of Sisterhood as an expression of political solidarity weakens and diminishes feminist movement. Solidarity strengthens resistance struggle. There can be no mass-based feminist movement to end sexist oppression without a united front—women must take the initiative and demonstrate the power of solidarity. Unless we can show that barriers separating women can be eliminated, that solidarity can exist, we cannot hope to change and transform society as a whole. The shift away from an emphasis on Sisterhood has occurred because many women, angered by the insistence on "common oppression," shared identity, sameness, criticized or dismissed feminist movement altogether. The emphasis on Sisterhood was often seen as the emotional appeal masking the opportunism of manipulative bourgeois white women. It was seen as a cover-up hiding the fact that many women exploit and oppress other women. Black woman activist lawyer Florynce Kennedy wrote an essay, published in the anthology *Sisterhood is Powerful,* voicing her suspicions about the existence of solidarity between women as early as 1970:

> It is for this reason that I have considerable difficulty with the sisterhood mystique: "We are sisters," "Don't criticize a 'sister' publicly," etc. When a female judge asks my client where the bruises are when she complains about being assaulted by her husband (as did Family Court Judge Sylvia Jaffin Liese), and makes smart remarks about her being overweight, and when another female judge is so hostile that she disqualifies herself but refuses to order a combative husband out of the house (even though he owns property elsewhere with suitable living quarters)—these judges are not my sisters.[1]

Women were wise to reject a false Sisterhood based on shallow notions of bonding. We are mistaken if we allow these distortions or the women who created them (many of whom now tell us bonding between women is unimportant) to lead us to devalue Sisterhood.[2]

Women are enriched when we bond with one another, but we cannot develop sustaining ties or political solidarity using the model of Sisterhood created by bourgeois women's liberationists. According to their analysis, the basis for bonding was shared victimization, hence the emphasis on common oppression. This concept of bonding directly reflects male supremacist thinking. Sexist ideology teaches women that to be female is to be a victim. Rather than repudiate this equation (which mystifies female experience—in their daily lives most women are not continually passive, helpless, powerless "victims"), women's liberationists embraced it, making shared victimization the basis for woman bonding. This meant that women had to conceive of themselves as "victims" in order to feel that feminist movement was relevant to their lives. Bonding as victims created a situation in which assertive, self-affirming women were often seen as having no place in feminist movement. It was this logic that led white women activists (along with black men) to suggest that black women were so "strong" they did not need to be active in feminist movement.[3] It was this logic that led many white women activists to abandon feminist movement when they no longer embraced the victim identity. Ironically, the women who were most eager to be seen as "victims," who overwhelmingly stressed the role of victim, were more privileged and powerful than the vast majority of women in our society. An example of this tendency is some writing about violence against women. Women who are exploited and oppressed daily cannot afford to relinquish the belief that they exercise some measure of control, however relative, over their lives. They cannot afford to see themselves solely as "victims" because their survival depends on continued exercise of whatever personal powers they possess. It would be psychologically demoralizing for these women to bond with other women on the basis of shared victimization. They bond with other women on the basis of shared strengths and resources. This is the woman bonding feminist movement should encourage. It is this type of bonding that is the essence of Sisterhood.

Bonding as "victims," white women liberationists were not required to assume responsibility for confronting the complexity of their own experience. They were not challenging one another to examine their sexist attitudes toward women unlike themselves or exploring the impact of race and class privilege on their relationships to women outside their race/class groups. Identifying as "victims," they could abdicate responsibility for their role in the maintenance and perpetuation of sexism, racism, and classism, which they did by insisting that only men were the enemy. They did not acknowledge and confront the enemy within. They were not prepared to forgo privilege and do the "dirty work" (the struggle and confrontation necessary to build political awareness as well as the many tedious tasks to be accomplished in day-to-day organizing) that is necessary in the development of radical political consciousness. The first task being honest critique and evaluation of one's social status, values, political beliefs, etc., they were seeking to avoid self-awareness. Sisterhood became yet another shield against reality, another support system. Their version of Sisterhood was informed by racist and classist assumptions about white womanhood, that the white "lady" (that is to say bourgeois woman) should be protected from all that might upset or discomfort her and be shielded from negative realities that might lead to confrontation. Their version of Sisterhood dictated that sisters were to "unconditionally" love one another; that they were to avoid conflict and minimize disagreement; that they were not to criticize one another, especially in public. For a time these mandates created an illusion of unity suppressing the competition, hostility, perpetual disagreement, and abusive criticism (trashing) that was often the norm in feminist groups. Today many splinter groups who share common identities (e.g., WASP working class; white academic faculty women; anarchist feminists, etc.) use this same model of Sisterhood, but participants in these groups endeavor to support, affirm, and protect one another while demonstrating hostility (usually through excessive trashing) toward women outside the chosen sphere. Bonding between a chosen circle of women who strengthen their ties by excluding and devaluing women outside their group closely resembles the type of personal bonding between women that has always occurred under patriarchy: the one difference being the interest in feminism.

To develop political solidarity between women, feminist activists cannot bond on the terms set by the dominant ideology of the culture. We must define our own terms. Rather than bond on the basis of shared victimization or in response to a false sense of a common enemy, we can bond on the basis of our political commitment to a feminist movement that aims to end sexist oppression. Given such a commitment, our energies would not be concentrated on the issue of equality with men or solely on the struggle to resist male domination. We would no longer accept a simplistic good girls/bad boys account of the structure of sexist oppression. Before we can resist male domination we must break out attachment to sexism; we must work to transform female consciousness. Working together to expose, examine, and eliminate sexist socialization within ourselves, women would strengthen and affirm one another and build a solid foundation for developing political solidarity.

Between women and men, sexism is most often expressed in the form of male domination, which leads to discrimination, exploitation, or oppression. Between women, male supremacist values are expressed through suspicious, defensive, competitive behavior. It is sexism that leads women to feel threatened by one another without cause. While sexism teaches women to be sex objects for men, it is also manifest when women who have repudiated this role feel contemptuous and superior in relation to those women who have not. Sexism leads women to devalue parenting work while inflating the value of jobs and careers. Acceptance of sexist ideology is indicated when women teach children that there are only two possible behavior patterns: the role of dominant or submissive being. Sexism teaches women woman-hating, and both consciously and unconsciously we act out this hatred in our daily contact with one another.

Although contemporary feminist activists, especially radical feminists, called attention to women's absorption in sexist ideology, ways that women who are advocates of patriarchy, as well as women who uncritically accept sexist assumptions, could unlearn that socialization were not stressed. It was often assumed that to support feminism was synonymous with repudiation of sexism in all its forms. Taking on the label "feminist" was accepted as a sign of personal transformation; as a consequence, the process by which values were altered was either ignored or could not be spelled out because no fundamental change had occurred. Sometimes consciousness-raising groups provided space for women to explore their sexism. This examination of attitudes toward themselves and other women was often a catalyst for transformation. Describing the function of rap groups in *The Politics of Women's Liberation*, Jo Freeman explains:

> Women came together in small groups to share personal experiences, problems, and feelings. From this public sharing comes the realization that what was thought to be individual is in fact common: that what was thought to be a personal problem has a social cause and a political solution. The rap group attacks the effects of psychological oppression and helps women to put it into a feminist context. Women learn to see how social structures and attitudes have molded them from birth and limited their opportunities. They ascertain the extent to which women have been denigrated in this society and how they have developed prejudices against themselves and other women. They learn to develop self-esteem and to appreciate the value of group solidarity.[4]

As consciousness-raising groups lost their popularity, new groups were not formed to fulfill similar functions. Women produced a large quantity of feminist writing but placed little emphasis on ways to unlearn sexism.

Since we live in a society that promotes fadism and temporary superficial adoptation of different values, we are easily convinced that changes have occurred in arenas where there has been little or no change. Women's sexist attitudes toward one another are one such arena. All over the United States, women spend hours of their time daily verbally abusing other women, usually through malicious gossip (not to be confused with gossip as positive communication). Television soap operas and nighttime dramas continually portray woman-to-woman relationships as characterized by aggression, contempt, and competitiveness. In feminist circles, sexism toward women is expressed by abusive trashing, total disregard for and lack of concern or interest in women who have not joined the feminist movement. This is especially evident at university campuses where feminist studies is often seen as a discipline or program having no relationship to feminist movement. In her commencement address at Barnard College in May 1979, black woman writer Toni Morrison told her audience:

> I want not to ask you but to tell you not to participate in the oppression of your sisters. Mothers who abuse their children are women, and another woman, not an agency, has to be willing to stay their hands. Mothers who set fire to school buses are women, and another woman, not an agency, has to tell them to stay their hands. Women who stop the promotion of other women in careers are women, and another woman must come to the victim's aid. Social and welfare workers who humiliate their clients may be women, and other women colleagues have to deflect their anger.
>
> I am alarmed by the violence that women do to each other: professional violence, competitive violence, emotional violence. I am alarmed by the willingness of women to enslave other women. I am alarmed by a growing absence of decency on the killing floor of professional women's worlds.[5]

To build a politicized, mass-based feminist movement, women must work harder to overcome the alienation from one another that exists when sexist socialization has not been unlearned, e.g., homophobia, judging by appearance, conflicts between women with diverse sexual practices. So far, feminist movement has not transformed woman-to-woman relationships, especially between women who are strangers to one another or from different backgrounds, even though it has been the occasion for bonding between individuals and groups of women. We must renew our efforts to help women unlearn sexism if we are to develop affirming personal relationships as well as political unity.

Racism is another barrier to solidarity between women. The ideology of Sisterhood as expressed by contemporary feminist activists indicated no acknowledgement that racist discrimination, exploitation, and oppression of multiethnic women by white women had made it impossible for the two groups to feel they shared common interests or political concerns. Also, the existence of totally different cultural backgrounds can make communication difficult. This has been especially true of black and white female relationships. Historically, many black women experienced white women as the white supremacist group who most directly exercised power over them, often in a manner far more brutal and dehumanizing than that of racist white men. Today, despite predominant rule by white supremacist patriarchs, black women often work in situations where the immediate supervisor, boss, or authority figure is a white woman. Conscious of the privileges white men as well as white women gain as a consequence of racial domination, black women were quick to react to the feminist call for Sisterhood by pointing to the contradiction—that we should join with women who exploit us to help liberate them. The call for Sisterhood was heard by many black women as a plea for help and support for a movement that did not address us. As Toni Morrison explains in her article "What the Black Woman Thinks About Women's Lib," many black women do not respect bourgeois white women and could not imagine supporting a cause that would be for their benefit.

> Black women have been able to envy white women (their looks, their easy life, the attention they seem to get from their men); they could fear them (for the economic control they have had over black women's lives); and even love them (as mammies and domestic workers can); but black women have found it impossible to respect white women. . . . Black women have no abiding admiration of white women as competent, complete people, whether vying with them for the few professional slots available to woman in general, or moving their dirt from one place to another, they regarded them as willful children, pretty children, mean children, but never as real adults capable of handling the real problems of the world.
>
> White women were ignorant of the facts of life—perhaps by choice, perhaps with the assistance of men, but ignorant anyway. They were totally dependent on marriage or male support (emotionally and economically). They confronted their sexuality with furtiveness, complete abandon, or repression. Those who could afford it gave over the management of the house and the rearing of children to others. (It is a source of amusement even now to black women to listen to feminist talk of liberation while somebody's nice black grandmother shoulders the daily responsibility of child rearing and floor mopping, and the liberated one comes home to examine the housekeeping, correct it, and be entertained by the children.) If Women's Lib needs those grandmothers to thrive, it has a serious flaw.[6]

Many perceived that the women's liberation movement as outlined by bourgeois white women would serve their interests at the expense of poor and working-class women, many of whom are black. Certainly this was not a basis for Sisterhood, and black women would have been politically naive had we joined such a movement. However, given the struggles of black women's participation historically and currently in political organizing, the emphasis could have been on the development and clarification of the nature of political solidarity.

White females discriminate against and exploit black women while simultaneously being envious and competitive in their interactions with them. Neither process of interaction creates conditions wherein trust and mutually reciprocal relationships can develop. After constructing feminist theory and praxis in such a way as to omit focus on racism, white women shifted the responsibility for calling attention to race onto others. They did not have to take the initiative in discussions of racism or race privilege but could listen and respond to nonwhite women discussing racism without changing in any way the structure of feminist movement, without losing their hegemonic hold. They could then show their concern with having more women of color in feminist organizations by encouraging greater participation. They were not confronting racism. In more recent years, racism has become an accepted topic in feminist discussions not as a result of black women calling attention to it (this was done at the very onset of the movement), but as a result of white female input validating such discussion, a process which is indicative of how racism works. Commenting on this tendency in her essay "The Incompatible Menage À Trois: Marxism, Feminism, and Racism," Gloria Joseph states:

> To date feminists have not concretely demonstrated the potential or capacity to become involved in fighting racism on an equal footing with sexism. Adrienne Rich's recent article on feminism and racism is an exemplary one on this topic. She reit-

> erates much that has been voiced by black female writers, but the acclaim given her article shows again that it takes whiteness to give even Blackness validity.[7]

Focus on racism in feminist circles is usually directed at legitimating the "as is" structure of feminist theory and praxis. Like other affirmative action agendas in white supremacist capitalist patriarchy, lengthy discussions of racism or lip-service to its importance tend to call attention to the "political correctness" of the current feminist movement; they are not directed at an overall struggle to resist racist oppression in our society (not just racism in the feminist movement). Discussions of racism have been implicitly sexist because of the focus on guilt and personal behavior. Racism is not an issue simply because white women activists are individually racist. They represent a small percentage of women in this society. They could have all been antiracist from the outset, but eliminating racism would still need to be a central feminist issue. Racism is fundamentally a feminist issue because it is so interconnected with sexist oppression. In the West, the philosophical foundations of racist and sexist ideology are similar. Although ethnocentric white values have led feminist theorists to argue the priority of sexism over racism, they do so in the context of attempting to create an evolutionary notion of culture, which in no way corresponds to our lived experience. In the United States, maintaining white supremacy has always been as great if not a greater priority than maintaining strict sex role divisions. It is no mere coincidence that interest in white women's rights is kindled whenever there is mass-based antiracist protest. Even the most politically naive person can comprehend that a white supremacist state, asked to respond to the needs of oppressed black people and/or the needs of white women (particularly those from the bourgeois classes), will find it in its interest to respond to whites. Radical movement to end racism (a struggle that many have died to advance) is far more threatening than a women's movement shaped to meet the class needs of upwardly mobile white women.

It does not in any way diminish the value of or the need for feminist movement to recognize the significance of antiracist struggle. Feminist theory would have much to offer if it showed women ways in which racism and sexism are immutably connected rather than pitting one struggle against the other or blatantly dismissing racism. A central issue for feminist activists has been the struggle to obtain for women the right to control their bodies. The very concept of white supremacy relies on the perpetuation of a white race. It is in the interest of continued white racist domination of the planet for white patriarchy to maintain control over all women's bodies. Any white female activist who works daily to help women gain control over their bodies and is racist negates and undermines her own effort. When white women attack white supremacy, they are simultaneously participating in the struggle to end sexist oppression. This is just one example of the intersecting, complementary nature of racist and sexist oppression. There are many others that need to be examined by feminist theorists.

Racism allows white women to construct feminist theory and praxis in such a way that it is far removed from anything resembling radical struggle. Racist socialization teaches bourgeois white women to think they are necessarily more capable of leading masses of women than other groups of women. Time and time again, they have shown that they do not want to be part of feminist movement—they want to lead it. Even though bourgeois white women liberationists probably know less about grassroots organizing than many poor and working-class women, they were certain of their leadership ability, as well as confident that theirs should be the dominant role in shaping theory and praxis. Racism teaches an inflated sense of importance and value, especially when coupled with class privilege. Most poor and working-class women or even individual bourgeois nonwhite women would not have assumed that they could launch a feminist movement without first having the support and participation of diverse groups of women. Elizabeth Spelman stresses this impact of racism in her essay, "Theories of Race and Gender: The Erasure of Black Women":

> This is a racist society, and part of what this means is that, generally, the self-esteem of white people is deeply influenced by their difference from and supposed superiority to black people. White people may not think of themselves as racists, because they do not own slaves or hate blacks, but that does not mean that much of what props up white people's sense of self-esteem is not based on the racism which unfairly distributes benefits and burdens to whites and blacks.[8]

One reason white women active in feminist movement were unwilling to confront racism was their arrogant assumption that their call to Sisterhood was a nonracist gesture. Many white women have said to me, "We wanted black women and other nonwhite women to join the movement," totally unaware of their perception that they somehow "own" the movement, that they are the "hosts" inviting us as "guests."

Despite current focus on eliminating racism in feminist movement, there has been little change in the direction of theory and praxis. While white feminist activists now include writings by women of color on course outlines, or hire one woman of color to teach a class about her ethnic group, or make sure one or more women of color are represented in feminist organizations (even though this contribution of women of color is needed and valuable), more often than not they are attempting to cover up the fact that they are totally unwilling to surrender their hegemonic dominance of theory and praxis, a dominance that they would not have established were this not a white supremacist, capitalist state. Their attempts to manipulate women of color, a component of the process of dehumanization, do not always go unnoticed. In the July 1983 issue of *In These Times*, a letter written by Theresa Funiciello was published on the subject of poor women and the women's movement which shows the nature of racism within feminist movement:

> Prior to a conference some time ago on the Urban Woman sponsored by the New York City chapter of NOW, I received a phone call from a NOW representative (whose name I have forgotten) asking for a welfare speaker with special qualifications. I was asked that she not be white—she might be "too articulate"—(i.e. not me), that she not be black, she might be "too angry." Perhaps she could be Puerto Rican? She should not say anything political or analytical but confine herself to the subject of "what the women's movement has done for me."

Funiciello responded to this situation by organizing a multiracial women's takeover of the conference. This type of action shows the spirit of Sisterhood.

Another response to racism has been the establishment of unlearning racism workshops, which are often led by white women. These workshops are important, yet they tend to focus primarily on cathartic individual psychological acknowledgment of personal prejudice without stressing the need for corresponding change in political commitment and action. A woman who attends an unlearning racism workshop and learns to acknowledge that she is racist is no less a threat than one who does not. Acknowledgment of racism is significant when it leads to transformation. More research, writing, and practical implementation of findings must be done on ways to unlearn racist socialization. Many white women who daily exercise race privilege lack awareness that they are doing so (which explains the emphasis on confession in unlearning racism workshops). They may not have conscious understanding of the ideology of white supremacy and the extent to which it shapes their behavior and attitudes toward women unlike themselves. Often, white women bond on the basis of shared racial identity without conscious awareness of the significance of their actions. This unconscious maintenance and perpetuation of white supremacy is dangerous, because none of us can struggle to change racist attitudes if we do not recognize that they exist. For example, a group of white feminist activists who do not know one another may be present at a meeting to discuss feminist theory. They may feel they are bonded on the basis of shared womanhood, but the atmosphere will noticeably change when a woman of color enters the room. The white women will become tense, no longer relaxed, no longer celebratory. Unconsciously, they felt close to one another because they shared racial identity. The "whiteness" that bonds them together is a racial identity that is directly related to the experience of nonwhite people as "other" and as a "threat." Often when I speak to white women about racial bonding, they deny that it exists; it is not unlike sexist men denying their sexism. Until white supremacy is understood and attacked by white women, there can be no bonding between them and multi-ethnic groups of women.

Women will know that white feminist activists have begun to confront racism in a serious and revolutionary manner when they are not simply acknowledging racism in the feminist movement or calling attention to personal prejudice, but are actively struggling to resist racist oppression in our society. Women will know they have made a political commitment to eliminating racism when they help change the direction of feminist movement, when they work to unlearn racist socialization prior to assuming positions of leadership or shaping theory or making contact with women of color so that they will not perpetuate and maintain racial oppression or, unconsciously or consciously, abuse and hurt nonwhite women. These are the truly radical gestures that create a foundation for the experience of political solidarity between white women and women of color.

White women are not the only group who must confront racism if Sisterhood is to emerge. Women of color must confront our absorption of white supremacist beliefs, "internalized racism," which may lead us to feel self-hate, to vent anger and rage at injustice at one another rather than at oppressive forces, to hurt and abuse one another, or to lead one ethnic group to make no effort to communicate with another. Often women of color from varied ethnic groups have learned to resent and hate one another, or to be competitive with one another. Often Asian, Latina, or Native American Indian groups find they can bond with whites by hating blacks. Black people respond to this by perpetuating racist stereotypes and images of these ethnic groups. It becomes a vicious cycle. Divisions between women of color will not be eliminated until we assume responsibility for uniting (not solely on the basis of resisting racism) to learn about our cultures, to share our knowledge and skills, and to gain strength from our diversity. We need to do more research and writing about the barriers that separate us and the ways we can overcome such separation. Often the men in our ethnic groups have greater contact with one another than we do. Women often assume so many job-related and domestic responsibilities that we lack the time or do not make the time to get to know women outside our group or community. Language differences often prevent us from communicating; we can change this by encouraging one another to learn to speak Spanish, English, Japanese, Chinese, etc.

One factor that makes interaction between multi-ethnic groups of women difficult and sometimes impossible is our failure to recognize that a behavior pattern in one culture may be unacceptable in another, that it may have different signification cross-culturally. Through repeated teaching of a course titled "Third World Women in the United States," I have learned the importance of learning what we call one another's cultural codes. An Asian-American student, of Japanese heritage, explained her reluctance to participate in feminist organizations by calling attention to the tendency among feminist activists to speak rapidly without pause, to be quick on the uptake, always ready with a response. She had been raised to pause and think before speaking, to consider the impact of one's words, a characteristic that she felt was particularly true of Asian-Americans. She expressed feelings of inadequacy on the various occasions she was present in feminist groups. In our class, we learned to allow pauses and appreciate them. By sharing this cultural code, we created an atmosphere in the classroom that allowed for different communication patterns. This particular class was peopled primarily by black women. Several white women students complained that the atmosphere in the class was "too hostile." They cited the noise level and direct confrontations that took place in the room prior to class starting as an example of this hostility. Our response was to explain that what they perceived as hostility and aggression, we considered playful teasing and affectionate expressions of our pleasure at being together. Our tendency to talk loudly we saw as a consequence of being in a room with many people speaking as well as cultural background; many of us were raised in families where individuals speak loudly. In their upbringing as white, middle-class females, the complaining students had been taught to identify loud and direct speech with anger. We explained that we did not identify loud or blunt speech in this way, and encouraged them to switch codes, to think of it as an affirming gesture. Once they switched codes, they not only began to have a more creative, joyful experience in the class, but they also learned that silence and quiet speech can in some cultures indicate hostility and aggression. By learning one another's cultural codes and respecting our differences, we felt a sense of community, of Sisterhood. Respecting diversity does not mean uniformity or sameness.[9]

A crucial concern in these multiracial classroom settings was recognition and acknowledgment of our differences and the extent to which they determine how we will be perceived by others. We had to continually remind one another to appreciate difference since many of us were raised to fear it. We talked about the need to acknowledge that we all suffer in some way but that we are not all oppressed nor equally oppressed. Many of us feared that our experiences were irrelevant because they were not as oppressive or as exploited as the experience of others. We discovered that we had a greater feeling of unity when people focused truthfully on their own experiences without comparing them with those of others in a competitive way. One student, Isabel Yrigoyei, wrote:

> We were not equally oppressed. There is no joy in this. We must speak from within us, our own experiences, our own oppressions—taking someone else's oppression is nothing to feel proud of. We should never speak for that which we have not felt.

When we began our communication by focusing on individual experiences, we found them to be varied even among those of us who shared common backgrounds. We learned that these differences mean we have no monolithic experiences that we can identify as "Chicana experience," "Black experience," etc. A Chicana growing up in a rural environment in a Spanish-speaking home has a life experience that differs from that of a Chicana raised in an English-speaking family in a bourgeois, predominantly white, New Jersey suburb. These two women will not automatically feel solidarity. Even though they are from the same ethnic group, they must work to develop Sisterhood. Seeing these types of differences, we also confronted our tendency to value some experiences over others. We might see the Spanish-speaking Chicana as being more "politically correct" than her English-speaking peer. By no longer passively accepting the learned tendency to compare and judge, we could see value in each experience. We could also see that our different experiences often meant that we had different needs, that there was no one strategy or formula for the development of political consciousness. By mapping out various strategies, we affirmed our diversity while working toward solidarity. Women must explore various ways to communicate with one another cross-culturally if we are to develop political solidarity. When women of color strive to learn with and about one another, we take responsibility for building Sisterhood. We need not rely on white women to lead the way to solidarity; all too often, opportunistic concerns point them in other directions. We can establish unity among ourselves with antiracist women. We can stand together united in political solidarity, in feminist movement. We can restore to the idea of Sisterhood its true meaning and value.

Cutting across racial lines, class is a serious political division between women. It was often suggested in early feminist literature that class would not be so important if more poor and working-class women would join the movement. Such thinking was both a denial of the existence of class privilege gained through exploitation as well as a denial of class struggle. To build Sisterhood, women must criticize and repudiate class exploitation. The bourgeois woman who takes a less privileged "sister" to lunch or dinner at a fancy restaurant may be acknowledging class but she is not repudiating class privilege—she is exercising it. Wearing second-hand clothing and living in low-cost housing in a poor neighborhood while buying stock is not a gesture of solidarity with those who are deprived or underprivileged. As in the case of racism in feminist movement, the emphasis on class has been focused on individual status and change. Until women accept the need for redistribution of wealth and resources in the United States and work toward the achievement of that end, there will be no bonding between women that transcends class.

It is terribly apparent that feminist movement so far has primarily served the class interests of bourgeois white women and men. The great majority of women from middle-class situations who recently entered the labor force (an entry encouraged and promoted by the feminist movement) helped strengthen the economy of the 1970s. In *The Two-Paycheck Marriage*, Caroline Bird emphasizes the extent to which these women (most of whom are white) helped bolster a waning economy:

> Working wives helped families maintain that standard of living through inflation. The Bureau of Labor Statistics has concluded that between 1973 and 1974 the real purchasing power of single-earner families dropped 3 percent compared with

> only 1 percent for families in which the wife was working. . . . Women especially will put themselves out to defend a standard of living they see threatened.
>
> Women did more than maintain standards. Working women lifted millions of families into middle class life. Her pay meant the difference between an apartment and a house, or college for the children . . . Working wives were beginning to create a new kind of rich—and . . . a new kind of poor.[10]

More than ten years later, it is evident that large numbers of individual white women (especially those from middle-class backgrounds) have made economic strides in the wake of the feminist movement's support of careerism and affirmative action programs in many professions. However, the masses of women are as poor as ever, or poorer. To the bourgeois "feminist," the million dollar salary granted newscaster Barbara Walters represents a victory for women. To working-class women who make less than the minimum wage and receive few if any benefits, it means continued class exploitation.

Leah Fritz's *Dreamers and Dealers* is a fine example of the liberal woman's attempt to gloss over the fact that class privilege is based on exploitation, that rich women support and condone that exploitation, that the people who suffer most are poor, underprivileged women and children. Fritz attempts to evoke sympathy for all upper-class women by stressing their psychological suffering, their victimization at the hands of men. She concludes her chapter "Rich Women" with the statement:

> Feminism belongs as much to the rich woman as to the poor woman. It can help her to understand that her own interests are linked with the advancement of all womankind; that comfort in dependency is a trap; that the golden cage has bars, too; and that, rich and poor, we are all wounded in the service of the patriarchy, although our scars are different. The inner turmoil that sends her to a psychoanalyst can generate energy for the movement which alone may heal her, by setting her free.[11]

Fritz conveniently ignores that domination and exploitation are necessary if there are to be rich women who may experience sexist discrimination or exploitation. She conveniently ignores class struggle.

Women from lower-class groups had no difficulty recognizing that the social equality women's liberationists talked about equated careerism and class mobility with liberation. They also knew who would be exploited in the service of this liberation. Daily confronting class exploitation, they cannot conveniently ignore class struggle. In the anthology *Women of Crisis,* Helen, a working-class white woman, who works as a maid in the home of a bourgeois white "feminist," expresses her understanding of the contradiction between feminist rhetoric and practice:

> I think the missus is right: everyone should be equal. She keeps on saying that. But then she has me working away in her house, and I'm not equal with her—and she doesn't want to be equal with me; and I don't blame her, because if I was her I'd hold on to my money just like she does. Maybe that's what the men are doing—they're holding on to their money. And it's a big fight, like it always is

> about money. She should know. She doesn't go throwing big fat pay checks at her "help." She's fair; she keeps reminding us—but she's not going to "liberate" us, any more than the men are going to "liberate" their wives or their secretaries or the other women working in their companies.[12]

Women's liberationists not only equated psychological pain with material deprivation to de-emphasize class privilege; they often suggested it was the more severe problem. They managed to overlook the fact that many women suffer both psychologically and materially, and for that reason alone changing their social status merited greater attention than careerism. Certainly the bourgeois woman who is suffering psychically is more likely to find help than the woman who is suffering material deprivation as well as emotional pain. One of the basic differences in perspective between the bourgeois woman and the working-class or poor woman is that the latter know that being discriminated against or exploited because one is female may be painful and dehumanizing, but it may not necessarily be as painful, dehumanizing, or threatening as being without food or shelter, as starvation, as being deathly ill but unable to obtain medical care. Had poor women set the agenda for the feminist movement, they might have decided that class struggle would be a central feminist issue; that poor and privileged women would work to understand class structure and the way it pits women against one another.

Outspoken socialist feminists, most of whom are white women, have emphasized class but they have not been effective in changing attitudes toward class in feminist movement. Despite their support of socialism, their values, behaviors, and lifestyles continue to be shaped by privilege. They have not developed collective strategies to convince bourgeois women who have no radical political perspective that eliminating class oppression is crucial to efforts to end sexist oppression. They have not worked hard to organize with poor and working-class women who may not identify as socialists but do identify with the need for redistribution of wealth in the United States. They have not worked to raise the consciousness of women collectively. Much of their energy has been spent addressing the white male Left, discussing the connections between Marxism and feminism, or explaining to other feminist activists that socialist feminism is the best strategy for revolution. Emphasis on class struggle is often incorrectly deemed the sole domain of socialist feminists. Although I call attention to directions and strategies they have not employed, I wish to emphasize that these issues should be addressed by all activists in feminist movement. When women face the reality of classism and make political commitments to eliminating it, we will no longer experience the class conflicts that have been so apparent in feminist movement. Until we focus on class divisions between women, we will be unable to build political solidarity.

Sexism, racism, and classism divide women from one another. Within feminist movement, divisions and disagreements about strategy and emphasis led to the formation of a number of groups with varied political positions. Splintering into different political factions and special interest groups has erected unnecessary barriers to sisterhood that could easily be eliminated. Special interest groups lead women to believe that only socialist feminists should be concerned about class; that only lesbian feminists should be concerned about the oppression of lesbians and gay men; that only black women or other women of color should be concerned about racism. Every woman can stand in political opposition to sexist, racist, heterosexist, and classist oppression. While she may choose to focus her work on a given political issue or a particular cause, if she is firmly opposed to all forms of group oppression, this broad perspective will be manifest in all her work irrespective of its particularity. When feminist activists are antiracist and against class exploitation, it will not matter if women of color are present or poor women, etc. These issues will be deemed important and will be addressed, although the women most personally affected by particular exploitations will necessarily continue in the forefront of those struggles. Women must learn to accept responsibility for fighting oppressions that may not directly affect us as individuals. Feminist movement, like other radical movements in our society, suffers when individual concerns and priorities are the only reason for participation. When we show our concern for the collective, we strengthen our solidarity.

Solidarity was a word seldom used in contemporary feminist movement. Much greater emphasis was placed on the idea of "support." Support can mean upholding or defending a position one believes is right. It can also mean serving as a prop or a foundation for a weak structure. This latter meaning had greater significance in feminist circles. Its value emerged from the emphasis on shared victimization. Identifying as "victims," women were acknowledging a helplessness and powerlessness as well as a need for support, in this case the support of fellow feminist activists, "sisters." It was closely related to the shallow notion of Sisterhood. Commenting on its usage among feminist activists in her essay "With All Due Respect," Jane Rule explains:

> Support is a much used word in the women's movement. For too many people it means giving and receiving unqualified approval. Some women are awfully good at withdrawing it at crucial moments. Too many are convinced they can't function without it. It's a false concept which has produced barriers to understanding and done real emotional damage. Suspension of critical judgment is not necessary for offering real support, which has to do instead with self-respect and respect for other people even at moments of serious disagreement.

Women's legacy of woman-hating, which includes fierce, brutal, verbal tearing apart of one another, has to be eliminated if women are to make critiques and engage in disagreements and arguments that are constructive and caring, with the intention of enriching rather than diminishing. Woman-to-woman negative, aggressive behavior is not unlearned when all critical judgment is suspended. It is unlearned when women accept that we are different, that we will necessarily disagree, but that we can disagree and argue with one another without acting as if we are fighting for our lives, without feeling that we stand to lose all self-esteem by verbally trashing someone else. Verbal disagreements are often the setting where women can demonstrate their engagement with the win-or-lose competitiveness that is most often associate with male interactions, especially in the arena of sports. Women, like men, must learn how to dialogue with one another without competition. Jane Rule suggests that women can disagree without trashing if they realize they do not stand to lose value or self-worth if they are criticized: "No one can discredit my life if it is in my own hands, and therefore I do not have to make anyone carry the false burden of my frightened hostility."

Women need to come together in situations where there will be ideological disagreement and work to change that interaction so communication occurs. This means that when women come together, rather than pretend union, we would acknowledge that we are divided and must develop strategies to overcome fears, prejudices, resentments, competitiveness, etc. The fierce negative disagreements that have taken place in feminist circles have led many feminist activists to shun group or individual interaction where there is likely to be disagreement that leads to confrontation. Safety and support have been redefined to mean hanging out in groups where the participants are alike and share similar values. While no woman wants to enter a situation in which she will be psychically annihilated, women can face one another in hostile confrontation and struggle and move beyond the hostility to understanding. Expression of hostility as an end in itself is a useless activity, but when it is the catalyst pushing us on to greater clarity and understanding, it serves a meaningful function.

Women need to have the experience of working through hostility to arrive at understanding and solidarity if only to free ourselves from the sexist socialization that tells us to avoid confrontation because we will be victimized or destroyed. Time and time again, I have had the experience of making statements at talks that anger a listener and lead to assertive and sometimes hostile verbal confrontation. The situation feels uncomfortable, negative, and unproductive because there are angry voices, tears, etc., and yet I may find later that the experience has led to greater clarity and growth on my part and on the part of the listener. On one occasion, I was invited by a black woman sociologist, a very soft-spoken individual, to speak in a class she was teaching. A young Chicana woman who could pass for white was a student in the class. We had a heated exchange when I made the point that the ability to pass for white gave her a perspective on race totally different from that of someone who is dark-skinned and can never pass. I pointed out that any person meeting her with no knowledge of her ethnic background probably assumes that she is white and relates to her accordingly. At the time the suggestion angered her. She became quite angry and finally stormed out of the class in tears. The teacher and fellow students definitely saw me as the "bad guy" who had failed to support a fellow sister and instead reduced her to tears. They were annoyed that our get-together had not been totally pleasurable, unemotional, dispassionate. I certainly felt miserable in the situation. The student, however, contacted me weeks later to share her feelings that she had gained new insights and awareness as a result of our encounter which aided her personal growth. Incidents like this one, which initially appear to be solely negative because of tension or hostility, can lead to positive growth. If women always seek to avoid confrontation, to always be "safe," we may never experience any revolutionary change, any transformation, individually or collectively.

When women actively struggle in a truly supportive way to understand our differences, to change misguided, distorted perspectives, we lay the foundation for the experience of political solidarity. Solidarity is not the same as support. To experience solidarity, we must have a community of interests, shared beliefs and goals around which to unite, to build Sisterhood. Support can be occasional. It can be given and just as easily withdrawn. Solidarity requires sustained, ongoing commitment. In feminist movement, there is need for diversity, disagreement, and difference if we are to grow. As Grace Lee Boggs and James Boggs emphasize in *Revolution and Evolution in the Twentieth Century:*

> The same appreciation of the reality of contradiction underlies the concept of criticism and self-criticism. Criticism and self-criticism is the way in which individuals united by common goals can consciously utilize their differences and limitations, i.e., the negative, in order to accelerate their positive advance. The popular formulation for this process is "changing a bad thing into a good thing . . ."

Women do not need to eradicate difference to feel solidarity. We do not need to share common oppression to fight equally to end oppression. We do not need antimale sentiments to bond us together, so great is the wealth of experience, culture, and ideas we have to share with one another. We can be sisters united by shared interests and beliefs, united in our appreciation for diversity, united in our struggle to end sexist oppression, united in political solidarity.

NOTES

1. Florynce Kennedy, "Institutional Oppression vs. The Female," pp. 438–446.
2. In early contemporary feminist writings (e.g., Redstockings Manifesto) the image of woman as victim was evoked. Joan Cassell's study of sisterhood and symbolism in the feminist movement, *A Group Called Women,* examines the ideology of bonding among feminist activists. Contemporary writers like Leah Fritz evoke an image of woman as victim to encourage woman bonding. Barbara Smith discusses this tendency in her introduction to *Home Girls.*
3. At the onset of contemporary feminist movement I (and many other black women) often heard white women in Women's Studies classes, consciousness raising groups, meetings etc., respond to questions about the lack of black female participation by stressing that this was not related to problems with the structure of feminist movement but an indication that black women were already liberated. The image of the "strong" black woman is evoked in the writings of a number of white activists (e.g., Sara Evans, *Personal Politics;* Bettina Aptheker, *Woman's Legacy*).
4. Jo Freeman, *The Politics of Women's Liberation,* p. 118.
5. Toni Morrison, "Cinderella's Stepsisters," p. 41.
6. Toni Morrison, "What the Black Woman Thinks About Women's Lib," p. 15.
7. Gloria Joseph, "The Incompatible Menage À Trois: Marxism, Feminism, and Racism," p. 105.
8. Elizabeth Spelman, "Theories of Race and Gender: The Erasure of Black Women," pp. 36–62.
9. My experience teaching "Third World Women in the United States" at San Francisco State has deeply enriched my understanding of women from diverse backgrounds. I am grateful to all the students I taught there, especially Betty and Susan.
10. Caroline Bird, *The Two-Paycheck Marriage,* p. 9.
11. Fritz, p. 225.
12. *Women of Crisis,* p. 266.

BIBLIOGRAPHY

Bird, Caroline. *The Two-Paycheck Marriage.* New York: Rocket Books, 1979.

Coles, Robert and Jane. *Women of Crisis.* New York: Dell Publishing Company, 1978.

Freeman, J. *The Politics of Women's Liberation.* New York: David McKay Company, 1975.

Fritz, Leah. *Dreamers and Dealers: An Intimate Appraisal of the Women's Movement.* Boston: Beacon Press, 1979.

Joseph, Gloria. "The Incompatible Menage À Trois: Marxism, Feminism, and Racism," *Women and Revolution.* Ed. Lydia Sargent. Boston: South End Press, 1981.

Kennedy, Florynce. "Institutionalized Oppression vs. the Female," in *Sisterhood Is Powerful.* Ed. Robin Morgan. New York: Vintage Books, 1970, pp. 438–46.

Morrison, Toni. "Cinderella's Stepsisters," in *Ms.*, September 1979, pp. 41–2.

______. "What the Black Woman Thinks About Women's Lib," in *The New York Times Magazine,* August 22, 1979.

Spelman, Elizabeth. "Theories of Race and Gender: The Erasure of Black Women," in *Quest,* Vol. V, No. 4, pp. 36–62.

A Manifesto for Cyborgs: Science, Technology, and Socialist Feminism in the 1980s

Haraway aims to extend the tradition of socialist feminism in a way that incorporates the insights of postmodernism without sacrificing the capacity to anticipate a gender-free feminist future. In a spirit that is both playful and iconoclastic, she invokes the idea of a cyborg—a being that is part machine and part organism—to characterize social reality and to provide a basis for socialist feminist critique and politics. Both human and animal, both organism and machine, both physical and spiritual—never altogether on one side or the other—the cyborg enables us to think beyond familiar and confining dichotomies and social theories.

Haraway observes that belonging in the category "female" does not make women into a cohesive political unit, and she examines the epistemological and political consequences of women's diversity. She critically examines the efforts of Marxist feminists and radical feminists to expand theoretical categories and to analyze social forces so as to accommodate women's lives and feminist imperatives. She then turns to her own account. In Haraway's view, modernity's concept of the person and its economic and political structures of domination are being replaced by a worldwide, high-tech system of production, reproduction, and communication that she dubs "the informatics of domination." In this postmodern world inhabited by cyborgs, the control and flow of information define power. Power is deployed to privatize work and leisure, to instrumentalize sexuality, and to maintain vast disparities in wealth and power between a technological elite and the technologically illiterate masses. Yet, Haraway is guardedly optimistic, for the pervasiveness of hardship under this system provides a basis for political coalitions that span race, gender, and class. The prime strategy for opposing this system of domination is intervention in communication networks. Thus, Haraway concludes with a series of reflections on the possibilities for feminist/cyborg discourses of subversion and transformation.

—D.T.M.

Chapter 27

Donna Haraway

A Manifesto for Cyborgs: Science, Technology, and Socialist Feminism in the 1980s

AN IRONIC DREAM OF A COMMON LANGUAGE FOR WOMEN IN THE INTEGRATED CIRCUIT

This essay is an effort to build an ironic political myth faithful to feminism, socialism, and materialism. Perhaps more faithful as blasphemy is faithful, than as reverent worship and identification. Blasphemy has always seemed to require taking things very seriously. I know no better stance to adopt from within the secular-religious, evangelical traditions of United States politics, including the politics of socialist-feminism. Blasphemy protects one from the moral majority within while still insisting on the need for community. Blasphemy is not apostasy. Irony is about contradictions that do not resolve into larger wholes, even dialectically, about the tension of holding incompatible things together because both or all are necessary and true. Irony is about humor and serious play. It is also a rhetorical strategy and a political method, one I would like to see more honored within socialist feminism. At the center of my ironic faith, my blasphemy, is the image of the cyborg.

A cyborg is a cybernetic organism, a hybrid of machine and organism, a creature of social reality as well as a creature of fiction. Social reality is lived social relations, our most important political construction, a world-changing fiction. The international women's movements have constructed "women's experience," as well as uncovered or discovered this crucial collective object. This experience is a fiction and fact of the most crucial, political kind. Liberation rests on the construction of the consciousness, the imaginative apprehension, of oppression, and so of possibility. The cyborg is a matter of fiction and lived experience that changes what counts as women's experience in the late twentieth century. This is a struggle over life and death, but the boundary between science fiction and social reality is an optical illusion.

Contemporary science fiction is full of cyborgs—creatures simultaneously animal and machine, who populate worlds ambiguously natural and crafted. Modern medicine is also full of cyborgs, of couplings between organism and machine, each conceived as coded devices, in an intimacy and with a power that was not generated in the history of sexuality. Cyborg "sex" restores some of the lovely replicative baroque ferns and invertebrates (such nice organic prophylactics against heterosexism). Cyborg replication is uncoupled from organic reproduction. Modern production seems like a dream of cyborg colonization of work, a dream that makes the nightmare of Taylorism seem idyllic. And modern war is a cyborg orgy, coded by C^3I, command-control-communication-intelligence, an $84 billion item in 1984's U.S. defense budget. I am making an argument for the cyborg as a fiction mapping our social and bodily reality and as an imaginative resource suggesting some very fruitful couplings. Foucault's biopolitics is a flaccid premonition of cyborg politics, a very open field.

By the late twentieth century, our time, a mythic time, we are all chimeras, theorized and fabricated hybrids of machine and organism; in short, we are cyborgs. The cyborg is our ontology; it gives us our politics. The cyborg is a condensed image of both imagination and material reality, the two joined centers structuring any possibility of historical transformation. In the traditions of "Western" science and politics—the tradition of racist, male-dominant capitalism; the tradition of progress; the tradition of the appropriation of nature as resource for the productions of culture; the tradition of reproduction of the self from the reflections of the other—the relation between organism and machine has been a border war. The stakes in the border war have been the territories of production, reproduction, and imagination. This essay is an argument for *pleasure* in the confusion of boundaries and for *responsibility* in their construction. It is also an effort to contribute to socialist-feminist culture and theory in a postmodernist, nonnaturalist mode and in the utopian tradition of imagining a world without gender, which is perhaps a world without genesis, but maybe also a world without end. The cyborg incarnation is outside salvation history.

The cyborg is a creature in a postgender world; it has no truck with bisexuality, pre-Oedipal symbiosis, unalienated labor, or other seductions to organic wholeness through a final appropriation of all the powers of the parts into a higher unity. In a sense, the cyborg has no origin story in the Western sense; a "final" irony since the cyborg is also the awful apocalyptic *telos* of the "West's" escalating dominations of abstract individuation, an ultimate self untied at last from all dependency, a man in space. An origin story in the "Western," humanist sense depends on the myth of original unity, fullness, bliss, and terror, represented by the phallic mother from whom all humans must separate, the task of individual development and of history, the twin potent myths inscribed most powerfully for us in psychoanalysis and Marxism. Hilary Klein has argued that both Marxism and psychoanalysis, in their concepts of labor and of individuation and gender formation, depend on the plot of original unity out of which difference must be produced and enlisted in a drama of escalating domination of woman/nature. The cyborg skips the step of original unity, of identification with nature in the Western sense. This is its illegitimate promise that might lead to subversion of its teleology as Star Wars.

The cyborg is resolutely committed to partiality, irony, intimacy, and perversity. It is oppositional, utopian, and completely without innocence. No longer structured by the polarity of public and private, the cyborg defines a technological polis based partly on a revolution of social relations in the *oikos*, the household. Nature and culture are reworked; the one can no longer be the resource for appropriation or incorporation by the other. The relationships for forming wholes from parts, including those of polarity and hierarchical domination, are at issue in the cyborg world. Unlike the hopes of Frankenstein's monster, the cyborg does not expect its father to save it through a restoration of the garden; i.e., through the fabrication of a heterosexual mate, through its completion in a finished whole, a city and cosmos. The cyborg does not dream of community on the model of the organic family, this time without the Oedipal project. The cyborg would not recognize the Garden of Eden; it is not made of mud and cannot dream of returning to dust. Perhaps that is why I want to see if cyborgs can subvert the apocalypse of returning to nuclear dust in the manic compulsion to name the Enemy. Cyborgs are not reverent; they do not remember the cosmos. They are wary of holism, but needy for connection—they seem to have a natural feel for united front politics, but without the vanguard party. The main trouble with cyborgs, of course, is that they are the illegitimate offspring of militarism and patriarchal capitalism, not to mention state socialism. But illegitimate offspring are often exceedingly unfaithful to their origins. Their fathers, after all, are inessential.

I will return to the science fiction of cyborgs at the end of this essay, but now I want to signal three crucial boundary breakdowns that make the following political fiction (political scientific) analysis possible. By the late twentieth century in United States scientific culture, the boundary between human and animal is thoroughly breached. The last beachheads of uniqueness have been polluted if not turned into amusement parks—language, tool use, social behavior, mental events, nothing really convincingly settles the separation of human and animal. And many people no longer feel the need of such a separation; indeed, many branches of feminist culture affirm the pleasure of connection of human and other living creatures. Movements for animal rights are not irrational denials of human uniqueness; they are clear-sighted recognition of connection across the discredited breach of nature and culture. Biology and evolutionary theory over the last two centuries have simultaneously produced modern organisms and objects of knowledge and reduced the line between humans and animals to a faint trace re-etched in ideological struggle or professional disputes between life and social sciences. Within this framework, teaching modern Christian creationism should be fought as a form of child abuse.

Biological-determinist ideology is only one position opened up in scientific culture for arguing the meanings of human animality. There is much room for radical political people to contest for the meanings of the breached boundary.[1] The cyborg appears in myth precisely where the boundary between human and animal is transgressed. Far from signaling a walling off of people from other living beings, cyborgs signal disturbingly and pleasurably tight coupling. Bestiality has a new status in this cycle of marriage exchange.

The second leaky distinction is between animal-human (organism) and machine. Precybernetic machines could be haunted; there was always the specter of the ghost in the machine. This dualism structured the dialogue between materialism and idealism that was settled by a dialectical progeny, called spirit or history, according to taste. But basically machines were not self-moving, self-designing, autonomous. They could not achieve man's dream, only mock it. They were not man, an author to himself, but only a caricature of that masculinist reproductive dream. To think they were otherwise was paranoid. Now we are not so sure. Late twentieth-century machines have made thoroughly ambiguous the difference between natural and artificial, mind and body, self-developing and externally designed, and many other distinctions that used to apply to organisms and machines. Our machines are disturbingly lively, and we ourselves frighteningly inert.

Technological determinism is only one ideological space opened up by the reconceptions of machine and organism as coded texts through which we engage in the play of writing and reading the world.[2] "Textualization" of everything in poststructuralist, postmodernist theory has been damned by Marxists and socialist feminists for its utopian disregard for lived relations of domination that ground the "play" of arbitrary reading.[3*] It is certainly true that postmodernist strategies, like my cyborg myth, subvert myriad organic wholes (e.g., the poem, the primitive culture, the biological organism). In short, the certainty of what counts as nature—a source of insight and a promise of innocence—is undermined, probably fatally. The transcendent authorization of interpretation is lost, and with it the ontology grounding "Western" epistemology. But the alternative is not cynicism or faithlessness, i.e., some version of abstract existence, like the accounts of technological determinism destroying "man" by the "machine" or "meaningful political action" by the "text." Who cyborgs will be is a radical question; the answers are a matter of survival. Both chimpanzees and artifacts have politics, so why shouldn't we?[4]

The third distinction is a subset of the second: the boundary between physical and nonphysical is very imprecise for us. Pop physics books on the consequences of quantum theory and the indeterminacy principle are a kind of popular scientific equivalent to the Harlequin romances as a marker of radical change in American white heterosexuality: they get it wrong, but they are on the right subject. Modern machines are quintessentially microelectronic devices: they are everywhere and they are invisible. Modern machinery is an irreverent upstart god, mocking the Father's ubiquity and spirituality. The silicon chip is a surface for writing; it is etched in molecular scales disturbed only by atomic noise, the

* A provocative, comprehensive argument about the politics and theories of "postmodernism" is made by Frederick Jameson, who argues that post-modernism is not an option, a style among others, but a cultural dominant requiring radical reinvention of Left politics from within; there is no longer any place from without that gives meaning to the comforting fiction of critical distance. Jameson also makes clear why one cannot be for or against postmodernism, an essentially moralist move. My position is that feminists (and others) need continuous cultural reinventing, postmodernist critique, and historical materialism; only a cyborg would have a chance. The old dominations of white capitalist patriarchy seem nostalgically innocent now: they normalized heterogeneity, e.g., into man and woman, white and black. "Advanced capitalism" and postmodernism release heterogeneity without a norm, and we are flattened, without subjectivity, which requires depth, even unfriendly and drowning depths. It is time to write *The Death of the Clinic.* The clinic's methods required bodies and works; we have texts and surfaces. Our dominations don't work by medicalization and normalization anymore; they work by networking, communications redesign, stress management. Normalization gives way to automation, utter redundancy. Michel Foucault's *Birth of the Clinic, History of Sexuality,* and *Discipline and Punish* name a form of power at its moment of implosion. The discourse of biopolitics gives way to technobabble, the language of the spliced substantive; no noun is left whole by the multinationals. These are their names, listed from one issue of *Science:* Tech-Knowledge, Genentech, Allergen, Hybritech, Compupro, Genen-cor, Syntex, Allelix, Agrigenetics Corp., Syntro, Codon, Repligen, Micro-Angelo from Scion Corp., Percom Data, Inter Systems, Cyborg Corp., Statcom Corp., Intertec. If we are imprisoned by language, then escape from that prison house requires language poets, a kind of cultural restriction enzyme to cut the code; cyborg heteroglossia is one form of radical culture politics.

ultimate interference for nuclear scores. Writing, power, and technology are old partners in Western stories of the origin of civilization, but miniaturization has changed our experience of mechanisms. Miniaturization has turned out to be about power; small is not so much beautiful as pre-eminently dangerous, as in cruise missiles. Contrast the TV sets of the 1950s or the news cameras of the 1970s with the TV wristbands or hand-sized video cameras now advertised. Our best machines are made of sunshine; they are all light and clean because they are nothing but signals, electromagnetic waves, a section of a spectrum. And these machines are eminently portable, mobile—a matter of immense human pain in Detroit and Singapore. People are nowhere near so fluid, being both material and opaque. Cyborgs are ether, quintessence.

The ubiquity and invisibility of cyborgs is precisely why these sunshine-belt machines are so deadly. They are as hard to see politically as materially. They are about consciousness—or its simulation.[5] They are floating signifiers moving in pickup trucks across Europe, blocked more effectively by the witch-weavings of the displaced and so unnatural Greenham women, who read the cyborg webs of power very well, than by the militant labor of older masculinist politics, whose natural constituency needs defense jobs. Ultimately the "hardest" science is about the realm of greatest boundary confusion, the realm of pure number, pure spirit, C^3I, cryptography, and the preservation of potent secrets. The new machines are so clean and light. Their engineers are sun-worshipers mediating a new scientific revolution associated with the night dream of postindustrial society. The diseases evoked by these clean machines are "no more" than the minuscule coding changes of an antigen in the immune system, "no more" than the experience of stress. The nimble little fingers of "Oriental" women, the old fascination of little Anglo-Saxon Victorian girls with doll houses, women's enforced attention to the small, take on quite new dimensions in this world. There might be a cyborg Alice taking account of these new dimensions. Ironically, it might be the unnatural cyborg women making chips in Asia and spiral dancing in Santa Rita whose constructed unities will guide effective oppositional strategies.

So my cyborg myth is about transgressed boundaries, potent fusions, and dangerous possibilities that progressive people might explore as one part of needed political work. One of my premises is that most American socialists and feminists see deepened dualisms of mind and body, animal and machine, idealism and materialism in the social practices, symbolic formulations, and physical artifacts associated with "high technology" and scientific culture. From *One-Dimensional Man* to *The Death of Nature*,[6] the analytic resources developed by progressives have insisted on the necessary domination of technics and recalled us to an imagined organic body to integrate our resistance. Another of my premises is that the need for unity of people trying to resist worldwide intensification of domination has never been more acute. But a slightly perverse shift of perspective might better enable us to contest for meanings, as well as for other forms of power and pleasure in technologically mediated societies.

From one perspective, a cyborg world is about the final imposition of a grid of control on the planet, about the final abstraction embodied in a Star Wars apocalypse waged in the name of defense, about the final appropriation of women's bodies in a masculinist orgy of war.[7] From another perspective, a cyborg world might be about lived social and bodily realities in which people are not afraid of their joint kinship with animals and machines, not afraid of permanently partial identities and contradictory standpoints. The political struggle is to see from both perspectives at once because each reveals both dominations and possibilities unimaginable from the other vantage point. Single vision produces worse illusions than double vision or many-headed monsters. Cyborg unities are monstrous and illegitimate; in our present political circumstances, we could hardly hope for more potent myths for resistance and recoupling. I like to imagine LAG, the Livermore Action Group, as a kind of cyborg society, dedicated to realistically converting the laboratories that most fiercely embody and spew out the tools of technological apocalypse, and committed to building a political form that actually manages to hold together witches, engineers, elders, perverts, Christians, mothers, and Leninists long enough to disarm the state. Fission Impossible is the name of the affinity group in my town. (Affinity: related not by blood but by choice, the appeal of one chemical nuclear group for another, avidity.)

FRACTURED IDENTITIES

It has become difficult to name one's feminism by a single adjective—or even to insist in every circumstance upon the noun. Consciousness of exclusion through naming is acute. Identities seem contradictory, partial, and strategic. With the hard-won recognition of their social and historical constitution, gender, race, and class cannot provide the basis for belief in "essential" unity. There is nothing about being "female" that naturally binds women. There is not even such a state as "being" female, itself a highly complex category constructed in contested sexual scientific discourses and other social practices. Gender, race, or class consciousness is an achievement forced on us by the terrible historical experience of the contradictory social realities of patriarchy, colonialism, and capitalism. And who counts as "us" in my own rhetoric? Which identities are available to ground such a potent political myth called "us," and what could motivate enlistment in this collectivity? Painful fragmentation among feminists (not to mention among women) along every possible fault line has made the concept of *woman* elusive, an excuse for the matrix of women's dominations of each other. For me—and for many who share a similar historical location in white, professional middle-class, female, radical, North American, midadult bodies—the sources of a crisis in political identity are legion. The recent history for much of the U.S. Left and U.S. feminism has been a response to this kind of crisis by endless splitting and searches for a new essential unity. But there has also been a growing recognition of another response through coalition—affinity, not identity.[8]

Chela Sandoval, from a consideration of specific historical moments in the formation of the new political voice called women of color, has theorized a hopeful model of political identity called "oppositional consciousness," born of the skills for reading webs of power by those refused stable membership in the social categories of race, sex, or class.[9] "Women of color," a name contested at its origins by those whom it would incorporate, as well as a historical consciousness marking systematic breakdown of all the signs of Man in "Western" traditions, constructs a kind of postmodernist identity out of otherness and difference. This postmodernist identity is fully political, whatever might be said about other possible post-modernisms.

Sandoval emphasizes the lack of any essential criterion for identifying who is a woman of color. She notes that the definition of the group has been by conscious appropriation of negation. For example, a Chicana or U.S. black woman has not been able to speak as a woman or as a black person or as a Chicano. Thus, she was at the bottom of a cascade of negative identities, left out of even the privileged oppressed authorial categories called "women and blacks," who claimed to make the important revolutions. The category "woman" negated all nonwhite women; "black" negated all nonblack people, as well as all black women. But there was also no "she," no singularity, but a sea of differences among U.S. women who have affirmed their historical identity as U.S. women of color. This identity marks out a self-consciously constructed space that cannot affirm the capacity to act on the basis of natural identification, but only on the basis of conscious coalition, of affinity, of political kinship.[10] Unlike the "woman" of some streams of the white women's movement in the United States, there is no naturalization of the matrix, or at least this is what Sandoval argues is uniquely available through the power of oppositional consciousness.

Sandoval's argument has to be seen as one potent formulation for feminists out of the worldwide development of anticolonialist discourse, i.e., discourse dissolving the "West" and its highest product—the one who is not animal, barbarian, or woman; i.e., man, the author of a cosmos called history. As orientalism is deconstructed politically and semiotically, the identities of the occident destabilize, including those of feminists.[11] Sandoval argues that "women of color" have a chance to build an effective unity that does not replicate the imperializing, totalizing revolutionary subjects of previous Marxisms and feminisms that had not faced the consequences of the disorderly polyphony emerging from decolonization.

Katie King has emphasized the limits of identification and the political/poetic mechanics of identification built into reading "the poem," that generative core of cultural feminism. King criticizes the persistent tendency among contemporary feminists from different "moments" or "conversations" in feminist practice to taxonomize the women's movement to make one's own political tendencies appear to be the *telos* of the whole. These taxonomies tend to remake feminist history to appear to be an ideological struggle among coherent types persisting over time, especially those typical units called radical, liberal, and social feminism. Literally, all other feminisms are either incorporated or marginalized, usually by building an explicit ontology and epistemology.[12] Taxonomies of feminism produce epistemologies to police deviation from official women's experience. And of course, "women's culture," like women of color, is consciously created by mechanisms inducing affinity. The rituals of poetry, music, and certain forms of academic practice have been pre-eminent. The politics of race and culture in the U.S. women's movements are intimately interwoven. The common achievement of King and Sandoval is learning how to craft a poetic/political unity without relying on a logic of appropriation, incorporation, and taxonomic identification.

The theoretical and practical struggle against unity-through-domination or unity-through-incorporation ironically not only undermines the justifications for patriarchy, colonialism, humanism, positivism, positivism, essentialism, scientism, and other unlamented-isms, but *all* claims for an organic or natural standpoint. I think that radical and socialist/Marxist feminisms have also undermined their/our own epistemological strategies, and that this is a crucially valuable step in imagining possible unities. It remains to be seen whether all "epistemologies" as Western political people have known them fail us in the task to build effective affinities.

It is important to note that the effort to construct revolutionary standpoints, epistemologies as achievements of people committed to changing the world, has been part of the process showing the limits of identification. The acid tools of postmodernist theory and the constructive tools of ontological discourse about revolutionary subjects might be seen as ironic allies in dissolving Western selves in the interests of survival. We are excruciatingly conscious of what it means to have a historically constituted body. But with the loss of innocence in our origin, there is no expulsion from the Garden either. Our politics lose the indulgence of guilt with the naïveté of innocence. But what would another political myth for socialist feminism look like? What kind of politics could embrace partial, contradictory, permanently unclosed constructions of personal and collective selves and still be faithful, effective—and, ironically, socialist feminist?

I do not know of any other time in history when there was greater need for political unity to confront effectively the dominations of "race," "gender," "sexuality," and "class." I also do not know of any other time when the kind of unity we might help build could have been possible. None of "us" have any longer the symbolic or material capability of dictating the shape of reality to any of "them." Or at least "we" cannot claim innocence from practicing such dominations. White women, including socialist feminists, discovered (i.e., were forced kicking and screaming to notice) the noninnocence of the category "woman." That consciousness changes the geography of all previous categories; it denatures them as heat denatures a fragile protein. Cyborg feminists have to argue that "we" do not want any more natural matrix of unity and that no construction is whole. Innocence, and the corollary insistence on victimhood as the only ground for insight, has done enough damage. But the constructed revolutionary subject must give late twentieth-century people pause as well. In the fraying of identities and in the reflexive strategies for constructing them, the possibility opens up for weaving something other than a shroud for the day after the apocalypse that so prophetically ends salvation history.

Both Marxist/socialist feminisms and radical feminisms have simultaneously naturalized and denatured the category "woman" and consciousness of the social lives of "women." Perhaps a schematic caricature can highlight both kinds of moves. Marxian socialism is rooted in an analysis of wage labor that reveals class structure. The consequence of the wage relationship is systematic alienation, as the worker is dissociated from his (sic) product. Abstraction and illusion rule in knowledge, domination rules in practice. Labor is the pre-eminently privileged category enabling the Marxist to overcome illusion and find that point of view that is necessary for changing the world. Labor is the humanizing activity that makes man; labor is an ontological category permitting the knowledge of a subject, and so the knowledge of subjugation and alienation.

In faithful filiation, socialist feminism advanced by allying itself with the basic analytic strategies of Marxism. The main achievement of both Marxist feminists and socialist feminists was to expand the category of labor to accommodate what (some) women did, even when the wage relation was subordinated to a more comprehensive view of labor under capitalist patriarchy. In particular, women's labor in the household and women's activity as mothers generally, i.e., reproduction in the socialist feminist sense, entered theory on the authority of analogy to the Marxian concept of labor. The unity of women here rests on an epistemology based on the ontological structure of "labor." Marxist/socialist feminism does not "naturalize" unity; it is a possible achievement based on a possible standpoint rooted in social relations. The essentializing move is in the ontological structure of labor or of its analogue, women's activity.[13]* The inheritance of Marxian humanism, with its pre-eminently Western

* The central role of object-relations versions of psychoanalysis and related strong universalizing moves in discussing reproduction, caring work, and mothering in many approaches to epistemology underline their authors' resistance to what I am calling postmodernism. For me, both the universalizing moves and the versions of psychoanalysis make analysis of "women's place in the integrated circuit" difficult and lead to systematic difficulties in accounting for or even seeing major aspects of the construction of gender and gendered social life.

self, is the difficulty for me. The contribution from these formulations has been the emphasis on the daily responsibility of real women to build unities, rather than to naturalize them.

Catharine MacKinnon's version of radical feminism is itself a caricature of the appropriating, incorporating, totalizing tendencies of Western theories of identity grounding action.[14] It is factually and politically wrong to assimilate all of the diverse "moments" or "conversations" in recent women's politics named radical feminism to MacKinnon's version. But the teleological logic of her theory shows how epistemology and ontology—including their negations—erase or police difference. Only one of the effects of MacKinnon's theory is the rewriting of the history of the polymorphous field called radical feminism. The major effect is the production of a theory of experience, of women's identity, that is a kind of apocalypse for all revolutionary standpoints. That is, the totalization built into this tale of radical feminism achieves its end—the unity of women—by enforcing the experience of and testimony to radical nonbeing. As for the Marxist/socialist feminist, consciousness is an achievement, not a natural fact. And MacKinnon's theory eliminates some of the difficulties built into humanist revolutionary subjects, but at the cost of radical reductionism.

MacKinnon argues that radical feminism necessarily adopted a different analytical strategy from Marxism, looking first not at the structure of class but at the structure of sex/gender and its generative relationship, men's constitution and appropriation of women sexually. Ironically, MacKinnon's "ontology" constructs a nonsubject, a nonbeing. Another's desire, not the self's labor, is the origin of "woman." She therefore develops a theory of consciousness that enforces what can count as "women's" experience—anything that names sexual violation, indeed, sex itself as far as "women" can be concerned. Feminist practice is the construction of this form of consciousness; i.e., the self-knowledge of a self-who-is-not.

Perversely, sexual appropriation in this radical feminism still has the epistemological status of labor, i.e., the point from which analysis able to contribute to changing the world must flow. But sexual objectification, not alienation, is the consequence of the structure of sex/gender. In the realm of knowledge, the result of sexual objectification is illusion and abstraction. However, a woman is not simply alienated from her product, but in a deep sense does not exist as a subject, or even potential subject, since she owes her existence as a woman to sexual appropriation. To be constituted by another's desire is not the same thing as to be alienated in the violent separation of the laborer from his product.

MacKinnon's radical theory of experience is totalizing in the extreme; it does not so much marginalize as obliterate the authority of any other woman's political speech and action. It is a totalization producing what Western patriarchy itself never succeeded in doing—feminists' consciousness of the nonexistence of women, except as products of men's desire. I think MacKinnon correctly argues that no Marxian version of identity can firmly ground women's unity. But in solving the problem of the contradictions of any Western revolutionary subject for feminist purposes, she develops an even more authoritarian doctrine of experience. If my complaint about socialist/Marxism standpoints is their unintended erasure of polyvocal, unassimilable, radical difference made visible in anticolonial discourse and practice, MacKinnon's intentional erasure of all difference through the device of the "essential" nonexistence of women is not reassuring.

In my taxonomy, which like any other taxonomy is a reinscription of history, radical feminism can accommodate all the activities of women named by socialist feminists as forms of labor only if the activity can somehow be sexualized. Reproduction had different tones of meanings for the two tendencies, one rooted in labor, one in sex, both calling the consequences of domination and ignorance of social and personal reality "false consciousness."

Beyond either the difficulties or the contributions in the argument of any one author, neither Marxist nor radical feminist points of view have tended to embrace the status of a partial explanation; both were regularly constituted as totalities. Western explanation has demanded as much; how else could the "Western" author incorporate its others? Each tried to annex other forms of domination by expanding its basic categories through analogy, simple listing, or addition. Embarrassed silence about race among white radical and socialist feminists was one major, devastating political consequence. History and polyvocality disappeared into political taxonomies that tried to establish genealogies. There was no structural room for race (or for much else) in theory claiming to reveal the construction of the category woman and social group women as a unified or totalizable whole. The structure of my caricature looks like this:

Socialist Feminism—
structure of class//wage labor//alienation
labor, by analogy reproduction, by extension sex, by addition race
Radical Feminism—
structure of gender//sexual appropriation//objectification
sex, by analogy labor, by extension reproduction, by addition race

In another context, the French theorist Julia Kristeva claimed women appeared as a historical group after World War II, along with groups like youth. Her dates are doubtful; but we are now accustomed to remembering that as objects of knowledge and as historical actors, "race" did not always exist, "class" has a historical genesis, and "homosexuals" are quite junior. It is no accident that the symbolic system of the family of man—and so the essence of woman—breaks up at the same moment that networks of connection among people on the planet are unprecedentedly multiple, pregnant, and complex. "Advanced capitalism" is inadequate to convey the structure of this historical moment. In the "Western" sense, the end of man is at stake. It is no accident that woman disintegrates into women in our time. Perhaps socialist feminists were not substantially guilty of producing essentialist theory that suppressed women's particularity and contradictory interests. I think we have been, at least through unreflective participation in the logics, languages, and practices of white humanism and through searching for a single ground of domination to secure our revolutionary voice. Now we have less excuse. But in the consciousness of our failures, we risk lapsing into boundless difference and giving up on the confusing task of making partial, real connection. Some differences are playful; some are poles of world historical systems of domination. "Epistemology" is about knowing the difference.

THE INFORMATICS OF DOMINATION

In this attempt at an epistemological and political position, I would like to sketch a picture of possible unity, a picture indebted to socialist and feminist principles of design. The frame for my sketch is set by the extent and importance of rearrangements in worldwide social relations tied to science and technology. I argue for a politics rooted in claims about fundamental changes in the nature of class, race, and gender in an emerging system of world order analogous in its novelty and scope to that created by industrial capitalism; we are living through a movement from an organic, industrial society to a polymorphous, information system—from all work to all play, a deadly game. Simultaneously material and ideological, the dichotomies may be expressed in the following chart of transitions from the comfortable old hierarchical dominations to the scary new networks I have called the informatics of domination:

Representation	Simulation
Bourgeois novel, realism	Science fiction, postmodernism
Organism	Biotic component
Depth, integrity	Surface, boundary
Heat	Noise
Biology as clinical practice	Biology as inscription
Physiology	Communications engineering
Small group	Subsystem
Perfection	Optimization
Eugenics	Population control
Decadence, *Magic Mountain*	Obsolescence, *Future Shock*
Hygiene	Stress management
Microbiology, tuberculosis	Immunology, AIDS
Organic division of labor	Ergonomics/cybernetics of labor
Functional specialization	Modular construction
Reproduction	Replication
Organic sex role specialization	Optimal genetic strategies
Biological determinism	Evolutionary inertia, constraints
Community ecology	Ecosystems
Racial chain of being	Neoimperialism, United Nations humanism
Scientific management in home/factory	Global factory/Electronic cottage
Family/Market/Factory	Women in the Integrated Circuit
Family wage	Comparable worth
Public/Private	Cyborg citizenship
Nature/Culture	Fields of difference
Cooperation	Communications enhancement
Freud	Lacan
Sex	Genetic engineering
Labor	Robotics
Mind	Artificial Intelligence
World War II	Star Wars
White Capitalist Patriarchy	Informatics of Domination

This list suggests several interesting things.[15] First, the objects on the right-hand side cannot be coded as "natural," a realization that subverts naturalistic coding for the left-hand side as well. We cannot go back ideologically or materially. It's not just that "god" is dead; so is the "goddess." In relation to objects like biotic components, one must think not in terms of essential properties, but in terms of strategies of design, boundary constraints, rates of flows, systems logics, costs of lowering constraints. Sexual reproduction is one kind of reproductive strategy among many, with costs and benefits as a function of the system environment. Ideologies of sexual reproduction can no longer reasonably call on the notions of sex and sex role as organic aspects in natural objects like organisms and families. Such reasoning will be unmasked as irrational, and, ironically, corporate executives reading *Playboy* and antiporn radical feminists will make strange bedfellows in jointly unmasking the irrationalism.

Likewise for race, ideologies about human diversity have to be formulated in terms of frequencies of parameters, like blood groups or intelligence scores. It is "irrational" to invoke concepts like primitive and civilized. For liberals and radicals, the search for integrated social systems gives way to a new practice called "experimental ethnography" in which an organic object dissipates in attention to the play of writing. At the level of ideology, we see translations of racism and colonialism into languages of development and underdevelopment, rates and constraints of modernization. Any objects or persons can be reasonably thought of in terms of disassembly and reassembly; no "natural" architectures constrain system design. The financial districts in all the world's cities, as well as the export-processing and free-trade zones, proclaim this elementary fact of "late capitalism." The entire universe of objects that can be known scientifically must be formulated as problems in communications engineering (for the managers) or theories of the text (for those who would resist). Both are cyborg semiologies.

One should expect control strategies to concentrate on boundary conditions and interfaces, on rates of flow across boundaries—and not on the integrity of natural objects. "Integrity" or "sincerity" of the Western self gives way to decision procedures and expert systems. For example, control strategies applied to women's capacities to give birth to new human beings will be developed in the languages of population control and maximization of goal achievement for individual decision makers. Control strategies will be formulated in terms of rates, costs of constraints, degrees of freedom. Human beings, like any other component or subsystem, must be localized in a system architecture whose basic modes of operation are probabilistic, statistical. No objects, spaces, or bodies are sacred in themselves; any component can be interfaced with any other if the proper standard, the proper code, can be constructed for processing signals in a common language. Exchange in this world transcends the universal translation effected by capitalist markets that Marx analyzed so well. The privileged pathology affecting all kinds of components in this universe is stress—communications breakdown.[16] The cyborg is not subject to Foucault's biopolitics; the cyborg simulates politics, a much more potent field of operations.

This kind of analysis of scientific and cultural objects of knowledge that have appeared historically since World War II prepares us to notice some important inadequacies in feminist analysis, which has proceeded as if the organic, hierarchical dualisms ordering discourse in "the West" since Aristotle still ruled. They have been cannibalized, or as Zoe Sofia (Sofoulis) might put it, they have been "techno-digested." The dichotomies between mind and body, animal and human, organism and machine, public and private, nature and culture, men and women, primitive and civilized are all in question ideologically. The actual situation of women is their integration/exploitation into a world system of production/reproduction and communication called the informatics of domination. The home, work place, market, public arena, the body itself—all can be dispersed and interfaced in nearly infinite, polymorphous ways, with large consequences for women and others—consequences that themselves are very different for different people and that make potent oppositional international movements difficult to imagine and essential for survival. One important route for reconstructing socialist-feminist politics is through theory and practice addressed to the social relations of science and technology, including crucially the systems of myth and meanings structuring our imaginations. The cyborg is a kind of disassembled and reassembled, postmodern collective and personal self. This is the self feminists must code.

Communications technologies and biotechnologies are the crucial tools recrafting our bodies. These tools embody and enforce new social relations for women worldwide. Technologies and scientific discourses can be partially understood as formalizations, i.e., as frozen moments, of the fluid social interactions constituting them, but they should also be viewed as instruments for enforcing meanings. The boundary is permeable between tool and myth, instrument and concept, historical systems of social relations and historical anatomies of possible bodies, including objects of knowledge. Indeed, myth and tool mutually constitute each other.

Furthermore, communications sciences and modern biologies are constructed by a common move—*the translation of the world into a problem of coding,* a search for a common language in which all resistance to instrumental control disappears and all heterogeneity can be submitted to disassembly, reassembly, investment, and exchange.

In communications sciences, the translation of the world into a problem in coding can be illustrated by looking at cybernetic (feedback controlled) systems theories applied to telephone technology, computer design, weapons deployment, or database construction and maintenance. In each case, solution to the key questions rests on a theory of language and control; the key operation is determining the rates, directions, and probabilities of flow of a quantity called information. The world is subdivided by boundaries differentially permeable to information. Information is just that kind of quantifiable element (unit, basis of unity) that allows universal translation, and so unhindered instrumental power (called effective communication). The biggest threat to such power is interruption of communication. Any system breakdown is a function of stress. The fundamentals of this technology can be condensed into the metaphor C^3I, command-control-communication-intelligence, the military's symbol for its operations theory.

In modern biologies, the translation of the world into a problem in coding can be illustrated by molecular genetics, ecology, sociobiological evolutionary theory, and immunobiology. The organism has been translated into problems of genetic coding and read-out. Biotechnology, a writing technology, informs research broadly.[17] In a sense, organisms have ceased to exist as objects of knowledge, giving way to biotic components, i.e., special kinds of information-processing devices. The analogous moves in ecology could be examined by probing the history and utility of the concept of the ecosystem. Immunobiology and associated medical practices are rich exemplars of the privilege of coding and recognition systems as objects of knowledge, as constructions of bodily reality for us. Biology is here a kind of cryptography. Research is necessarily a kind of intelligence activity. Ironies abound. A stressed system goes awry; its communication processes break down; it fails to recognize the difference between self and other. Human babies with baboon hearts evoke national ethical perplexity—for animal-rights activists at least as much as for guardians of human purity. Gay men, Haitian immigrants, and intravenous drug users are the "privileged" victims of an awful immune-system disease that marks (inscribes on the body) confusion of boundaries and moral pollution.

But these excursions into communications sciences and biology have been at a rarefied level; there is a mundane, largely economic reality to support my claim that these sciences and technologies indicate fundamental transformations in the structure of the world for us. Communications technologies depend on electronics. Modern states, multinational corporations, military power, welfare-state apparatuses, satellite systems, political processes, fabrication of our imaginations, labor-control systems, medical constructions of our bodies, commercial pornography, the international division of labor, and religious evangelism depend intimately upon electronics. Microelectronics is the technical basis of simulacra, i.e., of copies without originals.

Microelectronics mediates the translations of *labor* into robotics and word processing; *sex* into genetic engineering and reproductive technologies; and *mind* into artificial intelligence and decision procedures. The new biotechnologies concern more than human reproduction. Biology as a powerful engineering science for redesigning materials and processes has revolutionary implications for industry, perhaps most obvious today in areas of fermentation, agriculture, and energy. Communications sciences and biology are constructions of natural-technical objects of knowledge in which the difference between machine and organism is thoroughly blurred; mind, body, and tool are on very intimate terms. The "multinational" material organization of the production and reproduction of daily life and the symbolic organization of the production and reproduction of culture and imagination seem equally implicated. The boundary-maintaining images of base and superstructure, public and private, or material and ideal never seemed more feeble.

I have used Rachael Grossman's image of women in the integrated circuit to name the situation of women in a world so intimately restructured through the social relations of science and technology.[18] I use the odd circumlocution, "the social relations of science and technology," to indicate that we are not dealing with a technological determinism, but with a historical system depending upon structured relations among people. But the phrase should also indicate that science and technology provide fresh sources of power, that we need fresh sources of analysis and political action.[19] Some of the rearrangements of race, sex, and class rooted in high-tech-facilitated social relations can make socialist feminism more relevant to effective progressive politics.

THE HOMEWORK ECONOMY

The "new industrial revolution" is producing a new worldwide working class. The extreme mobility of capital and the emerging international division of labor are intertwined with the emergence of new collectivities and the weakening of familiar groupings. These developments are neither gender- nor race-neutral. White men in advanced industrial societies have become newly vulnerable to permanent job loss, and women are not disappearing from the job rolls at the same rates as men. It is not simply that women in third-world countries are the preferred labor force for the science-based multinationals in the export-processing sectors, particularly in electronics. The picture is more systematic and involves reproduction, sexuality, culture, consumption, and production. In the prototypical Silicon Valley, many women's lives have been structured around employment in electronics-dependent jobs, and their intimate realities include serial heterosexual monogamy, negotiating child care, distance from extended kin or most other forms of traditional community, a high likelihood of loneliness, and extreme economic vulnerability as they age. The ethnic and racial diversity of women in Silicon Valley structures a microcosm of conflicting differences in culture, family, religion, education, language.

Richard Gordon has called this new situation the homework economy.[20] Although he includes the phenomenon of literal homework emerging in connection with electronics assembly, Gordon intends "homework economy" to name a restructuring of work that broadly has the characteristics formerly ascribed to female jobs, jobs literally done only by women. Work is being redefined as both literally female and feminized, whether performed by men or women. To be feminized means to be made extremely vulnerable; able to be disassembled, reassembled, exploited as a reserve labor force; seen less as workers than as servers; subjected to time arrangements on and off the paid job that make a mockery of a limited work day; leading an existence that always borders on being obscene, out of place, and reducible to sex. De-skilling is an old strategy newly applicable to formerly privileged workers. However, the homework economy does not refer only to large-scale de-skilling, nor does it deny that new areas of high skill are emerging, even for women and men previously excluded from skilled employment. Rather, the concept indicates that factory, home, and market are integrated on a new scale and that the places of women are crucial—and need to be analyzed for differences among women and for meanings for relations between men and women in various situations.

The homework economy as a world capitalist organizational structure is made possible by (not caused by) the new technologies. The success of the attack on relatively privileged, mostly white, men's unionized jobs is tied to the power of the new communications technologies to integrate and control labor despite extensive dispersion and decentralization. The consequences of the new technologies are felt by women both in the loss of the family (male) wage (if they ever had access to this white privilege) and in the character of their own jobs, which are becoming capital intensive, e.g., office work and nursing.

The new economic and technological arrangements are also related to the collapsing welfare state and the ensuing intensification of demands on women to sustain daily life for themselves as well as for men, children, and old people. The feminization of poverty—generated by dismantling the welfare state, by the homework economy where stable jobs become the exception, and sustained by the expectation that women's wage will not be matched by a male income for the support of children—has become an urgent focus. The causes of various women-headed households are a function of race, class, or sexuality; but their increasing generality is a ground for coalitions of women on many issues. That women regularly sustain daily life partly as a function of their enforced status as mothers is hardly new; the kind of integration with the overall capitalist and progressively war-based economy is new. The particular pressure, for example, on U.S. black women, who have achieved an escape from (barely) paid domestic service and who now hold clerical and similar jobs in large numbers, has large implications for continued enforced black poverty *with* employment. Teenage women in industrializing areas of the third world increasingly find themselves the sole or major source of a cash wage for their families, while access to land is ever more problematic. These developments must have major consequences in the psychodynamics and politics of gender and race.

Within the framework of three major stages of capitalism (commercial/early industrial, monopoly, multinational)—tied to nationalism, imperialism, and multinationalism, and related to Jameson's three dominant aesthetic periods of realism, modernism, and postmodernism—I would argue that specific forms of families dialectically relate to forms of capital and to its political and cultural concomitants. Although lived problematically and unequally, ideal forms of these families might be schematized as (1) the patriarchal nuclear family, structured by the dichotomy between public and private and accompanied by the white bourgeois ideology of separate spheres and nineteenth-century Anglo-American bourgeois feminism; (2) the modern family, mediated (or enforced) by the welfare state and institutions like the family wage, with a flowering of a-feminist heterosexual ideologies, including their radical versions represented in Greenwich Village around World War I; and (3) the "family" of the homework economy, with its oxymoronic structure of women-headed households and its explosion of feminisms and the paradoxical intensification and erosion of gender itself.

This is the context in which the projections for worldwide structural unemployment stemming from the new technologies are part of the picture of the homework economy. As robotics and related technologies put men out of work in "developed" countries and exacerbate failure to generate male jobs in third-world "development," and as the automated office becomes the rule even in labor-surplus countries, the feminization of work intensifies. Black women in the United States have long known what it looks like to face the structural underemployment ("feminization") of black men, as well as their own highly vulnerable position in the wage economy. It is no longer a secret that sexuality, reproduction, family, and community life are interwoven with this economic structure in myriad ways that have also differentiated the situations of white and black women. Many more women and men will contend with similar situations, which will make cross-gender and race alliances on issues of basic life support (with or without jobs) necessary, not just nice.

The new technologies also have a profound effect on hunger and on food production for subsistence worldwide. Rae Lessor Blumberg estimates that women produce about fifty per cent of the world's subsistence food.[21]* Women are excluded generally from benefiting from the increased high-tech commodification of food and energy crops, their days are made more arduous because their responsibilities to provide food do not diminish, and their reproductive situations are made more complex. Green Revolution technologies interact with other high-tech industrial production to alter gender divisions of labor and differential gender migration patterns.

The new technologies seem deeply involved in the forms of "privatization" that Ros Petchesky has analyzed, in which militarization, right-wing family ideologies and policies, and intensified definitions of corporate property as private synergistically interact.[22] The new communications technologies are fundamental to the eradication of "public life" for everyone. This facilitates the mushrooming of a permanent high-tech military establishment at the cultural and economic expense of most people, but especially of women. Technologies like video games and highly miniaturized televisions seem crucial to production of modern forms of "private life." The culture of video games is heavily oriented to individual compe-

* The conjunction of the Green Revolution's social relations with biotechnologies like plant genetic engineering makes the pressures on land in the third world increasingly intense. AID's estimates (New York Times, October 14, 1984) used at the 1984 World Food Day are that in Africa, women produce about 90 percent of rural food supplies, about 60–80 percent in Asia, and provide 40 percent of agricultural labor in the Near East and Latin America. Blumberg charges that world organizations' agricultural politics, as well as those of multinationals and national governments in the third world, generally ignore fundamental issues in the sexual division of labor. The present tragedy of famine in Africa might owe as much to male supremacy as to capitalism, colonialism, and rain patterns. More accurately, capitalism and racism are usually structurally male dominant.

tition and extraterrestrial warfare. High-tech, gendered imaginations are produced here, imaginations that can contemplate destruction of the planet and a sci-fi escape from its consequences. More than our imaginations is militarized; and the other realities of electronic and nuclear warfare are inescapable.

The new technologies affect the social relations of both sexuality and of reproduction, and not always in the same ways. The close ties of sexuality and instrumentality, of views of the body as a kind of private satisfaction- and utility-maximizing machine, are described nicely in sociobiological origin stories that stress a genetic calculus and explain the inevitable dialectic of domination of male and female gender roles.[23] These sociobiological stories depend on a high-tech view of the body as a biotic component or cybernetic communications system. Among the many transformations of reproductive situations is the medical one, where women's bodies have boundaries newly permeable to both "visualization" and "intervention." Of course, who controls the interpretation of bodily boundaries in medical hermeneutics is a major feminist issue. The speculum served as an icon of women's claiming their bodies in the 1970s; that hand-craft tool is inadequate to express our needed body politics in the negotiation of reality in the practices of cyborg reproduction. Self-help is not enough. The technologies of visualization recall the important cultural practice of hunting with the camera and the deeply predatory nature of a photographic consciousness.[24] Sex, sexuality, and reproduction are central actors in high-tech myth systems structuring our imaginations of personal and social possibility.

Another critical aspect of the social relations of the new technologies is the reformulation of expectations, culture, work, and reproduction for the large scientific and technical work force. A major social and political danger is the formation of a strongly bimodal social structure, with the masses of women and men of all ethnic groups, but especially people of color, confined to a homework economy, illiteracy of several varieties, and general redundancy and impotence, controlled by high-tech repressive apparatuses ranging from entertainment to surveillance and disappearance. An adequate socialist-feminist politics should address women in the privileged occupational categories, and particularly in the production of science and technology that constructs scientific-technical discourses, processes, and objects.[25]

This issue is only one aspect of inquiry into the possibility of a feminist science, but it is important. What kind of constitutive role in the production of knowledge, imagination, and practice can new groups doing science have? How can these groups be allied with progressive social and political movements? What kind of political accountability can be constructed to tie women together across the scientific-technical hierarchies separating us? Might there be ways of developing feminist science/technology politics in alliance with antimilitary science facility conversion action groups? Many scientific and technical workers in Silicon Valley, the high-tech cowboys included, do not want to work on military science.[26] Can these personal preferences and cultural tendencies be welded into progressive politics among this professional middle class in which women, including women of color, are coming to be fairly numerous?

WOMEN IN THE INTEGRATED CIRCUIT

Let me summarize the picture of women's historical locations in advanced industrial societies, as these positions have been restructured partly through the social relations of science and technology. If it was ever possible ideologically to characterize women's lives by the distinction of public and private domains—suggested by images of the division of working-class life into factory and home, of bourgeois life into market and home, and of gender existence into personal and political realms—it is now a totally misleading ideology, even to show how both terms of these dichotomies construct each other in practice and in theory. I prefer a network ideological image, suggesting the profusion of spaces and identities and the permeability of boundaries in the personal body and in the body politic. "Networking" is both a feminist practice and a multinational corporate strategy—weaving is for oppositional cyborgs.

The only way to characterize the informatics of domination is as a massive intensification of insecurity and cultural impoverishment, with common failure of subsistence networks for the most vulnerable. Since much of this picture interweaves with the social relations of science and technology, the urgency of a socialist-feminist politics addressed to science and technology is plain. There is much now being done, and the grounds for political work are rich. For example, the efforts to develop forms of collective struggle for women in paid work, like SEIU's District 925, should be a high priority for all of us. These efforts are profoundly tied to technical restructuring of labor processes and reformations of working classes. These efforts also are providing understanding of a more comprehensive kind of labor organization, involving community, sexuality, and family issues never privileged in the largely white male industrial unions.

The structural rearrangements related to the social relations of science and technology evoke strong ambivalence. But it is not necessary to be ultimately depressed by the implications of late twentieth-century women's relation to all aspects of work, culture, production of knowledge, sexuality, and reproduction. For excellent reasons, most Marxisms see domination best and have trouble understanding what can only look like false consciousness and people's complicity in their own domination in late capitalism. It is crucial to remember that what is lost, perhaps especially from women's points of view, is often virulent forms of oppression, nostalgically naturalized in the face of current violation. Ambivalence toward the disrupted unities mediated by high-tech culture requires not sorting consciousness into categories of "clear-sighted critique grounding a solid political epistemology" versus "manipulated false consciousness," but subtle understanding of emerging pleasures, experiences, and powers with serious potential for changing the rules of the game.

There are grounds for hope in the emerging bases for new kinds of unity across race, gender, and class, as these elementary units of socialist-feminist analysis themselves suffer protean transformations. Intensifications of hardship experienced worldwide in connection with the social relations of science and technology are severe. But what people are experiencing is not transparently clear, and we lack sufficiently subtle connections for collectively building effective theories of experience. Present efforts—Marxist, psychoanalytic, feminist, anthropological—to clarify even "our" experience are rudimentary.

I am conscious of the odd perspective provided by my historical position—a Ph.D. in biology for an Irish Catholic girl was made possible by Sputnik's impact on U.S. national science-education policy. I have a body and mind as much constructed by the post–World War II arms race and cold war as by the women's movements. There are more grounds for hope by focusing on the contradictory effects of politics designed to produce loyal American technocrats, which as well produced large numbers of dissidents, rather than by focusing on the present defeats.

The permanent partiality of feminist points of view has consequences for our expectations of forms of political organization and participation. We do not need a totality in order to work well. The feminist dream of a common language, like all dreams for a perfectly true language, of perfectly faithful naming of experience, is a totalizing and imperialist one. In that sense, dialectics too is a dream language, longing to resolve contradiction. Perhaps, ironically, we can learn from our fusions with animals and machines how not to be Man, the embodiment of Western logos. From the point of view of pleasure in these potent and taboo fusions, made inevitable by the social relations of science and technology, there might indeed be a feminist science.

CYBORGS: A MYTH OF POLITICAL IDENTITY

I want to conclude with a myth about identity and boundaries which might inform late-twentieth-century political imaginations. I am indebted in this story to writers like Joanna Russ, Samuel Delany, John Varley, James Tiptree Jr., Octavia Butler, Monique Wittig, and Vonda McIntyre.[27] These are our storytellers exploring what it means to be embodied in high-tech worlds. They are theorists for cyborgs. Exploring conceptions of bodily boundaries and social order, the anthropologist Mary Douglas should be credited with helping us to consciousness about how fundamental body imagery is to world view, and so to political language.[28] French feminists like Luce Irigaray and Monique Wittig, for all their differences, know how to write the body, how to weave eroticism, cosmology, and politics from imagery of embodiment and, especially for Wittig, from imagery of fragmentation and reconstitution of bodies.[29]

American radical feminists like Susan Griffin, Audre Lorde, and Adrienne Rich have profoundly affected our political imaginations—and perhaps restricted too much what we allow as a friendly body and political language.[30] They insist on the organic, opposing it to the technological. But their symbolic systems and the related positions of ecofeminism and feminist paganism, replete with organicisms, can only be understood in Sandoval's terms as oppositional ideologies fitting the late twentieth century. They would simply bewilder anyone not preoccupied with the machines and consciousness of late capitalism. In that sense they are part of the cyborg world. But there are also great riches for feminists in explicitly embracing the possibilities inherent in the breakdown of clean distinctions between organism and machine and similar distinctions structuring the Western self. It is the simultaneity of breakdowns that cracks the matrices of domination and opens geometric possibilities. What might be learned from personal and political "technological" pollution? I will look briefly at two overlapping groups of texts for their insight into the construction of a potentially helpful cyborg myth: constructions of women of color and monstrous selves in feminist science fiction.

Earlier I suggested that "women of color" might be understood as a cyborg identity, a potent subjectivity synthesized from fusions of outsider identities. There are material and cultural grids mapping this potential. Audre Lorde captures the tone in the title of her *Sister Outsider*. In my political myth, Sister Outsider is the offshore woman, whom U.S. workers, female and feminized, are supposed to regard as the enemy preventing their solidarity, threatening their security. Onshore, inside the boundary of the United States, Sister Outsider is a potential amid the races and ethnic identities of women manipulated for division, competition, and exploitation in the same industries. "Women of color" are the preferred labor force for the science-based industries, the real women for whom the worldwide sexual market, labor market, and politics of reproduction kaleidoscope into daily life. Young

Korean women hired in the sex industry and in electronics assembly are recruited from high schools, educated for the integrated circuit. Literacy, especially in English, distinguishes the "cheap" female labor so attractive to the multinationals.

Contrary to orientalist stereotypes of the "oral primitive," literacy is a special mark of women of color, acquired by U.S. black women as well as men through a history of risking death to learn and to teach reading and writing. Writing has a special significance for all colonized groups. Writing has been crucial to the Western myth of the distinction of oral and written cultures, primitive and civilized mentalities, and more recently to the erosion of that distinction in "postmodernist" theories attacking the phallogocentrism of the West, with its worship of the monotheistic, phallic, authoritative, and singular world, the unique and perfect name.[31] Contests for the meanings of writing are a major form of contemporary political struggle. Releasing the play of writing is deadly serious. The poetry and stories of U.S. women of color are repeatedly about writing, about access to the power to signify; but this time that power must be neither phallic nor innocent. Cyborg writing must not be about the Fall, the imagination of a once-upon-a-time wholeness before language, before writing, before Man. Cyborg writing is about the power to survive, not on the basis of original innocence, but on the basis of seizing the tools to mark the world that marked them as other.

The tools are often stories, retold stories, versions that reverse and displace the hierarchical dualisms of naturalized identities. In retelling origin stories, cyborg authors subvert the central myths of origin of Western culture. We have all been colonized by those origin myths, with their longing for fulfillment in apocalypse. The phallogocentric origin stories most crucial for feminist cyborgs are built into the literal technologies—technologies that write the world, biotechnology and microelectronics—that have recently textualized our bodies as code problems on the grid of C^3I. Feminist cyborg stories have the task of recoding communication and intelligence to subvert command and control.

Figuratively and literally, language politics pervade the struggles of women of color; and stories about language have a special power in the rich contemporary writing by U.S. women of color. For example, retellings of the story of the indigenous woman Malinche, mother of the mestizo "bastard" race of the new world, master of languages, and mistress of Cortés, carry special meaning for Chicana constructions of identity. Cherrie Moraga in *Loving in the War Years* explores the themes of identity when one never possessed the original language, never told the original story, never resided in the harmony of legitimate heterosexuality in the garden of culture, and so cannot base identity on a myth or a fall from innocence and right to natural names, mother's or father's.[32] Moraga's writing, her superb literacy, is presented in her poetry as the same kind of violation as Malinche's mastery of the conqueror's language—a violation, an illegitimate production, that allows survival. Moraga's language is not "whole"; it is self-consciously spliced, a chimera of English and Spanish, both conquerors' languages. But it is this chimeric monster, without claim to an original language before violation, that crafts the erotic, competent, potent identities of women of color. Sister Outsider hints at the possibility of world survival not because of her innocence but because of her ability to live on the boundaries, to write without the founding myth of original wholeness, with its inescapable apocalypse of final return to a deathly oneness that Man has imagined to be the innocent and all-powerful Mother, freed at the End from another spiral of appropriation by her son. Writing marks Moraga's body, affirms it as the body of a woman of color, against the possibility of passing into the unmarked category of the Anglo father or into the orientalist myth of "original illiteracy" of a mother that never was. Malinche was mother here, not Eve before eating the forbidden fruit. Writing affirms Sister Outsider, not the Woman-before-the-Fall-into-Writing needed by the phallogocentric Family of Man.

Writing is pre-eminently the technology of cyborgs, etched surfaces of the late twentieth century. Cyborg politics is the struggle for language and the struggle against perfect communication, against the one code that translates all meaning perfectly, the central dogma of phallogocentrism. That is why cyborg politics insist on noise and advocate pollution, rejoicing in the illegitimate fusions of animal and machine. These are the couplings that make Man and Woman so problematic, subverting the structure of desire, the force imagined to generate language and gender, and so subverting the structure and modes of reproduction of "Western" identity, of nature and culture, of mirror and eye, slave and master, body and mind. "We" did not originally chose to be cyborgs, but choice grounds a liberal politics and epistemology that imagines the reproduction of individuals before the wider replications of "texts."

From the perspective of cyborgs, freed of the need to ground politics in "our" privileged position of the oppression that incorporates all other dominations, the innocence of the merely violated, the ground of those closer to nature, we can see powerful possibilities. Feminisms and Marxisms have run aground on Western epistemological imperatives to construct a revolutionary subject from the perspective of a hierarchy of oppressions and/or a latent position of moral superiority, innocence, and greater closeness to nature. With no available original dream of a common language or original symbiosis promising protection from hostile "masculine" separation, but written into the play of a text that has no finally privileged reading or salvation history, to recognize "oneself" as fully implicated in the world, frees us of the need to root politics in identification, vanguard parties, purity, and mothering. Stripped of identity, the bastard race teaches about the power of the margins and the importance of a mother like Malinche. Women of color have transformed her from the evil mother of masculinist fear into the originally literate mother who teaches survival.

This is not just literary deconstruction, but liminal transformation. Every story that begins with original innocence and privileges the return to wholeness imagines the drama of life to be individuation, separation, the birth of the self, the tragedy of autonomy, the fall into writing, alienation; i.e., war, tempered by imaginary respite in the bosom of the Other. These plots are ruled by a reproductive politics—rebirth without flaw, perfection, abstraction. In this plot women are imagined either better or worse off, but all agree they have less selfhood, weaker individuation, more fusion to the oral, to Mother, less at stake in masculine autonomy. But there is another route to having less at stake in masculine autonomy, a route that does not pass through Woman, Primitive, Zero, the Mirror Stage and its imaginary. It passes through women and other present-tense, illegitimate cyborgs, not of Woman born, who refuse the ideological resources of victimization so as to have a real life. These cyborgs are the people who refuse to disappear on cue, no matter how many times a "Western" commentator remarks on the sad passing of another primitive, another organic group done in by "Western" technology, by writing.[33] These real-life cyborgs, e.g., the Southeast Asian village women workers in Japanese and U.S. electronics firms described by Aiwa Ong, are actively rewriting the texts of their bodies and societies. Survival is the stakes in this play of readings.

To recapitulate, certain dualisms have been persistent in Western traditions; they have all been systemic to the logics and practices of domination of women, people of color, nature, workers, animals—in short, domination of all constituted as *others*, whose task is to mirror the self. Chief among these troubling dualisms are self/other, mind/body, culture/nature, male/female, civilized/primitive, reality/appearance, whole/part, agent/resource, maker/made, active/passive, right/wrong, truth/illusion, total/partial, God/man. The self is the One who is not dominated, who knows that by the service of the other; the other is the one who holds the future, who knows that by the experience of domination, which gives the lie to the autonomy of the self. To be One is to be autonomous, to be powerful, to be God; but to be One is to be an illusion and so to be involved in a dialectic of apocalypse with the other. Yet to be other is to be multiple, without clear boundary, frayed, insubstantial. One is too few, but two are too many.

High-tech culture challenges these dualisms in intriguing ways. It is not clear who makes and who is made in the relation between human and machine. It is not clear what is mind and what body in machines that resolve into coding practices. Insofar as we know ourselves in both formal discourse (e.g., biology) and in daily practice (e.g., the homework economy in the integrated circuit), we find ourselves to be cyborgs, hybrids, mosaics, chimeras. Biological organisms have become biotic systems, communications devices like others. There is no fundamental, ontological separation in our formal knowledge of machine and organism, of technical and organic.

One consequence is that our sense of connection to our tools is heightened. The trance state experienced by many computer users has become a staple of science-fiction film and cultural jokes. Perhaps paraplegics and other severely handicapped people can (and sometimes do) have the most intense experiences of complex hybridization with other communication devices. Anne McCaffrey's *The Ship Who Sang* explored the consciousness of a cyborg, hybrid of a girl's brain and complex machinery, formed after the birth of a severely handicapped child. Gender, sexuality, embodiment, skill: all were reconstituted in the story. Why should our bodies end at the skin, or include at best other beings encapsulated by skin? From the seventeenth century until now, machines could be animated—given ghostly souls to make them speak or move or to account for their orderly development and mental capacities. Or organisms could be mechanized—reduced to body understood as resource of mind. These machine/organism relationships are obsolete, unnecessary. For us, in imagination and in other practice, machines can be prosthetic devices, intimate components, friendly selves. We don't need organic holism to give impermeable wholeness, the total woman and her feminist variants (mutants?). Let me conclude this point by a very partial reading of the logic of the cyborg monsters of my second group of texts, feminist science fiction.

The cyborgs populating feminist science fiction make very problematic the statuses of man or woman, human, artifact, member of a race, individual identity, or body. Katie King clarifies how pleasure in reading these fictions is not largely based on identification. Students facing Joanna Russ for the first time, students who have learned to take modernist writers like James Joyce or Virginia Woolf without flinching, do not know what to make of *The Adventures of Alyx* or *The Female Man*, where characters refuse the reader's search for innocent wholeness while granting the wish for heroic quests, exuberant eroticism, and serious politics. *The Female Man* is the story of four versions of one genotype, all of whom meet, but even taken together do not make a whole, resolve the dilemmas of violent moral action, nor remove the growing scandal of gender. The feminist science fiction of Samuel Delany, especially

Tales of Neveryon, mocks stories of origin by redoing the neolithic revolution, replaying the founding moves of Western civilization to subvert their plausibility. James Tiptree Jr., an author whose fiction was regarded as particularly manly until her "true" gender was revealed, tells tales of reproduction based on nonmammalian technologies like alternation of generations or male brood pouches and male nurturing. John Varley constructs a supreme cyborg in his archfeminist exploration of Gaea, a mad goddess-planet-trickster-old woman-technological device on whose surface an extraordinary array of post-cyborg symbioses are spawned. Octavia Butler writes of an African sorceress pitting her powers of transformation against the genetic manipulations of her rival (*Wild Seed*), of time warps that bring a modern U.S. black woman into slavery where her actions in relation to her white master-ancestor determine the possibility of her own birth (*Kindred*), and of the illegitimate insights into identity and community of an adopted cross-species child who came to know the enemy as self (*Survivor*).

Because it is particularly rich in boundary transgressions, Vonda McIntyre's *Superluminal* can close this truncated catalogue of promising monsters who help redefine the pleasures and politics of embodiment and feminist writing. In a fiction where no character is "simply" human, human status is highly problematic. Orca, a genetically altered diver, can speak with killer whales and survive deep ocean conditions, but she longs to explore space as a pilot, necessitating bionic implants jeopardizing her kinship with the divers and cetaceans. Transformations are effected by virus vectors carrying a new developmental code, by transplant surgery, by implants of microelectronic devices, by analogue doubles, and other means. Laenea becomes a pilot by accepting a heart implant and a host of other alterations allowing survival in transit at speeds exceeding that of light. Radu Dracul survives a virus-caused plague on his outerworld planet to find himself with a time sense that changes the boundaries of spatial perception for the whole species. All the characters explore the limits of language, the dream of communicating experience, and the necessity of limitation, partiality, and intimacy even in this world of protean transformation and connection.

Monsters have always defined the limits of community in Western imaginations. The Centaurs and Amazons of ancient Greece established the limits of the centered polis of the Greek male human by their disruption of marriage and boundary pollutions of the warrior with animality and woman. Unseparated twins and hermaphrodites were the confused human material in early modern France who grounded discourse on the natural and supernatural, medical and legal, portents and diseases—all crucial to establishing modern identity.[34] The evolutionary and behavioral sciences of monkeys and apes have marked the multiple boundaries of late twentieth-century industrial identities. Cyborg monsters in feminist science fiction define quite different political possibilities and limits from those proposed by the mundane fiction of Man and Woman.

There are several consequences to taking seriously the imagery of cyborgs as other than our enemies. Our bodies, ourselves; bodies are maps of power and identity. Cyborgs are no exceptions. A cyborg body is not innocent; it was not born in a garden; it does not seek unitary identity and so generate antagonistic dualisms without end (or until the world ends); it takes irony for granted. One is too few, and two is only one possibility. Intense pleasure in skill, machine skill, ceases to be a sin, but an aspect of embodiment. The machine is not an *it* to be animated, worshiped, and dominated. The machine is us, our processes, an aspect of our embodiment. We can be responsible for machines; *they* do not dominate or threaten us. We are responsible for boundaries; we are they. Until now (once upon a time), female embodiment seemed to be given, organic, necessary; and female embodiment seemed to mean skill in mothering and its metaphoric extensions. Only by being out of place could we take intense pleasure in machines, and then with excuses that this was organic activity after all, appropriate to females. Cyborgs might consider more seriously the partial, fluid, sometimes aspect of sex and sexual embodiment. Gender might not be global identity after all.

The ideologically charged question of what counts as daily activity, as experience, can be approached by exploiting the cyborg image. Feminists have recently claimed that women are given to dailiness, that women more than men somehow sustain daily life, and so have a privileged epistemological position potentially. There is a compelling aspect to this claim, one that makes visible unvalued female activity and names it as the ground of life. But *the* ground of life? What about all the ignorance of women, all the exclusions and failures of knowledge and skill? What about men's access to daily competence, to knowing how to build things, to take them apart, to play? What about other embodiments? Cyborg gender is a local possibility taking a global vengeance. Race, gender, and capital require a cyborg theory of wholes and parts. There is no drive in cyborgs to produce total theory, but there is an intimate experience of boundaries, their construction and deconstruction. There is a myth system waiting to become a political language to ground one way of looking at science and technology and challenging the informatics of domination.

One last image: organisms and organismic, holistic politics depend on metaphors of rebirth and invariably call on the resources of reproductive sex. I would suggest that cyborgs have more to do with regeneration and are suspicious of the reproductive matrix and of most birthing. For salamanders, regeneration after injury, such as the loss of a limb, involves regrowth of structure and restoration of function with the constant possibility of twinning or other odd topographical productions at the site of former injury. The regrown limb can be monstrous, duplicated, potent. We have all been injured, profoundly. We require regeneration, not rebirth, and the possibilities for our reconstitution include the utopian dream of the hope for a monstrous world without gender.

Cyborg imagery can help express two crucial arguments in this essay: (1) the production of universal, totalizing theory is a major mistake that misses most of reality, probably always, but certainly now; (2) taking responsibility for the social relations of science and technology means refusing an antiscience metaphysics, a demonology of technology, and so means embracing the skillful task of reconstructing the boundaries of daily life, in partial connection with others, in communication with all of our parts. It is not just that science and technology are possible means of great human satisfaction, as well as a matrix of complex dominations. Cyborg imagery can suggest a way out of the maze of dualisms in which we have explained our bodies and our tools to ourselves. This is a dream not of a common language, but of a powerful infidel heteroglossia. It is an imagination of a feminist speaking in tongues to strike fear into the circuits of the supersavers of the new Right. It means both building and destroying machines, identities, categories, relationships, spaces, stories. Though both are bound in the spiral dance, I would rather be a cyborg than a goddess.

ACKNOWLEDGMENTS

Research was funded by an Academic Senate Faculty Research Grant from the University of California, Santa Cruz. An earlier version of the paper on genetic engineering appeared as "Lieber Kyborg als Gottin: Für eine sozialistisch-feministische Unterwanderung der Gentechnologie," in Bernd-Peter Lange and Anna Marie Stuby, eds., *1984* (Berlin: Argument-Sonderband 105, 1984), pp. 66–84. The cyborg manifesto grew from "New Machines, New Bodies, New Communities: Political Dilemmas of a Cyborg Feminist," The Scholar and the Feminist X: The Question of Technology conference, April 1983.

The people associated with the History of Consciousness Board of UCSC have had an enormous influence on this paper, so that it feels collectively authored more than most, although those I cite may not recognize their ideas. In particular, members of graduate and undergraduate feminist theory, science and politics, and theory and methods courses have contributed to the cyborg manifesto. Particular debts here are due Hilary Klein ("Marxism, Psychoanalysis, and Mother Nature"); Paul Edwards ("Border Wars: The Science and Politics of Artificial Intelligence"); Lisa Lowe ("Julia Kristeva's *Des Chinoises:* Representing Cultural and Sexual Others"); and Jim Clifford, ("On Technographic Allegory: Essays," forthcoming).

Parts of the paper were my contribution to a collectively developed session, Poetic Tools and Political Bodies: Feminist Approaches to High Technology Culture, 1984 California American Studies Association, with History of Consciousness graduate students Zoe Sofoulis, "Jupiter Space"; Katie King, "The Pleasures of Repetition and the Limits of Identification in Feminist Science Fiction: Reimaginations of the Body after the Cyborg"; and Chela Sandoval, "The Construction of Subjectivity and Oppositional Consciousness in Feminist Film and Video." Sandoval's theory of oppositional consciousness was published as "Women Respond to Racism: A Report on the National Women's Studies Association Conference," Center for Third World Organizing, Oakland, California, n.d. for Sofoulis's semiotic-psychoanalytic readings of nuclear culture, see Z. Sofia, "Exterminating Fetuses: Abortion, Disarmament and the Sexo-Semiotics of Extraterrestrialism," Nuclear Criticism issue, *Diacritics,* vol. 14, no. 2 (1984); 47–59. King's manuscripts ("Questioning Tradition: Canon Formation and the Veiling of Power"; "Gender and Genre: Reading the Science Fiction of Joanna Russ"; "Varley's *Titan* and *Wizard:* Feminist Parodies of Nature, Culture, and Hardware") deeply inform the cyborg manifesto.

Barbara Epstein, Jeff Escoffier, Rusten Hogness, and Jaye Miller gave extensive discussion and editorial help. Members of the Silicon Valley Research Project of UCSC and participants in SVRP conferences and workshops have been very important, especially Rick Gordon, Linda Kimball, Nancy Snyder, Langdon Winner, Judith Stacey, Linda Lim, Patricia Fernandez-Kelly, and Judith Gregory. Finally, I want to thank Nancy Hartsock for years of friendship and discussion on feminist theory and feminist science fiction.

NOTES

1. Useful references to Left and/or feminist radical science movements and theory and to biological/biotechnological issues include: Ruth Bleier, *Science and Gender: A Critique of Biology and Its Themes on Women* (New York: Pergamon, 1984): Elizabeth Fee, "Critiques of Modern Science: The Relationship of Feminist and Other Radical Epistemologies," and Evelyn Hammonds, "Women of Color, Feminism and Science," papers for Symposium on Feminist Perspectives on Science, University of Wisconsin, April 11–12, 1985 (proceedings to be published by Pergamon); Stephen J. Gould, *Mismeasure of Man* (New York: Norton, 1981); Ruth Hubbard, Mary Sue Henifin, and Barbara Fried, eds., *Biological Woman, the Convenient Myth* (Cambridge, Mass.: Schenkman, 1982); Evelyn Fox Keller, *Reflections on Gender and Science* (New Haven: Yale University Press, 1985); R. C. Lewontin, Steve Rose, and Leon Kamin, *Not in Our Genes* (New York:

Pantheon, 1984): *Radical Science Journal,* 26 Freegrove Road, London N7 9RQ; *Science for the People,* 897 Main St., Cambridge, Mass. 02139.

2. Starting points for Left and/or feminist approaches to technology and politics include: Ruth Schwartz Cowan, *More Work for Mother: The Ironies of Household Technology from the Open Hearth to the Microwave* (New York: Basic Books, 1983); Joan Rothschild, *Machina ex Dea: Feminist Perspectives on Technology* (New York: Pergamon, 1983); Sharon Traweek, "Uptime, Downtime, Spacetime, and Power: An Ethnography of U.S. and Japanese Particle Physics," Ph.D. thesis, UC Santa Cruz, History of Consciousness, 1982; R. M. Young and Les Levidov, eds., *Science, Technology and the Labour Process,* vols. 1–3 (London: CSE Books); Joseph Weizenbaum, *Computer Power and Human Reason* (San Francisco: Freeman, 1976); Langdon Winner, *Autonomous Technology: Technics Out of Control as a Theme in Political Thought* (Cambridge, Mass.: MIT Press, 1977); Langdon Winner, "Paths in Technopolis," esp. "Mythinformation in the High Tech Era" (forthcoming); Jan Zimmerman, ed., *The Technological Woman: Interfacing with Tomorrow* (New York: Praeger, 1983); *Global Electronics Newsletter,* 867 West Dana St., #204, Mountain View, CA 94041; *Processed World,* 55 Sutter St., San Francisco, CA 94104; *ISIS,* Women's International Information and Communication Service, P.O. Box 50 (Cornavin), 1211 Geneva 2, Switzerland, and Via Santa Maria dell'Anima 30, 00186 Rome, Italy. Fundamental approaches to modern social studies of science that do not continue the liberal mystification that it all started with Thomas Kuhn include: Karin Knorr-Cetina, *The Manufacture of Knowledge* (Oxford: Pergamon, 1981); K. D. Knorr-Cetina and Michael Mulkay, eds., *Science Observed: Perspectives on the Social Study of Science* (Beverly Hills, Calif.: Sage, 1983); Bruno Latour and Steve Woolgar, *Laboratory Life: The Social Construction of Scientific Facts* (Beverly Hills, Calif.: Sage, 1979); Robert M. Young, "Interpreting the Production of Science," *New Scientist,* vol. 29 (March 1979); 1026–1028. More is claimed than is known about room for contesting productions of science in the mythic/material space of "the laboratory"; the 1984 Directory of the Network for the Ethnographic Study of Science, Technology, and Organizations lists a wide range of people and projects crucial to better radical analysis; available from NESSTO, P.O. Box 11442, Stanford, CA 94305.
3. Frederic Jameson, "Post Modernism, or the Cultural Logic of Late Capitalism," *New Left Review,* July/August 1984, pp. 53–94. See Marjorie Perloff, " 'Dirty' Language and Scramble Systems," *Sulfur* 11 (1984); 178–183; Kathleen Fraser, *Something (Even Human Voices) in the Foreground, a Lake* (Berkeley, Calif.: Kelsey St. Press, 1984).
4. Frans de Waal, *Chimpanzee Politics: Power and Sex Among the Apes* (New York: Harper & Row, 1982); Langdon Winner, "Do Artifacts have Politics?" *Daedalus,* Winter 1980.
5. Jean Baudrillard, *Simulations,* trans. P. Foss, P. Patton, and P. Beitchman (New York: Semiotext(e), 1983). Jameson ("Post Modernism," p. 66) points out that Plato's definition of the simulacrum is the copy for which there is no original, i.e., the world of advanced capitalism; of pure exchange.
6. Herbert Marcuse, *One-Dimensional Man* (Boston: Beacon, 1964); Carolyn Merchant, *Death of Nature* (San Francisco: Harper & Row, 1980).
7. Zoe Sofia, "Exterminating Fetuses," *Diacritics,* vol. 14, no. 2 (Summer 1984); 47–59, and "Jupiter Space" (Pomona, Calif: American Studies Association, 1984).
8. Powerful developments of coalition politics emerge from "third world" speakers, speaking from nowhere, the displaced center of the universe, Earth: "We live on the third planet from the sun"—*Sun Poem* by Jamaican writer Edward Kamau Briathwaite, review by Nathaniel Mackey, *Sulfur* 11 (1984); 200–205. *Home Girls,* ed. Barbara Smith (New York: Kitchen Table, Women

of Color Press, 1983), ironically subverts naturalized identities precisely while constructing a place from which to speak called home. See esp. Bernice Reagan, "Coalition Politics, Turning the Century," pp. 356–368.

9. Chela Sandoval, "Dis-Illusionment and the Poetry of the Future: The Making of Oppositional Consciousness," Ph.D. qualifying essay, UCSC, 1984.
10. bell hooks, *Ain't I a Woman?* (Boston: South End Press, 1981); Gloria Hull, Patricia Bell Scott, and Barbara Smith, eds., *All the Women Are White, All the Men Are Black, But Some of Us Are Brave: Black Women's Studies* (Old Westbury, Conn.: Feminist Press, 1982). Toni Cade Bambara, in *The Salt Eaters* (New York: Vintage/Random House, 1981), writes an extraordinary postmodernist novel, in which the women of color theater group, The Seven Sisters, explores a form of unity. Thanks to Elliott Evans's readings of Bambara, Ph.D. qualifying essay, UCSC, 1984.
11. On orientalism in feminist works and elsewhere, see Lisa Lowe, "Orientation: Representations of Cultural and Sexual 'Others,' " Ph.D. thesis, UCSC; Edward Said, *Orientalism* (New York: Pantheon, 1978).
12. Katie King has developed a theoretically sensitive treatment of the workings of feminist taxonomies as genealogies of power in feminist ideology and polemic: "Prospectus," *Gender and Genre: Academic Practice and the Making of Criticism* (Santa Cruz, Calif.: University of California Press, 1984). King examines an intelligent, problematic example of taxonomizing feminisms to make a little machine producing the desired final position: Alison Jaggar, *Feminist Politics and Human Nature* (Totowa, N.J.: Rowman & Allanheld, 1983). My caricature here of socialist and radical feminism is also an example.
13. The feminist standpoint argument is being developed by: Jane Flax, "Political Philosophy and the Patriarchal Unconsciousness," in Sandra Harding and Merill Hintikka, eds., *Discovering Reality* (Dordrecht: Reidel, 1983); Sandra Harding, "The Contradictions and Ambivalence of a Feminist Science," ms.; Harding and Hintikka, *Discovering Reality;* Nancy Hartsock, *Money, Sex, and Power* (New York: Longman, 1983), and "The Feminist Standpoint: Developing the Ground for a Specifically Feminist Historical Materialism," reprinted here, Chap. 25; Mary O'Brien, *The Politics of Reproduction* (New York: Routledge & Kegan Paul, 1981); Hilary Rose, "Hand, Brain, and Heart: A Feminist Epistemology for the Natural Sciences," *Signs,* vol. 9, no. 1 (1983); 73–90; Dorothy Smith, "Women's Perspective as a Radical Critique of Sociology," *Sociological Inquiry* 44 (1974), and "A Sociology of Women," in J. Sherman and E. T. Beck, eds., *The Prism of Sex* (Madison: University of Wisconsin Press, 1979).
14. Catharine MacKinnon, "Feminism, Marxism, Method, and the State: An Agenda for Theory," reprinted here, Chap. 4. A critique indebted to MacKinnon, but without the reductionism and with an elegant feminist account of Foucault's paradoxical conservatism on sexual violence (rape), is Teresa de Lauretis, "The Violence of Rhetoric: Considerations of Representation and Gender," in Nancy Armstrong, ed., *The Violence of Representation: Literature and the History of Violence* (London: Routledge, 1989). A theoretically elegant feminist social-historical examination of family violence, that insists on women's, men's, children's complex agency without losing sight of the material structures of male domination, race, and class, is Linda Gordon, *Heroes of Their Own Lives: The Politics and History of Family Violence: Boston 1880–1960,* (New York: Viking, 1988).
15. My previous efforts to understand biology as a cybernetic command-control discourse and organisms as "natural-technical objects of knowledge" are: "The High Cost of Information in Post–World War II Evolutionary Biology," *Philosophical Forum,* vol. 13, nos. 2–3 (1979); 206–237; "Signs of Dominance: From a Physiology to a Cybernetics of Primate Society," *Studies in History of Biology* 6 (1983); 129–219; "Class, Race, Sex, Scientific Objects of Knowledge:

A Socialist-Feminist Perspective on the Social Construction of Productive Knowledge and Some Political Consequences," in Violet Haas and Carolyn Perucci, eds., *Women in Scientific and Engineering Professions* (Ann Arbor: University of Michigan Press, 1984); 212–229.

16. E. Rusten Hogness, "Why Stress? A Look at the Making of Stress, 1936–56," available from the author, 4437 Mill Creek Rd., Healdsburg, Calif. 95448.
17. A left entry to the biotechnology debate: *GeneWatch,* a Bulletin of the Committee for Responsible Genetics, 5 Doane St., 4th floor, Boston, Mass. 02109; Susan Wright,"Recombinant DNA: The Status of Hazards and Controls," *Environment,* July/August 1982; Edward Yoxen, *The Gene Business* (New York: Harper & Row, 1983).
18. Starting references for "women in the integrated circuit": Pamela D'Onofrio-Flores and Sheila M. Pfafflin, eds., *Scientific-Technological Change and the Role of Women in Development* (Boulder, Colo.: Westview Press, 1982); Maria Patricia Fernandez-Kelly, *For We Are Sold, I and My People* (Albany, N.Y.: SUNY Press, 1983); Annette Fuentes and Barbara Ehrenreich, *Women in the Global Factory* (Boston: South End Press, 1983), with an especially useful list of resources and organizations; Rachael Grossman, "Women's Place in the Integrated Circuit," *Radical America,* vol. 14, no. 1 (1980); 29–50; June Nash and M. P. Fernandez-Kelly, eds., *Women and Men and the International Division of Labor* (Albany, N.Y.: SUNY Press, 1983); Aiwa Ong, "Japanese Factories, Malay Workers: Industrialization and the Cultural Construction of Gender in West Malaysia," in Shelley Errington and Jane Atkinson, eds., *Power and Difference* (Stanford: Stanford University Press, 1990); Science Policy Research Unity, *Microelectronics and Women's Employment in Britain* (Sussex, UK: University of Sussex Press, 1982).
19. The best example is Bruno Latour, *Les Microbes: Guerre et Paix, suivi de Irreductions* (Paris: Metailie, 1984).
20. For the homework economy and some supporting arguments: Richard Gordon, "The Computerization of Daily Life, the Sexual Division of Labor, and the Homework Economy," in R. Gordon, ed., *Microelectronics in Transition* (Norwood, N.J.: Ablex, 1985); Patricia Hill Collins, "Third World Women in America," and Sara G. Burr, "Women and Work," in Barbara K. Haber, ed., *The Women's Annual, 1981* (Boston: G. K. Hall, 1982); Judith Gregory and Karen Nussbaum, "Race against Time: Automation of the Office," *Office: Technology and People* 1 (1982); 197–236; Frances Fox Piven and Richard Cloward, *The New Class War: Reagan's Attack on the Welfare State and Its Consequences* (New York: Pantheon, 1982); Microelectronics Group, *Microelectronics: Capitalist Technology and the Working Class* (London: CSE, 1980); Karin Stallard, Barbara Ehrenreich, and Holly Sklar, *Poverty in the American Dream* (Boston: South End Press, 1983), including a useful organization and resource list.
21. Rae Lessor Blumberg, "A General Theory of Sex Stratification and Its Application to the Position of Women in Today's World Economy," paper delivered to Sociology Board, UCSC, February 1983. Also Blumberg, *Stratification: Socioeconomic and Sexual Inequality* (Boston: Brown, 1981). See also Sally Hacker, "Doing It the Hard Way: Ethnographic Studies in the Agribusiness and Engineering Classroom," California American Studies Association, Pomona, *Humanity and Society,* vol. 9, no. 2 (1985); S. Hacker and Lisa Bovit, "Agriculture to Agribusiness: Technical Imperatives and Changing Roles," *Proceedings* of the Society for the History of Technology, Milwaukee, 1981; Lawrence Busch and William Lacy, *Science, Agriculture, and the Politics of Research* (Boulder, Colo.: Westview Press, 1983); Denis Wilfred, "Capital and Agriculture, a Review of Marxian Problematics," *Studies in Political Economy,* no. 7 (1982); 127–154; Carolyn Sachs, *The Invisible Farmers: Women in Agricultural Production* (Totowa, N.J.: Rowman & Allanheld, 1983). Thanks to Elizabeth Bird, "Green Revolution Imperialism," I & II, ms., UCSC, 1984.

22. Cynthia Enloe, "Women Textile Workers in the Militarization of Southeast Asia," in Nash and Fernandez-Kelly, *Women and Men;* Rosalind Petchesky, "Abortion, Anti-Feminism, and the Rise of the New Right," *Feminist Studies,* vol. 7, no. 2 (1981).
23. For a feminist version of this logic, see Sarah Blaffer Hardy, *The Woman That Never Evolved* (Cambridge, Mass.: Harvard University Press, 1981). For an analysis of scientific women's storytelling practices, especially in relation to sociobiology, in evolutionary debates around child abuse and infanticide, see Donna Haraway, "The Contest for Primate Nature: Daughters of Man the Hunter in the Field, 1960–80," in Mark Kahn, ed., *The Future of American Democracy* (Philadelphia: Temple University Press, 1983), pp. 175–208.
24. For the moment of transition of hunting with guns to hunting with cameras in the construction of popular meanings of nature for an American urban immigrant public, see Donna Haraway, "Teddy Bear Patriarchy," *Social Text,* forthcoming, 1985; Roderick Nash, "The Exporting and Importing of Nature: Nature-Appreciation as a Commodity, 1850–1980," *Perspectives in American History,* vol. 3 (1979); 517–560; Susan Sontag, *On Photography* (New York: Dell, 1977); and Douglas Preston, "Shooting in Paradise," *Natural History,* vol. 93, no. 12 (December 1984); 14–19.
25. For crucial guidance for thinking about the political/cultural implications of the history of women doing science in the United States, see: Violet Haas and Carolyn Perucci, eds., *Women in Scientific and Engineering Professions* (Ann Arbor: University of Michigan Press, 1984); Sally Hacker, "The Culture of Engineering: Women, Workplace, and Machine," *Women's Studies International Quarterly,* vol. 4, no. 3 (1981); 341–353; Evelyn Fox Keller, *A Feeling for the Organism* (San Francisco: Freeman, 1983); National Science Foundation, *Women and Minorities in Science and Engineering* (Washington, D.C.: NSF, 1982); Margaret Rossiter, *Women Scientists in America* (Baltimore: Johns Hopkins University Press, 1982).
26. John Markoff and Lenny Siegel, "Military Micros," UCSC Silicon Valley Research Project conference, 1983, forthcoming in *Microelectronics and Industrial Transformation.* High Technology Professionals for Peace and Computer Professionals for Social Responsibility are promising organizations.
27. Katie King, "The Pleasure of Repetition and the Limits of Identification in Feminist Science Fiction: Reimaginations of the Body after the Cyborg," California American Studies Association, Pomona, 1984. An abbreviated list of feminist science fiction underlying themes of this essay: Octavia Butler, *Wild Seed, Mind of My Mind, Kindred, Survivor;* Suzy McKee Charnas, *Motherliness;* Samuel Delany, *Tales of Neveryon;* Anne McCaffrey, *The Ship Who Sang, Dinosaur Planet;* Vonda McIntyre, *Superluminal, Dreamsnake;* Joanna Russ, *Adventures of Alyx, The Female Man;* James Tiptree Jr., *Star Songs of an Old Primate, Up the Walls of the World;* John Varley, *Titan, Wizard, Demon.*
28. Mary Douglas, *Purity and Danger* (London: Routledge & Kegan Paul, 1966), *Natural Symbols* (London: Cresset Press, 1970).
29. French feminisms contribute to cyborg heteroglossia. Carolyn Burke, "Irigaray Through the Looking Glass," *Feminist Studies,* vol. 7, no. 2 (Summer 1981); 288–306; Luce Irigaray, *Ce sexe qui n'en est pas un* (Paris: Minuit, 1977); L. Irigaray, *Et l'une ne bouge pas sans l'autre* (Paris: Minuit, 1979); Elaine Marks and Isabelle de Courtivron, eds., *New French Feminisms* (Amherst: University of Massachusetts Press, 1980); *Signs,* vol. 7, no. 1 (Autumn 1981), special issue on French feminism; Monique Wittig, *The Lesbian Body,* trans. David LeVay (New York: Avon, 1975; *Le corps lesbien,* 1973).
30. But all these poets are very complex, not least in treatment of themes of lying and erotic, decentered collective and personal identities. Susan Griffin, *Women and Nature: The Roaring Inside Her*

(New York: Harper & Row, 1978); Audre Lorde, *Sister Outsider* (New York: Crossing Press, 1984); Adrienne Rich, *The Dream of a Common Language* (New York: Norton, 1978).

31. Jacques Derrida, *Of Grammatology*, trans. and introd. G. C. Spivak (Baltimore: Johns Hopkins University Press, 1976), esp. part 2, "Nature, Culture, Writing"; Claude Lévi-Strauss, *Tristes Tropiques*, trans. John Russell (New York: Criterion Books, 1961), esp. "The Writing Lesson."
32. Cherrie Moraga, *Loving in the War Years* (Boston: South End Press, 1983). The sharp relation of women of color to writing as theme and politics can be approached through: "The Black Woman and the Diaspora: Hidden Connections and Extended Acknowledgments," An International Literary Conference, Michigan State University, October 1985; Mari Evans, ed., *Black Women Writers: A Critical Evaluation* (Garden City, N.Y.: Doubleday/Anchor, 1984); Dexter Fisher, ed., *The Third Woman: Minority Women Writers of the United States* (Boston: Houghton Mifflin, 1980); several issues of *Frontiers*, esp. vol. 5 (1980), "Chicanas en el Ambiente Nacional," and vol. 7 (1983), "Feminisms in the Non-Western World"; Maxine Hong Kingston, *China Men* (New York: Knopf, 1977); Gerda Lerner, ed., *Black Women in White America: A Documentary History* (New York: Vintage, 1973); Cherrie Moraga and Gloria Anzaldúa, eds., *This Bridge Called My Back: Writings by Radical Women of Color* (Watertown, Mass.: Persephone, 1981); Robin Morgan, ed., *Sisterhood Is Global* (Garden City, N.Y.: Anchor/Doubleday, 1984). The writing of white women has had similar meanings: Sandra Gilbert and Susan Gubar, *The Madwoman in the Attic* (New Haven: Yale University Press, 1979); Joanna Russ, *How to Suppress Women's Writing* (Austin: University of Texas Press, 1983).
33. James Clifford argues persuasively for recognition of continuous cultural reinvention, the stubborn nondisappearance of those "marked" by Western imperializing practices; see "On Ethnographic Allegory: Essays," forthcoming 1985, and "On Ethnographic Authority," *Representations*, vol. 1, no. 2 (1983); 118–146.
34. Page DuBois, *Centaurs and Amazons* (Ann Arbor: University of Michigan Press, 1982); Lorraine Daston and Katharine Park, "Hermaphrodites in Renaissance France," ms., n.d.; Katharine Park and Lorraine Daston, "Unnatural Conceptions: The Study of Monsters in 16th and 17th Century France and England," *Past and Present*, no. 92 (August 1981); 20–54.

Feminism, Citizenship, and Radical Democratic Politics

Mouffe rejects essentialist views of women on the grounds that they are inimical to a political practice that is both feminist and radically democratic. Recognizing the need to address many different forms of oppression, she formulates an alternative conception of identity that is designed to sustain an emancipatory politics. For Mouffe, a social agent is an "ensemble of 'subject positions' "—an intersection of many different, contingently related discourses. Through "articulatory practices"—discourses in which links are formed between diverse individuals and between different social groups—identities are partially and impermanently established.

Mouffe contends that this view of identity is necessary to understand the process through which concerns that were once regarded as apolitical have been politicized. Likewise, she urges that this view makes it possible to deconstruct the patriarchal conception of citizenship that prevails in democratic theory and to develop a conception of citizenship that is independent of group identifications, including sexual difference. For Mouffe, citizenship is constituted by identification with the principles of modern pluralist democracy—liberty and equality for all. Still, there are many interpretations of these principles. The radical democratic interpretation focuses on the many forms that domination takes and challenges them in the name of achieving liberty and equality. When the members of diverse groups share the aim of opposing domination, they gain a collective political identity as radical democratic citizens, but their distinctive needs and political objectives are not negated. Politics, on Mouffe's view, is a process of emancipatory "hegemonic articulation"—that is, a process of constructing new identities that transform existing subject positions. Feminist politics is the struggle against yoking the category "woman" to connotations of subordination. This struggle for women's equality must be waged as part of a larger struggle against all forms of oppression.

—D.T.M.

Chapter 28

Chantal Mouffe

Feminism, Citizenship, and Radical Democratic Politics

Two topics have recently been the subject of much discussion among Anglo-American feminists: postmodernism and essentialism. Obviously they are related, since the so-called postmoderns are also presented as the main critics of essentialism, but it is better to distinguish them since some feminists who are sympathetic to postmodernism have lately come to the defense of essentialism.[1] I consider that, in order to clarify the issues that are at stake in that debate, it is necessary to recognize that there is not such a thing as "postmodernism," understood as a coherent theoretical approach, and that the frequent assimilation between poststructuralism and postmodernism can only lead to confusion. Which is not to say that we have not been witnessing through the twentieth century a progressive questioning of the dominant form of rationality and of the premises of the modes of thought characteristic of the Enlightenment. But this critique of universalism, humanism, and rationalism has come from many different quarters and it is far from being limited to the authors called "poststructuralists" or "postmodernists." From that point of view, all the innovative currents of this century—Heidegger and the post-Heideggerian philosophical hermeneutics of Gadamer, the later Wittgenstein and the philosophy of language inspired by his work, psychoanalysis and the reading of Freud proposed by Lacan, American pragmatism—all have from diverse standpoints criticized the idea of a universal human nature, of a universal canon of rationality through which that human nature could be known as well as the traditional conception of truth. Therefore, if the term "postmodern" indicates such a critique of Enlightenment's universalism and rationalism, it must be acknowledged that it refers to the main currents of twentieth-century philosophy and there is no reason to single out poststructuralism as a special target. On the other side, if by "postmodernism" one wants to designate only the very specific form that such a critique takes in authors such as Lyotard and Baudrillard, there is absolutely no justification for putting in that category people like Derrida, Lacan, or Foucault, as has generally been the case. Too often a critique of a specific thesis of Lyotard or Baudrillard leads to sweeping conclusions about "the postmoderns" who by then include all the authors loosely connected with poststructuralism. This type of amalgamation is completely unhelpful when not clearly disingenuous.

Once the conflation between postmodernism and poststructuralism has been debunked, the question of essentialism appears in a very different light. Indeed, it is with regard to the critique of essentialism that a convergence can be established among many different currents of thought and similarities found in the work of authors as different as Derrida, Wittgenstein, Heidegger, Dewey, Gadamer, Lacan, Foucault, Freud, and others. This is very important because it means that such a critique takes many different forms and that if we want to scrutinize its relevance for feminist politics we must engage with all its modalities and implications and not quickly dismiss it on the basis of some of its versions.

My aim in this article will be to show the crucial insights that an antiessentialist approach can bring to the elaboration of a feminist politics that is also informed by a radical democratic project. I certainly do not believe that essentialism necessarily entails conservative politics and I am ready to accept that it can be formulated in a progressive way. What I want to argue is that it presents some inescapable shortcomings for the construction of a democratic alternative whose objective is the articulation of the struggles linked to different forms of oppression. I consider that it leads to a view of identity that is at odds with a conception of radical and plural democracy and that it does not allow us to construe the new vision of citizenship that is required by such a politics.

THE QUESTION OF IDENTITY AND FEMINISM

One common tenet of critics of essentialism has been the abandoning of the category of the subject as a rational transparent entity that could convey a homogeneous meaning on the total field of her conduct by being the source of her action. For instance, psychoanalysis has shown that far from being organized around the transparency of an ego, personality is structured in a number of levels that lie outside of the consciousness and the rationality of the agents. It has therefore undermined the idea of the unified character of the subject. Freud's central claim is that the human mind is necessarily subject to division between two systems of which one is not and cannot be conscious. Expanding the Freudian vision, Lacan has shown the plurality of registers—the Symbolic, the Real, and the Imaginary—which penetrate any identity, and the place of the subject as the place of the lack which—though represented within the structure—is the empty place that at the same time subverts and is the condition of constitution of any identity. The history of the subject is the history of his/her identifications and there is no concealed identity to be rescued beyond the latter. There is thus a double movement. On the one hand, a movement of decentering that prevents the fixation of a set of positions around a preconstituted point. On the other hand, and as a result of this *essential* nonfixity, the opposite movement: the institution of nodal points, partial fixations that limit the flux of the signified under the signifier. But this dialectics at nonfixity/fixation is possible only because fixity is not given beforehand, because no center of subjectivity precedes the subject's identifications.

In the philosophy of language of the later Wittgenstein, we also find a critique of the rationalist conception of the subject that indicates that the latter cannot be the source of linguistic meanings, since it is through participation in different language games that the world is disclosed to us. We encounter the same idea in Gadamer's philosophical hermeneutics in the thesis that there is a fundamental unity between thought, language, and the world and that it is within language that the horizon of our present is constituted. A similar critique of the centrality of the subject in modern metaphysics and of its unitary character can be found under several forms in the other authors mentioned earlier. However, my purpose here is not to examine those theories in detail but simply to indicate some basic convergences. I am not overlooking the fact that there are important differences among all those very diverse thinkers. But from the point of view of the argument that I want to make, it is important to grasp the consequences of their common critique of the traditional status of the subject and of its implications for feminism.

It is often said that the deconstruction of essential identities, which is the result of acknowledging the contingency and ambiguity of every identity, renders feminist political action impossible. Many feminists believe that, without seeing women as a coherent identity, we cannot ground the possibility of a feminist political movement in which women could unite as women in order to formulate and pursue specific feminist aims. Contrary to that view, I will argue that, for those feminists who are committed to a radical democratic politics, the deconstruction of essential identities should be seen as the necessary condition for an adequate understanding of the variety of social relations where the principles of liberty and equality should apply. It is only when we discard the view of the subject as an agent both rational and transparent to itself, and discard as well the supposed unity and homogeneity of the ensemble of its positions, that we are in the position to theorize the multiplicity of relations of subordination. A single individual can be the bearer of this multiplicity and be dominant in one relation while subordinated in another. We can then conceive the social agent as constituted by an ensemble of "subject positions" that can never be totally fixed in a closed system of differences, constructed by a diversity of discourses among which there is no necessary relation, but a constant movement of overdetermination and displacement. The "identity" of such a multiple and contradictory subject is therefore always contingent and precarious, temporarily fixed at the intersection of those subject positions and dependent on specific forms of identification. It is therefore impossible to speak of the social agent as if we were dealing with a unified, homogeneous entity. We have rather to approach it as a plurality, dependent on the various subject positions through which it is constituted within various discursive formations. And to recognize that there is no a priori, necessary relation between the discourses that construct its different subject positions. But, for the reasons pointed out earlier, this plurality does not involve the *coexistence*, one by one, of a plurality of subject positions but rather the constant subversion and overdetermination of one by the others, which make possible the generation of "totalizing effects" within a field characterized by open and indeterminate frontiers.

Such an approach is extremely important to understand feminist as well as other contemporary struggles. Their central characteristic is that an ensemble of subject positions linked through inscription in social relations, hitherto considered as apolitical, have become loci of conflict and antagonism and have led to political mobilization. The proliferation of these new forms of struggle can only be theoretically tackled when one starts with the dialectics and decentering/recentering described earlier.

In *Hegemony and Socialist Strategy*,[2] Ernesto Laclau and I have attempted to draw the consequences of such a theoretical approach for a project of radical and plural democracy. We argued for the need to establish a chain of equivalence among the different democratic struggles so as to create an equivalent articulation between the demands of women, blacks, workers, gays, and others. On this point our perspective differs from other nonessentialist views where the aspect of detotalization and decentering prevails and where the dispersion of subject positions is transformed into an effective separation, as is the case with Lyotard and to some extent with Foucault. For us, the aspect of articulation is crucial. To deny the existence of an a priori, necessary link between subject positions does not mean that there are not constant efforts to establish between them historical, contingent, and variable links. This type of link, which establishes between various positions a contingent, unpredetermined relation, is what we designated as "articulation." Even though there is no necessary link between different subject positions, in the field of politics there are always discourses that try to provide an articulation from different standpoints. For that reason every subject position is constituted within an essentially unstable discursive structure since it is submitted to a variety of articulatory practices that constantly subvert and transform it. This is why there is no subject position whose links with others is definitively assured and, therefore, no social identity that would be fully and permanently acquired. This does not mean, however, that we cannot retain notions like "working class," "men," "women," "blacks," or other signifiers referring to collective subjects. However, once the existence of a common essence has been discarded, their status must be conceived in terms of what Wittgenstein designates as "family resemblances," and their unity must be seen as the result of the partial fixation of identities through the creation of nodal points.

For feminists to accept such an approach has very important consequences for the way we formulate our political struggles. If the category "woman" does not correspond to any unified and unifying essence, the question can no longer be to try to unearth it. The central issues become: How is "woman" constructed as a category within different discourses? How is sexual difference made a pertinent distinction in social relations? How are relations of subordination constructed through such a distinction? The whole false dilemma of equality versus difference is exploded since we no longer have a homogeneous entity "woman" facing another homogeneous entity "man," but a multiplicity of social relations in which sexual difference is always constructed in very diverse ways and where the struggle against subordination has to be visualized in specific and differential forms. To ask if women should become identical to men in order to be recognized as equal, or if they should assert their difference at the cost of equality, appears meaningless once essential identities are put into question.[3]

CITIZENSHIP AND FEMINIST POLITICS

In consequence, the very question of what a feminist politics should be has to be posed in completely different terms. So far, most feminists concerned with the contribution that feminism could make to democratic politics have been looking either for the specific demands that could express women's interests or for the specific feminine values that should become the model for democratic politics. Liberal feminists have been fighting for a wide range of new rights for women to make them equal citizens, but without challenging the dominant liberal models of citizenship and politics. Their view has been criticized by other feminists who argue that the present conception of the political is a male one and that women's concerns cannot be accommodated within such a framework. Following Carol Gilligan, they oppose a feminist "ethics of care" to the male and liberal "ethics of justice." Against liberal individualist values, they defend a set of values based on the experience of women *as* women, that is, their experience of motherhood and care exercised in the private realm of the family. They denounce Liberalism for having constructed modern citizenship as the realm of the public, identified with men, and for having excluded women by relegating them to the private realm. According to this view, feminists should strive for a type of politics that is guided by the specific values of love, care, the recognition of needs, and friendship. One of the clearest attempts to offer an alternative to liberal politics grounded in feminine values is to be found in "Maternal Thinking" and "Social Feminism," principally represented by Sara Rudick and Jean Bethke Elshtain.[4] Feminist politics, they argue, should privilege the identity of "women as mothers" and the private realm of the family. The family is seen as having moral superiority over the public domain of politics because it constitutes our common humanity. For Elshtain "the family remains the locus of the deepest and most resonant human ties, the most enduring hopes, the most intractable conflicts."[5] She considers that it is in the family that we should look for a new political morality to replace liberal individualism. In women's experience in the private realm as mothers, she says, a new model for the activity of citizenship is to be found. The maternalists want us to abandon the male liberal politics of the public informed by the abstract point of view of justice and the "generalized other" and adopt instead a feminist politics of the private, informed by the virtues of love, intimacy, and concern for the "concrete other" specific to the family.

An excellent critique of such an approach has been provided by Mary Dietz,[6] who shows that Elshtain fails to provide a theoretical argument that links maternal thinking and the social practice of mothering to democratic values and democratic politics. Dietz argues that maternal virtues cannot be political because they are connected with and emerge from an activity that is special and distinctive. They are the expression of an unequal relation between mother and child which is also an intimate, exclusive, and particular activity. Democratic citizenship, on the contrary, should be collective, inclusive, and generalized. Sine democracy is a condition in which individuals aim at being equals, the mother/child relationship cannot provide an adequate model of citizenship.

Yet a different feminist critique of liberal citizenship is provided by Carole Pateman.[7] It is more sophisticated, but shares some common features with "Maternal Thinking." Pateman's tone bears the traces of radical feminism, for the accent is put, not on the mother/child relation, but on the man/woman antagonism.

Citizenship is, according to Pateman, a patriarchal category: who a "citizen" is, what a citizen does, and the arena within which he acts have been constructed in the masculine image. Although women in liberal democracies are now citizens, formal citizenship has been won within a structure of patriarchal power in which women's qualities and tasks are still devalued. Moreover, the call for women's distinctive capacities to be integrated fully into the public world of citizenship faces what she calls the "Wollstonecraft dilemma": to demand equality is to accept the patriarchal conception of citizenship, which implies that women must become like men, while to insist that women's distinctive attributes, capacities, and activities be given expression and valued as contributing to citizenship is to demand the impossible because such difference is precisely what patriarchal citizenship excludes.

Pateman sees the solution to this dilemma in the elaboration of a "sexually differentiated" conception of citizenship that would recognize women *as* women, with their bodies and all that they symbolize. For Pateman this entails giving political significance to the capacity that men lack: to create life, which is to say, *motherhood*. She declares that this capacity should be treated with equal political relevance for defining citizenship as what is usually considered the ultimate test of citizenship: a man's willingness to fight and to die for his country. She considers that the traditional patriarchal way of posing an alternative, where either the separation or the sameness of the sexes is valorized, needs to be overcome by a new way of posing the question of women. This can be done through a conception of citizenship that recognizes both the specificity of womanhood and the common humanity of men and women. Such a view "that gives due weight to sexual difference in a context of civil equality, requires the rejection of a unitary (i.e., masculine) conception of the individual, abstracted from our embodied existence and from the patriarchal division between the private and the public."[8] What feminists should aim for is the elaboration of a sexually differentiated conception of individuality and citizenship that would include "women *as* women in a context of civil equality and active citizenship."[9]

Pateman provides many very interesting insights into the patriarchal bias of the social contract theorists and the way in which the liberal individual has been constructed according to the male image. I consider that her own solution, however, is unsatisfactory. Despite all her provisos about the historically constructed aspects of sexual difference, her view still postulates the existence of some kid of essence corresponding to women *as* women. Indeed, her proposal for a differentiated citizenship that recognizes the specificity of womanhood rests on the identification of women *as* women with motherhood. There are for her two basic types of individuality that should be expressed in two different forms of citizenship: men *as* men and women *as* women. The problem, according to her, is that the category of the "individual," while based on the male model, is presented as the universal form of individuality. Feminists must uncover that false universality by asserting the existence of two sexually differentiated forms of universality; this is the only way to resolve the "Wollstonecraft dilemma" and to break free from the patriarchal alternatives of "othering" and "saming."

I agree with Pateman that the modern category of the individual has been constructed in a manner that postulates a universalist, homogeneous "public" that relegates all particularity and difference to the "private" and that this has very negative consequences for women. I do not believe, however, that the remedy is to replace it by a sexually differentiated, "bi-gendered" conception of the individual and to bring women's so-called specific tasks into the very definition of citizenship. It seems to me that such a solution remains trapped in the problematic that Pateman wants to challenge. She affirms that the separation between public and private is the founding moment of modern patriarchalism because

> the separation of private and public is the separation of the world of natural subjection, i.e. women, from the world of conventional relations and individuals, i.e. men. The feminine, private world of nature, particularity, differentiation, inequality, emotion, love and ties of blood is set apart from the public, universal—and masculine—realm of convention, civil equality and freedom, reason, consent and contract.[10]

It is for that reason that childbirth and motherhood have been presented as the antithesis of citizenship and that they have become the symbol of everything natural that cannot be part of the "public" but must remain in a separate sphere. By asserting the political value of motherhood, Pateman intends to overcome that distinction and contribute to the deconstruction of the patriarchal conception of citizenship and private and public life. As a result of her essentialism, however, she never deconstructs the very opposition of men/women. This is the reason that she ends up, like the maternalists, proposing an inadequate conception of what should be a democratic politics informed by feminism. This is why she can assert that "the most profound and complex problem for political theory and practice is how the two bodies of humankind and feminine and masculine individuality can be fully incorporated into political life."[11]

My own view is completely different. I want to argue that the limitations of the modern conception of citizenship should be remedied, not by making sexual difference politically relevant to its definition, but by constructing a new conception of citizenship where sexual difference should become effectively nonpertinent. This, of course, requires a conception of the social agent in the way that I have defended earlier, as the articulation of an ensemble of subject positions, corresponding to the multiplicity of social relations in which it is inscribed. This multiplicity is constructed within specific discourses that have no necessary relation but only contingent and precarious forms of articulation. There is no reason why sexual difference should be pertinent in all social relations. To be sure, today many different practices, discourses, and institutions do construct men and women (differentially), and the masculine/feminine distinction exists as a pertinent one in many fields. But this does not imply that it should remain the case, and we can perfectly imagine sexual difference becoming irrelevant in many social relations where it is currently found. This is indeed the objective of many feminist struggles.

I am not arguing in favor of a total disappearance of sexual difference as a pertinent distinction; I am not saying either that equality between men and women requires gender-neutral social relations, and it is clear that, in many cases, to treat men and women equally implies treating them differentially. My thesis is that, in the domain of politics, and as far as citizenship is concerned, sexual difference should not be a pertinent distinction. I am at one with Pateman in criticizing the liberal, male conception of modern citizenship, but I believe that what a project of radical and plural democracy needs is not a sexually differentiated model of citizenship in which the specific tasks of both men and women would be valued equally, but a truly different conception of what it is to be a citizen and to act as a member of a democratic political community.

A RADICAL DEMOCRATIC CONCEPTION OF CITIZENSHIP

The problems with the liberal conception of citizenship are not limited to those concerning women, and feminists committed to a project of radical and plural democracy should engage with all of them. Liberalism has contributed to the formulation of the notion of universal citizenship, based on the assertion that all individuals are born free and equal, but it has also reduced citizenship to a merely legal status, indicating the rights that the individual holds against the state. The way those rights are exercised is irrelevant as long as their holders do not break the law or interfere with the rights of others. Notions of public-spiritedness, civic activity, and political participation in a community of equals are alien to most liberal thinkers. Besides, the public realm of modern citizenship was constructed in a universalistic and rationalistic manner that precluded the recognition of division and antagonism and that relegated to the private all particularity and difference. The distinction public/private, central as it was for the assertion of individual liberty, acted therefore as a powerful principle of exclusion. Through the identification between the private and the domestic, it played indeed an important role in the subordination of women. Recently, several feminists and other critics of liberalism have been looking to the civic republican tradition for a different, more active conception of citizenship that emphasizes the value of political participation and the notion of a common good, prior to and independent of individual desires and interests.

Nevertheless, feminists should be aware of the limitations of such an approach and of the potential dangers that a communitarian type of politics presents for the struggle of many oppressed groups. The communitarian insistence on a substantive notion of the common good and shared moral values is incompatible with the pluralism that is constitutive of modern democracy and that I consider to be necessary to deepen the democratic revolution and accommodate the multiplicity of present democratic demands. The problems with the liberal construction of the public/private distinction would not be solved by discarding it, but only by reformulating it in a more adequate way. Moreover, the centrality of the notion of rights for a modern conception of the citizen should be acknowledged, even though these must be complemented by a more active sense of political participation and of belonging to a political community.[12]

The view of radical and plural democracy that I want to put forward sees citizenship as a form of political identity that consists in the identification with the political principles of modern pluralist democracy, namely, the assertion of liberty and equality for all. It would be a common political identity of persons who might be engaged in many different purposive enterprises and with differing conceptions of the good, but who are bound by their common identification with a given interpretation of a set of ethico-political values. Citizenship is not just one identity among others, as it is in Liberalism, nor is it the dominant identity that overrides all others, as it is in Civic Republicanism. Instead, it is an articulating principle that affects the different subject positions of the social agent while allowing for a plurality of specific allegiances and for the respect of individual liberty. In this view, the public/private distinction is not abandoned, but constructed in a different way. The distinction does not correspond to discrete, separate spheres; every situation is an encounter between "private" and "public," because every enterprise is private while never immune from the public conditions prescribed by the principles of citizenship. Wants, choices, and decisions are private because they are the responsibility of each individual, but performances are public because they have to subscribe to the conditions specified by a specific understanding of the ethico-political principles of the regime that provide the "grammar" of the citizen's conduct.[13]

It is important to stress here that if we affirm that the exercise of citizenship consists in identifying with the ethico-political principles of modern democracy, we must also recognize that there can be as many forms of citizenship as there are interpretations of those principles and that a radical democratic interpretation is one among others. A radical democratic interpretation will emphasize the numerous social relations in which situations of domination exist that must be challenged if the principles of liberty and equality are to apply. It indicates the common recognition by the different groups struggling for an extension and radicalization of democracy that they have a common concern. This should lead to the articulation of the democratic demands found in a variety of movements: women, workers, blacks, gays, ecological, as well as other "new social movements." The aim is to construct a "we" as radical democratic citizens, a collective political identity articulated through the principle of democratic *equivalence*. It must be stressed that such a relation of *equivalence* does not eliminate *difference*—that would be simple identity. It is only insofar as democratic differences are opposed to forces or discourses which negate all of them that these differences are substitutable for each other.

The view that I am proposing here is clearly different from the liberal as well as the civic republican one. It is not a gendered conception of citizenship, but neither is it a neutral one. It recognizes that every definition of a "we" implies the delimitation of a "frontier" and the designation of a "them." That definition of a "we" always takes place, then, in a context of diversity and conflict. Contrary to Liberalism, which evacuates the idea of the common good, and Civic Republicanism, which reifies it, a radical democratic approach views the common good as a "vanishing point," something to which we must constantly refer when we are acting as citizens but that can never be reached. The common good functions, on the one hand, as a "social imaginary": that is, as that for which the very impossibility of achieving a full representation gives to it the role of an horizon that is the condition of possibility of any representation within the space that it delimits. On the other hand, it specifies what I have designated, following Wittgenstein, as a "grammar of conduct" that coincides with the allegiance to the constitutive ethico-political principles of modern democracy: liberty and equality for all. Yet, since those principles are open to many competing interpretations, one has to acknowledge that a fully inclusive political community can never be realized. There will always be a "constitutive outside," an exterior to the community that is the very condition of its existence. Once it is accepted that there cannot be a "we" without a "them" and that all forms of consensus are by necessity based on acts of exclusion, the question cannot be any more the creation of a fully inclusive community where antagonism, division, and conflict will have disappeared. Hence, we have to come to terms with the very impossibility of a full realization of democracy.

Such a radical democratic citizenship is obviously at odds with the "sexually differentiated" view of citizenship of Carole Pateman, but also with another feminist attempt to offer an alternative to the liberal view of the citizen: the "group differentiated" conception put forward by Iris Young.[14] Like Pateman, Young argues that modern citizenship has been constructed on a separation between "public" and "private" that presented the public as the realm of homogeneity and universality and relegated difference to the private. But she insists that this exclusion affects not only women but also many other groups based on differences of ethnicity, race, age, disabilities, and so forth. For Young, the crucial problem is that the public realm of citizenship was presented as expressing a general will, a point of view that citizens held in common and that transcended their differences. Young argues in favor of a repoliticization of public life that would not require the creation of a public realm in which citizens leave behind their particular group affiliation and needs in order to discuss a presumed general interest or common good. In its place she proposes the creation of a "heterogeneous public" that provides mechanisms for the effective representation and recognition of the distinct voices and perspectives of those constituent groups that are oppressed or disadvantaged. In order to make such a project possible, she looks for a conception of normative reason that does not pretend to be impartial and universal and that does not oppose reason to affectivity and desire. She considers that, despite its limitations, Habermas's communicative ethics can contribute a good deal to its formulation.

Whereas I sympathize with Young's attempt to take account of other forms of oppression than the ones suffered by women, I nevertheless find her solution of "group differentiated citizenship" highly problematic. To begin with, the notion of a group that she identifies with comprehensive identities and ways of life might make sense for groups like Native

Americans, but is completely inadequate as a description for many other groups whose demands she wants to take into account like women, the elderly, the differently abled, and others. She has an ultimately essentialist notion of "Group," and this accounts for why, in spite of all her disclaimers, her view is not so different from the interest-group pluralism that she criticizes: there are groups with their interests and identities already given, and politics is not about the construction of new identities but about finding ways to satisfy the demands of the various parts in a way acceptable to all. In fact, one could say that hers is a kind of "Habermasian version of interest group pluralism," according to which groups are not viewed as fighting for egoistic private interests but for justice, and where the emphasis is put on the need for argumentation and publicity. So politics in her work is still conceived as a process of dealing with already-constituted interests and identities while, in the approach that I am defending, the aim of a radical democratic citizenship should be the construction of a common political identity that would create the conditions for the establishment of a new hegemony articulated through new egalitarian social relations, practices, and institutions. This cannot be achieved without the transformation of existing subject positions; this is the reason why the model of the rainbow coalition favored by Young can be seen only as a first stage toward the implementation of a radical democratic politics. It might indeed provide many opportunities for a dialogue among different oppressed groups, but for their demands to be construed around the principle of democratic equivalence, new identities need to be created: in their present state many of these demands are antithetical to each other, and their convergence can only result from a political process of hegemonic articulation, and not simply of free and undistorted communication.

FEMINIST POLITICS AND RADICAL DEMOCRACY

As I indicated at the outset, there has been a great deal of concern among feminists about the possibility of grounding a feminist politics once the existence of women *as* women is put into question. It has been argued that to abandon the idea of a feminine subject with a specific identity and definable interests was to pull the rug from under feminism as politics. According to Kate Soper:

> Feminism, like any other politics, has always implied a banding together, a movement based on the solidarity and sisterhood of women, who are linked by perhaps very little else than their *sameness* and "common cause" as women. If this sameness itself is challenged on the ground that there is no "presence" of womanhood, nothing that the term "woman" immediately expressed, and nothing instantiated concretely except particular women in particular situations, then the idea of a political community built around women—the central aspiration of the early feminist movement—collapses.[15]

I consider Soper here construes an illegitimate opposition between two extreme alternatives: either there is an already given unity of "womanhood" on the basis of some a priori belonging or, if this is denied, no forms of unity and feminist politics can exist. The absence of a female essential identity and of a pregiven unity, however, does not preclude the construction of multiple forms of unity and common action. As the result of the construction of nodal points, partial fixations can take place and precarious forms of identification can be established around the category "women" that provide the basis for a feminist identity and a feminist struggle. We find in Soper a type of misunderstanding of the antiessentialist position that is frequent in feminist writings and that consists in believing that the critique of an essential identity must necessarily lead to the rejection of any concept of identity whatsoever.[16]

In *Gender Trouble*,[17] Judith Butler asks, "What new shape of politics emerges when identity as a common ground no longer constrains the discourse of feminist politics?" My answer is that to visualize feminist politics in that way opens much greater opportunity for a democratic politics that aims at the articulation of the various different struggles against oppression. What emerges is the possibility of a project of radical and plural democracy.

To be adequately formulated, such a project requires discarding the essentialist idea of an identity of women *as* women as well as the attempt to ground a specific and strictly feminist politics. Feminist politics should be understood not as a separate form of politics designed to pursue the interest of women *as* women, but rather as the pursuit of feminist goals and aims within the context of a wider articulation of demands. Those goals and aims should consist in the transformation of all the discourses, practices, and social relations where the category "woman" is constructed in a way that implies subordination. Feminism, for me, is the struggle for the equality of women. But this should not be understood as a struggle for realizing the equality of a definable empirical group with a common essence and identity, women, but rather as a struggle against the multiple forms in which the category "woman" is constructed in subordination. However, we must be aware of the fact that those feminist goals can be constructed in many different ways, according to the multiplicity of discourses in which they can be framed: Marxist, liberal, conservative, radical-separatist, radical-democratic, and so on. There are, therefore, by necessity many feminisms, and any attempt to find the "true" form of feminist politics should be abandoned. I believe that feminists can contribute to politics a reflection on the conditions for creating an effective equality of women. Such a reflection is bound to be influenced by the existing political and theoretical discourses. Instead of trying to prove that a given form of feminist discourse is the one that corresponds to the "real" essence of womanhood, one should intend to show how it opens better possibilities for an understanding of women's multiple forms of subordination.

My main argument here has been that, for feminists who are committed to a political project whose aim is to struggle against the forms of subordination which exist in many social relations, and not only in those linked to gender, an approach that permits us to understand how the subject is constructed through different discourses and subject positions is certainly more adequate than one that reduces our identity to one single position—be it class, race, or gender. This type of democratic project is also better served by a perspective that allows us to grasp the diversity of ways in which relations of power are constructed and helps us to reveal the forms of exclusion present in all pretensions to universalism and in claims to have found the true essence of rationality. This is why the critique of essentialism and all its different forms: humanism, rationalism, universalism, far from being an obstacle to the formulation of a feminist democratic project is indeed the very condition of its possibility.

NOTES

1. See the issue of the journal *Differences*, 1 (September 1989), entitled "The Essential Difference: Another Look at Essentialism," as well as the book by Diana Fuss, *Essentially Speaking* (New York: Routledge, 1989).

2. Ernesto Laclau and Chantal Mouffle, *Hegemony and Socialist Strategy. Towards a Radical Democratic Politics* (London: Verso, 1985).
3. For an interesting critique of the dilemma of equality versus difference, which is inspired by a similar *problématique* from the one I am defending here, see Joan W. Scott, *Gender and The Politics of History* (New York: Columbia Univ. Press, 1988), part 4. Among feminists the critique of essentialism was first developed by the journal *m/f*, which during its eight years of existence (1978–1986) made an invaluable contribution to feminist theory. I consider that it has not yet been superseded and that the editorials as well as the articles by Parveen Adams still represent the most forceful exposition of the antiessentialist stance. A selection of the best articles from the 12 issues of *m/f* are reprinted in *The Woman In Question*, edited by Parveen Adams and Elisabeth Cowie (Cambridge, Mass.: MIT Press, 1990; and London: Verso, 1990).
4. Sara Ruddick, *Maternal Thinking* (London: Verso, 1989); Jean Bethke Elshtain, *Public Man, Private Woman* (Princeton: Princeton University Press, 1981).
5. Jean Bethke Elshtain, "On 'The Family Crisis,' " *Democracy* 3, 1 (Winter 1983); 138.
6. Mary G. Dietz, "Citizenship with a Feminist Face. The Problem with Maternal Thinking," *Political Theory* 13, 1 (February 1985).
7. Carole Pateman. *The Sexual Contract* (Stanford: Stanford University Press, 1988), and *The Disorder of Women* (Cambridge: Polity Press, 1989), as well as numerous unpublished papers on which I will also be drawing, especially the following: "Removing Obstacles to Democracy: The Case of Patriarchy"; "Feminism and Participatory Democracy: Some Reflections on Sexual Difference and Citizenship"; "Women's Citizenship: Equality, Difference, Subordination."
8. Carole Pateman, "Feminism and Participatory Democracy," unpublished paper presented to the Meeting of the American Philosophical Association, St. Louis, Missouri, May 1986, p. 24.
9. *Ibid.*, p. 26.
10. Carole Pateman, "Feminism and Participatory Democracy," pp. 7–8.
11. Carole Pateman, *The Disorder of Women*, p. 53.
12. I analyze more in detail the debate between liberals and communitarians in my article "American Liberalism and Its Critics: Rawls, Taylor, Sandel and Walzer," *Praxis International* 8, 2 (July 1988).
13. The conception of citizenship that I am presenting here is developed more fully in my "Democratic Citizenship and The Political Community," in *Community at Loose Ends*, edited by the Miami Theory Collective (Minneapolis, Minn.: University of Minnesota Press, 1991).
14. Iris Marion Young, "Impartiality and the Civic Public," in *Feminism as Critique*, edited by Seyla Benhabib and Drucilla Cornell (Minneapolis: University of Minnesota Press, 1987) and "Polity and Group Difference: A Critique of the Ideal of Universal Citizenship," *Ethics* 99 (January 1989).
15. Kate Soper, "Feminism, Humanism and Postmodernism," *Radical Philosophy* 55 (Summer 1990); 11–17.
16. We find a similar confusion in Diana Fuss who, as Anna Marie Smith indicates in her review of *Essentially Speaking, Feminist Review* 38 (Summer 1991), does not realize that the repetition of a sign can take place without an essentialist grounding. It is for that reason that she can affirm that constructionism is essentialist as far as it entails the repetition of the same signifiers across different contexts.
17. Judith Butler, *Gender Trouble: Feminism and the Subversion of Identity* (New York: Routledge, 1990), p. xi.

Part 6:
Care and Its Critics

In a Different Voice: Women's Conceptions of Self and of Morality

Throughout Western history, many philosophers, psychologists, and other thinkers have maintained that women's moral capacities are inferior to men's. They have claimed that women's virtues are less exalted than men's or that women are less principled than men. Doubting that women are morally inferior, psychologist Carol Gilligan sets out to demonstrate that there are two trajectories of moral development—the justice track, which is followed by many males and some females, and the care track, which is followed by some females.* In this essay, Gilligan describes the process of development within the care perspective.

There are three levels of development, and each level is divided into two stages. At the first level, called the preconventional level, morality is reduced to the question of individual survival. But in the transition to the second level, subjects come to see this preoccupation as selfish. At the second level, called the conventional level, morality is identified with self-sacrifice—a stereotype of femininity. But in the transition to level three, equating goodness to consuming altruism is seen as unfair to the person who is sacrificing herself for others. At the third level, called the postconventional level, subjects gain an expanded sense of responsibility. They treat themselves as equals and care for themselves. But since they remain committed to maintaining their interpersonal relationships, they strive to reconcile their own needs and aspirations with caring for other people.

According to Gilligan, autonomous moral reflection and judgment are possible within the ethic of care. However, autonomous choice within this framework is not based on separation from other people, does not invoke the value of objectivity, and does not equate fairness with noninterference. Care thinkers see themselves as fundamentally connected with other people, and they see attachment to others as a value. Thus, they construe moral ques-

---

* In "Moral Orientation and Moral Development," Gilligan indicates that care and justice are correlated with gender, but not in a simple or absolute way (see *Women and Moral Theory.* Ed. Eva Feder Kittay and Diana T. Meyers (Rowman and Littlefield, 1987), pp. 25–26). Her data show that one-third of her female subjects focus on care, one-third of her female subjects focus on justice, and one-third switch back and forth between justice and care. However, of her male subjects two-thirds focus on justice, one-third switch back and forth between justice and care, and none focus on care.

tions in terms of the injunctions to take responsibility for meeting people's needs and to avoid harm and exploitation. Gilligan concludes that it is necessary for developmental psychology to give equal recognition to the voice of care.

—D.T.M.

Chapter 29

Carol Gilligan

In a Different Voice: Women's Conceptions of Self and of Morality

The arc of developmental theory leads from infantile dependence to adult autonomy, tracing a path characterized by an increasing differentiation of self from other and a progressive freeing of thought from contextual constraints. The vision of Luther, journeying from the rejection of a self defined by others to the assertive boldness of "Here I stand," and the image of Plato's allegorical man in the cave, separating at last the shadows from the sun, have taken powerful hold on the psychological understanding of what constitutes development. Thus, the individual, meeting fully the developmental challenges of adolescence as set for him by Piaget, Erikson, and Kohlberg, thinks formally, proceeding from theory to fact, and defines both the self and the moral autonomously, that is, apart from the identification and conventions that had comprised the particulars of his childhood world. So equipped, he is presumed ready to live as an adult, to love and work in a way that is both intimate and generative, to develop an ethical sense of caring and a genital mode of relating in which giving and taking fuse in the ultimate reconciliation of the tension between self and other.

Yet the men whose theories have largely informed this understanding of development have all been plagued by the same problem, the problem of women, whose sexuality remains more diffuse, whose perception of self is so much more tenaciously embedded in relationships with others, and whose moral dilemmas hold them in a mode of judgment that is insistently contextual. The solution has been to consider women as either deviant or deficient in their development.

That there is a discrepancy between concepts of womanhood and adulthood is nowhere more clearly evident than in the series of studies on sex-role stereotypes reported by Broverman, Vogel, Broverman, Clarkson, and Rosenkrantz (1972). The repeated finding of these studies is that the qualities deemed necessary for adulthood—the capacity for autonomous thinking, clear decision making, and responsible actions—are those associated with masculinity but considered undesirable as attributes of the feminine self. The stereotypes suggest a splitting of love and work that relegates the expressive capacities requisite for the former to women, while the instrumental abilities necessary for the latter reside in the masculine domain. Yet, looked at from a different perspective, these stereotypes reflect a conception of adulthood that is itself out of balance, favoring the separateness of the individual self over its connection to others and leaning more toward an autonomous life of work than toward the interdependence of love care.

This difference in point of view is the subject of this essay, which seeks to identify in the feminine experience and construction of social reality a distinctive voice, recognizable in the different perspective it brings to bear on the construction and resolution of moral problems. The first section begins with the repeated observation of difference in women's concepts of self and of morality. This difference is identified in previous psychological descriptions of women's moral judgments and described as it again appears in current research data. Examples drawn from interviews with women in and around a university community are used to illustrate the characteristics of the feminine voice. The relational bias in women's thinking that has, in the past, been seen to compromise their moral judgment and impede their development now begins to emerge in a new developmental light. Instead of being seen as a developmental deficiency, this bias appears to reflect a different social and moral understanding.

This alternative conception is enlarged in the second section through consideration of research interviews with women facing the moral dilemma of whether to continue or abort a pregnancy. Since the research design allowed women to define as well as resolve the moral problem, developmental distinctions could be derived directly from the categories of women's thought. The responses of women to structured interview questions regarding the pregnancy decision formed the basis for describing a developmental sequence that traces progressive differentiations in their understanding and judgment of conflicts between self and other. While the sequence of women's moral development follows the three-level progression of all social developmental theory, from an egocentric through a societal to a universal perspective, this progression takes place within a distinct moral conception. This conception differs from that derived by Kohlberg from his all-male longitudinal research data.

This difference then becomes the basis in the third section for challenging the current assessment of women's moral judgment at the same time that it brings to bear a new perspective on developmental assessment in general. The inclusion in the overall conception of development of those categories derived from the study of women's moral judgment enlarges developmental understanding, enabling it to encompass better the thinking of both sexes. This is particularly true with respect to the construction and resolution of the dilemmas of adult life. Since the conception of adulthood retrospectively shapes the theoretical understanding of the development that precedes it, the changes in that conception that follow from the more central inclusion of women's judgments recast developmental understanding and lead to a reconsideration of the substance of social and moral development.

CHARACTERISTICS OF THE FEMININE VOICE

The revolutionary contribution of Piaget's work is the experimental confirmation and refinement of Kant's assertion that knowledge is actively constructed rather than passively received. Time, space, self, and other, as well as the categories of developmental theory, all arise out of the active interchange between the individual and the physical and social world in which he lives and of which he strives to make sense. The development of cognition is the process of reappropriating reality at progressively more complex levels of apprehension, as the structures of thinking expand to encompass the increasing richness and intricacy of experience.

Moral development, in the work of Piaget and Kohlberg, refers specifically to the expanding conception of the social world as it is reflected in the understanding and resolution of the inevitable conflicts that arise in the relations between self and others. The moral judgment is a statement of priority, an attempt at rational resolution in a situation where, from a different point of view, the choice itself seems to do violence to justice.

Kohlberg (1969), in his extension of the early work of Piaget, discovered six stages of moral judgment, which he claimed formed an invariant sequence, each successive stage representing a more adequate construction of the moral problem, which in turn provides the basis for its more just resolution. The stages divide into three levels, each of which denotes a significant expansion of the moral point of view from an egocentric through a societal to a universal ethical conception. With this expansion in perspective comes the capacity to free moral judgement from the individual needs and social conventions with which it had earlier been confused and anchor it instead in principles of justice that are universal in application. These principles provide criteria upon which both individual and societal claims can be impartially assessed. In Kohlberg's view, at the highest stages of development morality is freed from both psychological and historical constraints, and the individual can judge independently of his own particular needs and of the values of those around him.

That the moral sensibility of women differs from that of men was noted by Freud (1925/1961) in the following by now well-quoted statement:

> I cannot evade the notion (though I hesitate to give it expression) that for women the level of what is ethically normal is different from what it is in man. Their superego is never so inexorable, so impersonal, so independent of its emotional origins as we require it to be in men. Character-traits which critics of every epoch have brought up against women—that they show less sense of justice than men, that they are less likely to submit to the great exigencies of life, that they are more often influenced in their judgments by feelings of affection or hostility—all these would be amply accounted for by the modification in the formation of their super-ego which we have inferred above.

While Freud's explanation lies in the deviation of female from male developments around the construction and resolution of the Oedipal problem, the same observations about the nature of morality in women emerge from the work of Piaget and Kohlberg. Piaget (1932/1965), in his study of the rules of children's games, observed that, in the games they played, girls were "less explicit about agreement [than boys] and less concerned with legal elaboration." In contrast to the boys' interest in the codification of rules, the girls adopted a more pragmatic attitude, regarding "a rule as good so long as the game repays it." As a result, in comparison to boys, girls were found to be "more tolerant and more easily reconciled to innovations."

Kohlberg (1971) also identifies a strong interpersonal bias in the moral judgments of women, which leads them to be considered as typically at the third of his six-stage developmental sequence. At that stage, the good is identified with "what pleases or helps others and is approved of by them." This mode of judgment is conventional in its conformity to generally held notions of the good but also psychological in its concern with intention and consequence as the basis for judging the morality of action.

That women fall largely into this level of moral judgment is hardly surprising when we read from the Broverman et al. (1972) list that prominent among the twelve attributes considered to be desirable for women are tact, gentleness, awareness of the feelings of others, strong need for security, and easy expression of tender feelings. And yet, herein lies the paradox, for the very traits that have traditionally defined the "goodness" of women, their care for and sensitivity to the needs of others, are those that mark them as deficient in moral development. The infusion of feeling into their judgments keeps them from developing a more independent and abstract ethical conception in which concern for others derives from principles of justice rather than from compassion and care. Kohlberg, however, is less pessimistic than Freud in his assessment, for he sees the development of women as extending beyond the interpersonal level, following the same path toward independent, principled judgment that he discovered in the research on men from which his stages were derived. In Kohlberg's view, women's development will proceed beyond Stage Three when they are challenged to solve moral problems that require them to see beyond the relationships that have in the past generally bound their moral experience.

What then do women say when asked to construct the moral domain; how do we identify the characteristically "feminine" voice? A Radcliffe undergraduate, responding to the question, "If you had to say what morality meant to you, how would you sum it up?" replies:

> When I think of the world morality, I think of obligations. I usually think of it as conflicts between personal desires and social things, social considerations, or personal desires of yourself versus personal desires of another person or people or whatever. Morality is that whole realm of how you decide these conflicts. A moral person is one who would decide, like by placing themselves more often than not as equals, a truly moral person would always consider another person as their equal . . . in a situation of social interaction, something is morally wrong where the individual ends up screwing a lot of people. And it is morally right when everyone comes out better off.*

Yet when asked if she can think of someone whom she would consider a genuinely moral person, she replies, "Well, immediately I think of Albert Schweitzer because he has obviously given his life to help others." Obligation and sacrifice override the ideal of equality, setting up a basic contradiction in her thinking.

---

* The Radcliffe women whose responses are cited were interviewed as part of a pilot study on undergraduate moral development conducted by the author in 1970.

Another undergraduate responds to the question, "What does it mean to say something is morally right or wrong?" by also speaking first of responsibilities and obligations:

> Just that it has to do with responsibilities and obligations and values, mainly values. . . . In my life situation I relate morality with interpersonal relationships that have to do with respect for the other person and myself. [Why respect other people?] Because they have a consciousness or feelings that can be hurt, an awareness that can be hurt.

The concern about hurting others persists as a major theme in the responses of two other Radcliffe students:

> [Why be moral?] Millions of people have to live together peacefully. I personally don't want to hurt other people. That's a real criterion, a main criterion for me. It underlies my sense of justice. It isn't nice to inflict pain. I empathize with anyone in pain. Not hurting others is important in my own private morals. Years ago, I would have jumped out of a window not to hurt my boyfriend. That was pathological. Even today though, I want approval and love and I don't want enemies. Maybe that's why there is morality—so people can win approval, love, and friendship.
>
> My main moral principle is not hurting other people as long as you aren't going against your own conscience and as long as you remain true to yourself. . . . There are many moral issues such as abortion, the draft, killing, stealing, monogamy, etc. If something is a controversial issue like these, then I always say it is up to the individual. The individual has to decide and then follow his own conscience. There are no moral absolutes. . . . Laws are pragmatic instruments, but they are not absolutes. A viable society can't make exceptions all the time, but I would personally . . . I'm afraid I'm heading for some big crisis with my boyfriend someday, and someone will get hurt, and he'll get more hurt than I will. I feel an obligation to not hurt him, but also an obligation to not lie. I don't know if it is possible to not lie and not hurt.

The common thread that runs through these statements, the wish not to hurt others and the hope that in morality lies a way of solving conflicts so that no one will get hurt, is striking in that it is independently introduced by each of the four women as the most specific item in their response to a most general question. The moral person is one who helps others; goodness is service, meeting one's obligations and responsibilities to others, if possible, without sacrificing oneself. While the first of the four women ends by denying the conflict she initially introduced, the last woman anticipates a conflict between remaining true to herself and adhering to her principle of not hurting others. The dilemma that would test the limits of this judgment would be one where helping others is seen to be at the price of hurting the self.

The reticence about taking stands on "controversial issues," the willingness to "make exceptions all the time" expressed in the final example above, is echoed repeatedly by other Radcliffe students, as in the following two examples:

> I never feel that I can condemn anyone else. I have a very relativistic position. The basic idea that I cling to is the sanctity of human life. I am inhibited about impressing my beliefs on others.

> I could never argue that my belief on a moral question is anything that another person should accept. I don't believe in absolutes. . . . If there is an absolute for moral decisions, it is human life.

Or, as a thirty-one-year-old Wellesley graduate says, in explaining why she would find it difficult to steal a drug to save her own life despite her belief that it would be right to steal for another: "It's just very hard to defend yourself against the rules. I mean, we live by consensus, and you take an action simply for yourself, by yourself, there's no consensus there, and that is relatively indefensible in this society now."

What begins to emerge is a sense of vulnerability that impedes these women from taking a stand, what George Eliot (1860/1965) regards as the girl's "susceptibility" to adverse judgments of others, which stems from her lack of power and consequent inability to do something in the world. While relativism in men, the unwillingness to make moral judgments that Kohlberg and Kramer (1969) and Kohlberg and Gilligan (1971) have associated with the adolescent crisis of identity and belief, takes the form of calling into question the concept of morality itself, the women's reluctance to judge stems rather from their uncertainty about their right to make moral statements or, perhaps, the price for them that such judgment seems to entail. This contrast echoes that made by Matina Horner (1972), who differentiated the ideological fear of success expressed by men from the personal conflicts about succeeding that riddled the women's responses to stories of competitive achievement.

> Most of the men who responded with the expectation of negative consequences because of success were not concerned about their masculinity but were instead likely to have expressed existential concerns about finding a "non-materialistic happiness and satisfaction in life." These concerns, which reflect changing attitudes toward traditional kinds of success or achievement in our society, played little, if any, part in the female stories. Most of the women who were high in fear of success imagery continued to be concerned about the discrepancy between success in the situation described and feminine identity.

When women feel excluded from direct participation in society, they see themselves as subject to a consensus or judgment made and enforced by the men on whose protection and support they depend and by whose names they are known. A divorced middle-aged woman, mother of adolescent daughters, resident of a sophisticated university community, tells the story as follows:

> As a woman, I feel I never understood that I was a person, that I can make decisions and I have a right to make decisions. I always felt that that belonged to my father or my husband in some way or church, which was always represented by a male clergyman. They were the three men in my life; father, husband, and clergyman, and they had much more to say about what I should or shouldn't do. They were really authority figures which I accepted. I didn't rebel against that. It

> only has lately occurred to me that I never even rebelled against it, and my girls are much more conscious of this, not in the militant sense, but just in the recognizing sense. . . . I still let things happen to me rather than make them happen, than to make choices, although I know all about choices. I know the procedures and the steps and all. [Do you have any clues about why this might be true?] Well, I think in one sense, there is less responsibility involved. Because if you make a dumb decision, you have to take the rap. If it happens to you, well, you can complain about it. I think that if you don't grow up feeling that you ever had any choices, you don't either have the sense that you have emotional responsibility. With this sense of choice comes this sense of responsibility.

The essence of the moral decision is the exercise of choice and the willingness to accept responsibility for that choice. To the extent that women perceive themselves as having no choice, they correspondingly excuse themselves from the responsibility that decision entails. Childlike in the vulnerability of their dependence and consequent fear of abandonment, they claim to wish only to please but in return for their goodness they expect to be loved and cared for. This, then, is an "altruism" always at risk, for it presupposes an innocence constantly in danger of being compromised by an awareness of the trade-off that has been made. Asked to describe herself, a Radcliffe senior responds:

> I have heard of the onion skin theory. I see myself as an onion, as a block of different layers, the external layers for people that I don't know that well, the agreeable, the social, and as you go inward there are more sides for people I know that I show. I am not sure about the innermost, whether there is a core, or whether I have just picked up everything as I was growing up, these different influences. I think I have a neutral attitude towards myself, but I do think in terms of good and bad. . . . Good—I try to be considerate and thoughtful of other people and I try to be fair in situations and be tolerant. I use the words but I try and work them out practically. . . . Bad things—I am not sure if they are bad, if they are altruistic or I am doing them basically for approval of other people. [Which things are these?] The values I have when I try to act them out. They deal mostly with interpersonal-type relations. . . . If I were doing it for approval, it would be a very tenuous thing. If I didn't get the right feedback, there might go all my values.

Ibsen's play *A Doll House* (1879/1965) depicts the explosion of just such a world through the eruption of a moral dilemma that calls into question the notion of goodness that lies at its center. Nora, the "squirrel wife," living with her husband as she had lived with her father, puts into action this conception of goodness as sacrifice and, with the best of intentions, takes the law into her own hands. The crisis that ensues, most painfully for her in the repudiation of that goodness by the very person who was its recipient and beneficiary, causes her to reject the suicide that she had initially seen as its ultimate expression and chose instead to seek new and firmer answers to the adolescent questions of identity and belief.

The availability of choice and with it the onus of responsibility has now invaded the most private sector of the woman's domain and threatens a similar explosion. For centuries, women's sexuality anchored them in passivity, in a receptive rather than active stance, where the events of conception and childbirth could be controlled only by a withholding in which their own sexual needs were either denied or sacrificed. That such a sacrifice entailed a cost to their intelligence as well was seen by Freud (1908/1959) when he tied the "undoubted intellectual inferiority of so many women" to "the inhibition of thought necessitated by sexual suppression." The strategies of withholding and denial that women have employed in the politics of sexual relations appear similar to their evasion or withholding of judgment in the moral realm. The hesitance expressed in the previous examples to impose even a belief in the value of human life on others, like the reluctance to claim one's sexuality, bespeaks a self uncertain of its strength, unwilling to deal with consequences, and thus avoiding confrontation.

Thus women have traditionally deferred to the judgment of men, although often while intimating a sensibility of their own which is at variance with that judgment. Maggie Tulliver, in *The Mill on the Floss* (Eliot 1860/1965), responds to the accusations that ensue from the discovery of her secretly continued relationship with Philip Wakeham by acceding to her brother's moral judgment while at the same time asserting a different set of standards by which she attests her own superiority:

> I don't want to defend myself. . . . I know I've been wrong—often continually. But yet, sometimes when I have done wrong, it has been because I have feelings that you would be the better for if you had them. If *you* were in fault ever, if you had done anything very wrong, I should be sorry for the pain it brought you; I should not want punishment to be heaped on you.

An eloquent defense, Kohlberg would argue, of a Stage Three moral position, an assertion of the age-old split between thinking and feeling, justice and mercy, that underlies many of the clichés and stereotypes concerning the difference between the sexes. But considered from another point of view, it is a moment of confrontation, replacing a former evasion, between two modes of judging, two differing constructions of the moral domain—one traditionally associated with masculinity and the public world of social power, the other with femininity and the privacy of domestic interchange. While the developmental ordering of these two points of view has been to consider the masculine as the more adequate and thus as replacing the feminine as the individual movers toward higher stages, their reconciliation remains unclear.

THE DEVELOPMENT OF WOMEN'S MORAL JUDGMENT

Recent evidence for a divergence in moral development between men and women comes from the research of Haan (Note 1) and Holstein (1976) whose findings lead them to question the possibility of a "sex-related bias" in Kohlberg's scoring system. This system is based on Kohlberg's six-stage description of moral development. Kohlberg's stages divide into three levels, which he designates as preconventional, conventional, and postconventional, thus denoting the major shifts in moral perspective around a center of moral understanding that equates justice with the maintenance of existing social systems. While the preconventional conception of justice is based on the needs of the self, the conventional judgement derives from an understanding of society. This understanding is in turn superseded by a postconventional or principled conception of justice where the good is formulated in universal terms. The quarrel with Kohlberg's stage scoring does not pertain to the structural differentiation of his levels but rather to questions of stage and sequence. Kohlberg's stages begin with an obedience and punishment orientation (Stage One), and go from there in invariant order to instrumental hedonism (Stage Two), interpersonal concordance (Stage Three), law and order (Stage Four), social contract (Stage Five), and universal ethical principles (Stage Six).

The bias that Haan and Holstein question in this scoring system has to do with the subordination of the interpersonal to the societal definition of the good in the transition from Stage Three to Stage Four. This is the transition that has repeatedly been found to be problematic for women. In 1969, Kohlberg and Kramer identified Stage Three as the characteristic mode of women's moral judgments, claiming that, since women's lives were interpersonally based, this stage was not only "functional" for them but also adequate for resolving the moral conflicts that they faced. Turiel (Note 2) reported that while girls reached Stage Three sooner than did boys, their judgments tended to remain at that stage while the boys' development continued further along Kohlberg's scale. Gilligan, Kohlberg, Lerner, and Belenky (1971) found a similar association between sex and the moral-judgment stage in a study of high-school students, with the girls' responses being scored predominantly at Stage Three while the boys' responses were more often scored at Stage Four.

This repeated finding of developmental inferiority in women may, however, have more to do with the standard by which development has been measured than with the quality of women's thinking per se. Haan's data (Note 1) on the Berkeley Free Speech Movement and Holstein's (1976) three-year longitudinal study of adolescents and their parents indicate that the moral judgments of women differ from those of men in the greater extent to which women's judgments are tied to feelings of empathy and compassion and are concerned more with the resolution of "real-life" as opposed to hypothetical dilemmas (Note 1, p. 34). However, as long as the categories by which development is assessed are derived within a male perspective from male research data, divergence from the masculine standard can be seen only as a failure of development. As a result, the thinking of women is often classified with that of children. The systematic exclusion from consideration of alternative criteria that might better encompass the development of women indicates not only the limitations of a theory framed by men and validated by research samples disproportionately male and adolescent but also the effects of the diffidence prevalent among women, their reluctance to speak publicly in their own voice, given the constraints imposed on them by the politics of differential power between the sexes.

In order to go beyond the question, "How much like men do women think, how capable are they of engaging in the abstract and hypothetical construction of reality?" it is necessary to identify and define in formal terms developmental criteria that encompass the categories of women's thinking. Such criteria would include the progressive differentiations, comprehensiveness, and adequacy that characterize higher-stage resolution of the "more frequently occurring, real-life moral dilemmas of interpersonal, empathetic, fellow-feeling concerns" (Haan, Note 1, p. 34), which have long been the center of women's moral judgments and experience. To ascertain whether the feminine construction of the moral domain relies on a language different from that of men but one that deserves equal credence in the definition of what constitutes development, it is necessary first to find the places where women have the power to choose and thus are willing to speak in their own voices.

When birth control and abortion provide women with effective means for controlling their fertility, the dilemma of choice enters the center of women's lives. Then the relationships that have traditionally defined women's identities and framed their moral judgments no longer flow inevitably from their reproductive capacity but become matters of decision over which they have control. Released from the passivity and reticence of a sexuality that binds them in dependence, it becomes possible for women to question with Freud what it is that they want and to assert their own answers to that question. However, while society may affirm publicly the woman's right to choose for herself, the exercise of such choice brings her privately into conflict with the conventions of femininity, particularly the moral equation of goodness with self-sacrifice. While independent assertion in judgment and action is considered the hallmark of adulthood and constitutes as well the standard of masculine development, it is rather in their care and concern for others that women have both judged themselves and been judged.

The conflict between self and other thus constitutes the central moral problem for women, posing a dilemma whose resolution requires a reconciliation between femininity and adulthood. In the absence of such a reconciliation, the moral problem cannot be resolved. The "good woman" masks assertion in evasion, denying responsibility by claiming only to meet the needs of others, while the "bad woman" forgoes or renounces the commitments that bind her in self-deception and betrayal. It is precisely this dilemma—the conflict between compassion and autonomy, between virtue and power—that the feminine voice struggles to resolve in its effort to reclaim the self and to solve the moral problem in such a way that no one is hurt.

When a woman considers whether to continue or abort a pregnancy, she contemplates a decision that affects both self and others and engages directly the critical moral issue of hurting. Since the choice is ultimately hers and therefore one for which she is responsible, it raises precisely those questions of judgment that have been most problematic for women. Now she is asked whether she wishes to interrupt that stream of life which has for centuries immersed her in the passivity of dependence while at the same time imposing on her the responsibility for care. Thus the abortion decision brings to the core of feminine apprehension, to what Joan Didion (1972) calls "the irreconcilable difference of it—that sense of living one's deepest life underwater, that dark involvement with blood and birth and death," the adult questions of responsibility and choice.

How women deal with such choices has been the subject of my research, designed to clarify, through considering the ways in which women construct and resolve the abortion decision, the nature and development of women's moral judgment. Twenty-nine women, diverse in age, race, and social class, were referred by abortion and pregnancy counseling services and participated in the study for a variety of reasons. Some came to gain further clarification with respect to a decision about which they were in conflict, some in response to a counselor's concern about repeated abortions, and others out of an interest in and/or willingness to contribute to ongoing research. Although the pregnancies occurred under a variety of circumstances in the lives of these women, certain commonalities could be discerned. The adolescents often failed to use birth control because they denied or discredited their capacity to bear children. Some of the older women attributed the pregnancy to the omission of contraceptive measures in circumstances where intercourse had not been anticipated. Since the pregnancies often coincided with efforts on the part of the women to end a relationship, they may be seen as a manifestation of ambivalence or as a way of putting the relationship to the ultimate test of commitment. For these women, the pregnancy appeared to be a way of testing truth, making the baby an ally in the search for male support and protection or, that failing, a companion victim of his rejection. There were, finally, some women who became pregnant either as a result of a failure of birth control or intentionally as part of a joint decision that later was reconsidered. Of the twenty-nine women, four decided to have the baby, one miscarried, twenty-one chose abortion, and three remained in doubt about the decision.

In the initial part of the interview, the women were asked to discuss the decision that confronted them, how they were dealing with it, the alternatives they were considering, their reasons for and against each option, the people involved, the conflicts entailed, and the ways in which making this decision affected their self-concepts and their relationships with others. Then, in the second part of the interview, moral judgment was assessed in the hypothetical mode by presenting for resolution three of Kohlberg's standard research dilemmas.

While the structural progression from a preconventional through a conventional to a postconventional moral perspective can readily be discerned in the women's responses to both actual and hypothetical dilemmas, the conventions that shape women's moral judgments differ from those that apply to men. The construction of the abortion dilemma, in particular, reveals the existence of a distinct moral language whose evolution informs the sequence of women's development. This is the language of selfishness and responsibility, which defines the moral problem as one of obligation to exercise care and avoid hurt. The infliction of hurt is considered selfish and immoral in its reflection of unconcern, while the expression of care is seen as the fulfillment of moral responsibility. The reiterative use of the language of selfishness and responsibility and the underlying moral orientation it reflects sets the women apart from the men whom Kohlberg studied and may be seen as the critical reason for their failure to develop within the constraints of his system.

In the developmental sequence that follows, women's moral judgments proceed from an initial focus on the self at the *first level* to the discovery, in the transition to the *second level*, of the concept of responsibility as the basis for a new equilibrium between self and others. The elaboration of this concept of responsibility and its fusion with a maternal concept of morality, which seeks to ensure protection for the dependent and unequal, characterizes the *second level* of judgment. At this level the good is equated with caring for others. However, when the conventions of feminine goodness legitimize only others as the recipients of moral care, the logical inequality between self and other and the psychological violence that it engenders create the disequilibrium that initiates the *second* transition. The relationship between self and others is then reconsidered in an effort to sort out the confusion between conformity and care inherent in the conventional definition of feminine goodness and to establish a new equilibrium, which dissipates the tension between selfishness and responsibility. At the *third level*, the self becomes the arbiter of an independent judgment that now subsumes both conventions and individual needs under the moral principle of nonviolence. Judgment remains psychological in its concern with the intention and consequences of action, but it now becomes universal in its condemnation of exploitation and hurt.

Level 1: Orientation to Individual Survival

In its initial and simplest construction, the abortion decision centers on the self. The concern is pragmatic, and the issue is individual survival. At this level, "should" is undifferentiated from "would," and others influence the decision only through their power to affect its consequences. An eighteen-year-old, asked what she thought when she found herself pregnant, replies: "I really didn't think anything except that I didn't want it. [Why was that?] I didn't want it, I wasn't ready for it, and next year will be my last year and I want to go to school."

Asked if there was a right decision, she says, "There is no right decision. [Why?] I didn't want it." For her the question of right decision would emerge only if her own needs were in conflict; then she would have to decide which needs should take precedence. This was the dilemma of another eighteen-year-old, who saw having a baby as a way of increasing her freedom by providing "the perfect chance to get married and move away from home," but also as restricting her freedom "to do a lot of things."

At this first level, the self, which is the sole object of concern, is constrained by lack of power; the wish "to do a lot of things" is constantly belied by the limitations of what, in fact, is being done. Relationships are, for the most part, disappointing: "The only thing you are ever going to get out of going with a guy is to get hurt." As a result, women may in some instances deliberately choose isolation to protect themselves against hurt. When asked how she would describe herself to herself, a nineteen-year-old, who held herself responsible for the accidental death of a younger brother, answers as follows:

> I really don't know. I never thought about it. I don't know. I know basically the outline of a character. I am very independent. I don't really want to have to ask anybody for anything and I am a loner in life. I prefer to be by myself than around anybody else. I manage to keep my friends at a limited number with the point that I have very few friends. I don't know what else there is. I am a loner and I enjoy it. Here today and gone tomorrow.

The primacy of the concern with survival is explicitly acknowledged by a sixteen-year-old delinquent in response to Kohlberg's Heinz dilemma, which asks if it is right for a desperate husband to steal an outrageously overpriced drug to save the life of his dying wife:

> I think survival is one of the first things in life and that people fight for. I think it is the most important thing, more important than stealing. Stealing might be wrong, but if you have to steal to survive yourself or even kill, that is what you should do. . . . Preservation of oneself, I think, is the most important thing; it comes before anything in life.

The First Transition: From Selfishness to Responsibility

In the transition that follows and criticizes this level of judgment, the words selfishness and responsibility first appear. Their reference initially is to the self in a redefinition of the self-interest which has thus far served as the basis for judgment. The transitional issue is one of attachment or connection to others. The pregnancy catches up the issue not only by representing an immediate, literal connection but also by affirming, in the most concrete and physical way, the capacity to assume adult feminine roles. However, while having a baby seems at first to offer respite from the loneliness of adolescence and to solve conflicts over dependence and independence, in reality the continuation of an adolescent pregnancy generally compounds these problems, increasing social isolation and precluding further steps toward independence.

To be a mother in the societal as well as the physical sense requires the assumption of parental responsibility for the care and protection of a child. However, in order to be able to care for another, one must first be able to care responsibly for oneself. The growth from childhood to adulthood, conceived as a move from selfishness to responsibility, is articulated explicitly in these terms by a seventeen-year-old who describes her response to her pregnancy as follows:

> I started feeling really good about being pregnant instead of feeling really bad, because I wasn't looking at the situation realistically. I was looking at it from my own sort of selfish needs because I was lonely and felt lonely and stuff. . . . Things weren't really going good for me, so I was looking at it that I could have a baby that I could take care of or something that was part of me, and that made me feel good . . . but I wasn't looking at the realistic side . . . about the responsibility I would have to take on. . . . I came to this decision that I was going to have an abortion [because] I realized how much responsibility goes with having a child. Like you have to be there, you can't be out of the house all the time which is one thing I like to do . . . and I decided that I have to take on responsibility for myself and I have to work out a lot of things.

Stating her former mode of judgment, the wish to have a baby as a way of combatting loneliness and feeling connected, she now criticizes that judgement as both "selfish" and "unrealistic." The contradiction between wishes for a baby and for the freedom to be "out of the house all the time"—that is, for connection and also for independence—is resolved in terms of a new priority, as the criterion for judgment changes. The dilemma now assumes moral definition as the emergent conflict between wish and necessity is seen as a disparity between "would" and "should." In this construction, the "selfishness" of willful decision is counterposed to the "responsibility" of moral choice:

> What I want to do is to have the baby, but what I feel I should do, which is what I need to do, is have an abortion right now, because sometimes what you want isn't right. Sometimes what is necessary comes before what you want, because it might not always lead to the right thing.

While the pregnancy itself confirms femininity—"I started feeling really good; it sort of made me feel, like being pregnant, I started feeling like a woman"—the abortion decision becomes an opportunity for the adult exercise of responsible choice.

> [How would you describe yourself to yourself?] I am looking at myself differently in the way that I have had a really heavy decision put upon me, and I have never really had too many hard decisions in my life, and I have made it. It has taken some responsibility to do this. I have changed in that way, that I have made a hard decision. And that has been good. Because before, I would not have looked at it realistically, in my opinion. I would have gone by what I wanted to do, and I wanted it, and even if it wasn't right. So I see myself as I'm becoming more mature in ways of making decisions and taking care of myself, doing something for myself. I think it is going to help me in other ways, if I have other decisions to

> make put upon me, which would take some responsibility. And I would know that I could make them.

In the epiphany of this cognitive reconstruction, the old becomes transformed in terms of the new. The wish to "do something for myself" remains, but the terms of its fulfillment change as the decision affirms both femininity and adulthood in its integration of responsibility and care. Morality, says another adolescent, "is the way you think about yourself. . . . Sooner or later you have to make up your mind to start taking care of yourself. Abortion, if you do it for the right reasons, is helping yourself to start over and do different things."

Since this transition signals an enhancement in self-worth, it requires a conception of self that includes the possibility for doing "the right thing," the ability to see in oneself the potential for social acceptance. When such confidence is seriously in doubt, the transitional questions may be raised but development is impeded. The failure to make this first transition, despite an understanding of the issues involved, is illustrated by a woman in her late twenties. Her struggle with the conflict between selfishness and responsibility pervades but fails to resolve her dilemma of whether to have a third abortion.

> I think you have to think about the people who are involved, including yourself. You have responsibilities to yourself . . . and to make a right, whatever that is, decision in this depends on your knowledge and awareness of the responsibilities that you have and whether you can survive with a child and what it will do to your relationship with the father or how it will affect him emotionally.

Rejecting the idea of selling the baby and making "a lot of money in a black market kind of thing . . . because mostly I operate on principles and it would just rub me the wrong way to think I would be selling my own child," she struggles with a concept of responsibility that repeatedly turns back on the question of her own survival. Transition seems blocked by a self-image that is insistently contradictory:

> [How would you describe yourself to yourself?] I see myself as impulsive, practical—that is a contradiction—and moral and amoral, a contradiction. Actually the only thing that is consistent and not contradictory is the fact that I am very lazy which everyone has always told me is really a symptom of something else which I have never been able to put my finger on exactly. It has taken me a long time to like myself. In fact there are times when I don't, which I think is healthy to a point and sometimes I think I like myself too much and I probably evade myself too much, which avoids responsibility to myself and to other people who like me. I am pretty unfaithful to myself. . . . I have a hard time even thinking that I am a human being, simply because so much rotten stuff goes on and people are so crummy and insensitive.

Seeing herself as avoiding responsibility, she can find no basis upon which to resolve the pregnancy dilemma. Instead, her inability to arrive at any clear sense of decision only contributes further to her overall sense of failure. Criticizing her parents for having betrayed her during adolescence by coercing her to have an abortion she did not want, she now betrays herself and criticizes that as well. In this light, it is less surprising that she considered selling her child, since she felt herself to have, in effect, been sold by her parents for the sake of maintaining their social status.

The Second Level: Goodness as Self-Sacrifice

The transition from selfishness to responsibility is a move toward social participation. Whereas at the first level, morality is seen as a matter of sanctions imposed by a society of which one is more subject than citizen, at the second level, moral judgment comes to rely on shared norms and expectations. The woman at this level validates her claim to social membership through the adoption of societal values. Consensual judgment becomes paramount and goodness the overriding concern, as survival is now seen to depend on acceptance by others.

Here the conventional feminine voice emerges with great clarity, defining the self and proclaiming its worth on the basis of the ability to care for and protect others. The woman now constructs the world perfused with the assumptions about feminine goodness reflected in the stereotypes of the Broverman et al. (1972) studies. There the attributes considered desirable for women all presume an other, a recipient of the "tact, gentleness and easy expression of feeling," which allow the woman to respond sensitively while evoking in return the care that meets her own "very strong need for security." The strength of this position lies in its capacity for caring; its limitation is the restriction it imposes on direct expression. Both qualities are elucidated by a nineteen-year-old who contrasts her reluctance to criticize with her boyfriend's straightforwardness:

> I ever want to hurt anyone, and I tell them in a very nice way, and I have respect for their own opinions, and they can do the things the way that they want, and he usually tells people right off the bat. . . . He does a lot of things out in public which I do in private. . . . It is better, the other [his way], but I just could never do it.

While her judgment clearly exists, it is not expressed, at least not in public. Concern for the feelings of others imposes a deference which she nevertheless criticizes in an awareness that, under the name of consideration, a vulnerability and a duplicity are concealed.

At the second level of judgment, it is specifically over the issue of hurting that conflict arises with respect to the abortion decision. When no option exists that can be construed as being in the best interest of everyone, when responsibilities conflict and decision entails the sacrifice of somebody's needs, then the woman confronts the seemingly impossible task of choosing the victim. A nineteen-year-old, fearing the consequences for herself of a second abortion but facing the opposition of both her family and her lover to the continuation of the pregnancy, describes the dilemma as follows:

> I don't know what choices are open to me; it is either to have it or the abortion; these are the choices open to me. It is just that either way I don't . . . I think what confuses me is it is a choice of either hurting myself or hurting other people around me. What is more important? If there could be a happy medium, it would be fine, but there isn't. It is either hurting someone on this side or hurting myself.

While the feminine identification of goodness with self-sacrifice seems clearly to dictate the "right" resolution of this dilemma, the stakes may be high for the woman herself, and the sacrifice of the fetus, in any event, compromises the altruism of an abortion motivated by a concern for others. Since femininity itself is in conflict in an abortion intended as an expression of love and care, this is a resolution that readily explodes in its own contradiction.

"I don't think anyone should have to choose between two things that they love," says a twenty-five-year-old woman who assumed responsibility not only for her lover but also for his wife and children in having an abortion she did not want:

> I just wanted the child and I really don't believe in abortions. Who can say when life begins. I think that life begins at conception and . . . I felt like there were changes happening in my body and I felt very protective . . . [but] I felt a responsibility, my responsibility if anything ever happened to her [his wife]. He made me feel that I had to make a choice and there was only one choice to make and that was to have an abortion and I could always have children another time and he made me feel if I didn't have it that it would drive us apart.

The abortion decision was, in her mind, a choice not to choose with respect to the pregnancy—"That was my choice, I had to do it." Instead, it was a decision to subordinate the pregnancy to the continuation of a relationship that she saw as encompassing her life—"Since I met him, he has been my life. I do everything for him; my life sort of revolves around him." Since she wanted to have the baby and also to continue the relationship, either choice could be construed as selfish. Furthermore, since both alternatives entailed hurting someone, neither could be considered moral. Faced with a decision which, in her own terms, was untenable, she sought to avoid responsibility for the choice she made, construing the decision as a sacrifice of her own needs to those of her lover. However, this public sacrifice in the name of responsibility engendered a private resentment that erupted in anger, compromising the very relationship that it had been intended to sustain.

> Afterwards we went through a bad time because I hate to say it and I was wrong, but I blamed him. I gave in to him. But when it came down to it, I made the decision. I could have said, "I am going to have this child whether you want me to or not," and I just didn't do it.

Pregnant again by the same man, she recognizes in retrospect that the choice in fact had been hers, as she returns once again to what now appears to have been missed opportunity for growth. Seeking, this time, to make rather than abdicate the decision, she sees the issue as one of "strength" as she struggles to free herself from the powerlessness of her own dependence:

> I think that right now I think of myself as someone who can become a lot stronger. Because of the circumstances, I just go along like with the tide. I never really had anything of my own before. . . . [This time] I hope to come on strong and make a big decision, whether it is right or wrong.

Because the morality of self-sacrifice had justified the previous abortion, she now must suspend that judgment if she is to claim her own voice and accept responsibility for choice.

She thereby calls into question the underlying assumption of Level Two, which leads the woman to consider herself responsible for the actions of others while holding others responsible for the choices she makes. This notion of reciprocity, backwards in its assumptions about control, disguises assertion as response. By reversing responsibility, it generates a series of indirect actions, which leave everyone feeling manipulated and betrayed. The logic of this position is confused in that the morality of mutual care is embedded in the psychology of dependence. Assertion becomes personally dangerous in its risk of criticism and abandonment as well as potentially immoral in its power to hurt. This confusion is captured by Kohlberg's (1969) definition of Stage Three moral judgment, which joins the need for approval with the wish to care for and help others.

When thus caught between the passivity of dependence and the activity of care, the woman becomes suspended in an immobility of both judgment and action. "If I were drowning, I couldn't reach out a hand to save myself, so unwilling am I to set myself up against fate," begins the central character of Margaret Drabble's novel, *The Waterfall* (1971), in an effort to absolve herself of responsibility as she at the same time relinquishes control. Facing the same moral conflict that George Eliot depicted in *The Mill on the Floss*, Drabble's heroine proceeds to relive Maggie Tulliver's dilemma but turns inward in her search for the way in which to retell that story. What is initially suspended and then called into question is the judgment that "had in the past made it seem better to renounce myself than them."

The Second Transition: From Goodness to Truth

The second transition begins with the reconsideration of the relationship between self and other, as the woman starts to scrutinize the logic of self-sacrifice in the service of a morality of care. In the interview data, this transition is announced by the reappearance of the word selfish. Retrieving the judgment initiative, the woman begins to ask whether it is selfish or responsible, moral or immoral, to include her own needs within the compass of her care and concern. This question leads her to reexamine the concept of responsibility, juxtaposing the outward concern with what other people think with a new inner judgment.

In separating the voice of the self from those of others, the woman asks if it is possible to be responsible to herself as well as to others and thus to reconcile the disparity between hurt and care. The exercise of such responsibility, however, requires a new kind of judgment whose first demand is for honesty. To be responsible, it is necessary first to acknowledge what it is that one is doing. The criterion for judgment thus shifts from "goodness" to "truth" as the morality of action comes to be assessed not on the basis of its appearance in the eyes of others but in terms of the realities of its intention and consequence.

A twenty-four-year-old married Catholic woman, pregnant again two months following the birth of her first child, identifies her dilemma as one of choice: "You have to now decide; because it is now available, you have to make a decision. And if it wasn't available, there was no choice open; you just do what you have to do." In the absence of legal abortion, a morality of self-sacrifice was necessary in order to insure protection and care for the dependent child. However, when such sacrifice becomes optional, the entire problem is recast.

The abortion decision is framed by this woman first in terms of her responsibilities to others: having a second child at this time would be contrary to medical advice and would strain both the emotional and financial resources of the family. However, there is, she says, a third reason for having an abortion, "sort of an emotional reason. I don't know if it is selfish or not, but it would really be tying myself down and right now I am not ready to be tied down with the two."

Against this combination of selfish and responsible reasons for abortion is her Catholic belief that

> It is taking a life, and it is. Even though it is not formed, it is the potential, and to me it is still taking a life. But I have to think of mine, my son's, and my husband's, to think about, and at first I think that I thought it was for selfish reasons, but it is not. I believe that too, some of it is selfish. I don't want another one right now; I am not ready for it.

The dilemma arises over the issue of justification for taking a life: "I can't cover it over, because I believe this and if I do try to cover it over, I know that I am going to be in a mess. It will be denying what I am really doing." In asking "Am I doing the right thing; is it moral?" she counterposes to her belief against abortion her concern with the consequences of continuing the pregnancy. While concluding that "I can't be so morally strict as to hurt three other people with a decision just because of my moral beliefs," the issue of goodness still remains critical to her resolution of the dilemma:

> The moral factor is there. To me it is taking a life, and I am going to take that upon myself, that decision upon myself and I have feelings about it, and talked to a priest . . . but he said it is there and it will be from now on, and it is up to the person if they can live with the idea and still believe they are good.

The criteria for goodness, however, move inward as the ability to have an abortion and still consider herself good comes to hinge on the issue of selfishness with which she struggles to come to terms. Asked if acting morally is acting according to what is best for the self or whether it is a matter of self-sacrifice, she replies:

> I don't know if I really understand the question. . . . Like in my situation where I want to have the abortion and if I didn't it would be self-sacrificing, I am really in the middle of both those ways . . . but I think that my morality is strong and if these reasons—financial, physical reality, and also for the whole family involved—were not here, that I wouldn't have to do it, and then it would be a self-sacrifice.

The importance of clarifying her own participation in the decision is evident in her attempt to ascertain her feelings in order to determine whether she was "putting them under" in deciding to end the pregnancy. Whereas in the first transition, from selfishness to responsibility, women made lists in order to bring to their consideration needs other than their own, now, in the second transition, it is the needs of the self that have to be deliberately uncovered. Confronting the reality of her own wish for an abortion, she now must deal with the problem of selfishness and the qualification that she feels it imposes on the "goodness" of her decision. The primacy of this concern is apparent in her description of herself:

> I think in a way I am selfish for one thing, and very emotional, very . . . and I think that I am a very real person and an understanding person and I can handle

> life situations fairly well, so I am basing a lot of it on my ability to do the things that I feel are right and best for me and whoever I am involved with. I think I was very fair to myself about the decision, and I really think that I have been truthful, not hiding anything, bringing out all the feelings involved. I feel it is a good decision and an honest one, a real decision.

Thus she strives to encompass the needs of both self and others, to be responsible to others and thus to be "good" but also to be responsible to herself and thus to be "honest" and "real."

While, from one point of view, attention to one's own needs is considered selfish, when looked at from a different perspective, it is a matter of honesty and fairness. This is the essence of the transitional shift toward a new conception of goodness, which turns inward in an acknowledgment of the self and an acceptance of responsibility for decision. While outward justification, the concern with "good reasons," remains critical for this particular woman: "I still think abortion is wrong, and it will be unless the situation can justify what you are doing." But the search for justification has produced a change in her thinking, "not drastically, but a little bit." She realizes that in continuing the pregnancy she would punish not only herself but also her husband, toward whom she had begun to feel "turned off and irritated." This leads her to consider the consequences self-sacrifice can have both for the self and for others. "God," she says, "can punish, but He can also forgive." What remains in question is whether her claim to forgiveness is compromised by a decision that not only meets the needs of others but that also is "right and best for me."

The concern with selfishness and its equation with immorality recur in an interview with another Catholic woman, whose arrival for an abortion was punctuated by the statement, "I have always thought abortion was a fancy word for murder." Initially explaining this murder as one of lesser degree—"I am doing it because I have to do it. I am not doing it the least bit because I want to," she judges it "not quite as bad. You can rationalize that it is not quite the same." Since "keeping the child for lots and lots of reasons was just sort of impractical and out," she considers her options to be either abortion or adoption. However, having previously given up one child for adoption, she says: "I knew that psychologically there was no way that I could hack another adoption. It took me about four-and-a-half years to get my head on straight; there was just no way I was going to go through it again." The decision thus reduces in her eyes to a choice between murdering the fetus or damaging herself. The choice is further complicated by the fact that by continuing the pregnancy she would hurt not only herself but also her parents, with whom she lived. In the face of these manifold moral contradictions, the psychological demand for honesty that arises in counseling finally allows decision:

> On my own, I was doing it not so much for myself; I was doing it for my parents. I was doing it because the doctor told me to do it, but I had never resolved in my mind that I was doing it for me. Because it goes back to the fact that I never believed in abortions. . . . Actually, I had to sit down and admit, now, I really don't want to go the mother route now. I honestly don't feel that I want to be a mother, and that is not really such a bad thing to say after all. But that is not how I felt up until talking to Maureen [her counselor]. It was just a horrible way to feel, so I just wasn't going to feel it, and I just blocked it right out.

As long as her consideration remains "moral," abortion can be justified only as an act of sacrifice, a submission to necessity where the absence of choice precludes responsibility. In this way, she can avoid self-condemnation, since, "When you get into moral stuff then you are getting into self-respect and that stuff, and at least if I do something that I feel is morally wrong, then I tend to lose some of my self-respect as a person." Her evasion of responsibility, critical to maintaining the innocence necessary for self-respect, contradicts the reality of her own participation in the abortion decision. The dishonesty in her plea of victimization creates the conflict that generates the need for a more inclusive understanding. She must now resolve the emerging contradiction in her thinking between two uses of the term "right": "I am saying that abortion is morally wrong, but the situation is right, and I am going to do it." But the thing is that eventually they are going to have to go together, and I am going to have to put them together somehow." Asked how this could be done, she replies:

> I would have to change morally wrong to morally right. [How?] I have no idea. I don't think you can take something that you feel is morally wrong because the situation makes it right and put the two together. They are not together, they are opposite. They don't go together. Something is wrong, but all of a sudden because you are doing it, it is right.

This discrepancy recalls a similar conflict she faced over the question of euthanasia, also considered by her to be morally wrong until she "took care of a couple of patients who had flat EEGs and saw the job that it was doing on their families." Recalling that experience, she says:

> You really don't know your black and whites until you really get into them and are being confronted with it. If you stop and think about my feelings on euthanasia until I got into it, and then my feelings about abortion until I got into it, I thought both of them were murder. Right and wrong and no middle but there is a gray.

In discovering the gray and questioning the moral judgments that formerly she considered to be absolute, she confronts the moral crisis of the second transition. Now the conventions that in the past had guided her moral judgment become subject to a new criticism, as she questions not only the justification for hurting others in the name of morality but also the "rightness" of hurting herself. However, to sustain such criticism in the face of conventions that equate goodness with self-sacrifice, the woman must verify her capacity for independent judgment and the legitimacy of her own point of view.

Once again transition hinges on self-concept. When uncertainty about her own worth prevents a woman from claiming equality, self-assertion falls prey to the old criticism of selfishness. Then the morality that condones self-destruction in the name of responsible care is not repudiated as inadequate but rather is abandoned in the face of its threat to survival. Moral obligation, rather than expanding to include the self, is rejected completely as the failure of conventional reciprocity leaves the woman unwilling any longer to protect others at what is now seen to be her own expense. In the absence of morality, survival, however "selfish" or "immoral," returns as the paramount concern.

A musician in her late twenties illustrates this transitional impasse. Having led an independent life that centered on her work, she considered herself "fairly strong-willed, fairly in control, fairly rational and objective" until she became involved in an intense love affair and discovered in her capacity to love "an entirely new dimension" in herself. Admitting in retrospect to "tremendous naïveté and idealism," she had entertained "some vague ideas that some day I would like a child to concretize our relationship . . . having always associated having a child with all the creative aspects of my life." Abjuring, with her lover, the use of contraceptives because, "as the relationship was sort of an ideal relationship in our minds, we liked the idea of not using foreign objects or anything artificial," she saw herself as having relinquished control, becoming instead "just simply vague and allowing events to just carry me along." Just as she began in her own thinking to confront "the realities of that situation"—the possibility of pregnancy and the fact that her lover was married—she found herself pregnant. "Caught" between her wish to end a relationship that "seemed more and more defeating" and her wish for a baby, which "would be a connection that would last a long time," she is paralyzed by her inability to resolve the dilemma that her ambivalence creates.

The pregnancy poses a conflict between her "moral" belief that "once a certain life has begun, it shouldn't be stopped artificially" and her "amazing" discovery that to have the baby she would "need much more [support] than I thought." Despite her moral conviction that she "should" have the child, she doubts that she could psychologically deal with "having the child alone and taking the responsibility for it." Thus a conflict erupts between what she considers to be her moral obligation to protect life and her inability to do so under the circumstances of this pregnancy. Seeing it as "my decision and my responsibility for making the decision whether to have or have not the child," she struggles to find a viable basis on which to resolve the dilemma.

Capable of arguing either for or against abortion "with a philosophical logic," she says, on the one hand, that in an overpopulated world one should have children only under ideal conditions for care but, on the other, that one should end a life only when it is impossible to sustain it. She describes her impasse in response to the question of whether there is a difference between what she wants to do and what she thinks she should do:

> Yes, and there always has. I have always been confronted with that precise situation in a lot of my choices, and I have been trying to figure out what are the things that make me believe that these are things I should do as opposed to what I feel I want to do. [In this situation?] It is not clear cut. I both want the child and feel I should have it, and I also think I should have the abortion and want it, but I would say it is my stronger feeling, and that I don't have enough confidence in my work yet and that is really where it is all hinged, I think . . . [the abortion] would solve the problem and I know I can't handle the pregnancy.

Characterizing this solution as "emotional and pragmatic" and attributing it to her lack of confidence in her work, she contrasts it with the "better thought out and more logical and more correct" resolution of her lover who thinks that she should have the child and raise it without either his presence or financial support. Confronted with this reflected image of herself as ultimately giving and good, as self-sustaining in her own creativity and thus able to meet the needs of others while imposing no demands of her own in return, she questions not the image itself but her own adequacy in filling it. Concluding that she is not yet capable of doing so, she is reduced in her own eyes to what she sees as a selfish and highly compromised fight

> for my survival. But in one way or another, I am going to suffer. Maybe I am going to suffer mentally and emotionally having the abortion, or I would suffer what I think is possibly something worse. So I suppose it is the lesser of two evils. I think it is a matter of choosing which one I know that I can survive through. It is really. I think it is selfish, I suppose, because it does have to do with that. I just realized that. I guess it does have to do with whether I would survive or not. [Why is this selfish?] Well, you know, it is. Because I am concerned with my survival first, as opposed to the survival of the relationship or the survival of the child, another human being. . . . I guess I am setting priorities, and I guess I am setting my needs to survive first. . . . I guess I see it in negative terms a lot . . . but I do think of other positive things; that I am still going to have some life left, maybe. I don't know.

In the face of this failure of reciprocity of care, in the disappointment of abandonment where connection was sought, survival is seen to hinge on her work, which is "where I derive the meaning of what I am. That's the known factor." While uncertainty about her work makes this survival precarious, the choice for abortion is also distressing in that she considers it to be "highly introverted—that in this one respect, having an abortion would be going a step backward; going outside to love someone else and having a child would be a step forward." The sense of retrenchment that the severing of connection signifies is apparent in her anticipation of the cost which abortion would entail:

> Probably what I will do is I will cut off my feelings, and when they will return or what would happen to them after that, I don't know. So that I don't feel anything at all, and I would probably just be very cold and go through it very coldly. . . . The more you do that to yourself, the more difficult it becomes to love again or to trust again or to feel again. . . . Each time I move away from that, it becomes easier, not more difficult, but easier to avoid committing myself to a relationship. And I am really concerned about cutting off that whole feeling aspect.

Caught between selfishness and responsibility, unable to find in the circumstances of this choice a way of caring which does not at the same time destroy, she confronts a dilemma that reduces to a conflict between morality and survival. Adulthood and femininity fly apart in the failure of this attempt at integration as the choice to work becomes a decision not only to renounce this particular relationship and child but also to obliterate the vulnerability that love and care engender.

The Third Level: The Morality of Nonviolence

In contrast, a twenty-five-year-old woman, facing a similar disappointment, finds a way to reconcile the initially disparate concepts of selfishness and responsibility through a transformed understanding of self and a corresponding redefinition of morality. Examining the assumptions underlying the conventions of feminine self-abnegation and moral self-sacrifice, she comes to reject these conventions as immoral in their power to hurt. By elevating nonviolence—the injunction against hurting—to a principle governing all moral judgment and action, she is able to assert a moral equality between self and other. Care then becomes a universal obligation, the self-chosen ethic of a postconventional judgment that reconstructs the dilemma in a way that allows the assumption of responsibility for choice.

In this woman's life, the current pregnancy brings to the surface the unfinished business of an earlier pregnancy and of the relationship in which both pregnancies occurred. The first pregnancy was discovered after her lover had left and was terminated by an abortion experienced as a purging expression of her anger at having been rejected. Remembering the abortion only as a relief, she nevertheless describes that time in her life as one in which she "hit rock bottom." Having hoped then to "take control of my life," she instead resumed the relationship when the man reappeared. Now, two years later, having once again "left my diaphragm in the drawer," she again becomes pregnant. Although initially "ecstatic" at the news, her elation dissipates when her lover tells her that he will leave if she chooses to have the child. Under these circumstances, she considers a second abortion but is unable to keep the repeated appointments she makes because of her reluctance to accept the responsibility for that choice. While the first abortion seemed an "honest mistake," she says that a second would make her feel "like a walking slaughterhouse." Since she would need financial support to raise the child, her initial strategy was to take the matter to "the welfare people" in the hope that they would refuse to provide the necessary funds and thus resolve her dilemma:

> In that way, you know, the responsibility would be off my shoulders, and I could say, it's not my fault, you know, the state denied me the money that I would need to do it. But it turned out that it was possible to do it, and so I was, you know, right back where I started. And I had an appointment for an abortion, and I kept calling and cancelling it and then remaking the appointment and cancelling it, and I just couldn't make up my mind.

Confronting the need to choose between the two evils of hurting herself or ending the incipient life of the child, she finds, in a reconstruction of the dilemma itself, a basis for a new priority that allows decision. In doing so, she comes to see the conflict as arising from a faulty construction of reality. Her thinking recapitulates the developmental sequence, as she considers but rejects as inadequate the components of earlier-stage resolutions. An expanded conception of responsibility now reshapes moral judgment and guides resolution of the dilemma, whose pros and cons she considers as follows:

> Well, the pros for having the baby are all the admiration that you would get from, you know, being a single woman, alone, martyr, struggling, having the adoring love of this beautiful Gerber baby . . . just more of a home life than I have had in a long time, and that basically was it, which is pretty fantasyland; it is not very realistic. . . . Cons against having the baby: it was going to hasten what is looking to be the inevitable end of the relationship with the man I am presently with. . . . I was going to have to go on welfare, my parents were going to hate me for the rest of my life, I was going to lose a really good job that I have, I would lose a lot of independence . . . solitude . . . and I would have to be put in a position of asking help from a lot of people a lot of the time. Cons against having the abortion is having to face up to the guilt . . . and pros for having the abortion are I would be able to handle my deteriorating relation with S. with a lot more capability and

> a lot more responsibility for him and for myself . . . and I would not have to go through the realization that for the next twenty-five years of my life I would be punishing myself for being foolish enough to get pregnant again and forcing myself to bring up a kid just because I did this. Having to face the guilt of a second abortion seemed like, not exactly, well, exactly the lesser of the two evils but also the one that would pay off for me personally in the long run because by looking at why I am pregnant again and subsequently have decided to have a second abortion, I have to face up to some things about myself.

Although she doesn't "feel good about having a second abortion," she nevertheless concludes,

> I would not be doing myself or the child or the world any kind of favor having this child. . . . I don't need to pay off my imaginary debts to the world through this child, and I don't think that it is right to bring a child into the world and use it for that purpose.

Asked to describe herself, she indicates how closely her transformed moral understanding is tied to a changing self-concept:

> I have been thinking about that a lot lately, and it comes up different than what my usual subconscious perception of myself is. Usually paying off some sort of debt, going around serving people who are not really worthy of my attentions because somewhere in my life I think I got the impression that my needs are really secondary to other people's, and that if I feel, if I make any demands on other people to fulfill my needs, I'd feel guilty for it and submerge my own in favor of other people's, which later backfires on me, and I feel a great deal of resentment for other people that I am doing things for, which causes friction and the eventual deterioration of the relationship. And then I start all over again. How would I describe myself to myself? Pretty frustrated and a lot angrier than I admit, a lot more aggressive than I admit.

Reflecting on the virtues that comprise the conventional definition of the feminine self, a definition that she hears articulated in her mother's voice, she says, "I am beginning to think that all these virtues are really not getting me anywhere. I have begun to notice." Tied to this recognition is an acknowledgement of her power and worth, both previously excluded from the image she projected:

> I am suddenly beginning to realize that the things that I like to do, the things I am interested in, and the things that I believe and the kind of person I am is not so bad that I have to constantly be sitting on the shelf and letting it gather dust. I am a lot more worthwhile than what my past actions have led other people to believe.

Her notion of a "good person," which previously was limited to her mother's example of hard work, patience, and self-sacrifice, now changes to include the value that she herself places on directness and honesty. Although she believes that this new self-assertion will lead her "to feel a lot better about myself," she recognizes that it will also expose her to criticism:

> Other people may say, "Boy, she's aggressive, and I don't like that," but at least, you know, they will know that they don't like that. They are not going to say, "I like the way she manipulates herself to fit right around me." . . . What I want to do is just be a more self-determined person and a more singular person.

While within her old framework abortion had seemed a way of "copping out" instead of being a "responsible person [who] pays for his mistakes and pays and pays and is always there when she says she will be there and even when she doesn't say she will be there is there," now, her "conception of what I think is right for myself and my conception of self-worth is changing." She can consider this emergent self "also a good person," as her concept of goodness expands to encompass "the feeling of self-worth; you are not going to sell yourself short and you are not going to make yourself do things that, you know, are really stupid and that you don't want to do." This reorientation centers on the awareness that:

> I have a responsibility to myself, and you know, for once I am beginning to realize that that really matters to me . . . instead of doing what I want for myself and feeling guilty over how selfish I am, you realize that that is a very usual way for people to live . . . doing what you want to do because you feel that your wants and your needs are important, if to no one else, then to you, and that's reason enough to do something that you want to do.

Once obligation extends to include the self as well as others, the disparity between selfishness and responsibility is reconciled. Although the conflict between self and other remains, the moral problem is restructured in an awareness that the occurrence of the dilemma itself precludes nonviolent resolution. The abortion decision is now seen to be a "serious" choice affecting both self and others: "This is a life that I have taken, a conscious decision to terminate, and that is just very heavy, a very heavy thing." While accepting the necessity of abortion as a highly compromised resolution, she turns her attention to the pregnancy itself, which she now considers to denote a failure of responsibility, a failure to care for and protect both self and other.

As in the first transition, although now in different terms, the conflict precipitated by the pregnancy catches up the issues critical to development. These issues now concern the worth of the self in relation to others, the claiming of the power to choose, and the acceptance of responsibility for choice. By provoking a confrontation with these issues, the crisis can become "a very auspicious time; you can use the pregnancy as sort of a learning, teeing-off point, which makes it useful in a way." This possibility for growth inherent in a crisis, which allows confrontation with a construction of reality whose acceptance previously had impeded development, was first identified by Coles (1964) in his study of the children of Little Rock. This same sense of possibility is expressed by the women who see, in their resolution of the abortion dilemma, a reconstructed understanding that creates the opportunity for "a new beginning," a chance "to take control of my life."

For this woman,the first step in taking control was to end the relationship in which she had considered herself "reduced to a nonentity," but to do so in a responsible way. Recognizing hurt as the inevitable concomitant of rejection, she strives to minimize that hurt "by dealing with [his] needs as best I can without compromising my own . . . that's a big point for me, because the thing in my life to this point has been always compromising, and I am not willing to do that any more." Instead, she seeks to act in a "decent, human kind of way . . . one that leaves maybe a slightly shook but not totally destroyed person." Thus the "nonentity" confronts her power to destroy which formerly had impeded any assertion, as she considers the possibility for a new kind of action that leaves both self and other intact.

The moral concern remains a concern with hurting as she considers Kohlberg's Heinz dilemma in terms of the question, "Who is going to be hurt more, the druggist who loses some money or the person who loses their life?" The right to property and right to life are weighted not in the abstract, in terms of their logical priority, but rather in the particular, in terms of the actual consequences that the violation of these rights would have in the lives of the people involved. Thinking remains contextual and admixed with feelings of care, as the moral imperative to avoid hurt begins to be informed by a psychological understanding of the meaning of nonviolence.

Thus, release from the intimidation of inequality finally allows the expression of a judgment that previously had been withheld. What women then enunciate is not a new morality, but a moral conception disentangled from the constraints that formerly had confused its perception and impeded its articulation. The willingness to express and take responsibility for judgment stems from the recognition of the psychological and moral necessity for an equation of worth between self and other. Responsibility for care then includes both self and other, and the obligation not to hurt, freed from conventional constraints, is reconstructed as a universal guide to moral choice.

The reality of hurt centers the judgment of a twenty-nine-year-old woman, married and the mother of a preschool child, as she struggles with the dilemma posed by a second pregnancy whose timing conflicts with her completion of an advanced degree. Saying that "I cannot deliberately do something that is bad or would hurt another person because I can't live with having done that," she nevertheless confronts a situation in which hurt has become inevitable. Seeking that solution which would best protect both herself and others, she indicates, in her definition of morality, the ineluctable sense of connection which infuses and colors all of her thinking:

> [Morality is] doing what is appropriate and what is just within your circumstances, but ideally it is not going to affect—I was going to say, ideally it wouldn't negatively affect another person, but that is ridiculous, because decisions are always going to affect another person. But you see, what I am trying to say is that it is the person that is the center of the decision making, of that decision making about what's right and what's wrong.

The person who is the center of this decision making begins by denying, but then goes on to acknowledge, the conflicting nature both of her own needs and of her various responsibilities. Seeing the pregnancy as a manifestation of the inner conflict between her wish, on the one hand, "to be a college president" and, on the other, "to be making pottery and flowers and having kids and staying at home," she struggles with contradiction between femininity and adulthood. Considering abortion as the "better" choice—because "in the end, meaning this time next year or this time two weeks from now, it will be less of a personal strain on us individually and on us as a family for me not to be pregnant at this time," she concludes that the decision has

> got to be, first of all, something that the woman can live with—a decision that the woman can live with, one way or another, or at least try to live with, and that it be based on where she is at and other people, significant people in her life, are at.

At the beginning of the interview she had presented the dilemma in its conventional feminine construction, as a conflict between her own wish to have a baby and the wish of others for her to complete her education. On the basis of this construction she deemed it "selfish" to continue the pregnancy because it was something "I want to do." However, as she begins to examine her thinking, she comes to abandon as false this conceptualization of the problem, acknowledging the truth of her own internal conflict and elaborating the tension which she feels between her femininity and the adulthood of her work life. She describes herself as "going in two directions" and values that part of herself which is "incredibly passionate and sensitive"—her capacity to recognize and meet, often with anticipation, the needs of others. Seeing her "compassion" as "something I don't want to lose," she regards it as endangered by her pursuit of professional advancement. Thus the self-deception of her initial presentation, its attempt to sustain the fiction of her own innocence, stems from her fear that to say that *she* does not want to have another baby at this time would be

> an acknowledgement to me that I am an ambitious person and that I want to have power and responsibility for others and that I want to live a life that extends from 9 to 5 every day and into the evenings and on weekends, because that is what the power and responsibility means. It means that my family would necessarily come second . . . there would be such an incredible conflict about which is tops, and I don't want that for myself.

Asked about her concept of "an ambitious person," she says that to be ambitious means to be

> power hungry [and] insensitive. [Why insensitive?] Because people are stomped on in the process. A person on the way up stomps on people, whether it is family or other colleagues or clientele, on the way up. [Inevitably?] Not always, but I have seen it so often in my limited years of working that it is scary to me. It is scary because I don't want to change like that.

Because the acquisition of adult power is seen to entail the loss of feminine sensitivity and compassion, the conflict between femininity and adulthood becomes construed as a moral problem. The discovery of the principle of nonviolence begins to direct attention to the moral dilemma itself and initiates the search for a resolution that can encompass both femininity and adulthood.

DEVELOPMENTAL THEORY RECONSIDERED

The developmental conception delineated at the outset, which has so consistently found the development of women to be either aberrant or incomplete, has been limited insofar as it has been predominantly a male conception, giving lip-service, a place on the chart, to the interdependence of intimacy and care but constantly stressing, at their expense, the importance and value of autonomous judgment and action. To admit to this conception the truth of the feminine perspective is to recognize for both sexes the central importance in adult life of the connection between self and other, the universality of the need for compassion and care. The concept of the separate self and of the moral principle uncompromised by the constraints of reality is an adolescent ideal, the elaborately wrought philosophy of a Stephen Daedalus, whose flight we know to be in jeopardy. Erikson (1964), in contrasting the ideological morality of the adolescent with the ethics of adult care, attempts to grapple with this problem of integration, but is impeded by the limitations of his own previous developmental conception. When his developmental stages chart a path where the sole precursor to the intimacy of adult relationships is the trust established in infancy and all intervening experience is marked only as steps toward greater independence, then separation itself becomes the model and the measure of growth. The observation that for women, identity has as much to do with connection as with separation led Erikson into trouble largely because of his failure to integrate this insight into the mainstream of his developmental theory (Erikson 1968).

The morality of responsibility which women describe stands apart from the morality of rights, which underlies Kohlberg's conception of the highest stages of moral judgment. Kohlberg (Note 3) sees the progression toward these stages as resulting from the generalization of the self-centered adolescent rejection of societal morality into a principled conception of individual natural rights. To illustrate this progression, he cites as an example of integrated Stage Five judgment, "possibly moving to Stage Six," the following response of a twenty-five-year-old subject from his male longitudinal sample:

> [What does the word morality mean to you?] Nobody in the world knows the answer. I think it is recognizing the right of the individual, the rights of other individuals, not interfering with those rights. Act as fairly as you would have them treat you. I think it is basically to preserve the human being's right to existence. I think that is the most important. Secondly, the human being's right to do as he pleases, again without interfering with somebody else's rights. (p. 29)

Another version of the same conception is evident in the following interview response of a male college senior whose moral judgment also was scored by Kohlberg (Note 4) as at Stage Five or Six:

> [Morality] is a prescription, it is a thing to follow, and the idea of having a concept of morality is to try to figure out what it is that people can do in order to make life with each other livable, make for a kind of balance, a kind of equilibrium, a harmony in which everybody feels he has a place and an equal share in things, and it's doing that—doing that is kind of contributing to a state of affairs that go beyond the individual in the absence of which, the individual has no chance for self-fulfillment of any kind. Fairness; morality is kind of essential, it seems to me, for creating the kind of environment, interaction between people, that is prerequisite to this fulfillment of most individual goals and so on. If you want other people to not interfere with your pursuit of whatever you are into, you have to play the game.

In contrast, a woman in her late twenties responds to a similar question by defining a morality not of rights but of responsibility:

> [What makes something a moral issue?] Some sense of trying to uncover a right path in which to live, and always in my mind is that the world is full of real and recognizable trouble, and is it heading for some sort of doom and is it right to bring children into this world when we currently have an overpopulation problem, and is it right to spend money on a pair of shoes when I have a pair of shoes and other people are shoeless. . . . It is part of a self-critical view, part of saying, how am I spending my time and in what sense am I working? I think I have a real drive to, I have a real maternal drive to take of someone. To take care of my mother, to take care of children, to take care of other people's children, to take care of my own children, to take care of the world. I think that goes back to your other question, and when I am dealing with moral issues, I am sort of saying to myself constantly, are you taking care of all the things that you think are important and in what ways are you wasting yourself and wasting those issues?

While the postconventional nature of this woman's perspective seems clear, her judgments of Kohlberg's hypothetical moral dilemmas do not meet his criteria for scoring at the principled level. Kohlberg regards this as a disparity between normative and metaethical judgments, which he sees as indicative of the transition between conventional and principled thinking. From another perspective, however, this judgment represents a different moral conception, disentangled from societal conventions and raised to the principled level. In this conception, moral judgment is oriented toward issues of responsibility. The way in which the responsibility orientation guides moral decision at the postconventional level is described by the following woman in her thirties:

> [Is there a right way to make moral decisions?] The only way I know is to try to be as awake as possible, to try to know the range of what you feel, to try to consider all that's involved, to be as aware as you can be to what's going on, as conscious as you can of where you're walking. [Are there principles that guide you?] The principle would have something to do with responsibility, responsibility and caring about yourself and others. . . . But it's not that on the one hand you choose to be responsible and on the other hand you choose to be irresponsible—both ways you can be responsible. That's why there's not just a principle that once you take hold of you settle—the principle put into practice here is still going to leave you with conflict.

The moral imperative that emerges repeatedly in the women's interviews is an injunction to care, a responsibility to discern and alleviate the "real and recognizable trouble" of this world. For the men Kohlberg studied, the moral imperative appeared rather as an injunction to respect the rights of others and thus to protect from interference the right to life and self-fulfillment. Women's insistence on care is at first self-critical rather than self-protective, while men initially conceive obligation to others negatively in terms of noninterference. Development for both sexes then would seem to entail an integration of rights and responsibilities through the discovery of the complementarity of these of these disparate views. For the women I have studied, this integration between rights and responsibilities appears to take place through a principled understanding of equity and reciprocity. This understanding tempers the self-destructive potential of a self-critical morality by asserting the equal right of all persons to care. For the men in Kohlberg's sample as well as for those in a longitudinal study of Harvard undergraduates (Gilligan and Murphy, Note 5), it appears to be the recognition through experience of the need for a more active responsibility in taking care that corrects the potential indifference of a morality of noninterference and turns attention from the logic to the consequences of choice. In the development of a postconventional ethic understanding, women come to see the violence generated by inequitable relationships, while men come to realize the limitations of a conception of justice blinded to the real inequities of human life.

Kohlberg's dilemmas, in the hypothetical abstraction of their presentation, divest the moral actors from the history and psychology of their individual lives and separate the moral problem from the social contingencies of its possible occurrence. In doing so, the dilemmas are useful for the distillation and refinement of the "objective principles of justice" toward which Kohlberg's stages strive. However, the reconstruction of the dilemma in its contextual particularity allows the understanding of cause and consequence, which engages the compassion and tolerance considered by previous theorists to qualify the feminine sense of justice. Only when substance is given to the skeletal lives of hypothetical people is it possible to consider the social injustices that their moral problems may reflect and to imagine the individual suffering their occurrence may signify or their resolutions engender.

The proclivity of women to reconstruct hypothetical dilemmas in terms of the real, to request or supply the information missing about the nature of the people and the places where they live, shifts their judgment away from the hierarchical ordering of principles and the formal procedures of decision making that are critical for scoring at Kohlberg's highest stages. This insistence on the particular signifies an orientation to the dilemma and to moral problems in general that differs from any of Kohlberg's stage descriptions. Given the constraints of Kohlberg's system and the biases in his research sample, this different orientation can only be construed as a failure in development. While several of the women in the research sample clearly articulated what Kohlberg regarded as postconventional metaethical position, none of them were considered by Kohlberg to be principled in their normative moral judgments of his hypothetical moral dilemmas (Note 4). Instead, the women's judgments pointed toward an identification of the violence inherent in the dilemma itself, which was seen to compromise the justice of any of its possible resolutions. This construction of the dilemma led the women to recast the moral judgment from a consideration of the good to a choice between evils.

The woman whose judgment of the abortion dilemma concluded the developmental sequence presented in the preceding section saw Kohlberg's Heinz dilemma in these terms and judged Heinz's action in terms of a choice between selfishness and sacrifice. For Heinz to steal the drug, given the circumstances of his life (which she inferred from his inability to pay two thousand dollars), he would have "to do something which is not in his best interest, in that he is going to get sent away, and that is a supreme sacrifice, a sacrifice which I would say a person truly in love might be willing to make." However, not to steal the drug "would be selfish on his part . . . he would just have to feel guilty about not allowing her a chance to live longer." Heinz's decision to steal is considered not in terms of the logical priority of life over property which justifies its rightness, but rather in terms of the actual consequences that stealing would have for a man of limited means and little social power.

Considered in the light of its probable outcomes—his wife dead, or Heinz in jail, brutalized by the violence of that experience and his life compromised by a record of felony—the dilemma itself changes. Its resolution has less to do with the relative weights of life and property in an abstract moral conception than with the collision it has produced between two lives, formerly conjoined but now in opposition, where the continuation of one life can now occur only at the expense of the other. Given this construction, it becomes clear why consideration revolves around the issue of sacrifice and why guilt becomes the inevitable concomitant of either resolution.

Demonstrating the reticence noted in the first section about making moral judgments, this woman explains her reluctance to judge in terms of her belief

> that everybody's existence is so different that I kind of say to myself, that might be something I wouldn't do, but I can't say that it is right or wrong for that person. I can only deal with what is appropriate for me to do when I am faced with specific problems.

Asked if she would apply to others her own injunction against hurting, she says:

> See, I can't say that it is wrong. I can't say that it is right or that it's wrong because I don't know that the person did that the other person did something to hurt him . . . so it is not right that the person got hurt, but it is right that the person who just lost the job has got to get that anger up and out. It doesn't put any bread on his table, but it is released. I don't mean to be copping out. I really am trying to see how to answer these questions for you.

Her difficulty in answering Kohlberg's questions, her sense of strain with the construction that they impose on the dilemma, stems from their divergence from her own frame of reference:

> I don't even think I use the words right and wrong anymore, and I know I don't use the word moral, because I am not sure I know what it means. . . . We are talking about an unjust society, we are talking about a whole lot of things that are not right, that are truly wrong, to use the word that I don't use very often, and I have no control to change that. If I could change it, I certainly would, but I can only make my small contribution from day to day, and if I don't intentionally hurt somebody, that is my contribution to a better society. And so a chunk of that contribution is also not to pass judgment on other people, particularly when I don't know the circumstances of why they are doing certain things.

The reluctance to judge remains a reluctance to hurt, but one that stems now not from a sense of personal vulnerability but rather from a recognition of the limitations of judgment itself. The deference of the conventional feminine perspective can thus be seen to continue at the postconventional level, not as moral relativism but rather as part of a reconstructed moral understanding. Moral judgment is renounced in an awareness of the psychological and social determinism of all human behavior at the same time as moral concern is reaffirmed in recognition of the reality of human pain and suffering.

> I have a real thing about hurting people and always have, and that gets a little complicated at times, because, for example, you don't want to hurt your child. I

> don't want to hurt my child but if I don't hurt her sometimes, then that's hurting her more, you see, and so that was a terrible dilemma for me.

Moral dilemmas are terrible in that they entail hurt; she sees Heinz's decision as "the result of anguish, who am I hurting, why do I have to hurt them." While the morality of Heinz's theft is not in question given the circumstances that necessitated it, what is at issue is his willingness to substitute himself for his wife and become, in her stead, the victim of exploitation by a society which breeds and legitimizes the druggist's irresponsibility and whose injustice is thus manifest in the very occurrence of the dilemma.

The same sense that the wrong questions are being asked is evident in the response of another woman who justified Heinz's action on a similar basis, saying "I don't think that exploitation should really be a right." When women begin to make direct moral statements, the issues they repeatedly address are those of exploitation and hurt. In doing so, they raise the issue of nonviolence in precisely the same psychological context that brought Erikson (1969) to pause in his consideration of the truth of Gandhi's life.

In the pivotal letter, around which the judgment of his book turns, Erikson confronts the contradiction between the philosophy of nonviolence that informed Gandhi's dealing with the British and the psychology of violence that marred his relationships with his family and with the children of the ashram. It was this contradiction, Erikson confesses,

> which almost brought *me* to the point where I felt unable to continue writing *this* book because I seemed to sense the presence of a kind of untruth in the very protestation of truth; of something unclean when all the words spelled out an unreal purity; and, above all, of displaced violence where nonviolence was the professed issue.[6]

In an effort to untangle the relationship between the spiritual truth of Satyagraha and the truth of his own psychoanalytic understanding, Erikson reminds Gandhi that "truth, you once said, 'excludes the use of violence because man is not capable of knowing the absolute truth and therefore is not competent to punish.' " The affinity between Satyagraha and psychoanalysis lies in their shared commitment to seeing life as an "experiment in truth," in their being

> somehow joined in a universal "therapeutics," committed to the Hippocratic principle that one can test truth (or the healing power inherent in a sick situation) only by action which avoids harm—or better, by action which maximizes mutually and minimizes the violence caused by unilateral coercion or threat.[7]

Erikson takes Gandhi to task for his failure to acknowledge the relativity of truth. This failure is manifest in the coercion of Gandhi's claim to exclusive possession of truth, his "unwillingness to learn from *anybody anything* except what was approved by the 'inner voice.' " This claim led Gandhi, in the guise of love, to impose his truth on others without awareness or regard for the extent to which he thereby did violence to their integrity.

The moral dilemma, arising inevitably out of a conflict of truths, is by definition a "sick situation" in that its either/or formulation leaves no room for an outcome that does not do violence. The resolution of such dilemmas, however, lies not in the self-deception of rationalized violence—"I was" said Gandhi, "a cruelly kind husband. I regarded myself her teacher and so harassed her out of my blind love for her"—but rather in the replacement of the underlying antagonism with a mutuality of respect and care.

Gandhi, whom Kohlberg has mentioned as exemplifying Stage Six moral judgment and whom Erikson sought as a model of an adult ethical sensibility, instead is criticized by a judgment that refuses to look away from or condone the infliction of harm. In denying the validity of his wife's reluctance to open her home to strangers and in his blindness to the different reality of adolescent sexuality and temptation, Gandhi compromised in his everyday life the ethic of nonviolence to which in principle and in public he was so steadfastly committed.

The blind willingness to sacrifice people to truth, however, has always been the danger of an ethics abstracted from life. This willingness links Gandhi to the biblical Abraham, who prepared to sacrifice the life of his son in order to demonstrate the integrity and supremacy of his faith. Both men, in the limitations of their fatherhood, stand in implicit contrast to the woman who comes before Solomon and verifies her motherhood by relinquishing truth in order to save the life of her child. It is the ethics of an adulthood that has become principled at the expense of care that Erikson comes to criticize in his assessment of Gandhi's life.

This same criticism is dramatized explicitly as a contrast between the sexes in *The Merchant of Venice* (1598/1912), where Shakespeare goes through an extraordinary complication of sexual identity (dressing a male actor as a female character who in turn poses as a male judge) in order to bring into the masculine citadel of justice the feminine plea for mercy. The limitation of the contractual conception of justice is illustrated through the absurdity of its literal execution, while the "need to make exceptions all the time" is demonstrated contrapuntally in the matter of the rings. Portia, in calling for mercy, argues for that resolution in which no one is hurt, and as the men are forgiven for their failure to keep both their rings and their word, Antonio in turns forgoes his "right" to ruin Shylock.

The research findings that have been reported in this essay suggest that women impose a distinctive construction on moral problems, seeing moral dilemmas in terms of conflicting responsibilities. This construction was found to develop through a sequence of three levels and two transitions, each level representing a more complex understanding of the relationship between self and other and each transition involving a critical reinterpretation of the moral conflict between selfishness and responsibility. The development of women's moral judgment appears to proceed from an initial concern with survival, to focus on goodness, and finally to a principled understanding of nonviolence as the most adequate guide to the just resolution of moral conflicts.

In counterposing to Kohlberg's longitudinal research on the development of hypothetical moral judgment in men a cross-sectional study of women's responses to actual dilemmas of moral conflict and choice, this essay precludes the possibility of generalization in either direction and leaves to further research the task of sorting out the different variables of occasion and sex. Longitudinal studies of women's moral judgments are necessary in order to validate the claims of stage and sequence presented here. Similarly, the contrast drawn between the moral judgments of men and women awaits for its confirmation a more systematic comparison of the responses of both sexes. Kohlberg's research on moral development has confounded the variables of age, sex, type of decision, and type of dilemma by presenting a single configuration (the responses of adolescent males to hypothetical dilemmas of conflicting rights) as the basis for a universal stage sequence. This paper underscores the need for systematic treatment of these variables and points toward their study as a critical task for future moral development research.

For the present, my aim has been to demonstrate the centrality of the concepts of responsibility and care in women's constructions of the moral domain, to indicate the close tie in women's thinking between conceptions of the self and conceptions of morality, and, finally, to argue the need for an expanded developmental theory that would include, rather than rule out from developmental consideration, the difference in the feminine voice. Such an inclusion seems essential, not only for explaining the development of women but also for understanding in both sexes the characteristics and precursors of an adult moral conception.

NOTES

1. Haan, N. *Activism as Moral Protest: Moral Judgments of Hypothetical Dilemmas and an Actual Situation of Civil Disobedience.* Unpublished manuscript, University of California at Berkeley, 1971.
2. Turiel, E. *A Comparative Analysis of Moral Knowledge and Moral Judgment in Males and Females.* Unpublished manuscript, Harvard University, 1973.
3. Kohlberg, L. *Continuities and Discontinuities in Childhood and Adult Moral Development Revisited.* Unpublished paper, Harvard University, 1973.
4. Kohlberg, L. Personal communication, August 1976.
5. Gilligan, C., and Murphy, M. *The Philosopher and the "Dilemma of the Fact": Moral Development in Late Adolescence and Adulthood.* Unpublished manuscript, Harvard University, 1977.
6. Erikson, Erik H. *Gandhi's Truth.* NY: Norton, 1969, pp. 230–231.
7. Ibid., p. 247.

Maternal Thinking

Rejecting the view that mothering is simply a biologically programmed, instinctual activity, Ruddick maintains that practices of mothering shape and express maternal thinking. To grasp what maternal thinking is, Ruddick examines the predominantly female practice of mothering and draws out the virtues and values implicit in its ideal form. Ruddick does not idealize mothers—undeniably, no mother is perfect. However, she holds that maternal practice is based on a conception of achievement and that this goal sets standards for mothers. Ruddick's principal aim is to articulate these standards.

According to Ruddick, children need to have their lives protected, to have their growth fostered, and to have their development channeled in ways that will make them acceptable members of society. These three interests govern maternal practice and suggest a set of maternal values and disvalues. With respect to preserving a child's life, Ruddick identifies three values. She sees holding as a value and contrasts it with the disvalue of excessive control. She sees humility as a value and contrasts it with both assertiveness and self-effacement. She sees resilient cheerfulness as a value and contrasts it with both cheery denial and melancholy. With respect to fostering a child's growth, Ruddick identifies three additional values. Innovation, she urges, is a value that takes precedence over permanence. Disclosure and responsiveness are values that take precedence over clarity and certainty. With respect to nurturing a socially acceptable child, Ruddick argues that the value of appreciability supersedes conformism and inauthenticity. Finally, Ruddick endorses an overarching virtue that she calls love and that she contrasts with fantasy. It is crucial that caregivers register the unique individuality of children and refrain from projecting their experience and values onto their children. Guided by these values, maternal thinking unites intellect and emotion to yield judgment. According to Ruddick, these values should not be confined to childrearing—they should be applied to public policy issues, as well.

—D.T.M.

Chapter 30

Sara Ruddick

Maternal Thinking

We are familiar with Victorian renditions of Ideal Maternal Love. My own favorite, like so many of these poems, was written by a son.

> There was a young man loved a maid
> Who taunted him. "Are you afraid,"
> She asked, "to bring me today
> Your mother's head upon a tray?"
> He went and slew his mother dead,
> Tore from her breast her heart so red,
> Then towards his lady love he raced,
> But tripped and fell in all his haste.
> As the heart rolled on the ground
> It gave forth a plaintive sound.
> And it spoke, in accents mild:
> "Did you hurt yourself, my child?"[1]

Many of this story's wishes and fantasies are familiar. Our love for our sons is said to be dangerous to the "maid" who seeks to take him from us. Like the first mother, a mother-in-law is a maid's rival for the sexual possession of a man. We too were maids and lovers before we were mothers; we understand. We understand too that our love may jeopardize our sons' manhood. As "good" mothers we allow our sons contempt for our feelings ("the normal male contempt for women"),[2] if not for our lives, so that they may guiltlessly "separate themselves" from us. There is, however, an unfamiliar twist to the poem. The lady asked for our head, the son brought our heart. She feared and respected our thoughts. He believes only our feelings are powerful. Again we are not surprised. The passions of maternity are so sudden, intense, and confusing that we ourselves often remain ignorant of the perspective, the *thought* that has developed from our mothering. Lacking pride, we have failed to deepen or to articulate that thought. This is a paper about the head of the mother.

Central to our experience of our mothers and our mothering is a poignant conjunction of power and powerlessness. In any society a mother is unavoidably powerless. Nature's indifference—illness, death, and damage to the child or its closest loved ones—can frustrate the best maternal efforts. To unavoidable powerlessness is added avoidable social powerlessness. Almost everywhere the practices of mothering take place in societies in which women of all classes are less able than men of their class to determine the conditions in which their children grow. Throughout history, most women have mothered in conditions of military and social violence, as well as economic deprivation, governed by men whose policies they could neither shape nor control.

Powerless mothers are also powerful. "Most of us first know both love and disappointment, power and tenderness, in the person of a woman."[3] For a child, a mother is the primary, uncontrollable source of the world's goods; a witness and judge whose will must be placated, whose approval must be secured.[4] Some of a mother's power is avoidable if child care is shared, from infancy on, with other adults and older children. However, a mother has a residual power accruing from her capacity to bear and nurse infants. So long as she is able and chooses to utilize her reproductive body in her own and her children's interest, she will, in the predictable technological future, have power to give or deny children to men as well as to maintain some irreducible power over her children by dint of her unique and extraordinary physical intimacy with them.

In most societies however, women are socially powerless in respect to the very reproductive capacities that might make them powerful. The primary bodily experience of mothers is a poignant reminder that to think of maternal power is immediately to recall maternal powerlessness—and conversely. Freudians and feminists have made us aware of the unfortunate consequences of this lethal conjunction. Children confront and rely upon a powerful maternal presence only to watch her become the powerless woman in front of the father, the teacher, the doctor, the judge, the landlord—the world. A child's rageful disappointment in its powerless mother, combined with resentment and fear of her powerful will, may account for the matriphobia so widespread in our society as to seem normal. For whatever reasons, it seems almost impossible for older children or adults to construct a coherent, let alone a benign, account of maternal power.[5]

The conjunction of maternal power and powerlessness makes maternal practices oppressive to mothers and children alike. The oppression is real; much more could be said about it. However, to suggest that mothers are principally victims of a kind of crippling work is an egregiously inaccurate account of women's own experience as mothers and daughters. Although one can sympathize with the anger that insists upon and emphasizes the oppressive nature of maternal practices, an account that describes only exploitation and pain is itself oppressive to women.[6] Mothers, despite the inevitable trials and social conditions of motherhood, are often effective in their work.

In articulating those conditions of mothering that allow for happiness and efficacy, we need to remember some simple facts. Maternal practices begin in love, a love that for most mothers is as intense, confusing, ambivalent, and poignantly sweet as any they will experience. Although economic and social conditions, such as the poverty that is widespread and the isolation that is typical in America, may make that love frantic, they do not kill the love. For whatever reasons, mothers typically find it not only natural but compelling to protect and foster the growth of their children. Relatedly, mothers, especially those who have chosen or come to welcome parenthood, experience a social-biological pride in the function of their reproductive processes, a sense of activation of maternal power. In addition to a sense of reproductive power, many mothers early develop a sense of maternal competence, a sense that they *are* able to protect and foster the growth of their children.

That maternal love, pleasure in reproductive powers, and a sense of maternal competence survive in a patriarchal society where women are routinely derogated, makes one wonder at the further possibilities for maternal happiness in decent societies. Even in this relatively indecent society, mothers are usually socially rewarded for their work by the shared pleasure and confirmation of other women, by the gratitude and pride of grandparents, and frequently by the intense, appreciative paternal love of their mates. Moreover, mothers who work primarily at home often have more control over the details of their working day than is available to other workers.[7] Many mothers, whatever their work in the public world, feel part of a community of comothers, whose warmth and support are rarely equaled in other working relationships. Loving, competent, and appreciated, a mother need not experience her work as oppressive. When their children flourish, mothers have a sense of well-being.

On the other hand, no children flourish all of the time. The emotional and physical pains of their children are anguishing for mothers, inducing a sense of helplessness and guilt. Isolation, restricted options, and social devaluation can make mothering grim even for economically privileged women. It is difficult when writing about motherhood—or experiencing it—to be balanced about both its grim and its satisfying aspects.

Yet loving, competent well-being is an important element in our (my) memories of our mothers and mothering. We must bear these memories in mind if we are to understand that neither the world's misogyny nor our own related psychic dramas have totally prevented us from acquiring an image of benign maternal power. Whatever their scientific status, persistent interest in and positive response to myths of matriarchy show how avidly women search for a society in which mothers are powerful. Feminist utopias are apt to assign government to mothers. "You see we are *mothers,*" their authors seem to say, as if in saying that they have said it all.[8] Cultural myths and our own dreams tell of us a connection we would wish to make with a mother who is socially as well as personally powerful, powerful in adult as well as in infants' eyes. The construction of matriarchal pasts and futures signals longing and regret; longing for a powerful mother we remember and wish we could recognize; regret, often resentful and blaming, that she does not come again after the years of childhood.

My mama moved among the days
like a dreamwalker in a field;
seemed like what she touched was hers
seemed like what touched her couldn't hold,
she got us almost through the high grass
then seemed like she turned around and ran

right back in
right back on in.[9]

It is enormously difficult to come by an image of maternal power that is even coherent, let alone benign: it is easy to come by images of powerlessness and malign power. I consider my attempt to express and respect maternal thought one contribution to an ongoing, shared, feminist project: the construction of an image of maternal power that is benign, accurate, sturdy, and sane.

My particular project, the expression of maternal thought, connects to a general question. Do women, who now rightfully claim the instruments of public power, have cultures, traditions, and inquiries that we should insist upon bringing to the public world? If the "womanly" can be identified, should we respect it or attempt to surpass it? These questions divide feminists. The ideology of womanhood has been invented by men. It confines as it exalts us. On the other hand, the ideology of androgyny is often a disguised ideology of manhood that continues the disrespect for women shared by both sexes.

I am aware of the oppressive uses to which any identification of the "womanly" can be put. Our current gender dichotomies are rigid and damaging. Praising cultures of oppression comes close to praising oppression itself. Often we celebrate our mothers' lives only because we are afraid to confront the damage our past wrecked upon them and us. Despite these doubts, I am increasingly convinced that there are female traditions and practices out of which a distinctive kind of thinking has developed.

Maternal thinking is only one example of "womanly" thinking.[10] In articulating and respecting the maternal, I do not underwrite the still current, false, and pernicious identification of womanhood with biological or adoptive mothering of particular children in families.[11] For me, "maternal" is a social category; although maternal thinking arises out of actual child-caring practices, biological parenting is neither necessary nor sufficient. Many women and some men express maternal thinking in various kinds of working and caring with others. And some biological mothers, especially in misogynistic societies, take a fearful, defensive distance from their own mothering and the maternal lives of any women.

Maternal thought does, I believe, exist for all women in a radically different way than for men. It is because we are *daughters* that we early receive maternal love with special attention to its implications for our bodies, our passions, and our ambitions. We are alert to the values and costs of maternal practices whether we are determined to engage in them or to avoid them. Although some men do, and more men should, acquire maternal thinking, their ways of acquisition are necessarily different from ours.[12]

I do not wish to deny any more than I wish to affirm some biological bases of maternal thinking. The "biological body" (in part a cultural artifact) *may* foster certain features of maternal practice, sensibility, and thought. Neither our own ambivalence to our women's bodies nor the bigoted, repressive uses which many men, colonizers, and racists have made of biology, should blind us to our body's possibilities. In concentrating on what mothers do rather than upon what we are, I postpone biological questions until we have the moral and political perceptions to answer them justly.[13]

Along with biology, I put aside all accounts of gender difference or maternal nature that would claim an essential and ineradicable difference between female and male parents. However, I do believe that there are features of mothering experience which are invariant and nearly unchangeable, and others which, though changeable, are nearly universal.[14] It is therefore possible to identify interests that appear to govern maternal practice throughout the species. However, it is impossible even to begin to specify those interests without importing features specific to the class, ethnic group, and particular sex-gender system in which those interests are realized. I will be drawing upon my knowledge of the institutions of motherhood in middle-class, white, Protestant, capitalist, patriarchal America as these have expressed themselves in the heterosexual nuclear family in which I mother and was mothered. Although I have tried to compensate for the limits of my particular social and sexual history, I principally depend upon others to correct my interpretations and to translate across cultures.[15]

I speak about a mother's *thought*—the intellectual capacities she develops, the judgments she makes, the metaphysical attitudes she assumes, the values she affirms. A mother engaging in a discipline. That is, she asks certain questions rather than others; establishes criteria for the truth, adequacy, and relevance of proposed answers; and cares about the findings she makes and can act upon. Like any discipline, hers has *characteristic* errors, temptations, and goals. The discipline of maternal thought consists in establishing criteria for determining failure and success, in setting the priorities, and in identifying the virtues and liabilities which the criteria presume. To describe the capacities, judgments, metaphysical attitudes, and values of maternal thought does not presume maternal achievement. It is to describe a *conception* of achievement, the end to which maternal efforts are directed, conceptions and ends quite different from dominant public ones.[16]

In stating my claims about maternal thinking, I use a vocabulary developed in formulating theories about the general nature of thought.[17] According to these theories, *all* thought arises out of social practice. In their practices, people respond to a reality that appears to them as given, as presenting certain *demands*. The response to demands is shaped by *interests* which are generally interests in preserving, reproducing, directing, and understanding individual and group life. These four interests are general in the sense that they arise out of the conditions of humans-in-nature and characterize us as a species. However, these interests are always and only expressed as interests of people in particular cultures and classes of their cultures, living in specific geographical, technological, and historical settings. They are always and only responses to some realities—human and nonhuman, natural and supernatural—which present themselves to particular interested people as given. Thinking is governed by the interests of the practice out of which it arises. Thinking names and elaborates the "given" reality to whose demands practice is responding. It expresses, refines, and executes the interests of the practice in a way that is disciplined, directive, and communicable.

Maternal practice responds to the historical reality of a biological child in a particular social world. The agents of maternal practice, acting in response to the demands of their children, acquired a conceptual scheme—a vocabulary and logic of connections—through which they order and express the facts and values of their practice. In judgments and self-reflection, they refine and concretize this scheme. Intellectual activities are distinguishable, but not separable from disciplines of feeling. There is a unity of reflection, judgment, and emotion. It is this unity I call "maternal thinking." Although I will not digress to argue the point here, it is important that maternal thinking is no more interest governed, no more emotional, no more relative to its particular reality (the growing child) than the thinking that arises from scientific, religious, or any another practice.

Children "demand" that their lives be preserved and their growth be fostered. Their social group "demands" that their growth be shaped in a way acceptable to the next generation.

Maternal practice is governed by (at least) three interests in satisfying these demands for preservation, growth, and acceptability. Preservation is the most invariant and primary of the three. Because a caretaking mother typically bears her own children, preservation begins when conception is recognized and accepted. Although the form of preservation depends upon widely variant beliefs about the fragility and care of the fetus, women have always had a lore in which they recorded their concerns for the baby they "carried." Once born, a child is physically vulnerable for many years. Even when she lives with the father of her child or other female adults, even when she has money to purchase or finds available supportive health and welfare services, a mother typically considers herself and is considered by others to be responsible for the maintenance of the life of her child.

Interest in fostering the physical, emotional, and intellectual growth of her child soon supplements a mother's interest in its preservation. The human child is typically capable of complicated emotional and intellectual development; the human adult is radically different in kind from the child it once was. A woman who mothers may be aided or assaulted by the help and advice of fathers, teachers, doctors, moralists, therapists, and others who have an interest in fostering and shaping the growth of her child. Although rarely given primary credit, a mother typically holds herself and is held by others to be responsible for the *malfunction* of the growth process.

From early on, certainly by the middle years of childhood, a mother is governed by a third interest. She must shape natural growth in such a way that her child becomes the sort of adult that she can appreciate and others can accept. Mothers will vary enormously, individually and socially, in the traits and lives that they will appreciate in their children. However, a mother typically takes as the criterion of her success the production of a young adult acceptable to her group.

These three interests in preservation, growth, and acceptability of the child govern maternal practices in general. However, not all mothers are, as individuals, governed by these interests. Some mothers are incapable of interested participation in the practices of mothering because of emotional, intellectual, or physical disability. Severe poverty may make interested maternal practice and therefore maternal thinking nearly impossible. Then, of course, mothers engage in practices other than and often conflicting with mothering. Some mothers, aware of the derogation and confinement of women in maternal practice, may be disaffected. In short, actual mothers have the same sort of relation to maternal practice as actual scientists have to scientific practice, or actual believers have to religious practices. As mothers, they are governed by the interests of their respective practices. But the style, skill, commitment, integrity, with which they engage in these practices, differ widely from individual to individual.

The interest in preservation, growth, and the acceptability of the child are frequently and unavoidably in conflict. A mother who watches a child eagerly push a friend aside as she or he climbs a tree will be torn between preserving the child from danger, encouraging the child's physical skills and courage, and shaping a child according to moral restraints—which might, for example, inhibit the child's joy in competitive climbing. Although some mothers will deny or be insensitive to the conflict and others will be clear about which interest should take precedence, mothers typically will know that they cannot secure each interest, will know that goods conflict, will know that unqualified success in realizing interests is an illusion. The unavoidable conflict of basic interests is one objective basis for the maternal humility, which I will shortly describe.

A mother, acting in the interest of preserving and maintaining life, is in a peculiar relation to "nature." As a childbearer, she often takes herself and is taken by others to be an especially "natural" member of her culture. As a childtender, she must respect nature's limits and court its favor with foresightful actions ranging from immunizations to caps on household poisons to magical imprecations, warnings, and prayers. "Nature," with its unpredictable varieties of dirt and disease, is her enemy as much as her ally. Her children themselves are natural creatures, often unable to understand or abet her efforts to protect them. Because they frequently find her necessary direction constraining, a mother can experience her children's own liveliness as another enemy of the life she is preserving.

It is no wonder then that as she engages in preservation, a mother is liable to the temptations of fearfulness and excessive control. If she is alone with two or more young children as she tries to carry out her responsibilities, then control of herself, her children, and her physical environment is her only option, however rigid or excessive she looks to outsiders. Though necessarily controlling in their acts, *reflecting* mothers themselves identify rigid or excessive control as the likely defects of the very virtues they are required to practice. It is the identification of liability as such, with its implication of the will to overcome, that characterizes this aspect of maternal thought. The epithet "controlling mother" is often unsympathetic, even matriphobic. On the other hand, it may, in line with the insights of maternal thought, remind us of what maternal thinking *counts as* failure. To recognize excessive control as a *liability* sharply distinguishes maternal from scientific practice.[18]

To a mother, "life" may well seem "terrible, hostile, and quick to pounce on you if you give it a chance."[19] In response, she develops a metaphysical attitude toward "being as such," an attitude that I call "holding," an attitude that is governed by the priority of keeping over acquiring, of conserving the fragile, of maintaining whatever is at hand and necessary to the child's life. It is an attitude elicited by the work of "world-*protection*, world-*preservation*, world-*repair*... the invisible weaving of a frayed and threadbare family life."[20]

The recognition of the priority of holding over acquiring once again distinguishes maternal from scientific thought, as well as from the instrumentalism of technocratic capitalism. In recognizing resilient good humor and humility as achievements of its practices, maternal thought takes issue both with contemporary moral theory and with popular moralities of assertiveness.[21] Humility is a metaphysical attitude one takes toward a world beyond one's control. One might conceive of the world as governed by necessity and chance (as I do) or by supernatural forces that cannot be comprehended. In either case, humility implies a profound sense of the limits of one's actions and of the unpredictability of the consequences of one's work. As the philosopher Iris Murdoch puts it: "Every 'natural' thing, including one's own mind, is subject to chance. . . . One might say that chance is a subdivision of death. . . . We cannot dominate the world."[22] Humility that emerges from maternal practices accepts not only the facts of damage and death, but also the facts of the independent and uncontrollable, developing and increasingly separate existences of the lives it seeks to preserve. "Humility is not a peculiar habit of self-effacement, rather like having an inaudible voice, it is selfless respect for reality and one of the most difficult and central of virtues."[23]

If in the face of danger, disappointment, and unpredictability, mothers are liable to melancholy, they are also aware that a kind, resilient good humor is a virtue. This good humor must not be confused with the cheery denial which is both a liability and, unfortunately, a characteristic of maternal practice. Mothers are tempted to denial simply by the insupportable difficulty of passionately loving a fragile creature in a physically threatening, socially violent, pervasively uncaring, competitive world. Defensive denial is exacerbated as it is officially encouraged, when we must defend against perceptions of our own subordination. Our cheery denials are cruel to our children and demoralizing to ourselves.

Clear-sighted cheerfulness is the virtue of which denial is the degenerative form. It is clear-sighted cheerfulness that Spinoza must have had in mind when he said: "Cheerfulness is always a good thing and never excessive"; it "increases and assists the power of action."[24] Denying cheeriness drains intellectual energy and befuddles the will; the cheerfulness honored in maternal thought increases and assists the power of maternal action.

In a daily way, cheerfulness is a matter-of-fact willingness to continue, to give birth and to accept having given birth, to welcome life despite is conditions. When things fall apart, maternal cheerfulness becomes evident courage. There are many stories of mothers who, with resourcefulness and restraint, help their children to die well. The most common but disturbing stories concern mothers who accept their sons' wartime deaths, the most affecting, those which involve the deaths of small children in families.[25] These visible and accessible examples are but the manifestation of psychic strengths that have been developed in conditions of mothering that are invisible and frequently denied. Resilient good humor is a style of mothering "in the deepest sense of 'style' in which to discover the right style is to discover what you are really trying to do."[26]

Because in the dominant society "humility" and "cheerfulness" name virtues of subordinates, and because these virtues have in fact developed in conditions of subordination, it is difficult to credit them, easy to confuse them with the self-effacement and cheery denial, which are their degenerative forms. Again and again, in attempting to articulate maternal thought, language is sicklied o'er by the pale cast of sentimentality and through itself takes on a greeting card quality. Yet literature shows us many mothers who in their "holding" actions value the humility and resilient good humor I have described. One can meet such mothers, recognize their thoughts, any day one learns to listen. One can appreciate the effects of their disciplined perseverance in the unnecessarily beautiful artifacts of the culture they created. "I made my quilt to keep my family warm. I made it beautiful so my heart would not break."[27]

Mothers not only must preserve fragile, existing life. They also must foster growth and welcome change. If the "being" that is preserved seems always to be endangered, undone, slipping away, the "being" that changes is always developing, building, purposively moving away. The "holding," preserving mother must, in response to change, be simultaneously a changing mother. Her conceptual scheme in terms of which she makes sense of herself, her child, and their common world will be more the Aristotelian biologist's than the Platonic mathematician's. Innovation takes precedence over permanence, disclosure, and responsiveness over clarity and certainty. The idea of "objective reality" itself "undergoes important modification when it is to be understood, not in relation to the world described by science, but in relation to the progressing life of a person."[28]

Women are said to value open over closed structure, to eschew the clear-cut and unambiguous, to refuse a sharp division between inner and outer or self and other. We are also said to depend upon and to prize our private inner lives of the mind.[29] If these facets of the "female mind" are elicited by maternal practices, they may well be interwoven responses to the changeability of a growing child. A child is itself an "open structure" whose acts are irregular, unpredictable, often mysterious. A mother, in order to understand her child, must assume the existence of a conscious continuing person whose acts make sense in terms of perceptions and responses to a meaning-filled world. She knows that her child's fantasies and thoughts are not only connected to the child's power to act, but are often the only basis for her understanding of the child and for the child's self-understanding.[30]

A mother, in short, is committed to two philosophical positions: she is a mentalist rather than a behaviorist, and she assumes the priority of personhood over action. Moreover, if her "mentalism" is to enable her to understand and to love, she must be realistic about the psyche whose growth she fosters. *All* psyches are moved by fear, lust, anger, pride, and defenses against them, by what Simone Weil called "*natural* movements of the soul" and likened to laws of physical gravity.[31] This is not to deny that the soul is also blessed by "grace," "light," and erotic hungering for goodness.[32] However, mothers cannot take grace for granted, nor force nor deny the less flattering aggrandizing and consolatory operations of childhood psychic life. A mother must again and again "regain the sense of the complexity and the reality and the struggle . . . with some pity, some envy and much good will."[33]

Her realistic appreciation of a person's continuous mental life allows a mother to expect change, to change with change. As psychologist Jean Baker Miller puts it: "In a very immediate and day to day way women *live* for change."[34] Change requires a kind of learning in which what one learns cannot be applied exactly, and often not even by analogy, to a new situation. If science agrees to take as real the reliable results of *repeatable* experiments,[35] its learning will be quite different in kind from maternal learning. Miller is hopeful that if we attend to maternal practices, we can develop new ways of studying learning appropriate to the changing natures of all peoples and communities, for it is not only children who change, grow, and need help in growing. Most obviously those who care for children must change in response to changing reality. And we all might grow—as opposed to aging—if we could learn how. For everyone's benefit, "women must now face the task of putting their vast unrecognized experience with change into a new and broader level of operation."[36]

Miller writes of achievement, of women who have learned to change and respond to change. But she admits:

> Tragically in our society, women are prevented from fully enjoying these pleasures (of growth) themselves by being made to feel that fostering them in others is the only valid role for all women and by the loneliness, drudgery and isolated noncooperative household setting in which they work.[37]

Similarly, in delineating maternal thought, I do not claim that mothers realize in themselves the capacities and virtues that we learn to value as we care for others. Rather, mothers develop *conceptions* of abilities and virtues according to which they measure themselves and interpret their actions. It is no great sorrow that some mothers never acquire humility, resilient good humor, realism, respect for persons, and responsiveness to growth, that all of us fail often in many kinds of ways. What is a great sorrow is to find the task itself misdescribed, sentimentalized, and devalued.

Acting in the interests of preservation and growth, women have developed a maternal perspective. This perspective has its degenerative forms, such as the cheery denial that sometimes passes for cheerfulness. Preservation can turn into the fierce desire to foster one's *own* children's growth whatever the cost to other children. Holding—world-preservation and world-repair—can turn into frantic accumulating and storing, especially under the pressures of consumerism. Yet though liable to degenerative forms, this is a perspective that any moral or thinking person might profitably consider.

With regard to the third interest governing maternal practices, the interest in producing a child acceptable to the next generation, worthiness is quite problematic. Families and societies have an interest in reproducing their members in a manner and with a result they can appreciate. Women, themselves half of family and society, share that interest. Yet they act in a society in which they are relatively powerless in respect to men and governor-experts of both sexes. Powerlessness is exacerbated by the matriphobia I earlier described, by self-contempt, and by numerous demoralizing, frightening physical and psychological violences perpetrated against all women. In response to maternal powerlessness, to a society whose values it cannot determine, maternal thought has opted for inauthenticity and the "good" of others.

By "inauthenticity" I designate a double willingness—first a willingness to *travailler pour l'armée*,[38] to accept the uses to which others will put one's children; second a willingness to remain blind to the implications of those uses for the actual lives of woman and children. Maternal thought embodies inauthenticity by taking on the values of the dominant culture. Like the "holding" of preservation, "inauthenticity" is a mostly nonconscious response to Being as Such. Only this attitude is not a caretaker's response to the natural exigencies of childtending, but a subordinate's reaction to a social reality essentially characterized by the domination and subordination of persons. Inauthenticity constructs and then assumes a world in which one's own values don't count. It is allied to fatalism and to some religious thought, some version of Christianity, for example. As inauthenticity is lived out in maternal practice, it gives rise to the values of obedience and "being good"; that is, it is taken as an achievement to fulfill the values of the dominant culture. Obedience is related to humility in the face of the limits of one's powers. But unlike humility, which respects indifferent nature, the incomprehensible supernature, and human fallibility, obedience respects the actual control and preferences of dominant people.

Individual mothers, living out maternal thought, take on the values of the families and subcultures to which they belong and of the men with whom they are allied. Because some groups and many men are vibrantly moral, these values are not necessarily inadequate. However, even moral groups and men almost always accept the relative subordination of women, whatever other ideals of equality and autonomy they may hold. A "good" mother may well be praised for colluding herself and her own subordination with the destructive consequences to herself and her children that I've described. Moreover, most groups and men impose at least some values that are psychologically and physically damaging to children. A mother practiced in fostering growth will be able to "see" the effects of, for example, injurious stratification, competitiveness, gender stereotyping, hypocrisy, and conscription to war. Damage to a child is as clear to her as the effect of a hurricane on a young tree. Yet to be "good," a mother may be expected to endorse and execute inimical commands. She is also the person principally responsible for training her children in the ways and desires of obedience. This may mean training her daughters for powerlessness, her sons for war, and both for crippling work in dehumanizing factories, businesses, and professions. It may mean training both daughters and sons for defensive or arrogant power over others in sexual, economic, or political life. A mother who trains either for powerlessness or abusive power over others betrays the very life she has preserved, whose growth she has fostered. She denies her children even the possibility of being both strong and good.

The strain of colluding in one's own powerlessness, coupled with the frequent and much greater strain of betraying the children one has tended, would be insupportable if conscious. A mother under strain may internalize as her own values those values which are clearly inimical to her children. She has, after all, usually been rewarded for just such protective albeit destructive internalization. Additionally, she may blind herself to the implications of her obedience, a blindness that is excused and exacerbated by the cheeriness of denial. For precariously but deeply protected mothers, feminist accounts of power relations and their cost call into question the worthiness of maternal work and the genuiness of maternal love. Such women, understandably, fight insight as others fight bodily assault, revealing in their struggles a commitment to their own sufferings which may look "neurotic" but is in fact, given their options, realistic.

When I described maternal thought arising out of the interests in growth and preservation, I was not speaking of the actual achievement of mothers, but of a conception of achievement. Similarly, in describing the thought arising out of the interest in acceptability, I am not speaking of actual mothers' adherence to dominant values, but of a conception of their relation to those values in which obedience and "being good" is considered an achievement. There are many individual mothers who "fail," that is who insist on their own values, who will not remain blind to the implications of dominant values for the lives of their children. Moreover, I hope I have said enough about the damaging effects of the prevailing sexual arrangements and social hierarchies on maternal lives to make it clear that I do not blame mothers for their (our) obedience. Obedience is largely a function of social powerlessness. Maternal work is done according to the Law of the Symbolic Father and under His Watchful Eye, as well as, typically, according to the desires, even whims, of the father's house. "This is my Father's world / Oh let me ne'er forget / that though the wrong be oft so strong, / He is the ruler yet." In these conditions of work, inauthentic obedience to dominant patriarchal values is as plausible a maternal response as respect for the results of experiment is in scientific work.

On the other hand, interest in producing an acceptable child provides special opportunities for mothers to explore, create, and insist upon their own values, to train their children for strength and moral sensitivity. For this opportunity to be realized, either collectively or by individual mothers, maternal thought will have to be transformed by feminist consciousness.

> Coming to have a feminist consciousness is the experience of coming to know the truth about oneself and one's society. . . . The very *meaning* of what the feminist apprehends is illuminated by the light of what ought to be. . . . The feminist apprehends certain features of social reality *as* intolerable, as to be rejected in behalf of a transforming project for the future. . . . Social reality is revealed as deceptive. . . . What is really happening is quite different from what appears to be happening.[39]

Feminist consciousness will first transform inauthentic obedience into wariness, uncertain reflection, at times anguished confusion. The feminist becomes "marked by the experience of moral ambiguity" as she learns new ways of living without betraying her woman's past, without denying her obligations to others. "She no longer knows what sort of person she ought to be, and therefore she does not know what she ought to do. One moral paradigm is called into question by the laborious and often obscure emergence of another."[40]

Out of confusion, new voices will arise, voices recognized not so much by the content of the truths they enunciate as by the honesty and courage of enunciation. They will be at once familiar and original, these voices arising out of maternal practice, affirming its own criteria of acceptability, insisting that the dominant values are unacceptable and need not be accepted.

> How *does* the male child differentiate himself from his mother, and does this mean inevitably that he must "join the army," that is, internalize patriarchal values? Can the mother, in patriarchy, represent culture, and if so, what does this require of her? . . . What do we want for our sons? . . . We want them to remain in the deepest sense, sons of the mother, yet also to grow into themselves, to discover new ways of being men as we are discovering new ways of being women.
>
> What do we mean by the nurture of daughters? The most notable fact that the culture imprints on women is the sense of our limits. The most important thing one woman can do for another is to illuminate and expand her sense of actual possibilities. . . . The quality of the mother's life—however embattled and unprotected—is her primary bequest to her daughter.[41]

I have been arguing that maternal thought as it is governed by the interest in acceptability is clear and distinct enough to be expressed, but is not yet worthy of respect. The interest in acceptability will always shape maternal practices and provoke mothers to affirm and announce *some* values, their own or others.[42] The production of a child worthy of appreciation is a *real* demand which a mother would impose on herself even if it were not demanded of her by her community. The only question is whether that demand is met by acquiescence or the struggles of a conscience attending clearly to the good of children. When mothers insist upon the inclusion of their values and experiences in the public world which children enter, when they determine what makes their children acceptable, the work of growth and preservation will acquire a new gaiety and joyfulness.

Finally, I would like to discuss a capacity—attention—and a virtue—love—which are central to the conception of achievement that maternal thought as a whole articulates. This capacity and virtue, when realized, invigorate preservation and enable growth. Attention and love again and again undermine a mother's inauthentic obedience as she perceives and endorses a child's experience though society finds it intolerable. The identification of the capacity of attention and the virtue of love is at once the foundation and the corrective of maternal thought.

The notion of "attention" is central to the philosophy of Simone Weil and is developed, along with the related notion of "love" by Iris Murdoch, who was profoundly influenced by Weil. Attention and love are fundamental to the construction of "objective reality" understood "in relation to the progressing life of a person," a "reality which is revealed to the patient eye of love."[43] Attention is an *intellectual* capacity connected even by definition with love, a special kind of "knowledge of the individual."[44] "The name of this intense, pure, disinterested, gratuitous, generous attention is love."[45] Weil thinks that the capacity for attention is a "miracle," Murdoch ties it more closely to familiar achievement. "The task of attention goes on all the time and at apparently empty and everyday moments we are 'looking,' making those little peering efforts of imagination which have such important cumulative results."[46]

For both Weil and Murdoch, the enemy of attention is what they call "fantasy," defined not as rich imaginative play, which does have a central role in maternal thinking, but as the "proliferation of blinding self-centered aims and images."[47] Fantasy, according to their original conception, is intellectual and imaginative activity in the service of consolation, domination, anxiety, and aggrandizement. It is reverie designed to protect the psyche from pain, self-induced blindness designed to protect it from insight. Fantasy, so defined, works in the service of inauthenticity. "The difficulty is to keep the attention fixed on the real situation"[48]—or, as I would say, on the real children. Attention to real children, children seen by the "patient eye of love," "teaches us how real things [real children] can be looked at and loved without being seized and used, without being appropriated into the greedy organism of the self."[49]

Much in maternal practices work against attention love: intensity of identification, vicarious living through a child, daily wear of maternal work, harassment and indignities of an indifferent social order, the clamor of children themselves. Although attention is elicited by the very reality it reveals—the reality of a growing person—it is a discipline that requires effort and self-training. Love, the love of children at any rate, is not only the most intense of attachments; it is also a detachment, a giving up, a letting grow. To love a child without seizing or using it, to see *the child's* reality with the patient, loving eye of attention—such loving and attending might well describe the separation of mother and child from the mother's point of view. Of course, many of us who are mothers fail much of the time in attentive love and loving attention. Many mothers also train themselves in the looking, self-restraining, and empathy that is loving attention. They can be heard doing so in any playground or coffee klatch.

I am not saying that mothers, individually or collectively, are (or are not) especially wonderful people. My point is that out of maternal practices distinctive ways of conceptualizing, ordering, and valuing arise. We *think* differently about what it *means* and what it takes to be "wonderful," to be a person, to be real.

Murdoch and Weil, neither mothers themselves nor especially concerned with mothers, are clear about the absolute value of attentive love and the reality it reveals. Weil writes:

> In the first legend of the Grail, it is said that the Grail . . . belongs to the first comer who asks the guardian of the vessel, a king three quarters paralyzed by the most painful wound, "What are you going through?"
>
> The love of our neighbor in all its fullness simply means being able to say to him: "What are you going through?" . . . Only he who is capable of attention can do this.[50]

I do not claim absolute value but only that attention love, the training to ask, "What are you going through?" is central to maternal practices. If I am right about its place in maternal thought, and if Weil and Murdoch are right about its absolute value, the self-conscious inclusion of maternal thought in the dominant culture will be of general intellectual and moral benefit.

I have described a "thought" arising out of maternal practices organized by the interests or preservation, growth, and acceptability. Although in some respects the thought is "contradictory," that is, it betrays its own values and must be transformed by feminist consciousness, the thought as a whole, with its fulcrum and correction in attentive love, is worthy of being expressed and respected. This thought has emerged out of maternal practices that are oppressive to women and children. I believe that it has emerged largely in response to the relatively invariable requirements of children and despite oppressive circumstances. As in all women's thought, some worthy aspects of maternal thought may arise out of identification with the powerless and excluded. However, oppression is largely responsible for the defects rather than the strengths of maternal thought, as in the obedient goodness to which mothers find themselves "naturally" subscribing. When the oppressiveness of gender arrangements is combined with race, poverty, or the multiple injuries of class, it is a miracle that maternal thought can arise at all. On the other hand, that it does indeed arise, miraculously, is clear both from literature (Alice Walker, Tillie Olsen, Maya Angelou, Agnes Smedley, Lucille Clifton, Louisa May Alcott, Audre Lorde, Marilyn French, Grace Paley, countless others) and from daily experience. Maternal thought *identifies* priorities, attitudes, and virtues, *conceives* of achievement. The more oppressive the institutions of motherhood, the greater the pain and struggle in living out the worthy and transforming the damaging aspects of thought.

It is now widely argued that the most liberating change we can make in institutions of motherhood is to include men equally in every aspect of maternal care. I am heartened to read that "societies that do not elaborate the opposition of male and female and place positive value on the conjugal relationship and involvement of both men and women in the home seem to be most egalitarian in terms of sex role."[51] To prevent or excuse men from maternal practice is to encourage them to separate public action from private affection. Moreover, men's domination is present when their absence from the nursery is combined with their domination of every other room. To familiarize children with "natural" domination at their earliest age in a context of primitive love, assertion, and sexual passion is to prepare them to find equally "natural" and exhaustive the division between exploiter and exploited which pervades the world. Although daughter and son alike may internalize "natural" domination, neither, typically, can live with it easily. Identifying with and imitating exploiters, we are overcome with self-hate; aligning ourselves with the exploited, we are fearful and manipulative. Again and again family power dramas are repeated in psychic, interpersonal and professional dramas, while they are institutionalized in economic, political, and international life. Radically recasting the power-gender roles in those dramas just might revolutionize social conscience.[52]

Assimilating men into child care both inside and outside the home would also be conducive to serious social reform. Responsible, equal child-caring would require men to relinquish power and their own favorable position in the division between intellectual/professional and service labor as that division expresses itself domestically. Loss of preferred status at home might make socially privileged men more suspicious of unnecessary divisions of labor and damaging hierarchies in the public world. Moreover, if men were emotionally and practically committed to child care, they would reform the work world in parents' interests. Once no one "else" was minding the child, there would be good day-care centers with flexible hours, day-care centers to which parents could trust their children from infancy on. These day-care centers, like the work week itself, would be managed "flexibly," in response to human needs as well as "productivity," with an eye to growth, rather than measurable "profit." Such moral reforms of economic life would probably begin with professionals and managers servicing themselves. However, even in nonsocialist countries, their benefits could be unpredictably extensive.

I would not argue, however, that the assimilation of men into child care is the primary social goal for mothers to set themselves. Rather, we must work to bring a *transformed* maternal thought into the public realm, to make the preservation and growth of *all* children a work of public conscience and legislation. This will not be easy. Mothers are no less corrupted than anyone else by concerns of status and class. Often our misguided efforts on behalf of the success and purity of our children frighten them and everyone else around them. As we increase and enjoy our public effectiveness, we will have less reason to live vicariously through our children. We may then begin to learn to sustain a creative tension between our inevitable and fierce desire to foster our own children and the less compulsive desire that all children grow and flourish.

Nonetheless, it would be foolish to believe that mothers, just because they are mothers, can transcend class interest and implement principles of justice. All feminists must join in articulating a theory of justice shaped by and incorporating maternal thinking. Moreover, the generalization of attentive love to *all* children requires politics. The most enlightened thought is not enough.

Closer to home again, we must refashion our domestic life in the hope that the personal will in fact betoken the political. We must begin by resisting the temptation to construe "home" simple-mindedly, as a matter of justice between mothers and fathers. Single parents, lesbian mothers, and coparenting women remind us that there are many ways to provide children with examples of caring, which do not incorporate sexual inequalities of power and privilege. Those of us who do live with the fathers of our children will eagerly welcome shared parenthood—for overwhelming practical as well as ideological reasons. But in our eagerness, we mustn't forget that so long as a mother is not effective publicly and self-respecting privately, male presence can be harmful as well as beneficial. It does a woman no good to have the power of the Symbolic Father brought right into the nursery, often despite the deep, affectionate egalitarianism of an individual man. It takes a strong mother and father to resist the temptations to domination and subordination for which they have been trained and are socially rewarded. And whatever the hard-won equality and mutual respect an individual couple may achieve, so long as a mother—even if she is no more parent than father—is derogated and subordinate outside the home, children will feel angry, confused, and "wildly unmothered."[53]

Despite these reservations, I look forward to the day when men are willing and able to share equally and actively in transformed maternal practices. When that day comes, will we still identify some thought as maternal rather than merely parental? Might we echo the cry of some feminists—there shall be no more "women"—with our own—there shall be no more "mothers," only people engaging in child care. To keep matters clear I would put the point differently. On that day, there will be no more "fathers," no more people of either sex who have power over their children's lives and moral authority in their children's world, though they do not do the work of attentive love. There will be mothers of both sexes who live out a transformed maternal thought in communities that shape parental care—practically, emotionally, economically, and socially. Such communities will have learned from their mothers how to value children's lives.

NOTES

I began circulating an early draft of this paper in the fall of 1978. Since then, the constructive criticism and warm response of readers has led me to believe that this draft is truly a collective endeavor. I would like especially to thank Sandra Bartky, Gail Bragg, Bell Chevigny, Nancy Chodorow, Margaret Comstock, Mary Felstiner, Berenice Fisher, Marilyn Frye, Susan Harding, Evelyn Fox Keller, Jane Lilienfeld, Jane Marcus, Adrienne Rich, Amelie Rorty, William Ruddick, Barrie Thorne, Marilyn Blatt Young, readers for *Feminist Studies*, and Rayna Rapp.

1. From J. Echergray, "Severed Heart," quoted by Jessie Bernard, in *The Future of Motherhood* (New York: Dial, 1974), p. 4.
2. Ruth Mack Brunswick, "The Preoedipal Phase of Libido Development," quoted by Nancy Chodorow, in *The Reproduction of Mothering* (Berkeley: University of California Press, 1978), p. 196, footnote.
3. Adrienne Rich, *Of Woman Born* (New York: Norton, 1976), p. 11. My debt to this book is profound and pervasive.
4. For an extensive discussion of the power of mothers, see Dorothy Dinnerstein, *The Mermaid and the Minotaur: Sexual Arrangements and Human Malaise* (New York: Harper & Row, 1976). In expressing our fears of maternal power Dinnerstein sometimes, unfortunately and unwittingly, gives voices to the very matriphobia she decries.
5. In traditional heterosexual parenting, a returning father may distract even the nursing mother from her child, demanding attention and service which is frequently more alienating, more threatening to a mother's *self*-possession than children's demands. To the extent that the infant is sensitive to the gender of the mother, as Dinnerstein and others claim, to that extent it would be dimly aware of the gender-linked character of the interruption. In any case, the child will soon become aware that females are caretakers whose work and caring is endlessly interruptible.

   On the politics of interruption, see Michelle Cliff, "The Resonance of Interruption," *Chrysalis*, no. 8 (Summer 1979); Pamela Fishman, "Interaction: The Work Women Do," *Social Problems* 25, no. 4 (April 1978); and Don Zimmerman and Candace West, "Sex Roles, Interruptions and Silences in Conversations," in *Language and Sex: Difference and Dominance*, ed. Barrie Thorne and Nancy Henley (Rowley, Mass.: Newbury House, 1975).

   Many fathers are of course, socially unappreciated. Poor, declassed, or "failing" fathers know the pain of introducing their children to a world in which they do not figure. Sometimes their powerlessness is visited directly upon the mothers. Even when it is not, mothers suffer a double powerlessness when the "fathers" of her kind and cultural group are degraded by the Laws of the Ruling Fathers; the "world of the fathers" belongs neither to her sons nor to the men her daughters will live among.
6. I am indebted to Susan Harding for this point (personal conversation and lecture notes from the Residential College, University of Michigan).
7. For an analysis of the evil of factory work which emphasizes workers' loss of control of their time, see Simone Weil, "Factory Work," in *Simone Weil Reader*, ed. George A. Panichas (New York: McKay, 1977). For a similar comparison of mothers' control over time compared with that of other workers, see Barbara Garson, "Clerical," in *All the Livelong Day* (New York: Penguin Books, 1975). Of course, many mothers also work in factories, stores, and fields; and some mothers work in managerial, professional, and executive positions. The issue is whether mothers have more control over time and order of their work (in the Weil sense) in their maternal than in their other working hours. Mothers do not have control over their *lives*, and this relative absence of self-determination has consequences which I will specify.
8. Carol Pearson, "Women's Fantasies and Feminist Utopias," makes the general point that in several feminist utopias, "human kinship procedures can govern an entire society because the peo-

ple in the society are mothers." See *Frontiers* 2, no. 3 (Fall 1977). Pearson quotes extensively from *Herland* by Charlotte Perkins Gilman. "You see we are *mothers*" is taken from *Herland* (New York: Pantheon, 1979). For a clear discussion of the significance of matriarchy, see Paula Webster, "Matriarchy: A Vision of Power," in *Toward an Anthropology of Women*, ed. Rayna R. Reiter (New York and London: Monthly Review Press, 1975), pp. 141–56.

9. Lucille Clifton, "My Mama Moved Among the Days," in *Good Times* (New York, Random House, 1969), p. 2.
10. Among other possible aspects of women's thought are those that might arise from our sexual lives, from our "homemaking," from the special conflict women feel between allegiance on the one hand to women and their world, and on the other hand, to all people of their kin and culture. Any identifiable aspect of women's thought will be interrelated to all of the others. Because women almost everywhere are relatively powerless in relation to men of their class, all aspects of women's thought will be affected by powerlessness. Whether we are discussing the thought arising from women's bodily, sexual, maternal, homemaking, linguistic, or any other experience, we are faced with a confluence of powerlessness and the "womanly" whatever that might be.
11. The pervasive and false identification of womanhood and biological or adoptive motherhood injures both mothers and nonmothers. The identification obscures the many kinds of mothering performed by those who do not parent particular children in families. It frequently forces those labeled "nonmothers" to take a distance from their own mothers and the maternal lives of all women. Out of justified fear and resentment of the obligation to mother, these "nonmothers" may become caught up in socially induced but politically myopic efforts to divorce female identity from any connection with maternal practices. Meanwhile, mothers engage in parallel self-destructive efforts, which further divide women from each other. In their fight to preserve their nonmaternal aspirations and projects, mothers may belittle the importance of maternal experience in their lives. Or out of fear of their own anger at a limiting social identity as well as out of legitimate fury at the devaluation of mothers and motherliness, they may overidentify with the maternal identification foisted upon them, letting their nonmaternal working and loving selves die. Whichever we mothers do, and frequently we do both, the cost to our maternal and nonmaternal works and loves is enormous.
12. For the most complete and sensitive account of girls' special relation to mothers' mothering, see Chodorow, *The Reproduction of Mothering.* See also Jane Flax, "The Conflict Between Nurturance and Autonomy in Mother-Daughter Relationships and Within Feminism," *Feminist Studies* 4, no. 2 (June 1978): 171–89.
13. See Nancy Chodorow, "Feminism and Difference: Gender, Relation and Difference in Psychoanalytic Perspective," *Socialist Review*, no. 46 (July–August 1979). "We cannot know what children would make of their bodies in a nongender or nonsexually organized social world. . . . It is not obvious that there would be major significance to biological sex differences, to gender difference or to different sexualities" (p. 66).
14. Examples of the invariant and *nearly* unchangeable include: long gestation inside the mother's body; prolonged infant and childhood dependence; physical fragility of infancy; radical qualitative and quantitative change ("growth") in emotional and intellectual capacities from infancy to adulthood; long development and psychological complexity of human sexual desire, of memory and other cognitive capacities, and of "object relations." Features which are *nearly* universal and certainly changeable include: the identification of childbearing and child-caring, the consequent delegation of child care to natural mothers and other women, the relative subordination of women in any social class to men of that class.

15. To see the universal in particulars, to assimilate differences and extend kinship, is a legacy of the ecumenical Protestantism in which I was raised. I am well aware that even nonviolent, well-meaning Protestant assimilations can be obtuse and cruel for others. Therefore I am dependent on others, morally as well as intellectually, for the statement of differences, the assessment of their effects on every aspect of maternal lives, and finally for radical correction as well as for expansion of any general theory I would offer. However, I do not *believe* that the thinking I describe is limited only to "privileged white women," as one reader put it. I first came to the notion of "maternal thinking" and the virtues of maternal practices through personal exchange with Tillie Olsen and then through reading her fiction. My debt to her is pervasive. Similarly, I believe that "Man Child: A Black Lesbian Feminist's Response" by Audre Lorde, *Conditions*, no. 4 (Winter 1979): 30–36, is an excellent example of what I call "maternal thinking transformed by feminist consciousness." My "assimilation" of Olsen's and Lorde's work in no way denies the differences which separate us nor the biases that those differences may introduce into my account. These are only two of many examples of writers in quite different social circumstances who express what I take to be "maternal thinking."
16. Nothing I say about maternal thought suggests that the women who engage in it cannot engage in other types of intellectual discourse. A maternal thinker may also be an experimental psychologist, a poet, a mathematician, an architect, a physicist. I believe that because most thinkers have been men, most disciplines are partly shaped by "male" concepts, values, styles, and strategies. However, unless we have identified "male" and "female" aspects of thought, the claim of gender bias is an empty one. I do not doubt that disciplines are also shaped by transgender interests, values, and concepts, which women, whether or not they engage in maternal practices, may fully share. To the extent that the disciplines are shaped by "male" thought, mothers and other women may feel alienated by the practices and thinking of their own discipline. Correlatively, when thinkers are as apt to be women as men, thought itself may change.
17. I derive the vocabulary most specifically from Jurgen Habermas, *Knowledge and Human Interests* (Boston: Beacon Press, 1971). However, I have been equally influenced by other philosophical relativists, most notably by Peter Winch, Ludwig Wittgenstein, and Suzanne Kessler and Wendy McKenna. See, Winch, "Understanding a Primitive Society" and other papers, in *Ethics and Action* (London: Routledge & Kegan Paul, 1972); Wittgenstein, *Philosophical Investigations, Remarks on the Foundations of Mathematics, Zettel,* and *On Certainty* (Oxford: Blackwell, 1953, 1956, 1967, 1969); Kessler and McKenna, *Gender* (New York: Wiley, 1978). I am also indebted to the writings of Evelyn Keller, especially "Feminist Critique of Science: A Forward or Backward Move," "He, She and Id in Scientific Discourse" (unpublished manuscripts), and "Gender and Science," *Psychoanalysis and Contemporary Thought* 1, no. 3 (1978).
18. See Habermas, *Knowledge and Human Interests* for the view that scientific knowledge is organized by its interests in control.
19. The words are Mrs. Ramsay's in Virginia Woolf's *To the Lighthouse* (New York: Harcourt Brace & World, 1927), p. 92.
20. Adrienne Rich, "Conditions for Work: The Common World of Women," in *Lies, Secrets, and Silence* (NY: Norton, 1979, p. 205); first printed in *Working It Out.* Italics mine.
21. For the comparison, see Iris Murdoch, *The Sovereignty of Good* (New York: Schocken, 1971). Popular moralities as well as contemporary moral theory tend to emphasize decision, assertion, happiness, authenticity, and justification by principle.
22. Murdoch, *Sovereignty of Good,* p. 99.
23. Ibid., p. 95.

24. Spinoza, *Ethics*, Book 3, Proposition 42, demonstration. See also Proposition 40, Note and Proposition 45, both in Book 3.
25. For an example of the first, see Virginia Woolf's *Mrs. Dalloway* (New York: Harcourt, Brace & World, 1925), in which Lady Bexborough opens a bazaar holding the telegram announcing her son's death. Her action is simultaneously admirable, repellent, and politically disturbing, as I hope to show in the section on acceptability.
26. Bernard Williams, *Morality* (New York: Harper Torchbooks, 1972), p. 11.
27. The words are a Texas farmwoman's who quilted as she huddled with her family in a shelter as, above them, a tornado destroyed their home. The story was told to me by Miriam Schapiro.
28. Murdoch, *Sovereignty of Good*, p. 26.
29. These are differences often attributed to women both by themselves and by psychologists. For a critical review of the literature see Eleanor Maccoby and Carol Jacklin, *The Psychology of Sex Differences* (Stanford, Calif.: Stanford University Press, 1974). For a plausible account of women's valuing of inner life, see Patricia Meyer Spacks, *The Female Imagination* (New York: Knopf, 1975). Maccoby and Jacklin are critical both of the findings I mentioned and of adequacy of the psychological experiments they survey for testing or discovering these kinds of differences. I make little use of psychology, more of literature, in thinking about the kinds of cognitive sex differences I discuss. Psychologists are not, so far as I know, talking about women who have emphatically identified with and assimilated maternal practices, either by engaging in them or by identifying with their own or other mothers. It would be hard to identify such a subgroup of women without circularity. But even if one could make the identification, tests would have to be devised that did not measure achievement, but conception of achievement. Mothers, to take one example, may well prize the inner life, but have so little time for it to be so self-protectively defended against their own insights (as I will discuss shortly) that they gradually lose the capacity for inner life. Or again, a mother may not maintain sharp boundaries between herself and her child or between her child's "outer" action and inner life. However, she *must* maintain some boundaries. We value what we are in danger of losing (e.g., inner life); we identify virtues because we recognize temptations to vice (e.g., openness because we are tempted to rigid control); we refuse what we fear giving way to (e.g., either pathological symbiotic identification *or* an unworkable division between our own and our children's interests). It is difficult to imagine tests sophisticated and sensitive enough to measure such conceptions, priorities, and values. I have found psychoanalytic theory the most useful of psychologies and Chodorow's *The Reproduction of Mothering* the most helpful in applying psychoanalytic theory to maternal practices.
30. One reader has suggested that my account of a mother attuned to her own child's thoughts and fantasies is biased by my white, middle-class experience. By appreciation of a person's continuous mental life, I do not mean only the leisurely (and frequently intrusive) hovering over the child's psyche, hovering which is often the product of powerlessness and enforced idleness. The appreciation I think of is often a kind of pained groping for the meanings that a child is giving to its own experiences, including to its own sufferings. I believe I have heard these gropings both firsthand and in literary reflections of mothers who are not white and/or middle class. For two of many examples see Tillie Olsen's "I Stand Here Ironing" from *Tell Me a Riddle* (New York: Delacorte Press, 1956) and Audre Lorde's "Man Child." If my interpretation of others' experiences is wrong, other women with different lives will correct me. Expressing maternal thinking is necessarily a collective project.
31. Simone Weil, "Gravity and Grace," in *Gravity and Grace* (London: Routledge & Kegan Paul, 1952, p. 1; first French edition, 1947), passim.

32. Weil, "Gravity and Grace," and other essays in *Gravity and Grace.* Both the language and concepts are indebted to Plato.
33. Bernard's words in the summing up of Virginia Woolf's *The Waves* (New York: Harcourt, Brace & World, 1931), p. 294.
34. Jean Baker Miller, *Toward a New Psychology of Women* (Boston: Beacon Press, 1973), p. 54.
35. As Habermas argues in *Knowledge and Human Interest.*
36. Miller, *Toward a New Psychology of Women,* p. 56. This vast experience is unrecognized partly because psychologists assume that while mothers are responsible for preservation, fathers are responsible for growth. This view of psychologists "denies the possibility of a maternal nurturance which actually encourages autonomy. But what is nurturance if not the pleasure in the other's growth? if not the desire to satisfy the other's needs whether it be the need to cling or the need to be independent?" Jessica Benjamin, "Authority and the Family Revisited: or, A World Without Fathers?" *New German Critique,* no. 13 (Winter 1978): 35–57.
37. Miller, *Toward a New Psychology of Women,* p. 40.
38. I am indebted to Rich, *Of Woman Born,* especially chap. 8, both for this phrase and for the working out of the idea of inauthenticity.
39. Sandra Lee Bartky, "Toward a Phenomonology of Feminist Consciousness," in *Feminism and Philosophy,* ed. Mary Vetterling-Braggin, Frederick A. Elliston, and Jane English (Totowa, N.J.: Littlefield Adams, 1977), pp. 22–34, 33, 25, 28–29.
40. Bartky, "Phenomenology of Feminist Consciousness," p. 31. On the riskiness of authenticity and the courage it requires of women see also Miller, *Toward a New Psychology of Women,* chap. 9.
41. Rich, *Of Woman Born,* pp. 198, 211, 246, 247.
42. For a discussion of the relative weight of parents' and children's values in determining children's lives, see William Ruddick, "Parents and Life Prospects," in *Having Children,* ed. Onora O'Neill and William Ruddick (New York: Oxford University Press, 1979).
43. Murdoch, *Sovereignty of Good,* p. 40.
44. Ibid., p. 28.
45. Simone Weil, "Human Personality," in *Collected Essays,* chosen and translated by Richard Rees (London: Oxford University Press, 1962). Also, *Simone Weil Reader,* p. 333.
46. Murdoch, *Sovereignty of Good,* p. 43.
47. Ibid., p. 67.
48. Ibid., p. 91.
49. Ibid., p. 65.
50. Simone Weil, "Reflections of the Right Use of School Studies With a View to the Love of God," in *Waiting for God* (New York: G. P. Putnam's Sons, 1951), p. 115.
51. Michelle Zimbalist Rosaldo, "Woman, Culture and Society: A Theoretical Overview," in *Woman, Culture and Society,* ed. Michelle Zimablist Rosaldo and Louise Lamphere (Stanford: Stanford University Press, 1974).
52. Rich, *Of Woman Born*; Dinnerstein, *Mermaid and Minotaur,* passim.
53. Rich, *Of Woman Born,* p. 225.

Trust and Antitrust

"We inhabit a climate of trust," Baier remarks, "as we inhabit an atmosphere and notice it as we notice air, only when it becomes scarce or polluted." Without trust, people cannot flourish. Yet moral philosophers have paid surprisingly little attention to this topic. Baier explicates trust and argues that trust is a core feature of moral relations.

People entrust things to others because they need help in creating or caring for a wide range of things that they value. But trust is not the same as mere dependency or reliance on others. To trust is to let someone take care of something one values where taking care of involves discretionary powers. Thus, trust entails accepting vulnerability to another's possible, but not expected, ill will or incompetence. How, Baier asks, might trust get started? She rejects the view that explicit mutual agreements provide the foundation of trust. Instead, she urges that infants are innately disposed to believe in the good will of the adults on whom they must depend for their very survival, and that, as children grow up, they discover that their parents love them and regard harm to their offspring as harm to themselves. Thus, trust is initiated and sustained. Although many philosophers have overlooked its importance, trust is indispensable. Economic and social relations modeled on contracts presuppose domestic relations secured by trust. Moreover, voluntary agreements cannot substitute for trust, for contractual terms exhaust neither people's moral responsibilities to one another nor their expectations of one another. Still, trust can be misplaced, and it is necessary to ask when trust is morally warranted. Baier offers an "expressibility test" for the moral decency of trust relationships. If knowledge of what the other party is relying on to maintain trust—e.g., threats against the trusted person or concealment of breaches from the trusting person—would tend to undermine trust, the trust is corrupt. Baier concludes by cautioning against overuse of this test. Since trust is easily undermined and difficult to restore, it is best not to question it unless there is reason for distrust.

—D.T.M.

Chapter 31

Annette Baier

Trust and Antitrust

TRUST AND ITS VARIETIES

> Whatever matters to human beings, trust is the atmosphere in which it thrives.
>
> —Sissela Bok[1]

Whether everything that matters to us is the sort of thing that can thrive or languish (I may care most about my stamp collection) or even whether all the possibly thriving things we care about need trust in order to thrive (does my rubber tree?), there surely is something basically right about Bok's claim. Given that I cannot myself guard my stamp collection at all times nor take my rubber tree with me on my travels, the custody of these things that matter to me must often be transferred to others, presumably to others I trust. Without trust, what matters to me would be unsafe, unless like the Stoic I attach myself only to what can thrive, or be safe from harm, *however* others act. The starry heavens above and the moral law within had better be about the only things that matter to me, if there is no one I can trust in any way. Even my own Stoic virtue will surely thrive better if it evokes some trust from others, inspires some trustworthiness in them, or is approved and imitated by them.

To Bok's statement, however, we should add another, that not all the things that thrive when there is trust between people, and which matter, are things that should be encouraged to thrive. Exploitation and conspiracy, as much as justice and fellowship, thrive better in an atmosphere of trust. There are immoral as well as moral trust relationships, and trust-busting can be a morally proper goal. If we are to tell when morality requires the preservation of trust, when it requires the destruction of trust, we obviously need to distinguish different forms of trust, and to look for some morally relevant features they may possess. In this paper I make a start on this large task.

It is a start, not a continuation, because there has been a strange silence on the topic in the tradition of moral philosophy with which I am familiar. Psychologists and sociologists have discussed it, lawyers have worked out the requirements of equity on legal trusts, political philosophers have discussed trust in governments, and there has been some discussion of trust when philosophers address the assurance problem in Prisoner's Dilemma contexts. But we, or at least I, search in vain for any general account of the morality of trust relationships. The question, Whom should I trust in what way, and why? has not been the central question in moral philosophy as we know it. Yet if I am right in claiming that morality, as anything more than a law within, itself requires trust in order to thrive, and that immorality too thrives on some forms of trust, it seems pretty obvious that we ought, as moral philosophers, to look into the question of what forms of trust are needed for the thriving of the version of morality we endorse, and into the morality of that and other forms of trust. A minimal condition of adequacy for any version of the true morality, if truth has anything to do with reality, is that it not have to condemn the conditions needed for its own thriving. Yet we will be in no position to apply that test to the trust in which morality thrives until we have worked out, at least in a provisional way, how to judge trust relationships from a moral point of view.

Moral philosophers have always been interested in cooperation between people, and so it is surprising that they have not said more than they have about trust. It seems fairly obvious that any form of cooperative activity, including the division of labor, requires the cooperators to trust one another to do their bit, or at the very least to trust the overseer with his whip to do his bit, where coercion is relied on. One would expect contractarians to investigate the forms of trust and distrust parties to a contract exhibit. Utilitarians too should be concerned with the contribution to the general happiness of various climates of trust, so be concerned to understand the nature, roots, and varieties of trust. One might also have expected those with a moral theory of the virtues to have looked at trustworthiness, or at willingness to give trust. But when we turn to the great moral philosophers, in our tradition, what we find can scarcely be said to be even a sketch of a moral theory of trust. At most we get a few hints of directions in which we might go.

Plato, in the *Republic*, presumably expects the majority of citizens to trust the philosopher kings to rule wisely and expects that elite to trust their underlings not to poison their wine nor set fire to their libraries, but neither proper trust nor proper trustworthiness are among the virtues he dwells on as necessary in the cooperating parties in his good society. His version of justice and of the "friendship" supposed to exist between ruler and ruled seems to *imply* such virtues of trust, but he does not himself draw out the implications. In the *Laws* he mentions distrust as an evil produced by association with seafaring traders, but it is only a mention.[2] The same sort of claim can also be made about Aristotle—his virtuous person, like Plato's, must place his trust in that hypothetical wise person who will teach him just how much anger and pride and fear to feel with what reasons, when, and toward which objects. Such a wise man presumably also knows just how much trust in whom, on what matters, and how much trustworthiness, should be cultivated, as well as who should show trust toward whom, but such crucial wisdom and such central virtues are not discussed by Aristotle, as far as I am aware. (He does, in the *Politics*, condemn tyrants for sowing seeds of distrust, and his discussion of friendship might be cited as one place where he implicitly recognized the importance of trust; could someone one distrusted be a second self to one? But that is implicit only, and in any case would cover only trust between friends.) Nor do later moral philosophers do much better on this count.[3]

There are some forms of trust to which the great philosophers *have* given explicit attention. Saint Thomas Aquinas, and other Christian moralists, have extolled the virtue of faith and, more relevantly, of hope, and so have said something about trust in God. And in the modern period some of the great moral and political philosophers, in particular John Locke, looked at trust in governments and officials, and some have shown what might be called an obsessive trust in contracts and contractors, even if not, after Hobbes's good example here, an equal obsession with the grounds for such trust. It is selective attention then, rather than total inattention, that is the philosophical phenomenon on which I wish to remark, tentatively to explain, and try to terminate or at least to interrupt.

Trust, the phenomenon we are so familiar with that we scarcely notice its presence and its variety, is shown by us and responded to by us not only with intimates but also with strangers and even with declared enemies. We trust our enemies not to fire at us when we lay down our arms and put out a white flag. In Britain burglars and police used to trust each other not to carry deadly weapons. We often trust total strangers, such as those from whom we ask directions in foreign cities, to direct rather than misdirect us, or to tell us so if they do not know what we want to know; and we think we should do the same for those who ask the same help from us. Of course we are often disappointed, rebuffed, let down, or betrayed when we exhibit such trust in others, and we are often exploited when we show the wanted trustworthiness. We do in fact, wisely or stupidly, virtuously or viciously, show trust in a great variety of forms, and manifest a great variety of versions of trustworthiness, both with intimates and with strangers. We trust those we encounter in lonely library stacks to be searching for books, not victims. We sometimes let ourselves fall asleep on trains or planes, trusting neighboring strangers not to take advantage of our defenselessness. We put our bodily safety into the hands of pilots, drivers, doctors, with scarcely any sense of recklessness. We used not to suspect that the food we buy might be deliberately poisoned, and we used to trust our children to day-care centers.

We may still have no choice but to buy food and to leave our children in day-care centers, but now we do it with suspicion and anxiety. Trust is always an invitation not only to confidence tricksters but also to terrorists, who discern its most easily destroyed and socially vital forms. Criminals, not moral philosophers, have been the experts at discerning different forms of trust. Most of us notice a given form of trust most easily after its sudden demise or severe injury. We inhabit a climate of trust as we inhabit an atmosphere and notice it as we notice air, only when it becomes scarce or polluted.

We may have no choice but to continue to rely on the local shop for food, even after some of the food on its shelves has been found to have been poisoned with intent. We can still rely where we no longer trust. What is the difference between trusting others and merely relying on them? It seems to be reliance on their good will toward one, as distinct from their dependable habits, or only on their dependably exhibited fear, anger, or other motives compatible with ill will toward one, or on motives not directed on one at all. We may rely on our fellows' fear of the newly appointed security guards in shops to deter them from injecting poison into the food on the shelves, once we have ceased to trust them. We may rely on the shopkeeper's concern for his profits to motivate him to take effective precautions against poisoners and also trust him to *want* his customers not to be harmed by his products, at least as long as this want can be satisfied without frustrating his wish to increase his profits. Trust is often mixed with other species of reliance on persons. Trust which is reliance on another's good will, perhaps minimal good will, contrasts with the forms of reliance on others' reactions and attitudes that are shown by the comedian, the advertiser, the blackmailer, the kidnapper-extortioner, and the terrorist, who all depend on particular attitudes and reactions of others for the success of their actions. We all depend on one another's psychology in countless ways, but this is not yet to trust them. The trusting can be betrayed, or at least let down, and not just disappointed. Kant's neighbors, who counted on his regular habits as a clock for their own less automatically regular ones, might be disappointed with him if he slept in one day, but not let down by him, let alone had their trust betrayed. When I trust another, I depend on her good will toward me. I need not either acknowledge this reliance nor believe that she has either invited or acknowledged such trust since there is such a thing as unconscious trust, as unwanted trust, as forced receipt of trust, and as trust that the trusted is unaware of. (Plausible conditions for proper trust will be that it survives consciousness, by both parties, and that the trusted has had some opportunity to signify acceptance or rejection toward the trusting if their trust is unacceptable.)

Where one depends on another's good will, one is necessarily vulnerable to the limits of that good will. One leaves others an opportunity to harm one when one trusts, and also shows one's confidence that they will not take it. Reasonable trust will require good grounds for such confidence in another's good will, or at least the absence of good grounds for expecting their ill will or indifference. Trust then, on this first approximation, is accepted vulnerability to another's possible but not expected ill will (or lack of good will) toward one.

What we now need to do, to get any sense of the variety of forms of trust, is to look both at varieties of vulnerability and at varieties of grounds for not expecting others to take advantage of it. One way to do the former, which I shall take, is to look at the variety of sorts of goods or things one values or cares about, which can be left or put within the striking power of others, and the variety of ways we can let or leave others "close" enough to what we value to be able to harm it. Then we can look at various reasons we might have for wanting or accepting such closeness of those with power to harm us, and for confidence that they will not use this power. In this way we can hope to explicate the vague terms "good will" and "ill will." If it be asked why the initial emphasis is put on trusting's vulnerability, on the risks rather than the benefits of trust, part of the answer has already been given—namely, that we come to realize what trust involves retrospectively and posthumously, once our vulnerability is brought home to us by actual wounds. The other part of the answer is that even when one does become aware of trust and intentionally continues a particular case of it, one need not intend to achieve any particular benefit from it—one need not trust a person in order to receive some gain, even when in fact one does gain. Trusting, as an intentional mental phenomenon, need not be purposive. But intentional trusting does require awareness of one's confidence that the trusted will not harm one, although they could harm one. It is not a Hobbesian obsession with strike force that dictates the form of analysis I have sketched but, rather, the natural order of consciousness and self-consciousness of trust, which progresses from initially un-self-conscious trust to awareness of risk along with confidence that it is a good risk, on to some realization of why we are taking this particular risk, and eventually to some evaluation of what we may generally gain and what we may lose from the willingness to take such risks. The ultimate point of what we are doing when we trust may be the last thing we come to realize.

The next thing to attend to is why we typically do leave things that we value close enough to others for them to harm them. The answer, simply, is that we need their help in creating, and then in not merely guarding but looking after the things we most value, so we have no choice but to allow some others to be in a position to harm them. The one in the best position to harm something is its creator or its nurse-cum-caretaker. Since the things we typically do value include such things as we cannot singlehandedly either create or sustain (our own life, health, reputation, our offspring and their well-being, as well as intrinsically shared goods such as conversation, its written equivalent, theater and other forms of play, chamber music, market exchange, political life, and so on), we must allow many other people to get into positions where they can, if they choose, injure what we care about, since those are the same positions that they must be in in order to help us take care of what we care about. The simple Socratic truth that no person is self-sufficient gets elaborated once we add the equally Socratic truth that the human soul's activity is *caring* for things into the richer truth that no one is able by herself to look after everything she wants to have looked after, nor even alone to look after her own "private" goods, such as health and bodily safety. If we try to distinguish different forms of trust by the different valued goods we confidently allow another to have some control over, we are following Locke in analyzing trusting on the model of *en*-trusting. Thus, there will be an answer not just to the question, Whom do you trust? but to the question, *What* do you trust to them?—what good is it that they are in a position to take from you, or to injure? Accepting such an analysis, taking trust to be a three-place predicate (A trusts B with valued thing C) will involve some distortion and regimentation of some cases, where we may have to strain to discern any definite candidate for C, but I think it will prove more of a help than a hindrance.

One way in which trusted persons can fail to act as they were trusted to is by taking on the care of more than they were entrusted with—the babysitter who decides that the nursery would be improved if painted purple and sets to work to transform it, will have acted, as a babysitter, in an untrustworthy way, however great his good will. We are trusted, we are relied upon, to realize *what* it is for whose care we have some discretionary responsibility, and normal people can pick up the cues that indicate the limits of what is entrusted. For example, if I confide my troubles to a friend, I trust her to listen, more or less sympathetically, and to preserve confidentiality, but usually not, or not without consulting me, to take steps to remove the source of my worry. That could be interfering impertinence, not trustworthiness as a confidante. She will, nevertheless, within the restricted scope of what is trusted to her (knowledge of my affairs, not their management) have some discretion both as to how to receive the confidence and, unless I swear her to absolute secrecy, as to when to share it. The relativization of trust to particular things cared about by the truster goes along with the discretion the trusted usually has in judging just what should be done to "look after" the particular good entrusted to her care. This discretionary power will of course be limited by the limits of what is entrusted and usually by some other constraints.

Is it plausible to construe all cases of being trusted not merely as cases of being trusted by someone with access to what matters to the truster, but also as some control over that, expected to be used to take care of it, and involving some discretionary powers in so doing?[4] Can we further elaborate the analysis of a relationship of trust as one where A has entrusted B with some of the care of C and where B has some discretionary powers in caring for C? Admittedly there are many cases of trust where "caring for C" seems much more than A expects of B even when there is no problem in finding a fairly restricted value for C. Suppose

I look quickly around me before proceeding into the dark street or library stacks where my business takes me, judge the few people I discern there to be nondangerous, and so go ahead. We can say that my bodily safety, and perhaps my pocketbook, are the goods I am allowing these people to be in a position to threaten. I trust them, it seems, merely to leave me alone. But this is not quite right, for should a piece of falling masonry or toppling books threaten to fall on my head, and one of these persons were to leap into action and shove me out of this danger, I would regard that as more rather than less than I had trusted these strangers to do—a case for gratitude, not for an assault charge, despite the sudden, unceremonious, possibly painful, or even injurious nature of my close encounter with my rescuer. So *what* do I trust strangers in such circumstances to do? Certainly not anything whatever as long as it is done with good will, nor even anything whatever for my bodily safety and security of property as long as it is done with good will. Suppose someone I have judged nondangerous as I proceed into the stacks should seize me from behind, frightening but not harming me, and claim with apparent sincerity that she did it for my own good, so that I would learn a lesson and be more cautious in the future. I would not respond with gratitude but demand what business my long-term security of life was of hers, that she felt free to subject me to such unpleasant educational measures. In terms of my analysis, what I trusted her with was my peace and safety here and now, with "looking after" that, not with my long-term safety. We need some fairly positive and discretion-allowing term, such as "look after" or "show concern for," to let in the range of behavior that would not disappoint the library user's trust in fellow users. We also need some specification of what good was in question to see why the intrusive, presumptuous, and paternalistic moves disappoint rather than meet the trust one has in such circumstances. "Look after" and "take care of" will have to be given a very weak sense in some cases of trust; it will be better to do this than to try to construe cases where more positive care is expected of the trusted as cases of trusting them to leave alone, or merely safeguard, some valued thing. Trusting strangers to leave us alone should be construed as trusting them with the "care" of our valued autonomy. When one trusts one's child to one's separated spouse, it is all aspects of the child's good as a developing person that are entrusted to the other parent's care. Trusting him or her with our children can hardly be construed as trusting them not to "interfere" with the child's satisfactory development. The most important things we entrust to others are things that take more than noninterference in order to thrive.

The more extensive the discretionary powers of the trusted, the less clear-cut will be the answer to the question of when trust is disappointed. The truster, who always needs good judgment to know whom to trust and how much discretion to give, will also have some scope for discretion in judging what should count as failing to meet trust, either through incompetence, negligence, or ill will. In any case of a questionable exercise of discretion, there will be room both for forgiveness of unfortunate outcomes and for tact in treatment of the question of whether there is anything to forgive. One thing that can destroy a trust relationship fairly quickly is the combination of a rigoristic unforgiving attitude on the part of the truster and a touchy sensitivity to any criticism on the part of the trusted. If a trust relationship is to continue, some tact and willingness to forgive on the part of the truster and some willingness on the part of the trusted both to be forgiven and to forgive unfair criticisms seem essential.[5] The need for this will be greater the more discretion the trusted has.

If part of what the truster entrusts to the trusted are discretionary powers, then the truster risks abuse of those and the successful disguise of such abuse. The special vulnerability that trust involves is vulnerability to not yet noticed harm, or to disguised ill will. What one forgives or tactfully averts one's eyes from may be not well-meant but ill-judged or incompetent attempts to care for what is entrusted but, rather, ill-meant and cleverly disguised abuses of discretionary power. To understand the moral risks of trust, it is important to see the special sort of vulnerability it introduces. Yet the discretionary element that introduces this special danger is essential to that which trust at its best makes possible. To elaborate Hume: " 'Tis impossible to separate the chance of good from the risk of ill."[6]

It is fairly easy, once we look, to see how this special vulnerability is involved in many ordinary forms of trust. We trust the mailman to deliver and not tamper with the mail, and to some extent we trust his discretion in interpreting what "tampering" covers. Normally we do not expect him to read our mail but to deliver it unread, even when the message is open, on a postcard. But on occasion it may be proper, or at least not wrong, for him to read it. I have had friendly mailmen (in Greek villages and in small Austrian towns) who tell me what my mail announces as they hand it over: "Your relatives have recovered and can travel now, and are soon arriving!" Such interest in one's affairs is not part of the normal idea of the role of mailman and could provide opportunity for blackmail, but in virtue of that very interest they could give much more knowledgeable and intelligent service—in the above case, by knowing our plans, they knew when and where we had moved and delivered to the new address without instructions. What do we trust our mailmen to do or not to do? To use their discretion in getting our mail to us, to take enough interest in us and in the nature of our mail (compatibly with their total responsibility), to make intelligent decisions about what to do with it when such decisions have to be made. Similarly with our surgeons and plumbers—*just* what they should do to put right what is wrong is something we must leave to them. Should they act incompetently, negligently, or deliberately against our interests, they may conceal these features of their activities from us by pretense that whatever happened occurred as a result of an honest and well-meaning exercise of the discretion given to them. This way they may retain our trust and so have opportunity to harm us yet further. In trusting them, we trust them to use their discretionary powers competently and nonmaliciously, and the latter includes not misleading us about how they have used them.

Trust, on the analysis I have proposed, is letting other persons (natural or artificial, such as firms, nations, etc.) take care of something the truster cares about, where such "caring for" involves some exercise of discretionary powers. But not all the variables involved in trust are yet in view. One that the entrusting model obscures rather than highlights is the degree of explicitness. To entrust is intentionally and usually formally to hand over the care of something to someone, but trusting is rarely begun by making up one's mind to trust, and often it has no definite initiation of any sort but grows up slowly and imperceptibly. What I have tried to take from the notion of entrusting is not its voluntarist and formalist character but rather the possible specificity and restrictedness of *what* is entrusted, along with the discretion the trustee has in looking after that thing. Trust can come with no beginnings, with gradual as well as sudden beginnings, and with various degrees of self-consciousness, voluntariness, and expressness. My earlier discussion of the delicacy and tact needed by the truster in judging the performance of the trusted applied only to cases where the truster not merely realizes that she trusts but has some conscious control over the continuation of the trust relationship. The discussion of abuses of discretionary power applied only to cases where the trusted realizes that she is trusted and trusted with discretionary powers. But trust relationships need not be so express, and some important forms of them cannot be verbally acknowledged by the persons involved. Trust between infant and parent is such a case, and it is one that also reminds us of another crucial variable in trust relations to which so far I have only indirectly alluded. This is the relative power of the truster and the trusted, and the relative costs to each of a breakdown of their trust relationship. In emphasizing the toleration of vulnerability by the truster, I have made attitudes to relative power and powerlessness the essence of trust and distrust; I have not yet looked at the varieties of power of the trusted, both while the trust endures and in its absence. Trust alters power positions, and both the position one is in without a given form of trust and the position one has within a relation of trust need to be considered before one can judge whether that form of trust is sensible and morally decent. Infant trust reminds us not just of inarticulate and uncritical or blind trust, but of trust by those who are maximally vulnerable, whether or not they give trust.

TRUST AND RELATIVE POWER

I have been apparently preoccupied up to now with dimensions of trust that show up most clearly in trust between articulate adults who are in a position to judge one another's performance and who have some control over their degree of vulnerability to others. This approach typifies a myopia which, once noticed, explains the "regrettably sparse" attempts to understand trust as a phenomenon of moral importance.[7] For the more we ignore dependency relations between those grossly unequal in power and ignore what cannot be spelled out in an explicit acknowledgement, the more readily will we assume that everything that needs to be understood about trust and trustworthiness can be grasped by looking at the morality of contract. For it takes an adult to be able to make a contract, and it takes something like Hegel's civil society of near equals to find a use for contracts. But one has to strain the contractarian model very considerably to see infant-parent relations as essentially contractual, both because of the nonexpressness of the infant's attitude and because of the infant's utter powerlessness. It takes inattention to cooperation between unequals, and between those without a common language, to keep one a contented contractarian. To do more, I must both show how infant trust, and other variations along the relative power dimension, can be covered, and also indicate just where trust in contracts fits into the picture we then get.

Infant trust is like one form of non-contract-based trust to which some attention has been given in our philosophical tradition, namely, trust in God. Trust in God is total, in that whatever one cares about, it will not thrive if God wills that it not thrive. A young child too is totally dependent on the good will of the parent, totally incapable of looking after anything he cares about without parental help or against parental will. Such total dependence does not, in itself, necessarily elicit trust—some theists curse God, display futile distrust or despair rather than trust. Infants too can make suspicious, futile, self-protective moves against the powerful adults in their world or retreat into autism. But surviving infants will usually have shown some trust, enough to accept offered nourishment, enough not to attempt to prevent such close approach. The ultra-Hobbist child who fears or rejects the mother's breast, as if fearing poison from that source, can be taken as displaying innate distrust, and such newborns must be the exception in a surviving species. Hobbes tells us that, in the state of nature, "seeing the infant is in the power of the Mother, and is therefore obliged to obey her, so she may either nourish or expose it; if she nourish it, it oweth its life to the Mother and is therefore obliged to obey her rather than any other" (*Leviathan*, chap.

20). Even he, born a twin to fear, is apparently willing to take mother's milk on trust. Some degree of innate, if selective, trust seems a necessary element in any surviving creature whose first nourishment (if it is not exposed) comes from another, and this innate but fragile trust could serve as the explanation both of the possibility of other forms of trust and of their fragility.

Infant trust that normally does not need to be won but is there unless and until it is destroyed is important for an understanding of the possibility of trust. Trust is much easier to maintain than it is to get started and is never hard to destroy. Unless some form of it were innate, and unless that form could pave the way for new forms, it would appear a miracle that trust ever occurs. The postponement of the onset of distrust is a lot more explicable than hypothetical Hobbesian conversions from total distrust to limited trust. The persistent human adult tendency to profess trust in a creator-God can also be seen as an infantile residue of this crucial innate readiness of infants to initially impute goodwill to the powerful persons on whom they depend. So we should perhaps welcome, or at least tolerate, religious trust, if we value any form of trust. Nevertheless the theological literature on trust in God is of very limited help to us if we want to understand trust in human persons, even that trust in parents of which it can be seen as a nostalgic fantasy-memory. For the child soon learns that the parent is not, like God, invulnerable, nor even, like some versions of God, subject to offense or insult but not injury. Infant trust, although extreme in the discrepancy of power between the truster and the trusted, is to some extent a matter of mutual trust and mutual if unequal vulnerability. The parents' enormous power to harm the child and disappoint the child's trust is the power of ones also vulnerable to the child's at first insignificant but ever-increasing power, including power as one trusted by the parent. So not very much can be milked from the theological literature on the virtues of trust, faith, and hope in God and returned to the human context, even to the case of infant and parent. Indeed we might cite the theological contamination of the concept of trust as part of the explanation for the general avoidance of the topic in modern moral philosophy. If trust is seen as a variant of the suspect virtue of faith in the competence of the powers that be, then readiness to trust will be seen not just as a virtue of the weak but itself as a moral weakness, better replaced by vigilance and self-assertion, by self-reliance, or by cautious, minimal, and carefully monitored trust. The psychology of adolescents, not infants, then gets glorified as the moral ideal. Such a reaction against a religious version of the ethics of trust is as healthy, understandable, and, it is hoped, as passing a phenomenon as is adolescent self-assertive individualism in the life of a normal person.

The goods that a trustworthy parent takes care of for as long as the child is unable to take care of them alone, or continues to welcome the parent's help in caring for them, are such things as nutrition, shelter, clothing, health, education, privacy, and loving attachment to others. Why, once the child becomes at all self-conscious about trusting parents to look after such goods for her, should she have confidence that parents are dependable custodians of such goods? Presumably because many of them are also goods to the parent, through their being goods to the child, especially if the parent loves the child. They will be common goods, so that for the trusted to harm them would be self-harm as well as harm to the child. The best reason for confidence in another's good care of what one cares about is that it is a common good, and the best reason for thinking that one's own good is also a common good is being loved. This may not, usually will not, ensure agreement on what best should be done to take care of that good, but it rules out suspicion of ill will. However, even when a child does not feel as loved by a parent as she would like, or as she thinks her siblings or friends are, she may still have complete confidence that at least many of the goods she cares about can be entrusted to her parents' care. She can have plenty of evidence that, for reasons such as pride, desire to perpetuate their name, or whatever, they do care as she herself does about her health, her success, and her ties with them. She can have good reason to be confident of the continued trustworthiness of her parents in many regards, from what she knows of their own concerns.

As the child approaches adulthood, and as the parents draw nearer to the likely dependency of old age, the trust may approximate much more closely to mutual trust and mutual vulnerability between equals, and they may then make explicit or even formal agreements about what is to be done in return for what. But no such contractual or quasi-contractual agreement can convert the young child's trust and the parent's trustworthiness retrospectively into part of a contractual mutual exchange. At most it can transform what was a continuing relation of mutual trust into a contractual obligation to render some sort of service to one's parents. The previous parental care could become a moral *reason* for making a contract with parents, but not what one received as "consideration" in such a contract. At best that could be a virtual "consideration," perhaps symbolized by the parents' formal canceling of any until then outstanding "debt" of gratitude, in return for the rights the contract gives them. But normally whatever grateful return one makes to another is not made in exchange for a "receipt" that is proof against any outstanding "debt." Only those determined to see every proper moral transaction as an exchange will construe every gift as made in exchange for an IOU, and every return gift as made in exchange for a receipt. Only such trade fetishists will have any reason to try to construe the appropriate adult response to earlier parental care as part of a virtual contract, or as proper content for an actual contract. As Hume says, contract should not replace "the more generous and noble intercourse of friendship and good offices," which he construes as a matter of spontaneous service responded to by "return in the same manner."[8] We can resist this reduction of the more noble responses of gratitude to the fulfilling of contractual obligations if we focus our moral attention on other sorts of trust than trust in contracts. Looking at infant trust helps one do that. Not only has the child no concept of virtual contract when she trusts, but the parent's duty to the child seems in no way dependent on the expectation that the child will make a later return. The child or the parent may die before the reversal of dependency arrives. Furthermore, the parent's knowledge either that the child, or that he himself, or both, will die within say ten years, in itself (and disability apart) makes no difference to the parent's responsibility while he lives, as that is usually understood. Parental and filial responsibility do not rest on deals, actual or virtual, between parent and child.

TRUST AND VOLUNTARY ABILITIES

The child trusts as long as she is encouraged to trust and until the trust is unmistakably betrayed. It takes childhood innocence to be able to trust simply because of encouragement to trust. "Trust me!" is for most of us an invitation that we cannot accept at will—either we do already trust the one who says it, in which case it serves at best as reassurance,[9] or it is properly responded to with, "Why should and how can I, until I have cause to?"[10] The child, of course, cannot trust at will any more than experienced adults can—encouragement is a condition of not lapsing into distrust, rather than of a move from distrust to trust. One constraint on an account of trust which postulates infant trust as its essential seed is that it not make essential to trusting the use of concepts or abilities that a child cannot be reasonably believed to possess. Acts of will of any sort are not plausibly attributed to infants; it would be unreasonable to suppose that they can do at will what adults cannot, namely, obey the instruction to trust, whether it comes from others or is a self-instruction.

To suppose that infants emerge from the womb already equipped with some Ur-confidence in what supports them, so that no choice is needed to continue with that attitude until something happens to shake or destroy such confidence, is plausible enough. My account of trust has been designed to allow for unconscious trust, for conscious but unchosen trust, as well as for conscious trust the truster has chosen to endorse and cultivate. Whereas it strains the concept of agreement to speak of unconscious agreements and unchosen agreements, and overstrains the concept of contract to speak of unconscious or unchosen contracts, there is no strain whatever in the concept of automatic and unconscious trust, and of unchosen but mutual trust. Trust between infant and parent, at its best, exhibits such primitive and basic trust. Once it is present, the story of how trust becomes self-conscious, controlled, monitored, critical, pretended, and eventually either cautious and distrustful of itself, or discriminatory and reflexive, so that we come to trust ourselves as trusters, is relatively easy to tell. What will need explanation will be the ceasings to trust, the transfers of trust, the restriction or enlargements in the fields of what is trusted, when, and to whom, rather than any abrupt switches from distrust to trust. Even if such occurrences do ever occur (when one suddenly falls in love or lust with a stranger or former enemy, or has a religious conversion), they take more than the mere invitation "Trust me."

In his famous account of what a promise (and a contract) involves, Hume strongly implies that it is an artificially contrived and secured case of mutual trust. The penalty to which a promisor subjects himself in promising, he says, is that of "never being trusted again in case of failure."[11] The problem that the artifice of promise solves is a generally disadvantageous "want of mutual confidence and security."[12] It is plausible to construe the offer whose acceptance counts as acceptance of a contract or a promise as at least implicitly including an invitation to trust. Part of what makes promises the special things they are, and the philosophically intriguing things they are, is that we *can* at will accept *this* sort of invitation to trust, whereas in general we cannot trust at will. Promises are puzzling because they seem to have the power, by verbal magic, to initiate real, voluntary, short-term trusting. They not merely create obligations apparently at the will of the obligated, but they create trust at the will of the truster. They present a very fascinating case of trust and trustworthiness, but one which, because of those very intriguing features, is ill suited to the role of paradigm. Yet in as far as modern moral philosophers have attended at all to the morality of trust, it is trust in parties to an agreement that they have concentrated on, and it is into this very special and artificial mold that they have tried to force other cases of trust, when they notice them at all.

Trust of any particular form is made more likely, in adults, if there is a climate of trust of that sort. Awareness of what is customary, as well as past experience of one's own, affects one's ability to trust. We take it for granted that people will perform their role-related duties and trust any individual worker to look after whatever her job requires her to. The very existence of that job, as a standard occupation, creates a climate of some trust in those with that job. Social artifices such as property, which allocate rights and duties as a standard job does, more generally also create a climate of trust, a presumption of a sort of trustworthiness. On the Humean account of promises and contracts that I find more or less correct,[13] their establishment as a customary procedure also reverses a presumption concerning trustworthiness, but only in limited conditions. Among these is a special voluntary act by the promisor, giving it to be understood that what he offers is a promise, and another voluntary act by the promisee, acceptance of that promise. Promises are "a bond or security,"[14] and "the sanction of the interested commerce of mankind."[15] To understand them is to see what sort of sanction is involved, what sort of security they provide, and the social preconditions of each. Then one understands how the presumption about the trustworthiness of self-interested strangers can be reversed, and how the ability to trust them (for a limited time, on a limited matter) can become a voluntary ability. To adapt Hume's words, "Hence I learn to count on a service from another, although he bears me no real kindness."[16] Promises are a most ingenious social invention, and trust in those who have given us promises is a complex and sophisticated moral achievement. Once the social conditions are right for it, once the requisite climate of trust in promisors is there, it is easy to take it for a simpler matter than it is and to ignore its background conditions. They include not merely the variable social conventions and punitive customs Hume emphasizes, but the prior existence of less artificial and less voluntary forms of trust, such as trust in friends and family, and enough trust in fellows to engage with them in agreed exchanges of a more or less simultaneous nature, exchanges such as barter or handshakes, which do not require one to rely on strangers over a period of time, as the exchange of promises typically does.

Those who take advantage of this sophisticated social device will be, mainly, adults who are not intimate with one another and who see one another more or less as equal in power to secure the enforcement of the rules of the contracting game (to extract damages for broken contracts, to set in motion the accepted penalty for fraudulent promises, and so on). As Nietzsche emphasized, the right to make promises and the power to have one's promises accepted are not possessed by everyone in relation to everyone else. Not only can the right be forfeited, but it is all along an elite right, possessed only by those with a certain social status. Slaves, young children, the ill, and the mentally incompetent do not fully possess it. For those who possess it, whose offer or acceptance of a promise has moral force, the extent to which use of it regulates their relations with others varies with their other social powers. Women whose property, work, and sexual services became their husbands' on marriage did not have much left to promise, and what was left could usually be taken from them without their consent and without the formality of exchange of promises. Their right to promise anything of significance was contracted into the right to make one vow of fixed and non-negotiable content, the marriage vow, and even that was often made under duress. The important relationships and trust relationships that structured women's lives for most of the known history of our species, relations to spouse, children, fellow workers, were not entered into by free choice or by freely giving or receiving promises. They were, typically, relationships of which the more important were ones of intimacy, relationships to superiors or inferiors in power, relationships not in any strong sense freely chosen nor to chosen others. Like the infant, they found themselves faced with others to trust or distrust, found themselves trusted or not trusted by these given others. Their freely given and seriously taken promises were restricted in their content to trivialities. Contract is a device for traders, entrepreneurs, and capitalists, not for children, servants, indentured wives, and slaves. They were the traded, not the traders, and any participation they had in the promising game was mere play. It is appropriate, then, that Nietzsche, the moral philosopher who glorifies promise more even than contemporary contractarians, was also the one who advised his fellow male exchangers or givers of promises thus, "He must conceive of woman as a possession, as a property that can be locked, as something predestined for service and achieving her perfection in that."[17] Nietzsche faces squarely what Hume half faced, and what most moral philosophers have avoided facing, that the liberal morality that takes voluntary agreement as the paradigm source of moral obligation must either exclude the women they expect to continue in their traditional role from the class of moral subjects or admit internal contradiction in their moral beliefs. Nor does the contradiction vanish once women have equal legal rights with men, as long as they are still expected to take responsibility for any child they conceive voluntarily or nonvoluntarily, either to abort or to bear and either care for or arrange for others to care for. Since a liberal morality both *must* let this responsibility rest with women and yet cannot conceive of it as self assumed, the centrality of voluntary agreement to the liberal and contractarian morality must be challenged once women are treated as full moral fellows. Voluntary agreement, and trust in others to keep their agreements, must be moved from the center to the moral periphery, once servants, ex-slaves, and women are taken seriously as moral subjects and agents.

THE MALE FIXATION ON CONTRACT

The great moral theorists in our tradition not only are all men, they are mostly men who had minimal adult dealings with (and so were then minimally influenced by) women. With a few significant exceptions (Hume, Hegel, J. S. Mill, Sidgwick, maybe Bradley), they are a collection of gays, clerics, misogynists, and puritan bachelors. It should not surprise us, then, that particularly in the modern period they managed to relegate to the mental background the web of trust tying most moral agents to one another, and to focus their philosophical attention so single-mindedly on cool, distanced relations between more or less free and equal adult strangers, say, the members of an all-male club, with membership rules and rules for dealing with rule breakers, and where the form of cooperation was restricted to ensuring that each member could read his *Times* in peace and have no one step on his gouty toes. Explicitly assumed or recognized obligations toward others with the same obligations and the same power to see justice done to rule breakers then are seen as the moral norm.

Relations between equals and nonintimates will *be* the moral norm for adult males whose dealings with others are mainly business or restrained social dealings with similarly placed males. But for lovers, husbands, fathers, the ill, the very young, and the elderly, other relationships with their moral potential and perils will loom larger. For Hume, who had several strong-willed and manipulative women to cooperate or contend with in his adult life; for Mill, who had Harriet Taylor on his hands; for Hegel, whose domestic life was of normal complication; the rights and duties of equals to equals in a civil society which recognized only a male electorate could only be *part* of the moral story. They could not ignore the virtues and vices of family relationships, male-female relationships, master-slave, and employer-employee relationships as easily as could Hobbes, Butler, Bentham, or Kant. Nor could they as easily adopt the usual compensatory strategies of the moral philosophers who confine their attention to the rights and duties of free and equal adults to one another—the strategy of claiming, if pressed, that these rights are the *core* of all moral relationships and maybe also claiming that any other relationships, engendering additional or different rights and duties, come about only by an exercise of one of the core rights, the right to promise. Philosophers who remember what it was like to be a dependent child, or know what it is like to be a parent, or to have a dependent parent, an old or handicapped relative, friend, or neighbor, will find it implausible to treat such relations as simply cases of comembership in a kingdom of ends, in the given temporary conditions of one-sided dependence.

To the extent that these claims are correct (and I am aware that they need more defense than I have given them here),[18] it becomes fairly easy to see one likely explanation of the neglect in Western moral philosophy of the full range of sorts of trust. Both before the rise of a society that needed contract as a commercial device, and after it, women were counted on to serve their men, to raise their children to fill the roles they were expected to fill, and not to deceive their men about the paternity of these children. What men counted on one another for, in work and war, presupposed this background domestic trust, trust in women not merely not to poison their men (Nietzsche derides them for learning less than they might have in the kitchen), but to turn out sons who could trust and be trusted in traditional men's roles and daughters who would reduplicate their own capacities for trust and trustworthiness. Since the women's role did not include the writing of moral treatises, any thoughts they had about trust, based on their experience of it, did not get into our tradition (or did Diotima teach Socrates something about trust as well as love?). And the more powerful men, including those who did write the moral treatises, were in the morally awkward position of being, collectively, oppressors of women, exploiters of women's capacity for trustworthiness in unequal, nonvoluntary, and non-contract-based relationships. Understandably, they did not focus their attention on forms of trust and demands for trustworthiness that it takes a Nietzsche to recognize without shame. Humankind can bear only so much reality.

The recent research of Carol Gilligan has shown us how intelligent and reflective twentieth-century women see morality, and how different their picture of it is from that of men, particularly the men who eagerly assent to the claims of currently orthodox contractarian-Kantian moral theories.[19] Women cannot now, any more than they could when oppressed, ignore that part of morality and those forms of trust that cannot easily be forced into the liberal and particularly the contractarian mold. Men may but women cannot see morality as essentially a matter of keeping to the minimal moral traffic rules, designed to restrict close encounters between autonomous persons to self-chosen ones. Such a conception presupposes both an equality of power and a natural separateness from others, which is alien to women's experience of life and morality. For those most of whose daily dealings are with the less powerful or the more powerful, a moral code designed for those equal in power will be at best nonfunctional, at worst an offensive pretense of equality as a substitute for its actuality. But equality is not even a desirable ideal in all relationships—children not only are not but should not be equal in power to adults, and we need a morality to guide us in our dealings with those who either cannot or should not achieve equality of power (animals, the ill, the dying, children while still young) with those with whom they have unavoidable and often intimate relationships.

Modern moral philosophy has concentrated on the morality of fairly cool relationships between those who are deemed to be roughly equal in power to determine the rules and to instigate sanctions against rule breakers. It is not surprising, then, that the main form of trust that any attention has been given to is trust in governments, and in parties to voluntary agreements to do what they have agreed to do. As much as possible is absorbed into the latter category, so that we suppose that paying for what one takes from a shop, doing what one is employed to do, returning what one has borrowed, supporting one's spouse, are all cases of being faithful to binding voluntary agreements, to contracts of some sort. (For

Hume, none of these would count as duties arising from contract or promise.) Yet if I think of the trust I show, say, in the plumber who comes from the municipal drainage authority when I report that my drains are clogged, it is not plausibly seen as trust that he will fulfill his contractual obligations to me or to his employer. When I trust him to do whatever is necessary and safe to clear my drains, I take his expertise and his lack of ill will for granted. Should he plant explosives to satisfy some unsuspected private or social grudge against me, what I might try to sue him for (if I escaped alive) would not be damages for breach of contract. His wrong, if wrong it were, is not breach of contract, and the trust he would have disappointed would not have been that particular form of trust.

Contract enables us to make explicit just what we count on another person to do, in return for what, and, should they not do just that, what damages can be extracted from them. The beauty of promise and contract is its explicitness.[20] But we can only make explicit provisions for such contingencies as we imagine arising. Until I become a victim of a terrorist plumber, I am unlikely, even if I should insist on a contract before giving plumbers access to my drains, to extract a solemn agreement that they not blow me up. Nor am I likely to specify the alternative means they *may* use to clear my drains, since if I knew enough to compile such a list I would myself have to be a competent plumber. Any such detailed instructions must come from their plumbing superiors; I know nothing or little about it when I confidently welcome the plumber into the bowels of my basement. I trust him to do a nonsubversive plumbing job, as he counts on me to do a nonsubversive teaching job, should he send his son to my course in the history of ethics. Neither of us relies on a contract with the other, and neither of us need know of any contract (or much about its contents) the other may have with a third coordinating party.

It does not, then, seem at all plausible, once we think about actual moral relations in all their sad or splendid variety, to model all of them on one rather special one, the relation between promisor to promisee. We count on all sorts of people for all sorts of vital things, without any contracts, explicit or implicit, with them or with any third coordinating party. For these cases of trust in people to do their job conscientiously and not to take the opportunity to do us harm once we put things we value into their hands are different from trust in people to keep their promises in part because of the very indefiniteness of what we are counting on them to do or not to do. The subtlety and point of promising is to declare precisely *what* we count on another to do, and as the case of Shylock and Bassanio shows, that very definiteness is a limitation as well as a functional excellence of an explicit agreement.

Another functional excellence of contracts, which is closely connected with the expressness that makes breach easily established and damages or penalty decidable with a show of reasonable justice, is the *security* they offer the trusting party. They make it possible not merely for us to trust at will but to trust with minimal vulnerability. They are a device for trusting others enough for mutually profitable future-involving exchanges, without taking the risks trusters usually do take. They are designed for cooperation between mutually suspicious risk-averse strangers, and the vulnerability they involve is at the other extreme from that incurred by trusting infants. Contracts distribute and redistribute risk so as to minimize it for both parties, but trusting those more powerful persons who purport to love one increases one's risks while increasing the good one can hope to secure. Trust in fellow contractors is a limit case of trust, in which fewer risks are taken, for the sake of lesser goods.

Promises do, nevertheless, involve some real trust in the other party's good will and proper use of discretionary powers. Hume said that "to perform promises is requisite to beget trust and confidence in the common offices of life."[21] But performing promises is not the only performance requisite for that. Shylock did not welsh on an agreement, but he was nevertheless not a trustworthy party to an agreement. For to insist on the letter of an agreement, ignoring the vague but generally understood unwritten background conditions and exceptions, is to fail to show that discretion and goodwill which a trustworthy person has. To be someone to be trusted with a promise, as well as to be trusted as a promisor, one must be able to use discretion not as to when the promise has been kept but, rather, as to when to insist that the promise be kept, or to instigate penalty for breach of promise, when to keep and when not to keep one's promise. I would feel morally let down if someone who had promised to help me move house arrived announcing, "I had to leave my mother, suddenly taken ill, to look after herself in order to be here, but I couldn't break my promise to you." From such persons I would accept no further promises, since they would have shown themselves untrustworthy in the always crucial respect of judgment and willingness to use their discretionary powers. Promises *are* morally interesting, and one's performance as party to a promise is a good indicator of one's moral character, but not for the reasons contractarians suppose.

The domination of contemporary moral philosophy by the so-called Prisoner's Dilemma problem displays most clearly this obsession with moral relations between minimally trusting, minimally trustworthy adults who are equally powerful. Just as the only trust Hobbist man shows is trust in promises, provided there is assurance of punishment for promise breakers, so is this the only sort of trust nontheological modern moral philosophers have given much attention at all to, as if once we have weaned ourselves from the degenerate form of absolute and unreciprocated trust in God, all our capacity for trust is to be channeled into the equally degenerate form of formal voluntary and reciprocated trust restricted to equals. But we collectively cannot bring off such a limitation of trust to minimal and secured trust, and we can deceive ourselves that we do so only if we avert our philosophical gaze from the ordinary forms of trust I have been pointing to. It was not really that, after Hobbes, people *did* barricade their bodies as well as their possessions against all others before daring to sleep. Some continued to doze off on stagecoaches, to go abroad unarmed, to give credit in business deals, to count on others turning up on time for appointments, to trust parents, children, friends, and lovers not to rob or assault them when welcomed into intimacy with them. And the usual array of vicious forms of such trust, trustworthiness, and demands for them continued to flourish. Slaves continued to be trusted to cook for slaveowners; women, with or without marriage vows, continued to be trusted with the property of their men, trusted not to deceive them about the paternity of their children, and trusted to bring up their sons as patriarchs, their daughters as suitable wives or mistresses for patriarchs. Life went on, but the moral philosophers, or at least those we regard as the great ones, chose to attend only to a few of the moral relations normal life exhibited. Once Filmer was disposed of, they concentrated primarily *not* on any of the relations between those of unequal power—parent to child, husband to wife, adult to aged parent, slaveowner to slave, official to citizen, employer to employee—but on relations between roughly equal parties or between people in those respects in which they could be seen as equals.

Such relationships of mutual respect are, of course, of great moral importance. Hobbes, Locke, Rousseau, Hume, Kant, Sidgwick, Rawls, all have helped us to see more clearly how we stand in relation to anonymous others, like ourselves in need, in power, and in capacity. One need not minimize the importance of such work in moral philosophy in order to question its completeness. But a complete moral philosophy would tell us how and why we should act and feel toward others in relationships of shifting and varying power asymmetry and shifting and varying intimacy. It seems to me that we philosophers have left that task largely to priests and revolutionaries, the self-proclaimed experts on the proper attitude of the powerless to the powerful. But these relationships of inequality—some of them, such as parent-child, of unavoidable inequality—make up much of our lives, and they, as much as our relations to our equals, determine the state of moral health or corruption in which we are content to live. I think it is high time we look at the morality and immorality of relations between the powerful and the less powerful, especially at those in which there is trust between them.

A MORAL TEST FOR TRUST

The few discussions of trust that I have found in the literature of moral philosophy assume that trust is good and that disappointing known trust is always prima facie wrong, and meeting it always prima facie right. But what is a trust-tied community without justice but a group of mutual blackmailers and exploiters? When the trust relationship itself is corrupt and perpetuates brutality, tyranny, or injustice, trusting may be silly self-exposure, and disappointing and betraying trust, including encouraged trust, may be not merely morally permissible but morally praiseworthy. Women, proletarians, and ex-slaves cannot ignore the virtues of watchful distrust and of judicious untrustworthiness. Only if we had reason to believe that most familiar types of trust relationships were morally sound would breaking trust be any more prima facie wrong than breaking silence. I now turn to the question of when a given form of trust is morally decent, so properly preserved by trustfulness and trustworthiness, and when it fails in moral decency. What I say about this will be sketchy and oversimplified. I shall take as the form of trust to test for moral decency the trust that one spouse has in the other, in particular as concerns their children's care.

Earlier in discussing infant trust, I said that the child has reason to trust the parents when both child and parents care about the same good—the child's happiness, although the child may not see eye-to-eye with those trusted parents about how that is best taken care of. When one parent, say the old-style father, entrusts the main care of his young child's need to the old-style mother, there can be agreement on the good they both want cared for but disagreement about how best it is cared for. The lord and master who entrusts such care to his good wife, the mother, and so gives her discretionary power in making moment-by-moment decisions about what is to be done, will have done so sensibly if these disagreements are not major ones, or if he has reason to think that she knows better than he does about such matters. He should defer to her judgment, as the child is encouraged to do to the parents', and as I do to my plumber's. He sensibly trusts if he has reason to think that the discretionary powers given, even when used in ways he does not fully understand or approve of, are still used to care for the goods he wants cared for. He would be foolish to trust if he had evidence that she had other ends in view of her treatment of the child, or had a radically different version of what, say, the child's healthy development and proper relation to his father consisted in. Once he suspects that she, the trusted nurse of his sons and daughters, is deliberately rearing the daughters to be patriarch-toppling Amazons, the sons to be subverters of the father's values, he will sensibly withdraw his trust and dispatch his children to suitably chosen female relatives or boarding schools. What would properly undermine his trust would be beliefs he came to hold about the formerly trusted person's motives and purposes in her care of what was entrusted to her. The disturbing and trust-undermining suspicion is not necessarily that she doesn't care about the children's good, or cares only about her own—it is the suspicion that what she cares about conflicts with rather than harmonizes with what he cares about and that she is willing to sacrifice his concerns to what she sees as the children's and her own. Trusting is rational, then, in the absence of any reason to suspect in the trusted strong and operative motives that conflict with the demands of trustworthiness as the truster sees them.

But trusting can continue to be rational, even when there are such unwelcome suspicions, as long as the truster is confident that in those conflict of motives within the trusted the subversive motives will lose to the conformist motives. Should the wife face economic hardship and loss of her children if she fails to meet the husband's trust, or incurs too much of his suspicion, then she will sensibly continue as the dutiful wife, until her power position alters—sensibly, that is, given what she cares about. The husband in a position to be sure that the costs to the wife of discovered untrustworthiness are a sufficient deterrent will sensibly continue in trusting her while increasing his vigilance. Nor is he relying only on her fear, since, by hypothesis, her motives are conflicting and so she is not without some good will and some sympathy for his goals. Should he conclude that *only* fear of sanctions keeps her at her wifely duties, then the situation will have deteriorated from trust to mere reliance on his threat advantage. In such a case he will, if he has any sense, shrink the scope of her discretionary powers to virtually zero, since it is under cover of those that she could not really thwart his purposes for his children but work to change the power relations in her own favor. As long as he gives her any discretion in looking after what is entrusted to her, he must trust her, and not rely solely on her fear of threatened penalties for disappointing his expectations.

The trusted wife (who usually, of course, also trusts her husband with many things that matter to her) is sensible to try to keep his trust, as long as she judges that the goods which would be endangered should she fail to meet his trust matter more to her than those she could best look after only by breaking or abusing trust. The goods for the sake of whose thriving she sensibly remains trustworthy might include the loving relation between them, their mutual trust for its own sake, as well as their agreed version of their children's good; or it might be some vestiges of these plus her own economic support or even physical safety, which are vulnerable to his punitive rage should she be found guilty of breach of trust. She will sensibly continue to meet trust, even when the goods with whose case she is trusted are no longer clearly common goods, as long as she cares a lot about anything his punitive wrath can and is likely to harm.

Sensible trust could persist, then, in conditions where truster and trusted suspect each other of willingness to harm the other if they could get away with it, the one by breach of trust, the other by vengeful response to that. The stability of the relationship will depend on the trusted's skill in cover-up activities, or on the truster's evident threat advantage, or a combination of these. Should the untrustworthy trusted person not merely have skill in concealment of her breaches of trust but skill in directing them toward increasing her own power and increasing her ability to evade or protect herself against the truster's attempted vengeance, then that will destabilize the relation, as also would frequent recourse by the truster to punitive measures against the trusted.

Where the truster relies on his threat advantage to keep the trust relation going, or where the trusted relies on concealment, something is morally rotten in the trust relationship. The truster who in part relies on his whip or his control of the purse is sensible but not necessarily within his moral rights in continuing to expect trustworthiness; and the trusted who sensibly relies on concealment to escape the penalty for untrustworthiness may or may not be within her moral rights. I tentatively propose a test for the moral decency of a trust relationship, namely, that its continuation need not rely on successful threats held over the trusted, or on her successful cover-up of breaches of trust. We could develop and generalize this test into a version of an expressibility test, if we note that knowledge of what the other party is relying on for the continuance of the trust relationship would, in the above cases of concealment and of threat advantage, itself destabilize the relation. Knowledge of the other's reliance on concealment does so fairly automatically, and knowledge of the other's partial reliance on one's fear of his revenge would tend, in terms of normal pride and self-assertiveness, to prompt her to look for ways of exploiting her discretionary powers so as to minimize her vulnerability to that threat. More generally, to the extent that what the truster relies on for the continuance of the trust relation is something which, once realized by the truster, is likely to lead to (increased) abuse of trust, and eventually to destabilization and destruction of that relation, the trust is morally corrupt. Should the wife come to realize that the husband relies on her fear of his revenge, or on her stupidity in not realizing her exploitation, or on her servile devotion to him, to keep her more or less trustworthy, that knowledge should be enough to begin to cure these weaknesses and to motivate untrustworthiness. Similarly, should the truster come to realize that the trusted relies on her skill at covering up or on her ability to charm him into forgiveness for breaches of trust, that is, relies on *his* blindness or gullibility, that realization will help cure that blindness and gullibility. A trust relationship is morally bad to the extent that either party relies on the qualities in the other that would be weakened by the knowledge that the other relies on them. Where each relies on the other's love, or concern for some common good, or professional pride in competent discharge of responsibility, knowledge of what the other is relying on in one need not undermine but will more likely strengthen those relied-on features. They survive exposure as what others rely on in one, in a way that some forms of stupidity, fear, blindness, ignorance, and gullibility normally do not. There are other mental states whose sensitivity to exposure as relied on by others seems more variable: good nature, detachment, inattention, generosity, forgivingness, and sexual bondage to the other party to the trust may not be weakened by knowledge that others count on their presence in one to sustain some wanted relationship, especially if they are found equally in both parties. But the knowledge that others are counting on one's nonreciprocated generosity or good nature or forgiveness can have the power of the negative, can destroy trust.

I assume that in some forms of trust the healthy and desired state will be mere self-maintenance, while in others it will be change and growth. Alteration of the trust relationship need not take the form of destruction of the old form and its replacement by a new form, but of continuous growth, of slight shifts in scope of discretionary powers, additions or alterations in scope of good entrusted, and so on. Of course, some excitement-addicted persons may cultivate a form of trust in part for the opportunity it provides for dramatic disruption. Trust is the atmosphere necessary for exhilarating disruptions of trust and satisfyingly spectacular transfers of trust, as well as for other goods we value. For persons with such tastes, immoral forms of trust may be preferable to what, according to my test, are moral forms of trust.

It should be noted that my proposed test of the moral decency of trust is quite noncommittal as to what cases of reliance on another's psychology will be acceptable to the other. I have assumed that most people in most trust situations will not be content to have others rely on their fear, their ignorance, and their spinelessness. In some cases, however, such as trusting police to play their role effectively, and trusting one's fellows to refrain from open crime, some element of fear must play a role, and it is its absence—not its presence—that would destabilize trust in such contexts. In others, such as trust in national intelligence and security officers to look after national security, some ignorance in the trusting is proper, and awareness that such persons may be relying on one's not knowing what they know will not destabilize any trust one has in them to do what they are entrusted to do. What will be offensive forms of reliance on one's psychological state will vary from context to context, depending on the nature of the goods entrusted and on other relationships between the trusting and the trusted. Variations in individual psychology will also make a difference. Some are much more tolerant than others of having their good nature or preoccupation taken advantage of—not merely in that they take longer to recognize that they are victims of this, but they are less stirred to anger or resentment by the awareness that they are being deceived, blackmailed, or exploited in a given trust relation. I have used the phrase "tend to destroy" in the test for moral decency in the assumption that there is a normal psychology to be discerned and that it does include a strong enough element of Platonic *thumos.* Should that be false, then all sorts of horrendous forms of trust may pass my test. I do not, in any case, claim that it is the only test, merely an appropriate one. It is a test which amounts to a check on the will and good will of the truster and trusted, a look to see how good their will to one another is, knowing what they do about each other's psychology.

It may be objected that the expressibility test I have proposed amounts to a reversion, on my part, to the contractarian attitude which I have deplored.[22] Have I not finally admitted that we must treat trust relationships as hypothetical contracts, with all the terms fully spelled out in order to determine their moral status? The short answer is that contractualists do not have a monopoly on expressibility tests. In any case, I have applied it at a place no contractualist would, and *not* applied it where he does. Where he assumes self-interest as a motive and makes explicit what goods or services each self-interested party is to receive from the other, I have left it open what motives the trusting and trusted have for maintaining the relation, requiring only that these motives, insofar as they rely on responses from the other, survive the other's knowledge of that reliance, and I have not required that relied-on services be made explicit. What the contractualist makes explicit is a voluntary mutual commitment, and what services each is committed to provide. I have claimed that such explicitness is not only rare in trust relationships, but that many of them must begin inexplicitly and nonvoluntarily and would not do the moral and social work they do if they covered only what contract does—services that could be pretty exactly spelled out. My moral test does not require that these nonexplicit elements in trust should be made explicit but, rather, that something else survive being made explicit, one's reliance on facts about others' psychological states relevant to their willingness to continue serving or being served, states such as love, fear, ignorance, sense of powerlessness, good nature, inattention, which one can use for one's secret purposes. It is not part of contracts or social contracts to specify what assumptions each party needs to make about the other in respect of such psychological factors. Perhaps constraints regarding duress and fraud can be linked with the general offensiveness of having others rely on one's ignorance, fear, or sense of powerlessness, especially when these are contrived by the one who relies on them; but contracts themselves do not make express what it is in the state of mind of the other that each party relies on to get what he wants from the deal. What I have proposed as a general moral test of trust is indeed a generalization of one aspect of the contractarian morality, namely, of the assumptions implicit in the restrictions of valid contracts to those not involving fraud or duress. Whereas contracts make explicit the services (or service equivalent) exchanged, trust, when made express, amounts to a sort of exchange of responses to the motives and state of mind of the other, responses in the form of confident reliance. Contractualists and other exchange fetishists can see this as a spiritual exchange, if it pleases them to do so, but it is not voluntary in the way contracts are, nor does it presuppose any equality of need or of power in the parties to this "exchange." The relation of my account of the morality of trust to standard contractarian morality seems to me as close as it should be, and at roughly the right places, if, as I have claimed, trust in fellow contractors is a limited case of trust.

Nevertheless, there are two aspects of my test which worry me, which may indicate it is not sufficiently liberated from contractarian prejudices. One difficulty is that it ignores the *network* of trust, and treats only two-party trust relationships. This is unrealistic, since any person's attitude to another in a given trust relationship is constrained by all the other trust and distrust relationships in which she is involved. Although I have alluded to such society-wide phenomena as climates of trust affecting the possibilities for individual trust relationships, my test is not well designed for application to the whole network but has to be applied piecemeal. That is a defect, showing the same individualist limitations that I find in contractarianism. The second thing that worries me is that the test seems barely applicable to brief trusting encounters, such as those with fellow library frequenters. As the contractarian takes as his moral paradigm a relationship that has some but not a very complex temporal depth, assimilating simultaneous exchange to the delayed delivery which makes a contract useful, and treats lifelong mutual trust as iterated mutual delayed deliveries, so I have shown a bias toward the medium-length trust relationship, thereby failing to say or imply anything very helpful either about brief encounters or about cross-generational trust. Probably these two faults are connected. If one got a test for the whole network of trust, with all the dependencies between the intimate and the more impersonal forms properly noted, and had the right temporal dimensions in that, then both the morality of brief trusting encounters and the morality of trust between generations who do not encounter each other would fall into place.

Since I have thus oversimplified the problem of morally evaluating trust relationships by confining my attention to relationships one by one, my account of trusting as acceptance of having, as it were, entrusted my consequent expansion of trusting from a two-place into a three-place predicate will seem forced and wrong. For there are some people whom one would not trust with anything, and that is not because one has considered each good one might entrust to that one and rejected that possibility. We want then to say that unless we first trust them we will not trust them *with anything*. I think that there is some truth in this, which my account has not captured. For some kinds of enemy (perhaps class enemies?) one will not trust even with one's bodily safety as one raises a white flag, but one will find it "safer" to fight to the death. With some sorts of enemies, a contract may be too intimate a relation. If the network of relationships is systematically unjust or systematically coercive, then it may be that one's status within that network will make it unwise of one to entrust anything to those persons whose interests, given their status, are systematically opposed to one's own. In most such corrupt systems there will be limited opportunity for such beleaguered persons to "rescue" their goods from the power of their enemies—they usually will have no choice but to leave them exposed and so to act as if they trusted, although they feel proper distrust. In such conditions it may take fortitude to display distrust and heroism to disappoint the trust of the powerful. Courageous (if unwise) untrustworthiness and stoic withdrawal of trust may then be morally laudable. But since it usually will take such heroic disruptions of inherited trust relationships for persons to distance themselves from those the system makes their enemies, my test will at least be usable to justify such disruptions. In an earlier version of this paper I said that the ghost of plain trust and plain distrust haunted my account of goods-relativized or "fancy" trust. I think that I now see that ghost for what it is and see why it ought to continue to haunt. Still, such total oppositions of interest are rare, and one satisfactory thing about my account is that it enables us to see how we can salvage some respects in which we may trust even those whose interests are to some extent opposed to our own.

Meanwhile, my account of what it is to trust, and my partial account of when it is immoral to expect or meet trust, will have to be treated as merely a beginning (or, for some, as resumption, since there doubtless are other attempts at this topic that have escaped my notice). Trust, I have claimed, is reliance on others' competence and willingness to look after, rather than harm, things one cares about that are entrusted to their care. The moral test of such trust relationships which I have proposed is that they be able to survive awareness by each party to the relationship of *what* the other relies on in the first to ensure their continued trustworthiness or trustingness. This test elevates to a special place one form of trust, namely, trusting others with knowledge of what it is about them which enables one to trust them as one does, or expect them to be trustworthy. The test could be restated this way: trust is morally decent only if, in addition to whatever else is entrusted, knowledge of each party's reasons for confident reliance on the other to continue the relationship could in principle also be entrusted—since such mutual knowledge would be itself a good, not a threat to other goods. To the extent that mutual reliance can be accompanied by mutual knowledge of the conditions for that reliance, trust is above suspicion, and trustworthiness a nonsuspect virtue. "Rara temporum felicitas . . . quae sentias, dicere licet."[23]

This paper has an antiphonal title, and a final counterpoint may not be out of order. Although I think this test is an appropriate moral test, it is another matter to decide whether and when it should be applied to actual cases of trust. Clearly in some cases, such as infant trust and parental trustworthiness, which could in principle pass it, it cannot actually be applied by both parties to the relationship. That need not unduly worry us. But in other cases it may well be that the attempt to apply it will ensure its failing the test. Trust is a fragile plant, which may not endure inspection of its roots, even when they were, before the inspection, quite healthy. So although some forms of trust would survive a suddenly achieved mutual awareness of them, they may not survive the gradual and possibly painful process by which such awareness actually comes about. It may then be the better part of wisdom, even when we have an acceptable test for trust, not to use it except where some distrust already exists, better to take nonsuspect trust on trust. Luhmann says that "it is a characteristic mark of civilizing trust that it incorporates an element of reflexivity."[24] But to trust one's trust and one's distrust enough to refrain from applying moral tests until prompted by some distrust is to take a very risky bet on the justice, if not the "civilization," of the system of trust one inhabits. We may have to trade off civilization for justice, unless we can trust not only our trust but, even more vitally, our distrust.

NOTES

I owe the second half of my title to the salutary reaction of Alexander Nehamas to an earlier and more sanguine version of this paper, read at Chapel Hill Colloquium in October 1984. I also owe many important points which I have tried to incorporate in this revised version to John Cooper, who commented helpfully on the paper on that occasion, to numerous constructive critics at later presentations of version of it at CUNY Graduate Center, Brooklyn College, Columbia University, the University of Pennsylvania, and to readers for *Ethics.* I received such a flood of helpful and enthusiastic advice that it became clear that, although few philosophers have written directly on this topic, very many have been thinking about it. It is only by ruthlessly putting finis to my potentially endless revisions and researches into hitherto unfamiliar legal, sociological, psychological, and economic literature that any paper emerged from my responses to these gratifying and generous responses.

1. Sissela Bok, *Lying* (New York: Pantheon Books, 1978), p. 31n. Bok is one of the few philosophers to have addressed the ethics of trust fairly directly. The title of the chapter from which this quotation comes is "Truthfulness, Deceit and Trust."
2. Plato, *Laws* 4.705a. I owe this reference to John Cooper, who found my charge that Plato and Aristotle had neglected the topic of trust ungenerous, given how much they fairly clearly took for granted about its value and importance. (But taking for granted is a form of neglect.)
3. Besides Bok and Locke, whom I refer to, those who have said something about it include N. Hartmann, *Ethik* (Berlin: W. de Gruyer, 1962), pp. 468 ff.; Virginia Held, *Rights and Goods* (New York and London: Free Press, 1984), esp. chap. 5, "The Grounds for Social Trust"; D. O. Thomas, "The Duty to Trust," *Aristotelian Society Proceedings* (1970), pp. 89–101. It is invoked in passing by Aurel Kolnai in "Forgiveness," in *Ethics, Value and Reality*, ed. Bernard Williams and David Wiggins (Indianapolis: Macmillan Co., 1978): "Trust in the world, unless it is vitiated by hairbrained optimism and dangerous irresponsibility, may be looked upon not to be sure as the very starting point and very basis but perhaps as the epitome and culmination of morality" (p. 223); and by John R. S. Wilson in "In One Another's Power," *Ethics* 88 (1978): 303.
4. A reader for *Ethics* suggested that, when one trusts one's child to mail an important letter for one at the mailbox on the corner, no discretionary powers are given, although one is trusting him with the safe, speedy transfer of the letter to the box. But life is full of surprises—in Washington on inauguration day mailboxes were sealed closed as a security precaution, and in some parts of Manhattan mailboxes are regularly sealed after dark. One trusts the child to do the sensible thing if such an unforeseen problem should arise—to bring the letter back, not leave it on the ledge of the sealed mailbox, or go too far afield to find another.
5. This point I take from the fascinating sociological analysis of trust given by Niklas Luhmann (*Trust and Power* [Chichester, N.Y.: Ethics, 1979]), which I discovered while revising this paper. In many ways my analysis agrees with his, insofar as I understand the implications of his account of it as "reduction of complexity," in particular of complex future contingencies. He makes much of the difference between absence of trust and distrust, and distinguishes trust from what it presupposes, a mere "familiarity," or taking for granted. I have blurred these distinctions. He treats personal trust as a risky investment and looks at mechanisms for initiating and maintaining trust. Tact is said to play an important role in both. It enables trust-offering overtures to be rejected without hostility ensuing, and it enables those who make false moves in their attempts to maintain trust to recover their position without too much loss of face. "A social climate . . . institu-

tionalizes tact and knows enough escape routes for self presentation in difficult situations" (p. 84). It is important, I think, to see that tact is a virtue which needs to be added to delicacy of discrimination in recognizing *what* one is trusted with, good judgment as to whom to trust with what, and a willingness to admit and forgive fault, as all functional virtues needed in those who would sustain trust.

6. See David Hume, *Treatise*, ed. L. A. Selby-Bigge and P. H. Nidditch (Oxford: Clarendon Press, 1978), p. 497.
7. Luhmann, p. 8, n. 1. It is interesting to note that, unlike Luhmann and myself, Bernard Barber begins his sociological treatment of trust in *The Logic and Limits of Trust* (New Brunswick, N.J.: Rutgers University Press, 1983) not by remarking on the neglect of the topic but rather, by saying, "Today nearly everyone seems to be talking about 'trust' " (p. 1). He lists "moral philosophers" along with "presidential candidates, political columnists, pollsters, social critics and the man in the street" as among those talking so much about it but cites only two moral philosophers, Bok and Rawls (who by his own account is *not* always talking about it). Between Luhmann's work on trust, first published in Germany in 1973, and Barber's, sociologists had ten years to get the talk about trust going, but it has scarcely spread yet to most of the moral philosophers I have encountered.
8. Hume, p. 521.
9. My thoughts about the role of the words "Trust me!" are influenced by an unpublished paper on promising by T. M. Scanlon. Indeed Scanlon's talk on this topic to the University of Pittsburgh philosophy department in April 1984 was what, along with Hume's few remarks about it, started me thinking about trust in and out of voluntary changes.
10. Luhmann says, "It is not possible to demand the trust of others; trust can only be offered and accepted" (p. 43). I am here claiming something stronger, namely, that one cannot offer it or accept it by an act of will; that one cannot demand it of oneself or others until some trust-securing social artifice invents something like promise that *can* be offered and accepted at will.
11. Hume, p. 522.
12. Ibid., p. 521.
13. I have discussed and defended Hume's account in "Promises, Promises, Promises," in my *Postures of the Mind: Essays on Mind and Morals* (Minneapolis: University of Minnesota Press, 1985).
14. Hume, p. 541.
15. Ibid., p. 522.
16. Ibid., p. 521.
17. Nietzsche, *Beyond Good and Evil*, pt. 7, §238, trans. Walter Kaufman, *Basic Writings of Nietzsche* (New York, 1968), p. 357.
18. I defend them a little more in "What Do Women Want in a Moral Theory?" *Nous* 19 (March 1985): 53–64.
19. Carol Gilligan, *In a Different Voice* (Cambridge, Mass.: Harvard University Press, 1982).
20. Norbert Hornstein has drawn my attention to an unpublished paper by economist Peter Murrell, "Commitment and Cooperation: A Theory of Contract Applied to Franchising." Murrell emphasizes the nonstandard nature of franchise contracts, in that they typically are vague about what is expected of the franchisee. The consequent infrequency of contract termination by the franchisor is linked by him to the long duration of the contracts and to the advantage, to the more powerful proprietor of the trademark, of keeping the trust of the less powerful scattered franchisees and maintaining quality control by means other than punitive contract terminations. This, I persuade myself, is a case where the exception proves the rule, where the nonstandardness

of such inexplicit and trusting contracts points up to the explicitness and minimal trustingness of standard contracts.

21. Hume, p. 544.
22. Objections of this sort were raised by a reader for *Ethics.*
23. Hume placed on the title page of his *A Treatise of Human Nature* these words of Tacitus: "Rara Temporum felicitas, ubi sentire, quae velis, & quae sentias, dicere licet."
24. Luhmann, p. 69.

Feminism and Moral Theory

Held contends that traditional philosophical ethics fails to take women's moral experience seriously, and she undertakes to correct that oversight. For Held, moral experience is "experience of consciously choosing, of voluntarily accepting or rejecting, of willingly approving or disapproving, of living with these choices, and above all of acting and of living with these actions and their outcomes." Since women and men have traditionally been assigned different social roles, they have faced different moral problems, and they have had different moral experience. Feminist moral theory, in Held's view, focuses on women's moral experience and articulates its ethical significance.

Held examines women's moral experience as mothers. First, the mother's attentive, creative nurturance of her child may provide a better model for social relations than the fair contract in a free market provides. Second, the mother-child relationship highlights the domain of relationships between particular individuals, and it demonstrates that self-interest and egoism do not intrude in all relationships. Third, the vulnerability of children argues for respecting principles that protect individuals from caprice and domination, yet it is a mistake to suppose that a few general principles can resolve complex and diverse moral problems. Fourth, the choice to suffer the pain of giving birth together with women's comparatively limited capacity to reproduce gives mothers a distinctive reason for valuing children. Finally, Held concludes that mothers' moral experience represents a worthy alternative to traditional moral theory.

—D.T.M.

Chapter 32

Virginia Held

Feminism and Moral Theory

The tasks of moral inquiry and moral practice are such that different moral approaches may be appropriate for different domains of human activity. I have argued in a recent book that we need a division of moral labor.[1] In *Rights and Goods*, I suggest that we ought to try to develop moral inquiries that will be as satisfactory as possible for the actual contexts in which we live and in which our experience is located. Such a division of moral labor can be expected to yield different moral theories for different contexts of human activity, at least for the foreseeable future. In my view, the moral approaches most suitable for the courtroom are not those most suitable for political bargaining; the moral approaches suitable for economic activity are not those suitable for relations within the family, and so on. The task of achieving a unified moral field theory covering all domains is one we may do well to postpone, while we do our best to devise and to "test" various moral theories in actual contexts and in light of our actual moral experience.

What are the implications of such a view for women? Traditionally, the experience of women has been located to a large extent in the context of the family. In recent centuries, the family has been thought of as a "private" domain distinct not only from that of the "public" domain of the polis but also from the domain of production and of the marketplace. Women (and men) certainly need to develop moral inquiries appropriate to the context of mothering and of family relations, rather than accepting the application to this context of theories developed for the marketplace or the polis. We can certainly show that the moral guidelines appropriate to mothering are different from those that now seem suitable for various other domains of activity as presently constituted. But we need to do more as well: we need to consider whether distinctively feminist moral theories, suitable for the contexts in which the experience of women has or will continue to be located, are better moral theories than those already available, and better for other domains as well.

THE EXPERIENCE OF WOMEN

We need a theory about how to count the experience of women. It is not obvious that it should count equally in the construction or validation of moral theory. To merely survey the moral views of women will not necessarily lead to better moral theories. In the Greek thought that developed into the Western philosophical tradition,[2] reason was associated with the public domain from which women were largely excluded. If the development of adequate moral theory is best based on experience in the public domain, the experience of women so far is less relevant. But that the public domain is the appropriate locus for the development of moral theory is among the tacit assumptions of existing moral theory being effectively challenged by feminist scholars. We cannot escape the need for theory in confronting these issues.

We need to take a stand on what moral experience is. As I see it, moral experience is "the experience of consciously choosing, of voluntarily accepting or rejecting, of willingly approving or disapproving, of living with these choices, and above all of acting and of living with these actions and their outcomes. . . . Action is as much as part of experience as is perception."[3] Then we need to take a stand on whether the moral experience of women is as valid a source or test of moral theory as is the experience of men, or on whether it is more valid.

Certainly, engaging in the process of moral inquiry is as open to women as it is to men, although the domains in which the process has occurred have been open to men and women in different ways. Women have had fewer occasions to experience for themselves the moral problems of governing, leading, exercising power over others (except children), and engaging in physically violent conflict. Men, on the other hand, have had fewer occasions to experience the moral problems of family life and the relations between adults and children. Although vast amounts of moral experience are open to all human beings who make the effort to become conscientious moral inquirers, the contexts in which experience is obtained may make a difference. It is essential that we avoid taking a given moral theory, such as a Kantian one, and deciding that those who fail to develop toward it are deficient, for this procedure imposes a theory on experience, rather than letting experience determine the fate of theories, moral and otherwise.

We can assert that as long as women and men experience different problems, moral theory ought to reflect the experience of women as fully as it reflects the experience of men. The insights and judgments and decisions of women as they engage in the process of moral inquiry should be presumed to be as valid as those of men. In the development of moral theory, men ought to have no privileged position to have their experience count for more. If anything, their privileged position in society should make their experience more suspect rather than more worthy of being counted, for they have good reasons to rationalize their privileged positions by moral arguments that will obscure or purport to justify these privileges.[4]

If the differences between men and women in confronting moral problems are due to biological factors that will continue to provide women and men with different experiences, the experience of women should still count for at least as much as the experience of men. There is no justification for discounting the experience of women as deficient or underdeveloped on biological grounds. Biological "moral inferiority" makes no sense.

The empirical question of whether and to what extent women think differently from men about moral problems is being investigated.[5] If, in fact, women approach moral problems in characteristic ways, these approaches should be reflected in moral theories as fully as are those of men. If the differing approaches to morality that seem to be displayed by women and by men are the result of historical conditions, and not biological ones, we could assume that in nonsexist societies, the differences would disappear, and the experience of either gender might adequately substitute for the experience of the other.[6] Then feminist moral theory might be the same as moral theory of any kind. But since we can hardly imagine what a nonsexist society would be like, and surely should not wait for one before evaluating the experience of women, we can say that we need feminist moral theory to deal with the differences of which we are now aware and to contribute to the development of the nonsexist society that might make the need for a distinctively feminist moral theory obsolete. Specifically, we need feminist moral theory to deal with the regions of experience that have been central to women's experience and neglected by traditional moral theory. If the resulting moral theory would be suitable for all humans in all contexts, and thus could be thought of as a human moral theory or a universal moral theory, it would be a feminist moral theory as well if it adequately reflected the experience and standpoint of women.

That the available empirical evidence for differences between men and women with respect to morality is tentative and often based on reportage and interpretation, rather than on something more "scientific,"[7] is no problem at all for the claim that we need feminist moral theory. If such differences turn out to be further substantiated, we will need theory to evaluate their implications, and we should be prepared now for this possibility (or, as many think, probability). If the differences turn out to be insignificant, we still need feminist moral theory to make the moral claim that the experience of women is of equal worth to the experience of men and, even more important, that women themselves are of equal worth as human beings. If it is true that the only differences between women and men are anatomical, it still does not follow that women are the moral equals of men. Moral equality has to be based on moral claims. Since the devaluation of women is a constant in human society as so far developed, and has been accepted by those holding a wide variety of traditional moral theories, it is apparent that feminist moral theory is needed to provide the basis for women's claims to equality.

We should never forget the horrors that have resulted from acceptance of the idea that women think differently from men, or that men are rational beings, women emotional ones. We should be constantly on guard for misuses of such ideas, as in social roles that determine that women belong in the home or in educational programs that discourage women from becoming, for example, mathematicians. Yet, excessive fear of such misuses should not stifle exploration of the ways in which such claims may, in some measure, be true. As philosophers, we can be careful not to conclude that whatever tendencies exist ought to be reinforced. And if we succeed in making social scientists more alert to the naturalistic fallacy than they would otherwise be, that would be a side benefit to the development of feminist moral theory.

MOTHERING AND MARKETS

When we bring women's experience fully into the domain of moral consciousness, we can see how questionable it is to imagine contractual relationships as central or fundamental to society and morality. They seem, instead, the relationships of only very particular regions of human activity.[8]

The most central and fundamental social relationship seems to be that between mother or mothering person and child. It is this relationship that creates and recreates society. It is the activity of mothering that transforms biological entities into human social beings. Mothers and mothering persons produce children and empower them with language and symbolic representations. Mothers and mothering persons thus produce and create human culture.

Despite its implausibility, the assumption is often made that human mothering is like the mothering of other animals rather than being distinctively human. In accordance with the traditional distinction between the family and the polis, and the assumption that what occurs in the public sphere of the polis is distinctively human, it is assumed that what human mothers do within the family belongs to the "natural" rather than to the "distinctively human" domain. Or, if it is recognized that the activities of human mothers do not resemble the activities of the mothers of other mammals, it is assumed that, at least, the difference is far narrower than the difference between what animals do and what humans who take part in government and industry and art do. But, in fact, mothering is among the most human of human activities.

Consider the reality. A human birth is thoroughly different from the birth of other animals, because a human mother can choose not to give birth. However extreme the alternative, even when abortion is not a possibility, a woman can choose suicide early enough in her pregnancy to consciously prevent the birth. A human mother comprehends that she brings about the birth of another human being. A human mother is then responsible, at least in an existential sense, for the creation of a new human life. The event is essentially different from what is possible for other animals.

Human mothering is utterly different from the mothering of animals without language. The human mother or nurturing person constructs with and for the child a human social reality. The child's understanding of language and of symbols, and of all that they create and make real, occurs in interactions between child and caretakers. Nothing seems more distinctively human than this. In comparison, government can be thought to resemble the governing of ant colonies, industrial production to be similar to the building of beaver dams, a market exchange to be like the relation between a large fish that protects and a small fish that grooms, and the conquest by force of arms that characterizes so much of human history to be like the aggression of packs of animals. But the imparting of language and the creation within and for each individual of a human social reality, and often a new human social reality, seems utterly human.

An argument is often made that art and industry and government create new human reality, while mothering merely "reproduces" human beings, their cultures, and social structures. But consider a more accurate view: in bringing up children, those who mother create new human *persons.* They change persons, the culture, and the social structures that depend on them, by creating the kinds of persons who can continue to transform themselves and their surroundings. Creating new and better persons is surely as "creative" as creating new and better objects or institutions. It is not only bodies that do not spring into being unaided and fully formed; neither do imaginations, personalities, and minds.

Perhaps morality should make room first for the human experience reflected in the social bond between mothering person and child, and for the human projects of nurturing and of growth apparent for both persons in the relationship. In comparison, the transactions of the marketplace seem peripheral; the authority of weapons and the laws they uphold, beside the point.

The relation between buyer and seller has often been taken as the model of all human interactions.[9] Most of the social contract tradition has seen this relation of contractual exchange as fundamental to law and political authority as well as to economic activity. And some contemporary moral philosophers see the contractual relation as the relation on which even morality itself should be based. The marketplace, as a model for relationships, has become so firmly entrenched in our normative theories that it is rarely questioned as a proper foundation for recommendations extending beyond the marketplace. Consequently, much moral thinking is built on the concept of rational economic man. Relationships between human beings are seen as arising, and as justified, when they serve the interests of individual rational contractors.

In the society imagined in the model based on assumptions about rational economic man, connections between people become no more than instrumental. Nancy Hartsock effectively characterizes the worldview of these assumptions, and shows how misguided it is to suppose that the relationship between buyer and seller can serve as a model for all human relations: "The paradigmatic connections between people [on this view of the social world] are instrumental or extrinsic and conflictual, and in a world populated by these isolated individuals, relations of competition and domination come to be substitutes for a more substantial and encompassing community."[10]

Whether the relationship between nurturing person (who need not be a biological mother) and child should be taken as itself paradigmatic, in place of the contractual paradigm, or whether it should be seen only as an obviously important relationship that does not fit into the contractual framework and should not be overlooked, remains to be seen. It is certainly instructive to consider it, at least tentatively, as paradigmatic. If this were done, the competition and desire for domination thought of as acceptable for rational economic man might appear as a very particular and limited human connection, suitable perhaps, if at all, only for a restricted marketplace. Such a relation of conflict and competition can be seen to be unacceptable for establishing the social trust on which public institutions must rest,[11] or for upholding the bonds on which caring, regard, friendship, or love must be based.[12]

The social map would be fundamentally altered by adoption of the point of view here suggested. Possibly, the relationship between "mother" and child would be recognized as a much more promising source of trust and concern than any other, for reasons to be explored later. In addition, social relations would be seen as dynamic rather than as fixed-point exchanges. And assumptions that human beings are equally capable of entering or not entering into the contractual relations taken to characterize social relations generally would be seen for the distortions they are. Although human mothers could do other than give birth, their choices to do so or not are usually highly constrained. And children, even human children, cannot choose at all whether to be born.

It may be that no human relationship should be thought of as paradigmatic for all the others. Relations between mothering persons and children can become oppressive for both, and relations between equals who can decide whether to enter into agreements may seem attractive in contrast. But no mapping of the social and moral landscape can possibly be satisfactory if it does not adequately take into account and provide appropriate guidance for relationships between mothering persons and children.

BETWEEN THE SELF AND THE UNIVERSAL

Perhaps the most important legacy of the new insights will be the recognition that more attention must be paid to the domain *between* the self—the ego, the self-interested individual—on the one hand, and the universal—everyone, others in general—on the other hand. Ethics traditionally has dealt with these poles, trying to reconcile their conflicting claims. It has called for impartiality against the partiality of the egoistic self, or it has defended the claims of egoism against such demands for a universal perspective.

In seeing the problems of ethics as problems of reconciling the interests of the self with what would be right or best for everyone, moral theory has neglected the intermediate region of family relations and relations of friendship, and has neglected the sympathy and concern people actually feel for particular others. As Larry Blum has shown, "contemporary moral philosophy in the Anglo-American tradition has paid little attention to [the] morally significant phenomena" of sympathy, compassion, human concern, and friendship.[13]

Standard moral philosophy has construed personal relationships as aspects of the self-interested feelings of individuals, as when a person might favor those he loves over those distant because it satisfies his own desires to do so. Or it has let those close others stand in for the universal "other," as when an analysis might be offered of how the conflict between self and others is to be resolved in something like "enlightened self-interest" or "acting out of respect for the moral law," and seeing this as what should guide us in our relations with those close, particular others with whom we interact.

Owen Flanagan and Jonathan Adler provide useful criticism of what they see as Kohlberg's "adequacy thesis"—the assumption that the more formal the moral reasoning, the better.[14] But they themselves continue to construe the tension in ethics as that between the particular self and the universal. What feminist moral theory will emphasize, in contrast, will be the domain of particular others in relations with one another.

The region of "particular others" is a distinct domain, where it can be seen that what becomes artificial and problematic are the very "self" and "all others" of standard moral theory. In the domain of particular others, the self is already closely entwined in relations with others, and the relation may be much more real, salient, and important than the interests of any individual self in isolation. But the "others" in the picture are not "all others," or "everyone," or what a universal point of view could provide. They are particular flesh and blood others for whom we have actual feelings in our insides and in our skin, not the others of rational constructs and universal principles.

Relationships can be characterized as trusting or mistrustful, mutually considerate or selfish, and so forth. Where trust and consideration are appropriate, we can find ways to foster them. But doing so will depend on aspects of what can be understood only if we look at relations between persons. To focus on either self-interested individuals or the totality of all persons is to miss the qualities of actual relations between actual human beings.

Moral theories must pay attention to the neglected realm of particular others in actual contexts. In doing so, problems of egoism versus the universal moral point of view appear very different and may recede to the region of background insolubility or relative unimportance. The important problems may then be seen to be how we ought to guide or maintain or reshape the relationships, both close and more distant, that we have or might have with actual human beings.

Particular others can, I think, be actual starving children in Africa with whom one feels empathy or even the anticipated children of future generations, not just those we are close to in any traditional context of family, neighbors, or friends. But particular others are still not "all rational beings" or "the greatest number."

In recognizing the component of feeling and relatedness between self and particular others, motivation is addressed as an inherent part of moral inquiry. Caring between parent and child is a good example.[15] We should not glamorize parental care. Many mothers and fathers dominate their children in harmful or inappropriate ways, or fail to care adequately for them. But when the relationship between "mother" and child is as it should be, the caretaker does not care for the child (nor the child for the caretaker) because of universal moral rules. The love and concern one feels for the child already motivate much of what one does. This is not to say that morality is irrelevant. One must still decide what one ought to do. But the process of addressing the moral questions in mothering and of trying to arrive at answers one can find acceptable involves motivated acting, not just thinking. And neither egoism nor a morality of universal rules will be of much help.

Mothering is, of course, not the only context in which the salient moral problems concern relations between particular others rather than conflicts between egoistic self and universal moral laws; all actual human contexts may be more like this than those depicted by Hobbes or Kant. But mothering may be one of the best contexts in which to make explicit why familiar moral theories are so deficient in offering guidance for action. And the variety of contexts within mothering, with the different excellences appropriate for dealing with infants, young children, or adolescents, provide rich sources of insight for moral inquiry.

The feelings characteristic of mothering—that there are too many demands on us, that we cannot do everything that we ought to do—are highly instructive. They give rise to problems different from those of universal rule versus self-interest. They require us to weigh the claims of one self-other relationship against the claims of other self-other relationships, to try to bring about some harmony between them, to see the issues in an actual temporal context, and to act rather than merely reflect.

For instance, we have limited resources for caring. We cannot care for everyone or do everything a caring approach suggests. We need moral guidelines for ordering our priorities. The hunger of our own children comes before the hunger of children we do not know. But the hunger of children in Africa ought to come before some of the expensive amusements we may wish to provide for our own children. These are moral problems calling to some extent for principled answers. But we have to figure out what we ought to do when actually buying groceries, cooking meals, refusing the requests of our children for the latest toy they have seen advertised, and sending money to UNICEF. The context is one of real action, not of ideal thought.

PRINCIPLES AND PARTICULARS

When we take the context of mothering as central, rather than peripheral, for moral theory, we run the risk of excessively discounting other contexts. It is a commendable risk, given the enormously more prevalent one of excessively discounting mothering. But I think that the attack on principles has sometimes been carried too far by critics of traditional moral theory.

Noddings, for instance, writes that "To say, 'It is wrong to cause pain needlessly,' contributes nothing by way of knowledge and can hardly be thought likely to change the attitude or behavior of one who might ask, 'Why is it wrong?' . . . Ethical caring . . . depends not upon rule or principle" but upon the development of a self "in congruence with one's best remembrance of caring and being cared-for."[16]

We should not forget that an absence of principles can be an invitation to capriciousness. Caring may be a weak defense against arbitrary decisions, and the person cared for may find the relation more satisfactory if both persons, but especially the person caring, are guided, to some extent, by principles concerning obligations and rights. To argue that no two cases are ever alike is to invite moral chaos. Furthermore, for one person to be in a position of caretaker means that that person has the power to withhold care, to leave the other without it. The person cared for is usually in a position of vulnerability. The moral significance of this needs to be addressed, along with other aspects of the caring relationship. Principles may remind a giver of care to avoid being capricious or domineering. While most of the moral problems involved in mothering contexts may deal with issues above and beyond the moral minimums that can be covered by principles concerning rights and obligations, that does not mean that these minimums can be dispensed with.

Noddings's discussion is unsatisfactory also in dealing with certain types of questions, for instance those of economic justice. Such issues cry out for relevant principles. Although caring may be needed to motivate us to act on such principles, the principles are not dispensable. Noddings questions the concern people may have for starving persons in distant countries, because she sees universal love and universal justice as masculine illusions. She refrains from judging that the rich deserve less or the poor more, because caring for individuals cannot yield such judgments. But this may amount to taking a given economic stratification as given, rather than as the appropriate object of critical scrutiny that it should be. It may lead to accepting that the rich will care for the rich and the poor for the poor, with the gap between them, however unjustifiably wide, remaining what it is. Some important moral issues seem beyond the reach of an ethic of caring, once caring leads us, perhaps through empathy, to be concerned with them.

On ethical views that renounce principles as excessively abstract, we might have few arguments to uphold the equality of women. After all, as parents can care for children recognized as weaker, less knowledgeable, less capable, and with appropriately restricted rights, so men could care for women deemed inferior in every way. On a view that ethics could satisfactorily be founded on caring alone, men could care for women considered undeserving of equal rights in all the significant areas in which women have been struggling to have their equality recognized. So an ethic of care, essential as a component of morality, seems deficient if taken as an exclusive preoccupation.

That aspect of the attack on principles which seems entirely correct is the view that not all ethical problems can be solved by appeal to one or a very few simple principles. It is often argued that all more particular moral rules or principles can be derived from such underlying ones as the Categorical Imperative or the Principle of Utility, and that these can be applied to all moral problems. The call for an ethic of care may be a call, which I share, for a more pluralistic view of ethics, recognizing that we need a division of moral labor employing different moral approaches for different domains, at least for the time being.[17] Satisfactory intermediate principles for areas such as those of international affairs, or family relations, cannot be derived from simple universal principles, but must be arrived at in conjunction with experience within the domains in question.

Attention to particular others will always require that we respect the particularity of the context and arrive at solutions to moral problems that will not give moral principles more weight than their due. But their due may remain considerable. And we will need principles concerning relationships, not only concerning the actions of individuals, as we will need evaluations of kinds of relationships, not only of the character traits of individuals.

BIRTH AND VALUING

To a large extent, the activity of mothering is potentially open to men as well as to women. Fathers can conceivably come to be as emotionally close, or as close through caretaking, to children as are mothers. The experience of relatedness, of responsibility for the growth and empowerment of new life, and of responsiveness to particular others, ought to be incorporated into moral theory, and will have to be so incorporated for moral theory to be adequate. At present, in this domain, it is primarily the experience of women (and of children) that has not been sufficiently reflected in moral theory and that ought to be so reflected. But this is not to say that it must remain experience available only to women. If men came to share fully and equitably in the care of all persons who need care—especially children, the sick, the old—the moral values that now arise for women in the context of caring might arise as fully for men.

There are some experiences, however, that are open only to women: menstruating, having an abortion, giving birth, suckling. We need to consider their possible significance or lack of significance for moral experience and theory. I will consider here only one kind of experience not open to men but of obviously great importance to women: the experience of giving birth or of deciding not to. Does the very experience of giving birth, or of deciding not to exercise the capacity to do so, make a significant difference for moral experience and moral theory? I think the answer must be: perhaps.

Of course birthing is a social as well as a personal or biological event. It takes place in a social context structured by attitudes and arrangements that deeply affect how women experience it: whether it will be accepted as "natural," whether it will be welcomed and celebrated, or whether it will be fraught with fear or shame. But I wish to focus briefly on the conscious awareness women can have of what they are doing in giving birth, and on the specifically personal and biological aspects of human birthing.

It is women who give birth to other persons. Women are responsible for the existence of new persons in ways far more fundamental than are men. It is not bizarre to recognize that women can, through abortion or suicide, choose not to give birth. A woman can be aware of the possibility that she can act to prevent a new person from existing, and can be aware that if this new person exists, it is because of what she has done and made possible.

In the past we have called attention to the extent to which women do not control their capacity to give birth. They are under extreme economic and social pressure to engage in intercourse, to marry, and to have children. Legal permission to undergo abortion is a recent, restricted, and threatened capacity. When the choice not to give birth requires grave risk to life, health, or well-being, or requires suicide, we should be careful not to misrepresent the situation when we speak of a woman's "choice" to become a mother, or of how she "could have done other" than have a child, or that "since she chose to become a mother, she is responsible for her child." It does not follow that because women are responsible for creating human beings, they should be held responsible by society for caring for them, either alone, primarily, or even at all. These two kinds of responsibility should not be confused, and I am speaking here only of the first. As conscious human beings, women can do other than give birth, and if they do give birth, they are responsible for the creation of other human beings. Though it may be very difficult for women to avoid giving birth, the very familiarity of the literary image of the woman who drowns herself or throws herself from a cliff rather than bear an illegitimate child should remind us that such eventualities are not altogether remote from consciousness.

Women have every reason to be justifiably angry with men who refuse to take responsibility for their share of the events of pregnancy and birth, or for the care children require. Because, for so long, we have wanted to increase the extent to which men would recognize their responsibilities for causing pregnancy, and would share in the long years of care needed to bring a child to independence, we have tended to emphasize the ways in which the responsibilities for creating a new human being are equal between women and men.[18] But in fact, men produce sperm and women produce babies, and the difference is enormous. Excellent arguments can be made that boys and men suffer "womb envy"; indeed, men lack a wondrous capacity that women possess.[19]

Of all the human capacities, it is probably the capacity to create new human beings that is most worth celebrating. We can expect that a woman will care about and feel concern for a child she has created as the child grows and develops, and that she feels responsible for having given the child life. But her concern is more than something to be expected. It is, perhaps, justifiable in certain ways unique to women.

Children are born into actual situations. A mother cannot escape ultimate responsibility for having given birth to this particular child in these particular circumstances. She can be aware that she could have avoided intercourse, or used more effective contraception, or waited to get pregnant until her circumstances were different; that she could have aborted this child and had another later; or that she could have killed herself and prevented this child from facing the suffering or hardship of this particular life. The momentousness of all these decisions about giving or not giving life can hardly fail to affect what she experiences in relation to the child.

Perhaps it might be thought that many of these issues arise in connection with infanticide, and that if one refrains from killing an infant, one is responsible for giving the infant life. Infanticide is as open to men as to women. But to kill or refrain from killing a child, once the child is capable of life with caretakers different from the person who is responsible for having given birth to the child, is a quite different matter from creating or not creating this possibility, and I am concerned in this discussion with the moral significance of giving birth.

It might also be thought that those, including the father, who refrain from killing the mother, or from forcing her to have an abortion, are also responsible for not preventing the birth of the child.[20] But unless the distinction between suicide and murder, and between having an abortion and forcing a woman to have an abortion against her will, are collapsed completely, the issues would be very different. To refrain from murdering someone else is not the same as deciding not to kill oneself. And to decide not to force someone else to have an abortion is different from deciding not to have an abortion when one could. The person capable of giving birth who decides not to prevent the birth is the person responsible, in the sense of "responsible" I am discussing, for creating another human being. To create a new human being is not the same as to refrain from ending the life of a human being who already exists.

Perhaps there is a tendency to want to approve of or to justify what one has decided with respect to giving life. In deciding to give birth, perhaps a woman has a natural tendency to approve of the birth, to believe that the child ought to have been born. Perhaps this inclines her to believe whatever may follow from this: that the child is entitled to care, and that feelings of love for the child are appropriate and justified. The conscious decision to create a new human being may provide women with an inclination to value the child and to have hope for the child's future. Since, in her view, the child ought to have been born, a woman may feel that the world ought to be hospitable to the child. And if the child ought to have been born, the child ought to grow into an admirable human adult. The child's life has, and should continue to have, value that is recognized.

Consider next the phenomenon of sacrifice. In giving birth, women suffer severe pain for the sake of new life. Having suffered for the child in giving the child life, women may have a natural tendency to value what they have endured pain for. There is a tendency, often noted in connection with war, for people to feel that because sacrifices have been made, the sacrifice should have been "worth it," and, if necessary, other things ought to be done so that the sacrifice "shall not have been in vain." There may be a similar tendency for those who have suffered to give birth to assure themselves that the pain was for the good reason of creating a new life that is valuable and that will be valued.

Certainly, this is not to say that there is anything good or noble about suffering, or that merely because people want to believe that what they suffered for was worthwhile, it was. A vast amount of human suffering has been in vain, and could and should have been avoided. The point is that once suffering has already occurred and the "price," if we resort to such calculations, has already been paid, it will be worse if the result is a further cost and better if the result is a clear benefit that can make the price, when it is necessary for the result, validly "worth it."

The suffering of the mother who has given birth will more easily have been worthwhile if the child's life has value. The chance that the suffering will be outweighed by future happiness is much greater if the child is valued by the society and the family into which the child is born. If the mother's suffering yields nothing but further suffering and a being deemed to be of no value, her suffering may truly have been in vain. Anyone can have reasons to value children. But the person who has already undergone the suffering needed to create one has a special reason to recognize that the child is valuable and to want the child to be valued so that the suffering she has already borne will have been, truly, worthwhile.

These arguments can be repeated for the burdens of work and anxiety normally expended in bringing up a child. Those who have already borne these burdens have special reasons for wanting to see the grown human being for whom they have cared as valuable and valued. Traditionally, women have not only borne the burdens of childbirth, but, with little help, the much greater burdens of child rearing. Of course, the burdens of child rearing could be shared fully by men, as they have been partially shared by women other than natural mothers. Although the concerns involved in bringing up a child may greatly outweigh the suffering of childbirth itself, this does not mean that giving birth is incidental.

The decision not to have children is often influenced by a comparable tendency to value the potential child.[21] Knowing how much care the child would deserve and how highly, as a mother, she would value the child, a woman who gives up the prospect of motherhood can recognize how much she is losing. For such reasons, a woman may feel overwhelming ambivalence concerning the choice.

Consider, finally, how biology can affect our ways of valuing children. Although men and women may share a desire or an instinctive tendency to wish to reproduce, and although these feelings may be equally strong for both men and women, such feelings might affect their attitudes toward a given child very differently. In terms of biological capacity, a mother has a relatively greater stake in a child to which she has given birth. This child is about one-twentieth or one twenty-fifth of all the children she could possibly have, whereas a man could potentially have hundreds or thousands of other children. In giving birth, a woman has already contributed a large amount of energy and effort toward the production of this particular child, while a man has, biologically, contributed only a few minutes. To the extent that such biological facts may influence attitudes, the attitudes of the mother and father toward the "worth" or "value" of a particular child may be different. The father might consider the child more easily replaceable in the sense that the father's biological contribution can so easily and so painlessly be repeated on another occasion or with another woman; for the mother to repeat her biological contribution would be highly exhausting and painful. The mother, having already contributed so much more to the creation of this particular child than the father, might value the result of her effort in proportion. And her pride at what she has accomplished in giving birth can be appropriately that much greater. She has indeed "accomplished" far more than has the father.

So even if instincts or desires to reproduce oneself or one's genes, or to create another human being, are equally powerful among men and women, a given child is, from the father's biological standpoint, much more incidental and interchangeable: any child out of the potential thousands he might sire would do. For the mother, on the other hand, if this particular child does not survive and grow, her chances for biological reproduction are reduced to a much greater degree. To suggest that men may think of their children as replaceable is offensive to many men, and women. Whether such biological facts as those I have mentioned have any significant effect on parental attitudes is not known. But arguments from biological facts to social attitudes, and even to moral norms, have a very long history and are still highly popular; we should be willing to examine the sorts of unfamiliar arguments I have suggested that can be drawn from biological facts. *If* anatomy is destiny, men may be "naturally" more indifferent toward particular children than has been thought.

Since men, then, do not give birth, and do not experience the responsibility, the pain, and momentousness of childbirth, they lack the particular motives to value the child that may spring from this capacity and this fact. Of course, many other reasons for valuing a child are felt by both parents, by caretakers of either gender, and by those who are not parents; but the motives discussed, and others arising from giving birth, may be morally significant. The long years of child care may provide stronger motives for valuing a child than do the relatively short months of pregnancy and hours of childbirth. The decisions and sacrifices involved in bringing up a child can be more affecting than those normally experienced in giving birth to a child. So the possibility for men to acquire such motives thorough child care may outweigh any long-term differences in motivation between women and men. But it might yet remain that the person responsible for giving birth would continue to have a greater sense of responsibility for how the child develops, and stronger feelings of care and concern for the child.

That adoptive parents can feel as great a concern for an attachment to their children as can biological parents may indicate that the biological components in valuing children are relatively modest in importance. However, to the extent that biological components are significant, they would seem to affect men and women in different ways.

MORALITY AND HUMAN TENDENCIES

So far, I have been describing possible feelings rather than attaching any moral value to them. That children are valued does not mean that they are valuable, and if mothers have a natural tendency to value their children, it does not follow that they ought to. But if feelings are taken to be relevant to moral theory, the feelings of valuing the child, like the feelings of empathy for other persons in pain, may be of moral significance.

To the extent that a moral theory takes natural male tendencies into account, it would at least be reasonable to take natural female tendencies into account. Traditional moral theories often suppose it is legitimate for individuals to maximize self-interest, or satisfy their preferences, within certain constraints based on the equal rights of others. If it can be shown that the tendency to want to pursue individual self-interest is a stronger tendency among men than among women, this would certainly be relevant to an evaluation of such theory. And if it could be shown that a tendency to value children and a desire to foster the developing capabilities of the particular others for whom we care is a stronger tendency among women than among men, this too would be relevant in evaluating moral theories.

The assertion that women have a tendency to value children is still different from the assertion that they ought to. Noddings speaks often of the "natural" caring of mothers for children.[22] I do not intend to deal here with the disputed empirical question of whether human mothers do or do not have a strong natural tendency to love their children. And I am certainly not claiming that natural mothers have greater skills or excellences in raising children than have others, including, perhaps, men. I am trying, rather, to explore possible "reasons" for mothers to value children, reasons that might be different for mothers and potential mothers than they would be for anyone else asking the question: why should we value human beings? And it does seem that certain possible reasons for valuing living human beings are present for mothers in ways that are different from what they would be for others. The reason, if it is one, that the child should be valued because I have suffered to give the child life is different from the reason, if it is one, that the child should be valued because someone unlike me suffered to give the child life. And both of these reasons are different from the reason, if it is one, that the child should be valued because the continued existence of the child satisfies a preference of a parent, or because the child is a bearer of universal rights, or has the capacity to experience pleasure.

Many moral theories, and fields dependent on them such as economics, employ the assumption that to increase the utility of individuals is a good thing to do. But if asked *why* it is a good thing to increase utility, or satisfy desire, or produce pleasure, or *why* doing so counts as a good reason for something, it is very difficult to answer. The claim is taken as a kind of starting assumption for which no *further* reason can be given. It seems to rest on a view that people seek pleasure, or that we can recognize pleasure as having intrinsic value. But if women recognize quite different assumptions as more likely to be valid, that would certainly be of importance to ethics. We might then take it as one of our starting assumptions that creating good relations of care and concern and trust between ourselves and our children, and creating social arrangements in which children will be valued and well cared for, are more important than maximizing individual utilities. And the moral theories that might be compatible with such assumptions might be very different from those with which we are familiar.

A number of feminists have independently declared their rejection of the Abraham myth.[23] We do not approve the sacrifice of children out of religious duty. Perhaps, for those capable of giving birth, reasons to value the actual life of the born will, in general, seem to be better than reasons justifying the sacrifice of such life.[24] This may reflect an accordance of priority to caring for particular others over abstract principle. From the perspectives of Rousseau, of Kant, of Hegel, and of Kohlberg, this is a deficiency of women. But from a perspective of what is needed for late twentieth-century survival, it may suggest a superior morality. Only feminist moral theory can offer a satisfactory evaluation of such suggestions, because only feminist moral theory can adequately understand the alternatives to traditional moral theory that the experience of women requires.

NOTES

I am especially grateful to my daughter, Julia Held, for the suggestions she made concerning a draft of this paper and for the many insights she provided; she had given birth to Alexander Held White shortly before I began the paper. I am also grateful to many others who have expressed their thoughts about the issues involved. I especially thank Annette Baier, Brian Barry, Sandra Bartky, Larry Blum, Nancy Fraser, Marilyn Friedman, Ann Garry, Carol Gilligan, Jeffrie Murphy, Lucius Outlaw, and Carole Pateman for their early comments, and Marcia Baron, Louise De Salvo, Dorothy Helly, Nancy Holmstrom, Amélie Rorty, Sara Ruddick, Christina Hoff Sommers, Joan Tronto, and Diana T. Meyers and Eva F. Kittay, the editors of *Women and Moral Theory,* for additional later comments.

For financial support, I am grateful to the Center for Advanced Study in the Behavioral Sciences at Stanford, where I was a Fellow while writing the paper, to the Andrew Mellon Foundation, and to Hunter College of the City University of New York.

1. See Virginia Held, *Rights and Goods: Justifying Social Action* (New York: Free Press, Macmillan, 1984).
2. See Genevieve Lloyd, *The Man of Reason: "Male" and "Female" in Western Philosophy* (Minneapolis: University of Minnesota Press, 1984).
3. Virginia Held, *Rights and Goods,* p. 272. See also V. Held, "The Political 'Testing' of Moral Theories," *Midwest Studies in Philosophy* 7 (1982): 343–63.
4. For discussion, see especially Nancy Hartsock, *Money, Sex, and Power* (New York: Longman, 1983), chaps. 10, 11.
5. Lawrence Kohlberg's studies of what he claimed to be developmental stages in moral reasoning suggested that girls progress less well and less far than boys through these stages. See his *The Philosophy of Moral Development* (San Francisco: Harper & Row, 1981); and L. Kohlberg and R. Kramer, "Continuities and Discontinuities in Child and Adult Moral Development," *Human Development* 12 (1969): 93–120. James R. Rest, on the other hand, claims in his study of adolescents in 1972 and 1974 that "none of the male-female differences in the Defining Issues Test . . . and on the Comprehension or Attitudes tests were significant." See his "Longitudinal Study of the Defining Issues Test of Moral Judgment: A Strategy for Analyzing Developmental Change," *Developmental Psychology* (November 1975): 738–48; quotation at 741. Carol Gilligan's *In a Different Voice* (Cambridge: Harvard University Press, 1982) suggests that girls and women tend to organize their thinking about moral problems somewhat differently from boys and men; her subsequent work supports the view that whether people tend to construe moral problems in terms of rules of justice or in terms of caring relationships is at present somewhat associated with gender (Carol Gilligan, address at Conference on Women and Moral Thought, SUNY Stony Brook, March 21, 1985). Other studies have shown that females are significantly more inclined than males to cite compassion and sympathy as reasons for their moral positions; see Constance Boucher Holstein, "Irreversible, Stepwise Sequence in the Development of Moral Judgment: A Longitudinal Study of Males and Females." *Child Development* 47, no. 1 (March 1976): 51–61.

6. For suggestions on how Gilligan's stages, like Kohlberg's, might be thought to be historically and culturally, rather than more universally, based, see Linda Nicholson, "Women, Morality, and History," *Social Research* 50, no. 3 (Autumn 1983): 514–36.
7. See, e.g., Debra Nails, "Social-Scientific Sexism: Gilligan's Mismeasure of Man," *Social Research* 50, no. 3 (Autumn 1983): 643–64.
8. I have discussed this in a paper that has gone through several major revisions and changes of title, from its presentation at a conference at Loyola University on April 18, 1983, to its discussion at Dartmouth College, April 2, 1984. I will refer to it as "Non-Contractual Society: A Feminist Interpretation." See also Carole Pateman, "The Fraternal Social Contract: Some Observations on Patriarchy," paper presented at American Political Science Association meeting, August 30–September 2, 1984, and "The Shame of the Marriage Contract," in *Women's Views of the Political World of Men*, ed. by Judith Hicks Stiehm (Dobbs Ferry, N.Y.: Transnational Publishers, 1984).
9. For discussion, see especially Nancy Hartsock, *Money, Sex, and Power.*
10. Ibid., p. 39.
11. See Held, *Rights and Goods*, chap 5.
12. Ibid., chap. 11.
13. Lawrence A. Blum, *Friendship, Altruism and Morality* (London: Routledge and Kegan Paul, 1980), p. 1.
14. Owen J. Flanagan Jr. and Jonathan E. Adler, "Impartiality and Particularity," *Social Research* 50, no. 3 (Autumn 1983): 576–96.
15. See, e.g., Nell Noddings, *Caring: A Feminine Approach to Ethics and Moral Education* (Berkeley: University of California Press, 1984) pp. 91–94.
16. Ibid., pp. 91–94.
17. Participants in the conference on Women and Moral Theory offered the helpful term "domain relativism" for the version of this view that I defended.
18. See, e.g., Virginia Held, "The Obligations of Mothers and Fathers," repr. in *Mothering: Essays in Feminist Theory*, ed. by Joyce Trebilcot (Totowa, N.J.: Rowman and Allanheld, 1984).
19. See Eva Kittay, "Womb Envy: An Explanatory Concept," in *Mothering*, ed. by Joyce Trebilcot. To overcome the pernicious aspects of the "womb envy" she skillfully identifies and describes, Kittay argues that boys should be taught that their "procreative contribution is of equal significance" (p. 123). While boys should certainly be told the truth, the truth may remain that, as she states elsewhere, "there is the . . . awesome quality of creation itself—the transmutation performed by the parturient woman" (p. 99).
20. This point was made by Marcia Baron in correspondence with me.
21. In exploring the values involved in birth and mothering, we need to develop views that include women who do not give birth. As Margaret Simons writes, "We must define a feminist maternal ethic that supports a woman's right not to have children." See Margaret A. Simons, "Motherhood, Feminism and Identity," *Hypatia, Women's Studies International Forum* 7, 5 (1984): 353.
22. E.g., Noddings, *Caring*, pp. 31, 43, 49.
23. See Gilligan, *In a Different Voice*, p. 104; Held, "Non-Contractual Society: A Feminist Interpretation"; and Noddings, *Caring*, p. 43.
24. That some women enthusiastically send their sons off to war may be indicative of a greater than usual acceptance of male myths rather than evidence against this claim, since the enthusiasm seems most frequent in societies where women have the least influence in the formation of prevailing religious and other beliefs.

Gender and Moral Luck

Card defines luck as that which is beyond the control of the individual, and she stresses that luck includes the predictable consequences of social practices, including oppressive social practices. Thus, she takes up the question of how male dominance has affected women's moral luck—what responsibilities have fallen to women, whether the relationships women participate in, such as heterosexual relationships, are desirable to sustain, what moral insights are available from the vantage point of women's position under patriarchy, and what moral damage results from sex oppression.

Whereas Mary Wollstonecraft regards feminine virtues as vices that make it easier to dominate women and concludes that women are morally deformed under patriarchy, Carol Gilligan contends that women's virtues are different from and equal to men's. Card urges that although these positions conflict, both are plausible, and she suggests that this paradox indicates that oppressive relationships are distorting both women's and men's morality. Because women are not free to end bad relationships, they valorize assuming responsibility for maintaining whatever relationships they happen to be enmeshed in. It is important to recognize the moral damage attendant upon women's ethic of care and responsibility under patriarchy—especially women's unwarranted gratitude to men. Still, Card maintains that the theme of responsibility has been overlooked and is important to pursue. The concept of responsibility is pivotal to the morality of informal, personal relationships, and these relationships are fundamental to society.

—D.T.M.

Chapter 33

Claudia Card

Gender and Moral Luck

Pasts we inherit affect who be become.[1] As gendered beings in a society with a history of patriarchy, women and men inherit different pasts and consequently different social expectations, lines of communication, opportunities, and barriers. When these things influence character development, they make gender part of our "moral luck."[2] By "luck" I mean factors, good or bad, beyond the control of the affected agent: matters of chance and predictable results of social practice.[3]

I am interested in how gender-related moral luck illuminates biases in ethical theory. My special interest is character development under oppressive practices. In the present essay I question a view of women and care that proceeds as though women have no real damage to overcome, as though women's values and virtues need only to be appreciated and allowed to develop as they are, or at most, need to be supplemented by those more characteristically attributed to men. I then examine a more historically oriented view of women and ethics, preserving, without glorifying women's moral sensibilities, the idea that attention to women's lives can deepen and correct modern Western ethical thinking.

A number of feminist scholars are sympathetic to the idea, popularly associated with the work of Carol Gilligan, that an ethic of care is more characteristic of women or is more apt to be implicit in the experience and ideals of women and that an ethic of justice or rights, or abstract action-guiding principle, is more implicit in the experience of men.[4] If some such hypothesis were true, we might expect a bias in ethical theory toward justice or rights, or at least toward abstract action-guiding principles, given the history of sexism. Such a bias appears evident in the contractarianism and utilitarianism of modern Western ethics. Yet these theories have not always been dominant. A more modest hypothesis—less exciting, perhaps less romantic—also found in Carol Gilligan's work but often not distinguished from the "justice and care" hypothesis, is that *the responsibilities of different kinds of relationships* yield different ethical preoccupations, methods, priorities, even concepts.[5] Different kinds of relationships have been differently distributed among women and men in patriarchal society: a larger share of the responsibilities of certain personal and informal relationships to women, a larger share of the responsibilities of formal and impersonal relationships defined by social institutions to men. It is plausible that a result has been the creation of a significant difference in ethical orientation.[6] Putting it this way opens better to philosophical inquiry the questions of how good these relationships have been, what their virtues and vices are, their major values, their roles in a good life, in a good society. It allows us, for example, to explore the place of fairness in friendship and to note its absence as a flaw.[7]

The hypothesis in terms of *relationships* puts us into a better position than the justice and care hypothesis to identify moral damage resulting from and perpetuating sex oppression. We need to be sensitive to the possibility, easily disguised by the honorific language of "justice" and "care," that what often pass for virtues for both sexes are vices (see Houston 1987). Histories of oppression require us to read between the lines of what we say. The privileged are liable to arrogance with its blindness to others' perspectives. The oppressed are liable to low self-esteem, ingratiation, and affiliation with abusers ("female masochism"), as well as to a tendency to dissemble, a fear of being conspicuous, and chameleonism—taking on the colors of our environment as protection against assault. Histories of exploitation lead us to identify with service, to find our value in our utility or ability to please. Moral damage among both privileged and oppressed tends to be unself-conscious, mutually reinforcing, and stubborn. Where our identities are at stake, oppression is hard to face. Beneficiaries face guilt issues and are liable to defensiveness. The oppressed face damage to an already precarious self-esteem in admitting impotence.

It may also be our moral luck to develop special insights, even under oppressive institutions. I do not have in mind the *experience* of resisting oppressors. Temptations to romanticize resistance are sobered by the thought that so doing seems to glorify oppression (see Ringelheim 1985). Yet a priori, it seems plausible that divisions of responsibility divide opportunities for kinds of moral insight by unevenly distributing the decision-making experience that develops it. However, two cautions are in order. First, oppressive divisions of responsibility may encourage delusion more readily than insight. This suggests that insight is hard won. Second, the hypothesis that insights in the areas of *justice* and *care* might be unevenly distributed appears to assume uncritically that these are such different areas that insights in each are separable from insights in the other, assumptions that may be oversimple (Friedman 1987; Stocker 1986; Flanagan and Jackson 1987). Both cautions are themes in the present chapter.

The remainder of this chapter has two main tasks. First, I sketch a tension between the two kinds of feminist critique represented by Carol Gilligan and Mary Wollstonecraft, the former flattering both sexes, the latter flattering neither, and both focusing on maternal and adult heterosexual relationships.[8] I argue that correcting misperceptions of women identified by a care perspective, such as Carol Gilligan's, is not enough to vindicate women's characters, nor, therefore, to lend much support to the hypothesis that women's values and aspirations can deepen and correct defects in modern ethical theory.[9] My second task is to explore what more is needed to make that "corrective hypothesis" more plausible. To do so, I examine the sense of responsibility attaching to informal, often personal relationships, contrasting it with that of formal and impersonal ones, and attaching to it independently of a contrast between justice and care. I argue that taking only formal and impersonal relationships as paradigms of obligation and responsibility has produced arbitrarily biased and probably superficial theory. This idea, suggested also in recent work of Annette Baier (1986; see also Flanagan and Jackson 1987), is not that *justice* is superficial. I do not find justice superficial. The idea is rather that the ethical significance of basic informal and personal relationships is at least as much of the first order as that of basic social institutions. To the extent that the personal and informal underlie and circumscribe formal institutions, they are *more* basic. I argue throughout that a focus on formality is not the only bias in modern ethical theory, but that fairness has also been systematically ignored in personal and informal relationships, especially where women are involved.

1. WOMEN AND CARE

Sigmund Freud (1961) criticized women as deficient in the sense of justice. As Carol Gilligan (1982, 18) observes, the behavior underlying this common criticism of women by men is also often cited under different descriptions as evidence of women's "special goodness"—caring, sensitivity, responsiveness to others' needs, and appreciation of the concrete particular. Both the criticism and the praise are part of the tradition of modern Western moral philosophy. "The very thought of seeing women administer justice raises a laugh," said Arthur Schopenhauer. He thought women "far less capable than men of understanding and sticking to universal principles," yet also that "they surpass men in virtues of *philanthropy* and *lovingkindness* [*Menschenliebe*], for the origin of this is . . . intuitive" (1965, 151). On women and principles he followed Immanuel Kant, who exclaimed, "I hardly believe the fair sex is capable of principles," and speculated instead, "Providence has put in their breast kind and benevolent sensations, a fine feeling for propriety, and a complaisant soul" (1960, 81). The contradiction is acute in Immanuel Kant, whose views on women and on morality seem to imply that good women lack moral character.[10]

I refer loosely to the above views from the academic canon as "the patriarchal view." Women criticize this view from different angles. Some, like Carol Gilligan, defend the moral responses attributed to women as "different but also valuable," arguing that theories by which women appear deficient are faulty. I call this "the rosy view," because it presents a fairly romantic picture of the insights of women and men. Everyone comes out looking good though not perfect; the insights of each sex, basically sound, need to be supplemented by those of the other. Other critics, like Mary Wollstonecraft (1982), reject so-called women's goodness as a euphemism for vices that make it easier for women to be controlled by men. Mary Wollstonecraft argued that women under sexist institutions become morally deformed, neither loving nor just. Noticing similarities between the vices of women and those of the relatively powerless men in military service, she disagreed with her contemporaries, Jean-Jacques Rousseau and Immanuel Kant, on the gender relatedness of virtues. Her view was that *duties* might vary but *virtues* are the same for everyone. She ridiculed the idea that powerless, abused, uneducated women have a special kind of goodness. I call this view, generously, "the skeptical view," for it suggests skepticism about the likelihood that the perspectives of oppressed women yield special moral insights. The correlative idea, that oppressors' perspectives are no wiser, is not developed by Mary Wollstonecraft, who was writing in 1792 to an audience of men without benefit of a supporting women's community. It is implicit in her approach, however. In this view, the problem with "women's ethics" and "men's ethics" is not that they are incomplete or underdeveloped but that they are warped from the start.

However mutually incompatible they appear, the protests of both Carol Gilligan and Mary Wollstonecraft initially seem right. I have wanted to find more truth in the rosy view. Yet the skeptical view refuses to let go of me. If the two views are to be reconciled, it seems to me utterly crucial not to deny the truths of the skeptical view.

An observation documented in Carol Gilligan's recent essays is that nearly everyone interviewed seemed readily able to adopt both the care and justice perspectives but, as with incompatible gestalts, not simultaneously, and that most found one perspective more comfortable than the other (Gilligan et al. 1988). To me, these observations suggest the presence of something *other* than justice and care—such as an oppressive relationship—skewing both perspectives. For how can we judge ethical conflicts between considerations of justice and care if we cannot hold them in mind without a priori subordinating considerations of one sort to those of the other?[11] By looking at cases, Marilyn Friedman (1987) has convincingly argued that neither a priori ranking is plausible.

In friendship, both fairness and caring are valuable. Although friendship does not usually center on formulating rules and applying them to cases, it typically does involve, as Marilyn Friedman (1987) has pointed out, a division of responsibilities in a more or less extensive mutual support system. A good friendship is fair about such divisions. Such fairness may even be a requirement of caring. Fairness in friendship also requires responsiveness to personal deserts or worthiness.[12] If anything, to be a good friend one needs a *better* sense of fairness than to be a good citizen or soldier, an idea that makes good sense of Aristotle's report that people say that "when [we] are friends [we] have no need of justice, while when [we] are just [we] need friendship as well, and the truest form of justice is thought to be a friendly quality" (1925, 1155a). If "justice" here is meant to suggest enforcement, the idea seems sound. Responsiveness where enforcement is not forthcoming is a greater test of one's fairness than where there is possible recourse to sanctions. If the idea is that the values of justice are superficial, however, it seems confused. For what makes sense of friends not needing justice is that they have the relevant values so well internalized.

This interpretation suggests that it is *not* a mistake to evaluate the conduct of personal relationships by values associated with justice, such as fairness. Nevertheless, errors turn up in the patriarchal view of women and ethics, as Carol Gilligan has pointed out. Women's motives and intentions are often misperceived, misrepresented, oversimplified. The question arises whether righting these errors reveals virtues and values wrongly overlooked in patriarchal ethics.

In Lawrence Kohlberg's moral stages (Kohlberg 1981), for example, women may appear more concerned with approval, more conventional, when what they are actually doing is exhibiting a concern for maintaining relationships. In maintaining relationships, we respect points of view different from our own and attempt to empathize with them. Sigmund Freud found women to have "weak ego-boundaries," poor self-definition, problems with separation and autonomy, and a weaker sense of justice, at least a weaker "legal sense," and concluded that women were thereby deficient in moral reasoning. Carol Gilligan (1982, 43–45) responded that if women have a problem with separation, *men* have a problem with *connection.* She also responded that women judged deficient in justice may be resolving conflicts of interest by favoring inclusiveness over ranking or balancing claims. She illustrated the difference with the endearing story of "the pirate who lives next door."[13]

And yet despite the genuineness of such misperceptions and oversimplifications, disturbing facts remain. Women's political oppositions in misogynist environments complicate the assessment of women's moral responses. Institutionalized dependence on men for protection against male assault, for employment, promotion, and validation, have given women reasons to seek "approval," usually *male* approval. This approval is granted for conventional affiliations with men, respect for their views, empathy with them, etc. Just as there is no need to suppose that women value approval or conventionality *for its own sake* or that we confuse "right" with "conventional" (or "approved"), there is no need to assume on the basis of women's empathy that women value these connections for their own sake. Many women are prudent. Many are convinced that this exchange is what heterosexual love is about, since, after all, convention requires women to affiliate with masculine protectors out of "love." How many attachments are the product of what Adrienne Rich (1980) called "compulsory heterosexuality," the result of orientations molded at an age when our powers of assessment are morally undeveloped?

Speculation that many women are basically prudent about heterosexual relationships may strike some as ungenerous to women. However, where women are not respected, prudence is necessary. It is less generous to assume our readiness to be basically moved by attachment to those who do not respect us. If the distribution of power in society's basic structure is a clue to its members' level of respect for others, as is argued by John Rawls (1971, secs. 67, 82), a pervasive gender-related imbalance of power is evidence of widespread social disrespect for women. If so, what is at stake in evaluating heterosexual relationships is not simply the uses of power by those with more of it but also what it means that they have more of it. In such a context, reciprocity of respect might be extraordinary.

The variety of motives from which women may affiliate raises ethical questions that both the rosy view and the patriarchal view tend to bury. Male "disapproval" commonly reaches the pitch of harassment. What are some ethically honorable ways of avoiding, resisting, and stopping harassment? Entering into heterosexual relationships to purchase "protection" may be not only risky but also unfair to other women in further entrenching women's need for protection rather than combatting that need. Women are often surprised to hear that *they* are *unfair* if they reject sexual advances from men and similarly, when they bring accusations of rape, that expecting anything else was *not fair* under the circumstances. For patriarchy lacks a history of giving women *honorable* ways of invoking fairness to reject sexual overtures from men, especially from men from whom they cannot, or for various reasons do not wish to, sever connections altogether. Similar problems exist for the issues of self-definition and autonomy. Given women's inferior political position together with the lifelong message that a woman "alone" is "asking for it," who could be surprised that "studies show" women seeking to create and maintain affiliations? Again, cautions are in order: we need to look at why women affiliate and with whom. Women don't embrace just any affiliation. Many are terrified of lesbian connections and disdainful of interracial connections, for example. We who are women are taught that identifying ourselves in relation to certain men as sister, mother, wife, lover, etc., can reduce threats of assault. It does not follow that such a reduction amounts to *safety* or that women are under the illusion that it does. Nor does it follow that we do not know well where we leave off and men begin. We learn our places early.

Reciprocity is associated in modern ethics primarily with justice. Yet lack of reciprocity is probably a major cause of the breakup of friendships among peers. If, as Carol Gilligan noted early in her work (1982, 17), *at midlife* men come to see the value of intimacy, which women have seen all along, what does that say about the quality of heterosexual intimacy *prior to midlife*, and about the judgment of those who valued such relationships? Perhaps, as Phillippa Foot said of the villain's courage (1978, 14–18), women's caring here is not functioning as a virtue. It is also doubtful that paradigms of relationship in which women's choices are less than free represent women's values fairly or well.

Women's connectedness is not always a good thing. When our *primary* relationships lack reciprocity of valuing, we risk losing (or failing to develop) self-esteem. Valuing others independently of their utility is at the core of both respect and love, and being so valued is important to self-esteem. In respect we appreciate others as like ourselves in certain fundamental ways; in love we also cherish their particularities. Identifying and valuing ourselves in terms of relationships to others who likewise identify and value themselves in relation to us can leave us with enriched self-esteem. But when our primary attachments are to those who define and value themselves by what they take to be their own achievements while they define and value us in terms of our relationships to them, we are encouraged at best to assimilate, not really to affiliate. We risk becoming extensions, tools. Our caring does not have the same meaning that it has when it is valued because it comes from us. It is not the same source of self-esteem.

Failure to appreciate the value of others independently of utility has not been the failure of only those with the lion's share of power. In military boot camps, males of a variety of ages and political strata learn misogynist attitudes toward females in general.[14] Fear of the same phenomena seems to underlie Mary Wollstonecraft's opposition to boys' boarding schools, although she doesn't comment on military misogyny. When those who lack respect also come into the lion's share of power, affiliative relationships with them are not only impoverished but dangerous for those on the short end.

Recent work on women's conception of the self as rooted in relationships with others has led to speculations about men and violence. On the basis of fantasy studies, Carol Gilligan has suggested that violence in men's fantasies is rooted in men's fear of intimacy (Gilligan 1982, 39–45; Gilligan et al. 1988, chap. 12). She reported that in the studies in which subjects constructed stories in response to pictures, women tended to find safety in intimacy and danger in isolation, while men tended to find danger in intimacy and safety in independence. We should be skeptical, however, about the conclusion that women find safety in intimacy. The conclusion about men's fears may clarify why, if it is amplified and made more specific.

Many relationships women construct are informal, even personal, but not intimate. Like the nets that women test subjects supplied in response to a picture of trapeze artists, women's relationships with women are often for safety and protection—they are *networks* of connections, not sexual unions. Thus they are not the same as the relationships men seem to fear. The fantasies of both sexes may be compatible with *both* sexes fearing intimacy, each for different reasons. Fear of isolation is compatible with fear of intimacy; fear of isolation may be stronger for women. Women's networks are often cushions against the violence of intimate relationships. Where men do not construct such networks, perhaps they do not have a similar need. When men fear heterosexual intimacy, they usually have the power to avoid it.

If we examine fantasies for clues to our senses of danger, what do women's infamous rape fantasies tell us? Women are reluctant to articulate them, and not always because they reinforce stereotypes of female masochism. Rape fantasies are not only of attack *by* rapists but also of responsive attack *on* rapists, killing rapists, maiming them, etc. Intimacy has not cured the violence in women's lives. It has given the violent greater access to their victims. Rape is one of the most underreported crimes because it is committed more readily by acquaintances and intimates than by strangers (Amir 1971). Battery of women by intimates is a serious issue in misogynist environments.[15] Men's fears of rejection and entrapment by women in this context are not altogether misplaced. Men's fantasy violence may betray an appreciation of the implications of misogyny. Perhaps what men fear is *women's* historically well-grounded *fears of men*, which predictably issue in the tangle of women's clinging to men for acceptability and protection (against other men) and at the same time in their withdrawing sexually, engaging in manipulation, daily resentful hostilities, and eventual fantasies of widowhood.

Women's failure to value separation and autonomy is a genuine problem. But the problem is political, not simply psychological. Women are systematically penalized for not being available on demand to children, relatives, spouses, male lovers. A good example of women's moral luck may be that as a result of our political inability to end bad relationships, we have not learned to discriminate well between good ones and bad ones but have learned instead to assume responsibility for maintaining whatever relationships "fate" seems to throw our way. The great danger, as well as the great strength, of the method of inclusion is its presumption that there should be a way to satisfy everyone. Women are afraid to say no. But separation can be preferable to inclusion.

Inclusion brings us again to the sense of justice. Why contrast the search for inclusive solutions with justice or with *fairness*? Fairness is not only a matter of ranking, taking turns, or balancing claims—ways of distributing power among competing parties—but also a matter of recognizing who deserves what from whom, and deserts tend to bring the affects of sympathy and antipathy into the picture. Sometimes everyone deserves to be included. Although inclusion is an alternative to balancing claims, it is not necessarily an alternative to justice. The *difference principle* in John Rawls's theory of justice as fairness could favor inclusion over competition or taking turns. This principle directs that basic social institutions be so arranged that those least advantaged are as well-off as possible (Rawls 1971, secs. 11–12). If a more inclusive solution were more to the advantage of those least well-off, the difference principle would favor it. If methods of inclusion are *among* the methods of justice, women's reputation for a weak sense of justice may be undeserved in proportion to the accuracy of Carol Gilligan's observations. Where inclusion is unjust, it is unclear what can be said to recommend it.

Although women probably have more sense of justice than Freud thought, the truth that women are liable to misperception does not yet sustain the view that women's reasonings reveal virtues and values that can deepen and correct the ethics of those more privileged. Often our reasonings reveal survival strategies and, less flatteringly, vices complementary to those of the privileged. Still, I find the corrective potentialities of the data of women's lives to be genuine. To show how, I want to look at those data as giving us a domain of basic informal and personal relationships.

2. WOMEN'S LUCK AND MODERN ETHICAL THEORY

Women's care often takes the form of responsiveness to the needs of others. Thus in her 1982 writing, Carol Gilligan naturally moved from "an ethic of care" to "an ethic of responsibility," understanding responsibility as a capacity for responsiveness. The Kohlbergian tradition from which she began took over the Rawlsian view that the business of justice is to distribute rights. Hence her easy move from "justice perspectives" to "rights perspectives." However, two different views are conflated by these equations, one of which is more plausible, if less sweeping or dramatic, than the other. The thesis that women develop an ethic of care and men an ethic of justice is not logically tied to the thesis that women develop an ethic of responsibility and men an ethic of rights. The "responsibility and rights" thesis, or something like it, is more promising than the "justice and care" thesis.

Justice is not exhausted by rights. Justice is a far older concept. Nor does caring exhaust the responsibilities of women's relationships. By "an ethic of responsibility" what was more specifically meant was the ethics of informal and personal relationships; by "an ethic of rights," the ethics of formal or impersonal relationships. Both involve responsibilities, however, just as both involve relationships—different kinds of responsibilities and different kinds of relationships. That we can hear a "different moral voice" in the ethics of informal and personal relationships is plausible, even if it is not always the voice of "care" or the voice from which it diverges, that of "justice."

Modern moral philosophy has been preoccupied with power and control—its uses, its distribution, its forms (Hoagland 1988).[16] Attachment, in the sense that suggests emotion or feeling, has been downplayed, underrated, dismissed. In her more recent essays (Gilligan et al. 1988), Carol Gilligan emphasizes that power and attachment are two ways of defining relationships, two ways of defining responsibilities. She no longer contrasts rights with responsibilities or presents only women as focused on relationships, but sees women and men as often focused on different relationships and different responsibilities.

Contractarian and utilitarian ethics are preoccupied with control. They take formal and impersonal relationships as paradigms. Both kinds of theory reflect administrative practical wisdom. Ideal observers and veils of ignorance give versions of the perspective of an administrator (who may be a member of a board rather than a lone administrator). The data for these theories are drawn first of all from the public worlds of law and commerce, as are the concepts used in their analysis: *right* (or duty) and *good* (or interest). "Right" is rooted in law, the world of rights. "Good," in the relevant sense, suggests commerce, the world of goods. Ethics as normative theorizing about impersonal relationships is epitomized by John Rawls's theory of justice, by the current fascination with the prisoner's dilemma, and by consequentialist paradoxes concerning nuclear deterrence.

Responsibility in administration is a matter of supervision, management, accountability, and answerability. One who is responsible for something answers for it, takes whatever credit or blame is due. Those whose responsibilities go unfulfilled are expected to explain to others. This credit-and-blame sense of responsibility is the sense that figures in Nietzsche's obsession with the genealogy of morality as control. It is not at all what Carol Gilligan meant in attributing to women an ethic of responsibility. She had in mind responsiveness to needs, to situations. This is more congruent with the idea of *taking* responsibility *for* someone or something—committing oneself to look after its maintenance or well-being, preserve its value, even to make it good.[17] Here the focus is on well-being, not on control. When the focus is on well-being, responsiveness to needs comes to the fore. The administrative point of view is not noted for its responsiveness to needs.

The administrative point of view does not yield a theory of friendship. Philosophers in the last third of this century have begun remedying the relative lack of attention to friendship in modern ethics (Telfer 1970/1971; Stocker 1976; Blum 1980; Raymond 1986).

Friendship belongs to the larger area of personal relationships and informal practices—sexual intimacy, kinship, and a variety of networks loosely dubbed "friendships." As Annette Baier notes, historically, men have been able to take for granted a background of informal and personal relationships with women for the reproduction of populations and institutions, women have had less choice than men about participating in these relationships, and men have had material stakes in not scrutinizing such relationships morally (Baier 1986). It can be added that men also have stakes in not scrutinizing many informal relationships with one another underlying and circumscribing the formal ones on which attention is typically focused in their discussions of moral issues. If, as Annette Baier observes (1986), it has often been women's luck to have to make the best of involuntarily assumed personal relationships and to have to create networks of informal relationships in a world that has denied women a voice in law, men also have recourse to networks and relationships of varying degrees of informality—the Ku Klux Klan, gentlemen's agreements—when they want to *circumvent* the law.[18]

We need theories of the ethics of informal and personal relationships at least as well developed as administrative ethics. Informal relationships tend to *underlie* formal ones, circumscribe them, come into play when formal ones break down. On the view developed by John Rawls, obligations (or, we might say, responsibilities) require for their analyses references to criteria formulated specifically for evaluating public institutions. Perhaps *personal and informal* responsibilities require for their analyses references to criteria formulated *specifically for evaluating personal relationships and informal practices.*

What are "informal" and "personal" relationships? The informal and the personal are not the same. An informal agreement need not be personal. An interpersonal relationship is *personal* when it matters to the parties who the other parties are and when this mattering is important to the nature of the relationship.[19] "Personal" suggests closeness, intimacy. The personal introduces issues of attachment and antipathy. Informal relationships are characterized by responsibilities that can facilitate relationships of attachment.

A relationship is *formal* to the extent that it is well-defined, limited, in ways that are publicly understood and publicly sanctioned. Formality facilitates control where there would otherwise be a lack of trust or simply an inability to predict and plan. Formality is not the same as legality; both legal and nonlegal relationships have varying degrees of formality. Spousehood, for example, is a formally defined status in law, but the obligations of spouses to one another tend to be highly informal. Those of outsiders to spouses, on the other hand, become more formal in consequence of marriage.

Within limits, formality and personality are matters of degree. *Very* formal relationships, however, involve rights, which one either has or lacks. Friendship is personal and relatively informal. We may have formal relationships, such as contracts, with friends. But that can also create problems for friendship. Personal relationships tend toward informality. The relationships of clients and patients to physicians and other caretakers become more formal as clients and patients insist upon rights, which creates tensions for those who find it desirable that such relationships retain personal aspects. The relationship of judge to defendant, on the other hand, is (supposed to be) impersonal, not merely formal.[20]

Relationships defined by what John Rawls calls "the basic structure of society" are institutional. Institutions define responsibilities, or obligations, closely correlated with rights; the relationships are thus formal. They are also impersonal; persons are repeatedly presented as competing for positions defined by basic institutions. The perspective from which such responsibilities are ultimately analyzed and evaluated—the "Original Position"—is thoroughly impersonal (Rawls 1971, chap. 3).

The ethics of basic *institutions* is the subject of Rawls's theory of justice. Basic informal and personal relationships, however, are *like* basic institutions in possessing the three major features he identifies to support his view of those institutions as basic to the structure of society. Basic informal and personal relationships should therefore be also recognized as belonging to the basic structure of society. Goodness here is at least as important as justice in basic institutions.

The points of similarity are as follows. First, personal relationships are at least as important to our "starting places" in life as the institutions constituting the basic structure. Second, self-esteem, especially the conviction that one's life is worth living, is contingent not only on basic rights but also on informal practices and primary personal relationships. Third, personal relationships and informal practices create special responsibilities (but ones that are not closely correlated with rights), just as impersonal relationships and formal institutions create special responsibilities (which are closely correlated with rights). If such considerations support the moral importance of basic institutions, they support that of basic informal and personal relationships as well.

Consider starting places. The importance of justice as the first virtue of basic institutions rests heavily, in Rawls's theory, on the fact that these institutions determine our starting places in life. People born into different social positions have different expectations because these institutions work together in such a way as to favor certain starting points over others, and these inequalities, which tend to be deep, are not justifiable by appeal to merit or desert (Rawls 1971, 7). This is surely true. However, the profundity and pervasiveness of the effects of our personal and informal starting places is at least equal to those of our formal starting places. Our personal relationships with parents are a starting point. Parents who handle such relationships badly may leave us seriously disadvantaged for life. We have no more choice over these starting relationships than over participation in society's class structure or its basic economic institutions. Nor are they deserved or justifiable by appeal to merit. If involuntariness of participation and profundity of the effects upon health and well-being ground the ethical significance of social institutions, they can likewise ground the ethical significance of social institutions, they can likewise ground that of basic informal and primary personal relationships. Yet the latter are not defined by rights. They do not give us a "rights perspective," although they do give us a "responsibility perspective." Treating the monogamous family as an institution defined by rights does not adequately recognize the morality of family relationships.

Second, consider the effect of such relationships on self-esteem. The basis of self-esteem in a just society, according to Rawls (1971, 544), is a certain publicly affirmed distribution of basic rights and liberties. However, self-esteem is also contingent upon primary personal relationships, upon the sense we develop of ourselves in such relationships, our sense of ourselves as capable of faithfulness, understanding, warmth, empathy, as having the qualities we should want in a personal affiliate, not only the qualities that it is rational to want in a "fellow citizen." Our sense of these things can be destroyed, warped, or undeveloped if our starting affiliations in life are impoverished, and it can be undermined later by abusive primary affiliations. If the connection with self-esteem explains part of the ethical importance of justice in institutions, it also explains part of the ethical importance of the responsibilities of informal personal relationships.

Third, like the relationships defined by basic rights, informal personal relationships involve special responsibilities. They seem even to involve responsibility in a *different sense* from that of formal relationships: responsibilities that are *not duties* closely correlated with *rights*. Immanuel Kant attempted to capture such responsibilities with the concept of "imperfect duties" (Kant 1948, chap. 2) and later "ethical duties" in contrast with "juridical duties" (Kant 1964, 7–28). Intuitionists have also tried to cover them with the concept of duty (Ross 1930, chap. 2). To utilitarians, such responsibilities have seemed no more ethically fundamental than responsibilities correlated with rights, which also are not fundamental from the standpoint of utility (Mill 1957, chap. 5; Brandt 1984). What all of them have missed is the moral *relationship* between persons—literally, the *obligation* in its original sense of a *bond*—that grounds responsibilities.

The concept of obligation has paradigmatic use in two different contexts, as has been pointed out by Richard Brandt (1964): the context of promises or agreements and the context of accepting benefactions. The latter seems fundamental insofar as willingness to accept another's word manifests good will that does not itself rest on respect for contracts or promises. Such good will is, or can be, a benefaction. Promises and agreements ground duties correlated with rights, while accepting benefactions grounds responsibilities in relationships that are often highly informal. We commonly refer to both the responsibilities of carrying out duties and the responsibilities of informal and personal relationships as "obligations." But they differ from each other in *specificity* and in the *roles* they play in social relationships.

Formal obligations, like Immanuel Kant's "perfect duties," are to do some particular thing, often by a specified time and for or to some particular person. They are correlated with a right to that performance on the part of those to whom one is obligated. They are relatively well defined and often publicly sanctioned. They are the kind of obligation associated with the possible use of force or coercion, with a justification for limiting another's freedom. By contrast, as with "imperfect duties," when accepting a benefaction places us under obligation, there is often no specific thing we are obligated to do and no specific person to or for whom we are obligated to do it. There is consequently no correlated right to a specific performance on the part of the benefactor. We are typically responsible for determining what needs to be done (and when and how much), which requires initiative, imagination, and creativity. The most sympathetic way to interpret Carol Gilligan's method of inclusiveness is to see it as taking on a certain responsibility in this sense, the responsibility of *making it good* that everyone is included, of finding, creating, a *good* way to do that, thereby maintaining informal connections with everyone.

The different roles of the two kinds of obligation are suggested by differences in the consequences of fulfilling or failing to fulfill them. In fulfilling formal obligations, we *discharge* them, as in paying a debt. Discharging the obligation brings the relationship to a close, terminates that formal connection. Failing to fulfill responsibilities that are correlated with rights does not relieve us of the responsibility; it often makes us liable to penalties as substitutes for what we failed to do (sometimes in addition to making up what we failed to do). By contrast, with obligations incurred to a benefactor, we often think in terms of *living up to* them rather than of discharging them. Living up to them tends to *affirm* the relationship rather than to bring it to a close; the ties are extended, deepened. Putting pressure on those who are informally obligated to us can undermine the relationship on which the obligation depends. Failing to live up to an informal obligation likewise undermines the relationship in virtue of which the obligation existed. Formal obligations can thus facilitate good will between parties who are not intimate and perhaps have no wish to be, while informal ones can facilitate personal relationships.

Deontological ethics, especially contractarian, takes relatively formal, impersonal relationships as paradigmatic for moral theory, applying their metaphors and concepts to other relationships as well. This can yield farfetched results, as in Immanuel Kant's notion that ethical duties arise from a kind of contract with one's (bifurcated) self (Kant 1964, pt. 1, secs. 1–4). Modern teleologies, on the other hand, drop the idea of obligation as a *relationship* in favor of a looser idea of "obligation" as what one morally ought to do. Utilitarianism thus assimilates obligations constitutive of personal and informal relationships to the theory of impersonal moral choice, focusing on abstract action-guiding principles, albeit without taking rights as a fundamental concept.

The promising idea I find in the hypothesis that "women's ethics" can deepen and correct modern Western ethical theory is that the informal and personal relationships salient in women's lives raise issues of the ethics of attachment that are not reducible to the issues of control that have preoccupied contractualist and utilitarian theorists. Informal, personal relationships are as basic as any relationships in our lives. Acknowledging this does not imply that women have more or better knowledge of the ethics of such relationships. What women more clearly have had is more than our share of the responsibility for maintaining these kinds of relationships and less than our share of the responsibilities of participating in and defining formal institutions.

3. CONCLUSIONS

I have argued that attachment to individuals is not sufficient to yield caring as a virtue. However, without the values of attachment, there can be no satisfactory ethics of personal relationships. Utilitarian and contractualist theories recognize at best general benevolence, impersonal good will toward others, and a kind of general faith in others' ability to reciprocate such good will. But they do not recognize as ethically significant the caring partial to individuals. Carol Gilligan observed in her discussion of the fantasy study that "women . . . try to change the rules in order to preserve relationships," while "men, in abiding by these rules, depict relationships as easily replaced" (1982, 44). The sense of relationships as not replaceable recalls Immanuel Kant's insistence that individuals have a value for which nothing can satisfactorily take the place (Kant 1948, chap. 2). Kant was thinking of human dignity, attributed to everyone alike. What is irreplaceable here is what is distinctive, what sets individuals apart from others, not something they have in common.

An ethic of attachment is not necessarily an ethic of care, any more than an ethic of principle—such as utilitarianism—is necessarily one of justice. To sustain the view that the capacity for love, like the sense of justice, is part of character, we need an understanding of this capacity comparable in sophistication to Immanuel Kant's understanding of the capacity for acting on principle. Not every passionate attachment to persons is valuable, any more than every passionate espousal of principles is. The nature and basis of the attachment matters. Immanuel Kant missed the differences in attachment to persons in his dismissal of "pathological love." Yet he appreciated the differences in acting on principle. In a little-known passage in the same essay in which good women are presented as morally characterless, he wrote, "among men there are but few who behave according to principles—which is extremely good, as it can so easily happen that one errs in these principles, and then the resulting disadvantage extends all the further, the more universal the principle and the more resolute the person who has set it before himself" (Kant 1960b, 74). This danger did not deter him from searching for a devotion to principle having moral worth. Nor need present-day theorists be deterred by the danger of ill-founded personal attachments from recognizing the ethical value of others.

4. POSTSCRIPT

I have cautioned against minimizing women's bad moral luck in a society with a history of sex oppression. I end with examples of moral damage that a rosy view of women and care may disguise and that a sound ethic of personal and informal relationships should reveal.

When people are affiliated with "protectors," their affirmations of those affiliations may have little to do with love, though the language of love be the language of their discourse. Women's caretaking is often unpaid or underpaid labor performed from a variety of motives. More likely mistaken for a caring virtue is women's misplaced gratitude to men who take less than full advantage of their power to abuse or who offer women the privilege of service in exchange for "protection." Women have assumed caretaking responsibilities as a debt of gratitude for such "benefactions."[21]

Misplaced gratitude is a kind of moral damage women have suffered. There are others. Feminist thinkers are understandably reluctant to address publicly women's reputation for lying, cunning, deceit, and manipulation. (Arthur Schopenhauer did not have this problem.) But *are* these vices, one may ask, if they are needed for defense? They are surely not virtues, even if they are justified from the point of view of justice. Those who tell just the right lies to the right people on the right occasions may have a useful and needed skill. But it does not promote or manifest human good, even if needed for survival under oppressive conditions. Human good may be unrealizable under such conditions. Lying blocks the trust of friendship: though you are confident I lie only when justified, and you believe I am *often* justified, how can you know when to rely on me (Rich 1979)?

I have supported a view of the moral luck of the sexes more specific and less romantic than the view that justice and care are gender related. If informal practices and personal relationships are more salient in women's lives (and not only in women's discourse), women's characters may have a certain depth and complexity because of it. This does not imply that women are better; complexity is not virtue. Perhaps there *are* gender-related virtues, however, and perhaps they are best understood by the moral luck of the sexes. I have not argued that this idea is incoherent. My investigations suggest that some of our *vices* are gender related because of a history of sex oppression. If so, we might expect to find, as Mary Wollstonecraft did, similar vices in relation to other forms of oppression—oppression by class and by race, for example—and perhaps more complex vices where oppression is compounded.

Then why use the language of *gender*-relatedness, one may ask, rather than of *oppression*-relatedness? The answers are that gender is not incidental and that oppression is not everything. Those oppressed do not just happen to be female, brown-skinned, workers, or all of these. Social practices have made such aspects of our identities the bearers of fortune. Nor is all the fortune bad. Terms like "gender-related" enable us to call attention to these facts in order to clarify the myths and truths surrounding the moral luck of individuals.

NOTES

1. This essay has benefited from critical readings by Victoria Davion, Owen Flanagan, Nel Noddings, participants in a University of Wisconsin Women and Legal Theory Conference, and Joan Ringelheim's colleagues in a New York City women's discussion group; from the encouragement of Amélie Rorty for more than a decade; and from discussions with audiences at the philosophy department of the University of Wisconsin at Madison, the APA Central Division Meetings, and a University of San Diego conference on virtues. Part of the work on it was supported by a sabbatical from the University of Wisconsin at Madison.
2. My interest is in what Bernard Williams called *constitutive moral luck*, which enters into one's character. He contrasts this with *incident* moral luck (on which he focuses in the essay introducing the concept "moral luck"), which affects the morality of particular acts (Williams 1981).
3. In Card, 1996, I address the compatibility of luck with moral responsibility. In this essay I do not treat moral luck as a problematic concept but plunge into what we can learn from recognizable examples.
4. Carol Gilligan reports that nearly all those tested could readily adopt both justice and care orientations, although not simultaneously, but that two-thirds of each sex preferred one, and of these, almost all the men preferred the justice orientation, while half the women with a preference preferred the care orientation. Thus the care orientation might easily be overlooked in a study excluding women (Gilligan et al. 1988). Although she focuses on orientations rather than on their distribution, her recent essays describing testing across racial and class groups confirm her impressions about gender distribution. She sees a need for the care ethic where violence threatens but does not claim its superiority in all contexts.

   Nel Noddings (1984) has defended a care-based ethic *against* a justice-based one, arguing that abstract action-guiding principles have at best a subordinate role in care-based ethics.

   Sara Ruddick (1989) develops the idea of "maternal thinking" from ideals *implicit* in the practice of mothering and argues for their extension to international politics. Like Nel Noddings, she is not optimistic about the value of abstract action-guiding principles in general.
5. Focus on *differences in contexts and relationships* is more characteristic of the writings on women and care by Virginia Held (1984, 1987a, 1987b), Annette Baier (1985, 1986, 1987a, 1987b), and Sarah Hoagland (1988).
6. If oppression were at the root of the differences in moral preoccupation attributed to the sexes, such differences should have a more complex distribution. Benefits of sex privilege can be diluted or counteracted and burdens of sex oppression overwhelmed by racial or class oppression, and women can have race and class privilege.
7. Marilyn Friedman (1987), also concerned about underrating justice, urges similar shifts and likewise explores interconnections of justice and care.
8. I do not take up here, since I discuss in Card 1989, the lesbian care ethics developed by Sarah Hoagland (1988), which works from different paradigms, those of adult lesbians engaged in creating social alternatives to patriarchy.
9. I do not argue that women's development fares worse than that of men. My interest is more in women's characters than in such comparisons.
10. On the same page he says, "Women will avoid the wicked not because it is unright but, because it is ugly." Traits he calls women's virtues he called "merely adoptive virtues" in the preceding chapter, contrasting them with genuine virtues. That he never reconsidered shows in his anthropology lectures published late in his life (Kant 1974, part 2, B).

11. For an extended critique of the "gestalt view," see Flanagan and Jackson 1987.
12. On justice and personal desert, see Feinberg 1970 and Card 1972.
13. The story, which I first heard from her at a conference in 1984, is this: "Two four-year-olds—a boy and a girl—were playing together and wanted to play different games. . . . The girl said: 'Let's play next-door neighbors.' 'I want to play pirates,' the boy replied. 'Okay,' said the girl, 'then you can be the pirate that lives next door.' " Gilligan et al. write here of "comparing the inclusive solution of combining the games with the fair solution of taking turns" (1988, 9).
14. On military misogyny, see the first half (on U.S. Marine boot camp) of the film *Full Metal Jacket* (dir. Stanley Kubrick, 1987).
15. Violence is also a problem for lesbian relationships in a homophobic society (Lobel 1986; Card 1988b, 1989), which creates situations for same-sex intimacy analogous to those misogyny creates for heterosexual intimacy.
16. On Hume as an exception, see Baier 1985, 1987a.
17. I explore the concept of taking responsibility further in 1990 and further forward-looking senses of responsibility in Card 1996, Ch. 2.
18. Laura Hobson's 1947 novel, *Gentlemen's Agreement*, portrays persistence of anti-Semitism in the U.S. despite formal equality of rights, by way of such things as "gentlemen's agreements" to exclude Jews from country clubs and other "friendly" organizations.
19. So-called personal *obligations* do not always involve personal *relationships.* Obligations may be called "personal" to contrast them with other obligations of the same person in an official capacity. My interest here is in the obligations of personal *relationships.*
20. For further discussion of paradigms of obligation, see Card 1988a.
21. On the ethics of friendships between parties very unequal in power, see Card 1988a.

BIBLIOGRAPHY

Amir, M. 1971. *Patterns in Forcible Rape.* Chicago: University of Chicago Press.

Aristotle. 1925. *Nicomachean Ethics.* Translated by W. D. Ross. London: Oxford University Press.

Baier, A. 1985. "What Do Women Want in a Moral Theory?" *Noûs* 19: 53–63.

______. 1986. "Trust and Antitrust." Reprinted here, Chap. 31.

______. 1987a. "Hume, the Women's Moral Theorist?" In E. F. Kittay and D. T. Meyers (eds.), *Women and Moral Theory.* Totowa, N.J.: Littlefield, Adams.

______. 1987b. "The Need for More than Justice." In M. Hanen and K. Nielsen (eds.), *Science, Morality, and Feminist Theory.* Calgary: University of Calgary.

Blum, L. 1980. *Friendship, Altruism, and Morality.* London: Routledge and Kegan Paul.

Brandt, R. B. 1964. "The Concepts of Duty and Obligation." *Mind* 73: 373–393.

Card, C. 1972. "On Mercy." *Philosophical Review* 81: 182–207.

______. 1988a. "Gratitude and Obligation." *American Philosophical Quarterly* 25: 115–127.

______. 1988b. "Lesbian Battering." *American Philosophical Association Newsletter on Feminism and Philosophy* 88:3–7. (Review essay on Lobel 1986.)

______. 1989. "Defusing the Bomb: Lesbian Ethics and Horizontal Violence." *Lesbian Ethics* 3: 91–100.

______. 1990. "Intimacy and Responsibility: What Lesbians Do." In Martha Fineman and Nancy Thomadsen (eds.), *At the Boundaries of Law: Feminism and Legal Theory.* London: Routledge and Kegan Paul.

______. 1996. *The Unnatural Lottery: Character and Moral Luck.* Philadelphia: Temple University Press.

Feinberg, J. 1970. "Justice and Personal Desert." In *Doing and Deserving: Essays in the Theory of Responsibility.* Princeton: Princeton University Press.

Flanagan, O., and Jackson, K. 1987. "Justice, Care, and Gender: The Kohlberg-Gilligan Debate Revisited." *Ethics* 97: 622–637.

Foot, P. 1978. "Virtues and Vices." In Foot 1978a.

Freud, S. 1961. "Some Psychical Consequences of the Anatomical Distinction between the Sexes." In *The Standard Edition of the Complete Psychological Works of Sigmund Freud* (vol. 19), translated by J. Strachey. London: Hogarth. (First published in 1925.)

Friedman, M. 1987. "Beyond Caring: The De-Moralization of Gender," reprinted here, chap. 34.

Gilligan, C. 1982. *In a Different Voice: Psychological Theory and Women's Development.* Cambridge: Harvard University Press.

Gilligan, C., Ward, J. V., and Taylor, J. M., with Bardige, B., eds. 1988. *Mapping the Moral Domain: A Contribution of Women's Thinking to Psychological Theory and Education.* Cambridge: Harvard University Press.

Held, V. 1984. *Rights and Goods: Justifying Social Action.* New York: Free Press/Macmillan.

______. 1987a. "Feminism and Moral Theory," reprinted here, chap. 32.

______. 1987b. "Non-contractual Society." In M. Hanen and K. Nielsen (eds.), *Science, Morality, and Feminist Theory.* Calgary: University of Calgary.

Hoagland, S. L. 1988. *Lesbian Ethics.* Palo Alto, Calif.: Institute for Lesbian Studies.

Hobson, L. 1947. *Gentleman's Agreement.* New York: Grosset & Dunlap.

Houston, B. 1987. "Rescuing Womanly Virtues: Some Dangers of Reclamation." In M. Hanen and K. Nielsen (eds.), *Science, Morality, and Feminist Theory.* Calgary: University of Calgary.

Kant, I. 1948. *The Moral Law: Kant's Groundwork of "The Metaphysic of Morals."* Translated by H. J. Paton. London: Hutchinson. (First published 1785.)

______. 1960. *Observations on the Feeling of the Beautiful and Sublime.* Translated by J. T. Goldthwait. Berkeley: University of California Press. (First published 1764.)

______. 1964. *The Doctrine of Virtue: Part II of "The Metaphysic of Morals."* Translated by M. J. Gregor. New York: Harper & Row. (First published 1797.)

______. 1974. *Anthropology from a Pragmatic Point of View.* Translated by M. J. Gregor. The Hague: Nijhoff. (First published 1797.)

Kohlberg, L. 1981. *The Philosophy of Moral Development.* San Francisco: Harper & Row.

Lobel, K., ed. 1986. *Naming the Violence: Speaking Out about Lesbian Battering.* Seattle: Seal.

Mill, J. S. 1957. *Utilitarianism.* New York: Bobbs-Merrill. (First published 1861.)

Noddings, N. 1984. *Caring: A Feminine Approach to Ethics and Moral Education.* Berkeley: University of California Press.

Rawls, J. 1971. *A Theory of Justice.* Cambridge: Harvard University Press.

Raymond, J. 1986. A *Passion for Friends: Toward a Philosophy of Female Affection.* Boston: Beacon.

Rich, A. 1979. "Women and Honor: Some Notes on Lying." In *On Lies, Secrets, and Silence: Selected Prose, 1966–1978.* New York: Norton.

______. 1980. "Compulsory Heterosexuality and Lesbian Existence." *Signs* 5: 631–660.

Ringelheim, J. 1985. "Women and the Holocaust: A Reconsideration of Research. *Signs* 10: 741–761.

Ross, W. D. 1930. *The Right and the Good.* Oxford: Oxford University Press.

Ruddick, S. 1989. *Maternal Thinking.* Boston: Beacon Press.

Schopenhauer, A. 1965. *On the Basis of Morality.* Translated by E. F. J. Payne. Indianapolis: Bobbs-Merrill. (First published 1841.)

Stocker, M. 1976. "The Schizophrenia of Modern Ethical Theories." *Journal of Philosophy* 73: 453–466.

______. 1986. "Friendship and Duty: Toward a Synthesis of Gilligan's Contrastive Ethical Concepts." In E. Kittay and D. Meyers (eds.), *Women and Moral Theory.* Totowa, N.J.: Rowman and Allanheld.

Telfer, 1970/1971. "Friendship." *Proceedings of the Aristotelian Society* 71: 223–241.

Williams, B. 1981. "Moral Luck." In B. Williams, *Moral Luck.* Cambridge: Cambridge University Press.

Wollstonecraft, M. 1982. *A Vindication of the Rights of Women.* Harmondsworth: Penguin. (First published 1792.)

Beyond Caring: The De-Moralization of Gender

Friedman stakes out a complex position regarding the ethic of care. She points out that Gilligan's claim that differences in moral thinking are linked to gender difference has generated intense controversy in the social sciences. Yet many people find Gilligan's hypothesis intuitively plausible based on their personal experience. Friedman offers an explanation of why people believe that women use the ethic of care and men use the ethic of justice, regardless of whether rigorous empirical research bears out this gender difference. Gender stereotypes associate women with nurturance in the domestic sphere and men with law and productivity in the public sphere. Since perceptions of women and men are shaped by these stereotypes, people may fail to notice that many women and men violate these patterns, or they may dismiss exceptions as deviant instead of noticing gender diversity. This tendency to confirm stereotypes might not persist if there were no real gender difference in moral thinking and if care and justice were irreconcilably dichotomous modes of thought. However, Friedman argues that care and justice are conceptually compatible, indeed, necessary complements to one another. Justice is necessary to moral thinking about interpersonal relationships, and care is necessary to moral thinking about social policy.

Still, Friedman contends that Gilligan's work alerts us to an important difference between the ethic of care and the ethic of justice. Proponents of care have a primary moral commitment to particular admirable persons who serve as moral exemplars, whereas proponents of justice have a primary moral commitment to abstract rules, values, or principles. On Friedman's view, these moral orientations are distinct and cannot be combined into a unified approach.

—D.T.M.

Chapter 34

Marilyn Friedman

Beyond Caring: The De-Moralization of Gender

Carol Gilligan heard a "distinct moral language" in the voices of women who were subjects in her studies of moral reasoning.[1] Though herself a developmental psychologist, Gilligan has put her mark on contemporary feminist moral philosophy by daring to claim the competence of this voice and the worth of its message. Her book, *In a Different Voice*, which one theorist has aptly described as a best-seller,[2] explored the concern with care and relationships that Gilligan discerned in the moral reasoning of women, and contrasted it with the orientation toward justice and rights that she found to typify the moral reasoning of men.

According to Gilligan, the standard (or "male") moral voice articulated in moral psychology derives moral judgments about particular cases from abstract, universalized moral rules and principles that are substantively concerned with justice and rights. For justice reasoners: the major moral imperative enjoins respect for the rights of others (100); the concept of duty is limited to reciprocal noninterference (147); the motivating vision is one of the equal worth of self and other (63); and one important underlying presupposition is a highly individualized conception of persons.

By contrast, the other (or "female") moral voice that Gilligan heard in her studies eschews abstract rules and principles. This moral voice derives moral judgments from the contextual detail of situations grasped as specific and unique (100). The substantive concern for this moral voice is care and responsibility, particularly as these arise in the context of interpersonal relationships (19). Moral judgments, for care reasoners, are tied to feelings of empathy and compassion (69); the major moral imperatives center on caring, not hurting others, and avoiding selfishness (90); and the motivating vision of this ethic is "that everyone will be responded to and included, that no one will be left alone or hurt" (63).

While these two voices are not necessarily contradictory in all respects, they seem, at the very least, to be different in their orientation. Gilligan's writings about the differences have stimulated extensive feminist reconsideration of various ethical themes.[3] In this paper, I use Gilligan's work as a springboard for extending certain of those themes in new directions. My discussion has three parts. In the first part, I will address the unresolved question of whether a gender difference in moral reasoning is empirically confirmed. I will propose that even if actual statistical differences in the moral reasoning of women and men cannot be confirmed, there is nevertheless a real difference in the moral norms and values culturally associated with each gender. The genders are "moralized" in distinctive ways. Moral norms about appropriate conduct, characteristic virtues, and typical vices are incorporated into our conceptions of femininity and masculinity, female and male. The result is a dichotomy that exemplifies what may be called a "division of moral labor"[4] between the genders.

In the second part of the paper, I will explore a different reason why actual women and men may not show a divergence of reasoning along the care-justice dichotomy, namely, that the notions of care and justice overlap more than Gilligan, among others, has realized. I will suggest, in particular, that morally adequate care involves considerations of justice. Thus, the concerns captured by these two moral categories do not define necessarily distinct moral perspectives, in practice.

Third, and finally, I will propose that, even if care and justice do not define distinct moral perspectives, nevertheless these concepts do point to other important differences in moral orientation. One such difference has to do with the nature of relationship to other selves, and the underlying form of moral commitment which is the central focus of that relationship and of the resulting moral thought. In short, the so-called care perspective emphasizes responsiveness to particular persons, in their uniqueness, and commitment to them as such. By contrast, the so-called justice perspective emphasizes adherence to moral rules, values, and principles, and an abstractive treatment of individuals, based on the selected categories which they instantiate.

Let us turn first to the issue of gender difference.

I. THE GENDER DIFFERENCE CONTROVERSY

Gilligan has advanced at least two different positions about the care and the justice perspectives. One is that the care perspective is distinct from the moral perspective, which is centered on justice and rights. Following Gilligan,[5] I will call this the "different voice" hypothesis about moral reasoning. Gilligan's other hypothesis is that the care perspective is typically, or characteristically, a *woman's* moral voice, while the justice perspective is typically, or characteristically, a *man's* moral voice. Let's call this the "gender difference" hypothesis about moral reasoning.

The truth of Gilligan's gender difference hypothesis has been questioned by a number of critics, who cite what seems to be disconfirming empirical evidence.[6] This evidence includes studies by the psychologist Norma Haan, who has discerned two distinct moral voices among her research subjects, but has found them to be utilized to approximately the same extent by both females and males.[7]

In an attempt to dismiss the research-based objections to her gender difference hypothesis, Gilligan now asserts that her aim was not to disclose a statistical gender difference in moral reasoning, but rather simply to disclose and interpret the differences in the two perspectives.[8] Psychologist John Broughton has argued that if the gender difference is not maintained, then Gilligan's whole explanatory framework is undermined.[9] However, Broughton is wrong. The different-voice hypothesis has a significance for moral psychology and moral philosophy which would survive the demise of the gender difference hypothesis. At least part of its significance lies in revealing the lopsided obsession of contemporary theories of morality, in both disciplines, with universal and impartial conceptions of justice and rights and the relative disregard of *particular*, interpersonal relationships based on partiality and affective ties.[10] (However, the different-voice hypothesis is itself also suspect if it is made to depend on a dissociation of justice from care, a position I shall challenge in part II of this paper.)

But *what about* that supposed empirical disconfirmation of the gender difference hypothesis? Researchers who otherwise accept the disconfirming evidence have nevertheless noticed that many women readers of Gilligan's book find it to "resonate . . . thoroughly with their own experience."[11] Gilligan notes that it was precisely one of her purposes to expose the gap between women's experience and the findings of psychological research,[12] and, we may suppose, to critique the latter in light of the former.

These unsystematic, anecdotal observations that females and males do differ in ways examined by Gilligan's research should lead us either: (1) to question, and examine carefully, the methods of that empirical research which does not reveal such differences; or (2) to suspect that a gender difference exists but in some form which is not, strictly speaking, a matter of statistical differences in the moral reasoning of women and men. Gilligan has herself expressed the first of these alternatives. I would like to explore the second possibility.

Suppose that there were a gender difference of a sort, but one that was not a simple matter of differences among the form or substance of women's and men's moral reasonings. A plausible account might take this form. Among the white middle classes of such western industrial societies as Canada and the United States, women and men are associated with different moral norms and values at the level of the stereotypes, symbols, and myths that contribute to the social construction of gender. One might say that morality is "gendered" and that the genders are "moralized." Our very conceptions of femininity and masculinity, female and male, incorporate norms about appropriate behavior, characteristic virtues, and typical vices.

Morality, I suggest, is fragmented into a "division of moral labor" along the lines of gender, the rationale for which is rooted in historic developments pertaining to family, state, and economy. The tasks of governing, regulating social order, and managing other "public" institutions have been monopolized by men as their privileged domain, and the tasks of sustaining privatized personal relationships have been imposed on, or left to, women.[13] The genders have thus been conceived in terms of special and distinctive moral projects. Justice and rights have structured male moral norms, values, and virtues, while care and responsiveness have defined female moral norms, values, and virtues. The division of moral labor has had the dual function both of preparing us each for our respective socially defined domains and of rendering us incompetent to manage the affairs of the realm from which we have been excluded. That justice is symbolized in our culture by the figure of a woman is a remarkable irony; her blindfold hides more than the scales she holds.

To say that the genders are moralized is to say that specific moral ideals, values, virtues, and practices are culturally conceived as the special projects or domains of specific genders. These conceptions would determine which commitments and behaviors were to be considered normal, appropriate, and expected of each gender; which commitments and behaviors were to be considered remarkable or heroic; and which commitments and behaviors were to be considered deviant, improper, outrageous, and intolerable. Men who fail to respond to the cry of a baby, fail to express tender emotions, or fail to show compassion in the face of the grief and sorrow of others, are likely to be tolerated, perhaps even benignly, while women who act similarly can expect to be reproached for their selfish indifference. However, women are seldom required to devote themselves to service to their country or to struggles for human rights. Women are seldom expected to display any of the special virtues associated with national or political life. At the same time, women still carry the burden of an excessively restrictive and oppressive sexual ethic; sexual aggressiveness and promiscuity are vices for which women in all social groups are roundly condemned, even while many of their male counterparts win tributes for such "virility."

Social science provides ample literature to show that gender differences are alive and well at the level of popular perception. Both men and women, on average, still conceive women and men in a moralized fashion. For example, expectations and perceptions of women's greater empathy and altruism are expressed by both women and men.[14] The gender stereotypes of women center on qualities that some authors call "communal." These include: a concern for the welfare of others; the predominance of caring and nurturant traits; and, to a lesser extent, interpersonal sensitivity, emotional expressiveness, and a gentle personal style.[15]

By contrast, men are stereotyped according to what are referred to as "agentic" norms.[16] These norms center primarily on assertive and controlling tendencies. The paradigmatic behaviors are self-assertion, including forceful dominance, and independence from other people. Also encompassed by these norms are patterns of self-confidence, personal efficacy, and a direct, adventurous personal style.

If reality failed to accord with myth and symbol, if actual women and men did not fit the traits and dispositions expected of them, this might not necessarily undermine the myths and symbols, since perception could be selective and disconfirming experience reduced to the status of "occasional exceptions" and "abnormal, deviant cases." "Reality" would be misperceived in the image of cultural myth, as reinforced by the homogenizing tendencies of mass media and mass culture, and the popular imagination would have little foothold for the recognition that women and men were not as they were mythically conceived to be.

If I am right, then Gilligan has discerned the *symbolically* female moral voice, and has disentangled it from the *symbolically* male moral voice. The moralization of gender is more a matter of how we *think* we reason than of how we actually reason, more a matter of the moral concerns we *attribute* to women and men than of true statistical differences between women's and men's moral reasoning. Gilligan's findings resonate with the experiences of many people because those experiences are shaped, in part, by cultural myths and stereotypes of gender that even feminist theorizing may not dispel. Thus, both women and men in our culture *expect* women and men to exhibit this moral dichotomy, and, on my hypothesis, it is this expectation that has shaped both Gilligan's observations and the plausibility which we attribute to them. Or, to put it somewhat differently, *whatever* moral matters men concern themselves with are categorized, estimably, as matters of "justice and rights," whereas the moral concerns of women are assigned to the devalued categories of "care and personal relationships."

It is important to ask why, if these beliefs are so vividly held, they might, nevertheless, still not produce a reality in conformity with them.[17] How could those critics who challenge

Gilligan's gender hypothesis be right to suggest that women and men show no significant differences in moral reasoning, if women and men are culturally educated, trained, pressured, expected, and perceived to be so radically different?[18]

Philosophy is not, by itself, capable of answering this question adequately. My admittedly *partial* answer to it depends upon showing that the care/justice dichotomy is rationally implausible and that the two concepts are conceptually compatible. This conceptual compatibility creates the empirical possibility that the two moral concerns will be intermingled in practice. That they are actually intermingled in the moral reasonings of real women and men is, of course, not determined simply by their conceptual compatibility, but requires as well the wisdom and insight of those women and men who comprehend the relevance of both concepts to their experiences.[19] Philosophy does not account for the actual emergence of wisdom. That genders do not, in reality, divide along those moral lines is made *possible*, though not inevitable, by the conceptual limitations of both a concept of care dissociated from considerations of justice and a concept of justice dissociated from considerations of care. Support for this partial explanation requires a reconceptualization of care and justice—the topic of the next part of my discussion.

II. SURPASSING THE CARE/JUSTICE DICHOTOMY

I have suggested that if women and men do not show statistical differences in moral reasoning along the lines of a care/justice dichotomy, this should not be thought surprising since the concepts of care and justice are mutually compatible. People who treat each other justly can also care about each other. Conversely, personal relationships are arenas in which people have rights to certain forms of treatment, and in which fairness can be reflected in ongoing interpersonal mutuality. It is this latter insight—the relevance of justice to close personal relationships—that I will emphasize here.

Justice, at the most general level, is a matter of giving people their due, of treating them appropriately. Justice is relevant to personal relationships and to care precisely to the extent that considerations of justice itself determine appropriate ways to treat friends or intimates. Justice as it bears on relationships among friends or family, or on other close personal ties, might not involve duties that are universalizable, in the sense of being owed to all persons simply by virtue of shared moral personhood. But this does not entail the irrelevance of justice among friends or intimates.

Moral thinking has not always dissociated the domain of justice from that of close personal relationships. The earliest Greek code of justice placed friendship at the forefront of conditions for the realization of justice, and construed the rules of justice as being coextensive with the limits of friendship. The reader will recall that one of the first definitions of justice which Plato sought to contest, in the *Republic*, is that of "helping one's friends and harming one's enemies."[20] Although the ancient Greek model of justice among friends reserved that moral privilege for free-born Greek males, the conception is, nevertheless, instructive for its readiness to link the notion of justice to relationships based on affection and loyalty. This provides an important contrast to modern notions of justice, which are often deliberately constructed so as to avoid presumptions of mutual concern on the parts of those to whom the conception is to apply.

As is well known, John Rawls, for one, requires that the parties to the original position in which justice is to be negotiated be mutually disinterested.[21] Each party is assumed, first and foremost, to be concerned for the advancement of her own interests and to care about the interests of others only to the extent that her own interests require it. This postulate of mutual disinterestedness is intended by Rawls to ensure that the principles of justice do not depend on what he calls "strong assumptions," such as "extensive ties of natural sentiment."[22] Rawls is seeking principles of justice which apply to everyone in all their social interrelationships, *whether or not* characterized by affection and a concern for each other's well-being. While such an account promises to disclose duties of justice owed to all other parties to the social contract, it may fail to uncover *special* duties of justice that arise in close personal relationships, the foundation of which is affection or kinship rather than contract. The methodological device of assuming mutual disinterest might blind us to the role of justice among mutually interested and/or intimate parties.

Gilligan herself has suggested that mature reasoning about care incorporates considerations of justice and rights. But Gilligan's conception of what this means is highly limited. It appears to involve simply the recognition "that self and other are equal," a notion which serves to override the problematic tendency of the ethic of care to become *self-sacrificing* care in women's practices. However, important as it may be, this notion hardly does justice to justice.

There are several ways in which justice pertains to close personal relationships. The first two ways I will mention are largely appropriate only among friends, relatives, or intimates who are of comparable development in their realization of moral personhood, for example, who are both mature responsible adults. The third sort of relevance of justice to close relationships, which I will discuss shortly, pertains to families, in which adults often interrelate with children—a more challenging domain for the application of justice. But first the easier task.

One sort of role for justice in close relationships among people of comparable moral personhood may be discerned by considering that a personal relationship is a miniature social system, which provides valued mutual intimacy, support, and concern for those who are involved. The maintenance of a relationship requires effort by the participants. One intimate may bear a much greater burden for sustaining a relationship than the other participant(s) and may derive less support, concern, and so forth than she deserves for her efforts. Justice sets a constraint on such relationships by calling for an appropriate sharing, among the participants, of the benefits and burdens that constitute their relationship.

Marilyn Frye, for example, has discussed what amounts to a pattern of *violation* of the requirement of justice in heterosexual relationships. She has argued that women of all races, social classes, and societies can be defined as a coherent group in terms of a distinctive function which is culturally assigned to them. This function is, in Frye's words, "the service of men and men's interests as men define them."[23] This service work includes personal service (satisfaction of routine bodily needs, such as hunger, and other mundane tasks), sexual and reproductive service, and ego service. Says Frye, "At every race/class level and even across race/class lines men do not serve women as women serve men."[24] Frye is, of course, generalizing over society and culture, and the sweep of her generalization encompasses both ongoing close personal relationships as well as other relationships which are not close or are not carried on beyond specific transactions, for example, that of prostitute to client. By excluding those latter cases for the time being, and applying Frye's analysis to familial and other close ties between women and men, we may discern the sort of one-sided relational exploitation, often masquerading in the guise of love or care, which constitutes this first sort of injustice.

Justice is relevant to close personal relationships among comparable moral persons in a second way as well. The trust and intimacy that characterize special relationships create special vulnerabilities to harm. Commonly recognized harms, such as physical injury and sexual assault, become more feasible; and special relationships, in corrupt, abusive, or degenerate forms, make possible certain uncommon emotional harms not even possible in impersonal relationships. When someone is harmed in a personal relationship, she is owed a rectification of some sort, a righting of the wrong which has been done her. The notion of justice emerges, once again, as a relevant moral notion.

Thus, in a close relationship among persons of comparable moral personhood, care may degenerate into the injustices of exploitation, or oppression. Many such problems have been given wide public scrutiny recently as a result of feminist analysis of various aspects of family life and sexual relationships. Woman-battering, acquaintance rape, and sexual harassment are but a few of the many recently publicized injustices of "personal" life. The notion of distributive or corrective injustice seems almost too mild to capture these indignities, involving, as they do, violation of bodily integrity and an assumption of the right to assault and injure. But to call these harms injustices is certainly not to rule out impassioned moral criticism in other terms as well.

The two requirements of justice that I have just discussed exemplify the standard distinction between distributive and corrective justice. They illustrate the role of justice in personal relationships regarded in abstraction from a social context. Personal relationships may also be regarded in the context of their various institutional settings, such as marriage and family. Here justice emerges again as a relevant ideal, its role being to define appropriate institutions to structure interactions among family members, other household cohabitants, and intimates in general. The family, for example,[25] is a miniature society, exhibiting all the major facets of large-scale social life: decision making affecting the whole unit; executive action; judgments of guilt and innocence; reward and punishment; allocation of responsibilities and privileges, of burdens and benefits; and monumental influences on the life-chances of both its maturing and its matured members. Any of these features alone would invoke the relevance of justice; together, they make the case overwhelming.

Women's historically paradigmatic role of mothering has provided a multitude of insights that can be reconstructed as insights about the importance of justice in family relationships, especially those relationships involving remarkable disparities in maturity, capability, and power.[26] In these familial relationships, one party grows into moral personhood over time, gradually acquiring the capacity to be a responsible moral agent. Considerations of justice pertain to the mothering of children in numerous ways. For one thing, there may be siblings to deal with, whose demands and conflicts create the context for parental arbitration and the need for a fair allotment of responsibilities and privileges. Then there are decisions to be made involving the well-being of all persons in the family unit, whose immature members become increasingly capable over time of participating in such administrative affairs. Of special importance in the practice of raising children are the duties to nurture and to promote growth and maturation. These duties may be seen as counterparts to the welfare rights viewed by many as a matter of social justice.[27] Motherhood continually presents its practitioners with moral problems best seen in terms of a complex framework that integrates justice with care, even though the politico-legal discourse of justice has not shaped its domestic expression.[28]

I have been discussing the relevance of justice to close personal relationships. A few words about my companion thesis—the relevance of care to the public domain—is also in order.[29] In its more noble manifestation, care in the public realm would show itself, perhaps, in foreign aid, welfare programs, famine or disaster relief, or other social programs designed to relieve suffering and attend to human needs. If untempered by justice in the public domain, care degenerates precipitously. The infamous "boss" of Chicago's old-time Democratic machine, Mayor Richard J. Daley, was legendary for his nepotism and political partisanship; he cared extravagantly for his relatives, friends, and political cronies.[30]

In recounting the moral reasoning of one of her research subjects, Gilligan once wrote that the "justice" perspective fails "to take into account the reality of relationships" (147). What she meant is that the justice perspective emphasizes a self's various rights to noninterference by others. Gilligan worried that if this is all that a concern for justice involved, then such a perspective would disregard the moral value of positive interaction, connection, and commitment among persons.

However, Gilligan's interpretations of justice is far too limited. For one thing, it fails to recognize positive rights, such as welfare rights, which may be endorsed from a justice perspective. But beyond this minor point, a more important problem is Gilligan's failure to acknowledge the potential for *violence and harm* in human interrelationships and human community.[31] The concept of justice, in general, arises out of relational conditions in which most human beings have the capacity, and many have the inclination, to treat each other badly.

Thus, notions of distributive justice are impelled by the realization that people who together comprise a social system may not share fairly in the benefits and burdens of their social cooperation. Conceptions of rectificatory, or corrective, justice are founded on the concern that when harms are done, action should be taken either to restore those harmed as fully as possible to their previous state, or to prevent further similar harm, or both. And the specific rights that people are variously thought to have are just so many manifestations of our interest in identifying ways in which people deserve protection against harm by others. The complex reality of social life encompasses the human potential for helping, caring for, and nurturing others *as well as* the potential for harming, exploiting, and oppressing others. Thus, Gilligan is wrong to think that the justice perspective completely neglects "the reality of relationships." Rather, it arises from a more complex, and more realistic, estimate of the nature of human interrelationship.

In light of these reflections, it seems wise both to reconsider the seeming dichotomy of care and justice, and to question the moral adequacy of either orientation dissociated from the other. Our aim would be to advance "beyond caring," that is, beyond *mere* caring dissociated from a concern for justice. In addition, we would do well to progress beyond gender stereotypes which assign distinct and different moral roles to women and men. Our ultimate goal should be a nongendered, nondichotomized, moral framework in which all moral concerns could be expressed. We might, with intentional irony, call this project, "de-moralizing the genders."

III. COMMITMENTS TO PARTICULAR PERSONS

Even though care and justice do not define mutually exclusive moral frameworks, it is still too early to dispose of the different-voice hypothesis. I believe that there is something to be said for the thesis that there are different moral orientations, even if the concepts of care and justice do not capture the relevant differences and even if the differences do not correlate statistically with gender differences.

My suggestion is that one important distinction has to do with the nature and focus of what may be called "primary moral commitments." Let us begin with the observation that, from the so-called care standpoint, responsiveness to other persons in their wholeness and their particularity is of singular importance. This idea, in turn, points toward a notion of moral commitment, which takes *particular persons* as its primary focus.[32] A form of moral commitment which contrasts with this is one that involves a focus on general and abstract rules, values, or principles. It is no mere coincidence, I believe, that Gilligan found the so-called justice perspective to feature an emphasis on *rules* (e.g., p. 73).

In part II of this paper, I argued that the concepts of justice and care are mutually compatible and, to at least some extent, mutually dependent. Based on my analysis, the justice perspective might be said to rest, at bottom, on the assumption that the best way to *care* for persons is to respect their rights, and to accord them their due, both in distribution of the burdens and benefits of social cooperation, and in the rectification of wrongs done. But to uphold these principles, it is not necessary to respond with emotion, feeling, passion, or compassion to other persons. Upholding justice does not require the full range of mutual responsiveness that is possible between persons.

By contrast, the so-called ethic of care stresses an ongoing responsiveness. This ethic is, after all, the stereotypic moral norm for women in the domestic role of sustaining a family in the face of the harsh realities of a competitive marketplace and an indifferent polis. The domestic realm has been idealized as the realm in which people, as specific individuals, were to have been nurtured, cherished, and succored. The care perspective discussed by Gilligan is a limited one; it is not really about care in all its complexity, for, as I have argued, that notion *includes* just treatment. But it is about the nature of relationships to particular persons grasped as such. The key issue is the sensitivity and responsiveness to another person's emotional states, individuating differences, specific uniqueness, and whole particularity. The care orientation focuses on whole persons and de-emphasizes adherence to moral rules.

Thus, the important conception that I am extracting from the so-called care perspective is that of commitment to particular persons. What is the nature of this form of moral commitment? Commitment to a specific person, such as a lover, child, or friend, takes as its primary focus the needs, wants, attitudes, judgments, behavior, and overall way of being of that particular person. It is specific to that individual and is not generalizable to others. We show a commitment to someone whenever we attend to her needs, enjoy her successes, defer to her judgment, and find inspiration in her values and goals, simply because they are *hers*. If it is *who she is*, and not her actions or traits subsumed under general rules, which matters as one's motivating guide, then one's responsiveness to her reflects a person-oriented, rather than a rule-based, moral commitment.

Thus, the different perspectives that Gilligan called "care" and "justice" do point toward substantive differences in human interrelationship and commitment. Both orientations take account of relationships in some way; both may legitimately incorporate a concern for justice and for care, and both aim to avoid harm to others and (at the highest stages) to the self. But from the standpoint of "care," self and other are conceptualized in their *particularity* rather than as instances for the application of generalized moral notions. This difference ramifies into what appears to be a major difference in the organization and focus of moral thought.

This analysis requires a subtle expansion. Like care and justice, commitments to particular persons and commitments to values, rules, and principles are not mutually exclusive within the entire panorama of one person's moral concerns. Doubtless, they are intermingled in most people's moral outlooks. Pat likes and admires Mary because of Mary's resilience in the face of tragedy, her intelligent courage, and her good-humored audacity. Pat thereby shows a commitment *in general* to resilience, courage, and good-humored audacity as traits of human personality.

However, in Mary, these traits coalesce in a unique manner: perhaps no one will stand by a friend in deep trouble quite so steadfastly as Mary; perhaps no one petitions the university president as effectively as Mary. The traits that Pat likes, in general, converge to make *Mary*, in Pat's eyes, an especially admirable human individual, a sort of moral exemplar. In virtue of Pat's loyalty to her, Mary may come to play a role in Pat's life which exceeds, in its weightiness, the sum total of the values that Pat sees in Mary's virtues, taken individually and in abstraction from any particular human personality.

Pat is someone with commitments both to moral abstractions and to particular persons. Pat is, in short, like most of us. When we reason morally, we can take up a stance that makes either of these forms of commitment the focal point of our attention. The choice of which stance to adopt at a given time is probably, like other moral alternatives, most poignant and difficult in situations of moral ambiguity or uncertainty, when we don't know how to proceed. In such situations, one can turn *either* to the guidance of principled commitments to values, forms of conduct, or human virtues, *or* one can turn to the guidance that inheres in the example set by a trusted friend or associate—the example of how *she* interprets those same moral ambiguities, or how she resolves those same moral uncertainties.

Of course, the commitment to a particular person is evident in more situations than simply those of moral irresolution. But the experience of moral irresolution may make clearer the different sorts of moral commitment that structure our thinking. Following cherished values will lead one out of one's moral uncertainties in a very different way than will following someone else's example.

Thus, the insight that each person needs some others in her life who recognize, respect, and cherish her particularity in its richness and wholeness is the distinctive motivating vision of the care perspective.[33] The sort of respect for persons which grows out of this vision is not the abstract respect which is owed to all persons in virtue of their common humanity, but a respect for individual worth, merit, need, or, even, idiosyncracy. It is a form of respect which involves admiration and cherishing, when the distinctive qualities are valued intrinsically, and which, at the least, involves toleration when the distinctive qualities are not valued intrinsically.

Indeed, there is an apparent irony in the notion of personhood that underlies some philosophers' conceptions of the universalized moral duties owed to all persons. The rational nature that Kant, for example, takes to give each person dignity and to make each of absolute value, and, therefore irreplaceable,[34] is no more than an abstract rational nature by virtue of which we are all alike. But if we are all alike in this respect, it is hard to understand why we would be irreplaceable. Our common rational nature would seem to make us indistinguishable and, therefore, mutually interchangeable. Specific identity would be a matter of indifference, so far as our absolute value is concerned. Yet it would seem that only in *virtue* of our distinctive particularity could we each be truly irreplaceable.

Of course, our particularity does not *exclude* a common nature, conceptualized at a level of suitable generality. We still deserve equal respect in virtue of our common humanity. But we are also *more* than abstractly and equivalently human. It is this "more" to which we commit ourselves when we care for others in their particularity.

Thus, as I interpret it, there is at least one important difference in moral reasoning brought to our attention by Gilligan's "care" and "justice" frameworks. This difference hinges on the primary form of moral commitment which structures moral thought and the resulting nature of the response to other persons. For so-called care reasoners, recognition of and commitment to persons in their particularity is an overriding moral concern.[35]

Unlike the concepts of justice and care, which admit of a mutual integration, it is less clear that these two distinct forms of moral commitment can jointly comprise the focus of one's moral attention, in any single case. Nor can we respond to all other persons equally well in either way. The only integration possible here may be to seek the more intimate, responsive, committed relationships with people who are known closely, or known in contexts in which differential needs are important and can be known with some reliability, and to settle for rule-based equal respect toward that vast number of others whom one cannot know in any particularity.

At any rate, to tie together the varied threads of this discussion, we may conclude that nothing intrinsic to gender demands a division of moral norms that assigns particularized, personalized commitments to women and universalized, rule-based commitments to men. We need nothing less than to "de-moralize" the genders, advance beyond the dissociation of justice from care, and enlarge the symbolic access of each gender to all available conceptual and social resources for the sustenance and enrichment of our collective moral life.[36]

NOTES

1. *In a Different Voice* (Cambridge, MA: Harvard University Press 1982), 73. More recently, the following works by Gilligan on related issues have also appeared: "Do the Social Sciences Have an Adequate Theory of Moral Development?" in Norma Haan, Robert N. Bellah, Paul Rabinow, and William M. Sullivan, eds., *Social Science as Moral Inquiry* (New York: Columbia University Press 1983), 33–51; "Reply," *Signs* 11 (1986); 324–33; and "Remapping the Moral Domain: New Images of the Self in Relationship," in Thomas C. Heller, Morton Sosna, and David E. Wellberry, eds., *Reconstructing Individualism* (Stanford, CA: Stanford University Press, 1986) 237–52. Throughout this paper, all page references inserted in the text are to *In a Different Voice.*
2. Frigga Haug, "Morals Also Have Two Genders," trans. Rodney Livingstone, *New Left Review* 143 (1984); 55.
3. These sources include: Owen J. Flanagan Jr. and Jonathan E. Adler, "Impartiality and Particularity," *Social Research* 50 (1983), 576–96; Nel Noddings, *Caring* (Berkeley: University of California Press 1984); Claudia Card, "Virtues and Moral Luck" (unpublished paper presented at American Philosophical Association, Western Division meetings, Chicago, IL, April 1985, and at the Conference on Virtue Theory, University of San Diego, San Diego, CA, February 1986); Marilyn Friedman, *Care and Context in Moral Reasoning,* MOSAIC Monograph #1 (Bath, England: University of Bath, 1985), reprinted in Carol Harding, ed., *Moral Dilemmas* (Chicago: Precedent, 1986), 25–42, and in Diana T. Meyers and Eva Feder Kittay, eds., *Women and Moral Theory* (Totowa, NJ: Rowman and Littlefield 1987), 190–204; all the papers in Meyers and Kittay; Linda K. Kerber, "Some Cautionary Words for Historians," *Signs* 11 (1986); 304–10; Catherine G. Greeno and Eleanor E. Maccoby, "How Different is the 'Different Voice,'" *Signs* 11 (1986): 310–16; Zella Luria, "A Methodological Critique," *Signs* 11 (1986); 316–21; Carol B. Stack, "The Culture of Gender: Women and Men of Color," *Signs* 11 (1986): 321–24; Owen Flanagan and Kathryn Jackson, "Justice, Care, and Gender: The Kohlberg-Gilligan Debate Revisited," *Ethics* 97 (1987):

622–37. An analysis of this issue from an ambiguously feminist standpoint is to be found in: John M. Broughton, "Women's Rationality and Men's Virtues," *Social Research* 50 (1983): 597–642. For a helpful review of some of these issues, cf. Jean Grimshaw, *Philosophy and Feminist Thinking* (Minneapolis: University of Minnesota Press 1986), esp. chs. 7 and 8.

4. This term is used by Virginia Held to refer, in general, to the division of moral labor among the multitude of professions, activities, and practices in culture and society, though not specifically to gender roles. Cf. *Rights and Goods* (New York: Free Press 1984), ch. 3. Held is aware that gender roles are part of the division of moral labor but she mentions this topic only in passing, p. 29.
5. Gilligan, "Reply," 326.
6. Research on the "gender difference" hypothesis is very mixed. The studies which appear to show gender differences in moral reasoning for one or more age levels include: Norma Haan, M. Brewster-Smith and Jeanne Block, "Moral Reasoning of Young Adults: Political-social Behavior, Family Background, and Personality Correlates," *Journal of Personality and Social Psychology* 10 (1968): 183–201; James Fishkin, Kenneth Keniston and Catharine MacKinnon, "Moral Reasoning and Political Ideology," *Journal of Personality and Social Psychology* 27 (1973): 109–19; Norma Haan, "Hypothetical and Actual Moral Reasoning in a Situation of Civil Disobedience," *Journal of Personality and Social Psychology* 32 (1975): 255–70; Constance Holstein, "Development of Moral Judgment: A Longitudinal Study of Males and Females," *Child Development* 47 (1976): 51–61 (showing gender differences in middle adulthood but not for other age categories; see references below); Sharry Langdale, "Moral Orientations and Moral Development: The Analysis of Care and Justice Reasoning Across Different Dilemmas in Females and Males from Childhood through Adulthood" (Ed. D. diss., Harvard Graduate School of Education 1983); Kay Johnston, "Two Moral Orientations—Two Problem-solving Strategies: Adolescents' Solutions to Dilemmas in Fables," (Ed. D. diss., Harvard Graduate School of Education 1985). The last two sources are cited by Gilligan, "Reply," p. 330.

   Among the studies which show no gender differences in moral reasoning at one or more age levels are: E. Turiel, "A Comparative Analysis of Moral Knowledge and Moral Judgment in Males and Females," *Journal of Personality* 44 (1976): 195–208; C. B. Holstein, "Irreversible Stepwise Sequence in the Development of Moral Judgment: A Longitudinal Study of Males and Females" (showing no differences in childhood or adolescence but showing differentiation in middle adulthood; see reference above); N. Haan et al., "Family Moral Patterns," *Child Development* 47 (1976): 1204–6; M. Berkowitz et al., "The Relation of Moral Judgment Stage Disparity to Developmental Effects of Peer Dialogues," Merrill-Palmer Quarterly 26 (1980): 341–57; and Mary Brabeck, "Moral Judgment: Theory and Research on Differences between Males and Females," *Developmental Review* 3 (1983): 274–91.

   Lawrence J. Walker surveyed all the research to date and claimed that rather than showing a gender-based difference in moral reasoning, it showed differences based on occupation and education: "Sex Differences in the Development of Moral Reasoning," *Child Development* 55 (1984): 677–91. This "meta-analysis" has itself recently been disputed: Norma Haan, "With Regard to Walker (1984) on Sex 'Differences' in Moral Reasoning" (University of California, Berkeley, Institute of Human Development mimeograph, 1985); Diana Baumrind, "Sex Differences in Moral Reasoning: Response to Walker's (1984) Conclusion That There Are None," in Bill Puka, ed., *Caring Voices and Women's Moral Frames* (New York: Garland, 1994). The last two sources are cited by Gilligan, "Reply," p. 330.
7. Norma Haan, "Two Moralities in Action Contexts," *Journal of Personality and Social Psychology* 36 (1978): 286–305. Also cf. Norma Haan, "Moral Reasoning in a Hypothetical and an Actual

Situation of Civil Disobedience," *Journal of Personality and Social Psychology* 32 (1975): 255–70; and Gertrud Nunner-Winkler, "Two Moralities? A Critical Discussion of an Ethic of Care and Responsibility versus an Ethic of Rights and Justice," in William M. Kurtines and Jacob L. Gewirtz, *Morality, Moral Behavior, and Moral Development* (New York: John Wiley & Sons, 1984): 348–61.

8. Gilligan, "Reply," 326.
9. Broughton, "Women's Rationality and Men's Virtues," 636.
10. Gilligan's work arose largely as a critical reaction to the studies of moral reasoning carried on by Lawrence Kohlberg and his research associates. For the reaction by those scholars to Gilligan's work and their assessment of its importance to moral psychology, see Lawrence Kohlberg, "A Reply to Owen Flanagan and Some Comments on the Puka-Goodpaster Exchange," *Ethics* 92 (1982): 513–28; and Lawrence Kohlberg, Charles Levine, and Alexandra Hewer, *Moral Stages: A Current Reformulation and Response to Critics* (Basel: Karger 1983): 20–27, 121–50.

    In philosophy, themes related to Gilligan's concerns have been raised by, among others: Michael Stocker, "The Schizophrenia of Modern Ethical Theories," *Journal of Philosophy* 63 (1976): 453–66: Bernard Williams, "Persons, Character and Morality," in Amelie O. Rorty, ed., *The Identities of Persons* (Berkeley: University of California Press, 1976), reprinted in Bernard Williams, *Moral Luck* (New York: Cambridge University Press, 1982): 1–19; Lawrence Blum, *Friendship, Altruism and Morality* (London: Routledge & Kegan Paul, 1980); Alastair MacIntyre, *After Virtue* (Notre Dame Press, IN: University of Notre Dame, 1981), esp. ch. 15; Michael Stocker, "Values and Purposes: The Limits of Teleology and the Ends of Friendship," *Journal of Philosophy* 78 (1981): 747–65; Owen Flanagan, "Virtue, Sex and Gender: Some Philosophical Reflections on the Moral Psychology Debate," *Ethics* 92 (1982): 499–512; Michael Slote, "Morality Not a System of Imperatives," *American Philosophical Quarterly* 19 (1982): 331–40; and Christina Hoff Sommers, "Filial Morality," *Journal of Philosophy* 83 (1986): 439–56.
11. Greeno and Macroby, "How Different is the 'Different' Voice?" 314–15.
12. Gilligan, "Reply," 325.
13. For a discussion of this historical development, cf. Linda Nicholson, "Women, Morality and History," *Social Research* 50 (1983): 514–36; and her *Gender and History* (New York: Columbia University Press, 1986) esp. chs. 3 and 4.
14. Cf. Nancy Eisenberg and Roger Lennon, "Sex Differences in Empathy and Related Capacities," *Psychological Bulletin* 94 (1983): 100–31.
15. Cf. Alice H. Eagly, "Sex Differences and Social Roles" (unpublished paper presented at Experimental Social Psychology, Tempe, AZ, October 1986), esp. p. 7. Also cf: Alice H. Eagly and Valerie J. Steffen, "Gender Stereotypes Stem From the Distribution of Women and Men Into Social Roles," *Journal of Personality and Social Psychology* 46 (1984): 735–54.
16. The stereotypes of men are not obviously connected with justice and rights, but they are connected with the excessive individualism which Gilligan takes to underlie the justice orientation. Cf. Eagly, "Sex Differences and Social Roles," 8.
17. Eagly argues both that people do show a tendency to conform to shared and known expectations, on the parts of others, about their behavior, and that a division of labor which leads people to develop different skills also contributes to differential development; "Sex Differences and Social Roles," *passim.* It follows from Eagly's view that if the genders are stereotypically "moralized," they would then be likely to develop so as to conform to those different expectations.
18. Eagly and Steffen have found that stereotypic beliefs that women are more "communal" and less "agentic" than men, and that men are more "agentic" and less "communal" than women are based

more deeply on occupational role stereotypes than on gender stereotypes; "Gender Stereotypes Stem From the Distribution of Women and Men Into Social Roles," *passim*. In this respect, Eagly and Steffen force us to question whether the gender categorization which pervades Gilligan's analysis really captures the fundamental differentiation among persons. I do not address this question in this paper.

19. In correspondence, Marcia Baron has suggested that a factor accounting for the actual emergence of "mixed" perspectives on the parts of women and men may have to do with the instability of the distinction between public and private realms to which the justice/care dichotomy corresponds. Men have always been recognized to participate in both realms and, in practice, many women have participated, out of choice or necessity, in such segments of the public world as that of paid labor. The result is a blurring of the experiential segregation which otherwise might have served to reinforce distinct moral orientations.
20. Book I, 322–35. A thorough discussion of the Greek conception of justice in the context of friendship can be found in Horst Hutter, *Politics as Friendship* (Waterloo, ON: Wilfrid Laurier University Press, 1978).
21. Rawls, *A Theory of Justice*, 13 and elsewhere.
22. Ibid., 129.
23. Marilyn Frye, *The Politics of Reality* (Trumansburg, NY: The Crossing Press, 1983), 9.
24. Ibid., 10.
25. For an important discussion of the relevance of justice to the family, cf. Susan Moller Okin, "Justice and Gender," *Philosophy and Public Affairs* 16 (1987): 42–72.
26. For insightful discussions of the distinctive modes of thought to which mothering gives rise, cf. Sara Ruddick, "Maternal Thinking," reprinted here, chap. 30; and her "Preservative Love and Military Destruction: Some Reflections on Mothering and Peace," in Joyce Trebilcot, ed., *Mothering: Essays in Feminist Theory* (Totowa, NJ: Rowman & Allanheld 1983): 231–62; also Virginia Held, "The Obligations of Mothers and Fathers," in Trebilcot, ed., 7–20.
27. This point was suggested to me by L.W. Sumner.
28. John Broughton also discusses the concern for justice and rights which appears in women's moral reasoning as well as the concern for care and relationships featured in men's moral reasoning; "Women's Rationality and Men's Virtues," esp. 603–22. For a historical discussion of male theorists who have failed to hear the concern for justice in women's voices, cf. Carole Pateman, " 'The Disorder of Women': Women, Love, and the Sense of Justice," *Ethics* 91 (1980): 20–34.
29. This discussion owes a debt to Francesca M. Cancian's warning that we should not narrow our conception of love to the recognized ways in which women love, which researchers find to center on the expression of feelings and verbal disclosure. Such a conception ignores forms of love which are stereotyped as characteristically male, including instrumental help and the sharing of activities. Cf. "The Feminization of Love," *Signs* 11 (1986): 692–709.
30. Cf. Mike Royko, *Boss: Richard J. Daley of Chicago* (New York: New American Library, 1971).
31. Claudia Card has critiqued Gilligan's work for ignoring, in particular, the dismaying harms to which women have historically been subjected in heterosexual relationships, including, but by no means limited to, marriage ("Virtues and Moral Luck," 15–17).
32. Discussion in part III of my paper draws upon the insights of Claudia Card, "Virtues and Moral Luck" and Seyla Benhabib, "The Generalized and the Concrete Other: Vı́sions of the Autonomous Self," reprinted here, Chap 38.
33. This part of my discussion owes a debt to Claudia Card.

34. Cf. Immanuel Kant, *Groundwork of the Metaphysics of Morals*, trans. Lewis White Beck (Indianapolis: Bobbs-Merrill 1959): 46–47, 53–54.
35. For a helpful discussion on this topic, cf. Margaret Walker, "Moral Particularism," unpublished manuscript presented at the Pacific Division Meetings of the American Philosophical Association, March 1987.
36. I am grateful to Larry May, L.W. Sumner, Marcia Baron, and Christopher Morris for helpful comments on previous drafts of this paper. Earlier versions were presented to the Society for Women in Philosophy, Midwestern Division (USA), Madison, WI, October 1986; Society for Value Inquiry, Chicago, IL, April 1987; Seminar on Contemporary Social and Political Thought, University of Chicago, May 1987; Third International Interdisciplinary Congress on Women, Dublin, Ireland, July 1987; and Annual Conference of MOSAIC (Moral and Social Action Interdisciplinary Colloquium), Brighton, England, July 1987.

Gender and the Complexity of Moral Voices

Moody-Adams sees few redeeming features in Gilligan's work. Gilligan has done us a service by calling attention to the moral importance of care. But this contribution is vitiated by Gilligan's reduction of morality to two voices—care and justice. She should have discerned a multiplicity of moral voices. Thus, Moody-Adams criticizes Gilligan for race, class, religious, and ethnic bias and gender essentialism, and she traces these problems to weaknesses in the design of Gilligan's research.

Moody-Adams quotes a passage in which Gilligan notes that the prison population is largely male and that child care is largely provided by women and then attributes this difference to gender differences in moral reasoning. Moody-Adams objects that Gilligan is implying that women are superior moral thinkers. Also, since the prison population is disproportionately black, Gilligan's remark suggests that whites are better moral thinkers than blacks. However, there is little reason to believe that poor moral thinking leads to incarceration or that good moral thinking keeps people out of jail. Likewise, Moody-Adams objects that Gilligan is echoing gender stereotypes that have been damaging to women. She suggests that Gilligan's results reflect the kinds of moral problems she asked her subjects about. Gilligan might have obtained different results if, in addition to abortion, she had asked her subjects to discuss issues like sex discrimination in employment, rape, and pornography. Also, she might have obtained different results if she had included women with diverse class, race, religious, and ethnic backgrounds in her sample. In short, Gilligan's conclusions about gender difference and moral thinking are unwarranted, potentially harmful generalizations.

—D.T.M.

Chapter 35

Michele M. Moody-Adams

Gender and the Complexity of Moral Voices

On one very powerful conception, philosophical reflection about morality—like all moral reflection—is a species of *self*-reflection. It is a species of *sincere* and *rational* self-scrutiny that, if carried out in detail, could issue either in a clear account of a principle (or principles) for guiding reflection and action or in a general conception of the character traits, cognitive capacities, and emotions that ought to determine the shape of reflection and action. This kind of self-reflection has been at the center of philosophical reflection on the moral life at least since Plato reported Athenian resistance to Socrates's contention that the unexamined life is not worth living. Kant's moral theory provides a very different view of the kind of knowledge that results from the examined life. Kant believed that his account of the Categorical Imperative revealed the ideally rational and objectively valid structure of the ordinary moral consciousness. Indeed, he insisted that like Socrates he was making human reason "attend to its own principle" (Kant [1785] 1964, 71–72). Thus very different philosophical traditions have acknowledged the centrality of self-reflection to philosophical ethics.

On some versions of this conception of philosophical reflection, the self-scrutiny of an individual person engaged in moral reflection is crucially connected to the collective self-scrutiny of that person's culture. Socrates's activities as a "gadfly" on the neck of Athens might thus be viewed as attempts to encourage the collective (as well as individual) self-scrutiny that is inseparable from moral reflection. The same conception of philosophical reflection allows us to understand why Martin Luther King Jr. compared the nonviolent civil disobedience movement in the Untied States during the mid-twentieth century to the Socratic conception of philosophical reflection. King viewed that movement as a catalyst for the moral self-scrutiny of a culture as well as an instrument of social change (King 1964). Moreover, the importance of this connection between individual reflection and a culture's collective self-scrutiny is borne out by the fact that a person's self-conception is in part dependent upon that person's social experience. Of course there is much disagreement over what difference the self-conceptions of empirical persons ought to make to the shape and content of *philosophical* reflection about morality. Kant would have found the very question anathema; whatever we are to make of the Socratic vision, it seems clear that Plato himself would have done the same. My own view, though I will not argue for it here, is that the best philosophical reflection about morality will issue from a view that treats the self-conceptions of empirical persons (conceptions shaped by a variety of influences) as starting points for reflections, even though the ultimate aim of such reflection will typically be to encourage some revision of those self-conceptions.

On this model of philosophical reflection about ethics, if women do indeed speak about morality "in a different voice," recognition of this fact cannot leave such reflection unchanged. Of course we sometimes find it easier to avoid considerations that complicate moral reflection or require reflection on what we have always taken for granted. Like Plato's Euthyphro, we are sometimes resistant to the urgings of a newly audible moral voice. But figures such as Socrates and King are emblematic of the extent to which the voices that a culture seldom hears, or refuses to listen to, or even actively tries to silence, are most likely to serve as catalysts for sincere and rational self-scrutiny.

For many thinkers, the notion of a distinctively feminine moral voice has been given substance by Carol Gilligan's empirical research in developmental psychology. Yet I want to take issue with the confidence of the many theorists who believe that Gilligan's claims have been unequivocally established as fact. My aim in this essay is to inquire what we can make of Gilligan's claims to have found such a voice. In the first section I consider whether there can be any "disinterested" assertions of gender-specific differences in moral development, by specific reference to Gilligan's claims about her inquiry. In the second section, I consider how we might know whether there is a moral voice that is specifically female, and I ask whether the very idea might not lead us to miss the complexity of the moral domain—especially as women conceive of it. Finally, in the third section I consider the assumptions that underlie the design of Gilligan's research. I question whether Gilligan's results license some of the sweeping assertions many—including Gilligan—now make about women's patterns of moral thinking. I argue, ultimately, that we cannot discern the lessons of women's ways of thinking about morality unless we are sure that we have heard their *voices* correctly.

CAN THERE BE A DISINTERESTED ASSERTION OF SEX DIFFERENCES IN MORAL DEVELOPMENT?

In the introduction to *In a Different Voice*, Carol Gilligan initially seems decidedly reluctant to assert that there are sexual differences in the way people conceive of and talk about morality. She contends at first that the moral voice described in the book is "characterized not by gender, but theme," and that the association of this voice with women is "an empirical observation" and is "not absolute" (1982, 2). In these same passages she further asserts that the contrasts between male and female voices discussed throughout the book are intended to "highlight a distinction between two modes of thought . . . rather than to represent a generalization about either sex" (1982, 2). Just a few paragraphs later, however, the reluctance to make generalizations about the sexes gives way to claims that are emphatically about gender. She expressly states that the research detailed in the book is intended, among other things, to provide psychologists with the tools to come up with a "clearer representation of women's development" *and* to present the women readers in her audience with "a clearer representation of their thought" that will enable them to see that thought's integrity and validity (1982, 3). Indeed, many of the most important aims and ends of Gilligan's research clearly rest on empirical generalizations about the role of gender in moral discourse—specifically, patterns of emotion, thought, and action that most women allegedly articulate and defend in the process of reasoning about moral issues. Much of the response to Gilligan's research would be unintelligible were this not the case.

Gilligan's recent essays suggest that she has become increasingly confident of the legitimacy and importance of her claims about the patterns of women's moral thinking. Yet in at least one important essay, she acknowledges that some of her readers continue to find the project problematic. Although uneasiness about the implications of Gilligan's project has been expressed in many quarters, she pays particular attention to recent work in the psychology of moral development that seems to have "shied away" from noting sex differences in moral development. Gilligan attributes this resistance, quite rightly, to fears of "the dangers of stereotyping, the intimations of biological determinism, and the fact that in recent discussions of sex differences there is no disinterested position" (Gilligan and Wiggins 1987, 278). Yet her attempts to allay such fears provide little comfort to those who share such concerns. In a revealing passage, she contends that

> stereotypes of males as aggressive and females as nurturant, however distorting and however limited, have some empirical claim. The overwhelmingly male composition of the prison population and the extent to which women take care of young children cannot readily be dismissed as irrelevant to theories of morality or excluded from accounts of moral development. If there are no sex differences in empathy or moral reasoning, why are there sex differences in moral and immoral behavior? (Gilligan and Wiggins 1987, 279)

Not only does such a response fail to allay the relevant concerns, it also generates a host of doubts about whether it is possible to claim that there are sex differences in moral reasoning without at the same time organizing those differences hierarchically.

Note that in Gilligan's description, what purports to be a strictly empirical generalization about behavior abruptly turns into a claim about moral capacities. This claim about moral capacities, moreover, embodies two dubious presuppositions. First, it seems to presuppose that those who have not been imprisoned for a crime necessarily possess more highly developed moral sensibilities—a questionable assumption at best. Second, Gilligan's defense assumes that because women do not commit crimes at the same rate as men, they are somehow more moral than men—whatever the source of the tendency to behave more morally. To be sure, later in the same essay, Gilligan insists that she is not arguing for the moral superiority or inferiority of either sex. In fact, she contends that her research attempts to frame "the sex difference question" in such a way as to *reject* any suggestion that one sex is morally superior to the other (Gilligan and Wiggins 1987, 282). Yet how could the question about "sex differences in moral and immoral behavior" be relevant to the composition of the prison population unless one presupposes that these facts somehow point to the moral superiority of those who do not wind up in prison?[1] Now, let us grant for the sake of argument that at least in some circumstances it can be shown that women are more moral than men. In this instance, however, such a conclusion seems unjustified: Sex differences in "empathy and moral reasoning" may explain very little about the makeup of the prison population. People sometimes refrain from committing crimes simply for fear of going to jail. Indeed, a whole tradition of reflection on the nature of law—the classical legal positivism of Austin and Bentham—is built upon the assumption that, most of the time, fear of punishment can be a sufficient motive to obey the law. Moreover, it is certainly plausible that traditional social roles and conventions have simply given women fewer occasions to commit crimes and that changes in these roles and conventions might be accompanied by a rise in the number of women who commit serious crimes.

Equally problematic is Gilligan's failure to recognize that *precisely* the sorts of generalizations she invokes in this passage have historically been called upon to support theories about the biological "inevitability" of criminal behavior. Those of Gilligan's readers who are concerned about the dangers of racial stereotyping may wonder what one is to make, using Gilligan's logic, of the fact that the male prison population is disproportionately black. Such readers cannot overlook the uses of analogous generalizations about the *ethnic* or *socioeconomic* composition of the "overwhelmingly male" prison population to justify discrimination against certain males on the basis of race. To be sure, Gilligan does not wish to license any such appeals, but the passage is disturbing in its failure to acknowledge its affinities to such appeals. It simply is not clear why the makeup of the prison population could be relevant to reflection on "moral and immoral behavior" unless the intent of the passage is to suggest that not winding up in prison is evidence of superior moral capacities. Of course, the composition of the prison population may support generalizations about what groups of people display more criminal manifestations of aggression. But an adequate explanation of such data will certainly be far more complex than Gilligan's assumptions allow. Moreover, one must pause to reflect on the nature of aggression itself: Surely not all manifestations of aggression are either criminal or evidence of deficiencies in moral development. With the possible exception of the extreme pacifist, nearly everyone would agree that a woman who aggressively defends herself against rape, or a man who aggressively protects his children from an attacker, clearly behaves in a morally acceptable way. Indeed, a willingness to display aggression—in due measure and in appropriate circumstances—may be essential to revealing the depth of one's capacity to care for others.

It might be possible, of course, to provide a more sympathetic reading of the passage in question. One might simply argue, for instance, that it is an unintentional overstatement of the case. But the passage does more than take issue with existing hierarchies of alleged sex differences in moral development. The passage makes a claim of an altogether different kind: It asserts the moral deficiency of one sex. The juxtaposition of this view with Gilligan's insistence that she does not want to make hierarchical rankings of moral perspectives suggests a vacillation in her professed view of the equal worth of moral perspectives. This suggestion is borne out by one of the most striking passages in *In a Different Voice*—one in which Gilligan elaborates upon Erikson's criticism of Gandhi's treatment of his family. She first cites what she calls Gandhi's "blind willingness to sacrifice people to truth" as evidence of "the danger of an ethics abstracted from life." She then argues that "this willingness links Gandhi to the biblical Abraham, who prepared to sacrifice the life of his son in order to demonstrate the integrity and supremacy of his faith. Both men, in the limitations of their fatherhood, stand in implicit contrast to the woman who comes before Solomon and verifies her motherhood by relinquishing truth in order to save the life of her child" (1982, 104–105). Considerations of faith, this passage implies, cannot ground a moral perspective with as much integrity and importance as the perspective of care.[2] This implication is problematic enough. Even more problematic is the extent to which this passage confirms, as other commentators have noted, that Gilligan's account of sex differences in moral reasoning is *not* always disinterested (Flanagan and Adler 1983, 587). Here, Gilligan is clearly vulnerable to Debra Nails's objection that differences become deficiencies when we look through the lens of gender (1983, 643).

Some readers will no doubt respond that a suggestion of the moral superiority of women would not be a regrettable implication of Gilligan's research. They may note that much of the research to which Gilligan's project responds, at least in part, appeals to deprecatory generalizations about women's moral thinking. But we cannot ignore the worry expressed by some commentators that claims about women's allegedly superior moral capacities have been associated historically with the claim that these capacities best suit women for domestic pursuits—an association most vividly embodied in the Victorian conception of the "angel in the house." Nor can we ignore the extent to which, even apart from the problematic implication of women's moral superiority, the vision of morality that Gilligan believes to be dominant in women's thinking is bound up with rather limiting stereotypes (Williams 1989). Some of Gilligan's less sympathetic critics find the potential danger of this stereotype reason in itself simply to reject the theory (Nails 1983). Such a rejection is clearly problematic, however, since it avoids the question of whether Gilligan's generalizations might be true. But even if Gilligan has correctly described a predominantly female perspective on moral reasoning, a more important problem remains: Do the social, cultural, and economic conditions that generated that perspective place intrinsic limits on the normative value of that perspective? We must ask whether our conception of "the feminine" remains too entangled in a complex array of insufficiently disinterested assumptions to be a useful category for reflection.[3]

DOES THE NOTION OF A SINGLE GENDER-SPECIFIC VOICE MASK THE COMPLEXITY OF WOMEN'S MORAL REASONING?

The question of whether there is a distinctively feminine moral voice cannot be separated from the question of how we might discover such a voice and how we could be assured that we had correctly heard its distinctive urgings. If it is a fact that most women consistently give priority in their moral reasoning to considerations of care and responsibility in relationships, that they define themselves primarily in terms of their attachments to other persons, and that they tend to view moral problems "contextually" rather than "categorically," then we must be able to say how we know these claims about women's moral perspective to be true. Gilligan has of course offered her empirical research as evidence in support of these claims about women's moral voice. I am going to suggest, however, that there are some important difficulties with the design of Gilligan's research that may require us to reassess her claims.

In *In a Different Voice*, some of the relevant evidence comes from two studies of subjects' responses to hypothetical moral problems, as well as their responses to questions about how the subjects viewed themselves and what they considered to be moral problems. Gilligan refers to these two studies as the "college student study" (of students who had chosen to take a college course on moral and political choice) and the "rights and responsibilities" study (a comparative study of females and males of various ages and educational levels). But she seems to place the most importance upon the results of a third study, the abortion decision study, which generated data about the reasoning and actions of women deciding whether to undergo an abortion. One of the most striking features of Gilligan's research—in view of her claim to have revealed a distinctively feminine moral voice—is the absence of sustained discussion of many other concerns about which many women have become increasingly vocal. Of course the abortion decision study sought to elicit information about how women reason morally in one such circumstance. Yet other, very different circumstances confront women with equally difficult choices, though Gilligan does not consider them except in passing. Little or no attention is devoted to discussing how women think about, or act in response to, such problems as rape, physical or sexual abuse inflicted by a spouse, sexual harassment in the work place, or sexual discrimination in employment. My claim is not that these problems have greater moral significance than those concerns discussed in Gilligan's research. Rather, I want to suggest that women's responses to these problems might well reveal considerations discordant with some of Gilligan's findings. Considerations of care and responsibility in relationships might be important in some discussions of this sort, but it is possible that women's discussion of these problems would have very little to do with such concerns.

Moreover, reflection on such problems might reveal the limitations of a moral perspective that purports to place at the center of moral reflection the kind of considerations that Gilligan associates with a distinctively female moral voice. Three of the problems cited above—the problems of rape, sexual abuse, and sexual harassment—seem to focus moral reflection on duties of noninterference rather than duties of care. Further, duties of noninterference seem to have a special status in that they are duties owed to persons whatever the extent of our capacity to care for them, whatever our particular desires about how they ought to care for us, and whatever our beliefs about how they ought to lead their lives. As Kant might have argued, they are duties that require us to treat persons as objective ends (as ends-in-themselves), not merely as subjective ends ("whose existence as an object of our actions has value *for us*") (Kant [1785] 1964, 96). In less strictly Kantian language, such duties require respect for the integrity and worth of persons simply *as persons.* But this notion of respect for the integrity of persons—perhaps more than any other—is particularly resistant to reduction to the language of care.

To be sure, some of Gilligan's comments suggest that she thinks that this concept of the integrity of persons could simply be reinterpreted in terms of the concepts of care and responsibility in relationships.[4] But central elements of the care perspective turn out to be inadequate to the task of explaining or justifying the respect due to the integrity of individuals. A conception of the self as defined not through separation from but through interconnection with others is oddly unhelpful in deciding what is morally wrong with rape, abuse, and sexual harassment. Surely one of the principal features of such actions—what makes them so damaging beyond any physical harm they may or may not cause—is that they embody the perpetrator's refusal to respect the integrity and *separateness* of the victim. The rapist who says of his victim that "when she said 'no' she meant 'yes,' " fails to respect the integrity of this woman's expressed wishes, as well as her separateness as a person. Moreover, sexual discrimination in employment typically consists of actions that somehow treat women differently from men on the basis of characteristics that are arbitrary from the point of view of the requirements of the job. Moral condemnation of such conduct will typically stress that it rests on a failure to recognize that for reasons of employment, in most instances worth should be measured independently of gender. Sexual discrimination in employment embodies a failure to respect the integrity of an employee's desire to be judged on her ability to do the job. Gilligan argues at some length for the tendency of the female subjects in her studies to view moral problems "contextually" and not "categorically" (1982, 98–105). But surely most women would simply pronounce all of these actions, from rape to sexual discrimination in employment, categorically unacceptable. I am even willing to concede for the sake of argument that considerations associated with the care perspective might play a greater role in the typical woman's response to these actions. What I cannot concede is that this same woman would be unwilling to proclaim the absolute unacceptability of these actions.

One must also wonder what kinds of responses would have been generated by reflection on a topic less likely to reveal consensus—for instance, the topic of pornography. The question of the moral acceptability of pornography might have proven a particularly rich source of reflection on women's ways of reasoning, especially because it is a matter about which women disagree. Indeed, even those women who agree in condemning it cite a wide variety of moral considerations. Some allege a direct connection between pornography and specific instances of violence against women. Others argue that even if no such direct connection exists, pornography is intrinsically exploitative of women. Still others argue that independent of the possibilities of exploitation and violence, pornography embodies disrespect for the equal worth of persons. The voices of women who condemn pornography, especially those whose criticisms presume no direct connection between pornography and crime, sound quite different from the voices of those women who responded to Gilligan's abortion decision study. Moreover, the voices of those women who do not condemn pornography might surprise us in their willingness to cite the overriding importance of ideals such as liberty of conscience, thought, and speech. In short, these unexplored possibilities raise a crucial, persistent question: Might the dominance in her female subjects of what Gilligan describes as care reasoning be a function of the kinds of problems they were asked (or not asked) about rather than a function of the way they actually think?[5]

Just as the choice of questions might have affected the outcome of Gilligan's research, so, too, might her decisions about what kinds of women to interview. For instance, there are surely women whose vision of the moral landscape is shaped not by their understanding of the relation between the self and others but by their religious faith. Such women might even ground considerations of care (for self and others) in a religious conception on which a *command* to care issues from their faith. Still other women choose lives devoted to the perfection of their faith—even when that life requires that they place limitations on their capacity to care for others. A woman who chooses life in a religious community demanding celibacy is one such example. But we find an equally important example in the instance of a mother who believes that seeking medical treatment—even for her children—would violate the demands of faith. No doubt some such woman might choose to violate the demand on specific occasions. But surely even such a woman might take the choices of Gandhi or Abraham to illustrate much more than simply "the limitations of fatherhood" or "the dangers of an ethics abstracted from life." Surely women of strong religious convictions, even those who might bridle at conventional representations of femininity bound up with such convictions, can see those choices as the result of sincere and coherent moral reflection.

But religious faith is only one kind of ideal not discussed by Gilligan that might complicate our picture of women's moral reasoning. Other ideals—of personal integrity and courage, or aesthetic perfection, or scientific truth, for instance—might produce a vision of a moral landscape that would be dramatically different from that associated with considerations of faith. Interviews of women whose lives have been structured by such concerns might well have yielded a much more diverse picture of women's ways of reasoning about morality. A great writer, a diligent scientific researcher—even one whose choices included motherhood and family—might convince us that the moral domain consists of a diversity of goods. Even those women whose lives are not structured by the pursuit of such ideals might well be able to acknowledge the moral worth of lives devoted to them. Still further, few if any of the women interviewed in Gilligan's study seem to have undergone either the economic hardships or the racial and ethnic exclusion—or in some cases both—that are constants of some women's experience. Their experience might well make them more insistent than other women on the importance of respect for the equal worth of persons. At any rate, their experience would surely complicate one's account of the moral landscape—as women see it—even further.

WHY DOES GILLIGAN FIND UNITY WHERE WE MIGHT EXPECT TO FIND DIVERSITY?

One of the principal reasons Gilligan fails to discern the complexity of women's ways of reasoning morally is her decision to give the abortion decision study such a central place in her project. For though she cites the results of other studies, both in *In a Different Voice* and in later essays, the argument in the book suggests that the kind of response that emerges in the abortion decision study was indeed central. She framed the central problem of that project's design in clear terms: In order to discover "whether women's construction of the moral domain relies on a language different from that of men," it is necessary to find "places where women have the power to choose and thus are willing to speak in their own voice" (Gilligan 1982, 70). She then argues that the abortion decision study should play a central role because it yields important data about one of the "places where women have the power to choose." The legality of abortion (like the availability of birth control), she contends, affects women's power to make choices about "the relationships that have traditionally defined women's identities and frame their moral judgment." Moreover, she believes, the power to make these choices creates special kinds of conflicts for women: Although it can release them "from a sexuality that binds them in dependence," it also "brings them into conflict with the conventions of femininity" (Gilligan 1982, 70). In Gilligan's view, then, reproductive choice creates a framework within which women will be "willing to speak in their own voice."

But do women speak in their own moral voice *only* when they contemplate choices that might bring them into conflict with the cultural conventions of femininity? Even within these conventions, women have always been able to make choices about a variety of matters other than their capacity to reproduce. Suppose a woman at a supermarket, accompanied by her observant child, receives too much money back in change; even this outwardly simple situation might require the most serious exercise of moral judgment about the importance of honesty. Whether she decides to return the money or to keep it, justifications offered in support of the decision will surely have effects that transcend the situation itself. The child's understanding of this decision's coherence with other similar decisions; the child's understanding of the moral significance of the relation between what a parent says and what a parent does; even the child's eventual capacity to respect the moral authority of the parent—all these effects are surely implicated even in this apparently simple situation. The content of a woman's exercise of moral judgment in such a circumstance—not unlike the kinds of circumstances that frequently confront many women—is surely relevant to discerning women's patterns of moral reasoning.

More important, it is not only in deciding about birth control or abortion—or about reproduction in general—that women contemplate making choices that might bring them into conflict with cultural conventions of femininity. Gilligan is particularly concerned with the abortion decision study for the way it focuses women's thinking about cultural conventions according to which a woman's goodness is revealed in self-sacrifice (Gilligan 1982, 70). But other cultural conventions embody a very different view of the moral status of women. Cultural conceptions of female sexuality as an ever-present temptation to male immorality or of women as intrinsically forces of irrationality and disorder—sorely by virtue of their biology—underlie many people's belief that women are to blame for the sexual or physical violence to which they are sometimes subject. Moreover, a woman who decides to press charges in a rape case will almost certainly come into conflict with these conventions; she may even need to fight her own unreflective acceptance of them. This phenomenon is made manifest when women who are victims of rape find it difficult to convince others—sometimes even themselves—that they are not responsible for the wrongdoing of the attacker. Surely the voice of a woman who finds the courage to confront this dangerous conception is as distinctively a woman's voice as are the voices of the women in Gilligan's abortion decision study.

In a different but equally important way, some cultural conventions seek to define women's identity *solely* in terms of their capacity for reproduction and, as a consequence, in terms of their historically typical roles as primary caretakers of children. At least some women will come into conflict with this convention merely in *deciding* to pursue work that takes them outside of the domestic realm. Ironically, those women who historically have worked outside the home for reasons of economic necessity are usually "exempted" from this convention—at least so long as they occupy certain kinds of jobs. But nearly all women who decide to seek advancement in careers typically dominated by males will most certainly come into conflict with this stereotype. Some employers even now will argue that women should not be promoted to certain jobs because when they "go off to have babies," they will lose interest in the demands of a competitive career. Indeed, some employers even claim to find empirical confirmation for their conviction in the work of theorists such as Gilligan who assert an empirical association between women and the ethics of care (Williams 1989, 813–821).[6] Surely the voice of a woman who decides to protest her employer's decision not to promote her on such a basis is as distinctively a woman's voice as any of the voices in Gilligan's abortion decision study.

One of the most puzzling facts about Gilligan's use of the abortion decision study is that although she interviewed a variety of women, and although some chose to have abortions and others chose not to, she insists that the study could not really be used to reveal "the way women in general think about the abortion choice" (Gilligan 1982, 72). No effort was made, she explains, to ensure in advance that the women interviewed for the study amounted to a representative sample of women considering abortion. In fact, Gilligan even suggests that the women interviewed may have been referred to the study because counselors suspected them to be "in greater than usual conflict" over the decision (Gilligan 1982, 72). But it is extraordinary that although her subjects' decisions could not be relied upon to reveal general truths about the way women decide about abortion, they could nonetheless be relied upon to provide data about the way most women *as a whole* think about *morality in general.*

A woman considering abortion is surely confronted with a serious moral decision. But so, too, is a woman who must find the moral courage to confront her attacker—and the cultural conventions that threaten to excuse him. So, too, is a mother who must consider what to say to her child about why she decides one way or another when she receives too much money in change at the grocery. One can defend Gilligan's assumptions about the importance of the abortion decision study only if one accepts that women's decisions about their reproductive capacities—about motherhood—are the central morally significant fact of their experience. But in accepting such a view one endorses—knowingly or not—a set of assumptions about women that would make the biology of sex definitive of their identity. It is a short step from this to the view that a woman's biology is her destiny. Does not Gilligan herself continue to bind women in dependence to cultural conventions of femininity by assuming that women's distinctive moral voices will be heard most clearly in their judgments about reproduction?

CONCLUSION

There is a special irony in the fact that a project intended to make women's ways of reasoning about morality audible and intelligible should neglect the plurality of women's voices. For one of Gilligan's primary aims, of course, was to point out the respects in which previous developmental psychologists had failed to notice the complexity of moral discourse. Lawrence Kohlberg argues that detailed cross-cultural studies on the development of moral thinking support the thesis that there is a single invariant sequence of moral development for human beings. He also argues that ideally the right kind of moral education could, "without indoctrination," move the student's judgment toward higher stages in this sequence—toward reasoning that relied on ever more "adequate" principles (Kohlberg 1981, 27). Gilligan insists that Kohlberg's assumptions lead to an unacceptable picture of women's moral capacities as developmentally inadequate relative to the capacities of the typical male. Her research is thus in part a plea for a more complex understanding of the moral domain.

Gilligan is surely right to start from the presupposition that Kohlberg's view fails to do justice to the complexity of moral discourse. Indeed, Kohlberg is far from convincing in his claim to be able to account for moral discourse by reference to a single, universal sequence of stages of moral development. His conviction that there is some one set of structures of thought that underlies our moral reasoning abilities, as well as his caricature of Aristotle's view of morality as "the bag of virtues" view, both suggest a reluctance to acknowledge that moral reasoning might be an extraordinarily complex phenomenon. Kohlberg's resistance to Aristotle is of particular importance, since Aristotle defends a view on which what the ethical life requires of us cannot be codified or reduced to a single principle or set of principles. One need not accept Aristotle's theory of the virtues to understand the force of this view of the complexity of the moral domain. Moreover, Gilligan makes a strong case for the moral importance of considerations of care. As Lawrence Blum has suggested, in much of our daily lives, we find ourselves in circumstances where considerations of impartiality and justice seem simply irrelevant (Blum 1988, 479–480). Still further, in families and in friendships, for instance, concern for the integrity of persons *merely* as persons seems morally insufficient.

But Gilligan's tendency to assume that we could capture the complexity of moral discourse simply by arguing that there is an additional, primarily female voice—one that speaks the contextual language of care rather than the (alternative) abstract language of rights—does not avoid some of the misconceptions that cast doubt on the adequacy of Kohlberg's view. Even independent of the problems attending claims about gender-specific differences in moral reasoning, it is surprising that Gilligan would reproduce—in a different context—Kohlberg's unwillingness to allow for the diversity of moral discourse. To be fair, in some recent work Gilligan suggests (in passing) that there are "at least two" moral perspectives—apparently intending to posit more complexity in moral reasoning than her empirical research has led her to talk about (Gilligan 1987, 20 and 26). Yet at the same time, her own recent studies, as well as studies carried out by her collaborators, reveal an increased confidence that moral thinking is strictly "bimodal": that (1) moral reasoning is carried out in terms of justice or care or some mixture of the two, and that (2) the care perspective is the dominant perspective in women's moral reasoning.[7]

Yet there is a very good case for thinking that both women and men structure the moral domain in a variety of ways. There is also reason to believe that in the actual practice of moral reasoning, individual women and men—sometimes confronted with choices between seemingly incommensurable goods—would reject the notion that moral problems can all be reduced to some one or two measures of significance. A number of contemporary philosophical voices are attempting to convince us that the empirical practice of moral reasoning may here be considerably wiser than some in philosophy have thought (Taylor 1982; MacIntyre 1981). In varied contexts, Kohlberg and Gilligan have called attention to Piaget's notion that the child "is a philosopher" (Kohlberg 1981, 16; Kohlberg and Gilligan 1971). Women—in the empirical practice of moral reasoning as well as in the quiet of the study—can surely be philosophers, too. But we can understand what they are saying only if we let them speak in their distinctive moral voices.

NOTES

1. This presupposition is not an isolated instance in Gilligan's writings. Other commentators have noted in some of her essays a tendency to assert the moral superiority of the moral perspective she associates primarily with women (Flanagan and Adler 1983, 587).
2. Nel Noddings has taken an even more forceful stand on the biblical story of Abraham—especially on Kierkegaard's interpretation of that story; "For the mother . . . this is horrendous. . . . We love not because we are required to love but because our natural relatedness gives natural birth to love. It is this love, this natural caring, that makes the ethical possible. For us then, Abraham's decision is not only ethically unjustified but it is in basest violation of the supra-ethical—of caring" (1984, 43).
3. Genevieve Lloyd (1983, 1984) has asked whether the very idea of a distinctively feminine moral character is perhaps a *product* of the very intellectual traditions to which it purports to be a critical response. Moreover, Joan Williams (1989) attempts to show that it may be impossible to purge the vision of women's moral perspective defended by Gilligan, and others, of the socially and culturally limiting (and typically discriminatory) notions historically associated with it. My aim, of course, is to show why Williams may well be correct.
4. Gilligan is not entirely consistent on this point. Sometimes she suggests that she does not believe that all moral considerations could be reduced to the language of care. Sometimes she suggests

otherwise. Her use of the duck-rabbit image from the Gestalt psychology of perception (Gilligan 1987) does little to clear up this confusion. Even defenses of Gilligan on this point do little to clear up this confusion (see, for instance, Blum 1988, 474–476).

5. What Gilligan cites as an advantage of her study (1982, 2) may thus be something of a liability.
6. Joan Williams cites testimony in a Title VII class action lawsuit in which empirical research—like that done by Gilligan—is cited in support of a claim that men and women do not have "equal interests and aspirations regarding work" (Williams 1989, 813–820).
7. This is particularly true of the research in *Mapping the Moral Domain* (Gilligan, Ward, and Taylor 1988).

REFERENCES

Blum, Lawrence. "Gilligan and Kohlberg: Implications for Moral Theory." *Ethics* 98 (April 1988): 472–491.

Flanagan, Owen, and Jonathan Adler. "Impartiality and Particularity." *Social Research* 50 (Autumn 1983): 576–596.

Flanagan, Owen, and Kathryn Jackson. "Justice, Care, and Gender: The Kohlberg-Gilligan Debate Revisited." *Ethics* 97 (April 1987): 622–639.

Gilligan, Carol. *In a Different Voice: Psychological Theory and Women's Development.* Cambridge, Mass.: Harvard University Press, 1982.

______. "Moral Orientation and Moral Development." In *Women and Moral Theory*, edited by Eva Feder Kittay and Diana T. Meyers, 19–33. Totowa, N.J.: Rowman and Littlefield, 1987.

Gilligan, Carol, Janie Victoria Ward, and Jill McLean Taylor, with Betty Bardige. *Mapping the Moral Domain.* Cambridge, Mass.: Harvard University Graduate School of Education, 1988.

Gilligan, Carol, and Grant Wiggins. "The Origins of Morality in Early Childhood Relationships." In *The Emergence of Morality in Young Children*, edited by Jerome Kagan and Sharon Lamb, 277–305. Chicago: University of Chicago Press, 1987.

Kant, Immanuel. *Groundwork of the Metaphysics of Morals*, translated by H.J. Paton. New York: Harper and Row, 1964; first edition, 1785.

King, Martin Luther, Jr. "Letter from Birmingham Jail." In King, *Why We Can't Wait*, 76–95. New York: New American Library, 1964.

Kohlberg, Lawrence. "Indoctrination versus Relativity in Moral Education." In Kohlberg, *The Philosophy of Moral Development*, vol. 1, 6–28. San Francisco: Harper and Row, 1981.

Kohlberg, Lawrence, and Carol Gilligan. "The Adolescent as a Philosopher." *Daedalus* 100 (1971): 1051–1086.

Lloyd, Genevieve. *The Man of Reason.* London: Methuen, 1984.

______. "Reason, Gender, and Morality in the History of Philosophy." *Social Research* 50 (Autumn 1983): 490–513.

MacIntyre, Alasdair. *After Virtue.* Notre Dame, Ind.: University of Notre Dame Press, 1981.

Nails, Debra. "Social Scientific Sexism: Gilligan's Mismeasure of Man." *Social Research* 50 (Autumn 1983): 643–666.

Noddings, Nel. *Caring: A Feminine Approach to Ethics and Moral Education.* Berkeley: University of California Press, 1984.

Taylor, Charles. "The Diversity of Goods." In *Utilitarianism and Beyond*, edited by Amartya Sen and Bernard Williams, 129–144. Cambridge: Cambridge University Press, 1982.

Williams, Joan C. "Deconstructing Gender." *Michigan Law Review* 87 (February 1989): 797–844.

Part 7:
Women, Equality, and Justice

The Equality Crisis: Some Reflections on Culture, Courts, and Feminism

Under current interpretations of the U.S. Constitution and civil rights law, women's equality is protected in two respects. Statutory classification by sex is prohibited unless it bears a "substantial" relationship to an "important" government purpose. Moreover, discrimination against women in education and employment is prohibited. Still, questions remain about how feminists should interpret the goal of equality and how the courts should implement these prohibitions. Williams endorses a gender-neutral or androgynous conception of equality.

After reviewing the history of legal interpretation of women's status, Williams distinguishes two types of contemporary legal case. On the one hand, there are cases that concern compensating women for past injustices. On the other hand, there are "hard cases"—cases that raise fundamental questions about gender roles and that challenge us to imagine a gender-free society. Williams's discussion focuses on hard cases that address three issues—women in combat, teenage sexuality, and childbearing and employment. In each case, Williams defends gender-neutral egalitarianism. According to Williams, women should be subject to a military draft whenever men are. If women are exempt from defending their country (or conscientiously refusing to do so), gender stereotypes of aggressive males and nurturant females are perpetuated, and women's equality is undermined. Similarly, if teenage men can be charged with the crime of statutory rape, but teenage women are immune from prosecution, stereotypes of women as passive and men as predatory are reinforced, and women's agency and responsibility are denied. Finally, Williams endorses including pregnancy in the category of disabilities and refusing to grant any benefits to pregnant women that are not available to people with other disabilities. In order to ensure that neither the state nor employers will be free to impose liabilities on women as a class, Williams holds that feminists must not seek special benefits for women as a class.

—D.T.M.

Chapter 36

Wendy W. Williams

The Equality Crisis: Some Reflections on Culture, Courts, and Feminism

INTRODUCTION

To say that courts are not and never have been the source of radical social change is an understatement. They reflect, by and large, mainstream views, mostly after those views are well established, although very occasionally (as in *Brown v. Board of Education*, the great school desegregation case) the Court moves temporarily out ahead of public opinion. What women can get from the courts—what we have gotten in the past decade—is a qualified guarantee of equal treatment. We can now expect, for the most part, that courts will rule that the privileges the law explicitly bestows on men must also be made available to women.

Because courts, as institutions of circumscribed authority, can only review in limited and specific ways the laws enacted by elected representatives, their role in promoting gender equality is pretty much confined to telling legislators what they cannot do, or extending the benefit of what they have done, to women. In an important sense, then, courts will do no more than measure women's claim to equality against legal benefits and burdens that are an expression of white, male, middle-class interests and values.[1] This means, to rephrase the point, that women's equality as delivered by the courts can only be an integration into a preexisting, predominantly male world. To the extent that women share those predominant values or aspire to share that world on its own terms, resort to the courts has, since the early 1970s, been the most efficient, accessible, and reliable mode of redress. But to the extent that the law of the public world must be reconstructed to reflect the needs and values of both sexes, change must be sought from legislatures rather than the courts. And women, whose separate experience has not been adequately registered in the political process, are the ones who must seek the change.

Nonetheless, I am going to talk about courts because what they do—what the Supreme Court does—is extremely important, for a number of reasons. (1) The way courts define equality, within the limits of their sphere, does indeed matter in the real world. (2) Legal cases have been and continue to be a focal point of debate about the meaning of equality; our participation in that debate and reflection upon it has enabled us to begin to form coherent overall theories of gender and equality that inform our judgments about what we should seek from legislatures as well as courts. (3) The cases themselves, the participation they attract, and the debate they engender, tell us important things about societal norms, cultural tensions, indeed, cultural limits concerning gender and sexual roles.

My thesis is that we (feminists) are at a crisis point in our evaluation of equality and women and that perhaps one of the reasons for this crisis is that, having dealt with the easy cases, we (feminists and courts) are now trying to cope with issues that touch the hidden nerves of our most profoundly embedded cultural values. . . .

I. A BRIEF HISTORY OF GENDER EQUALITY AND THE SUPREME COURT

Just before the American Revolution, Blackstone, in the course of his comprehensive commentary on the common law, set forth the fiction that informed and guided the treatment of married women in the English law courts. When a woman married, her legal identity merged into that of her husband; she was civilly dead.[2] She couldn't sue, be sued,[3] enter into contracts,[4] make wills,[5] keep her own earnings,[6] control her own property.[7] She could not even protect her own physical integrity—her husband had the right to chastise her (although only with a switch no bigger than his thumb),[8] restrain her freedom,[9] and impose sexual intercourse upon her against her will.[10]

Beginning in the middle of the nineteenth century, the most severe civil disabilities were removed in this country by state married women's property acts.[11] Blackstone's unities fiction was for the most part replaced by a theory that recognized women's legal personhood but which assigned her a place before the law different and distinct from that of her husband. This was the theory of the separate spheres of men and women, under which the husband was the couple's representative in the public world and its breadwinner; the wife was the center of the private world of the family.[12] Because it endowed women with a place, role, and importance of their own, the doctrine of the separate spheres was an advance over the spousal unities doctrine. At the same time, however, it preserved and promoted the dominance of male over female.[13] The public world of men was governed by law, while the private world of women was outside the law, and man was free to exercise his prerogatives as he chose.

Perhaps the best-known expression of the separate spheres ideology is Justice Bradley's concurring opinion in an 1873 Supreme Court case, *Bradwell v. Illinois*, which begins with the observation that "civil law, as well as nature herself, has always recognized a wide difference in the respective spheres and destinies of man and woman"[14] and concludes, in ringing tones, that the "paramount destiny and mission of woman are to fulfill the noble and benign offices of wife and mother."[15] The separate spheres ideology was used in *Bradwell* to uphold the exclusion of women from legal practice. Thirty-five years later, in *Muller v. Oregon*,[16] it became the basis for upholding legislation governing the hours women were permitted to work in the paid labor force. Women's special maternal role, said the Court, justified special protections in the work place.[17] As late as 1961, in a challenge by a criminal defendant, the Court upheld a statute creating an automatic exemption from jury duty for all women who failed to volunteer their names for the jury pool, saying, "Woman is still regarded as the center of home and family life. We cannot say that it is constitutionally impermissible for a State . . . to conclude that a woman should be relieved from the civil duty of jury service unless she herself determines that such service is consistent with her own special responsibilities."[18]

The separate spheres ideology was repudiated by the Supreme Court only in the last twelve years. The engine of destruction was, as a technical matter, the more rigorous standard of review that the Court began applying to sex discrimination cases beginning in 1971.[19] By 1976 the Court was requiring that sex-based classifications bear a "substantial" relationship to an "important" governmental purpose.[20] This standard, announced in *Craig v. Boren*, was not as strong as that used in race cases,[21] but it was certainly a far cry from the rational basis standard that had traditionally been applied to sex-based classifications.

As a practical matter, what the Court did was strike down sex-based classifications that were premised on the old breadwinner-homemaker, master-dependent dichotomy inherent in the separate spheres ideology. Thus, the Supreme Court insisted that women wage earners receive the same benefits for their families under military,[22] social security,[23] welfare,[24] and workers compensation[25] programs as did male wage earners; that men receive the same child care allowance when their spouses died as women did;[26] that the female children of divorce be entitled to support for the same length of time as male children, so that they too could get the education necessary for life in the public world;[27] that the duty of support through alimony not be visited exclusively on husbands;[28] that wives as well as husbands participate in the management of the community property;[29] and that wives as well as husbands be eligible to administer their deceased relatives' estates.[30]

All this happened in the little more than a decade that has elapsed since 1971. The achievement is not an insubstantial one. Yet it also seems to me that in part what the Supreme Court did was simply to recognize that the real world outside the courtroom had already changed. [Women] were in fact no longer chiefly housewife-dependents. The family wage no longer existed; for a vast number of two-parent families, two wage earners were an economic necessity. In addition, many families were headed by a single parent. It behooved the Court to account for this new reality and it did so by recognizing that the breadwinner-homemaker dichotomy was an outmoded stereotype.

II. MEN'S CULTURE: AGGRESSOR IN WAR AND SEX

Of course, not all of the Supreme Court cases involved the breadwinner-homemaker stereotype. The other cases can be grouped in several ways; for my purposes I will place them in two groups. One group is composed of the remedial or compensatory discrimination cases—the cases in which a statute treats women differently and better than men for the purpose of redressing past unequal treatment.[31] The other group, the focus of this paper, consists of the cases that don't really seem to fit into any neat category but share a common quality. Unlike the cases discussed above, they do not deal with laws that rest on an economic model of the family that no longer predominates; rather, they concern themselves with other, perhaps more basic, sex-role arrangements. They are what I would call, simply, the "hard" cases, and for the most part, they are cases in which a sex-based classification was upheld by the Court.[32] There are a number of ways one could characterize and analyze them. I want to view them from one of those possible perspectives, namely, what they tell us about the state of our culture with respect to the equality of men and women. What do they say about the cultural limits of the equality principle?

In the 1980–81 term, the Supreme Court decided three sex-discrimination cases. One was *Kirshberg v. Feenstra*,[33] a case which struck down the Louisiana statute that gave husbands total control over the couple's property. That, to my mind, was an easy case. It falls within the line of cases I have already described which dismantle the old separate spheres ideology. The other two cases were *Rostker v. Goldberg*,[34] the case which upheld the male-only draft registration law, and *Michael M. v. Superior Court*,[35] the case upholding the California statutory rape law. They are prime candidates for my hard-cases category.

Justice Rehnquist wrote the opinion of the Court in both *Rostker* and *Michael M.* In *Rostker*, the draft registration case, his reasoning was a simple syllogism. The purpose of the registration, he said, is to identify the draft pool.[36] The purpose of the draft is to provide combat troops.[37] Women are excluded from combat.[38] Thus, men and women are not similarly situated with respect to the draft,[39] and it is therefore constitutional to register males only.[40] Of course, the problem with his syllogism was that one of the premises—that the purpose of the draft is exclusively to raise combat troops—was and is demonstrably false,[41] but the manipulation of the facts of that case is not what I mean to focus on here.

In *Michael M.*, a 17fi-year-old man and a 16fi-year-old woman had sexual intercourse. The 17fi-year-old man was prosecuted under California's statutory rape law, which made such intercourse criminal for the man but not the woman.[42] Rehnquist, for a plurality of the Court, accepted the utterly dubious proposition put forward by the State of California that the purpose of the statutory rape statute was to prevent teenage pregnancies. The difference in treatment under the statute is justified, he said, because men and women are not similarly situated with respect to this purpose.[43] Because the young woman is exposed to the risk of pregnancy, she is deterred from sexual intercourse by that risk. The young man, lacking such a natural deterrent, needs a legal deterrent, which the criminal statute provides.[44]

I think that perhaps the outcomes of these two cases—in which the sex-based statutes were upheld—were foregone conclusions and that the only question, before they were decided, was *how* the Court would rationalize the outcome. This is perhaps more obvious in the draft case than the statutory rape case, but applies, I think, to both. Let me explain.

Suppose you could step outside our culture, rise above its minutiae, and look at its great contours. Having done so, speculate for a moment about where society might draw the line and refuse to proceed further with gender equality. What does our culture identify as quintessentially masculine? Where is the locus of traditional masculine pride and self-identity? What can we identify in men's cultural experience that most divides it from women's cultural experience? Surely, one rather indisputable answer to that question is "war": physical combat and its modern equivalents. (One could also answer that preoccupation with contact sports is such a difference, but that is, perhaps, just a subset of physical combat.)

Not surprisingly, the Court in *Rostker* didn't come right out and say, "We've reached our cultural limits." Yet I [find] it significant that even the Justices who dissented on the constitutionality of the draft registration all seemed to concede the constitutionality of excluding women from combat.[45] When Congress considered whether women should be drafted, it was much more forthright about its reasons, and those reasons support my thesis. The Senate Armed Services Committee Report states:

> The starting point for any discussion of the appropriateness of registering women for the draft is the question of the proper role of women in combat. The principle that women should not intentionally and routinely engage in combat is *fundamental, and enjoys wide support among our people.*[46]

In addition, the committee expressed three specific reasons for excluding women from combat. First, registering women for assignment to combat "would leave the actual performance of sexually mixed units as an experiment to be conducted in war with unknown risk—a risk that the committee finds militarily unwarranted and dangerous."[47] Second, any attempt to assign women to combat could "affect the national resolve at the time of mobilization."[48] Third, drafting women would "place unprecedented strains on family life."[49] The committee envisioned a young mother being drafted leaving a young father home to care for the family and concluded, "The committee is strongly of the view that such a result . . . is unwise and unacceptable to a large majority of our people."[50] To translate, Congress was worried that (1) sexually mixed units would not be able to function—perhaps because of sex in the foxhole? (2) if women were assigned to combat, the nation might be reluctant to go to war, presumably because the specter of women fighting would deter a protective and chivalrous populace; and (3) the idea that Mom could go into battle and Dad keep the home fires burning is simply beyond the cultural pale. In short, current notions of acceptable limits on sex-role behavior would be surpassed by putting women into combat.

But what about statutory rape? Not such a clear case, you say. I disagree. Buried perhaps a bit deeper in our collective psyches but no less powerful and perhaps even more fundamental than our definition of man as aggressor in war is man as aggressor in sex. The original statutory rape laws were quite explicitly based on this view. Then, as is true even today, men were considered the natural and proper initiators of sex. In the face of male sexual initiative, women could do one of two things, yield or veto, "consent" or decline. What normal women did not, *should* not, do was to initiate sexual contact, to be the sexual aggressor. The premise underlying statutory rape laws was that young women's chastity was precious and their naivete enormous. Their inability knowingly to consent to sexual intercourse meant that they required protection by laws which made their consent irrelevant but punished and deterred the "aggressive" male.

The Court's opinion, I believe, is implicitly based on stereotypes concerning male sexual aggression and female sexual passivity, despite Justice Rehnquist's express denial of that possibility.[51] His recitation of the facts of the case sets the stage for the sexual gender-role pigeon-holing that follows: "After being struck in the face for rebuffing petitioner's advances, Sharon," we are told, "*submitted* to sexual intercourse with petitioner."[52] Although, in theory, coercion and consent are relevant only to the crime of rape, not to statutory rape, we are thus provided with the details of this particular statutory rape case, details that cast Michael and Sharon as prototypes of the sexually aggressive male and the passive female.

But it is Rehnquist's description of the lower court opinion that most clearly reveals sex role assumptions that led first to California high court and then the United States Supreme Court to uphold the legislation. He says, "Because *males alone* can 'physiologically cause the result which the law properly seeks to avoid [pregnancy], the California Supreme Court further held that the gender classification was readily justified as a means of identifying *offender* and *victim.*"[53] The statement is remarkable for two (related) reasons. The first and most dramatic is the strangeness of the biological concept upon which it is based. Do the justices still believe that each sperm carries a homunculus—a tiny person—who need only be planted in the woman in order to grow? Are they ignorant of ova? Or has sex-role ideology simply outweighed scientific fact? Since no one has believed in homunculi for at least a century, it must be the latter. Driven by the stereotype of male as aggressor/offender and woman as passive victim, even the facts of conception are transformed to fit the image.

The second is the characterization of man and woman as "offender" and "victim." Statutory rape is, in criminal law terms, a clear instance of a victimless crime, since all parties are, by definition, voluntary participants. In what sense, then, can Rehnquist assert that the woman is victim and the man offender? One begins to get an inkling when, later, the Justice explains that the statutory rape law is "protective" legislation: "The statute here protects women from sexual intercourse at an age when those consequences are particularly severe."[54] His preconceptions become manifest when, finally, Rehnquist on one occasion calls the statute a "rape" statute[55]—by omitting the word "statutory" inadvertently exposing his hidden assumptions and underlining the belief structure which the very title of the crime, "statutory rape," lays bare.

What is even more interesting to me than the Court's resolution of these cases is the problem they cause for feminist analysis. The notion that men are frequently the sexual aggressors and that the law ought to be able to take that reality into account in very concrete ways is hardly one that feminists could reject out of hand (I'm thinking here of sexual harassment and forcible rape, among other things); it is therefore an area, like the others I'm about to discuss, in which we need to pay special attention to our impulses lest we inadvertently support and give credence to the very social constructs and behaviors we so earnestly mean to oppose. Should we, for example, defend traditional rape laws on the ground that rape, defined by law as penetration by the penis of the vagina, is a sexual offense the psychological and social consequences of which are so unique, severe, and rooted in age-old power relationships between the sexes that a gender-neutral law would fail in important ways to deal with the world as it really is? Or should we insist that equality theory requires that we reorganize our understanding of sexual crime, that unwanted sexual intrusion of types other than male-female sexual intercourse can similarly violate and humiliate the victim, and that legislation that defines sexual offenses in gender-neutral terms, because it resists our segregationist urges and affirms our common humanity, is therefore what feminists should support? These are not easy questions, but they must be answered if feminist lawyers are to press a coherent theory of equality upon the courts in these hard cases.

As for *Rostker v. Goldberg*, the conflicts among feminists were overtly expressed. Some of us felt it essential that we support the notion that a single-sex draft was unconstitutional; others felt that feminists should not take such a position. These latter groups explicitly contrasted the female ethic of nurturance and life-giving with a male ethic of aggression and militarism and asserted that if we argued to the Court that single-sex registration is unconstitutional we would be betraying ourselves and supporting what we find least acceptable about the male world.

To me, this latter argument quite overtly taps qualities that the culture has ascribed to woman-as-childrearer and converts them to a normative value statement, one with which it is easy for us to sympathize. This is one of the circumstances in which the feeling that "I want what he's got but I don't want to be what he's had to be in order to get it" comes quickly to the surface. But I also believe that the reflexive response based on these deeper cultural senses leads us to untenable positions.

The single-sex laws upheld in *Michael M.* and *Rostker* ultimately do damage to women. For one thing, they absolve women of personal responsibility in the name of protection. There is a sense in which women have been victims of physical aggression in part because they have not been permitted to act as anything but victims.[56] For another, do we not acquire a greater right to claim our share from society if we too share its ultimate jeopardies? To me, *Rostker* never posed the question of whether women should be forced as men now are to fight wars, but whether we, like them, must take the responsibility for deciding whether or not to fight, whether or not to bear the cost of risking our lives, on the one hand, or resisting in the name of peace, on the other. And do we not, by insisting upon our differences at these crucial junctures, promote and reinforce the us-them dichotomy that permits the Rehnquists and the Stewarts to resolve matters of great importance and complexity by the simplistic, reflexive assertion that men and women "are simply not similarly situated?"

III. WOMEN'S CULTURE: MOTHER OF HUMANITY

We have looked briefly at the male side of the cultural equation. What are the cultural limits on women's side? Step outside the culture again and speculate. If we find limits and conflicts surrounding the male role as aggressor in war and sex, what will be the trouble spots at the opposite pole? What does the culture identify as quintessentially female? Where do our pride and self-identity lie? Most probably, I think, somewhere in the realm of behaviors and concerns surrounding maternity.

I would expect the following areas to be the places where the move toward equality of the sexes might come into collision with cultural limits, both in judicial opinions and in ourselves: treatment of maternity in the work place, the tender years presumption, and joint custody of children upon divorce. The issues surrounding pregnancy and maternity are the most difficult from a theoretical point of view and for that reason may be the best illustration of the conflict I am trying to explore.

Let me start again with a Supreme Court case. As discussed earlier, before 1971, the ideology of the separate spheres informed Supreme Court opinions; it allowed the courts to view men and women as basically on different life tracks and therefore never really similarly situated. That fundamentally dichotomous view which characterized man as breadwinner, woman as homemaker-childrearer, foreclosed the possibility that the courts could successfully apply an equality model to the sexes.

Once the Supreme Court took on the task of dismantling the statutory structure built upon the separate spheres ideology, it had to face the question of how to treat pregnancy itself. Pregnancy was, after all, the centerpiece, the linchpin, the essential feature of women's separate sphere.[57] The stereotypes, the generalizations, the role expectations were at their zenith when a woman became pregnant. Gender equality would not be possible, one would think, unless the Court was willing to examine, at least as closely as other gender-related rulemaking, those prescriptions concerning pregnancy itself. On the other hand, the capacity to bear a child is a crucial, indeed definitional, difference between women and men. While it is obvious that the sexes can be treated equally with respect to characteristics that they share, how would it be possible to apply the equality principle to a characteristic unique to women?

So what did the Court do? It drew the line at pregnancy. Of *course* it would take a more critical look at sex discrimination than it had in the past—but, it said, discrimination on the basis of pregnancy is not sex discrimination.[58] Now here was a simple but decisive strategy for avoiding the doctrinal discomfort that inclusion of pregnancy within the magic circle of stricter review would bring with it. By placing pregnancy altogether outside that class of phenomena labeled sex discrimination, the Court need not apply to classifications related to pregnancy the level of scrutiny it had already reserved, in cases such as *Reed v. Reed* and *Frontiero v. Richardson*, for gender classifications.[59] Pregnancy classifications would henceforth be subject only to the most casual review.

The position was revealed for the first time in 1974 in *Geduldig v. Aiello*,[60] a case challenging the equal protection clause exclusion of pregnancy-related disabilities from coverage by an otherwise comprehensive state disability insurance program. The Court explained, in a footnote, that pregnancy classifications were not sex-based but were, instead, classifications based upon a physical condition and should be treated accordingly:

> The California insurance program does not exclude anyone from benefit eligibility because of gender *but merely removes one physical condition*—pregnancy—*from the list of compensable disabilities.* While it is true that only women can become pregnant, it does not follow that every legislative classification concerning pregnancy is a sex-based classification. . . . Normal pregnancy is an objectively identifiable physical condition with unique characteristics. . . . [L]awmakers are constitutionally free to include or exclude pregnancy from the coverage of legislation such as this on any reasonable basis, *just as with respect to any other physical condition.*[61]

The second time the Supreme Court said pregnancy discrimination is not sex discrimination was in *General Electric Company v. Gilbert*,[62] decided in 1976. *Gilbert* presented the same basic facts—exclusion of pregnancy-related disabilities from a comprehensive disability program—but this case was brought under Title VII rather than the equal protection clause. The Court nonetheless relied on *Geduldig*, saying that when Congress prohibited "sex discrimination," it didn't mean to include within the definition of that term pregnancy discrimination.[63]

There was, however, an additional theory available in *Gilbert* because it was a Title VII case that was not available in the equal protection case. That theory was that if an employer's rule has a disparate effect on women, even though there is no intent to discriminate, it might also violate Title VII. And did the Court find that the exclusion of pregnancy-related disabilities had a disparate effect on women? It did not.[64] Men and women, said Justice Rehnquist, received coverage for the disabilities they had in common. Pregnancy was an *extra* disability, since only women suffered it. To compensate women for it would give them more than men got. So here there was no disparate effect—the exclusion of pregnancy merely insured the basic equality of the program.[65]

The remarkable thing about this statement, like Rehnquist's later assertion in *Michael M.* that only men can "cause" pregnancy, is its peculiarly blinkered male vision. After all, men received coverage under General Electric's disability program for disabilities they did not have in common with women, including disabilities linked to exclusively male aspects of the human anatomy.[66] Thus, the only sense in which one can understand pregnancy to be "extra" is in some reverse-Freudian psychological fashion. Under Freud's interpretation, women were viewed by both sexes as inadequate men (men *minus*) because they lacked penises.[67] In Rehnquist's view, woman is now man plus, because she shares all his physical characteristics except that she also gets pregnant. Under either of these extravagantly skewed views of the sexes, however, man is the measure against which the anatomical features of woman are counted and assigned value, and when the addition or subtraction is complete, woman comes out behind.

The corollary to *Gilbert* appeared in *Nashville Gas Co. v. Satty*,[68] decided in 1977. There the Court finally found a pregnancy rule that violated Title VII. The rule's chief characteristic was its gratuitously punitive effect. It provided that a woman returning from maternity leave lost all of the seniority she acquired *prior* to her leave.[69] Here, said Rehnquist, we have a case where women are not seeking extra benefits for pregnancy. Here's a case where a woman, now back at work and no longer pregnant, has actually had something taken away from her—her pre-pregnancy seniority—and she therefore suffers a burden that men don't have to bear.[70] This rule therefore has a disproportionate impact on women.

Roughly translated, *Gilbert* and *Satty* read together seemed to stand for the proposition that insofar as a rule deprives a woman of benefits for actual pregnancy, that rule is lawful under Title VII. If, on the other hand, it denies her benefits she had earned while not pregnant (and hence like a man) and now seeks to use upon return to her nonpregnant (male-like) status, it has a disproportionate effect on women and is not lawful.

In summary, then, the Court seems to be of the view that discrimination on the basis of pregnancy isn't sex discrimination. The Court achieves this by, on the one hand, disregarding the "ineluctable link" between gender and pregnancy, treating pregnancy as just another physical condition that the employer or state can manipulate on any arguably rational basis, and on the other hand, using woman's special place in "the scheme of human existence"[71] as a basis for treating her claim to benefits available to other disabled workers as a claim not to equal benefits but to special treatment. The equality principle, according to the Court, cannot be bent to such ends.

In reaction to *Gilbert* and, to a lesser extent, to *Satty*, Congress amended the definitions section of Title VII to provide that discrimination on the basis of pregnancy, childbirth, and related medical conditions was, for purposes of the Act, sex discrimination. The amendment, called the Pregnancy Discrimination Act (PDA),[72] required a rather radical change in approach to the pregnancy issue from that adopted by the Court. In effect, Title VII creates a general presumption that men and women are alike in all relevant respects and casts the burden on the employer to show otherwise in any particular case.[73] The PDA, likewise, rejects the presumption that pregnancy is so unique that special rules concerning it are to be treated as prima facie reasonable. It substitutes the contrary presumption that pregnancy, at least in the work-place context, is like other physical conditions which may affect workers. As with gender classifications in general, it places the burden of establishing pregnancy's uniqueness in any given instance on the employer. The amendment itself specifies how this is to be done:

> Women affected by pregnancy, childbirth, or related medical conditions shall be treated the same for all employment-related purposes, including receipt of benefits under fringe benefits programs, as other persons not so affected but similar in their ability or inability to work.[74]

Under the PDA, employers cannot treat pregnancy less favorably than other potentially disabling conditions, but neither can they treat it more favorably. And therein lies the crisis.

At the time the PDA was passed, all feminist groups supported it. Special treatment of pregnancy in the work place had always been synonymous with unfavorable treatment; the rules generally had the effect of forcing women out of the work force and back into the home when they became pregnant. By treating pregnancy discrimination as sex discrimination, the PDA required that pregnant women be treated as well as other wage earners who became disabled. The degree to which this assisted women depended on the generosity of their particular employers' sick leave or disability policy, but anything at all was better than what most pregnant women had had before.

The conflict within the feminist community arose because some states had passed legislation that, instead of placing pregnant women at a disadvantage, gave them certain positive protections. Montana, for example, passed a law forbidding employers to fire women who became pregnant and requiring them to give such women reasonable maternity leave.[75] The Miller-Wohl Company, an employer in that state, had a particularly ungenerous sick leave policy. Employees were entitled to *no* sick leave in their first year of employment and five days per year thereafter.[76] On August 1, 1979, the company hired a pregnant woman who missed four or five days over the course of the following three weeks because of morning sickness. The company fired her. She asserted her rights under the Montana statute. The company sought declaratory relief in federal court, claiming that Montana's special treatment statute was contrary to the equality principle mandated by the PDA and was therefore invalid under the supremacy clause of the constitution.[77]

Feminists split over the validity of the Montana statute. Some of us felt that the statute was, indeed, incompatible with the philosophy of the PDA.[78] Others of us argued that the PDA was passed to *help* pregnant women, which was also the objective of the Montana statute.[79] Underneath are very different views of what women's equality means; the dispute is therefore one of great significance for feminists.

The Montana statute *was* meant to help pregnant women. It was passed with the best of intentions. The philosophy underlying it is that pregnancy is central to a woman's family role and that the law should take special account of pregnancy to protect that role for the working wife. And those who supported the statute can assert with great plausibility that pregnancy is a problem that men don't have, an extra source of work-place disability, and that women workers cannot adequately be protected if pregnancy is not taken into account in special ways. They might also add that procreation plays a special role in human life, is viewed as a fundamental right by our society, and therefore is appropriately singled out on social policy grounds. The instinct to treat pregnancy as a special case is deeply imbedded in our culture, indeed in every culture. It seems natural, and *right*, to treat it that way.

Yet, at a deeper level, the Supreme Court in cases like *Gilbert*, and the feminists who seek special recognition for pregnancy, are starting from the same basic assumption, namely, that women have a special place in the scheme of human existence when it comes to maternity. Of course, one's view of how that basic assumption cuts is shaped by one's perspective. What businessmen, Supreme Court Justices, and feminists make of it is predictably quite different. But the same doctrinal approach that permits pregnancy to be treated *worse* than other disabilities is the same one that will allow the state constitutional freedom to create special *benefits* for pregnant women. The equality approach to pregnancy (such as that embodied in the PDA) necessarily creates not only the desired floor under the pregnant woman's rights but also the ceiling which the *Miller-Wohl* case threw into relief. If we can't have it both ways, we need to think carefully about which way we want to have it.

My own feeling is that, for all its problems, the equality approach is the better one. The special treatment model has great costs. First, as discussed above, is the reality that conceptualizing pregnancy as a special case permits unfavorable as well as favorable treatment of pregnancy. Our history provides too many illustrations of the former to allow us to be sanguine about the wisdom of urging special treatment.

Second, treating pregnancy as a special case divides us in ways that I believe are destructive in a particular political sense as well as a more general sense. On what basis can we fairly assert, for example, that the pregnant woman fired by Miller-Wohl deserved to keep her job when any other worker who got sick for any other reason did not? Creating special privileges of the Montana type has, as one consequence, the effect of shifting attention away from the employer's inadequate sick leave policy or the state's failure to provide important protections to all workers and focusing it upon the unfairness of protecting one class of worker and not others.

Third, as our experience with single-sex protective legislation earlier in this century demonstrated, what appear to be special "protections" for women often turn out to be, at best, a double-edged sword. It seems likely, for example, that the employer who wants to avoid the inconveniences and costs of special protective measures will find reasons not to hire women of childbearing age in the first place.[80]

Fourth, to the extent the state (or employers as proxies for the state) can lay claim to an interest in women's special procreational capacity for "the future well-being of the race," as *Muller v. Oregon* put it in 1908,[81] our freedom of choice about the direction of our lives is more limited than that of men in significant ways. This danger is hardly a theoretical one today. The Supreme Court has [shown a willingness] to permit restrictions on abortion in deference to the state's interest in the "potential life" of the fetus,[82] and private employers are adopting policies of exclusion of women of childbearing capacity in order to protect fetuses from exposure to possibly hazardous substances in the workplace.[83]

More fundamentally, though, this issue, like the others I discussed earlier, has everything to do with how, in the long run, we want to define women's and men's places and roles in society.

Implicit in the PDA approach to maternity issues is a stance toward parenthood and work that is decidedly different from that embodied in the special treatment approach to pregnancy. For many years, the prototype of the enlightened employer maternity policy was one which provided for a mandatory unpaid leave of absence for the woman employee commencing four or five months before and extending for as long as six months after childbirth.[84] Such maternity leaves were firmly premised on that aspect of the separate spheres ideology which assigned motherhood as woman's special duty and prerogative; employers believed that women should be treated as severed from the labor force from the time their pregnancies became apparent until their children emerged from infancy.[85] Maternity leave was always based upon cultural constructs and ideologies rather than upon biological necessity, upon role expectations rather than irreducible differences between the sexes.

The PDA also has significant ideological content. It makes the prototypical maternity leave policy just described illegal. In its stead, as discussed above, is a requirement that the employer extend to women disabled by pregnancy the same disability or sick leave available to other workers. If the employer chooses to extend the leave time beyond the disability period, it must make such leaves available to male as well as to female parents. Title VII requires sex neutrality with respect to employment practices directed at parents.[86] It does not permit the employer to base policies on the separate spheres ideology. Accordingly, the employer must devise its policies in such a way that women and men can, if they choose, structure the allocation of family responsibilities in a more egalitarian fashion. It forecloses the assumption that women are necessarily and inevitably destined to carry the dual burden of homemaker and wage earner.

Statutes such as the Montana statute challenged in the *Miller-Wohl* case are rooted in the philosophy that women have a special and different role and deserve special and different treatment. Feminists can plausibly and forcibly claim that such laws are desirable and appropriate because they reflect the material reality of women's lives. We can lay claim to such accommodations based on the different pattern of our lives, our commitment to children, our cultural destiny. We can even resort to arguments based on biological imperatives and expect that at least some members of the Supreme Court might lend a sympathetic ear. Justice Stevens suggested one such approach in a footnote to his dissent in *Caban v. Mohammed*,[87] a case invalidating a law that granted to unwed mothers but denied to unwed fathers the right to withhold consent to adoption of children. He observed:

> There is some sociological and anthropological research indicating that by virtue of the symbiotic relationship between mother and child during pregnancy and the initial contact between mother and child directly after birth a physical and psychological bond immediately develops between the two that is not then present between the infant and the father or any other person. [Citations omitted.][88] [Brackets in original.]

Justice Stevens's seductive bit of science is useful for making my point, although other illustrations might do as well. Many women who have gone through childbirth have experienced the extraordinary sense of connection to their newborn that the literature calls "bonding."[89] It may be, as some have contended, that the monolithic role women have so long played has been triggered and sustained by this phenomenon, that the effect of this bonding has made it emotionally possible for women to submit to the stringent limitations imposed by law and culture upon the scope and nature of their aspirations and endeavors.[90] On the other hand, it seems entirely possible that the concept of exclusive mother-infant bonding—the latest variation on "maternal instinct"—is a social construct designed to serve ideological ends.[91]

Less than a century ago, doctors and scientists were generally of the view that a woman's intellect, her capacity for education, for reasoning, for public undertakings, was biologically limited.[92] While men were governed by their intellect, women were controlled by their uteruses.[93] No reputable scientist or doctor would make such claims today. But if women are now understood to share with men a capacity for intellectual development, is it not also possible that mother-infant bonding is, likewise, only half the story? What Justice Stevens overlooks is the evidence of the capacity of fathers (the exploration of whose nurturing potential is as new as their opportunity actively to participate in the birth of their children) to "bond" as well.

Again, the question is, are we clinging, without really reflecting upon it, to culturally dictated notions that underestimate the flexibility and potential of human beings of both sexes and which limit us as a class and as individuals?

IV. CONCLUSION: CONFRONTING YIN AND YANG

The human creature seems to be constructed in such a way as to be largely culture bound. We should not, therefore, be surprised that the creaky old justices on the Supreme Court and we somewhat less creaky feminists sometimes—perhaps often—respond to the same basic characterizations of male and female—although, unquestionably, the justices tend sometimes to do different things with those basic characterizations than feminists would do. At this point, we need to think as deeply as we can about what we want the future of women and men to be. Do we want equality of the sexes—or do we want justice for two kinds of human beings who are fundamentally different? If we gain equality, will we lose the special sense of kinship that grows out of experiences central to our lives and not shared by the other sex? Are feminists defending a separate women's culture while trying to break down the barriers created by men's separate culture? Could we, even if we wanted to, maintain the one while claiming our place within the other? *Michael M.*, which yokes assumptions about male sexual aggression with the conclusion that the sexes are not similarly situated because of women's pregnancy, and the Senate report on the all-male draft, which suggests that what sends men to war and leaves women at home is a fundamental trade-off by which men are assigned to battle and women to childrearing, should give us pause. I for one suspect a deep but sometimes nearly invisible set of complimentaries, a yin-yang of sex-role assumptions and assignments so complex and interrelated that we cannot successfully dismantle any of it without seriously exploring the possibility of dismantling it all. The "hard cases"—cases like *Michael M., Rostker, Gilbert, Geduldig, Caban*—give us an opportunity to rethink our basic assumptions about women and men, assumptions sometimes buried beneath our consciousness. They allow us to ask afresh who we are, what we want, and if we are willing to begin to create a new order of things.

NOTES

1. This point is probably an obvious one. Until very recently, women were not represented among the lawmakers. S. Tolchin & M. Tolchin, *Clout: Womanpower and Politics* 17 (1973) (in 1973, women constituted 52% of the population and 53% of the voting population, but only 3% of the country's elected officials). A deliberative body made up exclusively of men—or whites, the rich, or Catholics—no matter how strong their desire to represent "all of the people," will, at least sometimes, inadequately discern, much less build into their laws, provisions that reflect the needs and interests of women—or nonwhites, the poor, or Protestants. This is not to say that there is a monolithic "women's viewpoint" any more than there is a monolithic "men's viewpoint." Plainly there is not. Rather, it is to suggest that women's life experiences still differ sufficiently from men's that a diverse group of women would bring a somewhat different set of perceptions and insights to certain issues than would a similarly diverse group of men. . . .
2. 2 *Blackstone's Commentaries* [444] (St. George Tucker ed. 1803). . . .
3. Ibid. at 442–43. The common law disability was not honored in the equity courts, where married women could sue and be sued in their own right. *See, e.g.*, 2 J. Story, *Commentaries on Equity Jurisprudence* 597–98 (1836) [hereinafter cited as Story, *Equity*].
4. At common law, marriage destroyed the general contractual capacity of a woman. Because marriage deprived her of ownership of her personal property and control over her real prop-

erty, she possessed nothing which could be bound by her contracts. R. Morris, *Studies in the History of American Law* 173 (1959) [hereinafter cited as Morris, *Studies*]. . . . As was the case with other disabilities, the contractual incapacity of married women was somewhat mitigated under equitable principles. . . . 2 Bishop, *Commentaries on the Law* at 418–20 §§ 528–32 (1875); . . . Story, *Equity*, supra note 4, at 626–28. . . .

5. At common law, the wife could not make a will with respect to her real property, 2 Bishop, *Commentaries on the Law of Married Women* § 535, at 422 (1875), although equity would compel the heir of the wife to make a conveyance to the party to whom she sought by will to leave her real property. Story, *Equity*, supra note 4, at 615–16. . . .
6. . . . Morris, *Studies*, supra note 5, at 166–67; Story, *Equity*, supra note 4, at 630. The wife's earnings, as personalty, became the husband's. Since the wife had a common law duty to provide services to her husband, see 1 J. Bishop, *Marriage, Divorce and Separation* §§ 1183–84, at 510 (1891), the fruits of her labors, including earned income, were his. Ibid. at § 1202, at 579.
7. 1 Bishop, *Marriage, Divorce and Separation* § 1202, at 579. Her husband acquired an estate in her real property by virtue of marriage, which entitled him to control the property as well as receive the profits from it. C. Moynahan, *Introduction to the Law of Real Property* 52–54 (1962). Again, equity modified the harshness of the common law by permitting the creation of an equitable estate under certain circumstances. Story, *Equity*, supra note 4, at 608–14.
8. See, e.g., 2 Blackstone, *Commentaries* 444–45 (St. George Tucker ed. 1803). . . .
9. 1 Blackstone, *Commentaries* 444 (St. George Tucker ed. 1803). . . .
10. The history of the common law rule that marriage was a defense to a charge of rape is traced in *State v. Smith*, 148 N.J. Super. 219, 372 A.2d 386 (Essex County Ct. 1977). Several states have abrogated this doctrine by statue. See generally Barry, "Spousal Rape: The Uncommon Law," 66 *A.B.A.J.* 1088 (1980).
11. . . . These early separate estate acts were limited measures; they did not grant women a right to their own earnings nor a general contractual capacity. Those developments emerged in the final third of the century. New York, for example, created such rights in an 1860 amendment to the 1848 act. [Johnston, "Sex and Property: The Common Law Tradition, The Law School Curriculum, and Developments Toward Equality," 47 *N.Y.U. L. Rev.* 1033, 1066 (1972)].
12. See, e.g., N. Cott, *The Bonds of Womanhood: "Woman's Sphere" in New England, 1780–1835*, at 197–200 (1977).
13. Separate spheres ideology was used, for example, to justify denial of the vote to women, E. Flexner, *Century of Struggle: The Women's Rights Movement in the United States* 306 (rev. ed. 1975); to exclude them from the practice of law, *Bradwell v. Illinois*, 83 U.S. 130 (1873); and to excuse them from participation in jury service, Hoyt v. Florida, 368 U.S. 57 (1961).

    The Court in *Muller v. Oregon*, 208 U.S. 412, 421–22, a case upholding limitations on the hours women were permitted to work, was quite explicit on the subject: "Still again, history disclosed the fact that woman has always been dependent upon man. He established his control at the outset by superior physical strength, and his control in various forms, with diminished intensity, has continued to present. . . . Though limitations upon personal and contractual rights may be removed by legislation, there is that in her disposition and habits of life which will operate against full assertion of those rights. She will still be where some legislation to protect her seems necessary to secure real equality of right."
14. 83 U.S. 130, 141 (1873).
15. Ibid.
16. 208 U.S. 412 (1908).

17. "Her physical structure and the proper discharge of her maternal functions—having in view not merely her own health, but the well-being of the race—justify legislation to protect her from the greed as well as the passion of man." Ibid. at 422.
18. *Hoyt v. Florida,* 368 U.S. 57, 62 (1961).
19. *Reed v. Reed,* 404 U.S. 71, 75 (1971). . . .
20. *Craig v. Boren,* 429 U.S. 190, 197 (1976). "[C]lassificatons by gender must serve important governmental objectives and must be substantially related to the achievement of those objectives."
21. *Reed* had required that the gender-based classification bear a "fair and substantial relationship to the object of the legislation." 404 U.S. at 76. The typical articulation of the standard applicable to racial classification was that the classification must be "necessary" to a "compelling state purpose." The effect of *Craig,* then, was to maintain the "substantial relationship" requirement of *Reed* and to add to it a heavier burden upon the state with respect to the state's purpose. The result was a standard consciously parallel in its elements to, but less stringent than, the racial classification standard.
22. *Frontiero v. Richardson,* 411 U.S. 677 (1973).
23. *Califano v. Goldfarb,* 430 U.S. 199 (1977).
24. *Califano v. Westcott,* 443 U.S. 76 (1979).
25. *Wengler v. Druggists Mutual Insurance Co.,* 446 U.S. 142 (1980).
26. *Weinberger v. Wiesenfeld,* 420 U.S. 636 (1975).
27. *Stanton v. Stanton,* 421 U.S. 7 (1975).
28. *Orr v. Orr,* 440 U.S. 268 (1979).
29. *Kirschberg v. Feenstra,* 450 U.S. 455 (1981).
30. *Reed v. Reed,* 404 U.S. 71 (1971).
31. See, e.g., *Kahn v. Shevin,* 416 U.S. 351 (1974) (Florida statute granting widows but not widowers property tax exemption constitutional because intended to assist sex financially most affected by spousal loss), and Califano v. Webster, 430 U.S. 313 (1977) (Social Security Act section creating benefit calculation formula more favorable to women than men held constitutional because intended to compensate women for wage discrimination). . . .
32. See, e.g., *Schlesinger v. Ballard,* 419 U.S. 498 (1975) (Court upheld [5–4] law that results in discharge of male officers if twice passed over for promotion, but guarantees female officers 13-year tenure before discharge for lack of promotion); *Rostker v. Goldberg,* 453 U.S. 57 (1981); *Michael M. v. Superior Court,* 450 U.S. 464 (1981); *Dorthard v. Rawlinson,* 443 U.S. 321 (1977); *Geduldig v. Aiello,* 417 U.S. 484 (1974): *General Electric Corp. v. Gilbert,* 429 U.S. 125 (1976); *Nashville Gas Co. v. Satty,* 434 U.S. 136 (1977). All of these cases were authored either by Justice Stewart or by Justice Rehnquist. . . .
33. 450 U.S. 455 (1981).
34. 453 U.S. 57 (1981).
35. 450 U.S. 464 (1981).
36. 453 U.S. at 75.
37. Ibid. at 76.
38. Ibid. The Court pointed out that the Navy and Air Force combat exclusions are statutory; the Army and Marine Corps "precludes the use of women in combat as a matter of established policy." Ibid.
39. Ibid. at 78–79.
40. Ibid.
41. See dissent of Justice White, joined by Justice Brennan, ibid. at 85.

42. 450 U.S. at 466, California's statute, which renamed the crime "illegal intercourse" in 1970, proscribed the act of sexual intercourse "accomplished with female not the wife of the perpetrator, where the female is under the age of 18 years." Cal. Penal Code § 261.5 (West Supp. 1982).
43. 450 U.S. at 471.
44. Ibid. at 473. . . .
45. 453 U.S. at 83 (White J., dissenting, joined by Brennan, J.: "I assume what has not been challenged in this case—that excluding women from combat positions does not offend the Constitution"). Ibid. at 93 (Marshall, J., dissenting, joined by Brennan, J.: "Had appellees raised a constitutional challenge to the prohibition against assignment of women to combat, this discussion in the Senate Report might well provide persuasive reasons for upholding the restrictions. But the validity of the combat restrictions is not an issue we need decide in this case").
46. Department of Defense Authorization Act of 1981. S. Rep. No. 826, 96th Cong., 2d Sess., reprinted in *U.S. Code Cong. & Ad. News* 2646, 2647 (emphasis added).
47. Ibid.
48. Ibid.
49. Ibid. at 2649.
50. Ibid.
51. "Contrary to [defendant's] assertions, the statute does not rest on the assumption that males are generally the aggressors." 450 U.S. at 475.
52. Ibid. at 467. Justice Blackmun, concurring, for some unknown reason graced posterity with extensive quotations from the transcript of the preliminary hearing (the actual details of the sexual liaison were not relevant to the constitutional issue presented to the court). The facts are a marvelous illustration of the cultural phenomenon of male initiator, female responder. But Justice Blackmun chose to delete (and Justice Rehnquist failed to mention) the young woman's specific response to the defendant's rather forceful request for sexual intercourse. Justice Mosk, of the California Supreme Court, supplies the detail: "In due course Michael told Sharon to remove her pants, and when at first she demurred he allegedly struck her twice. *Sharon testified she then said to herself, 'Forget it,' and decided to let him do as he wished.* The couple then had intercourse." Ibid. at 484–85; 25 Cal. 3d 616, 159 Cal. Rptr, at 345, 601 P.2d at 577 (emphasis added). Sharon was not entirely in a passive-responsive mode, however. After Sharon and the defendant, Michael, had spent some time hugging and kissing in the bushes, Sharon's sister and two other young men approached them. Sharon declined to go home with her sister, who then left with one of the two. Sharon thereupon approached and began kissing Bruce, the other young man. When Bruce left, Sharon then rejoined Michael, whereupon the events giving rise to his prosecution transpired. 450 U.S. at 486–87; 25 Cal. 3d at 616, 159 Cal. Rptr. at 345, 601 P.2d at 577.
53. 450 U.S. at 467 (emphasis added).
54. 450 U.S. at 471–72. . . .
55. Ibid. at 475.
56. Susan Brownmiller observes that "women are trained to be rape victims. . . . Rape seeps into our childhood consciousness by imperceptible degrees. Even before we learn to read we have become indoctrinated into a victim mentality." S. Brownmiller, *Against Our Will: Men, Women and Rape* 309 (1975).
57. See, e.g., *General Electric Co. v. Gilbert,* 429 U.S. 125, 161–62 (1976) (Stevens, J., dissenting).
58. *Geduldig v. Aiello,* 417 U.S. 484, 496, n.20 (1974).
59. In *Reed v. Reed,* 404 U.S. 17 (1971), the Court said that sex classifications were "subject to scrutiny," ibid. at 75, and that such classifications must be a "fair and substantial relation to the

object of the legislation." Ibid. at 76 (quoting *Royster Guano Co. v. Virginia,* 253 U.S. 412, 415 [1920]). In Frontiero v. Richardson, 411 U.S. 677 (1973), the Court came within one vote of deciding that sex classifications were "suspect" and that the state must prove that such classifications were necessary to a compelling state interest, the standard it applied in race cases. In *Geduldig,* the Court said, "The dissenting opinion to the contrary, this case is thus a far cry from cases like Reed . . . and Frontiero . . . involving discrimination based upon gender as such." 417 U.S. at 496 n.20.

60. 417 U.S. 484.
61. Ibid. at 496–97 n.20 (emphasis added).
62. 429 U.S. 125.
63. Ibid. at 135.
64. Ibid. at 136–40.
65. Ibid.
66. Ibid. at 152 (Brennan, J., dissenting).
67. See, e.g., Whitbeck, "Theories of Sexual Difference," in *Women and Philosophy* 68 (Gould & Wartofsky eds. 1976). . . .
68. 434 U.S. 136 (1977).
69. Ibid. at 137.
70. Ibid. at 142.
71. Gilbert, 429 U.S. at 139 n. 17. See also Satty, 434 U.S. at 142. . . .
72. 42 U.S.C. § 2000e(k) (Supp. IV 1980).
73. Thus, Title VII makes it an unlawful employment practice for an employer to classify on the basis of sex, 42 U.S.C. § 2000e-2(a), unless the employer can establish that sex is a "bona fide occupational qualification reasonably necessary to the normal operation of [the] particular business or enterprise," 42 U.S.C. § 2000e-2(e). The exception has been narrowly interpreted. See Dothard v. Rawlinson, 433 U.S. 321, 334 (1977) ("We are persuaded . . . that the bfoq exception was in fact meant to be an extremely narrow exception to the general prohibition of discrimination on the basis of sex"). Once the plaintiff establishes the existence of sex-based classification, the burden of persuasion shifts to the employer to establish that sex is a bfoq. See, e.g., *Weeks v. Southern Bell Tel. and Tel. Co.,* 408 F.2d 228, 235 (5th Cir. 1969).
74. 42 U.S.C. § 2000e(k) (Supp. IV 1980).
75. *Mont. code Ann.* §§ 39-7-201 to 209 (1981). The law also provided that an employee disabled as a result of pregnancy was entitled to her accrued disability or leave benefits. Ibid. at 39-7-203(3). . . .
76. *Miller-Wohl Co. v. Comm'r of Labor & Industry,* State of Montana, 414 F. Supp. 1264, 1265 (D. Mont. 1981), *rev'd on procedural grounds.* 685 F.2d 1088 (9th Cir. 1982).
77. Ibid. The trial court held that the statute did not conflict with the PDA because employers could comply with the state act and avoid discrimination by extending to persons disabled for other reasons the protections that act guarantees to pregnant women.
78. I did, for example.
79. See brief amicus curiae submitted on behalf of Equal Rights Advocates, Inc., Employment Law Center, and California Fair Employment Practice Commission in *Miller-Wohl.*
80. Title VII does not permit such practices. As a practical matter, however, proof of such motivations is difficult. Actions based on a class sufficiently large to illuminate the hidden motivation are prohibitively expensive and complex.
81. 208 U.S. 412, 422. . . .

82. See, e.g., Harris v. McRae, 448 U.S. 297, 325 (1980) . . . ; Maher v. Roe, 432 U.S. 464, 478–79 (1977). . . . See also *Poelker v. Doe,* 432 U.S. 519, 520–21 (1977).
83. See generally Williams, "Firing the Woman to Protect the Fetus: The Reconciliation of Fetal Protection with Employment Opportunity Goals Under Title VIII." 69 Geo. L.J. 641, 647–50 (1981).
84. . . . National Industrial Conference Board, "Maternity Leaves of Absence" 21 Management Record 232–34, 250–63 (1959). . . .
85. See, e.g., Meyer, *Women and Employee Benefits* 2, 4 (1978). (The reason many employers resist paying disability benefits for pregnancy related disabilities is that "a specific group—mothers-to-be— . . . is widely regarded as being made up of terminal employees whose loyalty will be to their homes and children rather than to the corporation.")
86. See *Phillips v. Martin Marietta Corp.,* 400 U.S. 542 (1971) (company policy prohibiting the hiring of mothers but not fathers of preschool-aged children violates section 703(a) of Title VII). . . .
87. 441 U.S. 380 (1979).
88. Ibid. at 405 n.10 (Stevens, J., dissenting).
89. I certainly number myself among those who have experienced this magical feeling and know, from many conversations with other mothers, that my experience is hardly unique. It seems apparent, however, that my reaction is not universal. See J. Bernard, *The Future of Motherhood* 35 (1974). More importantly, falling in love with a child is apparently not limited to mothers or even to biological parents. . . .
90. See, e.g., Rossi, "A Biosocial Perspective on Parenting," *Daedalus,* Spring 1977, at 3–5.
91. See, e.g., Arnay, "Maternal-Infant Bonding: The Politics of Falling in Love With Your Child," 6 *Feminist Studies* 546 (1980). Arnay reviews the bonding literature and concludes that its claims have not been adequately established. Ibid. at 548–56. He warns that "bonding theory lends legitimacy to the notion that women are the only appropriate attendants for children." Ibid. at 564. . . .
92. Both blacks and caucasian women were believed to have smaller and less convoluted brains and therefore restricted intellects. See, e.g., J. Haller & R. Haller, *The Physician and Sexuality in Victorian America* 53–61 (1978); S. Gould, *The Mismeasure of Man* 103–107 (1981). Women who did exert their intellects were thought to endanger their reproductive organs and even, if they pursued careers, to desex themselves and become "mannish" women. See Smith-Rosenberg and Rosenberg, "The Female Animal: Medical and Biological Views of Woman and Her Role in Nineteenth Century America," 60 *J. Am. Hist.* 332 (1973): Haller & Haller, supra at 60–61; B. Ehrenreich & D. English, *For Her Own Good: 150 Years of the Experts' Advice to Women* 125–31 (1979).

    Ehrenreich and English point out that men, too, were faced with a competition between their brains and their reproductive organs for the bodies' limited energy supply, but in the case of men, doctors recommended that they enhance their intellects by preserving their male fluids: "Since the mission of the male (the middle-class male, anyway) was to be a businessman, professor, lawyer, or gynecologist—he had to be careful to conserve all his energy for the 'higher functions.' Doctors warned men not to 'spend their seed' (the material essence of their energy) recklessly in marital relations, and of course not to let it dribble away in secret vice or prurient dreams." Ibid. at 126.
93. B. Ehrenreich & D. English, supra note 129, at 120–25. . . .

Reconstructing Sexual Equality

According to Littleton, "it is not gender difference, but the difference gender makes" that gives rise to a pernicious social divide between women and men. Thus, Littleton rejects "symmetrical" analyses of equality that require women's assimilation to men or that require women and men to adhere to androgyny. Likewise, she rejects "asymmetrical" analyses that retain a devalued view of women or that celebrate masculine values or norms. The special rights approach denies that women can be equal to men; the accommodation approach tinkers with the system enough to enable women to achieve traditionally masculine aims; the empowerment approach rests on the masculinist value of power. Littleton advocates the acceptance approach to equality.

The acceptance approach eliminates the unequal consequences of gender difference without seeking to eliminate gender. This analysis of gender equality aims to make gender difference "costless"—that is, to ensure that women are not penalized for their procreative capacities and that feminine qualities and values are not penalized in the work world. To implement equality based on acceptance of gender difference, Littleton recommends different strategies depending on the nature of the difference. Some differences are socially instilled; others are biological. On some axes of difference, there is considerable overlap between the class of women and the class of men; on others, there is none. For example, procreative differences between women and men are discontinuous and biological. Nevertheless, since women and men have an equal right to procreate, and since women and men are equal participants in the act of conception, women should not be subject to employment policies that penalize pregnancy and childbearing. But, according to Littleton, difference should not be denied to secure women's equality. Pregnancy should not be counted as a disability; it should be accepted and positively valued. Littleton maintains that this approach will create a social and economic context that is free of gender-based oppression and that a context in which gender is cost-free must be established before women can decide which, if any, aspects of femininity they want to retain and identify with and which, if any, they want to leave behind.

—D.T.M.

Chapter 37

Christine A. Littleton

Reconstructing Sexual Equality

DEVELOPMENT OF FEMINIST LEGAL THEORY

Feminist Responses

Feminist legal theory has been primarily reactive, responding to the development of legal racial equality theory. The form of response, however, has varied. One response has been to attempt to equate legal treatment of sex with that of race and deny that there are in fact any significant natural differences between women and men; in other words, to consider the two sexes symmetrically located with regard to any issue, norm, or rule.[1] This response, which I term the "symmetrical" approach, classifies asymmetries as illusions, "overboard generalizations," or temporary glitches that will disappear with a little behavior modification. A competing response rejects this analogy, accepting that women and men are or may be "different," and that women and men are often asymmetrically located in society. This response, which I term the "asymmetrical" approach, rejects the notion that all gender differences are likely to disappear, or even that they should.

1. Symmetrical Models of Sexual Equality. Feminist theorists frequently take the symmetrical approach to sexual equality, not as an ideal, but as the only way to avoid returning to separate spheres ideology. For example, in her highly compelling defense of symmetry in the law, Wendy Williams warns that "we can't have it both ways, we need to think carefully about which way we want to have it."[2]

There are two models of the symmetrical vision—referred to here as "assimilation" and "androgyny." Assimilation, the model most often accepted by the courts, is based on the notion that women, given the chance, really are or could be just like men. Therefore, the argument runs, the law should require social institutions to treat women as they already treat men—requiring, for example, that the professions admit women to the extent they are "qualified," but also insisting that women who enter time-demanding professions such as the practice of law sacrifice relationships (especially with their children) to the same extent that male lawyers have been forced to do.

Androgyny, the second symmetrical model, also posits that women and men are, or at least could be, very much like each other, but argues that equality requires institutions to pick some golden mean between the two and treat both sexes as androgynous persons would be treated. However, given that all of our institutions, work habits, and pay scales were formulated without the benefit of substantial numbers of androgynous persons, androgynous symmetry is difficult to conceptualize, and might require very substantial restructuring of many public and private institutions. In order to be truly androgynous within a symmetrical framework, social institutions must find a single norm that works equally well for all gendering characteristics. Part of my discomfort with androgynous models is that they depend on "meeting in the middle," while I distrust the ability of any person, and especially any court, to value women enough to find the "middle." Moreover, the problems involved in determining such a norm for even one institution are staggering. At what height should a conveyor belt be set in order to satisfy a symmetrical androgynous ideal?

Symmetry appears to have great appeal for the legal system, and this is not surprising. The hornbook definition of equal protection is "that those who are similarly situated be similarly treated,"[3] and many courts, following the Supreme Court's lead, have held that absent a showing of similarity, strict scrutiny is simply inapplicable.[4] Symmetrical analysis also has a great appeal for liberal men,[5] to whom it appears to offer a share in the feminist enterprise. If perceived difference between the sexes is only the result of overly rigid sex roles, the men's liberty is at stake too. Ending this form of sexual inequality could free men to express their "feminine" side, just as it frees women to express their "masculine" side.

2. Asymmetrical Models of Sexual Equality. Asymmetrical approaches to sexual equality take the position that difference should not be ignored or eradicated. Rather, they argue that any sexually equal society must somehow deal with difference, problematic as that may be. Asymmetrical approaches include "special rights," "accommodation," "acceptance," and "empowerment."

The special rights model affirms that women and men *are* different, and asserts that cultural differences, such as childrearing roles, are rooted in biological ones, such as reproduction. Therefore, it states, society must take account of these differences and ensure that women are not punished for them. This approach, sometimes referred to as a "bivalent" model,[6] is closest to the "special treatment" pole of the asymmetrical/symmetrical equality debate. Elizabeth Wolgast, a major proponent of special rights, argues that women cannot be men's "equals" because equality by definition requires sameness.[7] Instead of equality, she suggests seeking justice, claiming special rights for women based on their special needs.[8]

The second asymmetrical model, accommodation, agrees that differential treatment of biological differences (such as pregnancy, and perhaps breastfeeding) is necessary, but argues that cultural or hard-to-classify differences (such as career interests and skills) should be treated under an equal treatment or androgynous model. Examples of accommodation models include Sylvia Law's approach to issues of reproductive biology[9] and Herma Hill Kay's "episodic" approach to the condition of pregnancy.[10] These approaches could also be characterized as "symmetry, with concessions to asymmetry where necessary." The accommodations limit the asymmetry in their models to biological differences because, like Williams, they fear a return to separate spheres ideology should asymmetrical theory go too far.[11]

My own attempt to grapple with difference, which I call an "acceptance" model,[12] is essentially asymmetrical. While not endorsing the notion that cultural differences between the sexes are biologically determined, it does recognize and attempt to deal with both biological and social differences. Acceptance does not view sex differences as problematic per se, but rather focuses on the ways in which differences are permitted to justify inequality. It asserts that eliminating the unequal consequences of sex differences is more important than debating whether such differences are "real," or even trying to eliminate them altogether.

Unlike accommodationists, who would limit asymmetrical analysis to purely biological differences, my proposal also requires equal acceptance of cultural differences. The reasons for this are twofold. First, the distinction between biological and cultural, while useful analytically, is itself culturally based. Second, the inequality experienced by women is often presented as a necessary consequence of cultural rather than of biological difference. If, for instance, women do in fact "choose" to become nurses rather than real estate appraisers,[13] it is not because of any biological imperative. Yet, regardless of the reasons for the choice, they certainly do not choose to be paid less. It is the *consequences* of gendered difference, and not its sources, that equal acceptance addresses.

If, as it appears from Gilligan's studies,[14] women and men tend to develop somewhat differently in terms of their values and inclinations, *each* of these modes of development must be equally valid and valuable. In our desire for equality, we should not be forced to jettison either; rather, we should find some way to value both. That such different modes do not perfectly correspond to biological sex does not prevent them from being typed socially as "male" and "female," and neither should it prevent us from demanding that they be equally valued. Thus, if women currently tend to assume primary responsibility for childrearing, we should not ignore that fact in an attempt to prefigure the rosy day when parenting is fully shared. We should instead figure out how to assure that equal resources, status, and access to social decision making flow to those women (and few men) who engage in this socially female behavior.

The focus of equality as acceptance, therefore, is not on the question of whether *women* are different, but rather on the question of how the social fact of gender asymmetry can be dealt with so as to create some symmetry in the lived-out experience of all members of the community. I do not think it matters so much whether differences are "natural" or not; they are built into our structures and selves in either event. As social facts, differences are created by the interaction of person with person or person with institution; they inhere in the relationship, not in the person. On this view, the function of equality is to make gender differences, perceived or actual, costless relative to each other, so that anyone may follow a male, female, or androgynous life style according to their natural inclination or choice without being punished for following a female life style or rewarded for following a male one.

As an illustration of this approach, consider what many conceive to be the paradigm difference between men and women—pregnancy. No one disputes that only women become pregnant, but symmetrical theorists analogize pregnancy to other events, in order to preserve the unitary approach of symmetrical theory. Such attempts to minimize difference have the ironic result of obscuring more fundamental similarities.

In *California Federal Savings & Loan Association v. Guerra (Cal. Fed.)*,[15] Lillian Garland, a receptionist at California Federal, tried to return to her job after the birth of her child. The bank refused to reinstate her, and she sued under the California Fair Employment and Housing Act (FEHA).[16] That law requires that employees temporarily disabled by pregnancy be given an unpaid leave of up to four months, with guaranteed reinstatement in their original job or its equivalent.[17] The bank in turn sued in federal court, claiming that the FEHA was preempted by Title VII of the Civil Rights Act of 1964,[18] as amended by the Pregnancy Discrimination Act (PDA). The PDA requires only that employers treat pregnancy the same as any other disability.[19] California Federal argued that the PDA prevented California from enforcing its pregnancy disability leave requirements against firms that did not provide these benefits for disabilities unrelated to pregnancy.[20]

In addition to narrow questions of statutory interpretation, *Cal. Fed.* raised more fundamental questions about the meaning of equal employment opportunity for women. Citing the dangers of separate spheres ideology raised by "protectionist" legislation, the national ACLU filed an amicus brief arguing that the California law should be struck down, and that the remedy should provide for job-protected leave for all temporarily disabled employees, whatever the source of their disability.[21] California feminist groups, such as Equal Rights Advocates, filed on the other side of the debate, arguing that the California law guaranteed equality of opportunity, and was thus consistent with federal law and policy.[22]

Missing in these arguments, however, was any recognition that working men and women shared a more fundamental right than the right to basic disability leave benefits or job protection. The Coalition for Reproductive Equality in the Workplace (CREW) advanced the position that working women and men share a right to procreative choice in addition to an interest in disability leave.[23] In order to ensure equal exercise of procreative rights, it argued, an employer must provide leave adequate to the effects of pregnancy.

> The California statute eliminates barriers to equality in both procreation and employment faced by women who cannot afford to lose their jobs when they decide to become parents. Male employees who become fathers and female employees who become mothers are thus enabled to combine procreation and employment to the same extent.[24]

This form of acceptance, unlike those that analogize pregnancy to disability, emphasizes the basic commonality of procreation as a human endeavor involving both women and men. By recognizing pregnancy as "different" from other causes of disability, it supports efforts to equalize the position of working women and men with respect to this fundamental right.[25]

The foregoing asymmetrical models, including my own, share the notion that, regardless of their differences, women and men must be treated as full members of society. Each model acknowledges that women may need treatment different than that accorded to men in order to effectuate their membership in important spheres of social life; all would allow at least some such claims, although on very different bases, and probably in very different circumstances.

A final asymmetrical approach, "empowerment," rejects difference altogether as a relevant subject of inquiry.[26] In its strongest form, empowerment claims that the subordination of women to men has itself constructed the sexes, and their differences. For example, Catharine MacKinnon argues:

> It makes a lot of sense that women might have a somewhat distinctive perspective on social life. We may or may not speak in a different voice—I think that the voice that we have been said to speak in is in fact in large part the "feminine" voice, the voice of the victim speaking without consciousness. But when we understand that women are *forced* into this situation of inequality, it makes a lot of sense that we should want to negotiate, since we lose conflicts. It makes a lot of sense that we should want to urge values of care, because it is what we have been valued for. We have had little choice but to be valued this way.[27]

A somewhat weaker version of the claim is that we simply do not and cannot know whether there are any important differences between the sexes that have not been created by the dynamic of domination and subordination. In either event, the argument runs, we should forget about the question of differences and focus directly on subordination and domination. If a law, practice, or policy contributes to the subordination of women or their domination by men, it violates equality. If it empowers women or contributes to the breakdown of male domination, it enhances equality.

The reconceptualization of equality as antidomination, like the model of equality as acceptance, attempts to respond directly to the concrete and lived-out experience of women. Like other asymmetrical models, it allows different treatment of women and men when necessary to effectuate its overall goal of ending women's subordination. However, it differs substantially from the acceptance model in its rejection of the membership, belonging, and participatory aspects of equality.

3. The Difference That Difference Makes. Each of the several models of equality discussed above, if adopted, would have a quite different impact on the structure of society. If this society wholeheartedly embraced the symmetrical approach of assimilation—the point of view that "women are just like men"—little would need to be changed in our economic or political institutions except to get rid of lingering traces of irrational prejudice, such as an occasional employer's preference for male employees. In contrast, if society adopted the androgyny model, which views both women and men as bent out of shape by current sex roles and requires both to conform to an androgynous model, it would have to alter radically its methods of resource distribution. In the employment context, this might mean wholesale revamping of methods for determining the "best person for the job." Thus, while assimilation would merely require law firms to hire women who have managed to get the same credentials as the men they have traditionally hired, androgyny might insist that the firm hire only those persons with credentials that would be possessed by someone neither "socially male" nor "socially female."[28]

If society adopted an asymmetrical approach such as the accommodation model, no radical restructuring would be necessary. Government would need only insist that women be given what they need to resemble men, such as time off to have babies and the freedom to return to work on the same rung of the ladder as their male counterparts. If, however, society adopted the model of equality as acceptance, which seeks to make difference costless, it might additionally insist that women and men who opt for socially female occupations, such as childrearing, be compensated at a rate similar to those women and men who opt for socially male occupations, such as legal practice. Alternatively, such occupations might be restructured to make them equally accessible to those whose behavior is culturally coded "male" or "female."

The different models also have different potential to challenge the phallocentrism of social institutions. No part of the spectrum of currently available feminist legal theory is completely immune to the feminist critique of society as phallocentric. We cannot outrun our history, and that history demonstrates that the terms of social discourse have been set by men who, actively or passively, have ignored women's voices—until even the possibility of women having a voice has become questionable. Nevertheless, the models do differ with respect to the level at which the phallocentrism of the culture reappears.

Under the assimilationist approach, for example, women merit equal treatment only so far as they can demonstrate that they are similar to men. The assimilation model is thus fatally phallocentric. To the extent that women cannot or will not conform to socially male forms of behavior, they are left out in the cold. To the extent they do or can conform, they do not achieve equality *as women*, but as social males.

Similarly, empowerment and androgyny (an asymmetrical and symmetrical approach, respectively) both rely on central concepts whose current meaning is phallocentrically biased. If "power" and "neutrality" (along with "equality") were not themselves gendered concepts, the empowerment and androgyny approaches would be less problematic. But our culture conceives of power as power used by men, and creates androgynous models "tilted" toward the male. As Carrie Menkel-Meadow put it, the trouble with marble cake is that it never has enough chocolate; the problem with androgyny is that it never has enough womanness.[29] Similarly, empowering women without dealing with difference, like assimilation, too easily becomes simply sharing male power more broadly.

Equality as acceptance is not immune from phallocentrism in several of its component concepts. However, these concepts are not necessarily entailed by theory and may be replaced with less biased concepts as they reveal themselves through the process of equalization. For example, in discussing employment-related applications of the model, I use the measures already existing in that sphere—money, status, and access to decision making. These measures of value are obviously suspect. Nevertheless, my use of them is contingent. Acceptance requires only that culturally coded "male" and "female" complements be equally valued; it does not dictate the coin in which such value should be measured. By including access to decision making as part of the measure, however, the theory holds out the possibility that future measures of value will be created by women and men *together*. Thus, acceptance strives to create the preconditions necessary for sexually integrated debate about a more appropriate value system.

The various models of equality arise out of common feminist goals and enterprises: trying to imagine what a sexually equal society would look like, given that none of us has ever seen one; and trying to figure out ways of getting there, given that the obstacles to sexual equality are so many and so strong.

The perception among feminist legal thinkers that the stakes in the symmetrical versus asymmetrical debate are high is correct. Difference indeed makes a difference. Yet, the frantic nature of the debate about difference between the sexes makes the divergent views within feminist legal thought appear as a deadly danger rather than an exciting opportunity. The label "divisive" gets slapped on before the discussion even gets underway.

We need to recognize difference among women as diversity rather than division, and difference between women and men as opportunity rather than danger. Audre Lorde calls for the recognition of difference among women in terms that should apply to all human difference:

> As a tool of social control, women have been encouraged to recognize only one area of human difference as legitimate, those differences which exist between women and men. And we have learned to deal across those differences with the urgency of all oppressed subordinates. . . . We have recognized and negotiated these differences, even when this recognition only continued the old dominant/subordinate mode of human relationship, where the oppressed must recognize the masters' difference in order to survive.
>
> *But our future survival is predicated upon our ability to relate within equality.*[30]

There must be choices beyond those of ignoring difference or accepting inequality. So long as difference itself is so expensive in the coin of equality, we approach the variety of human experience with blinders on. Perhaps if difference were not so costly, we, as feminists, could think about it more clearly. Perhaps if equality did not require uniformity, we, as women, could demand it less ambivalently.

EQUALITY AND DIFFERENCE

Feminist Critique of Equality

The phallocentricity of equality is most apparent in the extraordinary difficulty the legal system has had in dealing with the fact that women (and *not* men) conceive and bear children. Indeed, it would not be necessary to go further than to establish that the legal system *has* had difficulty with this fact in order to ground the claim that equality analysis is phallocentric. It is, however, necessary to go beyond a simple recounting of the law in this area in order to lay out the particular ways in which the phallocentricity is manifested.

. . . [T]he Supreme Court's decision in *Reed v. Reed*[31] marked its acceptance of the "assimilationist" model of sexual equality. That decision was profoundly assimilationist in that the Court rejected as "irrational" the view that women might be different from men with respect to their ability to handle the traditionally "male" responsibilities of estate administration.

The first cases to reach the Supreme Court after its about-face in *Reed* did not present questions that challenged this assimilationist model. In *Craig v. Boren*,[32] for example, the Court saw the differences in driving patterns of male and female teenage drivers not as a significant difference but rather as one that could be readily ignored, thus failing to provide a substantial "fit" between the difference and the differential classification. Similarly, those classifications that were upheld by the Court were justified as temporary measures to reduce differences that were not intractable. Thus, in *Kahn v. Shevin*,[33] Florida's tax subsidy to widows (and not widowers) was upheld as a reasonable attempt to compensate the spouse who would most severely feel the economic loss of the other partner to the marriage, a difference that would disappear once sex discrimination is gone from our society. Temporary alleviation of socially created (and socially remediable) differences between the sexes is simple affirmative action. Its goal is symmetry of the sexes, achieved through temporary asymmetrical treatment. Under this view, had men been irrationally discriminated against in employment, it might just as easily have been the widowers rather than the widows who needed the tax break.

When challenges arose to pregnancy-based classifications, however, the Court was faced with a difference that it could not ignore or treat as created by irrational discrimination. In *Geduldig v. Aiello*[34] and *General Electric Co. v. Gilbert*,[35] the Supreme Court announced, apparently with a straight face, that singling out pregnancy for disadvantageous treatment was not discrimination on the basis of *sex.* Underlying both opinions was the unarticulated assumption that pregnancy was a real difference, and that equality was therefore simply inapplicable. As Justice Stewart stated in *Geduldig,* "There is no risk from which men are protected and women are not. Likewise, there is no risk from which women are protected and men are not."[36]

The Court's equality analysis could thus deal with overboard generalizations, questions of closeness of fit, and even temporary affirmative action, but a generalization of difference between the sexes that was accurate, and permanently so, was beyond the pale. The first strand of the feminist critique of equality addresses this failing, asserting that *equality analysis defines as beyond its scope precisely those issues that women find crucial to their concrete experience as women.*

Legal equality analysis "runs out" when it encounters "real" difference, and only becomes available if and when the difference is analogized to some experience men can have too. Legislative overruling of *Gilbert* by the Pregnancy Discrimination Act was thus accomplished by making pregnancy look similar to something men experienced as well—disability. Given the way employment is structured, pregnancy renders a woman unable to work for a few days to a few months, just like illness and injury do for men. However, what makes pregnancy a *dis*ability rather than, say, an additional ability, is the structure of work, not reproduction. Normal pregnancy may make a woman unable to "work" for days, weeks or months, but it also makes her able to reproduce. From what viewpoint is the work that she cannot do "work," and the work that she is doing *not* work? Certainly not from hers.

Thus, the second strand of the feminist critique of equality states: *Difference, which is created by the relationship of women to particular and contingent social structures, is taken as natural (that is, unchangeable and inherent), and it is located solely in the woman herself.* It is not impossible to imagine a definition of "work" that includes the "labor" of childbirth; nor is it impossible to imagine a workplace setting in which pregnancy would not be disabling.

Analogizing pregnancy to disability has created new difficulties for a legal system trying to apply an assimilationist model of equality. In *California Federal Savings & Loan Association v. Guerra*,[37] an employer challenged a mandatory pregnancy leave statute, arguing that the law could be regarded as equal treatment, rather than a special bonus for women, only where men already have a right to disability leave for other reasons. Underlying the employer's argument was the assumption that the workplace is itself a gender-neutral institution that must treat all workers evenhandedly. Evenhanded treatment requires treating each worker the same as her coworkers, which means extending leave to all workers regardless of cause or denying leave to all. This reasoning falls prey to the second strand of the critique by assuming that if women have other needs for disability leave, it is because *they* are different.

It also gives rise to a third objection: that an institution structured so that women are inevitably disadvantaged by its facially neutral policies is itself phallocentric. Thus, *the third strand of the critique challenges the assumed gender neutrality of social institutions, as well as the notion that practices must distinguish themselves from "business as usual" in order to be seen as unequal.*

The inability of traditional equality analysis to cope with difference is not limited to biological differences in the work place. Purporting to follow state constitutional equal rights amendments, many state courts have visited severe hardship on women in marital dissolution proceedings. In case after case, women who have spent most of the marriage as full-time homemakers and mothers are treated as "equal" to their male partners who have spent those years developing a career.[38] In setting alimony awards, courts have refused even to consider the possibility that the woman might find herself at a competitive disadvantage in the job market—a disadvantage directly related to the work she performed during the marriage. Instead, the parties are treated "equally," and any prior disadvantaging of the women vis-à-vis the workplace is completely ignored.[39]

To summarize, from a feminist viewpoint, current equality analysis is phallocentrically biased in three respects: (1) it is inapplicable once it encounters "real" differences; (2) it locates difference in women, rather than in relationships; and (3) it fails to question the assumptions that social institutions are gender neutral, and that women and men are therefore similarly related to those institutions. What the three strands of this critique share is their focus on "difference." A reconstructed equality analysis—one that seeks to eliminate, or at least reduce, the phallocentrism of the current model—must at some point deal with each strand of the critique. Thus, from a theoretical standpoint, symmetrical equality models, with their insistence that difference be ignored, eradicated, or dissolved, are not responsive to the feminist critique of equality.

Equality as Acceptance

The model of equality as acceptance responds to the first strand of the feminist critique of equality by insisting that equality can in fact be applied *across* difference. It is not, however, a "leveling" proposal. Rather, equality as acceptance calls for equalization across only those differences that the culture has encoded as gendered complements. The theory of comparable worth provides one example of this, and the field of athletics yields another.

Most proponents of comparable worth have defined the claim along the following lines: jobs that call for equally valuable skills, effort, and responsibility should be paid equally, even though they occur in different combinations of predominantly female and predominantly male occupations.[40] Thus, when an employer has defined two job classifications as gendered complements, the employer should pay the same to each. Equality as acceptance makes the broader claim that *all* behavioral forms that the culture (not just the employer) has encoded as "male" and "female" counterparts should be equally rewarded. Acceptance would thus support challenges to the overvaluation of "male" skills (and corresponding undervaluation of "female" ones) by employers, rather than limiting challenges to unequal application of an existing valuation or to the failure to make such a valuation.

In the sphere of athletics, equality as acceptance would support an argument that equal resources be allocated to male and female sports programs regardless of whether the sports themselves are "similar." In this way, women's equality in athletics would not depend on the ability of individual women to assimilate themselves to the particular sports activities traditionally engaged in by men.

Under the model of equality as acceptance, equality analysis does not end at the discovery of a "real" difference. Rather, it attempts to assess the "cultural meaning" of that difference, and to determine how to achieve equality despite it. This formulation responds to the second strand of the feminist critique by locating difference in the relationship between women and men rather than in women alone, as accommodation arguably does. Acceptance would thus provide little support for the claim that traditionally male sports (such as football) should be modified so as to accommodate women (or vice versa). Equality as acceptance does not prescribe the superiority of socially female categories, nor even the superiority of androgynous categories. It does, however, affirm the equal validity of men's and women's lives.

Finally, equality as acceptance responds to the third strand of the feminist critique by acknowledging that women and men frequently stand in asymmetrical positions to a particular social institution. It recognizes that women are frequently disadvantaged by facially neutral practices and insists that such asymmetries be reflected in resource allocation. To carry forward the athletics example, equality as acceptance would support an equal division of resources between male and female programs rather than dividing up the available sports budget per capita. Since women and men do not stand symmetrically to the social institution of athletics, per capita distribution would simply serve to perpetuate the asymmetry, diverting more resources to male programs, where the participation rate has been depressed both by women's exclusion from certain sports and by the subordination of those activities women have developed for themselves.

It may be apparent from the preceding paragraphs that equal acceptance as a legal norm does not automatically produce one and only one "right answer" to difficult questions of equality. Instead, it provides support for new remedial strategies as well as a method of uncovering deeper layers of inequality.

Acceptance, Not Accommodation

Asymmetrical equality theorists have usually been taken to mean that male institutions should take account of women's differences by accommodating those differences. "Reasonable accommodation" can be asked of a court (although the people usually being asked to be "reasonable" are those asking for accommodation), and if the choice truly is between accommodation and nothing, "half a loaf" *is* better than none.

The problem with accommodation, however, is that it implicitly accepts the prevailing norm as generally legitimate, even as it urges that "special circumstances" make the norm inappropriate for the particular individual or class seeking accommodation. In addition, it falls prey to the feminist critique of equality by labeling women as deviant from the norm, thus locating the difference in women. Assimilated women are particularly vulnerable to this misperception, and are all too often persuaded to drop valid demands for inclusion on their own terms by the response that they are asking for "an exception."

The distinction between accommodation and acceptance may be illustrated by a rather commonplace example. I remember a feminist lawyer walking up to a podium to deliver a speech. The podium was high enough that she could not reach the microphone. While arrangements were being modified, she pointedly noted, "Built for a man!" Accommodation is a step platform brought for her to stand on. Acceptance is a podium whose height is adjustable.

MAKING DIFFERENCE COSTLESS

Differently Gendered Complements

The problem of identifying gendered complements lies along two axes of difference. One axis measures the "source" of differences, ranging from the clearly biological to the clearly social (with a great deal of controversy in between). The other measures the degree of overlap between the sexes, and runs from more-or-less differences on one end to yes-or-no differences on the other.

For gender differences that are more-or-less, there is a significant degree of overlap between the sexes. Height is one of these. Not all women would have been disaffirmed by the too-high podium that was "built for a man," and not all men would have been affirmed by it. But more women than men in this society would have had the feminist lawyer's experience. Additionally, differences of the more-or-less variety are easier to deny, since there is always some woman over six feet or some man under five, and a great number of both in between. These differences are also easier to "match," because shorter and taller are both measures of the same concededly shared human characteristic of height.

For yes-or-no gender differences, there is no overlap at all. The primary example of this is, of course, pregnancy. No man can become pregnant, and most women can. However, women who have never had the capacity for pregnancy are not thereby made either biologically or socially male, even when the dominant culture has tended to view them as "not women." Thus, although it is useful for purposes of analysis to separate yes-or-no differences from more-or-less ones, they represent two poles of the same spectrum.

Disparate treatment analysis under Title VII allows individuals who are exceptions to the "rule" of their biological sex to be socially classed with the other sex. Thus, tall women must be treated the same as tall men, and short men the same as short women. As the podium example demonstrates, phallocentrism in such cases usually involves setting the norm by reference to the center of the male bell curve. When the norm is set by reference to the female bell curve, the same analysis applies; men who can type must be allowed into socially female secretarial positions.

To establish a prima facie case of discrimination under disparate treatment analysis, a plaintiff must show:

> (i) that [the plaintiff] belongs to a racial minority [or is a woman]; (ii) that he [or she] applied and was qualified for a job for which the employer was seeking applicants; (iii) that, despite [plaintiff's] qualifications, he [or she] was rejected; and (iv) that, after [plaintiff's] rejection, the position remained open and the employer continued to seek applicants from persons of complainant's qualifications.[41]

Requiring a female complainant to establish "qualifications" for a traditionally male job is to require her to establish that she is socially male, at least in this context.

Disparate impact analysis, on the other hand, allows socially female women to bring equality claims if the job qualification containing the gendered norm is irrelevant to the applicant's ability to perform the job. No showing of direct intent to discriminate is required.[42] Under disparate impact doctrine, then, a woman can establish discrimination by demonstrating that women as a class are more severely affected than men by a facially neutral employment practice, such as a height requirement. The employer can, however, justify the discriminatory impact by demonstrating that the practice is "job related" or necessary to the employer's business.[43] Moreover, the relevance of the practice is tested solely by reference to the way the job is already structured.[44] Thus, even disparate impact analysis—as currently practiced—does not allow for challenges to male bias in the structure of businesses, occupations, or jobs.[45]

Equality as acceptance would support challenges to government and employer policies and practices that use male norms even when such norms are considered job-related, necessary to the business, or "substantially related to an important governmental interest." Unlike the more radical version of the model of androgyny referred to above, however, acceptance would not necessarily require the *elimination* of such norms. Acceptance could instead be achieved by inventing complementary structures containing female norms. For example, assume an employer successfully defends its 5′9⊕minimum height requirement as necessary to the job of sorting widgets as they pass on a conveyor belt. Equality as acceptance could be achieved by restructuring the job itself—in this case, by changing the height of the conveyor belt or by adding a second belt. Alternatively, the employer could defend the requirement by demonstrating that equal job opportunities exist in the plant for applicants shorter than 5′9⊕ Acceptance would thus permit de facto sex segregation in the work place, but *only* if the predominantly male and predominantly female jobs have equal pay, status, and opportunity for promotion into decision-making positions.

Yes-or-no differences do not yield so readily to matching. This has helped focus the "equal treatment/special treatment" debate on pregnancy—specifically, on the question of whether requiring employers to grant pregnancy leaves for women violates the equal rights of men, who can never take advantage of such leaves. If pregnancy were a more-or-less difference, such as disabling heart trouble or child-care responsibility, it would be easy for the current legal system to answer this question. Since it is a yes-or-no difference, however, the legal system runs in circles: the Supreme Court in *Geduldig v. Aiello*[46] said pregnancy is different, so women can be punished for it; the federal district court in *Cal Fed.*[47] said pregnancy is not different, so women should not benefit from it; the Supreme Court, affirming the Ninth Circuit in *Cal Fed.*,[48] said pregnancy is different, so men are not hurt by taking account of it.

I think that the appropriate unit of analysis in yes-or-no cases is *interaction* of the sexes rather than comparison. Even with rapidly developing reproductive technology, it is still necessary for some part of a woman to interact with some part of a man to produce a pregnancy. In that interaction, the gendered complements are pregnancy for the woman and fewer sperm cells for the man. Since pregnancy almost always results in some period of disability for the woman, making the sex difference costless with respect to the work place requires that money, status, and opportunity for advancement flow equally to the womb-donating woman and the sperm-donating man (himself an equal contributor to the procreative act).[49]

Both average height and pregnancy lie near the biological pole of the source axis; these differences are clearly biological. Their existence and degree of overlap are less problematic as an empirical matter than are differences lying closer to the cultural pole. The clearly cultural differences, on the other hand, are more problematic, primarily because they are even more likely than biological differences to give rise to stereotypes that harm women. Arguments for ignoring difference are also more plausible with reference to the cultural axis. Because these differences are acquired, they can presumably be done away with, if not for us then for our children or grandchildren.[50] This combination of danger and plausibility has led several sex equality theorists to place themselves toward the middle of the symmetrical versus asymmetrical debate.[51] I am, however, either brave or foolhardy enough to believe that even cultural differences can be made accessible to equality analysis.

Cultural differences of the more-or-less variety can be dealt with along the same general lines as biological differences that overlap. Under acceptance, marital dissolution decrees, for example, could value the contributions of the nonearner spouse (usually, but not always, the woman), take into account services in the home performed after divorce, and treat realistically the expenses necessarily incurred by the custodial parent. These measures would go further toward reducing the potentially devastating economic impact of divorce for women than current experiments, such as presumptions in favor of joint custody.

Cultural differences of the yes-or-no variety are easier to identify than those of the more-or-less, but harder to deal with. Fortunately, there are relatively few of them (far fewer than there were a few decades ago). The most visible is employment in the armed services. Women are excluded from draft registration, and female volunteers are excluded from combat positions.

Just as gendered complements in the "biological" realm come from our current perceptions of biology, so must gendered complements in the "cultural" realm come from our current perceptions of culture. The traditional gender divide sets up "warrior" in its cultural sense directly opposite "mother" in its cultural sense.[52] The "cult of motherhood" resembles the "glory of battle" in a number of ways. Both occupations involve a lot of unpleasant work, along with a real sense of commitment to a cause beyond oneself that is culturally gussied up and glamorized culturally to cover up the unpleasantness involved. Both involve danger and possible death. And, of course, the rationale most frequently given for women's exclusion from combat is their capacity for motherhood.[53]

Making this gender difference less costly could mean requiring the government to pay mothers the same low wages and generous benefits as most soldiers.[54] It could also mean encouraging the use of motherhood as an unofficial prerequisite for governmental office. As a paying occupation with continuing status perks, many more men might be induced to stay home and raise their children. Alternatively, but less likely, making difference costless could mean ceasing to pay combat troops.

For example, in *Personnel Administrator v. Feeny*,[55] the Supreme Court upheld Massachusetts' lifetime veteran's preference against an equal protection challenge, reasoning that Massachusetts had not intended that preference to lock women into lower-level and dead-end civil service positions, regardless of the obvious effect. Under an equality as acceptance model, a state's failure to provide equal preference for the gendered female complement to military service would be evidence of intentional discrimination. Thus, even without additional constitutional or statutory enactment, a change in the Court's underlying model of equality could alter the result in actual cases.

Matching gendered complements in order to equalize across cultural differences may sound like marching directly into the valley of the stereotypes. Those who consider Carol Gilligan's discovery of "a different voice" sexist are not likely to find this appealing. Nevertheless, allow me to make two disclaimers. First, almost all cultural differences are, or could easily be, "more or less." Lots of biological men exhibit socially female characteristics (for which they are all too often punished); at least as many biological women exhibit socially male ones (for which they are often rewarded, although they are simultaneously punished for not having the biological form to match); and many more women and men fall in the middle, exhibiting no readily identifiable "male" or "female" behavior patterns. Second, what is objectionable about stereotypes is not that they are never true, but rather that they are not *always* true. Demonstrating that not every woman with children is primarily responsible for their care may help those women who do not have such responsibility to compete for certain jobs, but it does little to help those women struggling to hold down two jobs, only one of which is paid.

Disclaimers aside, what is relevant for this exercise is not the accuracy or inaccuracy of any set of gendered complements, but rather how the complements reward or punish those who are perceived to fall on one side or the other. Studies of sex-segregated work places tend to show that there is a high correlation between employer perceptions of gender differences and the segregation patterns themselves.[56] These perceived gender differences, such as lifting strength and small-muscle dexterity, are of the more-or-less type, and tend to fall toward the middle of the "source" axis.[57] Requiring individual testing alleviates segregation to some extent, but it only helps those women who do not fit the female stereotype (at the expense, of course, of those men who do not fit the male stereotype). However, the main problem with sex segregation is that promotion patterns and pay scales are determined by entry-level job classifications. Thus, those women who do fit the female stereotype (of, say, low lifting strength and high small-muscle dexterity) are stuck. They are not harmed by the "female" job classification as such; they are harmed by the disparity in pay and opportunity for promotion that goes along with it. And the disparity in promotion opportunities continues the cycle of overvaluation of "male" characteristics and undervaluation of "female" ones, because employers will continue to select those biological men and women who are socially male.

If, alternatively, both "male" and "female" entry-level positions paid the same and offered the same promotion opportunities, individual testing would not matter so much. Indeed, assuming proportionate numbers of openings, applicants might well self-select into the classification that better utilizes their particular strengths and minimizes their particular weaknesses. If so, the segregation pattern would gradually break down unless employers actively and, legally speaking, "intentionally" sought to maintain it. Moreover, even if self-selection by individual skills did not occur, a better sex mix at the management level would eventually have a significant impact throughout the firm.

As Frances Olsen sets forth in *The Sex of Law*, we tend to think in dichotomies, and those dichotomies are both sexualized (with one side masculine and the other feminine) and hierarchicized (with one side in each pair superior).[58] She argues that the sexualization and heirarchicization should be attacked simultaneously, to the end of deconstructing the dichotomies themselves. While I do not disagree with this goal, I do think Olsen's strategy is impractical. Dichotomies that purport to describe gender differences are, I think, only likely to fall apart once they no longer accurately describe differences in pay scales, hiring patterns, or promotion ladders. Additionally, since we presently think in these dichotomies, we may as well use them to help us in our struggle to discard them.

The rigidity of sexualized dichotomies does appear to be gradually breaking down in many areas. Whether the strategy I am suggesting would impede that breakdown is discussed below. With regard to the practical problem of implementation, however, the true breakdown of any particular male-female dichotomy is not a problem, but a benefit. It puts us one step closer toward eliminating them entirely.

Reifying Gender

The theoretical problem of the above discussion is, of course, the danger that using gendered complements overtly (I remain convinced that we use them covertly all the time) will strengthen the gender divide. This danger seems real, although perhaps overstated if the rest of my analysis holds. As I have urged throughout this article, it is not gender difference, but the difference gender makes, that creates a divide. Instead of division, there might easily be a continuum stretching beyond the current poles—the "polymorphous perversity" that Jeff Goldstein posits in the erotic arena[59] or the "reds and greens and blues" that Frances Olsen imagines within a liberated androgyny.[60] If the status of "victim" were not so debilitating in socially real terms, we would be able to laugh at the argument that the Minneapolis anti-pornography ordinance paints women as victims of male violence. Similarly, if the location of a person, action, or characteristic on the "female" side of the divide did not entail her/his/its immediate devaluation, then the mere identification of a law's beneficiaries as "women" would not divert us from a deeper and more practical analysis of its relative advantages and disadvantages.

There is yet another layer, however, to the critique of reifying gender. Not only is the socially female a constructed category, but that social construction was historically created in the absence of women, or at least without their participation. Therefore, runs the criticism, the socially female cannot be claimed as truly belonging to women, because it has been men who have done the defining. How, then, can I claim it as valuable on behalf of *women*?

I am not claiming that women's authentic voice would value everything that has been assigned to us by social definition. I literally do not know what I would say about my selfhood had I not been raised in a phallocentric culture—and neither does anyone else. However, as long as identification with socially female attributes is more "expensive" than identification with socially male ones—when taking parental leave shunts you off the partnership track, crying in a meeting shuts off the discussion, breastfeeding makes you unacceptable at the restaurant table—we are not ever going to be in a position to find out what women would value for themselves.

The social construction of "woman" has not just been a matter of men taking the best for themselves and assigning the rest to women. It has also been a matter of perceiving the "worst" as being whatever women were perceived to be.[61] This interaction can be disrupted either by revaluing what women have been perceived to be, or by reassigning the attributes that comprise the social sexes, or both. . . . So long as equality analysis takes place in [a phallocentric society], reassignment of social sex attributes must itself operate unequally. My claim is also based on the quasi-empirical observation that women are willing to pay an increasingly heavy price to maintain at least some socially female modes of being, and that men are unwilling, or unasked, to pay a similar price to take them on. To take one example, reassigning childcare has not thus far meant assigning it to men or even sharing it with them; it has meant assigning it to poorer women. Despite a rapid increase in the number of married women in the full-time labor force, men's contributions to household tasks have remained astonishingly low.[62] For the sexual dialectic to yield anything transformative, we have got to take our social finger off one end of the scale.

As indicated above, making gender difference costless, even in the skewed terms by which we now measure "cost," seems just as likely to decrease the overlap between biological and social sex as ignoring what we perceive as gender difference in the hope that it will disappear or be "transformed." If it costs most men and women the same to stay home with the baby, parenting is more likely to be shared. (Currently, women have less to lose than men by foregoing paid employment for unpaid childcare, since both women's salaries *and* expectations are generally lower.) And if the social rewards of childrearing are closer to those of what we now think of as employment, making the two compatible can proceed from two directions instead of one.

It is, of course, possible that "social transvestitism" will not occur to any great extent, even if it becomes relatively costless. Perhaps biological or cultural imperatives do play a larger role than power and economics. I doubt it. But if it does turn out that, given a flat cost curve, most biological women opt for social womanhood and most biological men opt for social manhood and very few explore new modes of social existence, I'm not sure I'd care very much. The modernists may enjoy mixing things up for its own sake; me, I'm only in it for the equality. . . .

NOTES

1. In the 1970s, the first wave of feminist litigators chose this approach, and this led to the rather counterintuitive use of male plaintiffs in most of the major constitutional sex discrimination cases of the 1970s. See, e.g., *Califano v. Goldfarb*, 430 U.S. 199 (1977); *Weinberger v. Weisenfeld*, 420 U.S. 636 (1975); *Kahn v. Shevin*, 416 U.S. 351 (1974). For a sympathetic interpretation of this phenomenon, see Cole, "Strategies of Difference: Litigating for Women's Rights in a Man's World," 2 *J.L. & Inequality* 33, 53–92 (1984).
2. Williams, "The Equality Crisis: Some Reflections on Culture, Courts, and Feminism," reprinted here, Ch. 36 (hereinafter Williams, "The Equality Crisis"). . . .
3. Tussman & tenBroek, "The Equal Protection of the Laws," 37 *Calif. L. Rev.* 341, 344 (1949). . . .
4. See e.g., *Rostker v. Goldberg*, 453 U.S. 57 (1981); *Michael M. v. Superior Court*, 450 U.S. 464 (1981) (both holding strict scrutiny inapplicable to classifications based on actual or legal differences between the sexes).
5. The least critical symmetrical approaches are found in the work of male legal theorists. Richard Wasserstrom, for example, envisions the sexually equal society as one in which biological sex is "no more significant than eye color," and in which asking whether a new baby is a boy or a girl is no more common than asking whether it has large or small feet. Wasserstrom, "Racism, Sexism, and Preferential Treatment: An Approach to the Topics," 24 *UCLA L. Rev.* 581, 606 (1977). . . .
6. See Scales, "Toward a Feminist Jurisprudence," 56 *Ind. LJ.* 375, 430–34 (1981); see also E. Wolgast, *Equality and the Rights of Women* 61–63 (1980).
7. E. Wolgast, supra note 6, at 122. . . .
8. . . . Ibid. at 157. . . .
9. Law, "Rethinking Sex and the Constitution," 132 *U. Pa. L. Rev.* 955, 1007–13 (1984) (calling for equal treatment in all areas *except* reproduction, where an analysis based on an empowerment approach . . . should be adopted).
10. Kay, "Equality and Difference: The Case of Pregnancy." 1 *Berkeley Women's L.J.* 1, 27–37 (1985) (sex differences should be ignored, *except* during the time a female is actually pregnant).
11. See, e.g., ibid. at 22 (distinguishing the author's approach from one that might support separate spheres).

12. At one time, I called this model of equality one of "affirmation." See C. Littleton, "Alternative Models of Sexual Equality," address delivered at the Clara Brett Martin Workshop, University of Toronto (1984) (on file with the author). I have changed the terminology, however, because I am not advocating a "celebration" of women's difference, or even pushing the subversive potential of "jouissance." See [*Introduction to New French Feminisms: An Anthology* 3 (E. Marks & I. de Courtivron, eds. 1980)]; D. Cornell, "Equality and Gender Difference: Towards a Critical Theory of Equality" 17 (1983) (unpublished manuscript on file with the author). Such celebrations look too much like embracing our oppression when women do it, and too much like condescension when men do. Nor am I calling for an inversion of the hierarchical ordering of male and female modes of being (although I might not object to one). It does, however, seem affirming to be simply (simply?) accepted for what one is, not pushed into one side or the other of the great gender divide by economic and social pressures. At the risk of making it sound like too little to ask, then, I have chosen to call the model one of "acceptance."
13. See *Lemons v. City & County of Denver*, 17 Fair Empl. Prac. Cas. (BNA) 906 (D. Colo. Apr. 17, 1978) (rejecting a comparable worth claim that paying nurses less tha[n] real estate appraisers violates Title VII).
14. See C. Gilligan, *In a Different Voice* (1982).
15. 107 S. Ct. 683 (1987).
16. *Cal. Gov't Code* §§ 12900–12996 (West 1980 & Supp. 1987).
17. § 12945(b)(2).
18. 42 U.S.C. §§ 2000e-10 to -17 (1982).
19. Pub. L. No. 95–555, 92 Stat, 2076 (1987) (codified at 42 U.S.C. § 2000e(k)). . . .
20. *Cal. Fed.*, 107 S. Ct. at 688, 692.
21. Brief for the ACLU as amicus curiae, *Cal. Fed.*, 107 S. Ct. 682 (1987) (No. 85–494). In this case, the Union did not represent the views of its largest affiliate, the ACLU of Southern California, which has consistently supported the pregnancy disability legislation. See ibid. at A-2. The National Organization for Women made a similar argument, suggesting that state and federal law could be reconciled by requiring the employer to provide leave for disability arising from any source. Brief for the National Organization for Women as amicus curiae. *Cal. Fed.*, 107 S. Ct. 683 (1987) (No. 85–494).
22. Brief for Equal Rights Advocates as amicus curiae, *Cal. Fed.*, 107 S. Ct. 683 (1987) (No. 85–595).
23. Brief for the Coalition for Reproductive Equality in the Workplace (CREW) as amicus curiae. *Cal. Fed.*, 107 S. Ct. 683 (1987) (No. 85–494). I was the attorney of record for CREW, and the principal author of the CREW amicus brief.
24. Ibid. at 36–37.
25. The *Cal. Fed.* opinion, authored by Justice Marshall, does much to bring together the asymmetrical and symmetrical equality arguments. As alternative holdings, the opinion first defends the California law as consistent with equal employment opportunity. "By 'taking pregnancy into account,' California's pregnancy disability leave statute allows women, as well as men, to have families without losing their jobs." 107 S. Ct. as 694. The Court then states that the employer can satisfy both California law and demands for symmetry by providing leave for all forms of disability. Ibid. at 694–95.
26. This model has been articulated most fully by Catharine MacKinnon, and draws heavily on the work of radical feminist theorists such as Andrea Dworkin. See C. MacKinnon *Sexual Harass-*

ment of Working Women (1979) (examining sexual harassment in context of male power structure); MacKinnon, "Feminism, Marxism, Method and the State: Toward Feminist Jurisprudence," reprinted here (examining how traditional theories of "the state" perpetuate male power to exclude women's perspective) . . . ; A. Dworkin, *Our Blood* 96–111 (1976); A. Dworkin, *Pornography: Men Possessing Women* 13–24 (1979). . . .

27. DuBois, Dunlap, Gilligan, MacKinnon, & Menkel-Meadow, "Feminist Discourse, Moral Values, and the Law—A Conversation," 34 *Buffalo L. Rev.* 11, 27 (1985) (emphasis added).
28. See Rossi, "Sexual Equality: The Beginning of Ideology," in *Beyond Sex Role Stereotypes* 80, 87 (A. Kaplan & J. Bean eds. 1976)].
29. A. Allen, C. Littleton & C. Menkel-Meadow, "Law in a Different Voice," 15th National Conference on Women and the Law, Address by C. Menkel-Meadow (Mar. 31, 1984) (tape on file with the author.)
30. A. Lorde, "Age, Race, Class and Sex: Women Redefining Difference," in *Sister Outsider* 114, 122 [1984] (emphasis added).
31. 404 U.S. 71 (1971).
32. 429 U.S. 190 (1976). . . .
33. 416 U.S. 351 (1974).
34. 417 U.S. 484 (1974).
35. 429 U.S. 125 (1976).
36. 417 U.S. at 496–97
37. 107 S. Ct. 683 (1987). . . .
38. Such "equality with a vengeance" has been exhaustively documented by Lenore Weitzman, a sociologist who spent several years studying the concrete effects of California's adoption of "no fault" divorce. L. Weitzman, *The Divorce Revolution* (1985).
39. Weitzman's findings indicate that one year after divorce, the standard of living of male ex-spouses rises 43%, while the standard of living of female ex-spouses falls 73%. Weitzman, "The Economics of Divorce: Social and Economic Consequences of Property, Alimony, and Child Support," 28 *UCLA L. Rev.* 1181, 1251 (1980). She blames this economic disaster not on the concept of "no fault" divorce itself, but on the state legislature's failure to take into account that male and female partners to marriage usually stand in asymmetrical positions with respect to the job market. See Stix, "Disasters of the No-Fault Divorce," *L.A. Times*, Nov. 7, 1985, § V, at 3, col. 1.
40. Note, "Comparable Worth—A Necessary Vehicle for Pay Equity," 68 *Marq. L. Rev.* 93, 98 n.33 (1984). . . .
41. *McDonnell-Douglas Corp. v. Green*, 411 U.S. 792, 802 (1973). . . .
42. *Griggs v. Duke Power Co.*, 401 U.S. 424 (1971).
43. *Griggs*, 401 U.S. at 429, 431.
44. A court might question an employer's *post hoc* characterization of a job, see *Diaz v. Pan Am. World Airways, Inc.*, 442 F.2d 385 (5th Cir.) (finding the purpose of the airline business to be safe transportation, not comforting passengers), *cert. denied*, 404 U.S. 950 (1971), but it will still evaluate the business as it is, not as it might be if it were not male-biased.
45. This does not mean that Title VII could not be interpreted to allow such challenges, only that its current interpretation does not, Wendy William's optimistic reading to the contrary. See Williams, "Equality's Riddle: Pregnancy and the Equal Treatment/Special Treatment Debate," 13 *N.Y.U. Rev. L. & Soc. Change* 325, 331 (1985) . . . (disparate impact analysis is a doctrinal tool useful for "squeez[ing] the male tilt out of a purportedly neutral legal structure").
46. 417 U.S. 484 (1974).

47. *California Fed. Sav. & Loan Ass'n v. Guerra.* 33 Empl. Prac. Dec. (CCH) ¶ 34,227 (1984), *rev'd* 758 F.2d 390 (9th Cir. 1985), *aff'd*, 107 S. Ct. 683 (1987). . . .
48. 107 S. Ct. 683 (1987).
49. Equality as acceptance does not itself dictate whether this acceptance should be accomplished by (1) female and male workers sharing the disadvantage that the work place now visits on women alone—perhaps through requiring male employees to take on without extra pay some portion of the work of the absent female employees; (2) eliminating the disadvantage to women through some form of pregnancy leave rights; or (3) reshaping the structure itself so that no disadvantage arises at all—through more radical time-shifting, time-sharing work schedules, or through elimination of the work place-home dichotomy. While equality as acceptance would support arguments for all three, option (2) is probably the most viable currently.
50. Why bother with making these differences costless relative to each other if we can get rid of them altogether? My response is similar to that given to androgyny as an equality model: getting rid of difference in a system of male dominance means getting rid of *women's* differences. For example, "equality" in private law firm practice seems to mean that both women and men who take parenting leave fail to make partner; "equality" in academia seems to mean that both women and men whose research field is women's studies are not considered "serious" scholars. Cf. *Lynn v. Regents of the Univ. of Calif.*, 656 F.2d 1337 (9th Cir. 1981) (university's disdain for women's studies is evidence of sex discrimination), *cert. denied.* 459 U.S. 823 (1982). Similarly, my female students are consistently counseled to wear gray or navy blue "power suits" to job interviews (often with little string or silk "ties").

    Until such time as "getting rid of sex differences" has some chance of operating equally, it is an empty (perhaps deadening) promise for women. Moreover, it does not seem particularly unfair for women to demand a little equality now, for ourselves, without waiting for our grandchildren to "grow up free." Nor does it seem unjustified for women to be accepted as equal members of this society in spite of our cultural skewing—after all, men are skewed too, albeit differently. Of course, there is the obligatory fallback position that the opportunity for "social transvestitism" I envision as a result of this strategy will actually hasten the day that sex differences cease to operate for most people. However, societies are not built by or for people who may never exist, nor even for the purpose of creating such people.
51. See e.g., Kay, supra note 10; Law, supra note 9 (both advocating a symmetrical model as the norm, with some area of asymmetry).
52. Williams, "The Equality Crisis," supra note [2], at 190.
53. See e.g., S. Rep. No. 826, 96th Cong., 2d Sess. 159, 161, reprinted in 1980 *U.S. Code Cong. & Admin. News* 2612, 2649–51. But see C. Enloe, *Does Khaki Become You?* 15 (1983) (women in combat would confuse men's certainty about their male identity).
54. Aid to Families with Dependent Children (AFDC) programs might be the culture's partial recognition of the importance of the occupation of childcare. However, that AFDC payments are seen as a response to need, rather than an earned income, makes them vulnerable to political windshifting. . . . In addition, social labeling of AFDC payments as "charity" rather than earnings has a necessary impact on recipients' self-image and sense of worth. Altering the basis and measurement of AFDC payments by making them the equivalent of military pay could go a long way toward alleviating both the feminization of poverty and the negative impact of social welfare programs on the purported beneficiaries. Additionally, the educational programs available in the military and by virtue of financial assistance following military service are far superior to the paltry "job training" programs currently available to welfare recipients.

55. 442 U.S. 256 (1979).
56. See W. Biebly & J. Baron, "Men and Women at Work: Sex Segregation and Statistical Discrimination" 27–28 (1985) (unpublished manuscript on file with the author). . . .
57. Ibid. at 22–33.
58. Olsen, "The Sex of Law 4–1" (1984).
59. Goldstein, "Pornography and Its Discontents," *Village Voice*, Oct. 16, 1984, at 19, 44.
60. Olsen, "The Family and the Market: A Study of Ideology and Legal Reform," 96 *Harv. L. Rev.* 1497, 1598 (1983). Olsen describes androgyny as arising from the synergism of male and female, rather than their union, and thus yielding characteristics not otherwise displayed by either. How this process is to take place is not explained.
61. Does the Dictionary of Occupation Titles rate childcare as unskilled work because it "really" is, or only because those speaking in the public discourse never saw or formalized the instruction that took place every day that we watched our mothers or cared for younger children ourselves? See Briggs, "Guess Who Has the Most Complex Job?," reprinted in B. Babcock, A. Freedman, E. Norton & S. Ross, *Sex Discrimination and the Law* 203 (1973). If the reply is that childcare is "instinctual," then so is tool use, but neither point is relevant. Modern human childrearing is as different from instinctual parental behavior as modern human tool use is different from its instinctual counterpart.
62. P. Roos, *Gender & Work* 13–19 (1985).

The Generalized and the Concrete Other: The Kohlberg-Gilligan Controversy and Moral Theory

Benhabib's project is to articulate an "anticipatory-utopian critique of universalistic moral theories from a feminist perspective." In pursuit of this aim, she briefly recounts the history of universalistic moral philosophy, pinpoints two major weaknesses in this view, and sketches an alternative account of moral inquiry and moral relations. Throughout her discussion, Benhabib reminds us of various ways in which conceptions of the person and moral thought are gender coded.

Benhabib presents a deflationary account of the rise of social contract theory. Charging that social contract theory treats the self as disembedded and disembodied, she urges that this approach to moral philosophy marginalizes women's experience and privileges the fantasies of advantaged men. According to Benhabib, contemporary universalistic moral theory is no improvement, for it conceives the moral subject as a generalized other. The generalized other represents persons as identical rational beings and thus eradicates individuality and difference among moral subjects. According to Benhabib, this view of the moral subject undercuts this theory's methods of moral inquiry. Reversibility or taking the viewpoint of the other is an empty exercise, since the other is indistinguishable from oneself. Universalizability or treating similar cases similarly is not feasible since one cannot identify similar situations unless one can individuate and characterize situations, but one cannot individuate and characterize situations unless one knows the people who are involved. Benhabib does not advocate repudiating the norms of formal equality and reciprocity and the moral feelings of respect, duty, worthiness, and dignity that are associated with universalistic moral theory. However, moral theory must recognize that every generalized other is also a concrete other—a person with interpersonal ties and a cultural background who is entitled to recognition as a distinctive individual. To achieve this balance, Benhabib urges, we should adopt Jürgen Habermas' communicative social ethic.

—D.T.M.

Chapter 38

Seyla Benhabib

The Generalized and the Concrete Other: The Kohlberg-Gilligan Controversy and Moral Theory

Can there be a feminist contribution to moral philosophy? Can those men and women who view the gender-sex system of our societies as oppressive, and who regard women's emancipation as essential to human liberation, criticize, analyze, and when necessary, replace the traditional categories of moral philosophy so as to contribute to women's emancipation and human liberation? By focusing on the controversy generated by Carol Gilligan's work, this essay seeks to outline such a feminist contribution to moral philosophy.

I. THE KOHLBERG-GILLIGAN CONTROVERSY

Carol Gilligan's research in cognitive, developmental moral psychology recapitulates a pattern made familiar to us by Thomas Kuhn.[1] Noting a discrepancy between the claims of the original research paradigm and the data, Gilligan and her coworkers first extended this paradigm to accommodate anomalous results. This extension then allows them to see some other problems in a new light; subsequently, the basic paradigm of the study of the development of moral judgment, according to Lawrence Kohlberg's model, is fundamentally revised. Gilligan and her coworkers now maintain that Kohlbergian theory is valid only for measuring the development of one aspect of moral orientation that focuses on the ethics of justice and rights.

In the 1980 article "Moral Development in Late Adolescence and Adulthood: A Critique and Reconstruction of Kohlberg's Theory," Murphy and Gilligan note that moral judgment data from a longitudinal study of twenty-six undergraduates scored by Kohlberg's revised manual replicate his original findings that a significant percentage of subjects appear to regress from adolescence to adulthood.[2] The persistence of this relativistic regression suggests a need to revise the theory. In this paper, they propose a distinction between "postconventional formalism" and "postconventional contextualism." While the postconventional type of reasoning solves the problem of relativism by constructing a system that derives a solution to all moral problems from concepts like social contract or natural rights, the second approach finds the solution in the following way: "While no answer may be objectively right in the sense of being context-free, some answers and some ways of thinking are better than others" (Murphy and Gilligan 1980: 83). The extension of the original paradigm from postconventional formalist to postconventional contextual then leads Gilligan to see some other discrepancies in the theory in a new light, especially women's persistently low score when compared to their male peers. Distinguishing between the ethics of justice and rights and the ethics of care and responsibility allows her to account for women's moral development and the cognitive skills they show in a new way. Women's moral judgment is more contextual, more immersed in the details of relationships and narratives. Women show a greater propensity to take the standpoint of the "particular other," and appear more adept at revealing feelings of empathy and sympathy required by this. Once these cognitive characteristics are seen not as deficiencies but as essential components of adult moral reasoning at the postconventional stage, then women's apparent moral confusion of judgment becomes a sign of their strength. Agreeing with Piaget that a developmental theory hangs from its vertex of maturity, "the point towards which progress is traced," a change in "the definition of maturity," writes Gilligan, "does not simply alter the description of the highest stage but recasts the understanding of development, changing the entire account."[3] The contextuality, narrativity, and the specificity of women's moral judgment is not a sign of weakness or deficiency, but a manifestation of a vision of moral maturity that views the self as being immersed in a network of relationships with others. According to this vision, the respect for each others' needs and the mutuality of effort to satisfy them sustain moral growth and development.

When confronted with such a challenge, it is common for adherents of an old research paradigm to respond by arguing (a) that the data base does not support the conclusions drawn by revisionists, (b) that some of the new conclusions can be accommodated by the old theory, and (c) that the new and old paradigms have different object domains and are not concerned with explaining the same phenomena at all. In his response to Gilligan, Kohlberg has followed all three alternatives.

A. The Data Base

In his 1984 "Synopses and Detailed Replies to Critics," Kohlberg argues that available data on cognitive moral development do not report differences among children and adolescents of both sexes with respect to justice reasoning.[4] "The only studies," he writes, "showing fairly frequent sex differences are those of adults, usually of spouse housewives. Many of the studies comparing adult males and females without controlling for education and job differences . . . do report sex differences in favor of males" (Kohlberg 1984: 347). Kohlberg maintains that these latter findings are not incompatible with his theory.[5] For, according to this theory, the attainment of stages four and five depends upon experiences of participation, responsibility, and role taking in the secondary institutions of society such as the work place and government, from which women have been and still are, to a large extent, excluded. The data, he concludes, do not damage the validity of his theory, but show the necessity for controlling for such factors as education and employment when assessing sex differences in adult moral reasoning.

B. Accommodation Within the Old Theory

Kohlberg now agrees with Gilligan that "the acknowledgement of an orientation of care and response usefully enlarges the moral domain" (Kohlberg 1984: 340). In his view, though, justice and rights, care and responsibility, are not two *tracks* of moral development, but two moral *orientations*. The rights orientation and the care orientation are not bipolar or dichotomous. Rather, the care-and-response orientation is directed primarily to relations of special obligations to family, friends, and group members, "relations which often include or presuppose general obligations of respect, fairness, and contract" (Kohlberg 1984: 349). Kohlberg resists the conclusion that these differences are strongly "sex related"; instead, he views the choice of orientation "to be primarily a function of setting and dilemma, not sex" (Kohlberg 1984: 350).

C. Object Domain of the Two Theories

In an earlier response to Gilligan, Kohlberg had argued as follows:

> Carol Gilligan's ideas, while interesting, were not really welcome to us, for two reasons . . . The latter, we thought, was grist for Jane Loewinger's mill in studying stages of ego development, but not for studying the specifically moral dimension in reasoning . . . Following Piaget, my colleagues and I have had the greatest confidence that reasoning about justice would lend itself to a formal structuralist or rationalist analysis . . . whereas questions about the nature of the "good life" have not been as amenable to this type of statement.[6]

In his 1984 reply to his critics, this distinction between moral and ego development is further refined. Kohlberg divides the ego domain into the cognitive, interpersonal, and moral functions (Kohlberg 1984: 398). Since, however, ego development is a necessary but not sufficient condition for moral development, in his view, the latter can be studied independently of the former. In light of this clarification, Kohlberg regards Murphy's and Gilligan's stage of "post-conventional contextualism" as being more concerned with questions of ego as opposed to moral development. While not wanting to maintain that the acquisition of moral competencies ends with reaching adulthood, Kohlberg nevertheless insists that adult moral and ego development studies only reveal the presence of "soft" as opposed to "hard" stages. The latter are irreversible in sequence and integrally related to one another in the sense that a subsequent stage grows out of and presents a better solution to problems confronted at an earlier stage.[7]

It will be up to latter-day historians of science to decide whether, with these admissions and qualifications, Kohlbergian theory has entered the phase of "ad-hocism," in Imre Lakatos's words,[8] or whether Gilligan's challenge, as well as that of other critics, has moved this research paradigm to a new phase, in which new problems and conceptualizations will lead to more fruitful results.

What concerns me in this paper is the question, what can feminist theory contribute to this debate? Since Kohlberg himself regards an interaction between moral philosophy and the empirical study of moral development as essential to his theory, the insights of contemporary feminist philosophy can be brought to bear upon some aspects of his theory. I want to define two premises as constituents of feminist theorizing. First, for feminist theory, the gender-sex system is not a contingent but an essential way in which social reality is organized, symbolically divided, and experienced. By the "gender-sex" system, I mean the social-historical, symbolic constitution, and interpretation of the differences of the sexes. The gender-sex system is the context in which the self develops an *embodied* identity, a certain mode of being in one's body and of living the body. The self becomes an *I* in that it appropriates from the human community a mode of psychically, socially, and symbolically experiencing its bodily identity. Societies and cultures reproduce embodied individuals through the gender-sex system.[9]

Second, the historically known gender-sex systems have contributed to the oppression and exploitation of women. The task of feminist critical theory is to uncover where and how this occurs and to develop an emancipatory and reflective analysis that aids women in their struggles to overcome oppression and exploitation. Feminist theory can contribute to this task in two ways: by developing an *explanatory-diagnostic analysis* of women's oppression across history, cultures, and societies; and by articulating an *anticipatory-utopian critique* of the norms and values of our current society and culture, which projects new modes of togetherness and of relating to ourselves and to nature in the future. Whereas the first aspect of feminist theory requires critical, social-scientific research, the second is primarily normative and philosophical: it involves the clarification of moral and political principles, both at the meta-ethical level, with respect to the *logic of justification*, and at the substantive, normative level with reference to their concrete content.[10]

In this chapter, I shall try to articulate such an anticipatory-utopian critique of universalistic moral theories from a feminist perspective. I want to argue that the *definition* of the moral domain, as well as of the ideal of *moral autonomy*, not only in Kohlberg's theory but also in universalistic, contractarian theories from Hobbes to Rawls, leads to a *privatization* of women's experience and to the exclusion of its consideration from a moral point of view. In this tradition, the moral self is viewed as a *disembedded* and *disembodied* being. This conception of the self reflects aspects of male experience; the "relevant other" in this theory is never the sister but always the brother. This vision of the self is incompatible with the very criteria of reversibility and universalizability advocated by defenders of universalism. A universalistic moral theory restricted to the standpoint of the "generalized other" falls into epistemic incoherencies that jeopardize its claim to adequately fulfill reversibility and universalizability.

Universalistic moral theories in the western tradition from Hobbes to Rawls are *substitutionalist*, in the sense that the universalism they defend is defined surreptitiously by identifying the experiences of a specific group of subjects as the paradigmatic case of all humans. These subjects are invariably white, male adults who are propertied or professional. I want to distinguish *substitutionalist* from *interactive* universalism. Interactive universalism acknowledges the plurality of modes of being human and the differences among humans, without endorsing all these pluralities and differences as morally and politically valid. While agreeing that normative disputes can be rationally settled, and that fairness, reciprocity, and some procedure of universalizability are constituents, that is, necessary conditions of the moral standpoint, interactive universalism regards difference as a starting point for reflection and action. In this sense, "universality" is a regulative ideal that does not deny our embodied and embedded identity, but aims at developing moral attitudes and encouraging political transformations that can yield a point of view acceptable to all. Universality is not the ideal consenses of fictitiously defined selves, but the concrete process, in politics and morals, of the struggle of concrete, embodied selves, striving for autonomy.

II. JUSTICE AND THE AUTONOMOUS SELF IN SOCIAL CONTRACT THEORIES

Kohlberg defines the privileged object domain of moral philosophy and psychology as follows:

> We say that *moral* judgments or principles have the central function of resolving interpersonal or social conflicts, that is, conflicts of claims or rights. . . . Thus moral judgments and principles imply a notion of equilibrium, or reversibility of claims. In this sense they ultimately involve some reference to justice, at least insofar as they define "hard" structural stages. (Kohlberg 1984: 216)

Kohlberg's conception of the moral domain is based upon a strong differentiation between justice and the good life.[11] This is also one of the cornerstones of his critique of Gilligan. Although acknowledging that Gilligan's elucidation of a care-and-responsibility orientation "usefully enlarges the moral domain" (Kohlberg 1984: 340), Kohlberg defines the domain of *special relationships of obligation* to which care and responsibility are oriented as follows: "the spheres of kinship, love, friendship, and sex that elicit considerations of care are usually understood to be spheres of personal decision-making, as are, for instance, the problems of marriage and divorce" (Kohlberg 1984: 229–30). The care orientation is said thus to concern domains that are more "personal" than "moral in the sense of the formal point of view" (Kohlberg 1984: 360). Questions of the good life, pertaining to the nature of our relationships of kinship, love, friendship, and sex, on the one hand, are included in the moral domain but, on the other hand, are named "personal" as opposed to "moral" issues.

Kohlberg proceeds from a definition of morality that begins with Hobbes, in the wake of the dissolution of the Aristotelian-Christian world view. Ancient and medieval moral systems, by contrast, show the following structure: a definition of man-as-he-ought-to-be, a definition of man-as-he-is, and the articulation of a set of rules or precepts that can lead man-as-he-is into man-as-he-ought-to-be.[12] In such moral systems, the rules that govern just relations within the human community are embedded in a more encompassing concept of the good life. This good life, the *telos* of man, is defined ontologically with reference to man's place in the cosmos at large.

The destruction of the ancient and medieval teleological concept of nature through the attack of medieval nominalism and modern science, the emergence of capitalist exchange relations, and the subsequent division of the social structure into the economy, the polity, civil associations, and the domestic-intimate sphere, radically alter moral theory. Modern theorists claim that the ultimate purposes of nature are unknown. Morality is thus emancipated from cosmology and from an all-encompassing world view that normatively limits man's relation to nature. The distinction between justice and the good life, as it is formulated by early contract theorists, aims at defending this privacy and autonomy of the self, first in the religious sphere, and then in the scientific and philosophical spheres of "free thought" as well.

Justice alone becomes the center of moral theory when bourgeois individuals in a disenchanted universe face the task of creating the legitimate basis of the social order for themselves. What "ought" to be is now defined as what all would have rationally to agree to in order to ensure civil peace and prosperity (Hobbes, Locke); or the "ought" is derived from the rational form of the moral law alone (Rousseau, Kant). As long as the social bases of cooperation and the rights-claims of individuals are respected, the autonomous bourgeois subject can define the good life as his mind and conscience dictate.

The transition to modernity does not only privatize the self's relation to the cosmos and to ultimate questions of religion and being. First, with western modernity the concept of privacy is so enlarged that an intimate domestic-familial sphere is subsumed under it. Relations of "kinship, friendship, love, and sex," indeed, as Kohlberg takes them to be, come to be viewed as spheres of "personal decision-making." At the beginning of modern moral and political theory, however, the "personal" nature of these spheres does not mean the recognition of equal, female autonomy, but rather the removal of gender relations from the sphere of justice. While the bourgeois male celebrates his transition from conventional to postconventional morality, from socially accepted rules of justice to their generation in light of the principles of a social contract, the domestic sphere remains at the conventional level. The sphere of justice, from Hobbes through Locke and Kant, is regarded as the domain wherein independent, male heads-of-household transact with one another, while the domestic-intimate sphere is put beyond the pale of justice and restricted to the reproductive and affective needs of the bourgeois *pater familias.* Agnes Heller has named this domain the "household of the emotions."[13] An entire domain of human activity, namely, nurture, reproduction, love, and care, which becomes the woman's lot in the course of the development of modern, bourgeois society, is excluded from moral and political considerations, and confined to the realm of "nature."

Through a brief historical genealogy of social contract theories, I want to examine the distinction between justice and the good life as it is translated into the split between the public and the domestic. This analysis will also allow us to see the implicit ideal of autonomy cherished by this tradition.

At the beginning of modern moral and political philosophy stands a powerful metaphor: the "state of nature." At times this metaphor is said to be fact. Thus, in his *Second Treatise of Civil Government,* John Locke reminds us of "the two men in the desert island, mentioned by Garcilaso de la Vega . . . or a Swiss and an Indian, in the woods of America."[14] At other times it is acknowledged as fiction. Thus, Kant dismisses the colorful reveries of his predecessors and transforms the "state of nature" from an empirical fact into a transcendental concept. The state of nature comes to represent the idea of Privatrecht, under which is subsumed the right of property and "thinglike rights of a personal nature" (*auf dingliche Natur persönliche Rechte*), which the male head of household exercises over his wife, children, and servants.[15] Only Thomas Hobbes compounds fact and fiction, and against those who consider it strange "that Nature should thus dissociate, and render men apt to invade, and destroy one another,"[16] he asks each man who does not trust "this Inference, made from the passions," to reflect why "when taking a journey, he arms himself, and seeks to go well accompanied; when going to sleep, he locks his dores; when even in his house he locks his chests. . . . Does he not there as much accuse mankind by his actions, as I do by my words?" (Hobbes, *Leviathan,* 187). The state of nature is the looking glass of these early bourgeois thinkers in which they and their societies are magnified, purified, and reflected in their original, naked verity. The state of nature is both nightmare (Hobbes) and utopia (Rousseau). In it, the bourgeois male recognizes his flaws, fears, and anxieties, as well as his dreams.

The varying content of this metaphor is less significant than its simple and profound message: in the beginning man was alone. Again, it is Hobbes who gives this thought its clearest formulation. "Let us consider men . . . as if but even now sprung out of the earth, and suddenly, like mushrooms, come to full maturity, without all kind of engagement to each other."[17] This vision of men as mushrooms is an ultimate picture of autonomy. The female, the mother of whom every individual is born, is now replaced by the earth. The denial of being born of woman frees the male ego from the most natural and basic bond of dependence. Nor is the picture very different for Rousseau's noble savage who, wandering wantonly through the woods, occasionally mates with a female and then seeks rest.[18]

The state-of-nature metaphor provides a vision of the autonomous self: this is a narcissist who sees the world in his own image; who has no awareness of the limits of his own desires and passions; and who cannot see himself through the eyes of another. The narcissism of this sovereign self is destroyed by the presence of the other. As Hegel expresses it:

> Self-consciousness is faced by another self-consciousness; it has come *out of itself.* This has a twofold significance: first, is has *lost* itself, for it finds itself as an *other* being; secondly, in doing so it has superseded the other, for it does not see the other as an essential being, but in the other sees its own self.[19]

The story of the autonomous male ego is the saga of this initial sense of *loss* in confrontation with the other, and the gradual recovery from this original narcissistic wound through the sobering experience of war, fear, domination, anxiety, and death. The last installment in this drama is the social contract: the establishment of the law to govern all. Having been thrust out of their narcissistic universe into a world of insecurity by their sibling brothers, these individuals have to reestablish the authority of the father in the image of the law. The early bourgeois individual not only has no mother but no father as well; rather, he strives to reconstitute the father in his own self-image. What is usually celebrated in the annals of modern moral and political theory as the dawn of liberty is precisely this destruction of political patriarchy in bourgeois society.

The constitution of political authority civilizes sibling rivalry by turning their attention from war to property, from vanity to science, from conquest to luxury. The original narcissism is not transformed; only now ego boundaries are clearly defined. The law reduces insecurity, the fear of being engulfed by the other, by defining mine and thine. Jealousy is not eliminated but tamed; as long as each can keep what is his and attain more by fair rules of the game, he is entitled to it. Competition is domesticized and channeled toward acquisition. The law contains anxiety by defining rigidly the boundaries between self and other, but the law does not cure anxiety. The anxiety that the other is always on the look to interfere in your space and appropriate what is yours; the anxiety that you will be subordinated to his will; the anxiety that a group of brothers will usurp the law in the name of the "will of all" and destroy "the general will," the will of the absent father, remains. The law teaches how to repress anxiety and to sober narcissism, but the constitution of the self is not altered. The establishment of private rights and duties does not overcome the inner wounds of the self; it only forces them to become less destructive.

This imaginary universe of early moral and political theory has had an amazing hold upon the modern consciousness. From Freud to Piaget, the relationship to the brother is viewed as the humanizing experience that teaches us to become social, responsible adults.[20]

As a result of the hold of this metaphor upon our imagination, we have also come to inherit a number of philosophical prejudices. For Rawls and Kohlberg, as well, the autonomous self is disembedded and disembodied; moral impartiality is learning to recognize the claims of the other who is just like oneself; fairness is public justice; a public system of rights and duties is the best way to arbitrate conflict, to distribute rewards, and to establish claims.

Yet this is a strange world: it is one in which individuals are grown up before they have been born; in which boys are men before they have been children; a world where neither mother, nor sister, nor wife exist. The question is less what Hobbes says about men and women, or what Rousseau sees the role of Sophie to be in Émile's education. The point is that in this universe, the experience of the early modern female has no place. Women are simply what men are not. Women are not autonomous, independent, and aggressive but nurturant, not competitive but giving, not public but private. The world of the female is constituted by a series of negations. *She* is simply what *he* happens not to be. Her identity becomes defined by a lack—the lack of autonomy, the lack of independence, the lack of the phallus. The narcissistic male takes her to be just like himself, only his opposite.

It is not the misogynist prejudices of early modern moral and political theory alone that lead to women's exclusion. It is the very constitution of a sphere of discourse that bans the female from history to the realm of nature, from public light to the interior of the household, from the civilizing effect of culture to the repetitious burden of nurture and reproduction. The public sphere, the sphere of justice, moves in historicity, whereas the private sphere, the sphere of care and intimacy, is unchanged and timeless. It pulls us toward the earth even when we, as Hobbesian mushrooms, strive to pull away from it. The dehistoricization of the private realm signifies that, as the male ego celebrates his passage from nature to culture, from conflict to consensus, women remain in a timeless universe, condemned to repeat the cycles of life.

This split between the public sphere of justice, in which history is made, and the atemporal realm of the household, in which like is reproduced, is internalized by the male ego. The dichotomies are not only without but within. He himself is divided into the public persona and the private individual. Within his chest clash the law of reason and the inclination of nature, the brilliance of cognition and the obscurity of emotion. Caught between the moral law and the starry heaven above and the earthly body below,[21] the autonomous self strives for unity. But the antagonism—between autonomy and nurturance, independence and bonding, sovereignty of the self and relations to others—remains. In the discourse of modern moral and political theory, these dichotomies are reified as being essential to the constitution of the self. While men humanize outer nature through labor, inner nature remains ahistorical, dark, and obscure. I want to suggest that contemporary universalist moral theory has inherited this dichotomy between autonomy and nurturance, independence and bonding, the sphere of justice and the domestic, personal realm. This becomes most visible in its attempt to restrict the moral point of view to the perspective of the "generalized other."

III. THE GENERALIZED VERSUS THE CONCRETE OTHER

Let me describe two concepts of self-other relations that delineate both moral perspectives and interactional structures. I shall name the first the standpoint of the "generalized"[22] and the second that of the "concrete" other. In contemporary moral theory, these concepts are viewed as incompatible, even as antagonistic. These two perspectives reflect the dichotomies and splits of early modern moral and political theory between autonomy and nurturance, independence and bonding, the public and the domestic, and more broadly, between justice and the good life. The content of the generalized as well as the concrete other is shaped by the dichotomous characterization, which we have inherited from the modern tradition.

The standpoint of the generalized other requires us to view each and every individual as a rational being entitled to the same rights and duties we would want to ascribe to ourselves. In assuming this standpoint, we abstract from the individuality and concrete identity of the other. We assume that the other, like ourselves, is a being who has concrete needs, desires, and affects, but what constitutes moral dignity is not what differentiates us from each other, but rather what we, as speaking and acting rational agents, have in common. Our relation to the other is governed by the norms of *formal equality* and *reciprocity:* each is entitled to expect and to assume from us what we can expect and assume from him or her. The norms of our interactions are primarily public and institutional ones. If I have a right to x, then you have the duty not to hinder me from enjoying x and conversely. In treating you in accordance with these norms, I confirm in your person the rights of humanity and I have a legitimate right to expect that you will do the same in relation to me. The moral categories that accompany such interactions are those of right, obligation, and entitlement; the corresponding moral feelings are those of respect, duty, worthiness, and dignity.

The standpoint of the concrete other, by contrast, requires us to view each and every rational being as an individual with a concrete history, identity, and affective-emotional constitution. In assuming this standpoint, we abstract from what constitutes our commonality. We seek to comprehend the needs of the other, his or her motivations, what he or she searches for and desires. Our relation to the other is governed by the norms of *equity* and *complementary reciprocity:* each is entitled to expect and to assume from the other forms of behavior through which the other feels recognized and confirmed as a concrete, individual being with specific needs, talents, and capacities. Our differences in this case complement rather than exclude one another. The norms of our interaction are usually private, noninstitutional ones. They are norms of friendship, love, and care. These norms require in various ways that I exhibit more than the simple assertion of my rights and duties in the face of your needs. In treating you in accordance with the norms of friendship, love, and care, I confirm not only your *humanity* but also your human *individuality.* The moral categories that accompany such interactions are those of responsibility, bonding, and sharing. The corresponding moral feelings are those of love, care, sympathy, and solidarity.

In contemporary universalist moral psychology and moral theory, it is the viewpoint of the "generalized other" that predominates. In his article on "Justice as Reversibility: The Claim to Moral Adequacy of a Highest Stage of Moral Judgment," for example, Kohlberg argues that

> moral judgments involve role-taking, taking the viewpoint of the others conceived as *subjects* and coordinating these viewpoints. . . . Second, equilibrated moral judgments involve principles of justice or fairness. A moral situation in disequilibrium is one in which there are unresolved, conflicting claims. A resolution of the situation is one in which each is "given his due" according to some principle of justice that can be recognized as fair by all the conflicting parties involved.[23]

Kohlberg regards Rawls's concept of "reflective equilibrium" as a parallel formulation of the basic idea of reciprocity, equality, and fairness intrinsic to all moral judgments. The Rawlsian "veil of ignorance," in Kohlberg's judgment, not only exemplifies the formalist idea of universalizability but that of perfect reversibility as well.[24] The idea behind the veil of ignorance is described as follows:

> The decider is to initially decide from a point of view *that ignores his identity* (veil of ignorance) under the assumption that decisions are governed by maximizing values from a viewpoint of rational egoism in considering each party's interest. [Kohlberg 1981: 200; my emphasis]

What I would like to question is the assumption that "taking the viewpoint of others" is truly compatible with this notion of fairness as reasoning behind a "veil of ignorance."[25] The problem is that the defensible kernel of the ideas of reciprocity and fairness are thereby identified with the perspective of the disembedded and disembodied generalized other. Now since Kohlberg presents his research subjects with hypothetically constructed moral dilemmas, it may be thought that his conception of "taking the standpoint of the other" is not subject to the epistemic restrictions that apply to the Rawlsian original position. Subjects in Kohlbergian interviews do not stand behind a veil of ignorance. However, the very *language* in which Kohlbergian dilemmas are presented incorporate these epistemic restrictions. For example, in the famous Heinz dilemma, as in others, the motivations of the druggist as a concrete individual, as well as the history of the individuals involved, are excluded as irrelevant to the definition of the moral problems at hand. In these dilemmas, individuals and their moral positions are represented by abstracting from the narrative history of the self and its motivations. Gilligan also notes that the implicit moral epistemology of Kohlbergian dilemmas frustrates women, who want to phrase these hypothetical dilemmas in a more contextual voice, attuned to the standpoint of the concrete other. The result is that

> though several of the women in the abortion study clearly articulate a post-conventional meta-ethical position, none of them are considered principled in their normative moral judgments of Kohlberg's hypothetical dilemmas. Instead, the women's judgments point toward an identification of the violence inherent in the dilemma itself, which is seen to compromise the justice of any of its possible resolutions. [Gilligan 1982: 101]

Through an immanent critique of the theories of Kohlberg and Rawls, I want to show that ignoring the standpoint of the concrete other leads to epistemic incoherence in universalistic moral theories. The problem can be stated as follows: according to Kohlberg and Rawls, moral reciprocity involves the capacity to take the standpoint of the other, to put oneself imaginatively in the place of the other, but under conditions of the "veil of ignorance," the *other as different from the self* disappears. Unlike in previous contract theories, in this case the other is not constituted through projection, but as a consequence of total abstraction from his or her identity. Differences are not denied; they become irrelevant. The Rawlsian self does not know

> his place in society, his class position or status; nor does he know his fortune in the distribution of natural assets and abilities, his intelligence and strength, and the like. Nor, again, does anyone know his conception of the good, the particulars of his rational plan of life, or even the special features of his psychology such as his aversion to risk or liability to optimism or pessimism.[26]

Let us ignore for a moment whether such selves who also do not know "the particular circumstances of their own society" can know anything at all that is relevant to the human condition, and ask instead, are these individuals *human selves* at all? In his attempt to do justice to Kant's conception of noumenal agency, Rawls recapitulates a basic problem with the Kantian conception of the self, namely, that noumenal selves cannot be *individuated.* If all that belongs to them as embodied, affective, suffering creatures, their memory and history, their ties and relations to others, are to be subsumed under the phenomenal realm, then what we are left with is an empty mask that is everyone and no one. Michael Sandel points out that the difficulty in Rawls's conception derives from his attempt to be consistent with the Kantian concept of the autonomous self, as a being freely choosing his or her own ends in life.[27] However, this moral and political concept of autonomy slips into a metaphysics according to which it is meaningful to define a self independently of *all* the ends it may choose and all and any conceptions of the good it may hold (Sandel 1984: 47ff.). At this point we must ask whether the *identity* of any human self can be defined with reference to its capacity for agency alone. Identity does not refer to my potential for choice alone, but to the actuality of my choices, namely, to how I, as a finite, concrete, embodied individual, shape and fashion the circumstances of my birth and family, linguistic, cultural, and gender identity into a coherent narrative that stands as my life's story. Indeed, if we recall that every autonomous being is one born of others and not, as Rawls, following Hobbes, assumes, a being "not bound by prior moral ties to another,"[28] the question becomes: how does this finite, embodied creature constitute into a coherent narrative those episodes of choice and limit, agency and suffering, initiative and dependence? The self is not a thing, a substrate, but the protagonist of a life's tale. The conception of selves who can be individuated prior to their moral ends is incoherent.

If this concept of the self as a mushroom, behind a veil of ignorance, is incoherent, then it follows that there is no real *plurality* of perspectives in the Rawlsian original position, but only a *definitional identity.* For Rawls, as Sandel observes, "our individuating characteristics are given empirically, by the distinctive concatenation of wants and desires, aims and attributes, purposes and ends that come to characterize human beings in the particularity" (Sandel 1984: 51). But how are we supposed to know what these wants and desires are independently of knowing something about the person who holds these wants, desires, aims and attributes? Is there perhaps an "essence" of anger that is the same for each angry individual; an essence of ambition that is distinct from ambitious selves? I fail to see how individuating characteristics can be ascribed to a transcendental self who can have any and none of these, who can be all or none of them.

If selves who are epistemologically and metaphysically prior to their individuating characteristics, as Rawls takes them to be, cannot be human selves at all; if, therefore, there is no human *plurality* behind the veil of ignorance but only *definitional identity;* then this has consequences for criteria of reversibility and universalizability said to be a constituent of the moral point of view. Definitional identity leads to *incomplete reversibility,* for the primary requisite of reversibility, namely, a coherent distinction between me and you, the self and the other, cannot be sustained under these circumstances. Under conditions of the veil of ignorance, the other disappears.

It is no longer plausible to maintain that such a standpoint can universalize adequately. Kohlberg views the veil of ignorance not only as exemplifying reversibility but universalizability as well. This is the idea that "we must be willing to live with our judgment or decision when we trade places with others in the situation being judged" (Kohlberg 1981: 197). But the question is, *which* situation? Can moral situations be individuated independently of our knowledge of the agents involved in these situations, of their histories, attitudes, characters, and desires? Can I describe a situation as one of arrogance or hurt pride without knowing something about you as a concrete other? Can I know how to distinguish between a breach of confidence and a harmless slip of the tongue, without knowing your history and your character? Moral situations, like moral emotions and attitudes, can only be individuated if they are evaluated in light of our knowledge of the history of the agents involved in them.

While every procedure of universalizability presupposes that "like cases ought to be treated alike" or that I should act in such a way that I should also be willing that all others in a like situation act like me, the most difficult aspect of any such procedure is to know what constitutes a "like" situation or what it would mean for another to be exactly in a situation like mine. Such a process of reasoning, to be at all viable, must involve the viewpoint of the concrete other, for situations, to paraphrase Stanley Cavell, do not come like "envelopes and golden finches," ready for definition and description, "nor like apples ripe for grading."[29] When we morally disagree, for example, we do not only disagree about the principles involved; very often we disagree because what I see as a lack of generosity on your part, you construe as your legitimate right not to do something; we disagree because what you see as jealousy on my part, I view as my desire to have more of your attention. Universalistic moral theory neglects such everyday, interactional morality and assumes that the public standpoint of justice, and our quasi-public personalities as right-bearing individuals, are the center of moral theory.[30]

Kohlberg emphasizes the dimension of ideal role-taking or taking the viewpoint of the other in moral judgment. Because he defines the other as the generalized other, however, he perpetrates one of the fundamental errors of Kantian moral theory. Kant's error was to assume that I, as a pure rational agent for reasoning for myself, could reach a conclusion that would be acceptable for all at all times and places.[31] In Kantian moral theory, moral agents are like geometricians in different rooms who, reasoning alone for themselves, all arrive at the same solution to a problem. Following Habermas, I want to name this the "monological" model of moral reasoning. Insofar as he interprets ideal role-taking in the light of Rawls's concept of a "veil of ignorance," Kohlberg as well sees the silent thought process of a single self who imaginatively puts himself in the position of the other as the most adequate form of moral judgment.

I conclude that a definition of the self that is restricted to the standpoint of the generalized other becomes incoherent and cannot individuate among selves. Without assuming the standpoint of the concrete other, no coherent universalizability test can be carried out, for we lack the necessary epistemic information to judge my moral situation to be "like" or "unlike" yours.

IV. A COMMUNICATIVE ETHIC OF NEED INTERPRETATIONS AND THE RELATIONAL SELF

In the preceding sections of this chapter, I have argued that the distinction between justice and the good life, the restriction of the moral domain to questions of justice, as well as the ideal of moral autonomy in universalist theories, result in the privatization of women's experience and lead to epistemological blindness toward the concrete other. The consequence of such epistemological blindness is an internal inconsistency in universalistic moral theories, insofar as these define "taking the standpoint of the other" as essential to the moral point of view. My aim has been to take universalistic moral theories at their word and to show through an immanent critique, first of the "state of nature" metaphor and then of the "original position," that the concept of the autonomous self implied by these thought experiments is restricted to the "generalized other."

This distinction between the generalized and the concrete other raises questions in moral and political theory. It may be asked whether, without the standpoint of the generalized other, it would be possible to define a moral point of view at all.[32] Since our identities as concrete others are what distinguish us from each other according to gender, race, class, cultural differentials, as well as psychic and natural abilities, would a moral theory restricted to the standpoint of the concrete other not be a racist, sexist, cultural relativist, discriminatory one? Furthermore, without the standpoint of the generalized other, it may be argued, a political theory of justice suited for modern, complex societies is unthinkable. Certainly rights must be an essential component in any such theory. Finally, the perspective of the "concrete other" defines our relations as private, noninstitutional ones, concerned with love, care, friendship, and intimacy. Are these activities so gender specific? Are we not all "concrete others"?

The distinction between the "generalized" and the "concrete" other, as drawn in this essay so far, is not a *prescriptive* but a *critical* one. My goal is not to prescribe a moral and political theory consonant with the concept of the "concrete other." For, indeed, the recognition of the dignity and worthiness of the generalized other is a *necessary*, albeit *insufficient*, condition to define the moral standpoint in modern societies. In this sense, the concrete other is a critical concept that designates the *ideological* limits of universalistic discourse. It signifies the *unthought*, the *unseen*, and the *unheard* in such theories. This is evidenced by Kohlberg's effort, on the one hand, to enlarge the domain of moral theory to include in it relations to the concrete other and, on the other hand, to characterize such special relations of obligation as "private, personal" matters of evaluative life choices alone. Urging an examination of this unthought is necessary to prevent the preemption of the discourse of universality by an unexamined particularity. Substitutionalist universalism dismisses the concrete other, while interactive universalism acknowledges that every generalized other is also a concrete other.

From a meta-ethical and normative standpoint, I would argue, therefore, for the validity of a moral theory that allows us to recognize the dignity of the generalized other through an acknowledgment of the moral identity of the concrete other. The point is not to juxtapose the generalized to the concrete other or to seek normative validity in one or another standpoint. The point is to think through the ideological limitations and biases that arise in the discourse of universalist morality through this unexamined opposition. I doubt that an easy integration of both points of view, of justice and of care, is possible, without first clarifying the moral framework that would allow us to question both standpoints and their implicit gender presuppositions.

For this task a model of communicative need interpretations suggests itself.[33] Not only is such an ethic, as I interpret it, compatible with the dialogic, interactive generations of universality, but most significant, such an ethic provides the suitable framework within which moral and political agents can define their own concrete identities on the basis of recognizing each other's dignity as generalized others. Questions of the most desirable and just political organization, as well as the distinction between justice and the good life, the public and the domestic, can be analyzed, renegotiated, and redefined in such a process. Since, however, all those affected are participants in this process, the presumption is that these distinctions cannot be drawn in such a way as to privatize, hide, and repress the experiences of those who have suffered under them, for only what all could consensually agree to be in the best interest of each could be accepted as the outcome of this dialogic process.

One consequence of this communicative ethic of need interpretations is that the object domain of moral theory is so enlarged that not only rights but needs, not only justice but possible modes of the good life, are moved into an anticipatory-utopian perspective. What such discourses can generate are not only universalistically prescribable norms, but also intimations of otherness in the present that can lead to the future.

In his current formulation of his theory, Kohlberg accepts this extension of his stage six perspective into an ethic of need interpretations, as suggested first by Habermas.[34] However, he does not see the incompatibility between the communicative ethics model and the Rawlsian "original position."[35] In defining reversibility of perspectives, he still considers the Rawlsian position to be paradigmatic (Kohlberg 1984: 272, 310). Despite certain shared assumptions, the communicative model of need interpretations and the justice model of the original position need to be distinguished from each other.

First, in communicative ethics, the condition of ideal role-taking is not to be construed as a *hypothetical* thought process, carried out singly by the moral agent or the moral philosopher, but as an *actual* dialogue situation in which moral agents communicate with one another. Second, it is not necessary to place any epistemic constraints upon such an actual process of moral reasoning and stipulation, for the more knowledge is available to moral agents about each other, their history, the particulars of their society, its structure and future, the more rational will be the outcome of their deliberations. Practical rationality entails epistemic rationality as well, and more knowledge rather than less contributes to a more rational and informed judgment. To judge rationally is not to judge as if one did not know what one could know, but to judge in light of all available and relevant information. Third, if there are no knowledge restrictions upon such a discursive situation, then it also follows that there is no privileged subject matter of moral disputation. Moral agents are not only limited to reasoning about primary goods, which they are assumed to want no matter what else they want. Instead, both the *goods* they desire and their *desires* themselves become legitimate topics of moral disputation. Finally, in such moral discourses, agents can also change levels of reflexivity, that is, they can introduce metaconsiderations about the very conditions and constraints under which such dialogue takes place and evaluate their fairness. There is no closure of reflexivity in this model as there is, for example, in the Rawlsian one, which enjoins agents to accept certain rules of the bargaining game prior to the very choice of principles of justice.[36] With regard to the Kohlbergian paradigm, this would mean that moral agents can challenge the relevant *definition* of a moral situation, and urge that this very definition itself become the subject matter of moral reasoning and dispute.

A consequence of this model of communicative ethics would be that the language of rights and duties can now be challenged in light of our need interpretations. Following the tradition of modern social contract theories, Rawls and Kohlberg assume that our affective-emotional constitution, the needs and desires in light of which we formulate our rights and claims, are private matters alone. Their theory of the self, and, in particular, the Rawlsian metaphysics of the moral agent, does not allow them to view the constitution of our inner nature in *relational* terms.

A relational-interactive theory of identity assumes that inner nature, while being unique, is not an immutable given.[37] Individual need interpretations and motives carry within them the traces of those early childhood experiences, phantasies, wishes, and desires as well as the self-conscious goals of the person. The grammatical logic of the word "I" reveals the unique structure of ego identity: every subject who uses this concept in relation to herself knows that all other subjects are likewise "I"s. In this respect, the self only becomes an "I" in a community of other selves who are also "I"s. Every act of self-reference expresses simultaneously the uniqueness and difference of the self as well as the commonality among selves. Discourses about needs and motives unfold in this space created by commonality and uniqueness, generally shared socialization, and the contingency of individual life histories.

The nonrelational theory of the self, which is privileged in contemporary universalist moral theory, by contrast, removes such need interpretations from the domain of moral discourse. They become "private," nonformalizable, nonanalyzable, and amorphous aspects of our conceptions of the good life. I am not suggesting that such concept of the good life either *can* or *should* be universalized, but only that our affective-emotional constitution, as well as our concrete history as moral agents, ought to be considered accessible to moral communication, reflection, and transformation. Inner nature, no less than the public sphere of justice, has a historical dimension. In it are intertwined the history of the self and the history of the collective. To condemn it to silence is, as Gilligan has suggested, not to hear that other voice in moral theory. I would say more strongly that such discourse continues women's oppression by privatizing their lot and by excluding a central sphere of their activities from moral theory.

As the second wave of the women's movement, both in Europe and the United States has argued, to understand and to combat woman's oppression, it is no longer sufficient to demand woman's political and economic emancipation alone; it is also necessary to question those psychosexual relations in the domestic and private spheres within which women's lives unfold, and through which gender identity is reproduced. To explicate women's oppression, it is necessary to uncover the power of those symbols, myths, and fantasies that entrap both sexes in the unquestioned world of gender roles. Perhaps one of the most fundamental of these myths and symbols has been the ideal of autonomy conceived in the image of a disembedded and disembodied male ego. This vision of autonomy was and continues to be based upon an implicit politics which defines the domestic, intimate sphere as ahistorical, unchanging, and immutable, thereby removing it from reflection and discussion.[38] Needs, as well as emotions and affects, become mere given properties of individuals, which moral philosophy recoils from examining, on the grounds that it may interfere with the autonomy of the sovereign self. Women, because they have been made the "housekeeper of the emotions" in the modern, bourgeois world, and because they have suffered from the uncomprehended needs and phantasies of the male imagination, which has made them at once into Mother Earth and nagging bitch, the Virgin Mary and the whore, cannot condemn this sphere to silence. What Carol Gilligan has heard are those mutterings, protestations, and objections that women, confronted with ways of posing moral dilemmas that seemed alien to them, have voiced. Only if we can understand why their voices have been silenced, and how the dominant ideals of moral autonomy in our culture, as well as the privileged definition of the moral sphere, continue to silence women's voices, do we have a hope of moving to a more integrated vision of ourselves and of our fellow humans as generalized as well as "concrete" others.

NOTES

An earlier version of this paper was read at the conference on Women and Moral Theory, SUNY at Stony Brook, March 22–24, 1985, and at the Philosophy and Social Science course at the Inter-University Centre in Dubrovnik, Yugoslavia, April 2–14, 1985. I would like to thank participants at both conferences for their criticisms and suggestions. Larry Blum, Eva Feder Kittay, and Diana T. Meyers have made valuable suggestions for corrections. Nancy Fraser's commentary on this essay, "Toward a Discourse Ethic of Solidarity," read at the Women and Moral Theory conference, has been crucial in helping me articulate the political implications of the position developed here.

1. Thomas Kuhn, *The Structure of Scientific Revolutions*, vol. 2, no. 2 of *International Encyclopedia of Unified Science* (Chicago: University of Chicago Press, 1970, second edition), pp. 52ff.
2. John Michael Murphy and Carol Gilligan, "Moral Development in Late Adolescence and Adulthood: A Critique and Reconstruction of Kohlberg's Theory," *Human Development* 23 (1980), pp. 77–104; cited in the text as Murphy and Gilligan 1980.
3. Carol Gilligan, *In a Different Voice: Psychological Theory and Womens' Development* (Cambridge: Harvard University Press, 1982), pp. 18–19; cited in the text as Gilligan 1982.
4. Lawrence Kohlberg, "Synopses and Detailed Replies to Critics," with Charles Levine and Alexandra Hewer, in L. Kohlberg, *Essays on Moral Development*, vol. II, *The Psychology of Moral Development* (San Francisco: Harper & Row, 1984), p. 341. This volume is cited in the text as Kohlberg 1984.
5. There still seems to be some question as to how the data on women's moral development is to be interpreted. Studies that focus on late adolescents and adult males and that show sex differences, include J. Fishkin, K. Keniston, and C. MacKinnon, "Moral Reasoning and Political Ideology," *Journal of Personality and Social Psychology* 27 (1973), pp. 109–19; N. Haan, J. Bock, and M. B. Smith, "Moral Reasoning of Young Adults: Political-Social Behavior, Family Background, and Personality Correlates," *Journal of Personality and Social Psychology* 10 (1968), pp. 184–201; C. Holstein, "Irreversible, Stepwise Sequence in the Development of Moral Judgment: A Longitudinal Study of Males and Females," *Child Development* 47 (1976), pp. 51–61. While it is clear that the available evidence does not throw the model of stage-sequence development into question, the prevalent presence of sex differences in moral reasoning does raise questions about *what* exactly this model might be measuring. Norma Haan sums up this objection to the Kohlbergian paradigm as follows: "Thus the moral reasoning of males who live in technical, rationalized societies, who reason at the level of formal operations and who *defensively intellectualize and deny interpersonal and situational detail*, is especially favored in the Kohlbergian scoring system," in "Two Moralities in Action Contexts: Relationships to Thought, Ego Regulation, and Development" *Journal of Personal and Social Psychology* 36 (1978), p. 287; emphasis mine. I think Gilligan's studies also support the finding that inappropriate "intellectualization and denial of interpersonal, situational detail" constitutes one of the major differences in male and female approaches to moral problems. This is why, as I argue in the text, the separation between ego and moral development, as drawn by Kohlberg and others, seems inadequate to deal with the problem, since formalist ethical theories do seem to favor certain ego attitudes like defensiveness, rigidity, inability to empathize, and lack of flexibility over others like a nonrepressive attitude toward emotions, flexibility, and presence of empathy.

6. L. Kohlberg, "A Reply to Owen Flanagan and Some Comments on the Puka-Goodpaster Exchange," in *Ethics* 92 (April 1982), p. 316. Cf. also Gertrud Nunner-Winkler, "Two Moralities? A Critical Discussion of an Ethic of Care and Responsibility Versus an Ethics of Rights and Justice," in *Morality, Moral Behavior and Moral Development*, edited by W.M. Kurtines and J. L. Gewirtz (New York: John Wiley and Sons, 1984), p. 355. It is unclear whether the issue is, as Kohlberg and Nunner-Winkler suggest, one of distinguishing between "moral" and "ego" development or whether cognitive-developmental moral theory does not presuppose a model of ego development that clashes with more psychoanalytically oriented variants. In fact, to combat the charge of "maturationism" or "nativism" in his theory, which would imply that moral stages are a priori givens of the mind unfolding according to their own logic, regardless of the influence of society or environment upon them, Kohlberg argues as follows: "Stages," he writes, "are equilibrations arising from interaction between the organism (with its structuring tendencies) and the structure of the environment (physical or social). Universal moral stages are as much a function of universal features of social structure (such as institutions of law, family, property) and social interactions in various cultures, as they are products of the general structuring tendencies of the knowing organism" (Kohlberg, "A Reply to Owen Flanagan," p. 521). If this is so, then cognitive-developmental moral theory must also presuppose that there is a *dynamic* between self and social structure whereby the individual learns, acquires or internalizes the perspectives and sanctions of the social world. But the mechanism of this dynamic may involve learning as well as resistance, internalization as well as projection and fantasy. The issue is less whether moral development and ego development are distinct—they may be conceptually distinguished and yet in the history of the self they are related—but whether the model of ego development presupposed by Kohlberg's theory is not distortingly *cognitivistic* in that it ignores the roles of affects, resistance, projection, phantasy, and defense mechanisms in socialization processes.
7. For this formulation, see J. Habermas, "Interpretive Social Science vs. Hermeneuticism," in *Social Science as Moral Inquiry*, edited by N. Haan, R. Bellah, P. Rabinow, and W. Sullivan (New York: Columbia University Press, 1983), p. 262.
8. Imre Lakatos, "Falsification and the Methodology of Scientific Research Programs," in *Criticism and the Growth of Knowledge*, edited by I. Lakatos and A. Musgrave (Cambridge: Cambridge University Press, 1970), pp. 117ff.
9. Let me explain the status of this premise. I would characterize it as a "second-order research hypothesis" that both guides the concrete research in the social sciences and that can, in turn, be falsified by them. It is not a statement of faith about the way the world is: the cross-cultural and transhistorical universality of the sex-gender system is an empirical fact. It is also most definitely not a normative proposition about the way the world *ought* to be. To the contrary, feminism radically challenges the validity of the sex-gender system in organizing societies and cultures, and advocates the emancipation of men and women from the unexamined and oppressive grids of this framework.
10. For further clarification of these two aspects of critical theory, see my *Critique, Norm, and Utopia: A Study of the Foundations of Critical Theory* (New York: Columbia University Press, 1986), part two, "The Transformation of Critique."
11. Although frequently invoked by Kohlberg, Nunner-Winkler, and also Habermas, it is still unclear *how* this distinction is drawn and how it is justified. For example, does the justice/good life distinction correspond to sociological definitions of the public versus the private? If so, what is meant by the "private"? Is women-battering a "private" or a "public" matter? Another way of drawing this distinction is to separate what is universalizable from what is culturally contingent,

dependent upon the specifics of concrete life forms, individual histories, and the like. Habermas, in particular, relegates questions of the good life to the aesthetic-expressive sphere; cf. "A Reply to My Critics," in *Habermas: Critical Debates,* edited by John B. Thompson and David Held (Cambridge: MIT Press, 1982), p. 262; "Moralbewusstsein und kommunikatives Handeln," in *Moralbewusstsein und kommunikatives Handeln* (Frankfurt: Suhrkamp, 1983), pp. 190ff. Again, if privacy in the sense of intimacy is included in the "aesthetic expressive" sphere, we are forced to silence and privatize most of the issues raised by the women's movement, which concern precisely the quality and nature of our "intimate" relations, fantasies, and hopes. A traditional response to this is to argue that in wanting to draw this aspect of our lives into the light of the public, the women's movement runs the risk of authoritarianism because it questions the limits of individual "liberty." In response to this legitimate political concern, I would argue that one must distinguish two issues: on the one hand, questioning life forms and values that have been oppressive for women, and making them "public" in the sense of making them accessible to reflection, action, and transformation by revealing their *socially constituted* character; and on the other hand, making them "public" in the sense that these areas become subject to legislative and administrative state action. The second may, but need not, follow from the first. Because feminists focus on pornography as an "aesthetic-expressive" mode of denigrating women, it does not thereby follow that their critique should result in public legislation against pornography. Whether there ought to be this kind of legislation needs to be examined in the light of relevant legal, political, or constitutional arguments. Questions of political authoritarianism arise at this level, but not at the level of a critical-philosophical examination of traditional distinctions that have privatized and silenced women's concerns.

12. Alasdair MacIntyre, *After Virtue* (Notre Dame: University of Notre Dame Press, 1981), pp. 50–51.
13. Agnes Heller, *A Theory of Feelings* (Holland: Van Gorcum, 1979), pp. 184ff.
14. John Locke, *The Second Treatise of Civil Government* in *Two Treatises of Government,* edited and with an introduction by Thomas I. Cook (New York: Haffner Press, 1947), p. 128.
15. Immanuel Kant, *The Metaphysical Elements of Justice,* translated by John Ladd (New York: Liberal Arts Press, 1965), p. 55.
16. Thomas Hobbes, *Leviathan* (1651), edited and with an introduction by C. B. Macpherson (Middlesex: Penguin Books, 1980), p. 186. All future citations in the text are to this edition.
17. Thomas Hobbes, "Philosophical Rudiments Concerning Government and Society," in *The English Works of Thomas Hobbes,* edited by Sir W. Molesworth, vol. 2 (Darmstadt, 1966), p. 109.
18. J. J. Rousseau, "On The Origin and Foundations of Inequality Among Men," in J. J. Rousseau, *The First and Second Discourses,* edited by R. D. Masters, translated by Roger D. and Judith R. Masters (New York: St. Martin's Press, 1964), p. 116.
19. G. W. F. Hegel, *Phänomenologie des Geistes,* edited by Johannes Hoffmeister (Hamburg: Felix Meiner, 1952), 6th ed., p. 141 (Philosophische Bibliothek, Bd. 114), translation used here by A. V. Miller, *Phenomenology of Spirit* (Oxford: Clarendon Press, 1977), p. 111.
20. Sigmund Freud, *Moses and Monotheism,* translated by Katharine Jones (New York: Vintage, Random House, 1967), pp. 103ff.; Jean Piaget, *The Moral Judgment of the Child,* translated by Marjorie Gabain (New York: Free Press, 1965), pp. 65ff. Cf. the following comment on boys' and girls' games: "The most superficial observation is sufficient to show that in the main the legal sense is far less developed in little girls than in boys. We did not succeed in finding a single collective game played by girls in which there were as many rules and, above all, as fine and consistent an organization and codification of these rules as in the game of marbles examined above" (p. 77).

21. Kant, "Critique of Practical Reason," in *Critique of Practical Reason and Other Writings in Moral Philosophy*, translated and edited with an introduction by Louis White Beck (Chicago: University of Chicago Press, 1949), p. 258.
22. Although the term "generalized other" is borrowed from George Herbert Mead, my definition of it differs from his. Mead defines the "generalized other" as follows: "The organized community or social group which gives the individual his unity of self may be called the 'generalized other.' The attitude of the generalized other is the attitude of the whole community." George Herbert Mead, *Mind, Self and Society: From the Standpoint of a Social Behaviorist*, edited with introduction by Charles W. Morris (Chicago: University of Chicago Press, 1955), tenth printing, p. 154. Among such communities, Mead includes a ball team as well as political clubs, corporations, and other more abstract social classes or subgroups such as the class of debtors and the class of creditors (ibid, p. 157). Mead himself does not limit the concept of the "generalized other" to what is described in the text. In identifying the "generalized other" with the abstractly defined, legal, and juridical subject, contract theorists and Kohlberg depart from Mead. Mead criticizes the social contract tradition precisely for distorting the psychosocial genesis of the individual subject, cf. ibid, p. 233.
23. Kohlberg, "Justice as Reversibility: The Claim to Moral Adequacy of a Highest Stage of Moral Judgment," in *Essays on Moral Development*, vol. I, *The Philosophy of Moral Development* (San Francisco: Harper & Row, 1981), p. 194, cited in the text as Kohlberg 1981.
24. Whereas all forms of reciprocity involve some concept of reversibility, these vary in degree: reciprocity can be restricted to the reversibility of actions but not of moral perspectives, to behavioral role models but not to the principles which underlie the generation of such behavioral expectations. For Kohlberg, the "veil of ignorance" is a model of perfect reversibility, for it elaborates the procedure of "ideal role-taking" or "moral musical chairs," where the decider "is to successively put himself imaginatively in the place of each other actor and consider the claims each would make from his point of view" (Kohlberg 1981, p. 199). My question is: are there any real "others" behind the "veil of ignorance" or are they indistinguishable from the self?
25. I find Kohlberg's general claim that the moral point of view entails reciprocity, equality, and fairness unproblematic. Reciprocity is not only a fundamental *moral* principle, but defines, as Alvin Gouldner has argued, a fundamental *social norm*, perhaps, in fact, the very concept of a social norm ("The Norm of Reciprocity: A Preliminary Statement," *American Sociological Review*, vol. 25 [April 1960], pp. 161–78). The existence of ongoing social relations in a human community entails some definition of reciprocity in the actions, expectations, and claims of the group. The fulfillment of such reciprocity, according to whatever interpretation is given to it, would then be considered fairness by members of the group. Likewise, members of a group bound by relations of reciprocity and fairness are considered equal. What changes through history and culture are not these formal structures implicit in the very logic of social relations (we can even call them social universals), but the criteria of inclusion and exclusion? Who constitutes the *relevant* human groups: masters versus slaves, men versus women, Gentiles versus Jews? Similarly, *which* aspects of human behavior and objects of the world are to be regulated by norms of reciprocity: in the societies studied by Levi-Strauss, some tribes exchange sea shells for women. Finally, *in terms* of what is the equality among members of a group established: would this be gender, race, merit, virtue, or entitlement? Clearly Kohlberg presupposes a *universalist-egalitarian* interpretation of reciprocity, fairness, and equality, according to which all humans, by virtue of their mere humanity, are to be considered beings entitled to reciprocal rights and duties.
26. John Rawls, *A Theory of Justice* (Cambridge: Harvard University Press, 1971; second printing, 1972), p. 137.

27. Michael J. Sandel, *Liberalism and the Limits of Justice* (Cambridge: Harvard University Press, 1982; reprinted 1984), p. 9; cited in the text as Sandel 1984.
28. Rawls, *A Theory of Justice*, p. 28.
29. Stanley Cavell, *The Claim of Reason* (Oxford: Oxford University Press, 1982), p. 265.
30. A most suggestive critique of Kohlberg's neglect of interpersonal morality has been developed by Norma Haan in "Two Moralities in Action Contexts: Relationships to Thought, Ego Regulation, and Development," pp. 286–305. Haan reports that "the formulation of formal morality appears to apply best to special kinds of hypothetical, rule-governed dilemmas, the paradigmatic situation in the minds of philosophers over the centuries" (p. 302). Interpersonal reasoning, by contrast, "arises within the context of moral dialogues between agents who strive to achieve balanced agreement, based on compromises they reach or on their joint discovery of interests they hold in common" (p. 303). For a more extensive statement see also Norma Haan, "An Interactional Morality of Everyday Life," in *Social Science as Moral Inquiry*, pp. 218–51. The conception of "communicative need interpretations," which I argue for below, is also such a model of interactional morality which, nonetheless, has implications for *institutionalized* relations of justice or for public morality as well, cf. note 37.
31. Cf. E. Tugendhat, "Zur Entwicklung von moralischen Begründungsstrukturen im modernen Recht," *Archiv für Recht und Sozialphilosophie*, vol. 68 (1980), pp. 1–20.
32. Thus a Rawlsian might object that while the epistemic information pertaining to the standpoint of the concrete other may be relevant in the application and contextualizing of general moral and political principles, it is unclear why such information need also be taken into account in the original choice or justification of such principles. For the moral point of view only concerns the constituents of our common humanity, not those differences which separate us from each other. I would like to distinguish here between the normative standpoint of *universalism*, which I share with Rawls and Kohlberg, and the methodological problem of *formalism*. Although the two have often gone together in the history of moral and political thought, they need not do so. A formalist method, which also proceeds via an idealized thought-experiment, is subject to certain epistemic difficulties which are well known in the literature critical of social contract theories. And as Rawls himself has had to admit in his later writings, the device of the "original person" does not justify the concept of the person from which he proceeds, rather it presupposes it (cf. "Kantian Constructivism in Moral Theory"). Once this admission is made, however, and the device of the "original position" with its "veil of ignorance" is said to presuppose a concept of the person rather than justify it, then the kinds of criticisms raised in my paper that concern moral identity and epistemology must also be taken into account. Rawls's concepts of the moral person and autonomy remain restricted to the discourse of the "generalized other." I would like to thank Diana T. Meyers for bringing this objection to my attention.
33. Although I follow the general outline of Habermas's conception of communicative ethics, I differ from him insofar as he distinguishes sharply between questions of justice and the good life (see note 11 above), and insofar as in his description of the "seventh stage," he equivocates between concepts of the "generalized" and the "concrete other"; cf. J. Habermas, "Moral Development and Ego Identity," in *Communication and the Evolution of Society*, translated by T. McCarthy (Boston: Beacon Press, 1979), pp. 69–95. The "concrete other" is introduced in his theory through the back door, as an aspect of ego autonomy, and as an aspect of our relation to inner nature. I find this implausible for reasons discussed above.
34. See Habermas, ibid., p. 90. and Kohlberg's discussion in Kohlberg 1984: 35–86.

35. In an earlier piece, I have dealt with the strong parallelism between the two conceptions of the "veil of ignorance" and the "ideal speech situation"; see my "The Methodological Illusions of Modern Political Theory: The Case of Rawls and Habermas," *Neue Hefte für Philosophie* (Spring 1982), no. 21., pp. 47–74. With the publication of *The Theory of Communicative Action*, Habermas himself has substantially modified various assumptions in his original formulation of communicative ethics, and the rendition given here follows these modifications; for further discussion see my "Toward a Communicative Ethics," in *Critique, Norm, and Utopia*, chap. 8.
36. Cf. Rawls, *A Theory of Justice*, pp. 118ff.
37. For recent feminist perspectives on the development of the self, cf. Dorothy Dinnerstein, *The Mermaid and the Minotaur: Sexual Arrangements and Human Malaise* (New York: Harper, 1976); Jean Baker Miller, "The Development of Women's Sense of Self," work-in-progress paper published by the Stone Center for Developmental Services and Studies at Wellesley College, 1984; Nancy Chodorow, *The Reproduction of Mothering* (Berkeley: University of California Press, 1978); Jessica Benjamin, "Authority and the Family Revisited: Or, A World Without Fathers?" in *New German Critique* 13 (1978), pp. 35–58; Jane Flax, "The Conflict Between Nurturance and Autonomy in Mother-Daughter Relationships and Within Feminism," in *Feminist Studies*, vol. 4, no. 2 (June 1981), pp. 171–92; and I. Balbus, *Marxism and Domination* (Princeton: Princeton University Press, 1982).
38. The distinction between the public and the private spheres is undergoing a tremendous realignment in late-capitalist societies as a result of a complicated series of factors, the chief of which may be the changing role of the state in such societies in assuming more and more tasks that were previously more or less restricted to the family and reproductive spheres, e.g., education, early child care, health care, care for the elderly, and the like. Also, recent legislation concerning abortion, wife battering, and child abuse, suggests that the accepted legal definitions of these spheres have begun to shift as well. These new sociological and legislative developments point to the need to fundamentally rethink our concepts of moral, psychological, and legal autonomy, a task hitherto neglected by formal-universalist moral theory. I do not want to imply by any means that the philosophical critique voiced in this paper leads to a wholly positive evaluation of these developments or to the neglect of their contradictory and ambivalent character for women. My analysis would need to be complemented by a critical social theory of the changing definition and function of the private sphere in late-capitalist societies. As I have argued elsewhere, these social and legal developments not only lead to an extension of the perspective of the "generalized other," by subjecting more and more spheres of life to legal norms, but also create the potential for the growth of the perspective of the "concrete other," that is, an association of friendship and solidarity in which need interpretations are discussed and new needs created. I see these associations as being created by new social movements like ecology and feminism, in the interstices of our societies, partly in response to and partly as a consequence of, the activism of the welfare state in late-capitalist societies; cf. *Critique, Norm, and Utopia*, pp. 343–53. I am much indebted to Nancy Fraser for her elaboration of the political consequences of my distinction between the "generalized" and the "concrete" other in the context of the paradoxes of the modern welfare state in her "Feminism and the Social State" (*Salmagundi*, April 1986). An extensive historical and philosophical analysis of the changing relation between the private and the public is provided by Linda Nicholson in her book, *Gender and History: The Limits of Social Theory in the Age of the Family* (New York: Columbia University Press, 1986).

Deconstructing Equality-Versus-Difference: Or, the Uses of Poststructuralist Theory for Feminism

Scott advocates poststructuralist feminism. She begins her essay by explicating several key poststructuralist concepts, namely, language, discourse, difference, and deconstruction. Then she undertakes to demonstrate the virtues of poststructuralist feminism by examining the controversial role of feminist expert witnesses in *EEOC v. Sears, Roebuck* & *Co.* (1979). In this case, lawyers for Sears successfully defended the company against the Equal Employment Opportunity Commission's sex discrimination charges by claiming that women are different from men. Since women are relational and noncompetitive, they lack interest in high-paying, commission sales positions. Women's preferences, as opposed to Sears's discrimination, were adduced to account for sex segregation in positions at Sears.

Attorneys for Sears and their witnesses cast the key issue as whether women and men are the same or different. Scott questions this formulation and points out that the EEOC did not assert that women and men have identical interests. Testifying for the EEOC, Alice Kessler-Harris sought to stake out a more nuanced position that emphasized the wide range of women's choices and the role of employers in enforcing gender segregation. The EEOC defined equality as the presumption that women and men have an equal interest in sales commission jobs—a presumption that would allow women to compete for these jobs without prejudice against them. But Sears prevailed, and the court concluded that women are different and that Sears did not discriminate.

Scott contends that this debacle shows that feminists must eschew equality versus difference as a false choice. According to Scott, difference does not entail inequality, nor does equality presuppose sameness. If equality is construed as ignoring differences between individuals for a particular purpose, e.g., hiring decisions, or in a particular context, e.g., at work, feminists can acknowledge difference and demand equality. The alternative to polar gender difference is not sameness, but rather diversity within gender categories. Thus, feminists must insist on women's diversity as the "very meaning of equality."

—D.T.M.

Chapter 39

Joan W. Scott

Deconstructing Equality-Versus-Difference: Or, the Uses of Poststructuralist Theory for Feminism

That feminism needs theory goes without saying (perhaps because it has been said so often). What is not always clear is what that theory will do, although there are certain common assumptions I think we can find in a wide range of feminist writings. We need theory that can analyze the workings of patriarchy in all its manifestations—ideological, institutional, organizational, subjective—accounting not only for continuities but also for change over time. We need theory that will let us think in terms of pluralities and diversities rather than of unities and universals. We need theory that will break the conceptual hold, at least, of those long traditions of (Western) philosophy that have systematically and repeatedly construed the world hierarchically in terms of masculine universals and feminine specificities. We need theory that will enable us to articulate alternative ways of thinking about (and thus acting upon) gender without either simply reversing the old hierarchies or confirming them. And we need theory that will be useful and relevant for political practice.

It seems to me that the body of theory referred to as poststructuralism best meets all these requirements. It is not by any means the only theory nor are its positions and formulations unique. In my own case, however, it was reading poststructuralist theory and arguing with literary scholars that provided the elements of clarification for which I was looking. I found a new way of analyzing constructions of meaning and relationships of power that called unitary, universal categories into question and historicized concepts otherwise treated as natural (such as man/woman) or absolute (such as equality or justice). In addition, what attracted me was the historical connection between the two movements. Poststructuralism and contemporary feminism are late twentieth-century movements that share a certain self-conscious critical relationship to established philosophical and political traditions. It thus seemed worthwhile for feminist scholars to exploit that relationship for their own ends.[1]

This article will not discuss the history of these various "exploitations" or elaborate on all the reasons a historian might look to this theory to organize her inquiry.[2] What seems most useful here is to give a short list of some major theoretical points and then devote most of my effort to a specific illustration. The first part of this article is a brief discussion of concepts used by poststructuralists that are also useful for feminists. The second part applies some of these concepts to one of the hotly contested issues among contemporary (U.S.) feminists—the "equality-versus-difference" debate.

Among the useful terms feminists have appropriated from poststructuralism are language, discourse, difference, and deconstruction.

Language. Following the work of structuralist linguistics and anthropology, the term is used to mean not simply words or even a vocabulary and set of grammatical rules but, rather, a meaning-constituting system: that is, any system—strictly verbal or other—through which meaning is constructed and cultural practices organized and by which, accordingly, people represent and understand their world, including who they are and how they relate to others. "Language," so conceived, is a central focus of poststructuralist analysis.

Language is not assumed to be a representation of ideas that either cause material relations or from which such relations follow; indeed, the idealist/materialist opposition is a false one to impose on this approach. Rather, the analysis of language provides a crucial point of entry, a starting point for understanding how social relations are conceived, and therefore—because understanding how they are conceived means understanding how they work—how institutions are organized, how relations of production are experienced, and how collective identity is established. Without attention to language and the processes by which meaning and categories are constituted, one only imposes oversimplified models on the world, models that perpetuate conventional understanding rather than open up new interpretive possibilities.

The point is to find ways to analyze specific "texts"—not only books and documents but also utterances of any kind and in any medium, including cultural practices—in terms of specific historical and contextual meanings. Poststructuralists insist that words and texts have no fixed or intrinsic meanings, that there is no transparent or self-evident relationship between them and either ideas or things, no basic or ultimate correspondence between language and the world. The questions that must be answered in such an analysis, then, are how, in what specific contexts, among which specific communities of people, and by what textual and social processes has meaning been acquired? More generally, the questions are: How do meanings change? How have some meanings emerged as normative and others have been eclipsed or disappeared? What do these processes reveal about how power is constituted and operates?

Discourse. Some of the answers to these questions are offered in the concept of discourse, especially as it has been developed in the work of Michel Foucault. A discourse is not a language or a text but a historically, socially, and institutionally specific structure of statements, terms, categories, and beliefs. Foucault suggests that the elaboration of meaning involves conflict and power, that meanings are locally contested within discursive "fields of force," that (at least since the Enlightenment) the power to control a particular field resides in claims to (scientific) knowledge embodied not only in writing but also in disciplinary and professional organizations, in institutions (hospitals, prisons, schools, factories), and in social relationships (doctor/patient, teacher/student, employer/worker, parent/child, husband/wife). Discourse is thus contained or expressed in organizations and institutions as well as in words; all of these constitute texts or documents to be read.[3]

Discursive fields overlap, influence, and compete with one another; they appeal to one another's "truths" for authority and legitimation. These truths are assumed to be outside human invention, either already known and self-evident or discoverable through scientific inquiry. Precisely because they are assigned the status of objective knowledge, they seem to be beyond dispute and thus serve a powerful legitimating function. Darwinian theories of natural selection are one example of such legitimating truths; biological theories about sexual difference are another. The power of these "truths" comes from the way they function as givens or first premises for both sides in an argument, so that conflicts within discursive fields are framed to follow from rather than question them. The brilliance of so much of Foucault's work has been to illuminate the shared assumptions of what seemed to be sharply different arguments, thus exposing the limits of radical criticism and the extent of the power of dominant ideologies or epistemologies.

In addition, Foucault has shown how badly even challenges to fundamental assumptions often fared. They have been marginalized or silenced, forced to underplay their most radical claims in order to win a short-term goal, or completely absorbed into an existing framework. Yet the fact of change is crucial to Foucault's notion of "archaeology," to the way in which he uses contrasts from different historical periods to present his arguments. Exactly how the process happens is not spelled out to the satisfaction of many historians, some of whom want a more explicit causal model. But when causal theories are highly general, we are often drawn into the assumptions of the very discourse we ought to question. (If we are to question those assumptions, it may be necessary to forgo existing standards of historical inquiry.) Although some have read Foucault as an argument about the futility of human agency in the struggle for social change, I think that he is more appropriately taken as warning against simple solutions to difficult problems, as advising human actors to think strategically and more self-consciously about the philosophical and political implications and meanings of the programs they endorse. From this perspective, Foucault's work provides an important way of thinking differently (and perhaps more creatively) about the politics of the contextual construction of social meanings, about such organizing principles for political action as "equality" and "difference."

Difference. An important dimension of poststructuralist analyses of language has to do with the concept of difference, the notion (following Ferdinand de Saussure's structuralist linguistics) that meaning is made through implicit or explicit contrast, that a positive definition rests on the negation or repression of something represented as antithetical to it. Thus, any unitary concept in fact contains repressed or negated material; it is established in explicit opposition to another term. Any analysis of meaning involves teasing out these negations and oppositions, figuring out how (and whether) they are operating in specific contexts. Oppositions rest on metaphors and cross-references, and often in patriarchal discourse, sexual difference (the contrast masculine/feminine) serves to encode or establish meanings that are literally unrelated to gender or the body. In that way, the meanings of gender become tied to many kinds of cultural representations, and these in turn establish terms by which relations between women and men are organized and understood. The possibilities of this kind of analysis have, for obvious reasons, drawn the interest and attention of feminist scholars.

Fixed oppositions conceal the extent to which things presented as oppositional are, in fact, interdependent—that is, they derive their meaning from a particularly established contrast rather than from some inherent or pure antithesis. Furthermore, according to Jacques Derrida, the interdependence is hierarchical with one term dominant or prior, the opposite term subordinate and secondary. The Western philosophical tradition, he argues, rests on binary oppositions: unity/diversity, identity/difference, presence/absence, and universality/specificity. The leading terms are accorded primacy; their partners are represented as weaker or derivative. Yet the first terms depend on and derive their meaning from the second to such an extent that the secondary terms can be seen as generative of the definition of the first terms.[4] If binary oppositions provide insight into the way meaning is constructed, and if they operate as Derrida suggests, then analyses of meaning cannot take binary oppositions at face value but rather must "deconstruct" them for the processes they embody.

Deconstruction. Although this term is used loosely among scholars—often to refer to a dismantling or destructive enterprise—it also has a precise definition in the work of Derrida and his followers. Deconstruction involves analyzing the operations of difference in texts, the ways in which meanings are made to work. The method consists of two related steps: the reversal and displacement of binary oppositions. This double process reveals the interdependence of seemingly dichotomous terms and their meaning relative to a particular history. It shows them to be not natural but constructed oppositions, constructed for particular purposes in particular contexts.[5] The literary critic Barbara Johnson describes deconstruction as crucially dependent on difference.

> The starting point is often a binary difference that is subsequently shown to be an illusion created by the working of differences much harder to pin down. The differences *between* entities . . . are shown to be based on a repression of differences *within* entities, ways in which an entity differs from itself. . . . The "deconstruction" of a binary opposition is thus not an annihilation of all values or differences; it is an attempt to follow the subtle, powerful effects of differences already at work within the illusion of a binary opposition.[6]

Deconstruction is, then, an important exercise, for it allows us to be critical of the way in which ideas we want to use are ordinarily expressed, exhibited in patterns of meaning that may undercut the ends we seek to attain. A case in point—of meaning expressed in a politically self-defeating way—is the "equality-versus-difference" debate among feminists. Here a binary opposition has been created to offer a choice to feminists, of either endorsing "equality" or its presumed antithesis "difference." In fact, the antithesis itself hides the interdependence of the two terms, for equality is not the elimination of difference, and difference does not preclude equality.

In the past few years, "equality-versus-difference" has been used as a shorthand to characterize conflicting feminist positions and political strategies.[7] Those who argue that sexual difference ought to be an irrelevant consideration in schools, employment, the courts, and the legislature are put in the equality category. Those who insist that appeals on behalf of women ought to be made in terms of the needs, interests, and characteristics common to women as a group are placed in the difference category. In the clashes over the superiority of one or another of these strategies, feminists have invoked history, philosophy, and morality and have devised new classificatory labels: cultural feminism, liberal feminism, feminist separatism, and so on.[8] Most recently, the debate about equality and difference has been used to analyze the Sears case, the sex discrimination suit brought against the retailing giant by the Equal Employment Opportunities Commission (EEOC) in 1979, in which historians Alice Kessler-Harris and Rosalind Rosenberg testified on opposite sides.

There have been many articles written on the Sears case, among them a recent one by Ruth Milkman. Milkman insists that we attend to the political context of seemingly timeless principles: "We ignore the political dimensions of the equality-versus-difference debate at our peril, especially in a period of conservative resurgence like the present." She concludes:

> As long as this is the political context in which we find ourselves, feminist scholars must be aware of the real danger that arguments about "difference" or "women's culture" will be put to uses other than those for which they were originally developed. That does not mean we must abandon these arguments or the intellectual terrain they have opened up; it does mean that we must be self-conscious in our formulations, keeping firmly in view the ways in which our work can be exploited politically.[9]

Milkman's carefully nuanced formulation implies that equality is our safest course, but she is also reluctant to reject difference entirely. She feels a need to choose a side, but which side is the problem. Milkman's ambivalence is an example of what the legal theorist Martha Minow has labeled in another context "the difference dilemma." Ignoring difference in the case of subordinated groups, Minow points out, "leaves in place a faulty neutrality," but focusing on difference can underscore the stigma of deviance. "Both focusing on and ignoring the difference risk recreating it. This is the dilemma of difference."[10] What is required, Minow suggests, is a new way of thinking about difference, and this involves rejecting the idea that equality-versus-difference constitutes an opposition. Instead of framing analyses and strategies as if such binary pairs were timeless and true, we need to ask how the dichotomous pairing of equality and difference itself works. Instead of remaining within the terms of existing political discourse, we need to subject those terms to critical examination. Until we understand how the concepts work to constrain and construct specific meanings, we cannot make them work for us.

A close look at the evidence in the Sears case suggests that equality-versus-difference may not accurately depict the opposing sides in the Sears case. During testimony, most of the arguments against equality and for difference were, in fact, made by the Sears lawyers or by Rosalind Rosenberg. They constructed an opponent against whom they asserted that women and men differed, that "fundamental differences"—the result of culture or long-standing patterns of socialization—led to women's presumed lack of interest in commission sales jobs. In order to make their own claim that sexual difference and not discrimination could explain the hiring patterns of Sears, the Sears defense attributed to EEOC an assumption that no one had made in those terms—that women and men had identical interests.[11] Alice Kessler-Harris did not argue that women were the same as men; instead, she used a variety of strategies to challenge Rosenberg's assertions. First, she argued that historical evidence suggested far more variety in the jobs women actually took than Rosenberg assumed. Second, she maintained that economic considerations usually offset the effects of socialization in women's attitudes to employment. And, third, she pointed out that, historically, job segregation by sex was the consequence of employer preferences, not employee choices. The question of women's choices could not be resolved, Kessler-Harris maintained, when the hiring process itself predetermined the outcome, imposing generalized gendered criteria that were not necessarily relevant to the work at hand. The debate joined then not around equality-versus-difference but around the relevance of general ideas of sexual difference in a specific context.[12]

To make the case for employer discrimination, EEOC lawyers cited obviously biased job applicant questionnaires and statements by personnel officers, but they had no individuals to testify that they had experienced discrimination. Kessler-Harris referred to past patterns of sexual segregation in the job market as the product of employer choices, but mostly she invoked history to break down Rosenberg's contention that women as a group differed consistently in the details of their behavior from men, instead insisting that variety characterized female job choices (as it did male job choices), that it made no sense in this case to talk about women as a uniform group. She defined equality to mean a presumption that women and men might have an equal interest in sales commission jobs. She did not claim that women and men, by definition, had such an equal interest. Rather, Kessler-Harris and the EEOC called into question the relevance for hiring decisions of generalizations about the necessarily antithetical behaviors of women and men. EEOC argued that Sears's hiring practices reflected inaccurate and inapplicable notions of sexual difference; Sears argued that "fundamental" differences between the sexes (and not its own actions) explained the gender imbalances in its labor force.

The Sears case was complicated by the fact that almost all the evidence offered was statistical. The testimony of the historians, therefore, could only be inferential at best. Each of them sought to explain small statistical disparities by reference to gross generalizations about the entire history of working women; furthermore, neither historian had much information about what had actually happened at Sears. They were forced, instead, to swear to the truth or falsehood of interpretive generalizations developed for purposes other than legal contestation, and they were forced to treat their interpretive premises as matters of fact. Reading the cross-examination of Kessler-Harris is revealing in this respect. Each of her carefully nuanced explanations of women's work history was forced into a reductive assertion by the Sears lawyers' insistence that she answer questions only by saying yes or no. Similarly, Rosalind Rosenberg's rebuttal to Alice Kessler-Harris eschewed the historian's subtle contextual reading of evidence and sought instead to impose a test of absolute consistency. She juxtaposed Kessler-Harris's testimony in the trial to her earlier published work (in which Kessler-Harris stressed differences between female and male workers in their approaches to work, arguing that women were more domestically oriented and less individualistic than men) in an effort to show that Kessler-Harris had misled the court.[13] Outside the courtroom, however, the disparities of the Kessler-Harris argument could also be explained in other ways. In relationship to a labor history that had typically excluded women, it might make sense to overgeneralize about women's experience, emphasizing difference in order to demonstrate that the universal term "worker" was really a male reference that could not account for all aspects of women's job experiences. In relationship to an employer who sought to justify discrimination by reference to sexual difference, it made more sense to deny the totalizing effects of difference by stressing instead the diversity and complexity of women's behavior and motivation. In the first case, difference served a positive function, unveiling the inequity hidden in a presumably neutral term; in the second case, difference served a negative purpose, justifying what Kessler-Harris believed to be unequal treatment. Although the inconsistency might have been avoided with a more self-conscious analysis of the "difference dilemma," Kessler-Harris's different positions were quite legitimately different emphases for different contexts; only in a courtroom could they be taken as proof of bad faith.[14]

The exacting demands of the courtroom for consistency and "truth" also point out the profound difficulties of arguing about difference. Although the testimony of historians had to explain only a relatively small statistical disparity in the numbers of women and men hired for full-time commission sales jobs, the explanations that were preferred were totalizing and categorical.[15] In cross-examination, Kessler-Harris's multiple interpretations were found to be contradictory and confusing, although the judge praised Rosenberg for her coherence and lucidity.[16] In part, that was because Rosenberg held to a tight model that unproblematically linked socialization to individual choice; in part it was because her descriptions of gender differences accorded with prevailing normative views. In contrast, Kessler-Harris had trouble finding a simple model that would at once acknowledge difference and refuse it as an acceptable explanation for the employment pattern of Sears. So she fell into great difficulty maintaining her case in the face of hostile questioning. On the one hand, she was accused of assuming that economic opportunism equally affected women and men (and thus of believing that women and men were the same). How, then, could she explain the differences her own work had identified? On the other hand, she was tarred (by Rosenberg) with the brush of subversion, for implying that all employers might have some interest in sex typing the labor force, for deducing from her own (presumably Marxist) theory, a "conspiratorial" conclusion about the behavior of Sears.[17] If the patterns of discrimination that Kessler-Harris alluded to were real, after all, one of their effects might well be the kind of difference Rosenberg pointed out. Caught within the framework of Rosenberg's use of historical evidence, Kessler-Harris and her lawyers relied on an essentially negative strategy, offering details designed to complicate and undercut Rosenberg's assertions. Kessler-Harris did not directly challenge the theoretical shortcomings of Rosenberg's socialization model, nor did she offer an alternative model of her own. That would have required, I think, either fully developing the case for employer discrimination or insisting more completely on the "differences" line of argument by exposing the "equality-versus-difference" formulation as an illusion.

In the end, the most nuanced arguments of Kessler-Harris were rejected as contradictory or inapplicable, and the judge decided in Sears's favor, repeating the defense argument that an assumption of equal interest was "unfounded" because of the differences between women and men.[18] Not only was the EEOC's position rejected, but the hiring policies of Sears were implicitly endorsed. According to the judge, because difference was real and fundamental, it could explain statistical variations in Sears's hiring. Discrimination was redefined as simply the recognition of "natural" difference (however culturally or historically produced), fitting in nicely with the logic of Reagan conservatism. Difference was substituted for inequality, the appropriate antithesis of equality, becoming inequality's explanation and legitimation. The judge's decision illustrates a process literary scholar Naomi Schor has described in another context: it "essentializes difference and naturalizes social inequity."[19]

The Sears case offers a sobering lesson in the operation of a discursive, that is, a political field. Analysis of language here provides insight not only into the manipulation of concepts and definitions but also into the implementation and justification of institutional and political power. References to categorical differences between women and men set the terms within which Sears defended its policies *and* EEOC challenged them. Equality-versus-difference was the intellectual trap within which historians argued not about tiny disparities in Sears's employment practices, but about the normative behaviors of women and men. Although we might conclude that the balance of power was against EEOC by the time the case was heard and that, therefore, its outcome was inevitable (part of the Reagan plan to reverse affirmative action programs of the 1970s), we still need to articulate a critique of what happened that can inform the next round of political encounter. How should that position be conceptualized?

When equality and difference are paired dichotomously, they structure an impossible choice. If one opts for equality, one is forced to accept the notion that difference is antithetical to it. If one opts for difference, one admits that equality is unattainable. That, in a sense, is the dilemma apparent in Milkman's conclusion cited above. Feminists cannot give up "difference"; it has been our most creative analytic tool. We cannot give up equality, at least as long as we want to speak to the principles and values of our political system. But it makes no sense for the feminist movement to let its arguments be forced into preexisting categories and its political disputes to be characterized by a dichotomy we did not invent. How then do we recognize and use notions of sexual difference and yet make arguments for equality? The only response is a double one: the unmasking of the power relationship constructed by posing equality as the antithesis of difference and the refusal of its consequent dichotomous construction of political choices.

Equality-versus-difference cannot structure choices for feminist politics; the oppositional pairing misrepresents the relationship of both terms. Equality, in the political theory of rights that lies behind the claims of excluded groups for justice, means the ignoring of differences between individuals for a particular purpose or in a particular context. Michael Walzer puts it this way: "The root meaning of equality is negative; egalitarianism in its origins is an abolitionist politics. It aims at eliminating not all differences, but a particular set of differences, and a different set in different times and places."[20] This presumes a social agreement to consider obviously different people as equivalent (not identical) for a stated purpose. In this usage, the opposite of equality is inequality or inequivalence, the noncommensurability of individuals or groups in certain circumstances, for certain purposes. Thus, for purposes of democratic citizenship, the measure of equivalence has been, at different times, independence or ownership of property or race or sex. The political notion of equality thus includes, indeed depends on, an acknowledgement of the existence of difference. Demands for equality have rested on implicit and usually unrecognized arguments from difference; if individuals or groups were identical or the same there would be no need to ask for equality. Equality might well be defined as deliberate indifference to specified differences.

The antithesis of difference in most usages is sameness or identity. But even here the contrast and the context must be specified. There is nothing self-evident or transcendent about difference, even if the fact of difference—sexual difference, for example—seems apparent to the naked eye. The question always ought to be, What qualities or aspects are being compared? What is the nature of the comparison? How is the meaning of difference being constructed? Yet in the Sears testimony and in some debates among feminists (sexual) difference is assumed to be an immutable fact, its meaning inherent in the categories female and male. The lawyers for Sears put it this way: "The reasonableness of the EEOC's *a priori* assumptions of male/female sameness with respect to preferences, interests, and qualifications is . . . the crux of the issue."[21] The point of the EEOC challenge, however, was never sameness but the irrelevance of categorical differences.

The opposition men/women, as Rosenberg employed it, asserted the incomparability of the sexes, and although history and socialization were the explanatory factors, these resonated with categorical distinctions inferred from the facts of bodily difference. When the opposition men/women is invoked, as it was in the Sears case, it refers to a specific issue (the small statistical discrepancy between women and men hired for commission sales jobs) back to a general principle (the "fundamental" differences between women and men). The differences within each group that might apply to this particular situation—the fact, for example, that some women might choose "aggressive" or "risk-taking" jobs or that some women might prefer high- to low-paying positions—were excluded by definition in the antithesis between the groups. The irony is, of course, that the statistical case required only a small percentage of women's behaviors to be explained. Yet the historical testimony argued categorically about "women." It thus became impossible to argue (as EEOC and Kessler-Harris tried to) that within the female category, women typically exhibit and participate in all sorts of "male" behaviors, that socialization is a complex process that does not yield uniform choices. To make the argument would have required a direct attack on categorical thinking about gender. For the generalized opposition, male/female serves to obscure the differences among women in behavior, character, desire, subjectivity, sexuality, gender identification, and historical experience. In the light of Rosenberg's insistence on the primacy of sexual difference, Kessler-Harris's insistence on the specificity (and historically variable aspect) of women's actions could be dismissed as an unreasonable and trivial claim.

The alternative to the binary constructions of sexual difference is not sameness, identity, or androgyny. By subsuming women into a general "human" identity, we lose the specificity of female diversity and women's experiences; we are back, in other words, to the days when "Man's" story was supposed to be everyone's story, when women were "hidden from history," when the feminine served as the negative counterpoint, the "Other," for the construction of positive masculine identity. It is not sameness *or* identity between women and men that we want to claim but a more complicated historically variable diversity than is permitted by the opposition male/female, a diversity that is also differently expressed for different purposes in different contexts. In effect, the duality this opposition creates draws one line of difference, invests it with biological explanations, and then treats each side of the opposition as a unitary phenomenon. Everything in each category (male/female) is assumed to be the same; hence, differences within either category are suppressed. In contrast, our goal is to see not only differences between the sexes but also the way these work to repress differences within gender groups. The sameness constructed on each side of the binary opposition hides the multiple play of differences and maintains their irrelevance and invisibility.

Placing equality and difference in an antithetical relationship has, then, a double effect. It denies the way in which difference has long figured in political notions of equality and it suggests that sameness is the only ground on which equality can be claimed. It thus puts feminists in an impossible position, for as long as we argue within the terms of a discourse set up by this opposition we grant the current conservative premise that because women cannot be identical to men in all respects, we cannot expect to be equal to them. The only alternative, it seems to me, is to refuse to oppose equality to difference and insist continually on differences—differences as the condition of individual and collective identities, differences as the constant challenge to the fixing of those identities, history as the repeated illustration of the play of differences, differences as the very meaning of equality itself.

Alice Kessler-Harris's experience in the Sears case shows, however, that the assertion of differences in the face of gender categories is not a sufficient strategy. What is required in addition is an analysis of fixed gender categories as normative statements that organize cultural understandings of sexual difference. This means that we must open to scrutiny the terms women and men as they are used to define one another in particular contexts—work places, for example. The history of women's work needs to be retold from this perspective as part of the story of the creation of a gendered work force. In the nineteenth century, for example, certain concepts of male skill rested on a contrast with female labor (by definition unskilled). The organization and reorganization of work processes was accomplished by reference to the gender attributes of workers, rather than to issues of training, education, or social class. And wage differentials between the sexes were attributed to fundamentally different family roles that preceded (rather than followed from) employment arrangements. In all these processes the meaning of "worker" was established through a contrast between the presumably natural qualities of women and men. If we write the history of women's work by gathering data that described the activities, needs, interests, and culture of "women workers," we leave in place the naturalized contrast and reify a fixed categorical difference between women and men. We start the story, in other words, too late, by uncritically accepting a gendered category (the "woman worker") that itself needs investigation because its meaning is relative to its history.

If in our histories we relativize the categories woman and man, it means, of course, that we must also recognize the contingent and specific nature of our political claims. Political strategies then will rest on analyses of the utility of certain arguments in certain discursive contexts, without, however, invoking absolute qualities for women or men. There are moments when it makes sense for mothers to demand consideration for their social role, and contexts within which motherhood is irrelevant to women's behavior; but to maintain that womanhood is motherhood is to obscure the differences that make choice possible. There are moments when it makes sense to demand a reevaluation of the status of what has been socially constructed as women's work ("comparable worth" strategies are the current example) and contexts within which it makes much more sense to prepare women for entry into "nontraditional" jobs. But to maintain that femininity predisposes women to certain (nurturing) jobs or (collaborative) styles of work is to naturalize complex economic and social processes and, once again, to obscure the differences that have characterized women's occupational histories. An insistence on differences undercuts the tendency to absolutist and, in the case of sexual difference, essentialist categories. It does not deny the existence of gender difference, but it does suggest that its meanings are always relative to particular constructions in specified contexts. In contrast, absolutist categorizations of difference end up always enforcing normative rules.

It is surely not easy to formulate a "deconstructive" political strategy in the face of powerful tendencies that construct the world in binary terms. Yet there seems to me no other choice. Perhaps as we learn to think this way solutions will become more readily apparent. Perhaps the theoretical and historical work we do can prepare the ground. Certainly we can take heart from the history of feminism, which is full of illustrations of refusals of simple dichotomies and attempts instead to demonstrate that equality requires the recognition and inclusion of differences. Indeed, one way historians could contribute to a genuine rethinking of these concepts is to stop writing the history of feminisms as a story of oscillations between demands for equality and affirmations of difference. This approach inadvertently strengthens the hold of the binary construction, establishing it as inevitable by giving it a long history. When looked at closely, in fact, the historical arguments of feminists do not usually fall into these neat compartments; they are instead attempts to reconcile theories of equal rights with cultural concepts of sexual difference, to question the validity of normative constructions of gender in the light of the existence of behaviors and qualities that contradict the rules, to point up rather than resolve conditions of contradiction, to articulate a political identity for women without conforming to existing stereotypes about them.

In histories of feminism and in feminist political strategies there needs to be at once attention to the operations of difference and an insistence on differences, but not a simple substitution of multiple for binary difference for it is not a happy pluralism we ought to invoke. The resolution of the "difference dilemma" comes neither from ignoring nor embracing difference as it is normatively constituted. Instead, it seems to me that the critical feminist position must always involve *two* moves. The first is the systematic criticism of the operations of categorical difference, the exposure of the kinds of exclusions and inclusions—the hierarchies—it constructs, and a refusal of their ultimate "truth." A refusal, however, not in the name of an equality that implies sameness or identity, but rather (and this is the second move) in the name of an equality that rests on differences—differences that confound, disrupt, and render ambiguous the meaning of any fixed binary opposition. To do anything else is to buy into the political argument that sameness is a requirement for equality, an untenable position for feminists (and historians) who know that power is constructed on and so must be challenged from the ground of difference.

NOTES

I am extremely grateful to William Connolly, Sanford Levinson, Andrew Pickering, Barbara Herrnstein Smith, and Elizabeth Weed for their thoughtful suggestions, which sharpened and improved my argument. This essay originally appeared in *Feminist Studies* 14, no. 1 (Spring 1988).

1. On the problem of appropriating poststructuralism for feminism, see Biddy Martin, "Feminism, Criticism, Foucault," *New German Critique* 27 (Fall 1982): 3–30.
2. Joan W. Scott, "Gender: A Useful Category of Historical Analysis," *American Historical Review* 91 (December 1986): 1053–75; Donna Haraway, "A Manifesto for Cyborgs: Science, Technology, and Socialist Feminism in the 1980s," *Socialist Review* 15 (March–April 1985): 65–107.
3. Examples of Michel Foucault's work include *The Archaeology of Knowledge* (New York: Harper & Row, 1976); *The History of Sexuality*, vol. 1, *An Introduction* (New York: Vintage, 1980); and *Power/Knowledge: Selected Interviews and Other Writings, 1972–1977* (New York: Pantheon, 1980). See also Hubert L. Dreyfus and Paul Rabinow, *Michel Foucault: Beyond Structuralism and Hermeneutics* (Chicago: University of Chicago Press, 1983).
4. The Australian philosopher Elizabeth Gross puts it this way: "What Derrida attempts to show is that within these binary couples, the primary or dominant term derives its privilege from a curtailment or suppression of its opposite. Sameness or identity, presence, speech, the origin, mind, etc. are all privileged in relation to their opposites, which are regarded as debased, impure variants of the primary term. Difference, for example, is the lack of identity or sameness; absence is

the lack of presence; writing is the supplement of speech, and so on." See her "Derrida, Irigaray, and Deconstruction," *Left-wright, Intervention* (Sydney, Australia) 20 (1986): 73. See also Jacques Derrida, *Of Grammatology* (Baltimore: Johns Hopkins University Press, 1976); Jonathan Culler, *On Deconstruction: Theory and Criticism after Structuralism* (Ithaca: Cornell University Press, 1982).

5. Again, to cite Elizabeth Gross's formulation: "Taken together, reversal and its useful displacement show the necessary but unfounded function of these terms in Western thought. One must both reverse the dichotomy and the values attached to the two terms, as well as displace the excluded term, placing it beyond its oppositional role, as the internal condition of the dominant term. This move makes clear the violence of the hierarchy and the debt the dominant term owes to the subordinate one. It also demonstrates that there are other ways of conceiving these terms than dichotomously. If these terms were only or necessarily dichotomies, the process of displacement would not be possible. Although historically necessary, the terms are not logically necessary." See Gross, 74.
6. Barbara Johnson, *The Critical Difference: Essays in the Contemporary Rhetoric of Reading* (Baltimore: Johns Hopkins University Press, 1980), x–xi.
7. Most recently, attention has been focused on the issue of pregnancy benefits. See, for example, Lucinda M. Finley, "Transcending Equality Theory: A Way Out of the Maternity and the Workplace Debate," *Columbia Law Review* 86 (October 1986): 1118–83. See Sylvia A. Law, "Rethinking Sex and the Constitution," *University of Pennsylvania Law Review* 132 (June 1984): 955–1040.
8. Recently, historians have begun to cast feminist history in terms of the equality-versus-difference debate. Rather than accept it as an accurate characterization of antithetical positions, however, I think we need to look more closely at how feminists used these arguments. A close reading of nineteenth-century French feminist texts, for example, leads me to conclude that they are far less easily categorized into difference or equality positions than one would have supposed. I think it is a mistake for feminist historians to write this debate uncritically into history, for it reifies an "antithesis" that may not actually have existed. We need instead to "deconstruct" feminist arguments and read them in their discursive contexts, all as explorations of "the difference dilemma."
9. Ruth Milkman, "Women's History and the Sears Case," *Feminist Studies* 12 (Summer 1986): 394–95. In my discussion of the Sears case, I have drawn heavily on this careful and intelligent article, the best so far of the many that have been written on the subject.
10. Martha Minow, "Learning to Live with the Dilemma of Difference: Bilingual and Special Education," *Law and Contemporary Problems* 48, no. 2 (1984): 157–211; quotation is from p. 160; see also pp. 202–206.
11. There is a difference, it seems to me, between arguing that women and men have identical interests and arguing that one should presume such identity in all aspects of the hiring process. The second position is the only strategic way of not building into the hiring process prejudice or the wrong presumptions about differences of interest.
12. Rosenberg's "Offer of Proof" and Kessler-Harris's "Written Testimony" appeared in *Signs* 11 (Summer 1986): 757–79. The "Written Rebuttal Testimony of Dr. Rosalind Rosenberg" is part of the official transcript of the case, U.S. District Court for the Northern District of Illinois, Eastern Division, *EEOC v. Sears*, Civil Action No. 79–C–4373. (I am grateful to Sanford Levinson for sharing the trial documents with me and for our many conversations about them.)
13. Appendix to the "Written Rebuttal Testimony of Dr. Rosalind Rosenberg," 1–12.

14. On the limits imposed by courtrooms and the pitfalls expert witnesses may encounter, see Nadine Taub, "Thinking about Testifying," *Perspectives* (American Historical Association Newsletter) 24 (November 1986): 10–11.
15. On this point, Taub asks a useful question: "Is there a danger in discrimination cases that historical or other expert testimony not grounded in the particular facts of the case will reinforce the idea that it is acceptable to make generalizations about particular groups?" (p. 11).
16. See the cross-examination of Kessler-Harris, *EEOC v. Sears*, 16376–619.
17. The Rosenberg "Rebuttal" is particularly vehement on this question: "This assumption that all employers discriminate is prominent in her [Kessler-Harris's] work. . . . In a 1979 article, she wrote hopefully that women harbor values, attitudes, and behavior patterns potentially subversive to capitalism" (p. 11). "There are, of course, documented instances of employers limiting the opportunities of women. But the fact that some employers have discriminated does not prove that all do" (p. 19). The rebuttal raises another issue about the political and ideological limits of a courtroom or, perhaps it is better to say, about the way the courtroom reproduces dominant ideologies. The general notion that employers discriminate was unacceptable (but the general notion that women prefer certain jobs was not). This unacceptability was underscored by linking it to subversion and Marxism, positions intolerable in U.S. political discourse. Rosenberg's innuendoes attempted to discredit Kessler-Harris on two counts—first, by suggesting she was making a ridiculous generalization and, second, by suggesting that only people outside acceptable politics could even entertain that generalization.
18. Milkman, 391.
19. Naomi Schor, "Reading Double: Sand's Difference," in *The Poetics of Gender*, ed. Nancy K. Miller (New York: Columbia University Press, 1986), 256.
20. Michael Walzer, *Spheres of Justice: A Defense of Pluralism and Equality* (New York: Basic Books, 1983), xii. See also Minow, 202–203.
21. Milkman, 384.

Permissions Acknowledgments

NANCY CHODOROW, "Gender, Relation, and Difference in Psychoanalytic Perspective." Reprinted from *Socialist Review* 46 9:4 (July–August 1979), pp. 51–70. Copyright © 1979, Center for Social Research and Education. Reprinted with permission. IRIS MARION YOUNG, "Is Male Gender Identity the Cause of Male Domination?" Reprinted from *Mothering* (1989), ed. Joyce Treibilcot, pp. 129–146. Copyright © 1983 Rowman and Littlefield Publishers. Reprinted with permission. ANN FERGUSON, "On Conceiving Motherhood." Reprinted from *Mothering* (1989), ed. Joyce Treibilcot, pp. 153–82. Reprinted with permission. CATHARINE A. MACKINNON, "Feminism, Marxism, Method, and State: An Agenda for Theory." Reprinted from *Signs* 7:3 (1982), pp. 514–544. Reprinted with permission of the University of Chicago Press and the author. SANDRA LEE BARTKY, "Foucault, Femininity, and the Modernization of Patriarchal Power." Reprinted from *Femininity and Domination* (1990), by Sandra Lee Bartky, pp. 63–82. Reprinted with permission of the author. JUDITH BUTLER, excerpts from *Gender Trouble: Feminism and the Subversion of Identity* (1990) by Judith Butler, pp. 128–149. Reprinted with permission of the author. NANCY FRASER AND LINDA J. NICHOLSON, "Social Criticism Without Philosophy." Reprinted from *Feminism/Postmodernism* (1990), ed. Linda J. Nicholson, pp. 19–38. Reprinted with permission of the authors. MARIA LUGONES, "Playfulness, 'World'-Travelling, and Loving Perception." Reprinted from *Hypatia* 2 (1987), pp. 3–19. Reprinted with permission of the author. ELIZABETH V. SPELMAN, excerpts from *Inessential Woman* (1988) by Elizabeth V. Spelman, pp. 133–159. Copyright © Elizabeth V. Spelman. Reprinted by permission of Beacon Press. ELIZABETH ABEL, "Race, Class, and Psychoanalysis? Opening Questions." Reprinted from *Conflicts in Feminism* (1990), ed. Marianne Hirsch and Evelyn Fox Keller, pp. 184–204. Reprinted with permission of the author. CHESHIRE CALHOUN, "Separating Lesbian Theory from Feminist Theory." Reprinted from *Ethics* 104 (1994), pp. 558–581. Reprinted with permission of the University of Chicago Press and the author. DEBORAH K. KING, "Multiple Jeopardy, Multiple Consciousness: The Context of Black Feminist Ideology." Reprinted from *Signs* 14:1 (1988), pp. 42–72. Reprinted with permission of the University of Chicago Press. KIMBERLE WILLIAMS CRENSHAW, "Beyond Racism and Misogyny: Black Feminism and 2 Live Crew." Reprinted from *Words That Wound: Critical Race Theory, Assaultive Speech, and the First Amendment* (1993), eds. Mari J. Matsuda, et al, pp. 111–132. Copyright © 1993 by WestviewPress. Reprinted by permission of WestviewPress. EVA FEDER KITTAY, "Woman as Metaphor." Reprinted from *Hypatia* 3 (1988), pp. 63–86. Reprinted with permission of the author. GENEVIEVE LLOYD, "Maleness, Metaphor, and the 'Crisis' of Reason." Reprinted from *A Mind of One's Own: Feminist Essays on Reason and Objectivity* (1992), eds. Louise Antony and Charlotte Witt, pp. 69–83. Copyright © 1992 by WestviewPress. Reprinted by permission of Westview Press. JULIA KRISTEVA, "Stabat Mater." Reprinted from *The Kristeva Reader* (1986), ed. Toril Moi, pp. 161–186. Copyright © 1986 by Columbia University Press. Reprinted with permission of the publisher. LUCI IRIGARAY, "And One Doesn't Stir Without the

Other." Reprinted from *Signs* 7 (1981), pp. 60–67. Reprinted with permission of the University of Chicago Press. PATRICIA J. WILLIAMS, excerpts from *The Alchemy of Race and Rights* (1991) by Patricia J. Williams, pp. 166–178. Reprinted by permission of the publisher from *The Alchemy of Race and Rights* by Patricia Williams, Cambridge, Mass.: Harvard University Press, Copyright © 1991 by the President and Fellows of Harvard College. NAOMI SCHEMAN, "Though This Be Method, Yet There is Madness in It: Paranoia and Liberal Epistemology." Reprinted from *Engenderings* (1993) by Naomi Scheman, pp. 75–105. Reprinted with permission of the author. SUSAN BABBITT, "Feminism and Objective Interests: The Role of Transformation Experiences in Rational Deliberation." Reprinted from *Feminist Epistemologies* (1993), eds. Linda Alcoff and Elizabeth Potter, pp. 245–264. Reprinted with permission of the author. ALISON M. JAGGAR, "Love and Knowledge: Emotion in Feminist Epistemology." Reprinted from *Gender/Body/Knowledge: Feminist Reconstructions of Being and Knowing* (1989), eds. Alison M. Jaggar and Susan R. Bordo. Copyright © 1989, Rutgers, The State University. Reprinted by permission of Rutgers University Press. MARILYN FRYE, "Some Reflections on Separatism and Power." Reprinted from *The Politics of Reality* (1983) by Marilyn Frye, pp. 132–138. Reprinted with permission of The Crossing Press, Inc. PATRICIA S. MANN, "Glancing at Pornography: Recognizing Men." Reprinted from *Micro-Politics: Agency in a Postfeminist Era* (1994) by Patricia S. Mann, pp. 62–89. Reprinted with permission of the University of Minnesota Press and the author. DIANA TIETJENS MEYERS, "The Family Romance: A *Fin-de-Siecle* Tragedy." Reprinted from *Feminism and Families* (1997), ed. Hilde Lindemann Nelson, pp. 235–254. Reprinted with permission of the author. NANCY HARTSOCK, "The Feminist Standpoint: Developing a Grounding for a Specificially Feminist Historical Materialism." Reprinted from *Discovering Reality* (1983), eds. S. Harding and M. Hintikka, pp. 283–310. Reprinted with permission of Kluwer Academic Publishers. BELL HOOKS, "Sisterhood: Political Solidarity Between Women." Reprinted from *Feminist Theory: From Margin to Center* (1984), by bell hooks, pp. 43–65. Reprinted by permission of the publisher, South End Press, 116 Saint Botolph Street, Boston, MA 02115. DONNA HARAWAY, "A Manifesto for Cyborgs: Science, Technology, and Socialist Feminism in the 1980s." Reprinted from *Socialist Review* no. 80 (1985), pp. 65–108. Reprinted with permission of the author. CHANTAL MOUFFE, "Feminism, Citizenship, and Radical Democratic Politics." Reprinted from *Feminists Theorize the Political* (1992), eds. Judith Butler and Joan W. Scott, pp. 369–384. Reprinted with permission of the author. CAROL GILLIGAN, "In a Different Voice: Women's Conception of the Self and Morality." Reprinted from *Harvard Educational Review* 47:4 (1977), pp. 481–517. Copyright © 1977 by the President and Fellows of Harvard University. All rights reserved. Reprinted with permission of *Harvard Educational Review.* SARA RUDDICK, "Maternal Thinking." Reprinted from *Feminist Studies* 6:2 (Summer 1980), pp. 342–367. Reprinted with permission of *Feminist Studies,* Inc., c/o Department of Women's Studies, University of Maryland, College, Park, MD 20742. ANNETTE BAIER, "Trust and Anti-Trust." Reprinted from *Ethics* 96 (1986), pp. 201–230. Reprinted with permission of the University of Chicago Press and the author. VIRGINIA HELD, "Feminism and Moral Theory." Reprinted from *Women and Moral Theory* (1989), eds. Eva Feder Kittay and Diana Tietjens Meyers, pp. 111–128. Reprinted with permission of Rowman and Littlefield. CLAUDIA CARD, "Gender and Moral Luck." Reprinted from *Identity, Character, and Morality* (1990), eds. Owen Flanagan and Amelie Oksenberg Rorty, pp. 199–218. Reprinted with permission of The MIT Press. MARILYN FRIEDMAN, "Beyond Caring: The De-Moralization of Gender." Reprinted from *The Canadian Journal of Philosophy,* Supplemental Volume 13 (1987), pp. 199–218. Reprinted with permission of the University of Calgary Press and the author. MICHELLE MOODY-ADAMS, "Gender and the Complexity of Moral Voices." Reprinted from *Feminist Ethics* (1991), ed. Claudia Card, pp. 195–212. Reprinted with permission of the University of Kansas Press and the author. WENDY W. WILLIAMS, "The Equality Crisis: Some Reflections on Culture, Courts, and Feminism." Reprinted from 7 *Women's Rights Law Reporter* 175 (1982), pp. 15–34. Copyright © 1983 by *Women's Rights Law Reporter.* CHRISTINE A. LITTLETON, "Reconstructing Sexual Equality." Reprinted from *California Law Review* 75:4 (1987), pp. 1279–1335. Reprinted with permission of the University of California Press and the author. SEYLA BENHABIB, "The Generalized and the Concrete Other: The Kohlberg-Gilligan Controversy and Moral Theory." Reprinted from *Praxis International* 5:4 (Jan. 1986), pp. 402–24. Reprinted with permission of Blackwell Publishers Limited. JOAN W. SCOTT, "Deconstructing Equality-Versus-Difference." Reprinted from *Feminist Studies* 14:1 (Spring 1988), pp. 35–50. Reprinted with permission of the Publisher, *Feminist Studies,* Inc., c/o Department of Women's Studies, University of Maryland, College Park, MD 20742.